Elevation

Feet	Meters
Over 6,561	Over 2,000
1,641–6,561	501–2,000
657–1,640	201–500
0–656	0–200
Below sea level	Below sea level

⊛ Capital city
• Major city

NORWAY
⊛ Oslo
SWEDEN
FINLAND
Helsinki
⊛ Stockholm
Tallinn ⊛
ESTONIA

SCOTLAND
• Edinburgh

North
Sea

NORTHERN
IRELAND

IRELAND
⊛ Dublin

DENMARK
Copenhagen ⊛

Baltic
Sea

Riga ⊛ LATVIA

UNITED
KINGDOM

WALES

ENGLAND

• Hamburg

LITHUANIA

RUSSIA
Vilnius ⊛

Min

BELAR

ATLANTIC
OCEAN

London ⊛

NETHERLANDS
Amsterdam ⊛

Elbe R.

Berlin ⊛

Vistula R.

Warsaw ⊛

English Channel

CHANNEL IS. (U.K.)

Brussels ⊛
BELGIUM

Rhine R.

GERMANY

POLAND

Seine R.

Paris ⊛

⊛ Luxembourg
LUXEMBOURG

• Frankfurt

Prague ⊛
CZECH REPUBLIC

Danube R.

Loire R.

FRANCE

LIECHTENSTEIN

SWITZERLAND

• Munich

SLOVAKIA
Bratislava •

⊛ Bern

Vienna ⊛

Geneva •

Vaduz ⊛

AUSTRIA

• Budapest

Rhône R.

Alps

HUNGARY

SLOVENIA
⊛ Ljubljana

• Milan

Zagreb ⊛

ROMANIA

PORTUGAL

Pyrenees

ANDORRA

CROATIA

Belgrade ⊛

Ebro R.

Andorra
la Vella

Madrid •

SPAIN

MONACO

SAN MARINO

BOSNIA AND
HERZEGOVINA

Bucharest ⊛

SERBIA

• Lisbon

Sarajevo ⊛

Danube R.

Barcelona •

Corsica
(France)

ITALY

KOSOVO

VATICAN
CITY

Podgorica ⊛

Pristina ⊛

BULGAR

Seville •

Rome ⊛

MONTENEGRO

Sofia •

Balearic Islands

Sardinia
(Italy)

Naples •

Tirana ⊛

Skopje •

MACEDONIA

GIBRALTER (U.K.)
CEUTA (Sp.)

ALBANIA

Tyrrhenian
Sea

Adriatic Sea

Rabat ⊛

Algiers •

GREECE

Tunis ⊛

Sicily

Athens ⊛

Aegean Sea

MOROCCO

Valletta •

TUNISIA

MALTA

Mediterranean Sea

Crete

| 0 | 100 | 200 mi |

| 0 | 100 | 200 km |

Tripoli ⊛

ALGERIA

LIBYA

THE WEST

A NEW HISTORY

ANTHONY GRAFTON
DAVID A. BELL

THE WEST

A NEW HISTORY

VOLUME TWO

W. W. Norton & Company

NEW YORK • LONDON

TO OUR STUDENTS

W. W. NORTON & COMPANY has been independent since its founding in 1923, when William Warder Norton and Mary D. Herter Norton first published lectures delivered at the People's Institute, the adult education division of New York City's Cooper Union. The firm soon expanded its program beyond the Institute, publishing books by celebrated academics from America and abroad. By midcentury, the two major pillars of Norton's publishing program—trade books and college texts—were firmly established. In the 1950s, the Norton family transferred control of the company to its employees, and today—with a staff of four hundred and a comparable number of trade, college, and professional titles published each year—W. W. Norton & Company stands as the largest and oldest publishing house owned wholly by its employees.

EDITOR Steve Forman
ASSOCIATE EDITORS Scott Sugarman and Justin Cahill
PROJECT EDITOR Melissa Atkin
EDITORIAL ASSISTANTS Lily Gellman, Kelly Rafey, and Travis Carr
DEVELOPMENTAL EDITORS Alice Vigliani and Harry Haskell
CARTOGRAPHIC EDITOR Charlotte Miller
COPYEDITORS JoAnn Simony and Alice Vigliani
MANAGING EDITOR, COLLEGE Marian Johnson
MANAGING EDITOR, COLLEGE DIGITAL MEDIA Kim Yi
ASSOCIATE DIRECTOR OF PRODUCTION, COLLEGE Benjamin Reynolds
MEDIA EDITOR Laura Wilk
MEDIA PROJECT EDITOR Rachel Mayer
MEDIA ASSOCIATE EDITOR Sarah Rose Aquilina
MEDIA ASSISTANT EDITOR Chris Hillyer
MARKETING MANAGER, HISTORY Sarah England Bartley
PHOTO EDITOR Stephanie Romeo
PHOTO RESEARCHER Lynn Gadson
DESIGNER Jillian Burr
PERMISSIONS MANAGER Megan Schindel
PERMISSIONS ASSOCIATE Elizabeth Trammell
LAYOUT ARTIST Brad Walrod/Kenoza Type, Inc.
CARTOGRAPHER AND ILLUSTRATOR Mapping Specialists—Fitchburg, WI
MANUFACTURING Transcontinental Interglobe Inc.—Beauceville QC

A catalogue record of the full edition is available from the Library of Congress.

This edition:
ISBN: 978-0-393-93799-2 (pbk.)

W. W. Norton & Company, Inc., 500 Fifth Avenue, New York, NY 10110

wwnorton.com

W. W. Norton & Company Ltd., 15 Carlisle Street, London W1D 3BS

1 2 3 4 5 6 7 8 9 0

ABOUT THE AUTHORS

ANTHONY GRAFTON is the Henry Putnam University Professor of History at Princeton University. A specialist in the cultural history of early-modern Europe, he is the author of many acclaimed books, including *The Footnote: A Curious History*, and *New Worlds, Ancient Texts: The Power of Tradition and the Shock of Discovery*, which won the Los Angeles Times Book Award in History, as well as intellectual biographies of Leon Battista Alberti, Girolamo Cardano, and Joseph Scaliger. Among his many honors from universities and cultural institutions around the world, Professor Grafton was awarded the Balzan Prize for History of the Humanities and the Andrew W. Mellon Foundation's Distinguished Achievement Award. At Princeton, where he regularly teaches the survey of Western Civilizations, he was honored with the President's Teaching Award. He is a member of the American Philosophical Society, the British Academy, and has served as president of the American Historical Association.

DAVID A. BELL is the Sidney and Ruth Lapidus Professor in the Era of North Atlantic Revolutions in the history department at Princeton University. His specialty is modern Europe with a focus on political culture in the age of revolutions. Among his recent works, *The First Total War: Napoleon's Europe and the Birth of Warfare As We Know It* was a finalist for the Los Angeles Times Book Award in History. Professor Bell regularly teaches undergraduate surveys of early-modern Europe, the Enlightenment, and the French Revolution. He is a regular contributor to *The Nation* and other general-interest periodicals. Professor Bell's current project is a transnational history of political charisma in the Atlantic revolutions of the late eighteenth and early nineteenth centuries.

CONTENTS IN BRIEF

10. RENAISSANCE EUROPE: A WORLD TRANSFORMED, 1400–1500   325

11. REFORMATIONS: PROTESTANT AND CATHOLIC, 1500–1600   371

12. THINGS FALL APART: A CONTINENT IN CRISIS, 1600–1640   409

13. ORDERING THE WORLD: NEW FORMS OF AUTHORITY AND KNOWLEDGE, 1640–1680   441

14. FROM COURT TO CITY: EMERGING CULTURES, 1680–1740   473

15. ENLIGHTENMENT: CHALLENGING THE PREVAILING ORDER, 1740–1780   505

16. REVOLUTION: LIBERTY AND TERROR, 1780–1799   539

17. THE AGE OF NAPOLEON: EMPIRE AND RESISTANCE, 1799–1820   571

18. ACCELERATION: THE AGE OF INDUSTRY, 1820–1845   601

19. GROWING PAINS: SOCIAL AND POLITICAL UPHEAVALS, 1845–1880   637

20. APOGEE: IMPERIAL RIVALRY AND GLOBAL POWER, 1880–1910   671

21. THINGS BLOW UP: WORLD WAR I AND THE RUSSIAN REVOLUTION, 1910–1922   705

22. IDEOLOGIES: THE TRIUMPH OF POLITICAL EXTREMES, 1922–1940   741

23. THE ABYSS: WORLD WAR II AND THE HOLOCAUST, 1940–1945   775

24. RECOVERY AND COLD WAR: REBUILDING A DIVIDED CONTINENT, 1945–1973   809

25. REUNION: EUROPEAN UNIFICATION AND THE END OF THE COLD WAR, 1973–1999   845

26. UNDER PRESSURE: EUROPE'S UNCERTAIN PRESENT, SINCE 2000   877

CONTENTS

MAPS   xxix
PRIMARY-SOURCE FEATURES   xxxi
PREFACE   xxxiii
ACKNOWLEDGMENTS   xxxvii
PEDAGOGY AND FEATURES   xxxix

10. Renaissance Europe: A World Transformed, 1400–1500   325

RENAISSANCE STATES   326

ITALY: TERRITORIAL STATES (1454–1494)   326
    Florence
    DOCUMENTING EVERYDAY LIFE Lorenzo Ghiberti's Declaration in the *Catasto* of 1427   328
    Milan • Venice • The Rise of Diplomacy: The Treaty of Lodi

MONARCHICAL STATES (1450–1494)   330
    Burgundy • France
    MAKING CONNECTIONS Poverty and the State: Cahier of the Estates General, "The Plight of the French Poor," and Juan Luis Vives, "Concerning the Relief of the Poor"   332
    England • Holy Roman Empire • Spain

THE OTTOMAN EMPIRE   335

THE TRANSFORMATION OF WARFARE   336

THE CAULDRON OF THE EARLY ITALIAN WARS (1494–1517)   337

CHRISTIANITY: CRISIS AND REFORM   339

THE GREAT SCHISM (1378–1417)   339

REFORM MOVEMENTS   340
    Lollards • Hussites • Conciliarists (1409–1449) • Orthodoxy in Ottoman Lands

"APPETITE FOR THE DIVINE"   342

NEW DIRECTIONS IN RELIGIOUS LIFE   342
    Beguines • Departures from Scholasticism • Witchcraft: Theory and Practice • Persecution of Non-Christians

EUROPE EXPANDS: NEW TECHNOLOGIES AND THEIR CONSEQUENCES   345

MARITIME ADVANCES   345

EARLY ATLANTIC EXPEDITIONS   345

TO THE INDIAN OCEAN   346

SLAVERY AND THE SLAVE TRADE 347

PRINTING: THE BOOK TRANSFORMED (1450–1517) 349

Gutenberg • The Immediate Impact of Book Printing

DISCOVERY: A NEW WORLD 351

COLUMBUS'S VOYAGES 351

EUROPEAN EXPLORATION AFTER COLUMBUS (1497–1522) 352

SPANISH CONQUEST 354

COLUMBIAN EXCHANGES 355

REDISCOVERY: RENAISSANCE CULTURE 356

PETRARCH 356

SALUTATI'S BREAKTHROUGH 357

HUMANISM 358

Politics • Society • Christine de Pizan

UNDERSTANDING VISUAL CULTURE Ghirlandaio's *Portrait of a Lady* 359

Understanding the Past

INNOVATION IN THE ARTS 361

Florence • Northern Europe • Patronage

CITY LIFE Renaissance Florence

Alberti: A New Vision • Leonardo, Michelangelo, Raphael

MACHIAVELLI: THE NEW POLITICS 367

CONCLUSION 368
CHAPTER REVIEW 369

11. Reformations: Protestant and Catholic, 1500–1600 371

MARTIN LUTHER AND THE CULTURE OF CHURCH REFORM 372

LUTHER'S BREAKTHROUGH (1515–1517) 373

CHRISTIANITY IN 1517 374

HUMANIST CRITICS OF THE CHURCH 375

Desiderius Erasmus • Thomas More's *Utopia* • Reforming the Bible •
Luther and Erasmus

LUTHER'S MESSAGE 377

THE DIET OF WORMS AND ITS AFTERMATH (1521) 378

THE REFORMATION MOVEMENT 379

THE MOVEMENT'S APPEAL 379

The Role of Print • Social Bases of Reform • Reform in the Cities

LUTHER'S CRITICS 381

Erasmus's Humanist Critique • Ulrich Zwingli

FISSURES IN THE MOVEMENT: ZURICH AND THE REFORMED TRADITION 382

TRANSFORMING SOCIETY: THE PEASANTS' WAR (1523–1525) 382

MAKING CONNECTIONS Martin Luther and the Peasants' War: Christoph Schappeler and Sebastian Lotzer, *Twelve Articles of the Peasants,* and Martin Luther, *Admonition to Peace Concerning the Twelve Articles of the Peasants*   383

RADICAL REFORMATION: THE ANABAPTISTS   385

RELIGIOUS EDUCATION   386

WOMEN AND THE REFORMATION   386

THE MESSAGE SPREADS   388

CALVINISM: THE CHURCH OF GENEVA   388

DOCUMENTING EVERYDAY LIFE Christmas in St. Andrews   389

CHURCHES AND MONARCHS: A CHANGING BALANCE   390

HENRY VIII AND THE CHURCH OF ENGLAND   390

FRANCIS I AND CHARLES V (1521–1546)   391
Foundations of State Power • Habsburg Control of Italy

STALEMATE: PEACE OF AUGSBURG (1555)   392

RENEWING CATHOLICISM   394

SOURCES OF RENEWAL   394
Holy Women • The Ursulines • Teresa of Ávila

THE SOCIETY OF JESUS   395

THE COUNCIL OF TRENT   396

RETHINKING THE NATURAL WORLD   396

OBSERVATION AND COLLABORATION   397

THE PERILS OF NEW THINKING   398

WAR ACROSS THE CONTINENT   398

GOVERNMENT AND WAR IN A NEW KEY: PHILIP II OF SPAIN   399

RELIGIOUS WAR, POLITICAL UPHEAVAL   399
The Dutch Revolt (1566–1648) • England: Anglicans and Puritans • The French Wars of Religion (1562–1589)

POLITICAL SETTLEMENTS   401

UNDERSTANDING VISUAL CULTURE De Witte's *The Interior of the Oude Kerk*   402

RUSSIA AND EASTERN EUROPE   403

A TIME OF DARKNESS   403

WITCH TRIALS   403

TWO RESPONSES TO POLITICAL AND RELIGIOUS CRISIS: JEAN BODIN AND MICHEL DE MONTAIGNE   404
Bodin • Montaigne

CONCLUSION   405
CHAPTER REVIEW   407

12. Things Fall Apart: A Continent in Crisis, 1600–1640   409

ECONOMIC CHANGE   411

    THE LITTLE ICE AGE   411

    STAGNATION ON THE CONTINENT   411

       Declining Trade • A Second Serfdom

    UNDERSTANDING VISUAL CULTURE   Bruegel the Elder's *Hunters in the Snow*   412

    GROWTH IN MARITIME EUROPE   413

       The Dutch Republic • Middle-Class Households

    OCEANIC TRADE   414

       The Early Transatlantic Slave Trade • Mercantilism

EUROPEAN EXPANSION IN THE ATLANTIC   415

    EARLY EUROPEAN SETTLEMENTS IN NORTH AMERICA   416

       Jamestown • Québec • New Amsterdam

    NEW ENGLAND   418

       A City upon a Hill • Settlers and Native Americans

STATES UNDER PRESSURE   419

    THE "MILITARY REVOLUTION"   419

    STATE BUILDING   420

       Unification of France • Divisions in Western and Central Europe

    REBELLIONS   421

A NEW SOCIAL DYNAMIC IN RELIGION   421

    RELIGION AND THE DISCIPLINE OF DAILY LIFE   421

       Elites and Commoners • The Church and Evangelization • The Inquisition • Religion and Gender • Witch Trials

    THE CONTINUING CATHOLIC RECONQUEST   424

CIVIL STRIFE   424

    INSTABILITY IN MUSCOVY AND THE OTTOMAN EMPIRE   424

    POLAND AND SWEDEN   425

    FRANCE   425

    TENSIONS IN THE GERMAN LANDS   426

THE THIRTY YEARS' WAR   426

    OUTBREAK OF WAR   427

    HABSBURG VICTORIES   428

    SWEDISH AND SPANISH INTERVENTION   428

    ATROCITIES AND MASS DEATH   429

    DOCUMENTING EVERYDAY LIFE   The Sack of Magdeburg   430

WAR AND ABSOLUTISM   430

    BREAKS WITH PRECEDENT   431

POWERFUL MINISTRIES 431

Richelieu • Olivares • Oxenstierna

THE DUTCH AND BRITISH EXCEPTIONS 432

ROYAL POWER AND CULTURE 433

BAROQUE ART 433

LANGUAGE AND LITERARY CULTURE 434

Don Quixote • Popular Culture

PATRONAGE AND ITS LIMITS 435

THE REPUBLIC OF LETTERS 435

EARLY STAGES OF THE SCIENTIFIC REVOLUTION 436

Galileo • Kepler • Bacon

MAKING CONNECTIONS Galileo and the Inquisition 437

DESCARTES 438

CONCLUSION 438
CHAPTER REVIEW 439

13. Ordering the World: New Forms of Authority and Knowledge, 1640–1680 441

THE CIVIL WARS IN THE BRITISH ISLES (1639–1649) 442

ORIGINS 442

INITIAL CONFLICTS (1637–1641) 443

PARLIAMENTARY VICTORY (1642–1645) 444

THE RADICAL TURN (1646–1649) 445

THE CONTINENTAL CIVIL WARS 446

THE FRONDE IN FRANCE (1648–1653) 446

IBERIA AND ITALY (1640–1659) 447

UKRAINE AND POLAND-LITHUANIA (1648–1668) 447

THE OTTOMAN EMPIRE (1640–1656) 448

RELIGIOUS QUESTIONING 448

MESSIANISM 448

PROTESTANT AND CATHOLIC DISSENTERS 449

The Quakers • The Jansenists

CATHOLIC DISCIPLINE AND RELIGIOUS WOMEN 450

The Ursuline Order • Marie Guyart

ORDER THROUGH REASON 451

HOBBES'S *LEVIATHAN* 451

BARUCH SPINOZA 452

BLAISE PASCAL 453

POULAIN DE LA BARRE AND EARLY FEMINISM   453

DOCUMENTING EVERYDAY LIFE   Gender Roles in
Seventeenth-Century England   454

SCIENCE, EXPERIMENTALISM, AND THE STATE   455

MAKING PEACE: CONSTRUCTING A NEW INTERNATIONAL
ORDER AFTER THE THIRTY YEARS' WAR   456

THE PEACE OF WESTPHALIA (1645–1648)   456

The Slow Waning of Religious Violence • Control of Power

THE ABSOLUTIST STATES   459

DENMARK AND BRANDENBURG   459

LOUIS XIV OF FRANCE (1643–1715)   460

Colbert's Reforms • The "Sun King" • Power and Culture at Versailles •
French Court Life • France at War

THE MERCANTILE STATES   464

BRITAIN: COMMONWEALTH, PROTECTORATE, RESTORATION
(1648–1688)   464

The Growth of Political Parties • Trade and the City

MAKING CONNECTIONS   Political Equality after the British Civil Wars   465

THE DUTCH "GOLDEN AGE"   466

Dutch Wealth • Toleration and Creativity • Decline

CITY LIFE   Golden Age Amsterdam

UNDERSTANDING VISUAL CULTURE   Rembrandt's *Anatomy Lesson
of Dr. Nicolaes Tulp*   469

CONCLUSION   470

CHAPTER REVIEW   471

14. From Court to City: Emerging Cultures, 1680–1740   473

INTOLERANCE INTENSIFIED   475

THE EDICT OF NANTES REVOKED   475

INTOLERANCE ACROSS EUROPE   475

THE GLORIOUS REVOLUTION AND ITS CONSEQUENCES   476

A CHANGE IN RULE   476

THE ENGLISH BILL OF RIGHTS   477

LOCKE'S *SECOND TREATISE*   477

CHANGES IN RELIGION   477

A NEW ECONOMIC DIRECTION   478

A PROTESTANT BASE IN IRELAND   478

PARLIAMENT AND POLITICS   478

ABSOLUTISM AT ITS HEIGHT 479

THE LAST YEARS OF LOUIS XIV 479
PETER THE GREAT OF RUSSIA 479
ABSOLUTISM IN PRUSSIA 480
PEASANT MISERIES 481
Russia and Ukraine • Famine in France

THE CONDUCT OF WAR 482

DOCUMENTING EVERYDAY LIFE Childhood in Rural France 483
DISCIPLINE AND VIOLENCE 483
ARISTOCRATS AT WAR 484

WAR AND THE BALANCE OF POWER (1680–1721) 485

FRENCH AGGRESSION 485
THE LAST GREAT OTTOMAN OFFENSIVE (1683) 485
THE WARS OF LOUIS XIV 486
The War of the League of Augsburg (1688–1697) • The War of the Spanish Succession (1702–1714) • The Peace of Utrecht (1713–1714)
NEW GREAT POWERS 488
Russia • England

AN ATLANTIC WORLD 489

BRITAIN'S MAINLAND COLONIES 489
SUGAR AND SLAVERY 489
The Atlantic Slave Trade • Slave Resistance
MAKING CONNECTIONS The Limits of Liberty 491
FRENCH EXPANSION IN NORTH AMERICA 492
French Louisiana • The French and Native Peoples
AMERICAN TRADE AND EUROPEAN ECONOMIES 493
UNDERSTANDING VISUAL CULTURE Mignard's *Portrait of Louise de Kérouaille, Duchess of Portsmouth* 494

CITY LIFE AND CULTURE 495

NEW CULTURAL INSTITUTIONS IN THE CITIES 495
The Coffeehouses • Salons • Periodicals
URBAN POVERTY, CRIME, AND REFORM 496
A NEW CULTURAL CLIMATE 497
Defoe • Swift
LEARNED PERIODICALS AND THE REPUBLIC OF LETTERS 498
THE CAMPAIGN FOR TOLERATION 498

A REVOLUTION IN THOUGHT 499

PIERRE BAYLE AND SKEPTICISM 499
CHALLENGING CHRISTIAN DOCTRINE 499
SKEPTICISM AND POLITICAL AUTHORITY 500
Montesquieu
ISAAC NEWTON'S UNIVERSE 501

LOCKE ON THE HUMAN MIND	502
THE INVENTION OF "SOCIETY"	502
CONCLUSION	502
CHAPTER REVIEW	503

15. Enlightenment: Challenging the Prevailing Order, 1740–1780   505

ECONOMIC CHANGE	506
AGRICULTURAL EXPANSION	506
INDUSTRIAL EXPANSION	507
The "Putting Out" System • New Technologies • New Infrastructure • Rising Inequality	
COLONIAL WEALTH AND SLAVERY	509
A NEW URBAN LANDSCAPE	510
The Urban Poor • The Growing Middle Classes	
WARFARE TURNED GLOBAL	511
THE WAR OF THE AUSTRIAN SUCCESSION (1740–1748)	512
THE SEVEN YEARS' WAR (1756–1763)	512
A CULTURAL TRANSFORMATION	514
EXPANDING LITERACY	514
The Rise of the Magazine and the Novel • Women as Readers	
DOCUMENTING EVERYDAY LIFE Coffeehouses and Newspapers in the Age of Enlightenment	515
PUBLIC CULTURE	517
New Social Settings • The Garden at Vauxhall	
UNDERSTANDING VISUAL CULTURE Lemonnier's *An Evening with Madame Geoffrin*	518
A BROADENING GLOBAL VIEW	519
Cook's Voyages • Cosmopolitanism • Anti-Cosmopolitanism	
RELIGIOUS CHANGE	521
THE DECLINE OF FORMAL OBSERVANCE	521
NEW "ENTHUSIASMS"	522
THE ENLIGHTENMENT AT ITS HEIGHT	523
THE CULT OF REASON	523
REASON AND RELIGION	524
SCIENCE AND PRACTICAL VALUE	524
THE SPREAD OF ENLIGHTENED THOUGHT	525
Writing for the Public • Underground Enlightenment • Voltaire the Philosophe	
MAKING CONNECTIONS Enlightenment Thinkers and Progress	526

THE SCIENCE OF SOCIETY   527

Montesquieu • The Scottish Enlightenment

SENTIMENT AND CITIZENSHIP   528

Social Exchange • Rousseau's *Social Contract* • Republicanism

THE POLITICS OF ENLIGHTENMENT   531

ENLIGHTENED ABSOLUTISM   531

The Case of Portugal • Germany and Austria • Catherine the Great • Enlightened Reform in France

BRITAIN AND THE WILKES AFFAIR   533

THE RIGHTS OF MAN   534

THE AMERICAN REVOLUTION (1776–1783)   535

CONCLUSION   536
CHAPTER REVIEW   537

16. Revolution: Liberty and Terror, 1780–1799   539

THE ORIGINS OF THE FRENCH REVOLUTION   540

SOCIAL TRANSFORMATIONS   541

THE IMPACT OF CULTURAL AND INTELLECTUAL CHANGE   541

AN APPROACHING FISCAL CRISIS   542

The Threat of Bankruptcy • Dutch Patriot Revolt (1781–1787)

THE REVOLUTION BEGINS (1788–1789)   543

THE QUESTION OF REFORMING THE ESTATES GENERAL   543

THE THIRD ESTATE TAKES POWER   545

THE INTERVENTION OF THE PEOPLE   545

UNDERSTANDING VISUAL CULTURE David's *The Tennis Court Oath*   546

RADICALIZATION (1789–1792)   547

THE OCTOBER DAYS   548

FORGING A NEW REGIME   548

THE REVOLUTION'S INTERNATIONAL IMPACT   549

Thwarted Reforms in Poland-Lithuania • Political and Ideological Responses • Slave Revolt in Saint-Domingue

MAKING CONNECTIONS Hopes and Fears of the French Revolution   551

FAILURE TO REACH CONSENSUS   552

Democracy and Violence • Counterrevolutionary Forces

THE KING'S FLIGHT AND ITS IMPACT   553

The Rush to War • Insurrection

THE BIRTH OF THE FIRST FRENCH REPUBLIC (1792–1793)   555

THE SEPTEMBER MASSACRES AND THE BATTLE OF VALMY   555

THE TRIAL AND EXECUTION OF THE KING   556

TOWARD CIVIL WAR   557
Renewed Economic Crisis • The Fall of the Girondins • The Committee
of Public Safety
DOCUMENTING EVERYDAY LIFE Bread Riots in Paris   558

THE REIGN OF TERROR (1793–1794)   559

THE MECHANISMS OF REPRESSION   560

THE ACHIEVEMENTS OF THE RADICAL REVOLUTION   561

THERMIDOR AND THE END OF THE TERROR   562

THE MEANING OF THE TERROR   562

THE INTERNATIONAL SYSTEM DISRUPTED   563

THE DIRECTORY AND RISE OF NAPOLEON BONAPARTE (1795–1799)   564

THE DIRECTORY   564

THE RISE OF NAPOLEON BONAPARTE   564
A Modern Caesar • The Egyptian Campaign • Further French Reverses •
A Military Coup

CONCLUSION   567
CHAPTER REVIEW   569

17. The Age of Napoleon: Empire and Resistance, 1799–1820   571

NAPOLEON BONAPARTE IN POWER (1799–1804)   573

EFFORTS TO RESTORE FRANCE'S INTERNATIONAL POSITION   573
Italy • Haiti

THE CONSULATE OF 1799–1804   574
Napoleon's Civil Code • Emperor of the French • Failed Attempts at Peace

THE CONQUEST OF EUROPE (1804–1807)   576

THE WHALE AND THE ELEPHANT   576

VICTORY IN CENTRAL EUROPE   576
The Remaking of Germany

THE EMPIRE CONTESTED (1807–1814)   578

THE SPREAD OF THE REVOLUTIONARY LEGACY   578
Reform in the Empire • Reforms in Prussia

RESISTANCE   579
Revolt in Southern Italy

THE IBERIAN TRAP   580
The Peninsular War (1808–1814) • Total War in Spain • Effects of the
Peninsular War
UNDERSTANDING VISUAL CULTURE The Colossus   582

EUROPE IN THE ERA OF NAPOLEON 583

A NEW ROMAN EMPIRE? 583
Imperial Culture • Imperial Society

SOCIAL AND ECONOMIC EFFECTS OF THE NAPOLEONIC WARS 586
France • Great Britain

NAPOLEON'S DOWNFALL (1812–1815) 587

THE RUSSIAN CAMPAIGN 587

DOCUMENTING EVERYDAY LIFE The Retreat from Russia 588

GERMAN NATIONAL RESISTANCE 589
The Origins of Romanticism • Prussia and Austria Switch Sides •
The Battle for Germany

THE BATTLE FOR FRANCE AND NAPOLEON'S FALL 590
Talleyrand • The Bourbon Restoration

MAKING CONNECTIONS European Attitudes toward Napoleon 591

THE CONGRESS OF VIENNA (1814–1815) 592

THE CONCERT OF EUROPE 593

THE HUNDRED DAYS 595

POST-NAPOLEONIC EUROPE 595

ABSORBING THE CHANGES 596

A NEW POLITICS 596

THE SURVIVAL OF REVOLUTIONARY RADICALISM 596
Reform and Repression in Britain

CONCLUSION 598
CHAPTER REVIEW 599

18. Acceleration: The Age of Industry, 1820–1845 601

THE INDUSTRIAL REVOLUTION 603

FIVE FACTORS PROMOTING INDUSTRIAL DEVELOPMENT 603

WHY GREAT BRITAIN? 604

COTTON: THE THREAD OF GLOBAL EXCHANGE 605

UNDERSTANDING VISUAL CULTURE Turner's *Rain, Steam and Speed—
The Great Western Railway* 606

NEW MEANS OF TRANSPORTATION AND COMMUNICATION 607

THE SURGING GROWTH OF CITIES 607

DAILY LIFE AND WORKING CONDITIONS 607
Child Labor • The Response to Industry

INDUSTRIAL EVOLUTION: THE PACE OF CHANGE 608
Variations across the Continent • A Mix of Technologies

DOCUMENTING EVERYDAY LIFE A Girl's Life in the Mines 609

SOCIAL CHANGE AND THE MIDDLE CLASSES — 611

DEFINING THE MIDDLE — 611
ROUTES TO THE MIDDLE CLASS: PROFESSIONS AND EDUCATION — 612
MIDDLE-CLASS CULTURE — 612
Organized Leisure • The Cult of Domesticity • The Middle Class as Model

CITY LIFE Middle-Class London, ca. 1850

THE INDUSTRIAL LOWER CLASSES — 615

THE WORKING POOR — 615
MAKING CONNECTIONS Industrial Promise and Social Misery — 616
URBAN DISEASE AND THE MEDICAL RESPONSE — 617
SOCIAL REFORM: POVERTY AND CRIMINALITY — 617
THE "UTOPIAN" REFORMERS — 618

RELIGIOUS REFORM AND ROMANTIC CULTURE — 619

NEW RELIGIOUS MOVEMENTS — 619
SPIRITUAL LONGING AND ROMANTICISM — 620
THE ROMANTIC MOVEMENT — 620
Britain and Eastern Europe • Germany • France • The Novel •
The Turn to History

NEW POLITICAL PATTERNS — 623

LIBERALISM AND CONSERVATISM — 623
REACTION AND RADICALISM — 624

REPRESSION AND REFORM — 624

SPAIN — 625
RUSSIA — 625
FRANCE AND THE REVOLUTION OF 1830 — 626
GREAT BRITAIN AND THE PATH OF REFORM — 627
The Reform Bill of 1832 • The Chartists • Repeal of the Corn Laws •
Trade Unionism

THE NEW INTERNATIONAL ORDER AND NATIONALISM — 628

THE PEACE KEEPERS — 628
TENSIONS IN THE OTTOMAN EMPIRE — 629
Greek Independence • Russian Expansion
THE RISE OF NATIONAL INDEPENDENCE MOVEMENTS — 629
The Emergence of Nationalism • Nationalism in Italy and Germany •
The Crisis of the Iberian Empires
IMPERIAL EXPANSION AND RESISTANCE — 632
The British Empire Ascendant • The French Conquest of Algeria •
Britain's Abolition of Slavery

CONCLUSION — 634
CHAPTER REVIEW — 635

19. Growing Pains: Social and Political Upheavals, 1845–1880   637

THE REVOLUTIONS OF 1848   639

  THE FRENCH SECOND REPUBLIC (1848–1852)   639

  THE SPREAD OF REVOLUTION   640
    Germany and Austria • Italy • Radicalism and *The Communist Manifesto*

  THE CONSERVATIVE REACTION   642
    The June Turning Point

  THE END GAME   644
    Austria and Prussia • Italy and France • Russia and Britain

BRITAIN'S ASCENDANCE   646

  THE VICTORIAN AGE (1837–1901)   646
    The Irish Famine • Indian War of Independence (1857–1858)

  DISRAELI AND THE POLITICS OF REFORM   648

POWER POLITICS   649

  CAVOUR, GARIBALDI, AND ITALIAN UNIFICATION   649

  BISMARCK AND THE FORMATION OF THE GERMAN NATION   651
    The Austro-Prussian War (1866) • The Crimean War (1853–1856)

  TURMOIL IN FRANCE   652
    The Franco-Prussian War (1870–1871) • German Unification •
    The Paris Commune and Third Republic

  RUSSIA UNDER ALEXANDER II   655
    Poland • Serfdom Abolished

  MAKING CONNECTIONS The Limits of Emancipation   656

ECONOMIC GROWTH AND SOCIAL CHANGE   657

  FORGING MORE UNIFIED NATIONS   657

  INDUSTRIAL GROWTH AND ITS IMPACT   658
    The Rise of Investment Banks • Continuing Urbanization

  CITIES AS A STAGE FOR THE MIDDLE CLASS   659
    Department Stores • The Crystal Palace

  UNDERSTANDING VISUAL CULTURE Vallotton's *Le Bon Marché*   661

CULTURE AND CLASS WARS   662

  CHALLENGES TO BOURGEOIS CULTURE   662
    Marxism and Anarchism • Tocqueville and Mill

  RETHINKING GENDER AND SEXUALITY   663

  DOCUMENTING EVERYDAY LIFE Women of the Paris Commune   664

  SCIENCE AND RELIGION   665
    Charles Darwin • Louis Pasteur • Religious Backlash

  NEW ARTISTIC DIRECTIONS   666
    Realism • New Forms of Romanticism • Antirealist Reaction

CONCLUSION   668
CHAPTER REVIEW   669

20. Apogee: Imperial Rivalry and Global Power, 1880–1910   671

ACCELERATING SOCIAL CHANGE   673

THE SECOND INDUSTRIAL REVOLUTION   673

An Increase in Scale • Technical Expertise • New Economic Opportunities for Women • Globalization • Changing Patterns of Migration • New Inventions

INCREASING RURAL DISTRESS   678

Population Pressure and Agricultural Production • Lower Birthrates in the West

INDUSTRIAL ARMAMENTS   679

LIBERALISM AT BAY   679

THE LIBERAL WORLDVIEW AND ITS CRITICS   679

FRANCE UNDER THE THIRD REPUBLIC   680

New Challenges from the Left and Right • French Anti-Semitism • The Dreyfus Affair

THE PERSISTENCE OF AUTOCRACY IN RUSSIA   682

The Russian Revolution of 1905

FIN DE SIÈCLE GERMANY AND AUSTRIA-HUNGARY   683

BRITAIN AND IRELAND   684

INCREASING SOCIAL PROTECTIONS   685

FIN DE SIÈCLE FEMINISM   685

DOCUMENTING EVERYDAY LIFE Feminism and Domestic Life   687

INTERNATIONAL RIVALRY AND THE NEW IMPERIALISM   686

THE SCRAMBLE FOR AFRICA   689

Partition of the Continent • The Boer War (1899–1902) • Violence against Africans • The "Civilizing" Mission

MAKING CONNECTIONS Discrimination against Indians in South Africa   693

THE GROWTH OF SETTLER COLONIES   694

EUROPE AND EAST ASIA   694

IMPERIALISM, RACE, AND CLASS   695

THE EFFECTS OF IMPERIALISM ON EUROPE   696

MODERNISM RISING   696

THE ROOTS OF ARTISTIC MODERNISM   697

Literature • Music • Painting

UNDERSTANDING VISUAL CULTURE Boccioni's *The City Rises*   701

PHILOSOPHY, SOCIAL SCIENCE, AND PSYCHIATRY   698

Durkheim and Weber • Sigmund Freud

THE PHYSICAL SCIENCES   700

The Curies • Albert Einstein

CITY LIFE **Fin de Siècle Vienna**

CONCLUSION   702
CHAPTER REVIEW   703

21. Things Blow Up: World War I and the Russian Revolution, 1910–1922   705

ORIGINS   706
   WAR PLANS   706
   GERMAN AMBITIONS   707
   NATIONALISM AND EMPIRE IN SOUTHEASTERN EUROPE   707
      Imperial Competition in the Balkans • Turmoil in Turkey
   ARMS RACES AND MILITARY MOBILIZATION   708
   MILITARISM AND THE MARCH TO WAR   709
      The Spark • The Move toward War • The Outbreak of War

INTO THE ABYSS (1914–1915)   711
   PUBLIC ATTITUDES   711
   EARLY GERMAN SUCCESSES   712
   BEGINNINGS OF THE STALEMATE   712
      Ypres • Trench Warfare
   ATTEMPTS AT BREAKTHROUGH   714

TOWARD TOTAL WAR (1915–1916)   715
   THE HOME FRONT   715
      Manpower • Economic Planning • War Finance • Propaganda • Women's Participation
   THE EXPANDING THEATER OF WAR   717
      The Eastern Front • The Gallipoli Campaign • The War at Sea
   NEW BATTLEFIELD WEAPONS AND OLD TACTICS   719
      The Continuing Bloodbath
   OPPOSITION TO THE WAR   721
      Life in the Trenches
   UNDERSTANDING VISUAL CULTURE Nash's *Over the Top* 722

BREAKING POINTS (1916–1917)   723
   THE BATTLE OF THE SOMME   723
   CENTRAL POWERS UNDER STRAIN   724
      American Intervention • Turmoil in the Middle East and Armenia
   RESISTANCE TO THE WAR   725
   MAKING CONNECTIONS Experiencing World War I   726
   LOSS OF HOPE   727

THE BEGINNING OF THE RUSSIAN REVOLUTION   727
   RUSSIA'S FEBRUARY REVOLUTION   727
   RUSSIA AND MARXISM   728
   LENIN AND THE BOLSHEVIKS   728
   THE OCTOBER REVOLUTION   729

THE WAR'S END	730

GERMANY'S SPRING OFFENSIVE   730

THE COLLAPSE OF THE CENTRAL POWERS   731

Wilson and Plans for Peace • Russia, Austria-Hungary, and the Threat of
Nationalism • Germany: Revolution and Surrender

THE RUSSIAN CIVIL WAR   733

The Hope and Promise of Communism • Birth of the USSR

DOCUMENTING EVERYDAY LIFE Peasant Criticism of the Bolsheviks   734

THE VERSAILLES PEACE SETTLEMENT   736

The Seeds of Future Conflict

CONCLUSION   738

CHAPTER REVIEW   739

22. Ideologies: The Triumph of Political Extremes, 1922–1940   741

A BLIGHTED RECOVERY   742

CONTINUING VIOLENCE AND INSTABILITY   743

POST-WAR GERMANY AND THE ORIGINS OF NAZISM   743

WEIMAR IN CRISIS   744

POST-WAR BRITAIN AND FRANCE   745

FRAGILE NEW STATES   745

Ethnic Tensions • Crumbling Democracies

THE SOVIET UNION AND RISE OF JOSEPH STALIN   747

MODERNIST CULTURE AND SOCIETY   748

MODERNIST CULTURE   748

Literature • Visual Arts • New Media • Architecture

UNDERSTANDING VISUAL CULTURE Grosz's The Pillars of Society   749

CITY LIFE   751

Paris and Berlin • Culture of Commemoration • Women in the City

A FRAGILE ORDER   754

ARMS CONTROL   754

ECONOMIC PLANNING   754

MAKING CONNECTIONS Communist and Fascist State Control   755

THE GREAT DEPRESSION   756

Faltering European Economies • Political and Cultural Effects of the Depression

THE COLONIAL EMPIRES   757

MIDDLE EASTERN MANDATES   758

NATIONALIST RESISTANCE   758

GANDHI AND INDIAN NATIONALISM   759

TOTALITARIAN DICTATORSHIPS   759

THE NAZI SEIZURE OF POWER   759

THE NAZI REGIME   760
Penetrating Society • Nazi Anti-Semitism

DOCUMENTING EVERYDAY LIFE German Racial Education   762

STALINISM: THE FIRST FIVE-YEAR PLAN   763
Building a New Society • Collectivization of Agriculture • Famine • The Great Terror

THE COMING OF WORLD WAR II   766

HITLER'S EARLY MOVES   766
Alliances • Rearmament

THE SPANISH CIVIL WAR   767

GERMAN AGGRESSION: AUSTRIA AND CZECHOSLOVAKIA   768
The Czech Crisis • Munich

PREPARING FOR WAR   769
Arms Race • The Nazi-Soviet Pact

INVASION OF POLAND   770

JAPANESE AGGRESSION   771

THE PHONY WAR   771

CONCLUSION   772
CHAPTER REVIEW   773

23. The Abyss: World War II and the Holocaust, 1940–1945   775

FROM BLITZKRIEG TO THE BATTLE OF BRITAIN   776

THE GERMAN OFFENSIVES IN SCANDINAVIA AND WESTERN EUROPE   776

THE FALL OF FRANCE   777

BRITAIN ISOLATED   777

THE BATTLE OF BRITAIN   779

OCCUPIED EUROPE   780

WESTERN EUROPE UNDER NAZI OCCUPATION   780
Vichy France

OCCUPIED POLAND AND THE JEWS   781

OCCUPATION OF EASTERN AND SOUTHERN EUROPE   782

BARBAROSSA   782

HITLER'S DECISION TO ATTACK THE SOVIET UNION   782

SOVIET CATASTROPHE   783

THE TURN TO MASS MURDER   783

TOTAL MOBILIZATION	784
THE STRUGGLES FOR LENINGRAD AND MOSCOW	785

CRUCIAL POINTS · 785

PEARL HARBOR AND THE GLOBAL WAR	786
A War of Empires	
NORTH AFRICA AND THE QUESTION OF A SECOND FRONT	788
Tensions in the Alliance	
STALINGRAD	788
MAKING CONNECTIONS Hunger on the Eastern Front	790
MIDWAY AND THE TURN IN THE PACIFIC	791

HOLOCAUST · 791

PLANNING GENOCIDE	791
THE DEATH CAMPS	792
DOCUMENTING EVERYDAY LIFE Deportation from the Lodz Ghetto	793

TOTAL WAR · 794

THE ALLIED ADVANTAGE	794
THE BOMBING CAMPAIGN	795
THE EASTERN FRONT	795
THE INVASION OF ITALY	796

HOME FRONTS · 796

WARTIME BRITAIN, GERMANY, AND THE USSR	796
UNDERSTANDING VISUAL CULTURE Women of Britain Come into the Factories	797
RESISTANCE MOVEMENTS	798

LIBERATION · 799

THE BEGINNING OF THE END	799
Building an Atomic Bomb • Planning a Cross-Channel Invasion	
D-DAY AND THE INVASION OF FRANCE	799
LIBERATION AND POWER STRUGGLES	800

A VIOLENT CONCLUSION · 801

BORDERS AND REFUGEES	802
THE GERMAN SURRENDER AND THE LIBERATION OF THE CAMPS	802
THE WAR IN ASIA AND THE POTSDAM CONFERENCE	804
UNPARALLELED VIOLENCE	805
UNDERSTANDING THE HOLOCAUST	805

CONCLUSION	806
CHAPTER REVIEW	807

24. Recovery and Cold War: Rebuilding a Divided Continent, 1945–1973

809

THE AFTERMATH OF WAR   810
  REFUGEES   810
  RECKONING WITH WAR CRIMES   811

REBUILDING   812
  THE ROLE OF THE STATE   812
    Industry over Consumers • The Rise of the Welfare State
  BRETTON WOODS AND THE MARSHALL PLAN   813

COLD WAR   814
  TENSIONS BETWEEN THE UNITED STATES AND THE SOVIET UNION   814
  THE SOVIETIZATION OF EASTERN EUROPE   815
    Yugoslavia and Poland • Western Reactions
  BERLIN   816
  A DIVIDED CONTINENT IN A DIVIDED WORLD   817

DECOLONIZATION: THE FIRST STEPS   818
  THE SUN SETS ON THE BRITISH EMPIRE   818
  THE DUTCH EMPIRE   819
  THE FRENCH EMPIRE AND THE FRENCH UNION   821

POST-WAR PROSPERITY   821
  STRUCTURAL CHANGE   821
  THE THIRTY GLORIOUS YEARS   822
  A CONSUMER REVOLUTION IN THE WEST   822
  NEW POSSIBILITIES FOR WOMEN   823
  DOCUMENTING EVERYDAY LIFE Women's Independence in West Germany   824
  COUNTRYSIDE AND CITY   825
  POPULATIONS ON THE MOVE   826
    Europeans • Guest Workers

POLITICAL STABILIZATION   826
  DESTALINIZATION IN THE EAST   826
  EASTERN BLOC REVOLTS   827
    East Germany and Poland • Hungary
  UNDERSTANDING VISUAL CULTURE "The Path from Earth to the Stars"   828
  WESTERN EUROPEAN STABILITY   829
  FIRST STEPS TOWARD EUROPEAN UNITY   829
  CULTURAL FERMENT   830

MAKING CONNECTIONS Europe's Others Write Back   831

DECOLONIZATION AND POLITICAL CHANGE   832

THE SUEZ CRISIS OF 1956   832

ALGERIA   832
The War for Independence • Algeria and the Fall of the French Fourth Republic

THE SCRAMBLE OUT OF AFRICA   833

SHIFTING COLD WAR DYNAMICS   834

COLD WAR CRISES   834

CITY LIFE Cold War Berlin

CHALLENGES TO COLD WAR IDEOLOGIES   836

THE DECADE OF YOUTH REVOLT   836

POST-INDUSTRIAL SOCIETY   837

THE DECLINE OF RELIGIOUS OBSERVANCE   837

YOUTH CULTURE   838

STUDENT REBELLIONS: 1968   838

SPAIN AND NORTHERN IRELAND   839

POLAND AND CZECHOSLOVAKIA   840

TOWARD NEW FORMS OF LIBERATION   841

CONCLUSION   841
CHAPTER REVIEW   843

25. Reunion: European Unification and the End of the Cold War, 1973–1999   845

SEASONS OF DISCONTENT   846

COUPS AND TERRORISM   846

THE OIL SHOCK OF 1973–1974   847

WELFARE STATES UNDER PRESSURE   847

SOUTHERN EUROPE'S BUMPY ROAD TO DEMOCRACY   848

SHIFTS IN THE POST-WAR SOCIAL CONSENSUS   849

MARGARET THATCHER'S ATTACK ON THE WELFARE STATE   849

IDEOLOGICAL SHIFTS   850
Communism in Decline

FRANCE'S "PARENTHESIS IN THE HISTORY OF SOCIALISM"   850

CULTURAL OPENINGS   851
The Arts

UNDERSTANDING VISUAL CULTURE Jahn's Messerturm   852
    Gender and Sexuality

EXTERNAL AND INTERNAL PRESSURES ON THE EASTERN BLOC   853

RONALD REAGAN AND THE EUROPEAN PEACE MOVEMENT   853

DISSIDENT MOVEMENTS IN THE EAST   854

MAKING CONNECTIONS The Individual against the State   855

"SOLIDARITY" IN POLAND   856

CRACKS IN THE EASTERN BLOC   856

DOCUMENTING EVERYDAY LIFE The Power of Lipstick   857

THE COLLAPSE OF COMMUNISM   858

NEW SOVIET LEADERSHIP: MIKHAIL GORBACHEV   858

THE END OF COMMUNISM IN POLAND AND HUNGARY   860

EAST GERMANY AND THE FALL OF THE BERLIN WALL   861

CZECHOSLOVAKIA, ROMANIA, AND BULGARIA   861

THE "THIRD WAY" REJECTED   862

THE REUNIFICATION OF GERMANY   862

THE END OF THE SOVIET EMPIRE   863

NATIONALIST CHALLENGES   863
    Nationalism in Perspective • Russian Nationalism

THE CRISIS OF 1990–1991   864

"RETURNING TO EUROPE"   865

THE NEW BALKAN WARS   867

YUGOSLAVIA'S COLLAPSE   867

THE WARS IN BOSNIA-HERZEGOVINA AND KOSOVO   868

CHECHNYA   869

CONNECTIONS   870

THE CHALLENGE OF ECONOMIC GLOBALIZATION   870

IMMIGRATION AND RIGHT-WING POLITICS   871

TOWARD EUROPEAN UNION   871

ECONOMIC CONNECTIONS   872

THE TRANSITION TO CAPITALISM IN THE FORMER EASTERN BLOC   873

RUSSIA'S DECADE OF DISRUPTION   873

CONCLUSION   874
CHAPTER REVIEW   875

26. Under Pressure: Europe's Uncertain Present, Since 2000   877

TERRORISM AND WAR   879

   SEPTEMBER 11 AND ITS AFTERMATH   879

   THE IRAQ WAR   880

   THE RESPONSE OF THE RIGHT   880

EUROPEAN CONSTRUCTION AND ITS DISCONTENTS   881

   THE EU AND NATO   881

   POLITICAL INTEGRATION   882

   SOCIAL AND CULTURAL CHANGE   883

   MAKING CONNECTIONS A Crisis in Unity   885

THE GREAT RECESSION AND THE EUROZONE CRISIS   884

   TENSIONS WITHIN THE EUROZONE   884

   THE CRISIS IN GREECE   886

CONFLICT IN THE FORMER SOVIET UNION   886

   PUTIN'S RUSSIA   887

   CRISIS IN UKRAINE   888

     The Crimean Peninsula • Eastern Ukraine

A RISING ILLIBERALISM   889

   HUNGARY AND POLAND   889

   WESTERN EUROPE   890

     France • Brexit

   UNDERSTANDING VISUAL CULTURE Erasing Britain from Europe   891

     Spain • Scotland

FROM FRICTION TO VIOLENCE: EUROPE AND ISLAM   893

   CULTURAL CONFLICT   893

   THE ISLAMIC STATE AND TERRORISM   893

   THE REFUGEE CRISIS   894

   DOCUMENTING EVERYDAY LIFE A Refugee's Perilous Journey   895

   A CENTRIST RESPONSE   896

CONCLUSION: The Present Moment in Historical Perspective   897

CHAPTER REVIEW   899

FURTHER READING   A1

GLOSSARY   A3

TEXT CREDITS   A15

PHOTO CREDITS   A17

INDEX   A20

MAPS

CHAPTER 10

Italian States at the Treaty of Lodi, 1454 329
European Monarchies, 1492 331
Early Italian Wars, 1494–1517 338
Portuguese Expeditions, 1415–1500 347
Portuguese Slave Trade, 1444–1500 348
The Spread of Printing, 1455–1500 350
European Explorations to the Western Hemisphere,
    1492–1550 353
Renaissance Florence, ca. 1500 363

CHAPTER 11

The Reformation Movement, 1521–1529 379
The Peasants' War, 1524–1525 384
Habsburg Lands, ca. 1556 392
Europe After the Peace of Augsburg 393
The Dutch Revolt and the French Religious Wars,
    1562–1598 400

CHAPTER 12

The Americas and the Triangle Trade, ca. 1640 416
Habsburg Possessions in the Holy Roman Empire,
    ca. 1600 420
The Thirty Years' War, 1618–1648 427

CHAPTER 13

The British Civil Wars, 1641–1645 445
Ukraine, 1648–1667 447
The Peace of Westphalia, 1648 457
Brandenburg-Prussia, 1618–1680 459
Louis XIV's Territorial Claims, 1662–1681 463
Golden Age Amsterdam 467

CHAPTER 14

The Russian Empire, 1689–1725 481
Europe, 1683–1721 487
The Great Northern War, 1700–1721 488
The Atlantic World, 1680–1740 490

CHAPTER 15

European Ports of Origin of the Atlantic Slave Trade,
    1642–1807 509
The War of the Austrian Succession, 1740–1748 511
The Seven Years' War and Associated Hostilities,
    1754–1763 513
The First Partition of Poland, 1772 514

CHAPTER 16

Counterrevolutionary Rebellion in France, 1793 560
Second and Third Partitions of Poland, 1793–1795 563
Revolutionary Wars, 1791–1799 565
Napoleon's Egyptian Campaign, 1798–1799 566

CHAPTER 17

Napoleon's Empire, 1812 584
Congress of Vienna, 1815 594
The Hundred Days, 1815 595

CHAPTER 18

Industrialization in Britain, 1800–1850. 604

Industrialization in Europe, 1800–1850 610

Middle-Class London, ca. 1850 613

Latin American Nations, 1800–1830. 631

British Expansion in Asia, 1843 632

CHAPTER 19

The Revolutions of 1848 641

British India, 1857–1880. 647

Unification of Italy, 1859–1870. 650

The Crimean War, 1853–1856. 652

Unification of Germany, 1862–1871 654

Europe in 1878. 658

CHAPTER 20

The Second Industrial Revolution, 1880–1914 674

Emigration from Europe, 1880–1910 677

Russia, 1910 682

European Imperialism, ca. 1800. 688

The Partition of Africa, 1880–1912 690

Fin de Siècle Vienna 695

CHAPTER 21

The Balkans, 1913 708

The Schlieffen Plan. 711

World War I, 1914–1916. 713

World War I, 1917–1918. 731

The Russian Civil War, 1918–1921 733

Europe, the Middle East, and Africa after
    World War I, 1922. 737

CHAPTER 22

National Minorities in Eastern Europe, 1920s 746

Middle Eastern Mandates, 1920s. 758

The Spanish Civil War, 1936–1939. 767

Aggression in Europe, 1936–1939. 771

CHAPTER 23

World War II in Europe and North Africa 778

World War II in the Pacific 786

The Holocaust 791

Europe at the End of World War II, 1945. 803

CHAPTER 24

European Refugees, 1945–1950. 811

Cold War Europe, 1950s 815

Decolonization in Asia 819

Decolonization in Africa 820

Cold War Berlin. 835

CHAPTER 25

Collapse of the Eastern Bloc, 1989–1990 860

The Former Soviet Union, 1992. 866

Yugoslavia, 1988–2000. 868

War in the Caucasus, 1998–1999. 870

The European Union, 1995 872

CHAPTER 26

Ukraine and Crimea, 2014–2017 889

The European Union, 2017 892

Refugee Crisis, ca. 2016. 897

PRIMARY-SOURCE FEATURES

CHAPTER 10

Making Connections Poverty and the State: Cahier of the Estates General, "The Plight of the French Poor," and Juan Luis Vives, "Concerning the Relief of the Poor"

Documenting Everyday Life Lorenzo Ghiberti's Declaration in the *Catasto* of 1427

Understanding Visual Culture Ghirlandaio's *Portrait of a Lady*

CITY LIFE Renaissance Florence

CHAPTER 11

Making Connections Martin Luther and the Peasants' War: Christoph Schappeler and Sebastian Lotzer, *Twelve Articles of the Peasants*, and Martin Luther, *Admonition to Peace*

Documenting Everyday Life Christmas in St. Andrews

Understanding Visual Culture De Witte's *The Interior of the Oude Kerk*

CHAPTER 12

Making Connections Galileo and the Inquisition: Galileo, from letter to the Grand Duchess Christina and The Inquisition, sentence against Galileo

Documenting Everyday Life The Sack of Magdeburg

Understanding Visual Culture Bruegel the Elder's *Hunters in the Snow*

CHAPTER 13

Making Connections Political Equality after the British Civil Wars: Gerrard Winstanley, from *The True Levellers Standard Advanced* and Anonymous, "The Protecting Brewer"

Documenting Everyday Life Gender Roles in Seventeenth-Century England: Margaret Cavendish, from *The World's Olio*

Understanding Visual Culture Rembrandt's *The Anatomy Lesson of Dr. Nicolaes Tulp*

CITY LIFE Golden Age Amsterdam

CHAPTER 14

Making Connections The Limits of Liberty: English Bill of Rights and The Black Code

Documenting Everyday Life Childhood in Rural France: from the Memoirs of Valentin Jamerey-Duval

Understanding Visual Culture Mignard's *Portrait of Louise de Kérouaille, Duchess of Portsmouth*

CHAPTER 15

Making Connections Enlightenment Thinkers and Progress: Marquis de Condorcet, *Sketch for a Historical Picture of the Progress of the Human Mind* and Louis-Sébastien Mercier, from *L'An 2440*

Documenting Everyday Life Coffeehouses and Newspapers in the Age of Enlightenment: from the journals of César de Saussure

Understanding Visual Culture Lemonnier's *An Evening with Madame Geoffrin*

CHAPTER 16

Making Connections Hopes and Fears of the French Revolution: The People of Marseilles, "Farewell to the Year 1790" and Edmund Burke, from *Reflections on the Revolution in France*

Documenting Everyday Life Bread Riots in Paris: from *Commissaire's* report on events of February 24, 25, 26, 1793

Understanding Visual Culture David's *The Tennis Court Oath*

CHAPTER 17

Making Connections European Attitudes toward Napoleon: William Cobbett, from the *Political Register*, January 16, 1814 and Madame de Rémusat, from *Memoirs*

Documenting Everyday Life The Retreat from Russia: from Adrien Bourgogne, *Memoirs of Sergeant Bourgogne, 1812–1813*

Understanding Visual Culture *The Colossus*

CHAPTER 18

Making Connections Industrial Promise and Social Misery: Andrew Ure, from *The Philosophy of Manufactures* and Friedrich Engels, from *The Condition of the Working Class in England*

Documenting Everyday Life A Girl's Life in the Mines: Patience Kershaw, *Testimony before the Parliamentary Committee on Mines, Parliamentary Papers*

Understanding Visual Culture Turner's *Rain, Steam and Speed—The Great Western Railway*

CITY LIFE Middle-Class London, ca. 1850

CHAPTER 19

Making Connections The Limits of Emancipation: Alexander II's Decree Emancipating the Serfs and Petition from Peasants in Podosinovka to Alexander II

Documenting Everyday Life Women of the Paris Commune

Understanding Visual Culture Vallotton's *Le Bon Marché*

CHAPTER 20

Making Connections Discrimination against Indians in South Africa: Henry Campbell, letter *Re* British Indians in Transvaal and Gandhi, Open Letter on Franchise Law

Documenting Everyday Life Feminism and Domestic Life: Millicent Garrett Fawcett, from "Home and Politics"

Understanding Visual Culture Boccioni's *The City Rises*

CITY LIFE **Fin de Siècle Vienna**

CHAPTER 21

Making Connections Experiencing World War I: Rupert Brooke, War Sonnets and Sidney Harold Baker, "Letter to his brother"

Documenting Everyday Life Peasant Criticism of the Bolsheviks: "Letter from a Peasant to the Bolshevik Leaders"

Understanding Visual Culture Nash's *Over the Top*

CHAPTER 22

Making Connections Communist and Fascist State Control: Nikolai Bukharin and Evgenii Preobrazhensky, from *The ABC of Communism* and Benito Mussolini and Giovanni Gentile, from "The Doctrine of Fascism"

Documenting Everyday Life German Racial Education: Melita Maschmann, from *Account Rendered: A Dossier on my Former Self*

Understanding Visual Culture Grosz's *The Pillars of Society*

CHAPTER 23

Making Connections Hunger on the Eastern Front: Willy Peter Reese, from *A Stranger to Myself* and Vasily Grossman, from *Life and Fate*

Documenting Everyday Life Deportation from the Lodz Ghetto: Josef Zelkowicz, from *In Those Terrible Days: Writings from the Lodz Ghetto*

Understanding Visual Culture *Women of Britain Come into the Factories*

CHAPTER 24

Making Connections Europe's Others Write Back: Simone de Beauvoir, from *The Second Sex* and Aimé Césaire, from "Discourse on Colonialism"

Documenting Everyday Life Women's Independence in West Germany: Note from a woman from an industrial region, in Walther von Hollander, "Women's Issues—Women's Worries," from *German History in Documents and Images*

Understanding Visual Culture "The Path from Earth to the Stars"

CITY LIFE **Cold War Berlin**

CHAPTER 25

Making Connections The Individual against the State: Václav Havel, from "The Power of the Powerless" and Margaret Thatcher, from "Speech in Finchley"

Documenting Everyday Life The Power of Lipstick, from Slavenka Drakulić, *How We Survived Communism and Even Laughed*

Understanding Visual Culture Jahn's Messerturm

CHAPTER 26

Making Connections A Crisis in Unity: Angela Merkel, from "Speech at the ceremony commemorating the 100th anniversary of the battle of Verdun, 5/29/16" and Nigel Farage, from "Speech to the European Parliament, 6/28/16"

Documenting Everyday Life A Refugee's Perilous Journey, from UNHCR Stories, "Hosein's Story, Greece"

Understanding Visual Culture Erasing Britain from Europe

The story of the West is an epic. This might seem strange to say, because there has never been a single, unified, easily defined place called "the West." Even the Roman Empire at its height did not control all of the territories that have come to form part of the West, and its hegemony lasted only a few centuries. The boundaries of the West have never been fixed or agreed upon. Moreover, whether in imperial Rome or Europe today, these borders have always been porous. People, goods, and ideas have constantly flowed across them in both directions, sometimes peacefully and often violently. What we today call "the West" is in significant measure a product of this unending process of exchange.

Even so, there is something we can call "the West." It is a web of societies, centered in Europe and its extensions, loosely linked by shared and interacting histories. These histories incorporate debts to other societies around the world and the results of conflicts both internal and global. At their core are ideas and institutions—cultural, political, social, and economic—that have outlasted the individual

societies that gave them birth and been developed and transformed to meet new needs. The story of the West is not one of repeated triumph or unbroken progress. It is not a story of a single tradition. But it is a story of epic proportions. It has been a story of hatred and intolerance, but also one of men and women fighting hatred and intolerance, and finding ways to rise above them. It has been a story of people who rejected the earth for heaven, and of people who wanted to build heaven on earth. It has been a story of breathtaking idealism and breathtaking cruelty, of innovation and competition, creation and destruction, new habits of thought, and of centuries-long conversations that we call "traditions."

The story is full of dramatic moments: moments when individuals and movements challenged established authorities and customs, when reformers transformed legal codes and religious practices, and when revolutionaries overturned governments. It is a story of individuals of titanic achievement: people who have given their names to ways of thinking and arguing, understanding the universe, and building and maintaining states. It is a story of blinding new insights into what justice really means, and one of blindness to the exploitation and persecution of others.

But it has also been a story of daily life: of men and women whose names we usually do not know who struggled to survive and raise children under the shadows of hunger and illness, war and displacement. It is the story of how daily life remained the same in many ways for thousands of years: of how most people lived close to the soil, trying to scratch out sustenance from it with their own muscle power and that of animals, according to the rhythm of the seasons. But it is also a story of how, starting in the seventeenth and eighteenth centuries, individuals and groups slowly developed new ways of wringing more food from the land—and how, by doing so, they changed the world.

Last, but by no means least, it is a story about how, in the last centuries, virtually everything about daily life changed, often at dizzying speed: factories rose, cities grew to sizes never seen before, gender roles were challenged and transformed, religion lost its commanding place in society, governments became newly pervasive, education spread, new technologies emerged, new media flourished, and vast new forms of wealth were created. It is a story of how modern nation-states were forged and of how populations migrated into and out of Europe.

The story was not the work of Europeans alone. Indeed, the civilization that took shape in Europe has arguably been more dependent than any other on what it could borrow, beg, or steal from the rest of the world. For much of its history—amid the competing city-states of ancient Greece and the fierce rivalries of the western Middle Ages and Renaissance—the West has been smaller, poorer in resources, more politically divided, and less sophisticated than rival civilizations elsewhere in the world. Only with the capture of the immense resources of the Americas in the early modern period, and the harnessing of fossil fuels during the Industrial Revolution, did the natural resources that Europe possessed make themselves fully felt in the worldwide balance of power. Yet precisely as a result of the West's relative poverty and political fragmentation, Western politicians and thinkers, soldiers and tinkerers were driven constantly to innovate with the resources they had and with the ideas and techniques they borrowed from other cultures. Writing came to the West from the Near East—from the Phoenicians, a Semitic people who lived in Palestine and the Fertile Crescent. So did the idea of setting down in writing massive works that described the adventures of humans and the hierarchies of gods. But the two Greek epics traditionally ascribed to the poet Homer are distinctively different from the great Near Eastern epic *The Song of Gilgamesh*, in the ways that they portray relations between gods and humans and in the voices that they give to their own societies.

Many elements of this story will seem strange to young people who live in the West today. The physical and mental worlds of an ancient Greek soldier, a medieval nun, or an African slave in an early-modern European colony were all enormously distant from those of today's students. Indeed, the scale of change in every area of life in modern times—political, economic, cultural, religious, technological—can easily lead to the conclusion that an unbridgeable gulf separates the more distant past from the present. Can a cohesive story encompass present-day Europeans, the poorest of whom can generally count on living to old age in conditions of relative physical comfort, and their predecessors of whom half did not live beyond adolescence, with the remainder at constant risk of death from infectious disease and possibly starvation, not to mention chronic, debilitating pain? Is it possible to draw connections between the Europeans of today, almost entirely literate and able instantly to summon vast libraries of text, image, and sound on devices they carry in their pockets, and predecessors who learned about the world principally from oral tradition, religious authority, and travel limited by the speed of wind, animals, or their own legs?

We think it is possible. If you live in the West today, and particularly if you are a student, this story is your story. It is not by any means the entirety of your story, but it is a critical part of it, and for two reasons. First, it is the story of how significant parts of your world came into being. The political systems that exist in the West today, nearly all of which claim the mantle of democracy, trace their origins back to the ancient Greek world in which the word "democracy" itself was invented. They are part of a tradition—a long process of evolution, debate, and conflict—in which the meaning of democracy has changed radically to include new conceptions of rights, political representation, civic and social equality, and a separation between the realms of politics and religion. This long process did not take place solely in the West, but it was centered there. It was also shaped by forms of political competition and fragmentation that have been characteristic of the West throughout most of its history and that distinguish the West from many other historical regions of the world.

Similarly, the capitalist system that most of the West lives under today has roots that reach far back: to the trading cities that developed in the ancient world, to patterns of commerce and banking that developed in medieval Europe, and to ideas about the organization of societies and the operations of markets that were formulated during the European Renaissance and Enlightenment. This system depended, from the start, on currents of trade, exploration, and exploitation and conquest that stretched far beyond the West, and it has subsequently developed strongly on a global scale. But at its core this system was centered in the West.

More broadly, the very ways in which we learn to read, think critically, devise arguments, innovate, and express ourselves creatively derive in significant measure from millennia-long conversations that began in the ancient Near East, were carried on throughout the classical Mediterranean world, and thence into other parts of Europe and the world. These conversations were rarely harmonious. Their basic assumptions were challenged, in fundamental ways, by new voices from both within and without. Their subjects and forms changed repeatedly. But as this book will show, important continuities can still be traced within these conversations.

And this is the second reason why the story of the West is your story. The habits and practices of learning, critical thinking, and effective expression that are necessary for citizens of contemporary Western industrial democracies are intimately related to the complex history that produced them.

History does not just help us better understand the world around us; it helps us function more effectively in it. This lesson, and this awareness, are themselves part of the Western story, and they lie at the heart of one of the most important Western traditions: the tradition of higher learning that is today carried on in colleges and universities. Ancient Romans trained for positions within their own society by learning Greek and studying important works of Greek philosophy and literature. During the Renaissance, so-called humanists sought to revive ancient Greek and Roman learning not just for the sake of learning, but in order to train young men as civil servants and diplomats, lawyers, and doctors. These systems of education could function as forms of social discrimination, excluding from desirable careers those who lacked the means to study Latin and Greek—a category that included virtually all women. But learning about Western history and traditions can also serve as a means of social inclusion, drawing diverse student populations into conversation with peers from all corners of their own society, with their own predecessors from centuries past, and with some of the most brilliant and creative minds the world has known.

As historians who have both taught Western history for decades, we recognize that the story of the West is complex and often challenging for introductory students. It ranges across the fields of politics, society, economics, war, religion, philosophy, science, culture, and much else. It is a story marked by discontinuities such as the sharp differences among different regions of the West, and by the many different forms of exchange and contact between the West and other areas of the globe. But precisely because of these complexities, we believe in the importance of integrating the history with strong narrative threads and telling the story in as cogent, engaging, and fluid a manner as possible.

We have therefore chosen to proceed in as close to a strictly chronological manner as possible, presenting subjects like the development of Christianity or the scientific revolution as they unfolded alongside other contemporary events, rather than cordoning them off into separate chapters. We believe it is important for the chronology of events to be clear and visible for beginning students. We wish also to show students the mutual interplay over time of politics and society, ideas, beliefs, and material conditions. These many overlapping layers of history should be understood together, developing over time, rather than as disconnected strands of the story. We have done our best to achieve the right balance in attending to these many dimensions of history. We have also tried to incorporate the best new scholarship in these fields along with the insights of previous generations of scholars.

The book covers as broad a sweep of history as is practical in two volumes designed for a year-long survey course. Volume One, written primarily by Anthony Grafton, begins with a Prologue on prehistory and takes the story from the ancient Near East up through the Reformation.

Volume Two, written primarily by David Bell, begins with the Renaissance and continues to the present day. Both volumes range in scope far beyond Europe. Volume One emphasizes the origins of the Western story in the Middle East and gives due attention to the societies around the Mediterranean basin during antiquity and the Middle Ages, including the rise, expansion, and cultural flourishing of Islam. It also deals with patterns of global exchange and the expansion of European political power that began in the fifteenth century. Volume Two centers its narrative on Europe and its extensions, focusing on the continuing dynamics of disorder and order, cohesion and fragmentation, as they played out in politics, culture, and society over the modern period.

THE WEST comes equipped with a full complement of illustrations (more than 500), newly drawn maps (more than 130), and useful pedagogical features described in the coming pages. But at the core of history is narrative, and we hope that *THE WEST* demonstrates our belief that clear, engaging prose remains the most effective means of introducing students to history.

Anthony Grafton
David A. Bell

ACKNOWLEDGMENTS

Heartfelt thanks to Steve Forman, our eagle-eyed and ever cheerful editor, and to his colleagues at W.W. Norton, who inspired me, prodded me, and turned sometimes inchoate drafts into a finished book; to my colleagues at Princeton, who have taught me so much about history; and, above all, to the students who have taken History 211. Many of the tales told here were first spun for them, and their lively responses, in class and out, to lectures, readings, and expeditions to the Rare Book Room have given me both pleasure and enlightenment over the years. It is a pleasure to join David Bell in dedicating this book to our students.
Anthony Grafton

Many thanks to all the colleagues at Johns Hopkins and Princeton who helped me over the years with suggestions and comments. I am grateful to the terrific staff at W.W. Norton, and especially our wonderful editor, Steve Forman, for everything they have done to bring this project to fruition. As always, my deepest gratitude to my wife, Donna Farber, and to my children, Elana and Joseph Bell, for their love and support. One of the greatest joys of the profession I am in comes in the moments of one's students' discoveries, watching them see into the past in a new way. It is in memory of these moments, and in gratitude to those who have passed through my classrooms, that I am delighted to join Anthony Grafton in dedicating this book to our students.
David A. Bell

THE WEST is a collective work in many respects, most pleasurably in its reflection of the commitment we share with many of our colleagues to the introductory course and its students. We would like to thank the following scholars for reading and commenting on our draft chapters. We have benefitted enormously from their criticisms and suggestions.

Megan Armstrong, McMaster University
Kenneth Bartlett, University of Toronto
Jean Berger, University of Wisconsin at Fox Valley
Hilary Bernstein, University of California, Santa Barbara
Nick Bomba, Northern Virginia Community College
Curtis V. Bostick, Southern Utah University
Jonathyne Briggs, Indiana University Northwest
Tobias Brinkmann, Pennsylvania State University
Bill Bulman, Lehigh University
Jeremy Caradonna, University of Victoria
Shawn Clybor, Utah State University
Susan Cogan, Utah State University
William Connell, Seton Hall University
Alix Cooper, State University of New York at Stony Brook
Mairi Cowan, University of Toronto at Mississauga
Andrew Daily, University of Memphis
Leah DeVun, Rutgers University
David Dorondo, Western Carolina University

Mary Duarte, Cardinal Stritch University

Bonnie Effros, University of Florida

John Eglin, University of Montana

Kyle Fingerson, University of Wisconsin, Rock County

Christopher Frank, University of Manitoba

Andrew Gallia, University of Minnesota

Phil Haberkern, Boston University

Amanda E. Herbert, Christopher Newport University

Rowena Hernández-Múzquiz, Broward College

Laura Hutchings, University of Utah

Bruce Janacek, North Central College

Erik Johnsen, Portland Community College

Donald Johnson, University of North Carolina at Wilmington

Edward Kolla, Georgetown University in Qatar

Jodie Kreider, Colorado State University

Greta Kroeker, University of Waterloo

Matthew Laubacher, Ashford University

Anne E. Lester, University of Colorado, Boulder

Yan Mann, Arizona State University

Benjamin Marschke, Humboldt State University

Bruce McCord, Aiken Technical College

Jeri McIntosh, University of Tennessee, Knoxville

Murat Menguc, Seton Hall University

John Patrick Montaño, University of Delaware

Rosemary Moore, University of Iowa

Seán Farrell Moran, Oakland University

George Munro, Virginia Commonwealth University

William Myers, University of Alaska, Anchorage

Lawrence Okamura, University of Missouri

Katrina Olds, University of San Francisco

John Powers, Virginia Commonwealth University

Jennifer Purcell, Saint Michael's College

Andrew Reed, Arizona State University

Walter Roberts, University of North Texas

Nicholas L. Rummell, Trident Technical College

Emily Rutherford, Columbia University

Linda B. Scherr, Middlesex County College

Edward Schoolman, University of Nevada, Reno

Colleen Shaughnessy Zeena, Endicott College

Linda Smith, University of Alabama at Birmingham

Ginger Smoak, University of Utah

John Swanson, University of Tennessee at Chattanooga

Emily Sohmer Tai, Queensborough Community College, CUNY

Paul Teverow, Missouri Southern State University

Corinna Treitel, Washington University in St. Louis

Liana Vardi, State University of New York at Buffalo

Corinne Wieben, University of Northern Colorado

PEDAGOGY AND FEATURES

The West offers an array of pedagogical features to guide students through the chapters and enrich their understanding of people and events.

All chapters open with a list of **focus questions** that correspond to the major section headings in the chapter. These questions, which appear also in the relevant running heads at the tops of pages, are meant to keep students alert to the key developments in each section. All chapters also open with a **chronology** of major events and an **immersive narrative vignette** to draw students into the reading. The chapters end with a review page that includes **study questions**, a list of the **key terms** (with page references) that appear in bold in the chapter, and a set of **Core Objectives**—key points that students should take away from the chapter. These Core Objectives are reinforced in the exercises provided in the online Student Site for *The West*. The key terms are all defined in the Glossary located in the Appendix, which also includes the authors' lists of **Further Reading** for each chapter.

Since one of the most important course goals in the introductory survey is to train students in the use of primary sources, each chapter also includes three **primary-source features** intended to introduce students to different types of documents and help build

their critical-thinking skills. The first of these features, **Making Connections**, consists of paired primary documents that connect to each other and the text itself. Brief headnotes and questions focus students on the issues to consider. The **Documenting Everyday Life** feature, comprising a source, a headnote, and questions, helps students understand an aspect of the everyday life of the period. The **Understanding Visual Culture** feature presents an image as a primary source to be examined critically by students.

The West also presents an innovative feature entitled **City Life**, intended to enhance the text's theme of cultural change and give students further work in developing history skills. We have eight of these full-page features in the text, four in Volume I and four in the non-overlap chapters of Volume Two. Each one focuses on a city at a critical moment, from Imperial Rome and Renaissance Florence to fin de siècle Vienna and Cold War Berlin. Through source quotations, images, a central map, and short questions that connect to text discussions, the features ask students to reflect on distinctive aspects of life in the cities, and to reach historical conclusions based on the feature sources. The digital resources connected to the City Life features further enhance student history skills.

Understanding Visual Culture

City Life

DIGITAL RESOURCES FOR STUDENTS AND INSTRUCTORS

W. W. Norton offers a robust digital package to support teaching and learning with *The West*. These resources are designed to make students more effective textbook readers and to develop their critical thinking and history skills.

RESOURCES FOR STUDENTS

Resources are available at digital.wwnorton.com/thewestv2 with the access card at the front of this text.

Norton InQuizitive for History

Norton InQuizitive for history is an adaptive quizzing tool that improves students' understanding of the themes and objectives from each chapter, while honing their critical analysis skills with primary-source, image, and map analysis questions. Students receive personalized quiz questions with detailed, guiding feedback on the topics in which they need the most help, while the engaging, gamelike elements motivate them as they learn. InQuizitive for *The West* was developed by Christopher Brooks, Portland Community College.

History Skills Tutorials

The History Skills Tutorials feature three modules—Images, Documents, and Maps—to support students' development of the key skills for the history course. These tutorials feature videos of the authors modeling the analysis process, followed by interactive questions that will challenge students to apply what they have learned.

Student Site

The free and easy-to-use online Student Site offers additional resources for students to use outside of class. Resources include interactive iMaps from each chapter, author videos, and a comprehensive Online Reader featuring more than 300 additional primary-source documents and images.

Ebook

Free and included with new copies of the text, **the Norton Ebook Reader** provides an enhanced reading experience that works on all computers and mobile devices. Features include intuitive highlighting, note-taking, and bookmarking as well as pop-up definitions and enlargeable maps and art. Direct links to InQuizitive also appear in each chapter. Instructors can focus

INQUIZITIVE

Analyze the two photographs below.

Click on the images to enlarge.

What new weapons and techniques used during World War I are reflected in these photographs?

Correct Answer(s)

Airplanes provided crucial intelligence, and soon fighter planes took to the sky to shoot down other planes.

The beginnings of trench warfare made it impossible for the armies to fight mobile, decisive campaigns.

Tanks became more agile and able to carry heavier artillary.

Chemical weapons became more widely used, and as a result troops were issued gasmasks.

Incorrect Answer(s)

Correct

The size, speed, range, and sophistication of warplanes all increased. By the war's end, the British, French, and Germans had produced over 150,000 planes, while "flying aces" became popular heroes.

Drag the rest of the items into the "Correct Answer(s)" or "Incorrect Answer(s)" areas to complete the question.

OK

---

student reading by sharing notes with their classes, including embedded images and video. Reports on student and class-wide access and time on task allow instructors to monitor student reading and engagement.

RESOURCES FOR INSTRUCTORS

All resources are available through digital.wnorton.com/books/instructors.

NORTON COURSEPACKS

Easily add high-quality digital media to your online, hybrid, or lecture course—all at no cost to students. Norton's Coursepacks work within your existing Learning Management System and are ready to use and easy to customize. The coursepack offers a diverse collection of assignable and assessable resources: **Primary-Source Exercises, Guided Reading Exercises, Review Quizzes, Flashcards, Map Exercises, and all of the resources from the Student Site.** The resources were developed by Matthew Mingus, University of New Mexico, Melanie Bailey, Piedmont Virginia Community College, and Gregory Vitarbo, Meredith College.

Test Bank

The Test Bank was authored by Rosemary Moore, University of Iowa, John Patrick Montano, University of Delaware, and Curt Bostick, Southern Utah University, and contains 2000 multiple-choice, true/false, and essay questions.

Instructor's Manual

The Instructor's Manual contains detailed Chapter Summaries, Chapter Outlines, Suggested Discussion Questions, and Supplemental Web, Visual, and Print Resources. This resource was authored by Craig Pilant, County College of Morris, Joel Anderson, University of Maine, and Mark Ruff, Saint Louis University.

Lecture and Art PowerPoint Slides

The Lecture PowerPoint sets authored by Nicholas Rummell, Trident Technical College, and Matthew Laubacher, Ashford University, combine chapter review, art, and maps.

CHRONOLOGY

1378–1417
Great Schism

1414–1418
Council of Constance

1415
Jan Hus burned at
the stake for heresy

1434
Medici family takes
power in Florence

1440s–1450s
Gutenberg invents
printing press

1453
Mehmed II conquers
Constantinople

1454
Treaty of
Lodi

1455–1487
Wars of
the Roses

1469
Isabella and Ferdinand
unite Castile and Aragon

1478
Spanish
Inquisition
begins

1482
Treaty of Arras

10

Renaissance Europe

A WORLD TRANSFORMED

1400–1500

1494–1517
Early Italian Wars

1494
Treaty of Tordesillas

1498
Savonarola is executed

Late 15th century
Leonardo da Vinci, Raphael, and Michelangelo begin their work

1508
Maximilian I becomes Holy Roman Emperor

1521
Cortés conquers the Aztecs

1492
Reconquista is achieved; Alhambra Decree

1492
Columbus's first voyage across the Atlantic

I n June 1502, a Florentine civil servant named Niccolò Machiavelli (1469–1527) reached the military camp of Cesare Borgia (1475/6–1507); Cesare was the son of Rodrigo Borgia, now Pope Alexander VI. Cesare had been campaigning successfully in central Italy, where he was working, with his father's support, to build a state for himself. Having taken Bologna and massacred a group of mercenaries who had plotted against him, Cesare was now contemplating a campaign against Florence. The city seemed vulnerable in the wake of a political crisis brought on by invading French forces and the actions of a charismatic Dominican preacher, Girolamo Savonarola, whom the Florentines, acting under papal pressure, had arrested, tortured, and executed a few years earlier.

Machiavelli spent several months with Cesare, reporting back to the Florentine government on the twists and turns of Cesare's policies, doing his best to sniff out the military leader's secrets and to reveal none of his own. He saw that Cesare's rule, dependent on his father's support, was much more vulnerable than it seemed. On this basis Machiavelli correctly predicted that Cesare would not be able to attack, much less conquer, Florence.

Renaissance: Art and War Around 1438–40, Paolo Uccello created this ten-foot-long painting of the battle of San Romano (1432) between Florence and Siena, a Florentine victory in the wars between Italian city-states that dominated the early fifteenth century. With Uccello's use of brilliant colors and linear perspective, the work is an early example of the characteristics that would later define the achievements of Italian Renaissance painting.

- How were states changing the ways they organized themselves and competed?
- What were the dynamics of change in religious life?
- How did new technologies and skills enable Europeans to expand their reach?
- What were the major effects of first contact between Europe and the Americas?
- How did Renaissance humanism encourage new ambitions in European culture and society?

Machiavelli was playing a new game: professional diplomacy, as conducted by ambassadors sent abroad by their states to live with and report on foreign rulers. Both this position and the skills that Machiavelli brought to it were the products of a transformation in European politics.

The period in which Machiavelli lived, now known as the Renaissance, witnessed spectacular creativity in many areas of life. Europeans devised more effective ways of organizing and governing states, waging war, and making peace. They found their way by sea to Asia and the Americas, altering patterns of trade that had existed for hundreds or even thousands of years, and opening the Old and New Worlds to a transforming exchange of goods, ideas, beliefs, practices, and pathogens. They began to study the ancients in new ways that also reshaped their understanding of the world. They turned painting and sculpture into learned arts, and invented a way to print books instead of copying them by hand. Across Europe, borders and barriers fell as institutions and disciplines took on radically different forms.

Machiavelli himself helped to create both a new kind of state and a new way of writing and thinking about politics. His most famous and influential work, *The Prince*, rested on his own experience of states, including his own, undergoing revolutionary change, and on his study of the Greek and Roman classics. In this chapter, we will watch Machiavelli and his contemporaries begin to create what we can recognize as modern Europe.

RENAISSANCE STATES

In the fifteenth century, states of a new kind took shape across Europe. They developed permanent powers for raising revenue and waging war. They built civil services that could handle the large amounts of documentation, verbal and numerical, required to exercise these powers. Thinkers—many of them directly involved as civil servants—developed political theories that described, and made sense of, the changing political world.

ITALY: TERRITORIAL STATES (1454–1494)

In Italy, the centuries-long political decline of the empire and the papacy had left individual cities effectively independent. Through the late thirteenth and fourteenth centuries, trade rivalry and warfare had raged. Many Italian cities had been republics during the Middle Ages: independent communes inefficiently governed by local merchants and bankers, who appointed outside officials to preside over them. In the fourteenth and fifteenth centuries, most of these republican states came under princely rule. Noble families supported by mercenaries built their own tiny courts, which imitated the French and Burgundian ones. In some cases—as in Naples—these families claimed ancient dynastic rights. In others, they simply took power.

As city-states struggled against one another, weaker territories could not maintain their independence and consolidation followed. By the early fifteenth century, most of Italy belonged to one of five major powers: Venice, still rich and still a fiercely independent republic, ruled by a well-defined group of patricians; Milan, the center of a vast territory ruled by the Visconti family; the Papal States, ruled by the pope, who relied on them for his economic and military power; Naples, where a Spanish court dominated the large capital city and the vast agricultural estates around it; and Florence, which transformed itself gradually from a republic into a territorial state under the **Medici family**. Locked in competition for territory and power, all of them found their governments under pressure and developed new ways of coping with it.

FLORENCE In the late fourteenth and early fifteenth centuries, Florence was a republic in reality as well as in name—even if participation in government was limited to a small group of wealthy citizens. Day-to-day governance was handled by the Signoria, the group of nine officials chosen by lot for two-month terms, who moved into the government palace and made the vital decisions. Other citizens served rotating terms on committees that made the major political decisions, such as whether to go to war, and if so, whether to raise taxes. A small group of families that belonged to the city's most powerful guilds, dominated by the Albizzi, held enough of these offices to shape most decisions. Paid officials—especially the chancellors and their assistants—drafted the city's official correspondence with other powers, maintained the archives, and wrote histories and propaganda pamphlets.

Warfare tested this system to its limits. To pay its professional soldiers, the state had traditionally relied on taxes assessed on the basis of neighbors' testimony and informers' accounts—an inefficient system, to say the least. In the 1420s, Florence faced a vast public debt, the result of a war with Milan. To deal with it, the government created a wealth tax based on a systematic census of the city's entire population, carried out household by household. The records of the *catasto,* as this census was called, provided the Florentine government with a detailed understanding of the city's resources. Today, they offer historians a vivid record of family structures. They show, for example, that relatively few Florentines lived for very long in a patriarchal family dominated by an elderly male. Since men married late, they often died before their children were independent, leaving the children in families headed by mothers. In these circumstances, widows often steered their families' economic and political enterprises, achieving considerable authority.

Despite these reforms, Florence's republic proved unstable. Cosimo de' Medici (1389–1464), head of his family's bank, was a prominent member of the city's oligarchy. Exiled in 1433 for his part in a disastrous war against a neighboring city, he returned to take power a year later. Working largely behind the scenes as a power broker, Cosimo retained the committees that had traditionally ruled the city but manipulated the selection of their members in order to dominate them. During his twenty-year rule, it was still possible to believe that Florence was a republic in the traditional sense. Those who praised Cosimo in public wrote with deliberate vagueness that he had brought peace to the city, without discussing how. When Cosimo died, his son Piero (1416–1469) borrowed troops from his fellow ruler in Milan, lined the central square—the Piazza della Signoria—with them, and only then called in the citizens to hear a public announcement of his succession to power.

Cosimo de' Medici The Florentine painter Agnolo Bronzino created this portrait of Cosimo de' Medici, probably in the mid-fifteenth century.

Using the influence and resources of the Medici bank, as Cosimo had, Piero ruled the city effectively and defeated Venice in 1467—thanks to his alliance with Milan and the Papal States.

Cosimo's grandson Lorenzo (1449–1492) continued the Medici rule of Florence through surrogates who held the traditional offices. He behaved in some ways like a prince, holding tournaments and encouraging the prominent families of the city to build enormous palaces. When under his direction the Medici bank began to encounter serious difficulties, Lorenzo and his friends exploited state finances to maintain their incomes. Though officially still a republic, Florence looked more and more like such princely states as Milan, and Lorenzo himself like a ruler. Still, as he noted with pride, he and his predecessors had given a great deal to their city, spending 663,000 florins (a brand new palace might cost 11,000 florins) on taxes, charity, and building projects between 1434 and 1471.

One major enterprise continued uninterrupted

LORENZO GHIBERTI'S DECLARATION IN THE *CATASTO* OF 1427

The *catasto*, a census of the population and wealth of Florence, enabled the government to collect precise records of all households in the city, from the poor to the rich. The first survey was conducted in 1427 by ten officials and their staff, who interviewed the heads of almost 10,000 households. Each household's record lists property held, including land, payments received, and investments; other business interests; deductions for dependents; and debts owed, which reduced the taxable amount.

This record lists the possessions and debts of the sculptor Lorenzo Ghiberti as declared in the catasto of 1427, when he was forty-nine. His assets include balances owed to him for the sale of works, including one purchased by Cosimo de' Medici. His debts offer insight into the diverse trades in Florence's bustling economy. Ghiberti's taxable assets, valued at 999 florins[1]—worth about $42,000 today—assured his family a comfortable lifestyle, but his wealth was far from that of the top 1 percent of Florentines, who were assessed at upward of 10,000 florins.

[Assets]
A house located in the parish of S. Ambrogio in Florence in the Via Borgo Allegri…with household furnishings for the use of myself and my family…   0

A piece of land in the parish of S. Donato in Franzano…   100-0-0

In my shop are two pieces of bronze sculpture which I have made for a baptismal font in Siena.…I estimate that they are worth 400 florins or thereabouts, of which sum I have received 290 florins; so the balance is 110 florins.   110-0-0

Also in my shop is a bronze casket which I made for Cosimo de' Medici; I value it at approximately 200 florins, of which I have received 135 florins. The balance owed to me is 65 florins.   65-0-0

I have investments in the *Monte*[2] of 714 florins.   714-0-0

I am still owed 10 florins by the Friars of S. Maria Novella the tomb of the General [of the Dominican Order, Lionardo Dati].

Obligations
Personal exemptions:
  Lorenzo di Bartolo, aged 46   200-0-0
  Marsilia, my wife, aged 26   200-0-0
  Tommaso, my son, aged 10 or thereabouts   200-0-0
  Vettorio, my son, aged 7 or thereabouts   200-0-0
I owe money to the following persons:
  Antonio di Piero del Vaglente and company, goldsmiths   33-0-0
  Nicola di Vieri de' Medici   10-0-0
  Domenico di Tano, cutler   9-0-0
  Niccolò Carducci and company, retail cloth merchants   7-0-0
  Papi d'Andrea, cabinet-maker   16-0-0
  Mariano da Gambassi, mason   7-0-0
  Papero di Mea of Settignano
  Simone di Nanni of Fiesole
  Cipriano di Bartolo of Pistoia
    (my apprentices in the shop)   48-0-0
  Antonio, called El Maestro, tailor   15-0-0
  Domenico di Lippi, culter   2-0-0
  Alessandro Allesandri and company   4-0-0
  Duccio Adimari and company, retail cloth merchants   8-0-0

Antonio di Giovanni, stationer   3-0-0
Isau d'Agnolo and company, bankers   50-0-0
Commissioners in charge of maintenance and rebuilding of the church of S. Croce   6-0-0
Lorenzo di Bruciane, kiln operator   3-0-0
Meo of S. Apollinare   45-0-0
Pippo, stocking maker   8-0-0
[Total of Lorenzo's taxable assets]   999-0-0
[Total obligations and exemptions]   1074-0-0

QUESTIONS FOR ANALYSIS

1. What does this declaration tell you about Ghiberti's personal life?
2. What do Ghiberti's debts and the balances owed to him suggest about the importance of banks and credit in Renaissance Florence?
3. What does the catasto suggest about Ghiberti's work as a sculptor and as a craftsman?

---

[1]**florin:** a skilled craftsman made slightly less than 1 florin for four days of work; a house in the upscale city center would rent for 20–50 florins per year
[2]**Monte:** a public fund

Source: Gene Brucker, ed., *The Society of Renaissance Florence: A Documentary Study* (Toronto: 1998), pp. 10–12.

throughout this period of institutional change: the city of Florence made itself the capital of a substantial state. Florentines proudly traced their city's origins back to republican Rome, and claimed that when they fought fiercely against the papacy in the late fourteenth century and against Milan and Naples in the early fifteenth, they were defending "Florentine liberty." Rather like the ancient Romans, the Florentines showed no reluctance to subject other states that had also been independent republics, such as Pisa, to their rule. Indeed, after the conquest of Pisa in 1406, the Florentines used it as a base for a state fleet of ten galleys. These ships made regular voyages between Florence and ports in the eastern Mediterranean, North Africa, and the North Sea, carrying Florentine wool and silk cloth to exchange for wool from England and spices from the East.

MILAN   Although Florence offered the smaller states it conquered relatively little compensation, other Renaissance states offered their new subjects significant advantages. The Visconti, who ruled Milan in the late fourteenth and early fifteenth centuries, sponsored canal-building projects that eased travel and transport. They also subsidized the introduction of mulberry bushes and silkworms. By the later fifteenth century, rich merchants, mostly from Florence, created an independent silk industry. The Milanese government encouraged these foreign entrepreneurs to settle, and allowed them to import skilled artisans. In the middle of the sixteenth century, silk manufacturing was Milan's major industry, along with the production of other luxury goods such as tapestries.

VENICE   Venice was also a self-governing republic ruled by an oligarchy: a small set of patrician families whose male members were eligible to sit in the representative assembly, or Great Council. Members of this body selected the doge, or chief of state, and elected the members of the smaller Senate and the Council of Ten, which did much of the work of governing the city. By the sixteenth century, more than 2,000 males had the right to take part in the meetings of the Great Council, ruling a city whose population was well over 100,000. Members of the Venetian oligarchy were expected to serve the city in multiple ways: representing Venice to foreign powers, governing cities that Venice had conquered on the mainland, or supervising communities of Venetians overseas. Few willingly left the city to serve. But those who did acquired knowledge about the world outside Venice, which they put to use in their commercial enterprises and in making laws and policies.

THE RISE OF DIPLOMACY: THE TREATY OF LODI

All of these Italian states, finally, developed a new way of conducting foreign affairs—one based on professional diplomacy, which would become a central institution in the rise of modern states. After a long series of wars and a transfer of power in Milan from the Visconti to the Sforza family had almost destroyed the Italian political system, Milan, Naples, and Florence made peace at Lodi, a city in Lombardy, in 1454. The Treaty of Lodi set permanent boundaries between Milanese and Venetian territory. Soon Venice and the Papal States also signed agreements with the other states. They pledged to maintain a balance of power, promising that they would all join in making war on any signatory that decided to attack another.

The Italian states devised a diplomatic system that they hoped could sustain this balance. They assigned resident **ambassadors** to one another's capitals: officials who

Italian States at the Treaty of Lodi, 1454 Despite their rivalries, the city-states that controlled the Italian Peninsula were tied together through mercantile relationships, with Florence at the center. The Medici bank had branches in Milan, Venice, Rome, and other cities, while Florentine trade routes conveyed luxury commodities such as silk from Milan, Venice, Genoa, and Naples to distant lands.

could represent their state's interests, gather information, and convey official communications. Governments developed systems for encoding dispatches to keep their communications safe and secret, and formulated rules for the treatment of ambassadors by hostile powers and during wartime. Diplomacy had existed for centuries, carried on by heralds and, often, through encounters between rulers. Now the Italian system of rapid interstate communication, run by political experts, gradually became a model for the rest of Europe.

Peace nevertheless remained precarious as limited wars broke out again and again. In 1478, when the Florentine Pazzi family conspired to assassinate Lorenzo de' Medici and his brother Giuliano and take over the state, the Pazzi had promises of help from the papacy and Naples. A mercenary captain in the papal service, Federigo da Montefeltro, was waiting outside Florence with his army, ready to move in and help the Pazzi consolidate their power. Though Giuliano was killed, Lorenzo survived the attempt and took brutal revenge on the Pazzi. The pope excommunicated Lorenzo, put Florence under the interdict, and went to war against the city with his ally, Naples. Offered little support by Milan, which was undergoing a political crisis of its own, Lorenzo eventually made his way to Naples, where, after a stay of months, he ultimately ended the crisis. In this case, as in many others, successful negotiations resulted as much from luck and determination as from skill. But in the sixteenth century, Lorenzo would be remembered—with some exaggeration—as the Magnificent, not only as a patron of the arts but also the master of balance-of-power politics. Italians had become—or so

many of them believed—the professional masters of politics, proud of the skill with which they manipulated powers both large and small to do their will.

MONARCHICAL STATES (1450–1494)

The Italians did not realize, however, that in the very decades in which they had been making politics into an art of feints and alliances, plots and proxy wars, the states of northern and western Europe had not only recovered from the crises of the fourteenth century but had developed stronger political and military resources. Improved military technology and large-scale forms of state organization gave them powers that dwarfed those available to the Italian states.

BURGUNDY During the wars that dominated the first half of the fifteenth century, as we have seen, the French royal house was challenged, for the last time, by the English, as well as by rivals of royal descent. These struggles left the French state weaker at times —and in control of less territory—than the rulers of some of its regions. The most important of these was Burgundy, a duchy in central and eastern France that was united by marriage, early in the fifteenth century, with Flanders and Brabant. These were the rich provinces of the **Low Countries**, the coastal region to the north and west whose cities, such as Bruges and Ghent, still ranked among Europe's most productive centers of industry and commerce. The Burgundians' French lands produced great wines. Their capital, Dijon, well located in eastern France, became a major trading center and the base of important commercial fairs.

For centuries, Burgundy had been ruled by branches of the same dynasties that ruled France—the Capetians and now the Valois. The last Valois dukes—especially Philip the Good (1396–1467) and Charles the Bold (1433–1477)— built Burgundy into a state that was, at its height, wealthier and more powerful than the kingdom of France itself, ruled by their Valois cousins. The Burgundian dukes pushed for independence, claiming prerogatives appropriate for a king. In 1423, for example, Philip the Good created a chivalric order—a small group of specially chosen noblemen, with their own meetings and rituals. Eventually Charles the Bold convinced the Holy Roman emperor to recognize him as the monarch of a separate kingdom, and had himself crowned. In 1465 he organized the League of the Public Weal—a group of powerful nobles, including the dukes of Brittany, Berry, and Lorraine, who demanded that the French king restore their ancient feudal prerogatives.

Federigo da Montefeltro In 1465, the artist Piero della Francesca painted this double portrait of Federigo and his wife, Battista Sforza.

European Monarchies, 1492 By the end of the fifteenth century, European monarchs ruled powerful and stable states. Louis XI achieved sovereignty over most of modern-day France; in England, Henry VII unified the country after defeating his rival Richard III at Bosworth. Maximilian I expanded the territory of the Holy Roman Empire and established new Habsburg claims, while Ferdinand and Isabella unified the Spanish kingdoms in 1469 and completed the Reconquista in 1492. Meanwhile, the Ottoman Empire under Mehmed I and II expanded dramatically.

FRANCE Yet the French monarchy had great residual strengths. Through the hard years of the fifteenth century, as fragmentation threatened, meetings of the **Estates General**—representatives of the Church, the nobility, and the Third Estate of urban merchants and traders—helped to preserve and enlarge the sense that France was a single nation. Although this assembly sometimes resisted individual kings, it also offered the monarchy essential help. As early as 1439, the Estates General conferred on King Charles VII (r. 1422–1461) the right to collect a permanent tax, the **taille**, from all those who were neither clerics nor nobles, and use it to support a permanent military formation, the Company of Ordinance. The taille rarely brought in enough to support all of the crown's military needs, especially as mercenaries played an increasingly

prominent role in warfare. The French kings supplemented their revenues with such problematic expedients as selling offices in the government, and the right to pass them on by inheritance. Still, the French monarchy had established its right to develop a standing army and to use the power of the royal purse to support it.

Louis XI (r. 1421–1483), known to his enemies as "the universal spider" for his skill at weaving webs of intrigue, managed to rebuild and extend the power of the monarchy. He made truces with most of his opponents, and when Charles the Bold, who unwisely invaded Switzerland, was defeated and killed, Louis dismembered much of Burgundy. In 1482, the Treaty of Arras gave him sovereignty over the historical duchy of Burgundy as well as Picardy, Artois, and Franche-Comté. An active ruler,

POVERTY AND THE STATE

Even as manufacturing and trade expanded in Renaissance Europe, poverty continued to afflict rural areas and cities alike. Farmers struggled against poor harvests, high taxes, and marauding bands of soldiers. In cities, abandoned children, the unemployed, and the sick begged on the streets. It had traditionally been the responsibility of the Church to ameliorate poverty, but as Renaissance states grew in scope and competence, people began to call on the state to harness its power to help the poor. The documents here address the problem of poverty in France and in Flanders.

Cahier of the Estates General, "The Plight of the French Poor"

This cahier, a catalog of grievances submitted to the king following the 1494 meeting of the Estates General, includes a plea for the relief of poor farmers from the demands of the taille and nobles' pensions.

When the poor labouring man has paid with great difficulty the quota he owes as tallage,[1] for the hire of the men of arms, and when he takes comfort in what is left to him, hoping it will be enough to live on for the year, or to sow, there suddenly come men of arms who eat up or waste this little reserve which the poor man has saved to live on....

While in the time of King Charles VII the quotas of the tallage imposed by the parish officials were counted only in the twenties, such as twenty, forty, sixty pounds, after his death they began to be levied by hundreds, and since, they have grown from hundreds to thousands....

Some have fled...others in great numbers have died of hunger, others in despair have killed their wives and children and themselves, seeing they had nothing left to live on. And many men, women, and children, having no animals, are forced to work yoked to the plough, and others labour at night out of fear that in daylight they will be seized and apprehended for the said tallage....

These things considered, it seems to the said estates that the king should take pity on his poor people, and relieve them of the said tallage and taxes.... And this they beg of him very humbly....

And may it please my lords who take pensions to content themselves with income from their own lords, without taking any extraordinary pensions or sums of money. Or at least if some receive them, let the pensions be reasonable, moderate, and bearable, out of regard for the afflictions and miseries of the poor people.... It is only the poor labourer who contributes to paying the said pensions.

Juan Luis Vives, "Concerning the Relief of the Poor"

In response to a request from the government of Bruges, longtime resident Juan Luis Vives proposed in 1526 a detailed plan for the state's improvement of living conditions in the city. This passage argues for the necessity of reducing poverty and teaching trades to the poor.

Surely it is a shame and disgrace to us Christians, to whom nothing has been more explicitly commanded than charity—and I am inclined to think that is the one injunction—that we meet everywhere in our cities so many poor men and beggars. Whithersoever you turn you encounter poverty and distress and those who are compelled to hold out their hands for alms. Why is it not true that, just as everything in the state is restored which is subject to the ravages of time and fortune—such as walls, ditches, ramparts, streams, institutions, customs, and the laws themselves—so it would be suitable to aid in meeting that primary obligation of giving, which has suffered damage in various ways?...

Some of the poor live in those institutions commonly called hospitals...; others beg publicly;...I call "hospitals" those places where the sick are fed and cared for, where a certain number of paupers is supported, where boys and girls are reared, where abandoned infants are nourished, where the insane are confined, and where the blind dwell. Let the governors of the state realize that all these institutions are a part of their responsibility....

Should the native poor be asked whether they have learned a trade? Yes; and those who have not, if they are of suitable age, should be taught the one to which they say they are most strongly inclined, provided it is feasible. If it is not feasible, let them be taught some similar trade.... But if this trade is too difficult, or he is too slow in learning, let an easier one be assigned to him, all the way down to those which anyone can learn thoroughly in a few days: such as digging, drawing water, bearing loads, pushing a wheelbarrow, attending on magistrates, running errands, bearing letters or packets, driving horses.

QUESTIONS FOR ANALYSIS

1. What are some of the sources of poverty for French farmers?
2. How does Vives recommend reducing poverty in Bruges?
3. According to these sources, what responsibilities do governments have for the poor?

---

[1]**tallage:** the taille

Source: "The Plight of the French Poor," *Journal des états généraux de France tenus à Tours en 1484*, ed. A. Bernier (Paris: 1835), quoted in J. B. Ross and M. Martin, eds., *The Portable Renaissance Reader*, trans. J. B. Ross (New York: 1953), pp. 215–18; Juan-Luis Vivès, "Concerning the Relief of the Poor," trans. M. M. Sherwood, *Studies in Social Work* 11 (New York: 1917), pp. 10–11, 14–15.

Louis traveled constantly. He rebuilt the king's traditional council of advisers, adding professional jurists who extended the jurisdiction of the royal courts, and developed a system of post roads so that news and messages could be transmitted rapidly across his kingdom. He promoted trade fairs, supported the silk industry, and saw the potential of the Mediterranean port of Marseilles, which belonged to Provence and was united with France in 1481. Above all, Louis was good at outliving other nobles of royal blood and inheriting their lands. By the end of his reign, he ruled most of what is now France.

ENGLAND In the second half of the fifteenth century, England was divided by the **Wars of the Roses** (1455–87), a protracted local appendix to the Hundred Years' War named for the white and red roses that symbolized the two warring parties. England's ruling family, the Plantagenets, was divided into two separate houses, both descended from Edward III and thus both with a claim to the throne. The Lancastrians were led by the ruling king, Henry VI (r. 1422–1461, 1470–1471), who suffered from bouts of insanity; the Yorkists by Richard, Duke of York. After war broke out in 1455, control passed repeatedly from house to house. The Yorkist victory in the bloody battle of Towton in 1461 made Richard's first son king. Edward IV (r. 1461–1470, 1471–1483) suppressed Lancastrian resistance and captured Henry, but eventually lost the support of his chief adviser, the powerful and wealthy earl of Warwick. Known as "the Kingmaker," Warwick decided to replace Edward by restoring Henry to the throne, but Edward defeated his opponents, killed Warwick in 1471, and had Henry murdered in the Tower of London. In this period of warfare, Warwick the Kingmaker was only one of many lords who hired retainers and built up their own military forces—sometimes, as in Warwick's case, to the point where they were able to challenge the crown itself.

When Edward IV died suddenly in 1483, his brother, Richard of Gloucester, seized the throne. As King Richard III (r. 1482–1485), he was an effective ruler with close ties to the city of London. He began to build new institutions—such as the Council of the North, an administrative body centered in the northern city of York—and to offer rapid and inexpensive justice through the Court of Requests. He also saw to it that the laws of England were translated, at long last, from Latin and French into English. But Richard was defeated and killed at the battle of Bosworth Field, in central England, by Henry Tudor, a Lancastrian claimant to the throne who founded the new dynasty of the Tudors.

Henry VII (r. 1485–1509), in his own way, introduced a

Wars of the Roses An illustration from the French historian Jean de Wavrin's 1471 chronicle of England shows a battle of the Wars of the Roses. Wavrin was from Burgundy, an ally of the House of York, which may explain the royal standards and white roses (representing York) that appear in the manuscript's margin.

model of kingship as novel as Louis XI's in France. Some of his policies were borrowed from the talented Richard III, whom he denounced as a usurper; others were created by his chief minister, John Morton, the archbishop of Canterbury. Henry relied heavily on the system of **justices of the peace**, unpaid local officials recruited from the ranks of local notables. They served for a year at a time, making them dependent on him for reappointment. Henry tasked them with overseeing the juries that decided cases, keeping public order, and ensuring that legislation was enforced. At the same time, he adopted new laws against "livery and maintenance"—the tradition by which powerful nobles had amassed armed retinues that amounted to private armies. These laws and the Court of Star Chamber, which Henry used to break the power of aristocrats suspected of plotting against him, established the monarchy as far more powerful than any potential rival.

In 1494 Henry engineered a boycott of the Flemish cloth industry that led, two years later, to an agreement favorable to British merchants trading in Antwerp—one of the industrial and financial centers of Europe. Over time, Henry became notorious for his demands for taxes and personal income. He went over financial records himself and annotated them in his own hand. And he used his gains not only to enrich the monarchy but also to begin the creation of a royal navy, with its own harbor, dockyard, and dry dock at Portsmouth. So in England, as in France, policies and institutions that would play essential roles in the creation of a modern state had their origins in the consolidation of monarchical power at the end of the fifteenth century.

HOLY ROMAN EMPIRE The Holy Roman Empire, which had undergone a sharp decline in power during the crises of the fourteenth and early fifteenth centuries, also began to recover. In 1440 Frederick of Habsburg, a member of the **Habsburg dynasty** that had long ruled Austria, was elected Holy Roman Emperor Frederick III, and in 1452 he was finally crowned by the pope. He married Eleanor of Portugal, establishing connections with other royal dynasties, and consolidated his power over the other members of the Habsburg family. Frederick's son and successor, **Maximilian I** (r. 1508–1519), was a true believer in the traditional codes of chivalry. He loved falconry and hunting, tournaments and chivalry—he famously took only 97 shots to bring down 100 birds—and nourished a special passion for splendidly decorated suits of armor.

Maximilian not only practiced the courtly arts of a medieval monarch; in some ways, he acted like one in politics as well. He saw himself not as creating a single, unified realm, but as pulling together multiple territories that he and his Habsburg successors could rule. Through advantageous marriages, both his own and that of his son

Maximilian's Power Artwork such as this 1526 woodcut by the printmaker Albrecht Dürer symbolizes Maximilian I's power and authority. The Holy Roman emperor and his wife, Mary, Duchess of Burgundy, ride a richly decorated chariot bearing a crest that represents the unification of their families. They are surrounded by admiring courtiers and mythological figures.

Philip, he established Habsburg claims over much of Burgundy, the kingdoms of Aragon and Castile, and Milan. Like the Italian rulers of his time, Maximilian believed in the powers of astrology and magic, and dispensed patronage to professors at Vienna whose predictions, he thought, could give him accurate information about the shifting fields of politics and war.

Yet Maximilian was also a modern prince. Lacking a single capital city and many of the other trappings of royalty found elsewhere, he wielded the powers of art and print—especially those of artists such as the brilliant Nuremberg painter and printmaker Albrecht Dürer (1471–1528)—to create images that emphasized the venerable antiquity of the Habsburg house and his own accomplishments. In an effort to create warmer support within the empire, Maximilian placed special emphasis on his German roots. In 1495, at a meeting of the Reichstag (the imperial general assembly) in Worms, he led an ambitious effort to reshape the empire, which was reorganized into a set of administrative districts and equipped, for the first time, with a supreme court. Imperial reform had only limited success, and Maximilian's early efforts to maintain authority over the Swiss and intervene in wars with the French elsewhere were unsuccessful. Nonetheless, he laid the foundations for what would remain, for centuries to come, the great power of the Habsburg family. The policy of creating alliances by marriage, at which he proved so successful, would continue to work well for his successors, and even gave rise to a famous proverb: "Let others wage war. You, happy Austria, need only marry."

SPAIN More dramatic still was the political transformation taking place on the Iberian Peninsula. In the fifteenth century, Spain had been divided into a number of states: chiefly the kingdoms of Castile, Aragon, and Portugal. From 1475 to 1479, Castile was torn by a war over succession, as France and England were. But the 1469 marriage of Isabella and Ferdinand, the so-called Catholic kings, connected Isabella's Castile, with its crusading traditions and military nobility, with Ferdinand's Aragon, the most economically advanced part of Spain. Valencia, a port city on the east coast of Aragon, had become wealthy in the fourteenth and fifteenth centuries as a center of banking, trade, and textile production. Politically, Aragon was oriented to the Mediterranean, and its rulers also claimed vast, productive agrarian lands in Sicily and southern Italy.

The energetic partnership of Aragon and Castile led to a renewal of the Reconquista, the effort, which began

Ferdinand and Isabella An anonymous fifteenth-century portrait depicts the Catholic monarchs of Castile and Aragon who united the Spanish kingdoms. They are dressed austerely, but wear jewelry that signifies their royal status.

as early as the eighth century, to restore all of the peninsula to Christian rule. The Reconquista culminated in 1492 when the last Muslim state—Granada, ruled from the magnificent eleventh-century Alhambra palace at the center of its splendid capital city—fell. The year 1492 also marked an end point for the Jews of Spain, who had long been pressured to convert to Christianity, and sometimes forced to do so. Now the **Alhambra Decree**, issued by Catholic monarchs Ferdinand and Isabella, gave Jews four months to convert or leave. Thousands fled, many of them to the rising empire of the Ottoman Turks. Tens of thousands of Jews converted to Christianity, but remained under suspicion of backsliding for decades to come.

Under Isabella and Ferdinand, each Spanish region retained its own name and individuality, and dealt with the crown through its own representatives, who met, as they had for centuries, in each region's Cortes. Still, a new system of government through royally appointed officers, the *corregidores* ("magistrates"), spread from Castile to the rest of the lands of the Catholic kings. Noble families cast their fate with the monarchy, serving—often for generations—as military officers and governors of settlements abroad.

The Spanish also developed their own formidable infantry, many of them professionals and veterans. They were organized in units called *tercios,* each with 1,500 to 3,000 soldiers armed with pikes, swords, and arquebuses, a new firearm. Their mastery of tactics and disciplined ability to dig in and repel attacks by formidable, numerically superior opponents enabled them to fight the Swiss and the German mercenaries on equal terms. Under the

leadership of Isabella's "Great Captain," the Castilian general Gonzalo Fernández de Córdoba (1453–1515), the Spanish became the most formidable army in Europe.

THE OTTOMAN EMPIRE

Even as the great monarchies of Europe were attaining new levels of political unity, a new empire in the eastern Mediterranean, that of the **Ottomans**, could muster even more resources than any of these Christian states. In 1261 the independent Greek state of Nicea, a remnant of the former Byzantine Empire, reconquered Constantinople from the so-called Latin empire established by the Fourth Crusade in 1204. The new Byzantine emperor, Michael VIII (r. 1261–1282), founded the Palaeologan dynasty and worked hard to repair the damage that had been done when the crusaders sacked the city. Michael also tried to restore parts of the ancient Byzantine Empire, but full restoration proved impossible.

Gradually, one of the small Muslim states near Constantinople, led by Osman I (1258–1326), began to expand. By the end of the fourteenth century, his Ottoman successors controlled most of Asia Minor. They had taken the ancient Greek city of Thessalonica from the Venetians in 1387, defeated the rival, rapidly growing Serbian empire, at the battle of Kosovo in 1389, and in 1396 routed a crusading army sent against them at the battle of Nicopolis in Bulgaria. They besieged Constantinople but were prevented from conquering the city itself when the Mongol leader Timur, who had already conquered vast amounts of territory in India, Persia, and Syria, invaded Asia Minor. Timur defeated the Ottoman sultan Bayezid I in 1402 at the battle of Ankara and imprisoned him. But Timur died only three years later, and his state collapsed.

Mehmed I (r. 1413–1421) restored the Ottoman lands and conquered new territory in Albania and the Crimea. Murad II (r. 1422–1451) and his son Mehmed II (r. 1451–1481) returned to the offense. The Byzantines appealed for help to the pope and the Latin powers. But the price of substantial aid was accepting papal primacy, and though the Byzantine emperor John VIII (r. 1425–1448) negotiated a union of the two churches, most of the Eastern Orthodox clergy rejected it. In 1453, Mehmed II conquered Constantinople. His soldiers killed the last Byzantine emperor, and after transforming the city into his capital, he went on to conquer the Morea peninsula (the Peloponnesus), Serbia, Albania, and Wallachia. In 1480, the Ottomans raided Italy itself. When Mehmed died in the next year,

Mehmed II This fifteenth-century Turkish portrait of the Ottoman sultan owes much to Italian artistic influence, particularly in the colors used and the subject's slightly turned pose. Yet his clothes and accoutrements—from the archer's ring on his right thumb to the scholar's turban—identify him as a Central Asian warrior and intellectual. The roses he holds in his right hand allude to his aesthetic and intellectual refinement.

still campaigning, the Ottoman Empire sprawled across much of Europe as well as Asia Minor.

Latin Europe knew that the Ottoman Empire was not only large but well administered. The sultans' special guard of Janissaries—boys taken from Christian families and trained to be professional soldiers—impressed observers with their loyalty to the ruler, their military skills, and their ferocity. The millet system—which allowed Christians and Jews to live in their own semiautonomous communities, with leaders approved by the state—kept the peace in the empire's massive European domains. Mehmed hired the best architects and artisans, Christian

as well as Muslim, to transform Christian Constantinople into the Muslim capital, which the Ottomans called Istanbul. Minarets were added to Justinian's church of Hagia Sophia, turning it into a spectacular mosque, and massive palaces and other public buildings went up rapidly. The Ottoman Empire was, in many ways, the most formidable of Europe's new states.

THE TRANSFORMATION OF WARFARE

Christian or Muslim, these new states acquired new kinds of military power. As early as the fourteenth century, the classic missile weapon of the Middle Ages, the British longbow, had proved its ability to decimate large armies of heavily armored knights. In the same period, European records begin to show the appearance of "fire-pots"—primitive metal cannon that used gunpowder to fire stone projectiles. The Chinese had invented gunpowder in the ninth century, and by the thirteenth they were using it in firearms. Knowledge of these devices reached Europe by unknown means—perhaps along the ancient routes of the Silk Road.

Between 1350 and 1450, guns developed in Europe with astonishing speed. Cannon—forged first of bronze, and then of iron—took multiple forms. Huge siege guns were made by expert iron founders such as Orban, the Hungarian Christian who built the cannon that Mehmed II used to breach Constantinople's legendarily impregnable walls. Smaller guns that could be pulled by horses or pivoted by their gunners also came into use, with devastating effect, on the battlefield and aboard ships. Projectiles themselves became more varied and effective, as metal balls replaced stones, and explosive shells came into use.

Poor regions—the cantons of Switzerland, the mountains of central Italy, some of the German states of the Holy Roman Empire—and areas torn by war such as England and France during the Hundred Years' War spawned professional soldiers, as landless young men left the homes that could not support them. Some mercenary units, such as the well-disciplined White Company led by the Englishman John Hawkwood (1320–1394), specialized in terrorizing civilian populations, burning villages, and destroying crops. Others—especially the Swiss—were skilled in fighting with long spears called pikes, with which they defeated the Burgundians in 1477.

Gunpowder gave these professional soldiers new possibilities. The arquebus—a muzzle-loading gun with a stock—became a standard infantry weapon. Aimed from

Arquebuses In an illustration from a 1517 German epic, opposing armies aim arquebuses at each other. In the foreground, a single soldier has wounded two enemy knights, indicating the new weapon's power.

the shoulder and fired with a new matchlock mechanism, the arquebus could penetrate the hardest armor at close range. Rulers soon realized that paid soldiers who could handle firearms could concentrate great force on their enemies. The king of Hungary built and trained a professional military force, the Black Army, from the 1450s on. Every fifth member of the force had an arquebus. Hungary and the German states became early centers of production, and during the course of the fifteenth century, the use of the arquebus spread from Portugal to Muscovy, a Russian monarchy that had taken shape in the late thirteenth century. Upholders of tradition hated these new weapons. Even more effectively than the longbow, they enabled men of low social position to kill their betters from a safe distance. Yet artisans such as Orban who built guns and cannon rose in stature—especially as illustrated texts about the new military devices began to circulate, and states competed for the services of the military engineers who wrote them.

The immediate impact of cannon, in particular, was dramatic. In Italy—where warfare was almost continuous in the fifteenth century—gunnery soon transformed the waging of war. The high stone walls that had traditionally protected cities and bastions against sieges proved too thin to withstand cannon fire. Within fifty years, Italian architects and their patrons had learned to replace the old style of fortification with a new one: low, thick walls of earth and stone designed to absorb the force of projectiles. These walls made it possible to resist a besieging army equipped with artillery. Projecting bastions served as gun platforms for defenders and enabled them to fire on attacks from the side. Ships equipped with cannon could engage in battle without having to draw alongside their opponents and engage in hand-to-hand combat. The European vessels that began to move outward into the Atlantic Ocean carried small crews, but they were far more formidably armed than any opposition they were likely to encounter, even in East Asia.

THE CAULDRON OF THE EARLY ITALIAN WARS (1494–1517)

The first to recognize how the political and military world had changed were the Italians—especially the Italian political classes—in the years around 1490. In 1492, Piero, the heir of Lorenzo de' Medici, succeeded his father as de facto ruler of Florence. Clumsier than the uniquely deft Lorenzo, Piero lost support in the city and failed to emulate his father in keeping a firm hand on foreign affairs. In 1494, Ludovico Sforza, Duke of Milan, worried that the Spanish forces in Naples threatened his rule, offered the French king Charles VIII (r. 1483–1498) free passage if he wished to take up the Valois family's ancient dynastic claim to the rule of Naples. Charles promptly invaded Italy. His massive army terrified the Italian rulers, who had honed their skills fighting on a far smaller scale and in less destructive and ruthless ways. Piero immediately surrendered Florence's fortresses to the French—only to find himself ejected from office and from the city. Girolamo Savonarola (1452–1498), a popular Dominican preacher, had reported visions in his recent sermons: he saw a sword over Italy, threatening divine vengeance, and Florence in triumph as the city of lilies—then as now the symbol of France. The invasion seemed to bear out his visions, and his prestige was enhanced when he helped to persuade Charles to move on from Florence without disturbing its inhabitants.

A believer in republican government, Savonarola used his influence to persuade the Florentines—split between wealthy patricians, many of whom still supported the Medici, and members of the craft guilds, who had been

Early Italian Wars, 1494–1517 The Italian Wars transformed the great powers of Europe and helped forge new, modern features of politics and war.

Christopher Columbus's sailors, broke out among them after they reached Naples. In 1498 the French invaded again, led by Charles VIII's successor Louis XII (r. 1498–1515). Though Sforza arrived with a Swiss army of his own, the French dispatched him easily. In 1501 Louis joined with the Spanish to conquer Naples. But they fell out, and the Spanish commander, "The Great Captain," Gonzalo Fernández de Córdoba, rapidly defeated the French. The Treaty of Lyon, signed in 1504, left the Spanish in Naples and the French in Milan. But the situation was highly unstable, and for more than five decades, the peninsula would be the site of what came to be called the Italian wars. This long series of conflicts established the modern form of warfare as a contest of professional soldiers armed with gunpowder weapons. Florence's republic, first put down in 1512, would revive for a last period of defiance from 1527 to 1530. In the end, the Spanish would control most of Italy, directly (in Milan, Naples, and Sicily) or indirectly.

The great powers transformed Italy, but they also were transformed by their experiences there. They learned to employ architects and build modern fortifications; to form and train a diplomatic corps and use it in the making of treaties and, even more important, the weaving of secret alliances; and to exploit propaganda of many kinds as a basic instrument of policy. By the 1530s, England, France, Spain, and the Holy Roman Empire all had chancellors and ambassadors who matched the Italians in craft and policy, but served their own, far more powerful states.

excluded from power and profit—to build a more open set of institutions than had been in place before the Medici took power. They preserved the traditional committee structure, but created a sovereign Great Council, in which more than 3,000 Florentines were eligible to serve—far more than had ever served actively in government before. Savonarola himself came into sharp conflict with Pope Alexander VI (r. 1492–1503). The threat of a papal interdict, which could have brought about the confiscation of Florentine goods everywhere, led to Savonarola's arrest and torture in 1498. He confessed that he had invented his visions, and was executed. But the republic he helped to bring into being survived him. Led by Piero Soderini, whom Machiavelli served as ambassador to Cesare Borgia, Rome, and France, the Republic lasted for another eighteen sharply contested years.

In 1494 French forces had moved down the Italian peninsula virtually unopposed—only to be driven back when syphilis, introduced by the Genoese mariner

Savonarola's Execution An unknown artist painted this picture of Girolamo Savonarola's 1498 execution by fire in the Piazza della Signoria in Florence. The cityscape includes the Palazzo Vecchio at right.

A new political and military world—one with distinctively modern features—was forged when Europe's revived territorial states were transmuted in the cauldron of the Italian Wars.

CHRISTIANITY: CRISIS AND REFORM

The papacy, once the most universal of European organizations, had lost power, resources, and spiritual authority during the thirteenth and fourteenth centuries. After seventy years of French domination in Avignon, the papacy returned to Rome in the 1370s. While in Avignon, the papacy had reorganized its central institutions, such as the supreme court of canon law, or Rota, and developed more efficient systems for collecting revenues. But its concentration on these practical matters had earned it a reputation for greed and corruption—one reinforced by its endless assertions of power over appointments to church offices (benefices), which were given out only in return for fees.

Antipope An illumination from a late-fourteenth-century French chronicle shows cardinals crowning the antipope Clement VII in Avignon.

THE GREAT SCHISM (1378–1417)

The return to Rome from Avignon was desired by many, from Italian members of the Curia itself to the influential writer Petrarch, who called Avignon "Babylon" and described the papal residence there as an exile like the Babylonian Captivity of the ancient Jews. Still, the return proved rough, even violent: the papacy waged war with Florence, traditionally a pro-papal city, over conflicting territorial claims in central Italy. And when the French pope Gregory XI (r. 1370–1378), who had brought the papacy back to Rome, died in 1378, the cardinals, pressed by the Roman populace, elected an Italian successor, Urban VI (r. 1378–1389). His conduct soon filled the cardinals with buyers' remorse. Urban insisted on the sole authority of the pope and demanded that the cardinals abandon their claims to a share of papal revenues. He called on them to live more simply and humbly, and continually abused them, exploding in fury at unpredictable intervals.

At the invitation of the French king Charles VI (r. 1380–1422), the French cardinals reconvened, deposed Urban, and elected Cardinal Robert of Geneva, who took the title of Pope Clement VII (r. 1378–1394) and set up his court in Avignon. Suddenly the universal church had two leaders, both apparently elected in the same way and by the same officials. Almost all of the Italian cardinals remained loyal to Urban. They declared Clement an antipope. Then the two popes excommunicated one another. For the next forty years, a period known as the **Great Schism**, Christians' allegiance was split, not between conflicting theologies but between two—and at one point among three—popes.

Much of Europe's business went on untroubled through this period. Bankers continued to transfer money and merchants to trade. Many Christians, having come to see the papacy as a purely administrative institution, paid little attention to which pope claimed ultimate authority over their sector of the Church, so long as masses were performed and the dead were buried. By the end of the 1380s, however, the Avignon church had increased its fiscal demands to even higher levels, while the Roman one campaigned to take control of Naples and southern Italy. The new Roman pope, Boniface IX (r. 1389–1404), became notorious for the financial pressures he exerted to maintain his political position. In 1390 alone, he excommunicated thirty bishops and sixty-five abbots for having fallen behind on the payments they owed the papacy for their offices. Savage attacks on the Roman papacy began to circulate, especially in northern Europe. More important, French clerics and theologians began to argue for other ways of defining the church. They identified it not with the pope but with the body of the faithful, represented by the bishops.

French kings and Burgundian dukes began to demand that both popes resign. A council held in Pisa from March through August 1409 declared both popes deposed for their grave sins. The popes struck back: they held councils of their own and eventually found successors. In 1417, at the **Council of Constance** (1414–18) in southern Germany, a Roman from the Colonna family, one of the noble clans that dominated the city of Rome, was elected Pope Martin V (r. 1417–1431). His international and financial positions were very weak. To gain the recognition of rulers and clerics across Europe, he had to give up many of his rights to bestow benefices and charge fees for doing so. His income amounted to a third of what his predecessors before the Great Schism had received. Accordingly, Martin used his local connections to begin the long process of reestablishing papal rule in Rome. From now on, there would be only one pope, and he would rule the Church from its ancient center, acting more and more like an Italian prince and drawing his chief power and revenues from Italy.

REFORM MOVEMENTS

Yet the Avignon Captivity and the subsequent Schism, together lasting from 1309 to 1417, had scratched and dented the aura of sanctity on which, in the end, papal authority rested. Signs of external resistance to papal authority accompanied these internal challenges. The English Parliament adopted the Statute of Provisors (1351), which prohibited papal interference in appointments to English benefices, and the Statute of Praemunire (1353), which forbade legal appeals outside the realm (i.e. to Rome). The latter also prohibited English subjects from obtaining bulls or other legal documents from the courts of the Roman Church, under penalty of expulsion from the king's protection and the forfeiture of property.

In England and Bohemia (now part of the Czech Republic), two vital centers of Christian culture, radical critics of the existing Church demanded that the Bible be translated from Latin and made available to all, and that religious services be held in the languages of ordinary men and women. Two theologians did much to form these movements. The Oxford theologian John Wycliffe (ca. 1330–1384) insisted on testing the institutions and practices of the Church against scripture. He found no support there for the idea that some Christians should lead a holier life than others as members of religious orders, or for many of the Church's practices, which he insisted were superstitious. Jan Hus (ca. 1372–1415), trained in theology at Prague, was inspired by Wycliffe as well as by his own study of the Bible. He denounced the immorality of the clergy and the wrong doctrines they taught. Both men found followers.

LOLLARDS John Wycliffe's message spread rapidly, at first primarily in England. His followers, who came to be known as Lollards, included a few men and women of high birth and a much larger number of small merchants, artisans, and peasants. Lollard beliefs spread mostly through personal ties: spouses converted spouses, parents instructed children, masters and mistresses taught servants. Lollards believed that every Christian, women as well as men, should read and interpret scripture—and in many cases spent long hours teaching basic literacy to members of their families. On the basis of their reading of the Bible, they rejected the whole hierarchy of the Church, from the pope on down, and demanded radical changes in religious services. They held their own religious meetings.

An initial period during which Lollards found some support at the universities gave way by 1400 to intense persecution by the Church and the English state. When a rebellion in England led by the Lollard Sir John Oldcastle failed in 1414 and another effort was repressed in 1439, Wycliffe's followers ceased to be an active force for a time. Still, they made their own editions of the Bible in English, copying them in secret scriptoria, and around 1,500 groups of them began to emerge from the shadows.

HUSSITES Dissent traveled with surprising speed and found more fertile ground on the Continent than it had in Britain. The kingdom of Bohemia was the richest part of central Europe in the fourteenth century. Its ruler, Charles IV (r. 1346–1378), who would later become Holy Roman emperor, built Prague, its capital, into a metropolis with some 40,000 inhabitants. He spanned the Vltava River with a magnificent stone bridge, began a cathedral, and founded a university. The countryside was relatively rich, cultivated by free peasants. Under his patronage, the Church became extraordinarily wealthy, controlling a third of the Bohemian lands. Reformers began to denounce the clergy for their wealth and worldliness. Czech scholars who studied in England brought back Wycliffe's new message.

Jan Hus, a young theologian who copied Wycliffe's works, developed his own reforming program, which he expounded in eloquent sermons. He believed that all lay Christians should join clerics in partaking of the wine

Jan Hus's Heresy In this fifteenth century manuscript illustration, a priest looks on as men—some stern, others celebratory—stoke the flames burning Hus at the stake. Hus wears the robe of a dissident cleric, while the sign on his hat condemns him as a heretic.

and bread during Communion, and that the Church must reform itself by giving up most of its wealth and power. At first, he found support from every level of the population, from nobles to artisans and peasants. Although a relative moderate who hoped to persuade the authorities to carry out necessary changes, Hus was imprisoned and condemned by the Council of Constance. In 1415 he was burned at the stake for heresy.

Hus's death turned his movement into a revolution. Hussites in Prague, most of them craftsmen, threw German nobles from the windows of the city hall in the Czech part of the city, and destroyed religious images and relics. Artisans and peasants in southern Bohemia, frightened by outbreaks of the Black Death, saw this movement as the beginning of the end of the world. They took up residence in a fortress south of Prague, to which they gave the biblical name Mount Tabor. Traveling when necessary in wagon trains that could be chained together in fortified camps, they abandoned all distinctions of clothing between priests and laypeople, demanded the abolition of courts and oaths, and fought off the crusades that the papacy sent against them. In 1434 the Taborites were defeated by more moderate Hussites, who negotiated a compromise treaty with the Latin Church, which allowed them to read their scriptures and practice their rites so long as they formally acknowledged papal supremacy. The wealth and power of the Church in Bohemia remained

greatly diminished, and the Hussites were allowed to use their own liturgy and give Communion with both bread and wine: a powerful exception to the long-established unity of the Latin Church.

CONCILIARISTS (1409–1449) Through the first decades of the fifteenth century, reforming cardinals and theologians, concerned about these threats to the Church as well as the problems of papal governance, continued to call councils. As early as the thirteenth century, some theologians—worried by increasing papal power and the possibility that its holder might become a heretic—theorized that although the pope was the steward of God, those who had elected him on behalf of the Christian people could also depose him when necessary. During the Great Schism, advocates of the councils—in later years they came to be called Conciliarists—argued that a representative body composed of cardinals, bishops, and others should hold supreme authority in the Church. The Council of Constance decreed that the authority of the council, since it came directly from God, was binding on all Christians, even the pope. Further councils met in Basel, Switzerland; Florence; and Ferrara, Italy, in the 1430s. All of these efforts, though attended with much powerful rhetoric and supported by some sincere believers, ran into the sand. Pope Pius II (r. 1458–1464), an Italian scholar and onetime Conciliarist, gained firm control of the Church in 1458 after he turned back a conspiracy of cardinals who hatched a plot against him in the Vatican lavatory, where they had gathered in the hope of electing a weaker Frenchman. Yet the papacy had lost much ground.

ORTHODOXY IN OTTOMAN LANDS Long before Pius became pope, he insisted that the whole Christian church was really one, and that Catholics had a duty to help the Orthodox Christians of Byzantium defend themselves against the Ottomans. Serious efforts were made to reunite the Greek and Russian Orthodox Churches with the Roman Church. At the Council of Florence in 1439, prelates from both eastern churches signed an act of union with Rome. But Vasily II (r. 1425–1462), the Grand Prince of Moscow, rejected the agreement. And though the Byzantine emperor John VIII Palaeologus accepted the union, the clergy and monks of the Greek Orthodox Church never did.

After Constantinople fell to the Ottomans in 1453, Pius proclaimed a crusade to retake the city. A brilliant writer of Latin, he did his best to appeal to all of the mixed groups of Europeans who held power and might take part, from feudal lords in northern Europe to merchants in Italy.

But only a small crusading force arrived in the port of Ancona on the eastern coast of Italy, most of which dissipated when the promised transport was slow to arrive. Pius himself died of fever, but the crusading ideal lived on, revived again and again, especially as Christian propaganda against the Ottomans.

A measure of coexistence developed in the Ottoman lands, where the Orthodox Church adapted to surviving under Muslim rule. Granted authority over all its churches and their property, the patriarchate of Constantinople was reestablished by Mehmed II in 1454 and conferred on a reliably anti-Catholic cleric. For centuries to come, the Greek Orthodox Church survived within the larger Ottoman framework. The Orthodox clergy were left in charge of powerful institutions, such as their many wealthy and massive monasteries. Gradually the Church was charged with legal as well as religious power over all of the sultan's Christian subjects. The patriarch collected taxes from Christians for the sultan, and handled all legal cases connected with marriage, divorce, or commercial relations between Christians and Muslims in the Ottoman lands.

"APPETITE FOR THE DIVINE"

The vast majority of western Europeans continued to be faithful Catholics, as their ancestors had been. If anything, in fact, they were more faithful than the generations that immediately preceded them. Most Christians made their yearly confession, attended their church each week, and followed the rituals of the Christian year, relatively austere in summer and fall but crammed with feast days in winter and spring. They attended the Latin Mass that was sung for them by cathedral or parish clergy, and viewed the stories of the Old and New Testaments rendered in sculpture, tapestry, or stained glass.

People who were neither rich nor saintly still showed—as the great French historian Lucien Febvre once remarked—a "boundless appetite for the divine." Plays and rituals based on the Bible continued to be staged before broad audiences. **Confraternities** (lay religious organizations) promoted active pursuit of Christian virtue in many ways. Hundreds of them flourished across Europe, especially in cities. Counting women as well as men as members, their activities ran the gamut, from doing penance together by flagellation, to visiting the sick, accompanying the condemned to execution, and writing letters to Saint Peter recommending fellow members, with whom they were buried.

A few saints continued to walk the streets, their

Christian Confraternities Members of the Florentine Compagnia dei Buonomini confraternity distribute clothes to the poor in this late-fifteenth-century fresco by the artist Domenico Ghirlandaio.

sanctity recognized by all. In the mid-fifteenth century, Rome was still largely vacant, with no more than 40,000 inhabitants wandering its streets and squares. Courtesans and merchants selling pilgrims' badges and other mementoes from small shops and outdoor tables crowded around the great Roman churches. Mingling among them was Saint Francesca Romana (1384–1440), the mystic who followed the course charted by her medieval predecessors as she made the ascent to spiritual union with God. Francesca had vivid visions and revelations, and worked, with the efficiency that only mystics and other supremely single-minded individuals enjoy, to create a hospital and a confraternity. She enjoyed such prestige that her very presence on the dark, violent streets of Rome could bring an end to feuds and, supposedly, heal mortal wounds.

NEW DIRECTIONS IN RELIGIOUS LIFE

Impresarios of the sacred created new ways of living a Christian life as deftly as Francis and Dominic had in the thirteenth century, when they called the mendicant orders into being. The Dutch cleric Geert Groot (1340–1384) founded houses for men and women who called themselves the Brothers and Sisters of the Common Life. They lived together, not taking vows. All of them—aristocrats and artisans, rich women and poor—worked for their living with their hands, in order to pursue poverty in a simpler, more literal way than that practiced by the powerful religious orders. Some members of this movement worked at first as scribes, then became printers when the new technology reached their city, using it to provide prayers and meditations for readers who shared their desire for a simple piety.

BEGUINES Across Europe, women experimented with new ways of life, inspired by religion. In the thirteenth century, beguines appeared in French and Netherlandish cities: women who lived in their own houses or in communities without taking vows, dressed simply, and did not marry. In the fourteenth and fifteenth centuries, beguine residences in Bruges and other cities in the Low Countries grew as women from poorer families joined, expanding into large courtyards lined by tiny houses in which the women lived. In the same period, religious houses of women living communally, but without a rule or, in some cases, male supervision, appeared in every Italian city. A new literature took shape: lives of the sisters who had created the houses and treatises on contemplation, written by and for women.

DEPARTURES FROM SCHOLASTICISM The energies of the Church went in other directions as well. In the twelfth and thirteenth centuries, scholastic theology had been a specialty of the universities of northern and western Europe. From the middle of the fourteenth century on, however, the effort to arrive at fundamental truths about God and the universe by formal argument spread into new parts of Europe. From Spain to Bohemia to Scotland, new universities popped up. And theologians were beginning to challenge the beautiful, coherent structures of doctrine that scholastics such as Thomas Aquinas had reared.

The Franciscan Roger Bacon (ca. 1214–ca. 1292), originally trained at Oxford, became an influential teacher at Paris in the mid-thirteenth century. He revised the scholastic program in multiple ways. It was wrong, he argued, to content oneself with word-for-word Latin translations from Aristotle, often hard to understand and sometimes inaccurate. Theologians must study Greek and other languages in which important forms of knowledge were preserved, and learn to read texts critically and correct them—or declare them spurious—when necessary. A believer in astrology, which he thought explained the course of world history, Bacon was also an engaged empiricist who devised experiments with lenses and argued that the university scholar needed to study the practical men who had learned to steer ships using a magnetic compass. In some ways, Bacon called for a return to the world of Aristotle and the Alexandrian scholars who had combined the study of texts with practical investigation of nature,

or that of the earlier House of Wisdom. But he believed that even more could be done. Someday, he claimed, magnificent technologies unknown in his day would make it possible for men to fly and transmute metals.

More radical, in some ways, than Bacon—and more influential in their time—was another Franciscan, William of Occam (ca. 1287–1347). Thomas Aquinas had believed, in a tradition going back to Plato, that general terms such as *beauty* and *goodness* referred to ideal forms that actually existed somewhere in the universe. Occam denied the existence of such abstract entities, and insisted that human language and argument could never prove the existence and justice of God. Fifteenth-century theologians took up and continued the debate between Occam and Aquinas; some shared Bacon's interest in astrology. And as the weighty issues about the structure of the Church and the location of its authority became the subjects of long, impassioned debates in the era of schism and councils, the French Conciliarist Jean Gerson and others began to devise ways of treating theological questions in shorter, more accessible forms such as pamphlets, which could be read by anyone literate, even if he or she did not have formal training in theology.

WITCHCRAFT: THEORY AND PRACTICE The most fertile of all the late-medieval approaches to the scholastic form of argument, tragically, was taken by German Dominicans. Since antiquity, Christians had determined that the devil not only existed but also regularly intervened in everyday life, hoping to lure Christians to their damnation and drawing on the help of lower devils. They had also accepted that some humans were witches—magicians who invoked the help of the devil to cast spells. But the theologians of the fifteenth century applied their full methods—for the first time—to the scattered anecdotes and sometimes-contradictory laws about witchcraft. They developed a coherent theory, which they laid out in systematic, cogently presented treatises. Devils, they argued, really walked the earth. They were replicas of human beings, which could take either male or female form and could speak and act. In their male form, they seduced human women, whom they persuaded to join the legions of the evil and to conjure harm by killing babies, drawing down hailstorms to destroy crops, and rendering men impotent. Worst of all, they produced diabolic offspring by injecting women with corrupted sperm that, in their female form, they had drawn from men they seduced. Every time a wife failed to conceive, a baby died in childbirth, crops failed, or livestock died, a witch might be to blame—and the devil with her.

Dominican theologians believed that only subtle, trained interrogators—backed, as always, by the threat and application of torture—could wring the truth from these enemies of the human race, avert their efforts to seduce their accusers, and combat the terrifying threat they represented. By the end of the fifteenth century, the first large witch trials were being held in Germany, Switzerland, and Italy. True, the real rage for holding them did not catch on until after 1560 or so, when a series of trials began that would eventually take some 30,000 to 70,000 lives across Europe, the majority of them female. But the belief in a conspiracy to destroy mankind—as neat and logical in its own way as the universe that Aquinas had built—made sense in a precarious world where plague endlessly returned and death threatened humans and animals alike. Every Christian baby, after all, was exorcized to remove the corruption of the devil before being baptized—a practice not abandoned until a Church council ended it in the 1960s. It made sense—the specialty of the scholastic theologian—to take seriously the idea of diabolic intervention in the world, and to draw out all of the ramifications it might have, one by one.

PERSECUTION OF NON-CHRISTIANS If witches did not materialize immediately on cue, however, other enemies did. In Trent, on the border between Italy and the Holy Roman Empire, Jews were accused in 1475, as they had been for centuries, of murdering Christian boys to use their blood for ritual purposes; several were condemned and executed. Further ritual-murder trials spread across the German world, and Jews were ejected from cities such as Regensburg, where they had lived since Roman times. The Jews of Spain, as we have seen, were forced in 1492 to convert or leave the country. In Italy, Jews were forced, far more systematically than ever before, to wear yellow patches—and in the case of women, earrings—to set them apart from Christians. Gradually they were confined to small, closed neighborhoods known as ghettos. Small groups of Ashkenazi Jews from western Europe and much larger communities of Sephardic Jews expelled from Spain and Portugal settled in cities across the Ottoman Empire, from Istanbul and Salonika in northern Greece to Jerusalem and Safed in Palestine. Like Orthodox Christians, the Jews lived as a protected nation in the Ottoman Empire, and many flourished in trade and banking.

Meanwhile, officials in Spain became increasingly expert in working out which supposed Christians not only had Jewish ancestors but continued to observe certain Jewish rituals, and which Moriscos, as Muslim converts were called, did the same with their traditions.

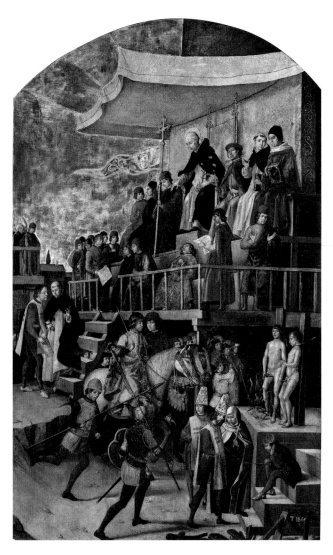

The Spanish Inquisition After ferreting out heretics, the Inquisition tribunal would pronounce judgment in a ceremony called the *auto da fé* (Portuguese for "act of faith") that would often include a procession, a mass, and a reading of the sentence in the town's piazza. Secular authorities would then carry out the sentence. In 1499, the tribunal asked painter Pedro Berruguete to depict Saint Dominic, the founder of the Dominican order, presiding over an *auto da fé*, as proof that the practice was a holy one.

From 1478, moreover, an official tribunal, the Spanish Inquisition, made the detection of crypto-Jews and, to a lesser extent, Moriscos its central business. Close inspection of genealogies and behavior, from eating to praying, enabled the inquisitors to detect the enemies of humanity. Modernity—as the history of the twentieth century shows—has brought with it both horrors and enlightenment. Both were amply present at the birth of the modern world, from the European settlements in the Iberian Peninsula to the heartlands of Catholic culture.

EUROPE EXPANDS: NEW TECHNOLOGIES AND THEIR CONSEQUENCES

Renaissance Europe was born under the signs of contraction and despair. The Black Death had devastated Europe in the mid-fourteenth century, and recurrences of the plague kept population levels low into the fifteenth century. And yet, beneath the turbulence, as we have seen in the areas of state formation and religion, Europeans were laying the foundations for recovery and transformation. The paired discoveries of a new world and an ancient past brought changes more startling than anything Europe—or the world—had previously experienced.

MARITIME ADVANCES

Even after 1453, when the Venetians lost the immense foothold in the eastern Mediterranean that Constantinople had provided, they and the Genoese continued to expand their mercantile empires. Venetian fleets, developed by state action, and Genoese ones, normally financed by private partnerships, ranged the Mediterranean. Venetians, Genoese, and other European mariners, moreover, continued to develop new techniques.

Although no one knows who invented the maps known as **portolan charts**, which came into widespread use in the fourteenth and fifteenth centuries, they were practical in a way that the scholars' schematic maps never had been. Portolan charts detailed the coastlines where European merchants mingled with the Asian and North African merchants with whom they could bargain for gold, spices, and silks. The new maps largely ignored the mainland interiors that Ptolemy and his Greek copyists had filled with rivers, mountains, and cities. Instead the maps traced, with ever-increasing precision, the primary routes that led from port to port. Equipped with portolans—and with magnetic compasses, the floating lodestones that also came into widespread use in the fourteenth and fifteenth centuries—European merchants could explore more widely than ever before.

The ships themselves, moreover, became capable of undertaking longer journeys. Alongside the low galleys, powered by oars and a single square sail, that had plied the Mediterranean since ancient times, new types of ships were developed with three or four masts. Equipped with complex rigging, they could both sail into the wind and tack before it, and could carry larger cargoes.

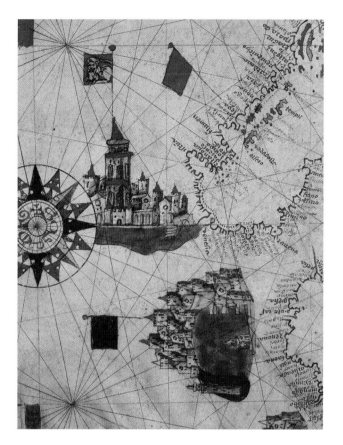

Portolan Charts New cartographic technology allowed navigators to follow the routes between ports. This fifteenth-century portolan chart of Italian trade routes includes illustrations of Venice and Genoa.

Caravels—small, slender, and maneuverable—navigated shallow coastal waters and explored rivers. Carracks—larger, with high, rounded sterns—were more stable and could carry more goods. The Europeans who sailed these ships mastered new navigation techniques. They learned, for example, that the Atlantic winds blew steadily back to the east. To return to Europe, ships entering the Atlantic from the Mediterranean or the western coastlines of Europe had to keep sailing west until they caught the wind, which brought them home.

EARLY ATLANTIC EXPEDITIONS

Support for these expeditions into the unknown came from more than one source. Henry the Navigator (1394–1460), fifth son of the king of Portugal, joined his father and brothers in 1415 in an attack on the Spanish city of Ceuta on the Moroccan coast, a convenient base for raids on Portugal across the narrow Strait of Gibraltar. Their success in taking the city encouraged Henry to organize

Henry the Navigator The Portuguese prince appears in a detail from a 1465 painting that shows the most important members of Portuguese society venerating Saint Vincent—hence Henry's pious posture and expression.

a series of further expeditions, which gradually pushed down the western coast of Africa and westward into the Atlantic. He was impelled by the hope of joining forces with a Christian ally in Africa, the king of Ethiopia, whose wealth and power were exaggerated by European reports. But possibilities of profit were also attractive.

The spice trade brought Europeans not only the sharp flavorings they demanded for their food but also a wider range of products, including such substances as opium, mummy (an aromatic exuded by embalmed bodies), and tutty (dried chimney scrapings), which were used in medicine. It yielded immense profits to the Muslim merchants who brought products to India and then across the Persian Gulf and Red Sea, where land routes continued to Europe. Venice had dominated the western end of these routes in the Mediterranean, but once Constantinople fell in 1453, the Ottomans controlled the trade and could raise taxes at will. Was it possible, the Portuguese and others now began to ask, to sail around Africa to reach the sources of spice directly?

By the beginning of the fifteenth century, the new techniques and vessels carried Spanish and Portuguese sailors and traders farther and farther from the known Mediterranean routes. Both groups found and settled massive island chains in the Atlantic: the Portuguese took the Azores, and the Spanish—after struggles with the Portuguese that ended only in 1479—the Canary Islands. These islands offered timber and land for cultivation. When the Madeira archipelago proved poor territory for grain production, Henry ordered the planting of sugarcane and sugar beets, both successful crops on the Mediterranean island of Cyprus. In the Mediterranean, Venice held a monopoly on the shipping of sugar. Genoese investors supported the building of sugar plantations on Madeira, which eventually surpassed Cyprus as a producer of sugar and brought great profits to Portugal.

TO THE INDIAN OCEAN

Gold, and ornaments made out of it, had always filtered north to Europe from Guinea, carried by Arab caravans across the Sahara to the ports of the North African region known as the Maghreb. But after the Portuguese established an African base in 1415, sailors made their way down Africa's west coast, where they came into direct contact with the kingdoms of Guinea. Their progress was often violent, combining trading with raiding. Slowly the Portuguese built forts, established trading posts, and staged a long series of expeditions that gradually charted the entire western coast of Africa.

Finally, the Portuguese navigator Vasco da Gama (ca. 1460–1524) rounded the Cape of Good Hope in an epic ocean journey that lasted from 1497 to 1499 and covered a greater distance than any previous European voyage. He touched down in eastern Africa, stunned by the quality and quantity of goods traded in the Indian Ocean. Da Gama was turned away, however, by the Muslim ruler of Mozambique, who found his gifts insultingly poor. With the help of an experienced Indian Ocean pilot, da Gama negotiated the monsoon winds and reached India in twenty-three days. He made land in Calicut, on the Malabar Coast, the center of the spice trade. Da Gama possessed only modest trading goods and found opposition at the hands of Muslim merchants, but he and his crew obtained some spices by bartering on the docks. Only a gift of meat and oranges from the ruler of Malindi enabled da Gama and his crew to make the voyage home, and fewer than a third of the crew survived. But when da Gama returned to Portugal in July 1499, it was clear that eastward voyages could yield extraordinary returns.

Further Portuguese voyages to Indian Ocean ports carried more extensive trading goods and were better prepared for the journey. The first was led by Pedro Álvares Cabral (1467/8–1520), who became the first European explorer to reach Brazil before he turned east to follow da Gama's route. But the Portuguese also came into sharp conflict with Muslim merchants, who killed fifty of Cabral's men. He retaliated by burning ten Muslim cargo vessels and killing almost 600 men, then moved on to establish a trading post at Cochin, also on the Malabar Coast. His return to Portugal, with seven of his original thirteen ships, showed that the old monopoly of Muslim traders on the spice trade was broken. Da Gama's next

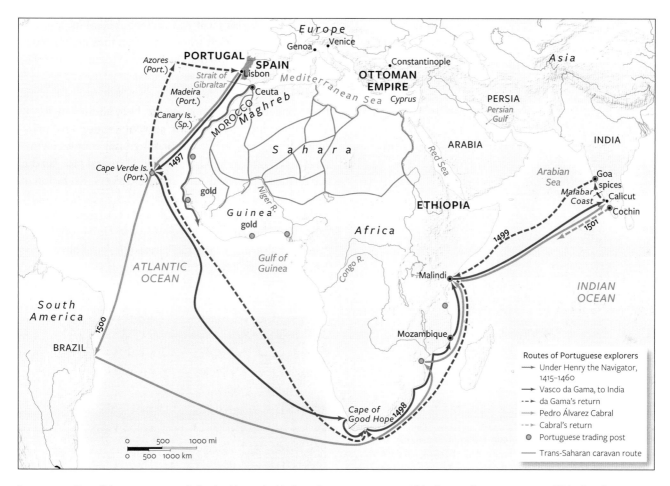

Portuguese Expeditions, 1415–1500 Following Henry the Navigator's voyage to western Africa in 1415, the Portuguese established trading posts along the coast and claimed the Azores and the Madeira archipelago. In 1497–99, Vasco da Gama's first voyage to western India opened up access to the spice trade, leading to expedition and Portuguese naval dominance in the Indian Ocean.

expedition amounted to a terror campaign against Muslim shipping, and he left a Portuguese naval force in Indian waters. Thanks to their superior military power, the Portuguese were soon able to establish a network of colonies that stretched from Mozambique to Goa, and to create a vastly profitable trade.

SLAVERY AND THE SLAVE TRADE

Europeans, Arabs, Africans, and others had traded for slaves for centuries. From the second half of the thirteenth century, Venetian and Genoese merchants bought slaves in markets around the Aegean and Black Seas. The high mortality induced by the Black Death helped to expand the market for this trade—most of whose victims were Mongols, Slavs, or Circassians, with a small number of Greeks and Christians from the Balkans. Practices differed according to local conditions. In Genoa, the number

of slaves doubled to 4,000 or 5,000—almost 10 percent of the population—during the fifteenth century. In Florence, by contrast, there were only 360 slaves in a population of 37,000 in 1427. These northern Italian slaves were mostly young women bought to serve as domestic workers. In the agricultural lands of southern Italy, by contrast, Muslim slaves were also sold, and men as well as women were bought to work in the fields.

Africa, like other parts of the world, had long been the scene of multiple forms of slavery: slaves included people captured in raids or in war, those who could not pay their debts, and people required for sacrifice in religious rituals. Slave women and children worked in the fields and households, men in the salt mines of the Sahara. Slaves were sold by Nubian, Ethiopian, and Funj masters, and brought by Arab merchants from the kingdoms of eastern and western Africa across the Sahara to markets in Algiers, Tripoli, and Cairo. The trans-Saharan slave trade supplied labor for the sugar plantations developed

Portuguese Slave Trade, 1444–1500 Enslaved Africans had long worked in the salt mines of the Sahara and had been sold in the Arab ports of Algiers, Tripoli, and Cairo. But the Atlantic slave trade began in 1444 when Portuguese traders brought slaves from western Africa to work on the sugar plantations on Madeira, the Canary Islands, and the Cape Verde Islands.

bought a house for meetings, and interceded successfully, in at least a few cases, when Christian masters set out to imprison or send into distant slavery African women who displeased them.

Black men and women moved into the rest of Europe, from Britain to Italy and beyond. They labored in dozens of occupations, as domestic servants, musicians, printing workers, and Venetian gondoliers. As couples formed and marriages took place, people of mixed race further diversified the crowds in European streets. Exclusionary practices spread: many guild statutes, such as those of the goldsmiths of Lisbon, prohibited slaves from becoming members. But these practices were not universal: Lisbon pie-makers, though they too banned slaves, explicitly proclaimed that free Christian black people from Africa and

by Moroccan entrepreneurs. In 1444, however, the Portuguese began to transport slaves by ship directly from western Africa to their homeland, eliminating the Arab middlemen of the Maghreb. Portuguese shipments of slave labor to the sugar plantations of Madeira, the Canary Islands, and the Cape Verde Islands formed the beginning of what would become the vast transatlantic slave trade, which the Portuguese extended to their colony in Brazil in the 1530s.

In Europe, more and more Africans, male and female, were brought to do every sort of work. Peoples and cultures mixed. Guinean artisans began to craft small sculptures of gold and ivory that included European objects (such as ships) and people, represented in styles that reflected European tastes. Enslaved and free black people entered Portugal—where, in some cities, they lived by the thousands, forming their own Christian congregations. In Valencia, a wealthy city on the Mediterranean coast of Spain, African slaves formed a religious confraternity,

Africans in Europe A portrait from the late sixteenth century, attributed to Italian painter Annibale Carracci (1560–1609), depicts an African woman in European clothing holding a clock of European manufacture, evidence of the presence of Africans in European society.

people of mixed European and African descent could be considered. The population on the streets of Europe was now, in part, nonwhite.

PRINTING: THE BOOK TRANSFORMED (1450–1517)

As transformative as the new ships and navigational techniques were, in some ways the most powerful—and potentially the most explosive—of all the new technologies that Europeans adopted in the fifteenth century was the printing press. For centuries, Asians had carved wood blocks and used them to print texts and illustrations. By the thirteenth century, Chinese printers were using wood blocks and moveable wooden type, which for the tens of thousands of Chinese characters were easier to produce and cheaper to replace than the cast metal type developed by the Koreans around the same time. Korea even developed a form of moveable type with a simplified alphabet rather than characters—though it was kept a royal monopoly and used only for official publications. Still, in the fifteenth and sixteenth centuries, bookshops in China and elsewhere in Asia brimmed with offerings of every kind, from official texts to pamphlets and gazetteers.

Europeans came later to the field, as the products needed for printing gradually reached the Continent. From the thirteenth century on, another Asian invention, paper made with cloth fibers from rags, came into wider use. It did not entirely replace parchment, made from the skin of calves and sheep, which had been the standard medium for centuries and continued to be used, especially for many types of legal documents. But paper sharply lowered the cost of writing materials and books. Through the first half of the fifteenth century, Europeans carried out experiments with printing single sheets from wood blocks and metal plates. These revolutionized the visual arts and yielded a fair number of illustrated books, printed page by page. They were narratives of biblical history and saints' lives, for the most part, reproduced in outline and then colored by hand, like graphic novels that combined a traditional faith in the old sacred narratives with an interest in new stories about the monsters that dwelled at the ends of the earth.

GUTENBERG In the 1450s, however, **Johannes Gutenberg** (1398–1468) created something that Europeans had not seen before. A craftsman—he seems to have been both a goldsmith and a blacksmith—Gutenberg came from a well-off merchant family in the German city of Mainz. His ancestors had worked in the mint of the local bishop, and Gutenberg may have learned about presses and molds from them. He spent the 1430s and 1440s tinkering with various projects, including a device for polishing metal mirrors. At least one of these efforts ended in bankruptcy. By the late 1440s he was borrowing money and working on something new. By bringing together old and new technologies, Gutenberg made it possible to produce books mechanically, rather than by hand.

Gutenberg himself may have devised one of the vital components: an oil-based ink that would stick to the metal type and then transfer neatly onto paper. He also crafted type for the Latin alphabet, molding the individual characters in sand. And he worked out how to set lines of type into a frame and lock them in place. This frame could be set into the existing technology of the hand press, long used for producing olive oil and metal badges. Simply

Gutenberg Bible Early printed books were often decorated with elaborate illustrations in the style of handwritten illuminated manuscripts, as on this page from a Gutenberg Bible. The large initial letter "P" surrounds a miniature portrait of King Solomon, and marks the beginning of the book of Proverbs.

by turning a large metal screw that pressed the frame down onto paper, Gutenberg's workers could print a whole series of pages at one time. Each sheet of paper would then be extracted from the press, dried, and folded so that its component pages appeared in the correct order.

In some ways, Gutenberg—like other early modern revolutionaries—was conservative. The first book that he printed—the enormous and beautiful book known as the Gutenberg Bible—faithfully reproduced, in larger format, what had been a standard form for manuscript Bibles since the early thirteenth century: a Latin Bible laid out in two columns of text per page. An observer who saw the book as it went through the press was struck by the neatness and legibility of its type, not by the novelty of its production. Manuscripts were not only written but illuminated (illustrated): decorated with very large initial letters, for example, that incorporated exquisite miniature paintings. Many copies of the Gutenberg Bible were also illustrated by hand, giving them the look of traditional manuscripts. Some were purchased for use in monasteries, probably for reading aloud, since their large, clear type would have been helpful for that purpose.

The Spread of Printing, 1455–1500

THE IMMEDIATE IMPACT OF BOOK PRINTING

Gutenberg's breakthrough did not so much revolutionize literacy in Europe as accelerate a revolution that was already under way. Medieval European society was already highly literate. Cities swarmed with notaries, accountants, and government clerks, all of them skilled in writing and computation. Religious dissidents copied their own Bibles, prayer books, and commentaries. More conservative Christians did the same. Many of the most popular books—the ones that printers immediately began to reproduce—were highly traditional: for example, the books of hours, which developed from the breviaries used by priests to recite the daily service in the mid-thirteenth century. Some of these, beautifully illuminated by such artists as Jan Van Eyck (ca. 1395–ca. 1441), were spectacular works of art reserved for the wealthiest patrons. But stationers in France and the Netherlands also mass-produced less-expensive versions without full-page illustrations. By 1500, a British female pauper was indicted for stealing a book of hours from a female servant—evidence that these functional books were available not only to the rich.

Printers rapidly transformed the existing networks of the book trade. Master printers found bankers to lend them capital so that they could obtain a house, type, a press, ink, and paper. Some printers formed partnerships with colleagues in other cities to exchange their products, so that each had a wider range of books to sell. Large and costly books, which required a great deal of paper, were produced by two or more printers working together in a syndicate. Universities, with their large student markets, proved especially welcoming. Two professors at the Sorbonne in Paris created a press in 1470, and then moved it to what became the center of the trade, the Rue Saint-Jacques. Other presses nested inside the colleges of the University of Paris, printing textbooks in small runs when the teaching staff needed them. Printing reached the University of Oxford by 1478.

Over time, printing proved to be, if anything, even more adaptable than the scribe's trade. Gutenberg printed not only his famous Bible, but also an almanac with instructions for bloodletting (a popular form of therapy) and a papal bull against the Turks in both German and Latin. Soon printers were turning out everything from editions of the Latin and Greek classics designed to please the educated elite, to theological and legal texts for the universities, to tiny pamphlets. Large books were designed to rest on wooden stands in university halls and scholars' studies. Books in the small octavo format—more or less the size of a modern mass-market paperback—could be carried in a bag or purse and dipped into at leisure. Broadsides—single sheets with vivid woodcut illustrations that described strange happenings and major battles—could be rapidly produced and peddled in city squares and village marketplaces. For the first time, people began to expect news to arrive regularly, in printed form.

Books multiplied faster than ever before, and as we well know, the speed with which messages travel can vastly increase their impact. By the end of the fifteenth century, some 27,000 distinct works had been printed—a flood of texts and images of every kind, ancient and medieval, Christian and Muslim, genuine and forged. One early media event makes clear their impact. At the beginning of the sixteenth century, almanac makers noticed that a conjunction of the planets would take place in 1524 in the zodiacal sign of Pisces, the Fish. They predicted that this

The Book Trade A French woodcut from around 1500 illustrates a Parisian street vendor hawking cheap books of hours and alphabet books for children, which the printing press made readily available to the public.

would cause a terrible flood, and the prediction went viral in almanacs and other small, inexpensive books. When 1524 came, the rains did not prove especially heavy. But thousands of Italians and Germans took to the hills, propelled by the rumors spread by the printing press. They and the astrologers became laughingstocks, mocked for years to come in another form of popular media, the comic plays performed in market squares.

It is difficult to assess the impact of printing in more general terms. It made books cheaper, though not cheap: prices for classical texts dropped by about half in Rome after a press was established there in 1470. The circulation of alphabet books, primers, and broadsides put literacy within the reach of more people across society than manuscript culture had. Print was provocative. Texts that had never been edited to ensure that they were factually accurate or theologically orthodox could now circulate in thousands of copies. Printing also gave publicity to figures whom the political and religious authorities would have liked to suppress. Thus small, elegant Italian editions of the works and doings of Savonarola, the rebellious

Dominican friar, helped to preserve his legacy and inspire his followers. Yet the traditional books of hours went through many more editions. Some of the first witnesses of presses in action praised the speed with which books could be produced. Others denounced printing as an invention of the devil. Even today, the effects of the first modern media revolution evade simple judgments.

DISCOVERY: A NEW WORLD

It was the products of the press—as well as the navigational skills and maritime technology that Europeans had amassed—that impelled the Spanish to undertake their extraordinary expansion to the New World and beyond. **Christopher Columbus** (1457–1506) was a skilled mariner from Genoa, who served in the 1470s and 1480s as a business representative for influential local families and helped to man armed convoys. By the late 1470s, he was sailing on a Portuguese ship and trading for Genoese backers at the Portuguese stations in western Africa. A passionate reader, he came across Latin texts by medieval and contemporary theologians that led him to believe that the world was approaching its end. All peoples, he thought, might soon be reunited as Christians. More important still, he read Ptolemy's *Geography*, the most detailed and technically precise ancient description of the surface of the earth, composed in second-century Alexandria. Ptolemy greatly overestimated the length of the continent of Asia and believed that only water separated it from Europe. Inspired by this ancient authority and filled with enthusiasm by his reading of theologians and prophets, Columbus became convinced that it must be possible to reach Asia relatively quickly by sailing due west.

COLUMBUS'S VOYAGES

Columbus persuaded the rulers of Spain, Ferdinand and Isabella, to support his enterprise by arguing—on the basis of Ptolemy—that the distance to Asia was far shorter than it actually is. On August 3, 1492, he set off with three ships. After stopping in the Canary Islands, he landed at a still unidentified island in the Bahamas. His mind stuffed with ancient reports of the strange races and gleaming treasures to be found in India, at the far eastern edge of the inhabited world, Columbus never worked out exactly what he had discovered. He described the natives he met as poor, naked, and generous, willing to swap treasures for

Columbus's Journeys This 1493 woodcut, from one of the earliest accounts of Columbus's first voyage to the Caribbean, shows King Ferdinand directing Columbus's ships to sail across the ocean. In the top half, the Spanish ships land in the New World, whose native inhabitants flee at the sight of them.

trinkets. But he also noted that some of them were "very fierce and eat human flesh," though he never explained how he had managed to learn this without knowing their languages.

This first trip took him to Cuba and Hispaniola, where one of his ships ran aground and had to be abandoned, and he left a small settlement behind. Using his mastery of the Atlantic winds, he sailed back to Europe, reaching Lisbon in March 1493 and Spain a week later. The news of his voyage spread rapidly, and the monarchs of Portugal and Spain both laid claim to the new discoveries. The dispute was eventually settled in 1494 by the **Treaty of Tordesillas**, which drew a boundary line 370 leagues (1,185 miles) west of the Cape Verde Islands, with Portugal controlling lands east of the line and Spain west.

Columbus set out again in September 1494, this time with seventeen ships and 1,200 men, planning to create settlements in the New World. Though his explorations were mostly confined to the Caribbean Islands—Guadeloupe, the Greater and Lesser Antilles and Hispaniola—on his third voyage in 1498 he reached the Orinoco delta at the northern edge of South America. Columbus correctly argued, from the vast amount of fresh water that the river sent out into the ocean, that he must have found an entire continent, but he believed then and for the rest of his life that the continent he had reached was Asia.

By the end of his third voyage, weakened by age and disease, Columbus found himself under attack by the colonists he had brought to the Americas. A fourth expedition launched in 1502 took him to Panama but ended with his ships beached in Jamaica, where he was stranded for a year. Beleaguered, criticized, and under heavy financial pressure, Columbus became convinced in the course of his later expeditions that he had actually discovered the Earthly Paradise, and believed that his discoveries were harbingers of the return of the Messiah. Bookishness could imprison as well as inspire readers.

EUROPEAN EXPLORATION AFTER COLUMBUS (1497–1522)

For all his illusions, however, Columbus was certain of one thing: the shores on which he landed offered resources of every kind for exploitation, from sheltered harbors to treasures of silver and gold to timber and spices. Expeditions set out from Europe in every direction. John Cabot (ca. 1450–ca. 1499), an Italian backed by King Henry VII of England, sailed straight west from Bristol in 1497 and made landfall in what was probably Newfoundland. By 1500 another Spanish fleet, led by the Florentine Amerigo Vespucci (ca. 1454–1512), had reached the mouth of the Amazon River. Portuguese expeditions, including a second one by Vespucci in 1501–2, found and explored the bulge of South America's eastern coast, and a French fleet landed in southern Brazil in 1504. In 1519, the Portuguese navigator Ferdinand Magellan (1480–1521) led a Spanish fleet of five ships on a voyage to circumnavigate the world. They sailed from Spain to South America and crossed through what is now called the Strait of Magellan into the Pacific Ocean, which they crossed on the way to the Spice Islands (now the Indonesian archipelago called the Moluccas). Though Magellan himself died in the Philippines, one ship returned to Seville in 1522.

Printing spread the news—often in the attractive if unreliable form of pamphlets, such as the short letters attributed to Vespucci that described both the Southern Cross and the cannibalism of American natives. Land expeditions began to fill in the vast blank spaces on the maps, as when Vasco Núñez de Balboa (1475–1519) crossed Panama in 1513 and became the first European to see the Pacific from the land side. Soldiers of fortune and missionary priests followed the first explorers. They spread

European Expeditions to the Western Hemisphere, 1492–1550 By the mid-sixteenth century, exploration and colonization linked Portugal and Spain to an expanse of new territory in the Americas and beyond. Christopher Columbus's voyages to the Caribbean first made Europeans aware of the resources of the Americas. Soon after, Amerigo Vespucci discovered the mouth of the Amazon River. Magellan crossed below the southern tip of South America into the Pacific, and one of his ships completed the first circumnavigation of the world. Later, Cortés travelled as far as central Mexico and conquered the Aztecs, and Pizarro pushed down into the Andes, where he overthrew the Inca. Once these ancient civilizations were defeated, the Spanish established control over much of the New World.

smallpox and other European diseases among the inhabitants of the New World, who had never been exposed to these pathogens and had no immunity. Millions died in the pandemics, radically weakening their states.

Exact statistics are impossible to provide, but many specialists believe that the population of the Americas fell from some 50 million in 1492 to as low as 6 million by 1650.

SPANISH CONQUEST

The pandemics made it possible for tiny groups of Europeans to conquer highly developed native civilizations. The Aztecs, for example, dominated much of Mesoamerica from their capital at Tenochtitlán, built on raised islands in Lake Texcoco—a setting unlike anything the Europeans had ever seen. The Aztecs and their allies used a combination of trade and conquest to extend their power, which rested on tribute paid by the other peoples of the Valley of Mexico. A caste of peasants who cultivated corn provided the material basis for a distinctive civilization. Magnificently armed and costumed warriors fought wars, regulated by an elaborate system of heroic values, to capture other brave men. War captives were sacrificed, their hearts cut out by priests atop the Aztecs' pyramids. The largest pyramid in Tenochtitlán had been the stage for tens of thousands of human sacrifices by the time the Spanish arrived.

Cortés and the Aztecs An illustration from a late-sixteenth-century Spanish history of the New World shows a tense meeting of Spanish and Aztec forces. The Aztec king Montezuma waves his finger angrily at Cortés and his soldiers, while an Aztec interpreter stands between the two parties.

Hernán Cortés (b. 1485–1547), who mounted an expedition to Mexico in defiance of his superior's orders to cancel it, reached Tenochtitlán by 1519. An adroit diplomat, by then he had made an alliance with the Tlaxcalans, enemies of the Aztecs. Though the Aztec ruler Montezuma admitted the Spanish and about a thousand Tlaxcalans to the city, strife broke out between the three parties. On July 1, 1520, the Spanish fought their way out of the city, across the raised causeways that gave access to it. In the spring of 1521 they returned to lay siege, and on August 13 they took the city, destroying it in the process. Cortés became the first governor of what was now New Spain. Another adventurous soldier, Francisco Pizarro (ca. 1475–1541), captured the emperor of the Incas, the people whose rich mountain empire stretched across the Andes, held together by astonishing roads and bridges. Though offered a huge bribe in gold, Pizarro found a pretext to execute the Inca ruler in 1533, making him master of another vast territory.

As the native kingdoms fell, great numbers of colonists emigrated from all regions of Spain to the New World—some 300,000 of them in the sixteenth century. The most successful of these migrants created *encomiendas*, large estates where they exercised near-absolute authority and used enserfed natives for labor. They rebuilt old cities and raised new ones on neat, systematic plans: Tenochtitlan, originally built on a grid, was reconfigured as Mexico City, capital of New Spain, one of two Spanish viceroyalties in sixteenth-century Latin America; Lima was built on a grid plan as the capital of the Viceroyalty of Peru. Vast lodes of silver in the sugarloaf-shaped mountain at Potosí, in modern Bolivia, founded as a mining town in 1545, became the site of the largest mining operation in the world. The treasure dug up at staggering human cost and shipped to Europe by the Spanish silver fleets made the rulers of Spain incomparably wealthier than their rivals, and strengthened Spain as a military power. New World silver gradually filtered through the European and Asian trade networks, exerting inflationary pressure on global prices and wages, and transforming China's economy.

Meanwhile, a historical struggle took shape in the Americas. Initially at Cortés's request, Franciscan and Dominican missionaries—many of them idealists—arrived in the New World nourishing high hopes for the American Indians, whom they saw as innocent and virtuous. They did their best to teach Christian doctrine and practice, and—as they became aware of the oppression many natives suffered as serfs of the colonists—tried to protect them against brutal exploitation. Bartolomé de Las Casas (1484–1566), a Dominican who became the first bishop of

Christianity in the New World In a set of 1531 legal documents drawn up by the Huexotzinco people, from an area near Mexico City, a pictographic rendering lists the taxes the Spanish colonial authorities demanded of them. The inclusion of a banner of the Virgin Mary and Baby Jesus indicates the influence of Spanish religion on indigenous perceptions only ten years after conquest.

Chiapas, in southern Mexico, actually to live and work in his diocese, pleaded with the Spanish crown to end the system of forced labor. He argued that the Indians were highly intelligent, as the complexity of their preconquest societies proved, and should enjoy decent living conditions and a chance to become believing Christians. Largely due to Las Casas's efforts, in 1542 the Spanish king promulgated the New Laws, which forbade the *encomenderos* to force Indians to work for them or to bequeath their estates to their children. Although the encomiendas were made heritable again in 1545, and *encomenderos* resisted the New Laws, the number of serfs fell. But the population decline continued, indicating that the majority of American natives who survived the Spanish conquest suffered in many ways for having done so.

COLUMBIAN EXCHANGES

The encounter between European and New World peoples was one of the great dramas of human history—a drama that continued long after the initial, catastrophic population loss unleashed by conquest and disease. Europeans brought with them all the elements of their civilization, from their domesticated dogs and horses and their

technical devices to their Christian religion and romance literature, which helped to inspire the conquistadores as they rode out to battle. In Latin America a new society took shape—one whose elite was often created by intermarriage between the conquerors and the descendants of native princes. Intermarriage was common at all levels: by the eighteenth century, the majority of Mexicans and Central and South Americans were so-called mestizos, people of mixed blood. They were served by a distinctive form of Christianity. Church architecture and religious images blended traditional Christian stories and teachings with native imagery. Indians took part with special enthusiasm, as the best-informed missionaries realized, in those Christian rites and festivals that fell on significant days in their own ancient calendars. Meanwhile, the horse—unknown in the New World before the conquerors arrived—spread throughout the Americas, transforming the lives of the Plains Indians, who had relatively little direct contact with either the Spanish or the inhabitants of Latin America.

In return, the New World had far more to offer the Old. Transported east across the Atlantic, staple agricultural products found acceptance in Europe at differing rates. Tomatoes and potatoes had little impact in the sixteenth century, but eventually they transformed Old World agriculture and diet. By contrast, tobacco and chocolate—both far stronger than their modern versions, and both central to American Indian religious rituals that fascinated Western observers and taught them how to consume these powerful stimulants—reshaped European social customs. In 1500, Europeans did not use tobacco or anything like it. A hundred years later, Europeans of all social ranks smoked or inhaled it. Taverns and other gathering places reeked of tobacco, as they would for centuries to come. Meanwhile, hot chocolate became a beloved luxury of elites, served at festive meals and sipped elegantly from tiny cups.

European sailors and soldiers also returned home with an unwelcome import: syphilis, a sexually transmitted disease that seems not have existed in Europe before 1492. It spread across the European continent, where it soon became an epidemic, with results that horrified sufferers and observers. The standard treatment involved drinking or applying a medicine made from the bark of the guaiacum tree, which—like the disease—came from the New World. The Fuggers, a prominent German banking family, soon established a monopoly on the sale of this bark, as they did with mercury, another treatment that could be effective but caused horrific side effects.

At the same time, the feather headdresses, jewels, and

illuminated codices of New World rulers were exhibited in the court museums of Europe. The skill of their makers won the admiration of such great artists as Albrecht Dürer, who saw what he described as a sun of gold and a moon of silver, along with other treasures and weapons from Mexico, in Brussels in 1520. "All the days of my life," he reflected, "I have seen nothing that rejoiced my heart so much as these things, for I saw among them wonderful works of art, and I marveled at the subtle intellects of people in distant lands."

REDISCOVERY: RENAISSANCE CULTURE

Like Dürer, the Florentine philosopher Marsilio Ficino (1433–1499) marveled at the cultural splendors of a world in discovery, this one located not across the ocean but in the ancient past. Ficino had these rediscovered riches in mind when he declared, "This century, like a golden age, has restored to light the liberal arts, which were almost extinct: grammar, poetry, rhetoric, painting, sculpture, architecture, music." Explorers claimed to have found a new world, but European thinkers came to believe that they had brought about a rebirth—a renaissance—of ancient Greece and Rome. The Italian cities had always supported communities of notaries and lawyers—practical men who used ancient texts and medieval contract forms with equal dexterity to meet the practical needs of merchants and bankers. In the fourteenth century, some of them developed new cultural ambitions. They began to study the classics of Latin literature: the prose of Cicero and Seneca, the epic poetry of Virgil, and even the love poetry of Catullus.

PETRARCH

The fourteenth-century Florentine writer Francesco Petrarca, or **Petrarch** (1304–1374), pulled these threads together and wove a new intellectual program from them. Pushed by his father to study law, Petrarch found himself repelled by the way in which contemporary jurists read the ancient texts. To make Roman laws fit modern cases, they assumed that every reference to a pagan temple must apply to Christian churches as well. Petrarch, by contrast, was thrilled by what he described as the "history" concealed in the legal texts. He saw them not as a set of timeless codes but as the revelation of a lost world, at once unfamiliar and

more powerful and attractive than his own. Leaving the law, he pursued literature. Petrarch's Italian lyric poems—in which he described, at meticulous length, the sufferings of lovers and the beauty of the women who refused their pleas—made him famous. He created the language used by writers of sonnets down to the time of William Shakespeare and John Donne.

Petrarch's Latin scholarship and writing made him the standard-bearer of a new intellectual movement. Networking with learned men in the papal offices in France and Rome, he collected, and corrected, as many classical texts as he could. He annotated everything he read, both responding to the texts and entering personal remarks: for example, we know from a note in his

Petrarch In Andrea del Castagno's early-fifteenth-century rendering, the poet holds a book—the symbol of his craft—and extends his right hand in a delicate, artistic gesture.

massive copy of Virgil's works that Laura, the woman who inspired Petrarch's sonnets, died during the Black Death in 1348. And he carved out a career as the most expert and eloquent Latinist of his day.

As he discovered new texts—such as the highly political letters that Cicero addressed to his friend Atticus—Petrarch responded to them with verve and passion, showing just how serious a matter reading was for him. In the Middle Ages, clerical readers had thought of Cicero above all as the author of his late, Stoical works on philosophy. Now it became clear that he had been an active participant in the final drama of the Roman Republic. Horrified, Petrarch dashed off a letter to Cicero in which he denounced the Roman for betraying the ideals of philosophy—only to soften his judgment in a second, follow-up note.

A pious Christian who often criticized the Church but never questioned basic doctrines, Petrarch knew that his love of ancient literature might seem questionable or worse—as it had to Saint Jerome, whose work he knew intimately. At times he reproached himself for loving the beauty of the ancients' books too much. But challenged by friends, he devised a powerful justification for studying the literary classics—one partly based on the thought of Augustine, whose books he loved even more than those of the Romans. Contemporary philosophers and theologians, Petrarch argued, tried to learn the truth, a quest that often led them into blind alleys. They wasted their energy seeking goals no human could reach, and ended up fiercely debating questions of no relevance to the ordinary person. The ancients, by contrast, thanks to their mastery of rhetoric, had known how to make their readers want to change their lives, to be better men and women. And in the end, he argued, for Christians in his own day as for pagans in antiquity, "it is more important to will the good than to know the truth." The study of the classics had an eminently practical goal: it was the best way to make oneself a moral agent and to persuade others to do so as well.

SALUTATI'S BREAKTHROUGH

Petrarch's fame, and the power of his work, persuaded many younger scholars to follow him in the middle of the fourteenth century and after. His fellow Florentine, Giovanni Boccaccio (1313–1375), emulated him in many ways. Boccaccio developed a cultivated Italian prose, comparable in purity to Petrarch's verse, in which he composed his *Decameron*, a magnificent set of 100 tales in Italian about sex and love, marriage and deception. But he also searched for manuscripts of ancient books that had remained hidden in monasteries, and compiled a massive Latin book in which he sorted out the complex genealogies of the pagan gods. Even more influential was Coluccio Salutati (1331–1406), a younger notary who became chancellor of Florence in 1375. A systematic scholar in the new manner, Salutati also wrote about ancient myths, revealing a clear sense that the ancient world had been very different from his own. Confronting the many loves of Hercules, he explained both simply and radically that pagans, unlike Christians, had not been bound to monogamy.

Many younger men came under Salutati's influence—notably two deft Latinists, Leonardo Bruni (ca. 1370–1444) and Gian Francesco Poggio Bracciolini (1380–1459), both of whom would serve after him as chancellor of Florence. Poggio, who wrote in an open, highly legible script, worked with Salutati to define a layout for books more appropriate to the classics than the spiky, highly abbreviated books used in the universities. The model they chose—a clear minuscule script, written with few abbreviations

Poggio Bracciolini An illuminated initial letter "C" on the first page of one of Poggio's translations gives an indication of what the Latinist might have looked like as a young man.

and presented on its own, rather than immersed in a sea of minute commentary—was actually Carolingian, not ancient. Adopted by the efficient stationers of Florence, it became, first in manuscripts and then in print, the basic form of the modern book: a book designed not to serve as a source of information but to be read for its own sake, whether chained to a library table or carried on a journey.

Most important, in 1397 Salutati persuaded an eloquent and learned Byzantine, Manuel Chrysoloras, (d. 1415) to teach Greek in Florence. Bruni and others who studied with him began to read the Greek historians and philosophers, and to translate their works into Latin. For the first time in a thousand years, Latin intellectuals could read the works of Plato and his followers as well as Aristotle, whom they had known for centuries in the Latin translations used in universities. Chrysoloras—who, like many Byzantine scholars, took as strong an interest in the sciences as in literature—explicated Ptolemy's *Geography*, which was soon translated into Latin, and thus provided part of the inspiration that would send Columbus on his voyage west. The encounter with these alien works from another world could be shocking: the first Latin translation of Plato's *Symposium* discreetly eliminated the references to same-sex love. Soon, however, it became clear that, as Petrarch had already suspected, Plato offered a vision of the universe and a method of writing philosophy that seemed closer to Christianity in substance and better fitted to the needs of ordinary readers than the more technical books of Aristotle.

When Marsilio Ficino spoke of a great revival of the arts in his own day, he referred partly to his own project to translate and comment on the complete works of Plato—a project that came to fruition in 1484, when his work was printed in Florence. In the larger sense, what he saw himself as living through was nothing less than a revolution—one that looked not forward, as revolutions have in the nineteenth and twentieth centuries, but backward, and that sought to rebuild culture on a basis of ancient texts properly established and understood.

HUMANISM

The scholars who set out on this new road to the ancient past—from Petrarch to Ficino—took a special interest in the arts of language, grammar, and rhetoric; in poetry; and in the further studies that would help to inform and improve the characters of men and women who played important roles in society. These studies came to be known as "the studies of humanity," and those who pursued them as "humanists"—not in the modern secular sense, since almost all of them were faithful Christians, but in a larger one. All of them recognizably adopted the same general intellectual program, called **humanism**.

POLITICS Becoming a humanist did not imply a commitment to a particular view of society or the state. Petrarch, and many humanists after him, saw monarchy, when carried out by just and virtuous rulers, as a laudable form of government. Drawing on Seneca, who had offered an idealistic version of Roman imperial government as created by Augustus (until he was forced by Nero to commit suicide), Petrarch praised the rulers of Milan for their justice, their clemency, and their own commitment to urban planning, which had made their city cleaner and more beautiful than any other. Many later humanists would write similar "mirrors of princes." Bruni and his successors in the Florentine chancery took the opposite course. They learned from Thucydides, Aristotle, and Polybius how to analyze Florence as a classical republic, and effusively praised the city's balanced government, tradition of defending liberty, and splendid architecture.

Humanism also found a niche, and a large one, in the papal court. The fifteenth-century popes who rebuilt the Roman Curia (the papal administration) as a going concern established that the papacy was as committed to classical learning as any secular monarchy, and surrounded themselves with bright young scholars of the sort Salutati had recruited. Humanists in papal employ translated many of the Greek classics, wrote new lives of the ancient saints in an up-to-date style, and made the liturgy classical. By the beginning of the sixteenth century, they drew up official documents for the popes that referred to God as Jupiter Optimus Maximus and avoided using the special vocabulary of Christian Latin. In 1475 the popes created a great library for these humanists to work in: not a religious collection, as is often wrongly thought, but a systematic assembly of Greek and Latin texts meant to be used by the members of the Curia when they too turned to the ancients for practical advice. The Vatican Library remains one of the world's great centers of scholarly research.

SOCIETY Studying the classics was eminently practical. The subjects that the humanists cultivated proved useful in the new states and societies that had taken shape in fifteenth-century Italy. Ambassadors, for example, needed to give speeches, write forceful memoranda, and use history to shed light on the difficult moments of the present—all humanist skills. The families that ruled the most powerful cities embraced them. Many appointed humanist teachers, opened schools that offered instruction to princes and aristocrats, and built libraries designed, as the Vatican's was, for quiet reflection.

Humanism also created new possibilities for women, even within the social traditions of Renaissance cities and courts. For the most part, marriage among members of the elite continued to be arranged by parents to promote family strategies, and women in the Renaissance married much younger than men in the expectation that they would produce as many children as possible. They and the dowries they brought with them in marriage were in their husband's power, and even when they were widowed, they were normally put under the guardianship of a male relative of their late husband. Yet as we saw in the catasto records of Florence, many widows achieved considerable authority as heads of families.

CHRISTINE DE PIZAN Christine de Pizan (1364–1430) was a humanist who, writing in French rather than Latin, posed new questions about women and their social position. Married at the age of fifteen and widowed with three children a decade later, Christine found support in the courts of Burgundy and France for her poetry. She created a circle of scribes and miniaturists who produced beautifully illuminated copies of her works; she took charge

GHIRLANDAIO'S *PORTRAIT OF A LADY*

In Renaissance Italy, portraits served as tokens of friendship, political alliance, and marital exchange between courts or powerful families. Domenico Ghirlandaio (1449–1494) was a successful painter who operated a workshop in Florence with his family; Michelangelo apprenticed in the workshop. Ghirlandaio most likely created his *Portrait of a Lady* (ca. 1490) to commemorate the sitter's marriage.

Italian portraits of the second half of the fifteenth century, especially those featuring women, expressed both the subjects' personal characteristics and the broad cultural values of the time. In this portrait, the young woman's golden hair, fair skin, and formal posture conform to a standard of female beauty present in many other portraits of the period, inspired by the medieval poetry of Dante Alighieri (1265–1321) and Petrarch (1304–1374). The orange blossom in the woman's hand, representing chastity, and the pearls on her necklace, symbolizing purity and associated with the Virgin Mary, also convey the subject's moral integrity. Her pearls and elegant dress communicate the wealth of the woman's family, always of importance in marriage negotiations. Ghirlandaio combined these elements to create an image of femininity that aligned closely with Florentine values.

QUESTIONS FOR ANALYSIS

1. What does this portrait suggest about the woman's social status?
2. How would you describe the image of femininity conveyed in the portrait?
3. Why would Ghirlandaio include Florence and the surrounding countryside in this portrait?

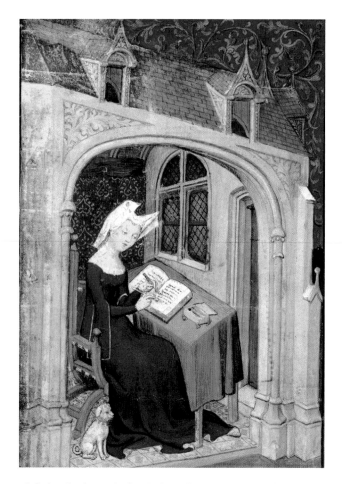

Christine de Pizan The frontispiece of a 1411 manuscript of her writings shows Christine de Pizan hard at work at her desk. She closely supervised the creation of this manuscript, which she presented to the queen of France in 1414.

of every detail, including the scripts that her scribes employed.

In her allegorical history of women, *The Book of the City of Ladies* (1405), Christine conjured up Lady Reason, who gave her a powerful lesson. Christine had believed, in a traditional way, in the evil character of women, which male authors such as Boccaccio had repeatedly confirmed. Lady Reason urged her to forget the slanders that had been heaped on women, and carry them away like "hods of earth" on her shoulders—a brilliant image of the woman writer as workmanlike scholar. "If it were customary to send little girls to school," Christine now argued, "and teach them the same subjects as are taught to boys, they would learn just as fully and would understand the subtleties of all arts and sciences." Marriage, she wrote, when unaccompanied by a spiritual connection, was no better than slavery.

UNDERSTANDING THE PAST Like the scholastics, the humanists developed a new and powerful set of technical skills—one based less on formal argument (though some did cultivate that) than on the knowledge that language, forms of writing, laws, customs, art, and religion all changed over time. Whereas scholastics enjoyed finding contradictions in arguments, humanists hunted anachronisms—errors and inconsistencies that showed that a given work could not have been written or painted by its supposed author or in its supposed period. The last thousand years, during which ancient books survived only when fallible individuals copied them in full, had left the canon in some confusion—a state rendered worse by the habit of many medieval writers and librarians of ascribing works they admired, whatever their origins, to particular ancient authors.

The most dramatic exposure of a medieval forgery involved the so-called Donation of Constantine. Old documents, produced by the papal chancery in the age of Charlemagne, purported to show that Pope Sylvester I (r. 314–335) had cured Constantine, the first Christian emperor of Rome, of leprosy, and that the emperor had given the popes the western empire in gratitude. Lawyers and theologians debated for centuries about whether this grant was legitimate. In 1440, Lorenzo Valla (1407–1457) a humanist who worked for the king of Naples, used the new scholarly tools to show that the documents in question were fakes that could not have been written at the time claimed. It did not matter whether Constantine's gift had been just or unjust—it had never taken place.

Humanists even created a new kind of history—one based on the material remains of the ancient world. Cyriac, a merchant from the Italian port of Ancona, revealed the ancient world vividly to his contemporaries. He traveled the Mediterranean for decades in the fifteenth century, sketchbook in hand, hopping from one Venetian or Genoese ship to another. Cyriac brought western Europeans their first news—and their first images—of the ancient temples of Greece, including the Parthenon, and of the obelisks and sphinxes of Egypt.

During the fifteenth century, humanists also revived every form of philosophy that the ancient world had known. Not only Aristotelianism and Platonism but Stoicism, Skepticism, and Epicureanism were reconstructed by scholars and exhaustively debated in Latin. New and varied syntheses took shape. Ficino, the translator of Plato, found connections between the works of Plato, a wide range of later Neoplatonic texts, and the learned tradition of natural magic and astrology that had taken shape in the medieval Islamic world. Ficino's younger friend Giovanni Pico della Mirandola, by contrast, believed that all serious schools of thought—Islamic as well as Christian, modern as well as ancient, scholastic as well as humanist—possessed distinctive elements of the truth. Humanism, which began as the discovery of the otherness of ancient Rome, gradually opened eyes and minds to the richness of a wide range of ancient traditions.

INNOVATIONS IN THE ARTS

Marsilio Ficino celebrated the revival of the visual arts as well as classical learning. Painting, sculpture, and architecture had flourished in the late thirteenth and fourteenth centuries in the most economically advanced parts of Europe—Italy and the Low Countries. But they had been seen as crafts. Those who practiced them learned their techniques as apprentices in masters' workshops and became journeymen once fully trained. They did not even have guilds of their own in most cities: sculptors joined and were regulated by the masons' guild, and painters by that of physicians and apothecaries. In the later fourteenth and

fifteenth centuries, however, what we now call the fine arts began to pull away from other crafts. Architects insisted that their work required knowledge not only of traditional building crafts, but also of mathematics and physical science. They found support in the ancient Roman handbook on architecture by Vitruvius (d. after 15 CE), who made the case that an architect needed to have encyclopedic knowledge of nature as well as building techniques in order to build healthy houses and cities.

FLORENCE   In 1418 Filippo Brunelleschi (1377–1446), a stunningly innovative Florentine sculptor and architect, told the committee responsible for finishing the city's Cathedral of Santa Maria del Fiore that he could build its enormous dome without any pillars to support it—as if deliberately mocking his predecessors, who had relied upon small forests of buttresses to support their cathedrals. The committee members treated him as insane at first, but eventually he convinced them. Brunelleschi worked with highly skilled craftsmen, but emphasized that he was responsible for their innovations. He designed the lifts, hoists, and scaffolds that enabled his crew to complete the dome in 1436—the biggest one built since the creation of the church of Hagia Sophia some

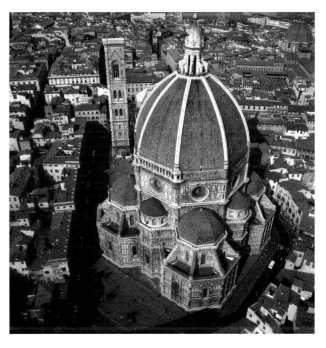

Brunelleschi and the Cathedral of Santa Maria del Fiore A 1427 fresco depicts Filippo Brunelleschi (right) alongside several contemporaries, including the painter Masaccio (left) and the writer and architect Leon Battista Alberti (center). Brunelleschi designed and built the magnificent dome of Florence's Cathedral of Santa Maria del Fiore using numerous architectural innovations, such as the rib-like support structure and an inner and outer dome.

Giotto's Frescoes In a vivid panel from Giotto di Bondone's frescoes narrating the Passion of Christ (1303–5), Jesus kisses Judas, who has betrayed him. The artist draws out the anger and tension of the scene through the facial expressions and gestures of the guards, disciples, and bystanders.

900 years earlier by the Roman emperor Justinian. As brilliant an engineer as he was an artist, Brunelleschi also devised war machines and transportation devices for the Florentines. He took out what amounted to the first modern patent to protect a piece of his intellectual property. He also created a new style of building that seemed classical, although, like the style of Renaissance books, it was medieval—in this case derived from churches of the twelfth century. He used it for the hospital built by the Florentines to accommodate foundlings.

Painters and sculptors also began to innovate. Giotto di Bondone (d. 1337), the most famous painter of the fourteenth century, used the large frescoes and mosaics that he was commissioned to create to find new ways of representing people, vividly and powerfully, as dominated by their emotions. Brunelleschi carried out experiments in linear perspective from the steps of the Florentine cathedral. He showed that by using a geometrical system of one-point perspective, he could produce an image of the octagonal Baptistery (the twelfth-century building across from the cathedral) that seemed genuinely three-dimensional.

Soon Florence became a center of artistic experiment. Brunelleschi's rival, the sculptor Lorenzo Ghiberti (ca.

1378–1455), experimented with foreshortening and perspective as he cast biblical scenes for the bronze doors of the Baptistery. Artists of the next generation—men such as Masaccio and Paolo Uccello, born around the year 1400—covered the walls of Florentine churches with vivid paintings: from a shrine, painted flat on the wall, that seemed to recede from the onlooker as if it were in three dimensions, to crowds and buildings that looked startlingly like their real-life counterparts. Uccello and other painters began to make systematic sketches, starting with nude figures and only later imagining them clothed. They depicted graceful men and women standing with their bodies curved symmetrically around vertical lines—figures as idealized, but also as apparently real, as the exquisite works of ancient Greeks like Phidias, whose sculptures filled the Parthenon.

NORTHERN EUROPE Innovation was just as rapid in the Low Countries, which produced a flood of illuminated manuscripts and tapestries as well as sculptures and paintings. Since the twelfth century, northern European artists had occasionally used oil as a painting medium, rather than the tempera (a mixture of pigment and a water-soluble binder such as egg yolk) that southern artists used when creating panels. In the fifteenth century, northern painters such as Jan van Eyck, who served his Burgundian master, Philip the Good, as diplomat as well as painter, learned how to apply oil paint in multiple thin layers. This technique enabled them to create rich, glowing colors and to produce microscopically faithful renditions of every sort of surface material, from stone to cloth, fur, and skin. They created many devotional pictures, but also specialized in painting portraits from life of prominent men and women. Works of art and techniques crossed the Alps and the Pyrenees. By the middle of the fifteenth century, Italian painters such as the Venetian Giovanni Bellini (ca. 1430–1516) were using oil as a medium, and the portrait was becoming a standard feature of Italian art.

PATRONAGE Support for the arts came from many sources. Committees of local notables oversaw the building and decoration of churches, such as the Florentine cathedral. Guilds also took part. The Florentine church of Orsanmichele, originally a grain market, was converted between 1380 and 1404 into the chapel of the Florentine craft and merchant guilds. Popes, princes, and patricians did their best to transform the built world. Merchant families and cardinals constructed huge palaces, drawing features from ancient structures like the Colosseum, in

RENAISSANCE FLORENCE

❝ WHO COULD EVER BE HARD OR ENVIOUS ENOUGH TO FAIL TO PRAISE PIPPO THE ARCHITECT ON SEEING HERE SUCH A LARGE STRUCTURE, RISING ABOVE THE SKIES, AMPLE TO COVER WITH ITS SHADOW ALL THE TUSCAN PEOPLE? ❞

LEON BATTISTA ALBERTI, *DE PICTURA*, ON FILIPPO BRUNELLESCHI'S DOME OF THE CATHEDRAL OF SANTA MARIA DEL FIORE

Map labels: City wall, 1284–1333; San Lorenzo church; Palazzo Medici; Hospital for foundlings; Santa Maria Novella church; Cathedral of Santa Maria del Fiore; Baptistery; Old market; Palazzo Rucellai; Palazzo Strozzi; Orsanmichele church; Piazza della Signoria; New market; Arno R.; Palazzo Vecchio; Santo Spirito church; Ponte Vecchio; Pazzi chapel

Scale: 0 600 1200 ft / 0 200 400 m

Through much of the fifteenth century, a painting's materials, selected by its patron, determined its value. In this work (ca. 1483) by Florentine painter Filippino Lippi, the ultramarine pigment of the Virgin Mary's mantle would have been many times more expensive than gold. But by the end of the century, many patrons valued artists' skills more than the materials they used.

❝ THIS CENTURY, LIKE A GOLDEN AGE, HAS RESTORED TO LIGHT THE LIBERAL ARTS, WHICH WERE ALMOST EXTINCT: GRAMMAR, POETRY, RHETORIC, PAINTING, SCULPTURE, ARCHITECTURE, MUSIC... AND ALL THIS IN FLORENCE. ❞

MARSILIO FICINO, "THE GOLDEN AGE IN FLORENCE"

This bronze relief panel (1425–1452) from the doors of the Baptistery, depicting a Biblical scene, displays Lorenzo Ghiberti's ingenious use of perspective. He took great pride in his ability to set himself demanding technical problems and solve them with virtuosity.

WORKSHOPS, 1472

54 marble workers and stonecutters
44 master gold- and silversmiths
at least 30 master painters

NOTABLE PATRONS & WORKS THEY COMMISSIONED

MEDICI FAMILY
Brunelleschi's church of San Lorenzo and various works by Michelangelo

FILIPPO STROZZI (BANKER)
Benedetto da Maiano's Palazzo Strozzi and Lippi's frescoes in the Strozzi Chapel at Santa Maria Novella

GIOVANNI RUCELLAI (MERCHANT)
Alberti's façade of Santa Maria Novella and his design of the Palazzo Rucellai

QUESTIONS FOR ANALYSIS

1. What innovations in the arts and learning appeared in Renaissance Florence?
2. In what ways did artists and their patrons embellish the city?
3. How did the city's artists resemble and also distinguish themselves from craftsmen?

Jan van Eyck One of van Eyck's notable portraits of prominent members of society is this 1434 painting of a newly married Italian merchant and his wife. The picture showcases in realistic detail the luxurious interior of the couple's house, while a mirror in the background allows the viewer to glimpse the scene from another perspective.

work of the best masters. Some 16,000 letters record her requests to the greatest artists of the time.

ALBERTI: A NEW VISION As artists' practices changed, so did their position in society. In the 1430s, a Florentine exile named **Leon Battista Alberti** (1404–1472), a humanist who worked in the service of the papacy, returned to his native city. What he saw astonished him. Cast off by his family and illegitimate, given to melancholy, Alberti had always believed that the course of history was downward, a process of degeneration, and that he and his contemporaries could never rival the accomplishments of the ancients. Now, he told Brunelleschi in a passionate letter, he realized he had been wrong: "I believe the power of acquiring wide fame in any art or

Isabella d'Este The Venetian painter Titian created this 1534–36 portrait of the influential art connoisseur and collector Isabella d'Este. She was in her early sixties at the time, but Titian portrayed her as she might have appeared in her youth.

which they walled themselves off from the turmoil of the streets and created private worlds of great splendor, decorated according to their owners' distinctive tastes.

Wealthy individuals also presented paintings and chapels to the churches they favored, and bought painted chests, tapestries, and other expensive items for their homes. These consumers of luxury goods became more discriminating in the fifteenth and sixteenth centuries: not only in choosing beautiful things but also in selecting the artists they employed. A few women forged careers that would have only been possible in this new world. At the highest social levels, noble and royal women became as expert as any man in the new skills of connoisseurship and collection. Isabella d'Este (1474–1539), Marchesa of Mantua, spent her large income on art objects and became renowned for her determination to pay for only the best

Alberti's Emblem This mid-fifteenth-century medallion bears Leon Battista Alberti's emblem, a winged eye, an allusion, perhaps, to the eye of the artist, as well as the precision to which new forms of art and learning aspired. The motto below the eye, "Quid tum," is more mysterious, possibly meaning "What then?" or "So what?"—a hopeful anticipation of future developments in human knowledge.

science lies in our industry and diligence more than in the times or in the gifts of nature." Brunelleschi's dome ("ample to cover with its shadow all the Tuscan people, and constructed without the aid of centering or great quantity of wood"), Ghiberti's bronze doors for the Baptistery, and other achievements of Florentine art showed that progress was still possible.

Recognizing these dramatic changes when they had only just begun, Alberti set out to give painting—and by extension the other arts—a new theoretical foundation. He argued that painters really resembled scholars. As the humanist wrote in order to move readers, the painter depicted dramatic scenes—such as the Annunciation and the Crucifixion—in order to achieve the same end. And as the humanist's mastery of a classical vocabulary proved his worthiness to take part in public discussion, so the painter's mastery of techniques—anatomy, perspective, foreshortening—proved his worthiness to tell great stories in visual form. Traditionally, the painter had needed to know where to find the best pigments. Now he needed to master the geometry of the picture plane and the bony and muscular structures of the body, especially if he wanted to challenge the great ancient artists, whose feats of creating illusion Alberti described at length.

Most painters continued to work as guild members (though Brunelleschi refused to do so, even when he was imprisoned for refusing to pay his dues). But the new vision of the painter that Alberti described—someone who crossed what had previously been rugged intellectual borders, combining skilled hands with the sort of knowledge that had once been the province of scholars—proved infectious to painters and convincing to patrons. Even at lower levels, contracts for paintings now specified that the master must execute all hands and faces. Some of what we now call the fine arts were being identified as different from other crafts, and their products were coming to be seen not as the collaborative work of many craftsmen but as that of especially brilliant individuals.

LEONARDO, MICHELANGELO, RAPHAEL Three of these individuals have seemed—in their own time and since—to epitomize the new intellectual and cultural standing of the artist: Leonardo da Vinci (1452–1519), Raphael Santi (1483–1530), and Michelangelo Buonarotti (1475–1564). Leonardo and Michelangelo both came from Tuscany, near the centers of artistic innovation; Raphael came from the hilltop court town of Urbino, where his father was a painter. All three learned their arts in the traditional way, as apprentices. All three established their fame by creating ambitious and spectacular paintings: Leonardo's *Last Supper*, his *Mona Lisa*, and *The Virgin of the Rocks*; Raphael's frescoes in the papal palace that depicted the School of Athens (a panorama

Michelangelo's Sistine Chapel Ceiling The famous frescoes Michelangelo painted on the Sistine Chapel's ceiling in 1508–12 illustrate scenes from the Old Testament, including Adam and Eve eating the forbidden fruit and being banished from Eden (top) and God's creation of Eve (center) and Adam (bottom).

The School of Athens This fresco by Raphael Santi in the Vatican palace conveys the Renaissance's reverence for the famous figures of classical philosophy and science: Plato and Aristotle converse (center), Pythagoras reads (bottom left), and Euclid points at a writing slate (bottom right). The seemingly receding arches in the background demonstrate Raphael's command of one-point perspective.

These men embodied—and still embody—a distinctive vision of the artist. Far grander figures than the humanists, the great artists of the years around 1500 fought for their independence even as they were fought over by the patrons whose tastes were most refined. Michelangelo waged endless battles with his chief patron, Pope Julius II (r. 1503–1513), even as he decorated the ceiling of the Sistine Chapel. Their quarrels became legendary, as did the bill the painter presented, in which he asked thousands of ducats for his work but only a small amount for pigments.

Traditionally, in European society, people trained for specialized occupations: craftsmen did the work that they had mastered as apprentices, and scholars wrote about the

of the great classical philosophers in disputation) and the Parnassus; Michelangelo's Sistine Chapel ceiling, with its panorama of the Old Testament, and his *Last Judgment* on the altar wall of the same chapel. And all three knew and responded to one another—especially in 1500 and just after, when Leonardo and Michelangelo were both creating masterpieces in the council chamber of Florence's town hall, the Palazzo Vecchio.

Yet they were much more than brilliant practitioners of a single art form. Leonardo and Michelangelo were as much sculptors as painters. Although Leonardo's enormous equestrian monument for Milan was never cast in bronze (and the clay original was destroyed when the city fell to the French), Michelangelo's figure of David dominated the Piazza della Signoria, Florence's central square. Both were also military engineers: Leonardo in the service of the Sforza family in Milan and then of Cesare Borgia; Michelangelo in that of the Florentine Republic. And all three were architects: Both Raphael and Michelangelo served as the official architect for St. Peter's Basilica in Rome, which was begun by Donato Bramante (1444–1514). Michelangelo finished the design for the church's dome, though he died before it was completed. Leonardo pursued the study of nature, reading and drawing with fantastic energy and compiling his results in enormous, fascinating notebooks. Michelangelo wrote brilliant Italian poetry.

The Virgin of the Rocks Leonardo da Vinci included this painting as part of an altarpiece for the church of San Francesco Grande in Milan in 1506–8. The Virgin Mary sits with the infant John the Baptist and Jesus, while an angel wearing a red cape watches over them.

subjects they had studied at universities. In the Renaissance, as Alberti noted, such barriers began to come down. These powerful artists seemed able to cross the boundaries between the worlds of craft and high learning, and between the crafts themselves. Leonardo challenged the learned physicians of his time in his notebooks. He argued that his knowledge of anatomy and his accurate drawings, with their minutely skillful perspective and foreshortening, enabled him to observe and describe the human body more precisely than they could. He and his two rivals came to be seen as geniuses—unique talents not subject to the rules or limitations that restricted others.

MACHIAVELLI: THE NEW POLITICS

And yet, even as Italian society seemed to reach its zenith of development during the Renaissance, and even as the monarchs and noblemen of France and Germany whose armies ravaged the Italian Peninsula were captivated by the new classical culture of scholarship and art—it seemed that all might be a dream. One of the most loyal servants of the Florentine Republic in the years from 1498 to 1512 was **Niccolò Machiavelli**, whom we met at the beginning of this chapter. Trained in the classics, he worked in the city's chancery and eventually became the right-hand man of Pietro Soderini, chief executive of the republic. Machiavelli went on diplomatic missions and wrote detailed reports about Florence's allies and enemies. He came to see, through the eyes of the other states he visited, just how weak the Italian ones were. Always a believer in the exemplary character of Rome, he organized a civic militia, with uniforms and systematic drill sessions, in the hope that it might provide Florence more protection than mercenary armies. After the republic fell once again to the Medici in 1512, Machiavelli came under suspicion of treason. He was tortured and then exiled from Florence. Settled on his farm outside the city, he pursued an understanding of the events he had been forced to witness: the easy destruction of the Italian states, including his own, by the powerful armies from the north.

Like a good humanist, Machiavelli went back to the ancients—above all to the historians—in the hope of understanding the crisis of his state. In a letter to a trusted member of the Medici regime that had replaced the republic, he described his life—one in which casual reading mingled with lower pursuits such as gambling. But after passing the day in trivialities, Machiavelli explained, he returned home and engaged in reading of a different kind: "I enter

Machiavelli The Florentine artist Rosso Fiorentino painted this early sixteenth-century portrait of the politician and diplomat Niccolò Machiavelli writing in a book.

the ancient courts of ancient men.... I am not ashamed to speak with them and to ask them the reason for their actions, and they in their kindness answer me."

The book Machiavelli was writing as he spoke with the ancients was *The Prince*—perhaps the most famous book written during the Renaissance. It represented a radical departure from convention. Earlier humanists from Petrarch on, following ancient precedent, had advised princes to practice virtue at all times and to show mercy and generosity whenever possible. But Machiavelli had watched real princes and other powerful men behave, and he had seen, with fury and contempt, how the princes of Italy and their humanist counselors collapsed before the foreign onslaught. Now he recorded what he saw as the savage truth: safety, for a prince like Ludovico Sforza of Milan, had to come not from his subjects' love, but from their fear; violence, rationally and economically dealt out, was the monarch's chief tool for dealing with both his subjects and his enemies. Machiavelli insisted that "how one lives is so far distant from how one ought to live, that he who neglects what is done for what ought to be done, sooner effects his ruin than his preservation.... Hence it is necessary for a prince wishing to hold his own to know how to do wrong, and to make use of it or not according to necessity." Seneca had warned monarchs to be human, not to imitate the cruel lion or the vicious fox. Machiavelli advised the monarch to imitate both, as circumstances demanded.

Machiavelli went even further. He demanded, more eloquently than any previous writer, that people shake themselves free of the comforting belief that God might help them, and create the only order they could. Unlike many other humanists, Machiavelli clearly saw that the ancient Romans had not been pious in the Christian way. He even praised their warlike religion, which he considered better than Christianity for the health of the state. Yet even Machiavelli, clear-eyed radical that he was, did not foresee the greater tensions and contradictions that would soon tear the fabric, not only of Italy, but of Europe as a whole.

CONCLUSION

The Renaissance was a transformative period. The balance of power in society began to tip away from the powerful noblemen who still played such important roles in later medieval society, and toward central governments, with their new revenue systems, fortifications, and professional soldiers. Merchants and navigators, soldiers and sailors began to turn outward, to explore and conquer parts of the world that had been unfathomably remote or entirely unknown. Scholars discovered in the ancient world new models for understanding the cosmos and human society. Christians experimented with new ways of gaining contact with the divine and some assurance of salvation. And artists devised brilliant and unexpected forms of painting, sculpture, and architecture, transforming the public spaces in cities across Europe. Machiavelli was more pessimistic than the other innovators who were his contemporaries, but he shared with many of them the capacity for seeing the world as it is, and the belief that central governments must prevail.

KEY TERMS

Medici family (p. 326)

ambassador (p. 329)

Low Countries (p. 330)

Estates General (p. 331)

taille (p. 331)

Wars of the Roses (p. 333)

justices of the peace
   (p. 333)

Habsburg dynasty (p. 334)

Maximilian I (p. 334)

Alhambra Decree (p. 335)

Ottomans (p. 335)

Mehmed I (p. 335)

Great Schism (p. 339)

Council of Constance
   (p. 340)

confraternity (p. 342)

portolan chart (p. 345)

Johannes Gutenberg
   (p. 349)

Christopher Columbus
   (p. 351)

Treaty of Tordesillas
   (p. 352)

Hernán Cortés (p. 354)

Petrarch (p. 356)

humanism (p. 358)

Leon Battista Alberti
   (p. 364)

Niccolò Machiavelli
   (p. 367)

REVIEW QUESTIONS

1. What were the primary models or structures of government in the city-states of Renaissance Italy?

2. How did the French, Spanish, and English monarchs of the fifteenth century consolidate their power and authority?

3. What were the most important innovations in warfare during the Renaissance?

4. Who were the leading religious reformers of the fourteenth and fifteenth centuries, and what changes did they champion?

5. Why did the European states intensify their efforts in maritime exploration?

6. How did the slave trade change Europe both economically and demographically?

7. How did the arrival of the printing press transform European society?

8. What are the some of the most significant elements of the Columbian Exchange?

9. In what ways was the humanism of the Renaissance revolutionary for its time?

10. What are some of the most important innovations of Renaissance art and architecture?

CORE OBJECTIVES

After reading this chapter, you should have a solid understanding of the following core objectives. To strengthen your grasp of the core objectives, use the resources on the Student Site for The West.

- Describe the political changes that took place in Renaissance Europe.

- Evaluate the crises and reforms that transformed the Church during the Renaissance.

- Trace the emergence of new technologies and areas of knowledge in the fourteenth and fifteenth centuries.

- Analyze the encounter between the Old and New Worlds that began with Columbus's voyages.

- Assess the intellectual and artistic breakthroughs of the Renaissance.

 GO TO inQuizitive TO SEE WHAT YOU'VE LEARNED—AND LEARN WHAT YOU'VE MISSED—WITH PERSONALIZED FEEDBACK ALONG THE WAY.

CHRONOLOGY

1511 Erasmus publishes *In Praise of Folly*	**October 31, 1517** Luther presents his Ninety-Five Theses for formal debate	**1524–1525** Peasants' War	**October 1529** Luther and Zwingli divide over Eucharist	**1536** Calvin publishes *Institutes of the Christian Religion*		**1543** Copernicus argues universe is heliocentric
1516 More publishes *Utopia*	**April 1521** Diet of Worms	**1527** Holy Roman Emperor Charles V's troops sack Rome	**1534** Henry VIII declares himself head of independent Church of England	**1540** Pope permits Loyola to found Jesuit order	**1545–1563** Council of Trent	**1555** Peace of Augsburg

Reformations

PROTESTANT AND CATHOLIC

1500–1600

1562–1598
French religious wars
1566–1648
Dutch Revolt
August 24, 1572
Saint Bartholomew's
Day Massacre

● ● ● ● ●

1580
Montaigne publishes
his *Essays*

1598
Edict of Nantes

On October 31, 1517, an obscure professor of biblical theology at Wittenberg, the capital of Saxony, changed the world. Martin Luther (1483–1546) published a series of ninety-five theses about indulgences (remissions of penalties for sins, granted by the Catholic Church) and presented them to his superior, the bishop of Brandenburg, and to the archbishop of Mainz. Luther intended to preside over a formal debate of the theses among theologians, a type of public discussion that had been a normal part of academic life for centuries.

But Luther's theses were more radical than most. He denied that Christians should confess to priests, that the pope could remit guilt, and that indulgences could help a dead sinner or a living one who was not repentant. Luther's first concern—confession—was one of the standard practices of the medieval church. To cleanse themselves of sin, Christians had to confess their actions to a priest, feel genuine contrition, and make satisfaction for what they had done by, for example, saying particular prayers or going on pilgrimage to a shrine. Indulgences—certificates that drew on the Treasury of Merit that Christ's sacrifice and the virtues of the saints had created for the church—could remit the actual penalties that the priest imposed. They worked, in theory, only if the sinner had confessed and was repentant. In practice, however, as Luther objected, pardoners sold indulgences not

---

Reformed Worship In 1564, in a Calvinist church in Lyon, France, attendees practice a new style of worship. Sitting on benches that line the round room, they listen as a preacher delivers a sermon, the central feature of services in many of the reformist movements that spread across Europe in the sixteenth century.

- Why were Luther's criticisms of the Church so influential?
- How did the Reformation movement spread and then splinter?
- How did political and religious allegiance become entangled?
- In what ways did Catholicism renew itself in the sixteenth century?
- What new understandings of the natural world were emerging at this time?
- Why were the religious wars so devastating?
- How did observers make sense of the disruptions of this period?

only to those who wanted to benefit from them after death but also to those who wanted to shorten the time that a dead relative might have to spend in the fires of purgatory to be cleansed of their sin. Some pardoners promised that "so soon as the penny jingles into the money-box, the soul flies out [of purgatory]." But Luther insisted that no human cleric could legitimately make such a promise: "It is certain that when the penny jingles into the money-box, gain and avarice can be increased, but the result of the intercession of the Church is in the power of God alone."

The particular indulgence to which Luther objected was intended to raise money for the construction of the greatest of Renaissance churches, Saint Peter's Basilica in Rome. Pope Leo X (r. 1513–1521) commissioned a Dominican, Johann Tetzel, to sell indulgences in the Holy Roman Empire. Student reports of Tetzel's abuses of the system aroused Luther to action. But it was not only the pardoners' excessive zeal and absurd promises that bothered Luther. The whole enterprise seemed wrong to him. It had made many laypeople worry about the pope and his concern for ordinary Christians. "Why does not the pope empty purgatory," so Luther paraphrased them, "for the sake of holy love and of the dire need of the souls that are there, if he redeems an infinite number of souls for the sake of miserable money with which to build a Church? The former reasons would be most just; the latter is most trivial."

In the end, what mattered most to Luther was not the purpose for which the indulgence was offered but the very idea of it. Christian repentance took place inside the soul. Anyone who preached that Christians could ease their consciences and reconcile themselves with God by paying money failed to understand that all Christians were called to suffer. Their optimistic message, which Luther summed up as "Peace, peace," could not simply be corrected; it must be replaced with the true teaching that Christians must follow Christ, "their Head, through penalties, deaths, and hell."

By early 1518, Luther's theses were being printed in Latin and translated into German so that ordinary people could understand them. Copies flew through the Holy Roman Empire and beyond. Luther himself became a celebrity, a bold German hero who had stood up for his fellow countrymen against the greedy Church of Rome. More important, he became the leader of a movement, one that put an end to the unified Catholic Church that had survived all challenges to its authority in the West for more than a thousand years, and did so not only in the Holy Roman Empire but also across the European world. The movement took its name—Protestantism—from the protest in 1529 of German princes against the Imperial Diet (assembly) in Speyer, which prohibited further religious reforms in the Holy Roman Empire. How did Luther's small act of defiance in a corner of northern Germany have such seismic consequences?

MARTIN LUTHER AND THE CULTURE OF CHURCH REFORM

Part of the explanation of Luther's influence lies in his character. The son of a hard man, a mining entrepreneur, **Martin Luther** joined a religious order at age twenty-two in gratitude to Saint Anne, who, he thought, had saved him from a lightning bolt that struck near him during a thunderstorm. He observed the rule of his order with absolute, almost fanatical devotion. He fasted, prayed, and made himself an expert on the Bible. Luther learned Greek and Hebrew so that he would be able to read the Old and New Testaments in their original languages. He printed special editions of the Psalms for his students, stripping them of commentaries to force the students to confront the original texts, but leaving wide margins so that they could enter their own reflections as they read.

Martin Luther The German artist Lucas Cranach the Elder, a friend of Luther's, painted his portrait in 1529, when Luther was forty-five.

LUTHER'S BREAKTHROUGH

From 1513 to 1517 Luther taught courses on the Psalms, on the apostle Paul, and on the works of Augustine. Meanwhile, he himself suffered from fear and at times paralysis. He worried that God's law, as stated in the Old Testament, was too harsh and demanding for anyone to follow. He continually reproached himself for failing to accomplish one religious duty or another, or for having done it only incompletely or halfheartedly. And then suddenly, one day, he found all his questions answered, all of his problems solved. By reading the Bible in a new way, he discovered, he could absolve himself of the need to follow a massive, arbitrary code of conduct without abandoning his search for grace.

Luther realized that Paul, the author of many of the New Testament epistles, had the answer to his problem. In Romans 1:17, Paul had written: "For therein is the righteousness of God revealed from faith to faith: as it is written, 'The just shall live by faith.'" Here, Luther thought, Paul's message was that the righteousness of God was not something that Christians had to seek endlessly, in a futile effort to curb their own bodies and cure their own vices, but something that Christ had earned for them by his sacrifice. They could share his righteousness if they wanted to: not by buying **indulgences**, not by endless pursuit of perfect obedience to a monastic rule, but simply by having faith in him. Because the New Testament verse contained an internal quotation from an Old Testament prophet, Luther argued, it encapsulated the meaning of the Bible as a whole. The Old Testament taught righteousness, the evil nature of mankind after the Fall, and the demands of God's law. But the New Testament taught faith: that Jesus, by sacrificing himself, had made it possible for all who believed in him to become just as well.

Luther's mastery of theology and his command of the Bible enabled him to view the basic problems of sin and damnation from a new perspective. As we will see, his

Sale of Indulgences A 1539 cartoon from Nuremberg mocks the proliferation of indulgences. The man is dressed in a costume made from letters of indulgences, and the caption explains that the letters are so ridiculous that the man had no choice but to join in the festivities of the Nuremberg carnival.

determination and abilities as a speaker and writer enabled him to bring his message to multiple audiences. Yet it was by no means obvious in 1517 and 1518 that Luther would create anything permanent, much less the first of many new versions of the Christian Church.

CHRISTIANITY IN 1517

In the first place, the world in which Luther lived—the world of late-medieval Christianity—seemed extremely solid. Serious, principled opposition to papal power in the Church had mostly come to an end with the conciliar movement by the middle of the fifteenth century. Girolamo Savonarola's defiance of papal authority in the 1490s had ended with his disgrace and death. The heretical movements of the decades around 1400 were fading slowly away by 1500. Even the once-defiant Hussites of Bohemia saw their movement as coming to an end. One compared it to a dying candle.

Wittenberg itself, where Luther taught, was a center of some of the traditions that he objected to most fiercely. Frederick the Wise (r. 1486–1525), Elector (ruler) of Saxony, believed in the Church's Treasury of Merit. He gained access to it by collecting relics—fragments of the True Cross and the Holy Spear that wounded Jesus on the cross, bones and garments that had belonged to saints, and many more, all encased in splendid vessels that displayed them discreetly through small windows. Frederick's subjects crowded into the local church every year on All Saint's Eve when the collection was put on display. In 1520, his secretary computed that the collection as a whole had earned Frederick and his subjects 1,902,202 years' and 270 days' indulgence from the time they would otherwise have had to spend in purgatory.

The popular response to Frederick's collection of relics showed that the Catholic Church still attracted affection and engagement from most believers, many of whom warmly valued the traditions that Luther challenged. Ordinary Christians crowded parish churches, finding deep rewards in hearing their priests perform the Mass. They embraced the rituals that celebrated the seasons of the agricultural year, such as the Harvest Home festival in the fall, and the yearly reliving of Christ's Passion in the Easter season. In cities, laypeople banded together in confraternities, religious organizations that among other benefits guaranteed their members proper burial.

Christians had always prayed. But the later Middle Ages saw the development of new, engaged forms of prayer. The

Thomas More's Family This 1593 copy of a painting originally by Hans Holbein shows Thomas More (far left) surrounded by his family, all holding books of hours.

rosary, for example—a devotion to the Virgin Mary that consisted of repetitions of the Lord's Prayer and ten Hail Marys—had been created in the thirteenth century. During the fifteenth century, it became normal to repeat the sequence fifteen times, with meditations on the mysteries of the Virgin added. Christians still saw the society of heaven as a hierarchical mirror of society on earth, and sought the help of the members of God's family and the larger community of saints. At the same time, though, worship became more intense and individual, as is clear from the spread of printed books of hours. A famous portrait of the family of Thomas More—English scholar, lawyer, and statesman— shows parents and children with their books of hours in hand, making their household a place of regular and intense devotion. Prayer seemed so precious that wealthy men and women endowed chantries—altars or chapels where masses would be said in perpetuity for their souls.

Serious efforts at reform continued to be made in the monastic and mendicant orders, some of which had become aristocratic preserves. The German Benedictine houses of the Bursfeld congregation, for example, came together for meetings at which the brilliant scholar Johannes Trithemius (1462–1516) called for a revival of the early monastic spirit. He laid out sensible rules for restoring discipline in houses for monks and nuns, and brought the rich spiritual writings of Hildegard of Bingen back into circulation. Franciscans and Dominicans, similarly, made serious efforts to restore their orders to the form that their founders had envisioned.

HUMANIST CRITICS OF THE CHURCH

Others found the Church, and the textures of Christian life, seriously problematic, and they helped to give Luther both the intellectual tools with which he set to work and a receptive audience. Some critics of the Church were rooted in the culture of humanism, which spread through northern Europe in the fifteenth century. As Italian humanists such as Aeneas Silvius Piccolomini (who became Pope Pius II) visited northern lands, and northern scholars such as the Englishman John Free visited Italy, the new methods of Italian humanism provoked increasing interest in the north. The scholarship of the humanists took on new forms, and showed new potentials, in the very different societies of England, France, and the Holy Roman Empire.

DESIDERIUS ERASMUS No one championed the humanism of the north more exuberantly or developed it more effectively than **Desiderius Erasmus** (1466–1536), and no one had a deeper impact on Luther. Born the

Erasmus Albrecht Dürer's 1526 engraving of Erasmus depicts the humanist priest in his element, surrounded by books and with pen in hand.

illegitimate son of a priest in the Netherlandish port city of Rotterdam, Erasmus studied in a school of the Brothers of the Common Life, whose members did not take vows but lived in community houses and earned their living as teachers, scribes, and early adopters of the new technology of printing. After joining a religious order, the Augustinian Canons, Erasmus became a priest. He found monastic life stifling, but never lost the taste he developed there for the meditative, gentle piety of the Brothers' and Canons' movement for religious reform known as Modern Devotion. Soon it became clear, to him and others, that he had unusual talents, especially for writing Latin. A French bishop employed him as a secretary and then gave him a stipend to study in Paris. Erasmus loathed the terrible food and squalid conditions of the Paris colleges, as well as what he considered the sterile pedantry of scholastic theology.

Gradually, however, he made the contacts that would determine the course of his intellectual life. Always a passionate classicist who hated what he called the "barbarians" of the university faculties with their inelegant Latin jargon, he turned out to have a wonderful knack for drawing up textbooks that could help aspiring Latinists become fluent and eventually find careers, as Erasmus had, in the employment of high-ranking clerics and government officials. In London in 1499, he met and was deeply impressed by John Colet (1467–1519), an austere senior scholar who loved the Platonist philosophy of Marsilio Ficino but insisted, at the same time, that Christians must study the New Testament directly. It was in the life, teachings, and death of Jesus, Colet insisted, not in formal theology and philosophy, that Christians would find the central principles of their faith. In 1504, Erasmus discovered a copy of the Italian humanist Lorenzo Valla's commentary on the New Testament. Valla taught him that just as the classics should be read in their original languages, so should the Christian scriptures. Erasmus, who had mastered Greek to support his secular scholarship, was delighted to apply his skills to the Bible.

From 1506 to 1509 Erasmus lived in Italy, where he earned a doctorate in theology from Turin. In Venice he found a home for several months in the printing shop of Aldus Manutius (1449–1515), whose handsome typefaces he admired. Manutius and the Byzantine exiles who corrected Greek texts for him made a wealth of Greek books available to this brilliant visitor. Even as Erasmus established himself as the first northern scholar who knew Greek and wrote Latin as well as any Italian, he continued to look for ways to connect his pursuit of learning with Christian piety.

As Erasmus steeped himself in the New Testament—especially the Gospels, with their vivid depiction of the life and teachings of Jesus—he found himself more and more at odds with society and the Church. The policies of the popes, with their pursuit of worldly power, seemed to contradict the message of Jesus, who had preached poverty and charity. So did the policies of most secular rulers. City burghers pursued wealth as passionately as kings, and nobles pursued power and glory. Their lives did not exemplify Christian principles in action—especially when they refused aid to the many poor people who lived in the streets outside their palaces.

Returning from Italy, Erasmus spent the years 1511 to 1514 in England, where he was professor of theology at the University of Cambridge and worked on the text of the New Testament. But he found other ways to try to reach and change public opinion. Imitating one of his favorite ancient writers, the second-century Greek satirist Lucian, Erasmus wrote a mock oration, *In Praise of Folly*, in which he ridiculed every order of Christian society—but reserved especially sharp mockery for the powerful. He couched criticisms of central features of Church practice in humorous form. Instead of denouncing the scholastic treatises on witches, for example, he made fun of a scholastic who defended them. He heaped ridicule on what he portrayed as the lifeless abstraction of scholastic theology. His book, which first appeared in Strasbourg in 1511, became a best-seller. It provoked furious protests from more traditional theologians.

THOMAS MORE'S *UTOPIA* Erasmus's wit made him friends, as well as enemies, across Europe. A brilliant young English lawyer named **Thomas More** (1478–1535), for example, learned from both Colet and Erasmus and applied their principles in his own highly original way. The Church of the first Christians, as the Gospels portrayed it, had been very different from its contemporary counterpart: not a wealthy, established institution with stiff hierarchies of officials, monks, and mendicants competing for recruits and bequests, but a frail, countercultural movement that had stood against war and tried to help the poor. A gifted student of Greek, More took inspiration from Plato's *Republic* and from contemporary reports of newly discovered lands. In his own book, More imagined a society that he called Utopia (Greek for "no place") and a brilliant, worldly traveler, Raphael Hythloday, who described it to More and other friends. On this pagan island, far from Europe, everyone worked, no one went hungry, and a rigorous system of

More's *Utopia* An illustration from the original 1516 edition of Thomas More's book shows a ship sailing to the island of Utopia.

discipline ensured that no one desired money, the root of all evil.

More's book did not confine itself to portraying an ideal society. In its opening sections More has Hythloday apply the lessons of Utopia and the other imaginary countries he has visited to contemporary England. More, who served in the Parliament and was an expert in international trade, made clear that he thought the society of his day deeply unchristian in Erasmus's sense. It was unfair to the soldiers who were cast off after being injured in its service, and to the peasants whom landlords were allowed to evict so their land could be used more profitably for raising sheep. The sheep, More's narrator complained, were eating the people of England. He was equally critical of Christian kings who wasted their subjects' money on wars meant to pursue their own narrow dynastic aims.

More's *Utopia* was published in 1516 and soon reprinted with approving prefaces by European scholars and enthusiastic marginal notes by Erasmus himself. Although More's narrator claims that work in a royal council would corrupt him rather than improve matters, More himself agreed to serve as a counselor to his young, dynamic king, Henry VIII. In the meantime, though, many readers saw *Utopia* and the *Praise of Folly* as the works not of isolated thinkers but of a more or less united European avant-garde, who were finding sharp new ways to show that classical scholarship and authentic Christian piety complemented one another.

REFORMING THE BIBLE Erasmus did more than remind European readers that Christ had told his followers to give all they had to the poor and turn the other cheek when violence was done to them. As a boy he had learned that true piety was not a matter of observances, of relics collected and indulgences bought, but of repentance and faith. Reading the New Testament in Greek, he found this central message in the words of Jesus and John the Baptist. In the Vulgate, the Latin translation of the Bible carried out in the late fourth century and used in all Catholic churches, Jesus tells Christians that they should "do penance." His command provided the foundation on which the complex system of confession, absolution, and remission of sin rested. In the Greek, however, Jesus instructs his hearers to "repent," meaning to come back to their right minds. Here and in many other passages, Erasmus held, the Latin Bible of the Church was clearly wrong.

Erasmus set out, accordingly, to reform the Vulgate itself. He prepared a revised Latin translation of the New Testament that made his new interpretations clear, and printed it with the Greek text to support it. Erasmus urged readers to refound theology, substituting direct study of the Bible for the logical arguments about doctrine that had traditionally formed the core of the field. His bold undertaking was flanked by even grander enterprises: an edition of the Psalms in Hebrew, Greek, and Arabic, as well as Latin; and a vast edition of the entire Bible, with the Old Testament in Hebrew, Greek, Aramaic, and Latin, and the New Testament in Greek and Latin. This polyglot Bible was sponsored by the Spanish cardinal and statesman Francisco Jiménez de Cisneros. A conservative, he compared the Vulgate text of the Old Testament, which his scholars printed between the Hebrew and the Greek, to Christ crucified between two thieves. But he still supported the study and publication of the originals. A massive controversy flared up in Germany over whether it was legitimate for Christians to learn from Jews and draw on their traditions of scholarship. The very identity of the Bible seemed debatable—just when Erasmus had placed its study at the center of theological inquiry.

LUTHER AND ERASMUS Luther came to maturity in the years when Erasmus and his friends attained the peak of their prestige. He followed Erasmus's teachings and example in making the New Testament the source for all Christian truths, and he used Erasmus's New Testament edition. His critique of indulgences began from the same point that Erasmus had made: that Jesus commanded not the doing of penance but repentance. Many of those who read Luther's theses and sent them on to colleagues and printers were clerics and officials who had read Erasmus's textbooks in their youth and shared his belief that Christians needed to return to their original principles. Like Erasmus himself, they saw Luther at first as an ally—as someone who continued the Christian humanist critique of the Church and offered the Bible as a template for its reform.

LUTHER'S MESSAGE

In fact, however, as Luther's message began to spread—and to encounter challenges—it became clear that his vision differed sharply from that of Erasmus: Luther represented not a movement to reform the existing Church but a challenge to its very existence. Between 1517 and 1521, he definitively stated most of his central doctrines in short, accessible books in Latin and German. Only scripture, Luther argued, contained the truths a Christian needed. Only divine grace made it possible to read scripture properly. And only faith in Jesus could win salvation. Everything else the Church did and believed, Luther now argued, was superfluous, and much of it harmful. The Church must be rebuilt on a solid foundation of scripture, correctly interpreted.

Traditional Catholic doctrine held that priests occupied a special spiritual as well as social position: they could intervene for other Christians, releasing them from the consequences of their sins. Luther argued that all Christians were priests who could pray for one another. Whereas Catholic priests offered seven distinct sacraments, Luther recognized only two: infant baptism and the Eucharist. And whereas the Catholic Church presented itself as a spiritual body that transcended mere political and linguistic borders and owed obedience only to the pope, Luther demanded that Christian rulers emulate Constantine, the emperor who had established Christianity as the religion of the Roman Empire and convoked the Council of Nicea to settle disputed points of doctrine. Secular rulers, Luther insisted, must take responsibility for the local churches that were under their political jurisdiction.

THE DIET OF WORMS AND ITS AFTERMATH (1521)

Luther's ideas now circulated in high official circles, especially after Albert of Brandenburg, Cardinal and Elector of Mainz, forwarded the **Ninety-Five Theses** to Rome. In July 1519, the eminent Catholic theologian Johann Eck (1486–1543) engaged Luther in a debate at Leipzig. Eck forced Luther to admit that he believed popes and even Church councils could err: only scripture was infallible. Eck pushed for a response from the Church, and in June 1520 Pope Leo X issued a bull condemning Luther.

Called to the **Diet of Worms**, a formal meeting of the Imperial Estates in April 1521, Luther accepted the invitation and stood before Holy Roman Emperor Charles V (r. 1519–1556) himself. Eck showed Luther a display of his writings and asked if he acknowledged them as his own. Luther requested time to reflect, but the next day he gave his opponents a sharp answer that expressed his conviction that he was acting as grace dictated:

> Unless I am convinced by the testimony of the Scriptures or by clear reason (for I do not trust either in the pope or in councils alone, since it is well known that they have often erred and contradicted themselves), I am bound by the Scriptures I have quoted and my conscience is captive to the Word of God. I cannot and will not recant anything, since it is neither safe nor right to go against conscience. May God help me. Amen.

Of Luther's extraordinary courage there can be no doubt. But his unflinching stance did not impress the emperor, who soon afterward delivered an impressive reply. He insisted on his duty, inherited from his ancestors, to defend the Catholic faith. On May 25, 1521, the emperor made Luther an outlaw. He forbade all subjects of the empire to give Luther food or water and permitted anyone to kill him without fear of consequences.

When Luther left the Diet, he was arrested by servants of Frederick the Wise, Elector of Saxony. They took him to the Wartburg castle in Eisenach, almost in the center of Germany, where he remained for several months under a loose form of house arrest. He used the time to translate the New Testament into German, realizing Erasmus's program to make the Bible available to all Christians. He poured out a series of pamphlets and treatises in which he began to draw the full consequences of his new theology. He argued, for example, that monks and nuns need not follow their vows of chastity, since marriage was a holy state, or of obedience, since obeying a superior would not bring them farther along the path to salvation.

By the end of 1521, Luther was hearing worrying messages from Wittenberg. Another minister who wished to reform the Church, Andreas Karlstadt (1486–1541), had taken over Luther's pulpit there. A radical by temperament, Karlstadt was inspired not only by Luther but also by miners from a nearby city, uneducated men who had visions and prophesied. Together they set out to transform the Church in Wittenberg beyond recognition. Whereas Luther argued that Christians should be able to understand the Bible for themselves, Karlstadt replaced the Latin Mass with a German-language service. And whereas Luther argued that Christians should not set too much store on images of saints, Karlstadt gained consent from the city council in 1522 to remove them from Wittenberg's churches.

Allowed to return to Wittenberg in March 1522, Luther appeared on his pulpit in the robes of his Augustinian Canons order. In a brilliant series of sermons, he convinced his fellow inhabitants of Wittenberg that it was wrong to move too quickly or to change things too radically, since by doing so they threatened the consciences of Christians who were not yet certain of the truth. Taking command of the situation, Luther began to create a new Church order. Soon cities across the Holy Roman Empire and beyond,

Diet of Worms A sixteenth-century history of Germany illustrates the dramatic scene of Luther's defense of his ideas to Holy Roman Emperor Charles V. The Catholic theologian Johann Eck (holding a book at center left) interrogates Luther as courtiers look on.

especially in Switzerland, were publicly joining the cause of reform. Luther himself was certain of what made his views—some of them highly abstract and difficult—take wing as they did. He and his dear friend and helper Philip Melanchthon simply sat in Wittenberg, he told his students much later, and drank the local dark beer. The Holy Spirit did the rest.

THE REFORMATION MOVEMENT

Between 1521 and 1529, Luther's challenge to the authority of the Church became a movement—the movement that became known, after the Diet of Speyer in 1529, as the **Protestant Reformation**. Princes and cities across the Holy Roman Empire and Switzerland, and individuals across a far wider area, found inspiration in Luther's writings to transform local churches. But they also encountered resistance—sometimes from Catholics faithful to the established order of things, sometimes from fellow Protestants who disagreed with them on basic questions of theology or Church discipline. By 1529, it was clear that the Protestant challenge would not soon disappear. But it was also clear that Protestantism would not take a single form or remain a unified movement. Luther's success was extraordinary—and partial.

THE MOVEMENT'S APPEAL

Many clearly identifiable features of Luther's world, beyond Wittenberg's dark beer, made his success possible. The power of print and the structures of authority in cities and states played vital roles in transforming a message into a movement.

THE ROLE OF PRINT Most important, the printing press gave Luther a megaphone that previous critics of the established Church lacked until the late fifteenth century, when the followers of Savonarola in Florence printed multiple editions of the Dominican's sermons. Luther used it with determination and brilliance. He became the master of the theological pamphlet, in both Latin and German. As a writer and translator, he developed a flexible German idiom that he could use both to render the word of God and to make his own arguments. He printed much of what he wrote—so much that, by the end of 1521, more than 100 editions of his works had already appeared. If each edition was produced in the period's standard quantity of 500 to 1,000 copies, then tens of thousands of copies of Luther's

The Reformation Movement, 1521–1529 By 1529, Lutheranism had spread from the central German cities where Luther's message first took hold to large states like Bohemia, Hessen, Prussia, and Sweden. In the area around Zurich, meanwhile, Zwingli's Reformed movement gained converts.

texts must have been in circulation four years after the outbreak of his movement. Luther and his printers developed a uniform format that became closely associated with him—some historians call this the first media brand.

Luther and his followers used illustrations as well as texts to appeal to their fellow Christians. Even before printing with moveable type was introduced in the West, collections of woodcut illustrations with some text, known as block books, brought graphic versions of the biblical narratives to readers of modest means and education. When printers learned to reproduce substantial texts with moveable type, they continued to adorn them with woodcut illustrations. Illustrated texts were far more accessible than unbroken blocks of type. A single

Printing Bibles A 1465 "pauper's Bible" demonstrates how printing technology could make the stories and ideas of the Bible accessible to all. Short excerpts from the text of the Latin Vulgate are set alongside woodcut illustrations of key stories, such as the birth of Jesus (center).

churches in their domains, he addressed princes and kings eager to enlarge their power and revenues, and city magistrates who believed that they were more qualified than any outsiders to see to the moral and spiritual health of their fellow citizens. When he addressed social and economic questions—such as bankers' practice of charging excess interest, which he denounced, or landlords' exploitation of their tenants—he seemed to offer hope to many that the message of the Gospel, as he defined it, would also change their position in life for the better. And when he told Christians that in so far as any of them were priests, all of them were, and all of them could intercede for one another, he seemed to offer women a religious position and role very different from anything that traditional Christianity in the West had provided. Support for Luther also came from master artisans and journeymen, printers and (in Saxony) miners—practitioners of new and expanding crafts.

REFORM IN THE CITIES Luther's message held special appeal in the imperial cities of the Holy Roman Empire—some sixty-nine cities such as Nuremberg, most in southern Germany, that acknowledged no authority below the Holy Roman emperor himself—and in the self-governing cities of Switzerland. City magistrates had long taken responsibility for settling disputes between such Catholic institutions as religious orders in their territory. Many cities had traditional shrines to which pilgrims came, bringing income; but many resented the need to pay ecclesiastical dues to the Roman Church every time a new bishop or abbot was inaugurated. Each city played out its own complex drama, following its own pace; in many, members of established elites—wealthy merchants, for example, and university professors—acted as a brake on both popular pressure and government action.

The case of Regensburg, an imperial city in Bavaria, illustrates the complexity of these processes. In 1519, the city expelled its Jewish community, which had been there since Roman times, and destroyed their synagogue. During the destruction a workman fell from a roof or was struck by a beam (accounts vary), but escaped harm. He claimed that the Virgin Mary had held his hand. Others ascribed his salvation to a medieval image of the Virgin in Regensburg. A wooden chapel was built on the site to hold it, with a statue of the Virgin outside. Crowds began to visit it. "'All sorts of people came,' one witness noted: 'some with musical instruments, some with pitchforks and rakes; women came with their milk cans, spindles, and cooking pots. Artisans came with their tools: a weaver with his shuttle, a carpenter with his square, a cooper with his measuring tape.'" More than 100,000 pilgrims visited within a year, buying

literate person could read them aloud to a circle of illiterate hearers, who could still appreciate the illustrations. And illustrations lent themselves to polemic. They could be used to contrast the poverty and humility of the Jesus of the New Testament to the arrogant, overstuffed clerics in Rome. They could also be used to spread news of portents, such as the fall of meteors or the birth of strangely deformed animals, which suggested that God was warning his people of important changes soon to occur. The artists who followed Luther—above all Lucas Cranach the Elder (1472–1553), the Wittenberg court artist—became expert at composing religious comic books and illustrating the Bible with polemical woodcuts that presented a bold challenge to the established Church.

SOCIAL BASES OF REFORM Luther's message would never have found the reception it did if he had not been speaking to the passions and interests of Christians, powerful and not, across the social spectrum. When Luther appealed to secular authorities to take control over the

The Virgin of Regensburg Printed at the height of enthusiasm for the Virgin at Regensburg, this woodcut image shows the statue in front of the wooden chapel, which is decorated with the arms of the city. Pilgrims line up to view the statue, with the most fervent collapsing in adoration.

badges to stick in their caps to show that they had done so. But by 1524, enthusiasm for the miracle-working image had ebbed. The city council busied itself trying to reform the local church while expelling Lutherans—clear evidence that Luther's message was being preached. By 1542, however, the council officially made the city Lutheran. A stone structure begun in 1525 to replace the wooden chapel was completed in 1542 and became the city's first Protestant church. Many cities experienced religious changes as rapid and unexpected as these in the 1520s.

LUTHER'S CRITICS

Yet Luther's success was anything but complete. In the first place, the radicalism of his challenge to the Church posed the question of authority in a new way. If the pope and his theologians had no right to determine the correct interpretation of the Bible or the theological doctrines that rested on it, then who did? Luther claimed that this power rested with the individual Christian. But even many of the humanists who had agreed that traditional Church structures and doctrines needed reform were shocked by the clean sweep that Luther proposed to make. Thomas More, for example, persisted in believing that the prayers of the living were needed by the souls who suffered in purgatory—a place whose very existence Luther denied. More lampooned Luther as an "infallible donkey" who proposed to replace the infallible pope of tradition with his own equally unquestionable authority.

ERASMUS'S HUMANIST CRITIQUE Erasmus, on the whole, agreed. As the contours of Luther's doctrines became clearer, Erasmus realized that the reformer really saw human nature as devoid of any value or virtue except what came to it through faith. By definition, men and women could play no active part in their own salvation. Ever the humanist, Erasmus believed that the best of the pagans had lived and thought in a virtuous way—so virtuous that they were almost Christians. And he could not accept the idea that God simply reached down and saved certain individuals. In a treatise against Luther published in 1524, Erasmus attacked him for claiming certainty on issues too difficult for human understanding. True Christians, he explained, preferred to avoid the sort of furious debates with colleagues that Luther's brand of theology required.

More important, Erasmus claimed, Luther was simply wrong about the relationship between humankind and God. A little child, Erasmus explained, cannot walk without the help of an adult—or be made to walk by that adult if he or she refuses to cooperate. This was also the situation of the Christian soul: too weak to save itself, but a vital participant in the drama of its own salvation. Luther—a far more rigorous theologian than Erasmus—devastated the humanist in his reply, but by the same token he made clear that he was now going down a road where some of those who had supported him would not follow.

ULRICH ZWINGLI Even those who dedicated themselves to reform in Luther's sense, moreover, did not always agree with him on vital details. What was the sacrament of the Eucharist, for example? Catholics believed that though the bread and wine of the Mass still looked like the original substances, the priest's words transformed them into the body and blood of Christ (the doctrine of transubstantiation). Luther argued that the Eucharist contained both sets of substances at once: bread and body,

Ulrich Zwingli An uncompromising reformer, Zwingli founded the Reformed church and transformed public conduct in Zurich and beyond.

wine and blood (a doctrine called consubstantiation). But **Ulrich Zwingli** (1484–1531), a former priest who led the transformation of the church in the Swiss city of Zurich, took a different view. Zwingli and others argued that the bread and wine remained themselves, rather than changing into a new substance, and represented the body and blood of Christ only as symbols. Luther denounced these views. After some polemical exchanges, the disagreeing parties met at Marburg Castle, in Hessen, in October 1529. When Luther chalked "This is my body" on a table, laid a cloth over the words, and defended his views forcefully, Zwingli insisted that "is," in this context, meant "stands for," as it did when Jesus said "I am the true vine" or "I am the road." Discussion soon broke down as the theologians traded insults. What had started out as a single movement began to fragment into multiple reformations.

FISSURES IN THE MOVEMENT: ZURICH AND THE REFORMED TRADITION

In Zurich, Ulrich Zwingli built a distinctive church. He was inspired not only by Luther, who taught him to insist that all believers were priests and to eliminate the old clerical estate, but also by Erasmus and other Christian humanists who had hoped to see Christianity transform society. Uncompromising in his reforms, Zwingli found support in the radical journeymen and women who, in Zurich, wielded a measure of political influence and power. Through two public disputations and a long series of sermons, he and his colleagues won over the Zurich population and their magistrates, who accepted the Reformation in 1523.

Zwingli's church—the first of the Protestant churches, based in Switzerland, that came to be called Reformed rather than Lutheran—differed from Luther's in both style and substance. Whereas Luther refused to eliminate all Catholic observances at once, Zwingli fought to reduce Christian ritual as soon as possible to the minimum clearly prescribed by the New Testament. Whereas Luther retained, and reformed, church music, Zwingli banned both instrumental music and singing. When Zwingli denounced religious images as a violation of divine law, the authorities had the great triptychs in Zurich's main churches closed. But their action inspired Zwingli's followers to tear down other shrines and images. In June 1524 the local authorities made Zwingli's position official, ordering that all churches be "cleansed" of their religious images and stained glass. Zwingli was delighted by the "white" and "luminous" look of the undecorated churches.

Zwingli also set out to impose Christian discipline on the citizens of Zurich. Here too differing from Luther, who held that what mattered to Christians was the condition of their souls, Zwingli argued that the Christian magistrate must reform public behavior as well as worship. Zurich adopted laws that regulated Sabbath observance and other forms of public conduct, while a new Marriage Court oversaw the making of marriages and the conduct of married life. By the mid-1520s, the church of Reformed Zurich looked very different from the one that Luther had built in Wittenberg.

TRANSFORMING SOCIETY: THE PEASANTS' WAR (1524–1525)

In the same decade, moreover, the messages of Luther and his rivals rippled through German society, sometimes joined to social and political grievances held by people across the social order. Early in the 1520s, for example, the German knights—a group of minor aristocrats who, like the governments of the imperial cities, recognized only

MARTIN LUTHER AND THE PEASANTS' WAR

The rebels who took part in the Peasants' War of 1524–25 were influenced by radical religious ideas as well as long-standing social grievances. Their demands are well stated in their manifesto, the Twelve Articles of the Peasants (1525), largely the work of the preacher Christoph Schappeler and a journeyman furrier, Sebastian Lotzer. Several Reformation theologians published responses to the Twelve Articles, notably Martin Luther, who in his *Admonition to Peace Concerning the Twelve Articles of the Peasants* (1525) urged lords and peasants to reach an understanding. Luther's position hardened into strong opposition to the peasants, however, as the uprising intensified.

Twelve Articles of the Peasants

The First Article. First, it is our humble petition and desire, indeed our will and resolution, that in the future we shall have power and authority so that the entire community should choose and appoint a minister, and that we should have the right to depose him should he conduct himself improperly. The minister thus chosen should teach us the holy gospel pure and simple, without any human addition, doctrine or ordinance....

The Second Article. Since the right tithe is established in the Old Testament and fulfilled in the New, we are ready and willing to pay the fair tithe of grain. Nonetheless, it should be done properly. The Word of God plainly provides that it should be given to God and passed on to his own. If it is to be given to a minister, we will in the future collect the tithe through our church elders, appointed by the congregation, according to the judgment of the whole congregation. The remainder shall be given to the poor of the place, as the circumstances and the general opinion demand....

The Third Article. It has been the custom hitherto for men to hold us as their own property, which is pitiable enough considering that Christ has redeemed and purchased us without exception, by the shedding of his precious blood, the lowly as well as the great. Accordingly, it is consistent with Scripture that we should be free and we wish to be so. Not that we want to be absolutely free and under no authority. God does not teach us that we should lead a disorderly life according to the lusts of the flesh, but that we should live by the commandments, love the Lord our God and our neighbor....

Conclusion ... If any one or more of these articles should not be in agreement with the Word of God, which we do not think, we will willingly recede from such article when it is proved to be against the Word of God by a clear explanation of the Scripture.

Martin Luther, *Admonition to Peace Concerning the Twelve Articles of the Peasants*

To the Princes and Lords

We have no one on earth to thank for this disastrous rebellion, except you princes and lords, and especially you blind bishops and mad priests and monks, whose hearts are hardened, even to the present day.... You do nothing but cheat and rob the people so that you may lead a life of luxury and extravagance. The poor common people cannot bear it any longer.... If it is still possible to give you advice, my lords, give way a little to the will and wrath of God.... Try kindness first, for you do not know what God will do to prevent the spark that will kindle all Germany and start a fire that no one can extinguish....

To the Peasants

In the first place, dear brethren, you bear the name of God and call yourselves a "Christian association" or union, and you allege that you want to live and act according to divine law. Now you know that the name, word, and cities of God are not to be assumed idly or in vain....

I say this, dear friends, as a faithful warning. In this case you should stop calling yourselves Christians and stop claiming that you have the Christian law on your side.... So again I say, however good and just your cause may be, nevertheless, because you would defend yourselves and are unwilling to suffer either violence or injustice, you may do anything that God does not prevent. However, leave the name Christian out of it....

If ... you will ... keep the name of Christian, then I must accept the fact that I am also involved in this struggle and consider you as enemies who, under the name of the gospel, act contrary to it, and want to do more to suppress my gospel than anything the pope and emperor have done to suppress it....

Admonition to Both Rulers and Peasants

Now, dear sirs, there is nothing Christian on either side and nothing Christian is at issue between you; both lords and peasants are discussing questions of justice and injustice in heathen, or worldly, terms.... For God's sake, then, take my advice! Take a hold of these matters properly, with justice and not with force or violence and do not start endless bloodshed in Germany....

QUESTIONS FOR ANALYSIS

1. How do the Twelve Articles interpret grievances according to religious principles?
2. What are Luther's greatest objections to the Twelve Articles?
3. Compare the ideals of the peasants and Martin Luther as articulated in these sources.

Sources: From "The Twelve Articles of the Peasants," in *Christianity and Revolution*, ed. Lowell Zuck (Philadelphia: 1975), pp. 14–16; from *Admonition to Peace Concerning the Twelve Articles of the Peasants*, in *Luther's Works*, vol. 46, eds. Robert C. Schultz and Helmut T. Lehmann (Philadelphia: 1967), pp. 19, 23–24, 32, 40.

the emperor as their superior—rebelled, claiming among other things that they meant to restore the true Church. They were soon put down. But during the **Peasants' War** of 1524–25, hundreds of thousands of peasants and craftsmen rebelled against their lords across central and southern Germany. This was not the first time, by any means, that peasants in these areas had risen. In 1476, thousands of them had converged on a town in southern Germany to hear the dramatic speeches of a former drummer turned prophet, Hans Böhm, who denounced the corruption of the clergy and demanded that all forests and waters be held in common. Others had followed a banner in the form of a peasant's rough shoe to denounce unjust taxes. In these earlier uprisings, peasants aimed generally for the restoration of traditional rights that had been taken from them.

The peasants who rose in 1524–25 also denounced

The Peasants' War, 1524–1525
Peasants' rebellions spread throughout a wide area of central and southern Germany, drawing thousands into pitched battles with royal forces from Bavaria, Hessen, and Saxony.

their landlords for depriving them of such traditional rights as gathering fallen firewood in the forests. Many of them were aggrieved by governments' and landlords' increasing use of written law and legal documents. But in the collections of articles drafted for them, they demanded much more. For the first time, peasants appealed to a fixed, printed text—that of the Gospels—to define their rights. As Christians, they claimed, they should be allowed to hear the true Gospel preached. As believers, moreover, they were free men and women, as Luther himself had written in a tract of 1521. Therefore, their lords had no right to make them serfs and bind them to the land.

The wave of peasant unrest and demands began in the countryside outside Zurich. Inspired by the transformation of the city, peasants and others called for a transformation of German society. The preacher Christoph Schappeler imagined that they might form a peasant republic, directly subject, as the imperial cities were, to the Holy Roman emperor. Schappeler defended their right, founded on the need to create a society of "brotherly love," to depose tyrants who opposed them. For a time, the princes and prelates seemed paralyzed as bands of peasants sacked castles and monasteries unopposed.

From Luther's standpoint, the peasant rebels were remaking his message of spiritual liberty into a charter for fundamental social change. Horrified by what he saw as a diabolic perversion of his enterprise, Luther called on the authorities to massacre the peasants. In May 1525, the princes of Bavaria, Hessen, and Saxony destroyed armed peasant bands in a series of pitched battles: in one encounter, 5,000 of the 6,000 peasants who took part were massacred in a single day.

The defeat of the peasants seemed total. Yet lords in much of the Holy Roman Empire came away from the uprising determined never to provoke another movement of the same kind. They changed the legal status of peasants to give them freedom of movement and of marriage, and peasants were accorded the clear right to long-term possession of their dwellings. Especially in the western parts of the Holy Roman Empire and in Switzerland, the successors of the massacred peasants enjoyed, from the sixteenth to the eighteenth centuries, many of the rights that they had demanded. By contrast, in eastern Germany,

Peasant Preaching Inspired by the writings of Martin Luther, peasants began to frame their sufferings and demands within the context of the Gospels. In this 1525 woodcut, a peasant preacher and follower of Luther gives a sermon to an attentive crowd.

Poland, and Russia during the same period, landlords succeeded in enserfing their peasants, building large estates, and tying their workforces to the land.

RADICAL REFORMATION: THE ANABAPTISTS

Even as the heaped corpses of the peasants were being buried, small groups, mostly in cities, were moving in what ultimately became an even more frightening direction for Luther, Zwingli, and other founders of reform. This movement began, like the Peasants' War, in Zurich, where Conrad Grebel (ca. 1498–1526) and other radical reformers were both inspired and infuriated by Zwingli. They agreed with him that the reform of religion meant the reform of society, and that scripture should serve as the rule for all changes. But they rejected Zwingli's defense of the tradition of infant baptism even though the New Testament always depicted baptism as for adults. When their ideas met resistance in Zurich, the radicals moved into the countryside. Peasants who found the city's rule oppressive were impressed by the denunciation of the tithes that they had to pay and the heavy hand of the city's government on areas outside the city walls. Others who heard these radicals preach, including merchants, craftsmen, and women, turned back to their own Bibles and found there a literal pattern for Christian life. They came to be known as **Anabaptists** ("re-baptizers"), because they believed that one could not properly join a church until one was an adult, like the adult converts of John the Baptist and Jesus.

Luther, in the tradition of Augustine, envisioned the Church as a universal community of the saved and the damned in this world. By contrast, the Anabaptists—like Augustine's ancient opponents, the Donatists—saw the Church as a small community of the saved, who had committed themselves to lead a Christian life. Luther accepted the need for private property, law, warfare, and all the other appurtenances of civil life in the world. The first Anabaptists refused to take oaths or fight, and they tried to live a literal version of the precepts of Jesus in the Gospels.

Luther was slow to turn against fellow reformers. Though he had helped to expel Andreas Karlstadt from the pulpit in Wittenberg and viewed him as a dangerous radical, he sheltered Karlstadt in his own house during the Peasants' War. But in the course of that conflict, as we saw, Luther had sided with the German princes—even Catholic princes—against the rebels. He and the secular

Persecution of Anabaptists A sixteenth-century engraving shows a crowd surrounding the cage containing the body of the Anabaptist leader John of Leiden, who was tortured and executed in Münster.

authorities responded to what they saw as the subversive program of the Anabaptists with special savagery. They made practicing or praising adult baptism and pacifism capital offenses. A number of the Anabaptists were executed for their beliefs. The ex-Benedictine monk Michael Sattler, who wrote the Anabaptist articles of faith known as the Schleitheim Confession and served as a roving missionary for his causes, was tortured and executed in 1527 while on a mission in southern Germany.

Many Anabaptists began to believe—as Luther himself did—that they were living through the last days of the world and that they were the holy martyrs whose lives and suffering were the central drama of the biblical book of Revelation. Divisions began to appear among them, and some of their leading figures, such as the one-time furrier-turned-preacher Melchior Hoffmann, predicted that the new era was about to start. Hoffmann was imprisoned in Strasbourg, the city where he had expected the

New Jerusalem to rise, and died in captivity in 1543. In Münster, in western Germany, groups of Anabaptists took up arms in 1534, expelled the bishop who ruled the city, and created a polygamous commune loosely modeled on the Israel of the Old Testament. After months of fierce resistance, they were crushed in June 1535, and their prophet, John of Leiden, was brutally executed some months later.

Surviving Anabaptists responded to this disaster in different ways. Pilgram Marpeck, a successful businessman from the Tirol, became an Anabaptist in 1527 and settled in Strasbourg in 1528. He became city engineer, first there and then in Augsburg, and his usefulness to governments protected him from violence. Weaving networks to bring his coreligionists together, he urged them to take oaths and pay taxes when the law required. Other Anabaptists, above all the Dutch ex-priest Menno Simons, insisted on the central importance of maintaining a communal life and the authority of the church. His followers, called Mennonites, became known for their commitment to pacifism. Thousands of Anabaptists took refuge in Moravia, now part of the Czech Republic, where they were eagerly sought as tenants by lords looking for reliable farmers. Some of the Moravian Anabaptists accepted the need of states to use force to defend themselves, while others rejected the use of arms on principle. The members of this latter group, which came to be known as Hutterites after their leader, Jacob Hutter (d. 1536), also decided to share all their property. Though the Anabaptists soon ceased to pose a serious challenge to the larger churches, they continued to be seen as a threat and were regularly persecuted. Their presence did much to make Luther and other reformers emphasize the need for central authority in church and state.

Lutheran Schools A 1516 painting illustrates the access to literacy that Lutheran Sunday schools provided. A schoolmaster directs a student in writing the alphabet, while other students read bound books.

RELIGIOUS EDUCATION

Luther and his allies saw education in the true principles of Christianity as one way to prevent further divisions, and did their best to ensure that all Lutherans knew the fundamentals of their faith. This view brought Philip Melanchthon, Luther's friend and a brilliant Greek scholar, to Wittenberg, where he created the curricula for what became Protestant secondary schools and universities. Luther's followers also established Sunday schools, where children learned the elements of literacy and the fundamentals of doctrine, which they memorized from catechisms. Bishops undertook regular visitations to ensure that ministers preached true doctrine and to oversee the quality of the schools. Luther loved music, and he and others wrote hymns that would become a cornerstone of Protestant religious practice. This was not complex music performed by professionals, as in the Catholic Church, but participatory singing in which the congregation could take part. In some Lutheran countries—especially in Denmark—male and female literacy seems to have become almost universal, and knowledge of religious doctrines with it. In Luther's own Germany, however, efforts at Protestant education met with varied levels of success. Some visitations reported orderly classes and knowledgeable parishioners; others described drunken mockers who scorned the Lord's Day. Building a new church was not easy.

WOMEN AND THE REFORMATION

Luther followed Paul in arguing that all Christians—women as well as men—were priests and could pray for one another. He himself married a former nun to show his rejection of celibacy as a human tradition. But he may have been surprised when he saw that some women were not only listening to and reading him but also imitating him. When a young man was imprisoned for Protestant heresy at Ingolstadt, a stronghold of traditional Catholicism, a Bavarian noblewoman, **Argula von Grumbach** (1492–ca. 1554), denounced what she considered to be the effort of Church authorities to attack the true Gospel.

A pious woman who had learned in her youth to pray to the Virgin Mary and to imagine herself conversing with angels, von Grumbach had also read the Bible—especially the Prophets and the New Testament. When she read the pamphlets that the Wittenberg presses were shipping in barrels across the Bavarian border, she was immediately convinced of the truth of Luther's message. She set out to defend the young man under accusation with all her strength. In a long letter to the theologians at Ingolstadt, she cited verse after verse from the Bible in support of Luther's new theology: "What do Luther and Melanchthon teach you but the word of God?" She used both the powerful language of the prophets and her own sharp idioms to tell the theologians that they were in the wrong: "The pot burns: and truly you and your university will never extinguish it."

Von Grumbach's letter to the Ingolstadt theologians circulated first in manuscript and then as a pamphlet, which was reprinted fourteen times. By the time she stopped writing, as many as 29,000 copies of that and other pamphlets by her may have been in circulation. She became a Protestant celebrity, who had the chance to share a meal with the legendarily busy Luther. She even gave him advice, for his wife, on how to wean her children. Von Grumbach and others—such as the former abbess Marie Dentière—rejected Paul's principle that women should not teach, arguing that Jesus had commanded all to preach his message. The British Protestant Anne Askew, who courted arrest by preaching, was tortured and then executed by burning at Smithfield in June 1546. She became one of the most famous Protestant martyrs; contemporary Protestant historians compared her to the early Christians who had died for their faith. Yet most of the women who set out to preach and write in public were silenced without winning fame.

Queens and noblewomen commanded the respectful attention of reformers—and were sometimes rewarded in special ways for doing so. Anna von Stolberg, abbess of Quedlinburg in the Black Forest, governed nine churches and two male monasteries. In the 1540s, when she converted to Protestantism, she ordered her priests to swear loyalty to Luther and turned her Franciscan monastery into an elementary school for boys and girls. Under her rule, Quedlinburg remained a convent even as it turned Protestant—as did many others.

Protestant women could leave convents and marry—as Katharina von Bora (1499–1552) did: after leaving her Cistercian monastery, she married Luther. Like earlier women we have encountered, von Bora participated actively in economic life even after finding a husband. The elector of Saxony gave her and Luther the property of the Augustinian cloister in Wittenberg. Teaching, preaching, and writing kept Martin busy. Accordingly, von Bora managed the estate, rising every day at 4:00 a.m. In addition to bearing Luther six children, she bred and sold cattle, brewed beer, and operated a hospital when epidemics struck. Yet von Bora always recognized Luther's supremacy in their

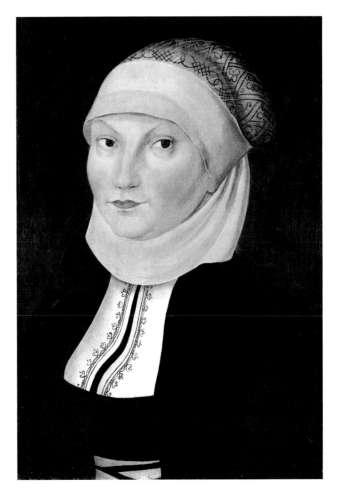

Katharina von Bora In 1528, Lucas Cranach the Elder painted this portrait of Katharina von Bora, the former nun who married Martin Luther.

marriage, calling him "Sir Doctor" and insisting that his calling was higher than hers.

As this case suggests, the larger position of women was not clearly transformed by the Reformation. The guildsmen who dominated cities that reformed their churches, such as Nuremberg, believed in the central importance of the patriarchal family. New legislation limited the roles that women could play—especially when, as happened in most Protestant cities, the convents were abolished and women could no longer live celibate lives as nuns. Sexual crimes were redefined: rape, for example, came to be treated less as a violent crime perpetrated by men than as evidence of licentious behavior by women. Male supremacy was reinforced in many ways: even Argula von Grumbach wrote with sorrow of the violence that she had suffered at the hands of her husband. Equality in the realm of the spirit did not bring with it the leveling of gender hierarchies.

THE MESSAGE SPREADS

By the later 1520s, Luther's period as the most influential spokesman of reform was coming to an end. But the messages of reform were spreading farther across Europe through efficient networks of exchange. Merchants and artisans—especially journeymen printers—carried the call for reform south to the Mediterranean and west and north to France, Britain, and Scandinavia. Hans Tauler, a former monk, preached the Reformation in Denmark and Norway. Though the king of Denmark and Norway, Frederick I (r. 1523–1533), claimed to oppose the Protestants, he protected Tauler and encouraged others to translate the Bible into the vernacular. Frederick was succeeded by Christian III (r. 1534–1559), who formally abolished the Mass, removed Catholic bishops, and installed Lutheran ones. Even in Spain, followers of Erasmus challenged and criticized traditional practices and beliefs. Some Italians—such as Bernardino Ochino, general of the Capuchin order, a branch of the Franciscans—realized that they agreed with the Protestants, and fled into exile in the north. Others continued to attend Catholic services but worshipped a Protestant God in secret. Germans in London made the Steelyard—the residence of merchants from the northern German trading cities that belonged to the Hanseatic League—a center of Protestant propaganda, to the fury of the British government. Even in France, traditionally "the most Christian nation" and loyal to the papacy, radical teachings spread. In 1534, in the Affair of the Placards, posters denouncing the Mass appeared all over Paris and other important cities—one of them on the king's bedroom door. These developments unleashed a vigorous effort to extirpate the new religion.

CALVINISM: THE CHURCH OF GENEVA

Many of the French Protestants who fled the campaign against them headed for Geneva, a small city in French-speaking Switzerland known chiefly for manufacturing kettles. One of the refugees, **John Calvin** (1509–1564), became the leading minister of Geneva and the second great intellectual leader of the Protestant movement. Trained as a humanist and Roman lawyer, Calvin initially encountered resistance in Geneva but overcame it by a combination of brilliant tactics and absolute commitment to his mission. By the early 1540s, Calvin and his allies dominated the city.

What Calvin devised there was, in the first place, the most rigorous version of Protestant theology, which he

John Calvin In this anonymous sixteenth-century portrait, Calvin appears as a determined young man, dressed somberly in black.

laid out in systematic form in his *Institutes of the Christian Religion*, a formal textbook of theology first published in 1536. In it he argued, more forcefully and consequentially than Luther, for the doctrine of predestination. Salvation was only God's affair, not man's. Human nature, Calvin explained, was vile, "a teeming horde of infamies." Only God could save humanity, and he did so by his own absolutely free choice, determining the fate of all—the damned as well as the saved. Evil as they were, human beings could not presume to question God's decision: "man falls by God's decree, but by his own fault." The rigor of this doctrine, which clarified points that Luther had not made clear, attracted many highly educated followers.

But Calvin did more than create a citadel of ideas. In Geneva, he also built up a church of a new kind—a Reformed church that went even further than Zwingli's in the imposition of discipline on all areas of life. He opened an academy to train ministers in Hebrew and Greek so that they could master the Bible in the original languages and learn its true doctrines as he had. Regular meetings and synods (formal meetings of all the clerics in a large district) oversaw the clergy once they were in the field, ensuring that they remained on message doctrinally

CHRISTMAS IN ST. ANDREWS

Kirk ("church") sessions were church courts in Scotland that, like the consistory in John Calvin's Geneva, enforced social discipline. They began to be established in Scottish towns during the Reformation, led in Scotland by John Knox, and within a generation had spread throughout much of the country. Ministers moderated weekly meetings of the courts, which focused largely on the morality of parishioners. Common charges ranged from fornication and adultery to popular but illegal Christmas customs such as singing carols. This excerpt is from the kirk session of St. Andrews in the winter of 1573/74.

The which day…upon Sunday the 24 day of January…Waltir Ramsay lorimer,[1] Waltir Lathangye cutler,[2] and Johne Smytht blacksmith in Ergail, being accused and convicted before for observing of superstitious days and especially of Yule Day,[3] became penitent and made open satisfaction therefore in the presence of the whole congregation then being present. And therefore the minister, at command of the assembly, publicly [an]nounced that all persons, within this parish, that observe superstitiously the said Yule Day or any other days, should be punished in like manner; and such like should be punished in like manner if they abstain from their work and labour that day more than any other day except Sunday, which only should be kept holiday. And hereupon the session interposed their decision.

The said day, James Clwny cutler and Waltir Zownger being accused for violating the Sabbath day by superstitious keeping of Yule Day holiday, and abstaining from their work and labour that day, James Clwny promised to desist and cease from keeping of Yule Day in time coming, under pain contained in the act immediately preceding. And Waltir Zownger…being accused…that [he] made his neighbors disobedient to the kirk, saying, in the Gallowlaik[4] that it does not become honest men to sit upon the penitent stool[5] which words he confessed: and also said that he is a young man and saw Yule Day kept as a holiday, and that the time may come that he may see the like yet; and therefore would not become obliged or restricted in time coming to abstain from work that day, but at his own pleasure. In respect of the aforesaid, the session decides and orders that him to be admonished by public admonition to make satisfaction upon the penitent stool under pain of excommunication, and also [because] he being required would give no other answer nor yet submit himself to the voice of the kirk.

QUESTIONS FOR ANALYSIS

1. What were the people in this record accused and convicted of having done?
2. What evidence does this record provide about how people marked Christmas in sixteenth-century Scotland?
3. These cases came before the kirk session more than ten years after the Reformation was accomplished in Scotland. Is their appearance evidence of the success or failure of the reformers' agenda?

[1]**lorimer:** maker of bits, spurs, and other small metal objects
[2]**cutler:** maker or seller of knives and other utensils
[3]**Yule Day:** Christmas Day
[4]**Gallowlaik:** a meeting place for craftsmen
[5]**penitent stool:** a seat used for public shaming rituals

Source: *Register of the Minister, Elders, and Deacons of the Christian Congregation of St. Andrews*, pt. 1, ed. David Hay Fleming (Edinburgh: 1889), pp. 387–89; text modernized by Mairi Cowan.

and that they dealt vigorously and honorably with their parishioners. Every Calvinist cleric had to take his turn presenting a sermon in French and then waiting for comments from his hearers on both style and content. The consistory—an institution, based on the model of the Zurich marriage court, which brought together elders and ministers—oversaw the behavior of Genevans. It summoned and punished individuals for everything from quarreling with spouses and failing to attend or listen to the sermons given by Geneva's ministers to adultery and gluttony. Some patricians resisted, but Calvin defeated them in 1555, after a long struggle, thanks to the support of French immigrants who became Genevan citizens and elected a city council that supported him.

By the time Calvin died in 1564, Geneva had become a startlingly disciplined town, where heads of households presided over family prayers. The city became a symbol of independent Protestantism, and many of the young intellectuals who went there emerged as effective clergymen, brilliant missionaries for the cause of reform. In France and the Low Countries, and to a considerable extent in England and the Holy Roman Empire, Protestantism was Calvinism—even if the Zwinglian citizens of Zurich would not have agreed.

CHURCHES AND MONARCHS: A CHANGING BALANCE

Rulers watched as city councils accepted the Reformation movement, abolished the Mass, and set their clergy to preaching the Gospel in the vernacular. Some rulers, such as the brilliant soldier Philip of Hesse (1504–1567), took action themselves. There were, after all, many advantages to be had. On becoming a Protestant, Philip abolished the rich monasteries in his territory, which no longer had any function. He used 41 percent of their wealth to found schools and the University of Marburg, and to provide dowries for the noble nuns whose world he had shattered. But he kept 59 percent of it for his own use.

HENRY VIII AND THE CHURCH OF ENGLAND

Henry VIII of England (r. 1509–1547), the king whom Thomas More served as a counselor, also broke with the Catholic Church. Henry, who feared and hated disorder, at first saw no reason to transform the practice of Christianity in England. For years, he and his ministers—above all Thomas More, who became his lord chancellor from 1529 to 1532—hunted British Protestants such as William Tyndale, who translated the Bible into English and was strangled and burned by Catholic authorities in Flanders. Henry himself published a treatise that defended the sacraments against Luther. Thomas More engaged in literary duels with heretics. He defended the souls in purgatory against Protestants who claimed that purgatory did not exist and that prayers for the dead were wasted.

But Henry wanted desperately to have his marriage to his brother's widow, Catherine of Aragon, annulled on religious grounds, and marry Anne Boleyn, a noble at

Henry VIII This painting shows Henry flanked by his only legitimate son to survive him, the future Edward VI, and his third wife, Jane Seymour.

court. Though Henry failed to convince the papacy that his cause was just, he married Boleyn in 1533. He then declared himself head of an independent national church in 1534. More and the others who retained a passionate commitment to the universal church, and who refused to acknowledge Henry's supremacy, found themselves in danger. In 1535 More was executed, as were the members of the London Charterhouse, the most rigorous of the old monastic orders. Boleyn herself was executed for adultery, incest, and treason in 1536.

Henry, like most other kings, was always in need of money. He also showed sympathy, as a young man, for humanists like Erasmus and their criticisms of the wealth of the Church. His chief minister, Thomas Cromwell (ca. 1485–1540), convinced him to disestablish the monastic orders and confiscate their property. Cromwell made serious efforts to ensure that the monasteries could never be reestablished. His men used explosives to demolish them, and looted the sites of everything of value. Efforts to restore the old religion—such as the 1536 Pilgrimage of Grace, a rebellious movement based in Yorkshire and sparked in part by high grain prices—were put down with remorseless violence. Protestant doctrines spread in the universities, and the tutors who brought up Henry's son Edward, a superbly educated young man, saw to it that he was grounded in what they took as the true doctrines.

Despite the passive resistance of parishioners and priests who loved their ancient rituals, England slowly became a Protestant land. In 1539 Myles Coverdale, a

Protestant trained originally in the Augustinian order, produced the Great Bible, which was for the most part a revision of Tyndale's translation of the Bible into English, and was approved for use in church services. Thomas Cranmer, the archbishop of Canterbury, changed Communion so that the laity as well as the priest received both wine and bread. And he oversaw the translation of one element after another of the liturgy until, in 1549, the entire service was in English. Clerics with reformed sympathies complained that too much of the tradition had been retained. John Hooper, a Calvinist, refused to be made a bishop if he had to wear the traditional vestments, which, he thought, derived from the practice of Jewish priests. Through the 1540s, the English church was taking shape as a great compromise between tradition and innovation.

FRANCIS I AND CHARLES V (1521–1546)

Religious reform spread through Europe at a time when states were rapidly developing their powers. The brilliant young monarchs who controlled England (Henry VIII), France (Francis I), and the Holy Roman Empire (Charles V) benefited from vast personal resources; so did the princes of smaller territories, such as the Wittelsbachs, who ruled Bavaria. The French monarchy, which had revived during the course of the fifteenth century, worked effectively with its Estates General. The French state also devised increasingly efficient systems of tax collection and continually looked for other forms of revenue. One of these—the sale of offices in the state administration—ultimately proved counterproductive, since state officers held their positions by right, as private property, and could resist royal orders. Nonetheless, French state revenues were large enough to enable Francis I (r. 1515–1547) to wage a long and exhausting series of wars in Italy, where he tried to make good on the French claim to rule over Naples and Milan.

Charles, son of the Habsburg king of Spain Philip I, became Holy Roman Emperor **Charles V** and the lord of a vast series of domains before he was twenty. Born in Flanders in 1500, at age six he inherited his paternal grandfather Maximilian's Burgundian territories in the Low Countries. His aunt, Margaret of Austria, acted as regent until Charles was fifteen, and went to war with France to establish that Flanders was not a French fief. At sixteen, when his maternal grandfather, Ferdinand II, died, he became King Charles I of Spain, though he had

little knowledge of it. Three years later, when Maximilian died, he inherited the Habsburg monarchy and became the natural candidate to become Holy Roman emperor. The vast expense of bribing the German electors to make him emperor and maintaining his costly Flemish court placed him under financial pressure.

FOUNDATIONS OF STATE POWER State power was sustained not only by taxation and conquest. In the decades around 1500, European economic life entered a new phase. Entrepreneurs, such as the banker **Jacob Fugger** of Augsburg, worked with the Habsburgs and other monarchs to which they lent money. For each loan he issued, Fugger extracted something more important in return—for example, the right to exploit minerals that belonged to the sovereign. At a time when mining technology was rapidly improving, Fugger secured permission to dig for silver in the Tirol, copper in Hungary, mercury in Spain, and even gold and silver in the New World. The metals he extracted were vital for everything from making bronze cannon to coining money, and Fugger made money from each use, which he then employed to seek out new business opportunities, such as the trade in pepper from Asia.

Charles V borrowed enormous amounts from Fugger, which he tried to repay by raising taxes. The Spanish kingdoms of Castile and Aragon were already in financial difficulties, having spent vast amounts on the destruction of the last Islamic emirate, in Granada, in 1492, and on maintaining their armies. Agitation against Charles began in Toledo and Segovia in 1520, and soon other cities joined. The *comuneros*, an unstable coalition of lesser nobles, urban artisans, and others who saw Charles as an outsider, rebelled against him. They formed a new government, recognizing Charles's mother as queen, and raised armies. But Charles's representative in Spain raised more effective armies of his own, in alliance with much of the landed aristocracy, and defeated the comuneros.

HABSBURG CONTROL OF ITALY Even as the Spanish authorities crushed the comuneros, the old war between France and the Habsburgs in Italy was revived by Charles V and Francis I. Charles mustered an enormous force, including German mercenaries as well as his Spanish armies. Employing superior tactics, Charles's forces pulled the French army apart at Pavia in 1525, and Francis himself was taken prisoner. Frightened by Charles's power, Pope Clement VII, a member of the Medici family, formed a coalition against the emperor, the League

Habsburg Lands, ca. 1556 At the height of his power, Charles V controlled much of Europe, including inherited kingdoms in the Low Countries and Spain, the Holy Roman Empire, and conquests in Italy. He sustained his power with military might, putting down rebellions in Spain and defeating the Protestant Schmalkaldic League and several Italian uprisings. But rebellions in Protestant central Europe and pressure from the French and the Ottomans at the borders limited Charles's total control of the continent.

of Cognac, allying himself with Venice, Florence, and other powers. But the Venetians refused to take an active part, and Charles, after defeating Florence, found himself unable to pay his troops. In 1527 his soldiers shocked the world by sacking Rome, including the Vatican. The pope was imprisoned, and Charles now commanded the Italian Peninsula.

The Florentines rose up in one last attempt to defend their republican tradition—a magnificent, doomed effort that won the warm support of Michelangelo. But after furious resistance, they were defeated in 1530. Though Venice remained independent—and though Francis would launch more Italian wars—Italy would remain under the

control of the Habsburgs for centuries, as the Spanish transformed the south and Sicily into the agrarian province of the Iberian kingdom.

STALEMATE: PEACE OF AUGSBURG

Charles V never managed to win the one decisive victory that would have enabled him to pacify all of his territories and defeat the Protestant princes of the empire definitively—a goal that he thought it his religious duty to pursue as Holy Roman emperor. The French challenged him again in 1536 and 1542—both times in league with the Ottomans, whose empire, under Sultan Suleiman the Magnificent (r. 1520–1566), reached from North Africa to Asia Minor and deep into Hungary—but both wars ended in stalemates. In 1547 Charles did manage to defeat the Schmalkaldic League of Protestant powers, created in 1531 by Philip of Hesse and John Frederick I, Elector of Saxony, and gradually enlarged to include other German states and imperial cities. Charles imprisoned Philip, the league's most formidable commander. But the overwhelming power Charles thus achieved terrified many, and in 1552 a Protestant rebellion, supported by the new French king, Henry II (r. 1547–1559), drove Charles out of the German

lands. Dogged by ill health, he gave his Spanish crown to his son Philip in 1555, while his brother Ferdinand succeeded him as Holy Roman emperor in 1556.

In 1555 the **Peace of Augsburg**, a formal treaty agreed by Charles and the members of the Schmalkaldic League, officially recognized that the empire no longer followed one religion. The principle *cuius regio, eius religio* ("his realm, his religion") acknowledged that each prince could decide which religion, Catholic or Protestant, to establish in his domain. Those who refused to go along had the right to leave—itself a major innovation. At the Diet of Worms long before, Charles had stated that he had an inherited

Europe after the Peace of Augsburg A complicated religious and political landscape followed the treaty: for the most part, northern Germany, Scandinavia, and Prussia were Lutheran, Scotland and Switzerland were Calvinist, England had its own state church, Muscovy and the European portion of the Ottoman Empire were Orthodox, and the rest of Europe remained Catholic. But religious minorities now had a foothold in many regions as well, from Catholics in northern Germany to Calvinists in France and Poland and Anabaptists in Germany and Hungary.

duty to defend the Catholic Church against innovators and rebels. Now it was clear that he had failed. Yet this religious and political settlement was highly provisional. The Anabaptists and vigorous Calvinists did not win acceptance from the rulers of Protestant and Catholic states, and they resented their precarious position. Meanwhile, the Catholic Church was beginning to regroup and even to go on the offensive against its critics and enemies.

RENEWING CATHOLICISM

Well before the sack of Rome by Charles V's forces in 1527, loyal Catholics had begun to push for the reform of their Church. The Venetian Gasparo Contarini (1483–1542), for example, experienced a spiritual awakening not unlike Luther's, but he pursued it in a different direction. He and others formed a movement to reform the Church from within, insisting on the spiritual, internal nature of true religion and denouncing the simony (payment for church offices) and courtly, hierarchical ways that, they believed, had corrupted the papal Curia. After Contarini's long and successful career as a diplomat in the Venetian service, Pope Paul III (r. 1534–1549), who wanted to harness the spiritual movement to the Church, made him a cardinal in 1535.

SOURCES OF RENEWAL

There were many others like him. The diplomat and bishop Gian Matteo Giberti, and Gian Pietro Carafa— later Pope Paul IV (r. 1555–1559)—founded the Oratory of Divine Love, a free association of clerics and laymen, in Rome in 1517. Its members practiced an intensive discipline of prayer and confession, visiting hospitals as a work of charity. Other new orders included the Theatines, founded in 1524, and the Capuchins, a branch of the Franciscans founded in 1525; both set out to provide preaching of high quality. Jacopo Sadoleto, a brilliant Latinist and elegant courtier, shocked his friends by leaving Rome after the sack in 1527. He moved to Carpentras, the distant, rural diocese in France that provided his income. There he improved the education of the clergy and tried to convert the remaining members of the medieval Waldensian church—in part to protect them from violent persecution.

HOLY WOMEN Women played a central role in the renewal of Catholicism. Many women did so through highly practical religious activities: Catherine of Genoa,

for example, who later became a saint, moved with her husband into a hospital, where she dedicated herself to the care of incurable victims of syphilis. Other women became known—as Hildegard of Bingen had in the Middle Ages—as living exemplars of holiness. Known for their deep penitence for their sins and their pursuit of mystical union with God, some also developed renown as prophetesses and reformers. Holy women inspired and mentored the founders of the new Theatine order.

THE URSULINES Other new orders—such as the Ursulines, founded by Angela Merici in 1535—forged new paths for the Church. Whereas Protestants looked back to the Christianity of the New Testament, Catholics often looked back to the Church of the late antique Fathers: Merici, for example, modeled a new community for women on the circle of learned Christian women that had assembled around Saint Jerome in the fourth century. The Ursulines taught girls and cared for the sick, originally without taking formal vows. In 1572, long after the death of Merici, Charles Borromeo, the archbishop of Milan,

Angela Merici An anonymous 1550 painting depicts an elderly Angela Merici, the founder of the Ursuline order.

insisted that the Ursulines become a religious order and live an "enclosed" life. Their houses spread through the New World as well as the Old.

TERESA OF ÁVILA As in the Middle Ages, mystics of the sixteenth century showed that their union with God gave them an energy and efficiency that others lacked. Teresa of Ávila (1515–1582), who came from a Spanish family partly made up of Jewish converts, wrote dazzlingly of her religious experiences, vividly evoking the pains and torments she suffered, as well as the ecstasy of her final union with God. She created a new model of female monasticism for the Carmelite order, to which she belonged, eliminating outside visits and insisting that members remain strictly confined and pursue sanctity. John of the Cross, another mystic who, like Teresa, later became a saint, collaborated with her to found new houses. In the later sixteenth century, the Catholic religious authorities would turn a more critical eye on many holy women, looking for possible cases of diabolic possession that mimicked true sanctity, and cutting down the areas of free action that religious women had found in the early period of Catholic renewal. But the movement for renewal itself was shaped in considerable part by female hands.

THE SOCIETY OF JESUS

Though different in many respects, all of these Catholics believed that their church was the true one, and remained ardently faithful to it. One of them in particular—Ignatius Loyola (1491–1556), a Spanish nobleman who was badly wounded in the Italian wars—showed as vividly as Luther how an individual with a spiritual vocation could change the world, especially a world divided over questions of belief. After a long period of preparation, which included years of meditation as a hermit and intensive study in Paris, Loyola went to Rome in 1535 with a few ragged followers, and gained papal permission to create a new order, the Society of Jesus, in 1540.

What made the **Jesuits** special was not their numbers, for there were never many of them, but the training on which Loyola insisted and the intense commitment that it both demanded and generated. To join the order, one had to go through a long preparation of studying, doing humble tasks as a novice, and—most important—making the Spiritual Exercises (a set of meditative exercises that Loyola designed) under the supervision of a Jesuit spiritual director. By undergoing these rigors, Loyola argued,

The Society of Jesus In a 1540 French engraving, Ignatius Loyola and a group of his fellow Jesuits kneel before Pope Paul III to offer him a copy of their rule. The pope raises his right hand in a gesture of benediction.

Jesuits would establish for certain that they possessed a religious vocation, a question that earlier orders had too often ignored. Equally important, they and their superiors would learn exactly which tasks they were best equipped to carry out for the order: teaching in schools, working in cities with the poor, or going on missions to Asia and other lands.

Although the rigorous Jesuit training resembled that of Calvinist ministers in some ways, its texture and content were completely different. Full members of the Jesuit order not only swore the traditional vows of poverty, chastity, and obedience but also pledged to go at once to the Holy Land if ordered to do so and preach the word of God. The Jesuits saw themselves as committed to everything that Calvin hated. They would obey the pope absolutely, "like a stick in the hand." They would defend the church fathers and the scholastic theologians of the Middle Ages against Protestant insistence that only scripture mattered. They would serve wherever the order or the pope sent them.

Many Jesuits went on missions to preach and find converts. Some missions took them into perils of every kind, especially in lands that had turned Protestant. In other cases, they followed the Catholic empires of Spain, Portugal, and France into the New World and Asia. As teachers, they founded schools across the globe and often induced the children of Protestant nobles, sent to them solely for an education, to convert back to their ancestral faith. As priests, they built shrines—including countless replicas of the house of the Virgin Mary at Loreto, which had supposedly been brought there from the Holy Land by angels. As spiritual directors, they counseled rulers and nobles, scholars and merchants through spiritual crises. And as historians, they documented every step they took, from recruiting novices to dying as martyrs in Japan. By the 1540s and 1550s, Jesuits were crossing Europe, ready to engage Protestants in a war for Christian souls.

THE COUNCIL OF TRENT

The reformers were never wholly isolated within the Church, and soon they found powerful allies. From 1545 to 1563, a broad, ecumenical council of the Church met at Trent, on the border between the Holy Roman Empire and northern Italy. After long deliberations, the **Council of Trent** settled disputed questions of doctrine: for example, it decreed that the true text of the Bible was "the old and Vulgate edition," by which it meant the Latin text on which the Catholic Church had long relied. It affirmed such traditional practices as the sacraments and the veneration of saints. It laid out a set of tasks for the popes, including revision of the Mass and new editions of the Bible. And it filled participants with a new energy.

As clerics left the council to return to their dioceses, they felt a new responsibility to the Christian laity and

Council of Trent A Dutch watercolor from 1560 illustrates a meeting of the Council of Trent. Cardinals, monks, priests, ambassadors, generals, and other laymen pack the galleries of a church in Trent, while speakers from these groups discuss matters of doctrine.

devised new ways to raise the standard of the clergy and improve the religious lives of laypeople. In Italy, determined archbishops imposed order on religious services and created seminaries to ensure that clerics were literate and able to do their jobs. They also reformed monastic orders and adopted new ways of instilling Catholicism with the vitality that Luther and so many others had missed. The archbishop of Milan, for example, devised the confessional: an enclosed, private space in which the Christian would confess to a priest and receive instructions for amendment. Confession, long a public, external ritual, as Erasmus and other Christian reformers had complained, became a private, internal matter: a frightening leap into the spiritual darkness, made safe only by the presence of the confessor.

Meanwhile, the papacy restructured its administrative apparatus, the Roman Curia. Cardinals remained courtiers, as they had long been: aristocratic clerics who lived in palaces. But they also found themselves assigned to committees tasked to oversee particular areas of Church life. One of these committees took charge of the censorship of the printing press, which—if it had been institutionalized more effectively in earlier years—might have made it possible to suppress the Reformation entirely. By the 1550s, the Church was issuing indexes of forbidden books: detailed lists of books that Catholics could not read at all, or that they could read only after designated passages had been removed.

A system of censorship took shape. Catholic authors had to submit their works before publication to Church censors, whose approbations must be included in the published books. Protestant librarians soon found these indices useful instruments for creating libraries of past heretical works, the products of movements that they saw as ancestors of their own. Catholic thinkers, however, found themselves subject to a partial but serious effort at thought control. In Spain, the Inquisition was repurposed as a mechanism for examining and punishing suspected critics of Church doctrine.

RETHINKING THE NATURAL WORLD

The bite of censorship was all the more painful to thoughtful Catholics because, in the middle decades of the sixteenth century, Europe experienced widespread intellectual ferment. For centuries, the universities, with their canonical texts and elaborate curricula, had dominated the study of the natural world and much more. Humanists and reformers challenged them. But so, even more, did the simple facts that now came to light. The existence of a sea route to Asia and the New World proved that ancient maps of the earth and the sky were erroneous and incomplete. Not until the seventeenth century would Europeans carry out something like intellectual iconoclasm, arguing that moderns knew far more than the ancients had. But the roots of that development lie in the Reformation period.

OBSERVATION AND COLLABORATION

One intellectual who embraced the new knowledge was the brilliant, irascible German doctor Theophrastus Bombastus Paracelsus (1493–1541). By the late 1520s, he had decided that the traditional medical textbooks were useless. Like Luther, who burned the bull of excommunication against him, Paracelsus publicly burned the standard textbook, *The Canon of Medicine* by Avicenna (Ibn Sina; d. 1037). Paracelsus told his readers that they should rely instead on the empirical knowledge of ordinary men and women, which was worth far more than the nonsense of "the high colleges," and he elaborated his own alchemical version of medical theory and practice.

Nicolaus Copernicus (1473–1543), a cathedral canon whose career unfolded in Poland, devised an even more radical theory. Though he observed the heavens himself and used observations made by others, he was looking not for greater accuracy but for greater simplicity. The universe, he argued in 1543, was not geocentric (centered on the earth), as practically every thinker since Aristotle had believed, but heliocentric (centered on the sun). The earth, moreover, was not at rest: it rotated on its axis once a day and revolved around the sun once a year. Copernicus's theory revolutionized the understanding not only of the cosmos but also of the earth, since it could no longer be assumed that when objects fell they were seeking the center of the universe. By accepting these views, Copernicus argued, astronomers could simplify their models for the motion of the planets—but to do so they had to imagine a universe much larger than they had traditionally believed.

Andreas Vesalius (1514–1564), who studied and taught medicine at the university in Padua, took a lesson from artists such as Leonardo da Vinci. Vesalius argued that the study of the human organism must rest on actual

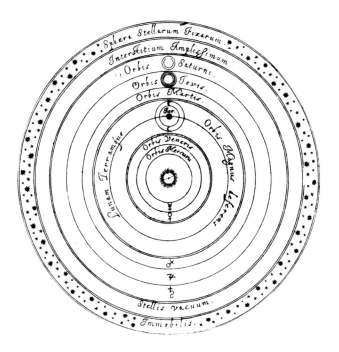

The Copernican Universe A 1647 scientific text includes this diagram of Copernicus's heliocentric theory of the cosmos. It shows the planets and Earth's moon orbiting the sun, surrounded by an immobile sphere of stars.

dissection of human bodies, as he thought it had in the ancient days of Greek physician and writer Galen, and the results recorded not only in writing but in detailed drawings. As Vesalius dissected the bodies of criminals, he discovered that Galen had committed many errors, some of them serious, because he had actually dissected apes rather than humans. In 1543, Vesalius brought out a magnificent study of the human body, illustrated by a Venetian artist. His work transformed medical study and laid the foundations for the further series of discoveries that would culminate, with William Harvey in 1628, in the demonstration that human blood circulated through the body, like the earth in the heavens.

Another sign of the radicalism of much—though not all—of the innovative thinking done in the sixteenth century is its collaborative character. Like Vesalius, many intellectuals found themselves changing the established body of knowledge by working with colleagues who were not learned at all. When the German botanist Leonhart Fuchs printed his illustrated guide to plants and their uses in 1542, he included portraits of the artists who had drawn the images and made and colored the printed woodcuts. It was a clear indication that knowledge was no longer, if it had ever been, the property of an elite trained to read canonical texts, but something to be discovered and

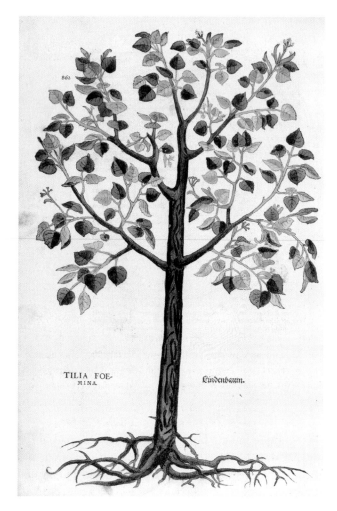

Fuchs's Botany One of the many painted woodcuts from Leonhart Fuchs's *De Historia Stirpium* (1542), this lime tree is labeled in Latin and German.

of Copernicus's work as the author was dying, added an anonymous preface in which he declared—contradicting the text that followed—that the author had meant only to advance a hypothesis, not to tell the truth about the universe. Though Copernicus's work was placed on the Church's indexes of forbidden books, this preface helped it survive, and annotated copies in libraries across Europe show that many were able to read it.

Not every book or author was so lucky. Michael Servetus (ca. 1511–1553), a Spanish theologian and medical specialist who speculated about the circulation of the blood, denied the doctrine of the Trinity. He managed to escape both Catholic and Protestant authorities for a time by using pseudonyms and moving frequently. In 1553, however, he made the fatal mistake of traveling to Geneva, even though Calvin was one of his harshest critics. Arrested and condemned, he was burned to death outside the city—a rare fate even for a heretic in the Protestant world—by Calvinists determined to show that they were no more lenient, when deadly heresies were concerned, than the Catholics.

WAR ACROSS THE CONTINENT

The peace established in the Holy Roman Empire by the Treaty of Augsburg (1555) did not extend to the rest of Europe. In England, Queen Mary I (r. 1553–1558), daughter of Henry VIII and his first wife, Catherine of Aragon, succeeded her half brother, Edward VI. A committed Catholic, Mary did her best to reestablish the Church. Hundreds of Protestants were forced to flee England; many sought refuge in Swiss cities. Almost 300 were burned, including the archbishop of Canterbury, Thomas Cranmer. In Italy, war had flared again in 1551, when a new French king, Henry II, declared war on Holy Roman Emperor Charles V, seeking to supplant Spanish control over the Italian Peninsula. After Charles abdicated, his son became King Philip II of Spain (r. 1556–1598) and opposed Henry.

Warfare was now completely professional, and both France and Spain had to borrow massive amounts to pay their troops. The capital came from banks and monarchs across Europe and beyond, including officials of the Ottoman Empire. Much of the capital flowed through Antwerp, the trading center of Europe. Its bourse, or financial exchange, founded in 1531, could broker enormous financial transactions. By late in the 1550s, neither

recorded by teams whose members crossed the boundaries of social orders and occupations to work together. In another example, Europeans learned from dozens of Native American informants, male and female, about the properties of New World plants and the products derived from them. Some of these products, such as chocolate and tobacco, were powerful stimulants whose use would transform Western society.

THE PERILS OF NEW THINKING

In a time of fear and censorship, ideas as radical as these could lead those who framed them into grave danger. Sometimes compromises were made: Andreas Osiander (1498–1552), the Lutheran cleric who oversaw the printing country could maintain interest payments on the loans. First Spain and then France reneged on these debts, bankrupting thousands of investors. Forced to negotiate an end to the conflict, Henry and Philip signed the Peace of Cateau-Cambrésis in 1559. Henry II died after a joust held to celebrate the treaty, when a splinter of the lance belonging to one of his guards penetrated his eye.

GOVERNMENT AND WAR IN A NEW KEY: PHILIP II OF SPAIN

Bankruptcy did not deter Philip II from his systematic effort to make Spain the dominant European power. Neither did the death of Queen Mary I of England, whom he had married, and whose efforts to bring England back into the Catholic fold he had encouraged. In 1559 Philip took the reins of power in Spain, assuming direct charge of the councils that dealt with finance, war, and the colonies. In his search for information about all his domains, he read and annotated thousands of documents every year. His habit of bringing memoranda to every meeting with his counselors won him the title "the paper king." Though he had to deal with separate assemblies, or estates, in Castile, Aragon, and Navarre, he established himself as a uniquely powerful monarch. He compensated for the debts that his father had left him with the immense wealth generated by the trade and industry of the Habsburg-controlled Low Countries, and the gold, silver, spices, tobacco, and sugar carried by Spanish convoys from its empire in the New World. These convoys, connecting Spain to its colonies in the Philippines, Mexico, Cuba, and elsewhere, began in 1565 and soon reached fifty or more ships at a time.

A passionate believer, Philip devoted himself to what he saw as the cause of Christendom—the defeat of the Ottoman Empire in the Mediterranean, the defeat of Protestantism in western Europe, and the final purification of Spain. No expense seemed to him too great, no effort too arduous, where this cause was concerned. When his efforts to suppress the Islamic customs still observed by some Moriscos (former Muslims) provoked a revolt in Granada in 1569, he had them expelled from the city and scattered throughout Spain. And when an Ottoman fleet took the Balearic Islands off Spain's eastern coast, he organized a Holy League of the Popes, the Venetians, the grand dukes of Tuscany, and others to oppose Sultan Selim II (r. 1566–1574). They eventually demolished the Ottoman navy at Lepanto, off the western coast of Greece,

in 1571. And when Mary's sister, Elizabeth, rejected his proposal of marriage, and Protestant leaders flocked back to England as it became clear that the new queen was one of them, Philip planned a gradual, massive campaign to defeat Protestantism, first in the Low Countries and then in England.

RELIGIOUS WAR, POLITICAL UPHEAVAL

In France and the Low Countries, the conflict between the Catholic Church and the Calvinists—known in French as **Huguenots**—soon blazed up in a new way. Reformed preachers and their congregations gathered at night, often in the fields outside towns and cities, with women and children protected by armed aristocrats. Calvinism had little appeal for peasants, but in the cities, workers, merchants, and members of the nobility all found its starkly clear message compelling. Catholic preachers, including many Jesuits, did their best to combat what they saw as this frightening development. After Henry II's death in 1559, his widow, Catherine de' Medici, served as regent, but she lacked the authority to impose order as violence broke out between Protestants—to whom, at first, she made concessions—and Catholics. Protestants destroyed religious images and interrupted Catholic processions, while Catholics preferred to massacre Protestants when they found them praying in groups. War erupted in France in 1562—followed, a few years later, by war in the Netherlands.

THE DUTCH REVOLT (1566–1648) Philip II's first representative as governor of the Netherlands was Margaret of Parma, the politically savvy and experienced illegitimate daughter of Philip's father, Charles V. She had tried to find some compromise that could preserve order, and when a group of noblemen formally requested that persecution of Protestantism come to an end, she agreed. But oppressive taxes, attempts to introduce the Inquisition, and a famine caused by poor harvests and rising wheat prices in 1565 led to increasing anger against the Spanish. Influential Dutch nobles withdrew from the government, and in 1566 religious statues, pictures, and stained glass windows were smashed across the Netherlands.

Philip's response in 1567 was to send his extremely effective general, the duke of Alba, with an army to quell the spreading revolt. But Alba's stern policies made matters worse—especially when two local noblemen who had remained loyal to Spain but opposed the introduction

The map legend reads:

The Dutch Revolt, 1566–1588
Spanish Netherlands
Rebel areas, 1588

The Spanish Armada, 1588
→ Route of the Armada
✕ Battle

North Sea

ENGLAND

London

HOLLAND

ZEELAND

Cherbourg

Calais

English Channel

Rhine R.

HOLY ROMAN EMPIRE

Seine R.

Paris
St. Bartholomew's
Day Massacre, 1572

ATLANTIC OCEAN

Loire R.

FRANCE

SWITZ.

Geneva

Rhône R.

SPAIN

NAVARRE

Garonne R.

Mediterranean Sea

French religious wars, 1562–1598
Areas of conflict
✕ 1562–1563
✕ 1567–1568
✕ 1568–1570
● Site of Huguenot massacre by Catholics
Large Huguenot minority
Holy League, 1585
● Huguenot stronghold, 1598

EUROPE

AFRICA

The Dutch Revolt and the French Religious Wars, 1562–1598
Violence between Protestants and Catholics flared throughout France in the 1560s and 1570s—particularly in southern areas with large Huguenot minorities—culminating in the St. Bartholomew's Day Massacre in Paris in 1572. In the Netherlands, Calvinists in the north rebelled against Catholic Spanish rule. Religious divisions also spurred Spain's naval conflict with England in 1588, ending with the English defeat of the Spanish Armada.

for more than eighty years, as we will see, and religious war spread across Europe.

ENGLAND: ANGLICANS AND PURITANS Even in England, where Queen Elizabeth I (r. 1558–1603) refused "to make windows into men's souls," conflict spread. On the one hand, the archbishops and bishops of the Church of England set out to create an Anglican church that combined stern Protestant doctrine with a rich and appealing liturgy. Against them were arrayed the Puritans—reformed believers who wanted to rid the church of all traditions not supported explicitly by the Bible. Anglicans and Puritans clashed over proper priestly vestments and central theological doctrines. Thanks to the political astuteness of Elizabeth and her closest friends, the dispute between these two sides, though often bitter, never broke out in actual civil or religious war.

THE FRENCH WARS OF RELIGION (1562–1589) On the Continent, however, savage wars erupted in 1562–63, 1567–68, and 1568–70. They were conflicts of a new kind, spawned by churches of a new kind. Both sides saw themselves as fighting for God against the devil. Violence became ritualized and almost normal as Catholics strove to cleanse the world of Protestant heretics, and Protestants sought to purify churches of the images, vessels, and incense that turned them into something like pagan temples.

The most famous atrocity of the French religious wars was the **Massacre of Saint Bartholomew's Day** in Paris on August 24, 1572. Catherine de' Medici, mother and regent of the young French king, Charles IX (r. 1560–1574), arranged a marriage between the Protestant Henry of Navarre and her daughter, the Catholic princess Margaret of Valois, and invited the Huguenot nobility to attend. This was provocative enough in a city that strongly favored the Catholic side. But on August 22, an assassin wounded the Protestant admiral Gaspard II de Coligny. Fearing reprisals from the Huguenots, the next day Charles ordered his own Swiss guards and other loyal troops to murder some 100 Protestant noblemen. The task was carried out, but instead of damping down violence, it ignited far more. Parisian civilians killed hundreds more Protestants—perhaps 2,000 in all. They mutilated the bodies of Coligny and others. Some were "tried" or "baptized" by being thrown into the Seine or soaked in the blood of their loved ones. These ritual parodies of the operations of courts and churches made clear that the Catholics saw themselves as carrying out an official act

of the Inquisition were arrested and executed. Another local nobleman, William the Silent (1533–1584), Prince of Orange, who had also served the Spanish state as a member of Margaret's council, fled and raised an army against Spain. Many of the Dutch—especially the Calvinists among them—renounced their loyalty to Philip II, whom they denounced as a tyrant. The **Dutch Revolt** continued of cleansing. Similar scenes took place in the provinces, where 3,000 more victims died—some of them, at Orléans, to the sound of serenades from musicians playing lutes and guitars.

The massacre put a stop to the expansion of the Huguenot church. Protestant numbers in northern and central French cities shrank. But in southern France, their stronghold, Protestants were, if anything, even more determined to resist what they saw as Catholic tyranny. Before the massacre, Protestant writers on politics had argued (following up a hint given by Calvin) that rebellion against a tyrannical monarchy might be legitimate if led by a lower official—since lower officials were appointed by God, just as higher ones were. Now they made open appeals for revolution, evoking a democratic French constitution. Soon the French Protestants had created their own, essentially independent kingdom in the south, close to Geneva, the capital city of Calvinism, and to Henry of Navarre's stronghold. The radical new temper of political thought—and politics—proved contagious. When Henry of Valois came to the French throne as Henry III (r. 1574–1589) and made concessions to the Protestants, a Catholic Holy League formed against him. Catholic political writers also claimed a right of resistance against tyranny, and in 1588 Henry fled Paris when the leader of the league, the duke of Guise, entered the city. Even political assassination became a tool of government. First, William the Silent, leader of the Dutch Revolt, was assassinated. Then Henry III, who had had the duke of Guise and his brother, a cardinal, murdered at the end of 1588, was himself killed in 1589 by a fanatical Dominican friar.

POLITICAL SETTLEMENTS

The Catholic forces of Spain, concentrated on the rebellious Netherlands, scored more successes at first. But for all their military superiority to the Dutch on land, the Spanish proved unable to suppress the Dutch Revolt, especially when many of its supporters took to the sea. Though Elizabeth infuriated some of her warlike subjects by her refusal to commit herself to a land war on the Continent in defense of European Protestantism, her privateers harried Spanish fleets and colonies. She gave modest but crucial assistance to the Dutch, and in 1588 the English fleet scattered and defeated the **Spanish Armada** that Philip II sent against her. Slowly it became clear on the larger European scale, as it had on the smaller German scale

Saint Bartholomew's Day Massacre The Huguenot painter François Dubois began this gory work shortly after the massacre took place in August 1572. Blood and corpses are strewn everywhere. Standing in front of the Louvre palace (in background at center) and dressed in black, Catherine de' Medici looks at a pile of bodies.

fifty years before, that neither party was strong enough to defeat the other definitively.

After witnessing the destruction caused by religious war, some influential French Catholics, including powerful lawyers and royal counselors, decided that it mattered more to have a unified state than a single religion. Known as *politiques*, these moderates often had valued Protestant as well as Catholic friends. They helped forge the brief alliance between Henry of Navarre—a Protestant but also a direct descendant of Louis IX—and the Catholic Henry III to fight the Spanish. After Henry III's assassination, Henry of Navarre renounced his Protestant faith (according to legend, he declared that "Paris is worth a mass"). Though his change of faith angered many Protestants, he was soon able to put an end to the resistance of the Holy League. In 1594 he was crowned King Henry IV, and in 1598, working from the principles of the politiques, he promulgated the **Edict of Nantes**, which gave Protestants limited religious freedom. Henry took up the tasks of restoring prosperity in France and rebuilding Paris, activities at which he proved very successful.

Though it took until 1609 for the Dutch to make a truce with the Spanish, the defeat of the Spanish Armada, repeated mutinies by Spanish troops, and the assumption of command by General Maurice of Nassau meant that the Dutch were able to conquer a number of major cities in the 1590s. Their independence secure, the counties of Holland and Zeeland, and the other states of Holland, reconfigured themselves as a Dutch republic, ruled by

DE WITTE'S *THE INTERIOR OF THE OUDE KERK*

John Calvin was even more rigorous than Martin Luther in his vision of reform. Whereas Luther expressed ambivalence toward religious images, which were sometimes retained in Lutheran churches, Calvin, like Zwingli, inspired Protestant reformers to shatter, burn, melt, or whitewash such images and decorations in their churches.

When Amsterdam's Oude Kerk (Old Church), built in the early fourteenth century, was transformed from a Roman Catholic to a Calvinist church in the late sixteenth century, Protestants destroyed its religious images. In this painting, *The Interior of the Oude Kerk* (ca.

1660), Emanuel de Witte portrays its clean columns, whitewashed walls, elegant arches, semicircular nave, and most important of all, its pulpit, where the word of God was preached.

The church was not only the community's religious center but also a popular meeting place where merchants conversed and sailors and their families prayed for the safe and successful conclusion of sea voyages. De Witte portrays scenes of everyday life in this unadorned setting: merchants discuss business (right), a mother nurses her child (far right), and a dog even urinates on a column (left). In the foreground, a burial is being prepared.

QUESTIONS FOR ANALYSIS

1. What does this depiction of a church's interior tell us about the influence of Calvinist theology in the Netherlands?
2. As indicated by this painting, what role did Reformed churches play in everyday life in the Netherlands?
3. How would you compare this scene to life in Calvin's Geneva as described earlier in the chapter?

their representative assemblies, or estates, and protected, but not ruled, by the House of Orange.

RUSSIA AND EASTERN EUROPE

More slowly than in the West, monarchs in Eastern Europe began to build up their states on modern lines. The power of Russian grand princes had been limited by the rival power of the boyars, or great noble families, and by their relatively old-fashioned armies, largely made up of mounted archers who offered their service in return for small grants of land. Ivan IV, known in Russian tradition as Ivan Grozny ("Ivan the Awesome"), was grand prince from 1533 to 1547, when he was crowned the first "Tsar of all the Russias," a title he held until he died in 1584. He thus claimed the status of an imperial ruler, like the early kings of Kiev and the emperors of Byzantium, and highlighted the existing claim that, after the fall of Constantinople, Moscow had become the third Rome.

Articulate and charismatic, Ivan rebuilt many Russian institutions. He established a council of advisers, forced the boyars to accept the duty of serving the tsar, regularized the system of taxation, and established a unified currency. He also gradually added well-trained musketeers and artillerymen to his armies. By conquering the Muslim Khanates of Kazan (1552) and Astrakhan (1556), he created a buffer against the Mongols and made Russia itself a multi-ethnic empire. Ivan celebrated these accomplishments by building a vast cathedral, St Basil's, in Moscow. In this and other ways he emulated the Renaissance rulers of Western Europe. Ivan built new fortresses, brought in foreign artists and craftsmen to improve Moscow, and engaged in elaborate diplomatic relations, especially with England. Though a formal alliance with Mary or Elizabeth eluded him, the Muscovy Company granted a monopoly, imported luxury goods and exported timber, tar, and other products needed to build English ships.

Like the western monarchies, Russia experienced crisis when Ivan's conduct became unpredictable. In 1564 he blackmailed his boyars into granting him absolute power, and used it to divide Russia. He established absolute control over a northern area, called the Oprichnina, in the former territory of Novgorod. A black-clad private army terrorized the inhabitants. On Ivan's orders they sacked Novgorod, already stricken by plague, in 1570. In 1572 he abolished the Oprichnina: his intentions in creating it remain unclear, though some historians believe he may have seen himself as creating a holy kingdom for the end of time. The Grand Duchy of Lithuania and the

Kingdom of Poland, both also expanding in resources and power, were joined in 1569 by the Union of Lublin, and in 1576 they joined the Ottomans in attacking Ivan's Empire. In 1581 he killed his son Ivan Ivanovich, apparently by accident. Expansion did not end. Toward the end of Ivan's reign, Cossacks —Slavic-speaking steppe dwellers, skilled in cavalry warfare, who served many lords— conquered Siberia and recognized him as Tsar. Famine, plague and war had exhausted Russia, which would fall into a crisis soon after Ivan's death. Yet he had established his country as the empire it would remain until the 20th century.

A TIME OF DARKNESS

The second half of the sixteenth century was—so many Europeans thought—a terrible age, perhaps uniquely terrible. The flow of silver and gold from the New World caused a slow but steady inflation of prices across the Continent. In a society that believed it possible to set fair prices and wages by statute, even a 2 percent rate of inflation was deeply unsettling. Harvest failures caused local spikes in the price of bread, which led to famines and often set off the most violent outbursts of religious rioting.

WITCH TRIALS

The famines also help to explain the outburst of witch trials across Europe during the period. The causes of

Burning Witches This woodcut illustration from a 1555 leaflet depicts witches being executed. Men stoke the flames, while a demon clings to one of the burning women. The women are shown again at right, descending into hell.

these trials varied, though they were always rooted in everyday events. Sometimes a woman who had difficulty giving birth, or whose baby was injured or died in the process, denounced her midwife; sometimes poor, older women who would have been objects of charity in traditional Catholic society provoked rage and denunciation from Protestants. In either case, the use of torture to interrogate those accused of witchcraft often led to further accusations. The largest witch hunts, sparked by famines, stopped only when members of the elite were accused.

The theory that witches conspired to attack Christian society took shape, as we have seen, in the fifteenth century. But it was in the age of religious war that the theory was applied in massive witch trials. By the time they came to an end in the late seventeenth century, some 30,000 to 70,000 people, 80 percent of them female, had been executed as witches. Thousands more were tried. The late sixteenth century genuinely was a time of darkness, and the fires that illuminated it too often consumed human beings.

TWO RESPONSES TO POLITICAL AND RELIGIOUS CRISIS: JEAN BODIN AND MICHEL DE MONTAIGNE

Jean Bodin (1530–1596) and Michel de Montaigne (1533–1592) both lived through the long series of religious wars unleashed in France by the Reformation; both were in their prime when the Massacre of Saint Bartholomew's Day took place. And both eagerly followed the intellectual revolutions of the mid-sixteenth century. Both realized that their world had changed, though they expressed their perceptions in different ways. Both were versed in the classics, trained in Roman law, and cosmopolitan in their interests and their reading. Bodin insisted that the only way to find the best constitution for one's country was to collect and compare laws from all over the world. He drew up one of the first guides to the study of history, which instructed the reader to pay as much attention to the East as to the West and as much to modern history as to ancient. Montaigne, who read Bodin's book, followed his instructions on how to read historians critically and fruitfully.

Both men took a deep interest in civilizations and religions other than their own, and regarded them with clear respect. Bodin wrote a provocative dialogue in which representatives of seven religions debate peacefully before parting from one another on terms of respect and affection. This work, with its suggestion that no religion could claim a monopoly on truth, could have endangered its author. It was not published, though manuscripts of it circulated widely. Montaigne, attending the circumcision of a Jewish baby in Rome, noted that Jewish babies cried "just as our babies do when they are baptized." Both Bodin and Montaigne, finally, were involved in trying to restore peace and stability to France.

BODIN But the solutions they arrived at differed radically. Bodin originally believed that constitutions could and should be mixed, as he thought the ancient Roman one, with its monarchical, aristocratic, and democratic elements, had been. He at first supported efforts by the French Estates General to limit the powers of the king, but in the late 1560s and 1570s he changed his mind. Only a ruler of absolute authority, he now insisted, could possibly maintain peace and order. Sovereignty—formal command over a state—could not be divided among contending parties but must rest with one of them: preferably the king, who should have the power of life and death over his subjects that the Roman head of household had held over his children. Bodin's doctrine, which came to be known as absolutism, proved highly attractive to monarchs and their ministers in the decades to come.

In the end, Bodin sided with the Catholic Holy League against the Huguenots and politiques, who included many of his former friends. More surprising still, he came to believe that witches, as well as heretics, threatened France. His treatise, *Of the Demonomania of Sorcerers*, made a powerful case for the prosecution of witches of both sexes. Its festering anecdotes of diabolic action in the world made it a reference book for two generations of witch-hunters.

MONTAIGNE Montaigne, by contrast, retired from public life as a lawyer in middle age to an estate outside Bordeaux. Reading and contemplating in his study, its rafters inscribed with classical proverbs, he tested the precepts of the ancients against his own experience. Although the Stoics, who had insisted that the wise must ignore pain and other distractions, had many followers in Montaigne's time, he found their precepts too demanding to be realistic. The ancient Skeptics, with their refusal to make dogmatic pronouncements, appealed to him more. Perhaps they offered a way out of the labyrinths of religious war. Gradually, Montaigne evolved a new literary form, the essay—literally, a trial or experiment. Whereas Bodin wrote formal treatises in Latin that propounded a single, absolute truth, Montaigne wrote short pieces in French that began from some supposed truth and subjected it to examination.

Dogmas of all kinds, Montaigne confessed, repelled and depressed him. He found it implausible that witches deserved to be burned for conspiring against humanity or that European culture, in its authoritarianism and violence, could claim ethical superiority to the so-called cannibals of the New World. Montaigne argued in a famous essay that New World natives practiced the arts with grace and subtlety, and had created an egalitarian society that put the supposed Christians of hierarchical, bloodthirsty Europe to shame. He expressed his horror at the Stoical hard men, Catholic and Protestant, who did not realize that knowing when to yield was a basic part of the moral life.

Montaigne's *Essays* (1580) spared few of the follies of his time. But Montaigne saw himself as a human brother, as much the prey of emotions and illusions as everyone else, and he made fun of his own tendency to draw radical conclusions. At the end of his essay on cannibals, for example, he told the story of how Brazilian natives brought to Europe to take part in royal ceremonies had exposed the un-Christian nature of Christian society to France's King Charles IX when he questioned them. Montaigne learned that they found two things odd: that grown men—strong, bearded, and armed—would obey a king who was still a child, and that the European poor did not kill the rich and take their goods. Montaigne's Indians sound like Thomas More's Raphael Hythloday denouncing the immorality of Europe. Unlike More, however, Montaigne immediately struck a comic note, conceding that he could not have understood everything he was told about the alien society he had tried to describe. He admitted that he had found it almost impossible to communicate with an Indian, even using an interpreter. And he summed up his elaborate, critical comparison of societies with rueful simplicity: "What's the use? They don't wear pants."

The first two books of the *Essays*, published in 1580, became best sellers. Now a celebrity, Montaigne traveled to Rome, examining the cities he passed through, their antiquities and customs. On his return to France, he continued writing essays, composing a third book in which he made himself, in all his own weaknesses and inconsistencies, his principal subject. But Montaigne also served as mayor of Bordeaux, political adviser to Henry of Navarre, and an intermediary in the negotiations between Catholics and Protestants that brought the French religious wars

Montaigne This portrait of a richly dressed Michel de Montaigne was painted during the writer's life by an anonymous artist.

to a close. The man who hated violence and intolerance did more than most to find a way to end what was, to that point, Europe's most violent and intolerant age. Neither Bodin nor Montaigne was an ordinary writer, typical of his time. But both shared their views with the thousands of readers who made their works so popular. And both, in their radically different ways, expressed the contradictions of a Europe torn by contending beliefs—and soon to be torn, in different ways, by new political, religious, and intellectual movements.

CONCLUSION

The Europeans of the sixteenth century lived through some of the most wracking changes in history. They became print professionals and skilled users of verbal and visual media, which could reproduce their ideas in hundreds, rather than dozens, of copies. They profited from the geographical discoveries of the late fifteenth century, and thought hard about what these discoveries implied about their traditional sense of Europe's central place in the universe. And they saw the unified Catholic Church, already more than one thousand years old, challenged by rivals that it could not defeat, even as its own powers revived.

Most Christians continued to believe that their own form of religion was the only true one. They saw it as reasonable—even virtuous—to persecute those who insisted on worshipping differently, or to rebel against political authorities that persecuted them. Only a few, such as Montaigne, shared the qualified belief in tolerance that had made Erasmus leery of persecuting heretics when the Reformation broke out. Eventually, however, the sheer human cost of religious conflict clearly outweighed any benefits, even in the eyes of many staunchly orthodox Catholics and Protestants. By the end of the sixteenth century, foundations had been laid for a development no one could have foreseen a century earlier: the creation not only of separate Catholic and Protestant churches but also of distinct Catholic and Protestant societies.

KEY TERMS

Martin Luther (p. 372)

indulgence (p. 373)

Desiderius Erasmus (p. 375)

Thomas More (p. 376)

Ninety-Five Theses (p. 378)

Diet of Worms (p. 378)

Protestant Reformation (p. 379)

Ulrich Zwingli (p. 382)

Peasants' War (p. 384)

Anabaptists (p. 385)

Argula von Grumbach (p. 386)

John Calvin (p. 388)

Henry VIII (p. 390)

Charles V (p. 391)

Jacob Fugger (p. 391)

Peace of Augsburg (p. 393)

Jesuits (p. 395)

Council of Trent (p. 396)

Nicolaus Copernicus (p. 397)

Huguenots (p. 399)

Dutch Revolt (p. 400)

Massacre of Saint Bartholomew's Day (p. 400)

Spanish Armada (p. 401)

Edict of Nantes (p. 401)

REVIEW QUESTIONS

1. What were Martin Luther's primary criticisms of the Catholic Church?

2. What factors spurred the expansion of the Reformation movement?

3. What were the most important differences in the thinking of Luther, Ulrich Zwingli, and John Calvin?

4. How did the Reformation inspire the Peasants' War in Germany?

5. How did the Reformation affect the lives of women?

6. What actions did Holy Roman Emperor Charles V take to expand and solidify his territories?

7. What were the most important outcomes of the Council of Trent?

8. What advances in scientific thinking took place during the Reformation?

9. Why did Europe's religious divisions lead to war in the sixteenth century?

10. What developments in the sixteenth century allowed for greater religious toleration?

CORE OBJECTIVES

After reading this chapter, you should have a solid understanding of the following core objectives. To strengthen your grasp of the core objectives, use the resources on the Student Site for The West.

- Analyze the intellectual and cultural context that influenced Martin Luther's ideas.

- Describe the major events of the Protestant Reformation.

- Compare the different Protestant movements inspired by Luther's message.

- Describe the social and political conditions that led to conflict between Protestants and Catholics.

- Explain the Catholic Reformation that arose in response to Protestantism.

- Identify the intellectual innovations and political conflicts that coincided with the Reformation.

 GO TO inQuizitive TO SEE WHAT YOU'VE LEARNED—AND LEARN WHAT YOU'VE MISSED—WITH PERSONALIZED FEEDBACK ALONG THE WAY.

CHRONOLOGY

17th century
Coldest point of
the Little Ice Age

1600
British East India
Company founded

1608
French found
Québec

1609
Dutch Republic gains
effective independence

1620
Pilgrims found Plymouth;
Bacon publishes
Novum Organum

1628
English Parliament's
Petition of Right

1602
Dutch East India
Company founded

1605
Cervantes publishes
first volume of
Don Quixote

1607
English establish Jamestown

1618–1648
Thirty Years' War

1625
Dutch found
New Amsterdam

1601–1603
Russia suffers
great famine

12

Things Fall Apart

A CONTINENT IN CRISIS

1600–1640

1629–1640
Charles I of Britain
rules without Parliament

1629
Edict of Restitution

1633
Inquisition condemns
Galileo for defense
of heliocentrism

1637
Descartes publishes
Discourse on Method

On December 26, 1606, a king watched a king go mad. As part of his annual Christmas festivities, King James I of England (r. 1603–1625) had invited his court to the first performance of a play by the fashionable author of the moment, William Shakespeare (1564–1616). The audience sat in crowded boxes in a sumptuously decorated London palace, watching a low stage on which the actors' company had erected a rudimentary set meant to evoke a wild, empty heath. The scent of hundreds of candles pervaded the drafty hall, and many of the courtiers wore heavy coats to protect against the cold and damp. With King James looking on, an actor portraying a much earlier English ruler, King Lear, raved and screamed. As men behind the makeshift stage rolled a metal ball on a metal sheet to simulate thunder and set off small firecrackers to mimic lightning, Lear tore off his clothes and howled:

> Blow, winds, and crack your cheeks! Rage! Blow! . . .
> Spit, fire! Spout, rain! . . . here I stand your slave,
> A poor, infirm, weak and despis'd old man
> . . . My wits begin to turn.

Velázquez and Domestic Life Early in his career, the Spanish painter Diego Velázquez (1599–1660), who would later be championed by the Spanish Count-Duke Olivares, was known for his paintings depicting domestic scenes. In his *Old Woman Cooking Eggs* (1618), the detailed portrayal of the titular subject and her kitchen seem to have been painted from life. A boy arrives with a melon and a flask of wine, luxuries amidst the widespread economic deprivation of the early seventeenth century.

- Why did parts of Europe stagnate and others surge economically?
- What were the first footholds for Europe in North America?
- How did European states respond to the new financial challenges they faced?
- How did Catholicism and Protestantism attempt to reform the daily lives of Europeans?
- What political tensions were destabilizing Europe?
- What caused the many smaller conflicts in Europe to become one major war?
- Why did royal ministers become so powerful at this time?
- How did the growth of absolutism affect major developments in culture?

Lear was no longer king, no longer the father of a family, no longer sane.

The scene would not have been altogether shocking to James and his court. Madness had featured prominently in tragic drama since the earliest days of the theater. English stages had long developed something of a specialty in depicting the overthrow of kings, and Shakespeare had made his reputation through a series of "history plays" that touched on examples from the more recent past.

Even so, there was something sublimely powerful and troubling about Shakespeare's treatment of Lear's fall. In this, the playwright's greatest tragedy, it is not merely a king who is overthrown. Rather, the collapse of order in the kingdom is mirrored by the collapse of order in every other possible domain. Lear's daughters Goneril and Regan—played by teenage boys since it was considered immoral for women to act on stage—turn against their father. The order of the natural world itself seems to collapse with the storms that wrack the heath on which Lear raves. Most frightening, the order of the mind collapses as well, as the imperious monarch from the first act turns before the audience's eyes into a naked, shuddering, incoherently babbling wreck. And in the midst of it all arises a terrifying character who seems to delight in this lack of order, scorning attempts to shore it

up with custom and tradition, driven by nothing but his own ambition and resentment, proud and cruel—"the bastard Edmund," illegitimate son of Lear's counselor Gloucester. "Thou, nature, art my goddess;" Edmund declares, "to thy law my services are bound." Watching in the flickering darkness of the palace, King James might well have taken comfort from the play's defense of order and legitimate rule. But he could not have helped but shudder at what Shakespeare showed about its terrible fragility, and the terrible allure of characters like Edmund, who strove to destroy it.

Hundreds of years later, it is almost irresistible to see *King Lear* foreshadowing the following decades of European history. Of course, Europe was hardly ignorant of horrific violence and had experienced tragic bouts of it within recent memory. In France, the bloody sixteenth-century religious wars remained at the forefront of civic consciousness. "O desolate France! O bloody earth. Not earth, but ash," as a French Protestant poet had recently written. In England, just one year before *King Lear*'s premiere, Catholic conspirators in the Gun-powder Plot (1605) had nearly succeeded in blowing up the Houses of Parliament and assassinating the Protestant monarch. James—the king of Scotland who had succeeded his cousin Elizabeth I on the English throne in 1603, thereby bringing the two kingdoms under the same crown—could hardly take the stability of his new Stuart dynasty for granted. It is no accident that nearly all of Shakespeare's plays with historical subjects feature the threat or reality of civil war.

Even so, in the decades that followed *King Lear's* premiere, a particularly concentrated, intense series of real-life tragedies took place in Europe. These were set against a literal change in the natural order—a period of exceptional and destructive cooling known as the Little Ice Age. The greatest of the tragedies was the murderous Thirty Years' War (1618–1648), whose human toll, measured as a proportion of the European population, dwarfs even that of World War II. Civil strife affected every major European state, from the Ottoman Empire to England itself. Just over four decades after the Christmas performance of *King Lear*, English revolutionaries would erect a scaffold outside the palace where he had viewed it, and there behead his son and heir, Charles I.

No single cause lay behind these tragic events. The Little Ice Age was compounded by a series of plagues and harvest failures that contributed to economic distress and broad social and political turmoil. Other economic changes, particularly associated with Europe's burgeoning overseas trade, fostered dangerous new rivalries. Innovations in military technology that had begun well before 1600 continued to drive up the human and material cost of warfare. Political factors such as turmoil within the Habsburg dynasty played a key role in the Thirty Years' War. And the ongoing divisions of Western Europe between Catholics and Protestants—as well as those between different Protestant churches—sharpened the strife and drove it forward.

But these tragedies did have one great, common result: a pressure on governments everywhere to strengthen and reform themselves. Everywhere, they faced the challenge of mobilizing resources more efficiently, above all for the purposes of warfare. This was a period in which patterns of competition in Europe turned increasingly violent and desperate, while peaceful exchange suffered. In many parts of the Continent, monarchs and their chief ministers sought new ways to streamline, subvert, or cooperate with traditional institutions and elites, and often provoked angry protests or even revolts. Some countries—notably France—emerged strengthened from the process; others—notably Spain—did far less well. And some were shattered altogether. In 1600 Europe was largely a continent of empires and what historians call "**composite monarchies**" in which a single monarch ruled largely separate and distinct states. By mid-century, this form of government was beginning to give way to cohesive nation-states capable of raising large, well-disciplined armies.

ECONOMIC CHANGE

The beginning of the seventeenth century saw extremely uneven patterns of economic development. Some parts of Europe not only experienced growth but technological innovation that would pay very long-term dividends. Others experienced only misery. And everywhere, the rates of growth were affected by climate and war.

THE LITTLE ICE AGE

Just a year after the performance of *King Lear* for King James, the River Thames at London froze so deeply that for only the second time on record, the city held a "Frost Fair" on the ice for several weeks, with shops, sports, theaters, and taverns being built in the middle of the river. Londoners were able to hold these fairs roughly one year in ten during the seventeenth century, less frequently in the eighteenth,

and for the last time ever in 1814. In 1622 a large part of the Bosphorus (the strait separating Europe from Asia at Constantinople) froze solid, and there were years in the century when portions of the Baltic Sea froze as well. The **Little Ice Age** began well before 1600 and lasted for centuries, but the seventeenth century was its coldest point.

The effects of the Little Ice Age were intensified in the years immediately after 1600 by the massive eruption of a Peruvian volcano that spewed enough sulfur and other particulate matter into the atmosphere to dim the sunlight and lower global temperatures even further. These conditions depressed crop yields and increased the chance of harvest failures. The freezing temperatures also lowered people's resistance to epidemics. For populations that even in good times lived on the edge of disaster, the results were catastrophic. The worst famine in Russian history occurred in 1601–03. In Spain between 1598 and 1602, poor harvests combined with an outbreak of bubonic plague to kill as much as 10 percent of the population. Grain production fell across the Continent, particularly around the Mediterranean and in central Europe. In Hungary, tithes collected by the Catholic Church (in theory a fixed percentage of the harvest) fell by 72 percent between 1570 and 1670.

STAGNATION ON THE CONTINENT

Overall, across Europe, the turn of the seventeenth century marked an end to the price increases that had taken place, more-or-less steadily, since the aftermath of the Black Death, and that serve as a rough indicator of economic growth. Although exact figures are elusive, it also seems as if the new century saw stagnation in the overall European population. And it saw an exponential increase in the number of Europeans forced across the line from poverty into indigence—the point at which they had to resort to begging, crime, prostitution, or migration simply to survive. Some migrants went great distances indeed, with 30,000 Scots ending up in Poland by the 1620s, and 40,000 French heading across the border into Catalonia (in northeastern Spain). To help the tribes of the destitute, reforming states and churches on both sides of the Catholic-Protestant divide continued to found institutions that gave charity in return for hard labor.

DECLINING TRADE Further harming the European economy was a Continent-wide slump in trade, provoked by the collapse of what had driven commercial expansion for more than a century: the Atlantic traffic of the Spanish

BRUEGEL THE ELDER'S *HUNTERS IN THE SNOW*

In its clear, sharp depiction of landscape and everyday life, *Hunters in the Snow* (1565) by the Dutch artist Pieter Bruegel the Elder allows us to see how villagers responded to the harsh conditions of winter during the Little Ice Age. Peasant villages are engulfed in deep snow and surrounded by frozen rivers and ponds, bare trees, and heavy skies. In the foreground, tired hunters and their hungry dogs return with a meager catch as women tend a fire and crows watch overhead. Beyond these necessities, a more joyful scene unfolds in the distance, as villagers and their children skate and play games on the ice. The painting captures both the power of nature and capacity of humans to cope with it.

QUESTIONS FOR ANALYSIS

1. What aspects of daily life does *Hunters in the Snow* depict?
2. How does the painting convey the challenges of the Little Ice Age?
3. What kind of relationships between humankind and nature does Bruegel show?

Peasants and Beggars The economic hardships experienced by many Europeans in the early seventeenth century are suggested by the French printer Jacques Callot's 1622 illustration of two beggar women. Dressed in ragged clothes and stooped over, bearing expressions of despair and exhaustion, they share a tiny bowl of food.

Empire. As Spain's New World colonies developed more complex economies of their own, they grew less dependent on trade with the mother country. At the same time, Spanish fleets increasingly fell prey to pirates and privateers (ships chartered to engage in piracy against a country's enemies). Spain's annual transatlantic trade dropped from 30,000 tons in the 1610s to 13,000 tons in the 1640s. In 1627/28, the Spanish government was forced to declare bankruptcy and devalue its currency by 50 percent. Soon after, Dutch privateers captured the entire Spanish silver fleet at sea. This combination of events created chaos in the international money markets and virtually destroyed the great banks of Genoa, which had financed the Spanish Empire's debt.

A SECOND SERFDOM In central and eastern Europe, falling harvest yields put pressure on large landowners to expand their farm holdings. With most fertile land already under cultivation by 1600, they could do so only

at the expense of peasant small-holders, many of whom were driven off their land and forced into serfdom. Central and eastern European states imposed particularly drastic restrictions on serfs to guarantee the labor supply, especially for profitable export crops. Between 1608 and 1653, seven major central and eastern European states, including Hungary and Muscovy (the grand duchy of which Moscow was the capital, a forerunner to modern Russia), took away serfs' freedom of movement and bound them to the land they farmed. Meanwhile, seigniorial lords—including the church and the state itself, which both had vast landownings—gained increased power to tax, judge, and discipline their serfs. Punishments could include lashes with the "knout," a powerful whip with wires or hooks woven into the leather to inflict maximum pain (100 lashes usually amounted to a death sentence).

By the late seventeenth century, particularly in Russian-speaking lands, this "second serfdom" (so called to distinguish it from the medieval variety) became effectively a form of slavery. Serfs in Muscovy lived in mostly miserable conditions, farming the hard soil in short summers with the most backward technology in Europe (metal plows, for instance, were almost unknown). These men and women, who amounted to nearly half the duchy's population, could be bought and sold at their lords' pleasure. To keep reproduction rates high, lords not only encouraged early marriage among serfs but sometimes paired them off by force. Serfs not working on the land had to pay their lords for the privilege of doing so.

GROWTH IN MARITIME EUROPE

The economic decline had harsh effects in southern and eastern Europe, but it was by no means uniform across the Continent. Even as southern and eastern Europe suffered and much of France and central Europe stagnated, the maritime regions of northwestern Europe grew strongly, as shown above all by the expansion of cities. The populations of 30 cities situated on an arc from Bordeaux in France to Copenhagen in Denmark increased at an average rate of close to 60 percent in the first half of the seventeenth century. Capital cities benefitting from the growth of state bureaucracies also grew rapidly, with newly-founded Madrid more than quadrupling in size between 1561 and 1630—from 30,000 to 130,000, despite the stagnation of the Spanish economy as a whole.

THE DUTCH REPUBLIC The greatest economic success story in the early seventeenth century belonged to the Dutch Republic. This new state, still fighting for independence from Spain in 1600, was the most urbanized in Europe, with more than a third of the population living in cities. Amsterdam, the capital, grew from 50,000 to 150,000 people between 1600 and 1650. In 1609 the Dutch took a large step toward creating a stable currency and strong national finance with the establishment of the Bank of Amsterdam. Chartered by the city's government, it was the precursor of today's national banks, which manage currencies and interest rates, and put the faith and credit of a national institution behind the value of a currency.

One other important measure of a modern economy is its overall energy usage, for manufacturing, agriculture, heating and lighting. Per capita, the Dutch in this period used more energy than any other people in Europe. Sources included the burning of peat and coal, horse- and water-powered mills, and of course, the country's iconic windmills—3,000 of them, each doing the work of forty or more horses. The Dutch also led the way in rural development. Between 1600 and 1639, they reclaimed more than 300 square miles of arable land from lakes and marshes. This land largely lay below sea level, so they built a complex series of dikes to protect it against flooding. During what one historian has called the "industrious revolution," rural workers processed raw materials delivered to them by urban merchants to produce textiles and other manufactures.

MIDDLE-CLASS HOUSEHOLDS The new wealth generated by these changes took on a striking physical expression in Dutch homes. More and more households—including among those we would now call the middle class—owned elaborately carved beds, cupboards, and other furniture. The cupboards were filled not only with local ceramics but with porcelain and china imported from Asia. Lottery prizes, which give a good idea of what aspiring families most desired, included engraved goblets, tankards, and ewers; mirrors; silver breadbaskets; candlesticks; and even sets of petticoats. Houses acquired sumptuously carved moldings, tapestries, and paintings on the inside, and elaborate gables on the outside. Pendulum-driven clocks made their appearance in middle-class homes, so that families of merchants and artisans no longer needed to depend on church bells or crude sundials to tell the time.

These economic changes also affected gender roles. The "industrious revolution" above all involved a form of labor—textile spinning—traditionally associated with women. But as it grew more important in northern European economies, men were increasingly seen behind the spinning wheel as well. They earned more money at it than

Domestic Luxuries A Dutch oil painting from the 1660s indicates the lavish interiors to which the newly wealthy could aspire. The light streams in through glass windows, which are covered, like the bed, in sumptuous textiles. While a servant sweeps in the background, the lady of the house plays a harpsichord in front of an extravagantly framed mirror.

their female counterparts, even as they were mocked for taking on women's work. Meanwhile, the growth of cities and of an urban middle class fueled an expansion in domestic service, one of the occupations most closely associated with women. Nearly all households with a modicum of disposable income—including those of merchants, clergymen, lawyers, doctors, and even moderately well-off artisans—kept servants. In the Netherlands, as throughout Europe, domestic service especially attracted young peasant women hoping to save money for a dowry or to purchase land.

OCEANIC TRADE

Even as the Dutch laid the groundwork for a more modern economy, they also increasingly came to dominate European trade. In the 1630s, the Dutch Republic's 2,500 merchant ships represented half of all European shipping. Each year 150 Dutch vessels sailed to the Caribbean. Hundreds more traded with Africa, Brazil, India, and the Far East. In 1599 a fleet of eight Dutch ships explored the Spice Islands in what is now Indonesia and returned with cargo that generated a 400 percent profit. Spices such as nutmeg and clove—which not only added diversity to the European diet but were believed to have health-giving properties—offered potentially huge wealth for Europeans. Nutmeg in particular sold in Europe for more than 100 times what it cost in Asia.

THE EARLY TRANSATLANTIC SLAVE TRADE

Another hugely profitable form of cargo, transported by all of the major maritime powers, was human beings. As we have seen, by the mid-fifteenth century the Portuguese had begun shipping African slaves to their overseas colonies. They and the Spanish enslaved Native Americans as well throughout the European colonies in the Americas in the seventeenth century, contributing to the decimation of native populations. But the Europeans rapidly discovered that Africans were better suited to the grueling regime required for labor-intensive crops such as sugar. (The first sugar refinery in the New World opened in the Portuguese colony of Brazil in 1601.) Under what is now called the transatlantic "**triangle trade**," Europeans transported cheap trade goods such as tools, cloth, weapons, and alcohol to Africa, where they exchanged them for slaves provided by local rulers and coastal Arab slave traders. From there the slaves were shipped across the Atlantic and sold in colonial port towns in the Americas, such as Port Royal in Jamaica, where the proceeds were used to purchase colonial goods such as tobacco for European markets. Between 1600 and 1640, Europeans—principally the Spanish and Portuguese—caused more than half a million Africans to be enslaved in this manner, more than two and a half times the number taken in the previous forty years.

Overseas trade remained a dangerous business. "Ships are but boards, sailors but men; there be land-rats and water-rats, water-thieves and land-thieves, I mean pirates, and then there is the peril of waters, winds and rocks," to quote Shakespeare's *The Merchant of Venice* (1598). In 1600, to spread out the risk, a large group of English merchants came together to form the East India Company, and won a charter from Queen Elizabeth I giving them a monopoly over trade with India and the Far East. The Dutch followed with their own East India Company two years later. In the early seventeenth century, these two competing enterprises engaged in frequent skirmishes on the high seas. Their representatives also meted out brutal treatment to indigenous populations, especially in the Spice Islands, where Dutch East India Company officials established plantations and hoped to found a large colony.

MERCANTILISM

The approach to trade taken by the English, the Dutch, and most other European states followed from the conviction that the world's economic resources were finite and that one country's commerce could grow only at the expense of another's. States therefore generally insisted on rigid control of trade, putting as much as possible in the hands of officially chartered monopoly companies and insisting that goods come to their home shores only in their own ships.

These policies, which have come to be known as **mercantilism**, were based on faulty evidence. Even in the crisis years of the seventeenth century, Europeans showed a remarkable ability to exploit ever-greater quantities of natural resources. Coal production on the Continent, for instance, increased from scarcely 200 tons a year in the early sixteenth century to nearly 3 million tons annually by the 1680s, an indication that the growing European population was using steadily more energy per capita for manufactures and heating. The first half of the seventeenth century also saw the opening up of new sources for another lucrative commodity, furs. The great sources of fur, namely Siberia and the French and English colonies in North America, provided some 200,000 pelts a year, principally for hats and coats. Even so, in the context of general economic decline, it seemed obvious to most Europeans that the growth of the Netherlands and England had come at the expense of other European countries, especially those on the Mediterranean.

EUROPEAN EXPANSION IN THE ATLANTIC

By 1600, the European powers had a massive overseas presence. They had established trading routes around the coasts of Africa to India and Southeast Asia, complete with networks of forts and trading posts. They were spreading east across Siberia toward China. Spanish conquistadores had overthrown the Aztec and Inca Empires in Mexico and Peru, and Spain and Portugal claimed sovereignty over nearly all of present-day Latin America. In the seventeenth century, the Spanish and Portuguese presence in Central and South America continued to grow, with changes that transformed even the physical environment. For example, at the start of the century, Spain's colonial authorities in Mexico City began one of the largest engineering projects of the early modern period: a series of canals that drained the lakes around the city and prevented its periodic flooding. The project would continue for centuries, and ultimately harm the indigenous population by depriving farmers of necessary irrigation water.

EARLY EUROPEAN SETTLEMENTS IN NORTH AMERICA

Yet one continent remained largely untouched by Europeans at the start of the seventeenth century: North America—or, rather, the portion of it north of Mexico. Several European powers had explored its coasts and attempted to establish small settlements in the late 1500s. The first English colony, on Roanoke Island in what is now North Carolina, vanished without a trace. The Spanish did succeed in establishing a small colony at St. Augustine, on the Atlantic coast of Florida, in 1565. Although nearly destroyed by French and British attacks, it remains the oldest continuously occupied European settlement in the continental United States. But it was not until three key events took place between 1607 and 1609 that permanent European colonization of the rest of North America began.

JAMESTOWN The first of these events involved three English ships that sailed into Chesapeake Bay in 1607 and

The Americas and the Triangle Trade, c. 1640 In the transatlantic "triangle trade," traders brought goods such as alcohol, cloth, tools, and weapons from Europe to the west coast of Africa and exchanged them for slaves bound for the plantations of the Americas. In destinations such as the Spanish West Indies, the ships picked up sugar and tobacco, which they transported to North America and back to Europe. New Dutch, French, and English colonies in northeastern North America also provided Europe with raw materials, such as furs.

established a fort called Jamestown. Although not the idle gentlemen of legend, the 240-odd colonists on board arrived with far too much optimism about the prospects for quick enrichment, and far too little knowledge of the region's climate, soil, resources (which included far fewer precious metals than they hoped), and native inhabitants. Disease, starvation, and hostilities with Algonquian Indians of the Powhatan tribe quickly killed off a majority of the colonists, and only the arrival of supply ships from England in 1610 saved Jamestown from Roanoke's fate.

Over the next few years, however, the surviving settlers discovered that they could grow a profitable cash crop: tobacco. King James I himself had railed against tobacco smoking in a 1604 essay, calling it a dangerous, addictive, "stinking suffumigation" that was particularly disgusting at the dinner table. But his condemnation did little to prevent the crop from finding a ready market in England and the rest of Europe. As a result, what soon became known as the Virginia Colony prospered. In 1619, following the example of the Spanish and Portuguese, the English colonists began to import African laborers to work the tobacco fields, and over the following decades the institution of North American slavery gradually took shape.

QUÉBEC One year after the founding of Jamestown, the second key event took place when the French explorer Samuel de Champlain (1567–1635) founded a fort and trading post at Québec, on the Saint Lawrence River, which became the capital of New France. Champlain traveled long distances around the region's river systems. In the course of establishing a flourishing trade in furs, he made contact both with tribes of Algonquian hunter-gatherers and with the more settled Huron. To cement his alliance with the Huron, Champlain took part in an expedition against their Iroquois enemies, and dispersed a 200-strong war party by killing two of its chiefs with firearms. New France also became the base for missionary efforts by French Franciscan and Jesuit clergy, with several Jesuits traveling hundreds of miles into the North American interior to preach the Gospel to Native Americans. The Jesuit Jean de Brébeuf (1593–1649) mastered the Huron language and impressed the Indians with his oratory, physical strength, and courage. But the Jesuits' efforts were undercut by European diseases, which, as so often in the past, decimated the native populations from the moment of sustained contact. The Huron, badly weakened by smallpox, were conquered and dispersed in the 1640s by the Iroquois, who tortured and killed Brébeuf along with several other missionaries.

The Tobacco Trade In a 1620 engraving, African slaves pack tobacco leaves, grown in the fields beyond, into barrels to be exported from Jamestown. English plantation owners watch from the shade.

NEW AMSTERDAM Meanwhile, in 1609, the third key event took place when a Dutch East India Company ship called the *Half Moon*, under the command of the Englishman Henry Hudson (ca. 1565–1611), explored the area now known as New York Harbor, and proceeded up the river that now bears his name as far as present-day Albany. The Dutch soon laid claim to the entire region. In 1624 they dispatched a group of settlers there in hopes of developing the fur trade. Soon after they purchased Manhattan Island from the local Indians and founded New Amsterdam, the future capital of New Netherland, at its southern tip. They paid with trade goods worth 60 Dutch guilders—perhaps $1,000 today.

Virginia Colony, New France, and New Netherland all had their origins in profit-seeking commercial enterprises and initially attracted colonists who, for the most part, intended to make money and return home, rather than settle permanently in North America. As a result, their populations grew only slowly. The French and Dutch colonies, dedicated to the fur trade and dependent on Native American trappers, remained particularly small and vulnerable. In each case, the population barely reached 2,000 in 1650. Virginia, with the rapid expansion of tobacco farming, attracted more settlers, numbering between 15,000 and 20,000 by mid-century. In all three colonies, European men greatly outnumbered European women. And unlike in the Spanish and Portuguese colonies, which tended to have much larger indigenous populations and where intermarriage quickly produced large communities of *mestizos*, relatively few of the European colonists in North America married native women.

NEW ENGLAND

The next English colony to be founded set a different pattern from its predecessors. In December 1620, a ship named the *Mayflower* sailed into Plymouth Harbor, in present-day Massachusetts. Its 102 passengers came, like the French and Dutch colonists, with financial backing from merchants back home hoping to develop the fur trade, but they themselves mostly had different goals in mind. Religious dissenters from Nottinghamshire, in east-central England, they favored a rigidly Calvinist variety of Protestantism that wanted to abolish priests, bishops, and liturgical practices not explicitly sanctioned by scripture. Persecuted by the English authorities, who practiced the Anglican variety of Protestantism that remained closer to Catholic beliefs, these men and women had initially fled to the Dutch Republic. Then, in 1619, the English authorities gave them permission to found a farming colony south of the Hudson River, which they envisaged as a model religious community "for the Glory of God and advancement of the Christian Faith," to quote their initial instrument of government, the Mayflower Compact. Having unexpectedly made initial landfall on Cape Cod, they settled in nearby Plymouth and eventually became known as the Pilgrims. Nearly half of them died in the first winter, including most of the adult women, but Plymouth survived with the help of local Indians. Their shared feast of thanksgiving is now celebrated as an American holiday.

A CITY UPON A HILL Other English dissenters followed, hoping, in the words of one of their leaders, to establish an exemplary "city upon a hill" in the New World. From 1630 on, they established colonies in Massachusetts Bay, Connecticut, and other areas of present-day New England. Like the Pilgrims, these settlers practiced a demanding form of Calvinism in which the community enforced rigorous moral norms and forbade many "worldly" pleasures, including dancing. Along with closely related Protestant communities in England, they would come to be known as "Puritans." They also came above all to farm, and despite the immense difficulty of clearing trees and rocks from the land, their new settlements quickly expanded. The Massachusetts Bay Colony alone saw the foundation of some fifty separate towns between 1630 and 1650. The population of what is now known as New England quickly dwarfed that of Virginia Colony, New France, and New Netherland combined, with more than 30,000 inhabitants by 1650. This number almost certainly exceeded that of the region's native populations, whose numbers fell rapidly from exposure to European diseases. By contrast, the Indian inhabitants of Latin America continued to outnumber the European settlers in those colonies.

SETTLERS AND NATIVE AMERICANS In New England, as in so many areas of the Americas previously, the European settlers quickly fell into violent conflict with the indigenous peoples. In the late 1630s, a dispute over the fur trade led to a brief but vicious war between the English colonies and the Pequot tribe, who were allied with the Dutch. In May 1637, an armed force of English and Narragansett Indian allies stormed a large Pequot village on the Mystic River (in present-day Connecticut) and massacred several hundred inhabitants. English Protestants, like the French Jesuits, did profess a desire to evangelize among the Indian tribes. The seal of the Massachusetts Bay Colony even included a Native American figure and

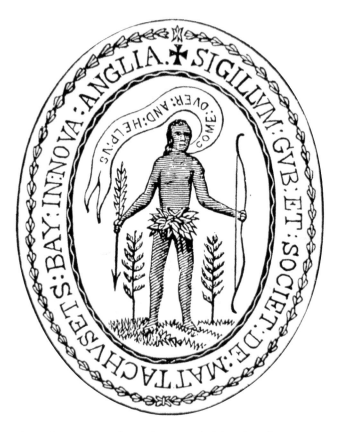

Massachusetts Bay Colony The 1630 seal of the colony shows a Native American wearing only leaves, an indication of the settlers' perception of the indigenous population as primitive. The Biblical quotation "Come over and help us" expresses the colonists' missionary intent.

the words "Come over and help us," a quotation from the biblical book of Acts. Several ministers struggled to learn the native languages. But they expected far more radical changes from their converts than the Jesuits in the French and Spanish colonies, insisting that Indians adopt European customs and learn to read scripture. As a result, the Protestants initially had far less success. The colonists also enslaved Native Americans, and brought African slaves to New England as well.

Overall, the colonies of New England and Virginia remained relatively small and vulnerable. Trade and settlement took place almost entirely along waterways, mostly near the Atlantic coast (it took enormous labor to clear roads through the thick eastern woodlands). European settlers remained highly vulnerable to disease, Native American raids, and attacks by other European powers. The same vulnerability and instability characterized other parts of Europe's overseas empires before 1650, even in the more well-established Spanish and Portuguese colonies. Throughout the New World, Europeans remained dependent on native allies. In 1623 and again in 1643, the Dutch sent fleets to the Pacific coast of South America in the hope of forging an alliance with the Indians there and fomenting a rebellion against their common enemy, Spain. But this idea came to naught, and the Spanish Empire continued to expand throughout the early seventeenth century. Its representatives explored the Pacific coast of North America and consolidated their authority in the Philippines, where they established a university in 1611.

STATES UNDER PRESSURE

Despite the relatively small scale of seventeenth-century imperialism, European overseas ventures were still expensive propositions. The Dutch fleet sent to South America in 1623 comprised eleven ships, 300 cannon, and 1,600 crew members, and took six years to prepare. When King Charles I of England (r. 1625–1649) decided to build a new fleet in the 1630s, it cost the equivalent of nearly a full year's state revenues. Looking for quick ways of raising money without having to ask Parliament for it, Charles hit on a medieval custom that obliged coastal towns to provide the crown with ships, or the money to build them. Charles was soon levying "**ship money**" on the entire kingdom, including areas far from any coast. It became one of the most important sources of royal income, as well as of grievances against him.

THE "MILITARY REVOLUTION"

But overseas ventures were just one source of financial pressure on European governments in the early seventeenth century. Others arose from the period's general economic and demographic crises, as shrinking and increasingly impoverished populations provided less tax revenue than they had in the past. Another factor was the impact of what some historians have misleadingly called the "military revolution," which refers to the changes in military technology and practice that took place in mostly evolutionary fashion over a long period.

We have already seen how the development of large-caliber gunpowder weapons affected warfare in the sixteenth century: it forced European powers to build much larger, stronger, and more elaborate fortifications, and put a new premium on siege warfare. It also transformed naval combat, as ship captains came to rely on broadsides from massed ranks of cannon to disable or sink opposing vessels. The trend toward bigger ships equipped with more cannon continued throughout the early seventeenth century. Whereas the vessels of the Spanish Armada in 1588 had roughly nineteen cannon each, the ships of the Dutch navy in 1665 averaged sixty-two.

One crucial set of innovations did come to fruition in a relatively short period in the early seventeenth century, thanks above all to the Dutch prince Maurice of Nassau (1567–1625). A keen student of ancient Roman military authors, Maurice placed new stress on intensive training and drill for common infantry, so that soldiers could maneuver in orderly fashion under fire. In combat, all the men in a line would fire their weapons in a single salvo and then march backward to reload, exposing a new line of soldiers who would fire in turn. In this way, despite the cumbersome procedures needed to load and discharge the muskets of the day (it took even a well-trained soldier up to a minute for each shot), a relatively rapid rate of fire could be maintained. Compared with the large, unwieldy square formations of infantry that had marched across typical sixteenth-century battlefields, these new, highly-trained units were far more expensive. Furthermore, the new requirements of training and constant drill effectively turned

Military Innovations A 1607 engraving from a Dutch manual of Maurice of Nassau's military drills shows a soldier lifting a smoking musket as well as the proper posture for balancing the formidable weapon. He also carries a sword, still necessary for fighting at close range.

the soldiers into full-time professionals, which pushed European states toward permanent standing armies. This development, in turn, only reinforced the long-term growth in army size.

STATE BUILDING

European states responded to the financial and administrative pressures by trying to wring as much revenue as possible from existing sources, as Charles I did with ship money. Another vivid example is the practice, developed most fully in France, called "**venality of office.**" Starting in the late fifteenth century, the French state had begun literally to sell some of the highest offices in the country—notably, judgeships in the high courts, or *parlements*. In return for the purchase price, the buyer (who needed a law degree, but few other qualifications) gained higher social status as well as the income from the office. By the sixteenth century, such "venal" offices were formally recognized as conferring nobility on their holders—and nobility, among other things, could provide exemptions from some of the heaviest forms of French taxation. This privilege made the offices highly desirable, and as their prices rose, the crown became increasingly dependent on their sale. By 1620, a special fee that allowed the owners of venal offices to pass them on to their heirs accounted for no less than 10 percent of the French state's total revenues. Law courts presided over by venal officeholders introduced new restrictions on women's property rights to ensure that the offices would pass to male heirs in perpetuity.

UNIFICATION OF FRANCE
The French state was able to exploit the practice of venality so effectively because of a crucial postmedieval development: the administrative unification of the French nation. To be sure, early-seventeenth-century France remained, in some ways, a patchwork kingdom. In a number of provinces, the local representative bodies and powerful noble families still possessed considerable autonomy. Law codes still varied from province to province, and the spoken language often varied from village to village, although by 1600 Parisian French had become the dominant written language almost everywhere. Under the Edict of Nantes issued by King Henry IV in 1598, French Protestants retained considerable rights, and even a number of military strongholds. Nevertheless, France formed a single political unit. The entire country acknowledged the king's word as law, even if the king himself was bound to respect tradition, religion, and the so-called fundamental laws (which forbade

him, for instance, from selling off parts of the kingdom or from passing on the throne to whomever he pleased). The number of judges, tax collectors, and other agents of the French crown rose from just 12,000 in the early sixteenth century to 80,000 by 1664.

DIVISIONS IN WESTERN AND CENTRAL EUROPE
In 1600 few other European monarchs could count on presiding over this degree of unity. Most of their domains remained composite monarchies, with each separate territory possessing its own government, laws, and customs. James I, who became king of both England and Ireland (r. 1603–1625), for instance, continued to rule the separate kingdom of Scotland as James VI (r. 1567–1625). The Spanish king Philip III (r. 1598–1621) was also Philip II of Portugal and held sovereignty over the Spanish Netherlands (modern Belgium). Even within Spain, several of the provinces retained greater autonomy than any in France.

The central European territories of the House of Habsburg existed in a particular state of confusion.

Habsburg Possessions in the Holy Roman Empire, c. 1600 The Habsburg dynasty controlled vast lands in western and central Europe, yet its territory was far from unified. The Spanish Habsburg king Philip III controlled the Spanish Netherlands, Milan, and part of present-day France, while independent Habsburg archdukes ruled over Lower Austria, Upper Austria, Inner Austria, and the Tirol. Hungary and the lands around Prague were under the jurisdiction of the Habsburg Holy Roman emperor Rudolf II, but were administered separately.

Separate governments and royal courts—under different, largely independent archdukes—existed in Lower Austria, Upper Austria, Inner Austria, and the Tirol. Holy Roman Emperor Rudolf II (r. 1576–1612) ruled directly over the rest, but the Hungarian lands answered to his government in Bratislava (today the capital of Slovakia), and the others to his capital in Prague. Rudolf also held ultimate sovereignty over the entire Holy Roman Empire, which remained divided into more than a thousand separate units, including several large, effectively independent German states, such as Saxony, Brandenburg, and Bavaria. In comparison with these composite monarchies, France held a definite advantage when it came to state building.

REBELLIONS

Yet in France, as in virtually all European states, rulers seeking to increase revenues faced multiple forms of resistance. Institutions from the kingdom's estates to village councils protested any supposed violations of their traditional rights and liberties. Under certain circumstances, moreover, protest could turn into revolt and violence directed against tax collectors and other agents of the central state. In 1593–95, as many as 50,000 peasants in southwestern France joined a rebellion that forced King Henry IV to lighten their tax burden. Similar revolts erupted in France through the first half of the seventeenth century.

In short, Europe at the beginning of the 1600s suffered from a sort of positive feedback loop in which the steadily rising costs of war and overseas ventures put governments under increasing financial strain, which the ongoing economic crisis only worsened. All of this drove them to take increasingly aggressive measures against their neighbors and competitors, which increased the cost of wars and overseas ventures further. Looking at Europe in the first decade of the century, it was all too easy to predict that this pattern might soon lead to a continental conflagration. In 1618 such a conflagration would arrive. But for it to do so, one other crucial factor was required: religious strife.

A NEW SOCIAL DYNAMIC IN RELIGION

The Thirty Years' War of 1618–48, which opposed largely Catholic forces to largely Protestant ones, has frequently been depicted as a direct offshoot of the large-scale, violent fragmentation of Western Christianity that followed the Protestant Reformation. Certainly, both sides had frequent recourse to religious language and imagery. Preaching to Catholic troops before the pivotal battle of White Mountain outside Prague in 1620, a Spanish friar denounced the Protestant forces as heretics, and started a frenzy by displaying an image of the Virgin and Child that the Protestants had supposedly desecrated. The Swedish king Gustavus Adolphus (r. 1611–1632), the great champion of the Protestant cause, wrote to the wavering ruler of Brandenburg: "This is a fight between God and the Devil. If His Grace is with God, he must join me. If he is for the Devil, he must fight me. There is no third way."

Yet it is simply wrong to imagine the war as a direct consequence of religious passions that had burned unchecked since the days of Martin Luther. The initial wars of the Reformation period in Germany ended with the Peace of Augsburg in 1555, which established the principle that all subjects should observe the religion of their ruler. The treaty ushered in a long period of relative tranquility in central Europe—one of the longest in the region's history. Although religious warfare ravaged France between 1562 and 1598, well before it ended the "Politique" party had emerged, which explicitly prized national unity and peace over confessional victory. Throughout the later sixteenth century, despite the principle established at Augsburg, many parts of Europe tolerated both Catholic and Protestant worship. Ordinary people of both faiths often managed to coexist in peace.

RELIGION AND THE DISCIPLINE OF DAILY LIFE

The faiths themselves continued to evolve during the first decades of the century, with effects that stretched well beyond the walls of churches. After the initial conflicts of the Reformation, nearly every church in western and central Europe undertook ambitious missionary efforts aimed at improving the religious knowledge and practices of ordinary men and women. Alarmist reports by clergy to their superiors depicted common people as in danger of falling victim to heresy through ignorance of the church's basic teachings. As an English Calvinist evocatively put it in the 1630s, "You meet with hundreds that had need be taught their very ABC in matters of religion." Both Protestant and Catholic clergy frequently compared European peasants to the "savages" of the Americas and Asia.

ELITES AND COMMONERS One important effect of these new attitudes was to deepen the cultural gulf between social elites and commoners, with elites now abandoning to the "barbaric" lower classes many traditional cultural practices they had previously engaged in themselves such as raucous local festivals. In the course of these shifts, churches on both sides of the confessional divide undertook what amounted to the most intensive educational effort ever aimed at ordinary Europeans. In the western French province of Brittany in the late sixteenth and early seventeenth centuries, the Jesuits conducted hundreds of month-long "missions," each involving a score of priests who spent as many as 8,000 hours instructing the laity in the basic elements of their religion. By 1650, the Jesuit order was teaching 150,000 students every year in 520 separate schools throughout Europe.

Everywhere, the religious authorities sought to impose new forms of social discipline by "reforming" and censoring the cultural practices of ordinary people. These practices ranged from ritual hazing and humiliations, to superstitious or magical beliefs, to bawdy festivals and songs. One favored strategy of the reformers was to write pious new verses for salacious songs. In the Scottish book *Gude and Godlie Ballatis*, published repeatedly between 1567 and 1621, the authors rewrote the main verses of a popular ballad but left the traditional chorus: "Johne, cum kis me now."

Folk Culture Flemish peasants take part in a *charivari*—a ritual intended to shame and humiliate members of the community who engaged in antisocial behavior, such as having an affair—in this seventeenth-century oil painting.

An unexpected effect of these missions was to foster the development of Europe's many minority languages, some of which had never existed in written form. The first important printed texts in Slovene were Protestant religious tracts from the 1580s. The Protestant emphasis on the believer's encounter with scripture led to the publication of the first New Testament in Welsh in 1567. On the Catholic side, where religious education remained mostly oral, the late sixteenth and early seventeenth centuries saw the publication of the first printed dictionaries and grammars in languages such as Breton and Basque, to serve clergy who wanted to preach in the native language of their flocks. A 1641 catechism from the French city of Toulouse, written in the local Occitan language, put the matter eloquently: "The poor of this country should be able to say, like the poor of other nations . . . : 'we dare to speak in our own language of the grandeurs of God and of the articles of our Faith.'"

THE CHURCH AND EVANGELIZATION These missionary activities had mixed results. Reports from clergy continued to lament the extent of ignorance and superstition throughout the early seventeenth century. Yet it was also the case that the Catholic Church, overall, tended to have greater success than either the Lutherans or the Calvinists. One reason was that for Protestants, true religious knowledge required literacy and the reading of scripture, and most of Protestant Europe, particularly in rural areas, simply lacked the necessary educational infrastructure. There were exceptions. In Sweden, by the later seventeenth century, literacy rates (at least measured by catechism-reading tests) had reached 50 percent, although some of the "literate" may simply have memorized the answers. Urban areas also did well, with adults in Amsterdam, for instance, having a 57 percent literacy rate by 1630.

The Catholic Church, by contrast, attached little importance to literacy, actively discouraged the reading of scripture by ordinary people, and was far more ready to simplify the beliefs and practices it demanded of them. In the southern Netherlands, the religious authorities specifically instructed local priests on the need for an "uncomplicated faith." Instructions to the clergy in the French city of Lyon urged priests to demand nothing more of their flocks than a knowledge of basic prayers, the Ten Commandments, and a short catechism. The Jesuit order, and many others in the Church, promoted a theology that tried to smooth over the complexities of Christian doctrine on the subject of salvation. Saint Augustine had taught that God predestines certain people for salvation and others for damnation, a doctrine that Luther and Calvin had

Expulsion of Moriscos A seventeenth-century Spanish painting shows Moriscos boarding ships bound for North Africa at the port of Vinaros, on the eastern coast of Spain.

developed further. In place of this teaching, Jesuit theologians insisted that men and women have the free will to choose between the paths of sin and salvation.

THE INQUISITION In much of Europe, the Church also backed up its evangelizing efforts with the threat of correction by its tried-and-true instrument for enforcing religious conformity and rooting out heresy: the Inquisition. The Spanish Empire counted no fewer than twenty-two separate Inquisition courts, which together handled 150,000 cases between 1550 and 1700. Some 75 percent of them concerned religious deviance; the remainder dealt with moral offenses such as adultery. Surviving documents suggest that at least 4,000 cases resulted in death sentences, with perhaps 2,000 actual executions. In another sign of increasing intolerance of anything that deviated from orthodox Catholic worship, in 1609 King Philip III of Spain ordered the expulsion of the Moriscos to North Africa. These Christian descendants of Spanish Muslims, now dispersed throughout the kingdom, were suspected of practicing the Islamic faith in secret, or of preserving vestiges of it.

RELIGION AND GENDER On both sides of western Europe's confessional divide, these changes in the religious sphere had important implications for women and their relations with men. Among Protestants, the need for all believers to read and understand scripture continued to drive efforts to provide primary education for both sexes, and the number of girls attending school in the Dutch Republic and Protestant Germany rose significantly. But the reform

of popular cultural practices often involved more stringent control over sexuality, and particularly female sexuality. Typical of the new spirit was a 1615 pamphlet by an English fencing master entitled *The Arraignment of Lewd, Idle, Forward, and Unconstant Women*. "Betwixt their breasts is the vale of destruction, and in their beds there is hell, sorrow, and repentance," the author warned his readers. Yet such outbursts were met with responses from women. including one named Rachel Speght, a well-educated Calvinist from London, who attacked this particular pamphlet and its author. She recalled Protestantism's promise that a man and a woman could find terrestrial happiness in a companionate marriage based on mutual respect. "Marriage," she put it eloquently, "is this world's Paradise, where there is mutual love."

WITCH TRIALS Such attempts to control sexuality helped feed a continuation of the European "witch craze" that had begun in the sixteenth century. The persecutions reached a height in the decades around 1600, above

Girls' Education At the Maison de St. Cyr, the first formal girls' school in France, girls were taught domestic arts as well as scripture. The students are learning to spin yarn in this seventeenth-century illustration, while the nuns, who ran the establishment, supervise.

all in Germany. In southwestern Germany alone, more than 300 witch trials took place between 1570 and 1630, leading to some 2,500 executions. Roughly four-fifths of those accused of witchcraft in the seventeenth century, and an even higher proportion of those put to death, were women. The persecutions often occurred in areas where one church or another had just established full control, and they tended to accompany precisely the sorts of intensive missionary enterprises that both Catholic and Protestant churches conducted. The torture and trials of suspected female witches were often highly sexualized, with investigators publicly stripping the accused to search their bodies for the devil's mark. The accused French witch Catherine Boyraionne was poked with needles to expose her mark, and died after her torturer poured burning lard into places it could be hidden.

THE CONTINUING CATHOLIC RECONQUEST

Although both Protestant and Catholic Europe experienced similar attempts at evangelization and social control in the early seventeenth century, the period also saw the continuation of the Catholic Reformation begun fifty years before. In 1590, Protestantism had commanded allegiance in roughly half of Europe west of Muscovy and the Ottoman Empire. In addition to Scandinavia, Britain, and northern Germany, it was a significant presence in France and the Habsburg German lands. Poland had hundreds of Protestant churches.

Two decades later, Protestant numbers across Europe had shrunk considerably. True, the highly disciplined Calvinists tended to be more resilient than the Lutherans, especially in Germany. In the Palatinate, a state in western Germany, Elector Frederick III (r. 1559–1576) had already converted to Calvinism from Lutheranism, and in the years around 1600 several other small Lutheran states followed suit. The numbers of Calvinist believers probably rose during this period. But in general, Protestants were increasingly on the defensive, which would quickly help to destabilize international politics.

CIVIL STRIFE

The fact that both the Protestant and Catholic populations had at least somewhat deeper religious knowledge and greater religious discipline than in earlier periods would prove highly conducive to religious militancy and even fanaticism. But many other factors could threaten the stability of states in these decades of crisis. Even as Catholicism and Protestantism continued to compete for authority in western Europe, large-scale civil strife shook the eastern part of the continent.

INSTABILITY IN MUSCOVY AND THE OTTOMAN EMPIRE

As seen in Chapter 11, soon after the death of Tsar Ivan IV (Ivan the Terrible) in 1584, effective power passed to his son-in-law, Boris Godunov (r. 1598–1605). Tsar Boris fought off attacks by Muslim Tatars from the southeast and continued Ivan's policy of imperial expansion into Siberia. But during the great famine of 1601–3, his authority weakened. He defeated a challenge from the powerful boyar (high-ranking noble) Fedor Romanov, whom he forced to become a monk. But in 1604 a Polish-backed army invaded, led by a man claiming to be Ivan the Terrible's younger son, Dmitri (who had actually died in 1591). In the ensuing turmoil, Boris himself died of illness, and Muscovy descended into a decade of chaos, featuring the tragicomic appearance of no fewer than nineteen further "false Dmitris" claiming the throne. A degree of order returned only when Michael Romanov, son of Fedor, became tsar in 1613, beginning a dynasty that would last three centuries. But Muscovy—now becoming known as Russia—lost considerable territory in what is now Belarus and Ukraine to Poland-Lithuania and along the Baltic

Wars in Muscovy In an episode characteristic of the instability in Muscovy in the early seventeenth century, Polish forces captured Vasili Shuisky, one of the many claimants to the Muscovite throne, and forced him to pay allegiance to the Polish king. In 1611, an Italian engraver imagined the scene of Vasili before the *Sejm*.

coast to Sweden, and its population declined by as much as a quarter between 1600 and 1620.

Although Muscovy set a high standard when it came to internal instability, the other great eastern power, the Ottoman Empire, offered some worthy competition. At its height in the mid-sixteenth century, the Ottoman sultans ruled some 15 million people across three continents. It won repeated victories over Christian powers, including a major victory over Poland-Lithuania in 1620–21. But the impressive Ottoman achievements in developing an efficient system of government administration—a crucial factor in their continuing military successes—coexisted periodically with brutal struggles for power at the highest level. Sultan Murad III (r. 1574–1595) had at least forty-nine children, and when his son Mehmet III (r. 1595–1603) succeeded to the throne, he followed Ottoman tradition by murdering all possible competitors, including many of his half brothers and at least twenty of his half sisters. He did so, in all likelihood, at the instigation of his Venetian mother, Sophia, who remained the power behind the throne until Mehmet's own death eight years later, in 1603. Over the next twenty years, the Ottoman Empire also descended into large-scale civil conflict, with one sultan deposed two separate times and another murdered. Famine and plague struck, and one chronicler wrote that "such hardship and misery appeared that it was thought the Day of Judgment had arrived or that it meant death for the entire people." Over the decades after 1620, Ottoman rulers would attempt again to reform the state, with considerable success, but uprisings and assassinations continued.

POLAND AND SWEDEN

The lands that bordered the Baltic Sea were not spared from civil strife either. Here, the dominant states were Poland and Sweden. The former, as we have seen, had expanded successfully towards the east and formally entered into a union with Lithuania in 1569. The latter, over the course of the sixteenth century, had emerged from under the shadow of Danish monarchs and German trading leagues to become a significant regional power. Then, in 1592, Poland's King Sigismund III (r. 1587–1632) inherited the Swedish throne, apparently putting the two states on the road to political union. But this brooding, artistically minded Catholic monarch failed to gain much support in Protestant Sweden, and his uncle and regent there, Charles, took advantage of the situation to seize real power, leading to decades of warfare between the two countries. Meanwhile, Sigismund's attempts to raise

Polish taxes and limit the authority of the representative body, the *Sejm*, led to a major noble revolt that lasted from 1605 to 1607. The revolt failed to overthrow the King, but nonetheless weakened the power of the monarchy to the advantage of the noble class. Since the late sixteenth century, this class had enjoyed the so-called "Golden Freedoms" that allowed it to elect the king and conferred large powers on the *Sejm*, in which individual nobles could veto legislation, including on taxation. Over the course of the following decades—indeed, into the eighteenth century—these freedoms would make it difficult for the Polish state to build up its military and administrative capacities, and to compete effectively with its principal rivals.

FRANCE

Western Europe as well was not spared from violence, even before the Thirty Years' War that began in 1618. France, which had just emerged from the worst civil war in its history, soon faced the prospect of renewed internal conflict. Under Henry IV (r. 1589–1610), a popular and effective king who worked with his chief minister, the duke of Sully, to improve the country's finances, France did enjoy a period of prosperity. In Paris, Henry sponsored several large projects that aimed to let light and air into the dark, narrow, foul-smelling medieval streets. Among them was the wide Pont Neuf (New Bridge) across the river Seine, the first bridge in the city not lined with houses. But in May 1610, a Catholic zealot stabbed the king to death, leaving his sickly eight-year-old son Louis XIII as the new king, and royal power in the hands of his Italian widow, Marie de' Medici. Over the next four years, Marie governed in her

Urban Improvements An architect's rendering of the Pont Neuf from 1577—shortly before construction began on the bridge—shows its stone arches standing out against the backdrop of the city.

son's name as regent and asserted his absolute authority in uncompromising terms, provoking a revolt by resentful grandees in 1615. Just when Marie seemed about to vanquish them, Louis demonstrated his independence by having her favorite counselor, a fellow Italian, murdered. Louis himself was an easily-influenced and indecisive man, but powerful ministers managed to introduce far-reaching changes to French government during his reign.

TENSIONS IN THE GERMAN LANDS

It was in the lands of the Holy Roman Empire, where early-seventeenth-century tensions had the most tragic and long-lasting ramifications. Before 1618 these lands saw much less actual violence, but they experienced a dangerous increase in religious conflict. This conflict challenged the stability of the Habsburg dynasty, which ruled its own collection of smaller territories while also providing the Holy Roman Empire with a long string of emperors. Back in 1599, Ferdinand of Styria, the young archduke of Inner Austria (1578–1637) and student of the Jesuits, expelled all Protestants from his lands. Holy Roman Emperor Rudolf II generally took a more conciliatory line, but found himself dragged into religious conflict against his will, time after time. A man subject to deep depressions, Rudolf had a deep fascination for the occult, for alchemy, and for esoteric wisdom. He dreamed of helping to forge a humanist "third way" that would move beyond both Catholicism and Protestantism. Yet in 1607 and 1609 he allowed the Catholics to retake several Protestant territories, provoking the formation of a defensive Protestant Union, which in time spurred the creation of a rival Catholic League.

Even as the religious conflict developed, the Habsburg dynasty itself was hobbled by vicious feuding, particularly between the childless Rudolf and his aggressive younger brother Matthias, Archduke of Upper Austria (1557–1612). Despite Rudolf's opposition, in 1606 the other Habsburg archdukes recognized Matthias as the heir to the Holy Roman throne. Over the next five years Matthias, who shared his brother's lack of religious enthusiasm, allied himself with powerful Protestant aristocrats, who helped him successfully claim the crowns of both Hungary and Bohemia. In return, he made significant political and religious concessions to these Protestants. A resurgent Catholicism therefore found itself facing off, throughout the empire, against a newly emboldened Protestant nobility, without being able to count on support from the supposed leaders of German Catholicism. Rudolf, driven further into insanity by his brother's successes, died a gibbering wreck in early 1612, but Matthias himself was already aging and ill.

Matters soon came to a head. Holy Roman emperors were elected, but sons generally succeeded fathers. Matthias, like Rudolf, was childless, so the question of succession again presented itself acutely. In 1617 the fervently Catholic Archduke Ferdinand came to a secret agreement with the Spanish Habsburgs to sponsor his candidacy for the imperial throne. He took the first step by winning election as king of Bohemia. With his support, the Catholic Bohemian government took aggressive measures against Protestants in the kingdom, provoking widespread protests and fear.

THE THIRTY YEARS' WAR

On the morning of May 23, 1618, some 200 Protestant deputies from the Estates of Bohemia burst into Prague's royal palace and rushed to a high floor where four Catholic members of Ferdinand's "regency council" were working. The Protestants angrily accused them of attacking Bohemian liberties and Protestant rights. They then opened the windows and threw two of the counselors out of the tower, followed by a secretary who very unwisely protested. All three men luckily fell into piles of garbage and survived, and the secretary was later rewarded with the noble title of Freiherr von Hohenfall (Lord of the High Fall). News of the event, known as the **Defenestration of Prague**, rapidly spread across Europe. Fighting broke out almost immediately in Bohemia itself, with the Protestant estates and their allies scoring several quick victories.

The Defenestration of Prague A 1640 engraving captures the chaotic scene of Bohemian Protestants throwing Ferdinand's deputies out of the windows of Prague's royal palace.

The Thirty Years' War, 1618–1648 When war broke out, fighting was confined to the Bohemian lands around Prague, but within a few years, it had spread across the entirety of central Europe. At first, Catholic Habsburg forces were successful, winning the Battle of White Mountain, invading the Palatinate, and reaching as far north as mainland Denmark. But when France and Sweden joined the war in the 1630s, it intensified and escalated—bringing particular devastation to the German states, which saw the bulk of the fighting.

OUTBREAK OF WAR

It was not clear at the start that a general war would follow. The Bohemian Protestants' most obvious allies, the English and Dutch, failed to provide significant aid. England's king, James I, was reluctant to challenge the authority of other rulers. The Dutch were distracted by simmering civil unrest between Calvinist factions. Moreover, they had little desire to break the peace treaty with Spain that they had signed in 1609, which had effectively recognized the Dutch Republic's independence.

Even in Germany, the largely Lutheran Protestant Union attempted to remain neutral.

The Bohemian nobles, however, soon took two decisive steps that made a general war more likely. In July 1619 they began to confiscate Catholic property in the kingdom. And in August they formally voted to depose King Ferdinand just as he was about to become Holy Roman Emperor Ferdinand II (r. 1619–1637), Matthias having died in March. In Ferdinand's place, they elected Frederick V—the twenty-three-year-old Calvinist elector of the Palatinate, and the son-in-law of England's James I—as King Frederick

I of Bohemia. This was a revolutionary and provocative step, as a Palatine official clearly recognized: "Let everyone prepare at once for a war lasting twenty, thirty or forty years. The Spaniards and the House of Austria will deploy all their worldly goods to recover Bohemia."

The Spanish did come to the aid of their Austrian cousins, and in August 1620 an army marched from the Spanish Netherlands deep into the Palatinate. The first battle of the Thirty Years' War took place just a few months later, at the White Mountain outside of Prague. Spanish and Catholic German forces, 27,000 men strong, attacked and destroyed a much smaller Protestant army while losing only 800 soldiers of their own. Soon most of Bohemia had fallen to the Catholics.

As the king of Sweden commented several years later, "All the wars that are afoot in Europe have become one war." Indeed, in the decade after the battle of White Mountain, the whirlpool of conflict centered on Bohemia dragged in one major power after another. The Thirty Years' War had begun.

HABSBURG VICTORIES

In 1621, with the Spanish Habsburgs already deeply involved in the war, the twelve-year truce between Spain and the Dutch Republic expired, and the Dutch came into the war as well on the side of the Protestant powers. The Spanish, by this point, recognized that it would be "seeking the impossible," in the words of Philip III's chief minister, to reconquer the powerful, prosperous Netherlands. But they also feared that a continuation of the truce would allow the Dutch further to develop their Atlantic trade to Spain's detriment, and to aid Spain's enemies in Italy.

The Habsburgs followed up their victory at the White Mountain with other successes. They occupied most of Bohemia and dealt harshly with its Protestant population. The Austrians and Spanish overran the Palatinate and forced Frederick into exile. Denmark, still a major Lutheran power, tried to stem the Catholic tide but failed. In 1628 a Catholic army led by the Bohemian noble Albrecht von Wallenstein (1583–1634) marched all the way to the Baltic, ultimately occupying all of mainland Denmark and forcing the Danes to sign a humiliating peace treaty. Wallenstein, who proved to be a superb organizer and military entrepreneur, was rewarded with a rich northern German duchy and briefly became one of the dominant and ambitious figures in central Europe before being assassinated by Habsburg officers after he came under suspicion of treason to the Habsburg cause.

But the more victories the Habsburgs won, the more they overreached. In March 1629 Emperor Ferdinand II signed the **Edict of Restitution**, which returned to the Catholic Church all the church property in the Holy Roman Empire that had come into Protestant hands since 1552. Over a hundred convents were forcibly "restituted" in this way, along with many large tracts of land. Nothing could have been better calculated to inflame Protestant fears across Europe. Wallenstein himself warned that the edict would "turn the entire Empire against us."

Within two years, the war had sucked in two additional major powers. France had remained relatively aloof during the 1620s, distracted by peasant revolts, murderous feuding between noble factions, and a major rebellion by French Calvinists that Louis XIII's government managed to contain only with great difficulty. But by 1631 the French crown had gone a long way toward reestablishing its authority, thanks in large part to Louis's brilliant chief minister, Cardinal Richelieu (1585–1642), who, when it came to the larger European war, placed French dynastic interest above confessional loyalty. Richelieu—though a prelate of the Catholic Church—was anxious to keep the Habsburgs from achieving total dominance over central Europe, and soon began to intervene more actively in the war on the Protestant side. As part of his strategy, he offered Lutheran Sweden large subsidies to join the fight against the Catholic Habsburgs.

SWEDISH AND SPANISH INTERVENTION

Sweden was the other major power whose intervention now changed the face of the conflict. King Gustavus Adolphus (r. 1611–1632) had forged a renewed partnership with the Swedish nobility, and in collaboration with his own brilliant chief minister, Axel Oxenstierna (1583–1664), rapidly built up state finances and the military. Sweden (which now also controlled most of the modern states of Finland, Estonia, and Latvia) gained from the travails of the other major Baltic powers: Russia was still recovering from its civil wars; Poland-Lithuania had recently been defeated by the Ottomans, and Denmark by the Habsburgs.

Despite the legends that cast Gustavus Adolphus as the great champion of the Protestant cause, the king's religious beliefs were not as passionate as those of Frederick of the Palatinate, or Emperor Ferdinand II. But he saw in the war a great opportunity to secure Sweden's new position. In 1630 he seized part of the southern Baltic coast, then pushed deep into Germany. In September 1631 he prevailed in the desperate battle of Breitenfeld, in Saxony, which decisively checked the Catholic "reconquest." A year later he died at the battle of Lützen, leaving the throne to his infant daughter, Christina. The Swedes remained in the war, albeit with less enthusiasm.

In response to these Swedish successes, Spain stepped up its role in the war. In 1621 the Spanish throne had passed to Philip IV (r. 1621–1665), a competent ruler who, unlike his French counterparts, placed the interests of religion above most secular matters. ("There is no affair of state for which the smallest danger to Religion should be adventured," he wrote in 1627.) He relied on the services of yet another enormously ambitious, energetic minister, Gaspar de Gúzman, Count-Duke Olivares (1587–1645), the great rival of Richelieu. Olivares originally focused his efforts on the Netherlands, where Spain's forces retook the key town of Breda in 1624. Then, in 1634, he managed to send a powerful army to Germany that crushed the Swedes, pushing them out of the war altogether. This defeat also forced many of the northern German Protestant states to sue for peace.

Yet, once again, Habsburg victories led to a strong reaction, pushing France to commit its own forces fully to the conflict on the Protestant side, beginning hostilities with Spain that would last for more than a decade beyond the general European conflict of the Thirty Years' War. French finances squealed under the strain, forcing Richelieu to double the principal French tax, the *taille*, between 1635 and 1643, which provoked violent resistance throughout the country. Spanish finances suffered even more, and Spain met with several important defeats. The Dutch briefly captured much of Brazil from the Spanish Empire in the early 1630s, and then won a major naval victory in 1639. By 1640, when revolts broke out against Philip IV in both Portugal and Catalonia, Spain—despite the expansion of its holdings in North America and Asia—was at the breaking point. While the war would last another eight years, the Habsburgs would never again come close to true victory, let alone regaining the dominant European position they had enjoyed under Charles V a century earlier.

ATROCITIES AND MASS DEATH

As the fighting escalated, it took an increasingly hideous toll on civilian populations. Even by the bloody standards of early modern European warfare, the Thirty Years' War quickly gained a reputation for atrocity. In 1637, to take an example almost at random, the Estates of Niederhessen, in central Germany, accused imperial Bavarian troops of raping women, throwing children into hot ovens, cutting

Horrors of the Thirty Years' War Jacques Callot's 1633 series of prints "The Miseries and Misfortunes of War" includes this famous image of soldiers hanging dozens of people.

off noses, ears, tongues, and breasts, and pouring molten lead or tin into mouths. Massacres were a regular occurrence. One of the worst occurred in May 1631 when the German city of Magdeburg was sacked by imperial forces. As many as 30,000 people—three-quarters of the city's population—died. The French printmaker Jacques Callot recorded the horrors allegedly committed by his country's troops in his 1633 series of etchings, "The Miseries and Misfortunes of War"—most famously a "hanging tree" with a score of corpses dangling from its branches.

In most cases, it is impossible to tell which atrocities actually happened and which were exaggerated or even invented by propagandists and fiction-writers. But it is clear that the Thirty Years' War led to a breakdown of order on an unprecedented scale, not simply exposing civilians to violence but destroying homes, disrupting harvests, and facilitating the spread of famine and plague, even as average temperatures probably dropped to their lowest point in the Little Ice Age. The overall demographic consequences were catastrophic. Between 1618 and 1648, the population of the Holy Roman Empire seems to have fallen at least 30 percent, from 15 million people to fewer than 11 million. Some areas suffered even more, including Pomerania on the Baltic coast, Württemberg in the southwest, and Bohemia, where losses exceeded 40 percent.

This astonishing loss of life resulted in part from the nature of early-seventeenth-century armed forces. These were no longer the relatively small, long-serving, largely mercenary groups that characterized so much of warfare in the Renaissance, before the revolution in military discipline and tactics described above. They were often of unprecedented size—Gustavus Adolphus's invasion force of the early 1630s numbered roughly 175,000 soldiers—and contained an uneasy mix of mercenaries, professional recruits, and (especially in the Swedish army) conscripts.

THE SACK OF MAGDEBURG

A mostly Protestant trade center in the central German state of Saxony, the city of Magdeburg declared for the Swedish emperor Gustavus Adolphus when he invaded northern Germany to support the Protestant cause. In 1631, the army of the Catholic League general Count von Tilly—some 20,000 unpaid and hungry soldiers dependent on plunder for survival—sacked the city. With neither wealth to bribe soldiers nor rank to command protection, Magdeburg's common citizens faced slaughter by the conquering soldiers. Otto von Guericke, a scholar and later mayor of Magdeburg, survived the invasion and recorded the chaos and violence.

[When] the city was lost... [there was] nothing but murder, burning, plundering, torment, and beatings. In particular, each of the enemies sought more and greater booty. When such a party of looters entered a house and the head of the household had something he could give them, then he could use this to save and preserve himself and his family until another soldier, who also wanted something, came along. Finally there was nothing left to give, then the misery really began.

For then the soldiers began to beat and threaten to shoot, skewer, hang, etc., the people, so that even if something had been buried under the earth or locked away behind a thousand locks, the citizens would still have been forced to seek it out and hand it over. Through such enduring fury... many thousands of innocent men, women and children were, with horrid, fearful screams of pain and alarm, miserably murdered and wretchedly executed in manifold ways, so that no words can sufficiently describe it. As to the common craftspeople, day laborers, servants, and apprentices, as well as soldiers who had served on the side of the Swedes and the city and could give nothing, they had to carry the booty and bundles of the enemy for a while, to do all kinds of service for them, or even to join the enemy's service, and so be supported by them. However, things went very badly for many of those women, girls, daughters, and maids who either had no men, parents, or relatives who could pay a ransom on their behalf, or could not appeal to high officers for help or advice; some were defiled and disgraced, and some were kept as concubines.

However, there were also many who similarly had no friends or no means, but who still, amazingly, kept their honor—partially due to honorable soldiers who, by dint of the decency of those they had taken prisoner, simply let them free or even married them.

QUESTIONS FOR ANALYSIS

1. How did wealth and influence help some inhabitants of Magdeburg survive the slaughter?
2. How might the besieging troops' need for plunder have driven some of the violence in Magdeburg?
3. Why were women especially vulnerable to violence in the sack of the city?

Source: Tryntje Helfferich, ed. and trans., *The Essential Thirty Years War: a Documentary History* (Indianapolis: 2015), pp. 47–49.

But they had not yet become the uniformed, tightly disciplined, professionally commanded, and relatively well-supplied armies of the eighteenth century. And they certainly did not receive regular pay. Simply to stay alive—and to provide for the wives, children, prostitutes, servants, and laborers who followed in their baggage trains, sometimes numbering in the tens of thousands—soldiers often had no choice but to plunder. As one historian has concisely put it, "Abuse did not simply undermine the system; abuse *was* the system." These conditions guaranteed that soldiers and civilians would see each other as enemies, even when they were supposedly on the same side.

WAR AND ABSOLUTISM

A war that caused this degree of devastation, lasted so long, and involved such huge armies and expenditures, forced all the states that participated to seek new ways of mobilizing their resources. We have already seen that throughout Europe rulers faced severe constraints—especially in this period of economic decline—in their ability to raise all-important tax revenues. They depended on the cooperation of their most powerful subjects to carry out most of the business of government, including tax collection. These subjects in turn enjoyed well-established privileges, including (for nobles and clergy) exemptions from many forms of taxation. Rulers could only challenge them at the risk of upsetting a delicate political balance and provoking revolts. Moreover, in most cases rulers had little desire to undermine such practices because they shared the culture and outlook of the aristocrats and prelates, participated in court life with them, and often considered themselves the "first gentlemen" of their realms. As a result, before the 1630s, when European rulers sought fiscal innovations, they generally tried to disguise them as mere expansions of supposedly "traditional" practices such as venality of office or England's "ship money."

BREAKS WITH PRECEDENT

Yet such were the pressures of the Thirty Years' War that many monarchs now attempted to bypass institutions such as estates and parliaments altogether, overrule the complaints of powerful nobles, and funnel revenue directly to the central state. These moves did not involve crushing nobilities in favor of the rising middle classes, as historians once assumed. They did not imply the wholesale elimination of traditional political institutions or the assumption of tyrannical, arbitrary powers by sovereigns. But they did imply the recognition of a monarch's absolute and indivisible sovereignty, and therefore reflect the political trend generally referred to as **absolutism**.

These breaks with precedent were not seen to the same extent everywhere. In Poland, where, as we have seen, King Sigismund Vasa (r. 1587–1632) had failed to limit the powers of the Sejm in the early seventeenth century, the king remained heavily dependent on his most powerful nobles. The Austrian Habsburg lands, meanwhile, were so fragmented and war-torn that the dynasty had to rely on military entrepreneurs to undertake the mobilization of resources that absolutist governments accomplished in other states. The most significant moves toward absolutism in the smaller German and Italian states tended to come after the middle of the seventeenth century.

POWERFUL MINISTRIES

In the major states of western Europe, however, important changes were already under way. Those driving the changes were most often not the rulers themselves, but powerful ministers: Oxenstierna in Sweden, Olivares in Spain, and above all Richelieu in France. They tended to have better educations than the monarchs they served, and also more energy to attend to administrative tasks. Olivares famously worked from five in the morning until eleven at night, while the French poet François de Malherbe said of Richelieu, "I swear there is something supernatural about that man." They were all zealous advocates of unquestioned royal authority, and cultivated intimate, intensely emotional relationships with the monarchs they served. They all recognized as well that royal power was something constructed not just through force but through magnificent display, including architecture and works of art. And they all sought ways of clearing out and simplifying the tangle of privileges and institutions that constituted early modern governments.

RICHELIEU   Richelieu had the greatest success. Well before he came to power in the 1620s, the French monarchy had begun to send agents known as **intendants** to the provinces with powers to advise, judge, and act as representatives of the king. But in 1635 Richelieu made

Cardinal Richelieu   This "Triple Portrait" of Richelieu, painted in 1642, was a sketch for a sculptor who intended to make a bust of the cardinal.

the intendants permanent fixtures in each of France's thirty-odd administrative districts. Over the next few years he granted them extensive powers, particularly over the collection of the principal land tax, the taille. They frequently clashed with local estates and high courts, and made a point of establishing their symbolic preeminence in local processions and church services. The new demands they made for revenue contributed directly to the ongoing peasant revolts, and to a wave of urban protests. But Richelieu did succeed in raising large sums for the central treasury. Gaunt, cunning, and enormously vain, he planned an entire new city (to be named after him) and built a magnificent palace in Paris, where a gallery of paintings of "Great Frenchmen" started with figures from the early Middle Ages and concluded with his own portrait.

OLIVARES   Olivares was a more tragic figure. Fat, red-faced, and given to dramatic outbursts, he too understood the importance of magnificent display, notably promoting the career of the painter Diego Velázquez (1599–1660), whose brilliant *Surrender of Breda* (1634–35) depicted the valor and magnanimity of the Spanish in one of their great victories over the Dutch. Despite the vast extent and wealth of the Spanish Empire, Olivares felt that it was hobbled by its patchwork division into different political units, each with its own customs and laws, and he pushed throughout his career for what he called "union and equality in the laws, customs, and forms of government." But while Olivares hoped to establish a more regular, uniform, rational administration, he did not have agents or financial resources adequate to the task. Even the Spanish government's basic knowledge of the kingdom was faulty: for example, it grossly overestimated the population of Catalonia, leading Olivares to demand more in taxes than the province could bear. In 1640 Catalonia revolted, as did Portugal, which had been ruled by the Spanish crown since 1580. Sick and exhausted, Olivares fell from power in 1642, sank into madness, and died three years later.

OXENSTIERNA   In northern Europe, fiscal innovations in government took different forms. Oxenstierna in Sweden promoted cooperation between the highest-ranking nobles and the crown, notably in fixing the composition of the Swedish estates (which were henceforth divided among nobles, prelates, commoners, and peasants). His success allowed Sweden to introduce a more intensive system of conscription than any other European power of the time, with some 55,000 men drafted between 1621 and 1632. But Sweden too found it impossible to sustain the necessary level of mobilization, particularly because roughly half of all conscripts could expect to be killed, wounded, or taken prisoner during their military service.

THE DUTCH AND BRITISH EXCEPTIONS

The Dutch Republic was an exception to the continental pattern of government. Each of its seven provinces exercised considerable autonomy and sent deputies to the powerful representative body known as the States General. Although the "stadholders" (essentially, executive officials of the republic) from the House of Orange did manage to extend their powers, they never came close to achieving absolute authority equivalent to that of the French king. But the republic did not need to copy Richelieu to raise the funds necessary for war, thanks to the profits of trade and its innovative new Bank of Amsterdam, which stabilized the currency and national debt. By the end of the century the Dutch had become the chief exporters of guns and other military supplies to the rest of Europe, further adding to the positive side of their balance sheets.

Britain was yet another distinct case. James I, an unusually cultivated monarch, not only believed in the divine right of kings but wrote extensively on the subject. "Kings," he pronounced, "are justly called gods, for that they exercise a manner or resemblance of divine power upon earth." James respected the limited rights of the English Parliament, which sat at his pleasure and could not countermand his decisions. He did depend on the gentry who sat in Parliament to collect his taxes and appropriate funds for military expeditions. But particularly after 1620 they frequently provoked his anger by failing to vote him the money he requested. The most remarkable legacy of this strife was the **Petition of Right** of 1628, in which Parliament declared that only it had the right to levy taxes, that the king could not declare martial law in peacetime, and that prisoners had the right to appeal their detention before a judge or court. These principles remain in the bedrock of Anglo-American government and law to this day.

James's son, the shy and hesitant **Charles I**, inherited his father's quarrels with Parliament and was increasingly attracted to the continental absolutist model. He dissolved three Parliaments in five years when they failed to vote him open-ended funds for the war. From 1629 to 1640, Charles tried to rule without Parliament altogether, raising money through expedients such as ship money. The conflicts raised the possibility of a civil war throughout the British Isles, even as Portuguese and Catalan revolts flared against Spain, the French stumbled toward their own civil war, and the Thirty Years' War approached its climax. While monarchs put on ever more grandiose displays of power, the disorder presaged in *King Lear* was sweeping over Europe in a torrent.

ROYAL POWER AND CULTURE

One way in which Charles's reign in England resembled that of Louis XIII in France and Philip IV in Spain involved his use of architecture and the other arts as an instrument of royal power. Once again, European rulers were reaching back to the example of the Roman emperors who used the arts to glorify themselves and solidify their power. The sheer quantity, size, and expense of the paintings, sculpture, and architecture produced to celebrate the early-seventeenth-century absolutist monarchs dwarfed the commissions of earlier periods. Figures such as Cardinal Richelieu used projects like his portrait gallery and planned city to shape the spaces of artistic display in minute detail, so as to control exactly how onlookers would see and interpret them.

BAROQUE ART

Peter Paul Rubens (1577–1640), a favorite of Charles I, was a brilliant and prolific Flemish painter whose sensual canvases, filled with bright color and movement, conveyed the splendor of monarchs and their courts. Rubens employed easily deciphered allegories to endow his subjects with mythical or divine characteristics. In 1621 the French queen, Marie de' Medici, hired Rubens to paint a grandiose series depicting her life, including the death and ascension to heaven of her husband Henry IV, and her tumultuous relationship with her son, Louis XIII. Fourteen years later, after a spell in Madrid, Rubens went to London, where Charles commissioned him to paint the ceiling of Whitehall Palace's new Banqueting House. The mural centered on the ascension to heaven of the king's father, James I. Rubens received knighthoods from both Spain and England.

Some of the period's best artists kept their distance from the style that Rubens's work exemplified. Notable among them was the French painter Nicolas Poussin (1594–1665), who developed a subdued, precise style. Nevertheless, **Baroque** art, with its dramatic, visceral appeal to the senses, perfectly suited the needs of the rulers who were its patrons. It also suited the needs of the aggressive, post-Reformation Catholic Church. Baroque

Rubens and Marie de' Medici The fourth painting in Rubens' 21-painting cycle about Marie de' Medici, made in 1621–25, shows angels presenting the future queen of France's portrait to King Henri IV. The couple did not meet before their marriage, but exchanged portraits. In this telling, the king reportedly fell in love with Marie at first sight.

works of religious art and architecture, like their secular counterparts, sought to overwhelm viewers—for instance in the grand, undulating church facades constructed by the Swiss-Italian Francesco Borromini (1599–1667). The Jesuits, with their mission of "propagating the faith" by all possible means, eagerly adopted the baroque style for their churches.

The Baroque especially contributed to the development of European sculpture, notably in the work of Gian Lorenzo Bernini (1598–1680). An excellent example is a piece he created for Santa Maria della Vittoria in Rome, a church rededicated to the Virgin Mary after the Catholic triumph at the battle of White Mountain in 1620. The sculpture, which recalls some of the masterpieces of Greek and Roman antiquity, illustrates an episode from the autobiography of Saint Teresa of Avila in which she imagines an angel piercing her heart with a spear, filling her with divine ecstasy. Bernini depicted the saint in a seated position, covered in flowing robes, her mouth open in rapture.

Ecstasy of Saint Teresa Bernini's dramatic sculpture of an angel piercing Saint Theresa's heart displays all the characteristics of the Baroque style: neoclassical forms, flowing fabrics, and expressive figures.

The angel is almost astride her as beams of golden sunlight shower down on them, and the whole composition is set amid lavish expanses of marble and polished stone.

LANGUAGE AND LITERARY CULTURE

Language and literature were just as important as the fine arts for the purposes of political and religious glorification. In 1635 Cardinal Richelieu presided over the foundation of the French Academy to serve as the official authority on the French language. Aiming to create a pure, stable French that could aspire to equality with classical Latin (still the language of scholarship and philosophy), its forty members worked to banish vulgar, mechanical, technical, and foreign terms and phrases from elite usage. When the playwright Pierre Corneille (1606-1684) had a massive success in 1637 with *Le Cid*, a story of medieval Spain whose hero is torn between love and honor, the Academy condemned him for not respecting the "classical unities" of space, time, and action, according to which stage dramas should take place within a single 24-hour period, in a single

place, with one single plot. In his later work, Corneille paid greater heed to the Academy's strictures: a good example of how the state managed to exercise authority over French literature, and to use it as an instrument of its glory.

DON QUIXOTE *Le Cid* itself was based on a Spanish original, and in the early seventeenth century the center of innovation in European literature and art remained very much in the Mediterranean region. In Spain, the period saw the production of some of the country's greatest works—above all the publication (starting in 1605) of Miguel de Cervantes' (1547–1616) *Don Quixote*, widely regarded as the first modern novel. Meandering, playful, full of puns and digressions and switches of perspective, it tells the story of an aging rural gentleman whose mind has been addled by the chivalric romances associated with aristocratic medieval knights. Don Quixote decides to go off on quests, but meets with all manner of pitfalls and humiliations, including a famous scene in which he charges with his lance at windmills that he mistakes for giants.

Don Quixote and the novels that followed it had much the same effect in Spain as Martin Luther's popular theological pamphlets had in Germany: they gave a permanent stamp to the written vernacular language and helped it achieve a more stable form. The genre quickly spread across Europe and was actively promoted for a time by the post-Reformation Catholic Church, which preferred the novel's realism (and the punishments it depicted befalling the wicked) to the sort of romances that had entranced Don Quixote. The only European literature to equal Spain's before 1640 was that of England, where Shakespeare kept writing until his death in 1616 and poets such as John Donne, George Herbert, and the young John Milton found receptive audiences.

POPULAR CULTURE The development of standard vernacular languages that we have seen promoted by both states and churches (above all, Protestant churches), and the flourishing of new genres such as the novel, helped to transform European literary culture more broadly. Although literacy rates remained low, most peasants could find neighbors to read to them, especially in evening village gatherings at which one neighbor might read aloud while others repaired tools, sewed clothing, and took care of children. Only a limited range of printed matter reached rural villages: mostly poorly-bound and poorly-printed religious tracts, almanacs, and small books known as "chapbooks" that consisted in great part of ballads, medieval romances (including, in England, tales of

Arthur and Robin Hood), and medicinal tracts. But while their appearance might be delayed by years or decades, novels and lyric poetry also arrived in chapbook form.

City-dwellers, however, had access to a larger range of printed material, especially in the economically expanding societies of Protestant northern Europe. There, the combination of prosperity and the religious imperative of literacy spurred the development of thriving book markets. In the Netherlands, books took their place alongside housewares as signs of increasing prosperity for merchants, professionals, and well-to-do artisans. It became increasingly popular for portrait painters to depict their subjects—men and women alike—holding books.

Meanwhile, in Italy, another new genre took shape, as attempts to revive classical Greek mixtures of instrumental and vocal music and drama coalesced into what we now know as opera. Based on popular and familiar stories, both sacred and profane, but using a combination of extravagant scenery, dance, and music to provide an impressive sensory experience in keeping with the century's Baroque style, opera quickly gained a popular as well as elite audience, with public opera theaters opening in Venice as early as the 1630s.

PATRONAGE AND ITS LIMITS

The demands of monarchs and patrons continued to influence powerfully the worlds of philosophy, natural philosophy (the origins of what we today call science), and scholarship. The Dutchman Hugo Grotius (1583–1645), one of the greatest political thinkers of the period, began his career writing works that justified the actions of the Dutch Republic in the international realm: a history of its struggle against Spain, a treatise insisting on the freedom of the seas and international trade, and a justification of privateering. Francis Bacon (1561–1626), one of the creators of the modern scientific method, served in a succession of high offices in the English state. The astronomer Galileo Galilei (1564–1642) avidly sought the patronage of Florence's House of Medici, to the point of naming the four moons of Jupiter he discovered after members of the Medici family (the moons ultimately became known by different names).

Yet it would be a mistake to assume that this influence was the determining factor in the period's intellectual developments. The lines of patronage did not always run smooth, as suggested by the fact that Grotius, Bacon, and Galileo all spent time in prison, although for different reasons. Grotius was an ally of the moderate Protestant party in the Dutch Republic and shared in its fall. Bacon was charged by enemies in Parliament with taking bribes in his official government position. As we will see, Galileo was put on trial by the Inquisition because of his defense of the Copernican view of the solar system.

But together, these cases show that important works could be written without direct patronage, or in defiance of powerful interests. It was during a ten-year exile in France that Grotius wrote his most important work, *On the Law of War and Peace* (1625), in which he tried to lay out rules, grounded in natural law, by which states could legitimately go to war, and propose rules for the legitimate conduct of hostilities. The book constituted an obvious, critical commentary on the Thirty Years' War then in progress. "Throughout the Christian world," Grotius commented, "I have observed a lack of restraint in war that even barbarous races should be ashamed of." And although it had little immediate impact, the book built on medieval and Renaissance precedents to become one of the founding works of modern international law.

THE REPUBLIC OF LETTERS

As in the late sixteenth century, the leading intellectual figures of the period, even in the midst of war, engaged in impressively voluminous correspondence with each other, in the still-universal language of scholarship and philosophy that was Latin. In this correspondence, some of it written for eventual publication, they not only exchanged information, engaged in criticism, and provided practical advice and recommendations. Together they built an international community—the so-called **Republic of Letters**—whose judgments were crucial to the success and esteem of individual members. Like any republic, this one had its share of quarrels and corruption. But at its best it defended principles of open, rational inquiry and held it a moral duty to defend and publicize the results, even when they ran contrary to the dictates of established authorities.

The Republic of Letters even proved open to contributions from women, who were excluded from universities and most other formal scholarly venues. For instance, in 1638 the learned Dutch

Anna Maria van Schurman
This 1657 portrait of the Dutch scholar and artist speaks to her accomplishments and involvement in the Republic of Letters. The tower in the background is perhaps a church or university, while a globe, books, paintbrushes, and other scholarly objects surround the portrait.

scholar Anna Maria van Schurman (1607–1678) published a Latin treatise on whether scholarly study befitted a Christian woman. As in the sixteenth century, some women worked as translators, while wealthy women influenced the direction of scholarship through the patronage they provided. Many members of the Republic hoped their researches would ultimately serve the greater glory of God or their royal patrons. As Bacon strikingly put it, "human knowledge and human power meet as one." But these ambitions did not diminish the importance of the standards they established and the subjects of inquiry they undertook.

EARLY STAGES OF THE SCIENTIFIC REVOLUTION

It was in large part under the aegis of the Republic of Letters that, between 1600 and 1640, there took place the crucial early developments in what historians now call the Scientific Revolution.

GALILEO Galileo and Bacon were the most important figures in this revolution. Galileo, born to a wealthy family in Pisa, was a professor at the University of Padua, teaching mathematics, geometry, mechanics, and astronomy. In 1609 he built a telescope, an instrument recently invented in the Netherlands, and began systematic astronomical observations. His discoveries challenged ancient ideas as to the perfect, unchanging nature of the heavens. Notably, he identified sunspots, which not only marred the supposedly pure surface of the sun, but changed over time, and moved in such a way as to suggest that the sun rotated around an axis. Galileo also discovered moons orbiting Jupiter, mapped the surface of the earth's moon, and showed that the sky contained a far greater number of stars than the ancients had suspected, opening the possibility that the universe was infinite in extent.

Galileo's observations of planetary motion also, crucially, confirmed Copernicus's theory that the earth and other planets revolved around the sun. He demonstrated empirically, in other words, that the earth was not the center of the universe, as scientific and religious thinkers had maintained since the time of Ptolemy and Aristotle. Galileo made a host of other observations and experiments, notably proving that all objects, no matter what their weight, fall to earth at the same rate. "Philosophy," he wrote beautifully in 1623,

> is written in this grand book—I mean the universe—
> which stands continually open to our gaze, but it

Galileo's Telescope The telescope and lens Galileo built in 1609, with which he made his revolutionary observations.

cannot be understood unless one first learns to comprehend the language in which it is written. It is written in the language of mathematics, and its characters are triangles, circles, and other geometric figures, without which it is humanly impossible to understand a single word of it; without these, one is wandering about in a dark labyrinth.

In 1633 the Inquisition condemned Galileo as a heretic for defending the "heliocentric" or sun-centered, vision of the universe, and Galileo reluctantly renounced it.

KEPLER Galileo received crucial support from his correspondent in the Republic of Letters, the German astronomer Johannes Kepler (1571–1630), whose careful calculations revealed that the planets moved around the sun in elliptical orbits. These findings were crucial for suggesting not only that the heavens shared the imperfections of the terrestrial sphere (otherwise the planets should have moved in perfect circles, as Copernicus thought), but obeyed the same basic laws that were found on earth. Kepler himself expressed the point clearly, and with deliberately loaded language: "The machine of the universe is not similar to a divine animated being, but similar to a clock." From the very beginning, then, the scientific revolution revolved around the idea of the machine—both as a metaphor for the universe and as a real-life means of probing its secrets.

GALILEO AND THE INQUISITION

Galileo issued an early defense of his theories in a 1615 letter to the Grand Duchess Christina of Tuscany—the mother of his patron, Cosimo II de' Medici. Christina had expressed misgivings about the Copernican view that the planets orbit a stationary sun, a seeming contradiction of Biblical passages in which the sun moves. Copies of Galileo's letter were widely distributed, but despite his argument that his findings could be reconciled with Catholicism, he was forbidden by the Church in 1616 to continue his heliocentric studies. Galileo initially obeyed this injunction, but the Inquisition placed him on trial for heresy in 1633 following the publication of his *Dialogue Concerning the Two Chief World Systems*, which delved further into Copernican views of the universe.

Galileo, from letter to the Grand Duchess Christina

In this passage, Galileo argues against critics in the Church that it is better to rely on sensory experience than the Bible to reveal the workings of the natural world.

The reason they advance to condemn the opinion of the earth's mobility and sun's stability is this: since in many places in Holy Scripture one reads that the sun moves and the earth stands still, and that Scripture can never lie or err, it follows as a necessary consequence that the opinion of those who want to assert the sun to be motionless and the earth moving is erroneous and damnable....

I think that in disputes about natural phenomena one must begin not with the authority of scriptural passages but with sensory experience and necessary demonstrations. For the Holy Scripture and nature derive equally from the Godhead, the former as the dictation of the Holy Spirit and the latter as the most obedient executrix of God's orders; moreover, to accommodate the understanding of the common people it is appropriate for Scripture to say many things that are different (in appearance and in regard to the literal meaning of the words) from the absolute truth; on the other hand, nature is inexorable and immutable, never violates the terms of the laws imposed upon her, and does not care whether or not her recondite reasons and ways of operating are disclosed to human understanding…and so it seems that a natural phenomenon which is placed before our eyes by sensory experience or proved by necessary demonstrations should not be called into question, let alone condemned, on account of scriptural passages whose words appear to have a different meaning.

The Inquisition, sentence against Galileo

This source details the Inquisition's charge of heresy against Galileo. Faced with the threat of torture and execution, Galileo agreed to disavow his theories.

We say, pronounce, sentence, and declare that you, the above-mentioned Galileo, because of the things deduced in the trial and confessed by you as above, have rendered yourself according to this Holy Office [Inquisition] vehemently suspected of heresy, namely of having held and believed a doctrine which is false and contrary to the divine and Holy Scripture: that the sun is the center of the world and does not move from east to west, and the earth moves and is not the center of the world, and that one may hold and defend as probable an opinion after it has been declared and defined contrary to Holy Scripture. Consequently you have incurred all the censures and penalties imposed and promulgated by the second canons and all particular and general laws against such delinquents. We are willing to absolve you from them provided that first, with a sincere heart and unfeigned faith, in front of us you abjure, curse, and detest the above mentioned errors and heresies, and every other error and heresy contrary to the Catholic and Apostolic Church, in the manner and form we will prescribe to you.

Furthermore, so that this serious and pernicious error and transgression of yours does not remain completely unpunished, and so that you will be more cautious in the future and an example for others to abstain from similar crimes, we order that the book *Dialogue* by Galileo Galilei be prohibited by public edict.

QUESTIONS FOR ANALYSIS

1. According to Galileo, why are sensory experience and demonstrations better tools for observing natural phenomena than scripture?
2. Why does the Inquisition view Galileo's theories as heresy?
3. How do Galileo and the Church differ in their perceptions of the relationship between religion and science?

Sources: *The Galileo Affair*, ed. and trans. Maurice A. Finocchiaro (Berkeley, CA: 1989), pp. 92–3 and 291.

BACON **Francis Bacon** did not share Galileo's readiness to tinker with telescopes and mechanical devices, but in his works—above all, the *Novum Organum* (*New Instrument*) of 1620—he justified the sorts of approaches Galileo employed, using both philosophical rigor and rhetorical skill. Bacon insisted on the importance of empirical research—to go to the facts themselves. One cannot accept ideas simply on the basis of ancient authority, no matter how exalted, he insisted. Investigation should start not with citations from Aristotle or Galen, but with skepticism: "If a man will begin with certainties, he will end in doubts; but if he will be content to begin with doubts, he will end in certainties." These certainties would emerge through a process of induction—finding a general rule that would fit the observed facts. Furthermore, Bacon defended experimentation as the best means to discover the necessary facts. In his wonderful description: "The nature of things betrays itself more readily under the vexations of art than in its natural freedom." It is in Bacon's work that we find the origins of the modern experimental scientific method.

DESCARTES

It was left to a Frenchman, the prolific **René Descartes** (1596–1650), to make scientific skepticism—the systematic questioning of received truths and values—the basis of a radically new philosophical system. In his *Discourse on Method* (1637), Descartes proposed that thinkers had to apply doubt as rigorously as possible, until they reached principles they could not doubt—in the first place, their own existence. In Descartes's famous formulation: *cogito ergo sum*. I think, therefore I am. Then, from first principles, one could deduce more complex ideas, on the model of mathematicians constructing logical proofs. It was a method at odds with Bacon's project of starting with the observation of facts and then inducing principles from them.

Descartes made the "dualist" argument that the entire universe was composed of two basic substances, mind and matter, and that all visible phenomena, in keeping with Kepler's earlier observations, fell into the latter category. He believed that the visible universe necessarily obeyed universal, knowable laws that human beings could discover by proper observation and reasoning. Descartes in no way denied the existence of God. But his work proposed that if God created the universe and set it in motion—like a giant, infinitely complex machine—then he did not need to involve himself to keep it functioning thereafter. Not surprisingly, Descartes feared persecution from the Christian churches, particularly after the condemnation

of Galileo. He lived much of his life as a wandering scholar, spending twenty years in a succession of Dutch towns and eventually serving as tutor to Queen Christina of Sweden, Gustavus Adolphus's daughter.

Even before Descartes, the consequences of the so-called New Philosophy were becoming evident to many observers. In 1611, the poet John Donne wrote:

And New Philosophy calls all in doubt . . .
'Tis all in pieces, all coherence gone;
All just supply, and all Relation.

It was just five years since Shakespeare had the bastard Edmund proclaim, "Thou, nature, art my goddess." But the proponents of the New Philosophy could not have differed more from Shakespeare's villain in *King Lear*. For where Edmund delighted in the collapse of a traditional order into chaos, they looked to the apparent chaos of the universe and found order in universal laws that could be discovered through observation and experimentation.

CONCLUSION

Although, in the early seventeenth century, the "New Philosophy" mattered principally to what we would now call "intellectuals," it had implications that stretched far beyond the intellectual realm. In the following decades, its proponents would explore the way that laws of nature could be applied to change the face of the world, while beginning to think that the same process of discovery they had initiated in the physical world might have a counterpart in human society as well. In principal, therefore, it might be possible to develop forms of political and social engineering to overcome the uncontrolled, violent forms of competition that had seemed, at so many points between 1600 and 1640, on the point of entirely engulfing the continent.

In this sense, the proponents of the New Philosophy had much in common with the architects of Europe's emerging absolutist monarchies, who also sought to rein in unbridled competition and channel social and political activity into more rational, harmonious forms. Yet the forces of disorder were still far from being vanquished. In the mid-seventeenth century they would prompt additional explosions of civil strife across Europe. Indeed, the combination of new and continuing conflicts between 1640 and 1680 would seem, to some, to herald nothing less than the end of the world. Would the new political and intellectual techniques for ordering the world allow Europeans to overcome these challenges?

KEY TERMS

composite monarchies
(p. 411)

Little Ice Age (p. 411)

triangle trade (p. 415)

mercantilism (p. 415)

ship money (p. 419)

venality of office (p. 420)

Defenestration of Prague
(p. 426)

Edict of Restitution
(p. 428)

absolutism (p. 431)

intendants (p. 431)

Petition of Right (p. 432)

Charles I (p. 432)

Baroque (p. 433)

Republic of Letters (p. 435)

Francis Bacon (p. 438)

René Descartes (p. 438)

REVIEW QUESTIONS

1. What were the causes of the economic hardships in some areas of Europe and progress in others?

2. What obstacles did early European settlements in North America face?

3. How did new technologies and tactics change the nature of western warfare in the 1600s?

4. What changes in Catholicism and Protestantism led to an increasing control of women?

5. What developments led to the outbreak of the Thirty Years' War?

6. Why did the Thirty Years' War expand beyond Bohemia to involve Protestant and Catholic forces across Europe?

7. How did the Thirty Years' War promote the growth of royal absolutism?

8. Why did royal ministers emerge as such strong figures in this period?

9. How did developments in art and literature relate to political changes?

10. What were the key breakthroughs during the early Scientific Revolution?

CORE OBJECTIVES

After reading this chapter, you should have a solid understanding of the following core objectives. To strengthen your grasp of the core objectives, use the resources on the Student Site for The West.

- Analyze the environmental and economic changes that affected European society in the early seventeenth century.

- Describe the evolution of European states in the first half of the seventeenth century.

- Trace the changes in religious education and practices before the Thirty Years' War.

- Assess the political instability across Europe leading up to the Thirty Years' War.

- Evaluate the events, patterns, and consequences of the Thirty Years' War.

- Describe the artistic, intellectual, and scientific innovations of the early seventeenth century.

 GO TO **inQuizitive** TO SEE WHAT YOU'VE LEARNED—AND LEARN WHAT YOU'VE MISSED—WITH PERSONALIZED FEEDBACK ALONG THE WAY.

CHRONOLOGY

1639–1649
British civil wars

1643
Louis XIV inherits
the French throne

1648–1652
Fronde revolt in France

1648
Peace of
Westphalia

1649
Charles I beheaded

1651
Hobbes publishes
Leviathan

1650s
Frederick William consolidates
power in Prussia

1650s–1670s
Anglo-Dutch Wars

1653–1658
Oliver Cromwell rules
England as Lord Protector

1656
Mehmet Köprülü
appointed Grand Vizier
of Ottoman Empire

1659
Treaty of the
Pyrenees

1657–1666
Florence's Experimental Academy,
Britain's Royal Society, and France's
Royal Academy of Sciences founded

1660
Restoration of the
English monarchy
under Charles II

Ordering the World

NEW FORMS OF AUTHORITY AND KNOWLEDGE

1640–1680

1666
Great Fire destroys much of London

1672
Dutch "disaster year" leads to civil war
1672–1678
Louis XIV's Dutch War

The painting shows a scene so unexceptional as to be almost banal: two children playing cards, the gap-toothed girl grinning as she displays her winning ace. True, the Dutch artist Dirck Hals (1591–1656) probably intended the picture to bear some moral weight. Dutch Protestant culture frowned on gambling, and the children's apparently innocent merriness can be seen as dramatically heightening the contrast with the cards themselves, suggesting the unnerving ease with which such tempting instruments of perdition can ensnare even the least likely victims. Yet at the same time, the artist's skill in capturing childhood as a distinct stage of life—from the happily disheveled clothing and hair, to the relaxed poses, to the detail, taken entirely for granted, of a chair suitable only for a young child—tells against this dark interpretation. Only the most hard-hearted of observers could look at the painting and see nothing but the devil at work.

Such depictions of ordinary life—executed in brilliant detail, from the buttons on a dress to the sheen on the scales of a dead fish—pervade Dutch painting of the seventeenth century. More than any previous school of art, Dutch painters of the country's so-called Golden Age—from talented journeymen such as Dirck Hals to masters such as Rembrandt and Vermeer—devoted themselves to meticulous renderings of the world around them. The streets, canals, marketplaces, and taverns of Amsterdam and other Dutch cities; the rooms where women spun and cooked, and children played; the places of government

Children Playing Cards Dirck Hals's detailed picture of a mundane scene is a characteristically Dutch view into daily life in the mid-seventeenth century.

- What lasting changes were brought about by the British civil wars?
- What was the significance of civil strife in the continental states of western and eastern Europe?
- What new religious movements proved important in this period?
- How were Europeans beginning to rethink the foundations of political authority?
- How did the Peace of Westphalia represent a new direction for Europe?
- How did absolutism seek to establish order in state and society?
- How did Britain and the Netherlands foster new forms of political and economic organization?

and business and work—these are the settings Dutch painters preferred. Conventional artistic subjects such as biblical stories and classical mythology, while hardly absent, were pushed somewhat to the side.

In one sense, this attention to ordinary life owed a great deal to the Protestant Reformation. Whereas pre-Reformation Catholics had detected visible marks of the divine throughout the world—in miracles, relics, saints, and the Church, supposedly founded by Jesus himself—Protestants tended to imagine a starker division between the realm of fallen humanity and that of the all-powerful Creator. And seeing the latter as forbiddingly distant, they turned their attention back to the human realm, seeing it as their mission to *create* holiness around them in their daily lives. As an English preacher wrote, "Whatsoever our callings be, we serve the Lord Christ in them."

By the middle years of the seventeenth century, however, such attention to the ordinary functioning of the world had moved well beyond the bounds of any particular Christian confession. Increasingly, not just in art, but in everything from political philosophy and the continuing developments of the scientific revolution to the construction of new forms of monarchy, Europeans devoted remarkable new energy to describing and understanding the natural and social realms, and the ways they functioned, without reference to divine

intervention. They sought to uncover the laws that governed these realms and to discover how those laws could be manipulated. This project constituted, in a sense, the great theme of mid-seventeenth-century European culture and politics.

It was a project undertaken against considerable odds, for in the 1640s and 1650s much of Europe remained sunk in disorder. As in the earlier years of the century, it was the wasteful, destructive side of competition that seemed to have gained the upper hand. Civil wars flared in all areas of the continent, the Thirty Years' War sputtered to its conclusion, and the hopes of the despairing fed widespread belief in the imminent arrival of the Messiah. But the 1660s and 1670s saw, if not an era of peace and stability, nonetheless a definite retreat from the brink of continental anarchy. Wars continued—indeed, in some areas, intensified—and yet the very size and disciplined structures of the period's armies testified to the new power of European states to contain and monopolize violence, and to direct it to specific, limited targets. And Europeans grew increasingly confident that if they could come to understand and manipulate the laws of nature and society, then they could also, in the future, prevent the spasms of bloodshed they had all witnessed far too often. These are the themes of this chapter.

THE CIVIL WARS IN THE BRITISH ISLES (1639–1649)

The 1640s plausibly deserve the title of Europe's most disorderly decade. Among the areas that experienced civil conflict were the British Isles, France, the Iberian Peninsula, several Italian states, Ukraine, and the Ottoman Empire. In many of these areas, there was not one war but several, fought in different theaters and different periods. Meanwhile, nearly every major European power took part in international conflict. In some parts of the continent, the strife had relatively few long-term consequences, despite all the sound and fury it generated. But in other areas, it brought about truly radical change, and nowhere more than in the British Isles.

ORIGINS

Although the civil wars in the British Isles were not the costliest of these conflicts in lives lost, their long-term impact on European affairs was unparalleled. Only in Britain did the form of government change fundamentally, with the temporary replacement of the monarchy by a republic that claimed to derive its legitimacy from the will of the sovereign people. Only in Britain did successful rebels dare to put a monarch on trial and execute him. And only in Britain did political groups emerge—and briefly gain prominence—that not only imagined a millennial transformation of the world—one that would bring it closer to a state of holiness, and, perhaps to the end times—but sought to bring about this new phase of human history themselves through drastic political and social reforms that would inspire revolutionary movements for centuries thereafter.

In the 1620s and 1630s, events had given relatively little indication that Britain stood on the brink of such a remarkable upheaval. As we have seen, King Charles I frequently came into conflict with his parliaments. Yet the strife was no worse than what many other European monarchies of the period were experiencing. During the eleven-year period known as Charles's "personal rule," in which he governed without calling Parliament into session, he did not try to impose new taxes but resorted to the manipulation of older practices such as ship money to raise funds. Here again the British story resembled that of the other European states of the period. In France, for instance, the kings did without the representative body known as the Estates General for some 175 years after 1614. In keeping with the concepts of Jean Bodin, European monarchs increasingly saw their rule in terms of absolute "sovereignty," which, Bodin believed, belonged to the prince alone and could not be shared with the people's representatives. Such ideas suited Charles I, a man convinced of his divine right to rule and his superiority to other mortals. An elegantly mannered and cultivated king, Charles fit an emerging European model of "absolutist" monarchy. "Remember," he remarked on one occasion, "that Parliaments are altogether in my power."

By itself, Charles's move toward absolutism would probably not have caused a civil war, and might well have transformed Britain into a monarchy on the continental model. But in the 1630s, two other factors turned a bad situation disastrous: religion and conflict among the different kingdoms ruled by Charles. The king, whose French queen was a devout Catholic, rejected the more austere elements of Protestantism. He liked neither the doctrine of predestination of souls beloved of the Calvinists nor militant Protestant attempts to forge a more holy society by banning traditional forms of entertainment such as dancing and card-playing. His handpicked archbishop of Canterbury, William Laud, reintroduced sumptuous religious services that often included the use of incense and music ("smells and bells"), ornately decorated altars, and priests in elaborate costumes. Laud and Charles also gave permission for popular entertainments to take place on Sundays, including archery, dancing, vaulting, and the setting up of Maypoles. To the rigidly Calvinist English Protestants who were now going by the name of Puritans these moves signaled dangerous backsliding toward Catholicism. But far from trying to placate the Puritans, Charles and Laud persecuted them mercilessly. In response, the Puritans began to develop arguments for religious toleration.

INITIAL CONFLICTS (1637–1641)

The final factor contributing to civil war was conflict among the kingdoms that Charles ruled. In 1637, Charles demanded that the Church of Scotland adopt the Church of England's *Book of Common Prayer*. It was a dangerously provocative step in light of Scotland's long tendency toward Calvinist beliefs and a system of ecclesiastical government by councils of elders, known as Presbyterianism, which stood in contrast to the more sharply hierarchical structure of the Anglican Church, with its bishops and archbishops. The king's move provoked riots in Scotland, mass adherence to a proclamation of resistance called the Scottish "National Covenant," and, in 1639, the formation of a rebel army, which a year later invaded northern England. Therefore, 1639 marks the start of the British civil wars.

To rally support and money for defense against the rebel invasion, Charles had no choice but to call two new parliaments in quick succession. The second of them, the so-called Long Parliament, elected in the autumn of 1640, would remain assembled in one form or another for thirteen years (and reassemble briefly in 1660). This new Parliament was more radical than any of its predecessors. From the start, it was dominated by a group of fervent Puritans who dreamed of remaking both the English Church and English society in line with Calvinist ideals, and defending them from the machinations of the king and his principal advisers, Archbishop Laud and Thomas Wentworth, the earl of Strafford (1593–1641). They envisaged a simplified church structure, shorn of bishops, a liturgy purified of what they considered Catholic corruptions, and the introduction of strict controls over public morality.

Initially led by the talented country squire and financier John Pym (1584–1643), the Long Parliament quickly took steps to counteract what it considered the abuses of Charles's reign. It banned the use of ship money and other such expedients, and abolished the widely hated

Court of Star Chamber, a long-established body subservient to the King which met in secret and had passed harsh and arbitrary sentences against Puritans and others accused of defying royal authority. The parliament passed a Triennial Act, demanding that parliaments meet at least every three years instead of at the monarch's pleasure. It tried to move the Church of England in a Puritan direction by proposing the elimination of bishops. And it voted a bill of attainder condemning Wentworth to death without trial, which it defiantly passed on to the king for his signature. Remarkably, the earl himself urged Charles to sign it "for the preventing of such massacres as may happen by your refusal." After two days of agonized indecision, Charles agreed. Wentworth was beheaded. The king also agreed to the other measures Parliament had passed in hopes of preventing further conflict and convincing the parliament to raise funds for him.

Events, however, quickly overwhelmed Charles's hopes. Wentworth had served as governor of largely Catholic Ireland, and although he had not been popular there, his execution led to Irish fears that the militant Protestants

Irish Revolt A contemporary illustration accused Irish rebels of the brutal tactics against English Protestant settlers. Above, the rebels force the Protestants to jump off a bridge to their deaths; below, they massacre women.

now ascendant in Britain might try to impose their religion on their neighboring island by force. The result was a revolt by Irish Catholics in 1641 and the massacre of at least 2,000 Irish Protestants, beginning a series of conflicts that would tear Ireland apart through the rest of the decade. The Irish revolt in turn strengthened English Puritan fears of Catholicism and so contributed to further radicalization in Parliament and among its supporters. In late 1641, Parliament narrowly passed a list of grievances known as the Grand Remonstrance accusing the king of hundreds of further offenses. Puritans gained control of the government of the City of London (the capital's commercial and financial district) and its powerful paramilitary forces.

PARLIAMENTARY VICTORY (1642–1645)

In January 1642, Charles finally broke with the Long Parliament. In a dramatic scene, he personally led eighty soldiers into the House of Commons to arrest its leaders. But, forewarned, they had escaped down the Thames River. "I see the birds have flown," the king snapped. But less than a week later, having failed to secure London, Charles himself fled the city, eventually joined by some two-fifths of the members of Parliament. The remaining members began to raise an army, which clashed with royal forces in September 1642. Civil war within England had begun.

Over the next four and a half years, the British Isles fell prey to some of the worst violence they have ever known. The civil wars were not a modern conflict with unbroken fighting between uniformed armies along well-defined front lines. Nor did they resemble the indiscriminate slaughter of the Thirty Years' War. Large pitched battles were rare, and no towns suffered the merciless sacking that took place so often in seventeenth-century Germany. But the death toll among the combatants was still high, and the civilian population suffered greatly from hunger and disease.

The Parliamentarians (also known as Roundheads because of the short haircuts some of them favored) ultimately prevailed in the first phase of the conflict. They controlled London, which had vast commercial wealth, a tenth of the English population, and the apparatus of government (including the navy). They had an advantage in manpower, outnumbering the Royalists (who were often called Cavaliers) by three to two in several key encounters. They had, at crucial moments, the support of the Scots. And although the Parliamentarians suffered both from internal divisions and from the death of their leader, Pym, in 1643, Charles's forces were even more fragmented and hard to control.

In the winter of 1644–45, Parliament reorganized its own armed forces into the disciplined New Model Army, whose cavalry was commanded by a forceful Puritan member of Parliament from a gentry background, **Oliver Cromwell** (1599–1658). It was a radically new sort of armed force for Europe—one created to advance an ideological agenda rather than a social or national one. It had a more centralized organization than most European armed forces of the period, accepted only soldiers and officers committed to the Puritan cause, and promised that talent, not social standing, would determine promotion (its leaders included a brewer and a butcher). It made particularly effective use of light cavalry and practiced strict discipline within the ranks. In June 1645, at the battle of Naseby some 115 miles northwest of London, the New Model Army crushed the Royalists, and the next spring King Charles surrendered.

Area held by Parliament, early 1645
Area gained by Parliament, late 1645
Area held by Royalists, late 1645
✕ Battle

The British Civil Wars, 1641–1645

THE RADICAL TURN (1646–1649)

As yet, very few people in England had any thought of doing away with the monarchy. But over the next two years, the situation remained dangerously unstable. The leading voices in Parliament wanted to transform the Church of England into a Presbyterian Church close to the Scottish model. However, an increasingly powerful group within the parliamentary forces, known as the Independents, which enjoyed particular support from the radical New Model Army and Cromwell, favored a much looser structure for religious life. Building on earlier Puritan arguments, the Independents demanded religious toleration for all Christian groups, even Catholics. The Army proved fertile soil for the emergence of other sorts of radicalism as well. Demands emerged for the reform of Parliament along egalitarian lines, with an extension of the vote from wealthy social elites to the male middle classes. A particularly vocal group of soldiers, frustrated by the social conservatism of Cromwell and the parliamentary leaders, went even further. Known as the **Levellers**, they suggested, for the first time in European history, that class privileges be "leveled" and that *all* adult men have the right to vote. In an extraordinary series of debates at Army headquarters in Putney during the fall of 1647, the

Levellers pressed their case eloquently. One Army officer declared:

> For really I think that the poorest he that is in England hath a life to live, as the greatest he; and therefore truly, Sir, I think it clear, that every Man that is to live under a Government ought first by his own Consent to put himself under that Government; and I do think that the poorest man in England is not at all bound in a strict sense to that Government that he hath not had a voice to put Himself under.

The Levellers drew their ideas from the English parliamentary tradition stretching back to Magna Carta, not from any engagement with classical democracy. Their example would have lasting importance in English politics, providing inspiration for many later generations of reformers. At the time, though, they never gained more than minority support.

These tensions within the victorious parliamentary camp eventually triggered what amounted to a second civil war. The Scots and the English Presbyterian opponents of Cromwell now made common cause with Charles, who, though held prisoner by the New Model Army, pledged that he would accept a Presbyterian Church if restored to power. Much of the navy went over to him, and several regional insurgencies in his favor began. But once again the New Model Army proved a superior fighting force and prevailed over its opponents. In 1648, it forcibly expelled 270 of 470 members of Parliament from the House of Commons, including most of the English Presbyterians. The remaining members, known derisively as the Rump Parliament, convened a High Court of Justice that put Charles on trial and sentenced him to death.

On January 30, 1649, on a scaffold erected just outside the Banqueting House in London, where his father had watched *King Lear*, Charles was beheaded. Like another Shakespearean character, *Macbeth*'s Thane of Cawdor, "nothing in his life became him like the leaving it." In his last hours, Charles showed supreme cool and courage, and was hailed by his supporters as a martyr. Soon after the execution, the Rump Parliament abolished the House of Lords and the monarchy, and in May declared England a Commonwealth—the English translation of *res publica*, a reference to the ancient Roman republic. The exhausted population greeted this momentous change without enthusiasm, hoping mostly for an end to the bloodshed.

THE CONTINENTAL CIVIL WARS

After these dramatic events, many in England feared that the continental European powers might unite and launch an invasion force across the Channel to address this threat to the institution of monarchy. They particularly feared France, whose recently deceased king, Louis XIII, had been Charles's brother-in-law. But no such invasion took place, in large part because so much of the European continent was itself in the grip of civil wars.

THE FRONDE IN FRANCE (1648–1653)

France itself briefly seemed as if it might imitate the British example. By the early 1640s, the costs of participating in the Thirty Years' War had again put the country's finances under terrible strain. Following the deaths of Cardinal Richelieu and Louis XIII, the throne passed in 1643 to a child king, Louis XIV (r. 1643–1715), with the regency held by his unpopular mother, Anne of Austria. Advised by her lover and chief minister, Cardinal Jules Mazarin (1602–1661), Anne increased the level of direct taxes and resorted to a series of stopgap revenue-raising measures that took a particular toll on the city of Paris. These included fines on building houses in certain zones where construction was prohibited, and the suspension of salaries for judges in the Paris high court (*parlement*), whose jurisdiction covered one-third of the kingdom.

In response, the high court judges, who owned their offices as a form of property, began to act as leaders of a national opposition. "The country has been ruined these past ten years," one judge daringly declared in the presence of Mazarin and the queen regent in January 1648, referring to the widespread misery that the Thirty Years' War had inflicted on France. "Millions of innocent souls are obliged to live on black and oat bread…the glory of conquered provinces cannot nourish those who have no bread." Four months later, the levying of yet another new tax led the magistrates from the capital's various courts to join together into a new, self-appointed assembly, which demanded the lowering of taxes, the abolition of the royal agents known as *intendants* (who were increasingly taking on the role of provincial governors), and, most important, veto power for themselves over all new royal taxes. When after several months Mazarin attempted to arrest the

The Fronde In this mid-seventeenth century engraving, a crowd is gathered in a field on the outskirts of Paris to listen to a speech from a leader of the Fronde. He urges his audience to revolt against the tyranny of Cardinal Mazarin.

movement's leaders, in August 1648 the city of Paris rose in revolt, with commoners building barricades that blocked streets throughout the city. The royal family eventually fled from Paris in what became known as the revolt of the **Fronde**, after the French word for the slingshots used as weapons by the Parisian crowd.

If the revolt began with a bang, it soon faded to a confused whimper. A French army led by the king's cousin, the prince of Condé (1621–1686), besieged Paris and forced the leaders of the Fronde to sign a truce in 1649. There followed four years of intermittent conflict as the magistrates, the supporters of Anne and Mazarin, and an independent-minded Condé schemed and fought against each other. Mazarin and the queen became the objects of a ferocious pamphlet campaign waged by a variety of opponents, including "Frondeurs" hoping to rekindle the spirit of the initial revolt and weaken the monarchy. The works cast the Italian-born cardinal as a corrupt sexual deviant plotting to enslave the people. But Mazarin and the queen outlasted their opponents. The fourteen-year-old Louis XIV returned to Paris in October 1652, followed by Mazarin four months later, while Condé fled into exile.

At no moment in the revolt of the Fronde did a coherent challenge to the social and political order emerge. Unlike the English rebels, the leaders of the movement's various factions continued throughout to protest their undying loyalty to the divinely ordained monarch. In Bordeaux, on the Atlantic Coast, Condé helped spur a popular movement against the city's high court. It tried to enforce limits on food prices and rent, and to expand participation in the municipal government. But when the English Commonwealth sent envoys to the city, armed with French translations of Leveller pamphlets, in the hope of securing a military alliance against the French monarchy, they were met with puzzlement.

IBERIA AND ITALY (1640–1659)

The germ of civil war not only touched France but spread to the Habsburg lands as well, with some of the worst strife coming in the northeast Spanish region of Catalonia. It began in the 1630s with attempts by the central government in Madrid to extract additional revenues from the region in defiance of its traditional constitutional privileges. "Better that the Catalans should complain, than that we should all weep," chief minister Olivares sneered in 1639. But the complaints soon turned violent as peasants and laborers began to attack royal troops, leading to savage reprisals. In June 1640, a popular Catalan insurgent force took the Catalonian capital of Barcelona, murdered the viceroy and several other royal officials, and sacked the homes of wealthy citizens. But as in France, the uprising did not lead in the direction of permanent social or political change. The Catalan ruling elites quickly moved to reinforce their privileges. They also sought French aid, with the result that the province became a battlefield in the ongoing Franco-Spanish War. Peace only returned in 1659, at which point France permanently annexed a slice of Catalonia and the rest returned to Habsburg rule.

The Catalans did not do as well as the Portuguese, whose revolt against Spain in 1640 remained firmly under the control of the country's nobility. The new king of Portugal, John IV (r. 1640–1656), quickly established his authority, leading to full Portuguese independence. Revolts against the Spanish Habsburgs also took place in southern Italy. A popular movement briefly seized control of Naples in 1647 and proclaimed the city a republic before the Spanish suppressed the uprising.

UKRAINE AND POLAND-LITHUANIA (1648–1668)

The bloodiest civil war of the period occurred in the east, in the lands now known as Ukraine, between Poland-Lithuania and Russia. Throughout the early seventeenth century, Catholic Poland had been expanding its territory to the east and south, challenging the Orthodox Church (which had separated from Roman Catholicism

in the eleventh century) in these regions. Opposition to this expansion grew, especially among the Orthodox clans known as Cossacks, who had strong martial traditions. In early 1648, the charismatic **Bogdan Chmielnicki** (1595–1657) emerged as overall Cossack leader, forged an alliance with the Muslims from the Ottoman province of the Crimea (on the north shore of the Black Sea), and began a massive uprising against the Poles, whom he accused of betraying his people. The rebels particularly targeted Jews, who often managed estates for the Polish nobility. As many as 100,000 of them, a high percentage of the Jewish population of the region, were slaughtered in the greatest tragedy for European Jewry between the massacres of the late medieval period and the twentieth-century Nazi Holocaust. Tens or even hundreds of thousands of Polish Christians also perished. (Historians continue to dispute the numbers.)

Ukraine, 1648–1667

For a time, it seemed as if an independent Cossack state might take shape in Ukraine. Chmielnicki marched into Kiev in triumph in 1648 and proclaimed himself the ruler of "Rus," the medieval name for the state centered in the region. The Poles initially had no choice but to acknowledge his authority there and allowed him to impose Orthodox Christianity. But the war resumed in 1651 and ultimately forced Chmielnicki to seek protective overlords. After first threatening to sign an agreement with the Ottoman Empire, he found a Christian protector in the Russian tsar, who agreed to an alliance that guaranteed Cossack liberties in return for accepting Russian sovereignty and the right to impose taxes.

The entire episode hugely weakened Polish-Lithuania, which faced further challenges in the following decades. In a costly war with Russia between 1654 and 1667 the Poles were unable to exploit their military victories, and ended up ceding territory in Ukraine. And only a year after this war broke out, another contender for supremacy in northeastern Europe—Sweden—invaded Poland-Lithuania and rapidly conquered much of the western part of the country (the Poles referred to the invasion as the "Swedish Deluge"). Only the fact that Sweden was soon drawn into fighting with Russia and Denmark allowed the Poles to regain most of the lost ground.

THE OTTOMAN EMPIRE (1640–1656)

The Ottoman Empire also remained prey to instability in the 1640s and 1650s. It still claimed authority over vast territories: not just southeastern Europe, but much of the Middle East and North Africa as well. It was wealthy, with a capital city, Constantinople, larger than any other European city of the age. It had a relatively effective and flexible system of government, but it was still dangerously weak at the center. The reign of Sultan Ibrahim I ("the Mad") from 1640 to 1648 was marked by a costly failure to seize the Mediterranean island of Crete from the declining Venetian Republic, and by rampant corruption. Faced with demands for massive new bribes by the sultan, the empire's religious leadership made common cause with the powerful military order known as the Janissaries—elite household guards staffed mostly at this period by European Christians taken as slaves, converted to Islam, and subject to strict discipline. With their help, the sultan was deposed and soon strangled to death.

Ibrahim's six-year-old son took his place as Sultan Mehmet IV (r. 1648–1693). But political chaos continued, with thirteen grand viziers (prime ministers) in just eight years and a religious revolt in Anatolia (today, Asian Turkey) that nearly toppled the government. Finally, in 1656, the capable Albanian official Mehmet Köprülü (1575–1661) was appointed grand vizier. He quickly consolidated his own power, convinced the young sultan to devote himself principally to hunting, and won a series of decisive victories at sea against Venice and on land in Transylvania (in modern Romania) against the Austrian Empire. For a brief moment, the Ottoman Empire enjoyed stability and again emerged as a potent threat to the western powers. But here, too, the mid-seventeenth-century crisis brought about little permanent political change.

RELIGIOUS QUESTIONING

Against this background of continent-wide unrest and civil strife, messianic voices were heard. In widely separated areas of the continent, figures arose who claimed to know the will of God and promised that God would soon intervene to bring solace to the suffering. Some promised that the disorder of human affairs would be swept away entirely and replaced with a new, divine order.

MESSIANISM

In 1648, as the horrific news of Chmielnicki's massacres of Jews spread through Europe, a twenty-two-year-old Greek Jew named **Shabbetai Sevi** (1626–1676) heard the voice of God and decided he was the Messiah—the divinely appointed Savior of the world. Sevi was soon excommunicated by the Jewish community in Smyrna, but during the 1650s and early 1660s, he traveled throughout the Ottoman-ruled eastern Mediterranean to proclaim the coming of God's kingdom. When, in 1665, Sevi announced that the biblical prophecies would be fulfilled the following year, thousands of Jews throughout Europe began fasting and selling their possessions in preparation for the Messiah's reign and their return to their ancestral homeland of Israel, or Zion.

Eventually, Sevi made the mistake of challenging the authority of the sultan. On a visit to Constantinople, he was arrested and given the choice of death or conversion to Islam. He chose the latter and as news of the apostasy spread, his movement quickly collapsed. During his lifetime, though, Christian commentators tried to incorporate Sevi into their own millenarian prophecies, on the grounds that the return of Jesus would be preceded by the Jews' return to Zion.

Janissaries This Janissary's elite status as the sultan's guard is signaled by his rich attire and horse's equipment, both decorated with large feather plumes.

Britain itself saw more than its share of millennial activity during the turmoil of its civil wars. The Puritans believed firmly that the end of the world would come, but generally saw it as blasphemous to assert that it would do so in their own lifetimes. A small sect called the Fifth Monarchy Men, however, rose to the challenge. They claimed that the eternal monarchy of Jesus Christ would imminently be established, and that they themselves, as God's elect, should hold sovereign political power. Another even smaller group, called the Diggers, claimed that by abolishing private property and all forms of human dependence, they would lift the curse of Adam and bring human beings back to God. The Diggers set up a communal settlement in southern England, which the Puritan government forcibly closed. Meanwhile, the so-called Ranters declared that the millennium had actually arrived, releasing them from all morality, especially sexual morality. These groups were all tiny (for instance, in comparison with the Levellers), and drew their supporters from a variety of social backgrounds. But later generations of British radicals would find considerable inspiration in their actions and writings.

PROTESTANT AND CATHOLIC DISSENTERS

These small millenarian groups did not, for the most part, outlast the period of the civil wars. But the middle of the seventeenth century also saw, both in Britain and the European continent, the emergence of several non-millenarian currents of belief that would have a larger effect on the future of Christianity.

THE QUAKERS In Britain the most important of these were the **Quakers**. George Fox (1624–1691), the son of a weaver, began during the Civil Wars to preach the message that a piece of the divine—the "inner light"—dwells within all souls. The idea drew on tensions in Christianity that went all the way back to Jesus's raising of the spirit over the letter of Old Testament law. Fox also drew on the radical challenges to spiritual authority formulated in the Reformation, rooted in Luther's insistence that Christians should read the Scriptures themselves. But Fox's ideas had unprecedented social and institutional consequences. He and his followers rejected the very idea of a clergy, preferring to come together as equals in "meetings" of "friends" that included women. They refused to engage in traditional forms of social deference or to take oaths, dressed in plain, drab clothes, and, most controversially, renounced armed force under any circumstances, refusing to fight

for their country. (Quakers have numbered among the most prominent "conscientious objectors" to military service in Britain and the United States down to the present day.) Despite persecution by successive English governments, the Quakers survived. Later in the century one of their leaders, William Penn (1644–1718), would found the Pennsylvania colony in America, ensuring the spread of Quakerism beyond the British Isles. Their egalitarianism and aversion to violence and persecution in all its forms led many Quakers to oppose slavery. Some of the earliest, most prominent leaders of anti-slavery movements of Britain and the United States were Quakers.

THE JANSENISTS Catholic Europe did not experience the same sort of messianism as the Jewish and Protestant worlds. Yet neither did it avoid turmoil, despite all the efforts the Church had made over the century since the Council of Trent to assert stronger control over its clergy and their congregations. In fact, in the middle of the seventeenth century, the Church's stance on the differences between Catholic and Protestant belief provoked such a strong reaction that some observers feared a new schism, similar to the Reformation. Whereas, Luther, and particularly Calvin, had stressed the utter sinfulness of mankind, and therefore the inability of any person to achieve salvation by good works, Jesuit theologians claimed that humans enjoyed a much larger degree of free will in the matter. But in doing so, they seemed to many to contradict the writings of Saint Augustine which sought to reconcile free will with God's infinite power and foresight, and even to challenge long-agreed interpretations of scripture.

The reaction to these developments occurred above all in France and the Low Countries, among a group of Catholics known as the **Jansenists** (for Cornelius Jansen, an influential Catholic bishop in the Spanish Netherlands). They criticized many aspects of the Catholic Reformation: the overly lavish, sensual decoration of Baroque churches; the "laxity" with which the Jesuits sought converts overseas; and the practice of "frequent communion" that allowed the faithful to shuffle off the burdens of sin on a weekly basis. Like the Calvinists, the Jansenists stressed both the depravity of humanity and its inability to know the plans of a distant and disapproving deity. But unlike the Calvinists, they counseled that where possible people should withdraw from the world to lives of ascetic deprivation and penance, similar to what monastic movements in Catholicism had long advocated for members of their orders. The Jansenists' writings appealed mostly to clerics and a small set of literate noble and middle-class laypeople. But their very existence terrified powerful interests in the

Jansenists In 1662, a French painter made this portrait of his daughter (right), a Jansenist nun, with the mother superior of her community. The sparse scene and somber, reverent attitude of the nuns speak to the ascetic and devoted values the Jansenists sought to uphold.

Catholic Church, who knew all too well the dangers of religious disputes and strove to suppress Jansenism.

These examples of religious fracturing throughout Europe, despite the obvious differences between them, did have some tendencies in common. They all involved attempts to undermine established religious authorities—whether the rabbinic ones of the eastern Mediterranean attacked by Sabbatai Sevi, the Anglican ones deemed unnecessary by the Quakers, or the Catholic hierarchy criticized by the Jansenists. Each sought to promote a more direct relationship between individual believers and God. And each stressed, in different ways, the difficulty of knowing God's will, whether because of his distance from a sinful humanity or because of his fundamentally mysterious nature. And so this moment in religious history, despite provoking fears of fanaticism and schism, did not lead to religious divides like those of the Reformation.

CATHOLIC DISCIPLINE AND RELIGIOUS WOMEN

Despite these new challenges, the established churches remained powerful—particularly the resurgent Catholic Church, which had recovered considerable territory in Germany despite the setbacks of the Thirty Years' War.

The attempts to strengthen Catholic religious institutions continued apace in the mid-seventeenth century and had particular implications for the roles of women in the Church.

THE URSULINE ORDER The Catholic Reformation had contradictory effects on women. On the one hand, it had spurred the creation of new women's religious orders such as the Ursulines, dedicated to work among the poor. Yet over time, suspicion grew in the male Church hierarchy over allowing the female members of such orders to live and work freely in the midst of secular society. To better control them, the Church transformed most of the orders into cloistered orders of nuns. By the mid-seventeenth century, Ursuline nuns mostly lived behind convent walls and could not even speak with nonreligious men except under strictly supervised conditions, generally from behind the bars of a grille.

Yet a few groups of religious women managed to escape these disciplinary strictures. The Daughters of Charity, founded by Saint Vincent de Paul (1581–1660) and Saint Louise de Marillac (1591–1660), the illegitimate daughter of a French nobleman, lived in small, non-cloistered urban communities that sustained themselves by taking in sewing, spinning, and laundry. Their members ministered to the sick and ran schools for poor girls. Formally recognized by the papacy as a confraternity, or lay religious organization, in 1668, the Daughters expanded significantly over the next half century, eventually establishing more than 250 separate communities throughout Europe.

Religious Women In this seventeenth-century engraving, nuns serve hot food to the patients of the Hôtel-Dieu hospital in Paris, an example of the vast array of charitable work undertaken by religious women of the period.

MARIE GUYART The spiritual satisfaction that such work could bring to ordinary women shows through in the life of Marie Guyart, better known as Marie of the Incarnation (1599–1672). Born in western France to a wealthy baker, she married at age seventeen and was widowed two years later. Over the following decade, she grew more and more fervent in her religious devotion. To scourge herself of sin, she whipped herself with nettles, wore chains and a hairshirt under her clothing, and slept on a plank. She prayed intensely, did charitable work, and found release and joy in confession and absolution.

Marie had visions of Jesus Christ and dreamed of

becoming a nun. To this end, she even tried to deny her young son tenderness, so he would not miss her when she finally entered a convent. She did so when he was just twelve, joining the Ursuline Order and effectively abandoning him. Yet even this step was not enough for her. Like many notable Catholic figures before her, she longed for Christian martyrdom, and courted it by traveling to the newly founded, precarious French colony in Canada and helping to instruct the Indians there:

> I saw, in inner certainty, demons triumphing over those poor souls, ravishing them from the domain of Jesus Christ ... I could not bear it. I embraced all these poor souls, I held them in my breast ... And the Holy Spirit, which possessed me, led me to say to the Eternal father, "... I am learned enough to teach of [Christ] to all the nations. Give me a voice powerful enough to be heard at the ends of the earth."

In 1639, Marie and several other religious women founded an Ursuline monastery in Quebec, and schools for Indian girls. She spent the next thirty-three years there, until her death.

ORDER THROUGH REASON

In the twenty-first century, "faith" is often opposed to "reason" and "science." Seventeenth-century Europeans, however, did not think in these terms. The religious ferment of the times in no way precluded the continuous development of rationalist, skeptical, scientific thought. Many thinkers we now remember as "scientific" were also fervent believers in the literal word of scripture. Christian churches did not condemn rationalist philosophy per se, but rather ideas that they believed contradicted their teachings, as we have seen in the case of Galileo. Yet even if the century's most advanced thought did not necessarily challenge traditional religious authority, it ultimately provided those who would mount such challenges with powerful intellectual tools.

HOBBES'S *LEVIATHAN*

In 1651, two years after the execution of Charles I, a book appeared in London with the curious title *Leviathan: Or the Matter, Forme and Power of a Commonwealth Ecclesiastical and Civill.* Long and difficult, it began with a detailed consideration of how the mind works and concluded with a long section entitled "The Kingdom of Darkness." But

Hobbes's Leviathan The original 1651 frontispiece of *Leviathan* provides a powerful visual representation of Hobbes's characterization of the state. The body of the sovereign is comprised of all the people of the state, while his twin authorities—the military sword and the ecclesiastical bishop's crook—loom over the land spread before him.

what immediately drew the attention of readers was the new theory of political authority that the book presented.

According to the author, the sixty-three-year-old **Thomas Hobbes** (1588–1679), humans living in a "natural condition," without the order imposed by a state and its laws, inevitably fall into bloody competition for limited resources— "a warre ... of every man against every man." Such violence made any sort of human social development impossible and, in Hobbes's memorable phrase, rendered "the life of man, solitary, poore, nasty, brutish and short." These words reflected Hobbes's horror at the period's civil strife, and in particular the near dissolution of the English state. (He himself spent the years from 1640 to 1651 in self-imposed exile in Paris.) But Hobbes then took a crucial step forward by suggesting that political authority initially arose as a solution to this state of affairs. People living in a state of nature entered into a "covenant," or contract, with each other, by which they surrendered their natural rights to a sovereign. In return, they received his protection and agreement to act on their behalf. The frontispiece of the book showed the members of a state coming together to form a single sovereign body.

Leviathan offered something to shock nearly all readers. Despite Hobbes's long sections on religion and earnest professions of faith, devout Christians recoiled from his secular account of the origins of sovereign political power. They also criticized him for limiting political obedience to subjects' actions, rather than insisting on conformity of beliefs, thus providing a rationale for toleration of dissent. And Hobbes's insistence that sovereign power depended on the initial consent of the governed shocked defenders of monarchy. More radical political voices, meanwhile, called him an apologist for royal tyranny. They rejected his claim that the transfer of rights from individuals to a sovereign was irrevocable and nearly total, leaving the governed no right to overturn an unjust ruler. In 1666, the House of Commons denounced *Leviathan* as a book that "tend[ed] to atheism, blasphemy and profaneness."

Despite the condemnation it aroused at the time, Hobbes's idea of a "social contract" would become one of the most important themes in the history of political philosophy, and *Leviathan* has become recognized as a founding text of modern political science. Its comprehensive theory largely provided the basic framework in which generations of later thinkers would try to understand political life. Many later secular thinkers discussed Hobbes and tried to refute him. Christian authors offered their own competing theories of politics in the mid-seventeenth century, but none of them had anything like Hobbes's enduring influence.

The power of Hobbes's work came above all from the fact that he approached politics in much the way the figures of the scientific revolution approached the physical universe. Just like them, he broke with classical and medieval theories of a preexisting, transcendent order in the universe. He too saw politics as a realm that obeyed fundamental, regular laws that could be observed or deduced from first principles. It was no accident that he began the work with an account of the operations of the mind and body that read like a work of anatomy, for *Leviathan* was a work of anatomy—the anatomy of the body politic. And it therefore offered the hope that the body politic's disorders could find a scientific cure, just like medical disorders. In the political context of the mid-seventeenth century, this was a powerful message. Could Europe finally escape from its seemingly endless cycles of turmoil and violence? To answer this question in the affirmative, as Hobbes did, meant abandoning traditional, religiously based theories of authority in favor of new theories based on reason—a leap into the unknown that few Europeans, as yet, were willing to make.

BARUCH SPINOZA

Hobbes had the most direct and immediate influence, but he was not the only author of the period to formulate ideas that defied prevailing Christian notions of politics and society. Another was his younger contemporary **Baruch Spinoza** (1632–1677), who, like him, read deeply in the scientific works of the time and studied the new scientific methods described above. Born in Amsterdam to a Jewish family descended from Portuguese exiles, Spinoza worked much of his adult life as a lens grinder, but eventually devoted himself full time to philosophy. His work, mostly written in Latin, was dense and difficult, but nonetheless aroused enough controversy to earn condemnations from Catholic, Protestant, and Jewish authorities alike.

Baruch Spinoza A mid-seventeenth-century portrait of the radical thinker.

Central to Spinoza's work is the idea that the universe is not divided between matter and spirit but consists of a single basic substance. This idea challenged Descartes's dualist philosophy and the basic Christian distinction between body and spirit. Furthermore, Spinoza maintained, everything in the universe is determined by an infinite chain of cause and effect. The true relations between things can be discovered only by reason, employing scientific observation, precise mathematical measurement, and logic. Spinoza wrote of a God, but his identification of God with the operations of the universe as a whole, and his refusal of the matter/spirit distinction, led his contemporaries to charge that he was really an atheist—at a time when atheism remained, in all European states, a crime.

Although Spinoza wrote extensively on ethics, he did not develop an explicit, formal system of politics in the manner of Hobbes. What he did write on politics, however, had even more corrosive implications than *Leviathan*. Spinoza advocated a political system in which most of the adult male population could vote for their rulers, calling it the "most natural form of state, approaching most closely to that freedom which Nature grants to every man." And while, like Hobbes, he defended the individual conscience, proclaiming that "everyone is by absolute natural right master of his own thoughts," he then went further and asserted a limited freedom of expression: "Utter failure will attend any attempt in a state to force men to speak only as prescribed by the sovereign despite their different and opposing opinions." Yet he also supported the right of states to impose forms of outward religious conformity on its subjects if this was necessary to ensure civil peace.

Spinoza was read in many different, often contradictory ways, and critics frequently used "Spinozism" as a blanket term for unorthodox beliefs. His works nonetheless helped inspire a current of radical thinking, particularly about the nature of the divine, that would later flow into the eighteenth-century Enlightenment.

BLAISE PASCAL

Another author of the period illustrated even more sharply how the confluence of the scientific revolution and new religious thought could contribute to fresh ways of thinking about society. **Blaise Pascal** (1623–1662), the son of a French tax collector, gained a reputation in his youth as a mathematician and made important contributions to probability theory and the study of fluids, pressure, and

Blaise Pascal Pascal's willingness to challenge conventional belief is hinted at in this mid-seventeenth-century portrait.

vacuum. In his twenties, he became an enthusiastic devotee of Jansenism, writing bitingly witty attacks on the Jesuits that the royal administration suppressed. Pascal died young but left an extraordinary, incomplete work called *Pensées* (*Thoughts*), which he intended as a defense of the Christian faith. It included a famous declaration that humans had nothing to lose by betting on the existence of God ("Pascal's Wager") and poetic meditations on the universe. "The eternal silence of these infinite spaces terrifies me," Pascal wrote, in an astonishing vision of a universe without end.

Pascal also wrote many passages that applied withering skepticism to conventional beliefs about society and the limits of human knowledge. For instance, he skewered the supposedly natural differences between national cultures, writing "We see neither justice nor injustice which does not change its nature with change in climate....Three degrees of latitude reverse all jurisprudence; a meridian decides the truth. Fundamental laws change after a few years of possession;...A strange justice that is bounded by a river! Truth on this side of the Pyrenees, error on the other side." Passages like this could have the effect of a

revelation, showing readers the essentially arbitrary and contingent character of arrangements they took as "natural" and even God-given.

POULAIN DE LA BARRE AND EARLY FEMINISM

In the 1670s, another French scholar—who remained largely unknown until the twentieth century—showed how such systematic, scientific skepticism could challenge even apparently fixed features of the social order. François Poulain de la Barre (1647–1725), a follower of Descartes, applied this skepticism to what we now think of as gender roles and produced a trio of works that asserted the equality of women to men. In a Pascalian vein of casting familiar subjects in new light, Poulain claimed that when it came to men and women's intellectual capacities, past philosophers had "attributed to nature a distinction that originates in custom." Grounding his arguments historically, he pointed out that customs changed over time and that "civil society," at present "governed and ordered by the male sex ... has not always and everywhere been organized in the same way."

Bringing in what we would now call anthropological evidence from outside Europe, Poulain insisted that despite European conventional wisdom, pregnancy and childbirth did not necessarily bar women from useful employment. At times in his work, Poulain even extended his arguments from gender to questions of race and social class. Were "Turks, Barbarians and Savages" less capable of learning than Europeans? In fact, "these peoples are human beings like us, with the same abilities, and ... if educated, they could equal us in any respect." Poulain's work—and a handful of other texts from the period that also deserve the label "proto-feminist"—had no immediate effect on European social practices, which continued to limit women's options for education and work. But they indicated clearly that new, skeptical, egalitarian forms of thinking about society had become possible and might eventually lead to real change.

A woman, who offered contemporaries a good illustration of Poulain's arguments for equality was Margaret Cavendish (1623–1673). An English aristocrat, she wrote plays, an

Margaret Cavendish In a 1650 portrait, Margaret Cavendish wears the elegant ermine robe and coronet to which she was entitled as the Duchess of Newcastle, her gaze boldly meeting the viewer's.

GENDER ROLES IN SEVENTEENTH-CENTURY ENGLAND

Opportunities for women remained limited in the seventeenth century. However, the growing interest in philosophy and science meant that the daughters of the elite often received a thorough education in all branches of human knowledge. A few continued on to careers as writers and scientists, corresponding with men of letters and writing their own poems, novels, and even scientific treatises.

Margaret Cavendish, the Duchess of Newcastle-upon-Tyne in northeastern England, was one of the better-known female intellects of the seventeenth century. She corresponded with Hobbes, Descartes, and other notable thinkers, and she was the author of a number of works of poetry, speculative fiction, philosophy, science, and drama. In *The World's Olio* (1655), Cavendish reflects on the differences between the genders and on women's capacity for knowledge.

And though it seem to be natural, that generally all Women are weaker than Men, both in Body and Understanding, and that the wisest Woman is not so wise as the wisest Man, wherefore not so fit to Rule; yet some are far wiser than some men, like Earth; for some Ground, though it be Barren by Nature, yet, being well mucked and well manured, may bear plentifull Crops, and sprout forth diverse sorts of Flowers, when the fertiller and richer Ground shall grow rank and corrupt, bringing nothing but gross and stinking Weeds, for want of Tillage; So Women by Education may come to be far more knowing and learned, than some Rustick and Rude-bred men. Besides, it is to be observed, that Nature hath Degrees in all her Mixtures and Temperaments, not only to her servile works, but in one and the same Matter and Form of Creatures, throughout all her Creations.

Again, it is to be observed, that although Nature hath not made Women so strong of Body, and so clear of understanding, as the ablest of Men, yet she hath made them fairer, softer, slenderer, and more delicate than they, separating as it were the finer parts from the grosser, which seems as if Nature had made Women as pure white Manchet,[1] for her own Table, and Palat, where Men are like coarse household Bread which the servants feed on; and if she hath not tempered Womens Brains to that height of understanding, nor hath put in such strong Species of Imaginations, yet she hath mixed them with Sugar of sweet conceits; and if she hath not planted in their Dispositions such firm Resolutions, yet she hath sowed gentle and willing Obedience, and though she hath not filled the mind with such Heroick Gallantry, yet she hath laid in tender

Affections, as Love, Piety, Charity, Clemency, Patience, Humility, and the like; which makes them neerest to resemble Angells, which are the perfectest of all her Works; where men by their Ambitions, Extortion, Fury, and Cruelty, resemble the Devill.

QUESTIONS FOR ANALYSIS

1. How does Cavendish compare women to men?
2. According to Cavendish, what can women contribute to human knowledge?
3. What can we learn about seventeenth-century conventions regarding gender, femininity, and women's roles from this excerpt?

[1] **manchet:** the highest-quality bread

Source: *Paper Bodies: A Margaret Cavendish Reader,* eds. Sylvia Bowerbank and Sara Mendelson (Peterborough: 2000), 141–42.

autobiography, and also six books on science, grounded in her own research in alchemy. She frequently defended the right of women to write, insisted they could do so as well as men, and pleaded for them to be judged on their merit: "Many of our Sex may have as much wit, and be capable of Learning as well as men, but since they want Instructions, it is not possible they should attain to it." Indeed, most women lacked the advantages that enabled Cavendish to contribute to the arts and sciences in this period.

SCIENCE, EXPERIMENTALISM, AND THE STATE

This flowering of skeptical thought took place against the background of the scientific revolution that had begun in the early years of the seventeenth century. In the middle of the century this revolution deepened, mainly through the use of special instruments that natural philosophers continued to develop in close partnership with skilled artisans. Blaise Pascal, for instance, had a primitive barometer carried up a mountain in 1648 to show that the weight of air varied at different elevations. A few years later, the Anglo-Irish aristocrat Robert Boyle (1627–1691) devised a special air pump that created a near-vacuum, and used it to demonstrate both the phenomenon of air pressure and the mathematical relationship between the pressure and volume of a gas at constant temperature (Boyle's Law). The Dutch tradesman Antonie van Leeuwenhoek (1632–1723) invented the microscope (or at least made crucial improvements in its design), and in the 1670s made the first observations of bacteria and other organisms invisible to the naked eye.

Just as important, the middle of the century marked the moment at which western European governments and social elites fully grasped the practical implications of the new science and created institutions to support and control it. Florence led the way with its Experimental Academy in 1657, followed by Britain's Royal Society in 1660 and France's Royal Academy of Sciences in 1666. These new bodies provided alternatives to the universities as sites of learning. While most European universities still concentrated on training theologians, lawyers, and doctors, these new societies emphasized the production of new knowledge. They not only hosted lectures and demonstrations but also—starting with the Royal Society in 1665—published journals to make the results of scientific research known as widely as possible. The societies immediately came to play a key role in the validation of scientific research. Leeuwenhoek, for instance, leaped to prominence when the Royal Society's journal published his account of his observations of micro-organisms in 1673. And when his claims about bacteria met with disbelief (could an ordinary drop of water really swarm with animals too small for the eye to see?), the Society sent observers to evaluate his work in person, declared it valid, and offered him a membership in its ranks. Over the next fifty

Scientific Academies In 1666, Louis XIV's adviser Jean-Baptiste Colbert suggested that the king create a Royal Academy of Sciences. In this grand painting of the following year, Colbert presents the members of the new academy to the king. They are surrounded by tools of their trade—globes, maps, and books.

years, Leeuwenhoek sent more than 500 letters recounting his observations to Europe's leading scientific societies. The new societies and publications also strengthened ties among scholars in the "republic of letters."

Although the societies promoted the new science, they would never have approved of the radical speculations of a Spinoza or a Poulain. After all, they were chartered—and, in some cases, lavishly supported—by national governments. Their memberships were dominated by social elites, as exemplified by Boyle, the son of one of Ireland's largest noble landowners. The bylaws of the French Academy of Sciences stated that "in the meetings there will never be a discussion of the mysteries of religion or the affairs of state," and the other national bodies observed similar caution. They helped enforce "gentlemanly" forms of behavior among their members and in the Republic of Letters at large. For all their efforts, they could not prevent the scientific method, and the systematic skepticism they promoted, from being applied in ways that they themselves disapproved of and to subjects that they considered off limits. Still, whatever their radical potential, in the mid-seventeenth century itself, they mostly helped promote order and stability.

MAKING PEACE: CONSTRUCTING A NEW INTERNATIONAL ORDER AFTER THE THIRTY YEARS' WAR

Order and stability were also the goals of most European political action in the middle of the century. Monarchs and ministers, whether inspired by Hobbesian social contract theory or by more traditional Christian concerns for peace, had as their most important goal ending the anarchic bloodshed that had convulsed the continent since the start of the Thirty Years' War in 1618. To a remarkable extent, they met with success. By the early 1650s the sheer level of violence in Europe had begun to diminish significantly.

THE PEACE OF WESTPHALIA (1645–1648)

In diplomacy, the great event was the end of the massively destructive Thirty Years' War and the foundation of a new international order to prevent anything like it from happening again. As we have seen, the 1630s had been marked by titanic struggles between the armies of the Catholic Habsburg dynasty on the one side, and, on the other, a coalition that included Protestant Sweden and Catholic France. In the early 1640s the course of the war, which remained enormously destructive, turned decisively against the Habsburgs. The Swedes again sent their armies deep into Germany and won a pivotal victory at Breitenfeld in 1642, the site of their earlier victory in 1631. A brief war with Denmark then distracted them, but by 1644 Danish strength collapsed entirely. The Swedes then pushed south again, all the way to Bohemia, while allies from Transylvania invaded Hungary. Meanwhile, French forces secured the right bank of the Rhine River while also defeating Catholic Bavaria. By 1645, the Habsburgs had been pushed far enough onto the defensive to enter into serious peace negotiations.

These negotiations took place in the German state of Westphalia between 1645 and 1648 and marked a turn in the history of European diplomacy. Thousands of delegates came from no fewer than sixty-six states belonging to the Holy Roman Empire and sixteen other independent European states. (Roughly 200 German states had participated in the war.) Many of the negotiators had little diplomatic experience and relied on guidance from seasoned Venetian and papal professionals. They spent months simply establishing the ground rules for their talks, including particularly the ceremonial honors they would pay one another.

Nonetheless, the treaties that emerged from the peace talks in 1648—the **Peace of Westphalia**—were carefully written and elaborate: the treaty between France and the Holy Roman Empire contained 128 separate articles. And they had ambitious aims. In theory, they meant to establish a "Christian, general, and permanent peace," and although few negotiators believed they could really do so, they did at least hope to set up a durable structure for containing future conflict and managing international affairs. This structure would be based on the principle of respect for the sovereignty of individual states. With Westphalia, in short, the parties to the Thirty Years' War rejected the ancient dream of a united Europe and a united Christendom. In its place came a vision of a continent of independent, secular states existing in a balanced constellation of power.

These "Westphalian" principles would help guide European international relations until the mid-twentieth century. They did not, of course, prevent new wars. They did not even end the war between France and Spain, which dragged on for another eleven years. But the idea of peace

Possessions, 1648
- Danish
- Dutch
- French
- Austrian Habsburg
- Spanish Habsburg
- Swedish
- Boundary of Holy Roman Empire

The Peace of Westphalia, 1648 The peace settled many of the territorial disputes of the Thirty Years' War: France now controlled areas of Alsace and Lorraine; Sweden acquired West Pomerania on the Baltic; and the Netherlands gained independence from the Habsburg territories in the Low Countries. The Spanish Habsburgs still controlled territory across Europe, but the war and its outcome had reduced their power.

conferences that would settle major existing disputes, and reestablish a balance of power, provided the precedent for a series of conferences that only ended with the one at Versailles in 1919, following World War I.

The Westphalia treaties also confirmed the major territorial and political changes of the war. France received formal control over new German-speaking territories in Lorraine and Alsace, which had previously belonged to the Holy Roman Empire, and solidified its position on the Rhine. Sweden gained Western Pomerania, giving it a foothold on the southern shore of the Baltic Sea. Borders changed for many German states. The peace also confirmed the independence of the Netherlands from the Habsburg Empire, thereby ending the eighty years' struggle of the Dutch for self-determination, and reducing the empire's size. The treaties helped, overall, to strengthen and streamline the empire's formal constitutional structure.

THE SLOW WANING OF RELIGIOUS VIOLENCE

As for the continent's religious divisions, the Peace of Westphalia confirmed the principle worked out nearly a hundred years earlier in the Peace of Augsburg: that the religion of the state follows the religion of the prince. In some areas of Europe, Catholic, Lutheran, and Calvinist minorities gained a limited degree of legal toleration, particularly regarding private worship. Jews and Orthodox Christians reaped no such benefits, however. Nor did the peace settlement mark an end to the violence of the Reformation. Large-scale, religiously inspired bloodshed between Catholics and Protestants, far from ceasing in 1648, flared up repeatedly over the following sixty years, both within and between many European states.

Yet the expression of intra-Christian violence in warfare on a continental scale had already ended *before* 1648, in the course of the Thirty Years' War itself. The alliance of Protestant states with Catholic France may have caused a scandal on both sides in the 1630s; but by the late 1640s, the combatants had come to take it for granted. The Westphalia treaties were drawn up between sovereign states, not between religious alliances. The war certainly played a decisive role in checking the spread of Protestantism. Whereas half of western Europe had lived under Protestant rule in 1590, a century later only a fifth of it did, with some of the most dramatic changes coming in the Habsburg lands. But at some point in the chaos and bloodshed of the Thirty Years' War, the major states of Europe finally gave up the dream of waging large-scale religious crusades on European soil.

CONTROL OF POWER For all these reasons, international politics in Europe after Westphalia took on a fundamentally new shape. Europeans increasingly saw the greatest threat to peace and stability as coming not from religious fervor, but from two other sources. First, there were those states whose excessive ambitions threatened the continent's overall balance of power. International alliances in the late seventeenth and eighteenth centuries would most often form not to protect coreligionists, or even to promote dynasties (although dynastic alliances remained important), but to restrain these ambitious states, France above all.

Second, there were the uncontrolled rampages of marauding soldiery that had caused so much of the war's devastation. *Simplicissimus*, a novel published in 1668 by Hans von Grimmelshausen (1621–1676), recounted these wartime atrocities in horrific detail. This and other postwar literary works testified to a new sensibility that refused to see large-scale, casual slaughter as an unavoidable part of war. In the major states, rulers tried to rely less than in the past on mercenaries or autonomous military contractors like Albrecht von Wallenstein. They strove to incorporate native and mercenary regiments alike into unified, uniform-wearing forces that fit into a well-defined chain of command—in other words, state armies. Gustavus Adolphus had set a powerful example in the 1630s with his Swedish force that numbered roughly 175,000 men. But within a few decades, France would field armies more than twice this size, organized into regiments and commanded by nobles who held their commissions from the king. Increasingly, those who wrote on the laws of war and peace focused less on what made a war just or unjust in the first place, than on the just or unjust *conduct* of war.

And so, although warfare continued after Westphalia, it did so with less destruction, and the contending powers generally fought for more limited and well-defined aims. The Protestant states of Britain and the Netherlands, for instance, clashed repeatedly from the 1650s through the 1670s. However, each of the Anglo-Dutch Wars was short and waged mostly at sea, in large part for commercial stakes. An English general, in defending the Navigation Acts by which the English sought to prevent Dutch ships from carrying goods to and from England, crudely asserted: "The Dutch have too much trade, and the English are resolved to take it from them." Yet the English failed to impose their will on the Netherlands. Both the Dutch Republic and France greatly improved their international positions in the middle of the seventeenth century. The Dutch reconfirmed their place in the constellation of European powers while increasing their naval and mercantile strength. The French, despite having to deal with the chaos of the Fronde, were rewarded for their interventions in German affairs with the consolidation of their eastern frontier.

But the period also had significant losers. Denmark, defeated once by the Habsburgs and once by Sweden, never again played a major international role in European affairs. Poland, torn apart by the Chmielnicki rebellion, lost territory to Russia and sank into political paralysis. Most important, Spain proved unable to regain its dominant position in Europe following the revolts in Catalonia and Italy, and the loss of Portugal. Instead, during the continuing warfare of the 1650s, it lost territory to France both in Catalonia and the Spanish Netherlands. The Treaty of the Pyrenees in 1659 marked Spain's eclipse as a major power on the continent. Its overseas empire, however, which still included vast territories in the Americas and stretched all the way to the Philippines, remained of crucial international importance.

THE ABSOLUTIST STATES

The search for political stability took European states in two broadly different directions. On the continent, the major monarchies for the most part followed the absolutist pattern set earlier in the century by ministers like Richelieu and Olivares. They pursued four major objectives: the further consolidation of royal authority, the weakening or elimination of independent political institutions, an assertion of greater state control over broad areas of social and economic life, and the transformation of the nobility from autonomous political actors to partners in a greater royal enterprise. The two great maritime powers of Britain and the Netherlands moved in a different direction. They experienced continuing political turmoil and a much less powerful role for the state. Commercial wealth in both countries helped shape new sorts of social relations and social institutions independent of the state. Overseas empire and trade had far greater importance in their cultures and politics than was the case in "absolutist" Europe, at least outside of Iberia.

DENMARK AND BRANDENBURG

The model absolutist power was not any of the larger monarchies, but tiny Denmark. The country had not only emerged badly battered from the Thirty Years' War, but also struggled with the exceptionally harsh winters of the Little Ice Age, in which the Baltic Sea itself sometimes froze over in part. Two unsuccessful campaigns against Sweden in 1657–60, as part of a larger northern alliance, only increased the pressures on the Danish government. King Frederick III (r. 1648–1670), a modest and reserved man, did not seem the sort to exploit these disasters to bring about major political change. But in 1660, advised by his brother-in-law Hannibal Sehestad (1609–1666), he managed to forge an alliance with the municipal elites of Copenhagen and the leaders of the Lutheran Church against the powerful

nobles of the Council of State. In a formal ceremony that autumn, the three Estates of the Kingdom recognized Frederick as the supreme sovereign power in Denmark and then dissolved, never to meet again. Sehestad brought non-nobles into a new Council of State, created a corps of official tax collectors in the provinces, and paid off the state's huge debt with grants of poor-quality royal land. New taxes and tariffs were imposed, including direct taxes on noble wealth. Frederick had gone a long way toward eliminating any independent authorities capable of challenging the monarchy.

To the south of Denmark, the German state of Brandenburg followed a somewhat different absolutist path. A small agricultural state situated in a particularly defenseless part of the north German plains, Brandenburg had survived in large part because its rulers had the privilege of helping elect the Holy Roman emperor. In 1618, it acquired the large Baltic duchy of Prussia, but took another forty years to gain full authority there. A large and powerful noble class, the Junkers, resisted any encroachment on their authority. But in the aftermath of the Thirty Years' War, during which Habsburg and Swedish armies had both treated Brandenburg as a parade ground, the canny "Great Elector" Frederick William (r. 1640–1688) convinced the Junkers to grant him the funds necessary to create a standing army that could protect the territory. In return, he agreed to consult with them regularly and to confirm their considerable feudal privileges over the peasantry, including, as we have seen, the imposition of serfdom. Frederick William also created a civil service modeled on the army, in which officials with military titles took charge both of maintaining troops and collecting taxes in particular districts, in collaboration with local nobles. The cooperation among monarchy, aristocracy, and militarized bureaucracy proved a sturdy basis on which to build the state that would, in the future, be known simply as Prussia.

Frederick III of Denmark
The Danish king's modesty is suggested in this mid-seventeenth-century portrait. He is dressed simply, with little of the pomp and grandeur associated with other European rulers of the time.

Brandenburg-Prussia, 1618–1680

LOUIS XIV OF FRANCE (1643–1715)

The absolutism of France's King **Louis XIV**, while often held up as the model followed by the rest of the continent, was actually unique in many respects. But because France reached the height of its power under Louis's reign, dominating the continent both politically and culturally, his story still deserves close attention.

Louis had an eventful childhood, to say the least. After losing his father and becoming king at age four in 1643, he had to flee his capital five years later during the popular turmoil of the Fronde. For five years after that he could do little more than watch as his mother, Anne of Austria, and her lover, Cardinal Mazarin, struggled to impose royal authority on the country's rebellious princes and high courts, only succeeding after all the sides were too exhausted to continue. For the rest of his life, Louis would have a visceral dislike for the common people of Paris who had rebelled against his mother.

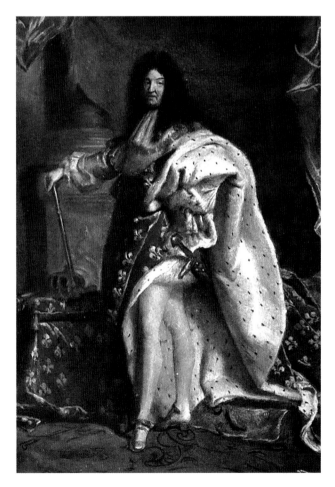

Louis XIV This 1701 portrait captures Louis XIV's grandiosity, showing him draped in ermine and the royal *fleur de lys* symbol.

Upon Mazarin's death in 1661, Louis decided to rule without a chief minister. And he quickly demonstrated, in an extraordinarily dramatic act, that he would never again let any mere functionary upstage him. Since the end of the Fronde, an experienced civil servant named Nicolas Fouquet (1615–1680) had acquired a huge fortune while serving as France's superintendent of finances. He built a magnificent Baroque château near Paris called Vaux-le-Vicomte, and in August 1661 entertained the king and thousands of other guests there, serving delicacies on plates of gold. A new comedy by the great playwright Molière was staged in the open air, amid elaborate fireworks and fountains. Had the minister upstaged the king himself? Three weeks later, Louis had Fouquet arrested, subjected to a long trial on corruption charges, and imprisoned for the rest of his life. Louis henceforth relied for advice and assistance upon Mazarin's talented protégé Jean-Baptiste Colbert (1619–1683). Even while amassing his own fortune, Colbert never forgot that he owed everything to the monarch who had raised him up from a merchant background to the highest rank of the French nobility.

COLBERT'S REFORMS Some critics complained that in promoting men like Colbert, and in shutting great aristocratic families out of the royal council, Louis was favoring the urban bourgeoisie, or middle class, over the nobility. But if anything, the reverse was true. Throughout his long reign, Louis sought to placate, co-opt, and cooperate with his nobles. He saw himself as the "first gentleman" of his realm. Though he continued and regularized Richelieu's policy of sending royal intendants to act as effective royal governors in the country's major provinces, he instructed them to work alongside the local elites to ensure smooth and reliable collection of taxes. Nobles in the 1680s kept for themselves a higher proportion of the taxes collected in their provinces than had been the case fifty years before. In short, they did well out of Louis's absolutism. The provincial estates, local assemblies that were dominated by nobles, actually gained influence and fiscal power during Louis's reign. And although the king made an effort to muzzle the noble magistrates, who constituted the most important institutional opposition to the monarchy, he also reaffirmed their judicial role and made sure to involve them in his administration. Finally, Louis took great care to associate nobles with the prestigious public works projects that he undertook, such as the 150-mile-long Canal du Midi waterway that joined the Mediterranean to the Garonne River and the Atlantic, facilitating the shipment of goods.

By contrast, Louis showed little consideration for

the urban middle classes and trades. In a series of major reforms, he stripped French cities of municipal independence and subjected them to the rule of the intendants. He and Colbert promoted French manufactures, particularly luxury goods such as tapestries, high-end textiles, and porcelain. They also extended the guild system that had been developing since the middle ages, organizing nearly all the French trades into closed "corporations" chartered by the monarchy, removing much of the autonomy they had previously enjoyed. In many professions and trades, ranging from wig making to the practice of law, would-be members of the corporation now had to buy the right to practice from the state—making them part of the system analogous to the selling of venal offices that also included high-court judgeships. Louis and Colbert repeatedly manipulated this structure of "offices" to extort even more money from the hapless practitioners. The practice became an alternate form of state finance at a time when the French state, thanks to repeated defaults on its debt caused by the steep rise in military spending, could borrow from the international credit markets only at very high rates.

Colbert, the well-educated descendant of merchants and accountants, had the ambition of turning absolutism into a systematic, even scientific form of government, collecting data about population and resources, and experimenting with new, more rational ways of managing them. Colbert's ambitions shine through in the advice he gave to his son in 1671, just before the latter left on a trip to Italy. In each state, Colbert instructed:

> look at . . . its situation, its military forces, the number of its peoples, the greatness of the state, the number and size of cities, towns, and villages, the quantity of the peoples that compose the whole; . . . Visit the public works, maritime and on the ground, all the palaces, public houses, and generally all that is remarkable.

Although Colbert's specific system of information gathering did not survive beyond his death, the principle that states needed to collect and organize as much information as possible about their subjects and territory would become broadly accepted by all modern European governments. This sort of information-gathering had been pioneered by Italian city-states in the Renaissance, but only now, in the seventeenth century, did large territorial states begin to employ the same methods in a systematic manner.

THE "SUN KING" At the heart of Louis's absolutist program—and what distinguished it from the models developed in Denmark or Brandenburg—was an intense

The "Sun King" The monarch was a master of style, using fashion and imagery to represent himself as the Sun King, radiating his grace throughout France. A ballet enthusiast, Louis even danced the role of the sun in an elaborate gold costume before his court in 1653.

and costly effort to glorify the monarch himself as a demigod. The sovereign's beneficence was seen as radiating outward from the royal person to embrace and ennoble his entire kingdom. As one philosopher wrote after Louis's death, "The prince stamps the character of his mind on the court, the court on the city, the city on the provinces. The sovereign's soul is a mould which gives its form to all the others."

In previous centuries, French royal ceremony had tended to stress the bonds between king and kingdom. Louis's predecessors had traveled extensively throughout the country, staging ceremonial "entries" into towns, in which they took part in elaborate processions with the local elites. Louis abandoned these practices in favor of distributing images that most often likened him to the sun. During his reign, the royal treasury paid for at least 700 engravings and some 300 statues of the "Sun King."

The equestrian statue of Louis in the Place Louis-le-Grand (Louis the Great) in central Paris was so large that during its installation, twenty workers could sit down for lunch inside of it. Dozens of French cities were adorned with Roman-style triumphal arches and churches dedicated to Louis's military victories.

POWER AND CULTURE AT VERSAILLES The centerpiece of this enterprise of glorification was the vast palace Louis built on the site of a small hunting lodge in **Versailles**, twelve miles west of Paris. Work began in the 1660s and continued for more than four decades. The finished palace—designed by the same architects who had worked on Fouquet's lavish château—had some 725,000 square feet of usable space and 2,000 sumptuously furnished rooms. Together with its adjoining buildings, it could house some 10,000 people. The vast, meticulously tended gardens covered an additional thirty square miles. They boasted fifty ornate fountains and a "Grand Canal" on which the king staged mock naval combats with specially designed flat-bottomed boats. Louis shifted his residence and much of the government to Versailles, removing them from the dangers of Parisian rebellion. Once there, he hardly ever returned to the capital city he hated.

Louis's ultimate ambition was for his reign to match in splendor and glory the greatest days of Greece and Rome; and to this end, he zealously promoted the arts. Versailles itself put grand, impressive examples of French Baroque art and architecture on display for the world. An

Versailles Inside the palace, magnificent rooms like the Hall of Mirrors displayed treasures and also reflected the opulence of the king and his courtiers back at them.

accomplished dancer, Louis participated in the elaborate ballets of Jean-Baptiste Lully (1632–1687), his Italian-born court composer.

Through his patronage, Louis encouraged the replacement of Latin with French in scholarship and supported the efforts of the French Academy to raise the French language to a level of purity and beauty that could, in theory, outshine the classical languages. The crown promoted the French theater, and during Louis's reign it marked its greatest triumphs with the works of the supremely witty playwright Jean-Baptiste Poquelin, known as Molière (1622–1673), and the tragedian Jean Racine (1639–1699). In *The Bourgeois Gentleman* and other plays, Molière skewered social pretentiousness and hypocrisy while subtly reinforcing norms of "sociable" and courtly behavior. Racine's verse tragedies, using material from ancient history, myth, and the Bible, focused on heroes and heroines driven by their passions into agonizing dilemmas.

FRENCH COURT LIFE At Versailles, an elaborate system of royal etiquette and ceremony developed, based on many different European precedents but going well beyond them. In the morning, for instance, specially designated courtiers were allowed to witness and participate in the royal *lever* (arising). As Louis got out of bed, his clothes would be ceremonially passed from one noble to another, with the role of actually assisting the king into them bestowed as a mark of special favor. Others would stand by, watching. In the evening, the king would eat in front of an audience, with the most important courtiers standing closest to the royal table. The courtiers themselves had to maintain high standards of self-control, using a rigorously defined repertory of acceptable movements, gestures, language, and even facial expressions, not to mention clothes. Reputation depended on always displaying proper behavior, and a single mistake could, in extreme cases, invite a lifetime of ridicule. Aristocratic hostesses, such as the marquise of Rambouillet (1588–1655), played a crucial role in this court society by performing in the rituals of etiquette and instructing men and women alike in their intricacies at social gatherings devoted to witty and sophisticated conversation. These gatherings, later known as "salons," became fertile ground for the sort of early feminist thought that Poulain de la Barre had developed.

The construction of Versailles dramatically changed the relationship between the monarchy and the aristocracy in France. Increasingly, the most powerful families in the kingdom spent much of the year at court, living in the palace and participating in its rituals, associating themselves with the Sun King's glory. Through his distribution of symbolic favors, Louis could manipulate aristocratic factions and thereby help ensure their obedience. The prince of Condé, the great rebel of the Fronde, was eventually pardoned by the king and spent his last days rowing on the Grand Canal at Versailles. But at the same time, the development of this new type of court bound the king himself more tightly than ever to the aristocracy, with whom he lived in such intimate contact. He also grew more isolated from the rest of his subjects, to whom he was no more than a name, an image, and a source of often unwelcome demands.

FRANCE AT WAR The single most important arena in which Louis both depended on and performed for his aristocracy was warfare. His twin goals throughout his reign were to secure France's international position—including especially its eastern and northern frontiers—and also to gain glory for himself. War was the means to both ends, and for the first part of his reign he had considerable success in it. Thanks in large part to Colbert's talent for raising revenue, he built up an army that numbered well over 100,000 in the 1670s and would eventually come to number some 400,000. Louis also employed brilliant military engineers who designed a series of massive fortifications for the French borders. Such demonstrations of military might not only enhanced the monarch's personal power and prestige, but bound him more closely to the aristocracy that commanded the expanded military.

Almost immediately, Louis put his forces to use. From 1667 to 1668, France attacked the Spanish Netherlands in the hope of annexing them. Very quickly, the new "balance of power" dynamic in European politics made itself felt. As France won dramatic victories, a broad coalition formed against it that included Sweden, Britain, and the Dutch Republic (the latter ending a war of its own to ally against France). Nonetheless, the French kept considerable territorial gains in the Spanish Netherlands. Louis then turned his attention to the Dutch Republic, which Colbert had long identified as a principal rival for France because of its growing commercial strength and large navy. From 1672 to 1678, Louis fought his "Dutch War," this time in alliance with the British, and sometimes leading his forces in person. To halt the French advance, the Dutch deliberately opened the dikes they had built over the previous century to reclaim land from the sea. The action flooded part of their country, literally bogging down Louis's troops.

Although France failed to conquer the Netherlands, it made gains on its eastern frontier at the expense of

Louis XIV's Territorial Claims, 1662–1681 Louis's commitment to warfare led to territorial expansion along France's northeastern border, bolstered by a series of new fortifications. After twenty years of war, his armies enlarged the French-controlled territory in the east, including in Alsace and Lorraine, but such gains came at the cost of huge debt.

German states. In a brilliant campaign, Louis's army occupied most of the German-speaking province of Alsace, along the Rhine. These limited successes came at a vast cost, however. In addition to burdening France with a hugely increased state debt, they practically guaranteed that any further wars would quickly cause large new alliances to form against Louis XIV. But all of this mattered little to the king, who grandly commemorated his victories by building the largest and most ornate gallery in Versailles: the 220-foot-long Hall of Mirrors, filled with paintings depicting the Dutch War and Louis's personal rule.

THE MERCANTILE STATES

To judge simply from the attention paid to Louis XIV (in the first place by his well-stocked stable of propagandists), it would seem that absolutism was the wave of the future in mid-seventeenth-century Europe, the "progressive" movement of its day. Here, it could be argued, was the solution that the most forward-looking Europeans had found to the chaos of civil and religious strife and unrestrained international war. Yet two countries in northwestern Europe, Great Britain and the Netherlands, offered a powerful alternative to absolute monarchy.

BRITAIN: COMMONWEALTH, PROTECTORATE, RESTORATION (1648–1688)

Britain remained for decades the weaker of the two, thanks to the effects of its brutal civil war, which had ended with the execution of King Charles I and the establishment of the Commonwealth. Though the fighting ended in England by 1648, it continued in Scotland and Ireland for much of the next decade, even if the royalists there soon lost any real hope of victory. Between 1649 and 1652, Oliver Cromwell, as commander of the New Model Army, undertook a savage, large-scale campaign to subjugate largely Catholic Ireland. His victory there resulted in the almost total dispossession of the Catholic land-holding elites and the establishment of large new Protestant "plantations" on the island.

Meanwhile, political turmoil continued in London. Cromwell and his Army could not find ways of cooperating with the Rump Parliament, and in 1653, Cromwell himself led soldiers into the House of Commons to dissolve it. After a new, handpicked parliament also proved uncooperative, Cromwell formally seized power as Lord Protector of England, Wales, Scotland, and Ireland—a king in all but name, although he refused an actual crown. A written constitution—the only one in English history—theoretically guaranteed religious toleration and triennial parliaments. In practice, however, Cromwell's Protectorate soon turned effectively into a dictatorship. He ruled without

Oliver Cromwell A 1653 portrait offers a heroic depiction of Cromwell. He wears armor and the plain white collar typically adopted by Puritans.

parliament and divided England into twelve military zones, each headed by a major general. He then tried to impose a Puritan social order on the country, banning alehouses, Maypoles, swearing, Sabbath-breaking, and the observance of Christmas as a holiday.

Upon Cromwell's death in 1658, his son Richard (1626–1712) briefly succeeded him, but by this point the Puritan revolution had grown both exhausted and hugely unpopular in the country. In May 1659, Richard Cromwell abdicated. Soon afterward the commander of British forces in Scotland, General George Monck, came south and staged a coup that led to the restoration of the Stuart dynasty in 1660. Charles I's son had lived in exile in France and the Low Countries after an attempt to reconquer England from his ancestral Scotland had failed in 1651. Now he returned to London and took the throne as Charles II (r. 1660–1685).

The poet John Dryden would later comment, acidly, on this period of British history that "thy wars brought nothing about." The conflicts that had toppled and killed one king ended with his son on the throne. Anglicanism was reestablished as the official state religion, and the country reverted to its traditional, unwritten constitution. A series of laws imposed penalties and loyalty oaths on Catholics and dissenting Protestants, and hundreds of Quakers who refused to swear oaths on principle were left to rot in prison. The bold experiments in parliamentary rule and religious toleration, and the calls for democracy and social equality, had all seemingly failed.

THE GROWTH OF POLITICAL PARTIES Yet the civil wars did prevent Britain from following the absolutist path of the continental monarchies. Charles II, a notoriously pleasure-loving monarch, did not imitate his father's repeated confrontations with Parliament. And although he secretly converted to Catholicism, and even pledged to Louis XIV that he would restore the religion in Britain, the new king did not dare make any serious moves in this direction. Parliament remained the active center of politics, and within it, two distinct factions emerged that in time would evolve into the world's first political parties. The Tories (originally an insult, from the Irish word for outlaw) generally supported the king. The Whigs (also originally an insult, meaning "cattle drivers") supported parliamentary supremacy and had greater sympathy for Protestant dissent. The Whigs, as we will see in the next chapter, failed to prevent Charles's Catholic brother and heir, James II, from succeeding to the throne in 1685 and reigning for three turbulent years. But in 1679 they passed the Habeas Corpus Act, which confirmed the

POLITICAL EQUALITY AFTER THE BRITISH CIVIL WARS

The British civil wars (1639–1649) ultimately became a dispute about the source of legitimate political power. For Royalists, the king was sovereign and his political authority derived from God. The Parliamentary view was more shifting and complicated. Some argued that men of property collectively held the right to rule, through their representatives in parliament. Radicals insisted that the right to vote be extended to all men. Oliver Cromwell's rise and the emergence of groups, such as the Levellers and the Diggers, clashed with the tradition of royal political authority. Despite the reestablishment of the monarchy in 1660, the questions the civil wars posed about power, equality, and the rights of Englishmen would persist through the eighteenth and nineteenth centuries.

Gerrard Winstanley, from *The True Levellers Standard Advanced*

Gerrard Winstanley, a former cloth merchant, led the Diggers—originally called the True Levellers for their adoption of a radical version of the Levellers' ideology. In this excerpt from his Digger manifesto, *The True Levellers Standard Advanced* (1649), Winstanley explores the origins of inequality and describes his plan to occupy and cultivate fallow land to provide for the poor and landless.

In the beginning of time, the great Creator Reason, made the Earth to be a Common Treasury, to preserve Beasts, Birds, Fishes, and Man, the lord that was to govern this Creation; for Man had Domination given to him, over the Beasts, Birds, and Fishes; but not one word was spoken in the beginning, That one branch of mankind should rule over another ... Then he [man] fell into blindness of mind and weakness of heart, and runs abroad for a Teacher and Ruler: And so selfish imaginations taking possession of the Five Sences, and ruling as King in the room of Reason therein, and working with Covetousnesse, did set up one man to teach and rule over another; and thereby the Spirit was killed, and man was brought into bondage, and became a greater Slave to such of his own kind, then the Beasts of the field were to him ...

The Work we are going about is this, To dig up Georges-Hill and the waste Ground thereabouts, and to Sow Corn, and to eat our bread together by the sweat of our brows.

And the First Reason is this, That we may work in righteousness, and lay the Foundation of making the Earth a Common Treasury for All, both Rich and Poor, That every one that is born in the land, may be fed by the Earth his Mother that brought him forth, according to the Reason that rules in the Creation ...

Take notice, That England is not a Free People, till the Poor that have no Land, have a free allowance to dig and labour the Commons,[1] and so live as Comfortably as the Landlords that live in their Inclosures.

Anonymous, "The Protecting Brewer"

This Royalist ballad (1662) lampoons the rise of Oliver Cromwell from brewer's son to Lord Protector and leader of the Commonwealth. The song questions whether commoners are capable and worthy of political rule.

A brewer may be a burgess grave, and carry
    the matter so fine and so brave,
That he the better may play the knave, Which
    nobody can deny.
A brewer may be a Parliament man, for there
    the knavery first began—
And brew most cunning plots he can, Which
    nobody can deny.
...
A brewer may make his foes to flee, and raise
    his Fortunes so, that he

Lieutenant-General may be, Which nobody
    can deny.
A brewer may be all in all, and raise his
    powers both great and small,
That he may be a Lord General, Which
    nobody can deny.
...
Methinks I hear one say to me, pray, why may
    not a brewer be,
Lord Chancellor o' th' University? Which
    nobody can deny.
A brewer may be as bold as *Hector*,[2] when as
    he had drunk off his cup of nectar,
A brewer may be a Lord Protector, Which
    nobody can deny.
Now here remains the strangest thing, how
    this brewer about his liquor did bring,
To be an Emperor, or a King, Which nobody
    can deny.
A brewer may do what he will, and rob the
    Church and State, to sell,
His soul unto the Devil in Hell, Which nobody
    can deny.

QUESTIONS FOR ANALYSIS

1. According to Winstanley, why are all men fundamentally equal and free?
2. How does the "Protecting Brewer" suggest that Cromwell is unworthy of political power?
3. How do *The True Levellers Standard Advanced* and "The Protecting Brewer" differ in their views of political equality?

[1] **commons:** shared public land
[2] **Hector:** a hero of the Trojan War

Sources: *The True Levellers Standard Advanced: Or, The State of Commonly opened, and Presented to the Sons of Men*, Gerrard Winstanley (London: 1649), pp. 6–7; 12; 15; *Constable's Miscellany of Original and Selected Publications in the Various Departments of Literature, Science, & the Arts*, Vol. 47, ed. Archibald Constable (Edinburgh, 1829), pp. 312–3.

1628 Petition of Right by guaranteeing speedy trials for those under arrest.

TRADE AND THE CITY During the Stuart Restoration (1660–88), trade and the overseas empire grew ever more important to Britain, as reflected in the bustling capital city of London. (Neither Charles II nor his successors ever tried to build a British equivalent to Versailles.) The population of the British colonies in North America grew roughly fourfold over the period of 1640 to 1680, to reach more than 200,000. As a result of the Anglo-Dutch Wars, Britain captured the New Netherland colony and transformed its strategically located capital, New Amsterdam, into New York. Henceforth, the British enjoyed unbroken possession of the Eastern Seaboard of North America from South Carolina to present-day Maine.

London, meanwhile, grew from a population of roughly 350,000 in 1640 to as many as 575,000 by the end of the century. It did so despite suffering two horrendous blows in the 1660s. First, the Great Plague of 1665—an episode of bubonic plague similar to the Black Death of 1348—caused widespread panic and a death toll that topped 7,000 a week in September. As in previous plague outbreaks, households touched by the disease had their doors and windows boarded up to prevent the infection from spreading. Then in 1666, the Great Fire destroyed some 13,200 buildings in the capital, leaving up to 70,000 people homeless. Yet by the 1670s, London had recovered from both disasters, with buildings rapidly reconstructed and new residents arriving to take advantage of the capital's commercial wealth.

THE DUTCH "GOLDEN AGE"

For all of Britain's economic dynamism, in the middle of the seventeenth century it still trailed behind its great mercantile rival, the Netherlands. The Dutch had a greater per capita income than the British until the 1670s, and Dutch artisans earned roughly two-thirds more than their counterparts in southern England. Dutch fishing and textile manufacturing (mostly from domestic wool) continued to prosper, while international trade in wine and other commodities boomed. Dutch traders shipped French Bordeaux wine to Germany and Sweden, French Burgundy to the Baltic countries, German Rhine wines to Russia and Spain, and Spanish Malaga and Italian Marsala to England. The Dutch were not only major importers of American tobacco and furs, but turned the former into a true consumer product, offering varieties flavored with

citron, aniseed, thyme, lavender, nutmeg, beer, rosemary, prunes, and much else. When the English diarist Samuel Pepys (1633–1703) boarded a Dutch ship docked in London in November 1665, he was astonished at the value of the cargo: "As noble a sight as ever I saw in my life, the greatest wealth in confusion that a man can see in the world. Pepper scattered through every chink. You trod upon it and in cloves and nutmeg I walked above the knees, whole rooms full. And silk in bales and boxes of copper plate." Much of this wealth, especially the spices, came from another burgeoning area of Dutch trade, East Asia, and especially what is now Indonesia, where the Dutch East India Company was establishing a series of forts and trading posts that would eventually evolve into full-fledged colonial rule.

DUTCH WEALTH Dutch mercantile wealth was not, for the most part, channeled into grand building projects like Versailles. It went into banks, which reinvested it in further commercial ventures. Following the example of the great Italian merchant banks of the late Middle Ages, these institutions built grandiose headquarters and exercised considerable social and political power. The wealth funded the building of solid homes in Amsterdam and the Hague; it bought the well-tailored clothes worn by Dutch burghers, and a great deal of it ended up as food. Even Dutch common sailors ate extraordinarily well by

Stock Exchange Emmanuel de Witte captured the Netherlands' financial prosperity in this 1653 painting of the Amsterdam stock exchange's lofty cloisters and the hustle and bustle of businessmen performing transactions.

GOLDEN AGE AMSTERDAM

> **WHAT IS THERE THAT'S NOT FOUND HERE / OF CORN; FRENCH OR SPANISH WINE / ANY INDIES GOODS THAT ARE SOUGHT / IN AMSTERDAM MAY ALL BE BOUGHT / HERE'S NO FAMINE...THE LAND IS FAT.**
>
> CONSTANTIJN HUYGENS (DUTCH COMPOSER AND POET), *CORN-FLOWERS*, 1672

Legend:

- City wall
- Road
- Dike
- Weigh house (for weighing goods)
- X Windmill
- Garden

BUILDINGS
1. Old Church
2. Meat market
3. Lombard Bank
4. Stock exchange
5. City Hall and Bank of Amsterdam
6. New Church

Salt warehouse — Area for drying herring

The Ij

Wharves

Grain exchange

Crane — Wharves

Dam Square — St. Anthony's market — Naval shipyard — Dutch East India Company

Market — National warehouse — Shipyards — Shipyards — Shipyard

Headquarters of Dutch East India Company — Fish market — New Canal — Warehouse

Hospital and almshouse — JEWISH QUARTER — Rope warehouse

Grain warehouse — Market — Synagogues — Garden of medicinal plants

Amstel R.

City stockyard

City wall, ca. 1663 — Cattle and pig markets

Jan Steen's *The Fat Kitchen* (ca. 1650–1655) may be an exaggerated representation of the Dutch appetite, but it is an exaggeration rooted in reality—feasts could stretch to twenty-five or thirty courses. Here a joyous family shares a meal, surrounded by kitchenware and hanging meats.

IMPORTS, JUNE 27, 1634

326,733 pounds of *Malaccan pepper*

297,446 pounds of *cloves*

292,623 pounds of *saltpeter*

141,278 pounds of *indigo*

75 pots of *spiced ginger* and other confections

3,989 rough *diamonds*

93 boxes of *pearls* and *rubies*

1,155 pounds of *Chinese silk*

199,800 pounds of unrefined *Sri Lankan sugar*

SOURCE: JOHAN DE BRUNE, *EMBLEMATA* (MIDDLEBURG: 1624), P. 9.

> **SWEETNESS AND EXCESS IS TODAY GROWN SO GREAT...THE MEN OF TODAY WOULD DEARLY LIKE TO HAIL COOKS AND OTHER SERVANTS OF THEIR GLUTTONY WITH TRUMPETS OF HONOR AND CROWNS OF LAUREL.**
>
> OTTO BELCAMPIUS, *THE LAST HOUR*, 1661

An intricate canal system supplied Amsterdam's vegetable markets with an abundance of fresh produce from farms. In Hendrick Martenszoon Sorgh's painting *The Vegetable Market* (1662), a woman working at her stall extends a gourd to the viewer. Her wares include cabbages, carrots, turnips, artichokes, squash, beets, and pumpkins.

QUESTIONS FOR ANALYSIS

1. How did the city life of Amsterdam revolve around food and its many dimensions?

2. What economic developments enabled the Dutch to enjoy such a rich selection of food?

3. How did food connect Amsterdam to the rest of Europe and the world?

POPULATION

1600: 60,000

1647: 140,000

Girl with a Pearl Earring This masterpiece from around 1665 conveys Vermeer's great genius for realistic depictions of people.

and then rejected Spinoza, numbered some 7,500 out of the city's population of 200,000. The British poet Andrew Marvell (1621–1678), in an anti-Dutch poem written on the eve of the First Anglo-Dutch War, condemned this "watery Babel," but could not help remarking on the spectacle. He likened the city's commerce in religious ideas to the other sort of commerce at which the Dutch excelled:

> Hence Amsterdam, Turk-Christian-Pagan-Jew,
> Staple of sects and mint of schism grew;
> That bank of conscience, where not one so strange
> Opinion but finds credit, and exchange.

The Netherlands also allowed an unprecedented degree of press freedom. Some of the first newspapers in the French and English languages were published there to avoid the state censorship imposed in France and Britain. Between 1650 and 1672, the Netherlands also enjoyed a tumultuous, relatively open, republican political system in which the elected representatives in the country's different provinces, gathered into legislative bodies called "states," were powerful political forces. And the Netherlands had a States General (in Dutch, Staaten Generaal, after which they named Staten Island in New Amsterdam), which dominated national political life.

It was in this wealthy, tolerant mercantile setting that the Dutch gave new attention to the contours and texture of ordinary life. Their artists increasingly found as much pleasure and beauty in everyday events and relationships as in the extraordinary, the mythical, and the world beyond. Dutch literature of the period celebrated companionate marriage and the joys of parenthood. Dutch Baroque architects devoted their most enduring efforts to intricately decorated town halls, marketplaces, and storehouses—not churches. And Dutch painters found their great subjects all around them: sober aldermen in their meeting halls, servants at work, children at play. Still-life and landscape painting flourished, even as religious and mythical themes faded. The painter Jan Vermeer (1632–1675) is known for his luminous depictions of such ordinary subjects as a girl wearing a pearl earring, and a simple street scene showing women at work. In Vermeer's hands, the sober, solid wealth of Dutch cities, fed by its trade and manufacturing, was vibrantly and memorably recorded. As for Rembrandt Harmenszoon van Rijn (1606–1669), perhaps the greatest painter of the age, he turned his mastery of color and brushwork to portraits of a militia company and to close studies of faces, as well as to biblical scenes. In many ways, Rembrandt, who came from a wealthy artisanal background in Leiden and became an apprentice painter at age sixteen, found his

European standards of the period. One Dutch ship with a crew of a hundred carried, for each month at sea, no less than 450 pounds of cheese, 5 tons of cured meat, 400 pounds of cured fish, several tons of pickled herring, and 8,960 gallons of ale. It all came to nearly 5,000 calories a day per sailor. All of this was made possible by the development of sophisticated new financial instruments that allowed credit to flow quickly to profitable enterprises. Building on the example of the Renaissance Italians who had invented modern methods of accounting, the Dutch kept reliable track of larger and more complex financial transactions than any previous society had done.

TOLERATION AND CREATIVITY As Amsterdam became the great warehouse of world trade, thronged with merchants and sailors from every continent, Dutch culture and politics changed. The severe, intolerant Calvinism that had still prevailed at the start of the century ceased to set the tone, and the Dutch Republic welcomed Protestant dissenters of many different stripes, as well as Jews from Germany and Portugal. By 1672, the flourishing Jewish community of Amsterdam, which had produced

REMBRANDT'S *ANATOMY LESSON OF DR. NICOLAES TULP*

Rembrandt's *The Anatomy Lesson of Dr. Nicolaes Tulp* (1632) conveys both his particular gifts as a painter and the intellectual curiosity developing in Amsterdam. The painting, commissioned by the city's guild of surgeons, captures a lesson during which a recently executed criminal's body was dissected. With the help of an anatomical textbook (bottom right), a group of surgeons observes Tulp's demonstration of the intricate workings of arm and hand muscles. Despite the seeming spontaneity of the figures, Rembrandt constructs a precisely arranged group portrait. His dramatic use of light and shadow emphasizes the surgeons' faces and the body's pale skin, and his careful rendering of the exposed muscles and tendons shows an interest in anatomic detail. As a whole, the painting serves as an example of the increasingly common realism of scenes in art and the new fascination with the pursuit of scientific knowledge.

QUESTIONS FOR ANALYSIS

1. How is this painting characteristic of Dutch Golden Age art?
2. What aspects of the painting contribute to its realism?
3. What attitudes toward science does this painting convey?

greatest subject in the mirror: he executed nearly ninety self-portraits over the course of his adult life, and never did a painter show greater fascination with wrinkles and the other ordinary marks of the aging, mortal self.

DECLINE The middle of the seventeenth century was the **Dutch "Golden Age,"** but by 1680 clear signs of decline were visible. The Anglo-Dutch Wars had hurt Dutch commerce and took away the promising New Netherland colony. Louis XIV's Dutch War, which lasted from 1672 to 1678, put the country under further pressure. Despite its naval and mercantile strength, the Netherlands was small (its population was less than 40 percent of England's) and its flat territory was difficult to defend. Internal political turmoil also took its toll. In the "disaster year" of 1672, the population again reached out to the country's leading noble dynasty, the House of Orange. The various Dutch provinces, which enjoyed considerable autonomy, now curtailed the power of their elected states general, the highest Dutch poitical authority, and chose the young Prince William III (r. 1672–1702) as executive "stadholder." "Orangist" mobs attacked members of the patrician elites who dominated in the states. There ensued a civil war lasting six years, from which the Dutch Republic emerged in a weakened state. For all the glories of the Golden Age, the next century would belong to the absolutist powers and to the Netherlands' great maritime rival, Great Britain.

CONCLUSION

At the end of the 1670s, despite continuing international rivalries that promised an indefinite future of warfare, something fundamental had changed in Europe. The wave of chaotic civil wars, which had swept over nearly every European country in the middle of the century, had receded. Throughout most of the continent, states were asserting more control over the use of force, both within their own territories and when directed at enemy states. These trends, in combination with a slowly improving climate and rapidly expanding overseas trade, were driving economic expansion. The 1670s, in comparison with what had come before in the century, were a decade of relative order and prosperity. The following decades would fall largely into the same pattern. As time passed, these changing conditions would open new political, social, and intellectual horizons for Europeans.

KEY TERMS

Court of Star Chamber (p. 444)

Oliver Cromwell (p. 445)

Levellers (p. 445)

Fronde (p. 446)

Bogdan Chmielnicki (p. 447)

Shabbetai Sevi (p. 448)

Quakers (p. 449)

Jansenism (p. 449)

Thomas Hobbes (p. 451)

Baruch Spinoza (p. 452)

Blaise Pascal (p. 453)

Peace of Westphalia (p. 456)

Louis XIV (p. 460)

Versailles (p. 462)

Dutch "Golden Age" (p. 470)

REVIEW QUESTIONS

1. What political and religious issues contributed to the outbreak of the British civil wars?

2. What were the causes of the civil wars on the Continent in the mid-seventeenth century?

3. What common tendencies linked the millenarian and other radical religious movements that emerged in the mid-seventeenth century?

4. During the 1600s, how did women contribute to efforts to re-energize the Catholic Church?

5. How did Thomas Hobbes's ideas on the origin of government challenge older assumptions about politics and religion?

6. How do the writings of Spinoza, Pascal, and Poulain de la Barre reveal the emergence of a more skeptical, egalitarian approach to society?

7. How did the Peace of Westphalia mark a new approach to international relations in Europe?

8. In what ways did Louis XIV expand the power of the French monarchy?

9. What were the effects of the dissolution of Oliver Cromwell's Protectorate?

10. What contributed to the commercial wealth and high standard of living of the Dutch Republic in the mid-1600s?

CORE OBJECTIVES

After reading this chapter, you should have a solid understanding of the following core objectives. To strengthen your grasp of the core objectives, use the resources on the Student Site for The West.

- Analyze the causes and effects of the civil wars that disrupted European politics and society in the mid-seventeenth century.

- Trace the rise in messianism and other radical religious movements that arose during the civil wars.

- Examine the evolution of new forms of political analysis and philosophy inspired by the emerging scientific worldview of the seventeenth century.

- Explain the new political order that emerged in Europe at the end of the Thirty Years' War.

- Describe the practices of absolutist states such as Prussia and France.

- Identify the key characteristics of the mercantile states of Great Britain and the Netherlands.

 GO TO **inQuizitive** TO SEE WHAT YOU'VE LEARNED—AND LEARN WHAT YOU'VE MISSED—WITH PERSONALIZED FEEDBACK ALONG THE WAY.

CHRONOLOGY

1682
Peter the Great ascends to the Russian throne

1683
Ottoman siege of Vienna

1684
Pierre Bayle begins editing *News from the Republic of Letters*

1685
France institutes "Black Code" in its overseas colonies

October 22, 1685
Louis XIV revokes Edict of Nantes

1687
Isaac Newton publishes *Principia Mathematica*

1688–1697
War of the League of Augsburg

1688–9
Glorious Revolution in England

1689
John Locke publishes *Second Treatise of Government* and *Essay Concerning Human Understanding*

July 12, 1690
Battle of the Boyne

1700–21
Great Northern War

1701
Kingdom of Prussia established

1702–14
War of the Spanish Succession

May 1703
Peter the Great founds Saint Petersburg

1707
Act of Union between England and Scotland

From Court to City

EMERGING CULTURES, 1680–1740

1714
Peace of Utrecht

1720
Financial bubbles
cause crises in
Britain and France

1719
Daniel Defoe publishes
Robinson Crusoe

1721
Montesquieu publishes
Persian Letters

I n 1697 Antonio de Vieira (1682–1745) experienced an unlikely twist of fate. Born into the same community of Amsterdam Sephardic Jews that had produced Baruch Spinoza, he was a fifteen-year-old cabin boy on a Dutch ship when Peter I, the young Tsar of Russia, came aboard for a sail during a tour of Western Europe. Peter, who spoke some Dutch, took a liking to Antonio and offered him a position as a page in his court. Over the next twenty years, the young Jew rose on the tide of the Tsar's favor, returning with him to Russia, converting to Russian Orthodoxy, winning the position of Adjutant-General of Police in the new capital city of Saint Petersburg, and even marrying into a princely family. In 1726 he became a Count of the Russian Empire.

The story is a revealing one for several reasons. First, it shows something about the occasionally spectacular opportunities for social advancement in a Europe that was growing more prosperous and settled. In an even more spectacular example, a Latvian serving maid named Marta Skawronska, who captured Tsar Peter's affections, ended up his empress and successor. As Tsarina Catherine I, she ruled the largest empire on earth, stretching from the Baltic Sea to the Pacific Ocean. The De Vieira story also points toward the growing cosmopolitanism of European elites, who over the next century would become increasingly

Sugar Cultivation A 1667 engraving from a French history of the Antilles depicts the industrial process that was sugar cultivation. Turning cane into products such as molasses, treacle, and refined sugar entailed vast quantities of slave labor as well as sophisticated machinery. The slaves of Europe's overseas colonies suffered from terribly cruel working and living conditions.

- Why did levels of religious intolerance increase in the late seventeenth century?
- What was the significance of the Glorious Revolution of 1689?
- In what ways did absolutism reach its height in this period?
- What major changes in the conduct of war occurred at this time?
- Why was war such a regular occurrence in this period?
- How did the Atlantic world affect Europe's trade and economy?
- Why did cities replace some courts as centers of culture in the early eighteenth century?
- How did skepticism influence European thought?

comfortable crossing borders and even living for years in foreign countries. And it hints at the growing possibilities for toleration in a Europe grown weary of religious conflict. Here, Peter led the way, allowing Catholics and Protestants to worship freely in his empire at a time when religious minorities in much of Western Europe remained ferociously persecuted.

De Vieira's story also matters because of what he did in Saint Petersburg. As late as 1700, the city did not yet exist. In the swamplands where the Neva River emptied into the Baltic Sea stood nothing but a small Swedish fort. But in May 1703, Tsar Peter captured the area, used lessons he had learned from the Dutch to drain the swamps, and laid the foundations for a new capital city that he saw both as a strategic port and a "window on the West." Entranced with Amsterdam, the Tsar planned Saint Petersburg as a city of broad canals and sober, sturdy stone buildings very different from the extravagant domes and towers (and rotting wood) of the old Russian capital, Moscow. He also vowed to make it a "well-policed" city in the broad, eighteenth-century sense of the word: not just a crime-free place, but an orderly, clean, and healthy one.

This is where de Vieira came in. Modeling his office

after the General Lieutenancy of Police created by French King Louis XIV for Paris in 1667, de Vieira issued regulations on everything from the freshness of the meat sold in Saint Petersburg markets to the moss used to fill cracks in wooden walls (he ordered that it be boiled to prevent cockroaches from feeding on it). He organized a trash collection service and a system of street lighting using candles. And he developed a force of policemen, night watchmen, barriers, and checkpoints to fight crime and keep tabs on the city's growing population. De Vieira's actions illustrated the social ideal of European absolutism: the well-ordered state, rationally managed by a single, central authority. To the European elites of Tsar Peter's day, a continent-wide system of such states seemed the best solution to the problem of managing competition among and within states, and preventing it from spinning out of control as it had done in the earlier years of the century.

Between 1680 and 1740, Europe seemed to belong more than ever to cultured, cosmopolitan servants of absolute monarchies like de Vieira. With the continuing exceptions of a few small republics including Venice, Switzerland, and the Netherlands, it remained a continent of monarchies. And while England took a strong move toward limiting its monarchy with its "Glorious Revolution" of 1688, no other country followed its trajectory. Indeed, during these years, as the destructiveness of European warfare waned and religious conflict, after briefly flaring anew, turned less strident, it seemed that absolute monarchs were more secure on their thrones than ever. When France's leading theologian wrote, around 1700, that monarchy was "the most common, oldest, and also the most natural form of government," it seemed to most of his readers that he was stating a self-evident truth.

Yet even as the placid, well-disciplined order envisaged by Tsar Peter seemed to be spreading, an intellectual revolution was beginning which would soon shake this order to its core. This revolution took place above all in Western Europe—particularly Britain, France, and Antonio de Vieira's home country of the Netherlands. And ironically, it was grounded in a principle also promoted by the advocates of the well-ordered police state, namely that reason should govern human affairs. The continuing spectacular progress of science—which served as a reference point for the absolutists as well—helped inspire this revolution, which took from it a vision of a universe that operated according to invariable, knowable laws. For the moment, the revolution remained largely limited to elite, learned circles, but it nonetheless marked a decisive break in European history: the beginning of the Enlightenment. This chapter will explore the conditions under which the Enlightenment was born, while also tracing the development of European politics, society, and culture in the late seventeenth and early eighteenth centuries.

INTOLERANCE INTENSIFIED

The road to the Enlightenment did not run smoothly, and the last decades of the seventeenth century actually brought heightened fears of renewed intolerance and religious strife. The intolerance did not, however, stem, as in earlier decades, from increased religious fervor. Now, it more often came from *fear of* religious fervor and the civil strife it could provoke. As European states continued to recover from the disruptions of the earlier decades, rulers felt that the best means of avoiding religious discord would be the strict enforcement of religious uniformity throughout their realms.

THE EDICT OF NANTES REVOKED

France offered the most spectacular example. Since 1598, King Henry IV's Edict of Nantes had offered French Protestants—known as Huguenots—limited toleration. It did not defend toleration as a principle: most French Catholics still saw Protestantism as a dangerous heresy, and tolerated it for the same reason the chronically ill tolerate the diseases they suffer from—because they felt they had no choice. The Edict did not grant even this limited toleration to Jews, who remained banished from most French territory. During the seventeenth century, Protestant privileges became increasingly restricted in France, and Louis XIV in particular undertook strong steps to encourage conversions to Catholicism (including forcing Protestant families to house unruly Catholic soldiers). Nonetheless, in practice the Edict allowed the Protestant community of some 850,000 to survive, and in many regions of France peaceful coexistence remained the norm.

On October 22, 1685, King Louis XIV finally felt the monarchy was strong enough to act against the so-called heretics, and formally revoked the Edict of Nantes. With the exception of recently annexed Lutheran territories

Flight of the Huguenots A Dutch engraving shows the Protestant families of La Rochelle, France hastily packing their belongings onto carts and leaving the city in 1661.

along the Rhine, Protestantism now became illegal on French soil. This action immediately posed French Protestants with the stark choice religious intolerance has always posed to its victims: conversion, exile, or death. A small number of Huguenots were executed for their beliefs. A large majority converted to Catholicism, although often with little or no sincerity. But approximately 200,000 fled France, joining others who had left earlier in the century. More than half of the refugees went to England and the Netherlands, but significant numbers settled in Germany and even farther afield. In 1700, London counted some 23,000 Huguenots among its population, and in Berlin they made up some 20 percent of the city's residents. In England's North American colonies, traces of Huguenot immigration still survive in towns like New Rochelle, New York (named for the Huguenot stronghold of La Rochelle), and in monuments to figures like Paul Revere (descended from Huguenots called De La Rivière).

INTOLERANCE ACROSS EUROPE

There were other examples of intensifying intolerance as well. Scarcely two months after Louis's action, the Catholic Duke of Savoy in northwest Italy revoked the toleration he had previously extended to 14,000 "Waldensian" Christians—spiritual descendants of a radical medieval reform movement that had embraced the Reformation. A joint French-Savoyard army massacred more than 1,000 of them, and imprisoned some 8,500 others in wretched prison camps. Even in the Netherlands, which had a reputation as the most tolerant state in Europe, only members of the Protestant Dutch Reformed Church could hold office or count on full freedom of worship. In England, the early 1680s marked a high point in the persecution of roughly 200,000 Protestants who "dissented" from the Church of England—predominantly Baptists, Quakers, and various sorts of Calvinists. If convicted of holding unsanctioned religious services, they ran the risk of heavy fines or imprisonment. The restored King Charles II, who flirted with Catholicism and converted secretly to it before his death, associated these denominations with the radicals who had cheered his father's execution during the civil wars.

THE GLORIOUS REVOLUTION AND ITS CONSEQUENCES

In England, these heightened religious tensions helped bring about one of the most consequential upheavals in the country's history. Although it did not make the country anything like a democracy in the modern meaning of the word, it established the supremacy of parliamentary representation, and guaranteed certain political rights more firmly than ever before.

A CHANGE IN RULE

In February 1685, just months before revocation of the Edict of Nantes would provoke outrage and fear across Protestant Europe, Charles II died and his brother, an open Catholic, took the English throne as King James II. Protestant preachers immediately labeled James another Queen Mary I in the making, and reminded their listeners (who needed no such reminders, so often had they heard the stories) of the Protestant martyrs who had bled and burned during her sixteenth-century reign. They predicted that James would abolish parliament and rule like an English Louis XIV—if, indeed, he did not actually surrender England to that autocratic monarch. James in fact initially tried to curry favor with dissenting Protestants (including Baptists, Quakers and Presbyterians) by relaxing the legal restrictions on them. But he also persisted in his advocacy of Catholicism, and in attempts to weaken Parliament. The dissenters' fear of "popery" quickly overwhelmed their hopes of toleration.

William and Mary This 1689 engraving emphasizes William and Mary's legitimacy as rulers of England. William carries the orb and scepter, symbols of the monarchy. At the bottom, the royal arms and pictures of other kings emphasize the monarchs' connections to the English royal lineage.

Almost as soon as James became king, the threat of a new civil war arose. In June 1685, Charles II's illegitimate Protestant son, the Duke of Monmouth, landed in western England and raised the flag of rebellion. James defeated him, had him beheaded, and meted out harsh justice to his supporters. These measures further alienated many Protestants. Three years later, James's Catholic queen gave birth to a son, who took precedence as the male heir over James's older Protestant daughters from an earlier marriage. Protestant opponents claimed that the birth had been fraudulent, with the real baby born dead and a substitute smuggled into the birthing chamber in a warming pan. Calls grew for James to be removed from the throne, and replaced by his adult Protestant daughter Mary (1662–1694).

Soon enough the calls were answered. Mary was married to William III of Orange (1650–1702), the Dutch Stadholder. Concerned above all to keep his country safe from another French invasion, William had initially resisted requests that he challenge James for the English throne. But when James signed a naval agreement with Louis XIV in 1688, posing a threat to the Netherlands, William changed his mind. On November 5, he successfully landed on the west coast of England, and issued a declaration in which he disingenuously claimed to be doing nothing other than ensuring the assembly of "a free and lawful Parliament . . . as soon as possible." The bulk of the English population quickly rallied to him, and within weeks, James II found his position untenable. The King fled to France, where he set up a court in exile. In the summer of 1689, a new Parliament declared King William III and Queen Mary II joint rulers, in what observers quickly dubbed the "**Glorious Revolution**."

THE ENGLISH BILL OF RIGHTS

This change of throne, which took place with almost no bloodshed in England itself, paved the way for important political reforms. In early 1689, the new Parliament, with overwhelming support from the population and from the grateful new monarchs, issued a "Bill of Rights." Through this act the Parliament effectively claimed sovereignty over the Kingdom, with the authority to approve taxes and laws and correct royal abuses up to and including removing unjust kings from office. In an effort to contain the scope of change, the revolutionaries themselves tried to play down what they had accomplished. They framed their reforms as a minimal, incremental set of changes that did little but correct King James's abuses, and introduce new constitutional safeguards in the spirit of an "ancient constitution" that supposedly traced its origins back to before the Norman Conquest of 1066. There could be no question, in other words, of confusing the events of 1688–1689 with the radical ones of 1649, which had toppled the monarchy and opened the door to religious millenarianism and radical theories of social equality. And in fact, the England of 1690 was no less dominated by large landowners and the Church of England than the England of 1685 had been.

The Glorious Revolution was not a social revolution. It was most definitely, however, a political one. While the Bill of Rights made few claims that Parliament had not made in the 1640s, this time they quickly became accepted as bedrock principles of the English constitution. After 1688, no English monarch ever dared imitate James II's absolutist ambitions or his insistence on a divine right to rule. Parliamentary rule had been established for good.

LOCKE'S *SECOND TREATISE*

This new political order also rested upon powerful, new intellectual bases. Just before the Revolution, the leading European political thinker of the age, **John Locke** (1632–1704), composed a powerful treatise that defended

just such action as Parliament would soon take. Locke, the brilliant son of Puritans, had read deeply in the political philosophy of the day, and especially in the work of Thomas Hobbes. But he broke with Hobbes in a significant way.

We have seen that Hobbes, writing during the turmoil of the mid-seventeenth century, had described mankind's natural state as a harsh one that amounted to the "war of all against all." For Hobbes, establishing social peace required the complete subjection of individuals to the sovereign power of the state, however tyrannical it might prove. Locke, by contrast, saw the "state of nature" as a relatively mild condition, which humanity evolved away from mostly out of the need to protect and preserve property. From this perspective, tyranny could not be justified so easily. In Locke's so-called *Second Treatise of Government* (1689), he offered a powerful theory of the people's right to oppose and even depose tyrannical rulers. Against unjust authority, he wrote, "the people are not [. . .] bound to obey; by which means they come again to be out of subjection, and may constitute themselves a new legislative [power]."

John Locke A late-seventeenth-century portrait made toward the end of the philosopher's life.

CHANGES IN RELIGION

The Glorious Revolution also marked a decisive change for England in matters of religion. Charles II and James II had favored the so-called "High Church" elements of the Church of England that most closely approached Catholicism, notably in its elaborate ritual and bishop-heavy church hierarchy. By contrast, William and Mary and the new Parliament favored the simpler, more egalitarian "Low Church" elements that were closer to Puritanism. The Toleration Act of 1689 instituted freedom of worship for all Protestants, including the "dissenting" groups marked by the radical spirit of the 1640s (although they could not hold office). The Act of Settlement of 1701 formally banned Catholics from inheriting the throne. Never again would British rulers flirt with the Church of Rome. After the 1690s, moreover, Catholics under British rule in Ireland (well over three quarters of the Irish population) suffered under some of the harshest restrictions of any religious community in Europe. They could not join the clergy, sit in parliament, teach, send their children overseas to university, purchase land, inherit from Protestants, or own a horse worth more than £5. Jews in Britain would not be able to vote or hold office until the nineteenth century.

A NEW ECONOMIC DIRECTION

Charles II and James II had also favored "mercantilist" economic policies similar to those of their patron and ally, Louis XIV of France. Taking land as the sole source of wealth, they promoted the interests of large landowners and sought to exploit the agricultural and mineral wealth of England's overseas colonies by means of state-chartered monopolies, such as the East India Company. They discouraged homegrown manufacturing—especially the textile industry—which depended on free trade with other countries to flourish. By contrast, the new regime followed the example of William of Orange's native Netherlands in favoring trade and manufacturing interests, lowering tariffs, and restricting the power of the great trading companies. The year 1694 saw the chartering by Parliament of an independent national bank, the Bank of England, on the model of the earlier Dutch Bank of Amsterdam. By providing stable, dependable credit to both the government and the manufacturing sector, the Bank supported a vast expansion of British trade in the following century.

A PROTESTANT BASE IN IRELAND

The final important effect of the Glorious Revolution came in foreign policy. After 1688–89, England quickly abandoned its alliance with France. War became inevitable when Louis XIV refused to acknowledge the change of government in London, and welcomed to Versailles the exiled James II as the legitimate king of England and Scotland. With French support, James sought to raise Ireland, with its large Catholic majority, against the Dutch "usurper" William. A year of brutal fighting in Ireland followed, ending the "bloodless" phase of the Glorious Revolution. On July 12, 1690, King William crushed a largely Irish and French force at the Boyne River. And by late 1691, his armies had driven James II's forces out of Ireland altogether. The victory guaranteed that the Protestant settlements initially implanted in northern Ireland by James I would remain in place. Indeed, these settlements established such deep roots that when the Catholic Irish finally achieved independence from Britain in the 1920s, their new state would be limited to the southern three-quarters of the island. The northern, Protestant-majority province of Ulster remains to this day part of the United Kingdom of Great Britain and Northern Ireland. Northern Irish Protestants continue to call themselves "Orangemen" in homage to William of Orange, and march in a triumphal parade every 12th of July, on the anniversary of the Battle of the Boyne.

PARLIAMENT AND POLITICS

In Britain, the changes wrought by the Glorious Revolution were cemented in the following decades. The principal change—parliamentary supremacy itself—owed at least something to the luck of monarchical succession. King William III was first and foremost a Dutchman, whose concern for domestic English politics centered on maintaining England as a powerful ally for the Netherlands. Queen Mary's sister, Anne (1655–1714), who succeeded to the throne after William's death in 1702, was a relatively weak monarch. When she died without heirs twelve years later, the new rules of Protestant-only succession meant that the crown again passed to a foreigner whose principal interests lay elsewhere. King George I (1660–1727), a descendant of James I, had previously been ruler of the north German state of Hanover. Even after becoming king, George spent as much time as possible in Germany and never learned more than rudimentary English. Under monarchs with little domestic interest or ambition, Parliament was able to consolidate the gains of the Glorious Revolution.

In Britain, this was also the period in which the first political parties in European history developed. The so-called Whigs supported the changes brought by the Revolution, while the Tories resisted them, remaining hostile to religious toleration, attached to High Church Anglicanism, and suspicious of England's new, commercially-oriented foreign policy. It took many decades for British observers to see party competition as legitimate rather than as selfish factionalism that detracted from the public good. The very words "Whig" and "Tory" were originally terms of abuse ("Whig," possibly drawn from Scottish Gaelic, originally meant "horse thief"). But over time, party organizations took shape, parliamentary elections became party contests, and the houses of parliament divided along party lines. The early eighteenth century became known as the period of Whig Ascendancy after the political party that dominated Parliament.

ABSOLUTISM AT ITS HEIGHT

Britain's mixed constitution and party system, however, represented an exception to the European rule. On the continent, the years 1680–1740 marked the high point of absolutism. The absolutist states did not, for the most part, engage in major reforms of the sort seen in France and Spain under Richelieu and Olivares. But monarchies consolidated their authority in important ways.

THE LAST YEARS OF LOUIS XIV

In France, despite the heavy financial burden imposed by warfare, the highly centralized system of rule developed by Louis XIV continued to unfold. The "intendants," who were appointed by the king and functioned as governors in France's provinces, steadily took on more responsibility, until by 1715 they and their cadre of bureaucrats had the final say over a large range of matters of public importance. Like Antonio de Vieira in Russia, they worked to regulate commerce and public hygiene, and to repress crime and corruption, without answering to any representative body. In 1715, when Louis died, the Estates General of France had not met for a full century. It would not meet again until 1789.

Louis did have to deal with some opposition to his rule. From abroad, French Protestants denounced him as a devil after the revocation of the Edict of Nantes. In France itself, during the last years of his reign, a circle of aristocrats around the duke of Saint-Simon (1675–1755) and the count of Boulainvilliers (1658–1722) discussed plans for government by a series of councils staffed by highborn men like themselves under a titular king. Meanwhile, several important religious figures deplored the human suffering, including epidemics and starvation, which followed upon Louis's wars. Archbishop François de Fénelon (1651–1715) condemned the King for living his "entire life apart from the paths of truth and justice [...] All France is nothing but a great, starving sick ward, and it is you yourself, Sire, who have brought all these troubles to pass." Such was Louis's stature, however, that nearly all these criticisms remained unpublished during the king's lifetime, circulating only in manuscript form among small numbers of like-minded critics.

So strong had Louis's system become that it even survived the near-extinction of the ruling Bourbon dynasty. In 1711–1712, Louis's son and grandson both died of infectious disease, leaving only a small, sickly great-grandson as heir to the French throne. On Louis's own death in 1715 a cousin, Philip of Orléans (1674–1723), became Regent. He brought the court back from Versailles to Paris, experimented with a series of aristocratic ruling councils of the sort that Saint-Simon and Boulainvilliers had proposed, and restored a measure of political autonomy to France's high courts (*parlements*). It seemed for a time that he might overturn Louis XIV's principal legacies. But he squandered any chances of serious reform with his support for his rakish financial advisor John Law, who, as we will see, nearly wrecked the French economy with a series of ambitious schemes. In the years after Philip died in 1723, power passed to Cardinal André-Hercule Fleury (1653–1743), the elderly tutor of King Louis XV (1710–1774). A cautious, intelligent minister who unexpectedly lived another twenty years, he reinforced Louis XIV's methods of rule.

Cardinal Fleury
This eighteenth-century portrait of Louis XV's tutor, adviser, and regent depicts him as a sagacious, elegantly-dressed older man.

The great weakness of French government, under Louis XIV and Fleury alike, remained its finances. In the 1690s, under the pressure of war, Louis introduced a head tax and an income tax that were payable by all his subjects, including the clergy and nobility. But to ward off opposition, he presented these as emergency wartime measures only. The principal tax on land, the *taille*, continued to be collected by a cumbersome bureaucracy. Excise taxes on goods—including heavy duties on salt in many parts of the country—were collected by private contractors known as tax farmers who pocketed a large share of the take as their commission. Louis and Fleury kept the treasury afloat through a series of familiar expedients, including devaluing the currency and borrowing on the international credit markets at ruinous rates of interest. These measures did raise additional revenue, but not nearly as much as the government needed. The situation contrasted strongly to the one in England, where the government also relied heavily on excise taxes (out of fear of alienating the great landed interests), but developed an efficient government service based on so-called "excisemen" to collect them.

PETER THE GREAT OF RUSSIA

In most other parts of Europe, the absolutist model continued to prevail. In Russia, **Peter I ("the Great,"** 1672–1725) had enormous admiration for Dutch technology (particularly ship-building and land drainage), but little desire to emulate Dutch republican form of government. Imposingly tall, Peter, the younger son of Tsar Alexei I, came to the throne in 1682, but the first ten years of his reign passed in bloody rivalry between him and various family members, including his own mother.

After emerging the victor of these feuds, Peter set about an ambitious program of reform aimed at reinforcing and streamlining his own rule. He eliminated the *boyar duma*, or council of nobles that had previously exercised considerable power, and also replaced semi-autonomous local authorities with a series of governorships controlled from the center. He created the first real Russian navy, and founded the new capital of Saint Petersburg. There, with the help of men like Antonio de Vieira—one of nearly a thousand Western European advisers whom he brought to Russia in the service of his Westernization projects—Peter aimed to realize the ideal of a well-ordered absolutist state on Russian soil.

As a crucial part of the program, he insisted on transforming his often recalcitrant nobility, the boyars, into a

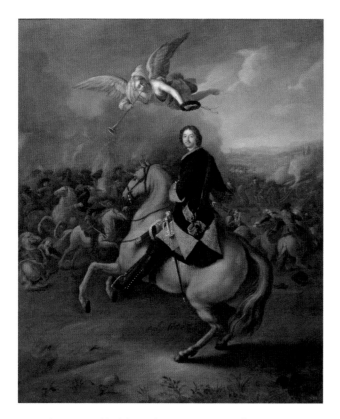

Peter the Great This eighteenth-century painting of Peter the Great winning the decisive battle of Poltava against Sweden in 1709 shows the monarch dressed in western European style. An angel descends from heaven to crown Peter with laurels, implying that his victory, like his rule, was divinely ordained.

true Western-style service elite. Russia's noble families had traditionally possessed high state offices as a hereditary right, and used them for their own self-interest. Peter introduced a "Table of Ranks" that opened these offices to all—including ambitious commoners. Peter further demanded that all aristocrats serve in the army or civil service, shave their traditional beards, and adopt Western clothing. Peter himself personally shaved the beards of several boyars. He did not, however, cure his own family of their tendency toward murderous feuding. He ended up executing his own son Alexei for treason, and at least two of his eighteenth-century successors died violent deaths. But Peter did permanently change the structures of Russian government and society, greatly curtailing the social influence of the high aristocracy while orienting Russian elites far more toward the West.

ABSOLUTISM IN PRUSSIA

The same notions of the well-ordered state and the aristocracy as a service elite took hold in the northern German state of Brandenburg, whose increasing strength and influence led to its transformation in 1701 into the Kingdom of Prussia. By the time the ruler of Brandenburg, Elector Frederick William, died in 1688, he had already done a great deal to make his scattered and largely indefensible territories a successful proposition—notably by inviting 20,000 industrious French Protestant exiles to settle there, and by building up its manufactures. His son, Elector Frederick III (1657–1713, known as King Frederick I after 1701) continued these pragmatic policies. Exhibiting a frugality that contrasted with French absolutist custom, he paid for his civil government entirely from the proceeds of his own lands, and could therefore use tax revenues almost exclusively for the army. In some regions of what was now Prussia, virtually every able-bodied nobleman served as a military officer. Officers, in turn, largely staffed the state bureaucracy. A famous eighteenth-century witticism held that while most states had armies, Prussia was an army that had a state. Frederick also granted the great landowning nobles known as Junkers greater authority over their serfs and nearly-total exemption from taxes, in return for their obedience and personal service. Soon after receiving his royal title, with very little opposition, he simply abolished Prussia's Estates General.

Frederick's son, King Frederick William I, who ruled from 1713 to 1740, faithfully continued these state-building policies. His frugality, in fact, became something of a European joke, as he cut the already-minimal expenses

The Russian Empire, 1689–1725 Peter the Great's early-eighteenth-century territorial acquisitions added little in landmass to the already vast Russian empire, but included key coastlines with access to the Caspian and Baltic Seas and the Pacific. The 1703 founding of his magnificent capital, Saint Petersburg, in newly conquered lands linked Russia much more closely to the rest of Europe.

of the royal household by 75 percent, dressed habitually in an old military uniform, and subjected his own family to strict military discipline. When his son rebelled against this harsh regime and tried to flee with a close male friend (possibly a lover), the king forced the future King Frederick the Great to watch as the man was executed. Frederick William lavished love and resources on one thing above all: the Prussian army, which he doubled in size. His pet project was a unit of exceptionally tall soldiers, many of whom were close to seven feet tall.

PEASANT MISERIES

The well-ordered absolutist state in theory promised a better life to all its inhabitants. It would crack down on internal violence, subject potentially rampaging soldiers

to better discipline, and limit the ways in which feudal lords exploited their peasant tenants and serfs. In France, for instance, in the early eighteenth century, the royal government frequently stepped in to help peasant villages sue their feudal overlords in court to protect their rights to common land, and to limit rents, fees for the use of mills, and other feudal charges.

RUSSIA AND UKRAINE In practice, however, whatever European peasants gained from these protections, they lost more through the increased taxes they paid to the central states and the stronger limits the state itself placed on their liberty. Russia's Peter the Great, for example, created a new class of "state peasants" who had more freedom to acquire property and move from place to place than ordinary serfs. In return, however, they had to pay heavy dues directly to the state. Peter also drafted thousands of serfs to work on state construction projects under horrific conditions, such as the swamp-draining necessary for the building of the new capital on the shores of the Baltic, in which many died from infectious disease. During Peter's rule, it became increasingly common for serfs to be bought and sold as near-slaves. Serfs who fled their masters faced the death penalty, as did any lords who harbored the fugitives.

In 1739, Russia imposed its version of serfdom on Ukraine as well. There most serfs belonged to great noble houses, such as the Potocki family, which had some 130,000 working on its estates. But nearly a million belonged to the Russian Orthodox Church, with the monastery of St. Sergei alone owning some 92,000. Ukraine's noble landowners, who themselves owed heavy duties to the state, demanded more and more compulsory labor from their serfs and reduced the amount of land that serfs could farm for their own benefit.

Even in Western Europe, where serfdom had largely disappeared by 1700, states increasingly drew on forced peasant labor for large-scale construction projects. In eighteenth-century France, peasants worked as much as a month a year building an ambitious new system of state roads.

FAMINE IN FRANCE Conditions generally grew worse for the peasantry in these last decades of the "Little Ice Age" as harvest failures and plagues continued to occur regularly. In France, the worst hit country in this period,

crises in 1693–1694 and 1709–1710 each killed as much as 5 percent of the population. Famine did not strike because of a complete absence of food, but because shortages drove up bread prices to unaffordable levels. The story of a typical family of five in the northern French village of Saint-Étienne brutally illustrates the point. In the early modern period, such a family relied on bread as its principal source of nutrition and energy, consuming together around 70 pounds a week. At the start of 1693, this peasant family needed to spend only a quarter of its income to purchase the needed amount of bread. But by the end of 1693, the price had more than doubled, forcing them to scrimp on all other expenses. And by mid-1694, the price had gone up another three-fold, so that the typical family of five could buy only 38 pounds of bread per week, even if they spent every penny on it. Starvation followed.

And there was worse to come. In the winter of 1709, one of the worst of the Little Ice Age, temperatures in northern France fell to as low as 40 degrees below zero. The Seine and Rhine Rivers froze, and as many as half a million people died of cold, disease, and starvation. No disasters of anywhere near this magnitude occurred after 1710, as the climate finally began to ease, and war moved largely away from French territory. Yet infectious disease remained a persistent threat. In 1720–1722, in one of the last great outbreaks of bubonic plague in Europe, over half of the 90,000 inhabitants of the great French port city of Marseilles died.

French Famine The French government was not adequately able to stem the grain shortage, as suggested by this contemporary image, in which crowds of peasants press against a bread distribution center in Paris.

THE CONDUCT OF WAR

The absolutist states used most of the additional revenue they extracted from their populations for the familiar purpose of fighting wars. Warfare of the late 1600s and early 1700s did not match the Thirty Years' War in ferocity and destruction, but it remained a common feature of European life. Religion drove some of this conflict. Yet even more than during the Thirty Years' War, European powers proved willing to forge alliances across religious lines when it suited their dynastic interests and helped offset French power. And while religious intolerance within states continued to cause considerable misery, it became much less frequent for states to go to war to protect religious minorities elsewhere. This was also a period in which Europe's increasingly powerful absolutist states continued to transform their armed forces into highly disciplined, professional organizations.

CHILDHOOD IN RURAL FRANCE

Despite new crops and advancements in agricultural techniques, the vast majority of France's population—some 90%—remained subsistence farmers in the early eighteenth century. Life was still hard: half of all children died before reaching adulthood, life expectancy was barely over 40 years, and hunger, even starvation, was a regular feature of rural life. Most peasants would never venture more than twenty miles from their place of birth.

One who did, however, was Valentin Jamerey-Duval. Born in 1695 in a poor rural commune, he eventually obtained an education and served the Holy Roman Emperor Francis I as a librarian. But despite his dramatic rise, his memoirs, published posthumously in 1784, make clear that he never forgot his humble origins. The following passage recounts the difficult conditions of his childhood in the French countryside.

I was born in France in a place that had once resembled a market town, but which the government's severity had in little time reduced to a poor village, thanks to the frequent storms of taxes. The house where I first saw the light of day had formerly been covered with tiles, but a heavy tax was raised, the tiles were sold to the benefit of the royal coffers, and soon the splendid roof was replaced by a modest covering of straw that could barely protect those it sheltered from the tempestuous weather of the seasons.

My upbringing hardly extended beyond my nourishment; I was raised in the way one cultivates plants, that is to say in a completely vegetative manner. My education consisted of learning the Lord's Prayer, in Latin and in poor French, along with a few other prayers that were explained to me in several elegant versions in dialect. About the same consideration was given to the catechism, and as a result of having fragments repeated to me, I arrived at a vague understanding that that there were a God, a Church, and some sacraments. I learned that there were a pope, the visible head of this Church, priests, and monks; I was taught to respect and even to fear them, and I do so still, although with some reservation.

Finding myself one day at a dinner held by our parish priest, I saw with astonishment that he was eating bread of a different color than that which I had lived on until then; this novelty struck me. I didn't dare ask for some, but the numerous circles I was making around the table and my watchful gaze made my wishes known, and my curious greed was satisfied; I had the pleasure, at the age of eight or nine, of eating white bread for the first time.

QUESTIONS FOR ANALYSIS

1. What challenges did Jamerey-Duval face as a child?
2. In this passage, what roles do the state and the Church play in peasant life?
3. Why do you think the memory of eating white bread for the first time is so vivid to Jamerey-Duval?

Source: Andrew Daily, trans., *Le XVIIIe siècle français au quotidien*, Roland Mortier, ed., (Brussels: 2002), p. 493.

DISCIPLINE AND VIOLENCE

As one example of the declining ferocity of warfare, consider an action widely denounced as one of the great atrocities of the age. In 1688–1689, Louis XIV, hoping to expand the borders of France eastward, invaded the western German region known as the Palatinate. When the Holy Roman Empire refused to yield to his demands, the French king coldly approved a plan that he hoped would intimidate the enemy and prevent it from undertaking offensive operations. In December, his armies began deliberately to destroy towns, villages, and manors throughout the Palatinate with fire and explosives, turning the inhabitants into refugees. A chorus of indignation rose up among France's enemies, and over the next century the scourging of the Palatinate remained a symbol of the Sun King's arrogance, and a permanent, ugly stain on his reputation.

The destruction was indeed severe. Yet in comparison to the vast slaughter of the Thirty Years' War, it was surprisingly mild. French troops remained largely under strict discipline, and concentrated their destructive activities on property, not humans. The fact that the episode became notorious speaks to the broadly lower levels of military violence against which it was measured.

Even when fighting one another, uniformed armies tended to maintain discipline far better than in the earlier part of the century. Commanders invested ever more time in drilling their troops and in maintaining discipline even in the most confusing moments of a battle, when thick clouds of greasy gunpowder smoke choked the soldiers and obscured their sight, and the overpowering roar of muskets and cannons made it difficult to hear orders. In most European states, common soldiers—drawn from the peasantry and urban poor—came to see the military as a long-term career.

Along with the disciplined men came a disciplined weapon, for the period 1660–1700 saw the perfection of the musket. Loaded with pre-packed cartridges, these long-barreled firearms could now be fired two or even three times per minute, allowing more controlled, continual fire than in the past. And a crucial late seventeenth-century addition to the musket—the removable bayonet—allowed infantrymen quickly to turn their guns into murderous edged weapons for use in hand-to-hand combat, eliminating the need for pikemen on the battlefield. But with a weapon of this sort, each of which cost the equivalent of an agricultural laborer's annual wages and demanded lengthy training, it became a priority for generals to preserve both the guns and the men who wielded them. Whereas the 1634 battle of Nördlingen, at the height of the Thirty Years' War, had cost the lives of one-third of the troops involved, a battle of similar importance six decades later—Malplaquet, during the War of the League of Augsburg—resulted in the deaths of only one-seventh of the combatants.

The end of the seventeenth century also saw a notable decrease in military violence against civilians. In siege warfare, commanders slowly evolved a code whereby a city or town would hold out until the first breaching of its defenses, but could then surrender honorably with the expectation of decent treatment. The initial siege could still bring widespread destruction—particularly if the besiegers shot red-hot cannonballs to start fires—but the wild sacking of towns and cities became far less frequent. Similarly, fewer and fewer armies allowed their soldiers to steal wantonly from civilians in their path. The armies of William and Mary developed a particular reputation

for discipline, and paying for the food and supplies they consumed.

ARISTOCRATS AT WAR

We have already seen some of the principal causes of the diminishing intensity of warfare: the logic of the "balance of power" that emerged after the 1648 Peace of Westphalia, the agonizing memory of the horrors of the Thirty Years' War, and a growing acceptance of religious differences among states, if not within states. Louis XIV, whatever his insistence on making France a wholly Catholic country, had little evangelical desire to make Europe a wholly Catholic continent. All of these trends, which first took shape in the mid-seventeenth century, continued in subsequent decades.

But the most important reason for the decreasing violence only made itself fully felt at the height of absolutism: the influence of the aristocracy in European societies in general, and in military leadership in particular. Louis XIV's Court of Versailles, with its complex etiquette and rigid attention to the smallest differences in rank, set the tone for the highest ranks of society, not only in France but also across much of the continent. Here, as we have seen, the ideal of the courtier saw its fullest flowering. This ideal described a man of splendid appearance, exquisite

The Versailles Court Courtiers kneel before Louis XIV to be inducted into the military Order of St Louis—one of the new institutions of court life—in a 1693 painting.

manners and speech, unblemished honor, perfect grace, and unquestioned devotion to the monarch, all undergirded by impeccable courage and self-discipline.

But at Versailles and its competitor courts, far more than in Renaissance Italy, the courtier was also a military officer, and a servant of the monarch. Noblemen, in fact, made little or no distinction between their social identity as nobles and their social identity as officers. And as a result, the twin theaters of the aristocracy that were the royal court and the military campaign were both governed by the courtly ideals that found their most intense expression at Versailles. War, like court life, ideally had to be conducted with self-control, restraint, and honor. Louis XIV's destruction of the Palatinate, which he barely even tried to justify, seemed shocking because it represented a violation of the aristocratic code of honor by the monarch who embodied that code. These ideals were widespread in absolutist continental Europe by 1700, and aligned with the insistence of monarchs from Versailles to Saint Petersburg that nobles become loyal servants of the state. Actual warfare, however, with its massive human and financial costs, never lived up to these ideals more than partially.

WAR AND THE BALANCE OF POWER (1680–1721)

Aristocratic officers wanted to limit the damage caused by war, but they did not want war itself to end. Since they saw war as their principal purpose, the source of their honor, prestige, and position within the state service, limiting its destruction above all offered them a means of engaging in it more often. For this reason, Europe did not see a single year of real peace between 1680 and 1721. France, the continent's most powerful nation, was at war for all but ten of these thirty-five years. France's ambitious king continued to drive the wars.

FRENCH AGGRESSION

In the mid-1680s, Louis XIV stood at the height of his power and glory. His palace of Versailles, now completed, awed and intimidated visitors from across Europe. As we have seen, he had restored internal order to France and presided over an unprecedented flourishing of the arts. Already by 1685, he had ruled far longer, and arguably more successfully, than any French king since Louis IX in the thirteenth century. On the international scene,

his immediate ambition was to expand France's frontier toward the Rhine in the north and east—the borders of the Roman province of Gaul—annexing the Dutch and German territories on the river's western bank. More generally, he hoped to establish France as the predominant power in Europe, and even to gain for himself and his heirs the crown of the Holy Roman Empire, making him the successor to the Roman Caesars.

In keeping with these ambitions, the period began with France trying to build on its territorial successes from the 1670s, annexing several Lutheran, German-speaking areas along the Rhine, including, in 1681, the city of Strasbourg. The Habsburg Holy Roman Emperor Leopold I (1640–1705), who ruled Austria and its Central European possessions, saw these moves as a direct threat. Despite Leopold's sickly appearance and cold, shy manner (until the death of his elder brother he had prepared for a career in the church), he had now ruled capably for a quarter of a century and saw himself as a serious rival to the French king.

THE LAST GREAT OTTOMAN OFFENSIVE (1683)

Leopold was distracted from this rivalry, however, in 1683, when his Austrian monarchy nearly fell to a renewed attack from the Ottoman Turks. Although the Ottomans no longer commanded the sort of military strength they had at the time of Suleiman the Magnificent in the sixteenth century, they still controlled the Balkans and much of present day Hungary. Leopold had unwisely renewed Austrian

Siege of Vienna This painting of the Ottoman siege of Vienna in July, 1683 shows the colorful tents and busy cavalry of the Ottoman army stationed in the hills above the city.

persecution of those Hungarian Protestants remaining under his rule, leading to a revolt by the largely Protestant Hungarian nobility, who called on the Turks for support. The Turks could not resist the temptation, and in 1683, Vizier Kara Mustafa (1635–1683) marched a 100,000-man army through Hungarian territory to besiege the capital of Vienna, raising fears that the Ottoman Empire might finally achieve its old ambitions and extend their rule into the heart of the European continent.

But Austria did not fall, for the threat prompted the quick formation of a Holy League financed by Pope Innocent XI and commanded by the dashing king of Poland, Jan III Sobieski (1629–1696), who routed the Ottoman army at Vienna in September 1683. Mustafa himself, after being stripped of his position by the sultan, was executed by strangulation with a silk cord. His defeat marked the last time the Turks would threaten Central Europe, and within a few years, nearly all Hungarian territory had again come under Habsburg rule. Even so, the war had shaken Austria, which remained in danger from revolt by the Hungarians and other subject peoples.

THE WARS OF LOUIS XIV

With Austria distracted by the Turks and England ruled by France's Catholic ally James II, Louis XIV felt all the more emboldened to push French expansion. But in 1688, when England's Glorious Revolution turned Louis's English ally into an enemy, the balance of power in Europe finally began to shift against him.

WAR OF THE LEAGUE OF AUGSBURG (1688–1697)
In the **War of the League of Augsburg**, France faced an alliance that drew other Catholic states (Austria, Spain, and Bavaria) and Protestant ones (Sweden, England, and the Netherlands) into a powerful coalition. The need to fight yet another European alliance pushed French resources to the breaking point. By 1693, the French armies had reached a strength of 400,000, the largest France had ever seen, but they still could not win a decisive victory. The catastrophic French harvest failures of 1693–1694 did not help. Finally, in 1697, the French and their enemies reached a compromise peace. It gave the combatants breathing time, but settled little, and everyone recognized that it had set the scene for another war to come.

WAR OF THE SPANISH SUCCESSION (1702–1714)
The most important issue left unsettled by the War of

the League of Augsburg involved Spain. During the late seventeenth century, its titular ruler was the Habsburg Charles II (1661–1700), who was physically and mentally disabled. Charles had no heirs, but his two sisters had married Louis XIV and the Emperor Leopold I, and both the French and Austrian monarchs claimed the Spanish succession for their families. As the seventeenth century drew to an end, the three rulers seemed close to reaching an agreement to split the Spanish empire between them, but Charles's ministers objected. Spain was no longer the great power it had been in the sixteenth century, but it still controlled vast territories, including more than half of South America, Central America stretching through California and Florida, islands in the Caribbean, the southern Netherlands (present-day Belgium), southern Italy, and various other Italian territories. Any hopes for a Spanish revival depended on keeping these far-flung territories together.

In November, 1700, Charles died, and it was discovered to everyone's surprise that he had left a will bequeathing this entire vast empire to Louis XIV's younger grandson, who was soon crowned Philip V (1683–1746). Philip renounced all claims to the French throne, thereby in theory ruling out any unification of the French and Spanish empires. But just the prospect of all Spanish domains coming under the control of the Bourbon dynasty was bad enough for both the Austrian Habsburgs and the British. It led almost immediately to the formation of yet another alliance against France, and the outbreak of the **War of the Spanish Succession**. The fighting lasted until 1713 and involved the Americas as well as Europe. Despite Louis XIV's best efforts to establish French supremacy on the seas, the French navy proved no match for its Anglo-Dutch rivals, while on the continent, French commanders were defeated in a series of major battles. These reverses again pushed the French state to the breaking point. Between 1683 and 1708, its budget deficit rose by a factor of 45.

And then, at the worst possible moment, the climate itself seemed to turn against France, with the terrible cold and famine of 1709–1710. King Louis XIV, now in his late sixties, suffered from a variety of painful, chronic conditions, and these events pushed him to despair. In an astonishing move for an absolute monarch, he wrote a letter, to be read from every pulpit in the kingdom, stressing the need for the people to support the nation in its hour of need. Over the next two years, the French managed to stave off military disaster, but the days of French aggression and expansion had come to an end.

Territory held before the War of the Spanish Succession, 1701 | Territorial gains by 1721
- Austrian Habsburg lands
- French Bourbon lands
- Great Britain
- Savoy/Kingdom of Sardinia
- Spanish Bourbon lands
- Prussian lands
- X Battle
- — Boundary of Holy Roman Empire, 1721

Claims in North America

Europe, 1683–1721 Defeat of Ottoman forces in 1683 allowed Austria to cement its claim to the Hungarian lands, including new possessions on the Ottoman border. In 1707, the English and Scottish crowns were formally joined, creating the new Kingdom of Great Britain. The Peace of Utrecht in 1713–14 inaugurated the greatest changes of the early eighteenth century: control of the Southern Netherlands and Sicily passed from the Spanish Habsburgs to the Austrian Habsburgs, the independent kingdom of Sardinia came to rule the French duchy of Savoy, and Britain acquired several French territories in North America.

THE PEACE OF UTRECHT (1713–1714) The war ended with the compromise **Peace of Utrecht**, a series of treaties negotiated in 1713–1714 that aimed to update and supplant the earlier Peace of Westphalia. Under its terms, France recognized the Protestant succession in England, pulled its remaining forces out of the southern Netherlands and Italy, and allowed the southern Netherlands and Naples to pass from Spain to Austria, thereby keeping them under the House of Habsburg. France also conceded to Britain the enormously profitable monopoly

Peace of Utrecht An illustration from the French royal almanac of 1714 shows diplomats signing a treaty at Utrecht. Images along the border and at the bottom of the image represent the royal families involved in the negotiations.

European great powers bore fruit. The great loser was Sweden's Charles XII (1682–1718), who came to the throne at age 15 in 1697, and who initially seemed to revive the conquering spirit of his predecessor Gustavus Adolphus. Taking advantage of his country's formidable system of conscription and powerful military tradition, Charles quickly delivered stinging blows to Denmark, Russia, and Poland-Lithuania, which combined had twenty times Sweden's population of 1.5 million. In 1707–1708, Charles's forces struck through Poland into Ukraine, threatening Russia again. But Tsar Peter, employing a strategy that Russian leaders would use many times against invaders in centuries to come, allowed his army to retreat unbeaten, drawing the Swedes farther and farther from their home base. Finally, in June 1709, Charles fought a much larger Russian force at the battle of Poltava, and his badly weakened forces were decimated. Even while fleeing for safety into Ottoman territory, Charles refused to give up. Over the next twelve years, Sweden fought desperately to hold off a broad coalition of Baltic powers, but never managed to recover its previous strength. The war took a particular toll on Sweden's Finnish provinces, which lost as much as half their population. Charles himself died in battle in Norway in 1718, and at the end of the Great Northern War in 1721, Sweden had to surrender considerable territory, above all to Russia, including much of present-day Estonia and Latvia.

ENGLAND Second came the astonishing rise of England. Under William and Mary, and then Queen Anne, it succeeded in checking France and establishing itself as a major military force on the continent. In 1707, in the middle of the War of the Spanish Succession, England further strengthened itself by entering into an Act of Union with Scotland. The court party in Scotland pushed the act through its Parliament despite widespread opposition in the population at large. While the two kingdoms had obeyed the same monarch since 1603, and the term "British" was already widespread, now a single government would formally rule the entire island as the Kingdom of Great Britain. (Ireland remained a separate kingdom, and only joined the union a century later.)

on selling slaves to the Spanish American colonies. And France gave Britain several of its colonies and settlements, including Acadia (Nova Scotia). Louis XIV did succeed in his single most important war aim, keeping his grandson on the Spanish throne, but the grandiose ambitions he had developed for France had been definitively checked. They would not revive again until the time of Napoleon, a century later.

NEW GREAT POWERS

The period from 1680 to 1715 saw two other major developments on the international scene. First, the Great Northern War of 1700–1721 marked the rise of a new great power—Russia—and the eclipse of Sweden.

RUSSIA In this conflict, Peter the Great's efforts to reform the Russian state and join the company of

The Great Northern War, 1700–1721

AN ATLANTIC WORLD

Britain's success derived not only from its gains in Europe, but also from the development of its colonial empire, especially in North America and the Caribbean. Between 1680 and 1740, the New World continued to grow in importance as a source of European wealth and a site of competition among the European powers. During this period, Britain emerged as by far the most dynamic colonial power, aided by its unsurpassed navy.

BRITAIN'S MAINLAND COLONIES

Britain's North American colonies grew almost five-fold in population between 1680 and 1740, to a total of over 900,000 inhabitants. Much of the growth was driven by immigration. As in earlier decades, both the British and French North American colonies were integrated into patterns of migration within Europe. The same routes that took Britons from the Midlands to London, and French migrants from the countryside to cities like Rouen or Paris, also extended across the Atlantic. Britain's colonies varied greatly in economy, social structure, and population. In New England, immigration came mostly from England itself, especially the dissenting Protestant groups related to the early Puritan settlers. Coastal fishing and inland farming communities predominated.

The mid-Atlantic British colonies had a much more diverse population. Settlers of the early Dutch and Swedish colonies, all taken over by England by 1670, lived alongside English migrants and a large number of Germans in what English observers routinely referred to as a "Babel" of cultures. Pennsylvania, a prosperous colony founded in 1682 by the Quaker William Penn (1644–1718), who offered religious liberty to all settlers, quickly drew particularly large numbers of migrants from Germany. In 1740, close to a third of the colony was German-speaking. In the Chesapeake and southern colonies, the plantation economy continued to expand, attracting poorer English settlers who initially came as indentured servants. Slavery, of both Africans and their descendants born in America, existed in all the colonies, and in the eighteenth century slaves largely supplanted indentured servants in plantation labor.

SUGAR AND SLAVERY

By 1740, the European colonies in the Caribbean were eclipsing those in mainland North America as sites of colonization and imperial competition. The huge profitability of Caribbean cash crops drove this change. Whereas Virginia relied on a single crop, tobacco, for its economic growth, the Caribbean islands provided different consumer products: coffee, indigo, and, especially, cane sugar. In the seventeenth century, Europeans who had previously relied on honey and fruit for sweets increasingly grew addicted to cane sugar from the tropics. The Portuguese began large-scale cultivation in Brazil, but by late in the century the center of sugar cultivation was moving north into the Caribbean. By 1700, Britain's island colonies, most importantly Barbados and Jamaica, had together outstripped Brazil, producing roughly 25,000 tons of sugar per year. By 1730, their capitals of Bridgetown and Port Royal had grown larger than any other city in British America except Boston. France began to catch up with Britain after the treaty ending the War of the League of Augsburg divided the large Caribbean island of Hispaniola (today, Haiti and the Dominican Republic) between France and Spain. The Spanish colony of Cuba was also an important source of European sugar.

The rise of sugar as a consumer product, and also, to a lesser extent, coffee, led to major changes in patterns of colonization. Both crops were hugely labor-intensive. The harvesting and processing of sugar cane into a form suitable for export could push work forces to the limit and beyond. During the harvest, the back-breaking labor of grinding and boiling cane went on day and night without cease. Colonial landowners quickly found it far more profitable to do this work with African slaves than with white indentured servants. In the 1640s, Barbados's population of 30,000 had included only a few slaves, and large numbers of European indentured servants. By 1700, however, the indentured servants had largely departed, and 15,000 free whites shared the island with 50,000 black slaves. Later in the eighteenth century, in some Caribbean colonies, black slaves would outnumber free whites by as much as twenty to one. Among the consequences of this demographic shift was that white colonists, fearful of slave rebellion, became tightly dependent on military force supplied by the imperial home country.

THE ATLANTIC SLAVE TRADE This shift also provided an enormous impetus to the Atlantic slave trade. As we have already seen, this trade developed in the sixteenth and early seventeenth century as a "triangle trade" in which Europeans used various goods, including textiles, metal tools, and guns, to purchase slaves in Africa, shipped the slaves across the Atlantic to the Americas, and then brought cash crops back to Europe. This pattern did not fundamentally change in the late seventeenth century, but

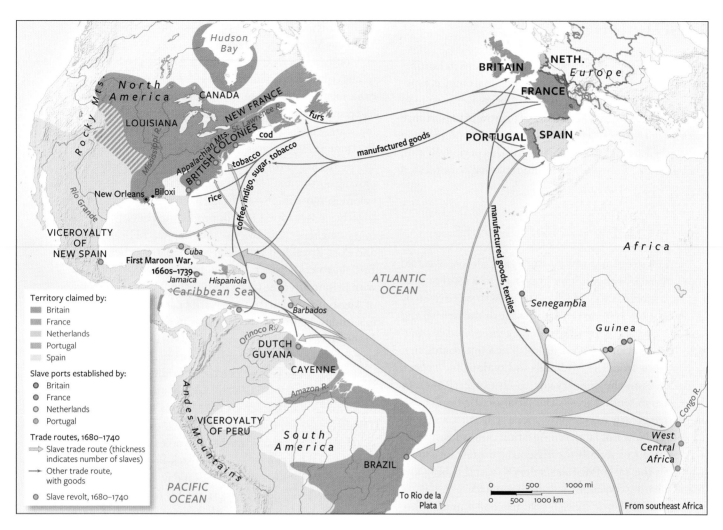

The Atlantic World, 1680–1740 A vast trading economy—particularly in enslaved people—linked European powers with their rapidly expanding colonies overseas. The slave trade moved staggering numbers of human cargo from Portuguese slave ports in west-central Africa to Brazil, and from Dutch, British, and French ports in Guinea and Senegambia to Dutch Guyana, the British colonies on the eastern coast of North America, and French colonies in North America and the Caribbean. There enslaved people produced huge quantities of trading goods such as sugar and tobacco to be sent back to Europe—although slave revolts in response to this violent economic system occurred frequently throughout the colonies.

it expanded enormously in scale. Between 1625 and 1650, Europeans transported roughly 7,000 Africans a year through the "middle passage." By 1700, this number had nearly quadrupled, and the growth continued through the following decades. Over its entire history, the slave trade shipped more than 11,000,000 Africans to the Americas, with 90 percent going to the Caribbean and South America. The **middle passage** across the Atlantic took place under horrific conditions for the slaves, who were shackled and crammed into filthy hulls, shaved of hair to reduce disease, and abused by the European crews (women, in particular, were routinely raped). Slave traders coldly calculated how many slaves they could cram into a single ship before the conditions led too many of them to die en route.

In the colonies, especially in the Caribbean, the slaves' condition could be equally cruel. In Jamaica and Saint-Domingue, the French territory of present-day Haiti, at some periods, newly arrived slaves could expect to live no more than ten years thanks to the terrible labor required of them. The death rates rose so high that the slave populations could not naturally reproduce, and the plantation owners needed to import more slaves just to keep up the numbers. There is some evidence that slave women deliberately avoided pregnancy by any means possible (including using their knowledge of plants to induce abortions) so as not to bring children into lives of slavery. Attempts to mitigate the horrors, such as a "Black Code" introduced in the French colonies in 1685 to prevent abuses

THE LIMITS OF LIBERTY

Though European governments granted greater rights and protections to the people, the expansion of liberty was limited: certain rights, like the right to property, reinforced European ownership of slaves. The differences between the English Bill of Rights and the Black Code of the French colonies demonstrate the contradiction between this increased liberty at home and slavery abroad. As the Bill of Rights extended the rights of white Europeans, the Code systematized the strict control of slaves' lives. These documents capture the ambiguous nature of liberty and equality in the late seventeenth century.

English Bill of Rights

The Bill of Rights (1689) made clear that while Parliament accepted the rule of William III and Mary II, their authority was limited by the rights of the English people.

And thereupon the said lords spiritual and temporal[1] and commons[2]…declare:

- That the pretended power of suspending the laws, or the execution of laws, by regal authority, without consent of parliament, is illegal…

- That the pretended power of dispensing with laws, or the execution of laws, by regal authority, as it hath been assumed and exercised of late, is illegal…

- That levying money for or to the use of the Crown by pretence of prerogative, without grant of parliament, for longer time, or in other manner than the same is or shall be granted, is illegal…

- That it is the right of the subjects to petition the king, and all commitments and prosecutions for such petitioning are illegal…

- That the raising or keeping a standing army within the kingdom in time of peace unless it be with consent of parliament, is against law…

- That the subjects which are Protestants, may have arms for their defence suitable to their conditions and as allowed by law…

- That election of members of parliament ought to be free…

- That the freedom of speech and debates or proceedings in parliament, ought not to be impeached or questioned in any court or place out of parliament;

- That excessive bail ought not to be required, nor excessive fines imposed; nor cruel and unusual punishments inflicted…

- That all grants and promises of fines and forfeitures of particular persons before conviction, are illegal and void;

- And that for redress of all grievances, and for the amending, strengthening, and preserving of the laws, parliaments ought to be held frequently.

The Black Code

While the following sections of the Code allow for rights for freed slaves, they also legalize harsh punishments.

XII. The children born of marriages between slaves will be slaves and will belong to the master of the female slaves, and not to those of their husbands, if the husband and the wife have different masters.

XIII. We wish that if a slave husband has married a free woman, the children, both male and girls, will follow the condition of their mother and be free like her, in spite of the servitude of their father; and that if the father is free and the mother enslaved, the children will be slaves for the same reason.…

XVI. In the same way we forbid slaves belonging to different masters to gather in the day or night…on pain of corporal punishment…frequent violations and other aggravating circumstances can be punished with death…

XXXI. Slaves cannot be party to either judgments or civil proceedings, nor can they be plaintiffs or defendants in civil or criminal proceedings…

XXXIII. The slave who will have struck his master or the wife of his master, his mistress, or their children and drawn to bring blood, or in the face, will be punished with death.…

LVIII. We command manumitted slaves to retain a particular respect for their former masters, their widows, and their children; and any insult that they make against them will be punished more severely than if it had been done to another person. However, we declare them free and absolved of any other burdens, services, and rights that their former masters would like to claim, as much on their persons as on their possessions and estates as patrons.

LIX. We grant to manumitted slaves the same rights, privileges, and liberties enjoyed by persons born free; desiring that they merit this acquired liberty and that it produce in them, both for their persons and for their property, the same effects that the good fortune of natural liberty causes in our other subjects.

QUESTIONS FOR ANALYSIS

1. In what ways does the Bill of Rights extend the rights of the English people?
2. How does the Black Code restrict the rights of slaves?
3. Do you see any similarities in the ways these documents approach the subject of rights?

[1] **lords spiritual and temporal:** bishops of the Church of England and secular members, respectively, in Parliament's House of Lords
[2] **commons:** Members of Parliament's lower House of Commons

Sources: *The Parliamentary History of England, from the Earliest Period to the Year 1803*, Vol. 5 (London: 1809), pp. 484–485; *Slave Revolution in the Caribbean, 1789–1804*, Laurent Dubois and John D. Garrigus, eds. (New York: 2006, pp. 51–54).

The First Maroon War An eighteenth-century oil painting shows British troops ending the Maroon revolt in Jamaica. Escaped slaves—depicted in exotic "native" dress—lay down their weapons, while a British officer reads the terms of surrender.

and encourage the slaves' conversion to Catholicism, were widely ignored.

SLAVE RESISTANCE The slaves themselves offered resistance to their condition. Slave revolts were common in the Caribbean, and brutally suppressed. In other cases, slaves fled and established fugitive communities in inaccessible regions of mountain or swamp. Known in English as "Maroons" (from an Indian word meaning "flight of an arrow"), these escaped slaves established some successful communities. During the "First Maroon War" in Jamaica, which lasted from the 1660s until 1739, the British authorities could not manage to suppress or capture the fugitives. In the end, they negotiated an agreement that allowed the Maroons to remain in their settlements under British supervision, provided that they not provide shelter to any other escaped slaves.

FRENCH EXPANSION IN NORTH AMERICA

The new wealth intensified imperial competition in the Americas, especially between France and Britain. The French, however, unwittingly sabotaged their own efforts, particularly on the North American mainland. While the English continued to allow religious dissidents to populate their colonies, the French maintained their policy of banning all Protestants from New France (in 1685 they banned Jews as well). As a result, the French Protestant emigration strengthened Massachusetts, New York, and South Carolina rather than French possessions. In Canada, Louis XIV's minister Colbert also limited growth by trying to rein in the French settlers who often travelled for months into the "Upper Country" of Canada to take part in the lucrative fur trade with the Indians. While tolerant of continuing Catholic efforts aimed at converting the Indians, Colbert insisted that all French subjects other than missionaries remain in a narrow, well-defined belt of territory along the Saint Lawrence River. There he tried to impose an idealized version of French absolutist society in which settlers were forced to pay heavy dues to feudal lords. As a result, relatively few French subjects opted to emigrate to Canada. Those who did mostly hoped to make money and return to France.

Nonetheless, the period 1680–1740 saw France expand its American colonies in new directions. In 1681–1682 the French explorer René-Robert Cavelier de La Salle (1643–1687) travelled from Montreal through the Great Lakes system into what is now Illinois, from where he followed the Mississippi River all the way to the Gulf of Mexico. Although encountering many Indian settlements along the way, La Salle followed the standard procedure of European explorers and claimed the entire vast Mississippi basin—from the Appalachians to the Rocky Mountains, roughly one-third of the present-day continental United States—for France, and named it Louisiana after Louis XIV.

FRENCH LOUISIANA In 1699, other French explorers established a settlement at Biloxi, near the mouth of the Mississippi (New Orleans followed in 1718). A large majority of the initial settlers died within months of infectious disease. Still, the French government was determined to colonize the Mississippi basin, so as to keep the major river system of North America out of British hands and fence off Britain's thirteen colonies with a thin ribbon of French settlement to the north and west. France deported prisoners to Louisiana (including roughly 1,000 female prostitutes), which pushed the colony's population to 3,000 by the 1740s. These settlers imported African slaves, who brought with them farming techniques well suited to the climate, particularly for rice. But while Louisiana developed into a slave colony, the food crops cultivated there did not require the sort of massive slave labor seen in the Caribbean, and did not generate the same profits.

THE FRENCH AND NATIVE PEOPLES Although the French could not compete in population with the British in America, they were adept at forging strategic alliances with the native peoples who lived across the British and French territories. Through these alliances, they managed to keep steady military pressure on the British colonies—often by raiding unprotected British towns. In early 1704, for instance, a force of French Canadians and Indians attacked the Massachusetts town of Deerfield, killing over fifty of its residents. French Jesuit missionaries continued their close study of the Indians and began to develop the elements of what we now know as anthropology. In his pioneering 1724 book *The Customs of American Savages Compared to the Customs of Early Times*, Joseph-François Lafitau (1681–1746) argued that American Indians resembled no one so much as the ancient Greeks. His work would follow the idea that *all* human societies evolve from similar "primitive" stages to more "advanced" ones. As we will see in later chapters, imperialists have often employed this idea to justify the subjugation of "primitive" peoples. Yet it also presupposes the essential similarity of all humans, whatever their social condition—a notion that would continue to resonate in Western social and political thought.

AMERICAN TRADE AND EUROPEAN ECONOMIES

The French and British both continued to govern their colonies according to strict mercantilist principles. They gave the monopoly of trade to government-chartered companies, and tried to forbid free exchange with Europe. When Spain passed to Bourbon rule under Philip V in 1700, its empire started to emulate the French, with more and more activity controlled by a series of new trading companies. Throughout the American colonies, overall economic growth rates remained surprisingly modest in the eighteenth century—as little as 1 percent per year per capita. The profits generated by the colonies did not stay in the colonies, but largely traveled back across the Atlantic to enrich European investors.

At the same time, European economies became increasingly powered by American trade, as twin financial crises in France and England illustrated in the years around 1720. Both crises derived from attempts to link state finances to the chartered companies that had monopolies over trade with the colonies. These "joint stock" companies sold shares to the public to raise money and spread the risk in their ventures. In France, the Scottish economist John Law (1671–1729), a gambling companion of the Regent Philippe d'Orléans, became effective finance minister in 1716, with unprecedented control over the country's economy. He founded a national bank, took over management of the huge national debt, and linked both to a new overseas trading corporation, the **Mississippi Company**. Convinced of Law's genius, the French public quickly bid up the price of shares in the company nearly twenty-fold. They did not recognize that their investments depended on reliable profits from the colonies, including especially Louisiana, where a few hundred disease-ridden colonists were at this point barely surviving. In 1720 the bubble burst, destroying the bank and company and sending Law fleeing from the country. In Britain, a similar situation developed with the South Sea Company, which had the right to supply Spanish South America with slaves. The company attempted to purchase the British national debt with its own shares, driving up their price. The bubble created by these inflated share prices burst in 1720 and precipitated a collapse in the English stock market as a whole.

Understanding Native Culture Lafitau's 1724 account of American Indians included these etchings depicting Native Canadian religious rituals, emphasizing the customs' exoticism and also their connection to the natural world.

MIGNARD'S *PORTRAIT OF LOUISE DE KÉROUAILLE, DUCHESS OF PORTSMOUTH*

Louise de Kérouaille, one of Charles II's favorite mistresses, used her position and influence to become the Duchess of Portsmouth in 1673. Located to the southwest of London, Portsmouth was a major port with strong ties to the burgeoning colonial trade of the seventeenth century.

The French painter Pierre Mignard's 1682 portrait of the Duchess emphasizes her legendary beauty, enhanced by delicate makeup, pearl earrings, and extravagant fabrics. But it also speaks to the importance of transatlantic trade to her wealth and standing: a black slave child kneels at her side, holding out a branch of red coral and a shell overflowing with pearls, expensive commodities from Britain's overseas colonies. The glimpse of the sea in the background alludes to the source of these luxuries. The Duchess—and Portsmouth—were increasingly dependent on the colonial trade represented by these symbols.

QUESTIONS FOR ANALYSIS

1. What impressions of the Duchess does Mignard convey?
2. Why do you think Mignard included a slave child in the portrait?
3. In what ways is the Duchess's physical beauty tied to colonial trade in this painting?

The story of these twin bubbles illustrates the increasing complexity and international character of the European economy in this period. The patterns of commercial development seen in the Netherlands earlier in the seventeenth century were spreading to neighboring states. Already in England by the time of the Glorious Revolution, only half the population was working directly in agriculture. Manufacturing, above all of textiles, increasingly drove the economies of England and northern France. Meanwhile, as colonial populations grew, they became not only a source of cash crops like tobacco, coffee, and sugar, but also a market for goods from the home country. In this world of increasingly sophisticated patterns of trade, merchants developed ever more intricate instruments of credit, and depended ever more on a stable currency. The founding of the Bank of England in 1694 proved an enormous boon to English merchants in this regard, preventing the South Sea bubble from doing long-term damage. In France, by contrast, the collapse of Law's system acted to delay the country's financial modernization—it would not acquire a true national bank until the nineteenth century.

CITY LIFE AND CULTURE

If the patterns set in the mid-seventeenth century had continued, the expanding economy would have fueled ever more opulent displays of courtly luxury by Europe's crowned heads. But after the 1680s, the drive for ostentation embodied in the construction of Versailles became less popular. In France, an increasingly influential Jansenist Catholicism, with its emphasis on simplicity and repentance, criticized the sensuality of court life as an invitation to sin. Louis XIV himself grew less fond of ostentation as he grew older, and started spending more time away from Versailles and its rigorous etiquette. After his death, the Regent moved the court to Paris, and while it later returned to Versailles, King Louis XV did not have his great-grandfather's taste for pageantry. In Russia, although Peter the Great built himself a magnificent palace on the Baltic in the style of Versailles, called Peterhof, he reserved his principal architectural energies for the new city of Saint Petersburg. In Prussia, as we have seen, Kings Frederick and Frederick William rejected the example of Versailles altogether in favor of a simpler, more frugal style of rule.

But as the courts declined in importance, cities rose. The decades around 1700 mark the period when cities—above all London and Paris—supplanted courts as the centers of gravity of European cultures. London, its port brimming with ships and products from around the world, had a particular attraction. Its population, probably around 575,000 in 1700, would grow to 750,000 over the next fifty years. More importantly, one in six inhabitants of England and Wales lived in the metropolis at some point in their lives. The ranks of middle-class merchants, professionals, and state officials all swelled.

NEW CULTURAL INSTITUTIONS IN THE CITIES

In keeping with these shifts, in the decades around 1700 new urban institutions began to draw people of different social backgrounds together.

THE COFFEEHOUSES The first Western European coffeehouses, copying Turkish models, had been founded in mid-seventeenth-century London. Their numbers then jumped from less than a thousand in 1675 to three thousand by 1710. Ranging from poorly furnished ground-floor rooms to large buildings decorated in a self-consciously

Saint Petersburg The towers of the new fortress Peter the Great built in his capital city rise out of the snow in this colored engraving of people promenading along the Neva River, made shortly after the fortress was completed in 1740.

London Coffeehouses Inside an early-eighteenth-century London coffeehouse, a landlady and boy serve coffee and other drinks and food to the male patrons, who gather around tables to read newspapers and discuss the issues of the day. Numerous pots of coffee boil on the fire.

"oriental" style with Turkish carpets and tapestries, these institutions attracted a broad, although mostly male social clientele, ranging from aristocrats to merchants, professionals, and well-off artisans.

SALONS In France, a key urban institution was what has come to be known as the **salon**: gatherings at aristocratic homes where writers read their works aloud or participated in discussions of literature and current events. As we have seen, the early salons had functioned principally as means of instructing newcomers in the customs and traditions of the court. However, particularly after the death of Louis XIV, they turned increasingly urban and literary in their focus.

Salons proved especially receptive to elite women, who not only attended them but frequently served as hostesses presiding over the discussions. For these women they offered new opportunities for self-expression. Consider, for instance, the remarkable case of Claudine Guérin de Tencin (1682–1749). Her father, a magistrate in Grenoble, destined her for the clergy, but before taking her vows, she secretly signed an affidavit stating that she was entering the convent against her will. When her father died, she used the affidavit to sue for release from her vows, and in 1712, was able to leave the convent. She joined her sister, already a notable hostess, in Paris, and within a few years had founded a salon of her own that welcomed some of the greatest writers of the day, including Montesquieu and Fontenelle. She herself became a published novelist. Her illegitimate son Jean Le Rond d'Alembert became a great philosopher and mathematician.

PERIODICALS These urban institutions flourished not just because of the period's economic development, but also thanks to important changes in western European printing and bookselling. In 1662, soon after the restoration of the Stuarts, the conservative Parliament passed the Licensing Act, which banned "heretical, schismatical, blasphemous, seditious, and treasonable books, pamphlets, and papers," and stipulated that all printed matter needed a government license. Just thirty-three years later, however, the post–Glorious Revolution parliament allowed the Act to lapse, and did not replace it. As a result, something approaching freedom of the press appeared for the first time in England, and printers found it far easier to disseminate works of all sorts. By 1700, London had several newspapers, and in 1702, a daily. Provincial newspapers quickly followed, as did a thrice-weekly satirical magazine called the *Tatler*. All these printed works stimulated the flow of coffee shop

conversation as surely as caffeine did (and many coffee shops provided newspapers free for their customers to read). While much harsher licensing rules remained in effect on most of the continent, periodicals began to appear there as well. By 1710, France had journals devoted to literary and scholarly matters as well as the formal, court-centered *Gazette de France*.

URBAN POVERTY, CRIME, AND REFORM

To be sure, most city dwellers did not patronize coffeehouses, visit salons, or read periodicals. The centers of most leading cities remained broadly similar to what they had been throughout the previous century and more: crowded warrens of narrow, unhealthy, dark streets, where many lived in poverty. In London, perhaps one in ten men, women, and children suffered from serious malnutrition. In moments of economic crisis, when servants, day laborers, and journeymen were turned out of work, the percentage could rise steeply. These men and women only survived thanks to what historians call an economy of makeshifts, which could include pawning possessions, hiring themselves out for whatever small jobs they could find, but also theft and prostitution. And despite Christian teachings on the subject of poverty, members of social elites often showed little sympathy for the poor in their midst. A member of the British parliament warned in 1741, speaking of London: "The filth, sir, of some parts of the town, and the inequality and ruggedness of others, cannot but in the eyes of foreigners disgrace our nation, and incline them to imagine a people, not only without decency, but without government, a herd of barbarians."

The report was not only exaggerated and unsympathetic, but an indication that the British government found it difficult to keep control over its capital, where crime was rampant. There the legendary Jonathan Wild, while supposedly acting as a "thief-taker" (catcher) on behalf of the government, actually ran one of the largest criminal enterprises in Europe. Contemporaries claimed that Wild had thousands of thieves reporting to him. Among the urban poor, Wild was a folk hero, and when finally put on trial and executed in 1725, he went to his death cheered by crowds of thousands.

The London poor themselves had a striking capacity for violence, especially when it came to reinforcing solidarity against a system of justice they saw, with some justification, as oppressive. In June of 1732, a crowd grabbed a man named John Waller, whom they resented for serving as a police informer and witness against a series of highway robbers. They stripped him naked, beat him to death, and abused the corpse. "My Son had neither Eyes, nor Ears, nor Nose to be seen," his mother piteously recounted. "They had squeezed his head flat."

British suspicions of over-powerful central government made effective policing more difficult. In the cities of absolutist continental states, however, the reforms introduced by officials like Antonio de Vieira achieved an unprecedented degree of social control. In Paris, as the office of the Lieutenant General of Police expanded its power, squads of watchmen reporting to neighborhood police "commissioners" sought to repress criminality and defend the moral and political order. They kept a particularly keen watch out for "bad speech" directed against the King or the Church, while also arresting men accused of homosexuality. City dwellers reacted with suspicion to these changes, and on occasions when order broke down—notably at times of bread shortages—the police watchmen found themselves the first target of rioters. To prevent such riots, which were often led by women, posing as guardians of the family breadbasket—they were also less likely to be attacked by soldiers or mounted police—the French crown and the Lieutenant General attempted to guarantee a supply of reasonably priced bread to Paris and other large cities. They did so by putting the entire process of bread production under greater government control. By the middle of the eighteenth century, a complex system controlled to whom farmers in the Parisian countryside could sell their grain and at what price; how millers would mill it into flour; how bakers would sell it to consumers and at what final price.

A NEW CULTURAL CLIMATE

In keeping with the general retreat from ostentation and the broadening consumption of culture, the fine arts and literature experienced a turn away from vast, epic productions in this period. Ambitious literary authors increasingly eschewed the epic poetic ambitions of Milton and Racine, and embraced forms of extended prose fiction that connected more directly with the experience of ordinary readers—including especially middle-class readers.

DEFOE Novels of a sort had existed in European culture since antiquity, and the sixteenth and early seventeenth centuries had seen the publication of such classic examples as *The Life of Gargantua and Pantagruel* by the French satirist François Rabelais (1494–1553) and especially *Don Quixote* by the Spanish writer Miguel de Cervantes (1547–1616). But in London in April, 1719, a new sort of novel appeared.

London Crime Eighteenth-century illustrations depict the violent world of crime and punishment in London. Pickpockets or highway robbers (left) might meet their comeuppance in a rowdy public hanging (right) attended by hundreds: robbery was punishable by death.

The preface to *Robinson Crusoe* proclaims that it is "a Just History of Fact; neither is there any appearance of Fiction in it." The narrative begins with the words "I was born in the Year 1632, in the city of *York*," and proceeds to tell the life story of a man from northern England who had gone to sea, nearly perished in a shipwreck, and washed up, alone, on a desert island: "I am divided from Mankind, a Solitaire." There Robinson Crusoe forges clothing, tools, and habitation for himself, and enlists in his service a pliable native he dubs his "man Friday."

In this book, Daniel Defoe (1660–1731)—the son of a wealthy candle-maker with a checkered career in business and a long record of political agitation—managed something remarkable. He presented a fictional tale of extraordinary individual initiative both as a "true" story and as something with which readers from many different backgrounds could identify. And they did. The 364-page novel sold some 20,000 copies in its first eight months, bringing its publisher unprecedented earnings. Still read today with pleasure, *Robinson Crusoe* arguably represents the first modern realist novel, and as we will see, in the later eighteenth century, it and its successors would have a decisive influence on European culture, society, and politics.

SWIFT The same literary climate also favored lighter works of fantasy, satire, and wit. In Britain, this was the age of the great Irish satirist Jonathan Swift (1667–1745), best remembered today for *Gulliver's Travels*, whose visions of lands inhabited by talking horses and humans both tiny and immense make it one of the earliest examples of science fiction. Among Swift's most brilliant satirical productions was his 1729 essay "A Modest Proposal," which drew attention to the miserable condition of Ireland's peasantry, and mocked overly ambitious projects for social improvement. It did all this by suggesting a simple solution to the problem of Irish food shortages: reducing the population by eating Irish children. "I have been assured by a very knowing American of my acquaintance in London," Swift wrote, "that a young healthy child well nursed is at a year old a most delicious, nourishing, and wholesome food, whether stewed, roasted, baked, or boiled . . . ."

LEARNED PERIODICALS AND THE REPUBLIC OF LETTERS

In the period 1680–1740, one other important new form of printed work appeared as well: the learned periodical. In 1684, in the Netherlands, an apparently modest French-language journal began publishing, with the unremarkable title *News from the Republic of Letters*. Edited and largely written by **Pierre Bayle**, a young Protestant exile from the France of Louis XIV, it contained book reviews, correspondence from different cities, the occasional letter to the editor, obituaries, and other literary tidbits, all bound together in a form that modern readers of a certain age will find remarkably familiar. It was soon joined by other, similar journals, but still had a very low circulation by modern standards (in the hundreds). Unlike *Robinson Crusoe*, it did not make anyone rich. But it and its successors had a critical effect on the community referred to in its title: the Republic of Letters.

The Republic of Letters had a long history. Networks of scholars who exchanged correspondence and manuscripts, engaged in reasoned criticism of each other's work, and provided assistance to each other, had existed at least since the days of Erasmus in the late fifteenth and early sixteenth centuries. By allowing authors to compare texts and identify where copyists had made mistakes or alterations, the emergence of the "republic" had spurred the development of modern standards of critical scholarship. By establishing standards of civil discussion by which scholars could admit mistakes or change their minds without shame, it laid the foundations for modern forms of scholarly debate. The Republic of Letters created a community of scholars and writers that could feel more real to its participants than the actual physical communities

in which they lived. As John Locke eloquently put it to a correspondent, "I draw breath everywhere but I live with my friends."

But in the late seventeenth century, periodicals like Bayle's changed the Republic of Letters in several ways. They gave it more visibility, a better-defined structure, and they associated it with a cause: religious toleration. The principal journals all came from the same place: the French Protestant refugee population in the Netherlands, which exploded in numbers after the revocation of the Edict of Nantes in 1685. In their reviews and discussions, the journals provided a forum for the strongest and most sustained arguments yet seen for religious toleration. *News from the Republic of Letters* and other French-language journals soon spawned English and Dutch imitators, but as French remained the most widely spoken vernacular language of the continent, it was the French Protestants who found the greatest audience.

THE CAMPAIGN FOR TOLERATION

The campaign for toleration came at precisely the moment that the need seemed greatest. Against Louis XIV's position that religious uniformity ensured civil peace, these writers insisted that such uniformity had driven civil strife and even civil war throughout history: thousands of years of "quarrels, blood and butchery," as John Locke put it. The Dutch theologian Philipp van Limborch wrote a magisterial *History of the Inquisition*, which cast that institution's

Religious Toleration European interest in learning about non-western religions is suggested by a 1724 illustration from an encyclopedia called *Religious Customs and Ceremonies of All the Peoples of the World*. At left a Hindu Brahmin wears an iron collar to raise money for a hospital; at right, another has suspended himself over a fire to show his faith.

campaigns against heresy as one of the great crimes of human history. The **tolerationists**, who remained, for the most part, believing Christians, ridiculed the idea that all subjects should follow the religion of their prince. Should the Christian subjects of the Ottoman sultan then mutely accept Islam, they asked? They also argued, most potently, that since heresy and other forms of religious deviance constituted crimes against God, not mankind, they should be punished by God alone. The tolerationists did not generally extend their good will to atheists, for they feared that without some sort of belief in the divine, humans would lose all conscience and turn completely amoral. But for everyone else, sometimes including even Jews, Muslims, and pagans, they defended a principle they called "liberty of conscience."

In adopting the cause of toleration, the Republic of Letters took on a political identity that it had previously lacked, and emerged as a potent critic of many of Europe's absolutist regimes. Still, absolute monarchy and toleration did not necessarily contradict each other. As we have seen, Peter the Great extended considerable toleration to Catholics and Protestants in Russia. Later in the eighteenth century, King Frederick II of Prussia would similarly embrace toleration. These monarchs were happy enough to let subjects follow their individual consciences in religious matters, so long as they remained unquestioningly obedient in others. It was particularly in France and Spain, where kings had retained a quasi-religious status, that monarchies remained wedded to an official ideal of religious uniformity, and were therefore most vulnerable to tolerationist critiques.

A REVOLUTION IN THOUGHT

But in a broader sense, the spread of tolerationist ideas in the Republic of Letters formed part of an intellectual upheaval that would ultimately shake all European regimes to the core. Centered in the Netherlands, France, and England, it would lead to a radical questioning, not just of religious intolerance, but also of Christianity itself, and the entire European social and political order.

This revolution in thought had many sides. Most generally, however, it involved the systematic application of a deep philosophical skepticism to all forms of authority, spiritual and secular alike. This skepticism owed a great deal to philosophical predecessors from the mid-century, especially Descartes and Spinoza, but it applied their inflammatory insights to particularly combustible timber.

PIERRE BAYLE AND SKEPTICISM

Although often presented as antireligious, this revolution also owed an enormous amount to the evolution of Christianity itself in the late 1600s and early 1700s. We have seen how Jansenism, with its search for a pure, uncompromising Catholicism, ended up casting doubt on the idea that sinful humans could really know anything of the mind of God and his influence on the world. As a result, some Jansenists started looking for ways to understand the world on its own terms, and to discover the regular natural laws by which it worked, thereby bringing them close to the natural philosophers of the day.

Similar tendencies were at work in the Calvinist churches. Pierre Bayle (1647–1706), the French Protestant founder of the *News from the Republic of Letters*, so strongly accepted the idea of the incomprehensibility of God, and so sharply attacked the idea that religion could be defended by reason, that some historians have taken him for an atheist. In fact, Bayle, an enormously influential figure in his time, remained religious all his life, but in an increasingly unorthodox manner. The son of a Calvinist minister, he fled from his native France to the Netherlands in 1681. His first major work, *Diverse Thoughts on the Comet of 1680* (published in 1682) debunked the idea that comets were a supernatural phenomenon, or harbingers of disaster. A few years later, he began his most famous project, an encyclopedic *Historical and Critical Dictionary*, which applied the same sharp skepticism, and a sly wit, to a wide range of historical figures and topics, including religious ones. To take just one example, the *Dictionary* called King David "a sun of holiness" only to add that "that sun had its spots," and then listed every one of David's crimes. And it concluded, mischievously, that "crowned heads" could take solace from the story of David, because it proved that even the worst kings could achieve salvation.

CHALLENGING CHRISTIAN DOCTRINE

While Bayle's *Dictionary* accepted the literal word of the Bible, some deeply observant Christian contemporaries did not. In 1685, the French priest Richard Simon (1638–1712) published, in Rotterdam, his *Critical History of the Old Testament*, which for the first time applied the techniques of textual criticism developed since the Renaissance to scripture itself. Through a careful analysis of the Hebrew texts, Simon argued that Moses could not have been the author of the many pieces of scripture attributed to him. The book aroused fierce opposition among both Catholics and Protestants. In the 1690s, Simon then dared apply the techniques to the New Testament, although insisting he was only trying to rescue the pure, original text of the Gospels from later corruption.

Other Christians went even further. In Britain, some radical dissenting Protestants rejected the Christian trinity (God, Jesus, and the Holy Ghost), insisting on God's fundamental unity. John Locke, in opposition to Bayle, attempted to reconcile Christianity with reason, but his efforts had unexpected consequences. In a 1695 essay, Locke argued that examples of divine revelation could only be accepted if they were fully supported by historical evidence, and accorded with reason and with principles of ethics derived directly from nature. Building on this work, Locke's compatriot Anthony Collins (1676–1729), one of the first self-proclaimed "free-thinkers," rejected prophecy and miracles altogether, and denied the proposition that the Jews had prophesied the coming of Christ. And from there, it was a short step for "deists" like Matthew Tindal (1657–1733) to dispense with Christianity altogether. Tindal did not dispute the existence of God, but presented the deity as a largely unknowable creator who had set the universe in motion, established a natural harmony, but thereafter had ceased to interfere with the world or manifest himself in it. The stories of the Bible were fiction, he maintained, and insights into the true "natural religion" could be found in many places, including Confucianism.

The figure of Baruch Spinoza, whom we met earlier, lurked behind many of these radical thoughts, and in the decades around 1700, Spinoza's work itself continued to gain readers and adherents. In the Netherlands, small circles of devoted followers circulated clandestine editions of his writings, along with biographical studies and commentaries. One of the most notorious, entitled *Treatise on the Three Impostors*—Moses, Jesus, and Mohammed—frankly made the case for atheism: "There are no such things in Nature as God or Devil or Soul or Heaven or Hell." Theologians, the anonymous treatise continued, were mostly "people of villainous principles who maliciously abuse and impose on the credulous populace." To be sure, views of this sort remained horrifying to the large majority of the European population, who continued to embrace the truths of Christianity.

SKEPTICISM AND POLITICAL AUTHORITY

The spirit of skepticism that pervaded all of these works corroded more than just religious authority. Pierre Bayle distrusted the claims of princes as much as those of prophets, and wrote scathingly about abuses of political authority, above all, those of Louis XIV. The Republic of Letters, by its emphasis on civil, rational interchange among its members, naturally encouraged a certain degree of egalitarian thinking. Its leading English representative, John Locke, exemplified this thinking with his insistence that government derives its legitimacy from the consent of the governed. Religious and political critiques tended to go hand in hand. When Prime Minister Fleury continued Louis XIV's persecution of the Jansenists in the name of religious uniformity, radical Jansenist lawyers began to circulate clandestine pamphlets that claimed for France's high courts (*parlements*), as heirs to the ancient councils of the kingdom, a position above the King himself. In the 1730s, the French crown perceived the greatest threat to its authority as coming from Jansenists who claimed to have experienced miraculous cures and revelations at the gravesite of a particularly pious Jansenist deacon (King Louis XV ordered the gravesite closed, thereby prompting one of history's great pieces of graffiti: "By the King's command God is forbidden to make miracles here.")

Compared to the Jansenist works, which enjoyed large audiences, the still more radical works of Bayle and Locke had limited influence at the time. Their readers largely belonged to the Republic of Letters, and numbered in the low thousands, perhaps even only in the hundreds. The number of true atheists in Europe in 1700 was also probably very low. Nonetheless, versions of these ideas did circulate more widely, often in the form of works of satirical fiction, which allowed more timid readers to encounter them without feeling required to fully accept or reject them.

MONTESQUIEU One of the greatest works of European fiction, first published (clandestinely, in the Netherlands) in 1721, exemplifies the use of fiction to convey such radical ideas. Its young author, **Baron Montesquieu** (1689–1755), regularly attended the Parisian salons of Madame de Tencin and others. His novel *Persian Letters* conveys the spirit of that institution, with its gentle stabs of wit, risqué allusions to sex, and short, easily digestible digressions. But despite this form, Montesquieu's work was no parlor tale. Cast as a series of letters between Persians traveling in Europe and correspondents back home, it initially provoked audiences by suggesting what Europe might look like to a Muslim visitor:

> The king of France ... is a great magician ... if there are only a million *écus* in his treasury and he needs two million, he simply tells his subjects that one is worth

two, and they believe him. . . . But there is another magician even stronger than him. . . . This magician is called the pope: he makes people believe that three equals one, or that bread is not bread, and wine is not wine, and a thousand other things of this sort.

This was bad enough. But underneath these jokes lay a profoundly seditious message. The bulk of *Persian Letters* followed the deteriorating relations between the leading traveler and his harem back in Persia, over which he ruled with despotic authority, but which he could not ultimately control. By the end of the book, it became clear to attentive readers that Montesquieu was using the harem as an allegory for despotic political authority in general. One short fable included in the novel presented a primitive republic of shepherds as the ideal political form, albeit one that was almost impossible to sustain over long periods. Another gave voice to the sort of women's longings that appeared in the early feminist literature discussed in Chapter 13—and not just for liberty and respect. In a daring reversal of the paradise reserved for male martyrs in Islam, it presented a female paradise where virtuous women would receive their reward in the form of sexual satiation from young, virile lovers. Not surprisingly, Montesquieu's novel was both immensely popular and immediately banned by authorities across Europe.

ISAAC NEWTON'S UNIVERSE

This revolution in European thought of around 1700 was greatly aided by the progress of natural science, and above all by the work of a toweringly important English physicist and mathematician, **Isaac Newton** (1642–1727). His scientific work ranged from seminal studies of optics to an obsession with the alchemists' Philosopher's Stone, which could supposedly turn base metals into gold. A devout Christian, Newton also spent many years trying to unravel the chronology of the ancient kingdoms of biblical times. But in all of his work Newton applied the principles of skepticism and systematic reasoning as elaborated by Francis Bacon and developed through the seventeenth century. He achieved undying fame with his stunning book on the motion of terrestrial and celestial bodies, *Principia Mathematica* (1687).

As we have seen, in the early seventeenth century, Galileo had demonstrated that objects moved along a straight line unless affected by a force, and that the earth exerted an identical pull on all objects. Meanwhile, the astronomer Kepler had perplexed learned Europeans with his discovery, based on careful observation through a telescope,

Isaac Newton The scientist made this sketch of one of his most important experiments about optics. It shows light from the sun being refracted through a series of prisms, which allowed Newton to understand that visible light is made up of many colors.

that the planets did not orbit the sun in perfect circular orbits, but in elliptical ones. Newton brought these works together, and resolved the puzzle that Kepler had raised, by proposing a law of universal gravitation: all bodies are attracted to other bodies by a force that is proportionate to the product of their mass and inversely proportionate to the square of their distance. In order to accomplish this crucial insight Newton had to invent a new sort of mathematics, differential calculus, which he did more or less simultaneously with the German philosopher Gottfried Wilhelm Leibniz (1646–1716). The resulting equations predicted precisely the orbits Kepler had observed for the planets. Newton's conclusions stood unchallenged until the twentieth century, and remain the basis for much of the science of physics today.

In the late seventeenth and early eighteenth centuries, Newton's work had a double significance. First, it seemed to restore to the physical universe the simplicity and perfection attributed to it by the ancient astronomical science of Ptolemy. We have seen that one early achievement of the "scientific revolution" was to challenge Ptolemaic conceptions of the perfection of the heavenly spheres, but as astronomers of the period peered more deeply into the skies, what they found proved difficult to account for. The systems they devised to explain the motion of celestial bodies were difficult to follow. Newton's theory of universal gravitation swept away the complexities, and restored perfection in the form of simple, easily understood equations that explained all the complex celestial motions the astronomers had observed. But this perfection seemed to derive directly from nature itself. Newton himself remained a devout Christian, but the only God needed in his scheme was a "watchmaker God" who built the machine, set it in motion, but thereafter let it run on its own. His physics was entirely compatible with this religious belief.

Secondly, Newton showed Europeans of the time the potential of the human mind to penetrate nature's mysteries. The idea was not simply that nature was governed by a set of clear, infallible laws, but also that these laws could be uncovered by humans of sufficient genius, given the proper conditions of observation. The national academies of science founded in the mid-1600s had already begun the public celebration of particularly talented natural philosophers, as those who studied the natural world were still called, but Newton, with his immense stature, raised this process to an entirely new level. As the English poet Alexander Pope wrote: "Nature and Nature's laws lay hid in night: / God said, Let Newton be! And all was light." It was in this period that the modern figure of the "genius" emerged. Previously, people were said to have genius—that is, innate talent—for various things, but not to *be* geniuses. Newton, with his immense prestige and seemingly superhuman intellect, exemplified for the eighteenth century what it meant to "be" a genius.

LOCKE ON THE HUMAN MIND

Just two years after Newton's *Principia*, John Locke published a massive book, *Essay Concerning Human Understanding,* which many contemporaries saw as a counterpart. Focused on the human mind, this work represented a decisive break with the philosophy of Descartes and his followers—especially with the notion that humans are imprinted from birth with certain innate ideas having to do with the nature of God or the physical properties of the universe. To the contrary, Locke presented the mind, in a famous formulation, as a "blank slate." Sense impressions struck this slate, and combined in various ways to form ideas and patterns of thought. All human thinking ultimately derived from the raw sense impressions received by particular minds. In short, the *Essay* seemed to offer what we would call natural laws of human thought, parallel to Newton's natural laws of physics. It was an approach that would dominate European philosophy for the next century.

THE INVENTION OF "SOCIETY"

The power and success of these ideas prompted Europeans of the day to look for yet another set of natural laws—the ones that governed society and politics. Did human society obey the same sort of fixed rules as the motions of the planets? Here, too, the ongoing transformations in the religious sphere made it easier to imagine a social world that existed apart from the heavenly one—a world in which God had no direct, on-going presence. It is around the year 1700 that large numbers of learned Europeans started to use the word "society" as we do today—that is, in the sense of a human formation that exists independently of and prior to political life. Only when Europeans stopped seeing God's presence constantly at work in the world—ordaining monarchs, rewarding the just and punishing the wicked—could such a notion of "society" emerge, and only then could it be thought of as possessing its own laws, equivalent to the laws of motion and gravitation elaborated by Newton. Only then could observers begin to contemplate the rational reform of society to put it in conformity with these natural laws.

CONCLUSION

Even when popularized by writers like Montesquieu, the skeptical ideas discussed in this chapter had little if any immediate impact on the lives of most Europeans. Most people encountered rational projects of social reform only through servants of the absolutist state like Antonio de Vieira, with his pragmatic plans for improving public hygiene, reducing crime, and keeping the population of Saint Petersburg under surveillance. De Vieira and other reformers were under no illusions that they were working in accordance with natural social laws. They were serving divinely ordained monarchs, and everything else faded before the priority of ensuring those monarchs' survival and success. And through the period 1680–1740, the absolutist ideal flourished, even amidst the financial challenges of war and the emergence of a counter-model represented by the supremacy of parliament in Great Britain after the Glorious Revolution.

But in the decades after 1740, the ideas circulating in the Republic of Letters would resonate far beyond the world of scholarship. The goal of reforming society in accordance with the dictates of reason would gain many thousands of adherents. And increasingly, in this age that historians now call the Enlightenment, Europeans would come to see the social and political structures that they had inherited from the past in a very different, more critical light.

KEY TERMS

Glorious Revolution (p. 477)

John Locke (p. 477)

Peter the Great (p. 479)

War of the League of Augsburg (p. 486)

War of the Spanish Succession (p. 486)

Peace of Utrecht (p. 487)

middle passage (p. 490)

Mississippi Company (p. 493)

salons (p. 496)

Robinson Crusoe (p. 497)

Pierre Bayle (p. 498)

tolerationists (p. 499)

Baron Montesquieu (p. 500)

Isaac Newton (p. 501)

REVIEW QUESTIONS

1. What new forms of religious persecution arose within some European states during the 1680s?

2. How did the Glorious Revolution reshape English government?

3. Under Peter the Great, how did Russia become more westernized?

4. How did military discipline and the conduct of war change in the late seventeenth century?

5. What forces contributed to the end of French expansion in the early eighteenth century?

6. How did the European balance of power change as a result of conflicts such as the War of the League of Augsburg and the War of the Spanish Succession?

7. How did imperial competition affect European colonies in North America and the Caribbean?

8. What cultural developments took place in cities during the early 1700s?

9. How did periodical journals and the Republic of Letters change the nature of scholarly exchange in Europe?

10. What is the evidence for the emergence of a greater skepticism regarding religious and political authority starting in the late 1600s?

CORE OBJECTIVES

After reading this chapter, you should have a solid understanding of the following core objectives. To strengthen your grasp of the core objectives, use the resources on the Student Site for The West.

- Consider the Glorious Revolution and its aftermath.
- Analyze absolutist monarchy at its height in France, Russia, and Prussia.
- Evaluate both the wars and the conduct of warfare in the absolutist period.
- Trace the development of the Atlantic World in the eighteenth century.
- Assess urban life and the emergence of new forms of culture.
- Compare the major themes of skepticism and reason in the thought of the period.

 GO TO **inQuizitive** TO SEE WHAT YOU'VE LEARNED—AND LEARN WHAT YOU'VE MISSED—WITH PERSONALIZED FEEDBACK ALONG THE WAY.

CHRONOLOGY

1730s
John Wesley founds
Methodism

1740–1748
War of the Austrian
Succession

1745
Charles Edward
Stuart invades
Scotland

1748
Montesquieu publishes
The Spirit of the Laws

1749
Handel's *Music for the
Royal Fireworks* performed
at Vauxhall Gardens

1751–1772
Diderot and d'Alembert
publish their *Encyclopedia*

1756–1763
Seven Years' War

1758–1779
Cook's three
expeditions

1759
Voltaire publishes
Candide

1760s
John Wilkes challenges
British government

1760s
Physiocrats advocate
economic reform in France

1762
Rousseau publishes
The Social Contract
and *Emile*

1771
Arkwright
develops
water frame

15

Enlightenment

CHALLENGING THE PREVAILING ORDER

1740–1780

O n a hot day in October 1749, a thirty-seven-year-old aspiring man of letters set out to walk the four miles from Paris to the nearby town of Vincennes. The largely self-educated son of a watchmaker from Geneva, he had knocked about France and northern Italy for years without much to show for it. Brilliant, and abrasive, he had a reputation as an eccentric.

As he walked, the man glanced through a magazine, his attention drawn to an advertisement announcing an essay competition. The theme was whether the revival of the sciences and the arts had contributed to the purification of public morals. As the man later described it, "The moment I read this, I seemed to behold another world, and became a different man." In his telling, he immediately saw that the answer to the question was "no," and feverishly composed an essay explaining why. Others would tell the story differently, claiming that the man had chosen to answer the question in the negative for cynical reasons, to distinguish himself from other contestants.

In any case, the final essay was a stunning piece of work. Thundering and impassioned, it denounced the arts and sciences for distracting men from their civic duties, weakening their character, and leading them into lives of constant pretense. It took the judges

1775–1783
American
Revolution
1778
1775 French enter **1781**
"Flour war" American Watt perfects
in France Revolution steam engine

1772 **1776**
First partition Adam Smith
of Poland publishes
*The Wealth
of Nations*

Vauxhall Gardens Londoners gather among the elaborate stone buildings, gazebos, and formal gardens at Vauxhall, near the river Thames, in this mid-eighteenth-century engraving. An orchestra plays from above. Events at the garden, such as the 1749 preview of Handel's *Music for the Royal Fireworks*, provided new venues for social classes to mix in public.

FOCUS QUESTIONS

- What was driving economic change in the period?
- How was warfare becoming more global?
- How was cultural change expanding in the period?
- How did religion reflect broader cultural and political change?
- What were the distinctive features of the Enlightenment at its height?
- What were the major political effects of the Enlightenment?

aback, but also impressed them deeply with its force and eloquence. After some heated debate, they awarded it the top prize, and it was soon published. The man, whose name was Jean-Jacques Rousseau, suddenly found himself an intellectual celebrity. A former king of Poland was just one of the many well-known Europeans who published replies to him. Over the next twenty-nine years, Rousseau (1712–1778) would build on this success to become one of the most famous writers in Europe, and a figure widely credited with inspiring the French Revolution.

This story reveals a great deal about the phenomenon now referred to as the European "Enlightenment," whose origins we have seen in the previous chapter. Its full flowering was the most significant European development of the years 1740–80. The Enlightenment followed naturally from the intellectual ruptures of the years around 1700, but it occurred in a rapidly changing social and cultural context that gave it a new sort of importance. The earlier great debates about science, the arts, and religion had taken place largely among a narrow, well-to-do, well-educated elite, many of whom participated in the scholarly networks of the Republic of Letters. If these controversies had powerful consequences, it was because powerful figures had paid attention to them. By contrast, during the mid- and later eighteenth century, a much wider spectrum of individuals not only read about but actively took part in intellectual debate. Through a variety of new and transformed institutions—newspapers, coffeehouses, learned academies, debating societies, libraries, public lecture series—serious intellectual conversation spilled out far beyond the bounds of the Republic of Letters. Writers increasingly made their livings and their reputations by appealing to that diffuse body known as the "public," rather than to a tiny number of wealthy and influential patrons. The public in turn became recognized as an increasingly significant force—and, by the end of the period, a revolutionary one.

The Enlightenment in its heyday broke from earlier European intellectual movements in another way as well. It involved a more sustained and well-informed curiosity about the non-European world. Its most important works—including Rousseau's—drew extensively on travel literature, early forms of anthropological observation, and historical works about Asia, the Americas, and Africa. The authors often offered wildly distorted pictures of non-European societies to suit their own purposes: using supposed, often imaginary, Polynesian sexual practices to criticize priestly celibacy, for instance, or casting Buddhism as an Eastern version of intolerant European churches. But increasingly the work made European readers more deeply aware of human diversity, and by the later part of the century some European authors were offering provocative critiques of slavery and imperialism.

ECONOMIC CHANGE

The development of this new, more wide-ranging Enlightenment could take place in large part because of favorable economic, social, and political circumstances. Most critically, the period 1740–80 saw a continuing improvement in the European climate and relatively few destructive epidemics. The most famous European natural disaster of the mid-eighteenth century was a great earthquake that destroyed 85 percent of the buildings in Lisbon in 1755 and may have killed as many as 90,000 people there. In the broader Western world this seismic shock had cultural repercussions, leading some intellectuals to question their faith in a beneficent nature. But overall a natural disaster on this scale was an exception in the period.

AGRICULTURAL EXPANSION

Under these largely favorable conditions, the European population and economy continued to experience impressive growth. Over the course of the eighteenth century, the population of the Continent rose by nearly 60 percent, to 190 million, with the most sustained growth between 1740 and 1780. Agricultural production rose as well. In most countries, the growth in output did not come as the result of any revolutionary change in farming techniques. Landowners expanded the areas under cultivation, notably through draining wetlands and consolidating small, inefficient strips of land into larger, more easily plowed ones. Yet in the northwestern corner of Europe, in a rough circle that included the Low Countries, southern England, and northern France, more striking improvements took place. In this "charmed circle," as we have seen, a culture of innovation and tinkering had already begun to spur economic growth in the seventeenth century, followed by dramatic agricultural improvements in the eighteenth. Where landowners and their tenants had once let fields lie fallow to restore their fertility, now many of them introduced into their agricultural cycle the planting of legumes that actively replenished the soil with nutrients.

In Britain, some wealthy landlords began "**enclosing**"—and taking for themselves—common lands that farmers had traditionally used to pasture animals, in a movement that would pick up speed toward the end of the eighteenth century. They farmed this land with tenants and applied the new innovations aggressively, earning significant profits. By the 1750s, farmers in some areas of Britain were more than twice as productive as their counterparts outside northwestern Europe, and Britain was exporting 15 percent of its agricultural product to the Continent. The potato, imported from the Americas in the sixteenth century, was rapidly gaining adherents throughout Europe as an efficient source of nutrition and caloric energy—and while it was consumed above all by laborers, social elites fully recognized its importance. One French queen even attached a small bouquet of potato flowers to her headdress at a royal ball.

INDUSTRIAL EXPANSION

In this charmed geographical circle of northwest Europe, increased productivity also led to changes that we now associate with the development of modern capitalism—notably an increased flow of private capital (money and credit) into non-agricultural investments, such as textiles manufacturing and mining of metals and coal, in the expectation that such investments would yield steadily stronger returns. Heightened agricultural productivity also allowed more and more poor country-dwellers (principally tenants and landless laborers) to diversify their activities. Foreign trade, notably with Asia, had increased the supply of finished textiles, resulting in cheaper prices, just as demand for these products rose. But finished textiles could be produced even more cheaply domestically, in country cottages where peasants devoted part of their time to handicrafts and part to farming. Thus there continued to develop what historians now call the "**putting out**" **system**, in which city-based merchants purchased wool and delivered it to these peasant producers, who processed and spun it into coarse cloth in their homes, receiving payment in cash or credit.

THE "PUTTING OUT" SYSTEM The roots of the putting out system go back to well before the eighteenth century, but it was only after 1740 that it took on its full economic importance. By 1780, half of all the inhabitants of certain rural areas in northern France abutting the Low Countries had abandoned full-time subsistence agriculture for part-time or full-time textile work. Most of these peasant men, women, and children remained in the countryside, in their own farmhouses. Yet the change profoundly affected the texture of their daily lives. Whereas earlier generations of peasants had spent winters in relative idleness, or left home to make money as laborers or servants elsewhere, now a cycle of work continued unbroken throughout much of the year. "Putting out" brought cash into the hands of peasants whose economies had previously consisted largely of barter and credit, although generally not enough cash to lessen significantly their dependence on large landowners. The system also put them in routine contact with city-dwellers who spoke and dressed differently, and brought news of the outside world more regularly than at any time in the past. In Britain, the changes were even more dramatic. By 1750, less than half the British population was employed full-time in agriculture, as opposed to 80 to 90 percent in most of eastern and central Europe.

NEW TECHNOLOGIES New technologies, and the accompanying flows of capital, brought other significant changes to rural life. In 1771, the British inventor Richard Arkwright (1732–1792) perfected a "water frame" technology that allowed large spinning wheels to be powered by flowing water. The invention quickly spread to river towns throughout Britain, increasing productivity and textile production, particularly of cloth made from cotton, imported increasingly from slave societies in the

Steam Engine An eighteenth-century watercolor offers a technical rendering of Watt's steam engine, which used a system of gears and shafts to harness the energy from burning coal to power machines.

Americas. And in the same period James Watt (1736–1819) perfected his steam engine, which allowed looms and wheels to be powered by burning wood or coal, and not just by flowing water, thereby freeing production from river-based locations. Throughout western Europe, large landowners, belonging mostly to the nobility, began to exploit the riches in coal and ore that lay beneath the surface of their estates. In the nineteenth century, these new technologies would make a full-scale Industrial Revolution possible.

NEW INFRASTRUCTURE This technological and economic change in turn helped drive the development of what we would now call "infrastructure," especially in western Europe. The French and British states invested large sums in road building, allowing for the development of far more rapid and reliable commercial coach service. To reach the port city of Bordeaux from Paris by horse-drawn coach in the mid-seventeenth century—a distance of some 360 miles—had taken over two weeks. By the 1780s, the same journey took less than six days. Travel time from London to Edinburgh (400 miles) fell even more dramatically, from nearly eleven days to under three. Schedules for coaches became more precise, forcing travelers to pay attention to minutes, not just hours; the London–Glasgow mail coach, for instance, gave passengers precisely thirty-five minutes for a dinner stop. The

same improvements allowed for more rapid and reliable mail service than ever before, making it possible for readers to subscribe to periodicals published hundreds of miles away.

RISING INEQUALITY Most of Europe, however, remained largely untouched by these developments. In southern Europe, and throughout most of France and Germany, the majority of peasants continued to farm the land in much the same way they had done two hundred years previously, and probably did not produce much more per acre than their distant predecessors at the time of the Roman Empire. In eastern Europe and the Russian Empire, as we have seen, great landowners were forcing more peasants than ever into conditions of serfdom that hardly differed from slavery. France was widely accounted a prosperous country and had rates of economic growth comparable to Britain's. Nonetheless, when the British agriculturalist Arthur Young (1741–1820) visited France in the late 1780s, he was shocked by the misery of the rural population, which he attributed to the small size of individual farms. At one stop in southern France, he wrote: "The poor people seem poor indeed; the children terribly ragged,—if possible, worse clad than if with no clothes at all; as to shoes and stockings, they are luxuries. A beautiful girl of six or seven years playing with a stick, and smiling under such a bundle of rags as made my heart ache to see her." In 1775 a rise in grain prices in France, caused in part by bad harvests, led to a massive series of rural riots called the "flour war." As in earlier riots, women often took the lead. The threat of famine remained very real. Meanwhile, outside of northwestern Europe travel remained almost as difficult and dangerous as a hundred years before. Crossing the relatively small but mountainous island of Sicily on land, for instance, could take nearly three weeks—longer than it took to traverse all of France.

Even in the most prosperous areas, the gap between rich and poor was vast. The city of London, among its rapidly expanding population, counted at least 15,000 full-time beggars, the large majority of them women and children. A woman named Elizabeth Evans, arrested for infanticide in 1740, insisted that her child had been still-born and defended herself with the heartbreaking argument that she would never kill a child she could use as a prop while begging. Eighteenth-century Britons fretted that poverty was generating an overpowering tide of crime. Smuggling gangs terrorized parts of the southern coasts, while in London pickpockets, thieves, and muggers gained a fearsome reputation. In response, Parliament quadrupled the number of offenses against property carrying the death penalty, although the courts exercised considerable discretion and actually sent fewer convicts to the gallows than in the previous century. One reason, though, is that they increasingly had the option of deporting convicts and debtors to overseas colonies. By the early 1770s, England and Wales were deporting over a thousand convicts and debtors a year just to the thirteen North American colonies. In 1795, local magistrates meeting in the town of Speenhamland, Berkshire, introduced a system of welfare payments for the rural poor that was widely adopted throughout England. In this "Speenhamland system," local landowners financed payments to the poor to ensure that they could buy bread.

COLONIAL WEALTH AND SLAVERY

Colonies, however, were far more than a dumping ground for convicts: they were probably the single most important source of the European economy's mid-eighteenth-century expansion. British trade, for instance, more than doubled between 1740 and 1780, mostly thanks to commerce with the colonies. British ports like Bristol saw over a hundred ships depart each year for destinations across the Atlantic, carrying manufactures and returning with tobacco, coffee, indigo, cotton, furs, molasses, and much else, all aimed at the developing mass market in Europe. Continuing a pattern begun earlier in the century, these ships plied a route that took them through the Caribbean and Latin America, where European plantation owners were making vast fortunes from sugarcane. By the 1780s the French territory of Saint-Domingue was the wealthiest colony in the world, by itself producing 40 percent of the globe's sugar. Its principal city, Le Cap François, had a population of 20,000—more than any North American city except Philadelphia or New York. The French port of Bordeaux saw 20 million pounds of sugar a year pass through its harbor in the 1730s; fifty years later the figure had grown fivefold.

But this wealth depended on the most brutal system of slave labor ever seen on the planet. Building on the "triangle trade" begun in the previous century, ships bound for the Americas would often make the slave markets of West Africa their first stop. Sugar production demanded tremendous physical effort in a hot, unhealthy climate— to plant and weed the cane, to chop down and transport it, and then to crush, mill, and boil it. All of this had to be done on the plantation, as the first stage of producing raw sugar. Without new arrivals, the slave populations of Saint-Domingue and Jamaica, the chief sugar colony of Britain, would have fallen between 2 and 5 percent

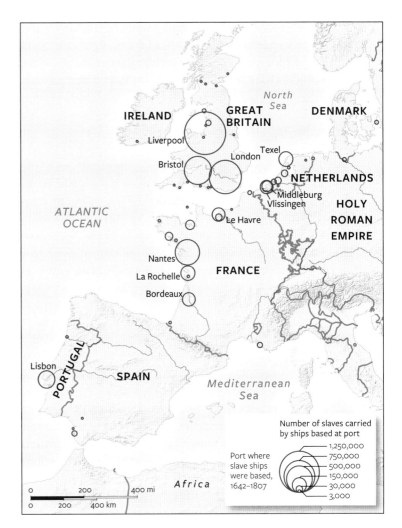

European Ports of Origin of the Atlantic Slave Trade, 1642–1807
Slave ships from over fifty coastal cities throughout Europe transported hundreds of thousands of slaves from Africa to the Americas, thoroughly transforming the fortunes of some of their ports of origin, such as Lisbon, Bordeaux, La Rochelle, Nantes, Texel, and above all, Bristol, Liverpool, and London.

every year because of premature death and the inability or unwillingness of the exhausted, traumatized, and largely male slave population to reproduce itself. But new slaves did come: traders brought well over 3 million from West Africa to the Caribbean during the years 1701–1810—far more than went to any other region. By 1789 Saint-Domingue alone had a population of 500,000 slaves, mostly African-born, who outnumbered whites and a growing population of free blacks and mulattoes (persons of mixed race) by roughly ten to one. The United States at the time had only 40 percent more slaves.

Europeans knew perfectly well of the horrors of the sugar industry. In 1759, in a scene of his masterpiece, *Candide*, the French writer Voltaire described a black slave whose master had cut off his leg when he tried to escape, and who had lost his hand when his finger got caught in a mill. "This is the price you pay," the slave explained to the novel's heroes, "for the sugar you eat in Europe."

A NEW URBAN LANDSCAPE

This Atlantic trade drove not only the expansion of the European economy but also a transformation of European cities. The ones that benefited most directly from this trade—ports such as Lisbon in Portugal, Bristol in England, or Nantes and Bordeaux in France—saw particularly dramatic growth and the building of lavish new homes for wealthy merchants. But other cities grew as well. London continued the spectacular growth seen earlier in the century. From 750,000 inhabitants in 1750, it would grow to nearly a million by 1800.

THE URBAN POOR Some aspects of urban life remained much as they had in earlier periods. For the poorest city-dwellers—indigent laborers, criminals, and prostitutes—the metropolis remained as much a source of death and despair as ever. In cities like Lyon in France, where thousands of young women toiled at the silk looms for pitifully low wages, babies were farmed out to poor wet-nurses in the nearby countryside under appalling conditions. Well over half of these babies did not survive to adulthood. Public streets remained the most common receptacle for trash and sewage, so that most city-dwellers lived in a world of powerful odors that we find hard to imagine today. (It did not help that most physicians continued to insist that bathing was dangerous to health.)

The traditional structure of the urban trades, with apprentices, journeymen, masters, and merchants organized into tight-knit "corporate bodies," continued to prevail throughout most of Europe. Organizations of artisans called "confraternities," which had elaborate initiation rituals, would offer raucous if ritual protests against the injustice of masters, and their rough brand of humor dominated popular urban culture. The Paris print worker Nicolas Contat recalled in his memoirs that by meowing loudly during the night next to a hated master's window, one of his fellow apprentices tricked the master into ordering all the cats in the neighborhood killed. The apprentices went about the task with glee, venting their frustrations over their work by trapping dozens of cats, smashing their spines with iron bars, and stringing them up on mock gallows, all the while convulsing with laughter. They took

particular delight when the master's hated wife saw the spectacle and feared—correctly—that her own beloved gray cat was among the victims.

THE GROWING MIDDLE CLASSES Yet overall, the tenor of urban life underwent some important changes in the period 1740–80. Writers in England frequently commented on the growing significance of what they called the "middling sorts" or "middle classes." They generally meant men and women who did not work with their hands and had moderate wealth, but who could not be considered wealthy or noble. Not all "middle-class" people lived in the cities, but most did. The group included merchants, low-ranking government officials, men and women living off investment income, and professionals such as lawyers, architects, and doctors. It could also include well-off master artisans. Such groups had existed since the Middle Ages but had rarely been seen as forming a discrete group and a fundamental element of the social order. Now their increasing numbers and prominence forced observers to start conceiving of the social order itself in different, and more complex, ways.

Already by the earlier years of the century, the urban middle classes in western Europe had established a distinct style of life, defined in large part by their education and by what they did with their money. This lifestyle resembled that of the urban elites of the seventeenth-century Netherlands, but now it spread much more widely. The middle classes generally had at least a primary education (men almost entirely, and women far more than in the past) and displayed recognizably modern patterns of consumer behavior. They tended to possess well-crafted furniture, mirrors, coffeepots, pocket watches, and china, along with wallpaper and framed prints. It also became common for even relatively modest families to accumulate savings and to make modest investments, usually not in risky business ventures such as the outfitting of ships or the building of mills, but in land or relatively safe annuities—financial instruments that guaranteed a regular stream of income, often paid by the state. In Britain, more and more companies offered life insurance, which in turn stimulated the development of actuarial science (how many years was a given individual likely to live?). Those lucky enough to enjoy a middle-class lifestyle—still a minority in Europe's largely rural societies—enjoyed a degree of social stability and physical comfort that their ancestors could not have counted on. In England, politicians increasingly argued that the well-being of the middle classes was crucial to the well-being of the nation as a whole.

The War of the Austrian Succession, 1740–1748 During the war, in which fighting ranged across the Austrian Habsburg lands, Prussia gained the formerly Austrian province of Silesia. Meanwhile, Prince Charles Edward Stuart took advantage of the conflict to march his Scottish army as far south in Great Britain as Derby, before a retreat and final defeat at Culloden.

WARFARE TURNED GLOBAL

Europe's increasing prosperity in this period was not threatened by warfare. The major powers continued to fight as often as before, and pitched battles remained devastating affairs in which one-quarter or more of the participants were left dead or wounded. But such battles took place relatively rarely, with most commanders preferring wars of attrition and maneuver. As one of France's most decorated mid-century commanders and best strategists wrote, "I am not at all for battles . . . and am convinced that a skillful general can go all his life without being forced to fight one." Some observers associated the slackening intensity of war with the rise of international trade. A Scottish author noted in 1769, "Commerce tends to wear off those prejudices which maintain distinction and animosity between nations." However, as overseas colonies and world trade became increasingly important to western European states, warfare itself turned increasingly global—requiring ever larger expenditures on navies and overseas armies.

THE WAR OF THE AUSTRIAN SUCCESSION (1740–1748)

The stakes of war were now almost entirely dynastic, territorial, and commercial, with very little armed conflict driven by religious passions. The War of the Austrian Succession began in 1740 when Holy Roman Emperor Charles VI of Austria (r. 1711–1740) died without a male heir and France, Prussia, and other German states challenged the right of his daughter, Maria Theresa, to inherit the Austrian throne. Britain came into the war on the Austrian side, which gave the Stuart dynasty of Britain (exiled since the Glorious Revolution of 1688) one last chance to regain its supposed birthright. In 1745, the dashing, French-backed grandson of the deposed James II, Charles Edward Stuart (known as "Bonnie Prince Charlie," 1720–1788), landed in Scotland, rallied an army, and marched to within 120 miles of London. For a moment the Protestant king George II feared for his throne. But lacking English support, the rebels retreated to Scotland, where, at the battle of Culloden, in April 1746, a British army under the duke of Cumberland annihilated them. There followed a merciless scourging of Highland Scotland, with thousands of poor farmers driven from their homes and left to starve. Charlie himself fled Scotland in a small boat, disguised as an Irish serving maid. It was the last foreign land invasion that England would experience to the present day.

As always, war tempted several powers with the prospect of territorial expansion. During the War of the Austrian Succession, Prussia, under its vigorous new king, Frederick II (r. 1740–1786), seized the wealthy eastern German province of Silesia from Austria. The event marked Prussia's emergence as a major power and left Austria eager for revenge. France and Britain dueled for territory across the globe. In North America, Britain's colonies were quickly expanding, their population doubling every twenty-five years through immigration and natural growth to reach over 1 million by the end of the 1750s. By contrast, the French colonies in Canada and "Louisiana" (a much larger area than the present state, stretching across the continent from present-day New Orleans to Montana) numbered well under 100,000, most of them concentrated along the shores of the Saint Lawrence River in Quebec. The French sought to hem in the British along the Atlantic seaboard by building chains of fortresses to the west of the thirteen colonies, and by forging a series of strategic alliances with Indian peoples. The North American war ended with the two sides still facing each other across the line of the Allegheny Mountains.

THE SEVEN YEARS' WAR (1756–1763)

Peace came in 1748, with Maria Theresa confirmed on the Austrian throne, but it amounted to little more than a temporary truce. Already in 1754 renewed fighting broke out between Britain and France in the Ohio Valley. (The young George Washington ordered the first shots fired while commanding a detachment of Virginia militia for the British.) Two years later, France, eager to improve its position in Germany, secretly negotiated an alliance with Austria, putting to an end a centuries-old competition between French Bourbons and Austrian Habsburgs, and forcing Prussia and Great Britain into each other's arms. Soon afterward, war began anew on the European continent.

This second major war of the period, misleadingly called the **Seven Years' War** (in North America it lasted from 1754 to 1763), was much larger in scale—and more expensive—than the War of the Austrian Succession. The fighting in North America, on the high seas, and also in French and British possessions in Africa and India, achieved such proportions that some historians call it the first true world war. Even so, the hostilities affected the daily lives of most people in western and central Europe less than the mammoth conflicts of the previous century.

Initially, the Franco-Austrian alliance did well. In North America, France and its Indian allies ambushed and destroyed a British army and took several key fortresses. In the Mediterranean, France took an important British naval base. But Britain soon struck back. Its ability to raise funds quickly and cheaply, thanks to its national bank and legendary army of excise tax collectors, allowed it to build ships and move armies more efficiently than its French enemies, who had to borrow money at high interest rates on the international markets. The well-equipped British navy in turn made it difficult for the French to resupply their forces in the Americas. In 1759, the British succeeded in capturing the French Canadian capital of Quebec City, putting an end to France's hopes of retaining colonies on the North American mainland. At the peace table in 1763, France ceded Canada to Britain and Louisiana to Spain in order to keep its valuable Caribbean sugar colonies—the French regime little understood the potential of Louisiana's millions of acres of forest and plain, which in another century would become the heartland of the United States. Meanwhile, halfway around the world, the British East India Company defeated French forces in India, reducing France's areas of influence to a small area and confirming Britain as the dominant European power on the Indian subcontinent.

The Seven Years' War and Associated Hostilities, 1754-1763 The Seven Years' War was concentrated in Europe, where Prussia achieved key victories and Britain blockaded France's access to the Atlantic, and also in North America, where despite early French victories, Britain and Spain gained control of enormous French territory. But the conflict was global in scope, with British victories around the world—most notably in India, beginning a century and a half of British dominance in the region.

In Europe, France and its allies did no better, with Frederick II (now known as Frederick the Great) crushing French forces in Germany. Prussia's fortunes did waver when Russia entered the war and routed Frederick's men in 1759 ("I believe everything is lost," the Prussian king wrote melodramatically after the defeat. "Farewell forever!"). But just when the Russians seemed poised to strike at Berlin, Russia's tsarina Elizabeth (r. 1741–1762) died unexpectedly and was replaced by the preening, unstable, German-born Peter III (r. Jan. 1762–July 1762), a great admirer of Frederick who promptly withdrew from the war. So Prussia, like Britain, emerged from the Seven Years' War a victor, and

Frederick solidified his reputation as a bold commander whose readiness to risk major battles contrasted with the cautious campaigns of maneuver favored by most contemporary strategists.

In the long run, the Seven Years' War would have significant consequences. Prussia's success marked the end of Austrian dominance in Germany. It also posed a threat to Poland, which had never fully recovered from the wars of the previous century against Sweden and Russia, and which had lost territory to Russia as that country expanded under Peter the Great. As we have seen, the enormous power enjoyed by Poland's nobility made it difficult for the monarchy to raise the funds necessary to compete effectively with its powerful neighbors. In 1772, the newly dominant Prussia came to an arrangement with Austria and Catherine the Great's Russia to carry out a "partition" in which each power carved off a large slice of Polish territory (two subsequent partitions in the last decade of the century would eventually dismember the Polish state completely). France, meanwhile, emerged from the war shorn of most of its overseas empire and loaded with a massive debt—one that would turn crippling when in 1778 it sent another army across the Atlantic to aid the newborn United States in its revolution against Britain. And while Britain emerged from the Seven Years' War triumphant on land and sea, it too had spent very heavily, running up ruinous budget deficits. After 1763, Parliament would demand that its colonies, although not possessing formal political representation in London, make much heavier contributions to their own defense, mostly in the form of new, stringently enforced taxes.

The First Partition of Poland, 1772

Map legend:
- - - Polish boundary, 1770
——— Boundaries, 1772
/// Polish territorial losses

RUSSIA, Baltic Sea, PRUSSIA, POLAND-LITHUANIA, AUSTRIA, OTTOMAN EMPIRE, Black Sea

A CULTURAL TRANSFORMATION

In the shadow of this limited but still continuous and increasingly global war, major cultural changes were under way. Before the eighteenth century, as we have seen, only a tiny minority of Europeans had had real access to a broad spectrum of information. Most peasants were illiterate and received news about the outside world principally from their clergy, traveling peddlers, and merchants, or from printed "chapbooks" that were read aloud to them. In the cities, by 1700, those above the level of the indigent poor had access to some primary education, and as adults they could attend theaters, official pageants and parades. Still, they probably had only a hazy idea of European history and geography. Even fully literate men and women in most cases had access only to a very small number of books, primarily religious in character, and no periodicals. Especially in Protestant countries, reading tended to be "intensive," involving the slow, repeated study of the same few, mostly sacred, texts.

EXPANDING LITERACY

In the eighteenth century, under the new conditions of relative social and political stability, this closed mental world burst open for millions of Europeans. To begin with, literacy grew impressively, especially in the cities. Primary schools, while still run mostly by the church, expanded in number and took on larger numbers of students—mainly boys. In London and Paris, virtually all adult males could

Schooling and Literacy Boys and girls sit on separate benches but are educated together in this eighteenth-century German engraving of a Berlin community primary school. Students learned by rote, with the schoolmaster reading aloud to them.

COFFEEHOUSES AND NEWSPAPERS IN THE AGE OF ENLIGHTENMENT

The Swiss writer César de Saussure traveled to London in the 1720s and was particularly struck by coffeehouses and their unique role in the city's daily life. He recorded in his letters many visits to London coffeehouses, noting the diverse clientele, the lively discussions, and the many kinds of business conducted in this new institution.

For Saussure, much of the appeal of the coffeehouses stemmed from the availability of the many newspapers, journals, and magazines that disseminated not only the new ideas of the era—which ranged from scientific discoveries to new theories about politics—but also local advertisements and gossip. Coffeehouses provided spaces in which patrons could read about and debate controversial ideas, open to all classes and trades—as long as you could afford the price of a cup.

In London there are a great number of coffee-houses, most of which, to tell the truth, are not over clean or well furnished, owing to the quantity of people who resort to these places and because of the smoke, which would quickly destroy good furniture. Englishmen are great drinkers. In these coffee-houses you can partake of chocolate, tea, or coffee, and of all sorts of liquors, served hot; also in many places you can have wine, punch, or ale.

What attracts enormously in these coffee-houses are the gazettes and other public papers. All Englishmen are great news-mongers.... About a dozen different papers appear in London—some every day, others twice a week or only once.... The article dated from London is always the most important.

In it you read of marriages and deaths, of the doings of distinguished personages, of the advancement of others in civil, military, and ecclesiastical employments, and in fact of everything interesting, comical and tragical, that has occurred in this big city. You can easily imagine of what amusing adventures you occasionally read, and the remaining part is filled up with advertisements. A lady will offer five guineas reward for a little lost dog worth five-pence. A husband will warn the public not to lend or sell his wife anything on credit.... Entertainments and spectacles are advertised; also offers of houses, domains, furniture, carriages, horses for sale or on hire, books, pamphlets, etc., and by reading these papers you know of all the gossip and

of everything that has been said and done in this big town....

Some coffee-houses are a resort for learned scholars and for wits; others are the resort of dandies or of politicians, or again of professional newsmongers.

QUESTIONS FOR ANALYSIS

1. According to Saussure, who patronized coffeehouses, and why?
2. What could coffeehouse customers learn from the newspapers and magazines they read?
3. How did coffeehouses represent a new type of social interaction?

Source: Madame Van Muyden, ed. and trans., *A Foreign View of England in the Reigns of George I. and George II.: The Letters of Monsieur Cesar de Saussure to His Family* (London: 1902), pp. 161–64.

read by the end of the century. The countryside lagged far behind, and even in England, one of the most literate of European countries, male literacy for the country as a whole barely reached 60 percent by 1800, and female literacy 40 percent.

Relatively open publishing climates permitted several dozen newspapers and magazines to circulate in Britain by the 1740s, and a similar number in the Netherlands. In France and most other continental states, the government continued to keep a much tighter watch on printed material, requiring works to pass a formal review by state censors before publication. But French-language newspapers printed in the Netherlands circulated widely in France, as did several illicit newspapers.

THE RISE OF THE MAGAZINE AND THE NOVEL

The number of books in print expanded even faster than the number of readers. But just as important, the nature of books changed as more people became literate, and as those people acquired more disposable income. In place of large, heavy, expensive tomes suitable for intensive, repetitive study, publishers found they could make a profit selling books in smaller, cheaper formats of just a few inches on a side, which could be carried around easily—even in a pocket—and read more casually. Magazines like the one Rousseau read while he was walking to Vincennes in 1749 were often specifically designed for portability. The most popular magazines provided a lively mixture of short, humorous essays, longer more serious essays, verse, and, increasingly, illustrations. The great prototype was the British magazine *The Spectator*, founded in 1711, which promised "to enliven morality with wit, and to temper wit with morality . . . to bring philosophy out of the closets and libraries, schools and colleges, to dwell in clubs and assemblies, at tea-tables and coffeehouses."

The subject matter of books changed as well over the eighteenth century. Religious works, while still an important part of publishers' catalogues, were challenged in popularity by histories, popular discussions of scientific topics, philosophical essays, travel narratives, and especially that most important literary genre of the period, the novel. Eighteenth-century novelists such as Daniel Defoe (1660–1731) presented their fictional worlds as slices of reality—as memoirs or letters that had fallen into their hands. Just as Defoe's *Robinson Crusoe* of 1719 purported to be the true story of a castaway, so *Pamela* (1740) and *Clarissa* (1748) by **Samuel Richardson** (1689–1761) adopted the form of letters written by young heroines trying to preserve their virtue from predatory men.

The new novel had a powerful impact on European culture. The brilliant French philosopher **Denis Diderot** (1713–1784) found Richardson's novels as realistic and absorbing as live acting. He said they drew him in so deeply that he continually wanted to shout warnings to the characters as he read. Novels offered an immersive experience in a form that readers could appreciate alone, at their leisure, rather than in a crowded, raucous theater. Thousands of men and women, moved as Diderot was by the compelling characters they encountered in these novels, wrote impassioned letters to their authors, sometimes with praise but often out of dismay that a cherished character had died. In the late 1760s Rousseau applied the psychological techniques and insights of the novel to his own life, and produced the first, and perhaps greatest, example of modern autobiography: the *Confessions*.

WOMEN AS READERS Women provided not only some of the most memorable characters in early novels but also the genre's most enthusiastic readers. Male critics soon came to complain that novels were distracting women from their domestic chores and filling their heads with dangerous fantasies. But novels opened new psychological horizons for middle-class and aristocratic women who, in many parts of Europe, did not work, could scarcely leave their homes without male escorts, and could only attend a fraction of the entertainments available to their husbands and fathers. Even if women's literacy rates remained far behind men's, and even if their formal educations remained far less developed, novels helped bring unprecedented numbers of them into the realm of literature. And by the end of the century, hundreds of women were becoming novelists themselves—and writing novels that explored the limits of women's freedom more explicitly than any previous works of art. The French writer Françoise de Graffigny (1695–1785) became one of the best known novelists of the century thanks to her 1747 *Letters from a Peruvian Woman*, which tells the story of an Inca

Women Readers A young woman reads attentively in a 1770 oil painting by the French artist Jean-Honoré Fragonard (1732–1806). The size of the book suggests that it is one of the novels that had recently become popular among women readers and writers alike.

princess kidnapped by Europeans, and which offers satirical observations on French society.

PUBLIC CULTURE

Beyond the novel, Europeans with sufficient education, leisure, and income could also sample a variety of other new or transformed cultural forms, at least in the larger cities. They could attend exhibitions of new paintings at the Royal Academy in London and the public displays of art held at the Louvre palace in Paris after 1737. And if they wanted paintings to decorate their own homes, they could find enterprising artists ready to supply them. One artist in London cleverly painted a continuous landscape on a long canvas and then sold off sections by the foot. Even more common in homes were cheaply produced engravings, predominantly depicting contemporary figures, including famous actors and writers as well as kings and queens. In Paris, dozens of new engravings appeared each year, and over half of all households possessed at least one. Great actors like London's David Garrick became celebrities on a level previously reached only by monarchs. He had his portrait painted or engraved at least 450 times.

Music played a particularly important role in the changing public culture. In addition to hearing it performed in public, at concerts, and at the opera, Europeans of the upper and middle classes played it more than ever before at home, thanks especially to a new instrument that had evolved out of the harpsichord in the early 1700s: the piano. Musical training became an especially important part of the education of middle- and upper-class women. Germany, Austria, and England particularly shone as sites of musical innovation, thanks to such figures as George Frideric Handel (1685–1759), Joseph Haydn (1732–1809), and the transcendently talented Wolfgang Amadeus Mozart (1756–1791). Mozart, who became known from early childhood as a musical prodigy (he composed his earliest keyboard pieces at the age of five), enjoyed a greater celebrity than any previous musician.

But there were also more academic entertainments, such as public scientific lectures and demonstrations, and exhibitions of curiosities brought from America and Asia. Constituting another window on the world were the subscription libraries that proliferated throughout Europe, modeled on the Library Company of Philadelphia that Benjamin Franklin founded in 1731. These quasi-public libraries allowed unlimited borrowing privileges to members, whose dues paid for the purchase of books. As all these cultural offerings multiplied, a new type of cultural

Musical Culture In a 1759 watercolor, an elegantly dressed woman identified as the wife of a war commissioner plays the piano—an example of the instrument's association with upper-class refinement.

figure emerged to help make sense of it all: the critic who reviewed new books, plays, music, and art exhibitions.

NEW SOCIAL SETTINGS In this expanded cultural world, the new venues for public socializing that had emerged in the late seventeenth century took on even greater importance. Coffee shops featured even more prominently in the daily life of middle-class and noble elites in major cities, and now could offer their patrons an expanded selection of periodicals to read (in Italy, one influential periodical even called itself *Il Caffè*). Paris and London each had well over a thousand of these institutions. In France and Germany, the aristocratic "salons," originally founded to encourage polite conversation and instruct nobles in the customs of royal courts, opened themselves ever more to serious intellectual pursuits. Often presided by women like Françoise de Graffigny, salons gave many key Enlightenment authors access to noble patrons and contributed to the circulation of their ideas in high society.

The number of scholarly academies multiplied too, with dozens in France by the mid-eighteenth century

LEMONNIER'S *AN EVENING WITH MADAME GEOFFRIN*

In this 1812 painting, Anicet-Charles-Gabriel Lemmonier depicts the celebrated salon of Madame Marie Thérèse Geoffrin, an important patron of the arts and learning in eighteenth-century Paris, as it might have looked in 1755. Despite encouraging discussion and including women, salons like Madame Geoffrin's nonetheless remained elite social gatherings, and as such were highly structured and mannered. While topics ranged across discoveries in the natural sciences to new techniques of manufacture, participants were expected to follow aristocratic norms of decorum and propriety, and wit and eloquence were highly prized.

Lemmonier's painting depicts the dual nature of the salon as intellectual gathering and as elite social event. Madame Geoffrin (in blue) sits at right, flanked by nobles and others of high rank, while many of the artists and intellectuals in attendance stand. A bust of Voltaire looks on as one of his works is read aloud. Though most of the attendees are men, women sit among them and speak freely.

QUESTIONS FOR ANALYSIS

1. How does Lemonnier's painting depict the social hierarchies that governed Madame Geoffrin's salon?
2. What opportunities did salons extend to women as shown in this painting?
3. How does Madame Geoffrin's salon reflect the tension between the Enlightenment ideals of inquiry and free thought and the aristocratic order of eighteenth-century Europe?

and an expanding number in Germany as well. They gave ordinary people the chance to participate actively in intellectual life by submitting responses to essay contests of the sort Rousseau won in 1749. Since entries were judged anonymously, hundreds of women felt free to submit entries, with several of them winning. The society of the **Freemasons**, which had its origins in seventeenth-century British confraternities of artisans, grew into a vast network of "lodges" throughout Europe and extended its social reach to the highest rank of society. The Freemasons developed complex rituals supposedly derived from ancient Egypt and Greece, and devoted themselves to a vision of the public good that descended from the radical ideas of the English Civil War, although it expressed itself publicly chiefly in charity. Salons, academies, and Masonic lodges all respected existing social hierarchies, but nonetheless facilitated new, loose forms of interactions between members from different social backgrounds.

THE GARDEN AT VAUXHALL A good example of the broad changes in European society and culture could be seen in 1749, when the British monarchy commissioned the composer Handel to write *Music for the Royal Fireworks* to commemorate the recent treaty that ended the War of the Austrian Succession. An ambitious entrepreneur named Jonathan Tyers secured the right to hold a public "rehearsal" of the work in his pleasure garden at Vauxhall, on the south bank of the river Thames. Since entrance was free, some 12,000 Londoners of all classes flocked to this popular amusement park to hear concerts, see exhibitions of art, eat, drink, and walk along carefully landscaped and illuminated pathways. For the performance of Handel's work, Tyers made full use of the garden to stage an extravagant spectacle for a socially mixed crowd that earned him gross receipts of over £1,500—a huge amount at a time when many urban laborers earned less than £20 per year. The event also caused a three-hour traffic jam on London Bridge, prompting many complaints. Such entertainments would soon become common throughout Europe.

A BROADENING GLOBAL VIEW

More than ever before, these new cultural venues exposed Europeans to the larger world. Earlier generations of Europeans had wondered at the "marvels" and "curiosities" brought back by explorers and colonizers in the sixteenth and seventeenth centuries. But the Europeans of the mid-eighteenth century looked at the rest of the world with more sustained attention, and with a greater sense that humanity was a single unit that stretched across national and religious borders. Travel literature enjoyed great popularity—and not just the religious, evangelizing varieties that highlighted the conversion of heathen "savages." As we will see, many of the Enlightenment's great works made serious use of this travel literature, comparative histories, and early works of anthropology.

COOK'S VOYAGES Voyages of scientific exploration, often large in scale and sponsored by national scientific academies, were particularly important in stimulating this new global view. The earliest of these dated back to the seventeenth century, but the mid-eighteenth again saw a significant increase in their scale, ambition, and prominence. The most important of these voyages were the three undertaken by Britain's Captain **James Cook** (1728–1779). Initially engaged by the Royal Society in 1766 to make astronomical observations in the South Pacific, Cook explored vast stretches of ocean over the next thirteen years. He ranged from the Nootka Sound in present-day British Columbia to just off the coast of Antarctica, and to Australia, where he made the first detailed observations of the indigenous population. Cook and his collaborator, the botanist Joseph Banks (1743–1820), brought back a trove of previously unknown flora and fauna, and sketches of the lands explored.

Cook's second expedition brought back a young Pacific Islander named Omai, who became a sensation in London and was introduced to King George III. Cook and explorers such as the French officer Louis-Antoine de Bougainville (1729–1811), whose scientific expedition sailed around the world in the late 1760s, reported a lack of sexual taboos or restrictions in Pacific islands such as Tahiti. These stories inflamed European imaginations and contributed to the idea that "noble savages"—men and women who lived in mankind's original, innocent state of nature—actually existed. Denis Diderot wrote a satirical *Supplement* to Bougainville's relation of his voyage that, among other things, contrasted the free-loving Tahitians to Catholic priests who unnaturally repressed their sexual urges. Having already spent time in prison for seditious writings, however, Diderot declined to publish the work.

European readers reacted more ambivalently to evidence that the sailors on the voyages were "going native"—marrying indigenous women, taking ritual oaths of friendship, and getting elaborate tattoos. And they were horrified when cultural misunderstandings turned violent, leading to the deaths of Europeans and sometimes

Views of Native Peoples A 1773 British travel narrative included this illustration of natives of Tahiti. The individual on the left is shown with a traditional facial tattoo; the one on the right is described as making an expression used to frighten enemies in battle.

even to ritual cannibalism. James Cook himself was killed by Hawaiians in 1779. Even as his killers, who continued to respect Cook, carefully cleaned and preserved his bones, the British reading public made him into a martyr and hailed him as a model of sensitive, enlightened masculinity.

COSMOPOLITANISM The sense of a common European identity fostered by this new global view, and by social interactions in spaces such as coffeehouses and Masonic lodges, contributed to another remarkable eighteenth-century phenomenon: growing homogeneity among social elites. In the age of Louis XIV, nobles and the wealthiest commoners might have taken on the speech and manners of royal courts, and read fashionable poetry and plays. Yet outside the courts, on the Continent, nearly all the population continued to speak local dialects and take part in traditional local entertainments, even if the elites increasingly condemned the excessive violence and obscenity they perceived in these entertainments. The middle classes continued to dress in traditional local fashion. Festivals and holidays also followed local custom.

But by the middle of the eighteenth century, a broad social elite—nobles, but also professionals (especially doctors and lawyers), the upper clergy, wealthy merchants and tradesmen, and their families—no longer participated in local cultural life in the same way. Now these men and

women increasingly took their cues from a small number of urban centers, which themselves were intensely aware of one another—London, Paris, Berlin, Milan, Naples, Vienna, Saint Petersburg. They read the same books and periodicals as their counterparts in the other cities, discussed the same plays and music—and performed this music themselves at home—and increasingly dressed and spoke in the same manner. This common high culture even extended to far-flung colonial locales: by the 1770s, in towns such as Philadelphia, and Le Cap François in Saint-Domingue, theaters and booksellers boasted the latest productions from Europe, while elegant men and women paraded in the latest European fashions. In Saint-Domingue, wealthy male planters ordered the same fashions for favored slave concubines, whose children they sometimes recognized as legitimate. Indeed, some of these mixed-race children became slave owners themselves.

Overall, then, Europe and its empires were becoming more cosmopolitan places, with the purveyors and products of culture alike readily crossing borders. Between 1675 and 1750, nearly 100 Italian composers took up residence in London. Between the 1720s and the 1770s, the British purchased from Italy, France, and Holland some 50,000 paintings and half a million etchings and engravings. Thousands of wealthy young Britons undertook "grand tours" of the Continent every year. There they visited public buildings and ancient ruins, studied modern languages, and developed social ties with continental Europeans of their own class.

But if the new high culture was international, it nonetheless had a clear focal point: France and the French language. Works in French were circulated and translated more widely than any others. Diplomats spoke French, and so did the nobles of Berlin and Saint Petersburg. King Frederick the Great of Prussia wrote in French and dismissed his mother tongue, German, as suitable only for addressing servants and dogs. In Russia, the tsars encouraged the use of French as well, in keeping with the "Westernization" policies first developed by Peter the Great. Noble Russian families hired French servants and tutors.

ANTI-COSMOPOLITANISM Some writers, however, began to lament the supposed disappearance of national differences. Jean-Jacques Rousseau, a Genevan-born French-speaker, wrote in 1772 that "today...there are no longer any Frenchmen, Germans, Spaniards, or even Englishmen: there are only Europeans. They all have the same tastes, the same passions, and the same customs." In England, by the 1750s a full-fledged cultural reaction was beginning, with influential critics decrying the supremacy of the French language and calling for a return to national, ethnic traditions. The years 1750–70 saw the foundation of a Society of Antiquaries devoted solely to the English past, and the publication of the first major English dictionary, biographical dictionary, and encyclopedia (the *Encyclopedia Britannica*). Aided by celebrities like the actor Garrick, a specifically English literary and dramatic canon was established, centering, of course, on Shakespeare. This cultural reaction was not politically conservative, however. In fact, in the appeal to a mythical national past, critics often sketched out a vision of a more egalitarian future.

Similarly, in Germany, a cohort of young writers challenged the dominance of French culture and urged Germans to rediscover the sources of their own literature by seeking out the supposedly unsullied speech and stories of the peasantry. The writer Johann Wolfgang von Goethe (1749–1832) rhapsodized about the peculiarly German splendors of Strasbourg Cathedral. The philosopher and critic Johann Gottfried Herder (1744–1803) developed the theory that each language and literature had its own particular character, which demanded protection from foreign influences. "Spew out the slime of the Seine," he urged his readers. "Speak German, O German."

These critiques would take on great importance in the early years of the nineteenth century, when they would help drive the emergence of nationalism as a major force in European politics and culture. But even in the cosmopolitan 1750s, Europeans frequently displayed remarkable intolerance toward foreigners. The British had the worst reputation, to the extent that one French visitor thought the English phrase for "foreigner" was "French dog." The Seven Years' War saw the French and British, for the first time, condemn entire enemy peoples for supposed war crimes. Yet even taking this intolerance into account, the mid-eighteenth century still stands, in most respects, as the period in history when European elites, including wealthy members of the middle class as well as nobles, had the most in common with each other. An educated traveler, assuming he or she spoke French, could find familiar institutions, and men and women who knew the same works of art, literature, and philosophy, in any major European city.

RELIGIOUS CHANGE

An additional element contributing to the emergence of a common European culture among elites was the declining public importance of religion. By the middle of the eighteenth century, the intense feelings that had led

Louis XIV of France to declare Protestantism illegal in 1685 had ceased to shape policy in most European states. True, Protestantism did remain illegal in many Catholic countries, while Catholics continued to suffer under a host of "penal laws" in Britain and other Protestant states. But just as religion had largely faded as a motive for international warfare, so the brutal religious violence that had claimed so many lives in previous times largely subsided. The place of religion in European public life was changing in important ways.

THE DECLINE OF FORMAL OBSERVANCE

For one thing, throughout much of western Europe, overt forms of Christian observance were declining. In France, dying men and women left less money to pay for masses for their souls in purgatory, while local elites abandoned religious confraternities in favor of secular Masonic lodges. The number of men choosing to enter the priesthood fell. Most strikingly, the birthrate declined measurably, pointing to the widespread adoption of primitive contraception (coitus interruptus and condoms made from linen or animal entrails) in defiance of religious teachings. But these changes remained uneven across Europe. Just across the French border in the northern Italian kingdom of Piedmont, bequests for masses, religious vocations, and the birthrate remained at the same rates as at the beginning of the century.

Where religious observance did decline, one reason was the growing influence of the skepticism and other new philosophical perspectives of the late seventeenth and early eighteenth centuries. Yet paradoxically, the churches themselves also helped drive the change. By the middle of the eighteenth century, the large-scale reform programs undertaken by both Protestant and Catholic churches since the late sixteenth century had reached fruition. Clergy had far better educations and lived under a greater degree of supervision than their predecessors. (Catholic clergy, in particular, observed much higher rates of celibacy.) They tended to participate in the cosmopolitan high culture and saw their parishioners' customs, and even language, as primitive. Throughout much of Catholic Europe, some clergy sought to impose a rigid, uncompromising form of Catholic practice that denied men and women many of the spiritual comforts they expected from religion. They decreased the frequency with which parishioners received absolution from their sins and took Communion. And so, especially in rural areas, a gap developed between the clergy and their own church members. "Let us regard ourselves," a French priest wrote to a colleague in 1731, "you and I, in these cantons, as if we were in China or in Turkey, even though we are in the middle of Christianity, where one sees practically naught but pagans." Not surprisingly, perhaps, the "pagans" in question reacted badly to such condescension.

NEW "ENTHUSIASMS"

The increasing distance from formal religious observance did not necessarily testify to a decline in religious belief itself. True atheists remained scarce, even in the most advanced intellectual circles. Many men and women seeking a more rational form of religion purged of what they saw as Christian "superstition" turned to some version of **deism**—a set of beliefs that envisioned a single, non-Christian God figure who was held to have created the universe and then left it to its own devices. Among those who embraced deism were prominent Enlightenment-era figures such as Rousseau and Voltaire.

Religious Revival A 1750 illustration of the Methodist leader George Whitefield (1714–1770) preaching on the outskirts of London is captioned "Enthusiasm Displayed," an indication of the kind of emotion that accompanied new religious movements in the period.

Many others, faced with what they saw as the cold, stultifying practices of the established churches, sought new, more vibrant forms of Christianity. In Protestant Germany, **pietism**, which had begun in the seventeenth century, flourished in the mid-eighteenth. Pietists insisted on the need for an enthusiastic religion of the heart, fed by intense Bible study and fervent "revival" meetings. In England, Pietism helped inspire the charismatic preacher John Wesley (1703–1791), who insisted on the redemptive power of ecstatic faith and founded the confession that has become known as Methodism. By the 1740s Wesley's followers had emerged as a mass movement, using every means at their disposal to excite and galvanize congregations, including a virtual obsession with the imagery of Christ's sacrificial blood:

> We thirst to drink Thy precious blood,
> We languish in Thy wounds to rest,
> And hunger for immortal food
> And long on all Thy love to feast.

In Britain's North American colonies, Methodism contributed to the Great Awakening of the 1730s and 1740s, in which preachers challenged their listeners to embrace a personal, passionate relationship with Christ to save them from hellfire. But Methodism remained frowned on by the established churches, with the result that Methodists often became advocates for religious toleration.

The mood of religious revivalism even reached the different setting of eastern European Judaism. In Poland and Lithuania in the 1740s and 1750s, a charismatic rabbi named Israel ben Eliezer (1698–1760) helped to found the movement known as Hasidism, which emphasized loud, joyful singing and prayer to stimulate ecstatic states in which believers would feel God's presence. Even as wealthier and better-educated Jews were embracing secular learning and the Haskalah (Jewish Enlightenment), the Hasids gained hundreds of thousands of followers among the poorer village Jews who remained the large majority of the European Jewish population.

In short, established religions across the Continent found themselves increasingly boxed in between the spread of radical freethinking or deism, on the one hand, and the new religious revival movements, on the other. But they retained their official status, their secular power stood undiminished, and despite the overall decline in religious violence, they could still strike out against supposed heretics in ways that recalled the persecutions of earlier years. Indeed, as examples of brutal intolerance became more rare, the ones that did occur seemed all the

Death of Calas An illustration from a late-eighteenth-century British pamphlet critical of the cruel punishment meted out to Jean Calas shows him being broken on the wheel. Armed guards keep a large crowd at bay in the background, and a priest triumphantly raises his arms.

more shocking. The most notorious example took place in 1761, in the southern French city of Toulouse, after a young Protestant named Marc-Antoine Calas was found dead in his home, a probable suicide. Rumors quickly spread that his father Jean had killed him to prevent him from converting to Catholicism, and on this flimsy basis the father was arrested. In March 1762 the high court of Toulouse, acting in concert with the Catholic authorities, found him guilty and condemned him to death by the gruesome traditional method known as "breaking on the wheel," in which the executioner tied the victim to a cart wheel, systematically broke his bones with an iron rod, inflicted other tortures on him, and left him to die. Episodes of religious rioting continued to occur as well, most notably in London in 1780. When Parliament considered an act to relieve Roman Catholics of some legal burdens, over 40,000 protesters ran amok in central London, forcing the government to call out the army to restore order in what became known, after one of the protest leaders, as the "Gordon riots." Nearly 300 died.

THE ENLIGHTENMENT AT ITS HEIGHT

It was against this broad backdrop of cultural and religious change that the great transformation of European thought and society known as the "**Enlightenment**" intensified. Unlike the Reformation, which Martin Luther had launched so spectacularly in 1517, the Enlightenment did not have a clear starting date. Nor did it take the shape of an organized movement. It spread through existing institutions and practices, including sites of sociability such as coffeehouses, salons and libraries, masonic lodges, printed periodicals, and the network of scholars known as "the Republic of Letters." But it had an enormous impact nonetheless, and also generated enormous opposition.

THE CULT OF REASON

Historians still have lively debates about how to judge the Enlightenment. Was it fundamentally a single phenomenon? Or can we talk about multiple "Enlightenments"— radical, moderate, conservative, even religious? How much do the national contexts matter? Did it arise out of the radical philosophical speculations of the seventeenth century, or did the mid-eighteenth century represent a new departure? Did the Enlightenment mark a step toward the liberation of humanity from the weight of tradition and superstition, or its imprisonment in a new mental straitjacket?

It is worth noting that the term "the Enlightenment" itself did not come into widespread use until the end of the eighteenth century, when Europeans looked back at the period and tried to make sense of it. Earlier attempts to define a single, great movement of thought in the mid-eighteenth century came largely from its self-declared enemies—from clergy, and from scandalized defenders of traditional political authority. Although the great German philosopher Immanuel Kant (1724–1804) wrote a path-breaking essay entitled "What Is Enlightenment?" in 1784, which did much to popularize the term, he omitted the definite article. He also largely avoided defining its specific intellectual content, focusing instead on the issue of how to allow the most profitable exchange of ideas, especially in print, which could in turn encourage "man's emergence from his self-imposed immaturity."

Overall, historians generally concede that "the Enlightenment" did not agree on any particular political program, any form of social organization, or any single view of aesthetics, economics, or metaphysics. Rather than defining the Enlightenment as a single current of thought, it makes most sense to associate it with a loose collection of characteristics shared by figures from a remarkable variety of political, social, and cultural backgrounds. Arguably the most important of these characteristics was inherited directly from radical thinkers of the late seventeenth century such as Baruch Spinoza and Pierre Bayle: this was a supreme confidence in the powers of reason.

REASON AND RELIGION

Intellectual leaders such as Denis Diderot of the mid-eighteenth century sought to remove divine revelation almost entirely from the discussion of things human. Consider the most emblematic work of the Enlightenment: the mammoth, innovative *Encyclopedia* that Diderot published between 1751 and 1772 with Jean le Rond d'Alembert (1717–1783), the son of the salonnière Madame de Tencin. The "tree of knowledge" that appears in this work—an attempt to map how all the branches of knowledge relate to one another—shows revealed religion banished from the central place it had possessed in earlier such exercises. Diderot and d'Alembert placed it instead on an upper branch, under the label "Superstition," next to the category "Black Magic." Some of the most radical thinkers of the mid-eighteenth century went beyond their predecessor Spinoza to offer a purely materialist view of human nature. Julien de La Mettrie (1709–1751) gained notoriety with a book entitled *Man: A Machine*.

Also in keeping with their radical seventeenth-century predecessors, Enlightenment thinkers generally downplayed or eliminated the idea of original sin that had weighed so heavily on the souls of previous generations of European Christians. Particularly important in this regard was **Jean-Jacques Rousseau**. He began his *Discourse on the Origins of Inequality* (1754) with a description of the characteristics humanity might have possessed in the "state of nature" that supposedly existed before civilization. According to Rousseau, primitive humans had two fundamental impulses: self-preservation, but also compassion for their fellows. This second impulse ensured that primitive humans had not existed in a state of permanent competition with one another, to say nothing of Thomas Hobbes's "warre . . . of every man against every man." They lived largely in isolation from one another, and when they first came together into families and societies, they dwelt in a condition of idyllic harmony—what contemporaries often called "noble savagery." In short, humans were fundamentally good, or at least benign, and only developed a capacity for evil as they grew corrupt, invented property rights, and started to exploit one another. While many contemporary thinkers challenged Rousseau's vision of human history, they largely shared his rejection of original sin and the deep pessimism about human nature that had informed European thought since the triumph of Christianity.

SCIENCE AND PRACTICAL VALUE

A broad faith in the scientific method marked one final major continuity with seventeenth-century thought. Enlightenment thinkers generally embraced John Locke's vision of the mind as a blank slate shaped by sense impressions. Their greatest heroes were Locke and especially Isaac Newton, whose work was translated and popularized by the French writer and philosopher **Voltaire** (1694–1778), who considered it a model of how human reason could penetrate nature's mysteries. In Voltaire's comic masterpiece *Candide* (1759), the characters discover a paradise called El Dorado in a remote South American mountain range. It lacks prisons and an established church, but does possess a massive Palace of Sciences full of ingenious instruments and machines.

Diderot and d'Alembert's *Encyclopedia* rejected the venerable notion that manual labor and machines belonged to a lesser order of nature than pure thought, a staple of European thinking since the ancient Greeks. The project devoted a large percentage of its 70,000-odd articles to careful expositions of technical disciplines, from watch-making to weaving to artillery, illustrated by meticulous diagrams and sketches. In keeping with this broad practical perspective, Enlightenment thinkers tended to measure value on the basis of what produced the greatest benefit for the greatest number of people—a concept soon to be known as "utilitarianism." As Rousseau remarked, "it is not a question of knowing what *is*, but only what is useful." Contrary to their opponents' vision of them as idle thinkers lost in the clouds, Enlightenment-era reformers devoted considerable effort to such practical matters as urban street lighting, improved sewage, the draining of marshes to reduce rates of malaria, and the use of street numbers on houses to help travelers navigate strange cities. In this way, their efforts echoed those of absolutist reformers such as Peter the Great and his servant Antonio de Vieira.

Jean-Jacques Rousseau
A portrait from 1753, when the philosopher was forty-one years old.

THE SPREAD OF ENLIGHTENED THOUGHT

The continuities of the Enlightenment with seventeenth- and early eighteenth-century thought are striking. Yet as the story of Rousseau's victory in the essay contest illustrates, these continuities were most important on the level of formal intellectual content. For a full understanding of the Enlightenment and the break it represented in European cultural history, we must consider how ideas were transmitted and their effects within the broad cultural and political context.

WRITING FOR THE PUBLIC To begin with, there was the question of audience. Spinoza and Newton had written in Latin for a small number of learned readers, mostly in the Republic of Letters. Locke's *Essay on Human Understanding* was a dry, technical piece of philosophical exposition that still defeats most readers. By contrast, when the French writer Montesquieu first attracted attention in 1721, it was with a scandalous, witty French-language novel called *Persian Letters*. As he himself commented in the book, "there are certain truths that you cannot simply persuade people of, but which you must make them feel." This sentence marked a clear shift to a new sort of intellectual enterprise, which came to fruition in the mid-century. Montesquieu was not writing for scholars or princely patrons, but for the emerging new public that attended salons and coffee houses and academies, read newspapers and novels, joined Masonic lodges, and even entered essay competitions. And to appeal to them—indeed, just to get their attention—he needed to do more than simply reason well. He needed to shock, titillate, and entertain.

Many of the most famous works of the Enlightenment similarly took the form of provocative entertainments, often set outside Europe. Voltaire's fable *Candide* presents a character named Dr. Pangloss (a spoof of the rationalist philosopher Leibniz), who hangs on to his belief in the pre-established harmony of the universe even after catching syphilis, losing an eye and an ear, nearly dying in an earthquake, barely escaping a hanging, and having been cut open by a surgeon, flogged almost to death, and forced to row in the Turkish galleys. The German intellectual Gotthold Lessing (1729–1781) made many of his most serious arguments for religious tolerance in the form of stage dramas like *Nathan the Wise*, set at the time of the Crusades. Even the deeply serious *Encyclopedia* was enlivened with constant small stabs of wit. For instance,

under the heading "Cannibalism," readers could find a learned discussion of the subject followed by a mischievous cross-reference to the article on Holy Communion.

UNDERGROUND ENLIGHTENMENT Not surprisingly, such deliberate provocations frequently ran afoul of the authorities—particularly in the absolute monarchy of France. Voltaire first achieved notoriety in 1734 with a series of *English Letters* that praised, and deliberately exaggerated, the political freedom and religious toleration found in Britain. The high court of Paris condemned the work, and Voltaire fled to Switzerland rather than face imprisonment. Montesquieu and Rousseau both had trouble with the French authorities as well, and the *Encyclopedia* was banned in 1759 for its irreligion, although the sympathetic director of the French book trade arranged for publication quietly to resume a few years later.

Few of the important works of the French Enlightenment actually appeared with the official permission in theory required of all books. Many were published clandestinely, sold "under the cloak" by booksellers willing to take the risk of imprisonment. Large publishing operations grew in Switzerland, the Netherlands, and Britain to feed the insatiable French appetite for illegal "philosophical" books—a genre that mixed true philosophy with provocative fiction, scurrilous gossip about figures at court, and explicit pornography. Smugglers carried them over remote mountain passes like any other sort of contraband. The authorities strove to suppress this booming trade, but their attempts proved counterproductive, for nothing spurred a book's sale like an official persecution. And authors gained heroic reputations for their defiance of censorship.

VOLTAIRE THE PHILOSOPHE Partly for this reason, the most successful Enlightenment authors enjoyed a public status unlike anything their seventeenth-century predecessors had known. They joined figures like the actor Garrick in the ranks of that new eighteenth-century phenomenon, the celebrity. Voltaire, the son of a Paris notary, had by the 1730s become the first of these—a true literary celebrity. Every educated person in Europe knew his name, and most had probably read something he had written. Even the public executioner charged with burning the *English Letters* on the steps

Voltaire A portrait of the philosophe in his study, at work on a piece of writing, shows him wearing his luxurious velvet housecoat.

ENLIGHTENMENT THINKERS AND PROGRESS

Many Enlightenment thinkers argued that properly directed, rational societies would liberate human genius and lead to the steady improvement of human life—or, in other words, to progress. Progress was a powerful idea, and it animated scientific and technological research and political and social reforms. Some thinkers, such as the French philosophe the marquis de Condorcet, believed that the gradual improvement of human life was inevitable, as one generation built on the work of the preceding generations. The idea of progress also had a utopian dimension, as in the French writer Louis-Sébastien Mercier's novel *L'An 2440* (*The Year 2440*, 1771), which suggested that progress would lead to the perfection of human society.

Marquis de Condorcet, *Sketch for a Historical Picture of the Progress of the Human Mind*

In this passage from his *Sketch* (1795), Condorcet foresees the gradual advancement of humanity through the progress of industry, science, and education.

As the progress of industry and welfare leads to a more advantageous ratio between human capacities and needs, each generation will be brought to greater enjoyments, as a result either of this progress or of the conservation of goods produced earlier...

The most enlightened peoples, reclaiming the right to expend their blood and their wealth, will gradually learn to see war as the deadliest scourge and the greatest of crimes. ...Peoples will know that they cannot become conquerors without losing their own liberty; that permanent confederations are the sole means of maintaining their independence; that they must seek security, not power. Commercial prejudices will gradually dissipate; false mercantile interests will lose their dreadful power to cover the earth with blood, ruining nations under the pretext of enriching them....

The progress of the sciences guarantees that of the art of instruction, which in turn accelerates scientific advance. The constant action of this reciprocal influence must be counted among the most dynamic and powerful causes of the amelioration of the human species. A young man leaving school today knows more mathematics than Newton acquired by profound study or discovered through his genius;...

Finally, can these same hopes be extended to intellectual and moral faculties? Our parents pass on to us the advantages and defects of their physical constitution, from which we derive distinctive bodily characteristics and dispositions to particular physical states. Can they not also pass on to us that part of physical organization governing intelligence, strength of mind, emotional energy, and moral sensibility? Is it not plausible that in improving these qualities education could affect this same physical organization, modifying and improving it? Analogy, analysis of the development of human faculties, and even some observed facts seem to prove the reality of these conjectures...

And how welcome to the philosopher is this picture of the human race freed from all its chains, released from the domination of chance and of the enemies of its progress, advancing with a firm and sure step in the path of truth, virtue, and happiness!

Louis-Sébastien Mercier, from *L'An 2440*

Mercier's popular utopian novel imagined an idealized Paris of the distant future. Here the narrator visits the ruins of Versailles.

I arrived at Versailles, and looked around for that superb palace, from whence issued the destiny of many nations. What was my surprise! I could perceive nothing but ruins, gaping walls, and mutilated statues; some porticos, half demolished, afforded a confused idea of its ancient magnificence. As I walked over these ruins, I saw an old man sitting upon the capital of a column. Alas! I said to him, what is become of this vast palace? "It is fallen."—How?—"It was crushed by its own weight. A man in his impatient pride would have here forced nature. He hastily heaped buildings upon buildings; greedy of gratifying his capricious will, he harassed his subjects; all the wealth of the nation was here swallowed up; here flowed a stream of tears to compose those reservoirs of which there are no traces. Behold all that remains of that colossus which a million of hands erected with so much painful labor.... O, may these ruins cry aloud to all sovereigns; that they who abuse a momentary power, only discover their weakness to future generations." At these words he shed a flood of tears, and turned his eyes to heaven with a mournful, repenting look. Why do you weep? I said. These ruins by no means declare any public calamity. He raised his voice and said: "Oh, how wretched is my fate! Know that I am Louis XIV who built this rueful palace. The Divine Justice has again illumined the torch of my days, to make me contemplate more nearly my deplorable enterprise. How transient are the moments of pride!..."

QUESTIONS FOR ANALYSIS

1. In Condorcet's essay, how does education contribute to the progress of humankind?
2. What do you think Mercier hopes to achieve by imagining the ruination of Louis XIV and Versailles?
3. What do Condorcet and Mercier see as obstacles to progress?

Sources: Marquis de Condorcet, *Sketch for a Historical Picture of the Progress of the Human Mind*, trans. Keith Michael Baker, *Daedalus* 133, no. 3 (Cambridge, MA: 2004), pp. 74, 77–78, 81; Louis-Sébastien Mercier, *Memoirs of the Year Two Thousand Five Hundred*, trans. W. Hooper (Dublin: 1772), pp. 198–99.

of the Palace of Justice in Paris secretly substituted a Spanish history book at the last minute, because he wanted Voltaire's work to read for himself. Voltaire's stories, plays, poetry, and histories sold well enough to equip the chalet where he lived in exile just across the border from France with six horses, four carriages, two footmen, a valet, two cooks, a secretary, and other servants. Voltaire himself wore a velvet housecoat that cost a year's wages for the average worker. Even before his death, biographers compared him to the greatest figures in French history. In fact, he was not just a celebrity but also the most successful of a new type of public intellectual—in the French term that will remain forever associated with the Enlightenment, a *philosophe*.

Yet despite this new status, Voltaire did not achieve a position of true independence. Operating in what was still a hierarchical, noble-dominated society, he continued to cultivate noble patrons and spent several years in Berlin as a sort of official philosophe at the court of the philosophically minded King Frederick the Great. Similarly, Diderot, the son of a cutler, paid visits to his own financial patron Catherine the Great of Russia. Even Rousseau, who enjoyed a degree of celebrity second only to Voltaire's, and who loudly deplored his colleagues' thirst for noble patronage as a sign of corruption, throughout his career accepted housing and financial support from a succession of bedazzled aristocrats.

Even as they received this support, the philosophes managed to remain at odds with the existing order. They continued to see their role as defending certain basic principles, most importantly those of religious toleration that nearly every European state continued to deny. When the Protestant Jean Calas was broken on the wheel in Toulouse in 1762, Voltaire quickly found out about the case. Soon convinced of Calas's innocence, he not only condemned what had happened but led a large-scale public campaign to have the verdict posthumously reversed and the family compensated, making use of pamphlets, newspaper articles, and a massive letter-writing campaign. He took to signing his letters "Crush that which is Infamous!"—meaning intolerance in general and the Catholic Church in particular. His efforts in the Calas case succeeded, showing the power inherent in the transformed, enlightened public sphere.

Opposition to the philosophes eventually crumbled in the face of their growing popularity. In 1772, just thirteen years after the condemnation of the *Encyclopedia* for irreligion, its co-editor d'Alembert became permanent secretary of the powerful French Academy. Six years after that, Voltaire, now eighty-four years old, returned to Paris for the first time in decades to attend a performance of his newest play. Admirers camped outside the house he was staying in to catch a glimpse of the great man, and crowds lined the street as he passed. At the theater, the author watched as the players solemnly crowned his bust with laurel leaves.

Critics in the Church still raged against the rising tide of irreligion in France, but they seemed to reach fewer and fewer listeners. Indeed, the Church itself was increasingly dominated by figures like Étienne Charles de Loménie de Brienne (1727–1794), archbishop of Toulouse from 1776, who eagerly corresponded with Voltaire and other philosophes. He was said to have every quality necessary for a prelate, with one small exception: he did not believe in God.

THE SCIENCE OF SOCIETY

The Enlightenment, then, was defined in large part by the changed relationship between its leading thinkers and the societies in which they lived. But this relationship was not limited simply to the new or transformed institutions and media through which Enlightenment ideas spread. The leading thinkers also came to see society itself in a new way—as an entity in its own right, which functioned according to its own complex laws and was susceptible to change through political action. The Enlightenment saw the emergence of a true, practical science of society, and it is in this respect that it moved beyond the thought of earlier periods.

MONTESQUIEU The key figure in this re-envisioning of society was Baron Montesquieu, who in 1748 published a massive, disorganized book entitled *The Spirit of the Laws*. Based on Montesquieu's extensive reading in the classics, French history, and especially travel literature from across the globe, *The Spirit of the Laws* offers a classification of governments, in much the way Aristotle had analyzed monarchy, aristocracy, and democracy in his *Politics*. But unlike Aristotle, Montesquieu grounded his analysis of governments in a classification of societies, which he saw as shaped above all by climate and history.

Montesquieu In an anonymous portrait of Montesquieu dated 1728, the thinker is portrayed in profile with a classical hairstyle and cloak—perhaps an allusion to the classical influences on his writing.

Here the new global perspective characteristic of the mature Enlightenment assumed crucial importance. Montesquieu drew a contrast between the supposedly despotic empires that arose in the lush, torpid climates of the South and East (such as China, in his view) and the small republics that flourished in allegedly hardier regions (such as Switzerland). He speculated on the "driving principles" that lay behind different forms of government, linking republics to the practice of virtue, monarchies to the idea of honor, and despotism to naked fear. He praised Great Britain's limited monarchy for its system of checks and balances, but also suggested that an absolute monarchy tempered by justice and restraint might prove best suited to France. The book remains the foundation stone of political sociology, and indeed of modern social science in general.

THE SCOTTISH ENLIGHTENMENT Montesquieu found readers not only in France but across the European world. In the American colonies, his theory of checks and balances helped inspire the authors of the United States Constitution of 1787. And he also had keen readers in a place far removed from the contentious atmosphere of Paris: Scotland, where a group of talented professors, lawyers, clergymen, and other professionals were developing their own version of the Enlightenment in the middle of the eighteenth century. These men, like their French counterparts, shared the radical inheritance of late-seventeenth-century thought. The most profound thinker among them, **David Hume** (1711–1776), a champion of rigorous philosophical skepticism, argued in his 1755 book *The Natural History of Religion* that belief in God had its origin in superstition and fear.

But unlike their French counterparts, these Scots mostly did not come into open conflict with the authorities, and many of them gained prominent positions at the universities of Glasgow and Edinburgh. There they developed sophisticated new approaches to history, deeply informed by readings in non-European history, tracing how "primitive" societies ruled by warrior classes and practicing subsistence agriculture evolved over the centuries into complex modern social organisms. They placed particular emphasis on the development of commerce, showing how it softened and moderated social relations, stimulating the development of politeness and the art of conversation, and also bringing women into public life.

Another great figure of the Scottish Enlightenment took the science of society in a new direction by pioneering the discipline that we now call economics. **Adam Smith** (1723–1790), a philosopher and professor, in 1776 published his great work *The Wealth of Nations*, which fundamentally broke with the mercantilist idea that a country's wealth was limited by its supply of precious metals and agricultural production. Smith proposed instead that countries could increase their economic productivity by adopting the division of labor, which organized the production process into particular tasks in which workers specialized. In making this recommendation, Smith was drawing on his own observations of the economic changes taking place in his lifetime, but also advocating their further spread and systematization. Smith also proposed abolishing barriers to trade, including across international borders. He believed firmly that each individual's drive to accumulate wealth would contribute to social harmony by a process that he dubbed the "invisible hand" of the free market. Prices would be set by the free interactions of producers who supplied goods, and the men and women who wielded a demand for them. If allowed to proceed without the interference of religious or secular authorities, the market itself would set prices and profits efficiently. In this system, which we refer to now as **laissez-faire** or free-market capitalism, private individuals and privately owned corporations control most economic activity.

Smith was not the first to make such arguments. Earlier in the century the British satirical writer Bernard Mandeville (1670–1733) had stressed the connection between "private vices" such as greed and "public benefits," while a variety of continental writers had challenged the conventional wisdom that luxury always had a corrupting effect. But Smith developed the ideas more systematically and with a greater understanding of how economic systems actually work. He also warned that unfettered freedom to pursue wealth would increase social inequities. Nonetheless, to the extent that modern free-market capitalism has a founding father, it is Adam Smith.

SENTIMENT AND CITIZENSHIP

Critics of the Enlightenment, from the eighteenth century to the present day, have often charged that its leading thinkers promoted a mechanistic view of human nature, coldly treating men and women like cogs in one of the machines so lovingly illustrated in the *Encyclopedia*. The Enlightenment's science of society put the lie to this claim. Although many eighteenth-century authors, including Voltaire, failed to recognize the degree of comfort people find in tradition, irrational belief, and even prejudice, others such as Montesquieu and the Scottish thinkers never insisted on managing human affairs by cold reason alone. They held a nuanced, careful view of human nature, grounded in empirical observation, and gave full scope to emotion and sentiment.

SOCIAL EXCHANGE The hallmark of modern civilization, from the perspective of these thinkers, was not that emotion had given way to reason, but that violent passion had given way to tender, gentle feeling that encouraged peaceful social intercourse. Women were key to this view of society. Not only was tender sentiment associated with femininity, but women were held to have a "civilizing" influence on men, calming their passions and teaching them how to be properly social. The role that women played in continental salons, and as patrons of Enlightenment writers, reinforced this argument. Many of the philosophes believed women could participate fully in Enlightenment culture. Emilie du Châtelet (1706–1749), a lover of Voltaire's who had studied and published on advanced physics and mathematics, collaborated with him on a translation of and commentary on Isaac Newton's *Principia Mathematica*.

An attention to sentiment runs through most Enlightenment writings. Readers often spoke of the tears they had shed on reading Voltaire's tragedy *Zaïre*—a combination love story and denunciation of intolerance, set in the time of the Crusades—or Rousseau's novel *The New Eloise*. Diderot and other critics openly praised the genre of melodrama, with its exaggerated sentimentality, for the tears it elicited, and tried their hand at writing such works themselves. The French painter Jean-Baptiste Greuze (1725–1805) made his name painting melodramatic scenes of family reconciliation and of tender rural virtue. Rousseau stressed the need to allow emotions and passions to develop naturally. He particularly praised the bond between mother and child and, in his popular educational treatise *Emile*, urged Europeans to return to the practice of breastfeeding. Such was the popularity of the book that thousands of them did, and continued to do so even after the eccentric Rousseau confessed to having unsentimentally abandoned five of his own children to orphanages.

ROUSSEAU'S *SOCIAL CONTRACT* While Rousseau championed sentiment in many works, in others he remained enthralled by the lure of the ancient Greek city of Sparta, whose citizens supposedly suppressed emotion the better to serve the common good. He himself recognized the dilemma. To cultivate the sort of stern patriotic

Sentiment in Art In this 1763 painting by Jean-Baptiste Greuze, a faithful family cares for a paralyzed man. Denis Diderot, who described Greuze's work as "morality in paint," appreciatively named this painting *The Benefits of a Good Education* and admired its expressive emotion.

loyalties expected of a Spartan, one had to suppress one's natural inclinations. Cultivating "tender" natural sentiments to the fullest made a person incapable of the bellicosity and self-sacrifice shown by Spartan citizens. Or, as he himself put it in *Emile*: "Forced to fight nature or social institutions, we must choose between making a man or making a citizen; we cannot do both." As the century wore on, figures associated with the Enlightenment increasingly opted for the latter course.

Rousseau himself did more than anyone to define the meaning of citizenship for the eighteenth century in *The Social Contract*, a powerful and enormously influential book he published almost simultaneously with *Emile* in 1762. Compared to *The Spirit of the Laws* or the works of the Scottish historians, this political treatise stood out for its relatively abstract language and frequent invocation of mathematics and geometry rather than history to describe forms of government. In its pages, Rousseau addressed the question that Hobbes had posed a century before in *Leviathan*: How could citizens live together in society without descending into civil war or tyranny? Like Hobbes, Rousseau argued that individuals must cede their rights to the sovereign power as part of a "social contract." But unlike Hobbes, he associated this sovereign power with the entire citizenry and insisted that true freedom could only be enjoyed collectively, by submission to what he called the "general will." Rousseau held out the enticing prospect that such submission would produce "a remarkable change in man, substituting justice for instinct in his behavior and endowing his actions with the morality they previously lacked." But he added, chillingly, that "anyone who refuses to obey the general will must be obliged to do so by the body [of citizens], which means nothing other than that he will be forced to be free."

The Social Contract represented a clear rejection of the science of society explored by Montesquieu and the writers of the Scottish Enlightenment. Whereas they had sought to explain political systems by reference to social conditions, and to find ways to harmonize society and politics, Rousseau insisted that "everything depended on politics," by which he meant that the nature of customs and social relations were fundamentally shaped by the form of a people's government. *The Social Contract* formulated a high standard of political virtue against which all existing political systems could only come up short. Rousseau himself believed that the principles set forth in his book could be implemented only in small city-states such as those of ancient Greece, and that in any case Europe's nations had nearly all grown too corrupt to establish the sort of democratic government he advocated. Nonetheless, by the 1780s many readers saw *The Social Contract* not as an intellectual exercise, but as a blueprint for political action.

REPUBLICANISM Even in the 1760s, the core theme of patriotic sacrifice for the common good that Rousseau helped to develop was already finding eager audiences. Because of the inspiration Rousseau and other authors took from the ancient republics, this current of thought is often called "**republican**," even if its adherents did not literally advocate the creation of republics in the place of the monarchies under which they lived. During the Seven Years' War, French and British propagandists alike presented their nations as the reincarnation of the virtuous Roman republic at war with its corrupt enemy, Carthage. After the war, many French writers blamed their defeat on their country's allegedly loose morals, and demanded a return to the strict standards of ancient Rome. The embrace of austerity even extended to painting, where

Neoclassical Art The French painter Jacques-Louis David's (1748–1825) *Oath of the Horatii* (1784) embodies the enthusiasm for antiquity and precise technique shared by neoclassical artists beginning in the late eighteenth century. The painting depicts three Roman brothers willing to sacrifice themselves in battle for their city.

the 1770s saw the flourishing of a neoclassicism that favored subjects of patriotic sacrifice rather than domestic tenderness.

Republican thinkers and artists signaled their critical stance toward their culture most clearly in their strict attitude toward women, whom they deemed unfit for public life on account of their supposed inability to overcome their emotions. In contrast to Montesquieu and the Scottish historians, who saw a prominent role for women in society as a sign of social progress, the classical republicans condemned it as a symptom of social collapse and corruption. Rousseau himself demanded a strict separation of the sexes, with women restricted to the domestic roles of wife and mother.

Expulsion of the Jesuits Clerics bemoan their fate—one even collapsing on the ground—as soldiers herd them toward waiting boats, in an engraving depicting the expulsion of the Jesuits from Spain in 1767.

THE POLITICS OF ENLIGHTENMENT

It should be clear that the major thinkers of mid-eighteenth-century Europe had widely varying political philosophies. The systems they advocated included both the collectivist republican democracy of Rousseau's *Social Contract* and the moderate, British-style representative politics advocated by Montesquieu and the young Voltaire. And especially in the 1760s and 1770s, the Enlightenment also appeared compatible with absolute monarchy, in a pattern that held remarkably steady across Europe. This period, indeed, might be called the brief golden age of "**enlightened absolutism**."

ENLIGHTENED ABSOLUTISM

It should not be surprising that Europe's absolute monarchs found much to appreciate in the Enlightenment. In the growing support for religious toleration and skepticism about revealed religion, they discovered an end to the doctrinal quarrels that had shaken their ancestors' thrones in the Reformation, and an excuse for curtailing the power and independence of established churches. In the growing embrace of utility ("the greatest good for the greatest number"), they saw the justification for the rational management of their societies by a single, controlling authority—their own. In the new concepts of economic productivity and free trade, later absolute monarchs saw a chance to increase their nations' wealth and their own tax revenues. While they continued to find individual

philosophes dangerously independent, they increasingly took the cause of Enlightened reform for their own. In Catholic Europe, they sought to exercise greater authority over the Church and to take greater control of education. This led, in several countries, to their expulsion of the Jesuit Order, which had previously dominated secondary education and which owed direct allegiance to the pope. Following these expulsions, the Order itself was dissolved, and only re-created in the nineteenth century.

THE CASE OF PORTUGAL Portugal offers one good example of the way monarchs could make use of Enlightenment ideas. In 1755 King José I (r. 1750–1777) appointed as prime minister the reform-minded Sebastião José de Carvalho e Melo, later known as the marquis of Pombal (1699–1782). During his twenty-four years in office, Pombal reduced the power of the Catholic Church, expelled the Jesuit Order from the country, instituted a degree of religious toleration for non-Catholic Christians, overhauled the tax system, and laid the basis for public primary and secondary education. He also did a great deal to limit the power of the high aristocracy, which hated him. Pombal governed ruthlessly, tolerated no dissent, and took every opportunity to increase the power of the central government. Neighboring Spain also saw considerable reform under King Charles III (r. 1759–1788), including the creation of a national bank, the streamlining of the central bureaucracy, an overhaul of the educational system, and a reduction of tariffs and price controls on basic commodities. These so-called Bourbon reforms also introduced efficiencies into the sprawling Spanish Empire.

GERMANY AND AUSTRIA The German states saw similar developments. As early as 1727, Prussia created the first university chairs in "cameralism"—the science of public administration—and other German states soon followed. Frederick the Great of Prussia cast himself as an enlightened ruler who reigned only for his subjects' happiness. He lightened the financial burdens of Prussian serfs, introduced greater religious toleration, and abolished torture and corporal punishment in the Prussian lands. Voltaire came to reside briefly at his court, under the mistaken impression that the king would treat him as something other than a servant. In fact, Frederick betrayed his true opinion of Voltaire when he wrote, "I shall have need of him for another year at most, no longer. One squeezes the orange and one throws away the peel." Yet unlike Pombal, Frederick identified thoroughly with the nobility. He promoted their interests and dedicated himself above all to the aristocratic vocation of war.

For a more thoroughgoing reform program, German-speakers had to look to Habsburg Austria, where Queen Maria Theresa (r. 1740–1780) and her son, Joseph II (r. 1780–1790), ruled in succession between 1740 and 1790. Joseph especially gained a reputation as a model of enlightened absolutism. He granted a degree of religious toleration to Protestants, Orthodox Christians, and Jews; banished the Jesuit order; and reorganized the Catholic Church in Austrian territories, confiscating much of its property in the process. Like Frederick, he lessened the financial and labor burden on the serfs, with the ultimate goal of turning them into rent-paying tenants. He also founded a public education system and relaxed censorship. But Joseph, too, saw reforms as a means of allowing the state to function more efficiently under the guidance of an unchecked, although impartial, monarchy. One of his advisers compared the state to a machine in which the ruler acted as the "mainspring," setting everything else in motion.

CATHERINE THE GREAT Even in Russia, the monarchy made some moves toward enlightened reform. Upon becoming tsar in 1762, the German-born Peter III alienated most of the Russian high aristocracy. After just six months a group of disaffected nobles killed him in a coup d'état and the throne passed to his German-born wife, who ruled as Catherine II ("the Great") until 1796. Catherine (r. 1762–1796) proved a very strong ruler. She fought and won two costly wars against the Ottoman Turks

Catherine the Great A portrait of the queen, dressed in the regal finery of a western European monarch, in 1770.

and annexed large territories in the south, including the Crimea, giving Russia warm-water ports on the Black Sea. She corresponded with Voltaire and Diderot, and even invited the latter to visit her court in Saint Petersburg. She convened a commission to produce a general statement of legal principles that included equality before the law for non-serfs, religious toleration, and an end to cruel punishments. But believing Russia not yet ready for such radical change, she did not try to put the principles into practice. Much of the Russian population remained in the virtual slavery that was Russian serfdom.

ENLIGHTENED REFORM IN FRANCE In France, despite the frequent conflicts between the philosophes and the monarchy, proponents of enlightened reform had some success as well. Although intelligent and energetic, King Louis XV had few of Frederick II's or Joseph II's ambitions. He spent much of his reign embroiled in disputes with the kingdom's high courts (*parlements*), which exercised their traditional right to protest royal decisions in order to protect Jansenist Catholics and block new forms of taxation. The high courts even forced the king to expel the Jesuit Order from France, a decision that helped persuade the pope—after similar expulsions in Portugal,

Spain, and Austria—to dissolve the order. In response to such obstructions, in 1770, in a hugely unpopular move, the king stripped the high courts of the right to protest and replaced the magistrates with pliant nominees of his own.

In the 1760s, however, a new school of philosophes arose in France who called themselves physiocrats, or "economists." They supported free markets, opposed mercantilist ideas, and argued for a streamlined, efficient monarchy in much the way Joseph II did. After Louis XV's death, his young grandson, Louis XVI (r. 1774–1792), named one of them, an ambitious official named **Anne-Robert Turgot** (1727–1781), to head his ministry. Turgot favored an innovative plan for a series of elected assemblies to advise the monarch, although not to legislate on their own. He freed price controls on grains and then moved to abolish the guilds, which still claimed a monopoly on virtually all trades. He also ended the conscription of peasants as road-builders. The edicts led to loud protests from leaders of guilds and the *parlements*, who feared the expansion of royal power. The edicts also spurred bread riots as prices began to rise. In the midst of this turmoil, enemies at court engineered Turgot's dismissal, but his efforts still amounted to the most ambitious reforms attempted by the French crown before the Revolution of 1789.

BRITAIN AND THE WILKES AFFAIR

Great Britain, while hailed by many on the Continent as a model of enlightened government, yet again stood out as an exception to the European pattern. Until 1760 and the death of King George II, British politics remained dominated by the Whig Party (descended from the victors of the Glorious Revolution of 1688) and a vast patronage system created by the party's leading figure, Robert Walpole. Until the 1760s, the Whigs controlled the principal government ministries. Thanks to the Bank of England and the well-organized tax-collection system, the British crown enjoyed a financial stability that its continental rivals could only envy. As a result, Britain could continue to build its navy into the force that ensured its triumph in the Seven Years' War. The king and his ministers saw little need for the sorts of reforms adopted by their continental counterparts.

The accession of George III (r. 1760–1820) in 1760 briefly seemed to alter the political equation, as the new monarch showed favor to the Whigs' opponents, the Tories, raising the fear that he might prove another would-be absolutist, like James II. Yet in fact, the major political conflicts of the 1760s and 1770s turned less around the monarchy than around Parliament, which still represented only a small, wealthy minority of adult British males. In 1763, Parliament refused to allow a radical critic of the government, John Wilkes, to take his seat. In the ensuing controversies, which dragged on over several years, there coalesced a movement for parliamentary reform (especially an end to the handpicking of some members by powerful aristocrats), an expansion of the franchise, and freedom of speech. This movement, while not seeking to create a fundamentally new political order, as had been the case with the Levellers and other mid-seventeenth-century radicals, nonetheless echoed some of the democratic aspirations of these earlier movements.

The **Wilkes affair** offered some of the most powerful evidence, before 1780, that the Enlightenment might ultimately have different political implications from what the absolute monarchs hoped. Wilkes himself had direct ties to the most daring thinkers of the Parisian Enlightenment. In the movement to seat him in Parliament, a newly assertive "public opinion," born out of the social and cultural transformations described above, especially the expansion of the press, claimed a formal voice in politics. Wilkes himself emerged as one of the first political celebrities, with followers delightedly following his escapades in the press. Engravings of him outsold those of famous actors, and the slogan "Wilkes and Liberty" appeared on many consumer products, including crockery and linens.

The Wilkesite movement had no direct counterpart on the Continent, where representative bodies had largely ceased to function. Still, the European public found other

"Wilkes and Liberty" This 1763 cream-colored ceramic teapot bearing the "Wilkes and Liberty" slogan exemplifies the types of consumer products that were popular with Wilkes's supporters.

venues to express itself. In a series of spectacular trials in France in the 1760s and 1770s, lawyers used the plight of persecuted Protestants, unjustly condemned prisoners, and children imprisoned at their parents' request, to highlight the flaws in the existing legal and political systems, and to call for enlightened reform.

THE RIGHTS OF MAN

More generally, the period 1740–80 saw the emergence of a broad new concept in European political life: "the rights of man," a phrase that dates to this period. The idea of natural rights had roots in the seventeenth-century political philosophies of Hobbes and Locke. But natural rights by definition arose out of the state of nature and did not necessarily apply to people once they had entered society. Indeed, the entry into society had implied, for many philosophers, the *surrender* of "natural rights" to the state. The rights of man (what we now call "human rights"), by contrast, belonged to people regardless of their social condition. They were unalienable.

The idea of the rights of man arose when it did because of the social and cultural changes we have seen. By the mid-eighteenth century, the men and women of

The Anti-Slavery Movement A 1780 French engraving from *The History of the Two Indies* pictures an Englishman selling a weeping African into slavery. Antislavery activists often highlighted such personal cruelties to bolster support for their cause.

cosmopolitan Europe and its colonial extensions had learned to feel a degree of sympathetic identification with people of different social ranks, whom they did not even know. This large, educated public mixed as equals in coffeehouses and other new settings, and learned through cultural forms like the novel to identify with servants, peasants—even criminals. The idea of human rights also received a boost from the enormous popularity of Rousseau's thought: his biting condemnations of inequality, his stirring evocations of the ancient republics (even if "the rights of man" had no place in such regimented societies), and the unforgettable opening words of *The Social Contract*: "Man is born free, but is everywhere in chains."

Although through 1780 the cause of the rights of man in continental Europe mostly stopped well short of calls for revolt against the monarchies, it had important political effects. In the 1760s, it helped inspire a movement for an end to official torture and horrific punishments such as breaking on the wheel. Voltaire had given little thought to the manner of Jean Calas's death when he started writing about the case in 1762, but within a few years he had come to denounce breaking on the wheel as a "barbaric" punishment. In his 1764 book *On Crimes and Punishments*, the Milanese reformer Cesare Beccaria (1738–1794) argued for swift, humane punishments, made the first sustained case in European history against the death penalty, and pointed the way toward imprisonment as the sole legitimate punishment for criminal offenses. Legal reform of this sort was compatible with enlightened absolutism because it tended to reduce the power of the noble magistrates who were defying the crown's power in France.

The cause of human rights also prompted some key thinkers to see the issue of slavery in a new light. In 1770 a group of philosophes led by Guillaume-Thomas-François Raynal (1713–1796) and including Diderot published a massive compendium entitled *The History of the Two Indies*, which took the long-standing Enlightenment interest in non-European societies to a new level. It surveyed the history of European imperialism, denounced the exploitation of indigenous peoples in scorching terms, protested slavery as one of the greatest human evils, and, invoking the leader of a great slave revolt in ancient Rome, called for a "Black Spartacus" to rise up and free the slaves in the Americas. The book went through some seventy printings before the French Revolution and helped inspire French societies promoting the abolition of slavery. Antislavery societies were also appearing in England, organized largely by the Quakers and other devout Christian opponents of the slave trade. The antislavery cause potentially threatened the economic well-being of Europe's American empires, but it did not yet represent a direct challenge to existing regimes.

THE AMERICAN REVOLUTION (1776–1783)

It was in the English-speaking world where the idea of "the rights of man" first posed a real threat to the ruling political order. The Wilkes affair, with its linking of human rights to parliamentary reform, set off tremors. But the first real earthquake occurred across the Atlantic Ocean, in Britain's colonies on the eastern seaboard of North America. There, in the 1760s, opposition to the British government swelled as Britain imposed new taxes to pay the enormous costs of defending the colonies in the Seven Years' War. But Britain did not give the colonists, who had no representation in Parliament, any say in the matter and furiously dismissed colonial protests on the issue.

These developments seemed to threaten the broad autonomy long enjoyed by the colonies. In addition, a strong strand of radical republicanism, especially in the northern colonies, had taught the American colonists to see government in general as prone to corruption and tyranny. The American cities had developed a public culture as vigorous and diverse as that in any European country—with higher literacy rates, more newspapers and books per capita, and an assortment of institutions in which people could gather to discuss politics and plan their actions. This provided the perfect setting for "public opinion" to be transformed into the "will of the people." Protests against the mother country swelled, and some of them turned violent. Patriotic societies, some of them taking the name "Sons of Liberty," organized boycotts of goods imported from Britain.

In the 1770s, these protests built into revolution. The unrest had led the British to send the army to Boston, and on March 5, 1770, troops opened fire on a hostile crowd there, killing five men and greatly increasing animosity toward the British government. In 1773, a new tax on imported tea led Sons of Liberty masquerading as Indians to storm a ship in Boston harbor and dump tea into the water (the original "Tea Party"). The British government responded with a series of punitive actions, including closing the city's port. In spring 1775, a Continental Congress drawn from all thirteen colonies raised a joint army and began moving toward independence.

Battle of Yorktown A French engraving shows the British surrendering to the large combined American and French force at the battle of Yorktown in 1781, ending the war.

From the very start, the **American Revolution** (1775–1783) justified itself in the new language of the rights of man. An enormously influential pamphlet written by Thomas Paine (1737–1809), a recent British arrival, helped establish a bedrock principle of modern democracies: *Common Sense* proclaimed in its very title that ordinary people, rather than kings, were the ultimate source of political authority. Thanks in large part to Paine's influence, colonial anger that had originally directed itself largely against the British Parliament, and had looked to King George III as a potential ally, turned republican and antimonarchical.

In July 1776, Thomas Jefferson (1743–1826)—a slaveholding lawyer and legislator from Virginia who was deeply influenced by Enlightenment thought—placed the concept of the rights of man at the heart of the American Declaration of Independence: "We hold these truths to be self-evident, that all men are created equal, that they are endowed by their Creator with certain unalienable Rights, that among these are Life, Liberty and the pursuit of Happiness. — That to secure these rights, Governments are instituted among Men, deriving their just powers from the consent of the governed."

In fact, securing the rights of Americans—or, at least, white Americans—also required a painful, grinding military conflict that lasted until 1781. The new United States faced heavy odds, fighting against a well-trained British military and also against many of their own number who remained loyal to Britain. But it benefited from steady, cautious leadership by George Washington, who quickly emerged as the greatest political hero of the age. And in

1778, a French government eager for revenge on Britain for the Seven Years' War came into the conflict on the American side, providing much-needed support. Finally, the United States defeated the British army on the ground. The new nation adopted a constitution that borrowed heavily from Montesquieu's theory of a mixed constitution, and enshrined human rights in its first ten amendments, known as the Bill of Rights.

CONCLUSION

These revolutionary events generated immense interest in Europe, especially for what they seemed to reveal about the liberationist potential of the Enlightenment. Documents such as the United States Constitution and especially the Declaration of Independence were quickly reprinted and translated, along with Paine's *Common Sense*. In the American Revolution, Europeans saw that the ideas they had been discussing for the past half century, in the transformed public culture of the Enlightenment, could have consequences far different from, and greater than, strengthening the hand of absolute monarchs against traditional opponents. They saw new outcomes to the trends of the previous four decades: increasing prosperity, increasing global communications and trade, a transformed cultural environment, and an intellectual movement committed to toleration and even to the "rights of man." And they grasped that Enlightenment—what the British thinker and politician Edmund Burke would soon castigate as "this new conquering empire of light and reason"—might soon strike at the very foundations of their own politics and societies.

KEY TERMS

enclosure (p. 507)

"putting out" system
(p. 507)

Seven Years' War (p. 512)

Samuel Richardson (p. 516)

Denis Diderot (p. 516)

Freemasons (p. 519)

James Cook (p. 519)

deism (p. 522)

pietism (p. 522)

Enlightenment (p. 523)

Jean-Jacques Rousseau
(p. 524)

Voltaire (p. 524)

philosophe (p. 527)

David Hume (p. 528)

Adam Smith (p. 528)

laissez-faire (p. 528)

republican (p. 530)

enlightened absolutism
(p. 531)

Anne-Robert Turgot
(p. 533)

Wilkes affair (p. 533)

American Revolution
(p. 535)

REVIEW QUESTIONS

1. What important developments lay behind the economic expansion and improved standards of living in eighteenth-century Europe?

2. Why did warfare reach a global scale during the mid-eighteenth century?

3. What new venues made the arts and intellectual pursuits more widely available to the public?

4. What evidence shows the emergence of a more cosmopolitan culture in eighteenth-century Europe and its colonies?

5. What religious movements developed in the eighteenth century?

6. What set the Enlightenment apart from earlier intellectual movements?

7. What roles did the philosophes play in the culture and society of the eighteenth century?

8. How did the philosophes change the meaning of citizenship?

9. What appeal did Enlightenment ideas hold for some of Europe's absolute monarchs? With what results?

10. In the later eighteenth century, how did the new concept of the rights of man lead to proposals for political reform?

CORE OBJECTIVES

After reading this chapter, you should have a solid understanding of the following core objectives. To strengthen your grasp of the core objectives, use the resources on the Student Site for The West.

- Analyze the economic, political, and social context of the Enlightenment.

- Describe the emergence of new cultural patterns contributing to the Enlightenment.

- Trace the development of a newly cosmopolitan worldview in the second half of the eighteenth century.

- Identify the essential intellectual elements of the Enlightenment.

- Assess the social and political themes of Enlightenment thought.

- Evaluate the political changes that were influenced by the Enlightenment.

 GO TO inQuizitive TO SEE WHAT YOU'VE LEARNED—AND LEARN WHAT YOU'VE MISSED—WITH PERSONALIZED FEEDBACK ALONG THE WAY.

CHRONOLOGY

May 1789
French Estates
General convene

August 1789
National Assembly issues
Declaration of the Rights
of Man and Citizen

October 1793
Execution of
Marie Antoinette

January 21, 1793
Execution of
Louis XVI

1795
Thermidorians
create Directory

1787
Prussians quell
Dutch Patriot Revolt

1790–1791
National Assembly
writes new constitution

1793
Second partition
of Poland

**Summer 1793–
Summer 1794**
Reign of Terror

1795
Third and last
partition of Poland

June 17, 1789
Formation
of National
Assembly

October 5, 1789
Bread rioters march
on Versailles

September 2–7, 1792
September Massacres in Paris

Summer 1794
Massacres in
the Vendée

July 14, 1789
Storming of
the Bastille

1791
Slave revolt in
Saint-Domingue
(Haiti)

September 20, 1792
French defeat
Prussians at Valmy

July 27–28, 1794
Ninth Thermidor revolt;
Robespierre is executed

April 1793
Committee of Public
Safety is formed

16

Revolution

LIBERTY AND TERROR

1780–1799

1798–1799
Napoleon's
Egyptian
campaign

November 9, 1799
Napoleon
launches coup

1797
Battle of Rivoli;
creation of French
"sister republics"
in northern Italy

High over the eastern edge of Paris, at the end of the eighteenth century, there loomed a bleak, eight-towered stone fortress known as the Bastille. The French monarchy had long used its jail cells to incarcerate notorious prisoners, and by the 1780s it had acquired a reputation as a place of horrid punishments. In fact, little torture or abuse had taken place for years, and as the French monarchy grew more concerned about its public image, the number of prisoners had declined. By July 14, 1789, only seven were actually in residence, including two suffering from mental illness.

The crowds who approached the Bastille that morning still mostly believed the fearsome legends. They had not, however, come to free the prisoners, but to take control of the large stocks of gunpowder kept at the fortress, so as to defend Paris against an expected attack. By mid-morning, around a thousand people had gathered outside the walls, many armed with guns or long, sharp pikes. They demanded that the Bastille's governor, Bernard-René de Launay, turn over all the powder and weapons at his disposal.

These ordinary Parisians—mostly artisans, shopkeepers, and laborers—were in a state of wild excitement and anxiety. Two months before, France's traditional representative body, the Estates General, had assembled for the first time since 1614–15 and had

Storming the Bastille The Bastille fortress rises high above a confrontation between revolutionaries and soldiers in this late-eighteenth-century painting, in which Parisian protesters have captured the prison and set fire to the surrounding buildings. From its outset, popular uprisings played a vital part in the Revolution's overthrow of authority and accelerating radicalism.

- What were the long-term and short-term causes of the crisis in France?
- How did the question of the Third Estate help bring on the Revolution?
- What drove the Revolution to become more radical, international, and violent?
- What pressures fractured the First French Republic?
- What was the significance of the Reign of Terror?
- How did the Directory channel the Revolution into war?

immediately fallen into paralyzing squabbles over organizational issues. Finally, in June 1789, the representatives of the Third Estate—that is, the common people and middle classes—had broken the deadlock by declaring themselves a "National Assembly" and announcing their intention to write a new constitution. The representatives of the other estates—the clergy and nobility—had eventually gone along, and the weak-willed, thirty-four-year-old king, Louis XVI, had apparently accepted the change. But even as the new Assembly set to work, rumors spread that the king and his advisers were preparing a military coup to restore full royal authority. On July 11, these rumors gained credibility when Louis abruptly dismissed a popular reforming minister and troops began to concentrate around the capital. On July 13, anxious crowds had gathered at various points in the city, then stormed a government arsenal and seized thousands of firearms. Now, on July 14, they had come to the Bastille in search of ammunition.

For a time, Governor de Launay tried to negotiate with them, but in the early afternoon the crowds, restless and frustrated, swarmed into the Bastille's undefended outer courtyard. Shots rang out (which side fired first remains a mystery), and soon a full-fledged battle was raging. Mutinous members of the French military soon joined the crowds, bringing guns and cannon along with them. At 5:00 p.m., de Launay surrendered, but he received no mercy. The crowds dragged him into the street outside and hacked him to death, after which an apprentice sawed off his head with a knife and stuck it on the end of a pike, to be paraded around Paris. The enraged crowd also killed several other officials,

including the city's top municipal official. The Bastille had fallen, and its gunpowder was in the hands of the insurgents. In Versailles the king, intimidated by this stunning expression of the popular will, quickly recalled the popular minister and dispersed the troops that had threatened Paris.

The fall of the Bastille did not mark the beginning of the French Revolution, which is usually dated to the meeting of the Estates General. But what happened on July 14, 1789, had an enormous and immediate effect on public opinion, not just in France but throughout the world. It was seen, rightly, as the moment when ordinary people forced their way into a political process hitherto dominated by well-educated elites. It was seen, also rightly, as the death knell of a royal power that had proclaimed itself "absolute." And it was seen, rightly once again, as the harbinger of spectacular and sometimes horrifying violence. Ever since, the date of July 14—now a French national holiday corresponding to the Fourth of July in the United States—has symbolized both the promise and the peril of modern politics. It stands not only for the revolutionary triumph of the people over undeserved social privilege and arbitrary rule, but also for the possible slide of revolutionary energy into bloodshed and terror.

In the last years of the eighteenth century, events in Europe as a whole took their lead from these tumultuous changes, which marked a more decisive break in the Continent's history than any since the Reformation. Prevailing patterns of thought, social interaction, and competition among and within states did not vanish, but they were now forever marked as belonging to the past, to tradition, to something that Europeans would soon call by the telling phrase "the Old Regime."

THE ORIGINS OF THE FRENCH REVOLUTION

How and why did the French nation come to this cross-roads? To answer this question, we must first recognize that the rising up of the people symbolized by the storming of the **Bastille** is by no means the whole story. An event as complex as the French Revolution simply did not have one single, dominant cause. Rather, it arose out of the confluence of a great many events and trends—some ranging over many years and involving millions of men and women, others almost absurdly small and arbitrary;

some involving the loftiest matters of philosophy, others turning on pressing questions of brute physical survival; some limited to France itself, and others involving large stretches of the globe. Taken individually, none of these factors would have led to revolution. But taken together, they triggered the great upheaval.

SOCIAL TRANSFORMATIONS

Many of these broader developments had affected other countries as well as France. As we have seen, most of northern Europe, including Britain and the Low Countries, had experienced a century of strong, if often stressful, economic growth, which in turn helped cause social disruption. "Middling" groups, which in France belonged to the Third Estate, had expanded enormously in wealth and prominence. Lawyers, for instance, more than tripled their numbers in France between 1700 and 1789. And in France, the boundaries between these middling groups and traditional social elites had grown more porous than ever, as the state sold noble titles by the thousands to wealthy commoners. Indeed, many historians argue that wealthy commoners and the nobility were consolidating into a single social class of "notables." Meanwhile, France, like the other major powers, also faced the challenge of financing warfare on a global scale. Its participation in victory over Britain in the American War of Independence, in particular, had come at a terrific price, for the cost of sending land and sea forces across the Atlantic to aid the American revolutionaries came close to doubling French public expenditures.

The French state, however, was much less well prepared to confront new social and economic challenges than some of its neighbors—Britain, in particular. France, it will be remembered, had no central bank to help finance its wars, and its baroque system of tax collection was much less efficient than that of the legendary "excisemen" who collected Britain's excise taxes. Nor did France possess a government capable of successfully implementing serious financial reforms, despite many attempts to do so. Before 1789, its closest equivalent to a national parliament, the Estates General, had not met for nearly 175 years (the so-called *parlements*, as we have seen, were not legislative bodies but courts of law). In theory, the king—as "absolute" executive, legislator, and judge all at once—had broad power to introduce change. But in practice, he had much more limited room for maneuver, depending as he did for much of his revenue on a massive system of social privilege that could not easily be dismantled. Indeed, tens of thousands of Frenchmen owned

their jobs or positions as a privileged form of property, and many of the wealthiest people in the kingdom enjoyed exemptions from key taxes. Any reform that sufficiently threatened social privileges might undermine confidence in the entire system. Desperate for new revenues, Louis XIV and Louis XV (who between them reigned from 1643 to 1774) had managed to introduce some new taxes on the privileged orders, but in the process they stirred up large-scale opposition, which contributed to the formation of a critical public opinion. In short, any piecemeal, gradual reform of the regime seemed practically impossible, raising the odds that problems would build up until explosive, radical change became the only course to follow.

THE IMPACT OF CULTURAL AND INTELLECTUAL CHANGE

The broad currents of cultural and intellectual change that now go by the name of the Enlightenment had, as we have seen, swept through nearly all of Europe in one form or another, but they had touched France most intensely. Religious belief and observance in France suffered more than elsewhere from "enlightened" criticism, and as it did the almost sacred respect long given to the king, supposedly anointed by God himself, began to ebb away. Still, taken together, the most popular works of Enlightenment thought did not offer anything like a coherent political philosophy. And while the American Revolution inspired great excitement in France, with its soaring promises of liberty and equality and its commitment to a republic that seemed to recall the days of ancient Greece and Rome, most French observers did not believe that the experiences of a "new people" across the Atlantic could be transplanted to Europe.

Before the summer of 1789, almost no one imagined that the calling of the Estates General might trigger anything other than moderate reforms—to say nothing of the replacement of the monarchy by a democratic republic. One elite observer, the future revolutionary Guy Target, sputtered that the very idea was ridiculous: "One hears tell, that . . . the kingdom (truthfully, I have heard this said) will degenerate into a democracy. Nothing of the sort is to be feared. . . . Democracy in a nation of twenty-five million . . . ! I confess in good faith that I have no idea what this means." French elites, with their impeccable classical educations, still associated "democracy" solely with the tumultuous city-states of ancient Greece.

Yet the Enlightenment's principal political effects did not take the form of constitutional blueprints implemented by politicians. Particularly in France, its most popular works were intensely moralizing: what some scholars have called the "age of reason" actually longed to be the "age of virtue." Authors like Rousseau held up ideal images of virtuous behavior, mostly inspired by accounts of ancient Greece and Rome, and with soaring eloquence contrasted them to the corruption that supposedly prevailed throughout Europe. In particular, they dismissed the difference between private and public morality. For them, a country where wives and husbands deceived each other, or where fathers oppressed sons, was a degenerate one in need of radical change. Public figures were to be judged by their private conduct.

From this perspective, the court of Versailles, with its intrigues, lavish displays of wealth, elaborate rituals, and biting cynicism, looked like the pinnacle of corruption and degeneracy. The eighteenth century's legions of newly minted authors and journalists liked nothing more than reporting on the lives and misdeeds, real and alleged, of courtly aristocrats. And what legal publications said with sly indirection and euphemism, illegal publications, sold "under the cloak" to avoid the formidable system of censorship then in place, said directly and with much use of obscenity. In both cases, they fastened on to the "unnatural" role played at court by powerful, pleasure-loving women, who should instead, according to the authors, have retired from public view to tend virtuously to their hearths and children.

AN APPROACHING FISCAL CRISIS

In 1774, these authors had received a stroke of good luck—and the French monarchy a bad one. In that year, when King Louis XV succumbed to smallpox, the vagaries of genetics and dynastic marriage brought to the French throne a couple perfectly suited to preside over catastrophe. **Louis XVI** (r. 1774–1792) was a well-meaning, timid, physically unimpressive young man who preferred tinkering in his workshop to deciding matters of policy. His queen, Marie-Antoinette (1755–1793), was a beautiful, naïve young woman who had been sent to France from her native Austria to seal the alliance the two countries had contracted at the time of the Seven Years' War. Louis, it appears, suffered from a genital condition that made sexual intercourse impossible, and for several years after his marriage he refused to undergo the minor operation needed to correct it. Rumors spread not only of his impotence but also of Marie-Antoinette's willingness to satisfy her lusts elsewhere. In short, not only did the monarchy

no longer enjoy quasi-sacral status, but the royal couple were now the butt of ridicule. In the queen's case, visceral hatred would soon follow.

Taken together, all of these circumstances differentiated France from its neighbors in a way that made a revolutionary explosion there possible. Still, it took a particular sequence of events to bring that explosion about. It started with the new king's hesitant attempts at reform. Upon taking the throne, in a show of reconciliation he restored the traditional position of the *parlements*, which Louis XV had largely stripped of their ability to obstruct royal legislation, and brought back the magistrates dismissed by the old king. This decision quickly brought him trouble when his ambitious minister Anne-Robert Turgot, a brilliant disciple of the *philosophes*, attempted a radical liberalization of the French economy. The *parlements* became the powerful voices of the entrenched interests threatened by Turgot, and in 1777 his opponents at court forced his departure. The episode set a pattern for the reign in which ambitious changes were proposed, criticized, and then withdrawn, leaving behind little but increased resentment.

Louis XVI In a portrait painted shortly after his coronation in 1774, King Louis XVI appears wearing his gold and ermine coronation robes, symbols of the lavish grandeur of the monarchy.

Meanwhile, in 1778 Louis decided to send French forces to aid the American revolutionaries. Their joint victory in 1783 weakened the British, but it did not restore France's lost colonies in the Americas, and the cost for France was the vast sum of over 1 billion French pounds, or roughly four times the state's entire annual peacetime budget. Instead of raising the necessary funds through taxation, the new finance minister, Jacques Necker (1732–1804), resorted to high-interest borrowing on international capital markets. He also published a self-serving account of the budgetary situation that disguised the enormous size of the debt. Necker, a brilliant and energetic Swiss banker, did try to simplify France's financial system and created the first of a projected series of provincial assemblies during his tenure as minister. But these reforms, like Turgot's, threatened entrenched interests, and Necker's opponents forced him out of office before he could achieve significant results.

THE THREAT OF BANKRUPTCY By 1786, France's fiscal situation had turned catastrophic, and government bankruptcy loomed. That year, yet another new finance minister, Charles-Alexandre de Calonne (1734–1802), proposed a complete overhaul of the tax system. Although nobles had paid a considerable amount since the start of the century, they still benefited disproportionately from France's complex system of fiscal privilege. In particular, they mostly enjoyed exemption from the hated land tax, the *taille*, which fell principally on rural commoners. Calonne's plan involved the abolition of the *taille* and the institution of a new tax that all landowners—nobles and clergy as well as commoners—would pay. He also suggested a show of national confidence by submitting the plan to a special Assembly of Notables comprising a small number of high-ranking nobles and prelates. But this body unexpectedly balked at undertaking such radical reform, leading the frustrated king to replace Calonne with the freethinking archbishop of Toulouse, Étienne Charles Loménie de Brienne.

Loménie tried to enact Calonne's plan by fiat, only to find himself challenged by the *parlements*, which deliberately paralyzed the French judicial system in protest and helped instigate riots in Paris and other major cities. In the spring of 1788, the king and his ministers raised the stakes even higher by trying to dissolve the *parlements* altogether, but this high-handed act of authority only led to even larger-scale violent disorders—above all, from the many people who depended financially upon the *parlements*. Finally, in August, the king gave in, dismissed Brienne, recalled the popular Necker (who would be dismissed and recalled once again in 1789), and agreed to assemble the Estates General in the hope that this older body might be able to introduce real financial reforms.

DUTCH PATRIOT REVOLT (1781–1787) The burgeoning French crisis caused powerful ripple effects throughout Europe, particularly in the Netherlands. In 1781, some eight years before the fall of the Bastille, the Dutch had begun a relatively moderate revolutionary movement of their own. A so-called Patriot Party had taken a stand against the country's aristocratic "Stadholder" chief executive, demanding an end to corruption and the enactment of democratic reforms inspired in part by the American revolutionary example. Conflict between the Patriots and the Stadholder's Orangist Party swelled over the next several years, with the Orangists backed by the new Prussian king, Frederick William II (r. 1786–1797), who was the Stadholder's brother-in-law. Finally, after a series of armed Patriot victories over the Orangists, a Prussian army invaded the Netherlands in September 1787, smashed the Patriots, and firmly cemented the Stadholder's authority. France had every interest in helping the

Dutch Patriot Revolt A 1787 satirical cartoon shows a disorganized band of Dutch rebels using a drawing of a Prussian soldier for target practice. It mocks the rebels as country bumpkins: their party even includes the armed frogs at their feet (bottom left).

Patriots and preventing the Netherlands from becoming a satellite of Prussia, its enemy since the Seven Years' War. But because of the crisis it could not intervene, and so suffered an international humiliation.

THE REVOLUTION BEGINS (1788–1789)

With Louis XVI's rapidly taken and somewhat desperate decision in August 1788 to convoke the Estates General, the entire French nation took a giant leap into the unknown. The Estates were a national representative body—but what did it mean, exactly, to "represent" the nation?

THE QUESTION OF REFORMING THE ESTATES GENERAL

Through their last meeting in 1614–15, the Estates had followed a classic medieval model of representation, which likened the different estates to different organs of a single body. In this way of thinking, it made sense for each estate to elect members to a chamber of its own, with each chamber having equal weight in deliberations. This arrangement, however, gave the first two estates—which, together, amounted to less than 2 percent of the population—an automatic majority. Yet in 1788 the French could look abroad and see other representative systems that gave equal voting rights to most white male adults (as in the United States) or that privileged wealth as much as inherited status (as in Great Britain). Well-to-do French commoners also knew that their Third Estate had increased tremendously in wealth and education since the Renaissance, and felt they should have a correspondingly greater say in national government. Yet the *parlements* feared that a larger Third Estate might join forces with the king to erode traditional privileges and long-standing barriers against royal "despotism." So in September 1788, the *parlement* of Paris declared that the Estates General would meet "according to the forms of 1614"—that is, one chamber per estate, with each chamber voting separately.

The result was a storm of protest, much of it in printed form. The king, in calling for elections to the Estates, had invited the people to express their views of what the Estates should discuss, and printers throughout the kingdom had taken these words as a de facto declaration of press freedom. Journalists and pamphleteers loudly denounced the nobility and demanded an Estates General in which half the deputies would come from the Third Estate and all deputies would vote "in common." The most powerful expression of the argument came from a clergyman named Emmanuel Sieyès (1748–1836) in a pamphlet he entitled **What Is the Third Estate?** Drawing not only on Enlightenment social science that placed new value on the economic productivity of commoners, but also on the political theory of Jean-Jacques Rousseau, he answered his title question in a single deafening word: "Everything." As the crushing majority, the Third Estate could stand in for the whole. Anyone who refused to join them effectively became an outsider to the nation.

The debate dragged on all through the winter of 1788–89. King Louis eventually decided to double the number of Third Estate deputies but did not allow deliberation or voting in common, which made the decision meaningless. As a result, the elections to the Estates took place in an atmosphere of bitterness and confusion, and produced an assembly doomed to fall into conflict. The Third Estate numbered many heroes of the protests of 1787–88, along with a host of lawyers, judges, and civil servants. Its chamber also included radical members of other estates, such as the clergyman Sieyès and the noble Honoré Riqueti de Mirabeau (1749–1791), who had made a reputation crusading against the laws that had allowed his own father, a notable political economist, to have him thrown in prison for filial disobedience. They chose to stand for election as commoners.

Among the clergy, a surprising number of poor parish

The Three Estates An eighteenth-century political cartoon provides a visual representation of Sieyès's argument. A farm laborer carries a clergyman and a nobleman on his back, just as the Third Estate holds up the two privileged orders.

priests emerged alongside the prelates. But in the ranks of the noble deputies, grand, wealthy old military families dominated. As part of the election process, local electors (themselves chosen in primary elections in which all adult male taxpayers could participate) also prepared petitions to redress "grievances," to present to the Estates General. These documents make for remarkable reading—the closest thing to a modern opinion survey produced anywhere in the eighteenth century. The most common demands included tax reform, judicial reform, religious toleration, and an end to fiscal privileges such as tax exemption for nobles. Collectively, the "grievances" called into question so many aspects of French government and society that the great nineteenth-century French thinker Alexis de Tocqueville would later claim that they amounted to a demand for the abolition of the entire Old Regime.

The Estates General faced almost insurmountable challenges. First came the unanswered question of its own organization, given the claims of the Third Estate to a greater share of representation. Second, there was the looming bankruptcy of the French state. And as if all this were not enough, national economic disaster and famine threatened as well. In the late summer of 1788, freakish cold, accompanied by hailstorms, had ruined much of the harvest. The price of bread—still the principal source of nourishment for most of the population—rose through the winter until it was devouring more than two-thirds of the income of even well-off artisans and workers. This inflation in turn choked off spending on everything else, leading to distress and unemployment throughout the economy. In late April 1789, just before the Estates met, unfounded rumors that a Paris wallpaper manufacturer was lowering wages led angry crowds to sack his house and factory, shouting "Down with the rich!" The riots were suppressed at the cost of twenty-five dead and hundreds wounded—the worst violence the capital had seen in many decades.

THE THIRD ESTATE TAKES POWER

The Estates General finally convened on May 5, 1789, with all the considerable pomp, ritual, and class prejudice that the Old Regime could muster. Gaudily attired lords and prelates paraded through the streets of Versailles, followed by the 600-odd deputies of the Third Estate, clad in basic black. Grandiose opening ceremonies took place, with the Third Estate confined to standing room at the back of the palace's Hall of Small Pleasures. But afterward, the three estates could not even agree on how to verify the members' credentials, let alone get down to business. The stalemate dragged on for a month. Angry emotions simmered.

Finally, in mid-June, a group of deputies decided to take action. They were led by the cold, precise Sieyès and by Mirabeau, a squat, ugly man (his face had been scarred by smallpox) whose natural talent for oratory was fortified by an extraordinary bass voice. Together, they convinced the Third Estate deputies that they could achieve their aims only by following Sieyès's argument to its logical conclusion. If the Third Estate was "everything"—that is, the entire nation—then logically its deputies constituted a **National Assembly** and should declare themselves such. On June 17, with considerable trepidation, the deputies did exactly that. And then they waited to see how the other estates and the king would react.

They did not have to wait long. As early as June 13, a number of parish priests who belonged to the First Estate by vocation but had been born into humble, commoner families had moved to join the Third Estate. Several

liberal-minded nobles followed their example, and the number of defectors swelled after the proclamation of the National Assembly. Then on June 20 came a particularly dramatic moment. The defiant deputies arrived at their meeting hall to find the doors barred. It was an accident, but the men, fearing a royal coup, immediately rushed to a large, nearby indoor tennis court, where they pledged—in what was later known as the **Tennis Court Oath**—not to disperse until they had provided France with a new, written constitution. Fully appreciating the historical significance of the moment, they chose to swear the oath with arms extended, like reborn versions of Roman heroes.

Louis XVI was not in fact ready to use force, even if a powerful faction at court (led by his brothers and Marie-Antoinette) already saw the Third Estate deputies as dangerous rebels. On June 23, he made an attempt at conciliation, addressing all three estates together in a "royal session" and proposing a broad reform program. A month earlier the speech might have won enthusiastic support from the Third Estate, but now it came too late. The deputies from all three estates would now settle for nothing short of truly fundamental changes in the political system. When the king had finished, most of the deputies stayed in place, refusing to disperse. The king sent an official to order them to leave. "We are here by the will of the people, and will only leave by the force of bayonets," declaimed Mirabeau. Unnerved by the defiance, and acutely conscious of the deputies' popular following, the king again retreated and ordered the deputies from all three estates to join together. The National Assembly had been born, and the French Revolution had begun.

THE INTERVENTION OF THE PEOPLE

There remained, however, the Revolution's baptism in blood and fire. Over the next few weeks, even as the Assembly began to deliberate over the form of a future constitution, the king dithered and doubted. The queen and his brothers tried to persuade him that he needed to reassert his authority by force. On July 11, 1789, Louis again dismissed Necker, replacing him with conservative aristocrats, and the new government began to concentrate troops around Paris. When the news reached Paris, thousands of people gathered in wild agitation in the center of the city, cheering orators who demanded immediate action. There followed the seizure of weapons and the fall of the Bastille on July 14.

In the wake of this extraordinary and symbolic event, royal authority throughout France seemed to evaporate.

DAVID'S *THE TENNIS COURT OATH*

Jacques-Louis David (1748–1825) was one of eighteenth-century France's greatest painters, a master of neoclassicism and also an enthusiastic participant in the French Revolution. Recognizing that the arts had long served to simultaneously represent the world and project rulers' authority and legitimacy, David turned his extensive talents to creating images that celebrated and mythologized the new revolutionary order.

His unfinished study *The Tennis Court Oath* (1789–91) emphasizes the passion, idealism, and egalitarianism of the oath that helped mark the start of the 1789 revolution. The emptiness of the upper half of the drawing draws the eye to the three deputies—a cleric, an aristocrat, and a member of the Third Estate—who have joined hands in the foreground. At the center, Jean-Sylvain Bailly, the soon-to-be mayor of Paris, leads the deputies in their oath to remain assembled until the ratification of a new constitution. The outstretched arms of the oath takers—many of them actual participants—echoes the pose of the patriotic, self-sacrificing Romans of David's earlier masterpiece *Oath of the Horatii* (page 530). In this new image, David sought to invest France's revolutionary birth with the dignity and grandeur of the world's great historical events.

QUESTIONS FOR ANALYSIS

1. What does the embrace of the three deputies at the center of David's drawing represent?
2. Why would David want to depict the participants in the Tennis Court Oath similarly to subjects from antiquity, such as the Romans of *Oath of the Horatii*?
3. How does David's image illustrate and celebrate the values of the Revolution?

In Paris and other major towns, the leaders of the Third Estate asserted their control over municipal governments. Middle-class men took up arms and began to form paramilitary units that would soon coalesce into a large new armed force controlled by the National Assembly: the National Guard. The king then reversed himself yet again, recalling Necker to office for a second time and visiting Paris on July 27. There the new mayor presented him with a cockade, a badge of ribbons in which the colors of Paris—blue and red—surrounded the white of the Bourbon dynasty. Reminiscent of the American and British national colors, this "tricolor" pattern would soon be used in the new French flag.

But the country remained deeply unsettled. On July 22, two royal officials were lynched in Paris. Anticipating many later endorsements of violence by leading revolutionaries, a young leader of the Third Estate remarked: "What, was their blood so pure?" In the countryside, the prevailing uncertainty and food shortages fueled wild rumors that spread at breakneck pace. In what became known as the "**Great Fear**," peasants throughout France became convinced that hordes of lawless brigands would soon descend on their villages. In response, they too took up arms and often ended up attacking noble property and destroying records of the heavy feudal obligations (including forms of rent and restrictions on movement and trade) that they owed their seigneurial overlords (the lords of the manor were called "*seigneurs*" in French). The movement forever altered the social structure of the French countryside, helping to end its domination by a tiny minority of wealthy landowners and thereby laying the foundation of a new, more democratic social order.

In the face of the continuing unrest, on the night of August 4, 1789, the new National Assembly took an unplanned, astonishing step. Prompted by a group of progressive deputies from Brittany, various noble members of the Assembly proposed the abolition of certain onerous seigneurial dues. As if on cue, other deputies then demanded that other forms of social privilege—hunting rights, private tolls, private courts of law—also be thrown onto the scrapheap. Deputy after deputy, swept up in the fervor, clamored to propose yet more abolitions of privilege. The tumultuous session dragged on through the night, and by the end virtually the entire "feudal regime" had been swept away. "There vanished that night," the great French historian Jules Michelet later wrote, romantically but not without a measure of truth, "the vast and toilsome dream of a thousand years of the Middle Ages. The dawn that would soon break was the dawn of liberty." Within days, the deputies would backtrack, insisting that the peasants reimburse their overlords for many of the abolished privileges. Nonetheless, the Assembly had swept aside the principles of hierarchy that had governed French society for centuries, and replaced them with a new, revolutionary ideal: civic equality, the principle that all are equal in law.

The summer of 1789 concluded with the publication of the French Revolution's most enduring and influential statement of principles: the Assembly's **Declaration of the Rights of Man and Citizen**. In its seventeen articles, it guaranteed the principles of freedom and civil equality, and the sovereignty of the entire nation. It established rights for criminal suspects and the presumption of innocence, and proclaimed freedom of the press, religion, and property. Strikingly, unlike the American Bill of Rights, it did not speak of one country alone but of "men" in general—women were nowhere mentioned, and the question of just which rights applied to them was left unposed. "Men are born free and equal in rights," it proclaimed. The Declaration was not simply a statement of principle, however. Through the very act of promulgating it, and particularly the statement that "no individual can exercise authority that does not expressly emanate from the Nation," the Assembly deliberately asserted its own role as the embodiment of national sovereignty, superior even to the king.

RADICALIZATION (1789–1792)

With the abolitions of privilege on the night of August 4 and the promulgation of the Declaration of the Rights of Man and Citizen a few weeks later, many observers, both inside and outside the Assembly, assumed that the "revolution" had now come to an end. They were using the word in the older, limited sense of a sudden, unpredictable whirling-about of human affairs. But as events would soon show, the French Revolution was a dramatically unprecedented sort of political phenomenon: again and again it would defy all attempts to bring it to an end, and lurch forward, often in an outburst of violence. Even the American Revolution had been relatively moderate in comparison, because while it led to vast changes in the political order, it always remained far more under the control of its original political leadership and the changes it prompted in the social order were more gradual and consensual. It was in France that the word "revolution" itself soon took on its modern meaning: as a deliberate, open-ended, and explosive expression of a people's collective will. A revolution was a process of continuous radicalization.

THE OCTOBER DAYS

In the fall of 1789, the immediate impetus for radical change again came from the common people of Paris. Despite the great symbolic victory of the Bastille, little had followed to relieve their difficulties. The price of bread remained dangerously high, and work dangerously scarce. The resulting popular anger was further stoked by fears that the king or his advisers might still try a military strike to restore royal authority. In early October, these fears seemingly received confirmation when news spread that at a banquet in Versailles military officers had pledged unlimited support to the embattled king and trampled tricolor cockades, the symbol of the revolution, underfoot.

On October 5, a huge crowd assembled spontaneously in front of the Paris City Hall, demanding food and action against enemies of the Revolution. Women, traditional defenders of the family breadbox, had often taken a leading role in bread riots in the seventeenth and eighteenth centuries, and now the market women of Paris, swept up in the same revolutionary fervor as their male relatives, led the greatest bread riot in history. The cry went up "To Versailles!" and thousands of women and men, without much obvious organization, set off on foot for the royal palace twelve miles away. The new revolutionary municipal government in Paris, unable to stop them, instead sent armed National Guards to attempt to keep the crowd in line. In the evening, drenched by rain and mud-spattered, the crowds reached Versailles, where a small delegation met with the king, who promised immediate shipments of grain to the capital.

Women's March on Versailles A dramatic contemporary engraving shows women—mostly poor—bearing weapons as they shout, "To Versailles!" In what may be creative license, several women pull a cannon; one also drags along a wealthy, well-dressed woman (left).

But as the hungry, wet, and cold Parisians camped outdoors throughout the night, their mood again darkened. At dawn, a group found the main gate of the palace unguarded and charged inside, killing guards, smashing their way through the ornate Hall of Mirrors, and shouting threats against the hated Marie-Antoinette (one woman declared she would cut out and cook the queen's liver). The queen barely escaped, shrieking and running barefoot to the king's apartments, her children in tow, and then pounding on the door for nearly ten minutes before someone heard and let her in. Finally, National Guards moved in to restore order, but the Parisians, by now as many as 60,000 strong, demanded that the royal family return with them to Paris, where it could be kept under permanent popular surveillance.

Fearing further violence, the king again gave in. On the afternoon of October 6, he and his family left Versailles in a hastily packed carriage, accompanied by the National Guard, listening to the crowd's wild songs and shouts. The magnificent palace of Versailles that Louis XIV had built as a refuge from Parisian turmoil stood abandoned, never again to have a king in residence. What had started as a crowd action closely related to many similar events under the Old Regime had turned into something very different: perhaps the most tangible and dramatic display of popular sovereignty in history.

FORGING A NEW REGIME

With the weakened king now removed to Paris, the Assembly set up shop there as well and began its work of drafting a written constitution—a task that would take the better part of two years. Unlike the American Constitutional Convention, which had concerned itself with the single task of constitution-writing and had only 55 active members, the National Assembly did its constitutional work while also attempting to govern the country, and numbered no less than 1,200 men. So not surprisingly, its debates—which took place in a long, narrow, foul-smelling, hastily converted indoor riding arena with abominable acoustics—were chaotic and often turned vituperative as well. Distinct liberal and conservative factions emerged, seated on the left and right sides, respectively, of the long, narrow meeting hall (thus giving rise to the modern political terms "left-wing" and "right-wing"). Indeed, it is at this moment in European history that we can begin, without anachronism, to distinguish between political "liberals" who favored individual rights and civic reforms such as the expansion of the suffrage, and "conservative" defenders of the traditional social order.

But despite the chaos and conflict, the Assembly was engaged in an unprecedented enterprise: dismantling a massively complex, inefficient, discriminatory system of government, and rebuilding it according to principles of reason and justice. Helen Maria Williams, a young British poet who attended in the spring of 1790, wrote of having seen history in the making with an enthusiasm that well conveys the emotions that the Revolution generated: "Those men now before my eyes are the men who engross the attention, the astonishment of Europe . . . and whose fame has already extended through every civilized region of the globe."

This momentous project was remarkably multifaceted. In less than two years, among other things, the National Assembly dissolved the guilds, implemented free trade, and replaced the uneven patchwork of French provinces with eighty-odd "departments" of equal size. It also offered membership in the national community to groups whose exclusion had previously been taken for granted. In the final days of the Old Regime, Louis XVI had already restored civil rights to Protestants. Then, in a series of measures adopted in 1790–91, the Assembly extended toleration, and full citizenship, to French Jews as well. In 1791, free men of color in France's Caribbean colonies were granted citizenship, while an influential Society of Friends of the Blacks campaigned for an end to slavery. The largest group of second-class citizens in the French population—women—made some tangible gains, notably with the legalization of divorce. An actress and playwright named Olympe de Gouges (1748–1793) even, optimistically, published a "Declaration of the Rights of Woman." Her demands mostly fell on deaf ears. Still, more voices were raised on behalf of women's rights than had been the case in previous Western upheavals. One prominent philosopher and political writer dismissed the argument that the burdens of menstruation and pregnancy should bar women from voting, noting mischievously that no one would impose such an exclusion on men suffering from gout.

THE REVOLUTION'S INTERNATIONAL IMPACT

Helen Maria Williams's prediction that the influence of the French Revolution would quickly spread through the globe was correct. In the Southern Netherlands—modern

Patriotic Women's Club In a 1793 illustration, women supporters of the Revolution discuss politics as one of their number reads aloud from a newspaper. Another woman (center) contributes coins to a charitable fund. This range of activities suggests the roles envisioned by some women themselves in the new republican France.

Belgium—events in France helped trigger revolutionary uprisings in the summer and fall of 1789. In one area, the independent principality of Liège, a popular movement overthrew the absolutist prince-bishop and issued a Declaration of the Rights of Man and Citizen on the French model. Elsewhere in the Southern Netherlands, the so-called revolution mostly took the form of relatively conservative protests against the territory's current overlords, the Austrian Habsburgs. In both cases, however, the movements were eventually crushed by troops from Austria and the Holy Roman Empire.

THWARTED REFORMS IN POLAND-LITHUANIA

The Polish-Lithuanian Commonwealth underwent a similarly abortive revolutionary experience. By the last decades of the eighteenth century, it had lost much of the influence it had possessed a century before and was increasingly vulnerable to the depredations of its powerful neighbors, Russia, Austria, and Prussia. As we have seen, in 1772 these neighbors carried out the so-called First Partition, each stripping away a slice of Polish territory. King Stanisław August Poniatowski (r. 1764–95) believed, along with many supporters, that the traditional Polish constitution was no longer workable. The so-called Golden Freedoms, which gave the nobility a dominant role in government, allowed it to block reforms while frequently causing political paralysis.

In 1791, even as excitement grew in Poland-Lithuania over the French Revolution, Stanisław August believed he had a chance to break the logjam. Russia had been weakened and distracted by wars against the Ottoman Empire and Sweden, and Austria had participated in the first of these. In May 1791, the king issued a new constitution that established a mixed government on the British model, but with a more powerful executive. It drew heavily on Enlightenment thinking, especially Montesquieu's theory of the separation of powers. But the events provoked the anger of the increasingly reactionary tsarina of Russia, Catherine the Great (r. 1762–1796). In 1792, after her army defeated the Turks, she invaded Poland-Lithuania and forced Stanisław August to abandon the reforms. The kingdom was now entirely at the mercy of the predatory great powers that surrounded it.

POLITICAL AND IDEOLOGICAL RESPONSES

Elsewhere in Europe, the news of the French Revolution prompted monarchs to fear for their own authority, while also driving hopes that they might profit from the turmoil in France. In 1790, Austria and Prussia signed an alliance and encouraged French nobles who had fled France to assemble a counterrevolutionary army in the hopes of restoring Louis XVI to his full powers. Austria, ruled by French queen Marie-Antoinette's brother, encouraged the French royal family to resist revolutionary change.

In Britain, opinions about the French Revolution were split. The *Times* of London spoke for many British observers when it praised the National Assembly as a collection of "Statesmen and Philosophers" and claimed to see in their actions nothing less than the "renovation of the golden age of society." The poet William Wordsworth, looking back on his youthful enthusiasm for the Revolution, memorably wrote: "Bliss was it in that dawn to be alive / But to be young was very heaven."

But in 1790, well before the outbreak of large-scale violence in France, the Whig parliamentarian **Edmund Burke** (1729–1797) delivered a blistering response to such views in a book that became the founding text of modern conservatism. His *Reflections on the Revolution in France* argued that political reform could succeed only if it was gradual, cautious, and built carefully upon existing tradition. The French revolutionaries, he charged, were instead trying to squeeze human beings into jarringly new, rigid shapes. Burke added that if the French, guided by their "barbarous philosophy," persisted in their blind enthusiasm for change, they would end up drowning in their own blood: "In the groves of their academy, at the end of every vista, you see nothing but the gallows."

In response to Burke's polemic, the great radical publicist Thomas Paine delivered a counterblast under the title *The Rights of Man* in which he argued that to defend their natural rights it was legitimate for a people to replace a tyrannical government. Paine, who was himself now living in France, treated Burke's eloquent praise of tradition with deadly scorn: "He pities the plumage, but forgets the dying bird." By 1791, the French Revolution had become a source of civil violence in Britain. That year, supporters of the Revolution, including the noted chemist Joseph Priestley, planned a banquet in Birmingham to commemorate the fall of the Bastille. A riot ensued, and Priestley's home was burned, along with two churches where many of the supporters had worshipped. Another English admirer of the Revolution, the writer Mary Wollstonecraft (1759–1797), followed her own response to Burke with the powerful *Vindication of the Rights of Women* (1792). Like Olympe de Gouges in France, she defended women's intellectual capacities and insisted that they enjoyed the same natural rights God had given to men.

SLAVE REVOLT IN SAINT-DOMINGUE

The French Revolution had even more direct effects in the Caribbean. It will be remembered that in the French colony of Saint-Domingue—modern Haiti—nearly 500,000 African slaves working under inhuman conditions drove highly profitable sugar and coffee production. In 1790–91, wealthy white planters persuaded the new French revolutionary government to give them their own assembly, with considerable control over colonial affairs. At the same time, free people of color demanded full citizenship rights,

Slave Revolt in Saint-Domingue A late-eighteenth-century engraving vividly depicts the unrest in Saint-Domingue, as enslaved people rise up against their masters and destroy property.

HOPES AND FEARS OF THE FRENCH REVOLUTION

The French Revolution profoundly divided Europe. Imbued with a new sense of political possibility, many observers looked to the upheaval in France with enthusiasm and pride, publishing pamphlets and newspapers in support of the ongoing changes. Opponents of the Revolution, however, including Edmund Burke, perceived this new order as harmful to civilization. They argued that Revolution threatened not just social and political structures but also the values and achievements that European culture had accumulated over the centuries. While some welcomed the promise and progress of the Revolution, others worried that such a break with the past would destroy all that they held dear.

The People of Marseilles, "Farewell to the Year 1790"

Issued by a group of citizens of Marseilles, this pamphlet was one of many that commemorated the revolutionary events of the year 1790. In this excerpt, the authors celebrate in particular the involvement of the citizenry.

Incomparable year! Never will any resemble you! Your older sister brought liberty and patriotism from her breast. (It was a child who had only just been born;) but you nourished him, weaned him, & he's beginning to walk unaided. What hopes don't we have, at the rate he's growing? His youth gives us the hidden premonition that he'll make rapid progress in the system of the revolution....

But you, dear year! You have triumphed over their weakness. It wasn't reasonable that ordinary Citizens were the victims of so many injustices; they [certain officials] have finally deserted the walls of this charming city, & their flight makes the Citizens' courage & patriotism bloom. Your older sister saw the demolition of the Bastille of the Capital... This is not enough; a new order must return authority to the people....

Fanaticism has contributed much to our fear, the rest arising from despotism as well; but despite the efforts of both, you triumph. Besides, you were almost assured of your glory; do you not remember the past fourteenth of July when you saw three million bayonets hurry to your defense, & close to eighteen million free Citizens, swearing to

preserve the right of all men? Well! that suffices to crown your victory.

Edmund Burke, from *Reflections on the Revolution in France*

In this passage from his famous book (1790), Burke bemoans the Revolution's destruction of European tradition and warns of the dangers ahead.

The age of chivalry is gone. That of sophisters, economists, and calculators, has succeeded; and the glory of Europe is extinguished forever.... Never, never more, shall we behold that generous loyalty to rank and sex, that proud submission, that dignified obedience, that subordination of the heart, which kept alive, even in servitude itself, the spirit of an exalted freedom....

But now all is to be changed. All the pleasing illusions, which made power gentle, and obedience liberal, which harmonized the different shades of life, and which, by a bland assimilation, incorporated into politics the sentiments which beautify and soften private society, are to be dissolved by this new conquering empire of light and reason....

On the scheme of this barbarous philosophy, which is the offspring of cold hearts and muddy understandings, and which is as void of solid wisdom, as it is destitute of all taste and elegance, laws are to be supported only by their own terrors, and by the concern which each individual may find in them from his own private speculations, or can spare to them from his own private interests. In the groves

of their academy, at the end of every visto, you see nothing but the gallows. Nothing is left which engages the affections on the part of the commonwealth....

To make a government requires no great prudence.... But to form a *free government*; that is, to temper together these opposite elements of liberty and restraint in one consistent work, requires much thought; deep reflection; a sagacious, powerful, and combining mind.... But when the leaders choose to make themselves bidders at an auction of popularity, their talents, in the construction of the state, will be of no service. They will become flatterers instead of legislators; the instruments, not the guides of the people....

Moderation will be stigmatized as the virtue of cowards, and compromise as the prudence of traitors; until, in hopes of preserving the credit which may enable him to temper and moderate on some occasions, the popular leader is obliged to become active in propagating doctrines, and establishing powers, that will afterwards defeat any sober purpose at which he ultimately might have aimed.

QUESTIONS FOR ANALYSIS

1. What made 1790 an "incomparable year" for the citizens of Marseilles?
2. What possible consequences of the Revolution does Burke fear?
3. What do the writers of these documents understand to be the political role of "the people"?

Sources: Andrew Daily, trans., *Les Adieux à l'année 1790*, le peuple Marseillais, (Marseille: 1790), pp. 5–7; Edmund Burke, *Reflections on the Revolution in France* (London: 1790), pp. 113–15, 352–53.

and some of them took to arms in pursuit of this goal. By August 1791, the colony had become the scene of a complex struggle between these different groups. And then, against this backdrop, the black slaves who made up the great majority of the population staged the largest and most successful slave revolt in history, burning rich plantations on the northern plain and threatening the colony's principal towns. Within two years the French commissioners on the island, desperate to retain control of events, issued an emancipation proclamation, which the revolutionary French government endorsed several months later and expanded upon by abolishing slavery throughout all French possessions. Another ten years of confused and vicious fighting followed, during which the former slave Toussaint Louverture took an increasingly important role. By 1798, with French support, he had become the de facto ruler of Saint-Domingue. Eventually, Haiti would join the United States as the second new independent state in the Americas—and would also be the first black republic in the world.

FAILURE TO REACH CONSENSUS

Back in France, violence remained more limited through 1791, but a national consensus over the Revolution stubbornly refused to take shape. Instead, as the National Assembly struggled to finish writing the constitution, the country split over fundamental issues of sovereignty. Where did ultimate political authority lie? With the people as a whole, as proclaimed in the Declaration of the Rights of Man and Citizen? With the people's representatives in the Assembly? Or with its traditional embodiment, the king? Few people in this long-standing European monarchy could yet imagine the country without a king, but it was unclear what role he should now play. His supporters demanded that the new constitution give him an absolute veto over legislative decisions, but the Assembly granted him only the power to suspend legislation temporarily.

The advocates of popular sovereignty demanded that all adult males receive the right to vote, but the Assembly's constitution of 1791 instead divided the citizenry into "active" and "passive" citizens, with only the former—those who possessed substantial property and income—enjoying the suffrage. Most divisively, the Assembly undertook a massive reform of the Catholic Church in France. In 1789 it had already confiscated the Church's vast landholdings and sold them off to ease the state's fiscal problems. The next year it attempted to subject the Church itself to state authority and to transform priests and bishops into elected officials on the public payroll. This act challenged both the king, in his role as the Church's protector, and the spiritual sovereignty claimed by the pope over all Catholics. Fully half the French priesthood refused to swear an oath of loyalty to the new Civil Constitution of the Clergy, leading to their dismissal from office, often over the indignant protests of their parishioners.

As these disputes dragged on, much of the country remained in an unsettled state, with frequent riots and clashes between revolutionary crowds and units of the royal army. On the first anniversary of the fall of the Bastille, the Assembly ordered a nationwide Festival of Federation, in which the army and the National Guard swore oaths of loyalty, accompanied by parading, fireworks, and revolutionary songs. But the grand and impressive symbolism did little to calm fears of civil war.

DEMOCRACY AND VIOLENCE From this point, the Revolution entered a new phase marked by increasing violence. It was a shift that still casts a forbidding shadow over the origins of modern democratic politics and poses an urgent question: Why did it happen? As with the origins of the Revolution itself, the reasons are not reducible to any single factor. Much of the reason, certainly, lies in what historians call the "political culture" bequeathed to the Revolution by the Old Regime. Unlike the American revolutionaries, with their long experience of various forms

The Jacobin Club A minister of the revolutionary government speaks to the crowded meeting room of the Jacobin Club in January 1792. Women crowd behind him (right) and soldiers stand guard (left), while club members shout back and one man even exposes his buttocks (center), leaving no doubt as to the club's lively political culture.

of self-government, the French revolutionaries had little familiarity with practical politics before 1789—especially the need to forge coalitions, negotiate compromises, and abide by the will of the majority. France's history of absolute, indivisible royal sovereignty made the prospect of parties competing for power, and one branch of the state checking another, seem unbearably discordant and disruptive. Political parties, or even independent popular movements of the sort that took shape in the American Revolution, seemed wholly illegitimate and dangerously anarchic.

In France, then, it was all too easy to perceive opposition as treason, and indeed, cries of treason resounded incessantly from right and left alike after 1789. They did so in the Assembly, in the streets, and in hundreds of political clubs and societies, the most important of which were the **Jacobins**, the name of the religious order in whose building they originally met. In the pages of a new, raucous newspaper press, writers competed to denounce their enemies in as eloquently vicious terms as possible. None did so more successfully than a Swiss doctor named Jean-Paul Marat (1743–1793), who published a wildly popular left-wing newspaper in Paris. "Your enemies need only to triumph for a moment," he warned in a typical outburst, "for blood to flow in torrents. . . . They will rip open the bellies of your wives, and their bloody hands will search the entrails of your children to find their hearts." Kill those enemies first, he demanded. "Sacrifice 200,000 heads, and you will save a million." Royalist, counterrevolutionary demagogues issued blood-curdling threats of their own. Meanwhile, in the major cities, and especially in Paris, independent popular movements developed, demanding that the revolutionary leadership take the demands of ordinary people into account—especially for food at a fair price.

COUNTERREVOLUTIONARY FORCES But it was not just these factors that drove the Revolution toward violent conflict. The very nature of revolutionary politics contributed powerfully as well. As different groups competed to pose as the true representatives of the people, the moderates who initially attracted the most support found themselves pushed to the side by others willing not just to oppose but also to demonize the aristocracy, recalcitrant priests, and counterrevolutionaries. In the Assembly, one of the most important of these was a deputy from the northern town of Arras named **Maximilien Robespierre** (1758–1794). Fussily dressed and a poor speaker, this former lawyer initially failed to impress his colleagues but gradually built up a reputation for coldly precise logic and compellingly absolute, unswerving dedication to the

Revolution. A British observer rightly saw in him "a character to be contemplated" who would shortly "be the man of sway . . . and govern the million." Between men like Robespierre and the supporters of the king, it soon became impossible to find common ground.

Still, if Marat and Robespierre built up a terrifying, nightmarish image of the counterrevolution, the better to advance their own program, the fact remains that the counterrevolution itself was no myth and its activities too drove the Revolution into violent conflict. In the Assembly, political clubs, and the press, a determined right-wing faction called for the reversal of the Revolution and the restoration of the king and nobility to their former powers and privileges. Thousands of nobles—including a large majority of France's army officers—fled the country to join the émigré army taking shape in Germany. And while the king and queen publicly professed support of the Revolution, privately they corresponded with the émigrés and hoped for their victory.

Maximilien Robespierre
An eighteenth-century portrait of the radical leader depicts him in the formal clothing he preferred.

THE KING'S FLIGHT AND ITS IMPACT

And then, in June 1791, Louis XVI showed his cards in an extraordinary—but, typically enough, botched—fashion. He and Marie-Antoinette plotted a dramatic escape from their quasi-captivity in Paris: in the dead of night they would sneak out of the Tuileries Palace in disguise and embark in a carriage for the eastern border. There troops were waiting, backed by the armed might of the Austrian Empire, now ruled by Marie-Antoinette's brother, Leopold II. The royal couple then planned to dissolve the Assembly and repeal most of its decisions. But they were undone by their genius for blundering. The bulky carriage, laden with baggage that the couple refused to do without, moved at a leaden pace, missing the rendezvous with loyal troops and arousing suspicions from local authorities, who detained them in the small eastern town of Varennes. Representatives of the Assembly who hoped to preserve a constitutional monarchy escorted the royal family back to Paris, claiming unpersuasively that the king had been "kidnapped." But their excuses could not prevent a wave of indignation from sweeping the country, as millions of

Capture of Louis XVI and Marie-Antoinette A colored etching dramatizes the moment at which revolutionaries apprehend the fleeing royal family in Varennes, as troops rush into an inn where the family are having dinner.

citizens realized that the fevered left-wing allegations of royal treason might actually be true.

The most virulent outcries against the monarchy came not only from left-wing journalists and deputies but also from revolutionary crowds in Paris and other cities. The same groups who had taken the Bastille and stormed Versailles had remained active participants in the Revolution. In Paris, they dominated many of the forty-eight "sections" into which the new municipal authorities had divided the city, each of which possessed its own, small, tumultuous "sectional assembly." With supplies of affordable bread still being in question and rumors of counterrevolutionary plots circulating feverishly (in part thanks to newspapers like Marat's), new, potentially violent crowd actions were a constant possibility.

By late 1791, the most active urban militants had started to be known as "*sans-culottes*"—those who wore full-length trousers instead of the calf-length breeches (*culottes*) of the upper classes. Although their leaders consisted largely of educated professionals and successful artisans, the rank-and-file came in large part from the urban working classes, and they preached hatred not only of aristocrats but of the wealthy in general. Their watchwords were bread for the people and death to counterrevolutionaries. In July 1791, less than a month after the king's flight, tens of thousands of *sans-culottes* flooded into Mars Field, a large open space in central Paris, to sign a petition demanding the replacement of the king by an executive

council. When a group of them killed two suspected spies, the mayor and Lafayette, a former hero of the American War of Independence now heading the National Guard, together ordered armed Guards into the field to restore order. A massacre of up to fifty crowd members ensued, further incensing radical opinion. The *sans-culottes* movement would continue to evolve, acquiring an effective organization and a hugely popular newspaper.

Despite these tumultuous events, for another year a delicate balance held. Louis remained king, and in the fall of 1791 the long-prepared new constitution finally came into effect. The Legislative Assembly that took office consisted entirely of new faces, for their predecessors had declared themselves ineligible for reelection. The deputies also came almost entirely from the former Third Estate, as the clergy and nobility had lost their old privileges. In fact, the nobility itself had legally ceased to exist, along with the system of estates—all French men were now equal.

THE RUSH TO WAR Although overt counterrevolutionaries were largely absent from the deputies' ranks, the new Legislative Assembly remained as prone to conflict as its predecessor, with radical Jacobins and more moderate deputies continuing heatedly to dispute the course of the Revolution. And almost immediately, the body found itself confronting the most divisive issue of all: war. The émigré counterrevolutionary army in Germany had continued to grow, while Austria and Prussia showed increasing hostility toward the revolutionary regime. In response, a group of French deputies known as the "**Girondins**" (who mostly belonged to the Jacobin Club) began agitating for an attack on Austria. Their leader was an ambitious deputy from Paris named Jacques-Pierre Brissot (1754–1793), who had struggled to establish himself as a *philosophe* under the Old Regime. As a journalist in the early Revolution, he gained a reputation for eloquent radicalism in the service of oppressed people. But once elected to the Legislative Assembly, he fastened on war as the issue that would bring him to power, presenting it as necessary both for quelling the threat of counterrevolution and for reinvigorating France itself. His allies eagerly echoed the message. As one wrote: "It is a cruel thing to think, but . . . peace is taking us backwards. We will only be regenerated by blood."

Not all members of the left agreed with the Girondins, but in the winter of 1791–92 they found it impossible to stop the rush to war. Robespierre, notably, distrusted Brissot's ambitions and considered war a distraction from the need to root out counterrevolution at home. Nor did he believe Brissot's promise that the revolutionary armies would bring liberation to oppressed peoples across Europe. "No one loves armed missionaries," Robespierre insisted in a speech at the Jacobin Club (to which he also belonged). Yet few of his colleagues listened, especially after the king and queen cynically threw their own weight behind Brissot's campaign, in the hope that a war would bring them back to full power ("these imbeciles don't see that they are helping us," Marie-Antoinette privately remarked). In April 1792, France declared war on Austria, and two months later Prussia joined the fight on the Austrian side.

INSURRECTION But far from strengthening the monarchy, the war helped ensure its final collapse. The French army, undermined by the emigration of much of the officer corps and heavily staffed by raw volunteers, fought poorly. Some troops fled at the first contact with Austrian regulars, and a few even massacred their own commanders. By early summer 1792, not only had the early French forays into the Austrian Netherlands been repulsed but France itself seemed dangerously open to invasion. At the same time, the Austrians and Prussians made the ideological stakes of the war perfectly clear. On July 25, the Prussian commander, the duke of Brunswick (1735–1806), issued a manifesto stating his intention to end the "anarchy" in France and to restore full powers to the king. And if the people of Paris offered violence to the royal family, he promised to take "ever memorable vengeance," including the "complete destruction" of the French capital. From this moment on, the Revolution's success depended on French military victory.

In this climate, the new French constitutional regime had no chance of solidifying itself. By now, a significant number of deputies, and radical journalists, were demanding the establishment of a republic, and they were backed by the increasingly assertive *sans-culotte* movement. On August 10, 1792, strengthened by detachments of radical National Guards from around the country, the *sans-culottes* attacked the royal palace in Paris. For the first time in the history of the Revolution, Paris itself witnessed a large-scale battle, as the king's loyal Swiss guards vainly tried to protect their master and were shot down. Finally, the royal family took refuge in the hall of the Assembly, whose members, faced with a popular fait accompli, took yet another leap into the unknown. Within days, they had abolished the monarchy and ordered the election of a **National Convention** to write a new, republican constitution. For the first time in European history, all of a nation's adult men would vote.

THE BIRTH OF THE FIRST FRENCH REPUBLIC (1792–1793)

If the first French revolutionary government had started its work in an atmosphere of crisis and violence in 1789, this second one—the First French Republic—came into being amid full-scale war and large-scale massacre. On August 19, 1792, the Prussian army crossed the eastern frontier into France, and two weeks later it took the key eastern fortress of Verdun. In Paris, a mood of panic soon found violent expression.

THE SEPTEMBER MASSACRES AND THE BATTLE OF VALMY

Between September 2 and 7, 1792, armed *sans-culottes* stormed prisons in the capital, where hundreds of suspected counterrevolutionaries had been detained. Setting up improvised courts, they dragged each prisoner in turn forward for a brief hearing, followed immediately by a pronouncement of innocence or guilt. In the latter case, the *sans-culottes* delivered the death sentence then and there, usually with clubs or knives to spare ammunition for the army. Lurid tales spread of tortures committed and bodies mutilated after death, most of which were likely invented. But between 1,100 and 1,400 men and women did die, mostly common criminals but including some 200 priests and many prominent nobles. The so-called

September Massacres Blood stains the revolutionaries' axes as they slaughter supposed counterrevolutionaries emerging from a prison. This 1790s engraving seeks to emphasize the carnage associated with the increasingly radical revolution.

September Massacres deeply shocked public opinion outside of France, with many observers renouncing their former approval of the Revolution to denounce the "monsters" in Paris.

Yet the same moment of extreme danger also saw the birth of a new, fervent revolutionary patriotism. In the dark, narrow streets of Paris, baking in the summer heat, bells rang constantly while soldiers marched to the sound of drums and cannon, calling for volunteers to defend the fatherland from the Prussians. Some 15,000 responded in a single week and were sent eastward in a disorganized mob, without training or even weapons. In the Convention, a new leader came to the fore—a former lawyer named Georges Danton (1759–1794) with a great mane of hair, prominent brows, a deep, bellowing voice, and an instinctive talent for rousing a crowd. On September 2, he gave his greatest speech, roaring that "To defeat our enemies, *Messieurs*, we need boldness, again boldness, forever boldness, and France is saved."

The volunteers, bold as they were, by themselves could not do much against well-drilled Prussian infantry. But the Prussians had problems of their own, their ranks having been decimated by an outbreak of dysentery that turned their line of march into one long, foul-smelling latrine. The French army confronted them on September 20 near the eastern town of Valmy, and the battle quickly turned into an artillery duel. Among the officers on the French side was a member of the royal family, Louis-Philippe (1773–1850), who had embraced the Revolution along with his father, the Duke of Orléans. The French artillery, which was staffed—unlike the infantry—by long-serving professionals, carried the day, and the weakened Prussians, commanded by the elderly, cautious duke of Brunswick, quickly withdrew. The revolutionaries hailed Valmy as a momentous victory that had saved France from invasion and that left the newly elected National Convention free to begin its work.

THE TRIAL AND EXECUTION OF THE KING

The Convention, though, was no freer from discord than its predecessors. The same dynamic of radicalization that had destabilized revolutionary politics from the start continued in this newest assembly, with different factions competing to pose as the purest, most determined representatives of the popular will. Now the principal division would come between two groups of Jacobins: Brissot and

the Girondins, on the one hand, and a group that came to be known as the "Mountain" because it occupied the upper seats in the Assembly hall. It included Danton, the wild journalist Marat, and Robespierre, now making his return to elected office. And Robespierre had a new ally: a pale, thin, intense man just twenty-five years of age named Louis-Antoine Saint-Just (1767–1794). Meanwhile, the restive, well-organized *sans-culottes* continued to put pressure on the Convention from the left.

The Convention also had no shortage of crises to deal with, of which the first and greatest was the question of the king. After the fall of the monarchy in the summer of 1792, the Convention had placed Louis under arrest. Should he be expelled from the country? Placed on trial? Killed? Saint-Just argued in his maiden speech that the people of France had already found Louis guilty by overthrowing him, but the deputies, who included a heavy proportion of lawyers, hesitated to condemn the king without due process of law. Finally, in December a trial took place before the Convention itself. The deputies found the king guilty of betraying the people by a wide margin and then, by a smaller one, sentenced him to die.

On January 21, 1793, Louis XVI was led to the large square in Paris that is today called the "Place de la Concorde." There awaited him one of the Revolution's most

Execution of Louis XVI Troops maintain order among massed spectators as a soldier displays the king's severed head to the crowd in this 1792 painting.

infamous inventions: the guillotine, whose heavy blade delivered the bloody but rapid punishment of decapitation. His hands bound behind him and his hair cut so as not to impede the blade, Louis was strapped to a board and thrust into the machine while continuous drumrolls drowned out the last words he tried to shout to the crowds. The blade fell, and the king of France perished. (Grotesquely, the guillotine did not cut cleanly through his pudgy neck, and the executioner had to pull the blade back up into position and drop it again.)

TOWARD CIVIL WAR

The king's trial and execution horrified social elites across Europe and ended any chance of the revolutionary regime conciliating with its enemies. Coupled as it was with revolutionary attacks on religion and promises of radical social equality not just for the French but for all humankind, Louis's death inspired even stronger opposition than the execution of England's Charles I had done in 1649. Britain and Spain soon opened hostilities against France, turning the war into a general European conflict—the first in nearly thirty years. In Britain, the government of Prime Minister William Pitt the younger undertook increasingly repressive actions. By the mid-1790s it had suspended the right of habeas corpus (which protects those arrested from indefinite, unlawful detention), put several dissidents on trial for treason, and passed laws banning "seditious" publications and meetings. British caricatures, especially those by the talented printmaker James Gillray, portrayed the French revolutionaries as cannibals.

The French, following their victory at Valmy, did well on the battlefield for a time, again invading the Austrian Netherlands and capturing Brussels. But the strains of war quickly took their toll on the new regime, which faced severe shortages of weapons, ammunition, and soldiers. In February 1793, the Convention decreed the conscription of 300,000 men, but the move met with massive resistance. Indeed, across western France, particularly in isolated rural areas where loyalty to the old Catholic priesthood ran strong, widespread resistance developed, and in several places crowds of peasants murdered revolutionary officials. The Convention managed to suppress most of these uprisings, but in the department of the **Vendée** peasant rebels put an ill-trained and badly led column of revolutionary soldiers to flight, and with the help of local nobles announced the formation of a "Catholic and Royal Army" pledged to fight for Louis XVI's young son, whom the Convention was

Anti-Revolutionary Cartoons Captioned "A Family of Sans Culotts [sic] refreshing after the fatigues of the day," Gillray's cartoon mocks the movement's name by portraying its members naked from the waist down as they eat a nobleman and sit on his riches. A woman roasts a child over the fire, and even the sans-culottes children feast on entrails.

holding prisoner in Paris. A true civil war had now begun, although it remained limited to the west.

RENEWED ECONOMIC CRISIS Meanwhile, the quality of life for ordinary French people, which had improved somewhat after 1789, again fell into a tailspin. A British blockade, coming hard on the heels of the slave revolt in Saint-Domingue, decimated French overseas trade, while internal conflict played havoc with the supply of bread to French cities. And the French had to face another, largely unprecedented economic crisis: a steep rise in the prices of goods, known today as "hyperinflation." The National Assembly of 1789 had temporarily eased the problem of the national debt by selling off the lands of the French clergy. But they did so by issuing paper notes called *assignats*, which could be redeemed for Church land. By 1791, the *assignats* had effectively become a paper currency, and within two years their value was in free fall, with prices rising out of control. In February 1793, *sans-culottes* rioted in Paris, calling for a "maximum" price on bread, and perhaps on other necessities as well, violating the principles of free trade declared after 1789.

Brissot and the Girondin faction in the Convention considered the *sans-culottes* a threat. They opposed the "maximum," called for an end to the popular movement's assemblies in the "sections" of Paris, and toyed with the idea of moving the government out of the capital

DOCUMENTING EVERYDAY LIFE

BREAD RIOTS IN PARIS

While the French revolutionary government debated the contours of the new legal and constitutional order, the common people challenged the state to ameliorate endemic poverty. The Parisian masses in particular, notably women, pressured successive revolutionary governments to cap food prices and even to distribute bread to the hungry. Bread riots and other civil disturbances were common throughout the revolutionary period, and merchants suspected of "hoarding" were beaten and even killed by angry crowds.

In February 1793, the Paris prefecture of police issued this report on the tense situation in the capital as the revolutionary government worked to maintain peace among its hungry and restive masses. For the poor, questions of liberty and equality were not simply abstract debates, but issues of real and pressing material needs.

The following day, the twenty-fifth of the same month, same year, at 7 A.M., we went, still assisted by the citizen-secretary-registrar, to the doors of the bakers in our Section to see whether bread deliveries were being made without incident and to take remedial action, if possible. We had the satisfaction of seeing that the measures we had taken the night before, in joint action with the Committee, had produced the full effect we were hoping for. Consequently, we returned to the Committee to find out whether there wasn't some new order, and finding none, we returned to our arrondissement.

There wasn't what you would call a tumult, but [rather] small groupings of citizens and citoyennes[1] at intervals. In some [of these groups] it was being said, "The bakers were rascals and deserved to be worked over." In others, "The grocers deserved the same, because they were hoarders," and finally, in others, "The majority of those who were directing the Republic were also rascals." And among others [there was] a drunk citizen who made himself conspicuous by saying, "We used to have only one king, and now there are thirty or forty of them." We did everything we could to restore calm in these groups. We succeeded in some; it was impossible in others; and lastly, it was folly in still others. All this [was happening] without our being able to arrest any of

the leaders, who were absolutely unknown to us and not from this Section.

QUESTIONS FOR ANALYSIS

1. Why was the revolutionary government so concerned with the distributions of bread and other staples?
2. What complaints did the citizens of Paris direct toward the commissioners who were dispatched to monitor the situation?
3. What does this source show about the Revolution's effect on France's poorest citizens?

[1] **citoyennes:** female citizens

Source: *Commissaire's* report on events of February 24, 25, 26, 1793, Section de l'Arsenal, in Archives de la Préfecture de Police de Paris, AA 69, nos. 296–97, in *Women in Revolutionary Paris*, eds. and trans. Darline Gay Levy, Harriet Branson Applewhite, and Mary Durham Johnson (Urbana: 1979), pp. 137–38.

---

altogether. One of their deputies threatened that if the Parisian movement were not curbed, one day passers-by would wander the banks of the Seine river "and ask where once Paris had stood." **The Mountain**, however, largely supported the *sans-culottes*, and on May 4 the Convention instituted a maximum on bread prices over Girondin protests. On May 30, in the major industrial city of Lyons, the conflict turned violent, as forces sympathetic to the Girondins overthrew the municipal government.

THE FALL OF THE GIRONDINS By the spring of 1793, the politics of the Revolution had once again reached an impasse, and yet again the impasse was broken by popular action. On May 31, alarm bells rang in Paris as the *sans-culottes* mobilized. On June 2, with tens of thousands of them surrounding the Convention's assembly hall, they demanded the expulsion and arrest of the principal Girondin deputies. The *sans-culotte* commander of the Paris National Guard aimed a cannon at the door and demanded that the Girondins be sent out—or else. Even some of the "Mountaineers" quailed at this direct assault on the Convention's democratic authority, but others argued that they had no choice if they were to save the infant republic from an even worse fate. Brissot and twenty-eight others were expelled and arrested.

The Convention would eventually restore its authority, but in the late spring and summer of 1793 both it and the Revolution seemed poised at the edge of disaster. In the west, the Vendéan revolt accelerated, as the Catholic and Royal Army captured one major town after another. Following the example of Lyon, several major cities sympathetic to the Girondins broke into open revolt against Paris. A young woman from Normandy, hoping to silence the loudest advocate of revolutionary violence, calmly walked into the Paris apartment of Jean-Paul Marat and stabbed him to death in his bathtub. The murder (for which the woman was quickly executed) led to bizarre scenes of mourning in which Marat's admirers hailed him as the Jesus of the *sans-culottes* and, at his funeral, placed his bathtub on an altar in place of Christ's crucifix. Meanwhile, French armies were driven back in the Austrian Netherlands and Germany, and the frontiers seemed open to invasion. In August, out of desperation, the Convention decreed a "mass levy"—a mobilization of the entire French population for the war effort, including the conscription of all unmarried young men. But thrusting yet more untrained and ill-equipped draftees into the firing line, for all its symbolic appeal, did not seem likely to save the Revolution from defeat.

THE COMMITTEE OF PUBLIC SAFETY It was at this moment, however, that the Revolution entered its most extraordinary phase—one that blended the most extravagantly utopian hopes with terrible violence, and whose events devoured almost everyone who tried to master them. It presented yet again, in the starkest terms, some of the promise and a great deal of the peril of modern revolutionary politics. Its dazed survivors would later compare it to an earthquake, or a volcanic eruption, or some other overpowering natural disaster.

Key to this phase of the Revolution, which lasted from the summer of 1793 through the summer of 1794, was a group of twelve men from the Convention, most famously Robespierre and Saint-Just, who made up the **Committee of Public Safety**. Originally created in April 1793, the committee had by late summer become the central organ of French government. The Convention itself retained ultimate authority, having first written and then almost immediately suspended a new constitution for the

Death of Marat Jacques-Louis David memorialized Marat in 1793 by depicting the journalist in his tub shortly after his stabbing. In David's vision, Marat was at work on his next article at the time of his death.

duration of the emergency. But its 700-odd members were far too unwieldy a body to govern, particularly in the midst of the numerous crises besetting the country. Effective authority quickly devolved upon the Committee, which used it to act as a collective executive in the emergency. Together, the Convention and the Committee set out to save the Revolution from destruction.

THE REIGN OF TERROR (1793–1794)

The leading revolutionaries of this period—Robespierre in particular—now operated according to ideas very different from what had prevailed in 1789. They were no longer concerned with devising constitutional means for translating the great abstraction of "popular sovereignty" into concrete forms of governance. Increasingly, they invoked the authority, not of the people or the nation, but of the Revolution itself—a form of irresistible historical progress that demanded total commitment from its followers. And increasingly, these revolutionaries placed their faith less in the institutions they governed through, and more in the moral strength and purity of their followers. It is not for nothing that so many commentators have compared the French Revolution to a religious movement, for in its fervent emphasis on the beliefs and righteousness of its adherents, it did indeed have this quality during its most radical moment. At the same time, alleged counterrevolutionaries became a species of heretic, damned as moral monsters—"enemies of the human race" who deserved nothing but extermination. And thus France entered into what historians now call the "**Reign of Terror**."

Counterrevolutionary Rebellion in France, 1793

THE MECHANISMS OF REPRESSION

The Terror, properly speaking, dates from the late summer of 1793. On September 5, Parisian crowds dramatically demanded that the Convention declare that "Terror is the order of the day." The deputies refrained from taking this step, but on September 17 they passed a Law of Suspects empowering revolutionary watch committees to arrest almost anyone suspected of counterrevolutionary sympathies. They followed that up on September 29 with a General Maximum law setting price controls on a wide range of necessities including wood, clothing, and tobacco. All these moves responded to the *sans-culotte* agenda, but at the same time the Mountain worked craftily to undercut *sans-culotte* influence. The Mountaineers ended the raucous "permanent sessions" of the *sans-culotte*–controlled district assemblies and also created several "revolutionary armies," drawn in large part from *sans-culotte* ranks, and sent them out into the countryside to maintain order.

To end the revolts against its authority and strengthen the armed forces, the Convention also sent its own members out into the country as "representatives on mission," entrusted with virtual dictatorial authority. Saint-Just, for instance, went to Strasbourg on France's eastern border. He extracted a huge forced loan from the city and demanded that the terrified citizenry supply the army with clothing from their own wardrobes. Some 17,000 pairs of shoes and 21,000 shirts quickly materialized. He also supervised a military tribunal as it handed down 27 death sentences against local officers and soldiers, mostly for the unforgivable crime of losing battles. During the Terror, no fewer than 84 generals went to the guillotine. In Lyons, meanwhile, another member of the Committee of Public Safety brought destruction on a terrible scale after the city finally fell to revolutionary forces in mid-October 1793.

By far the worst repression, however, came in the Vendée, in the west, where in June 1793 the Catholic and Royal Army finally met with competent revolutionary opposition and was soundly defeated outside the port city of Nantes. The revolutionaries pursued their new advantage through the summer and finally, in October, crushed the Vendéans in a pitched battle on their home territory. In December, the revolutionary forces wiped out what remained of the Vendéan army. "Following the orders you gave me," one commander wrote back to Paris, "I have crushed children under the hooves of horses, and massacred women who, these at least, will give birth to no more brigands. I do not have a single prisoner with which to reproach myself."

There then began slaughter on a scale unimagined in Europe since the wars of religion of the seventeenth century—far greater, for instance, than the September Massacres of 1792 in Paris. With the politicians in Paris feverishly demanding the "extermination" of the Vendée,

Nantes Drownings The Terror reached far outside Paris, as indicated by this 1793 lithograph, which depicts revolutionaries in the city of Nantes drowning suspected counter-revolutionaries, including Catholic priests and nuns, in the Loire estuary. As many as four thousand people, including women and children, were killed in this way.

the forces on the ground devised a plan to crisscross the territory with a series of armed columns, with orders to kill all suspected rebels and burn their villages. "We are going to be bearing iron and fire, a gun in one hand and a torch in the other," wrote one soldier to his family. "Men and women, all will be put to the sword. All must die, except the small children." In nearby Nantes, the revolutionaries lashed prisoners into barges, which were towed out into the Loire estuary and sunk. The killing in the region lasted for several months, and the total death toll probably ranged well over 100,000—most likely as high as 250,000.

THE ACHIEVEMENTS OF THE RADICAL REVOLUTION

Yet in a horrifying sense, the Terror worked. Although the western rebellion continued to smolder in places, it ceased to pose a mortal threat to the Revolution. The cities that had revolted against the Convention fell, one by one. And in the larger war as well, French forces recovered from the crisis of the summer of 1793. The Committee of Public Safety worked frantically to ensure adequate supplies for the army and to provide it with competent commanders. Volunteer units were molded together with the remnants of the old royal army and acquired proper training and weaponry. They were also taught new tactics: "The general rules are always to act *en masse* and offensively," stated a directive of the Committee of Public Safety. In key battles in the fall of 1793, French leaders concentrated the great mass of their troops against small weak spots in the Austrian lines and won narrow but significant victories in the Netherlands. By the beginning of 1794, the worst threats to France had been removed.

The military successes were extraordinary. But still more extraordinary was the ability of the deputies, in the midst of these terrible crises, to elaborate some of the most far-reaching plans in history for the betterment of society and the creation of a truly cohesive national community. In a new Declaration of Rights, issued in 1793, they proclaimed the rights of all citizens to primary education, subsistence, and work, and began to devise systems to guarantee these rights. They formulated an ambitious scheme for teaching the French language to all the citizens of what was still a typically European multilingual country, where only a minority of the citizens spoke standard French fluently. They designed a new calendar, numbering the years from the foundation of the First Republic in 1792 and dividing them into newly named months of

Cult of the Supreme Being A painting from around 1794 shows colorfully dressed citizens gathering at the foot of Robespierre's column in Mars Field to celebrate the Festival of the Supreme Being. The architecture of the column and the rings of laurel branches around the hill evoke the classical associations that Robespierre imagined for the new deist religion.

thirty days and weeks of ten. In these reforms they looked back, as their idol Jean-Jacques Rousseau had done, to the ancient world, seeing the Greek city-states and especially the Roman Republic as models of civic virtue.

In their most radical initiative the deputies, having already broken with the Catholic Church through the suppression of its privileges, the seizure of its land, and the attempt to make clergy into public functionaries, now attempted to suppress Christianity entirely. One group of deputies attempted to institute official atheism, with churches and cathedrals, including the Cathedral of Notre Dame in Paris, converted into "temples of reason" and signs posted over cemeteries reading "death is an eternal sleep." Robespierre, however, advocated the formation of a new religion: the "cult of the supreme being," which worshipped a God who had created the universe but did not personalize him or claim that he intervened in human affairs. In a grandiose festival in June 1794, Robespierre inaugurated it personally. Men and women paraded in white robes and sang hymns. In the center of Mars Field in Paris, an enormous plaster-and-cardboard mountain was erected, with a fifty-foot column near its summit bearing a tree and a statue of Hercules. Robespierre, dressed in a sky-blue coat, descended from the mountain in the manner of Moses, bearing a torch. In an ecstatic report drafted for the occasion, he hailed the event as a new beginning for the French people, whom the Revolution had advanced so far beyond other European countries (2,000 years' worth, in his estimation) that they "could practically be considered a new species."

THERMIDOR AND THE END OF THE TERROR

Yet neither these moments of extravagant hope, nor the Convention's real success in reasserting its authority, did anything to halt the Terror. Instead, the pace of executions redoubled. In mid-October 1793, Marie-Antoinette followed her husband to the guillotine after a grotesque trial in which prosecutors accused her of sexually molesting her young son. The Revolution was turning misogynistic, with the Jacobins associating public virtue with masculinity and insisting with new fervor that women remain outside the public eye, tending to the hearth, raising children, and certainly not claiming political rights. Pro-revolutionary women's political clubs were dissolved. Two weeks after the queen, the arrested Girondins died in their turn.

In the winter and spring of 1793–94, Robespierre and the Committee of Public Safety moved to purge both "ultra-revolutionaries" on the left and a party of supposedly over-moderate revolutionaries on the right. Here the increasingly erratic and allegedly corrupt orator Danton became the chief scapegoat, and after yet another show trial in April 1794 he and a number of others were also executed. In his trial, Danton bravely defied the Committee and denounced its "dictatorship," and in his last moments showed genuine bravura. "Show my head to the crowd," he instructed the executioner. "It deserves it. It is a fine head." In June, the Convention passed a law further streamlining the procedure for trying suspected traitors, and despite a decisive military victory over the Austrians, the executions continued. In June and July alone, fully 1,515 men and women were condemned to death in Paris, bringing the total for revolutionary courts to over 20,000. Many were convicted for the bad luck of having been born into the nobility or as the result of anonymous denunciations.

It was becoming clear that Robespierre and his allies had lost control of the Terror that they had set in motion. Robespierre himself seemed, to those around him, in the grip of paranoid suspicion. The Committee of Public Safety justified the executions with the argument that France's very success in defeating foreign enemies had given it the freedom to eliminate future internal threats and conspiracies. But in the Convention, many deputies

Thermidorian Reaction In this engraving from around 1794, chaos erupts at the National Convention as delegates fight one another and a group rushes to the podium to seize Robespierre.

feared for their lives, especially after Robespierre, on July 26, denounced a "conspiracy against public liberty" involving deputies yet to be named.

The very next day—9 Thermidor under the new calendar—numerous deputies, including several members of the Committee, finally attacked Robespierre on the floor of the Convention. Scores of others, seeing a chance for safety, joined in and managed to pass a motion calling for the arrest of Robespierre, Saint-Just, and their allies. The leaders of the *sans-culotte* movement tried to organize a new insurrection against the Convention in support of Robespierre, but the events of the previous year had weakened them, and their efforts succeeded only in giving the Convention a pretext to declare the Robespierrist deputies "outlaws," subject to immediate execution. Robespierre attempted to commit suicide but managed only to shoot himself in the jaw. The next day—July 28, 1794, by the Christian calendar—he and his allies went to the guillotine in their turn. The Terror was over, and with it the most radical phase of the French Revolution. The next phase of the Revolution would be known as the **"Thermidorian Reaction."**

THE MEANING OF THE TERROR

Ever since the Ninth of Thermidor, the Terror has appalled and amazed even sympathetic observers. Some have echoed Edmund Burke, seeing in it proof that the

French Revolution contained the seeds of tyranny and slaughter within it from the start—and that, perhaps, all radical revolutions do. Others view the Terror as an unfortunate deviation from the true spirit of the Revolution, as embodied, for instance, in the Declaration of Rights of 1789. And still others defend it as a necessary measure of self-defense by a revolution besieged on all sides by deadly enemies. Looking back in 1819, the great Swiss writer Benjamin Constant blamed the Terror on the revolutionaries' romantic but misguided desire to recover the "liberty of the ancients"—the practices of direct democracy and public austerity that they had read about in Greek and Roman authors, and that they saw as the key to "regenerating" a supposedly corrupt, effeminate, and weak society, even at the cost of individual rights. Such practices, Constant lectured, made no sense in modern commercial civilizations, in which individuals were far less willing to give up their individual rights and possessions in the name of the common good. Attempting to squeeze modern citizens into ancient molds could only cause frustration, resistance, and, if pushed too far, bloodshed.

Constant's interpretation of the Revolution remains one of the most powerful ever devised. Yet at the same time, he underplayed the Revolution's most important modern aspect, namely, the role of the French common people—urban artisans and shopkeepers, peasants and villagers—who had done as much as any learned deputy to drive events forward. In this, they did not resemble earlier generations of European lower-class rebels, who had generally fought either for a religious cause or to protest excessive rents or taxes. The French of 1789, like the Americans of 1776, fought for explicitly modern political goals—above all, those expressed by the two transcendent words "liberty" and "equality." In doing so, ordinary French people forced the wealthier and better-educated members of the Assemblies to adopt policies more radical than anyone had dreamed of before the Revolution. So in the end, the Terror stemmed not only from the dynamic of radicalization discussed above but also from the failure of successive revolutionary governments to contain the awesome political forces unleashed by the people of France themselves.

THE INTERNATIONAL SYSTEM DISRUPTED

The radical Revolution and the Terror had effects that spread far beyond France. It permanently disrupted the international system, which had been based on balance-of-power politics and restrained warfare since the reign of Louis XIV (r. 1643–1715). From as early as 1790, leading revolutionaries in France such as Brissot had extended the principle of popular sovereignty to international affairs, insisting that the will of the people trumped existing treaty law, even in determining international boundaries. They were proclaiming what would become known as the principle of "self-determination," and they implemented it by allowing the populations of various conquered territories to vote on whether they wanted to become part of France. Following the former papal territory of Avignon in southeastern France and the Piedmontese coastal city of Nice, a "Rhenish-German National Convention," governing western German territories conquered by French troops, also successfully appealed for annexation to France in March 1793.

The political initiative in the Rhineland came from groups—mostly middle-class journalists, lawyers, and clerics—who enthusiastically founded political clubs on the French Jacobin model. Scores of similar clubs sprung up throughout Germany, as well as in Italy, and as far afield as Poland, Greece, and Spain. In Britain and the United States, radical political societies "affiliated" themselves with the Jacobins, and even in India, French mercenaries in the service of the sultan of Mysore, an opponent of British expansion in the subcontinent, founded a Jacobin club. An international revolutionary movement, the first of its kind, was taking shape, and many of its members flocked to Paris, fervently proclaiming their belief in universal brotherhood and the coming end of all international divisions.

Yet these radical actions provoked equally radical reactions on the part of the states aligned against France. Now there was to be no question of limited warfare and balance-of-power politics. Each side was committing itself to the destruction of the enemies' political regimes. The French proclaimed as their slogan "peace to the cottages, war on the palaces." Now there would be no toleration of domestic opponents—"enemies within"—and when Prussia reoccupied the Rhineland capital of Mainz in the summer of 1793, it ferociously persecuted the local Jacobins in what amounted to a

Second and Third Partitions of Poland, 1793–1795

reverse Terror, although with a much smaller body count. And far from respecting national "self-determination," the central European powers took advantage of the war and disruption to gobble up new territory. Following Russia's defeat of Poland-Lithuania in 1792 and the dismantling of its liberal reforms, Prussia joined with Catherine the Great in carrying out a second, drastic partition of the Polish state. Afterward, only a third of the pre-1772 Polish population still lived under Polish sovereignty. And two years later, in a third and final partition, independent Poland-Lithuania would cease to exist altogether, only to be reborn more than a century later, after World War I.

THE DIRECTORY AND RISE OF NAPOLEON BONAPARTE (1795–1799)

Even before the fall of Robespierre on the Ninth of Thermidor (July 27, 1794), the popular forces that had done so much to spur revolutionary radicalization had suffered significant setbacks. But the men who took power on that date were even less tolerant than the Mountain of what they saw as dangerously anarchic and uncontrollable crowds. Their hostility quickly provoked an uprising by the remnants of the *sans-culottes*, who were also angered by a new bout of hyperinflation and food shortages in the spring of 1795. The so-called Thermidorians responded with a brutal military crackdown, breaking the movement forever, with hundreds sent to the guillotine or into exile in France's fever-plagued South American colony of Guyana. Along with ending the Terror and closing the Jacobin Club, the Thermidorians drew up yet another new constitution that restored property qualifications for voters and thereby ended France's brief experiment with universal manhood suffrage.

Hundreds of former Jacobin activists fell victim to an anarchic "White Terror" (as opposed to the radical "Red Terror" of 1793–94), particularly in southern France, where the settling of political scores from the period of Robespierre often degenerated into pure revenge-killing. A small group of ultra-revolutionaries, led by a former clerk named François-Noël Babeuf (1760–1797), who had renamed himself "Gracchus" Babeuf after the plebeian leader of the Roman Republic, also plotted to seize power in this period. Their plans called for communal ownership of all property. But the plotters were discovered and arrested. Babeuf died on the guillotine, and the last echoes of the radical revolution died with him.

THE DIRECTORY

The Thermidorians did not break with the revolutionary tradition altogether. When resurgent royalists tried to seize power in the fall of 1795, the Thermidorians responded every bit as brutally as they had done to the *sans-culottes*. A young army officer named Napoleon Bonaparte (1769–1821) made a reputation for ruthlessness by confronting an unruly crowd in central Paris and, so it was later claimed, ordering them dispersed with grapeshot (bullets and scrap metal fired from cannon at point-blank range). The regime the Thermidorians created in late 1795, called the "**Directory**" after its new five-man executive, remained very much a republic. When royalists who wanted to put Louis XVI's younger brother on the throne gained a majority in parliamentary elections in 1797, republican "directors" staged a coup with military backing, purging their enemies from all branches of the government.

The leading politicians and intellectuals associated with the Directory remained committed to republican ideas and did much to foster their development in France. But it was in war that the Directory showed its greatest commitment to continuing the Revolution, and also where revolutionary popular energy now expressed itself most strikingly. Many of the hundreds of thousands of young men drafted into the army in 1793 remained in uniform through the late 1790s, and with seasoning they became the most fearsome military force in Europe. Having eliminated threats to French territory in the spring of 1794, this revolutionary army conquered present-day Belgium and then pressed northward. In January 1795, the ruler of the Netherlands fled to Britain, and the French armies established a new regime there, with a constitution and institutions partly copied from France. In April, Prussia bowed out of the war in order to concentrate on its expansion to the east. Spain, which had lost a series of bloody encounters in the Pyrenees, made peace with France in July. Only Britain and Austria, of the major powers, were left in what we now call the "Revolutionary Wars."

THE RISE OF NAPOLEON BONAPARTE

In the spring of 1796, the Directory launched a triple thrust at Austria through central Germany, southern Germany, and northern Italy. The last of these attacks, involving only 38,000 French soldiers, was meant mostly as a diversion. No one in Paris expected much of the ill-fed and ill-equipped troops or of their commander, the inexperienced, twenty-seven-year-old **Napoleon Bonaparte**. It was not merely his youth that made him an unlikely French general. He had been born on the island of Corsica, to a minor noble family, just a year after France annexed it in 1768. He was slender and poorly dressed, had long greasy hair, and spoke with a thick Corsican accent. But he quickly proved a tremendous surprise to both his sponsors and his enemies.

After making heroic efforts to provide his tattered army with proper food and supplies, he invaded Italy in April and in a series of brilliant small battles crushed Austria's minor ally, Piedmont. He then carried out an ingenious campaign of maneuvers against the Austrians themselves, occupying the heart of northern Italy. In January 1797 the French won the crucial battle of Rivoli, forcing the Austrians to abandon the strategic citadel of Mantua, and by April Napoleon's men had crossed into the Austrian Alps and come within seventy-five miles of Vienna itself. Forced to the peace table, the Austrians allowed the French to set up dependent "sister republics" in northern Italy and to annex new territories to France itself. In scarcely more than a year, Napoleon had established the sort of dominance over the Italian peninsula that French rulers had been longing for, without success, since the fifteenth century. In doing so, he immediately established himself not merely as the most popular of French generals but as the most popular political figure in France itself.

A MODERN CAESAR In the politics of the revolutionary era, Napoleon represented something very new. Unlike Robespierre or Saint-Just, with their cold, high abstractions about national regeneration, he was a true populist who mixed easily with common soldiers and delighted in the nickname given him after he had allegedly helped aim artillery pieces himself during one of his Italian battles: "the little corporal." Unlike earlier revolutionary populists such as Mirabeau and Danton, he managed to present himself as above and removed from petty political squabbling—as a soldier who had risked his life for the Republic and cared solely about the common good. But unlike other French generals who had ventured into revolutionary politics, he also recognized the importance of not basing his appeal entirely on his military record. Since the earliest days of the French Revolution, astute observers—with the example of Rome very much in their minds—had expressed concerns that a new Caesar might arise to build a tyrannical empire on the ruins of the Republic. Napoleon cannily defused such fears by joining the civilian National Institute (a center for scholarship)

Revolutionary Wars, 1791–1799 After the battle of Valmy in 1792, France's wars with its European neighbors turned in its favor. Despite British naval blockades and Prussian and Austrian military opposition, France conquered several territories in the Rhineland, the Low Countries, and the Alps, and helped to install a republic in the Netherlands. Napoleon's brilliant campaigns later in the 1790s drove the Austrians from Italy. In addition to occupying Piedmont and Tuscany in 1799, the French established dependent "sister republics" throughout the Italian Peninsula.

and appearing at its public lectures in civilian clothes. In politics, he carefully navigated the treacherous politics of the Revolution, mostly by siding with the moderate republicans who had carried out the antiroyalist coup in 1797.

Napoleon also amounted to the world's first "media general." He sponsored newspapers to report on his and his army's exploits—including one called *Journal of Bonaparte and Virtuous Men*. He encouraged poets and playwrights to celebrate his victories. Several popular biographies embroidered his already-spectacular career by adding such feats as strategic victories in schoolboy snowball fights and

The Young Napoleon An 1801 portrait by Antoine-Jean Gros depicts Napoleon as a romanticized military hero, with flowing unkempt hair and wielding a banner and a sword, during a 1796 battle against Austrian forces.

capital. In his conquest of public opinion, he was aided by his glamorous wife, the aristocratic Joséphine de Beauharnais (1763–1814) whose first husband had died during the Terror.

THE EGYPTIAN CAMPAIGN For a time, Napoleon resisted temptations to put himself forth as a political leader. He judged the time not ripe. Instead, he decided to start a military campaign that might even eclipse his Italian victories. For some time, French strategists had dreamed of establishing a colony in Egypt to threaten Britain's supply routes to India and to start building a new colonial empire to replace the one they had lost to Britain in the 1760s. Napoleon easily gained the support of the Directory for the campaign, as the politicians in Paris already feared he might try to exploit his popularity by making a bid for power and were happy to see him leave the country.

In the summer of 1798, Napoleon landed with 25,000 men near the Egyptian city of Alexandria. The Mameluke military caste that ruled Egypt in the name of the decaying Ottoman Empire posed little serious resistance to him, and after a gruesome forced march of 120 miles through the North African heat, his men smashed the Mameluke army in a battle carried out within sight of the ancient pyramids. Napoleon, who became head of the new colony, made an effort to create enlightened Egyptian political institutions on the European model, while also founding hospitals and redistributing land to the peasantry. He also set to work 160 artists, scientists, and scholars he had brought with him from France. Among their achievements was the discovery of the Rosetta Stone, the ancient stele inscribed with a royal decree from 196 BCE that first enabled scholars to decipher the ancient Egyptian writing system known as hieroglyphs. The Egyptian campaign marked a new French commitment to overseas empire that would have important consequences for the nineteenth-century age of imperialism.

an epic balloon flight over Paris at age fifteen. As early as 1797, Napoleon appeared in scores of widely circulated popular engravings and the greatest painters of the day painted him as a glorious leader, his face shining with confidence as he led exultant troops into battle. "He flies like lightning, and strikes like thunder," wrote one over-excited journalist. "He is everywhere. He sees everything. Like a comet cleaving the clouds, he appears at the same moment on the astonished banks of two separate rivers." Police spies in Paris regularly reported on the "flood of praise" that the young general received from the common people of the

In the end, the Egyptian campaign turned into a fiasco. In a crucial naval battle on August 1, 1798, the British destroyed much of the French fleet, cutting off the newly born French colony from its supply base. Napoleon launched a campaign along the coast of Palestine to forestall an Ottoman attempt to retake their former possession, but failed

Napoleon's Egyptian Campaign, 1798–1799

to capture the crucial fortress of Acre (near present-day Haifa in Israel) and lost thousands of his troops to plague. Although he beat a Turkish army (and murdered hundreds of Turkish prisoners whom he had no means of caring for), he soon retreated to Cairo.

News of these failures took time to arrive in France, however, and the Napoleonic legend remained powerful. Indeed, in the winter and spring of 1798–99 it grew ever greater, as the French Republic seemed once again to totter on the edge of collapse. Not only did the unstable Directory experience two more coups by beleaguered directors against their own colleagues and legislature, but they could not even maintain basic law and order. In desperation, the Directory gave significant power to the military in close to 40 percent of French territory.

FURTHER FRENCH REVERSES Meanwhile, across the territories conquered in Italy, Germany, and the Low Countries, revolts broke out against French rule. A new allied coalition, with Russia adding its forces to those of Austria and Britain, drove the French back in Switzerland and the Netherlands. French territory itself seemed in danger, leading to calls for a renewal of the Terror. A law enacted by the Directory in 1798 created the first regular system of conscription in French history, institutionalizing the revolutionary concept of the people's army.

The French also failed in an attempt to cripple Great Britain by gaining a foothold in Ireland. There the hopeful echoes of the French Revolution had combined with resentment on the part of the disenfranchised Catholic majority to foster the emergence of a revolutionary society known as the United Irishmen, who wished to "break the connection with England." By 1797, it counted some 200,000 members. The British government carried out a very effective campaign of repression, spying upon and imprisoning suspected rebels, and the Royal Navy prevented a French fleet from landing in southern Ireland in 1796. But in 1798 a rebellion broke out, aided by a contingent of 1,000 French soldiers who landed in the northwest of the island. The Navy again prevented a larger contingent of French troops from arriving, and within months the rebellion had failed. The leader of the United Irishmen, Theobald Wolfe Tone (1763–1798), committed suicide in prison before his scheduled execution. Following the rebellion, in an attempt to bind Ireland more firmly to Great Britain, the British and Irish parliaments would pass Acts of Union in 1800, creating the United Kingdom of Great Britain and Ireland. The French had lost their best chance of undermining the British war effort.

A MILITARY COUP It was in the context of the French failures across Europe that Bonaparte left Egypt in the late summer of 1799, slipped past the British blockade, and landed back on the southern coast of France. As he headed north to Paris, crowds cheered him at every stop, and at Lyons the local theater celebrated him with a play entitled *The Return of the Hero*. Once in Paris in mid-October 1799, he quickly entered into a conspiracy with Emmanuel Sieyès, the early hero of the Revolution, who had survived the Terror and reemerged as a cynical and unscrupulous Director. The Directory, they agreed, should be terminated. Its assemblies should be prompted to dissolve themselves and place power in the hands of three interim "consuls": Napoleon, Sieyès, and a nonentity named Roger Ducos. Although several capable generals had driven back the new enemy coalition without any help from Napoleon, the plotters still judged the national crisis severe enough that the public—and especially wealthy property-owners—would support leaders committed to stability and security above all else. And Napoleon could also count on the support of the army, whose long-serving soldiers had grown increasingly disgusted with the Republic's endemic bickering and corruption.

The coup began on November 9, 1799—18 Brumaire under the new calendar. In the event, it did not take place with the smoothness Napoleon and Sieyès had hoped for. The lower house of the parliament refused to dissolve itself, and Napoleon, for once, found himself able to do little but bluster: "Don't forget, I walk with the God of war and the God of victory!" Instead of cheering, the deputies protested loudly, forcing him to flee the assembly and send soldiers in to clear out the hall ("Citizens," his subordinate Joachim Murat bellowed to them, "you are dissolved!"). The remaining handful cooperated with Napoleon's demands, but this did not change the fact that the coup had taken on a military character. For the first time in French history, the army had acted to put a general in power.

CONCLUSION

Napoleon himself continued to pose as a civilian leader and quickly gained the support of a large part of the population, especially as he acted effectively to restore law and order. Nonetheless, his coming to power marked the final extinguishing of the democratic flame that had burst out so brightly with the calling of the Estates General and the storming of the Bastille in 1789. Other aspects of the French Revolution would endure under his rule. These included civic equality, the end of the seigneurial system in the countryside, the confiscation of Church lands, the institution of religious toleration, and the administrative reforms that accompanied the breaking up of the old provinces. But many of the rights so proudly accorded to "man and citizen" in 1789 would now disappear, including freedom of the press and the right of the people to choose their own rulers. And from now on, what was left of the popular enthusiasm that had expressed itself so forcefully at the taking of the Bastille would be channeled above all in one direction: military conquest. As the year 1799 came to an end, the French Revolution did as well. The chapter of European history now beginning would be one of total war.

KEY TERMS

Bastille (p. 540)

Louis XVI (p. 542)

What Is the Third Estate?
(p. 544)

National Assembly (p. 545)

Tennis Court Oath (p. 545)

"Great Fear" (p. 547)

Declaration of the Rights
of Man and Citizen
(p. 547)

Edmund Burke (p. 550)

Jacobins (p. 553)

Maximilien Robespierre
(p. 553)

sans-culottes (p. 554)

Girondins (p. 554)

National Convention
(p. 555)

September Massacres
(p. 556)

Vendée (p. 557)

The Mountain (p. 558)

Committee of Public
Safety (p. 559)

Reign of Terror (p. 560)

Thermidorian Reaction
(p. 562)

Directory (p. 564)

Napoleon Bonaparte
(p. 565)

REVIEW QUESTIONS

1. How did long-term changes in French society and culture, combined with a shorter-term fiscal crisis, bring France to the point of revolution in 1789?

2. How did the meeting of the French Estates General in 1789 result in the formation of a National Assembly?

3. How did the National Assembly transform the nature of the Revolution?

4. From 1789 to 1791, in what ways did the French Revolution prove to be an event of international significance?

5. In what ways did the political culture of pre-revolutionary France, as well as the very nature of revolutionary politics, lead to violence?

6. What movements within the Revolution and the counterrevolution developed beginning in 1791?

7. How did the *sans-culottes* shape the Revolution?

8. What atrocities took place during the Reign of Terror, and in what ways did it succeed in preserving the Revolution?

9. How did the Revolution transform the model of warfare and diplomacy that had prevailed in Europe over most of the eighteenth century?

10. In the later 1790s, how did Napoleon Bonaparte establish himself as a popular political figure as well as a military leader?

CORE OBJECTIVES

After reading this chapter, you should have a solid understanding of the following core objectives. To strengthen your grasp of the core objectives, use the resources on the Student Site for The West.

- Analyze the origins of the French Revolution.
- Explain the radicalization of the French Revolution during its first few years.
- Evaluate the crises that shook the First French Republic.

- Describe the Reign of Terror and its consequences.
- Trace the establishment of the Directory and Napoleon Bonaparte's rise to power.

 GO TO **inQuizitive** TO SEE WHAT YOU'VE LEARNED—AND LEARN WHAT YOU'VE MISSED—WITH PERSONALIZED FEEDBACK ALONG THE WAY.

CHRONOLOGY

1800
Napoleon creates first
French National Bank

1800
Napoleon's second
Italian Campaign

1803
Louisiana Purchase

1804
Napoleon proclaimed
emperor of France

1804
Civil (Napoleonic)
Code established

1804
Republic of Haiti
gains independence

1805
Battle of Trafalgar

1805
Austria, Russia, Britain
form coalition against France

1805
Battle of Austerlitz

1806
Napoleon devises
Continental System

1806
End of Holy
Roman Empire

1807
Battle of Eylau

1807
Treaties of Tilsit

1808–1814
Peninsular War
in Iberia

1812
Napoleon's
Russian campaign

1812–1815
War of 1812 between
Great Britain and
United States

1813
"Battle of the
Nations" at Leipzig

1814–1815
Congress of Vienna;
Napoleon exiled
to Elba

1814
Bourbon Restoration
in France

1815
The Hundred Days;
battle of Waterloo

1815
Napoleon exiled
to Saint Helena

17

The Age of Napoleon

EMPIRE AND RESISTANCE

1799–1820

1821
Napoleon dies

1819
Peterloo Massacre

n December 1812, a twenty-four-year-old soldier from southern Germany named Jakob Walter stumbled in retreat westward across the border of the Russian Empire. Soon afterward, he caught sight of himself in a mirror and could not recognize the person who stared back at him. "The crusts on my hands, ears and nose had grown like fir-bark, with cracks and coal black scales," he recalled much later in life. "My face resembled that of a heavily bearded Russian peasant." Yet as Walter, a former stonemason, knew well, he was lucky to be alive. Just six months earlier, he had marched into Russia as one of over 650,000 soldiers whom Napoleon Bonaparte, emperor of France, had gathered into the Grand Army—the largest yet seen in European history. Less than a third were French; some 160,000 were Germans like Walter, from states allied to France. They marched hundreds of miles, in oppressive heat, through country stripped bare by their retreating Russian foes and the fleeing Russian peasantry. Walter would later recall that the desperately hungry soldiers did not even stop to cook a hog when they caught it, but ate the flesh raw, while drinking slimy, worm-infested water that they filtered as best they could through their handkerchiefs.

Napoleon himself did not want to occupy Russia, but to destroy its army and make it a pliable ally. But the Russian army retreated ahead of him. When the French finally

The Emperor Napoleon In this 1808 painting by Antoine-Jean Gros, Napoleon surveys the battlefield upon his narrow victory against the Russians and Prussians at Eylau in 1807. Despite the dead and maimed piled in the foreground, the work seems to glorify the emperor: a ray of sunlight shines on him, and wounded enemy soldiers reach out to him for mercy.

- What were the most important reforms enacted by Napoleon?
- How did Napoleon's conquests remake the map of Europe?
- What were the sources of resistance to Napoleon's empire?
- What were the main effects of the Napoleonic era?
- What were the pivotal events in Napoleon's downfall?
- How did the Concert of Europe attempt to bring the Napoleonic era to a close?
- What major political and social changes were reflected in the Europe of 1815?

notched up a major victory outside Moscow in early September, the bulk of the Russian force escaped. The French occupied Moscow, but as they did much of the city burned to the ground—most likely an act of Russian arson that went out of control. Napoleon himself would later recall: "It was the spectacle of a sea and billows of fire, a sky and clouds of flame—mountains of red rolling flames,…" It left the city largely uninhabitable, and after several weeks of dithering Napoleon decided to march back west.

There followed one of the most epic disasters in the history of warfare. Winter had come early. Snow, wind, and sub-zero temperatures assaulted soldiers who lacked proper coats and boots, and often had no tents to shelter in. Frostbite, disease, and starvation took ferocious tolls. Men went to sleep next to their comrades and woke up to find a field of snow-covered corpses. When horses died—and Napoleon lost some 200,000 of them during the campaign—they were immediately stripped for meat, after which the wounded took shelter in the still-steaming carcasses. On November 23, 1812, the Russians caught up to Napoleon's weakened force at the Berezina River, in modern Belarus. As panicked crowds of Grand Army soldiers and supporters rushed onto makeshift bridges, one bridge collapsed, sending hundreds into the freezing water. By the time Jakob Walter saw his transformed face in the mirror a month later, more than half the 650,000 men of the original force had died.

At the start of his Russian campaign in 1812, Napoleon Bonaparte had been at the apex of his power. In the almost uninterrupted series of wars he had fought since coming to power in 1799, he had vastly increased the territory of France, crowned himself its emperor, and defeated his major continental rivals. He had become arguably the greatest European conqueror since Alexander the Great in the fourth century BCE, outdoing even Julius Caesar and Charlemagne. But he could not defeat Great Britain, which had decimated his navy and tried to strangle French trade. In fact, it was Napoleon's vain attempt to close the European continent to British trade that ultimately led him toward the disastrous invasion of Russia.

The Russian catastrophe did not by itself spell the end of Napoleon's empire. His remarkable military talent, the institutions he had forged, and the wealth he had accumulated allowed him to survive as emperor for another two years and to come close to defeating his enemies yet again. But ultimately he fell from power (twice, as we will see). France lost its conquests, and the Bourbon dynasty toppled by the French Revolution returned to the throne.

Although historians often downplay the story of Napoleon's epic rise and fall, in fact the Napoleonic adventure led to many important changes and deserves close attention. The wars that reached their climax in the Russian campaign can be considered an early example of "total war"—one that drives entire nations, including their civilian populations, toward ever-greater mobilization, with the goal of utterly destroying an enemy. Indeed, the year 1812 marked a highpoint in the occurrence of organized violence throughout the Western world that would not be matched again for a century. The Napoleonic Wars not only exacted a massive human toll but also forced the victors—above all, Britain, Russia, and Austria—to realize that competition among states could no longer be trusted to remain within the bounds of eighteenth-century "balance of power" politics. From now on, maintaining peace would depend on continuous management of international disputes by a "concert"—a formal system of close cooperation—among great powers.

The wars also spurred the development of national independence movements that would flourish over the following decades, challenging the great multinational empires that had dominated the map of Europe before the French Revolution. By 1820, the revolutionary idea that Europeans should live in national states, whose governments' legitimacy derived at least in part from the consent of their citizens, had become widespread. The wars also shook the Spanish and Portuguese empires to the core and helped spread the national idea beyond Europe, notably to Latin America. They confirmed the supremacy of one great power—Great Britain—that would dominate the Continent in the nineteenth century while carving out for itself an unprecedented, worldwide empire. Finally, the wars marked the period in which a powerful new cultural movement, now known as romanticism, began to emerge.

This chapter will concentrate on Napoleon's rise and fall, and the immediate aftermath. It will also track the changes that continued in the shadow of the wars, particularly in the lives of ordinary men and women. And it will suggest that by 1820, these ordinary lives were becoming caught up in powerful new social, economic, and political forces that European elites were desperate to bring under control.

NAPOLEON BONAPARTE IN POWER (1799–1804)

The upheavals of this period, like those of the earlier revolutionary decade, had their center in France. They were tightly bound up with the continuing warfare that, by 1799, had raged over the Continent for seven years. And, to a degree unequaled in European history before or since, they revolved around a single man. Napoleon's formal rule began with the coup d'état that brought him to power in 1799 and ended with his abdication in 1815, but it took at least until 1820 for a post-Napoleonic order to stabilize.

EFFORTS TO RESTORE FRANCE'S INTERNATIONAL POSITION

Although other generals had removed the immediate threats to French territory even before Napoleon took power, he realized quite well that he would not remain long in power unless he restored France to the commanding position it had held before the military debacles of 1798–99.

ITALY In the spring of 1800, Napoleon decided to lead an invasion of northern Italy to gain back the territories he had first won in his electric campaign of 1796–97. In a

daring move, he decided to cross the Alps over the high, treacherous St. Bernard Pass, putting his army at risk in the hope of surprising the Austrians who had reoccupied the northern Italian plain. The French made it through, despite bitter cold, with Napoleon himself crossing on a mule, swathed in heavy blankets. Months went by without news of any obvious success, and in the French capital ambitious politicians and generals started to speculate on who might seize power next, if Napoleon failed.

But he did not fail. His army made it into Italy intact, surprising the Austrians and defeating them decisively at the Battle of Marengo. And Napoleon knew well how to exploit such a victory, organizing writers and artists to hail him as the hero of the new century and the savior of the French Republic. In Jacques-Louis David's great painting of him crossing the Alps, the heavy blankets are nowhere to be seen and a magnificent, rearing horse has taken the place of the mule. Napoleon himself, astride the horse, seems to command the very wind. By 1801, Austria had limped out of the war altogether, allowing France to

Crossing the Alps Painted in 1800–1801, Jacques-Louis David's portrait shows Napoleon—atop a horse, not a mule—leading his army across the Alps on his daring invasion of Italy. At bottom left, a stone engraved with "Bonaparte" lies ahead of rocks inscribed with the names of Hannibal and Charlemagne, casting Napoleon as the greatest conqueror of all.

establish a new satellite state in northern Italy and leaving Napoleon securely in power.

HAITI Outside of Italy, Napoleon did not immediately do so well. He had dreamed of retaking the wealthy Caribbean sugar colony of Saint-Domingue (modern-day Haiti), which had experienced the massive slave revolt of 1791. By 1801, the charismatic Haitian general Toussaint Louverture (1743–1803), while theoretically loyal to France, had established an autonomous regime there with its own constitution. To reassert firmer French control, in 1801 Napoleon dispatched an expeditionary force that succeeded in taking Louverture prisoner and deporting him to France, where he died in captivity. But yellow fever decimated the French army, forcing Napoleon to abandon his plans and to acquiesce, in 1804, in the colony's independence. The new nation took the name of the Republic of Haiti—the second independent state in the Americas after the United States, and the first independent black state.

As a result of the defeat, Napoleon also gave up on the idea of developing the Louisiana Territory of North America, which he had reacquired from Spain in 1800 and had hoped to use in large part as a supply base for Saint-Domingue. When representatives from the United States approached him with proposals to purchase New Orleans, he surprised them by offering the entire 530 million acres—nearly a third of the present-day continental United States—and eventually parted with it all for the sum of $15 million. France did retain the smaller Caribbean islands of Guadeloupe and Martinique. There, in 1802, Napoleon reversed the French Revolution's 1794 emancipation decree and forced free blacks back into slavery.

THE CONSULATE OF 1799–1804

Napoleon accomplished a great deal domestically during his first years in power. Shunting aside his partners in the 1799 coup, he asserted strong executive power as first consul and built upon emergency legislation of the previous Directory government to impose law and order with a heavy hand. He increased police powers and surveillance and dispensed harsh punishments, but dealt magnanimously with those former rebels who were willing to cooperate. The tactics proved effective at quelling the low-level revolts, brigandage, and simple disobedience that had plagued the country before his coup. In keeping with this increased social control, he imposed the strictest

censorship in French history and reduced the number of Parisian newspapers to four, from the hundreds that had appeared during the Revolution.

Drawing liberally on precedents from the Old Regime monarchy and eighteenth-century theories of "enlightened despotism," he developed a streamlined and centralized state administration. It placed government firmly in the hands of highly trained bureaucrats drawn from France's social elites, including "prefects" who would now govern each of France's "departments." Napoleon also worked to stabilize French finances, notably by creating the country's first permanent National Bank in 1800. He introduced a new constitution that confirmed his own executive role, although it also allowed for a three-chamber legislature. This body was theoretically elected by universal manhood suffrage, but the choice of representatives in practice lay largely in the hands of men loyal to Napoleon.

NAPOLEON'S CIVIL CODE Napoleon and his collaborators also began to prepare a revised, efficient national legal code to replace the patchwork quilt of laws inherited from the Old Regime. The new **Civil Code** (also known as the Napoleonic Code) reaffirmed the Revolution's abolition of formal social privilege and confirmed its large-scale transfer of property (especially Church lands) to new owners, including many peasants. In other respects, however, it was socially conservative. It greatly restricted the rights of women within marriage—for instance, by requiring that women receive their husbands' permission to work or to travel abroad. (The Code did not, however, repeal the revolutionary legislation that had introduced divorce.) In the same conservative vein, Napoleon negotiated a new agreement with the Vatican that recognized Catholicism as the dominant religion in France, although it stopped short of reestablishing it as an official religion. In short, Napoleon preserved some important features of the revolutionary heritage—especially formal legal equality of adult males— while also bringing back important aspects of the Old Regime. "I am the French Revolution," he boasted at one point. But he would also remark: "I picked the crown of France out of the gutter, and placed it on my head."

EMPEROR OF THE FRENCH In accomplishing all these tasks within less than five years, Napoleon impressed all who met him with his apparently boundless energy and intelligence. Rising at dawn, he would generally work straight through until eight or nine in the evening, sleep until midnight, wake up, and work an additional three or four hours. He could keep details of hundreds of military units, or provisions of laws, in his head and may indeed have had a photographic memory. As one of his subordinates remarked many years later, after he had led the French to disaster: "What a pity the man wasn't lazy."

The reforms Napoleon introduced quickly earned him real popularity among a French people left exhausted by political and social disorder. In fact, he was so popular that he did not even need to cheat to win several plebiscites (referendums) designed to legitimize his rule between 1800 and 1804. He did so anyway, and in one of them he supposedly received 3,000,000 "yes" votes and only 1,500 "noes." In 1802, he changed his title from "first consul" to "consul for life," and asserted the right to appoint a successor—a monarch in all but name. Two years later his tame Senate, one chamber of the new legislature, added the name by proclaiming him emperor. In the Paris cathedral of Notre Dame, now restored as a church from the godless "Temple of Reason" established there by the revolutionaries less than ten years before, the pope himself took part in an elaborate ceremony crowning Napoleon emperor of the French. Turning to his brother at one point in the festivities, Napoleon whispered, in his native Italian: "If only Papa could see us now."

FAILED ATTEMPTS AT PEACE In all these early reforms, Napoleon seemed intent on demonstrating that despite his military origins, he did not want to establish a military regime. His prefects and other top officials came mostly from civilian life, and he actually reduced the role of the army in maintaining law and order. He also attempted, between 1800 and 1803, to bring about a permanent European peace settlement. During this short period, he not only made peace with Austria but also negotiated treaties with the United States, Spain, Austria, Naples, Bavaria, Portugal, Russia, and the Ottoman Empire. And on March 25, 1802, he signed the Peace of Amiens with Great Britain, France's strongest and most determined opponent. For the first time in nearly a decade, Europe's guns fell silent.

But the peace did not last, and Napoleon's principal legacy remains one of bloodshed. True, his new administrative system forms the basis of French government to this day and has been widely imitated around the world. The same is true for his Napoleonic Code, which serves as the foundation for law codes in dozens of countries. The Code represents a rationalized, simplified version of Roman law and has particularly appealed to societies seeking to combine a strong centralized power with a recognition of equality before the law. But despite these achievements, Napoleon knew that staying in power would require more

The Corsican Spider In 1808, a British cartoonist satirized Napoleon's imperial ambitions by depicting him as a spider who has subdued most of the states of continental Europe like flies in his web. The Russian Fly and Turkish Fly (bottom) are afraid they will be dragged in as well, but the British Fly (top left) proudly insists, "I am not to be caught in your web."

than just thoroughgoing and popular domestic reform. "My power is dependent on my glory, and my glory on my victories," he once keenly remarked. "My power would fail if I did not base it on still more glory and still more victories."

But it was not just Napoleon's own thirst for glory that ensured the continuation of the European wars. Despite his coronation, relatively few Europeans outside of France perceived him as a legitimate ruler. In Britain in particular, he was still seen as "a stranger, a foreigner, and an usurper," to quote Prime Minister William Pitt (1759–1806) in 1800. The British remembered with fury that France had aided the rebellion against British rule in Ireland in 1798, which led Pitt two years later to dissolve Ireland's parliament and pass Acts of Union in 1800 to merge the country entirely into the "United Kingdom." The threat of French Jacobinism remained a strong presence in British politics, spurring both a powerful conservative turn and an upsurge of patriotism. The British press, meanwhile, railed with such vitriol against the "Corsican Ogre" that Napoleon protested to the British government and demanded the suppression of the offending articles.

The resumption of peace in 1802 therefore failed to end the tremendous hostility and suspicion that had characterized European international relations since 1789. While wealthy Britons flocked to Paris to catch up on a decade of French fashion, Napoleon continued to seethe against British plots. Meanwhile, the British protested France's continued military presence in the Netherlands, Napoleon's actions in the Caribbean, and his annexation of additional territories in Italy beyond the "natural frontier" of the Alps. Such disputes were inevitable, given how greatly the French Revolution had altered European borders after more than a century of slow, incremental change. And Napoleon continued to push for territorial reorganization, especially along his eastern frontier in Germany. Between 1800 and 1803, he eliminated most of the tiny statelets that had survived for centuries under the loose umbrella of the Holy Roman Empire, grouping them into larger entities. Not surprisingly, while Napoleon saw this move as a simple consolidation of what was already France's dominant position in Germany, his adversaries, in the prevailing atmosphere of hostility, perceived it as naked aggression.

THE CONQUEST OF EUROPE (1804–1807)

Given all these potential flashpoints, the peace could not hold. In 1803, scarcely a year after the agreement at Amiens, Napoleon decided that a resumption of hostilities was on the horizon. And so he declared war.

THE WHALE AND THE ELEPHANT

As soon as the war started, Britain seized all French ships in British ports, while Napoleon ordered the arrest and internment of all Britons on French soil. He also began to prepare for a full-fledged invasion of the British Isles. In French ports on the English Channel, he ordered the construction of a flotilla of small boats, while in the nearby countryside he assembled and trained an army filled with long-serving, seasoned professionals. With the French economy recovered from its earlier difficulties, and with

the government newly streamlined and efficient thanks to Napoleon's reforms, France could make full use of its abundant natural resources and large population—well in excess of 30 million, thanks to the recent annexations.

Napoleon's "Army of England" quickly emerged as the most formidable fighting force seen in Europe in centuries. And yet this great army could not reach its intended target. Great Britain remained under the protection of its own formidable military force, the Royal Navy, which kept the French fleet and its Spanish allies bottled up in port. Without cover from warships, Napoleon's invasion flotilla would have been blasted into so many floating splinters by the British navy. When Napoleon finally ordered the combined French and Spanish navies back to sea in 1805, the British annihilated them off Cape Trafalgar on the Spanish coast. The battle of Trafalgar ensured that Britain would remain safe from invasion and committed to France's defeat: the "whale" facing France's "elephant," as British wits put it.

VICTORY IN CENTRAL EUROPE

But the elephant soon found other enemies it could trample. Even as Napoleon planned his invasion of Britain, tensions had been rising once again with Austria and Russia, thanks above all to the changes Napoleon had engineered in Germany. Napoleon made matters worse in 1804 by sending French agents across the Rhine into the German state of Baden to capture a member of the old French royal family who had been plotting against him. The man's execution horrified public opinion across Europe and led one of Napoleon's counselors to remark famously that the event "was worse than a crime—it was a blunder."

Most horrified of all was the tsar of Russia, Alexander I (r. 1801–1825), who had come to the throne three years previously after the murder of his erratic father by disaffected officers and courtiers (Alexander himself had encouraged the plotters). Just twenty-five years old in 1804, Alexander was an ambitious, reform-minded, but mystically inclined man who believed he had a divine mission to redeem Europe. And although initially an admirer of Napoleon, by 1805 his mistrust of the "Corsican usurper" led him to join with Austria and Britain in a new anti-French coalition.

It was a disastrous decision. On August 23, Napoleon took what had been his Army of England out of its Channel-coast camps and headed toward Germany, marching over 200,000 men as much as thirty-five miles a day. Five weeks later they crossed the Rhine, and by

Invasion of Prussia An 1810 painting propagandistically shows townspeople cheering as Napoleon and his army march under the Brandenburg Gate into the center of Berlin.

mid-October they had reached the Danube. Napoleon was now at the height of his abilities and commanded the best army he was ever to have under his orders. In a complex campaign of brilliant, nimble maneuvers, he succeeded in crushing the Austrian army and occupying Vienna. Then, on the anniversary of his coronation, December 2, 1805, he confronted a combined Austro-Russian force near the small village of **Austerlitz**, in what is now the Czech Republic. Tsar Alexander and Austrian emperor Francis II (r. 1804–1835) were there in person, and Alexander rashly insisted on battle despite the advice of his experienced commander. Napoleon notched up another decisive victory, which left the tsar literally weeping under a tree.

THE REMAKING OF GERMANY After their previous defeats at Napoleon's hands, Austria's Habsburg rulers had survived relatively unscathed, but this time Napoleon showed little mercy. He stripped Austria of its remaining Italian possessions and undertook another round of territorial organization, forging the midsized western German states into a new organization called the "Confederation of the Rhine," dominated by France. And in the wake of these changes, he insisted on a further, heavily symbolic change. On August 6, 1806, the Holy Roman Empire formally came to an end. Although it had long since ceased to function as a real political unit, it remained, in many eyes, the legitimate heir to the throne of Charlemagne, and beyond that to the Roman Empire itself. Now, for the first time since Augustus, no European sovereign claimed the mantle of universal emperor. More important, in an immediate political sense, the Habsburg emperor lost the influence he had once wielded over Germany through the old institutions of the Holy Roman Empire. Germany had spun out of the orbit of Vienna and fallen into that of Paris.

Napoleon was soaring close to the zenith of his astonishing career but had still not quite reached it, for there remained one last German enemy to defeat. Prussia had remained out of the wars with France since making its separate peace in 1795. Its young and unsteady king, Frederick

William III (r. 1797–1840), had preferred to turn his attention toward Poland, whose heartland (including Warsaw) had fallen under Prussian rule in the successive partitions of 1772, 1793 and 1795, which, as we have seen, had wiped Poland from the map of Europe.

In 1806, with disastrous timing, Frederick William entered into a new coalition with Britain and Russia, which was still hoping to avenge its defeat at Austerlitz. In response, Napoleon took 180,000 superbly trained soldiers into the heart of Germany. He quickly won a pair of battles with overwhelming force and proceeded swiftly to capture one Prussian stronghold after another, finally marching triumphantly into Berlin in early November. Of the 171,000 soldiers that King Frederick William had sent against Napoleon, he lost 25,000 dead or wounded and 140,000 taken prisoner. The campaign had taken less time than Hitler's "Blitzkrieg" against France would take in 1940, and it eventually resulted in Prussia's losing half its territory and subjects, paying massive reparations to France, and seeing its army reduced to a token force. Even before the key battle, one of its witnesses, the German philosopher Georg Friedrich Hegel, wrote in amazement that the entire history of the world had been changed: "The connecting bonds of the world are dissolved and have collapsed like images in a dream."

And yet it took time to bring the Prussians to surrender, and the end of the campaign brought a hint that Napoleon's great streak of fortune might not last forever. The emperor chased the remaining Prussians north into East Prussia, where they had joined forces with the Russians. In the battle of Eylau, in February 1807, fought in the midst of a massive snowstorm, at least 30,000 men from the two sides fell dead and wounded. At the end, Napoleon controlled the battlefield. But he had failed to destroy the enemy armies and was left with little more than heaps of snow-covered corpses. "What a massacre—and with no result," commented a French field marshal. Although Napoleon finally overcame the last Prussian resistance, the days of his greatest victories were past.

THE EMPIRE CONTESTED (1807–1814)

In July 1807, Napoleon and Tsar Alexander met in person on a raft symbolically towed out into the middle of the Neman River, Russia's western frontier, near the town of Tilsit. Prussia's Frederick William was in attendance but was forced to wait on the shore, a poor supplicant. Napoleon concentrated on seducing the young tsar, whom he called his "brother monarch," and by showing a generosity that the dazzled Alexander did not expect, he at least partly succeeded. Together, he promised, the empires of France and Russia would henceforth dominate the Continent. Two **treaties of Tilsit** arranged a Franco-Russian alliance, drastically reduced Prussian territory, and established new French satellite states in Westphalia (in western Germany) and Poland. The latter, known as the "duchy of Warsaw," occupied only a portion of the former kingdom of Poland but did represent at least a partial rebirth of the Polish state.

Napoleon was already moving quickly to ensure French dominance of virtually all of continental Europe west of Russia. Having defeated the Bourbon kingdom of Naples (which included all of southern Italy and Sicily), he placed on its throne his older brother, Joseph Bonaparte (1768–1844), a dreamy man, far less ambitious than his brother, who before the Revolution had studied for the priesthood. Napoleon gave the new kingdom of Westphalia to his younger brother Jerome (1784–1860). He transformed the Netherlands into yet another kingdom under the rule of his younger brother Louis (1778–1846). And throughout Europe, he turned smaller areas into fiefdoms for his generals and ministers, who now became dukes and princes. From the list of titles now on display at the glittering French court—Duke of Ragusa, Duke of Otranto, Prince of Neuchâtel, Prince of Benevento—it might almost seem as if the French Revolution had never happened.

THE SPREAD OF THE REVOLUTIONARY LEGACY

Still, like Napoleon's Consulate and its administrative reforms, his French Empire remained true to the revolutionary tradition in several crucial ways. Napoleon himself did not abandon his commitment to the principles of civil equality and meritocracy: allocating offices to people on the basis of their talents and achievements. Although he welcomed Old Regime nobles to his court, he still did not move to undo the Revolution's redistribution of land and wealth, which had included the confiscation of émigré nobles' estates. He kept numerous former Jacobins among the ranks of his top advisers and ministers; and despite having made peace with the Catholic Church, he remained opposed to the influence of the clergy in secular affairs. Pope Pius VII, who had come to Paris to crown him in 1804, eventually excommunicated him, and Napoleon retaliated by keeping the pope prisoner in French territory for over six years. The French armies remained largely without chaplains.

REFORM IN THE EMPIRE Napoleon also helped spread the Revolution's legacy beyond France's old frontiers. Newly annexed imperial territories, notably in Italy and Germany, were transformed into French "departments." They were subjected to a full program of revolutionary reform, and their inhabitants received full French citizenship. These areas constituted the inner core of Napoleon's empire. The outer core of satellite kingdoms (including the former "sister republics" now ruled by members of the Bonaparte family) generally underwent a lesser but still important degree of revolutionary change, including the introduction of the Napoleonic Code and religious toleration. Jews in central and eastern Europe often remembered Napoleon as a liberator for granting them full civil rights. Notably, he eliminated the restrictions of ghetto life, allowing Jews to live and work where they wished. Thanks to these processes, which had the effect of reducing regional differences throughout the Continent, Napoleon was moving in the direction of founding a true European superstate. He told one subordinate: "I must make all the peoples of Europe one people, and Paris the capital of the world."

REFORMS IN PRUSSIA Even outside the areas of direct French influence, the Napoleonic upheavals led to rapid reform. In Prussia, after the humiliating defeat of 1806, two ministers in Frederick William's government—the pragmatic Karl von Hardenberg (1750–1822) and the aristocratic reformer Karl vom Stein (1757–1831)—began what has been called a "revolution from above." Their reforms imitated the French Revolution's assault on inefficient privilege but not its moves toward democracy; nor did the Prussians adopt the Revolution's emphasis on civil equality, which Napoleon defended. They abolished the last vestiges of rural serfdom in Prussia, instituted a more egalitarian tax system, introduced a measure of religious toleration, and pushed to make advancement in government service dependent on merit rather than favor. They promoted primary education and worked to transform the army into a more efficient, supple force. The upgrades to the Prussian military enraged Napoleon, who accused vom Stein of plotting a new war and put pressure on King Frederick William to restrain his minister. Fearful for his life, vom Stein fled to Russia.

RESISTANCE

Despite Napoleon's meeting with Tsar Alexander at Tilsit, a lasting peace settlement remained out of reach. Above all, Great Britain remained at war with France, its navy effectively blockading the Continent and strangling its foreign trade. In retaliation, in 1806 Napoleon began to devise what he would eventually call the "**Continental System**"—a Europe-wide boycott of British manufactures and British markets. Without European trade, he promised, the British would eventually be driven to economic collapse and would accept French dominance. But for the system to work, it would be necessary to impose it on literally tens of thousands of miles of European coastline. Napoleon had set himself an impossible task.

And then there was the specter of revolt. In France itself, the extension of the principles of the Revolution had provoked violent resistance, leading to the hideous guerrilla war in the Vendée. In the late 1790s, the imposition of the same principles on large areas of Italy, Germany, and the Low Countries had produced similar, if less bloody, results. The greatest source of resistance was the revolutionary practice of conscription (compulsory military service for all), which was imposed not only in territories that had become formally French but in the satellite republics and kingdoms as well. But there was also opposition to the huge new tax burdens imposed by the French and the new law codes that disrupted traditional patterns of social life by, for instance, legalizing divorce and imposing new rules for inheritance. Not surprisingly, where French authority seemed weak or uncertain, the population often seized the chance to revolt. Napoleon himself told his brother Joseph, on sending him to Naples in 1806: "Include in your calculations the fact that within a fortnight, more or less, you will have an insurrection. It is an event that constantly occurs in occupied countries."

REVOLT IN SOUTHERN ITALY The kingdom of Naples—the largest of the many independent states in Italy, covering the southern half of the peninsula and the island of Sicily—provided the first example of serious revolt against the empire. Although Napoleon's men had easily conquered the mainland portion of the kingdom, they could not overcome Sicily, which was protected by the British navy and where the Neapolitan royal family fled to rally resistance to the Bonapartes. Within months of Joseph Bonaparte's taking the throne in Naples, scores of towns rose up against him, especially in the remote, rocky region known as Calabria, at the tip of the Italian

Revolt in Calabria In 1806, a British force came to the aid of the rebels in Calabria against Joseph Bonaparte's rule. An English engraving shows the British (in red) victory over the French (in blue) at the battle of Maida, a small town in the region.

boot. The French had scarcely 9,000 soldiers there, many of them sick, and when it became clear that they could not restore order, dozens of bands of armed rebels sprang up under commanders known by such nicknames as "the Executioner," "the Monk," and "Brother Devil." Cutting French supply lines, swooping down on small detachments of French soldiers, and murdering supporters of the new regime, they quickly made it nearly impossible for the French to maintain control.

The insurrection never seriously threatened overall French control of Italy, and Joseph's regime eventually managed to suppress it, in part through sheer brutality. In July 1807, Joseph Bonaparte's Cabinet Council declared Calabria in a state of rebellion and warned that rebel villages would be sacked and burned. A month later, a town that continued to resist was burned to the ground, with at least 734 people killed. The French applied the same tactics—which strongly resembled the way French revolutionary forces had dealt with the Vendée in 1793–94—to many other villages in the rebel region, if not on so large a scale.

THE IBERIAN TRAP

The French managed to suppress rebellions elsewhere in Europe as well. But in one key location of southern Europe, the Iberian Peninsula (comprising Spain and Portugal), they failed. Here continuous resistance against Napoleon

became what contemporaries called "the Spanish ulcer," which ate away at the vitals of the French Empire and ultimately proved a key factor in its collapse.

Napoleon did not originally want to invade Iberia. Spain had made peace with revolutionary France in 1795, and later became Napoleon's ally. It shared in the naval debacle of Trafalgar in 1805. But the Spanish government seemed paralyzed by the unseemly and erratic behavior of its royal family. The unstable Bourbon king, Carlos IV (r. 1788–1808), had handed over much of his authority to his favorite, Manuel Godoy, who was also the lover of the queen. Carlos also squabbled incessantly with his vain twenty-three-year-old son and heir, Fernando (1784–1833). In October 1807, Carlos placed Fernando under arrest for plotting a coup against him. Still, Spain posed France no immediate danger.

Portugal was a different matter, at least in Napoleon's view. Long linked to Great Britain by strong trade ties and a naval alliance, Portugal quickly emerged after 1806 as the principal weak point in Napoleon's continental blockade—an entry point for British manufactures and an outlet for continental goods. Enraged, Napoleon invaded in the fall of 1807, with the Spanish allowing him to send an army through their territory. The French quickly defeated Portugal's small military and sent its royal family fleeing across the Atlantic to their colony of Brazil, although a British expeditionary force soon recaptured the capital of Lisbon. But Spain's continuing instability raised anxieties about supply lines to Portugal, while Napoleon's disgust at the Spanish royals' antics soon led him to think that the country might be a more effective ally if it had a Bonaparte rather than a Bourbon as king. The obvious candidate was Joseph, who was already ruling Naples but was eager to move to this larger and more prestigious throne.

In March 1808, the opportunity presented itself when riots against Godoy forced his dismissal and King Carlos's abdication. Napoleon refused to recognize Fernando as the new king, but instead ordered both father and son to meet him in the French-Spanish border town of Bayonne. There he overwhelmed them with threats until they *both* agreed to abdicate. With the Bourbons out of the way, he then summoned Joseph Bonaparte to Madrid, replacing him in Naples with their brother-in-law, Marshal Joachim Murat, a former greengrocer and army sergeant.

THE PENINSULAR WAR (1808–1814) Even before this game of musical thrones, the French had already moved 120,000 troops into Spain on a series of pretexts and taken control of strategic Spanish fortresses. They were hoping for a smooth transition of power. A large

number of Spaniards, especially from the urban middle classes and nobility, admired Napoleon and the French Revolution, believing that they embodied the ideas of the Enlightenment. These Spaniards were ready to support a new regime with enthusiasm. But soon after Napoleon browbeat the Bourbons into submission, an uprising took place in Madrid in May 1808, led by supporters of the old dynasty and backed by most of the common people. The French suppressed it with brutal force, executing hundreds of prisoners. The great Spanish painter Francisco de Goya (1746–1828) left an indelible, dreamlike image of the event in *The Third of May*, whose central figure—an illuminated, Christ-like victim, arms askew—draws the eye irresistibly.

Following this event, scores more Spanish cities and towns rose in open revolt against the new Bonapartist regime. The **Peninsular War** lasted for more than five years and badly drained French resources. In response to early Spanish victories, Napoleon himself took personal charge of the war, crushing the Spanish army, and by the fall of 1809 Joseph Bonaparte seemed secure on the Spanish throne. He imposed a revolutionary constitution that struck at long-entrenched feudal rights and also at the enormous power of the Catholic Church in the country. But the French still could not stamp out resistance. A legitimist government, loyal to Fernando, remained in operation, mostly in the southern port city of Cádiz. For a brief time there, Spanish liberals came to power and promulgated a constitution in 1812 that provided for a powerful parliament and a limited monarchy. The British, meanwhile, retained their base in Portugal, protected by massive fortifications around Lisbon and led by the brilliant, efficient Arthur Wellesley (later known as Lord Wellington and then the Duke of Wellington, 1769–1852). And throughout the peninsula, popular resistance remained powerful. In some areas, it was led by elements of the old Spanish and Portuguese armies. In others, it took the form of bands of insurgents fighting what was called "the little war"—or, in Spanish, *la guerrilla*, giving rise to the concept of **guerrilla warfare**.

TOTAL WAR IN SPAIN In places, the horrific fighting in Spain anticipated the massively destructive wars of the twentieth century. In June 1808, for instance, the city of Saragossa declared itself in revolt against the "intruder king" Joseph Bonaparte. To subdue it, the French fired thousands of explosive shells and then advanced street by street—often house by house—in some of the worst urban combat seen to date in Europe. Macabre scenes played out in the city's many religious establishments, where

The Third of May, 1808 Francisco de Goya's arresting, dark painting (1814) shows French soldiers executing defenseless Spanish prisoners, including a monk (left) and a laborer (in the white shirt).

explosions blew ancient skeletons out of their tombs and shattered containers holding thousands of gallons of sacramental oil and wine. It took until February 1809 for Saragossa to surrender, and at least 50,000 Spaniards died in its defense.

Elsewhere in Spain, the "guerrilla war" played itself out in a way quite similar to that of the rebellion in Calabria—but on a much larger scale. Bands led by charismatic leaders made it impossible for the French forces to operate in large areas. Contingents of French soldiers risked attack from groups of hundreds or even thousands of guerrillas, who would rely on sheer surprise and shock to overwhelm their enemies and then quickly melt back into the countryside. French soldiers themselves came to see every Spaniard as a potential guerrilla. They resorted to increasingly brutal counterinsurgency tactics, burning villages, taking and executing hostages, and generating ever-greater hatred on the part of the Spanish population.

EFFECTS OF THE PENINSULAR WAR In addition to showing how uncontrollable warfare had become—very different from the far more limited wars of the eighteenth century—the Peninsular War had another crucial consequence. Because of the conflict in Spain, its far-flung imperial territories—from the Philippines in Asia to all of Spanish-speaking South and Central America—found themselves cut off from the mother country. Colonial elites, often frustrated with Spanish restrictions on their economic and political actions, took advantage of the circumstances to assert greater rights. In some parts of the

THE COLOSSUS

In the Peninsular War (1808–1814), the Spanish army proved no match for Napoleon, but guerrillas constantly harassed French troops and supply lines. Their attacks in turn were met with violent reprisals that exacted a terrible toll on the Spanish population.

The violence and suffering of the war years influenced a dark turn in Spanish art, leading to works such as *The Colossus* (1808–12), previously attributed to Goya and possibly painted by one of his collaborators (the controversy is ongoing). In this painting, an imposing, nightmarish figure looms over a valley filled with a scattered caravan of fleeing people and their cattle. Against a tempestuous sky, the giant assumes a fighting stance, its left fist raised. The artist's technique is defined by dark tones and rough, thick paint-strokes, a style that perhaps reflected a visceral reaction to the agony and the uncertainty of the French occupation.

QUESTIONS FOR ANALYSIS

1. What do you think the colossus represents in this painting?
2. Who might the people in the valley represent?
3. What insight does this work provide into the horrors of the Peninsular War?

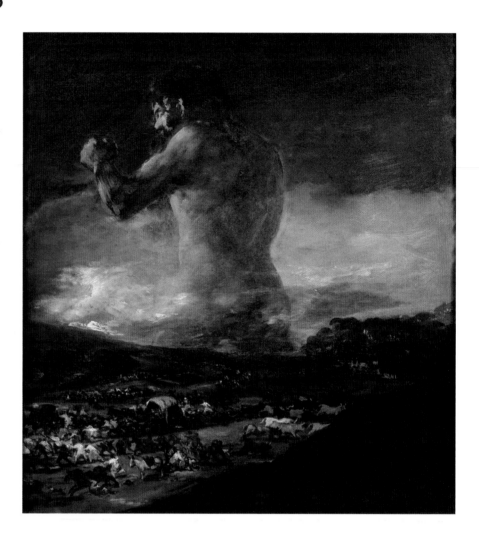

Spanish Empire, such as the future Argentina, these "creole" (that is, colonial-born) elites declared that they would function independently until the Bourbon king returned to the throne in Madrid. The liberal Cádiz constitution of 1812, which some creole representatives helped to draft, further encouraged these movements by giving the overseas possessions equal rights within the empire. In a stunning move, the constitution granted Spanish citizenship, if not voting rights, to indigenous peoples and more limited civil rights to free blacks and mulattoes. The Latin American revolutions of the 1810s and 1820s had their roots in the turmoil of this war.

The festering sore of the Peninsular War, and continuing British hostility, left Napoleon unable to turn the peace agreements reached at Tilsit into a permanent settlement for the Continent. Indeed, the Peninsular War provoked another conflict in central Europe when the Austrian Empire, trying to take advantage of the redeployment of French forces from central Europe to Spain, declared war on France yet again in 1809. At the same time, another major insurrection broke out in the Alpine region of the Tyrol, which had been annexed by France's ally, Bavaria. While it did not turn into a second Spain, the French were forced to come to Bavaria's aid. To deal with these emergencies, Napoleon drew on his efficient conscription system and managed an unprecedented mobilization of French strength. He soon defeated the Tyroleans and, after a decisive victory in the 1809 Battle of Wagram, forced Austria to sue for peace. But seasoned observers understood that continental conflict would continue.

EUROPE IN THE ERA OF NAPOLEON

Despite this turmoil, during the years 1809–12 Napoleon seemed more secure on his throne. Following the 1809 war with Austria, he not only reaffirmed his control over central Europe but also took the Austrian emperor's daughter, Maria-Louise (1791–1847), as his bride and empress. (Josephine continued her hold over Napoleon's affections, but her failure to produce an heir had led him to divorce her.) Brought to Paris in 1810, the new empress dutifully gave birth to a son the next year, apparently securing the future of the Bonaparte dynasty. Napoleon also continued apace with his annexations, even taking over territories he had previously delegated to members of his own family, such as the Netherlands. By 1812, France's borders extended over a greater territory than at any time since the reign of Charlemagne in the early Middle Ages. Indeed, when taking into account that France also maintained full control over the satellite regimes in Italy, Germany, and the Duchy of Warsaw, its empire dwarfed anything seen since Rome.

A NEW ROMAN EMPIRE?

Rome, indeed, served as the inspiration for Napoleon's grandiose dreams and plans. He imagined that just as Rome had supposedly melted the diverse peoples it ruled into a single, homogeneous polity, so Paris could now do the same. The French language would prevail as the language of government, trade, and scholarship from Gibraltar to the Baltic Sea. Europeans would use the same currency and the same weights and measures. A new system of broad, well-paved roads would improve communications and transportation. And this new, united Europe would in turn fulfill its destiny by conquering the whole world. "Europe is nothing but an anthill," Napoleon remarked to his secretary. "You have to go to the Orient— all the great glories come from there." He even proposed to Tsar Alexander that France and Russia combine forces to invade British India. The tsar prudently declined.

IMPERIAL CULTURE In Paris, to which he returned after each campaign, Napoleon began to sketch out plans for a capital city worthy of such a world empire. He imagined broad boulevards sweeping through the congested, dark, and filthy streets of the medieval city center (a plan eventually implemented by his nephew, Napoleon III, in the mid-nineteenth century). He commissioned grand buildings and monuments in the Roman style, including a Temple of Glory (today the Church of the Madeleine), a grand column cast from melted Russian cannon, and a huge triumphal arch at the city's western edge (the present-day Arc de Triomphe). In the empty space where the great fortress of the Bastille had stood before the French Revolution, he planned a grand statue of an elephant to embody "the Orient" and his planned conquests there. His regime did not get further than erecting a giant papier-mâché model of it, which quickly was dilapidated by rain and eaten from within by hordes of rats.

Like his Roman and French predecessors, Napoleon tried to harness the arts and literature to glorify himself and his regime. The works produced mostly belonged to the same neoclassical school that had flourished during

Napoleon's Paris Napoleon's vision for grand, neoclassical Paris included the Arc de Triomphe, which the emperor commissioned after his victory at Austerlitz. Though it was not completed until 1836, it memorializes the soldiers killed in the revolutionary and Napoleonic wars.

Napoleon's Empire, 1812 Despite some defeats—against the British at Trafalgar, in guerrilla war in Spain—by 1812 Napoleon had brought much of Europe under his control. French territory extended into the Pyrenees to the west and the Italian Alps and the Low Countries in the east and north. The Iberian and Italian Peninsulas, many of the German states, and much of Poland also fell under his control, and he reorganized them into new satellite states. This was Napoleon's empire at its height, before his retreat from Russia in 1812.

the late eighteenth century. Indeed, Napoleon had as his chief court painter Jacques-Louis David (1748–1825), who had previously inspired the French revolutionaries with his depictions of stern Roman virtue and the supposed martyrdom of the radical demagogue Marat. Now David and his students turned their talents to immortalizing the emperor of France. The contrast could not be greater between the sober, muted style of David's *Coronation of Napoleon* and the wild flourishes of color with which Goya rendered the suppression of the revolt in Madrid. Many other artists and writers turned away from Napoleon, accusing him of having betrayed the ideals of the Revolution. These included the French novelist Germaine de

Staël, whose initial flirtations with Napoleon quickly gave way to mutual loathing.

IMPERIAL SOCIETY Napoleon also imagined a new imperial society. It would be genuinely multinational: by 1813, nearly a third of the emperor's senate (the highest chamber of his new legislature) came from territories annexed to France since 1792. The empire would be rational and progressive, with the role of the Church reduced to a symbolic presence and far greater resources given over to research and education. Indeed, Napoleon laid the basis for the modern French university system. The society would be highly centralized under the rational management of the emperor and the experts gathered in his various councils. Orders would pass from them down through the various ministries to the prefects who ruled the individual "departments" into which the imperial territory was divided; thence to subprefects, town mayors, and eventually to ordinary citizens. Government would definitely *not* be democratic. Although there would be elected legislative bodies, in practice they would do little more than endorse the emperor's decisions.

Despite its supposedly progressive cast, the empire would also be distinctly patriarchal and hierarchical. Women would have no public role at all, but instead remain at home, dutifully bearing and raising children and managing the domestic sphere. The peasants who still made up the vast majority of the population would raise their crops, offer their sons to the armies, and otherwise remain distinctly in the background. Real power in French society would rest with the wealthy, property-owning men called "notables": members of the old nobility; contractors who had enriched themselves during the endless wars; other well-off financiers, merchants, and professionals; and above all the generals who had led France's armies to victory. The lives of ordinary people would be far more regimented, and placed under far greater surveillance, than in the past, especially in cities. In Paris, Napoleon's

ambitious interior minister organized a system whereby the caretakers of apartment buildings regularly spied on the tenants and reported on their activities to the police.

Napoleon did not set out to militarize his new imperial society, but a good deal of militarization took place nonetheless, in keeping with the overall ethos of regimentation and control. Military uniforms proliferated far away from the battlefield, becoming required dress in many government ministries. Schools took on a military cast as well, as students in new elite *lycées* (high schools) were formed into battalions of cadets and trained for the wars. Napoleon created a new "Legion of Honor" to reward citizens who had shown particular merit, and he promised at the outset that it would be open to men (not women) from all walks of life. But over 95 percent of those named to it during his reign came from the armies.

Indeed, of all the emperor's grand plans and hopes, the ones that came closest to fulfillment were his military ones. The most efficient arm of his new state administration was the gigantic system of conscription established to feed the endless hunger of the armies for men. All young men in the empire and most of the satellite kingdoms had to register at age eighteen for military service. Each year, the government decided what percentage of them actually to put into uniform, and sometimes took them all. An efficient

Napoleon's Coronation As depicted in David's grand commemorative painting (1806–7), Napoleon invited Pope Pius VII to his coronation but personally crowned Josephine and himself, showing that he did not recognize the Church's ultimate authority.

bureaucratic system ensured that few slipped out of the net. Still, wealthy young men had the option of paying someone else to serve in their place. Others sought to exploit loopholes in the law. Since married men enjoyed exemptions, the last years of the empire saw a rise in the marriage rate, including a suspicious number of unions between boys of age eighteen and widows in their sixties and seventies. The army was also plagued by large-scale desertion.

SOCIAL AND ECONOMIC EFFECTS OF THE NAPOLEONIC WARS

Events as destructive as the Napoleonic Wars could hardly fail to have massive economic and social consequences. The disruption of shipping caused by the wars, and the attempts by France and Britain to destroy each other's commerce, represented a major potential blow to European prosperity. But the blow was felt very unevenly.

FRANCE In France, the combination of the wars and the slave revolt in Saint-Domingue had already badly damaged trade in the 1790s. By 1807, French exports had finally come back to their 1787 levels. But thereafter, as the battle over Napoleon's Continental System took hold, they fell by half. French imports, meanwhile, remained well below the 1787 levels in 1807, and thereafter fell by two-thirds. Activity in the great French Atlantic ports such as Bordeaux, where slaves and sugar had generated dazzling wealth in the eighteenth century, now shriveled. The French economy turned inward. French textile centers such as Lyon did well for much of the period, but even here by 1810 shortages of imported raw material, such as cotton from India, caused a major downturn. Elsewhere on the European continent, effects were more mixed, but the fighting still caused major disruptions. In the Netherlands, the prices of imported goods such as sugar and coffee came close to tripling, while in Sweden imported textiles became almost impossibly expensive.

GREAT BRITAIN Great Britain also suffered disruptions during the Napoleonic Wars, but overall its economy performed far better. Despite Napoleon's attempt to blockade the Continent to British commerce, British merchants still found many European ports they could enter. The supple and sophisticated system of banking and credit in Britain handled the stresses of the wars better than its continental counterparts. The French national bank created by Napoleon did not entirely alter his reliance, in the manner of his Old Regime predecessors, on private financiers to manage state revenues, and they did so inefficiently.

And while the price of imported goods rose substantially in Britain, levels of imports and exports did not fall anywhere near as drastically as they did across the Channel. The price of grain rose, prompting many more landlords to enclose with fences, and farm for their own profit, fields that had previously been left for common use. Indeed, the acreage enclosed between 1800 and 1810 was nearly double that of the previous decade. The enclosure process, which had begun in the eighteenth century, hurt many agricultural workers but generated considerable profits for landowners. Capital remained available for investment. And while British wages were high compared to those on the Continent (and elsewhere in the world), the price of energy there remained far lower, the result of the abundance of coal. The price of transportation was also low, thanks in part to over 4,000 miles of serviceable canals, most of them built since 1750.

As a result, the wars did not materially slow the development of business and industry in Britain. Although the most dramatic developments would take place after 1820, in the years between 1800 and 1820 Britain continued to lay the groundwork for modern industry. The construction of steam engines continued apace. Already in 1800 there were more than 2,000 in operation—a quarter of them built by James Watt, the Scottish engineer who had developed the technology in the 1770s. Their numbers would increase steadily in the first two decades of the new century, while further technological advances resulted in the production of steam engines that could generate eight times the horsepower of earlier models. The number of steam-powered looms in operation went up by a factor of more than six in this period.

The spread of industrialization was uneven across Britain, with textile mills concentrated in the north of England around the city of Manchester, and in the south around London. And industrialization also brought disruption and opposition. Many observers were shocked by the noise and smoke that the textile mills generated, and found their functional architecture ugly. Already in 1804, the poet and artist William Blake decried the phenomenon in a poem about a supposed appearance of Jesus in England: "And was Jerusalem builded here, / Among these dark Satanic Mills?" A few years later, as textile manufacturers in the north introduced power looms in the mills, they began to dismiss large numbers of skilled, high-paid textile workers. Some of these workers—known as **Luddites** after Ned Ludd, a semi-mythical "captain" or "general" said to have smashed looms thirty years earlier—protested the use of

Ned Ludd An 1812 political cartoon depicts the semi-mythical figure of Ned Ludd—clad in rags and the kind of smock worn by pre-industrial agricultural laborers—encouraging his followers to rebellion.

such labor-saving machines by attacking workshops and destroying equipment. The British government, primed by twenty years of repressing radical activity associated with the French Revolution, responded harshly. In 1812, "machine breaking" was made a capital crime. Hundreds of Luddites were arrested, seventeen died on the scaffold, and many others were imprisoned or sentenced to penal transportation to Australia. In this sense, much like militarized France, Britain in this period saw moves toward a more disciplined, regimented society.

NAPOLEON'S DOWNFALL (1812–1815)

The wave of organized violence that had been building in the Western world since the French Revolution came to a climax in 1812. Following Napoleon's disruption of the Spanish Empire, independence movements and peasant revolts battled authorities in Latin America. Britain's attempts to keep the United States from trading with France, and to force American sailors into its overstretched navy (a practice known as "impressment"), helped provoke a declaration of war on Britain by the United States,

which also had designs on British Canada. The War of 1812 dragged on for two and a half years, with fighting in the Great Lakes region and on the eastern American seaboard, and ended in an unsatisfying draw. And in Europe itself, the cycle of violence spun completely out of control.

THE RUSSIAN CAMPAIGN

Despite Napoleon's stated desire for peace, France and its enemies could still not manage to acknowledge one another's legitimacy. Napoleon's men still tended to see the allied powers as the decrepit remains of Old Regime Europe, hobbled by religious superstition, unjust privilege, and blind obedience to tradition. The allies still tended to see Napoleon as a usurper, an ogre, and even the Antichrist, in a judgment formally pronounced by the Russian Orthodox Church. Together with the emperor's ambition and the inherent instability of the Continental System, these factors not only kept the wars going but led them to escalate. In 1800, at the battle of Marengo, roughly 60,000 soldiers had taken part in the fighting. Five years later, at Austerlitz, the number had grown to nearly 165,000. Four years after that, at Wagram, the largest battle yet seen in the gunpowder age since its start in the fifteenth century, some 300,000 men took part, with 80,000 of them dead and wounded. But such escalation could not continue indefinitely without pushing one side

Burning of Moscow In 1812, a German engraver made this dramatic image of smoke and flames lighting up the sky as the entire city of Moscow burns. A scattered band of French soldiers watches from the road.

THE RETREAT FROM RUSSIA

Napoleon's 1812 invasion of Russia was a massive undertaking, drawing soldiers from across his vast empire. One such soldier was Adrien Bourgogne, a sergeant in the elite Imperial Guard. Born into a merchant family in northern France, by the time of the invasion of Russia he was already a battle-hardened veteran who had served in Austria, Spain, and Portugal. Bourgogne's memoirs (ca. 1840s) of the retreat from Moscow captured both the wretched suffering and the fierce dedication of the Grand Army. In this excerpt, he recounts how under constant Russian harassment, soldiers starved and froze to death. Yet despite the brutal conditions, he also conveys the common soldier's proud sense of loyalty to Napoleon.

We were just then packed very closely together near a wood, and had a long time to wait before we could resume our march, as the road was narrow. As several of us sat together beating with our feet to keep warm, and talking of the fearful hunger we felt, all at once I became aware of the smell of warm bread. I turned round and behind me saw a man wrapped in a great fur cape, from which came the smell I had noticed. I spoke to him at once, saying, "Sir, you have some bread; you must sell it to me."… With one hand I seized the cake, while with the other I gave him five francs. But hardly had I the cake in my hand, when my companions threw themselves on it like madmen, and tore it from me. I only had the little bit I held between my thumb and two first fingers….

During this half-hour several men had lain down and died; many more had fallen in the column while marching. Our ranks were getting thinned already, and this was only the very beginning of our troubles. Whenever we stopped to eat hastily, the horses left behind were bled. The blood was caught in a saucepan, cooked, and eaten. But often we were forced to eat it before there was time to cook it. Either the order for departure was given, or the Russians were upon us. In the latter case we did not take much notice. I have sometimes seen men eating calmly, while others fired at the Russians to keep them off. But when the order was imperative and we were obliged to go, the saucepan was carried with us, and each man, as he marched, dipped his hands in and took what

he wanted; his face in consequence became smeared with blood.…

Those who went through this lamentable but glorious campaign proved, as the Emperor said, that they must have been made of iron to bear so many privations and so much misery; this was surely the very greatest test to which men were ever exposed.

QUESTIONS FOR ANALYSIS

1. What were conditions like for solders during Napoleon's retreat from Russia?
2. What does the excerpt reveal about the relationships among the soldiers?
3. Why does Bourgogne, despite the hardships he suffered, describe the Russian campaign as "glorious"?

Source: Adrien Bourgogne, *Memoirs of Sergeant Bourgogne, 1812–1813*, ed. Paul Cottin (New York: 1899), pp. 67–68, 351.

or another to collapse. In 1812, the collapse began with Napoleon's decision to invade Russia.

For Napoleon, there seemed to be good reasons to take this step. To begin with, Tsar Alexander had become a highly unreliable ally, resisting the Continental System and trying to assert new influence over central Europe. In 1809 he also seized Finland from Sweden—it would remain under Russian rule for more than a century. More broadly, Russia remained the only power with a sufficiently large army to challenge French domination over continental Europe. And Napoleon had already shown, in 1805–7, that

he could beat the Russians. Therefore, in June 1812 the French army of 650,000 men—including the young Jakob Walter, whom we met earlier—assembled on Russia's western frontier. Moscow lay some 600 miles to the east. There followed the epic disaster captured by the great Russian novelist Leo Tolstoy (1828–1910), who would later write in *War and Peace*, set in Russia during the Napoleonic era: "Assuming that Napoleon's object was to destroy his own army, the most expert strategist could hardly conceive of any other series of actions which would so completely and infallibly have accomplished that purpose."

In France, the rapidly rising human costs of the war strengthened discontent with Napoleon and his military adventures. Desertion and draft avoidance rose precipitously. During the Russian campaign, a general attempted a coup against Napoleon, which was quickly crushed. The liberal French writer Benjamin Constant offered a searching evaluation of Napoleon. Constant insisted that the emperor's "spirit of conquest," reminiscent of Alexander the Great and Julius Caesar, had no place in a modern, commercial world:

> In some ages of history, war was in the nature of man.... But the modern world is, in this regard, the opposite of the ancient world.... We have reached the age of commerce, which must necessarily replace the age of war ... war has lost both its utility and its charm.

Constant's anger, however, did not keep him from succumbing to Napoleon's charm and bribery a few years later and becoming one of the emperor's advisers.

Despite the scale of the Russian disaster, Napoleon's efficient conscription machine replenished his armies with appalling speed, quickly putting over 200,000 new French soldiers in uniform, although many were nearly past fighting age. It could not so easily replace the thousands of artillery pieces his men left behind in the Russian snows, or the horses—which remained key to any military operation in the period. Nor did fresh, ill-trained conscripts compare with the seasoned, capable soldiers who had died during the campaign. And at the other end of Europe, the "Spanish ulcer" continued to pin down hundreds of thousands of men who might have otherwise served Napoleon elsewhere. Still, by the spring of 1813 Napoleon again commanded a formidable fighting force and seemed poised, if not to reverse his recent losses, at least to force the allied powers to a draw. But could he keep his own coalition together? Before invading Russia, he had been able to count on the support of Austria, which he had defeated time after time, and Prussia, which he had crushed in 1806. Now both wavered.

GERMAN NATIONAL RESISTANCE

Even as Austria and Prussia hesitated, an influential group of German intellectuals were actively pushing for a break with France in the name of a powerful new idea: the unification of the multiple German-speaking states of central Europe.

THE ORIGINS OF ROMANTICISM As early as the 1770s, German writers like Johann Wolfgang von Goethe and Johann Gottfried Herder had begun to challenge the powerful Enlightenment idea that human societies differed from one another principally in the progress they had made along a scale that led from "savagery" to "civilization," with all savage peoples, and all civilized peoples—that is, those of western Europe—essentially alike. To the contrary, Goethe and Herder argued, peoples such as the Germans and the French had different spirits, which found expression in everything from the folktales told around their peasant hearths to the architecture of their greatest buildings. These writers advocated a return to nature, to the simplicity of the common people, and, as many of the Enlightenment authors had also urged, to sentiment. Out of these ideas would come the artistic, musical, and literary movement known as **romanticism**. Out of them would also come powerful new ways of inspiring devotion to that great abstraction that the French Revolution had already placed at the heart of European politics: the "nation." Napoleon himself broke with French revolutionary nationalism in his attempt to forge a multinational European empire. The same project, however, provoked the rise of explicitly nationalist feeling elsewhere, against him.

True, many of the German romantics initially swooned over Napoleon himself, seeing in him an elemental force of nature. Ludwig van Beethoven (1770–1827), greatest of romantic composers and an admirer of the French Revolution, initially wrote his Third Symphony to praise Napoleon, but he angrily changed his mind after the first consul crowned himself emperor. In 1808, Goethe and Napoleon met and exchanged fulsome compliments. But by 1812, to many onlookers Napoleon seemed less a force than a freak of nature: bloated, rapacious, and deadly. And the German intellectuals increasingly condemned him, while calling for all Germans to unite and forge a national spirit in opposition to him. The playwright Heinrich von Kleist (1777–1811), a veteran of the Prussian army, caused a sensation with a play in honor of the Germanic tribesmen who had risen up against the Roman emperor Augustus—its contemporary message was clear. The poet and historian Ernst Moritz Arndt (1769–1860) called for a single German fatherland, united by its common language, while preaching "hatred against the French forever.... This hatred glows as the religion of the German people."

PRUSSIA AND AUSTRIA SWITCH SIDES These ideas, it should be emphasized, had very limited resonance in German society as a whole. They did not spur peasants

Klemens von Metternich
A nineteenth-century portrait of Metternich shows the statesman richly adorned with medals and honors.

to rise from the plow in the name of the Fatherland. Nor did they prompt German princes to lay aside their thrones so as to forge a larger German nation. But they did have a great influence among well-educated young men, including a large portion of the Prussian officer corps. Emblematic in this regard was the young officer Carl von Clausewitz (1780–1831), the grandson of a theologian who began his military service in 1792, at age twelve, and spent two years as a prisoner of war in France following the terrible Prussian defeat of 1806. An enthusiastic supporter of the Prussian reforms introduced after this defeat, he could not bear serving in a diminished Prussian army subservient to France, and instead offered his services to Russia. In the last days of 1812, he helped negotiate an agreement under which a Prussian general commanding 30,000 men formally switched sides from France to Russia. Although Frederick William angrily denounced them as traitors, more and more officers followed their example, and pressure steadily built. Finally, in March 1813, Prussia renounced its alliance with Napoleon and entered the growing allied coalition against him.

Austria did not initially follow suit. After having sent a token force to join in the Russian campaign, it had subsequently taken its distance from France, but not so far as to enter the coalition against it. The key figure directing its diplomacy at this point was the Austrian foreign minister, Klemens Lothar von Metternich (1773–1859). A brilliant, vain man, he was also an incomparably skillful negotiator. Through early 1813, he still hoped for a peaceful settlement of the Napoleonic Wars. His hopes rose when Napoleon narrowly beat combined Russian-Prussian forces in two battles in Germany in May and then agreed to an armistice. Napoleon himself met with Metternich in June and agreed to a peace conference the next month. But the resulting discussions never came close to succeeding. Napoleon still hoped to divide the allies, while they—particularly the British—distrusted him too much to offer serious terms. Furthermore, they used the armistice to build up their own forces. In August the negotiations collapsed, and Austria, seeing itself with no choice, declared war on France in its turn.

THE BATTLE FOR GERMANY With this large coalition in place, Germany quickly became the theater of the largest-scale warfare it had seen since the Thirty Years'

War of the seventeenth century. Austria, and to a greater extent Prussia, made serious attempts to imitate French conscription methods and draft all available young men. In April 1813, Frederick William ordered all adult males under age sixty to serve in a Prussian Home Army and, taking inspiration from the Spanish guerrillas, encouraged "every citizen…to harm the enemy using all available means." In fact, Germany saw very little guerrilla activity, nor did the draftees add significantly to Prussia's military capacity. Nonetheless, the coalition forces were now benefiting from the spirit of patriotic enthusiasm that previously had mainly bolstered the French revolutionaries. And in October 1813, it helped carry them to victory in the mammoth "Battle of the Nations" at Leipzig, in central Germany. More than 500,000 soldiers took part, with 150,000 of them killed or wounded. And despite Napoleon's best efforts, it ended in a decisive French defeat.

THE BATTLE FOR FRANCE AND NAPOLEON'S FALL

Scenting victory, the coalition decided that it would settle for nothing less than the complete defeat of Napoleon's regime. As French forces fell back westward across the Rhine, a combined force of Russians, Prussians, and Austrians pushed the fighting onto French soil for the first time since the early 1790s. Meanwhile, as Napoleon desperately pulled men out of Spain, his brother's regime there collapsed. On June 21, 1813, Lord Wellington crushed the French at the battle of Vitoria in Spain. Joseph Bonaparte himself barely escaped back to France, while his carriages, loaded with Spanish gold, silver, and jewelry, were abandoned to whooping British redcoats. Seeing their rapacious behavior, Wellington denounced his own men in a letter as "the scum of the earth." By 1814, a combined British, Spanish and Portuguese army had pushed over the Pyrenees to invade France from the south, while the Bourbon king Fernando reclaimed his father's throne in Madrid. In the spring of 1814, Napoleon fought a brilliant campaign in eastern France, recapturing something of his old élan, with the help of soldiers desperate to protect their own homeland. But the combined forces of Russia, Prussia, Austria, and Britain simply proved too powerful for him. The fall of the empire appeared certain. But what would follow it?

TALLEYRAND At this point, a figure emerged who, along with Metternich, would prove crucial in determining the

EUROPEAN ATTITUDES TOWARD NAPOLEON

Napoleon's consolidation of many aspects of the French Revolution, along with his extensive military conquests, reshaped European society so profoundly that his influence became a matter of contentious debate among his contemporaries. For many observers, his Napoleonic Code, which established that all men were subject to a single legal order (women were subject to a plethora of civil disabilities), was an important step toward civil liberty and equality. Some saw his continued presence on the battlefield as a sign of bravery and self-sacrifice that brought glory to all who followed him. Yet others reviled Napoleon as a conqueror, usurper, and tyrant who had destroyed centuries-old traditions and practices. Napoleon would remain a polarizing figure throughout the nineteenth century: a tireless, courageous leader to some, and an iron-fisted, dangerous egoist to others.

William Cobbett, from the *Political Register*, January 16, 1814

A radical British journalist, Cobbett argued in this edition of his weekly newspaper for Napoleon's suitability as ruler for France.

Napoleon has many qualities…calculated to make him an object of respect with the people. Upon all occasions he shares the toils and the dangers of his armies. His attention to public business is almost incessant. He is sober. His associates…are men famed for their talents… for their wisdom, for their application to business. His hours of recreation are not spent at the gaming table, but in the manly exercises of the field. And yet this is the man whom our news-writers denominate a *monster*, though he is the son-in-law of our august ally, the Emperor of Austria!…

If indeed, Napoleon were a half-mad tyrant; if he were a sort of malignant idiot, who, while he kept his own worthless carcass safe…made it his sport to send forth armies to butcher or to be butchered; if he were a drunkard, a sot, a gambler, a swindler, a man, who, if in common life, would be kicked out of every hotel in Paris; if he were an emaciated creature, incapable of any sort of exertion bodily or mental…*then* might we *justly* accuse the people of France of *baseness* in patiently submitting to his sway.… But, if Napoleon be none of this; if he be *precisely the contrary* of the imaginary character that I have drawn, with what justice do we, or some of us, revile the people of France…for submitting to be ruled by him?

Madame de Rémusat, from *Memoirs*

Madame de Rémusat was a member of Napoleon's imperial court, a lady in waiting to Empress Josephine, and a noted diarist. In her memoirs (1802–8), she weighed Napoleon's capacity as a leader and criticized what she perceived as his self-centered ambition.

His [Napoleon's] reception by the troops was nothing short of rapturous. It was well worth seeing how he talked to the soldiers—how he questioned them one after the other respecting their campaigns or their wounds; taking particular interest in men who had accompanied him to Egypt.…He spoke to the subalterns in a tone of good fellowship, which delighted them all, as he reminded them of their common feats of arms.…Afterward… when he addressed his soldiers before leading them into battle, it was as a perpetually renewed posterity, to which the preceding and destroyed army had bequeathed its glory. But even this somber style of encouragement availed for a long time with a nation which believed itself to be fulfilling its destiny while sending its sons year after year to die for Bonaparte.…

If Bonaparte, who was so successful in conciliating individuals, had but gone a step further, and, instead of governing by force alone, had yielded to the reaction which longed for repose; if, now, that he had conquered the present moment, he had made himself master of the future, by creating durable institutions independent of his own caprice—there is little doubt but that his victory over our recollections, our prejudices, and our regrets would have been as lasting as it was remarkable. But it must be confessed that liberty, true liberty, was wanting everywhere; and the fault of the nation consisted in not perceiving this in time. As I have said before, the Emperor improved finances and encouraged trade, science and art; merit was rewarded in every class; but all this was spoiled by the stamp of slavery. Being resolved on ruling everything himself, and for his own advantage, he always put himself forwards as the ultimate aim. It is said that on starting for the first campaign in Italy, he told a friend who was editor of a newspaper: "Recollect in your accounts of our victories to speak of *me*, and always of *me*. Do you understand?" This "*me*" was the ceaseless cry of purely egotistical ambition.

QUESTIONS FOR ANALYSIS

1. Why does Cobbett support Napoleon's rule?
2. In Madame de Rémusat's estimation, what was Napoleon's great strength and his principal flaw?
3. What do Cobbett and Rémusat see as the French people's role in determining the nation's government?

Sources: William Cobbett, *Political Register*, Vol. XXV, from January to June (London: 1814), pp. 94–96; Madame de Rémusat, *Memoirs of Madame de Rémusat*, trans. Cashel Hoey and John Lillie (New York: 1880), pp. 86–87, 363–64.

Charles-Maurice de Talleyrand An early nineteenth-century engraving of Talleyrand as foreign minister, wearing splendid robes of state and imperial insignia.

shape of post-Napoleonic Europe. **Charles-Maurice de Talleyrand** (1754–1838) was a man whose subtlety, irony, and world-weary cynicism made him a perfect contrast to Napoleon Bonaparte. Born to great wealth and high rank before the Revolution, he had a club foot that kept him from his family's usual career of military service. Instead, he headed into the priesthood, where his connections, charm, and raw intelligence brought him to a key position—representative of the entire French clergy to the crown—by age twenty-six and earned him a bishopric at thirty-five. Siding with the Revolution, he first abandoned the Church and then abandoned France itself in 1792 when failure to keep up with the pace of political radicalization put his life in danger. He traveled in the United States, speculated on land in Pennsylvania and Ohio, and then returned home under the less radical Directorial regime of 1795–99, where his skills earned him the position of foreign minister. He quickly attached himself to Napoleon, who kept him in office after his 1799 coup.

Crafty and sophisticated, Talleyrand managed French diplomacy ably and was rewarded with huge wealth and an Italian principality. But even as Napoleon grew more ambitious, Talleyrand turned more cautious and warned that permanent expansion would lead France to disaster. He began private discussions with Tsar Alexander and with Metternich on how to control Napoleon, and these gradually developed into a conspiracy to ease the French emperor off his throne. When Napoleon discovered the plot in 1808, he banished Talleyrand, whom he cursed to his face as excrement "in a silk stocking"; but he could not bring himself to have the man executed, and allowed Talleyrand to return to Paris a few years later as a private citizen.

With the allied armies approaching Paris in 1814, Talleyrand, who had retained the trust of the allies, again began to scheme. For weeks, the situation remained chaotic as the allies explored different plans, including the abdication of Napoleon in favor of his young son, the king of Rome. But Talleyrand urged a different outcome. Ever since the heir to Louis XVI had died in prison in 1795, the executed king's younger brother had claimed the French throne as Louis XVIII. Although the British had given

him refuge and token support, most of the world had forgotten him. But as Napoleon's regime crumbled, the idea of a Bourbon restoration gained support in France. After all, it would be far more difficult for the allies to impose harsh terms on a Bourbon government that they recognized as legitimate, and an ally, than on a Bonapartist one that they considered the work of a dictatorial usurper. In southwestern France, a pro-Bourbon group called the "Knights of the Faith" engineered demonstrations in favor of Louis XVIII that impressed the advancing British. Talleyrand, meanwhile, worked to convince Metternich and Tsar Alexander of the Bourbons' merits, presenting their return to the throne as the beginning of a new age of stability in European politics.

THE BOURBON RESTORATION In the spring of 1814, the end appeared to come. Napoleon made a half-hearted attempt at suicide, taking a poison that had lost its potency. He survived and had to endure the humiliation of defeat, formally agreeing to abdicate. The Senate that had once done his bidding declared his reign at an end and welcomed the portly, faintly comical figure of Louis XVIII (1755–1824), who proceeded to "grant" a new constitution to the country that had rejected his family twenty-two years before. It seemed that French history had turned full circle—but in fact the new constitution represented anything but a return to the Old Regime. The new king knew perfectly well that the French would never accord the Church, the nobility, and the monarchy their old powers and privileges. As a result, France under the Bourbon Restoration looked very much like a compromise that retained many of the features of the Republic and Empire. The authority of the monarch was restrained by a legislature, although one elected by a tiny minority of wealthy male property-holders. The new regime also maintained the division of the country into departments, Napoleon's system of centralization, and his law code. It preserved the treaty with the Vatican that acknowledged Catholicism as the country's leading religion and gave the state a broad degree of control over religious life.

THE CONGRESS OF VIENNA (1814–1815)

Meanwhile, the allies prepared a peace settlement that, as Talleyrand had hoped, was relatively favorable to the loser. By the spring of 1814, the four major allied

Napoleon in Exile An 1814 British cartoon represents Elba as a tiny rock outcropping within sight of a European coast guarded against Napoleon's return. The former emperor sobs as crows and bats fly over his head, presumably waiting for his death.

powers—Britain, Austria, Russia, and Prussia—had agreed on the central points. France would have to surrender the major territorial conquests of the previous two decades, including Belgium (which would be joined to Holland in a new kingdom of the United Netherlands) and its annexations in northern and central Italy. Napoleon's satellite kingdoms such as Naples would revert to their original rulers, except for the quasi-independent duchy of Warsaw, most of which would become the autonomous "Congress Kingdom of Poland" under Russian rule. Although the allies did not want to restore the old Holy Roman Empire, they did plan for a loose German Confederation to take its place. But France would keep defensible borders and would not have to pay large reparations.

As for Napoleon himself, the allies agreed not to put him on trial. Instead, they gave him the tiny Italian island of Elba, within sight of his native Corsica, for a place of exile. He would even keep the title of emperor. To be sure, sending the man who had ruled most of Europe to reign over a flyspeck of territory had a measure of cruelty to it, and the English newspapers mercilessly quipped that in his new home Napoleon would not have much "Elba room." But all in all, it seemed that after the torrent of

blood spilled over the previous twenty-two years, the Napoleonic empire was coming to a surprisingly peaceful end.

THE CONCERT OF EUROPE

In the fall of 1814, the major powers gathered for a peace conference in the Austrian capital that would become known as the **Congress of Vienna**. In several ways, the Congress marked a break from earlier peace conferences, such as the one held in Westphalia in 1648. Rather than sending ambassadors, the major powers' foreign ministers came themselves, accompanied by large retinues of assistants. It was a dazzling social occasion for the city. Metternich and Wellington took part, and Tsar Alexander himself represented Russia. The participants had as their ambition not simply to finalize their earlier agreements but to settle *all* outstanding European conflicts, put in place a permanent peace settlement for the Continent, and prevent anything like the slaughter of the previous twenty years from ever repeating itself. The young tsar in particular dreamed of putting an end to warfare forever—much the same dream that had beguiled so many men and women of the Enlightenment—and joining all European states together into a grand Christian coalition. Metternich and Viscount Castlereagh (1769–1822), the British

Congress of Vienna An Austrian illustration from the early nineteenth century shows representatives of the major European powers poring over a map and globe as they establish new borders and seek to maintain the balance of power.

Congress of Vienna, 1815 The allied powers attempted to restore pre-French Revolution borders, seeking a balance of power that would maintain peace and stability. France's territorial conquests were either made into new kingdoms, like the United Netherlands, or given to other powers—like the parts of northern Italy ceded to Austria, or the Congress Kingdom of Poland, placed under Russian rule.

foreign secretary, had considerably less lofty visions but still hoped to devise a workable, long-lasting peace.

Recognizing that such a settlement could not succeed without active French support, the four allied powers quickly allowed France, in the person of Talleyrand, to join them at the Congress. (A grateful Louis XVIII had yet again appointed Talleyrand as foreign minister.) Many other rulers and foreign ministers from across Europe came to Vienna as well. Most important, the powers quickly came to realize that a durable settlement required the establishment of enforcement mechanisms. Although they did not specify exact mechanisms, they did agree to consult on disputes that might arise in the future and impose solutions, by force if necessary, before crises could spin out of control. This system would soon come to

be known as the "**Concert of Europe.**" During meetings that lasted for some nine months, the powers arbitrated disputes over borders throughout Europe, notably in the former territory of Poland-Lithuania, Italy, and Scandinavia. Russia was confirmed in its possession of Finland, which it had seized from Sweden in 1809.

The Congress of Vienna did succeed in laying the groundwork for the longest period of relative peace in European history before 1945. For forty years, although numerous small conflicts did arise, the major powers did not fight one another. And in the Crimean War of 1854–56, the operations would remain on a far more limited scale than during the Napoleonic Wars and were confined to a small region of the Russian Empire. Not until the Franco-Prussian War of 1870–71 would major European armies collide, in the western European heartland, with anything like the fury of the wars of 1792–1815, and even then the conflict was over in a matter of months. Only in 1914 would total war return to Europe.

THE HUNDRED DAYS

But the story of Napoleon Bonaparte did not come to an end without one great, last, surprising twist. At the end of February 1815, with the Congress of Vienna still in session, the emperor escaped from Elba and landed on France's Mediterranean coast with a handful of loyal supporters. The inhabitants of the villages where he first stopped found it almost impossible to believe that this balding, paunchy man in a bedraggled uniform was truly the emperor who had led France's armies across Europe. But once convinced of Napoleon's true identity, crowds quickly came to cheer him on. Disaffection with the new regime of Louis XVIII already ran high. The new Bourbon king not only lacked charisma but also seemed incapable of repairing the massive economic woes caused by the wars. Units of the French army disobeyed orders to capture Napoleon and, instead, joined him. On one occasion whose drama Napoleon savored, he stepped out in front of his men, opened his coat to the Royalist soldiers confronting them, and dared the soldiers to shoot (he had already received strong hints that they would not). Rather than do so, they promised to follow him. One field marshal who had declared his loyalty to the new regime initially promised to bring Napoleon back to Paris in a cage but then switched sides yet again. Louis XVIII pledged to die rather than leave Paris but quickly thought better of the idea and fled to Belgium.

Within three weeks of his escape, to the shock and consternation of the allies, Napoleon had returned to Paris amid scenes of frenzied enthusiasm. But could he, this time, remain in power? Although his feat excited admiration in the population, genuine support for Napoleon was fragile and thin. Very few people in France wanted a resumption of the wars, while the remnants of the revolutionary left sought a new Republic, not the return of Empire. In an attempt to gain their support, Napoleon quickly issued an amended constitution, with firm guarantees for freedom

The Hundred Days, 1815

of speech and real power for his previously rubber-stamp legislature. He also insisted that he had no desire to resume his program of conquest. But the allied powers quickly ruled out any idea of compromise, instead declaring Napoleon an outlaw. They began to reassemble their armies, even while continuing with the negotiations at Vienna for a general peace settlement.

This time, Napoleon's fate was decided in little more than three months, giving the bizarre episode the title of "**the Hundred Days.**" Frantically, Napoleon tried to raise a new army and to convert factories to the production of munitions. In June 1815, he marched north into Belgium to meet the allied armies, hoping against hope that a quick, decisive victory might bring them to the negotiating table, or at least divide them sufficiently to increase the chances of his political survival. On June 18, near the small Belgian village of Waterloo, he found himself pitted against a general he had never previously faced: Britain's Wellington, who had led the efforts to defeat him in Spain. Wellington deployed his red-coated infantry in a long firing line at the crucial moment to blast Napoleon's elite Imperial Guard. The timely appearance of Prussian forces helped win the day for the allies. The defeated French streamed back toward Paris, and after another brief period of confusion, Napoleon surrendered.

The allies did not prove as lenient in 1815 as in 1814. They quickly dispatched the emperor into exile on the tiny island of Saint Helena, in the South Atlantic, as a prisoner under the guard of the British army, with only a handful of loyal retainers by his side. There, in 1821 he died, probably of stomach cancer. In the hastily revised peace settlement, France lost additional small slices of territory and had additional reparations imposed upon it. Louis XVIII returned for a second time to Paris, where the exhausted population greeted him with muted acceptance. But because the episode had taken so little time, the Vienna peace settlement survived the shock.

POST-NAPOLEONIC EUROPE

At first glance, it might seem as if the new Europe of 1815 resembled nothing so much as the old Europe of 1788.

Nearly every European state remained a monarchy, and in most cases the same family sat on the throne as thirty years before. The most important exception was Sweden, where in 1809 the parliament had tried to placate Napoleon by appointing his marshal Jean-Baptiste Bernadotte to the throne (Bernadotte's descendants sit on the Swedish throne to this day). The overall apparent continuity, however, masked a break with the past that was almost as radical as the one that had occurred in 1789.

ABSORBING THE CHANGES

The French author François-René de Chateaubriand (1768–1848) did not exaggerate much when he commented, soon after 1815, about the period just ended, that "this quarter of a century contained many centuries." Just as Napoleon's glittery coronation as emperor in 1804 had concealed the continuing effects of the French Revolution, so too did the apparent restoration of the old order after his defeat. In fact, the Revolution had wrought immense changes even on those states that explicitly defined their policies *against* it. Most important, in the Europe of 1815 few European sovereigns still seriously claimed to rule by divine right. To one extent or another, they now mostly admitted the principle of the sovereignty of the nation. Even France's Louis XVIII, who claimed that he had only "granted" a constitution to the country, did not challenge the idea that an elected legislature would henceforth express the national will and make laws. The most important exception to this broad European rule was Russia, where Tsar Alexander had largely abandoned his earlier inclination toward reform. After 1815, he not only continued to claim absolute authority on the basis of divine ordination but also refused to allow for the possibility of an elected parliament. He also defended the system of serfdom that continued to keep the majority of the peasantry in a condition of effective slavery. Yet even in Russia, as we will see, a liberal opposition was beginning to take shape.

A NEW POLITICS

The very notion of a "**liberal**" opposition signified that throughout Europe political life as a whole was taking on a new shape, centered on the division between liberal and conservative movements. Before 1789, the very terms "liberal" and "**conservative**" had been largely unknown and

would have poorly described the politics of most European countries. But after 1815, starting in Britain and France, "liberal" became a common term, used to signify a desire for extending democratic representation to as large a swathe of the population as possible; defending the revolutionary principle of human rights; and breaking down the cumbersome systems of state-chartered corporate bodies that had previously characterized most European economies. At the same time, the term "conservative" came to signify an opposition to liberal and revolutionary politics. Some conservatives, following the great British political thinker Edmund Burke, venerated tradition for the stability and purpose it supposedly brought to society. Others did so in the name of Christian faith. In Britain, the pro-monarchical Tory Party of William Pitt would soon become known as the Conservative Party, a name it holds to this day.

Although the "liberal" agenda remained very far from fulfilled, a much greater degree of actual liberty prevailed in Europe in 1815 than in 1789. Throughout Germany and Italy, the French and their local allies had largely abolished the old guild systems that controlled artisanal work and trade. In most cases, these systems did not return in anything like their previous form. The French had also instituted religious freedom, and while several states (notably Spain) in 1815 moved to reestablish the hegemony of their traditional churches, most members of religious minorities faced fewer restrictions than before. In Germany and Italy, where the French tore down the walls of Jewish ghettos, anti-Semitism was restrained, at least for the time being. (By contrast, the Jews in the expanded Russian Empire faced continuing legal hardships.) In most European states, freedom of speech after 1815 was still highly restricted by modern standards, with Britain and the Netherlands being the main exceptions. But vigorous newspaper cultures were taking hold throughout nearly all of western and central Europe. In France, where Napoleon had shut down all but four national newspapers, a lively and combative press sprang back into operation upon his defeat.

THE SURVIVAL OF REVOLUTIONARY RADICALISM

As Alexis de Tocqueville astutely observed of the French Revolution, nothing stimulates demands for change like the beginnings of change, especially when governments then act to frustrate it. The years immediately after 1815, even while seeing both the triumph of a revitalized monarchical order in Europe and the subtle penetration of many French revolutionary values, also saw the birth of new, radical, and often nationalist revolutionary movements.

In Italy, these movements took the form of secret societies known as the **Carbonari** ("charcoal-burners"), organized into lodges with elaborate initiation rituals on the model of the freemasons, and originally formed to resist Napoleonic rule. After 1815, however, they quickly began to conspire against the restored regimes, particularly of the Austrian Empire in northern Italy and the Bourbon kingdom of the Two Sicilies (the name now taken by the kingdom of Naples) in the south. The Carbonari sought the establishment of a revolutionary democracy and a unified Italy. In France as well, pro-revolutionary sentiment remained strong, although mixed in with nostalgia for Napoleon. It deeply frightened the police, who diligently recorded even its smallest and most bizarre manifestations (including the appearance of Napoleon's

Carbonari Members of a Carbonari group crowd into a windowless room lit by a single lamp to listen to a speaker in this 1820 illustration. Some of the men read books in the low light, emphasizing the clandestine intellectual culture that accompanied the movement.

image in packs of cards, and a family who claimed to have seen his face on the surface of a flattened egg). In 1820, a radical artisan hoping for the overthrow of the monarchy fatally stabbed the duke of Berry, second in line to the throne. In Greece, where the Ottoman Turks had ruled since the fifteenth century, a radical nationalist movement began to take shape, led by a secret society of exiled Greeks founded in 1814 on the model of the Carbonari.

REFORM AND REPRESSION IN BRITAIN Vigorous radical movements also took shape in Britain. During the French Revolutionary and Napoleonic wars, a surge of popular patriotism curtailed much of the agitation for reform that had been developing in the 1760s and 1770s around such figures as John Wilkes. Some half a million men volunteered for military service in the event of a French invasion and underwent military training. Yet a number of notable radicals continued to press for an extension of the vote to all adult males and for a reform of the election system, which excluded millions of Britons from the suffrage and which, in many cases, left the choice of members of parliaments up to a handful of powerful local grandees. In 1815 a leading radical, the journalist William Cobbett, who had once been known for his anti-Jacobinism, even praised the hated Napoleon, saying: "Thy fame still lives in every Freeman's heart." Enough Britons shared Cobbett's views that when the ship bearing Napoleon to Saint Helena briefly stopped in Plymouth, the government rushed to move it out of British territorial waters, lest a sympathetic magistrate attempt to order the former emperor's release. Although in 1799 the government had outlawed the so-called corresponding societies—which had formed seven years earlier to press for parliamentary reform—their point of view was still regularly heard in the robust radical press.

On August 16, 1819, radical agitation and government repression collided violently in the northern English city of Manchester, which was then just beginning to change under the impact of industrialization. A crowd of some 60,000 to 80,000, mostly working people but well dressed and peaceful, gathered in St. Peter's Fields to demonstrate for parliamentary reform and the repeal of the so-called corn laws, which kept the price of cereals artificially high by restricting foreign imports. Local magistrates, fearing a riot, ordered out hundreds of police, infantry, and cavalrymen. When the crowd apparently resisted orders to disperse, the cavalrymen attacked, injuring hundreds and killing eleven. The episode immediately became known as

Peterloo Massacre The great British illustrator George Cruikshank (1792–1878) made this etching of cavalry, with swords drawn, trampling demonstrators at St. Peter's Fields. The illustration was addressed to a radical member of Parliament, urging him to condemn the attack.

the "**Peterloo Massacre**" and further galvanized British reformers, as we will soon see.

CONCLUSION

In a poem of savage beauty titled "England in 1819," inspired by the tragedy in Manchester, Percy Bysshe Shelley (1792–1822) memorialized "a people starved and stabbed in the untilled field" at the behest of

> Rulers who neither see nor feel nor know,
> But leechlike to their fainting country cling
> Till they drop, blind in blood, without a blow....

But Shelley also offered hope that from the graves of Peterloo and the desperate attempts of Britain's elites to hold on to their privileges, a "glorious Phantom" of hope might yet "burst, to illumine our tempestuous day."

The years that would follow 1819 indeed saw many such phantoms bursting forth in Europe. These movements inherited the passions of the Napoleonic years but did not equal the wars in their ferocity. The massive tide of organized violence that had reached its height in 1812 steadily receded. Napoleon Bonaparte himself, for all the enormous disruption he had caused, quickly faded into a faintly comic figure, mocked for his pretentious poses and allegedly small stature (actually, he was of average height). He became known as the man whose identity was most often claimed by the inmates of insane asylums. Yet his enormous impact on virtually every aspect of European society, politics, and culture could not be denied—it was greater than that of any other single individual of the eighteenth or nineteenth centuries. As his enemies attempted to impose newer, stricter forms of order on the Continent, new forms of resistance were germinating, thanks in large part to stunningly rapid economic change. It is to those that we now turn.

KEY TERMS

Civil Code (p. 574)

Austerlitz (p. 577)

treaties of Tilsit (p. 578)

Continental System (p. 579)

Peninsular War (p. 581)

guerrilla warfare (p. 581)

Luddites (p. 586)

romanticism (p. 589)

Charles-Maurice de Talleyrand (p. 592)

Congress of Vienna (p. 593)

Concert of Europe (p. 594)

the Hundred Days (p. 595)

liberalism (p. 596)

conservatism (p. 596)

Carbonari (p. 597)

Peterloo Massacre (p. 598)

REVIEW QUESTIONS

1. During his first five years in power, how did Napoleon restore French influence and prestige in Europe?

2. What were Napoleon's principal domestic accomplishments from 1799 to 1804?

3. What provoked resistance to French rule in Italy and Spain?

4. How did Napoleon design his capital and use the arts to reflect his ambition of creating a world empire?

5. In what ways did European society become more militarized during the Napoleonic age?

6. Why did Britain's economy outperform other European countries' economies during the Napoleonic age?

7. How did the Russian campaign contribute to Napoleon's downfall?

8. What led Prussia and Austria to break their alliance with France?

9. What were the principal elements of the agreement reached at the Congress of Vienna?

10. What major changes had taken place in European society and politics by 1815?

CORE OBJECTIVES

After reading this chapter, you should have a solid understanding of the following core objectives. To strengthen your grasp of the core objectives, use the resources on the Student Site for The West.

- Explain how Napoleon created his European empire.
- Evaluate the factors that undermined the stability of the Napoleonic order.
- Analyze the Napoleonic empire at its height.
- Assess the downfall of Napoleon and his empire.
- Describe the political order that emerged from Napoleon's defeat.

 GO TO inQuizitive TO SEE WHAT YOU'VE LEARNED—AND LEARN WHAT YOU'VE MISSED—WITH PERSONALIZED FEEDBACK ALONG THE WAY.

CHRONOLOGY

1833
Unrest in Spain
following
Fernando VII's
death

1831
Mazzini founds
Young Italy movement

1833
Abolition of
slavery in
British Empire

1810s–1820s
Latin American colonies
seek independence

September 27, 1825
First commercial
railroad opens in England

1828–1829
Russo-Turkish War

July 1830
July Revolution
in France

1819
First transatlantic
steamship crossing

December 1825
Decembrist revolt
against Nikolai I

1830
France begins
colonization of Algeria

1830–1832
Polish revolt against Russia

Early 1830s
Cholera epidemic
across Europe

1832
Greece gains
independence

1832
Reform Bill
in Britain

1835, 1840
Tocqueville publishes
Democracy in America

18

Acceleration

THE AGE OF INDUSTRY

1820–1845

1838–1848
Chartist movement
in Britain

1839–1842
First Opium War

1844
Morse invents telegraph

E arly on the morning of September 27, 1825, several thousand men and women converged on the small town of Brusselton, in northern England, to see an unusual spectacle. The starring role was played by a large, ungainly metal cylinder, resting on four hefty wheels and sporting a thick black funnel on one end. The whole contraption, including a coal-burning furnace, weighed eight tons. As the spectators watched, engineers lit the furnace, which powered a steam engine that turned the wheels. Slowly, the entire machine began to roll along two parallel metal tracks. It pulled thirty-six small wagons loaded with flour, coal, and six hundred passengers, everything together weighing over fifty tons. The spectators later went home, but the engine and wagons continued to roll, reaching a speed of over six miles per hour. On some downhill sections of the track, the speed increased to as much as fifteen miles an hour, panicking passengers, at least one of whom jumped off and badly injured himself. Four hours after leaving Brusselton, the train arrived safely at the port town of Stockton, twenty-four miles down the tracks. The world's first commercial railway had just staged its inaugural trip.

Despite the shock felt by some at the train's occasional high speed, there was nothing particularly new about the technology on view that September morning. Primitive steam

Industrial Innovations A lithograph celebrates the opening of the first railway in Italy, which ran from Naples to Portici, five miles to the south, in 1839. People of all classes watch from a distance, while a crowd on the platform rushes to board the train. The speed and accessibility of train travel completely transformed the lives of people across Europe.

- What were the most significant causes and effects of the Industrial Revolution?
- What were the key elements of middle-class life in this period?
- How was the industrial working class changing in this period?
- What were the major themes of the Romantic movement?
- What broad changes occurred in the politics of the period?
- In what ways was this a period of repression and reform?
- How did the rise of nationalism affect the international order?

engines dated back to more than a century earlier, and James Watt's commercially successful models had come into wide use by the 1770s. As early as 1801, the inventor Richard Trevithick (1771–1833) used a steam engine to power a moving coach he called the Puffing Devil. But Trevithick's invention did not immediately lead to commercial railroads. Despite the popular image of inventors changing the world and striking it rich simply by tinkering at workbenches, technological progress required a great deal more than just individual genius, even in the early nineteenth century. It also required capital—to develop and test prototypes, pay employees, purchase property and material, and build infrastructure. At a time when the average British agricultural laborer earned just £30 per year, the Brusselton–Stockton railway cost some £125,000 to build—tens of millions of today's dollars. The railway's promoters raised the money from wealthy investors who hoped to make a profit by moving coal efficiently from the mines around Brusselton to ships that would deliver it to port cities in Britain and around the world. And technological progress involved politics as well— just to build this first line required two separate acts of the British Parliament, to appropriate land for the train tracks and to charter the company.

The same factors also slowed the initial spread of railways, even after this first line proved successful. Investors were not always easy to find, especially since prominent British engineers were still dismissing as "ridiculous expectations" the idea that trains could ever reach the frighteningly high speed of even twelve miles per hour on an even grade. In 1830, a 35-mile-long railway opened between the emerging British industrial centers of Liverpool and Manchester. But proposals to connect London to the commercial city of Birmingham, some 112 miles away, met with ferocious opposition from landowners who did not want their property taken for tracks, and from road- and canal-builders who saw in the proposed railway a threat to their interests. It took Parliament three years to approve the project. The line itself cost £5,000,000, with construction lasting five years and involving 20,000 workers.

Still, the early experiments eventually spurred an explosion of railway building in Britain. Although in 1835 the country still had only 293 miles of railroad, by 1840 this number had risen to 1,435, and by 1850 to over 6,600. Other countries followed the British example. Russia opened its first passenger railroad in 1837 and had 3,000 miles of track by the mid-1860s. Rail transport became routine for cargo and passengers alike, with millions of people and millions of tons of goods traveling each year on journeys of tens or even hundreds of miles on regular schedules. And they did so at speeds that, as early as 1840, could reach as high as fifty miles per hour.

Historians today tend to dislike the term **Industrial Revolution**. It implies a sudden, violent break in patterns of economic and social activity, as if agricultural societies gave way in just a few years to systems of large-scale industrial production. Instead, historians stress that economic change in the nineteenth century occurred gradually, with a full-fledged industrial system first taking hold only in a few specialized zones. The system required many decades to become a major presence even in the most economically advanced European countries.

Yet we should not discount the immensity of the changes that did follow upon industrialization. The spectators who descended on Brusselton in 1825 knew that they were witnessing a historic event. And by the early 1840s, when it became clear that all corners of the Continent would soon be joined in one gigantic rail network, some farsighted observers already grasped the profound implications for the way human beings understood and experienced the world. Heinrich Heine (1797–1856), a German poet living in France, wrote in 1843: "Even the elementary concepts of time and space have begun to vacillate. Space is killed by the railways. …I feel as if the mountains and forests of all countries are advancing on Paris. Even now, I can smell the German linden trees, the North Sea's breakers are rolling against my door." And even as this transportation revolution disrupted concepts of space, the broader process of industrialization altered patterns of everyday life for people throughout Europe and the conduct of everything from warfare to novel-writing.

And industrialization represented only one form of the radical disorientation and sense of acceleration that Europeans experienced during the years 1820–45. In literature and the arts, the period saw the heyday of the romantic movement, which sought to overturn long-established stylistic practices and unsettle its audiences. In politics, it saw a revival of democratic, even revolutionary, energies that were often met by fierce, violent reaction. It saw the development of new forms of social thought. For the first time, writers and politicians, some radical but some conservative, began to define the most important forms of competition within European states as *social* competition that pitted different parts of society against one another. Meanwhile, with France's conquest of Algeria in 1830, the period saw the start of a new and unsettling phase in the history of European empire, involving the way European states both competed with one another abroad and dealt with non-European peoples.

Historians often isolate these different forms of disorienting change from one another. But the experience of what we now call "modernity" in fact derived in large part from the way they reinforced and interacted with one another. This chapter, therefore, will examine the period 1820–45 as a whole, exploring the parallels between these different, but connected, realms of human existence.

THE INDUSTRIAL REVOLUTION

Of the many disrupting and disorienting changes that occurred in Europe between 1820 and 1845, the most significant, in long-term perspective, were those connected with industrial development. As we have already seen, what historians now call the Industrial Revolution had begun well before 1820. But in these decades it accelerated dramatically, forever changing daily life for a large proportion of Europeans, and setting in motion a process that would eventually do the same for nearly all of the human race.

FIVE FACTORS PROMOTING INDUSTRIAL DEVELOPMENT

The revolution was driven by the same factors we have already seen at work in the eighteenth century. First came coal, whose combustion releases energy initially absorbed from the sun hundreds of millions of years ago by vegetation, and stored in what eventually hardened under pressure into sedimentary rock. When the steam engine made possible the conversion of this energy into mechanical power, humans gained the ability to do far more work, more efficiently, than with muscles alone (whether human or animal) and far more conveniently than with wind or water mills. To take just one example, a textile worker in the 1820s using a steam-driven spindle could produce a hundred times more thread per hour than his or her pre-industrial counterpart had managed. The only alternate fuel at this stage of technological development— charcoal from wood—simply did not exist in sufficient quantities. As a British writer put it in mid-century: "Coal in truth stands not beside, but entirely above, all other commodities. It is the material source of the energy of the country—the universal aid—the factor in everything we do. With coal almost any feat is possible; without it we are thrown back into the laborious poverty of early times."

Second, an engineering culture of constant, competitive innovation not only rewarded inventions but also quickly multiplied their efficiency. The spinning mule, for instance, was invented in 1779 and made possible mechanized cotton production. Then in 1825, the inventor Richard Roberts developed an automatic mule that did not require skilled workers to operate it. By 1837, some 500,000 mules based on this design were in operation in the British Isles. The steam engine itself underwent constant improvement. Richard Trevithick could only create his "Puffing Devil" because he had invented a high-pressure engine that operated with greater efficiency than James Watt's engine of the 1780s.

Financial innovations that made capital easily available for industrial expansion were also crucial. The early nineteenth century saw a rapid expansion of banks that provided loans to companies and helped them sell bonds, and of stock exchanges where shares of ownership could be offered up for sale. The driving force here was so-called railway mania, especially in Britain. By 1847, the total value of British railway shares had risen to some £126,000,000, far outstripping the level of investment in cotton or iron.

A fourth factor, agricultural productivity, also mattered greatly. The eighteenth century, as we have seen, brought a milder climate to Europe, while the destructive effects of war were limited in comparison to previous centuries. Meanwhile, farmers in northwestern Europe developed sophisticated crop rotation techniques, a better use of fertilizer, and the reclamation of marshland and heath previously deemed unsuitable for cultivation. The widespread adoption of potato cultivation helped the rural poor to raise their caloric intake significantly. Overall "yields" of wheat and other cereal crops (the amount produced for a given amount of seed) increased as well. All these trends continued in the decades after 1800, spurring greater agricultural profits, a rapidly rising population, and a larger overall food supply. The profits from these innovations produced capital that could be invested in industry, the rising population made available an industrial workforce, and the food supply ensured that this workforce had enough to eat.

Finally, while industrial capitalism is usually associated with the concept of free markets, the importance of state support must be acknowledged. States protected the rights of inventors with patent systems and helped provide a transportation and communications infrastructure. They projected diplomatic and military power abroad to open up export markets and to protect merchant shipping. The Industrial Revolution proceeded hand in hand with global trade, and it was European states and their armed forces that ensured this trade would be conducted to the advantage of Europeans.

WHY GREAT BRITAIN?

These five factors not only made the Industrial Revolution possible but also determined the place where it would begin: Great Britain. Rich seams of coal were more easily exploitable in Britain than almost anywhere else on earth. Britain's culture of innovation had flourished for centuries—thanks in part to the Protestant minority groups who valued gainful activity but were barred by law from government positions. Britain led the way in financial innovation as well. Between 1836 and 1845, stock exchanges were founded in most major British provincial cities, including Manchester, Liverpool, Birmingham, and

Industrialization in Britain, 1800–1850 By 1850, industrialization had changed the geography of Britain. Coal had been discovered in Wales, Scotland, and central northeast England. Though London remained a population center, workers also flocked to the factories in the booming industrial cities of Manchester, Leeds, and Birmingham, and dockworkers to the port of Liverpool. Railways increasingly linked far-flung parts of the country together, facilitating migration to the cities.

Edinburgh. The enclosure movement in Britain—which continued into the nineteenth century—favored the creation of large, market-oriented farms over small-scale subsistence farming. Already by the 1830s, England was producing three times as much grain as it had in the mid-eighteenth century. And the British state fully recognized the importance of commercial and industrial wealth to the nation's political fortunes, and acted accordingly. British merchant ships could bring raw materials to

Britain, and ship manufactured goods to the rest of the world, because they enjoyed the protection of the world's most formidable navy.

From its earliest years, the Industrial Revolution impacted many different sectors of the European economy. Given the centrality of coal, mining developed rapidly. Between 1800 and 1850, Great Britain's annual coal output increased fivefold. But soon Britain was not alone. By 1850, the Ruhr region of Germany had 300 coal mines, and the industry was expanding rapidly as well in Belgium. Iron had enormous importance as well, being necessary for engines, locomotives, railroad tracks, and bridges strong enough to bear the weight of trains. A series of technological innovations in the last decades of the eighteenth century in Britain allowed for the production of stronger steel at lower cost than in previous times, and production boomed. Annual production, which had stood at only 12,000 metric tons in Britain in 1700, reached 250,000 metric tons soon after 1800, and 2,000,000 by 1850.

COTTON: THE THREAD OF GLOBAL EXCHANGE

But the most important industry, overall, was textiles, and more specifically, cotton. A fabric lighter and more comfortable than wool, sturdier than linen, and easily dyed with bright colors, cotton grew in tropical climates and had long been imported into Europe. But its production had been time consuming and expensive, because of the need to separate seeds from the raw cotton by hand. Then in 1793 a young American inventor named Eli Whitney built a machine—the "cotton gin"—that could do the job faster and more efficiently than human hands could. Once regular Atlantic trade resumed in 1815 with the end of the Napoleonic Wars, cotton production expanded at a dizzying rate. British imports of raw cotton grew fortyfold between 1785 and 1850, by which date cotton goods accounted for two-thirds of British textile exports and a full 40 percent of British exports overall. The number of power looms in use in England rose nearly one hundredfold between 1813 and 1850.

Like sugar in the eighteenth century, cotton was a commodity that tied together European consumer capitalism and global trade. The production of cheap cotton did more than any other single factor to put fashion within the reach of non-elite social groups. Even poor people could now purchase outfits for pleasure as well as for practical use and change them before they wore out. As a moralizing contributor to a British magazine warned sternly in 1828: "The present low price of articles of dress naturally tempts persons to an improper fondness for show." Textile manufacturers eagerly took advantage of the trend, encouraging regular changes in women's fashions in particular, in the hope of stimulating consumption.

Cotton thread bound Europe more tightly than ever into global patterns of exchange. The need to import ever-greater quantities of raw cotton made Britain even more dependent on the slave economies of the Americas. Most of these slave economies no longer formed part of European empires, thanks to the independence of the United States followed by most of Latin America by the mid-1820s. Slavery in the remaining European colonies, particularly in the Caribbean, was overwhelmingly dedicated to sugar production, and while slave-produced sugar did not lose its profitability, it represented a shrinking proportion of European trade overall. But the expansion of cotton textile production strengthened the slave plantation system elsewhere, especially in the southern United States and Brazil. Fully 80 percent of all cotton spun in British mills was picked by slaves.

At the same time, the cotton boom had devastating consequences for other parts of the globe. Originally, Indians had manufactured most of the cotton fabric consumed in Europe. But competition with Britain, which colonial officials made harsher by imposing new financial burdens on indigenous production, turned the tables. Imports of manufactured cotton by south Asia from Europe increased

Textile Mills The scale of the new methods of textile production is evident in this 1830 illustration of a Lancashire cotton mill. Workers attend to rows and rows of power looms, which are attached to the shafts and belts that supply them with steam power.

TURNER'S *RAIN, STEAM AND SPEED—THE GREAT WESTERN RAILWAY*

J. M. W. Turner (1775–1851) was one of nineteenth-century Britain's leading painters. His work from the 1830s and 1840s reflected the effects of industrialization on Britain. In the course of a few decades, Britain was overlaid with a network of railways linking together the nation at speeds from 30 to 50 miles per hour, much faster than previous modes of transportation. Reflecting Turner's predisposition to experimenting on his canvases, his 1844 painting *Rain, Steam and Speed—The Great Western Railway* invented a new visual and painterly repertoire to capture the speed of rail transport and its transformation of the landscape. A train from London starts as a blurry dark streak against a pale white and blue background of steam and rain, with only the locomotive's chimney attaining a clear shape and form as it hurtles across a bridge over the Thames and toward the viewer. Turner's work illustrates how the industrial era both awed observers and stretched the bounds of human perception.

QUESTIONS FOR ANALYSIS

1. How does Turner attempt to represent the speed and movement of the train?
2. What effects of industrialization do you see in this painting?
3. How does Turner's painting capture the ways in which industrialization transformed humans' relationship to the natural world?

fifteenfold between 1820 and 1840, leading to an effective deindustrialization of this sector of the Indian economy.

NEW MEANS OF TRANSPORTATION AND COMMUNICATION

The new industrial technology did a great deal to facilitate faster and denser patterns of transportation and communication. Within Europe, railroads made it possible to transport coal, steel, and manufactured goods far more quickly and efficiently than in previous centuries. And nearly as important as the railroads was the introduction of steamships into maritime transport. The first steamships had come into commercial use in the 1810s, starting in the United States. In 1819, the first ship using steam to supplement sail power crossed the Atlantic from Savannah, Georgia, to Liverpool, England, and it was followed within a decade by ships that made the crossing on steam alone. By 1840, the Canadian Samuel Cunard (1787–1865) had a line of four steamships making trips across the Atlantic on a weekly schedule, carrying both passengers and cargo. In the same year, some eighty steamships were being used full-time to bring Irish cattle and dairy products to England.

In 1844, news came to Europe of a particularly astonishing invention. A dozen years before, a fashionable American painter, traveling in France, had come across a system first developed under Napoleon Bonaparte for quickly transmitting messages over long distances: a network of towers, spaced six miles apart, with mechanical arms or flags that could be seen through a telescope from the next tower down the line. The painter—his name was Samuel Morse (1791–1872)—became convinced that electric wires could transmit messages more quickly and efficiently using a simple binary code, and in 1844 he successfully demonstrated a prototype connecting Washington and Baltimore. An English-language newspaper in Paris quickly relayed an American journalist's verdict on Morse's "telegraph," which uncannily echoed Heine's comment on the railroads: "This is indeed the annihilation of space."

THE SURGING GROWTH OF CITIES

In Europe, the most visible effect of the Industrial Revolution was the spectacular and uncontrolled growth of cities—especially in Britain. The textile-manufacturing city of Manchester, whose population had barely exceeded

Steamships In this 1838 painting by the British artist J. M. W. Turner (1775–1851), an iron steamship belching smoke tows an old sailing ship to the dock where it will be demolished. The setting sun bathes the scene in a nostalgic glow, despite what a great many people would have viewed as progress.

15,000 in 1750, grew to over 70,000 inhabitants by 1800, and 185,000 by 1850. Cities involved in shipping and finance as well as textiles grew rapidly as well: in the same period, London's population more than doubled to 2.3 million, and Liverpool's more than quadrupled to 400,000. In 1850, for the first time in world history, fully half the population of a major territorial state—Great Britain—lived in large cities. And the very layout and appearance of these cities was undergoing drastic alteration. Rapidly built industrial housing in Britain most often used dark brick, each house virtually identical to the next. And now the largest and tallest buildings, visible from afar, were increasingly not cathedrals but factories with huge chimneys belching smoke. In 1842, a chemical manufacturer in Glasgow named Charles Tennant erected a chimney 435 feet tall—the highest in the world at the time, and higher than all but nine cathedral spires in Europe.

DAILY LIFE AND WORKING CONDITIONS

Daily life in this new industrial landscape differed from anything previously seen in world history. For the first time, most people no longer worked where they lived. Charles Tennant's chemical plant, for example, covered over a hundred acres, had 250,000 square feet of work space, and employed over a thousand people. Work itself became divorced from natural rhythms, with factories sometimes operating twenty-four hours a day to achieve greater efficiency. And the work was more intensive and repetitive than anything seen in pre-industrial workshops.

CHILD LABOR And it was not just adult men doing this work. In one survey of Lancashire cotton mills from 1833, 35 percent of all workers were under the age of sixteen, and 5 percent under eleven. In the 1840s, close to half of all workers in the British textile industry were female, and many now brought their children to work with them in factories. Factory owners insisted, in testimony to Parliament, that it was better to have small children usefully employed than running wild—the owners did not consider school as an alternative. They even claimed that the children's smaller fingers were necessary for some of the more delicate work on the great mechanical looms used to make cloth. But repeated investigations showed children working exhausting hours (as many as sixteen per day) in dangerous and unsanitary conditions. In response, Parliament passed a series of Factory Acts, starting in 1819, that put increasingly strict limits on working hours for children, banned those under age nine from the workplace, and mandated some degree of schooling. The same legislation prescribed limited working hours for women as well. Yet critics saw the acts as inadequate to the problem and complained that their provisions were frequently ignored.

Industrial Labor The new system of industrial labor affected people of all ages, who might previously have worked together on farms. This illustration of a London glassworks from 1842 shows small boys laboring alongside men in a hot and dangerous workshop.

THE RESPONSE TO INDUSTRY The rise of these new industrial landscapes horrified many observers. Consider, for instance, the reformer Ernest Jones's savage 1847 poem "The Factory Town." Whereas Jones's more famous predecessor William Blake had used the memorable phrase "dark satanic mills" to describe factories arising in supposedly pastoral settings, Jones sketched out an entire infernal landscape. In his description, "lurid fires" spring everywhere from chimneys so that the industrial town "like a cauldron bubbled"—and with "poison," no less. Within the factories' "reeking walls," amid "heavy, choking air" full of whirling dust, workers with "white, cracked, fevered lips" toiled day after day, alongside "half-naked infants" and spectral women. Even as the "bloated" factory owner boasted of his productivity to foreign visitors, his "crushed" masses, longing for the "dewy grasses" of their childhoods, cried out their misery:

> Hark! Amid the bloodless slaughter
> Comes the wailing of despair:
> "Oh! For but one drop of water!
> "Oh! For but one breath of air!"

A constant theme in the literature of the day was the contrast between the beauties of the British countryside, where men and women could lead "natural" lives, and the ugliness, artificiality, and filth of factory towns, along with the inhuman forms of exploitation, scarcely better than slavery, that prevailed there.

INDUSTRIAL EVOLUTION: THE PACE OF CHANGE

Nearly two centuries later, these criticisms retain their power to shock; but in some important ways they are also misleading. For all its importance, the Industrial Revolution did not transform all of European society at once. It affected different parts of the Continent at different times and at different rates. Even in the areas that were first and most sharply affected, not everyone experienced the changes in the same way. And despite factories like Charles Tennant's, the overall movement of the workforce into large factories took place more slowly than these spectacular examples might suggest. The "Industrial Revolution" was in many ways more of an "Industrial Evolution."

VARIATIONS ACROSS THE CONTINENT Before 1845, the new forces associated with industrialism barely touched large portions of the Continent. During this

A GIRL'S LIFE IN THE MINES

In the early nineteenth century, cotton mills, factories, and coal mines were only too happy to take on workers who would command a lower wage than adult male workers, and families desperate for income sent children to work. The sight of young girls and boys working in brutal conditions in the mines scandalized some—in particular, Lord Ashley, the earl of Shaftesbury, who introduced legislation in Parliament to regulate children's work. In 1841–42, he invited young workers to testify before his Parliamentary Commission. Their testimony painted a grim portrait of industrial labor.

Patience Kershaw was a coal "hurrier"—a worker who hauled coal from the pits to the surface—and she testified before Lord Ashley's Commission about the hard work in the mines. Testimony like Kershaw's helped spur Parliament to approve the Mines and Collieries Act of 1842, an early example of British workplace legislation.

My father has been dead about a year; my mother is living and has ten children, five lads and five lasses; the oldest is about thirty, the youngest is four; three lasses go to mill; all the lads are colliers,[1] two getters[2] and three hurriers; one lives at home and does nothing; mother does nought but look after home.

All my sisters have been hurriers, but three went to the mill. Alice went because her legs swelled from hurrying in cold water when she was hot. I never went to day-school; I go to Sunday-school, but I cannot read or write; I go to pit at five o'clock in the morning and come out at five in the evening; I get my breakfast of porridge and milk first; I take my dinner with me, a cake, and eat it as I go; I do not stop or rest any time for the purpose; I get nothing else until I get home, and then have potatoes and meat, not every day meat. I hurry in the clothes I have now got on, trousers and ragged jacket; the bald place upon my head is made by thrusting the corves[3]; my legs have never swelled, but sisters' did when they went to mill; I hurry the corves a mile and more under ground and back; they weigh three hundred pounds; I hurry 11 a-day; I wear a belt and chain at the workings, to get the corves out; the getters that I work for are naked except their caps; they pull off all their clothes; I see them at work when I go up; sometimes they beat me, if I am not quick enough, with their hands; they strike me upon my back; the boys take liberties with me; sometimes they pull me about; I am the only girl in the pit; there are about 20 boys and 15 men; all the men are naked; I would rather work in mill than in coal-pit.

QUESTIONS FOR ANALYSIS

1. According to Patience Kershaw's testimony, what kinds of work did children do in the coal mines?
2. What were conditions like in the mines, both for children and for adults?
3. What abuses did Kershaw suffer in the mines?

[1] **colliers:** coal miners
[2] **getters:** coal cutters
[3] **corves:** wagons

Source: Patience Kershaw, *Testimony before the Parliamentary Committee on Mines, Parliamentary Papers*, 1842, XV–XVII, Appendix 1; Appendix 2.

period, fully 70 percent of all the growth in European urban populations took place in a single country: Great Britain. Some **"factory towns"** sprang up in France, the Low Countries, and Catalonia, and by 1850 the Ruhr region of Germany counted hundreds of mills and foundries producing textiles, lumber, and iron. But most of eastern and southern Germany, along with most of southern France, remained heavily agricultural; and further east the Russian economy did not differ all that greatly from what it had been in the previous century, with over a third of the population living in the virtual slavery of serfdom. The Italian economy would likewise only see substantial increases in industrial production later in the century. Even in Britain, the rise of "factory towns" took place above all in a single rough geographical triangle, 100 miles or so on a side, between the cities of Birmingham,

Industrialization in Europe, 1800–1850 Industrialization was slower to take hold on the Continent than in Britain. Coal- and iron-producing regions were spread more sparsely, and along with railroads were concentrated in northern Europe. Though many areas, including in the south, retained historic strengths as ports or textile-producing regions, nowhere came close to Britain's concentration of large industrial cities.

Liverpool, and Leeds (and bulging up to the north over the county of Lancashire). This area had large coal deposits and, even before the railroads began, a robust transportation system in the form of canals.

A MIX OF TECHNOLOGIES Even in the industrial centers, factories did not simply replace older forms of home-based hand labor—instead, they complemented it. In the textile industry, for instance, weaving long remained the province of predominantly female and predominantly rural "piece workers," who now worked with factory-produced fibers. And even in 1850, even in Britain,

only a minority of industrial workers spent their days in factories. The massive installations employing thousands of workers in Manchester and Birmingham existed alongside hundreds of smaller workshops employing a few dozen workers each. And in many industries, older, artisanal forms of labor survived well into the industrial age, including wood- and metal-workers, clothes-makers, glaziers, barrel-makers, and many others. The London Census of 1841 listed no fewer than 840 separate crafts occupations in the city.

Still, industrialization produced significant effects even in areas hundreds of miles from the nearest factory.

Cheap industrial products made their way into the marketplace, often undercutting local production, while farmers now had large new urban markets to produce for. Most significant, overall western European economic growth increased from a rate of around 1 percent a year in 1820 to just under 2 percent by 1845, allowing for the fastest rise in per capita income in the Continent's history.

SOCIAL CHANGE AND THE MIDDLE CLASSES

It was long believed that the Industrial Revolution took place as part of a fundamental upheaval in social structure. It supposedly marked the rise of the capitalist **bourgeoisie**, or middle classes, at the expense of the old aristocracy, and the birth of a new class, the industrial **proletariat** (working class). The founders of socialism, Karl Marx and Friedrich Engels, put it this way in 1848: "The bourgeoisie has subjected the country to the rule of the towns. It has created enormous cities, has greatly increased the urban population as compared with the rural.... Modern Industry has converted the little workshop of the patriarchal master into the great factory of the industrial capitalist." Yet in fact, just as the Industrial Revolution itself took place in a slower and more uneven manner than the term "revolution" might suggest, the changes in social structure were also more gradual and complex than Marx and Engels believed.

To begin with, there was no simple correlation between a person's social class and economic role. Even in the most "middle-class" country of all, Great Britain, a high proportion of the investment capital crucial to industrialization actually came from the landed aristocracy, which had long been more open to entrepreneurial activity than its continental counterparts. Indeed, traditional landed interests literally fueled the process, for industry could not have developed without a massive increase in the supply of coal to power steam engines and looms—and British coal came mostly from land owned by the gentry. As we have seen with the railroads, industrialization also required the support of a Parliament that was still elected by a tiny sliver of male landowners—just 200,000 men in the 1820s. In the early nineteenth century, this Parliament commanded a British state that spent more, borrowed more, and employed more people than any other institution in the country.

In France, meanwhile, not only did the nobility still possess much of the country's wealth, despite the attacks on them during the French Revolution; it now provided one of the major sources of investment capital. And under the Bourbon monarchy restored to power in 1815, nobles and wealthy landed bourgeois dominated a state that had even more influence on economic development than its British counterpart. Despite incessant political turmoil, successive French governments carried on the industrial policies sketched out by Napoleon's interior minister, Jean-Antoine Chaptal (1756–1832). He believed in free markets but sought to stimulate them through close supervision and to temper their inegalitarian excesses. Elsewhere in the industrializing portions of the Continent, traditional elites generally stood in even more favorable positions, leading one historian to describe the history of nineteenth-century Europe with the phrase "the persistence of the Old Regime."

DEFINING THE MIDDLE

The "middle classes" themselves were a particularly tricky phenomenon to define. Even in Britain, supposedly the country with the strongest middle class in the nineteenth century, not all observers perceived society as divided neatly into upper, middle, and lower classes. Some saw it as a more complex social hierarchy, while others believed it really consisted mostly of poor workers and farmers pitted against a handful of wealthy aristocrats, with little of significance in between. In France, the word "bourgeois"—which had originally designated non-noble town-dwellers—most often functioned as a term of abuse, designating a grasping individual who put self-interest above the public good.

Yet even with these qualifications, it is clear that the "middle class," which had existed as a social phenomenon for centuries, did take on extraordinary new importance in the first half of the nineteenth century. In a rough, common-sense definition, the middle class had always been composed of people who on the one hand did not possess noble titles or extraordinary wealth, and on the other did not work with their hands but lived comfortably (something that generally required, even for a small household, at least one or two servants). In this period, the middle class expanded greatly in numbers and wealth. Although exact numbers are impossible to come by, somewhere between 15 and 20 percent of the British population could be classified as "middle class" by 1845—considerably more than in previous periods. In most of southern and eastern Europe, by contrast, the figure was closer to 5 percent. Beyond their numbers, the middle class was becoming more of a social force: in a world where aristocratic courts set fashions less and less, noble rank no longer conferred automatic legal privilege, and nobles now paid taxes like anyone else, the middle class no longer existed in a state of subservience to its social superiors.

ROUTES TO THE MIDDLE CLASS: PROFESSIONS AND EDUCATION

Much of the expansion of the middle class was driven by their participation in trade and industry, but it would be a mistake to associate the middle class only with these economic sectors. Even in an industrial city like Leeds, in England, fewer than half of all middle-class families in the 1840s derived their incomes from employment in trade and industry. More often, heads of middle-class families worked as professionals in fields that experienced expansion as they served the growing industrial sector: lawyers, doctors, architects, teachers, and clergymen. Teaching proved particularly accessible to women, with an almost three-to-one ratio of female to male teachers in London by the 1850s. Where states were expanding, more middle-class civil servants were recruited to work in them. French state expenditures, for instance, rose some 50 percent between 1822 and 1842, and as they did, the middle class expanded.

Because of the importance of the professions and state bureaucracies, entry into which generally demanded formal training, the most reliable route into the middle class was not wealth but education. Of course, education itself generally required some wealth, but well-to-do artisans, farmers, clerks, and (in Protestant Europe) clergymen gladly subsidized their children's schooling in the hope of securing their social advancement. Few European states in this period provided free public schooling, even at the primary level. France began to introduce such a system in 1833 but did not make schooling compulsory, and many poorer families withdrew their children from school as soon as they became old enough to work. In the early nineteenth century, only one out of two hundred French boys, and far fewer girls, completed secondary school. In the German states, the number of secondary-school graduates doubled from 1820 to 1830 but still only reached 2,000 per year and comprised nearly all men. Outside of northwestern Europe, the numbers were even smaller. In 1848, Russia, with a population of roughly 70 million, had only 5,000 students, all male, enrolled in higher education. However, unlike today, one did not need a university degree, or even to have completed secondary school,

to enter many middle-class professions. Across Europe, literacy rates for the peasants who still made up the large majority of the population remained low—with the exception of highly evangelized Protestant areas such as Prussia, where by the mid-nineteenth century illiteracy had fallen to just 5 percent for both sexes.

School curricula, after the primary years, remained heavily classical. In much of Europe, secondary students spent 50 percent of their time on Latin and Greek and less than 20 percent on math and science. Yet most educators still took the utility of classical instruction for granted. Britons saw in the study of ancient texts a source of mental rigor and the knowledge of people and institutions necessary to govern a steadily expanding empire. Still, especially in Britain the period 1820–45 also saw the creation of new educational institutes with a more practical focus. In 1826, the first unit of London University opened, along with its Department of Economics—the first in the world, for economics itself was emerging as a distinct area of study during this period. It was also the first British university to admit non-Anglicans, including Jews.

MIDDLE-CLASS CULTURE

Just as entry to the middle class depended heavily on education, so participation in middle-class life was in large part a matter of culture. There was no such thing as a "typical" middle-class family, but middle-class people did increasingly share a distinct set of cultural practices. At home, the young—especially young women—were expected to learn music (Paris had 60,000 pianos by the 1830s) and to perform at regular gatherings of families and friends. With most middle-class people in Europe literate by 1820, middle-class culture also involved reading newspapers, poetry, and especially novels. Here a technological innovation—the development of machines that produced paper cheaply in long rolls rather than expensive single sheets—played a significant part, allowing books and periodicals to sell at much lower prices. The price of printed material would plunge further when inventors discovered how to manufacture paper from cheap wood pulp in the 1840s. Novelists commonly serialized their work in newspapers, developing the technique of the cliffhanger to keep readers interested from one issue to the next. Charles Dickens (1812–1870) in Britain and Honoré de Balzac (1799–1850) in France proved particularly popular in Europe and America. In 1841, New Yorkers waited anxiously at the docks for an arriving ship to hear if one of the characters in Dickens's *The Old Curiosity Shop* was

MIDDLE-CLASS LONDON, ca. 1850

> **THE MIDDLE CLASSES ARE THE REAL TYRANTS OF SOCIETY... THEY SURPASS THE ARISTOCRACY IN ARROGANCE TOWARDS THE POOR, AND THE POOR THEMSELVES, IN OBSEQUIOUSNESS TOWARDS THE ARISTOCRACY.**
>
> THE POOR MAN'S GUARDIAN, AUGUST 17, 1833

Map legend:

- Road
- Mixed residential and commercial
- Industrial
- Park
- Factory
- Governmental or cultural institution
- Prison or workhouse
- School

Scale: 0–2 miles / 0–2 km

Map labels: Zoo, Regents Park, Cricket grounds, London University, British Museum, Pentonville Penitentiary, Regents Canal, Hyde Park, Thames R., London Docks, Zoo, Grand Surrey Canal

BUILDINGS

1. St. Paul's Cathedral
2. Post Office
3. Bank of England
4. East India House
5. Customs House
6. Parliament
7. Westminster Abbey
8. Buckingham Palace

The temperance movement targeted alcohol as a threat to the stable family, the middle-class ideal. In this etching by George Cruikshank, from a popular 1847 series of illustrations warning of the dangers of alcohol, a man offers his wife a drink for the first time, triggering their descent into homelessness, insanity, and death.

MIDDLE-CLASS OCCUPATIONS

TOTAL POPULATION	2,362,236

MALES	FEMALES
1,106,558	1,255,678

Occupation	Males	Females
GOVERNMENT OFFICERS	10,099	225
CLERGY AND CHURCH OFFICERS	2,393	529
LAWYERS AND LAW CLERKS	11,293	8
PHYSICIANS AND SURGEONS	5,331	0
TEACHERS	4,739	12,299
MERCHANTS AND SHOPKEEPERS	11,344	2,018
COMMERCIAL CLERKS	16,120	0

Source: *Census of England and Wales*, 1851, "Occupations of the People, London."

> **[THE POOR WORKER] IS... FREE... WHEN HE TAKES THE TEMPERANCE PLEDGE... WE INVITE HIM TO EXCHANGE HIS BEER... FOR A COMFORTABLE AND RESPECTABLE HOME.**
>
> SARAH STICKNEY ELLIS, *A VOICE FROM THE VINTAGE*, 1843

QUESTIONS FOR ANALYSIS

1. How did the professions of middle-class Londoners reflect the social and economic changes of the period?
2. In what ways did the family represent the ideal of middle-class life?
3. How did the middle class seek to establish its values throughout London society?

Leisure Activities Well-dressed middle-class families gather to admire exotic animals at the Regent's Park Zoo in London in this 1835 illustration.

still alive. Across Europe, middle-class people tended to belong to churches and to attend services regularly. Indeed, thanks in large part to the middle classes, in the late 1840s churchgoing rates reached their highest point of the century throughout western Europe.

ORGANIZED LEISURE Beyond religion, middle-class culture outside of the home centered on organized leisure: visits to public art museums (the Louvre in Paris had opened its doors during the French Revolution), concerts, lectures, holiday parades, and sporting events. The London Zoo, founded as a scientific institution, opened to the public in 1847. In the self-conscious linkage of leisure to "self-improvement" and cultivation, these pursuits stood in stark contrast to such traditional aristocratic entertainments as horse-racing and fox-hunting. Meanwhile, in part to control what was seen as the unruly behavior of the lower classes, middle-class British reformers worked to replace traditional popular entertainments like bear-baiting and cock-fighting with public soccer and cricket matches; they also closely regulated boxing. Rules for boxing published in 1838 formally forbade biting and hitting below the belt.

The early nineteenth century also saw the development of another modern form of leisure: the organized vacation. Already by the 1820s, an enterprising bookstore owner in Paris had begun to publish a guidebook for the city in English ("The English traveler must not expect to find on the continent all the cleanliness and comfort to which he has been accustomed..."). A decade later, the Englishman Thomas Cook (1808–1892) founded the first tourist agency, arranging excursions for hundreds of vacationers at a time and, increasingly, entire families traveling together, generally by railroad. The seashore became

a popular destination. Before the mid-eighteenth century, northern Europeans in particular tended to regard beaches as unattractive wasteland and the sea beyond as threatening and wild. But in the 1750s, doctors began to extol the health benefits of bathing in seawater, spurring the development of coastal resorts. The 1820s saw the construction of elaborate wooden pavilions in beach towns on both sides of the English Channel, as well as hotels and inns to house vacationers.

THE CULT OF DOMESTICITY Central to middle-class identity was the burgeoning **cult of domesticity**, centered on the idea of radically different roles for the sexes. Since the late eighteenth century, economic change in western Europe had brought steadily more rigid boundaries between workplaces and the "home." Male heads of household who had previously lived "above the shop" increasingly worked in offices, factories, and larger workshops,

Cult of Domesticity A profusion of advice manuals like *The Female Instructor or Young Woman's Companion* (1811) guided young women in the appropriate pastimes of a respectable wife and mother, such as sewing and educating children, as depicted on this title page.

away from their residences. Middle-class women were cut off from workplaces, and a growing body of "domestic" literature defined them as guardians of the home and hearth, subordinate to their husbands and devoted principally to the care of children. In Britain, a resurgent evangelical Christianity presented the middle-class home as the true source and model of morality, insisting on strict sexual continence for wives but paying much less attention to male infidelities.

At this point, little public support yet existed for what Queen Victoria (r. 1837–1901) would call the "mad, wicked folly of 'Woman's Rights.'" The brief upsurge in feminist demands by figures like Olympe de Gouges and Mary Wollstonecraft at the time of the French Revolution had not yet developed into a sustained movement. In France, and in other countries that had been swept into Napoleon's empire, the Napoleonic Code enacted strict limits on women's freedom, reversing much of the liberal legislation of the French Revolutionary period. It prohibited French wives from selling property or even publishing a book without their husband's written consent, and the latter law would remain in effect until the 1960s. The cult of domesticity was premised on an ideal of romantic love, and by the early nineteenth century the practice of arranged marriages had largely died out among the European middle classes. Yet middle-class families still expected their offspring to find socially acceptable partners and for the match to work to their economic benefit, with women providing dowries and men a regular income. The resulting tensions provided grist for some of the age's greatest fiction—particularly that of the British novelist Jane Austen (1775–1817).

THE MIDDLE CLASS AS MODEL Together, these middle-class ideals—of the home as a citadel of domestic bliss; of leisure activity as orderly and self-improving; and of work as meritorious—provided a model of behavior that reformers could also attempt to impose on the lower classes. During the 1820s and 1830s, as cities seemed to expand uncontrollably, fears had proliferated of the dangers supposedly posed by mobile, uprooted populations. Urban crime in the cities did increase during this period, and much middle-class fiction—Dickens's *Oliver Twist*, for example—depicted urban slums with some accuracy as lawless and threatening, to be avoided by unwary visitors. This fiction, in turn, helped spur reform movements aimed at transforming the lower classes into poorer copies of their social "superiors." In Britain, the single most powerful reform movement of this sort was temperance: the cause of restricting or even banning the consumption

of alcohol. In 1829, a Belfast professor and minister, John Edgar, poured all of his whiskey out of his window and went on to form the Ulster Temperance Movement. A British Society for the Promotion of Temperance followed in 1835, and working-class movements would soon adopt the cause as well in the hope of improving their own image. In short, middle-class culture increasingly served as the pattern to which reformers hoped lower-class life could be shaped.

THE INDUSTRIAL LOWER CLASSES

Middle-class reformers often had a fearful, exaggerated image of workers as drunken and uncontrollable. But they did recognize, however distortedly, an important social fact: that a coherent new social entity, the urban working class, was coming into being. In fact, the very term *working class* came into common usage in this period to denote people who worked for wages in the new industrial economy. The gap between the realities of life for the working class and the ideal sketched out by the middle-class reformers was vast.

THE WORKING POOR

A legislative report from 1832 on the English industrial center of Manchester spoke of the "dense masses of houses" lacking in decent light and ventilation, and barely furnished: "A whole family is often accommodated on a single bed, and sometimes a heap of filthy straw and a covering of old sacking hide them in one undistinguished heap." Sewers and running water were largely absent: "Among 579 streets inspected, 243 were altogether unpaved, 46 partially paved, 93 ill ventilated, and 307 contained heaps of refuse, deep ruts, stagnant pools, ordure. . . ." Diseases like typhoid, spread by poor sanitation, ran rampant. Similar conditions prevailed in even the wealthiest cities—including Paris, where fewer than one in five households had a connection to public sewers. Throughout western Europe, the death rate in large cities often ran twice as high as in rural areas.

Nothing could have been further from the middle-class cult of domesticity than the presence of small children and women laboring in factories in order to make ends meet for their families. But the pressures of industrialization led as well to many other dislocations in traditional patterns

INDUSTRIAL PROMISE AND SOCIAL MISERY

Industrialization unleashed tremendous productive and social forces, and transformed Europe's largely rural and agrarian society into an urban and industrial one. New machines and forms of work boosted production and efficiency. Many observers predicted that mechanization would liberate mankind from drudgery and labor. At the same time, the first industrial workers suffered incredible social dislocation and physical strain. Thousands poured into cities and settled in overcrowded districts where basic needs such as running water, heat, plumbing, and sanitation were scarce or nonexistent. Working hours were long, pay was poor, factories were often poorly heated and cooled, and accidents and injuries were commonplace. For many workers, these developments seemed less like the beginnings of a glorious new society than a different form of exploitation.

Andrew Ure, from *The Philosophy of Manufactures*

In his *Philosophy of Manufactures* (1835), the Scottish chemist and medical doctor Andrew Ure (1778–1857) pointed to machinery's capacity to make work less laborious.

The blessings which physico-mechanical science has bestowed on society, and the means it has still in store for ameliorating the lot of mankind, have been too little dwelt upon....

It has been said, for example, that the steam-engine now drives the power-looms with such velocity as to urge on their attendant weavers at the same rapid pace; but that the hand-weaver, not being subjected to this restless agent, can throw his shuttle and move his treddles at his convenience. There is, however, this difference in the two cases, that in the factory, every member of the loom is so adjusted, that the driving force leaves the attendant nearly nothing at all to do, certainly no muscular fatigue to sustain...whereas the non-factory weaver, having everything to execute by muscular exertion, finds the labour irksome, makes in consequence innumerable short pauses, separately of little account, but great when added together....

The constant aim and effect of scientific improvement in manufactures are philanthropic, as they tend to relieve the workmen either from niceties of adjustment which exhaust his mind and fatigue his eyes, or from painful repetition of effort which distort or wear out his frame. At every step of each manufacturing process described in this volume, the humanity of science will be manifest....

...The grand object therefore of the modern manufacturer is, through the union of capital and science, to reduce the task of his work-people to the exercise of vigilance and dexterity....

...It is, in fact, the constant aim and tendency of every improvement in machinery to supersede human labour altogether.

Friedrich Engels, from *The Condition of the Working Class in England*

The German philosopher Friedrich Engels (1820–1895) described the conditions of the industrial workplace as a system of oppression in this 1845 passage.

The consequences of improvement in machinery under our present social conditions are, for the working-man, solely injurious, and often in the highest degree oppressive. Every new advance brings with it loss of employment, want, and suffering, and in a country like England where, without that, there is usually a "surplus population," to be discharged from work is the worst that can befall the operative....

...We have seen, too, that this work affords the muscles no opportunity for physical activity. Thus it is, properly speaking, not work, but tedium, the most deadening, wearing process conceivable. The operative is condemned to let his physical and mental powers decay in this utter monotony, it is his mission to be bored every day and all day long from his eighth year. Moreover, he must not take a moment's rest; the engine moves unceasingly; the wheels, the straps, the spindles hum and rattle in his ears without a pause, and if he tries to snatch one instant, there is the overlooker at his back with the book of fines....

...Here ends all freedom in law and in fact. The operative must be in the mill at half-past five in the morning; if he comes a couple of minutes too late, he is fined; if he comes ten minutes too late, he is not let in until breakfast is over, and a quarter of the day's wages is withheld, though he loses only two and one-half hours' work out of twelve. He must eat, drink, and sleep at command....

...Here the employer is absolute law-giver.

QUESTIONS FOR ANALYSIS

1. In Ure's opinion, how will mechanization improve the lot of workers?
2. Why does Engels argue that the factory system represents a new form of exploitation of the working class?
3. What are the key differences between Ure's and Engels's arguments?

Sources: Andrew Ure, *The Philosophy of Manufactures* (London: 1835), pp. 7–8, 20–21, 23; Friedrich Engels, *The Condition of the Working-Class in England* (London: 1892), pp. 139, 177–79.

of lower-class social life. In the 1830s and 1840s, major western European cities saw illegitimacy rates rise to as much as one-half of all births, as compared to under 10 percent in most rural areas. In Paris, mothers unable to care for newborns abandoned as many as 33,000 of them per year. Women, who generally earned only a third to a half of what their male counterparts did, fared disproportionately badly in the process of industrialization. They also continued to have far worse access to education and higher rates of illiteracy. In general, despite middle-class gains in this area, overall illiteracy rates remained high for both men and women during this period.

Even so, it is wrong to describe the process of industrialization as an unremitting disaster for the men and women who toiled in its factories. In Britain, between the 1820s and the 1850s, the wages of non-agricultural workers rose 50 percent faster than those of agricultural ones. City-dwellers generally consumed more calories than their country cousins, even if a higher proportion of those calories came from sugar and alcohol. And city-dwellers did not live with the constant risk of famine or ruin from crop failures, such as the blights that struck Irish potato-growing with catastrophic results in the late 1840s, or the French silk industry a decade later. And as we will see, especially in Great Britain, workers in this period learned how to organize effectively to advocate for their collective interests.

URBAN DISEASE AND THE MEDICAL RESPONSE

Yet industrial cities were vulnerable to other natural threats, notably the **cholera** bacillus. This highly infectious water-borne disease struck cities across the Continent in the early 1830s with terrifying force, killing hundreds of thousands (50 percent of all afflicted persons died, usually within a day or two of infection). Parisians in 1832 reacted with macabre humor, one theater sponsoring a masquerade ball with a "cholera waltz" and an actor dressed up as the disease itself—in the words of a visiting American medical student, "with skeleton armor, bloodshot eyes, and other horrible appurtenances of a walking pestilence." Medical scientists did not yet associate disease with the bacteria they had been seeing in their microscopes since the seventeenth century, but they did notice that cholera outbreaks seemed to concentrate in areas of poor sanitation, and they called for the cleansing and purification of water systems and sewers.

These sanitary efforts themselves reflected a broader

Cholera Epidemic Patients suffering from cholera at the Hôtel-Dieu hospital in Paris beg a visiting nobleman for assistance in this artistic rendering (1832–1837) of the cholera epidemic of 1832.

turn in advanced European medical thought. Increasingly, progressive physicians were moving away from earlier models of diagnosis and treatment that concentrated on the physical and even moral constitution of individual patients. They were adopting more "epidemiological" approaches that looked for patterns of disease in large populations. In 1821, the French scientist Louis René Villermé (1782–1863) published a statistical study of the city of Paris demonstrating that contagious diseases flourished particularly in poor districts. French medical educators such as Pierre Louis (1787–1872) led the way in using aggregate data from hospitals to assess the effectiveness of medical treatments—a technique that led him to argue successfully in 1835 against the widespread (and counterproductive) practice of bleeding the sick. Foreign medical students flocked to Paris to hear his lectures.

SOCIAL REFORM: POVERTY AND CRIMINALITY

These new approaches in turn helped spur what could be called the growing medicalization of social thought in this period. Observers tended more and more to treat social problems such as poverty and criminality as medical in cause. Would the poor "always be with you," as was written in scripture (Matthew 26:11)? Was criminality too a permanent scourge of mankind? Or were these things social pathologies that might be treated in much the same way that doctors treated infectious disease? In keeping with this idea, and with the idea of the middle class as model, the period 1820–45 saw new efforts to "discipline" the poor and criminals alike.

For the former, the most spectacular example was England and Wales's **Poor Law Amendment of 1834**. Whereas the earlier Speenhamland system of poor relief had been based on individual parishes and involved income supplements for those in need, the new system operated on a national scale and centered on a network of residential "workhouses" for the indigent. Originally, the system's architects in Parliament had hoped to establish the workhouses as the sole source of poor relief and to make them such an unattractive, prison-like option that potential "inmates" would do almost anything to raise themselves out of poverty. In practice, the new law did not abolish all existing forms of poor relief, and while the workhouse environment usually proved grim and unhealthy—indeed, often brutal and dangerous—it still provided a welcome alternative to starvation. Although the total population of English and Welsh workhouses remained just under 200,000 in 1845, as many as ten times more had spent at least some time in the institution—roughly one out of every eight people, and a considerably higher proportion of city-dwellers.

As for criminal justice, early nineteenth-century western European states continued trends, begun in the Enlightenment, away from corporal punishment and toward imprisonment as the most common penalty. Theorists increasingly portrayed prisons as a way to quarantine prisoners entirely from society and from normal forms of human interaction. London's Pentonville Prison, opened in 1842 on the model of earlier institutions in the United States, kept prisoners rigidly separated from one another in individual cells. Guards referred to them by number, not name, and walked the corridors on padded shoes so as not to be heard. Although the "Pentonville model" proved too expensive and cumbersome for the Continent as a whole to copy, it had great influence. Meanwhile, French theorists in the 1840s began to speculate that criminality derived from the physical "degeneration" of criminals, perhaps because of alcoholism or sexual deviance. Like the insane, the criminally "degenerate" had to be forcibly separated from society, for its good and their own.

THE "UTOPIAN" REFORMERS

Despite this trend toward increasingly strict measures of social control, grounded in medicalized visions of society, the period also saw considerably more hopeful schemes for improving social conditions. The authors of these proposals had inherited the Enlightenment idea that society functioned according to knowable principles and could be reshaped by the scientific application of policy, but they had greater ambitions than the *philosophes* for actually accomplishing this reshaping in their own lifetimes. In France, Henri, Count Saint-Simon (1760–1825), published several works arguing that the rise of industry required the development of an entirely new social system, centralized and imposed from above, dominated by intellectuals (principally scientists) and the leaders of the productive industrial class, all working for the general good. Although his ideas had relatively little influence before his death in 1825, a group of devoted followers popularized them in the following decades.

Saint-Simon's countryman François-Charles Fourier (1773–1837) believed that reform had to start on a smaller scale, in individual communities, but the communities he sketched out represented a particularly radical departure: Fourier envisaged self-sustaining groups of, ideally, 1,620 men and women, each couple representing one of

Penal Reform As this illustration from around 1860 shows, London's model Pentonville Prison featured individual cells, with hammocks for sleeping and looms so that prisoners could pass their days in productive labor. The signs on the walls are probably Bible passages and lists of prison rules.

what he saw as 810 distinct human personality types. All 1,620 would live together in a single vast building, called a phalanstery, working harmoniously with one another and with equality between the sexes. Eventually, Fourier hoped, all humans would live in such communities. Yet another Frenchman, Pierre-Joseph Proudhon (1809–1865), openly advocated "communist" principles of common ownership of property, declaring in an 1840 tract that "property is theft." Such calls for a complete overhauling of the social order inspired women who saw in them a chance to overturn the subjugation of their sex. Flora Tristan (1801–1844), an early French feminist horrified by the conditions of the working class, traveled around France giving speeches in which she eloquently argued that workers could only achieve true emancipation if men and women were treated equally. But despite her efforts, a large-scale feminist movement would not coalesce in France until much later.

Across the English Channel, the Welsh industrialist Robert Owen (1771–1858) offered more practical ideas for self-governing communities in which all would work for the common good without poverty or misery. He tried to create an example in the Scottish mill town of New Lanark, centered on his own cotton mill, in which he built spacious, comfortable, and clean homes for his workers and a model school. Owen, who first popularized the word *socialism* to describe a social system that guaranteed decent living conditions and employment for all people, inspired several other such utopian communities in Europe and America, although he was frequently reproached for governing his own workers with a heavy hand.

New Lanark Robert Owens's model mill town included provision for respectable leisure pursuits for workers. In this 1825 engraving, young girls are given dancing lessons while well-dressed adults look on.

RELIGIOUS REFORM AND ROMANTIC CULTURE

These movements for social reform did not just aim to improve the material welfare of European populations. Reformers like Fourier and Owen were also centrally concerned with questions of spiritual welfare. Overall, the period experienced an important upsurge in religious revival movements, and, as in previous decades, the most popular of these took place outside of or against the established churches. It also saw the continued flowering of the romantic movement in the arts—a movement that, more than any previous European artistic school, explicitly sought to address the spiritual condition of the Continent.

NEW RELIGIOUS MOVEMENTS

Among Protestants in Britain, Switzerland, Germany, and the Low Countries, the most important religious reform movements of the decades after 1820 drew on Pietist and Methodist precursors, with open-air meetings of tens of thousands at which preachers insisted that believers develop an individual relationship with God. These movements offered roles to ordinary worshippers, including women, that the more established churches generally closed off. Within the Church of England, members of the dissident Oxford movement sought a more vivid, sensual form of religion, ultimately leading some of their leaders all the way back to Roman Catholicism. Among Catholics themselves, new strains of liberal observance developed, typified by the French priest Hugues de Lamennais (1782–1854), who became an advocate of popular sovereignty and social welfare policies. In 1834, he broke openly with the conservative Church hierarchy in a book that the pope condemned as "small in size, but immense in perversity."

These dissident movements proved all the more popular because, during this period, the balance of power between established churches and states shifted decisively in favor of the latter, across virtually all the Continent. The churches came to look increasingly like weak branches of the ruling political elites, unable to preserve the independent political power they had once possessed. In Britain, conservative Anglicans could not prevent the government from abolishing legal restrictions on Catholics and Protestant dissenters. In France the Restoration government resisted attempts by Catholic missionaries to "rechristianize" the country in massive rallies and to ban or burn offending books. In Russia, as we will see, Tsar Nikolai I cemented the transformation of the Russian Orthodox Church into essentially an obedient arm of the imperial state.

During these decades, Germany became the center of a series of movements that sought to make religion compatible with the liberal, post-Enlightenment social and political order. One key figure was the Protestant theologian and philosopher Friedrich Schleiermacher (1768–1834), who saw religion as intuition, experience, and feeling rather than the literal truth of scripture. His liberal Protestantism had an even more striking counterpart in Reformed Judaism, which coalesced in Germany in the 1820s. Building on the so-called Haskalah, or Jewish Enlightenment, the Reform movement removed the Hebrew language from most of the liturgy, deleted prayers for the return of the Jews to Israel, shortened religious services, and introduced organ music. Its leaders presented this new form of Judaism—the first competitor to Orthodox Judaism to emerge in the modern period—as rational and modern. It would permit Jews to integrate into the existing social and political order, and to assume their rights and responsibilities as equal citizens. To their detractors, both liberal Protestantism and Reform Judaism were overly rational forms of religion that lacked spiritual depth and emotional resonance.

SPIRITUAL LONGING AND ROMANTICISM

But in the early nineteenth century, it was not just to religion that Europeans turned to satisfy their spiritual longings: they also turned to art, music, and literature. More directly than in the past, painters, composers, and writers presented their work as spiritual guides that would help their audiences find a more profound connection with nature and God. In turn, these artists and writers found themselves worshipped by audiences, further encouraging what would become the modern cult of celebrity. The Hungarian composer and pianist Franz Liszt (1811–1886) had a reputation akin to that of modern rock stars. In the 1840s, he performed over a thousand times, mostly to sold-out crowds. Newspapers reported eagerly on his personal life, and thanks to the improvements in printing technology, thousands of engravings of him and other "virtuosi" were sold for framing and display in middle-class homes. Sometimes the work of these artists and writers was of an explicitly religious nature, as in the mystical, Catholic writings of François-René de Chateaubriand (1768–1848),

Franz Liszt In a nineteenth-century cartoon, women are enraptured by Liszt's performance. One releases butterflies in his direction and another, overcome, faints; all crowd around him, applauding wildly.

starting with his *Genius of Christianity*, first published in 1802. Sometimes it was clearly secular. Almost always, it evoked a sense of movement and speed that echoed the disorientations that accompanied industrialization.

THE ROMANTIC MOVEMENT

Nearly all of these artists were associated with the romantic movement. As we have seen, this movement began in the late eighteenth century with the reaction of figures like Goethe against the formal rules and decorous symmetries of neoclassical art and literature. Artists and writers associated with **romanticism** took inspiration from Jean-Jacques Rousseau's exaltation of sentiment and instinct, his worship of nature, and his denunciations of artifice and hypocrisy. Like the *philosophes* of the Enlightenment, the romantics saw their goal as exploring, in Goethe's words, "what holds the world together most deeply." But the romantics saw the path to this knowledge as lying not through the rationalism of science, but through exploration of their own, subjective perceptions, thoughts, and emotions. As the German romantic writer Novalis (1772–1801) put it: "We dream of travel through the universe, but is not the universe in us? We do not know the depths of our own souls. It is inwardly that the secret path leads." They also recognized the spiritual peril that accompanied the journey—the hero of Goethe's great poetic epic, Faust, thirsted for knowledge of the eternal mysteries. Finally, to achieve the desired knowledge, he sold his soul to the devil.

The romantics put new emphasis on their audiences' emotional reactions and tried to connect with them on a visceral level through a succession of vivid images. They often ridiculed reason, preferring to celebrate life in all its glorious disorder. The romantic sensibility emerges clearly in the British poet William Wordsworth's (1770–1850) evocation of the way a beautiful landscape fired his sense of deep connection to the natural world:

> And I have felt
> A presence that disturbs me with the joy
> Of elevated thoughts; a sense sublime
> Of something far more deeply interfused,
> Whose dwelling is the light of setting suns,
> And the round ocean and the living air,
> And the blue sky, and in the mind of man . . .

BRITAIN AND EASTERN EUROPE The romantic movement took different shapes across Europe. In England, where poetry was perhaps most important, Wordsworth's work was joined by John Keats's (1795–1821) beautiful evocations of love and melancholy, cut tragically short by his death at age twenty-five in 1821. George Gordon, Lord Byron (1788–1824), achieved the sort of celebrity enjoyed on the Continent by Liszt thanks to his famously good looks (he used curlers to keep his hair properly coiled) and his notoriously dissolute lifestyle, as well as his entertaining and accessible poetry. Competing with Byron for an "immoral" reputation was the master lyricist Percy Bysshe Shelley (1792–1822), whose radical political views inspired melodious imaginings of a better future. Shelley married Mary Wollstonecraft's daughter Mary (1797–1851), who at age eighteen wrote one of the great modern fables about science and technology: *Frankenstein*, featuring the monster created in a laboratory who runs amok. All of these works appealed deeply to the new, "self-improving" middle-class audiences for art and literature.

Romantic poetry had a crucial importance in eastern Europe as well. In Poland and Russia, the towering figures of Adam Mickiewicz (1798–1855) and Alexander Pushkin (1799–1837) helped define their countries' respective national literatures to such an extent that even today their works and lives remain crucial to Polish and Russian national identity. Mickiewicz's poetry, much of it composed in exile (the Russian authorities banished him from Poland in 1824), had a melancholy, elegiac tone, even as it celebrated the delights of Polish rural life. In his poem "The Grave of Countess Potocki," Mickiewicz mused on the "faded rose" who had died in exile from Poland and was now prey to the "worms of memories." As for Pushkin—the descendant, on his mother's side, of an African page raised by Peter the Great—he had literary genius that spilled over different genres and schools. Much of his work displays a precision and elegance that would become characteristic of realist writers in the decades to come. But in Pushkin's exaltation of the Russian nation, exemplified in his great narrative poem "The Bronze Horseman" (1833), and in his flamboyant life, which ended tragically in a duel with his own brother-in-law, he closely resembled the other great romantic poets of the day.

GERMANY Germany also held a commanding place in the pantheon of romantic poetry, thanks above all to the prolific genius of Goethe. Widely considered the most important figure in German cultural history, Goethe made brilliant and voluminous contributions to genres ranging from the novel to epic poetry to travel writing, history, art criticism, botany, and much else. But it is for his poetic works, especially *Faust*, that he is above all remembered.

Wanderer above the Sea of Fog It is the scene of sublime natural beauty, not the man, that is the focus of Caspar David Friedrich's (1774–1840) 1818 painting. Even the titular wanderer, as a good romantic should, turns away to admire the view.

Germany made another, particularly important contribution in the realm of music. The works of Ludwig van Beethoven (1770–1827), especially in the last years of his life, exemplified romantic principles: they challenged the classical harmonies beloved of earlier generations of composers; assaulted audiences with crescendos (as in the booming four notes that open the Fifth Symphony of 1807–1808); but then soothed them with the most delicate piano compositions (as in the "Moonlight" Sonata of 1801)—all of which proved uncannily able to elicit emotional responses. Beethoven's Austrian contemporary Franz Schubert (1797–1828), born of Moravian peasant stock, looked for inspiration in folk music for the more than 600 lieder (songs) he composed. As in the late eighteenth century, romantic artists and writers tended to believe in the "genius" or "spirit" of nations that was best preserved among simple rural people.

FRANCE   It was in France that romanticism prompted the most controversy. After the Restoration in 1815, the Comédie Française—the country's national theater and one of its most prestigious artistic institutions—remained in the hands of self-declared classicists who saw nothing in their own century to surpass the glories of an earlier age. But in early 1830, a group of young, self-declared partisans of the romantics finally managed to stage a contemporary play, *Hernani*, that deliberately challenged the strict canons of classical drama. Its author was a young writer of extravagant talent and ego: Victor Hugo (1802–1885),

the son of a Napoleonic general and a poet of extraordinary verbal facility (he claimed to compose verse in his dreams). At the first, hugely successful performances of *Hernani*, young supporters gleefully hurled insults at a bust of a seventeenth-century playwright in the theater's lobby. The same year, the French romantic composer Hector Berlioz (1803–1869) composed his masterpiece, the *Fantastic* Symphony, a "tone poem" that explored dream states in a fashion influenced by romantic verse. France also had great romantic painters such as Eugène Delacroix (1798–1863) and Théodore Géricault (1791–1824), who sought to stimulate the emotions of their viewers by using deep, vibrant, swirling colors to portray exotic subjects and extreme human experiences such as shipwrecks.

THE NOVEL   In England and France, the novel was the one great artistic and literary form that resisted the influence of romanticism. Writers like Jane Austen (1775–1817), Honoré de Balzac (1799–1850), Charles Dickens (1812–1870), and Stendhal (the pen-name of Henri Beyle, 1783–1842) were notable above all for their meticulous social and psychological observation. Austen, as we have seen, found drama in middle-class marriage practices, which she described with penetrating wit. Balzac produced a massive, panoramic series of works called *The Human Comedy* (after Dante's *Divine Comedy*) that savagely exposed the greed, selfishness, and delusions he saw at work in post-Napoleonic France. Dickens blended broad comedy with heart-rending melodramatic accounts of social injustice.

It was in Scotland, with Sir Walter Scott (1771–1832), that the romantic novel flourished most spectacularly. Scott's many works, starting with *Waverly* (1814), often called the first historical novel, sold astonishingly well. They displayed the characteristic romantic attention to sentiment and spiritual journeys, and to the reader's emotional response. However, as their principal setting they did not employ the natural environment, in the manner of Wordsworth, but rather human history. Scott's novels, many of them set in the Middle Ages, implied that people in earlier historical periods had experienced life differently, more deeply and vividly, than people of his own time. These works made Scott, alongside Dickens, one of the best-known English-language writers in the world.

THE TURN TO HISTORY   Scott's experiments with the historical novel illustrated another important shift in European thought taking place during the period. In many different realms of culture, Europeans were beginning to display a heightened sensitivity to the way

The Raft of the Medusa Contrasting light and shadows heighten the stark emotions conveyed by this 1818–1819 painting by Théodore Géricault. Survivors of a shipwreck reach out desperately for help, while dead bodies litter the foreground.

thought and behavior changed over the course of historical time, and an increasing attention to the historical roots of their own social and political practices and beliefs. We have already seen the way in which historical understanding developed during the Renaissance, but now an organized historical profession began to take shape. Specialized journals and institutions dedicated to history emerged, and universities, especially in Germany, added historians to their faculties. Scholars worked out systematic methods for organizing and analyzing archival documents. In Britain in 1838, Parliament passed the Public Record Office Act, which led to the establishment of formal government archives. European countries spent large sums to build museums displaying artifacts of the past, and the director of Denmark's national museum pioneered the division of "prehistory" into Stone, Bronze, and Iron Ages. By 1825, a Frenchman could write: "History is the Muse of our time; we are, I think, the first who have understood the past."

This "historical turn" had a particularly profound impact on European philosophy. The German philosopher Georg Wilhelm Friedrich Hegel wrote that in history the human spirit developed and became conscious of itself, and brought about human freedom. For him this "spirit," and human thought itself, did not exist in the abstract, outside of their historical context. Hegel saw the human spirit realizing itself above all within particular nation-states, with Germany as the most important and most advanced. Despite the difficult and abstract prose, educated Germans embraced Hegel's work with an almost religious enthusiasm.

The new philosophy of history joined hands with the religious and artistic movements of the period. Despite the differences among them, they all imparted to their followers a sense of participating in a process of revival and renewal. With the great political revolutions of the late eighteenth century now finished, and with socialist organizations still in their infancy, it was to these movements of inner, personal renewal that idealistic Europeans were now turning.

NEW POLITICAL PATTERNS

In the midst of these great economic, social, and cultural changes, and with the tumult of the revolutionary era still fresh in living memory, the 1820s saw political life across Europe take on new patterns. This was the first decade in European history in which we can accurately describe the principal political factions as "reactionary," "conservative,"

"liberal," or "radical." It was a period in which party systems, already well developed in Britain in the eighteenth century, began to spread to the Continent. And it was a period in which a great deal of political life began to turn around questions of what constituted a nation and where sovereign power within it lay.

LIBERALISM AND CONSERVATISM

Liberal politics in the period tended to center on claims to individual rights—especially the right to vote. Liberals inherited from older thinkers like Hobbes, Locke, and Rousseau the idea that sovereign authority derived from the consent of the governed and that citizens possessed certain inalienable, individual rights. From a later, predominantly British school known as **utilitarians** they developed a more insistent focus on the welfare of individuals as the ultimate measure of political good. The most famous of the utilitarians, Jeremy Bentham (1748–1832), held that governments should always pursue "the greatest good of the greatest number" and believed that this quality could be quantified through what he called a "felicific calculus." One basic assumption of liberalism was that people tended to act rationally, in their own economic self-interest, and that the market mediated these individual economic actions and desires to produce the best possible outcomes for society overall.

Liberals inspired by these principles campaigned for such goals as the expansion of the suffrage, legal protections for freedom of speech and religion, and promotion of free markets. They did not necessarily seek the vote for all adult men (still less women) and most had little quarrel with constitutional monarchy. Unlike modern American liberals, they generally distrusted strong government intervention in social and economic matters, even for the purpose of alleviating human misery. For this reason, they are now often referred to as classical liberals. They were poles apart from Saint-Simon, Fourier, and the other early utopian socialists, who were ready to curtail individual property rights and free markets in the name of the common good.

Liberals were particularly favorable to commercial and industrial interests. In Britain, the pioneering economic thinker David Ricardo (1772–1823) built upon the foundation established by Adam Smith in making a case for free trade, both within countries and between countries. His theory of "comparative advantage" held that countries should manufacture the products that they could produce most efficiently, and trade for the others. Elected to Parliament, Ricardo fought trade restrictions and supported industrial entrepreneurs.

Conservatives, in contrast, tended to stress the need for tradition and social order, and were prominent in support of monarchies across the Continent. The most important conservative ideas in the immediate post-Napoleonic period remained those of Edmund Burke. Like him, the later conservatives warned that too-rapid change, and too great an emphasis on individual desires and rights, could destroy the "organic" bonds that held nations together. Often hostile to commercial and industrial interests, they idealized monarchs, nobility, and rural society. Conservatives also insisted on the centrality of established, orthodox religion to the political and social order, praising the "union of throne and altar" despite the diminished power of the latter. They yearned for a mythical lost golden age when a pious peasantry dutifully followed the dictates of their religious leaders and social superiors.

One of the greatest thinkers in this period, the French noble Alexis de Tocqueville (1805–1859), combined aspects of liberal and conservative thought into one of the most profound bodies of work in European political thought. Descended from a grand noble family of the Old Regime, he openly lamented the passing of the aristocratic societies of the Old Regime. But having toured the United States in the early 1830s, he was impressed with the young nation's energy and returned to France to write a grand meditation entitled ***Democracy in America***. While most of his contemporaries still saw America as an "infant" society that trailed behind Europe in civilization and sophistication, Tocqueville presented it as an incarnation of modernity, which he associated with democracy, pluralism, and social equality. But at the same time, he saw these phenomena as mixed blessings at best, warning darkly about the "tyranny of the majority" over individuals in the United States. And more generally, he warned that in modern times, individuals needed to fear not only open despotism but also more subtle and insidious mechanisms of repression by the state. Over the citizens, he wrote, there

… is elevated an immense, tutelary power, which takes sole charge of assuring their enjoyment and of watching over their fate. It is absolute, attentive to detail, regular, provident, and gentle. It would resemble the paternal power if, like that power, it had as its object to prepare men for adulthood, but it seeks, to the contrary, to keep them irrevocably fixed in childhood [...] It works willingly for their happiness, but it wishes to be the only agent and the sole arbiter of that happiness.

It is a passage that remarkably anticipates later criticisms of excessive state power.

REACTION AND RADICALISM

Then there were the political extremes. At one end of the spectrum, reactionaries called for a full return to pre-Revolutionary social and political orders. French thinkers like Louis de Bonald (1754–1840) demanded the restoration of the old French Estates General, the abolition of press freedom, and the imposition of the death penalty for blasphemy. The Savoyard writer Joseph de Maistre (1753–1821) gained a wide influence with works that presented the French Revolution as fundamentally evil, but also part of God's plan for redeeming humanity. Monarchs like France's Charles X (r. 1824–1830) and Spain's Fernando VII (r. 1808; 1813–1833) eagerly subscribed to these ideas.

At the other end of the political spectrum, political radicals embraced a wide variety of goals. Some hoped above all for an expansion of the suffrage to all adult males; others advocated massive social and economic reforms, often taking inspiration from utopian socialists like Fourier and Owen. But not all of them limited themselves to Fourier's utopian fantasies of communal living or Owen's earnest blueprints for humane mill towns. As we will soon see, socialism took an important turn toward what its advocates considered a more scientific analysis of social forces and their direction. Other radicals formed secret societies to advance their goals through violence, of which the most famous, and strangest, was the Italian group known as the Carbonari ("charcoal-burners"), whom we met in the last chapter. One of their collaborators, Philippe Buonarotti, had worked with the French ultra-revolutionaries in the 1790s, and in an influential book he held them up as a model for a new generation to follow. The Carbonari themselves had imitators across the Continent.

Alexis de Tocqueville
Théodore Chassériau painted Tocqueville in 1850, when the latter was serving as foreign minister of France.

REPRESSION AND REFORM

The competition among liberals, conservatives, reactionaries, and radicals played out differently from country to country in this period. In Spain this competition led to open civil war; in France, to successful revolution. Elsewhere, violence was mostly limited to riots, sometimes on a large scale, and police repression. Indeed, throughout much of the Continent, the years between 1820 and 1845 marked a period of repression and reaction. Yet this repression itself helped generate new political forces that would soon coalesce into organized movements calling for power to the working classes.

In 1843, Prussian censors shut down a newspaper in the city of Cologne called the *Rheinische Zeitung* ("The Rhine Newspaper"), whose contributors included a young student of philosophy named Karl Marx (1818–1883). The paper advocated greater freedom of the press and campaigned for the rights of peasants against powerful landowners. The suppression helped convince Marx and other young Germans that a strategy of incremental liberal reform could not work, making revolution, perhaps even violent revolution, necessary. Marx began to read more deeply in the work of the early French and British socialists, and in 1845 he would proclaim that "the philosophers have only interpreted the world, the point is to change it." Even as many German liberals began to place their hope in a program of national unity, Marx and others began to envisage an international movement to combat social oppression.

SPAIN

Germany managed to avoid open civil war. The same was not true in Spain, which had barely recovered from its long and bloody struggle against Napoleon Bonaparte, and the loss of most of its overseas empire. On returning to Madrid after Napoleon's initial defeat in 1814, King Fernando VII repealed the liberal constitution that the national legislature in Cádiz had promulgated in 1812 under the influence of Enlightenment ideas and the French Revolution. In 1820, mutinous liberal soldiers put the king under virtual house arrest and forced him to implement the constitution, but his own followers soon revolted in turn. Fernando appealed to the European powers for help, and the Quadruple Alliance of Britain, France, the Netherlands, and Austria authorized the intervention of a French military force. With the Spanish far more divided than under Napoleon, the French won an easy victory and restored Fernando to full power.

Yet after Fernando's death in 1833, a quarrel over the succession led to new hostilities. The king had left the throne to his three-year-old daughter, with his liberal Italian queen as regent. But conservatives insisted that females could not inherit the throne and flocked to the standard of Fernando's brother Carlos, leading to the first of three nineteenth-century Carlist Wars that would last until 1876. Conservatives looked for their principal support in the countryside and in the northern Basque country, which feared for its traditional privileges under a liberal regime. But after six grinding years of conflict, and the death of as much as 3 percent of the entire Spanish population, in 1839 the liberals eked out a victory.

RUSSIA

Large-scale violence also broke out at the other end of Europe, in Russia. In 1825, Tsar Alexander I, the increasingly religious ruler who had led Russia in its defeat of Napoleon, died without legitimate offspring. Russia did not have much of a native liberal tradition, but since the French Revolution western European liberal ideas had found considerable support among intellectuals and in the army. These figures had watched with dismay as the tsar, increasingly fearful of revolution, had again ruled out any prospect of political reform. Now Russian liberals pinned their hopes on Alexander's brother Constantine. But unbeknown to them, Constantine had renounced his claim to the throne in favor of a third, far more autocratic brother, Nikolai. When Nikolai I (r. 1825–1855) took the throne in December 1825, the secret societies staged a massive protest in St. Petersburg aimed at sparking a popular revolution. But after a standoff lasting several hours,

Decembrist Revolt Crowds look on as a commander orders his troops to fire a cannon at protesters occupying a square in Saint Petersburg, in this watercolor depicting the suppression of the 1825 revolt.

Nikolai ordered his supporters to disperse the crowds with artillery, and the revolt crumbled. The leaders of the so-called **Decembrists** were hanged, and many of their followers banished to Siberia. Nikolai reigned for another thirty years as one of the most reactionary of European monarchs. The events drove idealistic young Russians to despair, and the romantic poet Mikhail Lermontov (1814–1841) made a grimly prescient prediction:

A year will come for Russia, a black year,
When its crowned head will fall into the mud,
When mobs will turn on all they once held dear
And Russians come to dine on death and blood.
. . .
Then shrouds will cover victims on the pyre
And famine will torment this wretched sphere,
While rivers glisten with reflected fire
—On this day will a mighty man appear.
And you will know him well, and understand
Why in his hand he holds a knife of steel.

Liberty Leading the People Delacroix's allegorical painting of the July Revolution shows Liberty, wearing the red revolutionary cap of 1789 and waving a tricolor flag, as she leads revolutionaries over the barricades into battle.

FRANCE AND THE REVOLUTION OF 1830

In France, the twice-restored monarchy of Louis XVIII tried, much like Napoleon himself, to plot a centrist course between reaction and liberalism. It had a written constitution and parliament, but a very small, wealthy, conservative electorate. Louis initially found himself opposed principally by the so-called ultras—ultraroyalist reactionaries—whose slogan "Long live the king in spite of himself!" expressed their dilemma of idealizing the monarchy while objecting to the actual monarch. But France's liberal moment came to an abrupt end in 1820, when an admirer of Bonaparte stabbed to death the king's nephew and heir to the throne, and public opinion turned sharply rightward. When Louis died in 1824, the throne passed to his younger brother Charles, whose instincts lay solidly with the ultras. King Charles X raised the specter of a broader restoration of the Old Regime, flirting with the possibility of reimbursing noble émigrés for property confiscated during the Revolution. And he staged a full Old Regime coronation for himself in Rheims Cathedral, where the kings of France were traditionally crowned. He even revived, to much ridicule, the medieval rite of trying to cure sufferers of scrofula by laying his royal hands on them.

Tensions with the liberal opposition finally came to a head in the summer of 1830, when Charles's government issued a series of ordinances that drastically reduced press freedom, dissolved a newly elected assembly, and culled opponents from the electoral rolls. In response, on July 27 a revolt broke out in Paris that quickly turned to revolution. Barricades sprang up in the city, and within four days the king had fled to London, leaving insurgents in command of the French state. The painter Eugène Delacroix immortalized this brief **July Revolution** in his grand tableau *Liberty Leading the People*.

For a moment, the return of a revolutionary republic seemed a possibility, but the leaders of the insurrection instead offered the throne to one of Charles's cousins, the fifty-six-year-old Louis-Philippe, duke of Orléans, who had served in the revolutionary army. Louis-Philippe (r. 1830–1848), popularly known as the Citizen King, took many symbolic steps aimed at reconciling monarchy more thoroughly with revolution. He dispensed with court etiquette, surrounded himself with bourgeois financiers, and restored the revolutionary tricolor as the national flag. He took the title "King of the French" (rather than "King of France"), signaling his respect for the sovereignty of the nation with the king as its agent. He also took more substantial measures, including more than doubling the size of the electorate and restricting the role of the executive in what became known as the July Monarchy of 1830–48. Radical workers were nonetheless disappointed by the limited scope of Louis-Philippe's reforms, particularly in regard to the suffrage and support for the poor. In the early 1830s several further uprisings took place, but the government violently suppressed them, and by the end of the decade a centrist and seemingly stable parliamentary regime had emerged. The king's most famous minister, François Guizot (1787–1874), dismissed queries from disenfranchised men demanding the vote with the words: "Get rich."

GREAT BRITAIN AND THE PATH OF REFORM

At several moments, revolution also seemed possible in Great Britain. In the 1820s, food riots and machine breaking continued across much of the kingdom. So did radical agitation against an electoral system that not only barred fourteen out of fifteen adult males from voting, mostly because of property requirements, but also left many parliamentary seats entirely in the control of powerful individual landowners. A series of acts dating to the seventeenth century had banned Catholics, Jews, and Protestant dissenters from serving in Parliament as well, and this effectively disenfranchised Ireland's large Catholic majority. In the late 1820s, the flamboyant Irish Catholic leader Daniel O'Connell (1775–1847) won election to Parliament but was barred from taking his seat. Even conservatives warned of serious unrest in Ireland unless the law was changed.

THE REFORM BILL OF 1832   But in the years around 1830 Britain's rulers, unlike Charles X of France, revealed a talent for compromise. The Tory and Whig Parties were used to shifting their positions in order to win elections, and both were fearful of revolution. Thus in 1829, faced with a deteriorating political situation in Ireland, a conservative government headed by the now duke of Wellington, the hero of the Napoleonic wars, repealed the measures barring Catholics from Parliament and allowed O'Connell and others to be seated. Then in 1830, a general election fought against the background of popular unrest brought a Whig government to power with a mandate to enact electoral reform. The failure of an initial attempt in 1831 prompted large-scale public protests, especially in northern industrial areas that still had little or no parliamentary representation despite huge increases in population. Finally, under pressure from his own conservative party and the new king, William IV (r. 1830–1837), Wellington agreed not to oppose the **Reform Bill of 1832**. It provided for elections in most parliamentary districts, redrew the country's electoral map more fairly, and expanded the electorate to include a large swathe of the middle classes—although still only 20 percent of the adult male population.

THE CHARTISTS   With the Reform Bill as a precedent, liberal and radical activity over the next sixteen years aimed at achieving a further, peaceful expansion of the franchise. In 1838, six liberal members of Parliament and six members of radical workingmen's associations published the "People's Charter," which called for universal adult male suffrage and annually elected parliaments. Although several of the so-called Chartists were arrested and jailed for sedition, they managed to organize a series of massive rallies, in London and other cities, and collected even more massive numbers of signatures on petitions calling for the Charter's enactment. In 1842, the National Chartist Association delivered to the House of Commons a giant scroll with no fewer than 3.3 million signatures, which Parliament summarily rejected as too threatening to its own rights. The **Chartist movement** was not entirely peaceful—a clash with authorities in Wales in 1839 left up to twenty-four people dead—but the movement never turned revolutionary, despite failing to achieve its goals. Full suffrage for men and women only arrived in Britain in the twentieth century.

REPEAL OF THE CORN LAWS   Radicals had greater success in another cause: repealing the Corn Laws, which imposed heavy tariffs on imported wheat, keeping domestic wheat prices high to the advantage of large landowners. The Anti–Corn Law League, founded in 1839 by Richard Cobden (1804–1865) and John Bright (1811–1889), united radicals with free-market liberals and a large portion of the urban middle classes. Bright, an evangelical and talented orator, cast the issue squarely as a contest between "the class of the great proprietors of the soil" and "trade and manufactures," and insisted that the time had come for the latter to prevail. In 1846 it did, when the Conservative government of Robert Peel agreed to the Corn Laws' repeal.

TRADE UNIONISM   A final area in which politics now turned increasingly around explicit questions of social class involved trade unionism. Prior to the 1830s, European industrial workers had engaged in relatively limited forms of collective action. On the Continent, journeymen's fraternities had sometimes tried to put pressure on masters and other employers—in Old Regime France, they had even initiated lawsuits for better wages and working conditions. In Britain, artisans had flocked to the radical corresponding societies of the 1790s, which agitated for political reform. And "friendly societies" that provided mutual aid for workers proliferated in the early nineteenth century, with over 200 in London alone. But legislation in many countries forbade the most direct and effective forms of workers' collective action, including formal unionization and strikes.

In 1824, however, Parliament repealed the principal British legislation on the subject, the so-called Combination Acts, and **trade unions** quickly came into existence. Robert Owen helped organize unions of skilled builders, and then a rickety Grand National Consolidated Trades Union, which collapsed a few months after it began in 1834. Unions in the individual crafts, however, developed successfully in the following decades. Unionism among unskilled, manual workers would not take hold until later in the century. Unionism nonetheless helped drive the various attempts by Parliament to alleviate working conditions in factories and to regulate the use of child labor. And British union members contributed to many of the great political causes of the day—particularly the call to expand the suffrage to all adult males.

THE NEW INTERNATIONAL ORDER AND NATIONALISM

At first glance, the years 1820–45 seem as turbulent, even violent, as any in European history. In addition to the upheavals already described in Spain, France, Russia, and Britain, the period saw revolutions in Belgium and Poland (the first successful; the second brutally repressed), civil strife throughout Germany and Italy, a successful independence struggle in Greece, and a new war between Russia and the Ottoman Empire. Yet in comparison with the bloody turmoil of 1789–1815, these struggles were relatively minor. Overall, the period was actually one of comparative calm, at least on the European continent, if not in Europe's overseas empires. The developments with the greatest potential for sparking international conflict were the stirrings of nationalist sentiment in Europe, driven in part by the cultural changes discussed above and the continuing expansion of overseas empires.

THE PEACE KEEPERS

The arrangements worked out at the Congress of Vienna after Napoleon's defeat were largely responsible for keeping the peace inside Europe for four decades after the battle of Waterloo in 1815. For the first time, the great powers—Britain, France, Austria, Prussia, and Russia—saw their role as not only maintaining a competitive balance of power, its terms worked out at successive peace conferences, but also actively managing the international order to prevent war through diplomacy—indeed, through a sort of joint security policy. The powers did not create a formal body analogous to the United Nations. However, the flurry of consultations among London, Vienna, St. Petersburg, Paris, and Berlin made this period a golden age of modern European diplomacy. The powers often disagreed—in general, the British felt more comfortable with adjustments to the order than did Metternich's Austria, particularly when it came to allowing new states to come into being in southeastern Europe. The "Holy Alliance" signed in 1815 by Austria, Russia, and Prussia also saw its mission as repressing social revolution throughout the Continent. But the diplomats generally managed to come to agreement.

Together, the powers repeatedly took steps to preserve monarchical authority. Recall that they authorized the French intervention in the Spanish civil war in 1823. Then, in the early 1830s, they ensured that Tsar Nikolai had a free hand when the autonomous kingdom of "**Congress Poland**" tried to claim full independence from Russia. This Polish revolt occurred when young Polish officers, inspired by the July Revolution in France and resentful of increasingly heavy-handed Russian rule, took up arms, leading to the establishment of a new revolutionary government that declared independence in January 1831. Russian troops finally crushed the revolt when they stormed Warsaw in the fall of 1832, driving tens of thousands of Poles into exile. The tsar then abolished the autonomous Polish Congress kingdom, revoking its constitution and dissolving its legislature and army.

In the same years, the powers similarly allowed Austria to crush a series of disorganized risings by liberal nationalists and radical secret societies elsewhere in Europe. The most important exception to the pattern occurred in 1830, when the Southern Netherlands declared independence from the Dutch government, which had ruled them since 1815 without giving its elites much say in the running of the newly enlarged kingdom. When it became clear that both Flemish and French speakers in the south supported the rebellion, the powers—driven by Great Britain—agreed to act as midwife for the newborn country of Belgium and to provide a German nobleman to sit on its new throne.

TENSIONS IN THE OTTOMAN EMPIRE

The order established by the Congress of Vienna came under greatest immediate pressure in eastern Europe. There, emergent nationalist movements and the strain put on the increasingly fragile Ottoman Empire by Russia led to repeated international crises.

GREEK INDEPENDENCE In 1821, Greeks living in the area of present-day Romania, led by a Russian prince of Greek descent, revolted against an Ottoman Turkish government that was struggling to reform its military and to keep its provincial officials in line. Although the Turks, with the initial support of the Congress powers, overcame these early rebels, the movement soon spread to Turkish-controlled Greece itself and gained the support of writers and artists like Byron, whose imaginations were captured by the largely fantastical idea of a revival

The Massacre at Chios Western outrage at Turkey is evident in Delacroix's painting of a scene from the Greek revolt. Women with their clothes torn off are at the mercy of Turkish soldiers on horseback, while other Greeks lie on the ground—some dead, some destitute.

of ancient Greek glory (Byron himself died on the way to help the rebels). Western European sympathy turned to anti-Turkish rage after the Turks massacred thousands of Greeks on the Aegean island of Chios and executed the Greek Orthodox patriarch of Constantinople.

By 1827, France and Britain had come to the conclusion that the hostilities could only be ended by Greek independence, and Russia, which had its own designs on the European possessions of the Ottoman Empire, including Constantinople, eagerly supported them. The Turks resisted, leading the allies to send a naval force that destroyed a Turkish fleet at the battle of Navarino, off the western Greek coast, in 1827. Five years later the Ottomans finally agreed to Greek independence, and the allied powers again dipped into Germany's large supply of under-employed princelings to find Greece a suitable monarch.

RUSSIAN EXPANSION After Navarino, Russia took advantage of the Turks' weakness to launch the only major war of the period and to pursue a dream of establishing itself as the preeminent power on the European continent by expanding to the Mediterranean—a key factor in the diplomatic and military history of the nineteenth century. The Russian army penetrated deep into the Balkans, occupying much of present-day Romania and Bulgaria. At this point Britain, France, and Austria grew nervous that the entire Turkish Empire might dissolve, with Russia reaping the spoils and gaining direct access to the Aegean. Thanks to their pressure, Russia made peace with the Ottomans in 1829. But it still gained effective control over the Romanian provinces of Moldavia and Wallachia, while the small Slavic principality of Serbia confirmed its autonomy from the Turks.

The Ottoman Empire would remain one of the most important sources of instability in Europe for the rest of the nineteenth century. Just a decade after the Russo-Turkish War of 1828–1829, the ambitious ruler of Egypt, Mehmet Ali (r. 1805–1848), attempted to declare independence for that country and conquered large portions of present-day Israel, Lebanon, and Syria. Although he hoped for support from France, the other major powers sent a naval expedition and forced him to withdraw.

THE RISE OF NATIONAL INDEPENDENCE MOVEMENTS

As the Greek, Polish, and Belgian events suggest, another important long-term threat to the stability of the 1815 settlement came from the growth of national independence movements. National sentiment itself was hardly a new phenomenon in Europe—even many medieval Europeans had a clear sense of the division of the Continent into separate nations. And as we have seen, **nationalism**—which is best defined as an explicit political program aimed at constructing nation-states—dates back to the French Revolution. During the Napoleonic Wars, the nationalist rhetoric deployed by the Jacobins to mobilize the French in the 1790s proved equally successful in spurring resistance against France, especially in Spain and Germany.

THE EMERGENCE OF NATIONALISM But in the 1820s, something changed: nationalism emerged for the first time as a potent, peacetime political force that posed particular dangers to Europe's multi-ethnic empires—the Austrian, Ottoman, and Russian. One reason for this emergence was that with the advent of liberalism and its priorities on individual rights, educated elites from Greece to Norway came to resent the denial of voting rights and constitutional protections by a regime controlled by another national group—and sought redress through their own national unity and independence. In addition, the romantic movement, with its emphasis on the individual character (or "genius") of different ethnic groups and its emotional appeal to national history, provided a powerful language for expressing nationalist aspirations and grievances.

The period 1820–45 saw only two large-scale nationalist revolts in Europe itself: the successful war for independence in Greece and the failed Polish uprising in 1830–32. But throughout the great European land empires, other nationalist movements started to take shape, as the case of the Czechs illustrates. Before 1800, most Czechs in the Austrian Empire lived in rural areas, often as serfs. The city of Prague was almost entirely German-speaking; the Czech language had largely disappeared from schools, the state administration, and print culture. But with the economic expansion of the early nineteenth century, Czechs began making their way back into the cities, and their levels of wealth and literacy rose. In 1809, the scholar and former Jesuit Josef Dobrovský (1753–1829) published a path-breaking grammar of the Czech language, and over the next twenty years lexicographers developed a modern Czech vocabulary. In the 1830s, large-scale Czech publishing began, and as it did, Czech politicians began pushing for greater autonomy within the Austrian Empire.

Similar developments occurred in Romania (still largely under Ottoman rule) and also Norway, which had passed from Danish to Swedish rule with the end of the Napoleonic Wars. In both Norway and Greece, scholars attempted to invent standard languages for the aspiring nation-states, combining different dialects and coining new words from traditional roots. In Hungary, which under Austrian rule had preserved many of its national institutions (including a parliament), as well as its literary language, nationalist leaders also began pushing for greater autonomy. Serbia continued its own gradual process of divorce from the Ottoman Empire, winning the right to hereditary rule by its own princes in 1833, and gaining its first constitution two years later.

NATIONALISM IN ITALY AND GERMANY An even more visible nationalist movement within the Austrian Empire took shape in Italy. Under the 1815 settlement, Austria claimed most of northern Italy east of Piedmont, including Venice and Milan. The remainder of the peninsula continued to be divided among a number of states, principally Naples (now called the kingdom of the Two Sicilies), the Papal States, and Tuscany. In 1831, a liberal Genoese lawyer named Giuseppe Mazzini (1805–1872) founded a group called Young Italy, which rejected the conspiratorial tactics of the Carbonari and envisioned a unification of the peninsula as a step in the creation of a peaceful Europe of federated, cooperative nation-states. "The map of Europe has to be remade," Mazzini would declare in 1852 after leading several failed insurrections, punctuated by spells in Austrian jails. Italian artists, including the composer Gioacchino Rossini (1792–1868), began to dramatize the cause of the Italian nation in their works.

In Germany as well, liberal aspirations began to drive calls for national unity in the years after the Congress of Vienna. Under the **German Confederation**, the largely toothless successor to the Holy Roman Empire, student groups in the German universities issued calls for uniting the fragmented German states. They even made one abortive attempt to storm the meeting place of the Confederation's parliament in Frankfurt. The dominant states in the Confederation—Prussia and Austria—feared anything that smacked of revolution and relentlessly repressed democratic activism.

In the end, developments in the years after 1815 suggested that German unification would follow a different model. With the Vienna settlement, Prussia gained significant territories in the western German area of the Rhineland, thereby becoming the dominant state in the German lands outside the Austrian Empire. Hoping that economic unity under autocratic Prussian leadership might foreshadow political unity under Prussia, its government then pushed through the creation of a customs union to facilitate intra-German trade. By 1835, it included a majority of the Confederation's member states. The ideal of a united Germany, hailed by writers and artists during the Napoleonic period, now seemed closer to institutional realization.

THE CRISIS OF THE IBERIAN EMPIRES Even with the emergence of nationalist sentiments and the destabilizing crises in the Ottoman Empire, the Congress arrangements still helped maintain an unprecedented degree of stability and peace in Europe itself during the period 1820–45. European overseas empires were a different story, however. Here the period saw considerable instability and violence, with setbacks as well as significant gains for imperialist causes. Much of the imperial instability was stirred by the spread of liberal and nationalist ideas from Europe to the Americas.

The greatest setbacks to the imperial cause took place in the Spanish and Portuguese empires. Revolts by settlers born in the Americas ("creoles") had occurred against Spanish rule in Latin America since the late eighteenth century. Napoleon's conquest of Spain allowed these scattered brushfires to explode into a continental conflagration, driven in large part by the resentment of creoles against Iberian-born officials. King Fernando then destroyed any hope for reconciliation with the heavy-handed absolutist policies he pursued upon his restoration in 1814. Spanish authorities initially won some victories over South American insurgents, but by 1818 the tide had definitively turned, and Spain had no choice but to give up most of its American empire.

Inspired above all by the leadership of the Argentinian general José de San Martín (1778–1850) and the Venezuelan leader Simón Bolívar (1783–1830), a constellation of independent nations emerged that would eventually stretch from Panama to Cape Horn in South America. They were joined by Mexico and a collection of smaller Central American states. The Congress powers, again concerned above all to maintain stability, refused Spanish requests for aid and soon granted diplomatic recognition to the newly independent nations. Britain played a particularly important role here and soon moved to establish a significant sphere of influence in South America, despite attempts by the United States to limit the role of European powers through the Monroe Doctrine of 1823. Spain preserved only a few island fragments of empire: principally the Philippines, Cuba, Puerto Rico, and some scattered Pacific territories.

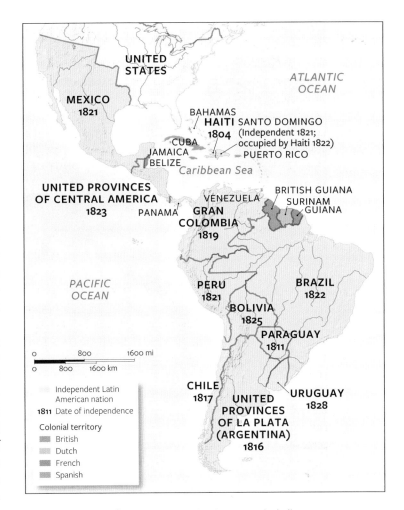

Latin American Nations, 1800–1830 By 1830, states including Argentina, Chile, Mexico, and Brazil achieved independence from the Spanish and Portuguese empires that had previously controlled the entirety of Central and South America. This map shows the initial borders of these new states. Spain only retained a few small colonies such as Cuba and Puerto Rico, while Britain, the Netherlands, and France also held small interests in Central and South America.

Meanwhile, in 1821, Brazil staged a successful, largely peaceful revolution against Portugal, which also found its empire reduced to a chain of trading posts and island territories, in this case stretching from Macao in China to India and southern Africa. In Latin America, the independence movements harkened back to the American Revolution. Many of the new nations quickly produced Declarations of Independence and Constitutions modeled on the American ones. Native Americans—a very large portion of the population in some of the new states—remained repressed and discriminated against, and in Brazil black slavery lasted until 1888.

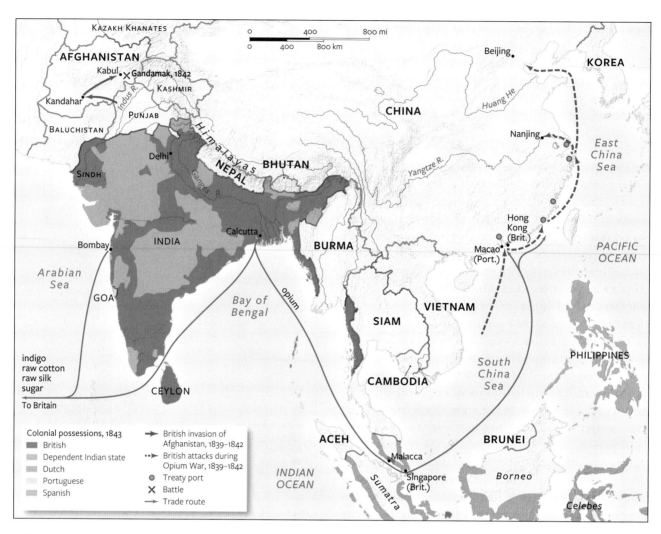

British Expansion in Asia, 1843 Despite Britain's failures in Afghanistan, the wars of the early 19th century made it an extremely powerful presence in Asia, eclipsing the other European empires in the region. Britain controlled the entire Indian subcontinent—either directly or through agreements with local rulers—as well as Hong Kong and parts of Burma and Siam. Also, it had established naval control over trade routes that brought Indian opium to China and Asian goods back to Britain.

IMPERIAL EXPANSION AND RESISTANCE

In these decades, European imperialism moved into a new phase. European empires shifted the principal theater of their activities from the Americas to Asia and Africa, and one empire in particular would far outstrip its rivals in establishing a worldwide colonial presence.

THE BRITISH EMPIRE ASCENDANT As the Iberian empires contracted, the British Empire expanded mightily. The British East India Company already ruled significant areas in India—partly on its own, and partly through dependent local princes. In the mid-1820s, a long

and costly war against the kingdom of Burma allowed the British to annex several rich eastern Indian provinces. And between the 1830s and 1843, the predominantly Muslim province of Sindh, covering much of present-day Pakistan and Afghanistan, fell under Company rule as well. Between 1839 and 1842, Britain also fought the short, decisive **Opium War** against China, forcing the Chinese to open ports to British trade—particularly the profitable trade in highly addictive Indian opium. The 1842 Treaty of Nanking gave Britain the port city of Hong Kong as well. In addition to this trade, the empire in this period increasingly supplied British factories with raw materials, notably cotton from the expanding cotton fields of India.

But the limits to British expansionism in Asia became

How did the rise of nationalism affect the international order?

633

apparent in that graveyard of empires, Afghanistan. Here the British had largely groundless strategic concerns—they worried that the expanding Russian Empire might eventually use the country as a base from which to threaten Britain's Indian possessions. British observers would come to refer to this competition between their country and Russia as the great game. Judging Afghanistan's king unreliable as an ally, they sent a 20,000-strong army north from India in 1839, which won a series of quick victories and set up camp in the capital of Kabul. But as the British presence in the city swelled, Afghans rallied to the king's son and carried out increasingly daring attacks on the British forces. The top British commander, after dithering for several months, finally decided to withdraw. But in the mountain passes leading back to India, Afghan tribesmen attacked the British, slaughtering all but a few of the soldiers and their family members. The news caused consternation in Britain, and dramatic images of the column's last stand at Gandamak proliferated. Afghanistan remained independent.

Last Stand at Gandamak This 1898 painting of the final moments of the British campaign in Afghanistan shows a small group of wounded soldiers, surrounded by dead comrades, preparing to face off against the enemy coming over the hill.

THE FRENCH CONQUEST OF ALGERIA The most important new theater of European imperialism in this period was Muslim north Africa. The local regimes along the southern Mediterranean coast, nominally loyal to the Ottomans, had fought with European regimes for centuries and frequently seized European ships, enslaving Christian passengers. In the late 1820s, the Restoration government in France, in part to distract public attention from its domestic troubles, decided to subdue what are now the coastal provinces of Algeria, the principal source of this piracy, and to bring them under French rule. The successful campaign, involving some 600 French ships and 34,000 soldiers, took place in June 1830, just days before the July Revolution. But the new king, Louis-Philippe, endorsed the conquest and began the transformation of Algeria into a French possession.

Local rebels resisted until well into the 1840s, but the French army eventually overcame them. French officials quickly developed the ambition of making Algeria a part of France. They also encouraged settlement by European colonists—unlike the British in India—and by 1845 over 100,000 had come from France, mostly to the temperate coastal cities. They were in a distinct minority, however, compared to the two million Algerian Muslims to whom the French denied equal rights. For the moment, Algeria had principally a strategic role for France, giving it effective control over the western Mediterranean, although in the future Algeria would develop considerable economic importance.

BRITAIN'S ABOLITION OF SLAVERY Overall, European imperialism in the period, from the conquests in Algeria and India to the Opium War in China, is often presented as an enterprise pursued without any moral checks whatsoever. But it is important to realize that from as early as Bartolomé de las Casas's condemnation of Spanish treatment of native Americans in the sixteenth century, moral critiques of imperialism had developed alongside imperialism itself. During the Enlightenment, influential works like the *History of the Two Indies*, composed by Parisian *philosophes*, had found large audiences with their arguments that supposedly "primitive" peoples had to be understood as social and cultural actors capable of developing their own path to modernity. Christian evangelical thought, Enlightenment conceptions of "the rights of man," and moralizing middle-class reform movements also spurred critiques of imperialism.

And in Britain, these critiques found important political expression. In 1807, Britain outlawed the slave trade throughout its possessions. Then in 1833 it proceeded to abolish slavery itself throughout most of the British Empire, with the notable exception of East India Company territories in South Asia and the Indian Ocean. Abolition was spurred by the strong opposition to slavery among dissenting Protestants, especially Quakers, who had a particularly strong presence in the middle-class electorate enfranchised by the Reform Bill. Still, slavery remained a profitable enterprise, especially on the sugar and coffee plantations of the French and Spanish Caribbean colonies, and the plantations of the United States. In the end, the spread of moralizing evangelical movements, and the rise of a liberal current of thought that was increasingly willing to attribute basic rights to all humans, won out over economic interests. Other than the abortive French Revolution emancipation decree of 1794, Britain's was the first major step to abolish slavery taken by a European power.

CONCLUSION

Some liberal British thinkers, including John Bright and Richard Cobden, wanted to go further than abolishing slavery. They proposed that Great Britain retreat from empire altogether, inviting opponents to brand them Little Englanders. But their efforts were unsuccessful. The heyday of European overseas empire was yet to come. In fact, between 1820 and 1845, and especially with the conquest of Algeria, Europe entered a second age of empire that differed in important ways from what had come before, even as it kept evolving through the rest of the nineteenth century.

The first age of European overseas empire, which had begun with the explorations of the fifteenth century, centered on the Americas and ended with the independence of most American territories during the half-century that followed 1776. The second age would above all involve Africa and Asia and would be shaped by the transformations Europe had undergone since the late eighteenth century. What the nineteenth century called imperialism would be powered by steam, plated with iron, and fed with a steady stream of raw materials awaiting their transformation into industrial manufactures and consumer goods. It would be a program carried out in large part by the new European middle classes. And it would be a program that inadvertently brought with it ideas of liberal democracy and national self-determination, which indigenous peoples would appropriate, adapt, combine with traditions of their own, and ultimately wield with destructive effect against the very countries that had sought to exploit them. In this way, the period 1820–45 set the stage both for the greatest global expansion of European power in history and for that expansion's ultimate end.

KEY TERMS

Industrial Revolution
  (p. 602)
factory towns (p. 609)
bourgeoisie (p. 611)
proletariat (p. 611)
cult of domesticity (p. 614)

cholera (p. 617)
Poor Law Amendment of
  1834 (p. 618)
socialism (p. 619)
romanticism (p. 620)
utilitarianism (p. 623)

Democracy in America
  (p. 624)
Decembrists (p. 626)
July Revolution (p. 626)
Reform Bill of 1832 (p. 627)
Chartist movement
  (p. 627)

trade unions (p. 628)
Congress Poland (p. 628)
nationalism (p. 630)
German Confederation
  (p. 630)
Opium War (p. 632)

REVIEW QUESTIONS

1. What factors established Britain's lead in industrial growth?

2. How did early industrialization transform Europe?

3. Describe some of the distinctive features of the family life and culture of the European urban middle classes of the mid-nineteenth century.

4. What made living and working conditions in cities during this period so unhealthy?

5. What social and religious reforms occurred during the first half of the nineteenth century?

6. How did romanticism shape the literature and arts of the early nineteenth century?

7. What did reactionaries, conservatives, liberals, and radicals, respectively, identify as the chief political problems of their time, and what solutions did each group propose?

8. What were the effects of the violent revolutions and uprisings that spread throughout Europe and Latin America during the first half of the nineteenth century?

9. How did national independence movements challenge the existing order?

10. What were the goals of the European overseas expansion that began in the 1830s?

CORE OBJECTIVES

After reading this chapter, you should have a solid understanding of the following core objectives. To strengthen your grasp of the core objectives, use the resources on the Student Site for The West.

- Identify the factors that led to the Industrial Revolution in the nineteenth century.
- Analyze the roles of the middle and lower classes in nineteenth-century industrial societies.
- Describe the negative impacts of industrialization and the responses to them.

- Assess the emergence of new religious movements and romanticism.
- Evaluate the emergent political ideologies and civil conflicts of the period.
- Consider the impact of nationalism and imperialism on Europe and the world in the first half of the nineteenth century.

 GO TO **inQuizitive** TO SEE WHAT YOU'VE LEARNED—AND LEARN WHAT YOU'VE MISSED—WITH PERSONALIZED FEEDBACK ALONG THE WAY.

1845–1849
Irish famine

1846
Repeal of Corn
Laws in Britain

1848–1849
Revolutions and
Counterrevolutions
throughout Europe

1848
Marx and Engels publish
The Communist Manifesto

1851
Great Exhibition in London

1852
Napoleon III
proclaims himself
emperor of France

1853–1856
Crimean War

1857–1858
Indian War of
Independence

1859
Charles Darwin publishes
On the Origin of Species

1860
Second
Opium War

1861
Alexander II
emancipates
Russian serfs

1866
Austro-Prussian War

19

Growing Pains

SOCIAL AND POLITICAL UPHEAVALS

1845–1880

1871
Unification
of Germany

March–May 1871
Paris Commune

1870
Unification of
Italy completed

1870–1871
Franco-Prussian War

1870s
Kulturkampf against
German Catholics

1876
Britain and its
colonies formally
become an empire

"The old Paris is no more. A city's shape changes more quickly, alas, than a human heart." When the author of these lines, the poet Charles Baudelaire, was born in 1821, the capital of France still had much the appearance of a medieval city. Although it had lost its medieval city walls, demolished well before the French Revolution, the city center remained a tangle of narrow streets and alleyways clustered tightly about the banks of the Seine River. Buildings seemed crammed into every available space: around the dozens of churches and convents that still dotted the urban landscape, right up against the walls of the old royal palace of the Louvre, now a museum, and even spilling into its massive courtyards. It was only in the late eighteenth century that the monarchy had cleared the last buildings off the city's bridges.

In the first decades of the 1800s, Paris had inadequate supplies of fresh water and a small, poorly maintained sewer system. Most inhabitants drew their drinking water from the filthy river, while human and animal waste collected in the streets. These conditions generated overpowering odors in warm weather and provided a fertile breeding ground for water-borne diseases like cholera. The city's narrow, winding streets also made it easy for insurgents to block off whole neighborhoods with impromptu but effective barricades, to the despair of successive governments. For centuries, reformers had dreamed

---

Haussmannization Gustave Caillebotte's 1877 painting *Paris Street; Rainy Day*, depicting elegantly dressed pedestrians walking along as if on display, as well as wide boulevards and gas lamps, perfectly illustrates the city's new character.

- What sparked the revolutions of 1848 across the continent?
- How did politics drive reform and imperial power in Britain?
- What drove national unification and international rivalry in this period?
- How did city life change over these years?
- What important challenges to bourgeois life emerged at this time?

of opening Paris up to light, air, fresh water—and to government authority—by constructing broad boulevards and leafy squares, aqueducts and proper sewers. Their efforts, however, had been limited.

But when Baudelaire reached his thirties, the old Paris, as he observed, was no more. The unlikely agent of change was a balding, portly civil servant with a passion for music who had spent his career avoiding the political storms of the century and steadily advanced up the ranks of the French national administration. Baron Georges-Eugène Haussmann (1809–1891) took office as prefect of Paris and the surrounding areas in 1853, with a mandate from Emperor Napoleon III to reshape the city of Paris. Napoleon, the nephew of Napoleon I, had originally come to power as an elected president of the French Republic, but in 1851 he staged a coup d'état against his own government, and a year later he proclaimed himself emperor. Now Napoleon III intended to use his power to achieve what the previous decades' constitutional monarchies and republics had not.

Under Haussmann's direction, the regime turned virtually the entire city into a dirt-clogged construction zone. Wide new boulevards were driven into Paris on north-south and east-west axes, facilitating, among other things, the movement of troops in case of rebellion. Napoleon I's Arc de Triomphe became the center of a spectacular intersection of twelve massive boulevards. To make room for these thoroughfares, and for imposing new government structures on the city's central island, thousands of old buildings were demolished. The process forced tens of thousands of Parisians to move out of their homes, in most cases to the city's gritty, expanding industrial suburbs.

Haussmann also took on the problem of sanitation. A new aqueduct system brought in plentiful fresh water from a source 80 miles to the east. Engineers added over 300 miles of sewer lines, including central "galleries" twelve feet high and twelve feet wide. As the most famous French writer of the century, Victor Hugo, would point out in the 1860s in *Les Misérables*: "Paris has another Paris under herself, a Paris of sewers; which has its streets, its crossings, its squares, its blind alleys, its arteries, and its circulation, which is slime, minus the human form." The organizers of the World Exposition of 1867, which aimed to show off the new Paris to the world, included guided tours of the sewer system.

The Paris that emerged from "Haussmannization," with its clean, broad streets flanked by stately apartment blocks, was now a middle-class showcase. A network of covered shopping arcades encouraged the conspicuous consumption of sophisticated pleasures. Horse-drawn taxis became a common sight, along with larger vehicles that carried passengers from both the middle and working classes along set routes. These vehicles took their name from the Latin word meaning "for all"—*omnibus,* or, in its more common abbreviation, *bus.*

More than a century and a half later, it is all too easy to look back on the transformation of Paris and imagine the middle years of the nineteenth century as ones of steady social and political progress. The middle classes became more prominent than ever before. Industrialization and urbanization continued apace, across more and more of Europe. Parliamentary democracy seemed ascendant as well, with western European countries mostly moving, by 1880, toward political systems in which all or most adult males voted for representative bodies with significant political power. Napoleon III himself left the scene for good in 1870, making way for the triumph of republicanism in France.

Nationalism seemed to be reshaping Europe into an orderly system of coherent nation-states. After centuries of division, both Italy and Germany unified, while the Austrian Empire devolved significant power to its largest ethnic minority, the Hungarians. Their partially autonomous kingdom took up more than half of the territory of what was now called the Austro-Hungarian Empire, extending well beyond the boundaries of the Hungarian ethnic group to include most of present-day Croatia and Slovakia, as well as parts of Poland, Serbia, Romania, and Ukraine. And the European powers flexed their muscles across the globe. Most telling, in October 1860, in the Second Opium War, a combined Anglo-French force crushed Chinese resistance and entered Beijing to force the Qing dynasty (1644–1912) to open more ports to Western trade—particularly the trade in opium.

Yet few of these developments were actually pointing in a clear, unambiguous direction. Industrialization provoked ever-sharper critiques and helped lead to the emergence of a coherent ideological movement committed to the wholesale transformation of European social structures—Marxist socialism. The period's greatest explosion of democratic and nationalist energies, in what came to be called the "springtime of nations" of 1848, was followed by a summer and autumn of reaction across much of the Continent, typified by Napoleon III. And Europe's expanding overseas empires remained fragile, capable not only of astonishing conquests but also of bloody reverses. British and French triumphs in China in 1860 nursed movements that would later emerge to oppose them. In short, even on the eve of Europe's greatest period of global power, the supposedly inevitable and irresistible advance of European civilization was anything but certain.

THE REVOLUTIONS OF 1848

At the end of the Napoleonic Wars in 1815, Europeans exhausted by carnage and instability had looked to politics principally for the maintenance of peace and order. Thirty years later, however, memories of the carnage had faded, and personalities and arrangements once praised as the height of rational security seemed crabbed and repressive. Once again, conditions were ripe for the outbreak of revolution across the Continent. The first sparks burst out in 1846, when Polish nationalists plotted simultaneous uprisings in the Polish regions of Prussia, Austria, and Russia, only to see them crushed by the police and, in Austria, by the army. In 1848, full-fledged revolutions again ignited, and as in the late eighteenth century, the flames burned brightest in France.

THE FRENCH SECOND REPUBLIC (1848–1852)

No person better illustrated the shift in political climate that brought about the revolutions than France's king,

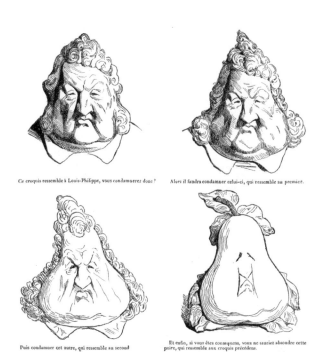

Louis-Philippe The caricaturist Charles Philipon made this illustration of Louis-Philippe turning into a pear, an enduring symbol of popular frustration with the monarch.

Louis-Philippe. At age eighteen, in 1792, he had been the dashing prince turned revolutionary who helped save the day for the newborn French Republic at the critical battle of Valmy. At age fifty-six, in 1830, he had been the reassuringly practical, unpretentious "citizen king" who seemed ideally suited for reuniting his country after the tumult and dissension of the Empire and the failed Restoration. But by age seventy-four, in early 1848, he seemed a corrupt curmudgeon whose jowly face lent itself all too easily to cruel caricature. Although Louis-Philippe's July Monarchy (named for the July Revolution that had brought it into being) had doubled the size of the electorate, the vote was still limited to just 200,000 men out of a total French population of 35,000,000, and real power lay with a small network of the king's cronies from the world of finance.

François Guizot, the talented Protestant historian and political writer who served as prime minister in the late 1840s, steadfastly resisted calls for universal suffrage and seemed for a time to command respect. But in 1846 and 1847, Louis-Philippe's regime came under new pressure from financial scandals, a severe industrial slump that started in the railroad sector, a banking panic, and an agricultural crisis that sent the price of grain soaring. Thanks to the radical centralization of the French state that had begun under the absolute monarchy and was completed by

Bonaparte, the regime's head—the central government in Paris—was also its Achilles' heel. As the French had seen in the Revolution of 1830 (which lasted just four days), whoever controlled Paris controlled the state.

The French Revolution of 1848 initially played out as a classic Parisian drama. With political rallies forbidden, opponents of the regime publicized their cause by holding a series of ostentatious public banquets. When Guizot banned the largest of these, scheduled for February 22, protesters thronged the streets of the capital, demanding his resignation. The next day the king dismissed Guizot, but by then the protests had taken on a momentum of their own. In the evening, a huge column of demonstrators from across the social spectrum literally collided with infantry and cavalry lined up on a major boulevard. Victor Hugo, an eyewitness, reported what happened next:

> At this moment a shot rang out, from which side is not known. Panic followed and then a volley. Eighty dead or wounded remained on the spot. A universal cry of horror and fury arose: "Vengeance!" The bodies of the victims were loaded on a cart lit with torches. The cortège moved back amidst curses at a funereal pace. And in a few hours Paris was covered with barricades.

The barricades, some built around the new "buses," blocked off scores of narrow, pre-Haussmann streets and proved effective. Louis-Philippe desperately sought to save the day, reshuffling his government and finally trying to abdicate in favor of his grandson. But by this point, insurgents—mostly skilled workers, students, and middle-class professionals—had captured key sites in central Paris and were proclaiming the Second Republic (the first was the regime that had lasted from 1792 to Napoleon's coronation in 1804). Rather than risk sharing the fate of his guillotined cousin Louis XVI, Louis-Philippe fled to London. A provisional government took power, on February 26, headed by nine republicans drawn from the liberal opposition to Louis-Philippe. At the insistence of the Parisian crowds, they then added two others to the list: the radical Louis Blanc and a worker by the name of Albert. Hopes were high that the new government would move toward extending the franchise to all adult men and institute social welfare policies to ease the lives of urban workers.

THE SPREAD OF REVOLUTION

Six decades before, the French Revolution of 1789 had not immediately provoked widespread imitations beyond the borders of France. It mostly took the arrival of aggressive, republican French armies to precipitate revolutionary action elsewhere. In 1848, things were different—in part because the telegraph now spread news instantaneously. Even before the 1848 Revolution in France, Sicilian nobles had revolted against the Bourbon government of the kingdom of the Two Sicilies (covering the southern half of the Italian peninsula). And afterward, revolutionary movements coalesced throughout the Continent, often led by university students inspired both by the news from Paris and by now-distant memories of the eighteenth-century revolutionary era.

The motivations of this new generation of revolutionaries were varied. In part, they reflected social tensions spurred by the disruptions of the Industrial Revolution. In many areas, they derived from nationalist sentiments and movements, with newly self-conscious national groups demanding greater sovereignty and independence. Partly they came from the spread of liberal political demands for greater freedom of expression and a wider suffrage, combined with frustration at what increasingly seemed an allergy to change on the part of stubborn ruling regimes. Examples of revolution in other countries both provided a model to follow and also provoked the anxiety that if the moment was not seized, the opportunity might disappear forever. All these factors combined to produce, in scarcely a month and a half, more sweeping political changes across Europe than at any time since 1815.

GERMANY AND AUSTRIA On March 3, scarcely a week after Louis-Philippe's abdication, protests and petitions began to proliferate in areas of western Germany that had belonged to Prussia since 1815. Demands from liberal groups included increased constitutional freedoms and the creation of new systems of social welfare to alleviate economic misery. On the same day, 650 miles to the east in Budapest, the nationalist lawyer Lajos Kossuth (1802–1894) established his leadership of Hungarian liberals with a fiery speech demanding representative government and additional rights for the Hungarians within the Austrian Empire, which remained a looser political entity than the hyper-centralized French state.

Ten days after that, in Vienna, it seemed as if the French events were repeating themselves. Students and radical artisans marched in the streets demanding expanded voting rights and the participation of the empire's German-speaking regions in a new pan-German federation. Troops opened fire, and the movement turned revolutionary. The dominant figure in Austrian political life had been the same man since early in the century: the

The Revolutions of 1848 Nationalist and liberal revolutions broke out in cities throughout Europe in the spring of 1848, from Paris to Budapest. But by 1849, conservatives had largely quashed the uprisings.

Montez. She fled the country, but soon afterward students took to the streets of Munich with liberal demands and forced Ludwig to abdicate in favor of his eldest son.

Elsewhere, princes remained on their thrones but only by promising substantial reforms. The most important events occurred in Prussia. Polish nationalists in the Polish-speaking region around Poznan revolted unsuccessfully in yet another attempt to unify their country and restore its sovereignty. Meanwhile, a revolution took place in Berlin itself, driven largely by urban artisans who feared both competition from outside the traditional guild structures and also the effects of mechanization. Violent crowds in the capital intimidated King Friedrich Wilhelm IV (r. 1840–1861) into conceding free elections, freedom of the press, and a new constitution. Like their counterparts in Vienna, the Berlin revolutionaries called for the creation of a united Germany.

In a proclamation to the Prussian nation on March 21, the king declared: "I have today ... placed myself and my people under the venerable banner of the German Empire. Prussia is from now on part of Germany." It seemed as if the German states, after their long centuries of fragmentation, were about to perform a spontaneous act of unification. At the end of March, a group of liberal reformers, mostly from southwestern Germany, met in Frankfurt to propose elections for a **pan-German parliament**, chosen by universal manhood suffrage, which would draw up a constitution for the entire country. The Diet, or assembly, of the weak German Confederation—which had replaced

conservative diplomat and politician Klemens von Metternich, one of the guiding spirits of the Congress of Vienna. But he was the same age as Louis-Philippe, and deeply unpopular. Now the Habsburg family, headed by the often incoherent emperor Ferdinand I (r. 1835–1848), prevailed upon Metternich to resign his position as chancellor and hoped that sweeping concessions would preempt further upheaval. Most important, they announced that all adult males would be able to vote for a new imperial Austrian parliament. This put the empire's German-speakers, still its largest ethnic group, in a distinct minority, outnumbered collectively by the empire's Hungarians, Czechs, Slovaks, and others.

The wave of revolutions continued in the second half of March 1848, sweeping over every major German state. In conservative, Catholic Bavaria, the unrest had begun a few weeks earlier with outraged protests against the mistress of King Ludwig I (r. 1825–1848), a flamboyant Irish adventuress named Eliza Gilbert who had previously enthralled London music hall audiences under the stage name Lola

Revolution in Berlin In a lithograph from the period, imperial troops fire upon revolutionaries on a barricade in Berlin in March 1848. The revolutionaries wave a new tricolor flag—first widely seen in the 1848 Revolution—that signals their support for a unified Germany.

the old Holy Roman Empire at the end of the Napoleonic Wars—approved the plan, and elections to the new united parliament in Frankfurt began almost immediately.

ITALY At the same moment, it seemed as if a drive for unification might overtake Italy as well. In mid-March, nationalist crowds skirmished with troops in the streets of Austrian-ruled Lombardy and Venice, leading to open revolts and proclamations of independence. Further south, protests elicited promises of reform from the rulers of Tuscany and the kingdom of the Two Sicilies. Newspapers from across Italy called on the prosperous northwest Italian state of Piedmont-Sardinia to take a more active role in uniting the peninsula, despite the initial reluctance of King Carlo Alberto (r. 1831–1849). Anxious about the movement taking too radical a direction, the king finally sent his army into Lombardy, defeating the aged but canny Austrian general Josef Radetzky, a veteran of the wars against Napoleon. But Piedmont-Sardinia didn't follow up on the victory, and the Austrians retreated into a chain of well-defended Italian fortresses. Not until 1859 would the drive toward Italian unification regain its momentum.

RADICALISM AND *THE COMMUNIST MANIFESTO*

The question was now whether, in fulfillment of Carlo Alberto's fears and those of conservatives across the Continent, the revolutions of 1848 would follow the example of the original French Revolution and descend into an uncontrolled spiral of radicalization—perhaps even leading to their own Reigns of Terror. Would long-standing forms of privilege crumble and churches be overturned? Would the short-lived urban street violence of February and March beget more widespread bloodshed or full-fledged civil war? Indeed, given the progress of radical utopian ideas over the previous decades, would the new revolutions give rise to movements even *more* radical than Jacobinism?

Karl Marx A portrait of the German socialist from around 1865. Marx's hugely influential writings on society, including his collaboration with Engels, *The Communist Manifesto*, foresaw a class struggle in which the proletariat would overthrow the bourgeoisie.

Some revolutionaries certainly hoped so. In February 1848, two German writers issued a summary of their political program that began with these dramatic words: "A specter is haunting Europe: the specter of Communism." We have already met one of these men, the socialist writer and organizer **Karl Marx**. Marx's early work explored, among other things, the contradictions between the universal rights theoretically on offer in liberal bourgeois societies, and the economic forces that he claimed limited effective enjoyment of these rights to the wealthy and the middle class. Unlike the utopian thinkers we have seen such as Saint-Simon, Marx did not believe that the solution to social problems lay in new schemes of social organization imposed from above by well-meaning reformers. Instead, he was developing a powerful new philosophy of history, derived from German thinkers such as Hegel and early economists like David Ricardo, that predicted social change would take place largely on its own propelled by the operation of ineluctable economic forces.

In the early 1840s, Marx met the well-born German thinker and journalist **Friedrich Engels** (1820–1895), author of a scathing account of the condition of the working class in England under the industrial system. Now the two men distilled their thought into a short, accessible, enormously influential pamphlet known as ***The Communist Manifesto*** (1848). It laid out in stark terms an all-encompassing vision of history and politics: "All history is the history of class struggle." Just as the bourgeoisie had supposedly overcome the feudal order during the French Revolution, so, Marx and Engels argued, the industrial working class, which they called the **proletariat**, would eventually rise up and overcame the bourgeoisie. This upheaval would yield an egalitarian worker's paradise in which property would be owned communally and a truly representative government would equitably manage all resources: "from each according to his abilities, to each according to his needs." The revolution of the working class would also eliminate international competition, for the proletariat's interests were the same everywhere. To quote the most famous Marxist slogan, taken from the conclusion to the *Manifesto*: "Workers of the World, unite! You have nothing to lose but your chains."

THE CONSERVATIVE REACTION

In France, there were signs that the Second Republic was moving in radical directions. The provisional government quickly drew up plans for new elections based on universal manhood suffrage. It set up a series of National Workshops, proposed by the socialist Louis Blanc, to provide the unemployed with work and a minimum income. On April 27, 1848, declaring slavery an "offense against human dignity," the government abolished the practice throughout France's overseas possessions, finally delivering on the promise originally made by the First French Republic and betrayed by Napoleon Bonaparte. Although coming fifteen years after the abolition of slavery in the British Empire, the measure anticipated abolition in the United States by over fifteen years. As in the early 1790s, calls were heard to extend the suffrage to women, and women's political clubs formed. In March, a group petitioned the government—in vain—to grant women equal political rights with men, and Eugénie Niboyet, a prolific author, founded the world's first feminist newspaper, a short-lived venture called *Womens' Voice*.

But if the fires of revolution spread far more quickly in 1848 than in 1789, they burned less hot, and in many cases soon blew out. The month of March turned out to be their high point, not their starting point. In most cases, the revolutionary movements, mainly comprising urban skilled artisans, professionals, and students, simply could not muster sufficient strength in their respective countries to cement their initial victories. The peasants who still made up the majority of the population in nearly every European state, and whose material interests often diverged considerably from those of urban workers, proved particularly resistant. So what followed these victories was not a new Terror, but months of frustration and confusion that could not resist, in most of the affected states, a well-organized and violent conservative reaction.

Even while radical hopes remained alive in France, the Austrian authorities in Vienna quickly discovered that the way to prevent liberal nationalism from threatening the empire was to play its different nationalities against one another. They began to exploit the resentment felt by Croats and Slovaks toward the Hungarians who claimed authority over their territories. As early as March 1848, the Austrian government appointed a Croat as governor of Croatia, knowing full well he would refuse to cooperate with the Hungarian authorities. Kossuth and the other Hungarian leaders, in no mood to compromise, passed a series of discriminatory measures against non-Hungarians, leading to an uprising in Slovakia and considerable tumult elsewhere. Meanwhile, the traditional Diet in Bohemia (now part of the Czech Republic) remained dominated by German-speakers who, with support from Vienna, resisted the calls by the region's Czech majority for greater autonomy within the empire. A Pan-Slav Congress made up of representatives from the empire's different Slav nationalities (including Czechs, Slovaks, Slovenes, Croats, and Ukrainians) convened in Prague in June but nearly fell apart as the delegations squabbled about how best to reorganize the imperial government.

THE JUNE TURNING POINT Just as March 1848 had been the crucial month for revolution, June proved the crucial one for counterrevolution. In Prague, even as the Pan-Slav Congress got under way, frustrated workers and artisans built barricades and tried to wrest control of the city away from the hated Austrian governor. He did not hesitate to bombard Prague with artillery, and managed to suppress the insurrection within four days.

Barely a week later, similar events occurred in Paris. In April, some 9 million newly enfranchised French men had gone to the polls and elected a Constituent Assembly charged with the task of writing a new constitution. But France was still a heavily rural country, and most peasant voters did not support a program of drastic social reforms. Few of the new deputies had much sympathy for the economic difficulties of Parisian workers. They saw the reforms implemented by February's provisional government as a dangerous drain on the national purse, even as the unemployed flooded to Paris to take advantage of the National Workshops there.

On June 23, the new government ordered the Workshops closed and called on General Eugène Cavaignac (1802–1857) to maintain order. In the so-called June Days, Cavaignac brutally suppressed a workers' insurgency, his forces killing over 1,500 and taking 12,000 prisoners.

June Days A supporter of the revolution, the painter Ernest Meissonier (1815–1891) depicted the outcome of the June Days as a bloodbath. The corpses of revolutionaries pile up in a narrow Paris street amid the rubble of a demolished barricade.

The government exiled more than 4,000 of the prisoners to French Algeria. Cavaignac became provisional chief executive, and the Assembly finalized plans for a new conservative republican regime that would give significant powers to an elected president. The elections took place in December 1848, and a surprising candidate emerged victorious: Louis-Napoleon Bonaparte (1808–1873), the nephew of Napoleon Bonaparte, who promised to restore stability and moderation to the shaken country.

Even as the barricades were being blasted apart by cannon fire in the streets of Paris and Prague, the new pan-German Parliament was meeting in Frankfurt to devise a constitution for a united German state. But while the deputies, largely representing the legal profession, indulged in high-flown rhetoric, they quickly found they had little ability to translate the rhetoric into reality. The two most powerful German states, Prussia and Austria, had no desire to surrender authority to a new national government; and, following the spring's shift in the European winds, they discovered new confidence that they could resist doing so. Nor did the Frankfurt deputies make a serious attempt to garner support among the urban and rural masses. In particular, they balked at endorsing measures to protect artisans against the twin threats to the traditional trades: industrial mechanization, and competition from outside the old guild structure. In September 1848, the Parliament had to call on Prussian and Hessian soldiers to protect them from workers who had stormed into their meeting hall to demand radical action.

THE END GAME

The final act of the 1848 revolutions was the longest and most tragic, stretching through 1849 and into the early years of the next decade. In country after country, the forces of "order" continued to reassert themselves, violently suppressed liberal and radical movements, and restored autocratic monarchy as the continental status quo.

AUSTRIA AND PRUSSIA In August and October 1848, the Austrian government quelled new rebellions in Vienna—the second time at a cost of more than 3,000 dead. Martial law was declared and censorship reestablished, even as the erratic emperor, Ferdinand, abdicated in favor of his pliable eighteen-year-old grandson Franz Josef (r. 1848–1916). In 1849, when the Austrian assembly elected the previous year completed work on a new

constitution, the new Austrian minister-president, Prince Felix von Schwarzenberg (1800–1852), paid little heed. He dissolved the body and imposed his own, more autocratic constitution which, among other things, made no concessions to non-German nationalities. These actions pushed the Hungarians under Kossuth into launching a full-scale war for independence. But in response, Schwarzenberg and Franz Josef appealed to Russia's reactionary tsar, Nikolai, who feared nationalist rumblings within his own multi-ethnic empire. With the help of a large detachment of Russian troops, the Austrians stamped out the Hungarian resistance and sent Kossuth fleeing for his life.

In Prussia as well, the tide quickly turned against the revolutionary movement. In May 1848, King Friedrich Wilhelm IV had acquiesced in the election, by universal male suffrage, of a liberal Berlin Assembly that was charged with writing a new Prussian constitution (this Prussian body was different from the Frankfurt pan-German Parliament). But after the failure of the June insurrection in Paris, the king dismissed the liberal cabinet that had been serving since March. In December, he proclaimed martial law and dissolved the Berlin Assembly, and then, like Schwarzenberg, promulgated a monarchist, conservative constitution of his own. In April of the next year, he imposed new restrictions on voting that would give conservatives the upper hand for decades.

Despite these events in Austria and Prussia, the men elected to the new pan-German parliament in Frankfurt were still hoping against hope to achieve the unification of Germany under a liberal constitution. In December 1848, they issued a grand document: the Fundamental Rights of the German People, which insisted on equality before the law and freedom of speech and religion. Four months later, they completed work on a constitution that would provide for a hereditary German emperor, an upper house composed of representatives from the individual German states, and a lower house elected by universal manhood suffrage. They limited membership in the new state to areas with German-speaking majorities, meaning that most of the Austrian Empire would be ineligible.

But the proposal won no support from ruling German sovereigns. The Habsburgs refused even to consider splitting their empire. And King Friedrich Wilhelm IV of Prussia rejected the constitution as well, even when the Frankfurt Parliament offered him the German crown— he scorned it as a "crown from the gutter" and dissolved his own Prussian assembly so its members would have no chance to defy him on the issue. In despair, the Frankfurt Parliament broke up, and in September 1849 the German states revived the German Confederation of 1815.

ITALY AND FRANCE   The revolutionary movements also largely failed in Italy and France. In 1849, the war resumed between Austria and Piedmont-Sardinia, and this time Radeztky's forces took the upper hand. King Carlo Alberto of Piedmont-Sardinia abdicated in favor of his son Vittorio Emmanuele II (r. 1849–1861), and the Austrians returned to rule in Milan. In August 1849, after a long blockade and bombardment, they also reoccupied Venice.

In late 1848, one of the most radical and ambitious Italian revolutions had begun in Rome. It was launched against Pope Pius IX (r. 1846–1878), who ruled the extensive Papal States of central Italy, which had existed in one form or another since the eighth century. After making some initial concessions to the liberal rebels, Pius fled to Naples disguised as a simple parish priest. The new liberal government confiscated Church property and, in early 1849, held elections for an assembly that quickly proclaimed a Roman Republic. But a coalition of Catholic powers—including Louis-Napoleon's France—marched on Rome in support of the pope. A ragtag army of volunteers from across Italy briefly held them off, but eventually the Republic capitulated and the pope returned to reimpose autocratic rule. This Roman revolution brought to prominence one of the most important figures in modern Italian history: a former merchant-sailor named **Giuseppe Garibaldi** (1807–1882). Garibaldi's work for Mazzini's Young Italy had led to a prolonged exile in South America, where he gained military experience in Brazilian and

Napoleon III A painting from the late 1850s by Edouard Detaille shows Louis Napoleon at a French military camp flanked by his officers. He is dressed as a general, with metals and epaulets—and a meticulously waxed mustache.

Giuseppe Garibaldi The revolutionary (seated in the carriage with hat in hand) and his Red Shirts triumphantly enter Naples after capturing the city in September 1860 in this contemporary illustration.

Uruguayan civil wars. Returning to Italy, he led the Roman Republic's volunteer force and became a hero by himself leading them in bayonet charges against the French.

It was in France that history seemed to repeat itself most closely. Until 1848, Louis-Napoleon had been seen largely as a joke. Although nostalgia for his uncle remained surprisingly strong, few saw the pompous, grandstanding nephew as a worthy heir. His two attempts to imitate the adventure of the Hundred Days by invading France with a handful of supporters failed miserably, the second time landing him in a French prison, from which he escaped by exchanging clothes with a workman. But by late 1848, nearly every major political figure in France had been discredited by the year's tumultuous events, and Louis-Napoleon, now directly imitating his uncle, posed as a figure above politics, capable of uniting a bloodied country. After winning the presidential election in December, he initially governed as a moderate, positioning himself against a largely monarchist assembly but also reaching out to the Catholic Church by restoring the dominant role in the educational system that it had possessed before 1848.

In 1851, faced with an Assembly that refused to amend the constitution to allow him to run for a second presidential term, Louis-Napoleon staged his coup d'état. It met significant resistance, particularly from peasants who favored the so-called démoc-soc (that is, democratic-socialist) program of lowering rural taxation and increasing access to property ownership, which had gained some support in the Assembly. But Louis-Napoleon prevailed, and in December 1852 he completed the rewriting of his uncle's story by declaring himself **Napoleon III**, emperor of the French. From the Second Republic, France had moved to the Second Empire. Even before this action, Karl Marx delivered a devastating verdict on the history of France since 1848 in one of his most famous lines: "Hegel remarks somewhere that all great world-historical facts and personages appear, so to speak, twice. He forgot to add: the first time as tragedy, the second time as farce."

RUSSIA AND BRITAIN Only two of the major European powers did not see significant disruptions of their politics in 1848 and 1849. One was Russia, where Tsar Nikolai had constructed a powerful apparatus of police repression and dreamed of building a literal wall around the country to protect it from revolutionary "contagion." The other was Britain, where the parliamentary system and the extended franchise adopted in the Reform Act of 1832 proved sufficiently flexible to forestall moves toward revolution.

For a brief moment in early 1848, the last great gasp of the democratic Chartist movement did stir fears that Britain might yet follow the path of the Continent. In April, after one of the largest mass meetings in British history, in London, the Chartist leadership presented a petition with 6 million signatures to Parliament, which scornfully rejected it. But the Chartists disavowed any action that might lead to violence, while the government mobilized thousands of troops and volunteer "special constables" against possible threats. A British revolution failed to materialize. As the great Whig historian Thomas Macaulay (1800–1859) wrote, comparing Britain's stability to the Continent's tumult: "We have order in the midst of anarchy."

BRITAIN'S ASCENDANCE

Between 1815 and 1848, European politics had been shaped largely by the domestic and international frameworks constructed by the victors of the Napoleonic Wars to ensure peace and stability on the Continent. Between 1848 and 1852, they were shaped largely by the dynamics of revolution and counterrevolution. But between 1852 and 1880, with powerful states less constrained than before by the international system, European politics came to be influenced, to a remarkable degree, by strong personalities. These belonged both to sovereigns and to talented ministers who managed, even in parliamentary systems, to retain power for many years and to change the map of Europe. This pattern was especially true of Great Britain, which was now approaching the zenith of its power and influence. There, by the mid-nineteenth century, it was the prime minister who headed the government and set policy, while the monarch served largely as a figurehead. The office of prime minister now went, in most cases, to the leader of the largest party in Parliament.

THE VICTORIAN AGE (1837–1901)

Despite the weakness of her office, the single most famous British personality was undoubtedly **Queen Victoria** (r. 1837–1901). Born when the British monarchy's popularity was at an especially low ebb, she became queen at age eighteen in 1837. In 1840, she married the German prince Albert von Saxe-Coburg (1819–1861), whose personal stiffness and inexperience with British politics contributed to the royal couple's initial unpopularity. However, over the next two decades Victoria bore nine children and survived several assassination attempts, while Albert helped organize the hugely successful Great Exhibition of 1851, and their image was transformed.

Albert's death, at age forty-two in 1861, plunged the queen into an extended period of grief and despair, but by the 1870s she had nonetheless gained lasting support from the population. Victoria was legendarily rigid in matters sexual—she refused to believe in the possibility of lesbianism, frowned deeply on sex outside of marriage, and saw sex within marriage as a duty to be endured. The adjective *Victorian* is today often synonymous with a repressive Puritanism. But in 1851, the word referred rather to a country and an empire moving toward the height of confidence and power. That confidence was still tested, however, in the early decades of Victoria's exceptionally long reign, when Great Britain faced several large challenges, including a devastating famine in Ireland and a war of independence in India.

THE IRISH FAMINE In Ireland, a rural Catholic peasantry subsisting on tiny farms had become dangerously dependent on a single crop, the potato, originally imported from the Americas. Potatoes were easy to grow, had a high caloric and nutritional value, and did not require special preparation (such as milling into flour) before being cooked. The Irish population had expanded more than twice as fast as that of England or Scotland in the nineteenth century, reaching 8 million by 1845 and putting a strain on the food supply. In that year, a "wet rot" struck the potato crop and two successive harvests failed almost completely. Soon widespread starvation set in, which the British government proved miserably incapable of alleviating. It was the **Irish famine** that in 1846 finally helped liberal forces in the British Parliament to repeal the Corn Laws, which since 1815 had obstructed a free market in grains and corns, including imported ones. But lower prices for imported corn proved of only limited help to the starving Irish.

The Irish death toll, caused mostly by the diseases that struck the emaciated population, reached at least 800,000, one-tenth of the population. A further million Irish followed what was by now a longstanding pattern of dealing with hard times: they emigrated, principally to North American cities such as Boston and New York. This movement in turn marked the beginning of a massive overall increase in emigration from Europe that would involve tens of millions of people by the end of the nineteenth century. In the 1850s, for example, fully 1 million Germans emigrated to the United States, driven by economic turbulence, the promise of greater wealth on the other side of the Atlantic, cheaper and safer transoceanic travel, and the failure of the revolutions of 1848.

INDIAN WAR OF INDEPENDENCE (1857–1858)

In the 1850s, another crisis struck Britain, this time in what was becoming the crown jewel of the empire: India. Over the first half of the century, the officially chartered East India Company, through which Britain ruled in the subcontinent, had greatly increased its territory and influence, stirring resentment among supporters of native authorities. It long had its own army, staffed largely by native Indian troops known as sepoys. India served as a large and growing market for British goods, while exporting significant quantities of rice, spices, silks, tea, and raw cotton. But in April 1857, in the unlikely setting of a military exercise in the small city of Meerut, northeast of the capital Delhi, a revolt began. The exercise was meant to train some 4,500 Company troops, a large majority of them Indian, in the use of a new rifle. But when ordered to load the guns, all but five of the men refused. They protested that their cartridges were greased with beef and pork fat—the one considered unclean by Hindus, the other by Muslims.

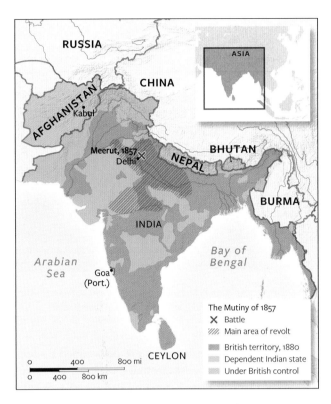

British India, 1857–1880 The uprising that began in Meerut in 1857 soon spread throughout a wide area of northern India. But the British army successfully repressed the Mutiny and affirmed the influence of the British Empire, which by 1880 controlled the entire subcontinent and Afghanistan.

The British officers in charge insisted—truthfully—that the cartridges had no animal fat on them. But the soldiers remained defiant. Finally, the regiment's lieutenant colonel, who had spent his entire, undistinguished career in India, ordered the protesting soldiers placed under arrest. They were stripped of their ranks and almost all sentenced to ten years of hard labor after a ceremony of public humiliation. Soon afterward, members of the regiment turned on their British superiors, and soldiers from other Indian regiments in Meerut followed their example. They attacked officers' homes; tore through the city bazaar; killed roughly fifty British men, women and children, and a similar number of Indians; and called for a march on Delhi. Within weeks, Indian troops of the East India Company throughout northern India had revolted in what the British referred to simply as **the Mutiny**. For a time, it seemed Britain might lose its most important colonial territory.

As one of the more farseeing British politicians of the Victorian period, Benjamin Disraeli (1804–1881), insisted: "The decline and fall of great empires are not affairs of

The Indian Mutiny In an 1884 painting, British soldiers execute Indian rebels by tying them to cannons and firing through their bodies.

DISRAELI AND THE POLITICS OF REFORM

Disraeli (1804–1881) was the most eloquent exponent of British imperialism. A descendant of Jews who had migrated to Britain from Italy in the previous century, he made a very unlikely British leader. Although baptized at his father's request in 1817, he still had to contend with the anti-Semitism that pervaded British society. As a young man, moreover, he earned a reputation for flamboyant dress and risky behavior, including ruinous financial speculations. He also wrote a series of skillfully executed, popular novels. Elected to Parliament as a Conservative in 1837, he spent three decades, in his own words, "climbing the greasy pole," maneuvering against rivals until in 1868 he began the first of his terms as prime minister.

Britain at the time remained a deeply unequal society. A mere 1,200 people owned a quarter of all the land in England, and even after the Reform Act of 1832 a majority of adult men remained disenfranchised. The Conservative Party seemingly existed to protect this status quo. Indeed, this period in British politics is often seen as one of polarization between the Conservatives and the Liberals, who had gradually taken over from the Whigs. Formally founded in 1859, the Liberal Party carried on the Whig tradition of supporting free trade and parliamentary reform, although it was tied far more to middle-class and business interests than to the landed interests that had dominated the earlier party. It was shaped into a powerful political force by William Ewart Gladstone (1809–1898). But Disraeli was no reactionary. Like the Liberals, he, too, had reforming impulses, but he wanted to move reforms in a paternalistic direction.

In 1867, as party leader, Disraeli, fearing social unrest if the franchise did not expand, sponsored a second major Reform Act that for the first time gave the vote to every male householder. (The Liberals under Gladstone also supported the act.) As prime minister for a second time, between 1874 and 1880, Disraeli also pushed through a Health Act that mandated improved public sanitation and a Trade Union Act that removed most of the last restrictions on labor organizing. He and Gladstone competed for the new, working-class voters with increasingly modern electoral techniques, including Gladstone's novel campaigning by railroad in the election of 1879. And Disraeli competed effectively, even as many voters rejected the Liberals' often-rigid laissez-faire program, which aimed to limit poor relief. "It is not by the State that man can be regenerated," Gladstone famously proclaimed, to which

greased cartridges. Such results are occasioned by adequate causes." These causes included increasingly intrusive proselytism by British missionaries, which offended both Hindu and Muslim religious sensibilities. They also included increasingly aggressive attempts by the East India Company to annex Indian territory by dispossessing native ruling families. With Indian resentment of the British already so volatile, the affair of the cartridges was simply the spark that set off an almost inevitable explosion.

Indians now celebrate the events of 1857–58 as a war of independence, presaging their country's eventual twentieth-century achievement of independent sovereignty. In the shorter run, however, the events arguably strengthened not only British rule in India but also the British Empire as a whole. Throughout 1857, atrocities multiplied on both sides, with the British press giving sensationalist treatment to the deaths of British civilians. These accounts helped justify savage forms of retaliation, including executing rebels by tying them to the mouths of cannon and firing. Spurred to undertake a massive military effort aided by 35,000 additional troops brought in from Britain, imperial forces eventually retook all the cities captured by the "mutineers" and dispersed their forces. The conflict finally ended in June 1858, after which the British government dissolved the East India Company and took over direct rule of its Indian possessions. A new era of British imperialism, in which the London government made sure to back its ventures with large-scale military force, had begun. Great Britain did not face another colonial challenge on the scale of the Mutiny for many decades.

one labor leader responded in 1879: "The Conservative party have done more for the working classes in five years than the Liberals have in fifty."

Disraeli's most important legacy, however, came in the imperial realm, which he saw not simply as a means of increasing his country's power and wealth but also as a source of unity for its often-divided population. In 1872, he declared that "the people of England . . . are proud of belonging to a great country, and wish to maintain its greatness—. . . they are proud of belonging to an Imperial country, and are resolved to maintain, if they can, the empire of England." As prime minister, Disraeli moved to protect Britain's valuable possessions in Asia by confronting Russia as it moved to expand its rule in Central Asia. He also avenged the previous British debacle in Afghanistan by defeating the Afghans in 1878–80 and securing the country in the British sphere of influence.

In India, Disraeli moved to consolidate Britain's possessions into a single vast colony. In 1876, he put the capstone on these policies by persuading Queen Victoria

"New Crowns for Old Ones!" This British cartoon from 1876 shows a caricatured Disraeli presenting the crown of empress of India to Queen Victoria, conveying suspicion of Disraeli's offer.

to take the title "empress of India"—it was with this act that the British state and its colonies formally became an empire. And Disraeli's Britain bought out Egypt's share of the Suez Canal. Constructed in the 1860s by a French company to connect the Mediterranean to the Red Sea, the canal greatly facilitated travel and trade with India. Although many Liberals also supported imperialist policies in this period, breaking in practice with their earlier "Little England" rhetoric, it was Disraeli's Conservatives who did the most to define the British imperialist mission for the rest of the century. British imperial power did continue to receive challenges—notably in 1879, by an uprising in what is now South Africa when a massive Zulu army overwhelmed a small British force at the battle of Isandlwana. Even so, by 1880 the British Empire had expanded enormously in influence and power.

POWER POLITICS

The rest of Europe also had more than its share of dominant political personalities. In an age where political success accrued increasingly to leaders who could appeal to mass audiences through the mass media of the day (above all, newspapers), the ability to craft a striking image for oneself mattered as never before. The most successful of these images were often those associated with strong nationalist or imperialist programs.

CAVOUR, GARIBALDI, AND ITALIAN UNIFICATION

One of the most unlikely of these personalities was Italian: a nearsighted, impulsive Piedmontese named **Camillo di Cavour**, who spoke French better than Italian but nonetheless ended up the architect of Italian unity. In the 1850s, Italy's unification movement was driven more by statesmen such as Cavour than by pressure from below. It drew support largely from intellectuals, middle-class professionals, and business figures, who had the most to gain from the creation of a single, Italian-speaking nation free of the internal borders and tariffs that blocked the movement of people and goods. In 1852, Cavour became the dominant political figure of Piedmont-Sardinia, which was still reeling from its defeat by Austria in the aftermath of the revolutions of 1848. A classical liberal, he opened up markets by working to abolish guilds and remove price controls, and as prime minister he oversaw a period of significant economic growth. Hostile to anything that smacked of radical revolution, he did not hesitate on one occasion to betray the leading Italian nationalist militant, Giuseppe Mazzini, to the Austrians to forestall a new revolution in Lombardy.

Cavour also maneuvered skillfully on the international scene, drawing close to Napoleon III of France. In 1859, France and Piedmont-Sardinia signed a formal alliance with the aim of forcing Austria out of northern Italy and increasing France's sphere of influence at Austria's expense. Soon afterward, war broke out. Austria was decisively defeated, while Cavour's agents provoked revolts in several northern Italian states, including Tuscany

Unification of Italy, 1859–1870 In 1860, with Italian unification seemingly unattainable, Garibaldi and the Red Shirts sailed to Sicily to wage their campaign against the Neapolitan army. Marching to Naples, they claimed much of the Italian peninsula for the Piedmontese king Vittorio Emanuele. Battles in 1859 had already joined Lombardy to Piedmont; when Venice and Rome joined the kingdom in 1866 and 1870, the unification of Italy was complete.

and Modena, with the goal of having them annexed to Piedmont-Sardinia. Napoleon III, suddenly anxious that a united Italy might be more a rival than an ally, moved quickly to sign a peace treaty with the Habsburgs that left Venice under Austrian control, and the Papal States and the kingdom of the Two Sicilies as separate, independent states. For the moment, the prospect of Italian unification seemed blocked.

But at this point yet another remarkable personality took a hand in Italian events: Giuseppe Garibaldi. After the defeat of his Roman volunteers in 1849, the former sailor had returned to the high seas, touching land everywhere from Nicaragua to Peru, the Philippines, and even Staten Island, New York, where he briefly worked in a candle factory. But in the mid-1850s he returned to Italy, and during the 1859–60 war with Austria he offered his services to Piedmont-Sardinia, seeing no path to Italian unity other than a monarchy headed by the Piedmontese Vittorio Emmanuele II. Cavour, although leery of Garibaldi's republican, revolutionary tendencies, accepted the offer.

In April 1860, seeing the movement toward Italian unity stalled, Garibaldi took the initiative. A rural revolt had broken out on the island of Sicily against the Bourbon government in Naples and the burdensome feudal regime it enforced. Garibaldi raised a legion of 1,000 volunteers from around the peninsula, known as the Red Shirts after the men's informal uniforms. Landing on the westernmost point of Sicily, it defeated the Neapolitan army in a dashing engagement (charging uphill with bayonets fixed) and then marched into the island's capital of Palermo, where Garibaldi announced he was taking power in the name of Vittorio Emmanuele. He then crossed the Strait of Messina and marched on Naples itself, capturing it with the help of a Piedmontese army. Garibaldi's forces also occupied most of the Papal States, although the pope retained control over the city of Rome itself until 1870. Cavour praised Garibaldi's extraordinary expedition as "the most poetic fact of the century," but at the same time he instructed the Piedmontese forces to keep a watchful eye on the Red Shirts.

In April 1861, with nearly all the peninsula under Piedmont-Sardinia's control, Vittorio Emmanuele declared himself king of Italy, with Cavour as his prime minister. The so-called Risorgimento, or rebirth of Italy, was nearly complete, at least as far as political boundaries were concerned. Venice would be added in 1866, while the last piece, Rome and its surrounding area, would join the new kingdom in 1870, leaving the pope sovereign only over the 109 acres of the Vatican in central Rome. Cavour himself, however, had little chance to savor his triumph, as he died of a stroke in June 1861.

BISMARCK AND THE FORMATION OF THE GERMAN NATION

Just as a single state, Piedmont-Sardinia, drove Italian unification, so Prussia did the same in Germany. But if the Italian process required, among its driving factors, the efforts of Mazzini, Cavour, and Garibaldi with his movement of volunteers, German unification is associated above all with one dominant personality: **Otto von Bismarck** (1815–1898). The descendant of Prussian military nobles (known as Junkers), Bismarck was described unforgettably by an English journalist in the 1880s: "strong-willed, choleric, utterly unscrupulous, pitiless towards such as cross his path, though ready enough to forgive a vanquished foe; in a word, a splendid heathen." But Bismarck was also superbly educated, speaking several languages and writing crisp, elegant German. He spent many years as a diplomat, representing Prussia in the German Confederation and then serving as ambassador to Russia. Wilhelm I (r. 1861–1888), who became king of Prussia in 1861, had little love for Bismarck but reluctantly appointed him minister-president (that is, prime minister) of Prussia in 1862.

Bismarck originally feared that German unification might destroy Prussian independence. By the early 1860s, however, he had become convinced that if Prussia could play the role of Piedmont-Sardinia, it could unify the nation on its own terms and make Germany a Prussia writ large. He took diplomatic steps toward this goal but insisted that the final process would depend on force, not negotiation. As he declared in his most famous speech, in 1862: "The great questions of the day will not be decided by speeches or majority votes—that was the great mistake of 1848 and 1849—but by iron and blood."

Bismarck took advantage of Prussia's strong industrial base, which by 1860, although far behind Britain's, could provide its soldiers with high-quality, machine-tooled weapons, especially rapid-firing rifles. And Prussia had a dense railroad network that enabled it to mobilize soldiers quickly. Throughout the 1860s, Bismarck played the game of European power politics with ruthless skill, focusing on Prussia's advantage to the exclusion of moral or ideological concerns, exemplifying what German writers were beginning to call **Realpolitik**. He helped the new tsar of Russia, Alexander II, defeat another Polish uprising in 1863, and

thereby gained Russian goodwill for his ambitions. The next year, Prussia fought a decisive war with Denmark and moved toward annexing the large border province of Schleswig-Holstein, ending a diplomatic tangle whose complexities had befuddled diplomats for a generation.

THE AUSTRO-PRUSSIAN WAR (1866) Then, in 1866, there came a confrontation with Prussia's major rival in Germany, the Austrian Empire, in which Prussia drew on long-standing military tradition and ethos as well as its newfound industrial advantages. The Austro-Prussian War lasted just seven weeks and ended with major changes to the European balance of power. Prussia emerged greatly strengthened and on a clear path to unifying a "small Germany," excluding the German-speaking regions of Austria, under its rule. It soon established a North German Confederation as one step toward this goal and, as another, expanded the Zollverein, the German customs union it had long been promoting. Austria itself emerged from the war badly weakened. It was forced to surrender Venice to the new Italian state, which had backed Prussia, and in 1867 had to confirm a much greater degree of autonomy for Hungary. Austria now acknowledged that the empire was a dual monarchy, the Austro-Hungarian Empire.

With hindsight, it can seem puzzling that the other major European powers—Britain, France, and Russia—did not work harder to prevent the rise of a united, aggressive, militarized Germany. But Britain in particular still saw Russia, not Germany, as its greatest potential enemy, in part because of what British officers called the "great game" that the two powers were playing against each other in central Asia (driven largely by British fears that Russian expansion might eventually threaten India). Furthermore, because of a bitter recent experience, Britain was reluctant to be dragged into another European conflict. That experience was to be the **Crimean War**, the first major conflict among the great powers since the battle of Waterloo in 1815, if also one of the least decisive of modern European history.

THE CRIMEAN WAR (1853–1856) The war had begun in 1853, when Tsar Nikolai fell into another of his country's long series of wars against the Turks. He wanted to protect the increasingly fragile interests of Orthodox Christians in the unstable Ottoman Empire, to assert Orthodox authority over Christian holy sites in Palestine (then still under Ottoman rule), and also to resume the Russian drive into the Balkans that the western powers had halted twenty years before. Russia hoped eventually to take control of the city of Constantinople, still the symbolic heart of Eastern Orthodox Christianity despite its centuries under Muslim rule, and to gain access to the Mediterranean Sea. Britain and France both decided to help Turkey, so as to block this threatened Russian expansion, and sent their armies to invade Russia's Crimean Peninsula in the Black Sea. After the capture

The Crimean War, 1853–1856

of the Crimean town of Sebastopol in 1855, the war stuttered to a limited allied victory, which left British public opinion—at least as expressed in the newspaper press—deeply frustrated at the inability of the most powerful nation on earth to impose its will more forcefully.

Thanks to the telegraph and the development of the newspaper press, especially in Britain, the Crimean War was the first major conflict in which journalists filed regular reports from the front lines. These dispatches brimmed with patriotic fervor, but they also exposed the blundering and disorganization of the allied campaign, and the wretched condition of wounded and sick soldiers. "The worn-out pensioners who were brought out as an ambulance corps are totally useless," the London *Times* reported to its readers. "And not only are surgeons not to be had, but there are no dressers or nurses . . . to attend on the sick."

Partly as a result, the war saw the first concerted attempts at battlefield nursing, led by the famous British nurse and writer **Florence Nightingale** (1820–1910), who had defied her family by taking up a career that they deemed unsuitable for a woman. In calling additional attention to the abominable treatment given to sick and wounded soldiers, Nightingale helped to establish nursing as a profession and improve standards of healthcare on and off the battlefield. The war also led to the founding of the Red Cross in 1859. Falling military death rates, however, owed just as much to the British army's own improving sanitary practices, including a prefabricated hospital facility designed by the engineer Isambard Kingdom Brunel (1806–1859).

TURMOIL IN FRANCE

Despite its frustrations, the Crimean War did not dissuade Napoleon III's France from playing a steadily more aggressive role beyond its borders. In 1859, as we have seen, it sided with Piedmont-Sardinia against Austria and was rewarded with the Alpine province of Savoy and the city of Nice. During the same period, France also sent its troops

Battlefield Nursing Florence Nightingale, pictured at left in a photograph from around 1860, pioneered the nursing of soldiers on the battlefield. At right, a nurse cares for a wounded soldier during the Crimean War.

to help Britain in the Second Opium War in China. In the 1860s, Napoleon III committed his country to two further major overseas adventures. In the successful one, French forces defeated the kingdom of Vietnam in 1858, allegedly to protect Catholic missionaries but in reality to project French power abroad and to match Britain's efforts in India. It ultimately annexed several southern Vietnamese provinces as a French colony. In the other, disastrous adventure, aimed at establishing a French presence in the Americas, a French army installed an Austrian archduke, Maximilian, as emperor of Mexico in the early 1860s. The episode ended after several years with a humiliating French withdrawal and Maximilian's execution.

Yet even then Napoleon III still longed to play a more decisive role in world politics. By the late 1860s, he had ruled France for longer than any other figure since Louis XV a century before. He felt secure enough to bring some liberal reforms to his regime, including greater freedom of the press and a larger role for the legislature. But he still dreamed of equaling his famous uncle's reputation and establishing France firmly as the dominant power on the Continent. A confrontation with Bismarck's aggressive Prussia, which saw a confrontation with France as a way of completing its unification of Germany, therefore became all too likely.

THE FRANCO-PRUSSIAN WAR (1870–1871) This confrontation arrived quickly. Napoleon III hoped to annex the small country of Luxembourg, strategically located between France, Germany, and Belgium, but was blocked by Bismarck's shrewd diplomacy. Then in 1870, the emperor worked feverishly to ensure that the throne of Spain, which had become vacant, would not go to a member of Prussia's royal family, the Hohenzollerns. When a French ambassador pressed Prussia's King Wilhelm to renounce his family's claims to Spain in perpetuity, the king reported his annoyance to Bismarck in a telegram, which Bismarck himself edited to make it seem as if both parties to the conversation had grievously insulted each other—and then released to the press.

A week later, France declared war. It was a major blunder, for few wars in European history were as one-sided as the **Franco-Prussian War** of 1870–71. Prussia had its dense railroad network, its increasingly formidable steelworks, its long-standing military tradition, and a well-seasoned, superbly trained military that was managed far better than its French rival, owing to a General Staff headed by the brilliant strategist Helmuth von Moltke (1800–1891). It also had secret alliances with the southern German states, the momentum toward German

unity that derived from the recent victory over Austria, and even the tacit support of Russia, which remained grateful for Bismarck's earlier support against the Poles.

France had a large but markedly less efficient and less mobile army, and its leader was, so to speak, no Napoleon. In early September 1870, the Prussians crushed the French at the battle of Sedan, in eastern France, and captured the emperor himself, who had tried to imitate his far more talented uncle by accompanying his troops into the field. In Paris, an uprising took place almost immediately, leading to the overthrow of Napoleon III and the proclamation of a Third Republic. But while its leaders continued the war, the Germans moved toward Paris and put it under siege. Further French defeats followed, while the capital ran dangerously short of food. With gastronomic flair, the Parisians butchered the animals in the city zoo and traded recipes for rat pâté (it was generally agreed that brewery rats tasted better than sewer rats). Finally, in the winter, France surrendered, agreeing to the loss of its wealthy eastern regions of Alsace and Lorraine, which to French public opinion seemed an almost unbearable humiliation.

GERMAN UNIFICATION In a ceremony designed to highlight France's humiliation, a united German Empire or Reich—a German nation-state—was proclaimed in the former French royal palace of Versailles on January 18, 1871. Prussia's King Wilhelm now became Emperor Wilhelm, reviving the German title *Kaiser*, derived from the

German Unification King Wilhelm is proclaimed kaiser of the German Reich at Versailles in this 1885 painting. At right, in white uniform, Bismarck looks on approvingly.

Unification of Germany, 1862–1871 Prussia achieved control over a united Germany both through military campaigns against Austria and clever diplomatic negotiations that joined Prussia economically and politically with states such as Saxony and Bavaria. Finally, the end of the Franco-Prussian War in 1871 marked the birth of a unified German Empire.

But the Prussian elites could not control the new state as closely as they wanted. While Prussia had been very largely Lutheran, fully one-third of the united German population was Catholic and used to taking guidance in social issues from the Church. Bismarck saw these German Catholics as potentially seditious, since most of them had favored Catholic Austria over Prussia. In the 1870s, he waged a *Kulturkampf* ("culture struggle") aimed at banishing Catholics from positions of influence in German society and reducing the role of the Church in education. Hundreds of priests were imprisoned or dismissed from their positions. Eventually, though, Bismarck softened the campaign in order to win Catholic support against another perceived threat: socialism, which was gaining adherents among the rapidly growing German industrial working class, as well as among the educated middle classes. Bismarck strove to banish and imprison socialists but could not prevent the Social Democratic Party, founded in 1875 under the influence of Marx and Engels's writings, from steadily gaining adherents.

THE PARIS COMMUNE AND THIRD REPUBLIC

France, meanwhile, lurched directly from defeat into the horror of civil war. In early 1871, soon after the armistice, with a German occupation army still present on French soil, the provisional government of the new Third Republic organized elections for a National Assembly. But just as in 1848, a political gulf opened up between the new deputies—elected by a still heavily rural, relatively conservative country—and the city of Paris, where, despite Baron Haussmann's renovations, the working class still had a heavy presence outside the wealthy central districts. In fact, a majority of the Assembly favored the return (yet again) of the Bourbon monarchy. In mid-March, the radical Parisian National Guard violently resisted the new national government's attempts to confiscate its artillery, seized control of Paris, and organized elections for a municipal authority, or Commune, to govern in defiance of that government.

With a heavy representation of socialists, anarchists, and self-proclaimed Jacobin republicans, the **Paris Commune** passed measures to protect workers, decreed the total separation of church and state, encouraged participatory democracy, and even brought back the revolutionary calendar of the French Revolution (under which it was now Year 79). The national government, headed by the veteran politician and historian Adolphe Thiers (1797–1877), who had first been prime minister under Louis-Philippe, laid siege to the city and then in May 1871 carried out a full-scale assault. Even as the Commune

Roman *Caesar*. Bismarck's ambitions had been realized. The next ten years saw Germany peacefully consolidate its position as a major European power. Bismarck himself saw little need for further military adventures in Europe, commenting that the Balkans—where war threatened at the end of the 1870s—were not worth "the bones of a single Pomeranian grenadier." Bismarck became the first chancellor (prime minister) of the new, united Germany.

In this new Germany, which included every German-speaking state except Austria-Hungary, the monarchy and the Junker aristocracy held the predominance of power, with the latter controlling the high positions of the army and civil service. Although all adult males did gain the right to vote for the parliament, the Reichstag, it had limited legislative powers and could do little without the assent of the emperor and a Federal Council (Bundesrat) consisting of aristocratic representatives of the different German states. And while the former non-Prussian states, including Bavaria and Saxony, retained some autonomy, Prussia made up two-thirds of German territory.

Execution of Communards In this 1871 engraving from an American newspaper, soldiers of the French army execute members of the Commune.

executed hostages, including the archbishop of Paris, the army swept bloodily through working-class neighborhoods, shooting thousands of "Communards" out of hand. After Thiers's forces had finally restored order, thousands more Parisians were imprisoned or exiled, including small French colonies in the South Pacific.

In the coming decades, the Commune, although not strictly Marxist in its politics and in many ways closer to the Jacobin tradition of the French Revolution, became a symbol around which socialist movements rallied. Karl Marx praised "the self-sacrificing heroism with which the population of Paris" had acted, while commenting bitterly about the Commune's defeat that "the civilization and justice of bourgeois order comes out in its lurid light whenever the slaves and drudges of that order rise against their masters." For its part, France slowly recovered from this debacle over the next decade. Its form of government remained uncertain for several years, with the return of the monarchy a real possibility. But the heir to the Bourbon dynasty, the count of Chambord, proved to be a most uninspiring potential king. Petulant and stiff-necked, he refused to reach out to moderate republicans, rejecting the tricolor flag of the French Revolution. Despite the best efforts of Marshal Patrice MacMahon (1808–1893), who served as head of state for much of the 1870s, a monarchist consensus never coalesced, and the republican Assembly, elected by universal manhood suffrage, ended up establishing itself as the dominant power. Léon Gambetta (1838–1882), a flamboyant, anti-clerical

lawyer and politician, emerged as its leading figure. The Third Republic would have frequent elections and a revolving-door series of unstable coalition governments but nonetheless became the longest-lived regime in modern French history, lasting until 1940.

RUSSIA UNDER ALEXANDER II

At the other end of Europe, Russia in the mid-nineteenth century did not have outsize political personalities like Cavour or Bismarck. When the harshly autocratic Tsar Nikolai died in 1855, during the Crimean War, power passed to his son, **Alexander II**, who was liberal in comparison. But Alexander (r. 1855–1881) proved almost as aggressive as his father when it came to the empire's territorial integrity and its international position.

POLAND In 1863, a move to conscript 30,000 Poles into Russian military service prompted another Polish nationalist revolt. Russian forces crushed it, publicly hanged ringleaders in Warsaw, exiled thousands of political prisoners to Siberia, closed Polish universities, and began a program of Russification. The Russian authorities removed the last traces of Poland's autonomous Congress kingdom, even renaming the territory Vistula Land after its principal river. In 1877, Alexander launched the fourth Russo-Turkish war of the century and forced the Ottoman Empire to grant full independence to the Balkan countries of Serbia, Montenegro, Romania, and Bulgaria. In reaction—in a move that recalled the Congress of Vienna—the other European powers convoked the Congress of 1878 and forced Russia to scale back the territorial gains for the new states.

SERFDOM ABOLISHED Although Alexander remained committed to this program of Russian expansionism and absolute monarchy, he did carry out the most important Russian social reform of the nineteenth century. In 1861, he abolished serfdom and freed over 23 million men, women, and children from virtual slavery. Various forms of resistance by the serfs themselves, including violent protests, had grown over the preceding decades. Between 1857 and 1861 alone, the army had to muster over 900 times to quell the disorder. Furthermore, Russia's defeat in the Crimean War exposed the poor condition of the serfs, who supplied a large percentage of the army's forces. By 1861, the Russian elites had broadly accepted that serious reform of the country required the institution's abolition. The measure therefore took place peacefully and with little resistance,

THE LIMITS OF EMANCIPATION

Alexander II's emancipation of the serfs in 1861 constituted a significant gain for the millions of Russians laboring in extreme poverty in rural areas. But although the tsar's decree granted land-ownership rights to the serfs, it also forced them to repay their former masters for land and their freedom, and it preserved the superiority of nobles, who retained ownership over the most valuable properties. As expressed in petitions such as the second document excerpted below, peasants who protested this arrangement were often brutally punished by government officials.

Alexander II's Decree Emancipating the Serfs

Here the tsar describes the "obligations" owed by the serfs in exchange for their freedom.

When word of the Government's plan to abolish the law of bondage [serfdom] reached peasants unprepared for it, there arose a partial misunderstanding. Some [peasants] thought about freedom and forgot about obligations. But the general good sense [of the people] was not disturbed in the conviction that anyone freely enjoying the goods of society correspondingly owes it to the common good to fulfill certain obligations, [a conviction held] both by natural reason and by Christian law, according to which "every soul must be subject to the governing authorities."... Rights legally acquired by the landlords cannot be taken from them without a decent return or [their] voluntary concession; and that it would be contrary to all justice to make use of the lords' land without bearing the corresponding obligation.

And now We hopefully expect that the bonded people, as a new future opens before them, will understand and accept with gratitude the important sacrifice made by the Well-born Nobility for the improvement of their lives.

Petition from Peasants in Podosinovka to Alexander II

This May 1863 petition from peasants in western Russia describes the flogging of hundreds of members of their community after they rejected unfair land allotment.

The most merciful manifesto of Your Imperial Majesty from 19 February 1861, with the published rules, put a limit to the enslavement of the people in blessed Russia. But some former serfowners—who desire not to improve the peasants' life, but to oppress and ruin them—apportion land contrary to the laws, choose the best land from all the fields for themselves, and give the poor peasants...the worst and least usable lands.

To this group of squires must be counted our own, Anna Mikhailovna Raevskaia.... Of our fields and resources, she chose the best places from amidst our strips.... But our community refused to accept so ruinous an allotment and requested that we be given an allotment in accordance with the local Statute.... The peace arbitrator...and the police chief...slandered us before the governor, alleging that we were rioting and that it is impossible for them to enter our village.

The provincial governor believed this lie and sent 1,200 soldiers of the penal command to our village.... Without any cause, our village priest Father Peter—rather than give an uplifting pastoral exhortation to stop the spilling of innocent blood—joined these reptiles, with the unanimous incitement of the authorities.... The provincial governor—without making any investigation and without interrogating a single person—ordered that the birch rods be brought and that the punishment commence, which was carried out with cruelty and mercilessness. They punished up to 200 men and women; 80 people were at four levels (with 500, 400, 300 and 200 blows); some received lesser punishment....

We dare to implore you, Orthodox emperor and our merciful father, not to reject the petition of a community with 600 souls, including wives and children. Order with your tsarist word that our community be allotted land...as the law dictates (without selecting the best sections of fields and meadows, but in straight lines).

QUESTIONS FOR ANALYSIS

1. How does Alexander justify the limitations on the serfs' newly granted rights?
2. What injustices do the peasants of Podosinovka suffer?
3. In what ways do these sources demonstrate Alexander's consolidation of the Russian government's power?

Sources: James Cracraft, ed., Major Problems in the History of Imperial Russia (Lexington, MA: 1994), pp. 340–44; Gregory L. Freeze, ed., From Supplication to Revolution: A Documentary Social History of Imperial Russia (New York: 1988), pp. 170–73.

very much unlike the abolition of slavery at the same time during the American Civil War.

Yet Alexander II was no promoter of social equality. The emancipation measures required the serfs themselves to make redemption payments to their masters for the lost labor, over a period of no less than forty-nine years. To these masters, Alexander also cannily argued that it was better to free the serfs from above than wait for them to free themselves from below. Meanwhile, advocates of a more efficient, modernized state bureaucracy knew that the reform would diminish the political power of the landowners, to the benefit of the monarchy. Above all, they hoped to create a more flexible labor force that would accept agricultural innovations and help feed a still-nascent Russian industrial revolution. And while a few former serfs had managed to rise well above their station even before 1861, most remained mired in desperate poverty for the rest of the century.

ECONOMIC GROWTH AND SOCIAL CHANGE

"Italy is made. Now it remains to make Italians." When the Piedmontese statesman Massimo d'Azeglio wrote these words in the mid-1860s, he pointed to one of the most paradoxical features of nineteenth-century European social and political change. On maps, by the 1870s the Continent now seemed divided into a tidy collection of well-delineated nation-states—some mapmakers rendered them satirically as jostling men and animals. But in reality, the borderlines disguised tremendous cultural, social, political, and even linguistic diversity within states.

FORGING MORE UNIFIED NATIONS

In Italy, scarcely any of the population spoke standard, literary Italian at home, preferring native dialects that were often mutually unintelligible such as Piedmontese, Tuscan, Venetian, Roman, and Sicilian. A 70 percent illiteracy rate made these dialects all the more durable. Similar diversity prevailed in Germany and Spain. Even in France, with its long history of state centralization, a large number of Romance (derived from Latin) and non-Romance regional languages survived, including the Celtic Breton (a close cousin of Welsh) in the west and Basque (which has no linguistic relatives) in the southwest. Urban visitors

Europe after 1870 Widely reprinted, this map, originally designed by a French cartoonist, took a humorous approach to the geopolitical changes of the mid-nineteenth century. Prussia stretches out its hands to grab more of Europe while France fends it off. In the meantime, Italy seems ready to leap into the fray. Russia waits expectantly for its chance, and Britain isolates itself.

to remote rural areas of almost every European country reported with dismay that the population often had little knowledge of or loyalty to the larger nation. They casually referred to the peasants as "savages" or "our Indians."

In truth, these perceptions were often exaggerated. An illiterate Sicilian or Provençal peasant might not be able to carry on an extended conversation with a middle-class person from Rome or Paris, but he or she could probably engage in a basic business transaction and understand a simple sermon or speech in standard Italian. And while such peasants might well seem to be shirking the call of patriotic duty when it came to paying taxes or doing military service, on many other national issues they expressed themselves forcefully. When Louis-Napoleon Bonaparte staged his coup d'état against the French Second Republic in 1851, peasants across much of the country rose up in insurrection, despite their supposed disinterest in national issues. Yet the condescension of city-dwellers was itself a significant historical fact. In 1870, more than 70 percent of all Europeans still lived in the country. But the educated classes, increasingly, saw these men and women as irrelevant to the great currents of European history, which seemed now to turn on the social tensions in cities between the middle and working classes. Karl Marx, who believed in a great coming battle between the bourgeoisie and the proletariat, devoted little thought to the peasants of his own day and wrote scornfully of the "idiocy of rural life."

Europe in 1878 By the late nineteenth century, new borders divided Europe. The resulting states now included the newly unified Germany and Italy, the major eastern empires of Russia, Austria-Hungary, and the Ottomans, countries with significant overseas empires such as Britain and France, and smaller nation-states such as the Netherlands, Belgium, Denmark, and Switzerland.

INDUSTRIAL GROWTH AND ITS IMPACT

These perceptions were fueled by the progress of industrialization. In the 1850s, the English inventor Henry Bessemer (1813–1898) devised a radically cheaper method of producing high-quality steel. In 1867, German and English inventors produced the first dynamo capable of generating electricity in the quantities necessary for industrial usage. And levels of coal and iron production continued to leap upward. Iron output in Britain quintupled between 1840 and 1870, while in Germany it rose nearly eightfold in an even shorter period, from 1850 to 1871. European railway construction continued apace, reaching a high point around 1880 thanks in part to a huge expansion of the railroad network in Russia. These developments made

mobility within nations easier than ever before, while increasing the importance of major industrial centers to national economies.

THE RISE OF INVESTMENT BANKS But it was not just industrialization that continued to develop in this period. This degree of industrial growth also required the development of more sophisticated forms of capitalist finance. Investment banks with close links to national governments arose, with the highly centralized French state taking the lead. In 1852, Napoleon III's French government approved the founding of a private investment bank on a new scale. Called the Crédit Mobilier, it had an initial capital of 60 million francs, which quickly multiplied through investments from industrialists and the general public. It and other French banks established on its model provided huge loans to the French government during the Crimean War and helped finance major transportation and infrastructure projects throughout the country, including Baron Haussmann's rebuilding of Paris. The model rapidly spread, and by 1880 forty large investment banks had been created in Europe.

CONTINUING URBANIZATION Industrial growth helped drive the continuing urbanization of Europe. By 1870, despite the overall European rural majority, the most industrialized areas of England, Scotland, Belgium, and the Netherlands already had a population density of over 200 people per square kilometer—well more than could be supported by farming the land in question. Already by 1851, nearly 40 percent of the British population lived in towns of 20,000 or more people. London, which had long been the biggest city in Europe, tripled in population between 1815 and 1860 to reach a total of 3.2 million. Many other cities experienced tremendous growth, and not just in the most heavily industrialized northwestern

Paris Opéra In this 1877 painting of the grand staircase of the Paris Opéra, gas-lit lamps flood the ornately decorated room with light. Fashionable men and women in evening dress promenade up and down the stairs, becoming part of the spectacle of the opera.

portion of the Continent. Budapest, for instance, went from a population of just 180,000 in 1848 to over 280,000 in 1867, and by 1914 would reach fully 900,000, fed by a movement from the countryside that included significant numbers of Jews.

The poorer portions of these expanding urban populations still endured the deplorable living conditions that early critics of industrial society had condemned in the 1830s and 1840s. Yet at the same time, the greater attention to public hygiene that also began in this earlier period started to pay dividends. Paris in the period of Haussmannization provides one of the clearest examples, with the building of the new aqueducts and sewer systems that we have already described. As a result of such measures, which had imitations across Europe, overall mortality rates finally began to drop steeply in the mid-nineteenth century. In the Netherlands, they fell from 26.6 per thousand per year in the 1840s to just 15.7 per thousand per year in 1900. And largely owing to this change (and also, by the 1870s, to higher levels of food consumption), the European population as a whole continued its steep nineteenth-century rise, from 274 million in 1850 to 423 million in 1900. The population of Russia doubled in the same period to nearly 120 million.

CITIES AS A STAGE FOR THE MIDDLE CLASS

Cities like Haussmann's Paris provided a new stage for the performance of middle-class life. Elegant shopping arcades that catered to the tastes of the urban bourgeoisie were constructed using the same techniques and materials that went into railroad stations and other grand public buildings. Middle-class men and women could attend the theater, museums, concerts, and the single most magnificent public entertainment of the century: the opera. The grandest new Parisian building of the mid-century was the new opera house built between 1861 and 1875. It was widely copied elsewhere in Europe.

Middle-class life in the later nineteenth century involved far more formality than it does today. Attending a performance at the Opéra required what we would now call formal dress—tuxedos and gowns. Novels and diaries of the period offer many examples of stern father figures who would rarely leave home without a top hat or appear in their own parlor except in jacket and tie. Indeed, the middle-class parlor, where family gathered and guests were received, was itself a stage of middle-class life, expensively furnished with elaborately designed furniture. By the 1870s, middle-class homes were lit by the brightest source of interior illumination yet developed, gas light, which had already been in use in streetlights and theaters for several decades. Middle-class furnishings also reflected Europe's increasing dominance in the world economy, often featuring decorative pieces of Asian porcelain and china, as well as vast new buffets and bookcases that were only affordable because of supplies of cheap wood from overseas.

As we have seen, according to many writers from earlier in the century, middle-class life also demanded a strict delineation between the "public" world of men and the "private," domestic sphere of women. The distinction was never fully followed in practice. By mid-century, middle-class life had in fact come to involve a great deal of public display for women as well as men. Although the wealthiest and highest-born European women remained relatively out of sight—transported in private carriages, having their shopping done for them by servants, and viewing operas and plays from the privacy of boxes—middle-class urban women were visible as never before on the boulevards, in stores, in theaters and museums. As we will see, however, the education of middle-class women still lagged far behind that of middle-class men, and the large-scale entry of middle-class women into the workforce would not take place until later in the nineteenth century.

DEPARTMENT STORES One of the most prominent sites for middle-class display were the new temples of consumerism called department stores, where all manner of household goods, furniture, and clothing were laid out on vast surfaces for the largely female clientele to inspect and purchase. The Bon Marché department store, founded in Paris in 1869, had 15,000 customers a day by the late 1880s. It also provided free meals for its largely lower-middle-class, largely male staff, along with free language classes, lectures, a small library, medical services, and regular evening concerts. To attract customers, stores also began to develop the art of advertising, filling urban streets with massive printed posters hawking their wares and resorting to other, more theatrical ways of attracting attention. One London hat-maker had a custom-made, seven-foot-tall hat carried through the streets with his name prominently affixed to it.

THE CRYSTAL PALACE The most conspicuous venue for middle-class display, as well as British power, may have been the great World Exhibition held in London in 1851.

Crystal Palace A contemporary lithograph shows how the engineering marvels of the Crystal Palace created a huge, light-filled open space, crammed with displays from lands as far away as Turkey and the British West Indies.

The Exhibition showcased technological and industrial progress—Britain's in the first instance, but more generally the Western world's. Its centerpiece was the so-called Crystal Palace, a massive structure built of steel (3,300 columns and 2,300 girders) and glass (nearly 1 million square feet, the most ever used in a single building). Six stories tall, 400 feet wide, and 1,850 feet long, it had 100,000 separate items on display and welcomed no fewer than 6 million visitors. Huge water towers designed by the engineer Isambard Kingdom Brunel held 1,200 tons of water and delivered a flow of 120,000 gallons per minute to some 12,000 water jets in the Palace's fountains.

Entrepreneurs constructed special rail lines and bus routes to bring visitors to the Crystal Palace, where organizers steered them past the displays in carefully designed pedestrian traffic patterns. What struck visitors above all was the sheer sense of abundance. The American editor and politician Horace Greeley described it in this way:

How magnificent the prospect! Far above is the sober sky of canvas-covered glass, through which the abundant light falls gently and mellowly. Spacious and richly decorated galleries, some sixty feet apart, overhang all the ground floor but the grand aisle, and are themselves the depositories of many of the richest and most tempting fabrics and lighter wares exhibited.

VALLOTTON'S *LE BON MARCHÉ*

The second half of the nineteenth century was a period of increasing material security for an expanding middle class of Europeans who could afford goods that a few decades earlier were only available to elites. The Bon Marché department store in Paris catered to this growing consumerism, gathering a wide variety of goods into a modern steel-and-glass retail space. The store also pioneered new business techniques—advertising, sales, and tea salons and dressing rooms—that retailers from London to Chicago soon copied.

Parisian urban life fascinated the artist Félix Vallotton (1865–1925), and his prints, engravings, and paintings often depict everyday scenes from the modern metropolis. This panel from an 1898 set of paintings of the Bon Marché casts the crowd of shoppers in dark shadow, in strong contrast to the bright gleam of the shop's lights, goods, and placards. Clerks wait attentively on the well-dressed customers, who carefully browse displays of jewelry, works of art, and fine fabrics. The painting captures the Bon Marché's bustle, glitter, and abundance.

QUESTIONS FOR ANALYSIS

1. What can you tell about the clientele of the Bon Marché from this painting?
2. What does the painting reveal about public life in Paris in the second half of the nineteenth century?
3. Why might Vallotton have decided to emphasize the shop's product displays, using light and color?

CULTURE AND CLASS WARS

Although middle-class culture had its origins well before the mid-nineteenth century, it reached extraordinary new prominence in this period, tied to the new political and economic power of people identified as *bourgeois*, a term that implied both membership in a class and also a well-defined set of cultural practices. An awareness of social class suffused European culture, shaping political, artistic, and even scientific debates and discussion. The brilliant British political theorist and philosopher John Stuart Mill (1806–1873) put the idea well: "Wherever there is an ascendant class, a large portion of the morality of the country emanates from its class interests, and its feelings of class superiority." It was generally believed that the middle class had finally and definitively supplanted the old aristocracy as the Continent's dominant social group.

CHALLENGES TO BOURGEOIS CULTURE

Not everyone born to the comforts of bourgeois, middle-class life willingly embraced it, however. Even as Haussmann's Paris became a stage for the top-hatted men and silk-draped women of Caillebotte's *Paris Street; Rainy Day*, it also gave birth to the rebellious stepchild of modern middle-class life: Bohemian life (the term *Bohemian* was often used in the nineteenth century for gypsies and had connotations of poverty and vagabondage). In the 1830s and 1840s, this word came to designate an ill-defined

Bohemians A nineteenth-century French illustration shows the proprietor of a cafe complaining to a Bohemian man about how little the man and his friends spend.

world of struggling writers and artists who deliberately defied middle-class conventions of dress, domesticity, sexual morality, and ambition. As the French novelist Amantine-Lucile-Aurore Dupin (1804–1876), who wrote under the pen name George Sand, proclaimed: "The artist's country is the whole world, the great Bohemia, as we say.... Let us mock the pride of the great, laugh at their foolishness, spend our wealth gaily when we have it, accept poverty without worry when it comes. Above all let us preserve our liberty, enjoy life whatever happens, and *vive la Bohème*!" Gathering in a constellation of clubs, artists' studios, cabarets, and cafes, criticized by more conventional observers as unsanitary, dangerous vagabonds, **Bohemians** loudly proclaimed their alienation from middle-class culture. In most of Europe, their challenge never coalesced into any sort of political program, but it did help to inspire the Paris Commune of 1871, whose somewhat diffuse rebel program consisted in part of simple hostility to bourgeois society.

MARXISM AND ANARCHISM Overlapping Bohemian critiques of the bourgeoisie, but far more serious in its radical ambitions, was the world of revolutionary political parties devoted to the overthrow of bourgeois power. During the decades of the mid-century, Karl Marx and Friedrich Engels remained its most important figures, organizing international meetings of representatives from working-class movements in different European countries. Persecuted by the police, especially in Germany, they and other socialist leaders often had to go into hiding, and Marx himself lived from 1849 onward in exile in London. There he wrote his massive masterwork, *Capital* (published between 1867 and 1894), which analyzed the economic contradictions that he believed were undermining the capitalist system and leading inevitably to a working-class revolution.

Marxian socialists had considerable company, however, on the revolutionary left. Although Marx's followers held that a "dictatorship of the proletariat" was necessary to advance working-class goals and believed that this historical stage would eventually enable the state itself to "wither away," anarchists disputed the need for states at all. They called for the immediate replacement of organized states by various forms of social cooperative. The Russian anarchist Mikhail Bakunin (1814–1876), one of Marx's principal rivals, argued both for revolutionary uprisings and for spectacular acts of violence to inspire them—this "propaganda of the deed" included political assassinations. Violent conspiratorial groups, composed heavily of students, had particular prominence in Russia, and in 1881 one of them succeeded in assassinating Tsar Alexander II.

TOCQUEVILLE AND MILL Not all the important political thinkers of the mid-century were radicals, however. The traditions of political thought that traced back to John Locke, Edmund Burke, and Jeremy Bentham in Britain, as well as Montesquieu and Rousseau in France, remained very much alive. In France, the great aristocratic liberal Alexis de Tocqueville, who had particular debts to Montesquieu and Burke, followed up his earlier *Democracy in America* with the brilliant historical study *The Old Regime and the French Revolution* (1856). In it, he blamed state centralization for weakening social bonds, thereby paving the way for revolution and Napoleonic tyranny. To Tocqueville, though, a free society—not anarchism—was the solution. He was little more sympathetic to the bourgeoisie than the radicals, however, and decried the increasing power of money in the social order.

In England, **John Stuart Mill** (1806–1873) published the incisive study *On Liberty* (1859), which argued for granting citizens the greatest possible freedom in all their actions. Unlike most modern libertarians, however, Mill did not advocate restricting the government's role to an absolute minimum. He did not have complete faith in capitalism and believed that the state should assist workers in forming cooperative enterprises to mitigate the harmful effects of the market. He shared with Tocqueville—and the radicals and Bohemians—a scorn for the middle classes. He warned against the social power of public opinion, which he associated above all with the middle classes and disdained as a "collective mediocrity."

RETHINKING GENDER AND SEXUALITY

Both radical and liberal thought in this period had long-term implications for the status of women. During the 1848 revolutions, feminists such as **Jeanne Deroin** (1805–1894) in France founded women's clubs and newspapers. Deroin even tried, without success, to present herself as a candidate for election to the Assembly in 1849, arguing that "an Assembly entirely composed of men is . . . incompetent to pass laws regulating our society, which is composed of men and women." Women (including Deroin) played a prominent role in the emerging socialist movements as well, hoping that under socialism women would obtain equal rights. An estimated 12 percent of the members of underground revolutionary groups in Russia in the 1870s were women—and the Russian government targeted them

Jeanne Deroin A French engraving from 1848 shows the feminist leader and socialist activist carried on women's shoulders. She bears a vase inscribed, "Universal suffrage for women."

disproportionately in arrests and show trials. John Stuart Mill was a prominent advocate for women's rights, owing in part to his long-term intellectual and romantic partnership with the feminist writer Harriet Taylor (1807–1858). Mill's 1869 essay *The Subjection of Women* argued the case with particular force: "The legal subordination of one sex to another . . . is wrong in itself, and now one of the chief hindrances to human improvement . . . it ought to be replaced by a system of perfect equality, admitting no power and privilege on the one side, nor disability on the other."

The questioning of sex roles in these works, along with the changing status of women in bourgeois society, contributed to a broad rethinking of human sexuality in the middle of the century. This rethinking was neither entirely repressive—despite popular modern images of Victorian culture—nor necessarily liberating. Rather, it provided new languages for both the regulation and the expression of sexuality. In Britain, for example, the 1860s saw the passage of harsh Contagious Diseases Acts, which gave police broad powers to intimately examine and imprison prostitutes suspected of carrying venereal diseases. But the same

WOMEN OF THE PARIS COMMUNE

The Commune was a laboratory for many forms of political and cultural expression, including experiments in radical feminism. The women of Paris organized in their communities, establishing soup kitchens, orphanages, and other aid services, serving on local councils, and fighting in the streets and on the barricades. When the Commune was suppressed in May 1871, the ferocity of women activists in working-class neighborhoods led anti-Commune politicians to blame them for the fires that broke out across Paris as government forces stormed the city. Paris's women were not spared the reprisals that followed: hundreds were executed or exiled alongside their male counterparts.

Prominent women activists pressured the Commune government to grant female suffrage and support initiatives for gender equality. In the following excerpt, from April 14, 1871, a women's group argues for the necessity of women's participation in the defense of the Commune.

Address by the Female Citizens to the Executive Commission of the Commune of Paris:

Considering:

That since it is everyone's duty and right to fight for the great cause of the people, for the Revolution;

That since the peril is imminent and the enemy is at the gates of Paris;

That since strength comes from unity, in the hour of danger all individual efforts need to fuse together into the collective resistance of the entire population, which is itself irresistible;

That since the Commune represents the great principle of the annihilation of all privileges, and all inequality—and is therefore is pledged to take into account the just claims of the entire population, without distinctions of sex—distinctions that were created and maintained by the governing classes whose privileges depend on antagonism amidst the people they govern;

That since victory in the current struggle—which aims at an end to abuses, and in due course a complete social regeneration that will ensure the reign of labor and justice—is equally of interest to female and male citizens;

That since the massacre of the defenders of Paris by the assassins of Versailles has enormously inflamed the mass of female citizens and driven them to seek vengeance;

That since a great number of these female citizens have resolved, in the event that the enemy should breach the gates of Paris, to fight and conquer or die for the defense of our common rights;

That since a serious effort to organize this revolutionary element into a force capable of effectively and vigorously supporting the Commune of Paris can only succeed with the help and cooperation of the government of the Commune;

Consequently,

The delegates of the female citizens of Paris request that the executive commission of the Commune

1. Order each of the district governments in Paris to provide a meeting hall for the local committees, as well as for the Central committee formed by female citizens for the defense of the city; or, if this is impossible, a separate location where these committees can meet in permanent session;

2. For the same purpose to set aside a large location where the female citizens can hold public meetings;

3. To have printed, at the Commune's expense, whatever circulars, posters and notices that these committees judge necessary to send out.

QUESTIONS FOR ANALYSIS

1. What do the women citizens of Paris demand from the Commune government?
2. In what ways do you think that the requested assistance would enable women to defend the Commune?
3. How do the authors of this request link their fight for women's equality to the Commune's fight for economic freedom and equality?

Source: "Adresse Des Citoyennes," in *Réimpression du Journal officiel de la République française sous la Commune, du 19 mars au 24 mai 1871*, ed. V Brunel (Paris: 1871), p. 260. Translated by David A. Bell.

acts also prompted a spirited feminist reaction that called attention, among other things, to the sexual double standard under which society policed female sexuality while turning a blind eye to male infidelity. In the 1860s, doctors such as the German-Austrian Richard von Krafft-Ebing (1840–1902) began to diagnose sexual "pathologies" such as sadism and masochism, and to define sexual attraction to a member of the same sex as a form of identity rather than behavior—the origins of modern understandings of homosexuality. In 1861, Great Britain abolished the death penalty for sodomy, substituting a prison term of ten years.

SCIENCE AND RELIGION

Sexuality was hardly the only area in which the biological sciences gained new social and political prominence in this period. These decades also saw astonishing changes in the way that scientists understood the world of living things, and their work had immediate, powerful resonance far beyond the walls of laboratories and universities.

CHARLES DARWIN   In the early 1830s, a young English naturalist named **Charles Darwin** (1809–1882) had spent several years on board the HMS *Beagle*, making geological and biological observations along the coast of South America. The species he saw in the remote Galápagos Islands—in particular, several varieties of finch—especially fascinated him, and after returning to Britain he began to formulate a theory that species might over time mutate or go extinct through a process of what he called natural selection. He worked on the theory over the next twenty years, and in 1859—prompted by the competing work of Alfred Russel Wallace (1823–1913), who had come to very similar conclusions—he published his book *On the Origin of Species*. Here Darwin made the case for biological evolution, presenting a "general law, leading to the advancement of all organic beings, namely multiply, vary, let the strongest live and the weakest die." Species that mutated in a way useful to their survival would thrive and displace others, and over the long history of the earth they would therefore mutate out of all recognition. The theory made sense of the fossil remains of extinct species—especially dinosaurs—that had long puzzled observers.

Darwin did not initially take the logical step of asserting the evolution of humans from other animals, but in 1871, in his book *The Descent of Man*, he made this case as well. The fossil evidence supported Darwin's claim: in 1856, bones from a primate ancestor of modern humans had been discovered in the Neander Valley of Germany (in German, *Neanderthal*). Nonetheless, Darwin's books generated the greatest controversy around science seen since Galileo in the seventeenth century, if not before. Christians who took the book of Genesis as literal, sacred truth fulminated against Darwin's theory and the implication that humankind did not have a specially ordained role in the universe, but had evolved in a seemingly random process from creatures that resembled apes. This controversy remains alive today.

But in an imperialist, bourgeois Europe increasingly obsessed with race and class, Darwin's work had other effects as well. Almost immediately, social theorists began speculating on its possible application to human affairs: Did what Darwin called natural selection influence the competition among different human races the way it influenced the competition among different species? In 1855, the French writer Arthur de Gobineau (1816–1882) had published an *Essay on the Inequality of Human Races,* which insisted on the existence of rigid, biologically grounded differences among races and the innate superiority of Caucasians over Asians, Africans, and Native Americans. While Darwin's work did not support such conclusions, many thought it did. Other writers, known as social Darwinists, began to argue that human progress depended on a merciless competition in all spheres of life—including among social classes. Darwin's compatriot Herbert Spencer (1820–1903) memorably referred to this competition as "the survival of the fittest." Darwin himself speculated on whether the "civilized races" would eventually exterminate the "savage" ones.

LOUIS PASTEUR   Even as the theory of evolution captured European imaginations, other advances in biology promised increased survival rates for all humans. Although microscopes had permitted observation of microorganisms since the late seventeenth century, scientists had so far reaped relatively little practical benefit from their use. Many continued to believe erroneously that bacteria were generated spontaneously in processes of decay, fermentation, and disease. But in the 1840s, German and Italian scientists had begun to speculate that microorganisms might actually *cause* disease.

In the 1850s, the great French biologist Louis Pasteur (1822–1895), working in the French university system, carried out experiments that demonstrated the role these organisms played in fermentation. By the 1870s, this work led to the isolation of the bacterium that caused anthrax, and soon of the tuberculosis bacterium as well. Pasteur was soon able to develop vaccines against several bacterial and viral diseases and also to develop techniques to kill bacteria in food products, giving them a much longer shelf-life (we now call it pasteurization). Combined with the discovery of crude forms of anesthesia in the 1840s, which significantly increased the survival rate from surgical operations, these biological discoveries began to contribute to Europe's declining mortality rates. Already in his lifetime, Pasteur was hailed by his contemporaries as one of the geniuses of the day and treated to the sort of public adulation usually reserved for great writers.

RELIGIOUS BACKLASH In the face of these challenges from science, the Christian churches and particularly the Catholic Church strongly reasserted the claims of faith. In 1858, one opportunity arose when a young girl in the southern French town of Lourdes, Bernadette Soubirous, had visions of the Virgin Mary. The Church authorities, aided by Louis-Napoleon's Second Empire, soon confirmed the occurrence of miracles at the site, including miraculous cures for those treated with its spring water. Within a decade, a vast basilica had been built and Lourdes was attracting hundreds of thousands of visitors annually, including thousands of the desperately ill. A gushing account of the miracles by a Catholic journalist sold more than a million copies, becoming one of the greatest bestsellers of the century.

Priests insisted that Lourdes showed the superiority of faith to Pasteur's biology. Some even went so far as to drink water from the springs contaminated by the scabs, pus, and blood of sick pilgrims; one visitor commented that "the water of the good mother of Heaven is always delicious." In 1868, Pope Pius IX convened the first Church Council since the sixteenth century, specifically to combat the dangers of "rationalism." Among other things, the Council established the doctrine of papal infallibility in matters of dogma—a deliberate challenge to those who wished to reconcile the Church with ideas of scientific skepticism.

NEW ARTISTIC DIRECTIONS

Artists and writers responded to the cultural changes of the mid-century in different ways, with some building on the heritage of romanticism and others reacting against it. The criticism of middle-class society voiced so directly by political radicals and Bohemian critics found many sorts of artistic expression. In the theater, the Norwegian playwright Henrik Ibsen (1828–1906) wrote a series of dark, piercing dramas that sought to expose the hypocrisy and constraints that afflicted intimate relationships in small-town and

middle-class Scandinavia. Britain's Mary Ann Evans, writing under the pen name George Eliot (1819–1880), brought piercing psychological insight and wit to her novels set in English towns buffeted by social change. The French novelist Gustave Flaubert (1821–1880) brought the art of the novel to perhaps the highest point yet reached in western Europe with several meticulously constructed, perfectly executed accounts of middle-class life. His *Madame Bovary* (1857) earned him a legal prosecution for immorality because of its surgical dissection of life in small-town Normandy, where the title character seeks relief from the tedium of her existence in extramarital affairs.

REALISM Ibsen, Eliot, and Flaubert are often labeled leaders of realism in nineteenth-century literature, not only because of their attention to accuracy and detail but above all because of the probing psychological insight they brought to their characters. **Realism** marked a clear break with the romantic movement in the arts and literature, and it reflected a sense that modern times required from the arts a stern, unvarnished depiction of society and social problems. The term also describes much of the painting of the mid-century, with artists such as Jean-François Millet (1814–1875) and Gustave Courbet (1819–1877) giving pride of place to ordinary, imperfect, and sometimes visibly bored subjects, including peasants and workers, in grand canvases that some observers perceived as mocking classical traditions.

Realism developed in different directions in Russia, particularly in the sublime novels written by Fyodor Dostoyevsky (1821–1881) and Leo Tolstoy (1828–1910). The young Dostoyevsky's attraction to liberal politics earned him a terrifying mock execution and a prison sentence, during which he underwent something of a conversion to Slavophile positions that rejected the influence of the West on Russia. The Slavophile writer Nikolai Gogol famously boasted that "we are a backward people, and therein lies our salvation." Dostoyevsky's novels, especially *Crime and Punishment* (1866) and *The Brothers Karamazov* (1880), employed meticulous attention to detail and psychology, much like Flaubert's, but did so to explore alienation and evil in modern society. *The Demons* (1872) was a searingly critical portrait of Russian revolutionaries. Tolstoy, meanwhile, wrote massive, panoramic descriptions of Russian life—his *War and Peace* (1869), for instance, has some 580 characters and over a thousand pages in most editions. Set against the background of Napoleon's wars against Russia, this grand novel focuses on the quest for spiritual fulfillment of a young Russian aristocrat, who finally finds it in the simple, contented life of ordinary Russian peasants.

Realist Art Characteristic of Millet's realism, *The Gleaners* (1857) shows in detail women agricultural laborers during one of the everyday tasks of the harvest, gleaning—collecting small pieces of hay left behind in a reaped field.

NEW FORMS OF ROMANTICISM Yet not all the art and fiction of this exceptionally brilliant period in European culture can be considered realist. In France, Victor Hugo continued to publish lush romantic poetry and intensely melodramatic novels such as *Les Misérables* (1862), which left readers across the West weeping at a series of tragic scenes designed to expose and condemn social injustice. Also in France, the immensely popular writer Jules Verne (1828–1905) became the king of European escapist fiction, with early ventures in science fiction such as *20,000 Leagues under the Sea* (1870) and *From the Earth to the Moon* (1865), which satisfied the reading public's growing fascination with the impact of technology on modern society. If novel-reading had once been associated with middle-class women, it was now—thanks to improving literacy rates, serialization in newspapers, and the availability of cheap editions—a universal practice among middle-class people of both sexes, and among an increasing proportion of the working class as well.

Finally, opera developed further in the long, lushly orchestrated, and dramatic works of composers such as the German Richard Wagner (1813–1883) and the Italian Giuseppe Verdi (1813–1901). Both composers were associated with the romantic nationalism that accompanied

their countries' unifications. Wagner drew on traditional German mythology for his greatest works, especially the Ring cycle, a four-part epic that integrated music, drama, and stagecraft in an innovative "artwork of the future." Verdi, working in a more populist but still recognizably romantic style, became an icon of what the new Italian nation could accomplish. His very name was used as a nationalist acronym against the Austrians: "Viva VERDI" stood for "Viva Vittorio Emmanuele Re d'Italia," or "Long live Vittorio Emmanuele, king of Italy."

ANTIREALIST REACTION As early as the 1850s and 1860s, some European artists and writers were explicitly revolting *against* realism. A group of young French painters that included Édouard Manet (1832–1883), Claude Monet (1840–1926), and Pierre-Auguste Renoir (1841–1919) began producing experimental works that included deliberately shocking juxtapositions (such as the nude woman next to two fully clothed men in Manet's *Le Déjeuner sur l'herbe* of 1863), and canvases that seemed to blur or obscure the persons and objects depicted so as to draw attention to the play of light and color. Derided as "**impressionists**," some of the group eventually adopted the label as their own and gloried, in language similar to that of the Bohemians, in their exclusion from the annual exhibition of officially approved French works in Paris. In an era in which photography could produce perfectly accurate images, these artists seemed to be saying, visual art needed to find new frontiers.

An important advocate of this revolt against realism was the French poet Baudelaire, who, like several of the impressionist painters, closely observed the changes that transformed Paris in his lifetime. Baudelaire's own works shockingly challenged the older conventions of European poetry in subject and form. Some read like opium-induced fantasies. Others evoked corpses or filthy beggars. Some rejected poetic meter and rhyme, presenting themselves as prose poems. Baudelaire could directly scold his audience ("hypocritical reader—my likeness—my brother!") or produce a whirlwind of fragmentary images to capture the hubbub of the Parisian boulevards. "Plunge into the Abyss," he wrote famously; "—heaven or hell, it makes no difference—to the depths of the unknown to find what is NEW!" This was Baudelaire's creed, and from it would burst forth the artistic modernism of the late nineteenth and early twentieth centuries.

CONCLUSION

This ferment in the world of the arts and letters testified to the disorientation that many Europeans felt at the rapid social and political change they were experiencing in the mid-nineteenth century. The progress of industrialism and the triumph of bourgeois culture were the most important of these changes. Many artists and writers also expressed the widespread conviction—shared in radically different ways by revolutionaries, Bohemians, and religious reactionaries—that these changes had come at a very high human price, destroying older forms of community and eroding many different forms of faith. Yet others saw these changes as dynamic and energetic, capable of begetting new forms of social organization and cultural expression. Despite the political legacy of failed revolutions between 1845 and 1880, and the continued existence of conservative monarchies, Baudelaire's thirst for the "new" remained widely shared, along with the belief that it was attainable. It was this belief that would help drive Europe to its greatest heights of power and worldwide influence in the decades that followed.

Antirealist Art Manet's *Le Déjeuner sur l'herbe* shocked viewers not only for its juxtaposition of the nude woman and two clothed men, but also because of the woman's bold stare out of the painting to meet the viewer's gaze.

KEY TERMS

pan-German parliament (p. 641)

Karl Marx (p. 642)

Friedrich Engels (p. 642)

The Communist Manifesto (p. 642)

proletariat (p. 642)

Giuseppe Garibaldi (p. 645)

Napoleon III (p. 646)

Queen Victoria (p. 646)

Irish famine (p. 647)

The Mutiny (p. 647)

Camillo di Cavour (p. 649)

Otto von Bismarck (p. 651)

Realpolitik (p. 651)

Crimean War (p. 651)

Florence Nightingale (p. 652)

Franco-Prussian War (p. 653)

Paris Commune (p. 654)

Alexander II (p. 655)

Bohemians (p. 662)

John Stuart Mill (p. 663)

Jeanne Deroin (p. 663)

Charles Darwin (p. 665)

realism (p. 666)

impressionism (p. 667)

REVIEW QUESTIONS

1. What events catalyzed the revolutions throughout Europe in 1848?

2. Why did the 1848 revolutions generally lose momentum by the summer?

3. What people and forces increased British power and influence in the second half of the nineteenth century?

4. How did Cavour and Garibaldi succeed in unifying Italy?

5. Under Otto von Bismarck, how did Prussia create and assume leadership over a unified German Empire?

6. From about 1840 to 1880, what lay behind a new wave of European economic and urban growth?

7. How did city life change during this period, especially for the middle class?

8. In what very different ways did Bohemians, socialists, and liberals such as Tocqueville and Mill challenge middle-class culture and values?

9. How did discoveries by Darwin and Pasteur affect society?

10. What new artistic movements developed in the second half of the nineteenth century?

CORE OBJECTIVES

After reading this chapter, you should have a solid understanding of the following core objectives. To strengthen your grasp of the core objectives, use the resources on the Student Site for The West.

- Trace the course of the revolutions of 1848 across Europe.

- Analyze the events that shaped British politics as the British Empire expanded.

- Describe the new power politics of the mid-nineteenth century, including the Crimean War and the unifications of Italy and Germany.

- Assess the social and cultural changes associated with middle-class life in the nineteenth century.

- Identify the political, scientific, and artistic achievements and controversies of the second half of the nineteenth century.

 GO TO **inQuizitive** TO SEE WHAT YOU'VE LEARNED—AND LEARN WHAT YOU'VE MISSED—WITH PERSONALIZED FEEDBACK ALONG THE WAY.

CHRONOLOGY

1881–1882
Officially tolerated
pogroms in Russia

1884–1885
Berlin Conference
partitions Africa

1889
Universal Exposition of 1889;
Eiffel Tower completed

1896
Marie and Pierre
Curie isolate radium

1899–1902
Boer War

1899
Freud publishes
*The Interpretation
of Dreams*

1882
Germany, Austria-Hungary,
and Italy form Triple Alliance

1883–1885
Nietzsche publishes
Thus Spoke Zarathustra

1894–1906
Dreyfus Affair

1898–1899
Spanish-American War

1900
Labour Party
founded
in Britain

1900–1901
Boxer Rebellion
in China

Apogee

IMPERIAL RIVALRY AND GLOBAL POWER

1880–1910

1903
Emmeline Pankhurst
founds the Women's
Social and Political Union

1904–1905
Russo-Japanese War

1904
Massacre of Herero and
Nama people in German
Southwest Africa

1905
Einstein publishes his
theory of relativity

1905
Revolution in Russia

1907
Picasso paints
*The Young Ladies
of Avignon*

1907
Finland extends voting
rights to women

1907
Britain, France, and Russia
form Triple Entente

The first genocide of the twentieth century took place in 1904. In January of that year, around 7,000 well-armed Herero tribesmen in German Southwest Africa (present-day Namibia), which Germany had ruled since 1884, rose up in revolt against the colonial administration. Enraged by German confiscation of their land and a series of epidemics they blamed on German colonists, they killed around 125 Germans, almost all of them adult males. But in Germany itself, wild reports circulated of massacres of German women and children. Kaiser Wilhelm II ordered reinforcements and placed the campaign under the direct control of the General Staff in Berlin. When the colonial governor, Theodor Leutwein, began negotiations with the Herero, an outraged Berlin newspaper insisted that although "humanity" had its claims, "national honor and the future of the colony require punishment and suppression of the rebels via force of weapons and the superiority of the white man."

Leutwein's forces drove most of the nomadic Herero population of 80,000 onto an encampment on the Waterberg plateau, at the edge of the Omaheke desert. But after Leutwein began a strategic withdrawal, his superiors replaced him with an aggressive general

---

Modernism and City Life The turn of the century saw the rise of modernism—new forms of art, literature, music, and thought that challenged tradition and captured the rapid changes taking place in urban life. Included in this movement were the German expressionists, who depicted abstracted, distorted street scenes in vivid color. In this 1912 painting, the German artist Ernst Ludwig Kirchner shows the frenetic convergence of city dwellers and streetcars in a busy Berlin intersection.

- How did the Second Industrial Revolution affect economic and social life?
- What challenges did liberalism face across Europe?
- What were the major characteristics of the new imperialism?
- How did modernism reflect changes in society and politics?

committed to a policy of total destruction. On August 11, 1904, the Germans attacked the Waterberg encampment and drove the Herero into the desert, where tens of thousands died of thirst. Survivors were forced into military prison camps, where the death rate reached 45 percent. In October, another ethnic group in the territory, the Nama (whom the Germans called Hottentots, after their clicking language), rose up in turn and were repressed with similarly ghastly casualties. At the start of 1904, there had been roughly 100,000 Herero and Nama living in southwestern Africa. Four years later, 75,000 of them were dead.

Germany's actions were all the more horrific because they seemed so utterly senseless. Just a quarter-century earlier, few if any Germans would have seen any need for their country to have a strategic presence, let alone a colony, in southern Africa. Even in 1904, the future Namibia provided only a tiny market for German goods, and, with its rich diamond mines yet to be discovered, it generated little wealth for the mother country. The German army caused the deaths of 75,000 Africans in order to protect just 4,500 German settlers.

But starting in the 1880s, all the major western European powers had entered a ferocious drive for colonial expansion that dwarfed anything they had attempted in previous centuries, even at the height of the slave trade. This expansion amounted to a new imperialism in which major European powers competed with one another for colonies meant not for settlement but for the plunder of material resources and for their use as markets for European goods. Focused on Asia and Africa, the new imperialism subjected indigenous populations to severe racial discrimination, reflecting ideas and practices that were also operative at home.

During the last two decades of the century the European powers carried out a massive land grab—the so-called scramble for Africa—while also expanding their overseas colonies elsewhere. Although Europe itself covers barely 7 percent of the world's land mass, by 1900 European countries and their former settler colonies ruled 84 percent of the globe. Great Britain itself claimed domination over a quarter of the world's population. Germany, a country without any tradition of overseas settlement to speak of, in the thirty years after its unification in 1871 increased the land area under its rule sixfold through imperial annexations, principally in Africa. German Southwest Africa alone was considerably larger than Germany itself. King Leopold II of Belgium (r. 1865–1909) had acquired, essentially as his personal fiefdom, a central African colony, the Congo, eighty times the size of Belgium.

This expansion had important effects on the European countries: on everything from the character and population of their major cities, to the products available in their markets, to the careers followed by men and women of every social class, to the themes explored in their art, literature, and philosophy. This **new imperialism** made for a crude but effective sign of the economic and technological superiority that Europe had gained over the rest of the world by the late nineteenth century. In fact, in the period 1880–1914, in terms of raw power, wealth, and cultural influence, Europe had reached its apogee. And the arrogance shown by the great powers abroad was matched by their apparent confidence and strength at home. Despite continuing social strife, wars, and one major revolution—in Russia in 1905—Europe nonetheless seemed in this period to have attained an unprecedented degree of social and economic integration.

The major European powers showed such self-satisfaction that in 1897 the poet most closely associated with the imperial enterprise—Britain's Rudyard Kipling—felt obliged to offer a stern warning against hubris, albeit in the accents of the period's pervasive racism:

> If drunk with sight of power we loose
> Wild tongues that hold not Thee in awe—
> Such boastings as the gentiles use
> Or lesser breeds without the Law—
> Lord God of Hosts be with us yet,
> Lest we forget, lest we forget!

In fact, anxieties about Europe's future and premonitions of a coming apocalypse rose strikingly in the decades around

1900, not least in the period's art and philosophy. Liberalism, with its promise of steady, benign progress toward ever-greater prosperity, faltered and found itself increasingly on the defensive from political forces prophesying titanic political struggles that would lead to the violent birth of a better world. Even so, liberal self-satisfaction remained strong.

The German campaign in southwest Africa, even while demonstrating Europe's crushing military superiority over "natives," showed why the premonitions of strife were all too accurate, and why the age of European dominance would soon be cut brutally short. For the most important factor driving the European powers into empire—and driving Germany into genocide—was dangerously unstable international competition. Like all the great powers, Germany hoped to exploit its new colonies' resources and to use them to expand the markets for its own goods. But above all, it plunged into Africa to keep abreast of its geopolitical rivals—for what the German newspaper quoted above called "national honor." And while sheer racism has its part in explaining the genocide of the Herero and the Nama, it was probably not the most important cause. Rather, the Germans' policies reflected German military practices, as worked out in the wars Prussia had fought for German unification and continuously refined thereafter in preparation for an eventual showdown with Russia, France, and Britain. The German military had the ability to operate with almost no civilian oversight. And the German General Staff put a strong emphasis on relentless offense, on rapid movement that did not allow for the taking of prisoners in large numbers, and on wagering everything on massive battles of annihilation. Above all, as Governor Leutwein put it: "In Germany what counts as a success is not a simple victory, but only the destruction of the enemy."

ACCELERATING SOCIAL CHANGE

The rise of Europe in the late nineteenth century took place with a speed and intensity that has few parallels in history. But unlike the cases of the Roman or imperial Chinese empires, this process did not see one power eventually vanquish its principal rivals. Instead, the competition continued even as all the powers participated in an increasingly intertwined global economy. And always, therefore, the danger lurked of this competition spinning out of control and becoming self-destructive, as the Continent had previously seen with such conflicts as the Thirty Years' War of the seventeenth century. In the age of European apogee, the danger was avoided. But soon enough, competition would break loose from its chains.

THE SECOND INDUSTRIAL REVOLUTION

The heightened international competition of the years after 1880 developed in the context of accelerating economic and social change. The years around 1900 marked the completion of what historians call the **Second Industrial Revolution**, which brought fundamental shifts in the structures of European economic life. Steel, because of its strength, durability, and flexibility, was the key industrial material in this expansion.

By 1914, nearly all of northern and central Europe possessed full-fledged industrial economies, with Germany making the most spectacularly rapid progress. German coal production rose sixfold between 1880 and 1910, almost up to the British level, and German steel production rose tenfold in the same period, surpassing Britain's own impressive eightfold increase. Russian industry also

The Factory System Workers at the Krupp Steel Works in Essen, Germany, run machines and stack piles of their finished product— wheels for railway locomotives—in a photograph taken around 1900.

The Second Industrial Revolution, 1880–1914 By 1914, industrialization spread across Europe, drawing on new materials and technologies. Discovery of coal and oil transformed formerly rural areas such as eastern Europe and northern Italy. Railway networks knit together towns and cities from Lisbon to Moscow. Germany, in particular, was able to draw on its resources of coal and iron to rival Britain for industrial supremacy.

expanded furiously. Its steel production, minimal before the 1870s, shot up by a factor of 50 by the start of World War I. The Russian urban working class expanded by 50 percent, from 2 to 3 million, just in the years 1900–14, although its peasantry of 100 million still dwarfed that number. Among European cities, only Paris and London had had populations in excess of 1 million in the mid-nineteenth century; by 1914, they had been joined by Berlin, Vienna, Saint Petersburg, and Moscow, among others. For men and women in these and other cities, lit by electric light, resounding with the noise of heavy machinery, trains, and cars, and stinking of coal smoke, the world in 1910 seemed to have changed beyond recognition.

AN INCREASE IN SCALE With the vast expansion of industry in this period came a new scale of operation. By 1900, a majority of workers in the industrialized countries labored in a true factory system. Industrial firms now employed hundreds or thousands of people in plants whose complex infrastructure often resembled that of a small city. The greatest example in 1900 was the Krupp Steel Works, based in Essen, in northwest Germany, which employed over 25,000 people. Founded in 1816, it was run by a merchant dynasty that had been producing weapons since the seventeenth century. The company's property included 100 miles of private rail lines, 60 factory buildings, 7 electrical power stations, and 130 miles of electrical power lines. Its steelworks processed some 685,000 tons of iron ore per year and used as much water as the entire city of Frankfurt. Companies like Krupp increasingly tried to control all the different phases of the production process, from raw materials to finished goods. Critics, notably from the emerging socialist parties, charged these companies with amassing unhealthy degrees of power, but the firms certainly contributed to the vast increases in overall industrial capacity of European societies.

Illustrating this overall capacity was the gigantic scale on which Europeans now built things. Consider Paris's 1,000-foot-tall Eiffel Tower, the tallest structure in Europe at the time, completed in 1889. It used 18,000 separate pieces of steel, together weighing some 7,000 tons, and was held together by 2.5 million rivets. More important economically were the vast ships that, by 1900, carried passengers and cargo between Europe and the rest of the world. The *Lusitania* and the *Mauritania*, ships of the British Cunard Line launched in 1907, featured steel hulls and each displaced some 45,000 tons of water. Each one could carry some 2,400 passengers, including 500 who traveled in luxurious first class and a larger number of poor emigrants in the crowded, airless quarters at the bottom of the ship known as steerage. To feed the passengers on a single voyage across the Atlantic (usually requiring six days), a similar ship carried some 13,000 pounds of butter, 30,000 pounds of sugar, 240,000 eggs, and 80 tons of meat, including geese, turkeys, ducks, pheasants, pigeons, grouse, quail, and partridges. Over the sixty years from 1850 to 1910, the overall capacity of the world's merchant fleets nearly quadrupled.

TECHNICAL EXPERTISE The Second Industrial Revolution required considerably more scientific expertise than the first, and hence higher levels of education in the skilled workforce. Industries increasingly made use of complex processes that had to be managed by engineers with sophisticated knowledge of chemistry, mechanics, electricity, and metallurgy. Electricity was particularly important. As the Krupp example shows, while European manufacturing remained powered by coal, the coal increasingly was burned to generate electricity rather than to drive machines directly by steam power.

One reason for Germany's rapid advance in the late nineteenth century was its university system, which by mid-century had made engineering and scientific research central activities. While Britain saw the founding of several new universities and institutes devoted to engineering and science, the older, more prestigious universities of Oxford and Cambridge remained focused on providing a classical education to future civil servants, lawyers,

and clergymen. In 1900, Germany spent 12 percent of its annual budget on education at all levels, as opposed to 10 percent in Britain, 8 percent in France, and just 1.5 percent in Spain. German universities served as a model around the world—notably in the United States, where Johns Hopkins University (founded in 1876) and the University of Chicago (1890) built German-style degree programs and filled their first faculties with German-trained professors. Germany also benefited from coming later to industrialization than other European countries. German factories such as the Krupp Works were designed to make use of the new industrial processes; there was no need to rebuild older, less suitable facilities.

The larger, more complex industries of the late nineteenth century required larger, more complex organizations to manage them. Rather than belonging exclusively to a single person or family, large firms became impersonal corporations owned by stockholders and run by trained executives chosen by boards of directors. These firms were organized into many different departments, from mail rooms to personnel offices, and required trained staffs of managers and accountants: among its 25,000 employees in 1900, Krupp counted some 2,207 such white-collar workers. All of them needed a high level of literacy, and across Europe firms like Krupp benefited from the steadily rising proportion of men and women receiving secondary education. The companies also needed messengers, telephone operators, deliverymen, and secretaries.

NEW ECONOMIC OPPORTUNITIES FOR WOMEN
In the 1870s, another new invention, the typewriter, became common in European offices, and schools arose to train young women in secretarial skills such as typewriting and shorthand. Between 1881 and 1901, the number of secretaries in Britain rose twelvefold. This increase in secretarial labor points to a broader shift in patterns of European work. As we have seen, in pre-industrial societies women and children had composed a large part of the labor force. Women could not generally become masters or journeymen in the early trades, but they made up a majority of domestic servants, worked in many capacities in shops and doing piece work at home, and filled early textile factories in cities like Lyon, in France. And of course they performed back-breaking labor on farms and spent countless hours maintaining their own families.

The first Industrial Revolution did not deviate greatly from this pattern. Women and children initially made up a large portion of the labor force in factory towns like Manchester. But over the course of the nineteenth century, progressive legislators, starting with Britain's 1833 Factory

Act, had succeeded in curtailing child labor. Meanwhile, in industries such as metalworking and munitions, the factory became increasingly a male preserve. But new positions opened up for women as clerical workers, both in private industry and in government. In Britain, women filled fewer than 10 percent of government and post office clerical jobs in 1861, but more than half of them by 1911. In Germany, a popular women's magazine published nineteen articles on business opportunities for women just in the years 1893–94. Among the possible professions recommended were honey cultivation, bookselling, gardening, interior decoration, and photography. Women's professional organizations were founded in major German cities such as Berlin and Hamburg.

This move by women into the labor force often met with considerable resistance from white-collar male workers, who felt their jobs threatened and sometimes used their professional unions to advocate discriminatory measures. In 1904, Austria's Conference of White-Collar Workers declared that "it has never been considered cultural progress but rather a product of necessity for women to earn their livelihood; it is a sign of disease in the social body." A year later, the Austrian union of postal employees unsuccessfully demanded the exclusion of all married women from employment, the exclusion of women in general from skilled jobs, and the separation of women and men in the workplace.

The same shifts caused widespread anxieties that women's work would destroy traditional family life. In Germany, newspapers and books lamented a supposed epidemic of "surplus women," especially in the so-called

Telephone Exchange The rapid spread of the telephone created a need for skilled operators, many of whom were women. Here women operators at a telephone exchange in London in 1910 manually connect callers across the network.

better classes. Some pamphlets alleged that as many as 50 percent of educated women never married, in part as a result of changes in patterns of work. But these allegations had little basis in fact. In one north German city closely studied by historians, the proportion of women who never married in fact actually dropped slightly between 1890 and 1910. Patterns of family life changed more slowly than the critics feared. Yet cultural panics about marriage and motherhood, then as now, could have a life of their own. The newspaper press gave inordinate attention to actresses and women writers whose "disruptive" lifestyles seemed to confirm fears about the breakdown of family life. The French actress and journalist Marguerite Durand (1864–1936), who founded a women's newspaper and campaigned for women's rights while divorcing her husband and raising an illegitimate son, exemplified figures of this sort.

GLOBALIZATION Expansion in the industrial economy was powered not only by these changes in the workforce but also by the rising flow of capital, facilitated by the kinds of free-trade policies introduced in Britain earlier in the century. By 1900, unprecedented amounts of capital were flowing within Europe, and between Europe and the rest of the world. From 1850 to 1910, the volume of world trade rose tenfold. Facilitating this increase, between 1880 and 1914 most Western countries adopted the gold standard, pegging the value of their currencies to a fixed amount of gold. The effect was to create fixed exchange rates between currencies and easily convertible prices throughout the world economy. **Globalization**, or the integration of world economies, accelerated remarkably in the wake of the economic slump in 1896. An increasingly sophisticated banking system, with London as its world center, facilitated loans and payments. The British pound sterling functioned as the international currency of choice.

European investors increasingly saw other continents as the source of their most profitable investments. British capital helped to finance the building of American railroads, and by 1914 Britain exported more than half of all its capital. These capital flows contributed to a growing European trade deficit with the rest of the world, but European control of shipping and the international insurance market helped make up for it. The capital flows also helped labor and goods cross international borders with unprecedented ease.

CHANGING PATTERNS OF MIGRATION The economic developments of the period had very real effects on ordinary lives, mainly through the impetus they gave to

Emigration from Europe, 1880–1910 At the turn of the twentieth century, huge numbers of Europeans—including eastern European Jews fleeing persecution—emigrated to North America, but also to a wider range of destinations. Spanish and Portuguese speakers led migration to South America, Russians moved within the vast Russian Empire, Jews emigrated to Palestine, and French and southern European people settled in the French colonies in North Africa.

migration. With cheap steamship tickets and few formal barriers to movement, emigration from Europe accelerated dramatically at the end of the nineteenth century: to the British "settler" colonies (Australia, New Zealand, Canada, South Africa), to Latin America, and above all to the United States, with the emigrants coming increasingly from eastern and southern Europe. In the period 1880–1910, for instance, fully one-seventh of the Greek population emigrated, as did one-third of the Jews in the Russian Empire. As these Jews moved across the Atlantic, the Jewish population of New York City rose more than sevenfold. In one example that typified emigration patterns to the United States, Avrom-Meir Bolotsky, in 1904, left a small village in present-day Belarus to join three of his brothers already in New York. After finding work driving a cart, delivering coal in winter and ice in summer, he sent for his wife and seven children, one member of the family coming over each year until all were reunited in America. Another important form of European migration took place within a single country: the movement of between 7 and 10 million people from European Russia to Siberia, to work in mines, expanding cities, and to build

the Trans-Siberian Railroad linking Moscow and Saint Petersburg to the Pacific.

NEW INVENTIONS Other changes in ordinary life were a result of technological advances. Sometimes they had very humble beginnings. In 1887, for instance, an inventor in northern Ireland named John Boyd Dunlop (1840–1921) puzzled over how he might equip his son's tricycle with more comfortable wheels. He developed a process for shaping rubber into inflatable tires. Although Dunlop himself earned very little money from it, rubber tires were an immediate sensation and made the use of new sorts of wheeled vehicles practical. Within a few years, rubber consumption in the United States and Europe had jumped to hundreds of thousands of tons a year. As we will see, this change had disastrous implications for the inhabitants of the principal source of world rubber, the Belgian Congo.

Even more important, in the 1880s a German engineer named Karl Benz (1844–1929) made decisive steps in perfecting an internal combustion engine that could power a new wheeled vehicle: the "horseless carriage," or automobile. Benz's first models in fact looked like carriages, with huge, rigid wheels. They moved at less than ten miles an hour and could not climb hills unaided. Nonetheless, in 1888 Benz's wife managed to drive sixty-five miles in one of them. Improvements to the engine and a move toward smaller wheels equipped with rubber tires, along with improvement in road surfaces, soon allowed automobiles to travel more rapidly over ever-longer distances. They faced some initial resistance—an early British law mandated a speed limit of two miles per hour and insisted that each car be accompanied by three men on foot waving red flags—but by the late 1890s they had become common sights in many European cities. In Paris, between 1896 and 1914 the number of cars on the street tripled. The same streets also thronged with bicycles, another recent invention facilitated by Dunlop's pneumatic tires. By 1914, the French alone were producing 3.5 million bicycles per year.

The rise of internal combustion engines powered by gasoline, along with the popularity of kerosene as a source of lighting, drove yet another new industry: petroleum. In the second half of the nineteenth century, engineers developed techniques for extracting oil from deep wells and then refining it. Important early centers of oil production included Pennsylvania, Mexico, and Romania.

Daily life in the cities changed in other largely beneficial ways during the last two decades of the nineteenth century. The cities literally grew brighter as electricity began to replace gas lighting in urban homes and public places—although kerosene and other oils remained important until well into the twentieth century. At the same time, telephones, invented in the United States in the 1870s, spread rapidly, with owners in London, Paris, and Berlin placing millions of calls per year (telephone exchanges became another heavily female workplace). French inventors perfected "moving pictures," and between 1908 and 1914 the first European movie theaters opened. The Italian Guglielmo Marconi (1874–1937) invented long-distance radio transmission. And in London, the first true underground subway lines opened in 1890, marking the beginning of rapid transit systems in European cities. At surface level, slower-moving streetcars, also running on rails, supplemented the bus systems developed earlier in the century.

Improved water and sewer systems in cities helped to reduce the incidence of water-borne diseases. Between these changes and the invention of the first vaccines against the disease, the scourge of cholera began to vanish from European cities, with the last major outbreak in western Europe occurring in Hamburg in 1892. In eastern Europe, the disease remained a major killer into the early twentieth century. In a more sinister vein, the terrorists

of the period made all-too-effective use of the new forms of high explosives devised by the period's chemists, especially dynamite, invented by a Swede named Alfred Nobel (1833–1896); he left the vast fortune he compiled as a result to fund the Nobel Prizes. Overall, these developments distinguished urban from rural life more than ever before.

INCREASING RURAL DISTRESS

Rural areas in industrial countries were the principal losers during the Second Industrial Revolution. In rural settings, electricity and the telephone—which, like the earlier telegraph, required the installation of vast networks of wires—remained relative rarities early in the twentieth century. Yet rural populations benefited from other technological innovations. For example, agricultural productivity continued to increase, thanks to improved fertilization and harvesting techniques. In some countries, including Germany, the wheat yield per acre in 1900 had more than doubled from a century earlier. In eastern and southern Europe it remained stagnant, contributing to the strong emigration rates from these regions, but European wheat production as a whole continued to rise impressively.

POPULATION PRESSURE AND AGRICULTURAL PRODUCTION Yet even so, the increase in agricultural productivity could not keep up with the rise in population, which led to increased demand for food and kept prices high. Robust rates of population growth continued in southern and eastern Europe during these decades, with the Russian population rising more than 36 percent. Furthermore, the integrated world economy meant that European agriculture increasingly faced competition from North America, Australia, and Argentina. By 1900, Britain was importing 80 percent of its grain, a development that enriched urban merchants and middlemen but contributed to an agricultural depression at home and diminished the power of the country's great landowners. By the early twentieth century, 80 of Britain's 100 greatest family fortunes came from manufacturing, not land. England, where less than 10 percent of the population now worked on the land, was an extreme case. But even Germany, with a much larger and healthier agricultural sector, was importing more than 10 percent of its grain by 1900. Russia exported grain on a large scale, and partly as a result its foreign trade tripled between 1885 and 1913, but the gain came from a relatively small number of efficiently managed farms. Overall, the precarious situation of European agriculture in this period contributed to a prolonged business depression in the 1870s and 1880s. It also fed the accelerating stream of emigration.

LOWER BIRTHRATES IN THE WEST The travails of agriculture, coupled with urbanization, in turn contributed to an ongoing change in demographic patterns in the western half of the Continent. Even as population growth remained strong in southern and eastern Europe, the birthrate was already falling in France early in the nineteenth century, leading Germany to move past it in population by 1870, followed by the British Isles twenty-five years later. The French feared that the trend pointed to national decline, which the government answered with largely unsuccessful economic incentives for bearing children. But a low birthrate, coupled with a low mortality rate, is typical of modern industrial societies. Between 1890 and 1910, the French population rose by only 3 percent, and by the end of the century other northern and central European countries were moving in this direction. So in addition to all the other changes they were experiencing, Europeans had to get used to smaller numbers of children in families less likely to have lost children and young adults to infectious disease.

INDUSTRIAL ARMAMENTS

Overall, the strong growth of European industry in these decades held the promise of a new age of prosperity and peaceful international exchange. And yet observers could hardly fail to notice that the industries benefiting most directly from Europe's remarkable economic developments were the armaments industries. The same shipyards that turned out the huge new commercial steamships also turned out battleships. The same manufacturing processes that produced textiles, bicycles, rubber tires, and electric lights also produced guns and cannon. Chemical factories could turn out the high explosives developed by Alfred Nobel. Europe's robust industrial capacity could easily be turned to purposes of destruction. And despite the developing networks of global economic integration and the growing numbers of newly founded international organizations (on which more below), the intense competition among the great powers made such a turn increasingly likely.

LIBERALISM AT BAY

The intensity of international competition at the century's end did not strike all observers as necessary. To the contrary, many liberals hoped that a new era of peace and international cooperation was arriving, and they failed to see that liberalism itself would increasingly come under pressure from across the political spectrum. Much like Enlightenment thinkers before them, they argued that commerce was binding the powers of Europe closer together. As the British politician Richard Cobden had written in 1843: "Commerce is the grand panacea, which … will serve to inoculate with the health and saving taste for civilization all the nations of the world." His fellow liberal John Bright agreed, calling war sheer "madness" for commercial nations and insisting that "any peace is better than the most successful war." The fact that the European powers had not fought a truly large-scale, unlimited war since 1815 seemed to lend credence to these ideas.

Other Europeans felt that the progress of industry had made war so potentially destructive that no sane leader would ever again dare to begin one. And they seemingly had a point, for in the 1880s Britain's Sir Hiram Maxim (1840–1916) perfected a machine gun that could shoot more than 600 rounds a minute, while in 1900 the Krupp firm in Germany began to produce a howitzer cannon that could fire 800-pound shells over a distance of five miles.

Between 1890 and 1910, the threat of war led the major powers to sign a number of agreements meant to enhance international cooperation, of which the most important were the Hague Conventions of 1899 and 1907. These treaties aimed to regulate the conduct of war, including the treatment of prisoners of war, and to prohibit abuses such as the use of poison gas. They even set up a permanent court of arbitration to rule on international disputes and prevent the outbreak of violent conflict. The conventions were welcomed as a further sign that liberal cooperation would in the future take the place of war. In 1910, the Anglo-American journalist Norman Angell (1872–1967) made this case in *The Great Illusion,* a compellingly written book that sold 2 million copies, was translated into twenty-five languages, and earned its author a knighthood.

THE LIBERAL WORLDVIEW AND ITS CRITICS

But at the so-called fin de siècle ("end of the century"), the liberal worldview was increasingly on the defensive in Europe. On one side, a variety of socialist movements were gaining strength and advocating policies that ranged from expanded suffrage and a stronger social safety net to the wholesale expropriation and redistribution of property by revolutionary dictatorships. The socialist Second

International (an alliance of workers' organizations and political groups committed to the overthrow of capitalism), which succeeded the earlier International Working-men's Association, held nine internationalist congresses between 1889 and 1912. On the other side, a variety of right-wing movements were condemning liberal society as soulless and decadent, and insisting on a return—often a violent one—to a more "organic," "spiritual" form of society. Very often these latter movements grounded their claims in theories of inevitable conflict between nations and races, in which only the "fittest" would survive. And increasingly, they defined their chief enemies as the supposedly rootless, money-obsessed, and God-hating "race" they associated with the worst evils of market liberalism: the Jews.

FRANCE UNDER THE THIRD REPUBLIC

The pattern showed through even in the countries that were apparently most hospitable to moderate liberalism, such as France. There the 1880s saw the consolidation of the Third Republic, a stable regime that had beaten back challenges both from the left-wing Paris Commune of 1871 and from right-wing monarchists. In 1881–82, the French minister for public instruction, Jules Ferry, instituted an ambitious system of free, universal, secular primary education. The Third Republic enforced religious toleration, allowing French Jews to attain high positions in the universities, business, and even the army well ahead

Trade Trade Unions A room of somber men, women, and children stage a peaceful strike in Limoges, France in 1910.

of their counterparts elsewhere in Europe. The economy expanded, with the French taking a lead in new industries such as automobiles. Railroads penetrated formerly isolated parts of the countryside. Soon the Republic celebrated itself in a massive world's fair—the Universal Exposition of 1889—marking the centenary of the French Revolution. The fairgrounds covered a portion of central Paris, their centerpiece being that preeminent symbol of industrial modernity, the Eiffel Tower.

NEW CHALLENGES FROM THE LEFT AND RIGHT

Yet despite this apparent success, the Third Republic remained embattled throughout the late nineteenth and early twentieth centuries. On the left, the fin de siècle saw a resurgence of trade union activity in industry. The movement culminated in 1895 with the foundation of the General Confederation of Labor, which was committed to the overthrow of capitalism by means of general strikes. While its membership initially included only a minority of industrial workers, the Confederation expanded rapidly and by 1912 boasted over 600,000 members. Its 1906 charter explained that "the working class ... can expect nothing from men, powers and forces exterior to itself, but must create its own conditions for struggle and find in itself the means of acting." Militant political action by unions came to be known in France as **syndicalism**. Its chief exponent was the French philosopher Georges Sorel (1847–1922), who in 1908 dramatized the idea of the general strike in 1908 as an event that would lead to the violent cleansing and regeneration of society as a whole. Although the Confederation never managed to bring a general strike about, the principal French unions continued to pursue the ideal.

Meanwhile, in 1905, France's fractious socialist political parties united into the French Section of the Workers' International, referring to the Second International discussed above. Although it refused to participate in "bourgeois" governments, the socialist group nonetheless quickly became one of the most important players in French political life. Standing apart from the socialist movements, and excluded from the International, were anarchist groups, often inspired by Mikhail Bakunin. In the 1890s, anarchist groups increasingly reoriented their terrorist tactics toward random persons rather than prominent political figures, prefiguring contemporary forms of terrorism. They called the use of violence "propaganda of the deed." In 1894, an anarchist named Emile Henry threw a bomb in a crowded cafe in a Paris train station, killing one person and wounding many more.

An even more significant challenge to the French

Republic in this period came from the right. Despite the failure of conservatives to restore the monarchy in the 1870s, they never accepted the new regime's legitimacy. The religious fervor associated with sites like Lourdes was channeled into political directions through a host of popular associations and periodicals, reinforcing the message that a corrupt Republic was undermining the French nation. In the 1880s, an apparent right-wing savior came to the fore: a general named Georges Boulanger, who openly challenged the regime and came close to staging a coup d'état. But his career collapsed spectacularly amid charges he had embezzled from the war ministry, and in 1891, overcome with grief at the death of his mistress, Boulanger blew his brains out at her graveside. But even without him, anti-Republican activity continued apace. The novelist Maurice Barrès (1862–1923) dramatized the supposed decadence of the Third Republic in his hugely popular novel *The Uprooted* (1897), and soon afterward a powerful right-wing periodical and political movement committed to monarchism, Action Française ("French Action"), came into being.

FRENCH ANTI-SEMITISM In the 1880s, anti-Republican sentiment became tightly bound up with a virulent wave of anti-Semitism. France was of course hardly alien territory for anti-Semitism, and it flourished on the left as well as the right. Despite the political emancipation of Jews in the French Revolution and their entry into the army, universities, and professions, the small French Jewish community (less than one-quarter of 1 percent of the population, concentrated in the eastern province of Alsace and large cities) remained the regular target of discrimination, and of caricatures and attacks in the press and popular culture. But through the mid-nineteenth century, anti-Semitism in France remained relatively low-key compared with Russia, which as we will see subjected its much larger Jewish population to heavy legal burdens and frequent, officially tolerated popular violence.

After the foundation of the Third Republic, however, this began to change. In 1886, a journalist named Édouard Drumont (1844–1917) published an anti-Semitic tract entitled *Jewish France*, which became one of the greatest bestsellers in French history, going through 140 editions in just two years and making the fortune of the Flammarion publishing house. Drumont and his followers spun out bizarre conspiracy theories about a Jewish plot for world domination and about a Jewish role in various French financial scandals. Drumont's message spread throughout the country, relayed especially by Catholic clergy: "We are being pillaged, dishonored, exploited, and emptied by the Jew,"

one Church newsletter declared. "Servile, slithering, artful, filthy, and vile when he is the weaker one, he becomes arrogant when he has the upper hand, as he does now. The Jew is our master."

THE DREYFUS AFFAIR In this hateful climate, it is hardly surprising that when the French intelligence services found evidence of a highly placed German spy in the French army in 1894, suspicion immediately fell on a Jewish officer, Alfred Dreyfus (1859–1935). Army officials quickly conducted a perfunctory court martial, in which they failed to disclose evidence that supported Dreyfus's innocence. Dreyfus received a life sentence, to be served on Devil's Island off the coast of South America, where life sentences were usually short.

And then what had started as a simple albeit outrageous miscarriage of justice turned into a full-blown political crisis. As the extent of Dreyfus's innocence became clear, largely through the efforts of Dreyfus's family, desperate officers forged further evidence against him. They

The Dreyfus Affair This 1899 caricature uses anti-Semitic imagery to demonize Dreyfus, depicting him as a horrific, traitorous monster threatening the state.

even went so far as to protect the real spy when his guilt became apparent, so as to protect the honor of the army. The **Dreyfus Affair** dominated headlines and public discussion, divided families, and seemed to threaten the Republic's survival.

In 1898, the novelist Émile Zola published one of the great political polemics of all time in defense of Dreyfus: a lengthy newspaper article entitled simply "J'accuse" ("I accuse"). But on the other side there flowed a torrent of venom. Jews throughout France were vilified and threatened, and mobs paraded in the street calling for their deaths, while Dreyfus was caricatured as a treasonous monster. An Anti-Semitic League founded by Drumont flourished broadly, with hundreds of branches throughout France.

It took many years, a long series of trials, and an unprecedented campaign for public opinion before Dreyfus finally won exoneration in 1906. In theory, this exoneration meant a victory for the secular, liberal Third Republic. It was quickly followed by the removal of the Roman Catholic Church's privileged status in France, and the separation of church and state—although the government continued to fund many religious activities. But to most observers the Republic looked weaker, not stronger, after the Affair. And as many historians have suggested, simply based on the extent of public anti-Semitism, the European country that looked, in 1900, most likely someday to attempt a violent extermination of the Jews was not Germany or Russia, but France.

Already in the 1880s, a Jewish nationalist movement known as Zionism had begun to take shape in response to the rising threat of anti-Semitism in Europe. Most of its adherents hoped to found a new Jewish state in their ancestral homeland of Palestine, and in the 1880s and 1890s tens of thousands of Jews, mostly from the Russian Empire, migrated to Palestine, which still belonged to the Ottoman Empire. The horror aroused in European Jewry by the Dreyfus Affair enormously strengthened the movement and led to a second wave of emigration to Palestine. The Austrian Jewish journalist Theodor Herzl (1860–1904) saw Dreyfus's ordeal as confirmation that Jews could only live normal lives in a homeland of their own and went on to convene a worldwide Zionist conference and to found a formal Zionist organization.

Russia, 1910

THE PERSISTENCE OF AUTOCRACY IN RUSSIA

Liberalism was even more embattled in Russia. The assassination of Tsar Alexander II in 1881 by a revolutionary group called The People's Will led to the accession of his staunchly autocratic son, Alexander III (r. 1881–1894). In a country with no parliament of any sort, one of the new tsar's first actions was to retract a tentative move toward creating political assemblies that would have been dominated by large landowners and wealthy townspeople. And in a burgeoning Russian Empire that by 1905 would contain some 200 nationalities speaking 145 separate languages, Alexander III dreamed of a homogenous Russian nation-state. He pursued vigorous Russification policies that prompted the Russian language, the Russian Orthodox Church, and ethnic Russians. He also gave free rein to anti-Semitic elements who wanted to force on the Empire's Jews the stark choice between conversion, emigration, or death, so as to eliminate them entirely from Russian soil. In 1881–82, a series of officially tolerated anti-Jewish **pogroms** (riots) took place, leaving hundreds dead and thousands wounded, and spurring the massive Jewish emigration to America and Palestine.

Alexander III did preside over a rapid expansion of the Russian economy. Between the 1880s and 1910, foreign trade and railroad lines tripled in size (with the Trans-Siberian Railroad reaching all the way from Moscow to the Pacific by 1916), and coal and steel production grew exponentially. But even though the urban working class was some 2 million strong by 1900, mostly concentrated in the two great cities of Saint Petersburg and Moscow, the vast majority of the population of 100 million still lived as peasants. The Russian peasants were no longer tied to the land as serfs, and this new freedom spurred emigration abroad, particularly from Ukraine. Still, most of the peasantry continued to live near their places of birth.

Alexander died prematurely in 1894, and initially liberals—mostly professionals living in cities—placed great hopes in his son, Nikolai II (r. 1894–1917). The nephew, on his mother's side, of Britain's future queen Alexandra (r. 1901–1910), he had traveled to Britain and pronounced himself impressed with its institutions. But upon taking the throne he too quickly returned to a defense of autocracy. In 1903, his government sanctioned another series of bloody pogroms against Russia's Jews. The Russian state also renewed its persecution of socialists. When a united and largely urban Russian Social Democratic Workers' Party formed in 1898, the police quickly moved against it and its members had to continue their work in exile. In 1903, the party split into two factions: the more moderate **Mensheviks** ("minority") and the radical **Bolsheviks** ("majority"), who insisted on violent revolution leading to a dictatorship of the proletariat. The names of the factions were misleading as the Mensheviks were actually more numerous.

THE RUSSIAN REVOLUTION OF 1905 An opening for change in Russia only arrived with the disastrous Russo-Japanese War of 1904–1905 (see below), in which the Japanese largely destroyed two of the three Russian fleets and took considerable territory. The Russians had to face the humiliation of losing a conflict to a people they considered to be inferior non-Europeans.

In the midst of this crisis, Russian liberals—rather like their French predecessors in 1848—organized a series of public banquets to draw attention to their calls for political representation. The movement, launched in the fall of 1904, brought together opponents of the regime ranging from Marxist groups to liberal professionals who hoped above all for the creation of a Russian political democracy—but who were hampered by their lack of strong leadership. The local Moscow assembly issued a series of demands that included a national legislature, freedom of religion, and freedom of the press. Grudgingly, the tsar promised some limited reforms.

Then, on so-called Bloody Sunday, January 22, 1905, a huge crowd of workers led by a charismatic priest converged on the Winter Palace in Saint Petersburg, only to be met by gunfire from the army. Hundreds died, and again, as in the 1848 revolutions, the horrific spectacle led to a much larger groundswell of protest. The Marxists and the liberal Constitutional Democrats (called the Kadets) now competed to organize the opposition, with the former helping to form workers' councils, or soviets, in the major cities. In October, the Saint Petersburg soviet led a successful general strike. Tsar Nikolai desperately issued an October Manifesto promising a new constitution that would guarantee civil liberties and create a national parliament, or **Duma**.

But in the end, the revolutionaries could not preserve their momentum against relentless counterattacks from the tsarist state. The principal socialist parties, including the Bolsheviks and Mensheviks, refused to participate in

Bloody Sunday This oil painting from 1905 dramatizes the victims of Bloody Sunday at the Winter Palace in Saint Petersburg. Protestors look on in horror as some of them are hit by the army's gunfire, their blood staining the snow.

the initial elections for the Duma, while a complex system of proportional representation limited the influence of peasants and workers. The Kadets swept into the Duma by default but found their powers starkly limited. The tsar insisted on reserving control over the executive, the military, and foreign policy; retaining the right to legislate in the Duma's absence, and on placing it below a State Council that he controlled. Even so, the Duma proved insufficiently pliant, and he dissolved it in 1906. He did the same the next year with its successor, which this time included socialist deputies. And he followed the second dissolution with a campaign of savage repression against political opponents, with several thousand imprisoned or executed. A new electoral law ensured an even more conservative, compliant third Duma, and for the remaining few years of the Russian Empire political opposition was effectively stifled. The Bolsheviks and Mensheviks largely went underground or organized abroad.

FIN DE SIÈCLE GERMANY AND AUSTRIA-HUNGARY

Germany as well proved inhospitable territory for liberalism in the fin de siècle. Just as in Russia, liberals, especially in the universities and the professions, placed great hopes in a new ruler, Friedrich III (r. March–June 1888), who succeeded his father, Wilhelm I, as kaiser in 1888. Although a hero of the wars of German unification, Friedrich, like

Nikolai of Russia, had close ties to Britain—his wife was the eldest daughter of Queen Victoria. He supported an expansion of the franchise and a greater role for the Reichstag (the lower house of parliament) in state affairs. But his ambitions were thwarted by his father's longevity—Wilhelm I lived to age ninety, and just before Friedrich finally came to the throne a fatal throat cancer struck him. He ruled for just ninety-nine days.

Friedrich's own son, Wilhelm II (r. 1888–1918), had a very different character. Intelligent and well educated, Wilhelm was also temperamental and aggressive. He had a strong, paternalist sense of obligation to ordinary Germans, but was also deeply militarist, with a fetish for elaborate uniforms, and he despised democracy. "We Hohenzollerns," he declared once, "are answerable only to heaven." He was obsessed above all with surpassing Great Britain and did everything he could to expand Germany's armed forces—in particular, sponsoring aggressive expansion of the navy. Within a couple of years of his accession, anxious to rule without rivals, he dismissed the aging Bismarck from office and thereafter oversaw a series of much weaker chancellors.

During the decades around 1900, Germany, like other European countries, saw its political culture increasingly dominated by the language of racial conflict. German militarists insisted that the country's racial destiny was to dominate Europe through violent competition. Influential writers such as the historian Heinrich von Treitschke (1834–1896) rejected the liberal idea of perpetual peace among nations, calling it "not just impossible, but immoral as well." War, Treitschke declared, was something "sacred." Ardent nationalists such as the composer Richard Wagner, who had attacked "Jewishness in Music" in a notorious 1850 article, insisted that German culture had to be preserved from "alien" and "artificial" influences—above all, Jewish ones. In 1892, the German Conservative Party officially added anti-Semitic positions to its platform, calling for limiting the Jewish presence in broad areas of German public life.

At the same time, pressuring German liberals from the other side of the political spectrum, the Social Democratic Party experienced remarkable growth, drawing support from German workers to become the largest and best-organized socialist party in Europe. Although in 1891 it adopted a hard-line Marxist revolutionary program, calling for the nationalization of major industries, it thereafter moved in a more moderate direction, cooperating with other parliamentary forces. But in an authoritarian system dominated by the Kaiser, the socialists could exercise only limited influence.

Ethnic conflict was even more pronounced in the polyglot Habsburg Empire. Czechs agitated successfully for their language to be put on an equal footing with German, and when pressure from German-speakers forced a reversal of the policy in 1893, they protested so energetically that the government had to impose martial law on the Czech regions. In Bosnia-Herzegovina, which Austria-Hungary had acquired from the Ottoman Empire in 1878, the sizable Serbian Christian population there demanded union with the newly independent Serbian state. Croats and Slovenes bristled at the policies of Magyarization (imposition of the Hungarian language) that had followed the creation of the Austro-Hungarian dual monarchy in 1867. And in the empire's vibrant, multi-ethnic capitals of Vienna and Budapest, Austrian and Hungarian politicians increasingly strove to appeal to the workers and middle classes by inciting resentment against a group that supposedly exploited them and blocked their social advancement: the Jews. A self-professed admirer of the French anti-Semite Drumont, Karl Lueger (1844–1910) routinely denounced Jewish conspiracies and the unfair business practices that Jews supposedly used to compete with Christians. In 1895, he won election as mayor of Vienna. Anti-Semitism reached a fever pitch in Austria-Hungary at much the same time as it did in France with the Dreyfus Affair.

BRITAIN AND IRELAND

In Great Britain, ethnic and religious tensions put liberalism under pressure in a different way. Here these tensions involved above all the country's oldest and closest overseas possession: Ireland. As we have seen, the early nineteenth century witnessed significant political agitation in Ireland, as the Catholic majority pushed for full civil rights. But the end of legal discrimination only emboldened Catholic activists to demand the repeal of the 1801 Act of Union between Ireland and Britain. The push for **home rule**, or Irish self-government, was led by the Irish National League and its flamboyant chief, Charles Stewart Parnell (1846–1891), whose career was cut short when he died of a heart attack at age forty-five. But in the early 1880s, more radical forces tried to take matters into their own hands, with the violent Irish Republican Army murdering two British officials in Dublin. Home rule nonetheless won significant support in Britain, including that of Liberal Party leader William Ewart Gladstone. But it provoked white-hot opposition from many others in Britain, not to mention the Protestants who held the majority in several

Home Rule A 1912 political cartoon representing the perspective of the northern Irish province of Ulster, whose Protestant majority supported continued union with Great Britain. It shows England holding on to Ulster by a rope to prevent Ireland from floating off and running aground on the symbolic "Home Rule Rocks."

counties of northern Ireland and feared oppression from a future Catholic majority.

In 1886, Britain's Liberal Party split over the issue of Irish home rule, with the Birmingham politician Joseph Chamberlain (1836–1914) dominating a new Liberal Unionist Party (named for its support of continuing union with Ireland), which would soon ally with the Conservatives and eventually merge with them. The original Liberals remained strong enough to win one last election in 1906, and the party accomplished some major reforms—notably, forcing the House of Lords to give up its veto over legislation. This put far more power in the hands of the House of Commons, elected by nearly all adult males.

But the Liberal Party would soon be reduced to marginal status, and not just because of Ireland. In 1893, a group of socialists dissatisfied with them, and hoping to introduce social welfare policies and checks on the power of business, founded an Independent Labour Party, which successfully contested several parliamentary seats. In the new century, the British trade union movement then helped sponsor the creation of a larger Labour Party, which gradually overtook the Liberals as one of two major British parties, along with the Conservatives.

INCREASING SOCIAL PROTECTIONS

Liberalism's difficulties throughout Europe at the end of the century did not mean the end of social reform. To the contrary, continuing labor activism and right-wing paternalism both drove forward the extension of social protections for the working classes and the very poor. By 1914, fully 3 million British workers and 1.5 million German ones belonged to labor unions—although even in Britain the number still amounted to just 25 percent of the workforce, concentrated in industries such as metallurgy. In France, the year 1904 saw more than a thousand strikes. But the country that made the greatest progress on social reform was neither liberal Britain nor republican France, but the more authoritarian Germany whose government had paternalist plans to strengthen and modernize the state. Starting with a sickness insurance act passed in 1883, Germany went on, by 1900, to provide workers with national insurance programs for accidents and disability. It also enacted a pension system, although it required forty-eight years of contributions, and workers did not draw full pensions until age seventy. Britain did not match Germany's social policies, but between 1875 and 1910 a series of laws reduced the length of the workweek, put in new regulations against unsanitary housing, and provided limited pensions for the desperately poor who had no other sources of income. France also limited the workweek and began to regulate working conditions more thoroughly.

FIN DE SIÈCLE FEMINISM

In many ways, the most important liberal movements in Europe between 1880 and 1910 were those advocating women's rights. By 1910, Britain, France, and Germany all had something close to universal adult male suffrage; several other European countries, including Greece (1864) and Norway (1898), did as well. But only the Grand Principality of Finland, an autonomous area within the Russian Empire, gave the vote, in 1907, to women as well. Laws throughout Europe restricted women's control of property and many other rights. In France, husbands had the right to their wives' salaries. The calls for woman suffrage in the 1789 and 1848 revolutions had had little effect. Women in much of southern Europe still had no right to divorce, owing to the influence of the Catholic Church.

While women did move rapidly into some new economic sectors, the professions (for example, law, medicine, architecture) remained largely barred to them. Figures such as Marie Curie (see below), a French scientist who won two Nobel Prizes, were very much the exception. Male scientists in the period routinely argued that men innately possessed greater intelligence than women.

Nonetheless, during the fin de siècle, women's groups

Woman Suffrage A 1914 photograph shows Emmeline Pankhurst, leader of the militant wing of the British woman suffrage movement, being arrested outside Buckingham Palace in London while trying to present a petition to the king.

Like the Chartists of the previous generation, they gathered petitions with hundreds of thousands of signatures in favor of their cause. **Emmeline Pankhurst** (1858–1928), founder of the Women's Social and Political Union in 1903, urged civil disobedience in the hope of drawing attention to the cause of woman suffrage and ultimately persuading Parliament to enact it. She was a charismatic leader whose speaking style was memorably described by the writer Rebecca West: "Trembling like a reed, she lifted up her hoarse, sweet voice on the platform, but the reed was of steel and it was tremendous." She called herself a "soldier" engaged in a "civil war" and justified her "trouble-making" with eloquent language:

> You have two babies very hungry and wanting to be fed. One baby is a patient baby, and waits indefinitely until its mother is ready to feed it. The other baby is an impatient baby and cries lustily, screams and kicks and makes everybody unpleasant until it is fed. Well, we know perfectly well which baby is attended to first. That is the whole history of politics. You have to make more noise than anybody else, you have to make yourself more obtrusive than anybody else, you have to fill all the papers more than anybody else, in fact you have to be there all the time and see that they do not snow you under.

Some of her supporters took her martial language literally and resorted to bomb-throwing in their frustration at Parliament's failure to act in their favor. More of them engaged in forms of peaceful protest, such as chaining themselves to fences. Upon arrest, they demanded to be treated as political prisoners, and when denied the right, went on hunger strikes. In response, prison authorities had them violently force-fed. These tactics did have the effect of drawing enormous attention to the issue of suffrage, and sympathetic declarations from both Liberal and Labour politicians. In 1912, the Labour Party came out in favor of votes for women. But British women would not actually gain the right to vote until after World War I.

INTERNATIONAL RIVALRY AND THE NEW IMPERIALISM

The struggles of liberalism against both socialist and right-wing opponents throughout Europe, coupled with the growing nationalist passions that we have seen developing on the Continent, helped to foster a climate of ever-more-intense international competition at the end

throughout Europe gained in numbers and influence. In Germany, the Socialist leader August Bebel's 1879 book *Women under Socialism* became something of a feminist bible and helped foster a powerful feminist socialist movement led by Clara Zetkin (1857–1933). But many women's groups favored "spiritual motherhood" rather than political equality. Many French Catholic women's groups had a similar focus, engaging in charitable work (particularly in connection with the pilgrimage to Lourdes) rather than political organizing. In 1889, however, an International Congress on Women's Rights and Feminine Institutions convened in Paris. It would prove influential in forging ties among mostly middle-class feminist leaders and in developing common agendas among the different national movements.

British suffragists—whom male politicians patronizingly dubbed suffragettes—provided particularly forceful and eloquent voices in favor of women's right to vote.

FEMINISM AND DOMESTIC LIFE

Feminism gained strength in the late nineteenth and early twentieth centuries as women used the language of liberalism to argue for equal rights. In Britain, the suffrage campaign united feminists, but the movement was remarkably diverse. While some feminists argued that men and women were essentially equal, others, like the English suffragist Millicent Garrett Fawcett, drew on the ideology that men belonged in the public sphere and women in the household. In the following passage from her speech "Home and Politics" (1894), Fawcett argues that women's experience with domestic life is crucial to effective governance.

With regard to the differences between men and women, those who advocate the enfranchisement of women have no wish to disregard them or make little of them. On the contrary, we base our claim to representation to a large extent on them. If men and women were exactly alike, the representation of men would represent us; but not being alike, that wherein we differ is unrepresented under the present system.

The motherhood of women, either actual or potential, is one of those great facts of everyday life which we must never lose sight of. To women as mothers, is given the charge of the home and the care of children. Women are, therefore, by nature as well as by occupation and training, more accustomed than men to concentrate their minds on the home and the domestic side of things. But this difference between men and women, instead of being a reason against their enfranchisement, seems to me the strongest possible reason in favour of it; we want the home and the domestic side of things to count for more in politics and in the administration of public affairs than they do at present. We want to know how various kinds of legislative enactments bear on the home and on domestic life. And we want to force our legislators to consider the domestic as well as the political results of any legislation which many of them are advocating....

Depend upon it, the most important institution in the country is the home.

QUESTIONS FOR ANALYSIS

1. What makes men and women different, according to Fawcett?
2. Why is the difference between men and women not an argument against, but in fact an argument for, women's suffrage?
3. How does women's command of the home contribute to the well-being of the nation?

Source: Millicent Garrett Fawcett, "Home and Politics," in *Before the Vote Was Won: Arguments for and against Women's Suffrage, 1864–1896*, ed. Jane Lewis (London: 1987), pp. 419–20.

of the nineteenth century. In France, rage and humiliation at the country's defeat in the Franco-Prussian War fed steady calls for revenge and for recovery of the "lost provinces" of Alsace and Lorraine. In Germany, rivalry with Britain was zealously stoked by Kaiser Wilhelm II and military leaders. A Navy League that they sponsored, to support the rapid expansion of German naval power, counted over 300,000 paying members by 1900. Russia chafed at the way the other great powers, particularly Germany, had tried to limit its influence in the Balkans at the 1878 Congress of Berlin. And Great Britain sought to retain its status as the preeminent imperial power. To strengthen their positions, the great powers squared off in alliances, with Germany, Austria-Hungary, and Italy forming the **Triple Alliance** in 1882. In response, France and Russia eventually negotiated an alliance of their own, and in 1907 Russia signed an accord with Britain as well, effectively creating the **Triple Entente**.

International competition was hardly a new phenomenon in Europe, but between 1880 and 1910 it assumed a new form. Once before, in the mid-eighteenth century, an important European rivalry, between Britain and France, had played out in large part overseas. But France's defeat in the Napoleonic Wars largely ended this phase of international relations. And particularly after most Latin American nations gained independence in the early

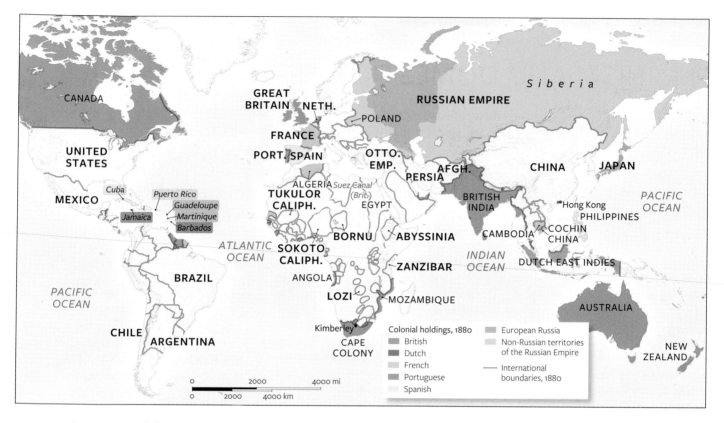

European Imperialism, ca. 1880 In the late nineteenth century, several older imperial powers—Spain, Portugal, the Netherlands—retained control of territories on the other side of the world. Other European empires were just beginning to expand, such as France in North Africa and Southeast Asia. Russia also controlled an extensive landmass across Europe and Asia. But the most powerful empire, Britain, controlled territories on five continents, ranging from the vast land expanses of Canada and Australia to the economically significant Egypt, Cape Colony, and India.

nineteenth century, Britain remained by far the most significant European imperial power. True, the Netherlands preserved its far-flung colonies in present-day Indonesia. Spain held on to Cuba, Puerto Rico, the Philippines, and a few other territories. Portugal had colonies in southern Africa and trading posts throughout Asia. And France by the mid-nineteenth century had established a significant presence in Algeria, kept some small island colonies in the Caribbean, and was moving to take over most of southeast Asia.

But these empires paled in comparison with Britain's, which by the 1880s included all of south Asia from present-day Pakistan to Burma; significant and strategic colonies at the southern tip of Africa; Jamaica, Barbados, and other island possessions in the Caribbean and elsewhere; and the large, autonomous British settler states of Canada, Australia, and New Zealand. Massive emigration from the British Isles (one million people just in the 1850s) led to stunning growth in these settler states.

In New Zealand in 1842, just 2,000 white settlers lived among some 80,000 native Maori. By 1896, disease and violent conflict had reduced Maori numbers by half, while the white population had exploded to 700,000. In China, Britain controlled the most important trading port, the city of Hong Kong, although other European powers also enjoyed trade concessions from the ruling Qing dynasty.

And the British Navy continued to exercise unquestioned dominance on the high seas. As a result, competition among European states overseas had remained limited for many decades. Until the late nineteenth century, Britain's most important competitor in areas outside of Europe had been Russia, whose land empire extended west from Poland to the Pacific Ocean. In the mid-nineteenth century, the tsarist regime extended its control from Russia and Siberia south into present day Turkmenistan, Uzbekistan, and Tajikistan, and threatened to proceed into Afghanistan and thence toward

British India. Russia was now the largest territorial state in the world.

THE SCRAMBLE FOR AFRICA

In the 1880s and 1890s, the so-called **scramble for Africa** upset the European states' previous calculations. As late as 1880, the European powers had a relatively minimal presence in Africa: the French colony of Algeria in the Arab north; the British at the Cape; the Portuguese in Angola, Mozambique, and a series of trading posts along the coasts. Altogether, Europeans claimed less than 10 percent of Africa and were relatively inactive in the areas they did claim. After the end of the slave trade in the early nineteenth century, the economic significance of the continent for Europeans had actually declined. Infectious disease—especially malaria—dissuaded Europeans from venturing into the African interior, and transportation away from the coast remained hugely expensive. It has been estimated that to move 50 tons of freight a distance of 20 miles in many parts of Africa, in the absence of water transport, required over 13,000 porters.

But as the nineteenth century unfolded, technological advances made African exploration and conquest far more practical. Europeans discovered how to extract quinine efficiently from tree bark and to use it to prevent malaria. Railroads and newly cheap shipping enabled the affordable extraction of natural resources from the continent's interior. And the new military technology—especially the deadly machine gun—dramatically increased Europeans' military advantages over indigenous Africans.

With these new tools of empire in hand, throughout the century Europeans explored and mapped vast areas of Africa that had been previously unknown to them. Sponsored by both Protestant and Catholic churches hoping to establish African missions, by governments interested in natural resources and colonial markets, and by newspapers hoping for good stories, a series of colorful explorers such as David Livingstone (1813–1873), Pierre Savorgnan de Brazza (1852–1905), and Henry Morton Stanley (1841–1904) captured European imaginations. In 1871, when Livingstone went missing in central Africa, the founder of the *New York Herald* hired the Welsh-born Stanley to venture into unknown territory to find him; Stanley succeeded, allegedly uttering the words "Dr. Livingstone, I presume," and went on to chart the course of the Congo River.

The expeditions helped make European rulers aware of the tremendous resources available in Africa: gold and other precious metals; crops like cotton and cocoa; and plant extracts such as rubber and palm oil for which the Second Industrial Revolution was finding increasingly profitable uses. Particularly spectacular was the discovery of diamonds at Kimberly in southern Africa in 1871—it led to a diamond rush in which tens of thousands of immigrant European miners transformed a small hillock into a vast hole a quarter of a mile across and up to 700 feet deep, producing some 6,000 pounds of diamonds between 1871 and 1914.

Such wealth also made Europeans aware of Africa's potential as a market for their own manufactured goods, such as textiles, at a time when shrinking domestic markets and overproduction were leading to dangerously lower prices. With the European powers already primed for competition, the realization of this potential set off the

Explorers in Africa An illustration from a late-nineteenth-century biography of David Livingstone shows his famous meeting with Henry Stanley in East Africa in 1871. The event was a publicity stunt devised by the *New York Herald*—hence the American flag carried by one of the expedition's native facilitators.

The Partition of Africa, 1880–1912 From 1880, European powers moved in from the African coast to claim large tracts of land in the interior. Resistance to colonization was fierce, leading to violence throughout the continent. But by 1912, major imperial possessions—such as the French in northwest Africa, the British claims that stretched "from Cape to Cairo," and the Belgian Congo—meant that Africa was a theater of European conflicts such as the Boer War (1899–1902). Only Abyssinia remained independent of European rule.

scramble, which developed quickly. The British statesman Lord Salisbury remarked in 1891: "When I left the Foreign Office in 1880, nobody thought about Africa. When I returned to it in 1885 the nations of Europe were almost quarreling with each other as to the various portions of Africa which they should obtain." He correctly called the event a "sudden revolution."

PARTITION OF THE CONTINENT In the early 1880s, a fear of being left behind overcame Britain, France, and Germany. Smaller powers such as Belgium and Italy also started to see an advantage in pursuing their own African empires through military force. In 1882, Britain, taking advantage of chaos in Egypt and acting to ensure that its Asia-bound ships could pass through the new Suez Canal, established a **protectorate** in Egypt. This was a form of imperial rule supposedly intended to protect the indigenous population but in fact designed to assert significant control for the imperial power. France established a similar protectorate over Tunisia and made claims in the Congo. Germany, initially reluctant to pursue an overseas expansion for which its history offered no precedent, became convinced that it had to join in or cede a crucial strategic and economic advantage to its rivals. It claimed German Southwest Africa and soon moved to establish protectorates in the future states of Togo, Cameroon, and Tanzania. Seeking to make their scramble more orderly, the European powers convened the **Berlin Conference of 1884–1885** to draw borders. Delegates divided the vast area of the Congo between France and Belgium, and gave free rein to France in much of West Africa, particularly the future Ivory Coast. Britain had its interests in Egypt recognized and received effective authority over large areas of East Africa as well.

By 1911, the European partition of the continent had been completed. The French consolidated their empire by seizing the vast western African territories between Algeria and the Ivory Coast, while also moving into central Africa, taking the large island of Madagascar, and establishing a protectorate over Morocco. Italy entered the race late, establishing the colony of Eritrea on the Red Sea and fighting a successful war against the Ottoman Empire for Libya in 1911. It failed, however, in an earlier, more ambitious war against the independent kingdom of Abyssinia (Ethiopia). In a campaign marked by remarkable incompetence, the Italians lost a crucial battle in 1896, leaving the Abyssinians in possession of one of two significant independent states in Africa. The other was the Republic of Liberia, which had been settled in the 1840s by former American slaves.

For the most part, the scramble for Africa took place without significant violence between Europeans. A crisis briefly developed between Britain and France over the Sudan in the mid-1890s, with British gunboats confronting a small French expedition at the remote river fort of Fashoda in 1898. But the French simply did not have the resources to challenge the British presence, and eventually backed down in return for British acknowledgment of their positions in West Africa and the hope of future British support against Germany.

THE BOER WAR (1899–1902) The largest exception to the pattern of peaceful competition came in South Africa, where, by the mid-nineteenth century, the descendants of the early Dutch colonists (with a fair admixture of French Huguenots and other Protestants) had carved out two independent states: the Transvaal and the Orange Free State. In both, small white minorities dominated much larger populations of Africans and mixed-race "coloreds," who lacked the vote and any meaningful civil rights. These states resisted attempts at British annexation (with a Liberal government in London confirming the Transvaal's independence), but the discovery of rich deposits of gold and diamonds, particularly in the Transvaal town of Johannesburg, triggered an inrush of English-speaking immigrants from throughout the British Empire and put new pressure on the relationship. In 1895, the British-born South African politician and entrepreneur Cecil Rhodes (1853–1902) sponsored a botched attempt to take the Transvaal for Britain by force.

Four years later, open war broke out between Britain and the two **Boers** (from the Dutch word for "farmer") republics. The Boers shocked the British army with unexpectedly effective resistance by both regular troops and guerrillas. In response, the British shipped in hundreds of thousands of soldiers and adopted increasingly harsh tactics. They executed guerrillas and drove Boer families off their farms into dangerous, unsanitary compounds referred to—in a foreshadowing of the horror of the century to come—as concentration camps. The tactics caused enormous controversy in Britain, with a faction of pro-Boers defending the Boer cause against their own country, and the leader of the Liberal Party denouncing "methods of barbarism in South Africa." Finally, in 1902 the Boers sued for peace but soon afterward had their states admitted into a Union of South

British Concentration Camps During the Boer War, social investigators visited South Africa to document what they argued were the atrocities of the British concentration camps. Their work included this 1900 photograph of a child who died of malnutrition in one such camp.

Africa, which quickly achieved self-governing dominion status similar to that of Canada within the British Empire. This arrangement also signified official British approval of South Africa's policies of racial inequality, inherited from the Boer republics, which subordinated the African population to whites, depriving them of the vote and civil rights.

VIOLENCE AGAINST AFRICANS The relative lack of violence between Europeans in Africa was more than offset by the massive violence inflicted on native African populations. When armed with European weapons, African forces could still sometimes defeat European armies. Abyssinia's triumph over Italy was one example; another was the victory in 1885 of Muslim Sudanese rebels over an Anglo-Egyptian force, and the killing of the British general Charles Gordon (1833–1885). But more typical was Britain's revenge on the Sudanese at the battle of Omdurman in 1898, when a larger Anglo-Egyptian force under Field Marshal Herbert Kitchener (1850–1916), armed with Maxim machine guns, killed 10,000 Sudanese and wounded 13,000, while losing only 47 dead and 382 wounded of their own. A popular verse of the period ended with the words "Whatever happens, we have the Maxim Gun and they do not."

The worst violence inflicted on Africans, however,

Belgian Congo A white overseer poses with his forced African laborers and their bountiful rubber harvest in this photograph from 1899.

happened off the battlefield. We have already seen how in 1904 the Germans deliberately slaughtered the Herero and Nama peoples in Southwest Africa. But even that example of mass killing was overshadowed by the horrifying exploitation of the Congo by Belgium after it became the private fiefdom of King Leopold II in 1885. The king's agents forced Congolese to work for little or no pay harvesting rubber, gathering ivory, and mining valuable ores. Many died as a result of the appalling work conditions; others perished in the epidemics that spread through the disrupted territory (as in Latin America three hundred years before, the indigenous population often had little immunity to European diseases); still others starved to death after Leopold's army had carted off the available foodstuffs for itself. And huge numbers were simply shot for disobeying orders.

In a particularly terrible turn of events, Belgian military leaders insisted that to save on ammunition, soldiers turn in a severed hand of a Congolese native for every bullet they fired. The Belgians took to hacking hands off defenseless women and children if a bullet missed the mark. All in all, as many as 8 million Congolese—half the population—lost their lives between 1885 and 1908, while King Leopold himself reaped over a billion dollars in today's money in profits. Finally, international protests led him to give up his fiefdom and in effect sell his private colony to the Belgian government. The Congo became the setting for the most powerful European novel about the horrors of imperialism in Africa, by the Polish-born British novelist Joseph Conrad (1857–1924): *Heart of Darkness*.

THE "CIVILIZING" MISSION Despite the naked power politics and economic impulses that prompted the new imperialism, the European powers nonetheless justified their conduct by stressing the beneficial effects of their rule for native peoples. Non-Europeans, it was explained, were in desperate need of "civilization"—in the words of Rudyard Kipling's 1897 poem "The White Man's Burden," they were "half-devil and half-child." The same Universal Exposition of 1889 that led to the construction of the Eiffel Tower in Paris also featured a so-called negro village—a literal human zoo featuring some 400 Africans in a re-creation of their "native" habitat, reinforcing the message that indigenous peoples needed European teaching to learn everything from proper hygiene and manners to civics and Christianity.

In practice, what became known as Europeans' civilizing mission in Africa came to focus on the building of schools, the teaching of European languages, and the provision of elementary medical services, as well as attempts

DISCRIMINATION AGAINST INDIANS IN SOUTH AFRICA

By the 1890s, tens of thousands of Indians had immigrated to South Africa, often to work as indentured servants—contracted for a fixed period, after which they could return to India or settle permanently—on sugar plantations, railways, or mines, or as independent merchants. Most lived in the southeastern British colony of Natal, others in the independent state of the Transvaal to the north. As the Indian presence in these regions continued to grow, settlers of European origin increasingly passed legislation to deny them rights. However, some merchants and lawyers, including the future Indian independence leader Mohandas Gandhi, fought to expose the injustice of these discriminatory measures.

Henry Campbell, *Re* British Indians in Transvaal

Although British subjects living in the Transvaal could own property and engage in commerce, an 1885 law severely restricted these rights for all Asians, including Indians. In response, a lawyer representing a group of Indian merchants, Henry Campbell, wrote the following letter in 1890 requesting intervention from Britain's Colonial Office.

The ordinary license to trade is now being refused to the Indian Merchants....

Owing to the refusals now notified to me the whole of the Indians are in fear that at the end of the year they will be refused licenses for 1891 in all districts simultaneously.

I fear such is the view held by officials and their intent likewise. As the law providing for the licenses sets out, any person trading without a license is liable to fine and imprisonment.

In all probability licenses will not be issued, their tender of money on January 1st 1891 will be refused, and they will be brought face to face with closed doors and a ruined business, or, opening their doors, being [hauled] to prison....

Some two hundred mercantile firms and businesses are thus threatened....

Their capital sum invested totals a quarter of a million sterling in the Transvaal alone. The paralysis of this quarter of a million sterling would react on the Head Offices in India amongst their commercial and financial banking in Bombay and the other Presidencies....

Capital invested by those people in the Transvaal on the security of their status as British subjects is made the sport of a local law which has given the power to compel them to leave the towns where alone business can be done, and go into a semi-leper isolation into a so-called "location, ward, or street" removed from the centres of traffic and from the towns, markets, bazaars, or marts.

This position is alike cruelly unjust and intolerable; either those people have the right of British subjects to "full liberty with their families to enter, travel, or reside in any part of the South African Republic; entitled to hire or possess houses, manufactories, warehouses, shops, and premises; to carry on their commerce either in person or by any agents whom they may think fit to employ or not." They either have the right to do all this or they have not.

Gandhi, Open Letter on Franchise Law

In 1894, the colony of Natal passed a law stripping Indians of the right to vote. Shortly thereafter, Gandhi wrote an open letter to the legislature in protest.

I suppose there can be no doubt that the Indian is a despised being in the Colony, and that every opposition to him proceeds directly from that hatred.

If that hatred is simply based upon his colour, then, of course, he has no hope. The sooner he leaves the Colony the better. No matter what he does, he will never have the white skin. If, however, it is based upon something else, if it is based upon an ignorance of his general character and attainments, he may hope to receive his due at the hands of the Europeans in the Colony.

The question what use the Colony will make of the 40,000 Indians is, I submit, worthy of the most serious consideration....

It is for you to say whether you will lower them or raise them in the scale of civilization, whether you will bring them down to a level lower than what they should occupy on account of heredity, whether you will alienate their hearts from you, or whether you will draw them closer to you—whether, in short, you would govern them despotically or sympathetically....

Withdraw the Indian from the sugar estate, and where would the main industry of the Colony be?

QUESTIONS FOR ANALYSIS

1. According to Campbell, what makes the treatment of Indians in the Transvaal unjust?
2. What does Gandhi see as the root cause of British discrimination against Indians in the Natal colony?
3. What economic arguments do both Campbell and Gandhi make for the fair treatment of Indians in South Africa?

Sources: Henry Campbell, letter, in *India: A Journal for the Discussion of Indian Affairs* (London: 1890), p. 281; Mahatma Gandhi, *The Collected Works of Mahatma Gandhi*, vol. 1 (New Delhi: 1958), pp. 171–72.

to limit the use of native law, reduce the influence of tribal chiefs, and eradicate slavery. In the British and German colonies, much of the educational mission was left up to Christian missionaries. In the French empire, and especially in the extensive territories that made up French West Africa, the republican state took the leading role, while proclaiming as its goal the assimilation of Africans to French values and customs. But the fundamental tension—indeed, the hypocrisy—of the civilizing mission showed through in the reluctance of the French administration to grant full citizenship to anyone outside a tiny indigenous elite.

THE GROWTH OF SETTLER COLONIES

The scramble for Africa was the most striking and visible aspect of European imperialism between 1880 and 1910, but it was not the whole story. Several European empires, particularly the British, expanded through Asia and other parts of the world during this period. The growing British presence in India can be measured in miles of track. British rail networks in the country grew from 300 miles in 1857 to 25,000 in 1900. Europeans continued to flow to settler colonies and dominions, which were former settler colonies that now had self-rule, such as Canada and Australia. By 1900, close to 500,000 white French citizens were living in Algeria and had direct representation in the French parliament. Large parts of the capital Algiers had become, in effect, a European city.

But it was not just Europeans who took part in new global migrations. Within the British Empire, Indian laborers migrated to Burma, to the future Malaysia, to South Africa, and to British colonies in the Caribbean. By 1914, there were 250,000 Indians in Guyana and 134,000 in Trinidad. The French facilitated the immigration of Chinese into French Southeast Asia. The French would also soon begin using black officials from their Caribbean territories of Martinique and Guadeloupe to help them administer their empire in Africa.

The one great exception to the story of imperial expansion in the period was Spain, which lost its principal remaining colonies—Cuba, Puerto Rico, and the Philippines—to the United States in the Spanish-American War of 1898. This war also marked the rising international power of the United States, which increasingly saw itself in competition with Europeans in the race for empire. U.S. senator Albert Beveridge, a promoter of the outright annexation of the Philippines, made a daring call for America to establish its own overseas empire: "We will not renounce our part

Colonial Cities A view of the Algiers railway station in 1894 shows the influence of French colonization. Besides the newly developed infrastructure, European-style buildings rise to the left, reminiscent of the apartment buildings of Paris.

in the mission of our race, trustee, under God, of the civilization of the world." The British poet Rudyard Kipling agreed, calling on the United States to "take up the white man's burden."

EUROPE AND EAST ASIA

As the European empires expanded across the globe, they came into conflict with the two most prominent East Asian nations, Japan and China, but with different results. Japan was making a concerted effort to Westernize in the Meiji Restoration that began in 1868. It modeled large parts of its government and law on that of the German Empire, and its military on the French army. By the end of the nineteenth century, it had increased its power sufficiently to deliver a decisive defeat to China in the Sino-Japanese War of 1894–1895 and then to Russia in the Russo-Japanese War of 1904–1905. Russia's humiliation contributed to the Revolution of 1905 and persuaded Russia to bring Britain into its alliance with France, for protection against the rising power of Germany.

The Chinese story was different. In the last decades of the nineteenth century, the Western powers continued to press China to open its markets to their goods and to allow them to establish trading ports, building on the

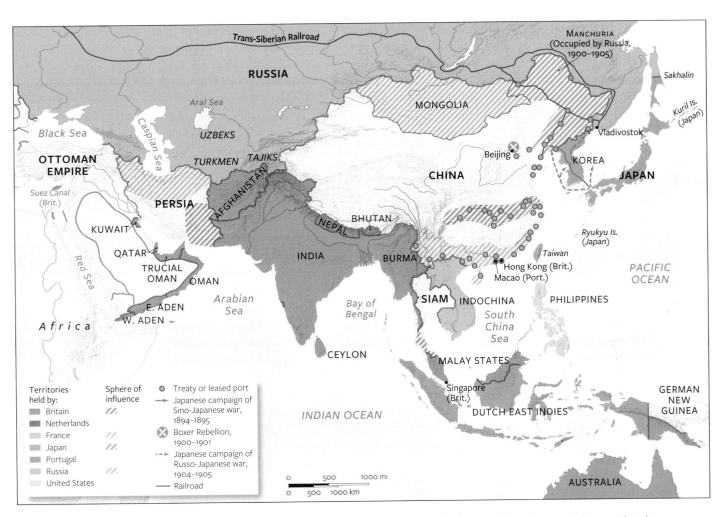

Imperialism in Asia, 1880–1910 By the end of the nineteenth century, Asia had become a key site for the negotiation of geopolitical power. Though Britain remained dominant, controlling South Asia, Malaysia, Australia, and key territories in the Persian Gulf (including the Suez Canal), France was becoming increasingly powerful in Southeast Asia, controlling key ports on the South China Sea. The Trans-Siberian Railroad enabled Russia to extend its reach eastward, but the Russian Empire reached its limit with defeat by the Japanese Empire in the Russo-Japanese War. China was surrounded on all sides by other empires, which exerted their power over it through punishing trade deals and the defeat of the Boxer Rebellion.

precedents established in the mid-century Opium Wars and the "unequal treaties" that the Chinese acquiesced in. Many Chinese felt outraged and humiliated by these events and by the proselytizing activities of Christian missionaries in China. In 1900, a secret Chinese nationalist society known as the Boxers carried out attacks on European missionaries, merchants, and soldiers, killing several hundred. In response, a combined force of British, French, German, Russian, Japanese, and American troops landed in China, put down the Boxer Rebellion, and forced the Chinese government to pay crushing reparations. The Europeans thereby preserved their commercial advantages in China, but at the cost of further destabilizing China's teetering Qing Empire and helping to bring about the country's first modern revolution, in 1911.

IMPERIALISM, RACE, AND CLASS

As they built their empires, Europeans were deeply influenced by what many at the time thought of as the "science" of race. Since mid-century, biologists and anthropologists had attempted to apply Charles Darwin's theory of evolution to human racial differences, and in the decades around 1900 these efforts multiplied. Scientists posited differences in brain types and intelligence not only between Europeans and non-Europeans, but also among Europeans themselves—usually to the advantage of northern (Teutonic or Aryan) Europeans, and to the disadvantage of Mediterraneans, especially Jews.

In Britain, Darwin's cousin Francis Galton (1822–1911) coined the term **eugenics** to describe a supposedly scientific program of improving the human race through selective breeding. Eugenicists especially worried about the falling European birthrates and the supposed degeneration of European physical stock as a result of the unhealthy conditions of industrial society. These concerns helped spur new attention to children's health and physical training, and especially to motherhood, which imperialists sometimes cast as a sacred racial duty. A prominent British gynecologist in 1903 promoted health education for new mothers in these terms: "By instruction leading to the improvement of the individual we shall aid in preserving women for their supreme purpose, the procreation and preservation of the race, and at the same time promote that race to a better standard, mentally and physically." In the colonies, such racial thinking helped to justify the brutal treatment of indigenous peoples. The quote also expresses a prevailing view of women's roles at the time.

Class distinctions also came into play for Europeans overseas. In settings from formal receptions to courts of law, British officials in particular often accorded to native royalty a status well above that of common British soldiers. The wife of the British governor of Fiji described high-ranking Fijians as "an undoubted aristocracy." She added, in a letter home, that "their manners are so perfectly easy and well bred.... Nurse can't understand it at all, she looks down on them as an inferior race. I don't like to tell her that these ladies are my equals, which she is not!" In these circumstances, one might say, the class prejudices of the British trumped their racial prejudices.

THE EFFECTS OF IMPERIALISM ON EUROPE

Overall, the imperialism of this period had powerful effects on the European countries themselves as well as on their colonial territories. Economically, it opened up new sources of raw materials for European industry and new markets for manufactured goods, including textiles and metals. By 1900, one-third of all Britain's exports were to its empire. Even by 1914, however, the equivalent figure for Germany, which had yet to develop the full economic potential of its new empire, was just 1 percent. Important new career paths also opened up. In 1900, for instance, fully one-quarter of the graduates of Oxford University's elite Balliol College had left Britain for positions somewhere in the empire, often as administrators of vast territories. Imperial trade and military service brought non-Europeans to Europe by the thousands, thronging the streets of port cities and capitals, while also moving men and women between different parts of the empire. The future Indian independence leader Mohandas Gandhi studied law in London from 1888 to 1891, and in 1893 moved to the Natal colony in South Africa. He participated as a stretcher-bearer at the battle of Spion Kop during the Boer War, where his future political adversary, Winston Churchill, was present as a journalist.

Interactions with non-Europeans both challenged and supported European racial ideas and left a deep impression on European popular culture. In the popular Sherlock Holmes stories written by Arthur Conan Doyle (1859–1930), most of the famous detective's adventures involve some form of significant contact between Britain and its empire. The first novel, *A Study in Scarlet*, begins with the return of the narrator, Dr. Watson, from military service in central Asia, and Holmes's first words to him are: "You have been in Afghanistan, I perceive." The imperialist poet of empire, Rudyard Kipling (1865–1936), born in Bombay, India, was the most popular British writer of the period.

In this heyday of global integration and European imperialism, with its ceaseless movement of peoples among continents, non-Europeans began to exert a greater influence on European scholarship and science than at any time since the Middle Ages. The physician Frederick Akbar Mahomed (1849–1884), born in Brighton, England but descended on his father's side from Bengalis, did pioneering work on the effects of hypertension. The historian Romesh Chunder Dutt (1848–1909) published fundamental works on Indian economic history—showing, among other things, how British colonialism had inhibited Indian economic development.

MODERNISM RISING

The newly intense engagement with overseas peoples also contributed to the astonishing developments in European art, literature, and thought that now go by the name of **modernism**, which represented a conscious break with earlier styles of art. To take one of the most prominent examples, in the 1880s the French painter Paul Gauguin (1848–1903), dazzled by the example of the impressionists such as Monet and Renoir, increasingly moved away from representational art toward the expressive use of brilliant color and coarse brushwork. In 1891, seeking inspiration, he traveled to the French colony of Tahiti in the South Pacific, where he was overcome by the vibrant native art. Its strong colors, shapes, and departures from realistic representation strongly influenced his development as a painter.

During the next two decades, one of the greatest

modernist artists, the Spaniard **Pablo Picasso** (1881–1973), discovered African sculpture, with its emphasis on simple shapes, dramatic angles and planes, and expressive treatment of the human form. It influenced many of his works, including his 1907 masterpiece *The Young Ladies of Avignon*. In 1913, the Russian composer Igor Stravinsky (1882–1971) shocked Parisian audiences with the jarring, unfamiliar harmonies and jagged rhythms of the music he wrote to accompany a ballet called *The Rite of Spring*. Although the ballet depicted pre-Christian Russia, the music, especially in its rhythms, bore the strong influence of non-European cultures, including West African ones.

THE ROOTS OF ARTISTIC MODERNISM

Modernism had many other, complex roots. Modernist artists, writers, and composers sought to capture something of the fractured, frantic, whirling existence they associated with urban life in the fin de siècle. They sought to give artistic expression to what was often perceived as the destruction of traditional certitudes by heady advances in science. With photography now enabling amateurs to make precise images of physical reality, artists increasingly turned toward exploring the pure play of color, light, and shape, without representing any recognizable object. And so-called avant-garde artists and writers deliberately sought to assert the value of their work by differentiating it from the unchallenging, sentimental compositions, artworks, and literature that were being churned out in ever greater numbers to satisfy the demands of burgeoning middle-class audiences. The French phrase *épater la bourgeoisie* ("shock the bourgeoisie") became the avant-garde's watchword, and the easiest way to do so was through art that was seen as morally questionable or simply alien and bizarre. Avant-garde artists challenged the standards of rationalism that they associated with middle-class culture and sought to unlock hidden depths of the human psyche.

LITERATURE Before World War I, the most important modernist innovations in literature took place in poetry. There, especially in France, a rapid evolution occurred from the hauntingly strange verse of Baudelaire (see Chapter 19) toward more difficult symbolist experiments with pure sound, with the vivid depiction of momentary, discontinuous sensations, and invocations of a mysterious realm of human transcendence that had distinct pagan accents. Symbols, the advocates of this school argued, represented the way to bridge the gap between the world of nature and the world of spiritual exploration. Symbolist poets such

The Young Ladies of Avignon Picasso's 1907 masterpiece bears the influence of African sculpture and is characteristic of the angular, abstract cubist style he pioneered.

as Stéphane Mallarmé (1842–1898) were criticized for the impenetrability of their work, but nonetheless emerged as dominant poetic voices. Outside of France, more popular poets such as the American-born Ezra Pound (1885–1972), the German Rainer Maria Rilke (1875–1926), and the Irish William Butler Yeats (1865–1939) were developing a distinctive modernist style that would flourish after 1914. Fiction-writing did not experience such dramatic changes, but the great novelists of the fin de siècle, such as Thomas Hardy (1840–1928) in England and Émile Zola (1840–1902) in France, often generated controversy with unsparing depictions of the underside of bourgeois society, including especially its sexual mores.

MUSIC Music saw, in some ways, the most radical break with earlier standards. Some composers, while seeking to create dreamscapes in sound, nonetheless remained tied to a melodic late-romantic tradition. But the French composers Erik Satie (1866–1925) and Claude Debussy (1862–1918) moved further away from traditional tonalities, harmonies, and rhythms with wildly playful, if sometimes remarkably gentle, pieces that involved unfamiliar chords, scales, and forms of modulation. Stravinsky's modernist experiments in *The Rite of Spring* caused the greatest public controversy; but even before they did, the Austrian composer Arnold Schoenberg (1874–1951) attracted criticism for experimental atonal music that avoided ordinary melodies and key signatures altogether.

Modernists like Schoenberg had an enormous influence on twentieth-century music, but their difficult pieces never attracted anything like the audiences for the music of Wagner, Verdi, and other late romantic composers. As a result, the modernist moment in music, more than in any other art form, opened up a stark divide between a relatively small, heavily academic realm of "serious" composition and a much larger sector of performance and instruction that remained tied mostly to the classical canon of eighteenth- and nineteenth-century composers.

PAINTING By contrast, modernism in painting—while also subject to fierce criticism—was wildly popular. Its most important figures, Pablo Picasso first and foremost, became wealthy, universally recognized celebrities.

The evolution of painting in the fin de siècle began with the innovations of the impressionists but soon moved beyond them. Painters of the 1880s and 1890s such as Gauguin, the Dutch Vincent Van Gogh (1853–1890), and Paul Cézanne (1839–1906) left far behind the goal of producing accurate reproductions and experimented with color combinations unseen in nature. "Instead of trying to render what I see before me," wrote Van Gogh, who cut off part of his own ear in a psychotic rage, "I use color in a completely arbitrary way to express myself powerfully." Van Gogh produced some of the most glorious and popular works of the period. These artists in turn inspired a younger group of painters, whom critics labeled the *fauves* ("wild beasts") for their spirited use of bright colors and simple, geometrical shapes (one opponent compared them to small children who had uncovered a paint box).

Most of these artists, whether French or not, soon gravitated to Paris, still the undisputed capital of Western art. Its principal competition as a center of modernist painting was Vienna, where the clash of cultures and politics from across the Austro-Hungarian Empire, along with the liberal cultural tradition associated with the city's large Jewish minority, created a whirling, intensely attractive milieu for artistic experimentation. There Gustav Klimt (1862–1918) experimented with deliberately shocking works that melded classically erotic imagery with abstract shapes and color combinations, as in his 1905 masterpiece *The Kiss*.

Soon painters began daring to move away from representational art altogether. Picasso, who first visited Paris in 1900, declared: "I paint objects as I think them, not as I see them." Works such as *The Young Ladies of Avignon* deliberately violated the traditional rules of perspective and plane, reduced its distorted figures to the essentials

The Kiss Klimt's groundbreaking painting (1905) depicts a man leaning down to kiss a woman in a field; the clothing of the two figures and the background are painted in abstract designs of shimmering gold.

of shape, and placed them at unconventional angles to one another. Critics blasted Picasso for painting as a child might, and Picasso's defenders retorted that he was trying precisely to recapture a child's view of the world and to move beyond the staid conventions of realism. But soon Picasso and his colleagues went even further, painting so-called cubist works that seemed to break up images and reassemble them into arbitrary, geometric patterns, as if seen through a series of prisms or kaleidoscopes. Russian artists even moved toward entirely abstract works. One of them, Cazimir Malevich (1879–1935), would take the process to its logical conclusion in 1915 with the painting *Black Square*, which was exactly that.

PHILOSOPHY, SOCIAL SCIENCE, AND PSYCHIATRY

The exploration of the unconscious, irrational, and "primitive" by modernist artists, writers, and composers had its counterpart in European thought between 1880 and 1910. The German philosopher **Friedrich Nietzsche** (1844–1900), himself chronically plagued by mental and physical illness, delivered one of the most powerful challenges to European rationalism. Nietzsche defined the human by reference not to reason or morality, but to a mysterious,

FIN DE SIÈCLE VIENNA

> *... [T]HE NATURE OF OUR EPOCH IS MULTIPLICITY AND INDETERMINACY.*
>
> HUGO VON HOFMANNSTHAL, *THE POET AND THIS AGE, 1905*

Legend:
- Road
- City rail line
- Tram line
- Railroad
- Government or significant building
- Industrial or military building
- Plaza
- Middle and upper class district
- Working class district
- Park or open area
- Café

**Map labels:**
General hospital
Main building of University of Vienna
Neustiftgasse 40
Neustiftgasse 40
Secession building
College of Technology
Karlsplatz
Music Society Hall
Schwarzenberg Palace
Belvedere Palace
Ringstrasse
Danube R.
Danube Canal

BUILDINGS
1. City Hall
2. Parliament
3. Palace of Justice
4. Natural history museum
5. Art museum
6. State Opera House
7. Hofburg Palace
8. Burg theater
9. Exchange
10. Office of Sigmund Freud

When liberal, constitutional rule came to Vienna, its leaders built a ring road lined with monumental public buildings in the center of the city. The University building shown here was Renaissance in style to proclaim its alignment with rational, secular culture.

Otto Wagner's apartment building (Neustiftgasse 40, built in 1910) shows the unornamented, functional uniformity characteristic of modernist design. Stores occupy the ground floor, with residences in the floors above.

POLITICS AND CULTURE

1859
Development of the Ringstrasse begins

1860s–1880s
Austria ruled by a liberal, constitutionalist regime

1880s–1900s
Liberal rule defeated by nationalist and socialist mass movements

1893
Otto Wagner's modernist plans win competition for new urban development

> *THE ONLY POSSIBLE POINT OF DEPARTURE FOR OUR ARTISTIC CREATION IS MODERN LIFE.*
>
> OTTO WAGNER, *MODERN ARCHITECTURE, 1895*

QUESTIONS FOR ANALYSIS

1. In what ways is the modernist style of Otto Wagner's apartment building a rejection of the Renaissance style embodied in the University building?

2. How was the apartment building a fitting reflection of modern life?

3. What connections can you draw between political and cultural change in Vienna at this time?

creative, irrational life force. As his work developed, he tried to show how rationalist philosophy and Christian morality had shackled that life force. He challenged Europeans, to cite the title of one of his best-known works, to think "beyond good and evil." In his most lyrical book, *Thus Spoke Zarathustra* (1883–1885), he prophesied a "superman" who could destroy the "slave morality" of the "herd" and release the life force. Nietzsche did not describe this superman in racial terms, but following his death many interpreters and opportunistic German politicians did so.

DURKHEIM AND WEBER Nietzsche's celebration of the irrational was not, however, typical of European thought in this period. Far more common was a recognition of the power of the irrational by thinkers who nonetheless sought to harness reason to analyze large-scale social problems and thereby develop more effective social policies. Thinkers such as France's Émile Durkheim (1858–1917) explored how traditional forms of social cohesion, especially religious ones, had broken down in modern industrial society, producing the isolated individual, alienation, and despair. Durkheim proposed powerful models for how society shaped individual consciousness and religious thought. Max Weber (1864–1920) traced the origins of modern capitalist society to Reformation Calvinism and its emphasis on living a productive, active, worldly life. Weber also argued that the growth of rationality in modern society led to the creation of large, efficient, but impersonal and soulless bureaucracies in business and government. The work of Durkheim and Weber, among others, made the period 1880–1910 the golden age of European social theory and, building on the work of older thinkers such as Montesquieu, Adam Smith, and Karl Marx, led to the rise of the discipline of sociology.

Sigmund Freud This 1921 photo shows the psychoanalyst posing with his trademark cigar.

SIGMUND FREUD Just as social scientists sought to analyze the problems of society, so the Austrian doctor **Sigmund Freud** (1856–1939) aspired to develop rational, scientific methods for understanding and treating mental disorders. After having studied in France with the great neurologist Jean Charcot (1825–1893), Freud adopted Charcot's technique of using hypnosis and also began exploring the way that dreams expressed unconscious desires. His 1899 book *The Interpretation of Dreams* marked a milestone in modern psychological understanding.

Then, six years later, Freud shocked the medical community with a book of essays arguing that even very young children were not innocent of sexuality and that childhood experience could have a deep influence on adult sexual desire. These ideas, and practical work with women suffering from hysteria, led Freud to develop methods of treatment based on sustained conversation with an analyst who could uncover the formative experiences at the root of a person's condition.

Freud's methods were anything but foolproof. In one famous case, of a young patient named Ida Bauer (whom he referred to as Dora), he attributed her suicidal, depressive tendencies to her difficulty in dealing with her sexuality, rather than to the abuse she suffered when her father tried to make her sexually available to the husband of his own mistress. Yet Freud's theories, and the key they seemed to offer to understanding human behavior—including even the most apparently irrational, primitive drives— had a powerful impact on European culture. Observers immediately detected deep connections between Freud's work and the modernist movement in literature and the arts. Freud himself saw his work as liberating and rational. However, his evocation of powerful, deep, perhaps uncontrollable urges that manifested themselves even in childhood, and that included what he referred to as a death drive, struck many readers as deeply frightening and expressive of a world that seemed to be spinning about madly, without a fixed frame of reference.

THE PHYSICAL SCIENCES

Those disturbed by Freud's theories might once have looked to the natural sciences for such a fixed frame of reference. Yet in the period 1880–1910 even developments in natural science seemed to be conspiring to unmoor Europeans from their certainties.

THE CURIES In Paris, in 1896, the Polish-born scientist Marie Curie (1867–1934), along with her French husband, Pierre Curie (1859–1906), isolated the element of radium and thereby discovered the phenomenon of radioactivity. Scientists built on this work to describe the structure of the atom and to prove what ancient alchemists had asserted and modern science had strongly denied—namely, that one element could transmute into another. The German scientist Max Planck (1858–1947) challenged earlier understanding of light and other forms of radiant energy, showing that it was not emitted as a single constant wave but in discrete tiny packages, or quanta.

BOCCIONI'S *THE CITY RISES*

Umberto Boccioni (1882–1916) was an Italian painter who believed that artistic form had to accord to the conditions of modern life. His career was short—he was killed during World War I—but his canvases and sculptures expressed the increasingly abstract modernist aesthetic that transformed European art and culture in the early twentieth century.

In his large painting *The City Rises* (1910), originally titled *Work*, Boccioni celebrates the dizzy activity of the construction of a new electric plant, visible in the background, in Milan. The moving lines, splashes of color, and blurring of figures combine to convey the chaotic dynamism of a city street, where workers struggle to control a horse. Boccioni emphasizes the collective nature of work, with the men and horses heaving together in an energetic mass. Just as life in a modern city never stood still, neither, the painter suggests, could an art that hoped to capture that life.

QUESTIONS FOR ANALYSIS

1. In what ways is this painting representative of modernism?
2. What attitudes toward work and the modern city does Boccioni convey?
3. How does this painting suggest the ways in which the modern city transformed people's experience of the world in the late nineteenth and early twentieth centuries?

ALBERT EINSTEIN   Most unsettling, however, was the work of an obscure German physicist working as a patent clerk in Switzerland: **Albert Einstein** (1879–1955). Like other physicists of the period, Einstein had observed with dissatisfaction the results of a series of experiments involving light and electromagnetic radiation. But whereas other physicists tried to find where the experiments had gone wrong, Einstein accepted the experiments as valid and asked where the underlying theories had gone wrong. In 1905, he published a revolutionary paper with the modest title "On the Electrodynamics of Bodies in Motion." It postulated that time itself could flow at different rates for different bodies, depending on their relative motion; that the speed of light is always constant for all observers, regardless of their motion; and that there exists no absolute state of rest in the universe.

And then, after linking space and time in this manner, in another paper the same year Einstein also linked mass and energy, suggesting that as a body's relative speed increases, so does its mass. Einstein concisely expressed this connection in the formula $e = mc^2$ (energy equals mass times the speed of light squared). It asserted the essential equivalency of mass and energy, and also the potential for transforming small quantities of the former into massive quantities of the latter, thereby opening the door, theoretically, to nuclear fission and fusion. Einstein's theory of relativity arguably had a greater impact than the work of any scientist since Isaac Newton in the seventeenth century.

CONCLUSION

Of all the creative works of this period, one of the most eerie is a painting: the German artist Ludwig Meidner's 1913 work *Apocalyptic Landscape*. It belongs to the modernist school generally referred to as German expressionism, which favored violent, clashing colors and tortured images, and seemed to be reaching into the darkest corners of the human psyche. *Apocalyptic Landscape* is not the most distinguished work of the school, but it uncannily seems to predict the horrific destruction that would break out just a year after its composition, with the beginning of World War I.

To many Europeans, Meidner's premonitions must have seemed absurd. As we have seen in this chapter, in

Apocalyptic Landscape   The thickly applied paint and jagged lines of Meidner's 1913 painting indicate a new departure for abstract art in the early twentieth century—and seem to suggest the approaching chaos of World War I.

1913 Europeans collectively enjoyed a greater degree of wealth, material comfort, health, leisure, and social security than ever before in history, and they dominated the globe as never before. Global commerce seemed to be binding humanity closer together than ever before, and the development of science and industry seemed to many to confirm the power of reason to better the human condition, even if voices had arisen protesting the ways industry had produced disruption and exploitation.

Yet at the same time, despite this "progress" (to use a word then much in vogue), national rivalries remained as strong as ever and were fueled more than ever before by poisonous ideologies of racial superiority. Scientific and industrial progress expressed itself not only in material comfort but also in massive new levels of destructive armaments. The developments in art, philosophy, and social science that we have just discussed highlighted the frightening power of the irrational. And with Einstein's work on relativity, science itself seemed to be breaking apart the comfortingly stable, predictable, Newtonian vision of the universe that had prevailed since the scientific revolution. From this perspective, it seemed all too likely that the vast energies Europeans were now capable of harnessing could be turned to purposes of destruction. In 1914, with stunning speed, Meidner's premonitions would come terrifyingly to life.

KEY TERMS

new imperialism (p. 672)

Second Industrial Revolution (p. 673)

globalization (p. 676)

syndicalism (p. 680)

Dreyfus Affair (p. 682)

pogroms (p. 682)

Mensheviks (p. 683)

Bolsheviks (p. 683)

Duma (p. 683)

home rule (p. 684)

Emmeline Pankhurst (p. 686)

Triple Alliance (p. 687)

Triple Entente (p. 687)

scramble for Africa (p. 689)

protectorate (p. 691)

Berlin Conference of 1884–1885 (p. 691)

Boers (p. 691)

eugenics (p. 695)

modernism (p. 696)

Pablo Picasso (p. 697)

Friedrich Nietzsche (p. 698)

Sigmund Freud (p. 700)

Albert Einstein (p. 702)

REVIEW QUESTIONS

1. How did the Second Industrial Revolution change European economies?

2. Why did emigration increase during this period?

3. During the period 1880–1910, how did technological advances widen the differences between rural and urban life?

4. What tensions between liberal and conservative movements developed in the late nineteenth century?

5. What factors led to the Russian Revolution of 1905, and what were the revolution's effects?

6. What feminist movements developed during the fin de siècle?

7. By the 1880s, what gave Britain the greatest global influence of any power?

8. What accounts for the tremendous expansion of European control of Africa between 1880 and 1914?

9. What effects did the new imperialism have on Europe?

10. What were the principal characteristics of modernist culture?

CORE OBJECTIVES

After reading this chapter, you should have a solid understanding of the following core objectives. To strengthen your grasp of the core objectives, use the resources on the Student Site for The West.

- Analyze the rapid technological and economic changes in European societies around the turn of the twentieth century.
- Describe the shifts in social roles, demographics, and emigration during the period.

- Trace the challenges to the liberal worldview in the major European countries.
- Identify the characteristics of the new imperialism in Africa and Asia.
- Assess the intellectual and artistic innovations of the period.

 GO TO **inQuizitive** TO SEE WHAT YOU'VE LEARNED—AND LEARN WHAT YOU'VE MISSED—WITH PERSONALIZED FEEDBACK ALONG THE WAY.

CHRONOLOGY

June 28, 1914
Archduke Franz
Ferdinand assassinated

1915–1917
Armenian
genocide

August 1914
Battle of
Tannenberg

1915
Gallipoli
Campaign

Feb.–Dec. 1916
Battle of Verdun

March 1917
Tsar Nikolai II
abdicates

October 1917
Bolshevik (October)
Revolution

March–July 1918
German Spring
Offensive

March 3, 1918
Treaty of
Brest-Litovsk

November 11, 1918
Armistice officially
ends war

September 1914
Battle of the Marne

July 28, 1914
World War I
begins

May 7, 1915
Sinking of the
Lusitania

April 24, 1916
Easter Rising
in Dublin

July–Nov. 1916
Battle of the Somme

April 1917
United States
enters the war

January 1918
Wilson outlines
Fourteen Points

1918–1921
Russian Civil War

Oct.–Nov. 1918
Revolution breaks
out in Germany

21

Things Blow Up

WORLD WAR I AND THE RUSSIAN REVOLUTION

1910–1922

March 1921
Kronstadt rebellion

1919
Soviet Union forms the Comintern

1919
Versailles Peace Conference

K atikati, New Zealand, is a small agricultural town with a lively arts community and tourist business on the country's northern island. Settled by migrants from northern Ireland in 1875 on land confiscated from the native Maori, it is a quiet, peaceful, ordinary place. And with no less than 11,500 miles separating it from Belgium and northern France, it seems as remote as any spot on earth from the blood-soaked battlefields of 1914–18.

Yet at the center of Katikati stands a War Memorial Hall. A nearby bay is named for the Australian and New Zealand Army Corps (ANZAC) and its disastrous landing on Turkey's Gallipoli Peninsula in 1915. In a nature park a quarter-mile out of town, beneath a kauri tree, lies a plaque commemorating the armistice of 1918. And at the park's entrance stand memorial gates bearing the names of ten men who left Katikati between 1915 and 1918 and never returned home. Henry Pritt fell at Gallipoli in August 1915. Albert Squinobal, a twenty-six-year-old farmer, died at the Somme fifteen months later and was buried "in a grave known only to God." Otto Diggelmann, age twenty-two, also a farmer and of German ancestry, was shot in the head in October 1918 and died in England just two weeks before the war's end. There are seven more, including two grandsons of the town's founder. Fifty other men from Katikati went off to the war and survived, but nineteen of

---

No-Man's-Land The British war artist Paul Nash uses modernist forms and stark color to depict the unprecedented destruction of World War I in his 1919 painting *The Menin Road*. Soldiers trek across a barren battlefield littered with debris and shattered trees. Smoke rises from artillery fire in the background.

them were wounded, four more than once. And all this from a town that in 1915 had just 400 inhabitants. A war fought on the opposite side of the globe remains, by far, the most traumatic event in Katikati's history, and vividly illustrates why it deserves to be called the First World War. In its aftermath, many simply called it the Great War.

Katikati's experience was a tragically typical one. In New Zealand, fully 42 percent of men between the ages of nineteen and forty-five went to fight in Europe, and over half of these—58 percent—were killed or wounded. Katikati's war memorial is just one of 500 in the country. And although New Zealand, as a loyal dominion of the British Empire, sent an exceptionally large proportion of its young men to the European slaughterhouse, similar monuments appear throughout the Western world: in remote cattle towns on the Canadian plains; in Oxford colleges; in industrial city centers in Germany; in the villages of Serbia. The bodies of the fallen lie in cemeteries throughout Europe, under endless rows of white crosses or simple headstones, or crammed namelessly into ossuaries. The vaults of the ossuary of Douaumont, near the battlefields of Verdun in eastern France, contain the bones of 130,000 unidentified French and German soldiers.

If Europe between 1880 and 1910 had seemed to reach its apogee, dominating the globe and attaining unprecedented levels of wealth and comfort, one can say that between 1914 and 1918 it fell bloodily to earth. Historians generally dislike making large-scale generalizations about collective psychology, but they agree that what took place on the Continent in these years inflicted a brutal, collective trauma on populations throughout the world, and especially in Europe. Most immediately, the war killed and maimed a higher proportion of that population than any other European catastrophe since the Thirty Years' War of the seventeenth century, and it did so more quickly than anything since the Black Death three hundred years before that. It left the survivors shocked, dispirited, and cynical—with a sense of living in what the future British leader Winston Churchill called "a crippled, broken world." It destroyed two empires, the Ottoman and the Habsburg, and toppled the regimes of two others, in Russia and Germany. It was a decisive factor behind the most significant—and, ultimately, the most violent—of modern European revolutions, in Russia. It helped give birth to the rise of fascist regimes, most immediately in Italy and later in Germany and elsewhere. Although defined by many of its participants as "the war to end all wars," it created the conditions under which the world would go to war again, even more horrifically, just two decades later.

The First World War was, quite simply, one of the greatest disasters in world history. And while Europeans on all sides justified their participation in grandiose terms, calling it a war for peace and for civilization, even at the time those justifications rang hollow. Today very few people think the war was worth the cost.

ORIGINS

The war's horrors have long overshadowed and distorted the search for its origins. How, it is asked agonizingly, could rational, responsible statesmen possibly have led their peoples into such a cataclysm? The question has obsessed generations of historians, who have pored over every scrap of paper pertaining to pre-war planning and every link in the chain of decisions that led to the outbreak of hostilities. But the question presumes that the statesmen had at least a premonition of the horrors to come. Not all of them did.

WAR PLANS

Upon the outbreak of the war in August 1914, the British foreign secretary, Sir Edward Grey (1862–1933), uttered a lament that has become famous: "The lamps are going out all over Europe. We shall not see them lit again in our time." Yet Grey was in a minority. Far more states-men had the attitude of Germany's Kaiser Wilhelm II, who thought the conflict would take the form of a quick, invigorating adventure and who told troops departing for the front that they would be home again before the leaves fell. The German General Staff based its war strategy on the so-called **Schlieffen Plan**, finalized by Count Alfred von Schlieffen (1833–1913) in 1905, which laid out steps to achieve victory over France in just forty-two days, with a longer campaign against Russia to follow. All of the major countries involved based their military planning on the assumption that a war would move at industrial speed and be decided by a handful of monumental offensives. The recent history of the West seemed to support that assumption: with the exception of the American Civil War (1861–1865), it offered several compelling examples of quick and decisive wars, such as Prussia's victories over Austria in 1866 and France in 1870, or Japan's over Russia in 1904–5.

And while the outbreak of war in 1914 dismayed many, few found it mysterious. Most observers took it for granted that ambitious, aggressive nations will naturally come to blows. Nonetheless, the outbreak of war was not inevitable. If most statesmen anticipated a quick and deci-sive conflict, they knew they were taking large risks. The years, months, and days before the fighting were marked by incessant calculation and recalculation of these risks, and the final decisions to move ahead rested in part on the classic gambler's mixture of faith and hope that the odds had turned in the right direction. Other factors of course mattered too, including national pride, sheer chance, pure blundering, the structures of European diplomacy, and the codes of honor whose obligations ensnared elites across the Continent.

GERMAN AMBITIONS

The story starts with Germany. Its unification and emer-gence as a major power were the most important Euro-pean geopolitical developments of the late nineteenth and early twentieth centuries. Germany's rapidly increasing economic and military strength, and its leaders' obvious ambitions, upset the European balance of power that had largely prevailed since the Congress of Vienna in 1815. Fearing that Germany, with its large population and industrial capacity, could come to dominate the Conti-nent, Britain and France put aside their age-old rivalry for good. As we have seen, the two countries had nearly gone to war over competing ambitions in Sudan as late as 1898; now they became steadfast allies. The same dynamic also

eventually drove both these democracies into the arms of autocratic Russia, which the British had long seen as their principal rival on the international stage. By 1907, Europe had split into two antagonistic blocs: the Triple Alliance of Germany, Austria-Hungary, and Italy; and the Franco-British-Russian Triple Entente.

For the latter, a fear that Germany would continue to rise generated a willingness to go to war sooner rather than later. But the Germans themselves were anything but confident about their future, and continually worried that the odds against *them* were increasing. Thus came about the Moroccan Crises of 1905 and 1911, in which the Ger-mans challenged France's right to establish a protectorate over the North African state in the hope of checking any further expansion of French power on the African conti-nent. The Germans also hoped that casting France as an aggressor might isolate it diplomatically and put pressure on the Franco-British partnership. But in both episodes, the British stood by their allies and international media-tion averted a conflict. By now, a thick web of diplomatic connections existed between the major powers, as well as close family relationships between the major royal houses (Germany's emperor Wilhelm II and Tsarina Alexandra of Russia were both grandchildren of Britain's Queen Vic-toria). Still, at both of these moments, war seemed more likely than it did to most observers in the spring of 1914.

NATIONALISM AND EMPIRE IN SOUTHEASTERN EUROPE

A second set of long-term causes of the war involved nationalism and the threat it posed to two empires that the war ultimately smashed to pieces: Austria-Hungary and Ottoman Turkey. Neither empire was as fragile as is sometimes thought, especially before 1900. The Aus-trian Habsburgs had developed a workable relationship with the empire's largest national minority, the Hun-garians, and affection for the dynasty went beyond the German-speaking minority. As for the Ottomans, their long practice of providing a degree of autonomy and pro-tection for different ethnic and religious communities, combined with opportunities for groups such as Albanians and Greeks in the Ottoman military, administration, and commerce, continued to keep the empire viable long after its military weakness had made it known as the Sick Man of Europe. But by 1908, tensions in both empires reached dangerous levels. And in both cases, the center of tension was the Balkan Peninsula.

IMPERIAL COMPETITION IN THE BALKANS The Balkan Peninsula had a long tradition of violence stemming partly from its volatile mix of religious and ethnic groups and partly from its strategic position in relation to the Austro-Hungarian, Ottoman, and Russian empires. As we have seen, Ottoman control over the Balkans had begun to crumble in the 1820s with the war for Greek independence. By 1900, Greece, Romania, Serbia, Montenegro, and Bulgaria were all independent, leaving Turkey with a narrow strip of territory cutting through the peninsula's heart to predominantly Muslim Albania on the Adriatic coast.

The triangular territory of Bosnia-Herzegovina, to the west of Serbia—divided then as now between Muslim Bosnians and Christian Orthodox Serbs, with a smaller admixture of Catholic Croats—had come under Austro-Hungarian occupation in 1878, although it remained theoretically still under Ottoman sovereignty. Its acquisition proved problematic for the Habsburgs, for it spurred the resentment of Serbian nationalists who hoped to join all the "Yugoslav" (southern Slav) territories into a single Serbian-led nation. The revolutionary Serb group the Black Hand resisted Austro-Hungarian rule in the name of this cause and wielded enormous influence in Serbia itself. In 1903, its members staged a coup there, assassinating the king and queen. Russia, meanwhile, lent support to Serbia in the name of pan-Slavism (the brotherhood of Slav peoples) and the hope that any new Yugoslav state would become its ally. In 1908, the Habsburgs decided formally to annex Bosnia-Herzegovina so as to integrate its population as swiftly as possible into the empire.

TURMOIL IN TURKEY In the Ottoman Empire, tensions came in large part from the capital, Constantinople. In the 1870s, a new sultan, Abdulhamid II (r. 1872–1909), had come to the throne and raised hopes in Europe that his regime would move toward Western democratic practices. A new constitution established parliamentary rule and equality before the law. But Abdulhamid reneged on his promises and, in a break with Ottoman precedent, initiated brutal persecution of non-Muslims, especially Armenian Christians living in what is now Armenia and eastern Turkey. In response, forward-looking opponents of the regime founded a Committee of Union and Progress in Paris. And in 1908 its members, known as the **Young Turks**, staged a coup, forcing the reintroduction of Abdulhamid's constitution but causing further disruption. Exploiting the situation, Italy undertook its successful conquest of Ottoman-ruled Libya in 1911. Soon afterward

The Balkans, 1913 By 1913, a number of Balkan states had established their independence, and in the Balkan wars of 1912–13 they almost entirely ejected the Ottoman Empire from the peninsula. But continued Ottoman and Austro-Hungarian interest in the Balkans—including the Austro-Hungarian annexation of Bosnia-Herzegovina—contributed to the volatile political situation that led to World War I.

Serbia, Bulgaria, Montenegro, and Greece formed a Balkan League and defeated Turkey in the short First Balkan War of 1912. After dividing up nearly all the rest of the Ottomans' European territory, however, the victors fell out, leading to a Second Balkan War (1913) in which Serbia and Greece took territory from Bulgaria, and Albania saw its independence (proclaimed the year before) confirmed.

ARMS RACES AND MILITARY MOBILIZATION

The two Moroccan crises, the Bosnian crisis, and the two Balkan wars, all driven by nationalist rivalries and occurring within just eight years, amplified anxieties about a general European war. These anxieties also drove a massive, unprecedented arms race. In just the five years from 1908 to 1913, the six countries that made up the Triple Alliance and Triple Entente collectively increased their military spending by 50 percent. Factories turned out guns and ammunition, armies stockpiled supplies, and shipyards rushed to build Dreadnoughts—a new class of battleship almost as long as two football fields, bristling with heavy artillery and protected by metal armor up to eleven inches thick. A single vessel cost the British the then-enormous sum of over 1.5 million pounds. But at this moment in history, warfare had not yet become entirely mechanized. The major powers also still relied heavily on a very longstanding auxiliary of Western armies—horses—to transport men and supplies where train tracks did not reach (although, as we will see, they did build tracks in some areas of the front).

Alongside these vast expenses, the process of mobilizing a country's military—calling up reserve soldiers from civilian life, getting them equipped, and transporting them to the right places, along with the necessary weaponry and supplies—was costly and time-consuming. Even before the war, the combatants realized they would need to put tens of millions of men into uniform (together, they ultimately deployed no fewer than 74 million). German mobilization plans involved a schedule of some 11,000 train trips, calculated down to the minute. So if one country mobilized, its adversaries faced enormous pressure to do the same or risk getting caught unprepared. The same factors put ever-greater pressure on the European alliances to coordinate their actions during a crisis, to ensure that if one country entered into war, its partners would be ready to support it.

MILITARISM AND THE MARCH TO WAR

The general population's attitudes toward a possible war remained distinctly mixed. Socialists and pacifists throughout Europe insisted that class solidarity should trump nationality. French and German Socialist leaders traveled to each other's countries to pledge that their members would not take up arms if a conflict broke out. Keir Hardie (1856–1915), a founder of Britain's radical Independent Labour Party, organized a massive peace demonstration in London shortly before Britain's declaration of war in 1914. Yet at the same time, the idea that a society might purge and cleanse itself through warfare remained frighteningly powerful. In 1909, the Italian

Dreadnoughts A postcard shows the British battleship HMS *Dreadnought*, in 1906, leaving the shipyard where it was built. Employing the very latest developments in steam power and weaponry, it was indicative of increases in military spending during the pre-war arms race.

writer Filippo Tommaso Marinetti (1876–1944) composed a manifesto for the so-called Futurist group of artists in which he called war "the only hygiene of the world ...we want to glorify war." Similarly, the London *Daily Mail* argued in 1912 that "peace may and has ruined many a nationality with its surfeit of everything except those tonics of privation and sacrifice." Modernist critiques of "decadent" bourgeois society all too easily fed the perception that only a purifying war could save the West from inevitable decline.

With many Europeans seeing war as inevitable, national leaders not surprisingly looked for the best moment to start it on their own terms. As early as 1911, the chief of the German General Staff, Helmuth von Moltke, openly expressed his belief that a war would come soon. During the Second Moroccan Crisis he pressed his government "to make an energetic demand which we are prepared to enforce with the sword." Many other statesmen and soldiers across the Continent shared von Moltke's point of view to some degree. "We shall have a war. I will make it, and I will win it," declared France's marshal, Joseph Joffre (1852–1931), in 1911. It only required the right combination of circumstances for these men's collective calculations to unleash an inferno.

THE SPARK In the summer of 1914, these circumstances materialized. On June 28, Archduke Franz Ferdinand (1863–1914), heir to the throne of the Austro-Hungarian Empire, paid a visit to Sarajevo, capital of Bosnia-Herzegovina. The city's appearance itself vividly expressed the tensions of the region, with traditional Ottoman market streets leading into broad new boulevards equipped with tramways in which the western Latin script had displaced the older Cyrillic. Franz Ferdinand, although a temperamental, unpopular figure, was more favorable to South Slav aspirations than most Austrian leaders. But his relatively liberal political views did not stop a motley group of Bosnian Serb terrorists from hatching a plot to kill him. These terrorists were not skilled commandos but young, half-trained, excitable men. Their initial attempt to bomb the archduke's motorcade on the morning of June 28 turned into something of a farce. Two assassins failed to throw their bombs, while a third bounced his bomb off the back of Franz Ferdinand's car, leaving it to detonate under the following vehicle.

But what the terrorists lacked in competence was made up for by the incompetence of their enemies and by sheer dumb luck. Following the failed bombing, Franz Ferdinand and his wife decided to visit wounded victims in the hospital. His car turned by mistake onto a side street, tried to reverse, and stalled. By chance, one of the terrorists, Gaurilo Princip (1894–1918), a twenty-year-old, was in the

Assassination of Franz Ferdinand In a contemporary illustration from an Italian newspaper, Gavrilo Princip emerges from a crowd with his pistol drawn. Soldiers lunge forward, but they are unable to stop him from shooting the archduke and his wife.

street having stopped at a nearby delicatessen for a bite to eat. He whipped out a pistol, pushed his way forward, and fired two shots into the car. One pierced Franz Ferdinand's jugular vein, and the other hit his wife in the stomach. Within an hour, both were dead.

THE MOVE TOWARD WAR The assassination of Archduke Franz Ferdinand caused a furor in Austria and led to calls for revenge on Serbia, whose secret police was immediately suspected of complicity. In fact, the Black Hand, which still wielded influence in Serbia, particularly in the secret police, had provided supplies and advice to the assassins. Germany's Kaiser Wilhelm shared in the outrage and urged Austria-Hungary to take forceful measures against the Serbs. The Germans and Austrians knew the risks involved. Russia might intervene to protect Serbia, and hostilities between Russia and Austria-Hungary might oblige their allies to fight as well, leading to a general war. But even while hoping that Russia would hesitate before taking sides with terrorists and assassins, the two German-speaking powers were prepared to fight. "If we must go under, we had better go under decently," the Austrian emperor Franz Josef reportedly remarked.

There followed weeks of tense diplomatic exchanges during which Austria-Hungary quietly recalled soldiers who had taken leave to work on their family farms. As usual in summer, European elites departed on vacation. General von Moltke enjoyed a few days at a Bohemian spa. But the appearance of normality was deceptive. Even as Austria prepared to present Serbia with harsh terms, the Russians made clear that they would not stand by and see their fellow Slavs overrun. Nonetheless, on July 23, Austria-Hungary demanded that Serbia take immediate action to suppress anti-Austrian activity, including censoring publications, banning independence organizations, and—most provocatively—giving Austrian officials free rein to interrogate and arrest Serbian citizens on Serbian soil. Even as the diplomatic exchanges reached a desperate crescendo, Serbia refused this last demand and ordered its forces to mobilize. Austria mobilized in turn, and Germany refused a last-minute offer of British mediation. On July 28, Austrian gunboats opened fire from the Danube River on the Serbian capital of Belgrade.

THE OUTBREAK OF WAR At this point, fears of being caught unprepared began to overwhelm all other considerations. The transformation of an Austro-Serbian skirmish into World War I took just one week. After two days of anxious vacillation, Tsar Nikolai II ordered a general mobilization on July 30 against both Austria-Hungary and Germany—a step that in practice would have been enormously difficult to reverse. Germany nonetheless demanded that Russia step down and, upon receiving no response, declared war against Russia on August 1. France now acted to fulfill its treaty of alliance with Russia, rejecting German requests that it remain neutral.

The Germans prepared to implement an updated version of the 1905 Schlieffen Plan, which called on the German army to make a great arc through neutral Belgium and sweep into France from the north. When the Germans demanded Belgium's permission to cross its territory, the Belgians refused and Germany invaded. Britain had so far hesitated to fulfill its own treaty promises to France and Russia. Prime Minister Herbert Asquith (1852–1928) wrote to a friend that the country might yet remain a "spectator," even while warning that "we are within measurable … distance of a real Armageddon." But German aggression against Belgium, a country the British had long regarded as belonging to its sphere of influence, smashed hopes for British neutrality. On August 4, Britain declared war on Germany. All the combatants now completed their mobilization, and as early as August 5 fighting had started along a long arc from southern Alsace to central Belgium.

The Schlieffen Plan

INTO THE ABYSS (1914–1915)

For nearly a hundred years, starting with the Congress of Vienna, Europe had avoided a war involving all of the major powers. Despite the many smaller wars that had occurred, the diplomatic safeguards set in place by the exhausted victors of the struggle against Napoleon had continued, more or less, to function. But in 1914, diplomatic considerations crumbled before fears that restraint—a delay in mobilization, a reluctance to strike first—might lead to quick defeat. And so Europe hurtled into the abyss.

PUBLIC ATTITUDES

Popular reactions to the outbreak of war were anything but uniform. The pacifists and socialists who dreamed of workers defying the call to arms met with bitter

disappointment. Only 1.5 percent of French reservists did not report when mobilized—far fewer than the government feared. The percentage was barely different in Austria-Hungary, despite the nationalist turmoil there. In Britain, 750,000 men, including over half the undergraduates at Oxford and Cambridge, voluntarily enlisted in the armed forces just in the months of August and September 1914, overwhelming recruiting offices. Emmeline Pankhurst, leader of the British woman suffrage movement, broke off contact with her pacifist daughter Sylvia and ordered members of the Women's Social and Political Union to suspend political protests in the name of national unity. The one antimilitarist leader in Europe who might have rallied significant numbers against the war was the charismatic French Socialist leader Jean Jaurès (1859–1914). And on July 31, 1914, just as France prepared to enter the war, a nationalist militant shot him dead in a Parisian cafe.

Many onlookers and participants in fact saw the war as a welcome release from peacetime frustrations. Adolf Hitler (1889–1945), an indigent and sometimes homeless Austrian artist, had failed to meet the physical requirements for Austrian military service in February 1914. In August, in Munich, he joined a crowd cheering Germany's declaration of war. "I sank to my knees and thanked heaven that it had given me the good fortune to live at such a time," the future dictator who would lead Germany into World War II wrote a decade later. (Hitler enlisted in the German army and spent the entire war at the front.) The young British poet Rupert Brooke (1887–1915) spoke for many when he compared his war-bound generation to "swimmers into cleanness leaping / Glad from a world grown old and cold and weary." (Less than a year later, he died of an infected mosquito bite while on service with the Royal Navy.)

Even so, true war fervor was most often brief and did not extend to entire populations. Especially outside of major urban centers, a sense of patriotic duty and grim determination predominated. Some writers, like Britain's H. G. Wells (1866–1944), hoped that the war would prove a last great spasm of violence before an age of perpetual peace: it was he who coined the phrase *the war to end all wars*. Politicians on both sides—the so-called Allies (France, Britain, and Russia, soon to be joined by Italy) and the Central powers (Germany, Austria-Hungary, Turkey, and, belatedly,

Bulgaria)—appealed for public support with lofty speeches about fighting for "civilization" against "barbarism" or (in the case of German rhetoric) "decadence." And many people looked upon the coming conflict with nothing but dread. The Russian poet Anna Akhmatova wrote that in the month of July 1914 "we grew a hundred years older." And she continued, describing the moment:

> Out of the mind, like a burden now fled,
> There vanished all traces of passion and song.
> And in their place the Almighty now read
> From a book of portents, horrific and long.

EARLY GERMAN SUCCESSES

Early in the war, the German army gave Allied propagandists altogether too much material to support the idea that Germans were a new barbarian horde threatening civilization. In order to have any hope of prevailing against enemies on both east and west, German strategy, as formulated in the Schlieffen Plan, called for a victory over France in just six weeks, before the vast but lumbering Russian military could fully mobilize. Furthermore, the German army was committed to carrying out what its tactical doctrine referred to as "absolute destruction" against civilian populations to reach its objectives. When in August 1914 the Belgians put up unexpectedly stiff resistance to German forces, the Germans shot over 5,000 Belgian hostages, burned whole sections of Belgian towns, and turned a blind eye to their troops raping women and despoiling civilian property. Lurid atrocity stories circulated in the French and British press and were relayed personally by Belgian refugees, of whom a quarter of a million fled across the English Channel.

Despite the Belgian resistance, the first weeks of the conflict went well for Germany and fit the pattern of rapid, mobile warfare, punctuated by massive battles, that its General Staff had expected. On August 23, the German First Army fought the British Expeditionary Force around the Belgian town of Mons, near the French border, and forced it into a two-week-long retreat. But the same day, more than eight hundred miles to the east, a Russian army over 400,000 strong, which had mobilized with unexpected speed, approached German East Prussia. In a week-long struggle that became known as the battle of Tannenberg, the well-organized and well-equipped Germans, commanded by Paul von Hindenburg (1847–1934), massacred the Russian force and a week later forced it back over the Russian border. The battle cost the Russians dear:

German Atrocities in Belgium An apelike German soldier clutching a smoking rifle menaces a defenseless Belgian woman in this French cartoon (1915). The illustration is representative of Allied perceptions of the German army's brutal treatment of Belgian civilians.

They lost close to 200,000 men killed and wounded in the battle, and over 100,000 prisoners. Russia would not again threaten German territory during the war. The despairing Russian commander committed suicide. But the battle also helped, at a crucial moment, to relieve pressure on the Western Allies in Belgium and France by diverting German troops east.

BEGINNINGS OF THE STALEMATE

German strategy dictated quick victory over France, but in 1914 this victory failed to materialize. The Germans closed to within thirty miles of Paris in the first week of September. But they had deployed crucial troops away from the western front to hold back the Russians, and more to defend Alsace against a French attack. They were plagued by hesitation and poor communications among their generals. French scorched-earth tactics disrupted their supply chain. And Italy, the supposed ally of Germany and Austria-Hungary, failed to enter the war, allowing the French to redeploy troops from its southern

World War I, 1914–1916 The war remained a stalemate on the western front in France and Belgium, with neither army advancing despite several protracted, bloody battles. Conflict in the Balkans saw an Austro-Hungarian invasion of Serbia and the failed invasion of Gallipoli by British imperial troops. Successive waves of invasion on the German-Russian border saw territory change hands frequently, as well as high casualty rates. Meanwhile, German use of submarines won victories of a different kind, cutting off Allied supply lines in the Atlantic Ocean and the North Sea.

Alpine border to the north. Finally, at a crucial moment, a twentieth-century innovation—aerial reconnaissance—enabled the French to identify a weak spot on the Germans' flank as they crossed the Marne River. French commanders rushed troops into the line, even commandeering

600 Parisian taxis to help carry them, and the Germans retreated.

YPRES In late October and early November, the Germans made one last attempt to sweep around the British and French toward the English Channel, in the so-called Race to the Sea. A desperate battle ensued around the town of Ypres in western Belgium (the British troops, not knowing how to pronounce the name, called it Wipers), where the Germans again found their way blocked. And this time, in the mud and rain, the combatants' great industrial war machines locked gears with one another and stalled. Over half the Germans' trucks broke down, while horses died for lack of adequate feed (they required 2 million pounds of it per day). Meanwhile, the use of high-powered machine guns and high-explosive shells against infantry in the open field—and even more against the brightly uniformed cavalry to which the generals on both sides remained stubbornly attached—was causing insupportable carnage. By the end of 1914, fully 300,000 French and German soldiers had died, along with one-third of the original British Expeditionary Force.

TRENCH WARFARE   And so the front lines froze in place, and both sides began to fortify them with deep trenches, fronted with sandbags or walls of earth. Quickly they learned to build several rows of trenches and to lay impenetrable thickets of barbed wire, up to 100 feet wide and 5 feet high, in front of them. As 1915 began, such trench systems ran for hundreds of miles through Belgium and northern France. Sheltering in the trenches, troops were safe from gunfire and anything but a direct hit from artillery. And from the trenches, they could sweep the battlefield in front of them with machine gun fire, cutting down enemies floundering through barbed-wire barriers. So the fighting continued, but neither side could advance.

ATTEMPTS AT BREAKTHROUGH

At this point, the war took a tragic turn. Stabilization of the western front, and the beginnings of **trench warfare**, made it impossible for the armies to fight mobile, decisive campaigns. But neither the generals nor the civilian leaderships could accept the new circumstances. Commanders like Sir John French (1852–1925), who led the British Expeditionary Force, remained stubbornly attached to the old tactics. He insisted that the moment would soon come to release the British cavalry, which he imagined charging triumphantly past the trenches, across ranks of dazed Germans, as if in a replay of the battle of Waterloo. Faced with trench warfare, the generals became obsessed with the idea of a breakthrough that would allow a return to these older and supposedly more honorable forms of combat. And they assumed that only brute force would allow them to achieve it: first bombarding the enemy trenches with the greatest possible quantity of explosive shells, and then sending wave after wave of infantry to attack through the barbed wire until the enemy crumbled. But such was the advantage enjoyed by the defenders that these tactics accomplished little. Most of the shells burst harmlessly outside the trenches, and the infantry smashed against the enemy machine guns like so much human porcelain.

All too typical was the British attempt to break through German lines near the French village of Neuve Chapelle in mid-March 1915. The British commanders planned an early-morning artillery barrage, to be followed by an infantry assault by 40,000 British and Indian troops. They hoped that once the lead German trenches had fallen, the cavalry could follow. But the barrage accomplished little, and the infantry found themselves trapped in the open, caught on barbed wire, and easy prey. Just two German machine guns killed a thousand men, and by the time Sir John French suspended the attack two days later, the British had suffered 13,000 casualties (that is, killed, wounded, and missing) in exchange for less than a mile of

Trench Warfare In this photo from 1917, German troops stand shoulder-to-shoulder in narrow, neck-deep trenches during a break between battles.

ground. An offensive directed by Marshal Joffre in Champagne did scarcely better and cost 145,000 French killed and wounded. But the British, French, and Germans all continued to try variant after variant on the same plan, turning the front into a slaughterhouse. In the year 1915 alone, total casualties on the western front surpassed 2 million. And total Allied gains amounted to exactly 8 of the nearly 20,000 square miles of France and Belgium occupied by Germany.

TOWARD TOTAL WAR

The sheer scale of the war, and the ghastly tactics developed on the western front, imposed a brutal logic on the war efforts of both sides: strategic skill mattered less than sheer volume. Whoever managed to put the most men, weaponry, and ammunition into the field would have the advantage. And this logic put enormous pressure on what was being called the home front—the millions of civilian men and women who were not in uniform but who were nonetheless called on to sacrifice and contribute to the war effort.

THE HOME FRONT

From the earliest periods of European history, warfare had taken a ferocious toll on noncombatants, and by the time of Napoleon the notion of mobilizing an entire society for war had become firmly established. But in World War I, governments could exercise considerably more control over economies and societies than in previous centuries, and they did so with remarkable results. The goal of **total war**—the phrase itself first appeared toward the end of the conflict—was coming closer to realization.

MANPOWER The most pressing concern was military manpower. Most countries employed conscription at the start of the war, subjecting all young men to military service without possibility of substitution, and backed it up with intensive government recruitment drives. Britain only resorted to conscription in 1916 as its own need for manpower increased, but even before that an enormous stigma attached to young British men who did not volunteer. The British novelist Mary Ward (1851–1920) helped found the Order of the White Feather, whose female members presented this traditional symbol of cowardice to healthy young men they saw in civilian clothes. In every country, the numbers of people in military service

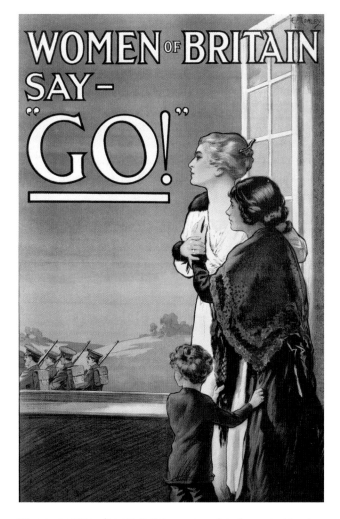

Women and Recruitment British women such as those who joined the Order of the White Feather played a significant role in promoting patriotism and commitment to the war effort. The government also capitalized on women's influence, as in this 1915 recruitment poster that shows both a wealthy woman and a working-class woman united in urging men to enlist.

set records, with Russia calling up an astonishing 14.6 million—over a quarter of all adult men. Sometimes overly intensive recruitment efforts could actually hurt the war effort—in 1915, France had to release half a million skilled workers from the army to aid in munitions production at home.

ECONOMIC PLANNING As in France, governments everywhere took larger and more direct roles in their economies. They worked with industrialists to optimize production for the war effort and spent overall far more than they had before 1914. In Britain, government spending as a percentage of gross domestic product (the total value of goods and services) rose nearly fivefold, from 8.1 percent in

1913 to 38.7 percent in 1917. In both France and Germany, by 1918 the figure topped 50 percent. The British government founded a Munitions Ministry in 1915, which took over management of much of the armaments industry and even built its own factories. The government also took control of the railroads and shipping, and restricted industrial output unrelated to the war effort. The huge increase in the proportion of munitions manufacturing caused the production of consumer goods and services to fall. In 1918, with supplies of food from the Americas threatened by German submarines, the British government imposed food rationing. Families were issued weekly ration cards with which the could buy limited quantities of meat, milk, sugar, flour, and other basic products—but no more. Even the king and queen received ration cards. Similar measures were taken by the other Allies.

Among the Central powers, the need for economic coordination was even greater. At the start of the war, their combined economic output stood at just one-quarter that of the Allies, making it even more necessary for them to direct every possible resource to the war effort. In Germany, coordination between the state and private industry (notably the Krupp firm) grew so tight that Russian Communists later took it as a model for their own central planning. With food imports largely cut off by a British blockade, Germany began a strict regime of food rationing in 1915.

WAR FINANCE Paying for the war also became a critical challenge for all of the combatants. Every country carried out strenuous propaganda campaigns urging its population to buy war bonds, which amounted to loans to the government. Taxes were increased. In Britain, the standard rate of income tax rose from 6 percent in 1914 to 30 percent in 1918. Governments also resorted to printing money, resulting in high inflation rates (up to 400 percent over the course of the war in the case of Italy). To do so, they had to abandon the gold standard to which they had pegged their currencies since the late nineteenth century. The three major Allied powers—Britain, France, and Russia—used their combined gold reserves as collateral on a massive series of loans from American banks, above all the firm of J. P. Morgan, which enabled them to purchase food and war materiel from American firms. Well before the entry of the United States into the war in 1917, these loans effectively tied America to the Allied side.

PROPAGANDA The propaganda campaigns launched by all the combatant nations made use of both literature and the visual arts. Garish war posters proliferated on city and

Wartime Propaganda Recruitment posters drew on the latest advertising techniques, including eye-catching, colorful illustrations and bold slogans, to encourage participation in the war. This German poster from the war reads: "Your Fatherland is in danger: Enlist!"

town walls urging citizens to purchase war bonds, to avoid "loose talk" that might reveal military secrets to enemy spies, and above all, if they were young men, to enlist. The Allies exploited accounts of rapes committed by Germans in occupied Belgium and France, depicting the enemy as horrific wild beasts. Germany's execution of a British nurse, Edith Cavell, for helping Allied soldiers escape from Belgium became central to British propaganda efforts. In Russia, propaganda activities were accompanied by government programs aimed at identifying and surveilling "suspect" ethnic groups, including the German-speakers who lived along the Volga River and also the Russian Jewish population. Civilian institutions added fervent voices to the bellicose chorus as well—including churches. In 1915, the bishop of London gave a sermon urging his listeners to "Kill Germans! Kill them!...Not for the sake of killing, but to save the world. . . . Kill the good as well as the bad."

WOMEN'S PARTICIPATION Although only Russia of the belligerent nations permitted women to fight alongside men—and that only in 1917—the war brought major changes to women's lives. At the front, they served as nurses, ambulance drivers, and cooks. Back home, with virtually all able-bodied men away at war, women entered the labor force in vast numbers: over a million in Austria-Hungary by war's end, and 400,000 in Britain just in the war's first year. In Britain, the proportion of adult women earning wages rose from 24 percent to 37 percent over the course of the war. Governments encouraged this shift, as did most women's movements. Women particularly took on jobs in munitions factories. As we have seen, after constituting a considerable proportion of the industrial workforce early in the nineteenth century, women had gradually been driven from the factory floor. But in World War I, they came back in force, as well as taking up more of what now seemed "conventional" female jobs such as nursing and secretarial work.

Women and the War A remarkable photo from the summer of 1917 shows Maria Bochkareva embracing the British suffragist leader Emmeline Pankhurst: two very different faces of European feminism. Pankhurst even wears a military decoration, suggestive of their common dedication to the war effort.

The long-term implications of these shifts can be exaggerated. Once the war ended, the percentage of female participation in the workforce returned to pre-war levels in most countries. Yet the wartime experiences showed women capable of a wider range of work than most pre-war observers had allowed for, including jobs as mechanics and factory workers in sectors such as munitions production. Female membership in trade unions rose to record levels. In Russia, women entered the most stereotypically male profession of all when the government approved the creation of several battalions of women soldiers in 1917. One of them, the Women's Battalion of Death, led by a former laborer named Maria Bochkareva (1889–1920), briefly saw action in the summer of 1917 and made a lasting impression on European women's movements.

The wartime sacrifices and contributions made by women in Britain played a major role in leading Parliament to grant the vote to most women over age thirty (with all British adult women finally enfranchised in 1928). Germany, too, and several other European countries, including Russia, would give women the vote at the war's end. Woman suffrage occurred in the United States with ratification of the Nineteenth Amendment to the Constitution in 1920.

THE EXPANDING THEATER OF WAR

As the fighting dragged on, the Allies and the Central powers put ever-greater demands on their colonial empires, turning the European war into a global war. France extended conscription to men in some of its African colonies, while Britain urged its former white settler colonies, now autonomous dominions, to help the mother country. Young men from Katikati and the rest of New Zealand willingly volunteered, as did millions of others in Australia, Canada, and South Africa. Meanwhile, the fighting itself extended abroad. British, French, and Belgian troops attacked German colonies in East Africa, where German troops engaged in stubborn guerrilla resistance until 1918. The Union of South Africa overran German Southwest Africa, putting an end to that tragic chapter in German colonial history. In East Asia, Japan had already entered the war on the Allied side in 1914, fighting naval battles with the Germans and capturing German outposts in China.

The geographical scope of the war increased within Europe as well. Even as hostilities were breaking out in the summer of 1914, Ottoman Turkey, now ruled by the Young Turks, signed a treaty with Germany that promised

Turkey rich rewards in the Balkans and German economic help in return for its entry into the war. In response, the Allies began greedily to plot the partition of the Ottoman Empire, with France and Britain secretly promising Russia control of Constantinople and allotting themselves spheres of influence in the Arab world. In 1915, another ally joined the Central powers: Bulgaria, which hoped to regain territory taken by Serbia in the Second Balkan War. And the same year Italy, having abandoned the Central powers, entered the war on the Allied side, leading to long and costly battles with Austria-Hungary in difficult, mountainous terrain. So by 1915 the war had four separate European fronts: western, Italian, Balkan, and eastern.

THE EASTERN FRONT Of these four fronts, the eastern and Balkan remained the most volatile and rarely bogged down into the sort of trench warfare seen in the west. While Russia's early assault on East Prussia failed spectacularly at Tannenberg, the country did better against Austria-Hungary in 1914, advancing into Galicia (a region straddling the border between modern Poland and Ukraine) and occupying the strategic city of Lvov. A Habsburg attempt to repel the Russians early in 1915 failed, costing Austria-Hungary some 350,000 dead and wounded. But then in May the Germans came to the aid of their allies. In a successful six-month offensive, they drove the Russians back 300 miles along a front that stretched for twice that distance. By autumn, all of present-day Poland, most of Lithuania, and large portions of Latvia, Belarus, and Ukraine had fallen under German and Austrian occupation. Meanwhile, in the fall of 1915 Austria-Hungary and Bulgaria managed to overrun most of Serbia.

These campaigns, like the ones we have seen in the west, took an enormous toll. Not only did Russia suffer a staggering 1.4 million casualties in the 1915 German offensive alone; it carried out a scorched-earth policy, destroying its own towns, farms, railroads, and food stockpiles to keep them from falling into German hands. The Russian army also forced local populations—especially non-Russians such as Ukrainians and Jews who the army feared might collaborate with the enemy—to flee east deeper into Russia: some 3 million people in 1915 alone became internal refugees. But Russia did not suffer as badly as Serbia, where a brutal Austrian occupation, widespread famine, and one of the worst typhus epidemics in history produced a human catastrophe. Estimates of the total loss of life in Serbia during the war vary from one-sixth to well over one-fifth of the entire population. Casualties among adult males ran over 50 percent.

THE GALLIPOLI CAMPAIGN In 1915, the British tried to open up a front in Turkey. The initiative here belonged to the boisterous, forty-year-old Winston Churchill (1874–1965), who served as first lord of the Admiralty. A direct descendant of the duke of Marlborough and veteran of numerous adventures as a soldier and war correspondent, Churchill pressed for an Allied assault on the Dardanelles, the narrow strait west of Constantinople that, together with the Bosphorus, links the Black Sea to the Mediterranean and separates mainland Europe from Asia. He believed that such a campaign could knock Turkey out of the war, divert German forces from the western front, protect the Suez Canal (which Turkey, as the principal power in the eastern Mediterranean, could potentially threaten), and thereby preserve Britain's all-important passage to India.

But the **Gallipoli Campaign**, organized with excessive speed and insufficient care, turned disastrous. An initial naval attack failed when the British lost six out of nine battleships to Turkish mines. In April and May, the British managed to land on the Gallipoli Peninsula, but the Turkish army, while under strength and of mixed quality, had dug in well and used machine guns to the same frightening effect seen on the western front. Thousands of men died in the water and on the beaches, and the survivors remained pinned down. More than half the 400,000 soldiers under British command had become casualties before Britain decided to evacuate in early 1916. The 400,000 included a particularly large contingent of Australians and New Zealanders in the ANZAC corps, and their heavy losses spurred a resentment against Britain that has never quite faded in either nation.

THE WAR AT SEA Britain put pressure on the Central powers more effectively through its use of naval power. Despite all of Kaiser Wilhelm's efforts to develop the German navy before the war, it was no match for the Royal Navy on the high seas—partly because British intelligence had broken the German navy's codes and knew its plans. In 1914, Britain won sea battles in the Indian Ocean and the South Atlantic, and effectively forced the German fleet back into harbor. The Germans attempted naval breakouts, but despite bloodying the British off the coast of Denmark in 1916 at the battle of Jutland, in which some 250 ships participated, they could not break the British blockade, which was slowly strangling the German economy.

German naval hopes increasingly focused not on massive battleships but on submarines, which had been under development since the 1860s. Both Britain and Germany had substantial numbers of submarines at the start of the war, but the Germans augmented their use against the merchant shipping that brought crucial supplies, including oil and food, to Britain. By the war's end, Germany had put some 375 of its torpedo-carrying U-boats (*Untersee*, or underwater boats) with crews of as many as 60 men, into service. The British had no means of detecting them while submerged, and they inflicted huge damage. U-boats sank over 5,000 merchant ships by the end of the war, killing tens of thousands of sailors and destroying massive quantities of foodstuffs and industrial goods. Initially, however, the Germans refrained from targeting the vessels of neutral countries. The most important of these countries was the United States, which had not formed part of any European alliance before 1914.

But the expanding German submarine campaign also raised the chance that the United States, already increasingly tied to the Allies because of the massive loans made to them, might join the war on the Allied side. On May 7, 1915, a U-boat torpedoed and sank the British ocean liner *Lusitania* off the coast of Ireland. The ship had been carrying munitions and therefore amounted to a legitimate military target. But the huge loss of life—1,195 out of 1,959 passengers, including 128 of 139 U.S. citizens—caused outrage in America. One magazine denounced "a deed for which a Hun would blush, a Turk be ashamed, and a Barbary pirate apologize." American president Woodrow Wilson (1856–1924) sent a series of protest notes to the German government, warning that the United States would see any further German attacks on merchant vessels carrying American citizens as "deliberately unfriendly." Wilson also ordered an increase in American military spending, although he continued to promise the American public that he would keep the country out of war.

NEW BATTLEFIELD WEAPONS AND OLD TACTICS

Submarines were not the only technological innovation as the combatants searched desperately to break the stalemate on the western front. As early as the fall of 1914, the British used airplanes to drop small bombs on German strongholds. In May 1915, a large German blimp appeared over London and released incendiary devices in a deliberate if ineffective attack on civilians. Airplanes provided crucial intelligence, and soon fighter planes took to the sky to shoot down other planes. Throughout the war

Fighting in the Air British (circular insignia) and German (cross insignia) planes engage in a dogfight, a form of airborne close combat.

the size, speed, range, and sophistication of warplanes all increased. By the war's end, the British, French, and Germans had produced over 150,000 planes, while "flying aces" became popular heroes.

And toward the end of the war, the Germans made another advance with striking implications for aeronautics. The Krupp steel and munitions works developed a railroad-mounted artillery piece with a 100-foot-long barrel that could fire a 210-pound shell a distance of over eighty miles. The shells took three minutes to reach their targets and rose to the greatest height yet attained by a man-made projectile: twenty-five miles above the ground. From a position in Champagne, in eastern France, the Germans managed to bombard the city of Paris for several weeks with the giant field cannon known as the Paris Gun. On Good Friday, 1918, one shell collapsed the roof of the Church of Saint-Gervais, killing eighty-eight members of the congregation.

Earlier in the war, the Germans had begun to use a much more sinister weapon. In April 1915, they released

Chemical Weapons British soldiers at the battle of Ypres wear gas masks for protection as they stand in a trench, awaiting a German advance.

suit. The British war poet Wilfred Owen (1893–1918) wrote unforgettably about the horrifying experience of a gas attack:

> Gas! GAS! Quick, boys!—An ecstasy of fumbling,
> Fitting the clumsy helmets just in time;
> But someone still was yelling out and stumbling
> And flound'ring like a man in fire or lime ...
> Dim, through the misty panes and thick green light,
> As under a green sea, I saw him drowning.
>
> In all my dreams, before my helpless sight,
> He plunges at me, guttering, drowning.

Yet the cruel fact was that none of these technological innovations could relieve the terrible stalemate on the western front. Although poison gas was terrifying and frequently deadly, it remained far less effective than machine guns and artillery. One other new weapon did have the potential to change the nature of the war. A fast-moving, heavily armored tank could cross the no-man's-land between the trenches, roll over barbed wire, and use its heavy guns to destroy enemy machine-gun positions from close range. But while the British began to deploy primitive tanks in 1916, until the very end of the war they made little difference: they were as yet too slow, unreliable, poorly shielded, and not organized into the concentrated units that would have made the greatest difference. Lacking a technological solution, the generals on the western front therefore felt they had to stick with the same gruesome tactics they had deployed from the start of the stalemate. And millions of soldiers paid the price.

THE CONTINUING BLOODBATH The years 1915 and 1916 brought repeated Allied efforts to achieve the longed-for breakthrough via sheer force, but these efforts failed. The Germans meanwhile followed a different strategy. Faced with fighting on two fronts, and increasingly plagued by the British blockade, they doubted their ability to assemble the force necessary for a major offensive in the west. Much of their high command now believed that they could and should drive the Russians from the war first—a sort of Schlieffen Plan in reverse.

But the new German commander in chief, Erich von Falkenhayn (1861–1922), still believed the western Allies could be brought to sue for a negotiated peace. The method was to be a grisly campaign of attrition, aimed less at capturing territory than at inflicting the maximum number of casualties. In early 1916, he opened a major attack against a series of fortresses in eastern France, around the town of Verdun, making use of massive artillery and hoping to

thick chlorine gas from their trenches near Ypres, Belgium. It blew into French positions, choking the soldiers and sending them into convulsions. Heavier than air, the chlorine settled into the trenches, forcing men out into the unprotected open ground. It even killed the rats that infested nearly all the trenches. By September, British general Douglas Haig (1861–1928) was ordering chlorine containers as well for yet another failed attempt at a breakthrough on the western front. In some cases, the poison gas blew back over British positions.

Soon both sides were issuing gas masks as standard equipment, leading the Germans to yet another escalation. In 1916, they started using mustard gas, which was not only far more concentrated and easier to deploy than chlorine but also could enter the body through the skin, rendering gas masks ineffective. The international conventions signed at the Hague in 1899 and 1907 had prohibited these chemical weapons (along with aerial bombing), but once one country had violated them, the others followed inflict five casualties on the French defenders for every two of his own. The French held out and then, in the fall, counterattacked. But in the process they lost 540,000 men killed and wounded. The Germans, unable to stick to Falkenhayn's desired ratio, lost 430,000. The flood of corpses at the **battle of Verdun** overwhelmed attempts to bury them. As late as the 1930s, it was possible to stumble across bones of the dead in the hills near Verdun.

OPPOSITION TO THE WAR

It is remarkable that despite the relentless killing, popular opinion throughout Europe remained largely committed to the war effort, and few soldiers spoke out against their commanders. Propaganda helped nurture this support, but so did the genuine sense of patriotic duty felt in each of the countries, coupled with outrage at the enemy for the damage already inflicted. And of course characterizing the war as a pointless and obscene mistake was to suggest that millions of men were dying for nothing.

In Britain, a small antiwar movement did consistently express its opposition to the continuing hostilities, despite legislation that curtailed freedom of speech for the duration of the war emergency. One prominent member was the country's greatest living philosopher, Bertrand Russell (1872–1970), who lost his university position and briefly went to prison for his pacifist writings. Another was the leading suffragist and socialist Charlotte Despard (1844–1939), sister to none other than the British commander in chief Sir John French (the siblings remained close despite their totally opposed positions on the war). Britain did permit men to qualify as conscientious objectors, especially Quakers, whose pacifist convictions dated back to the beginning of their movement. In Germany, a handful of socialists publicly protested the war, and after two of their leaders were jailed in 1916, 50,000 munitions workers in Berlin staged a one-day strike. But overall, antiwar activity had tragically little effect.

LIFE IN THE TRENCHES For most front-line soldiers, the flames of patriotic zeal quickly sputtered out in the mud of the trenches. That mud was everywhere, along with pools of stagnant water, mice, rats, frogs, slugs, insects, human waste, and, worst of all, the dead. The British soldier George Coppard (1898–1984) recalled, in a memoir of the war:

> Every square yard of ground seemed to be layered with corpses, producing a sickening stench. We

would curtain off protruding parts with a sandbag, pinned to the side of the trench with cartridges. A swollen right arm, with a German eagle tattooed on it, used to stick out and brush us as we squeezed by; once a head appeared which wasn't there an hour before.

In the winter, food and water froze solid. In the fall and spring, the men could spend hours standing in the water, which often led to a dangerous, painful swelling called trench foot that sometimes destroyed the limb altogether. Post-traumatic stress disorder affected an unknown but very large number of soldiers. The British army alone diagnosed 80,000 men as suffering from what was called "shell shock," supposedly induced by artillery barrages.

Fortunately, battlefield medical care had improved markedly since the reforms of the Crimean War, when field hospitals and organized nursing care had been introduced. The field hospitals were now equipped with surgical theaters where soldiers could be operated on under anesthesia. The use of antiseptics to prevent the spread of infection (although true antibiotics only arrived after 1940) meant that serious wounds were no longer an almost-certain death sentence. Vaccinations now protected soldiers from many common illnesses, with the result that in the war, for the first time in European history, more soldiers died from battle wounds than from

Field Hospitals New medical technology could increasingly save lives close to the front. In this photograph, doctors at a French field hospital use a brand-new X-ray machine to locate a bullet in a soldier's abdomen.

NASH'S *OVER THE TOP*

As soldiers tried to make sense of the violent and alienating experience of World War I, they produced a large body of visual art that expressed the horrors of life in the trenches. A successful painter before the war, the Englishman John Nash (1893–1977) was one such artist.

Nash was one of only twelve men from a regiment of eighty who avoided death or injury while participating in a British counterattack during the battle of Cambrai, in northern France, in late 1917. His painting *Over the Top* (1918) depicts the first minutes of the unit's tragic assault, capturing in bold forms and colors the carnage, confusion, tedium, and futility of the fighting. Against a backdrop of smoke and shellfire, the men of the regiment clamber out of their trench, past the bodies of their comrades, and trudge toward enemy lines and almost certain death.

QUESTIONS FOR ANALYSIS

1. What does Nash's painting reveal about conditions on the western front?
2. What do the expressions and postures of the men convey about their feelings regarding the war?
3. What does the painting suggest about interaction among soldiers in battle?

disease. Yet soldiers now had to deal with the psychological trauma of battles that lasted not for hours or even days but for months on end, keeping them at risk of death the entire time.

During attacks, battle police ensured that no one stayed behind in the trenches, and those who refused to go "over the top" risked arrest and even execution. As is frequent in wartime, the soldiers often felt the greatest loyalty not to their officers, or even to their country, but to their fellow soldiers. The common experience of the trenches could even, on occasion, create a form of camaraderie with the enemy. In a famous incident, on several parts of the western front on Christmas Day 1914, soldiers managed to organize informal truces, exchanging food and cigarettes and arranging impromptu soccer games in the no-man's-land. Commanders on both sides were horrified and worked hard to ensure that nothing of the sort would happen again.

BREAKING POINTS (1916–1917)

At this point in the war, victory—to say nothing of planning for the postwar world—seemed further away than ever to nearly all the participants. But this was total war, in which each side attempted to mobilize every possible resource to achieve destruction of the enemy. As the losses on each side mounted into the millions, it became increasingly difficult for either the Allies or the Central powers to imagine any end to the war short of complete victory for their side.

THE BATTLE OF THE SOMME

In the summer of 1916, following the massive German offensive at Verdun, the Allies made the largest and most intensive effort yet to achieve a breakthrough on the western front. The so-called Big Push, planned for a sector of the front near the Somme River in northern France, did not differ greatly in form from earlier offensives. It was to start with an artillery bombardment to destroy the German defenses, to be followed by a massed infantry attack. Once the infantry had captured the German trenches, the Allies would begin a rapid, triumphant advance through the open country beyond.

What was new about the Big Push was above all the plan's scale, which dwarfed anything previously seen in this or any other war. The **battle of the Somme** was scheduled to last five full days and involve 21,000 tons of

Lochnagar Crater The explosions of the mines with which the Allies began the battle of the Somme left giant craters like this one on the battlefield. Today Lochnagar Crater—named after the type of British mine used—is a memorial site.

explosives—1.5 million shells—all directed at a strip of land 14 miles long and slightly more than 1 mile wide, or nearly 150 shells per acre. The infantry attack would begin with the detonation of enormous mines under or near German trenches, containing as much as 30 tons of high explosives each (one of them blew a crater that still measures 55 feet deep and 220 feet wide). The British infantry attacks alone would involve 120,000 men. Just to bring the necessary men and materiel to the front, the Allies set about building 55 miles of railroad track.

Yet the Allied commanders were deluding themselves in thinking that an increase in scale could make the difference, for nothing had changed in the implacable logic that gave such a tremendous advantage to the defense. Over long months, the Germans had dug themselves deep at the Somme, building a chain of reinforced, ventilated bunkers thirty feet or more below ground. For all the fury of the initial artillery barrage, two-thirds of the shells were shrapnel, which mostly spent itself in the earth or pinged harmlessly off steel and concrete fortifications. Of the remaining high-explosive shells, very few hit close enough to bunkers or machine-gun emplacements to destroy them. And a quarter of all the shells did not detonate at all.

At 7:28 on the morning of July 1, 1916, the Allies set off their massive mines. Two minutes later (the time it took for the mine debris to fall back to earth), officers blew whistles to send their first waves of infantry "over the top" and advance. Even as they climbed ladders to exit their trenches, Allied infantry heard the ominous sound of bugles from the German trenches, summoning the defenders into position. And as the troops started across no-man's-land, they found the German positions virtually unscathed, the barbed wire uncut, and machine-gun fire cutting through their ranks like giant scythes. The slaughter was almost unimaginable. One Newfoundland regiment suffered 90 percent casualties in the space of forty minutes. Every one of its twenty-six officers was killed or wounded. And yet the Allied commanders, having staked so much on the attack, could not bring themselves to call it off, and they continued to send wave after wave of soldiers to their deaths. On this single day, nearly as many British soldiers died as during the entire Crimean War—some 19,000 with another 2,000 mortally wounded. Total British casualties for this one day came close to 60,000, or nearly half the 120,000 men who took part in the attack. Nearly all of them fell onto territory the British had already held.

And still the offensive continued. All through the summer and early fall, the British and French battered on the Somme defenses with human hammers and succeeded in doing little but smashing those hammers to pieces. In only a few spots did the Allies manage to advance more than a mile or two. In mid-November, when they finally admitted failure, their casualties had risen to 620,000 for this campaign alone. General Haig, now the British commander in chief, began to adopt the viewpoint of his German counterpart Falkenhayn, coming to see the struggle as one of attrition. It led him to the perverse logic of treating massive British casualty figures as a sign of success in their own right, confident that the Germans must be suffering even more. "The total losses of this division are under a thousand!" he exclaimed with frustration in his diary after yet another failed advance. On January 1, 1917, King George V (r. 1910–1936) promoted him to field marshal, the highest rank in the army.

CENTRAL POWERS UNDER STRAIN

In 1917, the colossal strain the war had placed on all the combatants made itself felt more strongly. Germany had ceased to make headway against Russia, which in 1916 carried out another successful offensive against Austria-Hungary. It did not knock Austria-Hungary out of the war, as the Russian commanders had hoped, and it put further strain on the Russian army, which was suffering ever-higher rates of desertion. But it inflicted ghastly casualties (over 2 million total), severely damaged Austria-Hungary's military capacities, and helped relieve the pressure on the western front.

AMERICAN INTERVENTION Germany now faced the prospect of indefinite stalemate on both fronts and slow strangulation from the British blockade. The so-called turnip winter of 1916–17 (so named because Germans had little else to eat) was one of the coldest on record. Hundreds of thousands of Germans died of malnutrition and exposure. Paul von Hindenburg, who now succeeded Falkenhayn as commander in chief, and Hindenburg's powerful deputy Erich von Ludendorff (1865–1937), both realized the need for a drastic gamble. They convinced the government to allow unrestricted submarine warfare in the Atlantic, targeting neutral as well as British vessels carrying food and war materiel across the Atlantic, with the goal of starving Britain out of the war. They understood correctly that the move would probably provoke American intervention, but they hoped to overcome the British before the Americans could make a difference. They also hoped that political turmoil in Russia (discussed below) would weaken the Russian war effort and allow them to concentrate on the western front.

The gamble failed. The German submarine campaign initially succeeded, with hundreds of ships sunk—in March 1917 a quarter of all those bound for Britain, principally from the Americas. British food reserves dwindled. But by the summer, the Allies had begun organizing their transatlantic shipping into convoys, escorted by warships, and the losses fell back to manageable proportions. Meanwhile, the submarine campaign indeed stirred American outrage, as did the exposure of a farcical German attempt to distract America by provoking a war with Mexico. President Woodrow Wilson angrily cut off diplomatic relations with Germany. In April 1917, he convinced Congress to declare war.

It took the United States many months to mobilize, but its involvement promised the Allies a decisive advantage in the long run. The American economy had expanded enormously over the previous decades, and in 1916 it became the largest in the world, surpassing Great Britain's. The United States could also draw on a large population of military-age men.

TURMOIL IN THE MIDDLE EAST AND ARMENIA Meanwhile, Turkey also stumbled toward the brink of collapse. Although the British attempt to knock it out of the war at Gallipoli had failed, the British succeeded at the other end of the Ottoman Empire, where by 1916 they had taken possession of Mesopotamia, the heart of the future state of Iraq. With oil, as we have seen, emerging as a steadily more crucial fuel for the Western world, the Allies made it a priority to capture control of the rich Middle Eastern oil fields. The British also attacked the Turks in the Arabian Peninsula, with the aid of nationalists seeking an independent Arab state. In 1917, a British army fought its way from Egypt up the Mediterranean coast into Palestine, Syria, and Lebanon, and for the first time since the Crusades a European army took possession of Jerusalem. And in contradiction to earlier promises to Arab nationalist leaders, the British foreign secretary, Arthur Balfour (1848–1930), declared his government's support for the establishment of a Jewish national state in Palestine.

In eastern Turkey, where the Turks came into conflict with Russia, Turkish setbacks provided the immediate cause for a campaign of horrifying repression by the Turks against Christian minorities, above all Armenians. Already in the late nineteenth century, several Armenian nationalist groups in the empire had campaigned for the foundation of an independent Armenian state. The rise of the nationalist Young Turks, and the Ottoman's humiliating defeat in the Balkan Wars, had led to increasing resentment and suspicion of the Christian minorities by Muslim Turks (Balkan Christians were accused of treacherously siding with the Ottomans' enemies). In 1915, a crushing Russian victory of the Ottomans at the Battle of Sarıkamış in eastern Anatolia led to outright accusations of treason against Armenians. The government demobilized Armenian soldiers, many of whom it subsequently executed. Resistance by Armenians then provided a pretext for the Ottoman government to order the mass deportation of virtually the entire Armenian population under Ottoman rule to desert camps in present-day Syria. Without

Armenian Genocide A group of Armenian refugees fleeing the genocide in the winter of 1915 stands next to a house or shelter covered in snow, bundled up against the cold of the Caucasus Mountains.

food and water, Armenians died by the thousands during the forced march south, while Ottoman irregular forces carried out numerous massacres. The campaign ended up causing the deaths of at least 600,000 people, and possibly more than a million. Most scholars consider it a genocide: a deliberate, systematic attempt to exterminate an entire people. Like the German campaign of extermination against the Herero and Nama in Southwest Africa at the beginning of the century, but on a much larger scale, the **Armenian genocide** foreshadowed further such crimes in the twentieth century, eventually leading, after World War II, to international covenants recognizing genocide as the worst of all crimes against humanity.

RESISTANCE TO THE WAR

The increased strain of the war on all the combatants called forth unprecedented forms of resistance in 1916 and 1917. In the British Isles, resistance found its sharpest expression in Ireland, where nationalists felt outrage at the sacrifices demanded of them for a British war. Although conscription was never introduced in Ireland during World War I, some 200,000 Irishmen served in the military and some 30,000 died. Nationalists also saw an opportunity to achieve independence while British forces were pinned down in Europe. In Dublin at Easter 1916, some 1,000 nationalists led by Pádraig Pearse (1879–1916), a poet, lawyer, and teacher, staged a badly organized uprising that British forces quickly suppressed. The British executed the ringleaders, but in the long run they succeeded only in creating martyr-heroes and ensuring that if given the choice, the southern, Catholic provinces of Ireland would settle for nothing less than national independence. As the poet William Butler Yeats wrote in a haunting poem about the Easter Rising, the ringleaders—and by extension, all of Ireland—had been "changed, changed utterly. / A terrible beauty is born."

In France, the moment of crisis arrived in the spring of 1917, after commander in chief Robert Nivelle (1856–1924) led yet another failed attempt at a decisive breakthrough. The battle of the Chemin des Dames, along the Aisne River, repeated many elements of the previous summer's Somme offensive, and while in some areas the French forces succeeded in advancing several miles, they did not achieve their objective and casualties were again enormous. In early May, tens of thousands of French soldiers began refusing commands to attack, and mutinies spread through the French army. Desertion rates soared.

EXPERIENCING WORLD WAR I

Following the outbreak of war, many young men rushed to enlist in the British army, whether out of a sense of patriotic duty or in search of a glorious adventure. However, the realities of industrialized warfare—machine guns, high explosives, tanks, the trenches, poison gas—proved a bitter revelation. As the war ground on, the expectant and even enthusiastic mood that had driven many young men to enlist, energetically captured by the British poet Rupert Brooke—who never saw combat—in his War Sonnets (1914), gave way to resignation, fatalism, and anger. Many letters home penned later in the war, including the following message sent from Major Sidney Harold Baker to his brother, exposed the horrors of the war and the disenchantment of the young men who were sent to fight it.

Rupert Brooke, War Sonnets

In "Peace," the first of the two War Sonnets presented below, Brooke embraces the opportunity for action brought by the war. In "The Soldier," he finds comfort in patriotic self-sacrifice.

I. Peace

Now, God be thanked Who has matched us
     with His hour,
          And caught our youth, and wakened
               us from sleeping,
With hand made sure, clear eye, and
     sharpened power,
          To turn, as swimmers into cleanness
               leaping,
Glad from a world grown old and cold and
     weary,
          Leave the sick hearts that honour
               could not move,
And half-men, and their dirty songs and
     dreary,
          And all the little emptiness of love!

Oh! we, who have known shame, we have
     found release there,
          Where there's no ill, no grief, but sleep
               has mending,
               Naught broken save this body,
                    lost but breath;
Nothing to shake the laughing heart's long
     peace there
          But only agony, and that has ending;
               And the worst friend and
                    enemy is but Death.

V. The Soldier

If I should die, think only this of me:
          That there's some corner of a foreign
               field
That is for ever England. There shall be
          In that rich earth a richer dust
               concealed;
A dust whom England bore, shaped, made
     aware,
          Gave, once, her flowers to love, her
               ways to roam,
A body of England's, breathing English air,
          Washed by the rivers, blest by suns of
               home.

And think, this heart, all evil shed away,
          A pulse in the eternal mind, no less
               Gives somewhere back the
                    thoughts by England given;
Her sights and sounds; dreams happy as
     her day;
          And laughter, learnt of friends; and
               gentleness,
               In hearts at peace, under an
                    English heaven.

Sidney Harold Baker, "Letter to his brother"

Baker was a frontline officer stationed in northern France who was killed in action in March 1918. In this November 1917 letter, he describes a night spent watching over a wounded fellow soldier.

I found myself trying to comfort a wretched wounded man till the stretcher-bearers should somehow scramble through the torn branches and cross the shell holes and get him back to the Aid Post. Poor fellow, I found him there by his cries; he had been calling, calling, calling, hour after hour, ever since a shell had knocked him out in the darkness, long before the dawn, and now it was night again. He had crept into a hole for shelter, alongside a ruined pill-box,[1] and was utterly helpless and numbed with cold. I could get no warmth into him at all, but a drink and a cigarette and yet another drink helped him a bit, till at last four stretcher-bearers stumbled and scrambled back with him. Poor chap, I doubt if he comes through....

'Tis a horrible business—enough to make a strong man weep. It seems to me just one long degradation; it is the enemy who has "willed it," and we have to go through with it.

QUESTIONS FOR ANALYSIS

1. Why does Brooke describe the war in such a poetic, even celebratory, tone?
2. Whom does Baker blame for the war, and why?
3. What do you think accounts for the dramatic differences between Brooke's poem and Baker's letter in their attitudes toward the war?

[1]**Pill-box:** bunker

Sources: Rupert Brooke, "Peace" and "The Soldier," in *New Numbers*, vol. t, no. 4 (Ryton, UK: 1914), pp. 165, 169; Sidney Harold Baker, letter, in *War Letters of Fallen Englishmen*, ed. Laurence Housman (New York: 1930), pp. 35–36.

For the most part, the rebellious soldiers had no desire to overthrow the French state or even to end the war. They wanted the war prosecuted in a more effective manner. Even so, French authorities held some 23,000 courts martial, which ended up condemning hundreds of mutineers to death, although only fifty or so were actually executed. But at least partly in reaction to the mutinies, in mid-May Nivelle was replaced by the more cautious Philippe Pétain (1856–1951), the general who had prevailed at Verdun and who had a reputation (even if, in World War I, these things were sadly relative) for keeping soldiers alive.

LOSS OF HOPE

Despite the strains, throughout 1917 the leaderships in the warring countries remained unable to break out of the gruesome pattern of combat in which the western front was still tragically locked. In July, General Haig launched another major offensive, in Belgium. The new campaign featured the first mass attacks by British tanks, which were slowly gaining in efficiency, and took place in such heavy mud that hundreds, perhaps thousands, of soldiers died by drowning far from the sea. But this latest offensive accomplished little more than earlier ones. Among the soldiers the mood turned ever more cynical, despairing, and numb. Already in January, an Indian soldier in British service had written to his family: "Now I write the truth. ... Consider us as having died today or tomorrow. There is absolutely no hope of our ever returning.... None will survive." In October, the British poet Wilfred Owen, who would die on the western front a year later, wrote his poem about comrades dying from poison gas, and concluded:

> If you could hear, at every jolt, the blood
> Come gargling from the froth-corrupted lungs,
> Obscene as cancer, bitter as the cud
> Of vile, incurable sores on innocent tongues, —
> My friend, you would not tell with such high zest
> To children ardent for some desperate glory,
> The old lie: *Dulce et decorum est*
> *Pro patria mori.*

The last two lines translate to "How sweet and fitting it is to die for one's country," as Latin poet Horace had written in the first century BCE, lines familiar to every educated European of the period. By late 1917, the experience of World War I had come close to scorching such traditional notions of patriotism and glory out of Western culture altogether.

THE BEGINNING OF THE RUSSIAN REVOLUTION

The first of the combatants to break, and in the most spectacular fashion, was Russia. Of all the major powers, it had suffered most from the war. Some of its wealthiest western provinces, with a population of over 65 million, spent much of the war under German occupation. Six million refugees from these provinces overwhelmed the state's severely limited resources. Of over 14 million soldiers mobilized, nearly a quarter were killed or disappeared—a far larger number than in any previous Russian war. Unable to pay for the war with taxes and loans, the tsarist government ended up printing money, which started an inflationary spiral. Between 1914 and 1916, real wages in Russia fell by a third, as did overall gross domestic product. The fierce winter of 1916–17 intensified the misery beyond anything even the Germans were experiencing. Worst of all, the antiquated and autocratic Russian state was far less capable of dealing with such strains than its counterparts to the west.

RUSSIA'S FEBRUARY REVOLUTION

By 1914, Tsar Nikolai had rolled back nearly all the liberal gains made during the Revolution of 1905. As a result, Russia had nothing like an independent parliament or civil service. Corruption was rampant, and the Romanov court continued its displays of luxury. Critics charged that Tsarina Alexandra increasingly dominated the weak-willed tsar. Both she and her husband had fallen under the spell of an erratic Russian Orthodox holy man named Grigori Rasputin (1869–1916). In December 1916, a group of nobles at court attacked Rasputin. After a massive dose of cyanide failed to kill him, they shot him, clubbed him, and then tied him into a carpet and threw him into the freezing Neva River. Still, he nearly escaped before finally drowning. By the end of 1916, public loyalty to the tsarist government was collapsing, especially among the urban working classes. The secret police, the Okhranka, was warning the government that a revolutionary situation was brewing.

Despite the government's calls for patriotic unity and sacrifice, waves of strikes and protests broke out. In early March 1917 (February by the Julian calendar then followed in Russia), they intensified, leading to a general strike in the capital, now called Petrograd rather than the German-sounding Saint Petersburg. The tsar ordered troops to disperse the protests by force, and demonstrators were killed, including women. The soldiers reacted with dismay; thousands of them switched sides and stormed arsenals to obtain weapons. Rebels in Petrograd and elsewhere created their own **soviets** (councils), prominently including workers as members. Moscow fell into the hands of insurgents, and within days the army leadership abandoned the hapless ruler. On March 15, 1917, a panicked Nikolai abdicated, and his brother, whom he had named to succeed him, refused the throne. The centuries-old Russian monarchy had, in a matter of days, come to an inglorious end.

Over the following months, the political situation in Russia turned even more chaotic. A **Provisional Government** appointed by the old parliament, the State Duma, took power but had to compete for authority with the increasingly influential soviets. Owing partly to continuing close ties between urban workers and the peasant communities where many still had relatives, most of the peasants who dominated the army rank-and-file increasingly saw the prominent Petrograd soviet as the country's legitimate government. Through the early spring of 1917, the eastern front remained calm, with the Germans happy to look on as Russia fell apart. They contributed to the disorder by bringing leaders of the Bolsheviks, the most radical Russian revolutionary faction, back to Russia from Swiss exile in a special train across German territory.

Finally, in June the Russian Provisional Government, now effectively led by the moderate Socialist Alexander Kerensky (1881–1970), attempted another offensive against Austria-Hungary, hoping to rally the people patriotically behind the government. The offensive, which failed disastrously, had the opposite effect. The Provisional Government now lost even more credit with the population. The writer Maxim Gorky wrote: "Everybody agrees that the Russian state is splitting apart like an old barge in a flood." In August, a right-wing coup failed, and expectations mounted that the Bolsheviks would try to seize power.

RUSSIA AND MARXISM

In the fall of 1917, the Russian revolutionary turmoil reached a dramatic climax that brought greater long-term consequences for Europe than anything since the French Revolution of 1789. A radical Marxist regime came to power, led by a political party possessing dictatorial authority, committed to common ownership of the means of production and to the abolition of all or most private property. It was the world's first successful communist revolution.

According to orthodox Marxist thinking, communism, as the most advanced stage of human society, should have properly come first to the most economically advanced industrial countries: Great Britain, Germany, and the United States. Russia, whose 100-million-strong peasantry vastly outnumbered its fledgling urban working class, and where political and social power still lay largely in the hands of an aristocratic, quasi-feudal elite, seemed an unsuitable candidate. Even during the Russian Revolution itself, many Russian socialists continued to argue that the time for direct action had not yet arrived.

And yet, as we have seen, these theories had not stopped a small but hardy socialist revolutionary movement from emerging in Russia in the late nineteenth century, led by disaffected intellectuals who seethed with hatred of the tsarist regime. Some of them were committed to revolutionary change in Russia as part of a world revolution. Many endorsed the idea that in a "backward" country like Russia, the liberal bourgeoisie would never succeed in bringing about a sufficient level of industrialization for a spontaneous proletarian revolution, so historical progress depended on the efforts of a revolutionary party.

LENIN AND THE BOLSHEVIKS

Vladimir Ilich Ulyanov (1870–1924)—better known by his revolutionary alias, **Lenin**—was the son of a school inspector in the central Russian town of Simbirsk and was fairly typical of the revolutionary intelligentsia. Trained as a lawyer, short, balding, bearded, and unkempt, he was given to long, intense pronouncements on the fine points of revolutionary social theory. The American journalist John Reed (1887–1920) memorably described him as "a leader purely by virtue of intellect: colorless, humorless, uncompromising and detached... but with the power of explaining profound ideas in simple terms." He had turned to revolutionary activity after his adored older brother died on the gallows for participating in an assassination attempt on Tsar Alexander III. But at age thirty, after release from internal exile in Siberia, Ulyanov left Russia for Switzerland and spent the next seventeen years living in a succession of shabby apartments, spied on by the Russian secret services, writing for and speaking to tiny audiences, wrapped up in factional quarrels that often seemed of little interest to anyone outside his small circle of like-minded zealots. But he was anything but a fool. He was hardheaded, ruthless, relentless, and shrewd.

In his years abroad, as leader of the Bolshevik faction of Russian socialists, Lenin developed the theory of

Vladimir Lenin A photo from October, 1917, captures Lenin addressing a crowd of Bolsheviks in Red Square, Moscow, marking the collapse of the Russian government and the rise of Soviet rule.

revolution centered on the role of a secretive, highly centralized, tightly organized party. He strove to shape the Bolsheviks into such a party, both in Russia and abroad. To raise funds, its members sometimes resorted to armed robbery. Slowly, it gained influence in the Russian trade unions. After 1914, Lenin attacked socialists who supported the Russian war effort and also those calling for peace. Instead, he demanded immediate violent revolution and the establishment of a communist state.

In April 1917, when the Germans delivered him back to Russia, Lenin again called for an immediate uprising of workers and peasants to place power in the hands of the soviets, which had already established themselves as an alternate foundation of authority. He demanded an end to Russia's involvement in the war and to the massive privations Russians had suffered since 1914. Petrograd workers welcomed the message, and the Bolsheviks capitalized on their increasing popularity in the city to recruit volunteers for a militia. In July, the Provisional Government cracked down on them, and Lenin fled to nearby Finland. But Kerensky, now prime minister, needed Bolshevik support to resist the attempted right-wing coup in August, and by early fall the party was recovering its strength. In the fall, Kerensky attempted to form a new, more left-wing coalition to outflank the Bolsheviks, but it was too late. The Bolsheviks were ready to seize power.

THE OCTOBER REVOLUTION

The **Bolshevik Revolution** (or October Revolution), for all the violence it ultimately caused, was itself surprisingly

rapid and relatively bloodless. Its success was owed above all to Lenin, who through sheer strength of argument persuaded doubtful Bolshevik colleagues that the time had come to act. In particular, he persuaded his brilliant and charismatic fellow party-member, Leon Trotsky (1879–1940)—as with Lenin, the surname was a revolutionary alias; he was born into a prosperous Ukrainian Jewish family named Bronstein. On October 24 and 25, 1917 (by the Julian calendar), the Bolsheviks seized key sites in Petrograd and surrounded the Provisional Government's headquarters in the tsar's Winter Palace. As the cruiser *Aurora* fired blank warning shots at the palace from the Neva River, the Bolsheviks prepared for a drawn-out conflict. But Kerensky had lost popular support, and his government collapsed without a struggle. By telegraph, the Bolsheviks sent word across Russia that power had passed to the soviets, which immediately cast an aura of legitimacy over what might otherwise have seemed a simple coup d'état. It seemed incredible to many that men with little experience of politics beyond revolutionary pamphleteering and conspiracy, and little popular support outside of Petrograd and Moscow, could assert control over the vast Russian Empire. But owing to the almost complete vacuum of power that had opened up following the tsar's abdication, and the failure of the Provisional Government and Kerensky to fill it, Lenin and his party had their chance.

Trotsky, in fact, cleverly timed the insurrection to take place on the eve of a national congress of soviets. Many of its moderate socialist deputies criticized the Bolsheviks for acting independently and walked out when it became

Bolshevik Revolution Bolshevik fighters take aim with rifles during the short-lived military confrontation at the Winter Palace in Petrograd in late October 1917.

clear the Bolsheviks had an effective majority. Trotsky, in one of his most famous lines, scornfully quipped that they had tossed themselves into the "dustbin of history." The Bolsheviks then brusquely sidestepped the soviets, announcing that control of the central government would not pass to the soviets' Central Committee, which had representatives from several parties, but to a new, all-Bolshevik Council of People's Commissars. Lenin himself was now the head of government, and Trotsky was responsible for foreign affairs. Russia was moving toward one-party rule.

During the winter of 1917–18, the Bolsheviks moved to establish a revolutionary communist dictatorship. They nationalized the banking system, suppressed hostile newspapers, banned the liberal Kadet Party, and unleashed a powerful new police apparatus known by its Russian acronym as the Cheka—the forerunner to the KGB. They allowed elections to take place for a Constituent Assembly that would in theory write a new constitution, but when they lost heavily to the more moderate Socialist Revolutionaries, they adjourned the new body after a single day. In February 1918, the government nationalized the great landed estates and church lands. Peasant support surged even as armed opposition crystallized, setting the stage for civil war.

A few weeks later, Soviet Russia agreed to the exceptionally harsh peace terms offered by Germany in the Treaty of Brest-Litovsk. Although Germany had facilitated Lenin's return to Russia in hopes of adding to the country's chaos, it had not controlled him or sponsored the Bolshevik coup. Germany reaped the benefit, however, because the Bolshevik leadership desperately wanted peace—in order to deliver on its promises to the Russian population and to concentrate fully on its domestic program. By the terms of Brest-Litovsk, the Russians gave up 1.3 million square miles of territory to Germany and to a new, German-dominated independent state of Ukraine. This territory included a quarter of Russia's population, a third of its grain fields, and a third of its heavy industry. The treaty also meant that for the first time in the war Germany did not have to fight on two fronts, but could concentrate all of its efforts against the western Allies.

THE WAR'S END

At the start of 1918, even with the Russian Revolution scrambling everyone's calculations, Europeans could be forgiven for thinking of the ongoing war as a nightmare that would never end. But finally in 1918 the stubborn balance of destruction that had prevailed since 1914 burst apart. The war did not end with the long-hoped-for breakthrough in the trenches. But it finally did end.

GERMANY'S SPRING OFFENSIVE

One key factor upsetting the balance was Russia's exit from the war. Not only did the armistice with the Bolsheviks allow the Germans to concentrate all their efforts in the west—it also provided them with crucial new resources to gamble everything on a final cataclysmic western offensive. Even before Germany and Soviet Russia signed the Treaty of Brest-Litovsk, the German army had marched far beyond the old eastern front lines and was busily shipping foodstuffs, manufactured goods, and even whole factories westward. At the same time, the German high command knew that with American soldiers steaming toward Europe, they had to act quickly. As General Ludendorff put it, they would either win or "go under."

In March 1918, the Germans launched a Spring Offensive along a forty-mile stretch of the western front extending south from the English Channel through Belgium and northern France. It was the most massive offensive of the entire war, involving some 1.6 million soldiers and 10,000 field guns. They began by firing an unprecedented 1 million shells in just five hours, many loaded with a mixture of explosives and poison gas (at the Somme in 1916, the British had taken almost a week to fire 1.5 million shells). The barrage was audible a hundred miles away in southern England. And after three years in which the Germans had mostly remained on the defensive, British forces in the sector were complacent and unprepared. They did not break altogether, but the offensive came closer than any other of the war to achieving true breakthrough.

In May, the Germans made another massive push, preceded by an even larger artillery barrage (2 million shells in less than five hours), and came within less than forty miles of Paris. But at this crucial moment, with Parisians fleeing south, the French government evacuating its offices, and the Allies contemplating defeat, two other factors came into play. First, the Germans reached the end of their resources, both materiel and human—they had taken half a million casualties in the offensive and simply had few fresh troops left. Second, the arrival of hundreds of thousands of soldiers from the United States gave critical support to the Allies. In June and July 1918, the Americans held their ground at the battles of Château-Thierry and

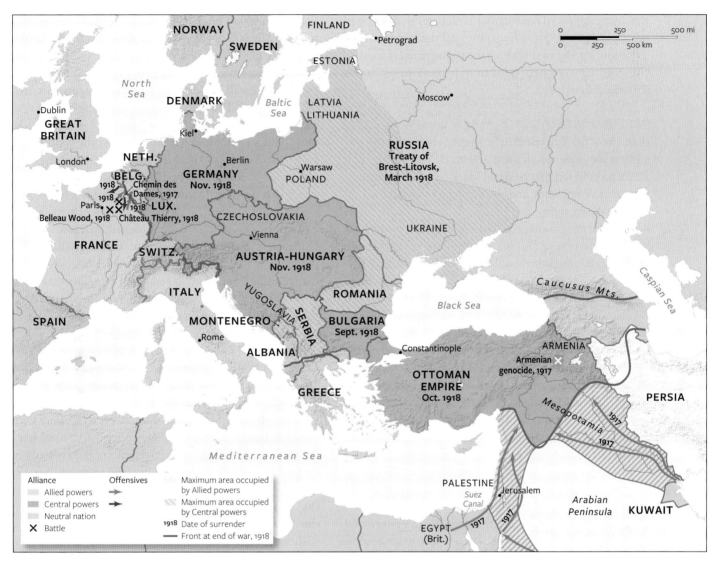

World War I, 1917–1918 Events in 1917–18 brought the war to a swift conclusion. The British invasion of the Arabian Peninsula meant that Allied powers surrounded the Ottoman Empire, while the Bolshevik Revolution led to Russia pulling out of the war, ceding large territories in eastern Europe to Germany. Finally, in 1918, American resistance to the German Spring Offensive broke the stalemate on the western front, leading to Germany's surrender.

Belleau Wood, and the great German push finally stalled. Ludendorff had lost his gamble.

THE COLLAPSE OF THE CENTRAL POWERS

In the summer and fall of 1918, the Central powers, bled white by four years of total war, fell to pieces. In July, the Allies opened a counteroffensive, pushing the Germans out of the territory they had gained in the spring. For the

first time, in a sign of wars to come, the Allies made effective use of tanks, manufactured primarily by automobile and tractor firms, which neither barbed wire nor machine guns could easily stop. Meanwhile, the Austrian armies were collapsing on the Italian front. In September, an exhausted Bulgaria sued for peace and was followed the next month by Turkey. Allied forces occupied Constantinople. Ludendorff, now the effective leader of the German armed forces, showed signs of incipient madness, sometimes falling to the floor in convulsions. In September, he declared that defeat was imminent. Soon afterward, the

Reichstag approved constitutional changes that stripped significant powers from the kaiser and the army, making Germany for the first time a true parliamentary monarchy. A new government tried to start peace negotiations with the Allies.

It was Wilson, more than any other individual, who shaped the end of the war and the subsequent peace settlement. He was both an idealist who believed that he could function as a peacemaker, not just as a combatant, and also a firm believer in American destiny who thought America should take the lead in determining the new world order. In keeping with both these ambitions, he outlined his goals for the post-war world more explicitly than any other wartime leader. In January 1918, he spoke to a joint session of the U.S. Congress and outlined the so-called **Fourteen Points** that he hoped would form the basis for a new European order. Among other things, he called for the creation of a League of Nations to settle international disputes. He also insisted on the redrawing of European borders according to the principle of national self-determination: individual nationalities, such as those within the Austro-Hungarian Empire, should have the right to decide what nation they should belong to. Only with the satisfying of legitimate national grievances, he claimed, could a lasting peace take hold.

Unfortunately, Wilson, who knew the western half of Europe far better than the eastern one, underestimated how difficult it would be in practice to respect this principle. What of the many areas, especially in eastern and southeastern Europe, whose demographic maps resembled a crazy quilt of different ethnic groups? And how narrowly should "national groups" be defined? Did the Croats constitute a nation of their own, or a branch of a larger Yugoslav one? Could Ukraine, the ancient heartland of the Russian monarchy, split off from Russia? None of these questions had obvious or uncontroversial answers.

RUSSIA, AUSTRIA-HUNGARY, AND THE THREAT OF NATIONALISM Wilson's defense of national self-determination only encouraged national groups to push for independence from the great multi-ethnic empires; and as the war sputtered to an end, nationalist groups took matters into their own hands. In the winter of 1917–18, Ukraine, Lithuania, and Estonia all proclaimed independence from Russia, with Latvia soon to follow. In 1917, Croat and Slovene nationalists in Austria-Hungary had announced their intention to fulfill Serbia's pre-war dreams and merge into a larger state of Yugoslavia. Czechs and Slovaks pushed for their own joint independence.

Poles in Austria-Hungary, Russia, and Germany prepared to revive the independent Poland that had vanished at the end of the eighteenth century.

The Austrian emperor Karl I (r. 1916–1918) desperately tried to forestall the dissolution of his empire, promising to give his Polish territories independence and to reconstitute the rest as a loose federation of peoples. In mid-October 1918, he sued for peace on the basis of the Fourteen Points. But the Allies had already endorsed the idea of full Czechoslovak and Yugoslav independence, and the new states now formally declared their sovereignty. On October 31, the Hungarian government tried to follow suit by dissolving the dual monarchy. However, the Hungarians' success in gaining equal status in the empire in 1867 now told against them, for the Allies considered them enemies and made it clear that Hungary could not hope to preserve its pre-war borders. On November 3, Austria-Hungary laid down its weapons.

GERMANY: REVOLUTION AND SURRENDER The war's last act played out in the country that had done the most to bring it about: Germany. After having accepted the inevitability of defeat in September, General Ludendorff suddenly changed his mind and, along with some civilian politicians, called explicitly for "total war." But the Germans had reached the limits of their resources. Desertion from the army had become rampant. Strikes spread throughout the country. In defiance of the army, the new government tried to open negotiations with the Allies on the basis of what Wilson had called "peace without victory"; but France and Britain, after so much sacrifice, refused to contemplate anything but a decisive victory.

On October 28, the German navy ordered its ships to sea for a final, suicidal battle against the British. In response, sailors in the northern port city of Kiel mutinied and prevented the departure. When the authorities imprisoned the ringleaders, a wider rebellion began, with workers' unions and the Social Democratic Party joining the struggle. The commander of the Baltic Fleet—none other than the kaiser's brother—snuck out of Kiel in disguise. Within days, the rebellion became a revolution. Troops in Berlin mutinied, and parliamentary liberals and socialists joined to proclaim a republic and sue for peace. Kaiser Wilhelm, informed that he had "abdicated," fled across the border to the Netherlands.

At 5:00 a.m. on November 11, 1918, the German commanders signed an armistice with the Allies in a railway car in eastern France. It went into effect six hours later. Not a long space of time, and yet, during those six hours, a further 8,000 soldiers were wounded and 2,738 killed. It was a cruel and pointless end to a war that had long lost its point for all but its most fervent participants.

THE RUSSIAN CIVIL WAR

Even as hostilities elsewhere in Europe sputtered to their dispiriting end, civil war raged as fiercely as ever in Russia. In 1918, several White armies emerged to oppose the "red" Bolsheviks, and in response Trotsky organized a new Red Army, partly commanded by former tsarist officers. The resulting conflict saw atrocities, terror, and mass murder on both sides. In the summer of 1918, after holding Niko-lai II and his family prisoners, the Bolsheviks murdered them, probably on Lenin's orders, to prevent them from becoming a White rallying point. The Russian Civil War of 1918–1921 pushed the Bolsheviks toward the more radical position known as **war communism**, which involved nationalization of all heavy industry and the development of a centrally planned, largely money-free economy.

In addition to the Whites, the Reds had to fight against independence movements in Ukraine and the Caucasus, and against the newly independent state of Poland, which sought to exploit the chaos in Russia to expand its own territory. The Red Army managed to drive the Poles back to the outskirts of Warsaw but ultimately made peace when their final offensive failed. Meanwhile, the Allied powers sent supplies and small, largely ineffective armed contingents of their own to aid the Whites, in hopes of containing what they considered to be the communist threat to Western democracy and capitalism. Americans landed in Russia's far north, and also the far east, near Vladivostok. The presence of these foreign contingents made it easier for Lenin and the Communists to portray themselves as patriots fighting against hostile outsiders.

THE HOPE AND PROMISE OF COMMUNISM

Despite this violence, revolutionary Russia, like revolutionary France before it, was also producing extraordinary outbursts of utopian hope. The Bolsheviks did not just promise a more equitable society; they promised a transformation in human relations. Women would be liberated not just from domestic drudgery and political repression but from the confines of traditional gender roles. The Communist Party (as the Bolsheviks formally became known in 1918) supported legal divorce and legal abortion, and some leaders hinted that marriage itself could be abolished. The party also supported the vote for women, although suffrage would become mostly symbolic

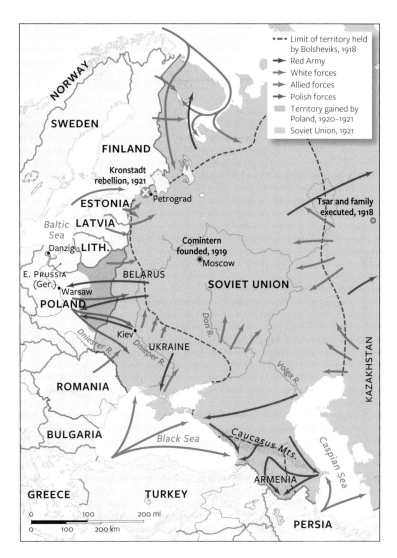

The Russian Civil War, 1918–1921 Fighting occurred at all the borders of the territory that the Bolsheviks controlled from Moscow. The Red Army fought White forces in the east and west and pushed back British, Japanese, and American forces in the north and south. It also engaged an independent Polish invasion, ultimately ceding territory to Poland. By 1921, though, the Red Army had established stable borders for an expansive USSR.

under the party dictatorship. The new regime would not only break the political power of the Russian Orthodox Church; it would also free men and women from their addiction to religion, which Karl Marx had famously called "the opium of the people."

Bolshevik agents in the countryside mocked Jesus and publicly dared God to strike them dead. Avant-garde, non-representational art received official support and flourished more strongly than elsewhere in Europe. And in a utopian tract entitled *The ABC of Communism* (1919), two Bolshevik leaders promised that once the dictatorship of

PEASANT CRITICISM OF THE BOLSHEVIKS

The Bolsheviks launched their revolution in the name of the Russian people, but the Russian people were not always enthusiastic about the Bolshevik leaders or the course of the Revolution. Hundreds of ordinary Russians wrote letters to the Bolshevik government criticizing its land policies, political program, and suppression of competing revolutionary groups, and addressing other topics that touched the lives of ordinary Russians.

While many of these letters sought to draw attention to specific injustices, others denounced the entire Revolution as a threat to Russian society and its values. The following 1918 letter, from a Russian peasant, attacks the Bolshevik leaders in indignant and colorful terms, accusing them of betraying Russia and overseeing myriad crimes against its people.

TO YOU!

Rulers, plunderers, rapists, destroyers, usurpers, oppressors of Mother Russia, citizens Lenin, Trotsky…and Co.

Allow me to ask you how long you are going to go on degrading Russia's millions, its tormented and exhausted people. Instead of peace, you signed an armistice with the enemy, and this gave our opponent a painful advantage, and you declared war on Russia. You moved the troops you had tricked to the Russian-Russian front and started a fratricidal war. Your mercenary Red Guards[1] are looting, murdering, and raping everywhere they go. A fire has consumed all our dear Mother Russia. Rail transport is idle, as are the plants and factories; the entire population has woken up to find itself in the most pathetic situation, without bread or kerosene or any of the other essentials, unclothed and unshod in unheated houses. In short: hungry and cold…. You have strangled the entire press, and freedom with it, you have wiped out the best freedom fighters, you have destroyed all Russia. Think it over, you butchers, you hirelings of the Kaiser. Isn't your turn about up, too? For all you are doing, we, politically aware Great Russians, are sending you butchers, you hirelings of the Kaiser, our curse. May you be damned, you accursed one, you bloodthirsty butchers, you hirelings of the Kaiser—don't think you're in the clear, because the Russian people will sober up and that will be the end of you. I'm writing in red ink to show that you are bloodthirsty…. I'm writing these curses, a Great Russian native of Orel Province.[2]

QUESTIONS FOR ANALYSIS

1. What crimes and abuses does the peasant accuse the Bolsheviks of perpetrating?
2. What does the letter writer mean when he calls the revolutionary leaders "hirelings of the Kaiser"?
3. What does this letter suggest about the political engagement of Russian peasants during the Russian Revolution?

[1] **Red Guards:** volunteer groups of armed workers
[2] **Orel Province:** province south of Moscow in western Russia

"Letter from a Peasant to the Bolshevik Leaders (1918)," in *Voices of Revolution, 1917*, ed. Mark D. Steinberg, trans. Marian Schwartz (New Haven: Yale University Press, 2001), pp. 302–303.

the proletariat had completed its work, the state would wither away, just as Marx had promised: "There will be no need for special ministers of State, for police or prisons, for laws and decrees—nothing of the sort. Just as in an orchestra all the performers watch the conductor's baton and act accordingly, so here all will consult the statistical reports and will direct their work accordingly."

These hopes extended well beyond the borders of Russia. Across the world, many socialists cheered the Bolsheviks' seizure of power and formed Communist Parties explicitly aligned with them. In 1919, the Soviet Union formally gathered these parties into a Communist International, or **Comintern**, on the model of the older Workers' Internationals, but largely under soviet control. European leaders waited nervously to see if the "plague bacillus" of communist revolution, as Churchill called it, would spread to their own countries. But it did not, thanks in part to effective resistance from national

Women and Communism A 1920 Russian propaganda poster shows the sun shining on a triumphant woman worker, who gestures to other women streaming into social or cultural institutions such as a day care center, library, and a social club. Celebrating the Revolution's gains for women, the caption reads: "What the October Revolution gave to the woman worker and the woman peasant."

armies and right-wing paramilitary forces. Proclamation of a Soviet Republic in Berlin, in November 1918, by German Communist Party co-founder Karl Liebknecht (1871–1919), went nowhere, and Liebknecht and his charismatic colleague Rosa Luxemburg (1871–1919) were later assassinated by right-wing militants. In Bavaria, socialists actually did establish a short-lived Soviet Republic, but it was suppressed by German soldiers aided by right-wing paramilitary groups. A Hungarian Soviet Republic, which nationalized all private property in the country, lasted for several months in 1919 under the leadership of the communist Béla Kun (1886–1938). But it quickly found itself at war with Czechoslovakia and Romania, which had strong backing from the Allies, and within months Kun, too, had been overthrown.

BIRTH OF THE USSR In 1919–21, Russia lurched through one of the most devastating phases of its history. Partly owing to the disruptions of the Civil War, a massive famine struck, killing as many as 7 million people. Reports circulated of cannibalism. Yet eventually, the Bolsheviks and the Red Army, which Trotsky, despite his lack of military experience, had forged into an effective fighting force, managed to eke out a victory and restore order. The Whites, suffering from disunity and poor communications, could only mobilize 300,000 men, counting the small western expeditionary forces. The Reds mobilized 800,000 and benefited from controlling the traditional power centers of the rigidly centralized Russian state: Petrograd and Moscow. They could also count on support from urban workers and a large portion of the peasantry.

The end of the Civil War in 1921 left little doubt about the sort of regime that would now rule the Union of Soviet Socialist Republics (USSR), as the former Russian Empire became known. In theory, a new federal structure gave considerable autonomy to the most important ethnic groups, such as Ukrainians, Belorussians, and Kazakhs, each now gathered into a separate Soviet Republic of their own. In practice, however, local authorities remained subordinate to the party bosses in Moscow.

Lenin proved willing to compromise, temporarily, on economic issues. To deal with the effects of the famine and wartime disruption, he proclaimed the New Economic

Rosa Luxemburg Co-founder of the German Communist Party, Luxemburg is photographed here at a meeting of the Second International Social Democratic Congress in 1907. The highly educated Luxemburg argued for a party committed to revolution—though she later criticized Lenin's power-centralizing approach in the wake of the Bolshevik Revolution.

Kronstadt Mutiny Sailors salute the commander of the rebels who took control of a battleship during the 1921 mutiny of sailors at the Kronstadt naval base.

Policy, which retreated from the severe measures of war communism by allowing limited free trade in food and services, although it left the central state firmly in control of the economy's "commanding heights." But the Bolsheviks would not compromise on the issue of their own political power. They refused to allow free elections, a free press, or free trade unions. The Cheka quickly evolved into a much-feared secret police. And in March 1921, the regime demonstrated it would not even brook opposition from its most legendary supporters. After strikes broke out in Petrograd, sailors at the Kronstadt naval base near Petrograd, who had provided key support for the Bolsheviks in 1917, mutinied in support of the strikers. They demanded that Bolshevik commissars cede power and allow the creation of a truly popular soviet republic, controlled by peasants and workers. Trotsky sent Red Army and Cheka units to slaughter them. A wave of disillusionment spread across Russia and among its supporters in the West. But Lenin remained securely in power.

THE VERSAILLES PEACE SETTLEMENT

At the other end of Europe, the victorious western Allies were trying to resolve a host of questions that the war had left dangerously unsettled. How would Wilson's principle of national self-determination be put into practice? What would happen to the Central powers' colonial possessions? What about questions of responsibility for the war? Would some sort of international body come into being to prevent further outbreaks of war? To settle these questions, representatives from thirty-one countries gathered for six months in 1919 in the vast palace complex of Versailles outside of Paris. The meeting fell squarely into the tradition of peace conferences that stretched back to the 1648 Peace of Westphalia. It was by far the largest and most ambitious of these conferences. And it was also, by most measures, the least successful.

President Wilson, who attended, hoped that the **Versailles Peace Conference** would inaugurate an era of peaceful international cooperation, overseen by a new **League of Nations**. The League indeed came into being in 1919–20. But the American's idealism collided with the desire of France and Britain to exact revenge on the Germans. Both countries were just beginning to come to terms with their appalling losses in the war. France had buried nearly 1.4 million of its young men, and fewer than a quarter of the nearly 8 million it mobilized had come home unscathed. Britain had lost nearly a million men, and the grief touched every part of its vast empire and dominions. In both countries, social elites accounted for a disproportionate number of the dead. The two countries' prime ministers, the canny republican centrist Georges Clemenceau (1841–1929) and the Welsh Liberal David Lloyd George (1863–1945), came to Versailles convinced of the Germans' guilt for the war. They insisted that Germany accept full responsibility and pay mammoth reparations—equivalent to hundreds of billions of dollars today—while reducing its army to a token force of 100,000.

Guided in theory by the principle of self-determination, the participants at Versailles signed a series of treaties that radically redrew the map of Europe. The Austro-Hungarian Empire vanished, with Austria and Hungary reduced to small, ethnically homogenous republics. Its remaining territory was parceled out to the new states of Yugoslavia (initially called the Kingdom of Serbs, Croats, and Slovenes) and Czechoslovakia, to an expanded Romania, to Italy, and to the newly independent Poland. The four centuries in which Habsburgs had helped shape the fortunes of a continent had come to an abrupt end. Meanwhile, Germany lost significant territory to Poland, returned Alsace-Lorraine to France, and accepted the demilitarization of the German Rhineland. Although the situation within the former Russian Empire remained enormously unstable, the independence of Finland and the

Europe, the Middle East, and Africa after World War I, 1922 At the Versailles Peace Conference, Allied leaders divided up the territory of the defeated powers. Germany had to return Alsace-Lorraine to France, with the Rhineland established as a demilitarized zone; Poland regained its independence; other parts of eastern Europe and the Austro-Hungarian Empire were divided into independent states. The newly founded League of Nations designated former German colonies in Africa and parts of the Ottoman Empire as mandates to be administered by Britain, France, and other Allied powers.

three Baltic states was recognized. Turkey was reduced to the ethnically Turkish areas of Europe and Anatolia. The Young Turks now formally abolished the sultanate and proclaimed a republic. The Ottoman Empire was no more.

THE SEEDS OF FUTURE CONFLICT Yet at Versailles and a number of sucessor conferences, the Allies applied the principle of self-determination very unevenly. In some areas, they staged plebiscites (referenda) to determine the new borders. But they assigned

the mountainous Sudetenland region of western Bohemia to the new Czechoslovak state, despite its heavily German population, and stranded large Hungarian populations within Romania and Yugoslavia. Large Greek and Turkish minorities remained within each other's countries. And the principle completely failed to apply to non-Europeans. The former German overseas colonies such as Southwest Africa (now Namibia) and Tanganyika (now Tanzania), and most of Turkey's Middle Eastern possessions (Lebanon, Syria, Palestine, Iraq), were given the status of "mandates" theoretically subject to the League of Nations. But their administration fell principally to Britain and France, which treated them largely as additions to their own colonial empires. Calls by national movements within those empires for representation at Versailles were ignored.

Even as the representatives returned home from Versailles, it was clear that the conference had done more to provoke future conflicts than to prevent them. In the early 1920s, Greece and Turkey carried out a massive, bloody population exchange to "resolve" the issue of their reciprocal minorities. Greeks were expelled from the new Turkish Republic, and Turks from Greece. Traditionally Greek cities in Asia Minor were transformed into almost entirely Turkish ones: Smyrna, for instance, became the Turkish Izmir. Along the new borders and existing ethnic divides, violence and political instability remained endemic. And the new League of Nations, while hardly toothless, proved tragically inadequate to the task of managing the peace, especially after an isolationist U.S. Senate rebuffed a broken-hearted and incapacitated President Wilson and rejected American membership. Worst of all, in Germany the same conservative, militarist forces that had done the most to bring the war about now blamed the new, left-leaning German Republic for the humiliating peace terms, even alleging that Germany had not been defeated but "stabbed in the back" by disloyal socialists, liberals, and Jews. (The point seemed superficially plausible, since Germany surrendered without having had its own territory invaded.) Already in 1919, the raucous German political sphere was filled with strident calls for revenge.

An exhausted continent suffered one additional body blow. In 1918–19, as soldiers returned home in crowded, unsanitary railroad cars and refugees streamed across newly erected borders, they carried with them deadly invisible passengers: a new and virulent flu virus. Within months, the so-called Spanish flu had killed 21 million Europeans and 40 million people world-wide, deepening the oceans of grief left by the war. It was a tragic end to what had been, arguably, the most tragic decade yet seen in European history.

CONCLUSION

Overall, a war fought in the name of civilization had produced unprecedented barbarism. The hopes for quick victory, and the claim that war would have a cleansing effect like swimmers leaping into pure water, died choking and screaming in the muck of the trenches. So did ancient ideals of military glory and honor. All the contending powers had discovered, to their horror and grief, what total war looked like when driven by the full force of modern industry. Since World War I, and in direct reaction to its horrors, the West has had a fundamentally different attitude toward war from what often prevailed before. While accepted as a grim necessity, it is no longer something to be glorified for its own sake. Since World War I, nearly all serious war literature has been antiwar literature.

A war fought to make the world "safe for democracy," in Woodrow Wilson's words, had left democracy somewhat more widespread than in 1914, but also deeply imperiled. Everywhere in the new regimes of central Europe, fragile democratic constitutions swayed under the attacks of angry nationalist and ideological militants. In Russia, the greatest European revolution since the eighteenth century had produced, after ghastly civil war, an increasingly repressive ideological dictatorship. And in one other country, soon after the war, democracy failed as well. In the fall of 1922, after a period of extended political and social turmoil, the Italian parliament granted its new prime minister the power to rule by decree for a year. His name was Benito Mussolini, the head of a party that had not only an expanding membership but also a dangerous paramilitary force: the Fascists. Many in Europe saw him as a role model. The stage was set for a battle of ideological extremes.

KEY TERMS

Schlieffen Plan (p. 707)
Young Turks (p. 708)
trench warfare (p. 714)
total war (p. 715)
Gallipoli Campaign (p. 718)

Lusitania (p. 719)
battle of Verdun (p. 721)
battle of the Somme (p. 723)
Armenian genocide (p. 725)

soviets (p. 728)
Provisional Government (p. 728)
Lenin (p. 728)
Bolshevik Revolution (p. 729)

Fourteen Points (p. 732)
war communism (p. 733)
Comintern (p. 734)
Versailles Peace Conference (p. 736)
League of Nations (p. 736)

REVIEW QUESTIONS

1. By the early 1900s, why was there an increased likelihood of war in Europe?

2. Why did the assassination of Franz Ferdinand spark World War I?

3. What factors contributed to the bloody stalemate that persisted on the western front?

4. In what ways did civilians become involved in the war effort?

5. How did governments mobilize their societies and economies for total war?

6. How did the war expand into a global conflict?

7. In what ways did new technologies change the conduct of war?

8. Following the collapse of the tsarist government in Russia, what led to the October Revolution in Russia?

9. How did the Bolsheviks change Russian government and society?

10. How did the peace settlements established at the Versailles Peace Conference reshape Europe and set in motion future conflicts?

CORE OBJECTIVES

After reading this chapter, you should have a solid understanding of the following core objectives. To strengthen your grasp of the core objectives, use the resources on the Student Site for The West.

- Identify the factors and events that led to the outbreak of World War I.

- Outline how and why the war developed into a horrific stalemate.

- Analyze the war's impact on the home front and on overseas colonies.

- Describe the major events of the late period of the war.

- Explain the causes and main events of the Russian Revolution of 1917.

- Evaluate the aftermath of the war around the world.

 GO TO INQUIZITIVE TO SEE WHAT YOU'VE LEARNED—AND LEARN WHAT YOU'VE MISSED—WITH PERSONALIZED FEEDBACK ALONG THE WAY.

CHRONOLOGY

1919–1933
Bauhaus School
active in Germany

1919
Weimar Republic
established

1922–1925
Benito Mussolini
consolidates
power in Italy

November 9, 1923
Munich Beer Hall Putsch

1925–1926
Hitler publishes
Mein Kampf

1928–1932
First Five-Year
Plan in Russia

1932
Iraq gains
independence
from Britain

February 1933
Reichstag fire

1923
Inflation skyrockets
in Germany

1924
Lenin dies

1927
Stalin consolidates power
in the Soviet Union

October 24, 1929
Wall Street crashes;
Great Depression begins

1933
Hitler appointed
chancellor of Germany

Ideologies

THE TRIUMPH OF POLITICAL EXTREMES

1922–1940

1936–1939
Spanish Civil War

1936–1938
Great Terror in Soviet Union

Sept. 1, 1939
Germany invades Poland

1936
Nazi Germany and Fascist Italy sign alliance

Aug. 23, 1939
Nazi-Soviet non-aggression pact

1935
Nazi regime passes Nuremberg Laws

Nov. 9, 1938
Kristallnacht

1935
Italy invades Ethiopia

1938–1939
Germany gains control of Czechoslovakia

March 1938
Germany annexes Austria

In the late afternoon of May 18, 1933, four large barges anchored on the shores of the island of Nazino, in the Ob River in Siberia, some 1,500 miles east of Moscow. The island was desolate and uninhabited—a flat, wet expanse of swamp grass and poplar trees. A light snow was falling as the barges unloaded their cargo: some 5,000 human beings. A local official described them as "these injured and ill people, these poor wretches with deathly pale faces, most of them in rags, a few dressed in city clothes, with shoes and a coat, but all of them without even a bag. All these people got off the boat—if they could still stand up—with nothing, without any provisions at all, empty-handed." It had taken the barges four days to reach Nazino from the Siberian city of Tomsk, during which time the passengers had received little or nothing to eat. The barges also carried twenty tons of flour, most of which was dumped into wet sandbags on the riverbank.

Over the next several days, official reports described scenes of chaos as the men and women abandoned on the shore tried to make fires and primitive shelters, and fought for flour that they lacked the means to bake into bread. Those who ate raw flour mixed with river water developed dysentery. Hundreds died of hunger, exposure, or violence. Hundreds more drowned attempting to cross the frigid, swiftly flowing river in primitive

Political Upheaval The Surrealist artist Max Ernst (1891–1976) painted his *Fireside Angel* in 1937. The grotesque image is a protest against the successes of Fascist forces against leftist Republicans in the Spanish Civil War. The creature's hideousness and its rampage over the landscape are suggestive of the rise of totalitarian regimes and the threat of war that haunted Europe in the 1930s.

rafts, or were shot by guards. And the survivors resorted to the most desperate possible measures. One official wrote: "They told us that people had begun eating the dead bodies, that they were cooking human flesh." On May 27, more barges brought thousands more helpless men and women to the island. They suffered the same fate as their predecessors. Within two months, two-thirds of those delivered to Nazino—what historians have since dubbed Cannibal Island—in late May had died.

Who were these people? Most had been rounded up off the streets of Moscow and Leningrad (the former Saint Petersburg) because they lacked proper documentation, or were suspected of counterrevolutionary activity, or belonged to the class of kulaks (rich peasants) that the Soviet government was bent on eradicating. Soviet officials had no intention of actually killing these people and the others who died on Nazino. They were part of a planned deportation of nearly 500,000 "socially undesirable elements" whom the Soviet regime expelled from its cities in 1933.

But a high proportion of these 500,000 did die. They, in turn, represent only a small proportion of the total victims of the government of Joseph Stalin, who came to power in the 1920s and ruled until his death in 1953. The best estimates of the total number range as high as 10 to 15 million Soviet citizens.

In 1918, the victorious Allies of World War I had hoped that their success would bring a better world into being. Instead, for too many Europeans the 1920s and 1930s became an age of ideological dictatorship, totalitarianism, terror, and mass murder, of which the horrors on Nazino were just one extreme example. In the two largest European states, the Soviet Union and Germany, there came to power two of the most repressive regimes in the history of the world. Dictatorships spread across more than half of all European states, and in many of the rest, democracy seemed on the verge of extinction. It was an age of intrusive surveillance of civilian populations, of arrests and executions of innocent victims, of vast archipelagos of prison camps, and, ultimately, of genocide. And it led directly into the most murderous and horrific conflict in human history: World War II, which began in 1939.

Today, in the West, we tend to associate the word *totalitarianism* with the idea of a ruthlessly efficient government that controls every aspect of its citizens' lives. Yet as the Nazino example suggests, the reality of the USSR in these years was considerably more chaotic and disorganized, a bizarre mixture of frightening power and shocking weakness. The Soviet officials who brought the deportees to the island were cogs in a fatally dysfunctional system that could not handle the massive strains put upon it, and they feared disobeying orders lest they, too, become victims. Yet, as we will see, neither Stalin's regime, nor Adolf Hitler's in Germany, can be reduced to repression, brutality, and fear alone. Both regimes enjoyed, for a long time, the support of millions of people who participated willingly in what they considered to be experiments to create a new, superior sort of human society. The Soviet system remained dedicated, in theory, to socialist ideals that continued to inspire millions around the globe.

The story of Europe in the 1920s and 1930s is not just a story of ideological extremism. It is also a story of remarkable artistic energies in the heyday of modernism. It is a story of continued economic and technological development, even amid the worst economic slump of modern times. It is a story of western European countries struggling to retain their overseas empires in the face of a floodtide of nationalism that they themselves helped to inspire. And it is a story of the western democracies bending, almost breaking, but eventually being forced to confront the worst of the dictators, Adolf Hitler.

A BLIGHTED RECOVERY

The men and women who, in 1914, believed that war would have a cleansing, regenerative effect on European society were proven wrong, not merely by the war itself but by its chaotic aftermath. Recovery from the bloodletting and destruction of 1914–18 would be a difficult, painful process.

CONTINUING VIOLENCE AND INSTABILITY

Indeed, the end of the war did not even bring relief from mass violence. Hundreds of thousands—possibly millions—died in the aftermath of the Armenian genocide, the Russian Civil War and accompanying famine, and border conflicts between Poland and Russia. Hundreds of thousands more lost their lives in the expulsions of populations in Greece and Turkey; the suppression of the communist revolutions in Hungary and Germany; and the more small-scale violence that accompanied Mussolini's Fascist takeover in Italy.

The British Isles as well experienced a small civil war after a majority of Irish voters chose the pro-independence Sinn Féin Party in the 1918 general election, following the failed Easter Uprising of 1916. After a year and a half of sporadic fighting, the British recognized the southern, Catholic-majority provinces of the island as an independent Irish Free State. In northern Africa, Spain suffered a humiliating defeat by Moroccan Berber insurgents in the so-called Rif War, with half its army of 20,000 killed or wounded in a single battle in the summer of 1921. The defeat led to a military coup in Spain two years later.

Although less destructive than the massive battlefield clashes of the world war, these outbreaks were dangerously destabilizing. The battles between the Irish Republican Army and Protestant forces, the orchestrated street thuggery of Mussolini's Fascists, and the fighting in the former Russian Empire brought violence directly into the heart of European cities. They made a return to anything Europeans saw as normal life almost impossible, while creating a yearning in many places for strong executive power that could enforce civil peace—even at the cost of human rights. While most European countries—including the newly independent states of central and eastern Europe—began the 1920s as nominal democracies, in relatively few states did democratic practice have a firm anchor.

POST-WAR GERMANY AND THE ORIGINS OF NAZISM

This pattern held true particularly in the country whose stability mattered most to post-Versailles Europe:

Germany. In 1919, a convention in the town of Weimar produced a constitution for the Republic proclaimed the previous November. It gave the vote to all adult men and women, and it included provisions for a powerful elected president who had the ability to dissolve the Reichstag (parliament) and, in certain situations, rule by decree.

But despite the attempts to ground the new regime in popular sovereignty, many Germans considered it illegitimate. They associated the **Weimar Republic** with the malevolent conspirators—above all, socialists and Jews—who had supposedly stabbed the country in the back, precipitating the defeat and the 1918 revolution. German military leaders resisted the demilitarization demanded by the Versailles treaty, and supported the formation of paramilitary Freikorps ("free corps"). In Berlin and other major cities, these right-wing groups fought street battles with police and with Communists and Socialists throughout the early 1920s. And in early 1920, they supported army and navy officers who attempted an unsuccessful coup d'état in Berlin.

Among the radical groups that proliferated in Germany at this time was the tiny, Munich-based German Workers' Party. Its members were racist, nationalist, and generally hostile to capitalism, and some had occult beliefs related to traditional Nordic mythology. In September 1919, the German army sent a low-ranking soldier to observe and report on the party. The man duly showed up for a meeting at a beer hall and promptly fell into an argument with one of the members. Impressed with the soldier's debating skills, the party leader invited him to join, and he accepted, becoming member number 55. His name was **Adolf Hitler**.

At this point in his life, Hitler struck many people as a crank. Born in 1889 in the small Austrian town of Braunau-am-Inn, the son of a minor customs official, he was a poor and rebellious student who left school at age sixteen. Dreaming of a career as an artist, he applied to the Academy of Fine Arts in Vienna, but it rejected him. He spent most of the next nine years in the Austrian capital, making a poor living painting postcards and hanging wallpaper, living mostly in flophouses, and absorbing the venomous anti-Semitism that permeated so much of Viennese life at the time. Pale-skinned, with lank dark hair and poor teeth, badly dressed and given to obsessive ranting, he cut a strange, unimpressive figure. He found salvation of a sort in the war. Joining the German army in the summer of 1914, he beat considerable odds by surviving more than four years at the front.

In the German Workers' Party, Hitler found his true calling. To all who would listen, he expounded a political

Hyperinflation A banknote for 100 trillion ("billion" in German) marks, issued by Germany's national bank in February 1924, indicates the extent of inflation during the economic crisis of the early 1920s.

theory hammered together out of spare boards of socialism, tales of worldwide Jewish conspiracy, and an extreme racial nationalism. He also spoke with a mesmerizing intensity and conviction that led others to follow him. Soon he had risen to head the party, which he renamed the National Socialist German Workers' Party, nicknamed the **Nazis** (from the first two syllables of the German word for *national*). Under his leadership, membership quickly increased. By the fall of 1923, it had reached nearly 20,000 and acquired a paramilitary arm known as the brown shirts in echo of Italy's black shirts, the followers of the Fascist leader Mussolini. With a genius for effective symbolism, Hitler had also chosen a striking visual emblem for the party: the ancient Indian twisted cross known as the swastika.

WEIMAR IN CRISIS

Conditions in Germany seemed almost perfect for the rise of just such a fanatical, antidemocratic party. Resentment against the Weimar government for accepting Allied demands remained high. In particular, the massive reparations imposed on Germany at Versailles threatened to smother the economy before a recovery from the war could even start. To put some pressure back on the Allies, Foreign Minister Walter Rathenau negotiated a treaty of military and economic cooperation with the Soviet Union in 1922, the Rapallo Treaty. But the Allies remained rigid in their demands, and when an inflation-plagued Germany failed to meet its payment schedule in late 1922, the Belgian and French armies moved in to occupy the rich industrial territory of the Ruhr, enraging German public opinion. It was a climate in which political violence continued to fester—the Jewish Rathenau himself was shot

and killed by anti-Semitic assassins in 1922. The German government printed money to finance a strike of Ruhr miners against the occupation forces, thereby feeding a catastrophic inflationary spiral and economic collapse.

The great German inflation of 1923 was not the first incident of post-war hyperinflation: that honor belonged to Austria and Hungary, which had inherited the crushing war debt of the entire Austro-Hungarian Empire. But the German inflation remains emblematic of the phenomenon. The reichsmark, which had traded at a little over 4 to the dollar in 1914, and 400 to the dollar in the early summer of 1922, fell to a rate of some 4 trillion to the dollar by November 1923. On November 15, a 100-billion-mark bill bought just one loaf of bread. The national and local governments alike frantically issued new banknotes by the day or reprinted new values on old ones. Hapless shoppers carried their money to the shop in large baskets, returning home with their purchases in their purses and wallets. The inflation wiped out both savings and debt, and impoverished anyone living on a fixed income. Germany's economy had effectively collapsed.

At precisely this moment, the Nazi Party attempted to seize power. Hitler had managed to enlist the support of General Erich von Ludendorff, who had served under the aged Paul von Hindenburg as effective commander of German forces at the end of the war. On November 9, 1923, the Nazis assembled in a Munich beer hall with plans to seize the government of Bavaria and then march on Berlin. However, local police and military units remained loyal to the Republic and quickly squelched the so-called **Beer Hall Putsch**. Hitler and Ludendorff were put on trial, and Hitler received a five-year sentence, of which he served less

Beer Hall Putsch Hitler stands at the front of a crowd during the Beer Hall Putsch in Munich on November 9, 1923. He is flanked by Alfred Rosenberg (left), head of the Nazis during Hitler's stint in jail, and Friedrich Weber (right), one of the architects of the Putsch.

than a year in comfortable conditions. Despite the failure, the incident raised the party's profile and did not greatly damage Hitler's political credibility. He used his time in prison to write a ranting, rambling book called *Mein Kampf* ("My Struggle"), which was animated by a vicious anti-Semitism and insisted on the need for Germany to find "living space" (*Lebensraum*) to the east, at the expense of its Slavic neighbors.

POST-WAR BRITAIN AND FRANCE

Although other western European countries did not experience the same degree of political instability as Germany, the early 1920s were everywhere years of difficulty and disruption. In Britain, unemployment exceeding 10 percent belied Prime Minister David Lloyd George's campaign slogan about making a country "fit for heroes to live in." As returning soldiers swelled the labor force, industrial employers tried to lengthen the working day while reducing pay—especially in the key coal-mining sector. Working-class frustration swelled the ranks of the Labour Party, now led by the charismatic orator Ramsey MacDonald (1866–1937). In 1924, Labour won its first election. The party's platform called for public ownership of major industries and an expanded social welfare net, including subsidized low-income housing, unemployment insurance, and pensions for the elderly and war widows. But Labour also rejected the Soviet model, and the Communist Party itself only attracted a small minority of the British electorate.

Things were different in France, where the Communist Party had split off from the Socialists in 1920 and quickly outstripped their membership numbers. The Communists did well in the industrial, working-class suburbs that had sprung up around major French cities, taking over a large number of municipalities in the 1920s. There they worked to enact ambitious social programs on a local level, such as a series of free holiday camps for children—who were thereby exposed to both a healthier climate and a degree of ideological indoctrination. Conservatives feared with some justification that the French Communist Party was taking orders directly from Moscow and might place Soviet interests above their own national ones. In France, as in Britain, conservatives stayed in office throughout most of the 1920s, initially benefiting from nationalist enthusiasm at the military victory. But in 1924, France suffered a bout of destabilizing inflation (although nothing to compare with the German experience), which helped propel a Radical-Socialist "cartel of the left" into power, but only for a short time.

FRAGILE NEW STATES

The new European states created in the wake of World War I came into being amid waves of national pride and hopes that democracy might now take root in the heart of the Continent. And just like many countries to the west, the new states—Austria, Hungary, Czechoslovakia, Yugoslavia, Poland, Turkey, and the Baltic states Lithuania, Latvia, and Estonia—mostly embraced an expanded, "social" vision of democracy, which counted subsistence and even work as a basic right. In localities where socialist parties came to power, they tried to pursue ambitious social welfare policies. Social Democratic officials in Red Vienna, as the capital of the new, shrunken Austrian republic quickly became known, offered perhaps the best example. They built public housing to relieve a housing crisis, imposed stringent taxes on luxury goods, and gave generous assistance packages, including clothes, to all needy new parents. At the same time, the city supervised its residents more carefully than before, moving quickly, for instance, to remove children from families it deemed irresponsible.

Turkey emerged as a new state following the Versailles conference, when in 1920 the Treaty of Sèvres dismantled the Ottoman Empire, leaving it with only a small foothold in Europe and reducing its Asian possessions to Anatolia. A charismatic Ottoman general, Mustafa Kemal (1881–1938), successfully drove foreign forces out of this territory, and in 1923 he became the first president of the new Republic of Turkey. Taking the name of Atatürk ("Father of the Turks"), he pursued a radical policy of Westernization, secularization, and Turkish nationalism, seeking to transform the Republic into a modern, ethnically homogeneous nation-state. He abolished the Muslim caliphate that had been associated with the Ottoman sultanate and separated civil law from Islamic law. He advocated integrating women more fully into Turkish society through education, a greater degree of legal equality, and the adoption of Western dress. He also supported the replacement of the Arabic alphabet by a new Turkish alphabet derived from the Latin.

ETHNIC TENSIONS All of the new states that emerged from the post-war conferences faced a thicket of challenges, with nationalism first among them. The Versailles agreement had given some 60 million inhabitants of the former Austro-Hungarian, Russian, and Ottoman Empires nation-states of their own. But at the same time it left 25 million more Europeans living as members of "national minorities" within these new states. The newly

National Minorities in Eastern Europe, 1920s The new countries of eastern Europe were far from the ethnically homogeneous nation-states that had been imagined by western diplomats. Poland and Hungary, for instance, contained significant German minorities; Czechoslovakia was split evenly between two ethnic groups; and Romania and Yugoslavia were a mix of many different groups. Many cities—especially in Poland and the Soviet Union—contained large Jewish populations. This would all have consequences for the nationalisms of the 1930s and the outbreak of World War II.

independent Poland, for instance, included 18 million ethnic Poles and nearly 9 million others, including some 4 million Ukrainians, 1 million Germans, and 3 million Jews. And despite an international treaty that made the new League of Nations the formal protector of Poland's

minority groups, the Polish government repeatedly trod on minority rights. During the inter-war period, it shuttered almost all Ukrainian-language schools and violently repressed Ukrainian nationalist activity.

In Czechoslovakia, the dominant Czechs and Slovaks had to deal not only with each other but also with large, homogeneously German and Hungarian territories, whose populations felt little allegiance to the new state. And Yugoslavia (initially called the Kingdom of Serbs, Croats and Slovenes) was a wild ethnic and religious stew of Serbs, Croats, Bosnian Muslims, Slovenes, Germans, Hungarians, and Albanians, to name only the largest groups, and of Roman Catholics, Eastern Orthodox Christians, and Muslims. By contrast, the newly independent state of Hungary had a far more ethnically homogeneous population, but over 30 percent of Europe's Hungarians lived outside its newly shrunken borders, leading to resentments of a different sort.

The ethnic tensions in turn worsened the urban-rural divide in the new states. Most of them still had large peasant majorities who looked with suspicion on capital cities like Warsaw, Budapest, and Riga, where a large proportion of the businesses and visible wealth belonged to Jews, Germans, and other minority groups. Many of the new states, including Poland and the Baltic countries, immediately implemented land reform, breaking up large estates (especially those owned by Germans and Russians) and turning the descendants of serfs into property owners for the first time. But lingering disputes over land ownership led to the spread of "smallholder" political parties that had little loyalty to democratic institutions and were often virulently anti-Semitic.

CRUMBLING DEMOCRACIES Already by the mid-1920s, many of the frail new democracies were crumbling. In Poland and Lithuania, the armed forces carried out coups against elected governments in 1926. In Poland, they brought to power Marshal Józef Piłsudski (1867–1935), the leader of Polish forces in the recent war against the Soviet Union, who called for a "healing" of the Polish body politic. Although Poland never veered entirely into dictatorship, democratic rights remained starkly curtailed. In Yugoslavia, a Serbian member of parliament himself shot dead the leader of a major Croatian political party in 1928. A year later, King Alexander (r. 1921–1934) banned all political parties. Of all the new states, only Czechoslovakia managed to remain democratic throughout the inter-war period, and that with some difficulty.

In Italy, **Benito Mussolini** and his Fascist movement consolidated their hold on the country between 1922 and

1925 with considerable help from the social and political elites. Mussolini, a former editor of the official Italian Socialist newspaper, had come to prominence because of his skill in using the press, and by developing a program that combined an insistence on social order with considerable promises to the working class and peasantry (including an eight-hour work day and free public education). His National Fascist Party grew, and in October 1922 he staged a "March on Rome" with 20,000 of his paramilitary black shirts. With the political system in a state of paralysis, King Vittorio Emmanuelle III (r. 1900–1946) named Mussolini Prime Minister. Mussolini presented himself to the social elites as the only possible bulwark against Russian-style revolution, and presented himself to the people (and particularly to embittered war veterans) as their advocate against the ruling oligarchy. He deployed his black shirts to intimidate or even kill his political opponents, and by 1925 he and the Fascists had a commanding majority in Parliament and were moving toward total control of the Italian state.

The only large European region where democracy survived without serious threats between the wars was Scandinavia. There, in contrast to the new central and eastern European states, urban social democrats managed to work out alliances with rural voters and introduced robust social welfare programs. Sweden, ruled by the Social Democratic Party after 1932, introduced particularly generous social insurance and pension programs, supported by high levels of income tax.

THE SOVIET UNION AND RISE OF JOSEPH STALIN

The newly founded Soviet Union, no more democratic than its tsarist predecessor, remained as dangerously unstable as central and eastern Europe. Although the Communists had won the Civil War, and the New Economic Policy had saved the economy from meltdown and preserved a partial market system, the regime's future direction remained uncertain. Leon Trotsky, the charismatic leader of the Red Army, argued that the USSR should continue to promote revolution abroad (using the Comintern to coordinate the actions of foreign Communist parties) and also begin a process of rapid, forced industrialization. Others in the party suspected Trotsky of Bonapartist tendencies—nearly all the party leaders had read deeply in the history of the French Revolution and feared that the Revolution of 1917 would degenerate into militarism along the lines of the Revolution of 1789. When

Stalin and Lenin Stalin (right) visited an ailing Lenin at his estate in 1922. This photo of their meeting was heavily doctored to conceal Lenin's illness. In later years, the photo was used to demonstrate Stalin's supposed closeness to the founder of the Soviet Union.

Lenin, who had already barely survived an assassination attempt, suffered a stroke in 1922, it became clear that he would not be able to retain control of the party for long.

The man who quickly emerged as Trotsky's most effective challenger for the succession was almost as unlikely a leader for this new version of the Russian Empire as Adolf Hitler would be for Germany. Josef Dzhugashvili (later changing his name to **Joseph Stalin**) had been born in 1879 in Georgia, in the Caucasus region. The son of a violently hard-drinking artisan and a devout mother, he had initially hoped to enter the priesthood, only to rebel against the conservatism of the Eastern Orthodox churches. Joining the Bolsheviks, he became known both for organizing ability and for violence; at one point, he personally took part in a bank robbery to raise funds. He then took on the Russian name Stalin ("steel"). Repeated spells in prison and in Siberian exile won him a high reputation and Lenin's favor. He even became editor of the Bolshevik newspaper *Pravda*, despite never speaking Russian with complete fluency.

Stalin served as one of Lenin's most important deputies in the Bolshevik takeover in 1917 and thereafter had a place in the highest circles of the party. In 1922, he became its general secretary—a position that gave him control over the all-important party bureaucracy. As general secretary, he argued against too heavy a focus on fomenting revolution elsewhere, suggesting instead that the Soviet government first build "socialism in a single country." And he opposed Trotsky's ambitious program of industrialization.

At the end of 1922, Lenin suffered a second, even more debilitating stroke. In a testament that circulated soon afterward and was attributed to Lenin (the authorship remains disputed), the Soviet leader warned of the "boundless power" Stalin was accumulating and suggested that the Georgian be removed from the position of general secretary. But by this point, Stalin had placed too many allies in key positions in the party. And when Lenin died in early 1924, Stalin had his followers ready to hail him as Lenin's hand-picked successor.

Trotsky tried to organize a so-called Left Opposition to Stalin. He even argued for allowing a degree of freedom to non-Communist organizations. But Stalin ruthlessly outmaneuvered him and by 1927 had won a decisive victory. Trotsky and his allies were expelled from the Communist Party. Understanding all too well the need for a cult of leadership in a country with such powerful autocratic traditions, Stalin's propagandists presented him as an almost superhuman genius, working tirelessly to promote the welfare of the Soviet people. Lenin, meanwhile, was virtually deified, his body carefully preserved and put on permanent display in a mausoleum in Red Square next to the Kremlin.

MODERNIST CULTURE AND SOCIETY

The highly unsettled political, social, and economic conditions of the 1920s gave new inspiration to the modernist movement in art and literature, and encouraged new ways of living in cities such as Paris and Berlin.

MODERNIST CULTURE

Many artists and writers in the 1920s, particularly those who had experienced the trenches, testified to the cultural impact of the war. The British painter and author Wyndham Lewis (1882–1957), a veteran of the western front, referred to the war as a "dividing wall in time, a thousand miles high and a thousand miles thick." Yet in many ways,

the war simply gave further impetus to modernist tendencies clearly visible before 1914.

LITERATURE Much post-war poetry continued to experiment with the whirling, fragmentary, disorienting forms of verse that were already common in pre-war Paris and Vienna. Here one of the greatest examples was provided by the Anglo-American poet T. S. Eliot (1888–1965). The opening section of his 1922 masterpiece, "The Waste Land," consisted mostly of apparently disconnected shards of speech, the effect being rather like scanning rapidly through different radio stations. The poem mixed figures out of classical mythology, stray invocations of Shakespeare and Dante, and caustic images of passionless sex to create a tableau of a fragmented, sterile civilization, although the conclusion contained a faint promise of renewed fertility and hope amid the ruins. The Irish poet William Butler Yeats (1865–1939) evoked the horrifying image of a monstrous "second coming" in a 1919 poem that seemed to lament the continuing political turmoil of the post-war period:

> Things fall apart; the centre cannot hold;
> Mere anarchy is loosed upon the world,
> The blood-dimmed tide is loosed, and everywhere
> The ceremony of innocence is drowned;
> The best lack all conviction, while the worst
> Are full of passionate intensity.

The post-war period also saw the triumph of modernist prose fiction. The greatest single example (as well as one of the longest) was *In Search of Lost Time* by the French novelist Marcel Proust (1871–1922), whose publication in seven large volumes stretched from 1913 to 1927. Unlike the great novels of the nineteenth century, its plot, set in the aristocratic world where Proust himself had grown up, mattered much less than the narrator's delicate exploration of his own memories and emotions and ruminations on the nature of art. In 1922 the Irish writer James Joyce (1882–1941) published his monumental novel *Ulysses*, devoted to chronicling a single day seen through the eyes of a Dubliner named Leopold Bloom. The novel is fiercely difficult: a tangle of classical allusions, abrupt breaks in the narrative, long digressions, and numerous puns, and requiring intimate familiarity with the topography of early twentieth-century Dublin. Its use of obscenity led to several attempts to ban it. But its stream-of-consciousness technique was widely hailed for capturing something essential about the operations of the human mind, and Joyce was widely imitated. Further east, the Prague writer Franz Kafka (1883–1924) published stories and novels that

GROSZ'S *THE PILLARS OF SOCIETY*

The German painter George Grosz (1893–1959) was a major figure in German art circles and a prominent left-wing activist. During the 1920s, he produced scathing canvases, such as *The Pillars of Society* (1926), that blended satiric critiques of Weimar society with an absurdist black humor that he developed during his time in Berlin's Dada movement. Borrowing from the caricatures and cartoons of the popular press, *The Pillars of Society* expresses Grosz's view that the German elite was complicit with right-wing extremism and responsible for the nation's economic collapse.

In the foreground, a trio of bourgeois figures drink together: a businessman brandishing a sword and wearing a tie decorated with a swastika; an editor clutching bloodstained newspapers; and a politician bearing a German flag and a placard reading "Socialism is work," his head topped with a pile of excrement. Behind them, a smug priest delivers a blessing, seemingly blind to the burning building in the top-left corner, a symbol of the dire conditions in Germany. At top right, advancing soldiers suggest a renewed militarism. Together, these elements present a harsh condemnation of the elite's control of German society.

QUESTIONS FOR ANALYSIS

1. How does Grosz use symbolism to criticize German society?
2. What aspects of the painting refer to the rise of Nazism?
3. What do you think Grosz meant by titling this painting *The Pillars of Society*?

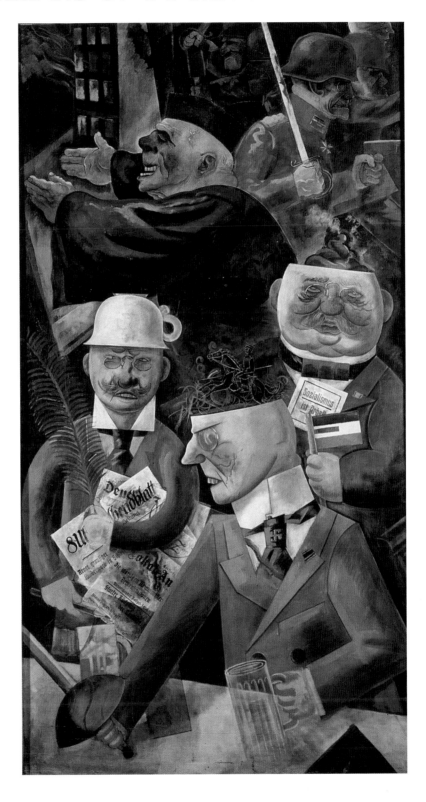

featured bizarrely surreal situations (most famously, a man waking up to find himself transformed into a giant insect) and highlighted the absurdity—and often, the hopelessness—of modern life.

Among them, Proust, Joyce, and Kafka greatly expanded what prose fiction was capable of—but at the price of reinforcing the separation between high art and popular art that we have already seen at work in the world of music. While these modernists found readers in all social classes, they did not attain the popularity of nineteenth-century writers like Charles Dickens or Victor Hugo. Modernist authors, like their Bohemian predecessors but in a much more influential manner, tended to disdain the mass societies produced by large-scale industrialization and urbanization. They considered these societies smotheringly conformist and often deliberately sought to produce works at odds with popular tastes.

VISUAL ARTS During this period of high modernism, the same attitudes were evident in visual art. Painters like the Dutch Piet Mondrian (1872–1944) experimented with wholly abstract compositions of lines and colors in a grid pattern. The so-called Dada group of artists, formed in Zurich in 1916, argued that the entire mental world of bourgeois Europe needed to be turned upside down, to eradicate the ideas that had brought about the war's destruction. To do so, they called for challenging supposed common sense by an explicit celebration of nonsense— which they tried to represent both visually and in prose. Marcel Duchamp (1887–1968), a French artist, memorably challenged the privileged status of art objects by submitting a urinal as his contribution to a 1917 art exhibit. More accessible were the so-called surrealists, who emerged as a distinct group, complete with manifestos, in the late 1920s. They also sought to challenge ordinary ideas of rationality and common sense, but did so in hauntingly strange, distorted images and verse seemingly drawn directly from the human unconscious analyzed by Sigmund Freud. The school also had an important influence on the Spaniard Pablo Picasso, the great pioneer of modernism who remained through the inter-war period probably the best-known visual artist in the world as well as the most highly paid.

NEW MEDIA Even as the modernists repeatedly challenged conventional standards of art and literature, the very boundaries of culture were shifting with the rise of new media. Just as the initial spread of print had led to new cultural forms such as the Republic of Letters in the sixteenth and seventeenth centuries, and the use of

photography had changed everything from journalism to high art to family life in the nineteenth century, two equally powerful new technologies now had a significant cultural impact. By the 1920s, Britain, France, and Germany each possessed thousands of movie theaters, with a large proportion of the population seeing silent films on a regular basis. In the 1930s, the introduction of sound to film would change the landscape yet again. The importance of Hollywood imports, even at this early date, signaled a new role for American culture in Europe that would only grow through the century. However, European directors such as the Russian Sergei Eisenstein, the German Fritz Lang, and the French Abel Gance also directed major works that convinced Europeans to take cinema seriously as an art form. With Robert Wiene's 1920 German film *The Cabinet of Doctor Caligari*, which mostly took place in a surreal dreamscape, high modernism established its presence in the movies. Commercial radio stations opened in most of western Europe in the early 1920s, and by the 1930s most middle-class families owned a radio receiver—an innovation that enabled political leaders to speak directly into private homes. Magazines illustrated with photographs proliferated, and all these new media served as effective vehicles for commercial advertising.

ARCHITECTURE The 1920s also saw one of the most important shifts in the history of European architecture, one with major implications for the shape of European

The Bauhaus School The campus of the Bauhaus School in Dessau (in the east of Germany) itself exemplifies the use of straight lines, rows of grid-like windows, and application of reinforced concrete pioneered by Bauhaus architects.

Potsdamer Platz A 1929 photo of Berlin's famous square conveys its buzzing commercial activity. Storefronts and large, vivid advertisements face the streets, which are crisscrossed by trams, buses, automobiles, and pedestrians.

cities and the texture of urban life. The influential **Bauhaus School**, founded in 1919 and active until 1933 in Germany, advocated a strictly functional design for buildings. Bauhaus structures showed no ornamentation and emphasized clear, clean geometrical forms with muted colors. The architects—notably the school's founder, Walter Gropius (1883–1969), and Mies van der Rohe (1886–1969)—favored steel-reinforced concrete as a building material, while opening up whole sides of buildings to natural light through striking, floor-to-ceiling windows. It was the start of the modernist architecture that now dominates nearly all major cities around the world.

CITY LIFE

European cities of the inter-war period were transformed by Bauhaus-style buildings and cinemas and much else. The continuing spread of automobiles—which had now largely edged out horse-drawn carriages from the centers of major metropolises—along with expanding systems of public transportation, made it easier than ever for members of all social classes to live in distant suburbs and travel to city centers for both work and leisure. These now bustled with a newly intense sort of commercial urban life, lit not only by electrical lamps but—from the mid-1920s on—by neon signs.

Consider the Potsdamer Platz, the large square at the center of Berlin. By the 1920s, up to 60,000 cars a day were passing through it, along with hundreds of trams. To manage the traffic flow required the services of eleven policemen, and then, in 1924, the construction of a tower with traffic lights—one of Europe's first. Within easy walking distance were scores of cafes and beer halls, five major hotels, the mammoth Wertheim department store, and an establishment called Haus Vaterland ("Fatherland House"), opened in 1928, that included a dozen national-themed restaurants, one of them named the Wild West Bar. There was also space for half a dozen orchestras and a 1,400-seat movie theater. Nothing like it had ever been seen in Europe. All this was joined in 1932 by an ultra-modernist, nine-story office block called Columbushaus, one of the largest Bauhaus-style projects yet completed. Piccadilly Circus in London and the Champs-Élysées in Paris had similar roles as the gaudy centerpieces of inter-war commercial culture. But despite the growing popularity of modernist architecture, European cities did not follow the lead of New York and permit the large-scale construction of modern skyscrapers.

The new urban consumer culture did have its dangers. In most major European cities, a large majority of men and close to 40 percent of women smoked (mostly unfiltered) cigarettes, raising the levels of heart disease and cancer. And the automobile brought other dangers. In Britain in 1930, with only a million cars on the road, 7,000 people died in auto accidents. Today Britain has 33 million private cars, but only 3,000 annual road deaths.

PARIS AND BERLIN Paris and Berlin served as joint capitals of modernist culture in the 1920s. Paris continued to draw the greatest artists and writers of the Western world—not only Spaniards like Picasso and Dalí, but American writers such as Ernest Hemingway, F. Scott Fitzgerald, the songwriter Cole Porter, and Gertrude Stein. Paris also teemed with immigrants and political refugees who gave it a renewed cosmopolitan atmosphere. The groups included White Russian exiles from the Soviet Union; Greeks and Turks fleeing the bloodshed in the eastern Mediterranean; and Italians, Poles, Belgians, Spaniards, and Portuguese in search of work. Between the wars, France welcomed a higher percentage of immigrants than any other Western country.

Berlin gained a reputation for its raucous and daring cabarets (immortalized in Christopher Isherwood's stories, the basis for the musical *Cabaret*) and for its wildly experimental music, painting, and film. The playwright Berthold Brecht (1898–1956) combined biting Marxist social commentary with surrealist motifs that aimed to defamiliarize their subjects. In *The Three-Penny Opera* (1928), Brecht's words were set to the jagged, modernist rhythms of the composer Kurt Weill to produce a masterpiece that appeared thousands of times on European stages before World War II. In an increasingly common pattern, popular plays and novels were also adapted for the cinema and the radio. In both Paris and Berlin, the whirl of modernist culture—with the new freedoms embraced by women and the open depictions of both straight and gay sexuality—was loudly condemned as "degenerate" by political and religious conservatives.

CULTURE OF COMMEMORATION Modernism did not entirely dominate European culture in the inter-war period. Particularly in their intense efforts to commemorate the war dead of 1914–18, most of the former combatant nations also reached back to traditional—indeed, classical—cultural forms. Poets and novelists continued to condemn the war as a ghastly blunder, most famously in the shockingly explicit 1929 novel about the trenches, *All Quiet on the Western Front*, written by German novelist Erich Maria Remarque (1898–1970). But the designers of war memorials such as the sober Cenotaph in London struggled to find ways to endow the wartime sacrifices with meaning. Commemorations of the war, especially on the anniversary of the November 11 armistice, played a key role in public culture of all the major states with the exception of the Soviet Union. But in one sense, these regular outpourings of grief reinforced rather than contradicted the message of the modernist antiwar works. They

Memorializing the War A color photograph shows the Cenotaph war memorial in central London shortly after it was completed in 1920. Mourners who might not have been able to recover their own loved ones' bodies gather to pay their respects.

strengthened the widespread public conviction, particularly in Britain and France, that their countries must avoid future war at any cost.

WOMEN IN THE CITY In such new urban spaces, women could experiment with new roles. The end of the war had brought mixed results for women's rights, as demobilized soldiers flooding back into the job market displaced women from wartime employment. The large numbers of men killed at the front left many widows and single women whose lack of family attachment raised anxieties. But at the same time, women finally won the right to vote in Britain (although not fully until 1928) and in Germany, Austria, and most of the countries of northern Europe. As early as 1919, women took seats in the British House of Commons. In France and much of southern Europe, the battle for woman suffrage continued.

Relatively small-scale technological changes had a large impact on urban women's lives in this period. The spread of sewing machines, gas stoves, electric irons, and running hot water, even in the upper segment of working-class homes, reduced the time spent on domestic chores. Leisure time increased correspondingly, with women taking advantage of the sort of attractions now found in urban centers like Potsdamer Platz. The fashion industry rushed to supply them with clothing and cosmetics, and sales boomed, driven by a flood of new advertising aimed at women. So did the number of European beauty parlors. Women's clothing styles, especially in the cities, shifted toward shorter, less constraining dresses and skirts, and shorter, simpler hairstyles that bespoke a more liberated social role for women—and a more liberated sexuality.

In these years, birth control became more easily available in some European countries. In Britain, in 1920, the scientist and author Marie Stopes (1880–1958) founded the first public birth-control clinic in Europe, dispensing advice and contraceptives that included the cervical cap and spermicides. But like many early birth-control campaigners in both Europe and America, Stopes was motivated as much by the pseudo-science of eugenics as by concern for the quality of women's lives. In one pamphlet, she lamented "reckless breeding" as "the worst end of our community," which supposedly led to higher rates of mental disability. The German feminist Helene Stöcker (1869–1943) similarly touted birth control as a means "to prevent the incurably ill or degenerate from reproducing." In nearly all of Catholic Europe, birth control remained illegal.

All of these changes in women's lives reactivated familiar anxieties about gender and national health.

Changing Fashions A 1927 tabloid photograph of a French aristocrat gives an indication of the new women's fashions, including shorter skirts, silk stockings, and cropped hairstyles.

Conservative cultural critics condemned the opening up of new cultural and social roles for women, and, as in previous centuries, pointed to declining birthrates to support their claims. After a brief post-war jump, birthrates did in fact fall throughout most of Europe during the inter-war period, due above all to the increasing availability of birth control and the prevailing economic uncertainty. In countries as diverse as Norway, Italy, and France, birthrates fell by close to a third during the 1920s. Mussolini's relentless promotion of domesticity and motherhood ("Maternity," to quote one Fascist slogan, "is the patriotism of women") made little difference.

In the cinema and especially literature, sexuality itself was represented far more openly than before the war. In 1928, the British novelist D. H. Lawrence (1885–1930) published *Lady Chatterley's Lover*, about a high-born woman who finds sexual and emotional satisfaction with a gamekeeper, her husband having lost his sexual function as a result of war injuries. Because of its highly explicit language, the British government banned the book, and it did not appear in an unexpurgated British edition until

1960. The British modernist author Virginia Woolf (1882–1941) used such literary tools as stream of consciousness to explore the inner lives of female characters. In a landmark 1929 essay entitled "A Room of One's Own," she analyzed the barriers to women's ability to write. In France, the novelist Colette (1873–1954) explored female emotions and sexuality, and made no secret of her own lesbian relationships. Several novelists risked prosecution by openly describing male homosexuality, including Proust and the Frenchman André Gide (1869–1951).

A FRAGILE ORDER

In the mid-1920s, the chaos and disruptions of the immediate post-war period finally seemed to recede. Following the collapse of the German currency in 1923, a League of Nations commission negotiated a new, less severe schedule for German reparations. And a series of international conferences took place with the goal of ensuring that the vast bloodshed of the war would never repeat itself.

ARMS CONTROL

Following the first international arms control conference, in Washington, D.C., in 1921–22, a series of treaties effectively limited the size of the great powers' navies and ended the construction of new battleship fleets. The Locarno Treaty of 1925 stabilized relations between Germany and its western neighbors, and paved the way for the country's entry into the League of Nations a year later. In 1928, all the major European powers, including the Soviet Union, formally adhered to the Kellogg-Briand Pact (named for the U.S. secretary of state and the French foreign minister), which attempted to ban war as "an instrument of national policy" altogether. It seemed that a new comity had finally entered into international relations. Yet in Germany, resentment against the post-war settlement remained strong, as shown by the election of former military chief Paul von Hindenburg—the embodiment of the old Prussian military spirit—as president in 1925.

ECONOMIC PLANNING

The economies of most European countries also strengthened in the mid-1920s. Unemployment levels dropped, industry expanded, and by 1925 in most cases production

had returned to its pre-war levels. By 1927, many European countries had returned to the gold standard and its promise of economic stability.

Yet growth remained hampered by a number of factors. High tariffs, introduced to protect emerging industries, particularly in the new central and eastern European states, slowed trade. The war's disruption of foreign investment in European economies continued in the 1920s. France had lost nearly half its foreign investment, and Germany nearly all of it. Britain did better, but London still effectively surrendered the title of the world's financial center to New York, and the United States attracted much of Europe's available investment capital. Labour leader Ramsey MacDonald was just one of the prominent Europeans expressing fears that the United States had become a "super-national power." Meanwhile, reduced peacetime demand for certain commodities—particularly those related to the military—created painful dislocations. In Britain, in 1926, an attempt to cut wages and hours for miners led to the most ambitious attempt at a general strike in the country's history, spearheaded by the Trades Union Congress, but it achieved relatively little.

European governments responded to economic unpredictability by embracing concepts of scientific management and planning, and by relying more heavily on advice from university-trained economists. The theories of the American engineer Frederick Winslow Taylor (1856–1915), who sought to maximize productivity by applying various forms of standardization, labor discipline, and supposedly scientific rules to work flow, gained popularity. Even more important was the work of **John Maynard Keynes** (1883–1946), the most influential economist of the twentieth century. Keynes argued that free markets by themselves would not necessarily produce high economic growth and low unemployment. To combat economic slumps, he advocated government action to stimulate overall economic demand through public spending. Even industrialists generally agreed that governments needed to take a role in coordinating economic production. A similar message came to Europe from the United States, where even the chief executive of General Electric called for the formation of state-coordinated industrial cartels. In the Western world, the idea of an unrestricted market system had few champions in the 1920s and 1930s.

Although state planning went furthest in the Soviet Union, a form of it also developed in Fascist Italy, where Benito Mussolini promoted a type of social organization generally called **corporatism**. To coordinate the needs of business owners, industrial workers, peasants,

Communist and Fascist State Control

Amid the economic and social instability left in the wake of World War I, the new governments of Communist Russia and Fascist Italy claimed to offer political systems that could energetically and efficiently restore order. To many people, both communism and fascism seemed to represent a cathartic reinvigoration of society through strict state control. And leaders of both movements offered confident visions of how these new ideologies would transform their nations, as expressed in the following two sources.

Nikolai Bukharin and Evgenii Preobrazhensky, *The ABC of Communism*

Bukharin (1888–1938) and Preobrazhensky (1886–1937), notable Bolshevik leaders, originally wrote their *The ABC of Communism* (1919) to convince Russian citizens— particularly those with little education—to support the Communist Party. Though the book was written before Stalin's rise, this passage hints at the absolute control that he would come to have over the state in the name of the proletariat.

The basis of communist society must be the social ownership of the means of production and exchange. Machinery, locomotives, steamships, factory buildings, warehouses, grain elevators, mines, telegraphs and telephones, the land, sheep, horses, and cattle, must all be at the disposal of society. All these means of production must be under the control of society as a whole, and not as at present under the control of individual capitalists or capitalist combines....

For the realisation of the communist system the proletariat must have all authority and all power in its hands. The proletariat cannot overthrow the old world unless it has power in its hands, unless for a time it becomes the ruling class. Manifestly the bourgeoisie will not abandon its position without a fight.... Precisely because the opposition will inevitably be so embittered, it is necessary that the workers' authority, the proletarian rule, shall take the form of a dictatorship. Now "dictatorship" signifies very strict methods of government and a resolute crushing of enemies.

It is obvious that in such a state of affairs there can be no talk of "freedom" for everyone. The dictatorship of the proletariat is incompatible with freedom for the bourgeoisie.... In extreme cases the workers' government must not hesitate to use the method of the terror. Only when the suppression of the exploiters is complete, when they have ceased to resist, when it is no longer in their power to injure the working class, will the proletarian dictatorship grow progressively milder.

Benito Mussolini and Giovanni Gentile, "The Doctrine of Fascism"

In 1932, Mussolini and the Italian philosopher Giovanni Gentile (1875–1944) published the essay "The Doctrine of Fascism," which in the following passage describes the central ideas of the all-controlling Fascist state.

Against individualism, the Fascist conception is for the State; and it is for the individual in so far as he coincides with the State, which is the conscience and universal will of man in his historical existence.... For the Fascist, everything is in the State, and nothing human or spiritual exists, much less has value, outside the State. In this sense Fascism is totalitarian, and the Fascist State, the synthesis and unity of all values, interprets, develops and gives strength to the whole life of the people....

Therefore Fascism is opposed to Socialism, which confines the movement of history within the class struggle and ignores the unity of classes established in one economic and moral reality in the State....

Fascism is opposed to Democracy, which equates the nation to the majority, lowering it to the level of that majority....

The Fascist State, the highest and most powerful form of personality, is a force, but a spiritual force, which takes over all the forms of the moral and intellectual life of man....

Fascism...thus repudiates the doctrine of Pacifism—born of a renunciation of the struggle and an act of cowardice in the face of sacrifice. War alone brings up to their highest tension all human energies and puts the stamp of nobility upon the peoples who have the courage to meet it....

In the Fascist State the individual is not suppressed, but rather multiplied, just as in a regiment a soldier is not weakened but multiplied by the number of his comrades. The Fascist State organizes the nation, but it leaves sufficient scope to individuals; it has limited useless or harmful liberties and has preserved those that are essential. It cannot be the individual who decides in this matter, but only the State.

QUESTIONS FOR ANALYSIS

1. What are the methods of control that must be used by "dictatorship of the proletariat," as described by Bukharin and Preobrazhensky?
2. Why are Mussolini and Gentile opposed to socialism, democracy, and pacifism?
3. What are the key differences between communism and fascism as described in these sources, and how do they resemble each other?

Sources: Nikolai Bukharin and Evgenii Preobrazhensky, *The ABC of Communism*, trans. Eden and Cedar Paul (London: 1922), pp. 70, 80–81; Benito Mussolini and Giovanni Gentile, "The Doctrine of Fascism," in *The Social and Political Doctrines of Contemporary Europe*, ed. Michael Oakeshott (Cambridge: 1939), pp. 166–68, 170–71, 177–78.

shopkeepers, and others, the Fascist government divided the economy into sectors managed by corporations that bore a superficial relationship to medieval guilds. As Mussolini himself explained in 1932: "Fascism recognizes the real needs which gave rise to socialism and trade unionism, allowing them due weight in the guild or corporative system in which divergent interests are coordinated and harmonized in the unity of the State." The state would therefore intervene to set production targets in particular industries, and it would also determine wages and benefits.

In practice, the system replaced Adam Smith's "invisible hand" of free markets with the heavily visible hand of government, leading to the creation of huge government bureaucracies. It was typical of the contradictions of Italian **fascism**, which combined brutal repression of opposition (mostly political, but also including the infamous criminal organizations of southern Italy) with sporadic displays of efficiency (often referred to by the phrase "making the trains run on time") and considerable bombast. Mussolini contrasted fascism to democracy, which he blasted for its "spirit of collective irresponsibility, and the myth of happiness and indefinite progress."

THE GREAT DEPRESSION

Despite the economic growth of the late 1920s, the European economy remained fragile. Wartime disruptions, the huge war debts incurred to the U.S. government, and investments in the booming American economy had combined to yoke Europe's economic fate to that of the United States, which in 1916 had become the world's largest economy. During the later 1920s, a full-fledged financial bubble developed on Wall Street, with companies hugely overvalued in the stock market. When the United States fell into recession in 1929, a financial panic ensued and Wall Street crashed, destroying vast quantities of paper wealth and severely cutting demand for goods and services. The result was the **Great Depression** of the 1930s. American unemployment rates soared to nearly 25 percent, while industrial production plunged by nearly 50 percent in 1932.

FALTERING EUROPEAN ECONOMIES As the American economy sank, it dragged European ones down. The hardest-hit country was Germany, whose banks were tied to American ones through a thick web of loans linked to wartime reparations. There, too, unemployment quickly hit 20 percent, and industrial production fell sharply. Fears of a new bout of hyperinflation kept the German

government from trying to stimulate economic demand in line with Keynes's theories, making the situation even worse. Central European countries such as Austria and Hungary, whose economies were tied to Germany's, experienced similar conditions. The downward pressure in the international financial system led most major countries finally to go off the gold standard altogether in order to gain more control over their own currencies.

The British economy suffered badly as well, although not on the same scale. A new Labour government under MacDonald briefly tried to stimulate demand through public works and higher unemployment benefits, as Keynes urged. The writer George Orwell (1903–1950) brilliantly described the plight of the unemployed in a study of a northern English mining community, *The Road to Wigan Pier*, which addressed the filth, crowding, and general ugliness produced by poverty that eroded basic decency and hope. Commenting on what he believed capitalism had wrought, Orwell wrote: "We are living in a world in which nobody is free, in which hardly anybody is secure, in which it is almost impossible to be honest and to remain alive."

The Depression played out differently in the other industrial countries. France initially seemed more resistant, owing to an economic self-sufficiency rooted in the continuing importance of the rural sector and small businesses. But ultimately the downturn affected France as well, and the refusal of successive governments to devalue the franc hurt exports and made France one of the last countries to recover. The European country that best resisted the Depression was Sweden, where, in keeping with Keynesian economics, the government made up for investment shortfalls with its own spending and continued its ambitious central planning and social welfare programs. In Sweden, productivity grew by 20 percent between 1929 and 1935.

POLITICAL AND CULTURAL EFFECTS OF THE DEPRESSION In some ways, the Depression did not have worse social and economic effects than several nineteenth-century economic crises. Although many Europeans went hungry in the early 1930s or experienced crowded, unhealthy living conditions, very few starved or were forced to live on the streets. Europe had no real equivalent to the so-called Hoovervilles of shacks and tents that sprang up in American cities. But the Depression arrived in Europe at a moment of exceptional political and cultural instability. Democracies had begun to fail even before 1929, and the Depression hastened this process. In Portugal, General António de Oliveira Salazar

Economic Crisis Crowds line up outside a Berlin bank in July 1931 in order to withdraw their money. Such bank runs became common during the economic crisis that began in 1929.

(1889–1970) consolidated a conservative, corporatist dictatorship that would survive from the 1930s until the mid-1970s. And in the 1930s, the remaining democracies of central and eastern Europe succumbed to authoritarianism, one by one, until only Czechoslovakia was left.

Britain and France, with their much deeper democratic traditions, survived the Depression with their political systems intact, but not without significant bruising. In Britain, Oswald Mosley (1896–1980) founded the British Union of Fascists, modeled on Mussolini's party, although with a stronger anti-Semitic tinge. Membership for a time reached the tens of thousands, but Mosley never established a major electoral presence, and a string of Conservative Party governments remained comfortably in power. In 1936, Britain even survived a potential constitutional crisis when the government successfully pressured the new king, Edward VIII (r. Jan. 1936–Dec. 1936), to abdicate after he refused to break off a relationship with an American divorcée.

France came much closer to the brink of real political instability, enduring no fewer than eighteen separate governments in the 1930s. As the Depression worsened, so did attacks on the Republic from both the extreme left and the extreme right. On the night of February 6, 1934, a huge protest organized by right-wing leagues descended on the Place de la Concorde, in central Paris, and threatened the National Assembly just across the river. In the wake of the incident, the French Socialists and Communists partly reconciled and eventually formed a Popular Front that won elections in 1936. The Jewish Socialist Léon Blum (1872–1950) became prime minister, heightening right-wing and anti-Semitic outrage. But the Popular Front itself, despite passing important social reforms, could not stay in power for long. Caught between Communist allies who wanted to proceed with the nationalization of key industries, and a financial sector that threatened to undermine even much more mild steps toward socialism, Blum could not keep his fractious coalition intact.

THE COLONIAL EMPIRES

In some ways, both Britain and France emerged from World War I with their empires stronger than ever. Thanks to the addition of former German colonies and Ottoman territories in the form of League of Nations **mandates**, British officials now ruled in Palestine and Iraq, and French officials in Syria and Lebanon. Large new African territories such as Southwest Africa, Tanzania, and Cameroon also became British and French possessions.

MIDDLE EASTERN MANDATES

As oil became ever more important to run automobiles, ships, and planes, the Middle Eastern mandates, with their rich oil reserves, gained particular importance. The British somewhat cavalierly cobbled together several former Ottoman provinces, divided by religion and ethnicity (Shia Muslim Arabs, Sunni Muslim Arabs, and Sunni Muslim Kurds), into the new state of Iraq. According to one story, Winston Churchill first sketched out its borders on a napkin during a dinner party. They placed on its throne a member of a family that had contended unsuccessfully for control of independent Saudi Arabia, and they granted the new state independence in 1932. But they ensured that Iraq's policies continued to benefit British oil companies. Another member of the family installed to rule in Iraq

Middle Eastern Mandates, 1920s Through the mandates system, Britain and France became dominant powers in the Middle East. The creation of the Iraq mandate allowed Britain control of key oil reserves in Iraq and on the Persian Gulf, in addition to numerous other territories throughout the region.

ended up as king of Transjordan (later changed to Jordan), which the British carved out of the original Palestine mandate. In the rest of that mandate, immigration from Europe swelled the Jewish population in the 1920s and 1930s, leading to conflict with Palestinian Arabs.

NATIONALIST RESISTANCE

By the 1920s, many British and French colonial and mandate territories had growing middle classes, some of whose members had studied in Europe, spoke English or French fluently, and—crucially—had appropriated European ideas of national self-determination for themselves. These ideas had fertile soil to grow and change in, given native traditions of patriotism and self-respect, plus resentment against a colonial system that obviously benefited the European powers at the colonies' expense, and a well-justified sense of entitlement deriving from the importance of colonial troops to the Allied war effort.

The result, across the globe, was the rise of potent independence movements in which European patterns of national competition now turned against Europe itself. Already during the Versailles Peace Conference, some nationalists from European colonies, such as Vietnam's Ho Chi Minh, had attempted, without success, to receive a hearing from the negotiators. Men and women in the mandate territories did somewhat better after the peace, when they could send petitions to the League of Nations. They thereby gained publicity and the possibility of League pressure to give indigenous peoples a greater role in their own government.

Subjects of the French Empire did not fare so well. In the 1920s and 1930s, France faced nationalist agitation—sometimes violent—in Southeast Asia, North Africa, and Madagascar. In response, the French government cracked down brutally on more moderate organizations seeking merely to obtain equal rights for colonial subjects, and it further restricted the rights these subjects already enjoyed. In a reversal of earlier, more liberal policies, it restricted the access to French citizenship once offered to certain African elites. This repression pushed moderates toward advocating full independence—and also, in France's Caribbean and African possessions, toward the development of a new literary and political movement of black pride that went by the name of Négritude. The movement included among its most prominent voices the Senegalese poet and future national leader Léopold Senghor (1906–2001) and the Martinique poet Aimé Césaire (1913–2008).

The British faced a variety of independence movements

as well, some of which adopted violent means. In Palestine, it faced two such movements at once. One came from the Jews, seeking to make good on former foreign minister Arthur Balfour's promise that the country would become a Jewish national home. The other came from Palestinian Arabs desperate to prevent the establishment of a Jewish state in what they considered Arab land.

GANDHI AND INDIAN NATIONALISM

The most important anti-imperial resistance, however, came in India, where resentment at British rule predated the failed War of Independence of 1857. In 1919, the British abandoned the use of juries in Indian political trials, and when indignant protesters rallied in the city of Amritsar, British soldiers panicked and massacred over 400 men and women.

Over the next decade, a powerful independence movement developed under the leadership of **Mohandas Gandhi** (1869–1948), who had first become involved in civil rights agitation while working as a lawyer in South Africa. Abandoning his prim suits for traditional Hindu garb, adopting an ascetic lifestyle, and preaching a philosophy of nonviolent resistance that he drew from Indian sources and the writings of Christian authors such as Leo Tolstoy, Gandhi stood as a living rebuke to British imperialism. On being asked by a reporter what he thought of Western civilization, he famously replied: "It would be a good idea."

In 1930, Gandhi staged the most important symbolic protest yet against British rule, leading thousands of

Mahatma Gandhi The Indian nationalist leader, clad in minimalist clothing, spins cotton on a traditional spinning wheel in 1931. Reclaiming indigenous methods of production could be an important way of demonstrating independence from colonial rule and customs.

followers on a 240-mile march to the sea to gather salt, a commodity on which the British claimed a monopoly. Gandhi and tens of thousands of other Indians were arrested by the British authorities; and while he did not win concessions on the salt issue, he attracted massive attention and sympathy worldwide—including in Britain itself. But through the 1930s, India remained firmly under British control.

TOTALITARIAN DICTATORSHIPS

While democracy managed to survive the troubled years of the Depression in some of central Europe and much of western Europe, in Germany it did not. As unemployment worsened and industrial production plummeted, the parties of the extreme surged in public support.

THE NAZI SEIZURE OF POWER

Hitler and his deputy, Joseph Goebbels (1897–1945), proved geniuses in the use of propaganda: visual, oral, and in the form of well-orchestrated rallies. In September 1930, the Nazi party gained 18 percent of the vote in a national election. Two years later, the Nazis and Communists together won a majority of German votes, and the Nazis emerged as the largest party in the Reichstag. At the same time, some of the most powerful institutions in German life, notably the army and big business, lost what little commitment they had to the Weimar Republic. Under these conditions, the Social Democratic–led coalition that had governed through much of the 1920s collapsed, and no credible successor emerged. As early as 1930, many of the functions of government were being carried out by presidential decree. And unlike in France after 1934, in Germany the Communists and Socialists failed to join forces to defeat the right. Indeed, with encouragement from the USSR, the Communists in the early 1930s attacked the German Socialists as "Social Fascists," undercutting them just when they most desperately needed popular support.

Nonetheless, right up to the Nazi seizure of power in 1933, few Germans imagined that their country would follow Italy's path toward fascist dictatorship. Hitler's vicious anti-Semitic rhetoric, and the brutal tactics of the Nazi paramilitary forces, repelled many Germans who saw their country as a "land of poets and thinkers." Influential businessmen, soldiers, and politicians had little but contempt for a man and a movement they considered ignorant and vulgar. But fatally, some of them thought they could control him, particularly after Nazi support slipped in new parliamentary elections held in November 1932. In December, President von Hindenburg appointed as chancellor a general, Kurt von Schleicher, who tried to form a government that would include some Nazis, but not Hitler. When the attempt floundered, the political initiative passed to the previous chancellor, the conservative Franz von Papen, who proposed giving the top spot in government to Hitler but keeping him on a short leash by reserving most of the Cabinet posts for non-Nazis. Von Hindenburg agreed, boasting that he had put Hitler in a box.

In fact, all of Germany was about to become a Nazi prison. Von Papen and the men around the failing president had not counted on Hitler's ruthlessness and how he might abuse the state power now in his hands. At the end of February 1933, a mysterious fire destroyed much of the Reichstag building. It remains unclear who started it (the most recent research suggests it was the Nazis themselves), but Hitler blamed it on a Communist conspiracy to seize power. He convinced the deputies to suspend civil rights throughout Germany, allowing him to arrest the leadership of the Communist Party and other opponents. Less than a week later, with the voters cowed by increasing Nazi control of the police, a new election took place that made the Nazis by far the largest party in Germany, although they still won only 44 percent of the popular vote. Hitler then convinced conservative and Catholic parties to vote with him, the latter in return for guaranteeing the rights of the Catholic Church in Germany.

Hitler thereby had the two-thirds of the Reichstag necessary to pass the so-called Enabling Act of March 23, which gave him and his party unlimited "emergency" powers. By July, he had used these powers to ban all other political parties, arrest thousands of political opponents, impose strict censorship on the press, and allow his party's paramilitary forces to grow into an inviolable state-within-the-state. Germany had become a fascist dictatorship. A few figures inside the party retained enough of a power base to challenge Hitler—especially Ernst Röhm, the head of the powerful Nazi paramilitary. But in June 1934, Hitler had Röhm and eighty other potential opponents savagely murdered in the so-called Night of the Long Knives. Two months later, upon the death of von Hindenburg, Hitler assumed the title of Führer—supreme leader. Political opposition was entirely silenced, with dissidents arrested and imprisoned in special camps, such as Dachau on the outskirts of Munich.

THE NAZI REGIME

Over the next few years, Hitler and his allies created a regime that, while sharing some features with both Italian fascism and Stalinism, represented something new on the European scene. To begin with, it was grounded in an extreme racial science, loyally propagated by schools and government-controlled media. Nazi race theorists exalted the blond, northern ("Aryan") races, while alleging the physical and moral inferiority of other races, including especially Slavs and the supposedly subhuman, vermin-like Jews. It was the destiny of the Aryans to dominate other races, the Nazis argued, and they therefore required their new "living space" in the vast Slavic territories to the east. The British biologist Julian Huxley (1887–1975) was one of many European scientists who ridiculed the Nazis' racial ideas, invoking Hitler's portly deputy Hermann Goering and the 5'4" propaganda chief Goebbels:

> Our German neighbors have ascribed to themselves a teutonic type that is fair . . . tall and virile. Let us make a composite picture of a typical Teuton from the most prominent exponents of this view. Let him be as blond as Hitler . . . as tall as Goebbels, as slender as Goering. . . . How much would this resemble the German ideal?

However, the Nazi ideas in fact came all too close to those popularized since the late nineteenth century by influential racial theorists and eugenicists, and they enjoyed considerable legitimacy, even outside of Germany.

PENETRATING SOCIETY In Germany, the Nazis began organizing social life into new, highly ideological forms that challenged long-standing Western distinctions between public and private life. Boys were pressured into joining the Hitler Youth, which combined activities drawn from scouting with rudimentary military training and heavy ideological indoctrination. Although the Nazis favored the elimination of women from most public life, preferring to restrict them to the home, they also started women's organizations that provided ordinary housewives with new forms of social recognition. The Nazis staged food drives for the poor and encouraged young men to join the military or the paramilitary organizations called the SA and SS. Uniforms and parades became ubiquitous.

A massive propaganda apparatus, led by Goebbels, everywhere saluted the Nazi revival and hailed Hitler as the infallible genius saving Germany from ruin. The party staged mammoth rallies every year in the city of

Nazi Propaganda A 1938 propaganda poster shows a member of the girls' wing of the Hitler Youth holding a collecting tin. The caption reads, "Build youth hostels and homes," referring to the kinds of social welfare programs that the Nazi regime promised to the Germans.

Nuremberg and filmed them so that the rest of the country could watch. The Nazis even required Germans to replace ordinary greetings with the words *Heil Hitler!* A remarkable number of prominent Germans—including the country's most prominent philosopher, Martin Heidegger (1889–1976)—gave the regime their enthusiastic support. This insistence on popular participation, the exaltation of the supreme leader, the suppression of civil liberties, and the unleashing of the Gestapo secret police are all considered hallmarks of **totalitarianism**. This concept, first invented by Italian Fascists to describe the state they saw Mussolini as building, generally denotes a system in which the state aims at a far greater, more deliberate, more ideologically driven control over all aspects of public and private life than any earlier state had achieved.

Although foreign observers sometimes found it hard to believe, particularly in these early years, the Nazis enjoyed significant popularity. Despite its brutality, the party exuded a strength that the war and defeat otherwise seemed (in the eyes of many) to have scorched out of German life. It imposed a strict civil order that showed no mercy to criminals and enforced a new efficiency in public services. Middle-class Germans who were horrified by the open sexuality of the Weimar period and its experimental cultural life looked on with pleasure as the Nazis reimposed strict forms of sexual morality, imprisoned homosexuals, and staged bonfires of supposedly degenerate books and art. In the depths of the Depression, the Allies had already cancelled the remaining German reparations, but Hitler still repeatedly decried British and French "oppression" and won applause for doing so. Many Germans felt that he was making the country great again after the horrors of the war and the turbulence of Weimar and the Depression. In 1936, Hitler put his new Germany on display to an international audience by hosting the Olympic Games in Berlin. Germany won the most medals, but in a blow to the Nazis' racial theories, the African-American Jesse Owens was the single most successful athlete of the games, with four gold medals in track and field events.

NAZI ANTI-SEMITISM With their long-standing traditions of anti-Semitism now endorsed and strengthened by the Nazis' racial pseudo-science, many Germans also applauded the regime's implementation of an anti-Semitic program without precedent since the Middle Ages. In 1933, the Jews constituted well under 1 percent of the German population (barely 500,000 out of 67 million people) but enjoyed disproportionate prominence in many fields, including the universities, the arts, and retail business. They were also highly visible in the Socialist and Communist parties. With malign skill, the Nazi propaganda machine focused all the anger that had built up in Germany since the war—anger over the defeat and subsequent national humiliation, over the economic disasters and frustrations, over the corrupt spectacle of Weimar politics, over the supposed excesses of Weimar culture—on this one, vulnerable scapegoat.

The Nazi propaganda sheet *Der Stürmer* ("The Stormer," or "Attacker") exemplified the campaign, every week unleashing a new torrent of abuse, lies, and conspiracy theories about the Jewish threat to Germany, sometimes associating it with capitalism, sometimes with socialism. "Who Is the Enemy?" asked one typical issue

GERMAN RACIAL EDUCATION

Melita Maschmann (1918–2010) was born into a wealthy and conservative German family just after World War I. She joined the Hitler Youth over her family's objections and worked as a propagandist in a Nazi women's organization before taking part in the colonization of Poland following Germany's invasion of the country in 1939.

In this passage from her memoir, *Account Rendered* (1963), Maschmann recounts the racial propaganda and education that shaped her perceptions of the Poles. Well before the outbreak of World War II, racist beliefs were firmly entrenched in German society.

I must have been still at primary school the day I pulled a map out of our letter box which pleased me because of its gaiety. The countries of Europe stood out from one another in bright colours and on each country sat, crawled or stood a naked baby. I showed the map to my father because I wanted to know the significance of the babies. He explained to me that each of these children was a symbol of the birthrate of the country. The German families had on the average far less children than, say, Polish families. That was why only a frightened little girl sat on the patch of blue that meant Germany. On the yellow patch, just next door to the right, a sturdy little boy was crawling on all fours aggressively in the direction of the German frontier.

"Look at the boy," said my father. "He is bursting with health and strength. One day he will overrun the little girl."

The picture map stuck in my memory. It kept alive in me the feeling that the Poles were a menace to the German nation.

Later in "racial science" classes in the upper school the emotional lesson was "scientifically" reinforced. [Previously] we compared the birth rates of the Slavonic nations with those of the German nation and were instructed about the "average qualities of the east European races." Amongst them, so we heard, the intellectual and particularly the creative element came to the fore much more rarely. The noble, refined and intellectual qualities were everywhere in danger of being suppressed by the brutality of the primitive. That was why the Nordic nations were threatened with annihilation by…the Slavs. Primed with these views I came to the region which had been for generations a battlefield in the nationalist struggle between Poles and Germans. What I saw and heard seemed to confirm the National Socialist theories: the foreign nation seemed to consist only of manual workers, poor peasants and lower middle class townspeople, and the few Polish families I had a chance to study had substantially more children than corresponding German families.

QUESTIONS FOR ANALYSIS

1. In what ways did propaganda expose Maschmann to racist thinking as a child?
2. What supposedly scientific evidence of the Slavs' inferiority was taught to Maschmann in school?
3. What does Maschmann's memoir tell us about the importance of race to Nazi ideology?

Source: Melita Maschmann, *Account Rendered: A Dossier on my Former Self*, trans. Geoffrey Strachan (London: 1964), p. 66.

from 1934, and answered the question with a grotesque caricature of a Jew. "The Jews Are Our Misfortune," ran the paper's weekly motto, quoting from Hitler's *Mein Kampf.* The Nazis called for the boycott of Jewish business as early as April 1933, and party members defaced storefronts with signs and graffiti reading "Don't Buy from Jews."

The anti-Semitic campaigns stunned German Jews themselves. Numbering among the most secular, integrated, and best-educated Jewish populations in all of Europe, they generally took intense pride in their German culture. A high proportion of middle-aged Jewish men were war veterans. Although part of the Jewish community—especially those with strong ties abroad—emigrated soon after Hitler's seizure of power, many others did not. But conditions quickly grew worse.

In 1935, the Nazis passed the so-called **Nuremberg Laws**, which stripped Jews of citizenship and obliged them to wear large yellow stars of David on their clothing.

Nazi Anti-Semitism The headline of the Nazi newspaper *Der Stürmer* asks, "Who is the enemy?" The answer, as suggested by the grotesque cartoon, is the Jews, whom the article blames for World War I and the German defeat.

Jews were banned from most professions—often with the enthusiastic support of those professions' governing bodies. In November 1938, after an unbalanced, stateless Polish Jew shot and killed a German diplomat in Paris, the Nazis staged a massive pogrom, encouraging ordinary Germans and the paramilitaries to attack Jewish businesses and synagogues. Hundreds of synagogues were burned. The event came to be known as Kristallnacht—"Crystal Night"—after the shards of glass left in the street. At this point, another stampede for emigration began in the remaining Jewish population, but in some cases it was too late—Western governments, fearful of losing favor with their own populations by seeming too favorable to Jews, had started to close their doors.

And yet, despite the savage repression and anti-Semitism, the Nazi regime had not—at this point—made Germany into a land of mass murder. In some ways the Nazis were highly legalistic, passing no fewer than 4,000 laws during their first three years in power. Finding many enthusiastic collaborators in the conservative German judiciary, and purging other judges, they found it easy to twist the court system to their ends. Before 1939, Hitler's murder victims still numbered in the thousands, not the millions—and the large majority of them were political opponents. The same generalization holds for the other right-wing authoritarian states in Europe as well, including Mussolini's Italy. Stalin's USSR was different. There, already in the late 1920s, totalitarianism had taken a new, catastrophic turn.

STALINISM: THE FIVE-YEAR PLAN

After consolidating his power in the years around 1930, Stalin quickly adopted as his own the plan for rapid industrialization that he had previously opposed. The survival of the Soviet state, he declared, demanded that the Communists "put an end to backwardness in the shortest possible time." The party's central planners drew up a so-called **Five-Year Plan** (1928–32) to drag what was still largely a peasant country into the industrial age.

BUILDING A NEW SOCIETY Labor would be harnessed not just to build and staff factories, but also to construct entirely new industrial cities. The ambition of the plan was staggering. During these five years, Soviet officials put more people on the move (mostly, without their consent) than any other country in the world had seen for centuries, outside of wartime. The population of Moscow ballooned from 2 million in 1926 to 3.3 million just seven years later, causing severe housing shortages. In the same period, the Ural city of Sverdlovsk exploded by 346 percent after the Soviets designated it a center of heavy industry. In 1929, the Soviets set up a camp and railhead in the southern Ural Mountains, where hundreds of millions of tons of iron ore were easily accessible. Just three years later, Magnitogorsk ("Magnetic Mountain Town") had become a city of 250,000 people, most still housed in barracks and tents. Enduring temperatures that ranged from forty below zero Fahrenheit in winter to over a hundred in summer, these men and women struggled to build a massive steel works, completed in 1937.

Despite the harsh conditions, the workers in Magnitogorsk and other, similar industrial sites in some ways enjoyed a special, elite status in the Soviet Union. Stalin hailed them as the pioneers building socialism—indeed, building a new civilization—and elaborate propaganda campaigns treated them as heroes. The planners made every effort to ensure adequate supplies of food and fuel for Soviet proletarians. Workers who exceeded their production quotas won special rewards and recognition, including medals for "labor valor." In Moscow, the state built a lavish underground metro system, with many of the stations lined with marble. It was intended as a sign that under communism, beautiful things would be provided to the masses rather than restricted to the rich. In practice, the party elites themselves grew into a new upper class, enjoying access to the best apartments and special stores where they could purchase goods unavailable to ordinary citizens. Yet historians have found that in this early period, the Soviet industrialization project called forth a great deal of popular enthusiasm and willing participation. Ordinary citizens felt themselves engaged in constructing a new and better form of society.

COLLECTIVIZATION OF AGRICULTURE But city-dwellers and industrial workers were not the only Soviet citizens on the move, and if they enjoyed relative privilege, others suffered grievously. The Five-Year Plan depended on reliable supplies of cheap grain to feed the swelling numbers of industrial workers. Yet Lenin's New Economic Policy had left over 95 percent of arable land in the hands of individual proprietors, who could choose how much grain to sell on the open market. Even as the new industrial cities were coming into being, Stalin therefore decreed, in 1928, a larger-scale transformation in the countryside: the forcible replacement of private agriculture with vast, state-run collective farms.

The decision immediately provoked peasant resistance,

Anti-Kulak Propaganda Stalin's government sought to generate resentment against kulaks with propaganda like this cartoon, which shows a fist descending to push an evidently well-fed farmer off land that is instead to be farmed collectively.

which Stalin blamed on wealthy peasants, called kulaks. But it was not just kulaks who objected to **collectivization**, particularly when it meant handing over what was often their principal form of wealth: farm animals. Across the Soviet Union, peasants sold or slaughtered their animals rather than give them up to the collective. In response, the government forcibly expelled nearly 2 million people from their homes, sending them into internal exile, often thousands of miles away to inhospitable conditions in Siberia, the Urals, and Soviet Kazakhstan.

FAMINE The campaign to collectivize agriculture quickly caused other forms of disruption. Grain production dropped, and the products of the collective farms themselves were diverted to the cities. By early 1930, famine spread through the countryside. Foreign travelers in Ukraine, formerly known as the breadbasket of the Russian Empire, were shocked to see children with distended bellies, the telltale sign of starvation, and even corpses lying unburied in fallow fields. In the towns and cities, endless lines outside bakeries from before dawn became a common sight.

In March 1930, Stalin signaled a reversal of course in an article in the official newspaper, *Pravda* ("Truth"), disingenuously titled "Dizzy with Success." The collectivization drive had succeeded brilliantly, he declared: "A radical turn of the countryside toward socialism may be considered as already achieved." But some lower-level functionaries, he continued, were committing excesses, and so it was time to slow the process down. But the famine did not end, and in at least some areas of the Soviet Union, the state prevented the starving peasants from fleeing to the cities, which were themselves facing food shortages, or across the border to neighboring provinces or countries. The death toll mounted. By 1937, the collectivization program had largely succeeded, with roughly 93 percent of all arable land now in collective farms. But at least 6 million people had died of hunger.

No area suffered more from collectivization than the western Soviet republic of Ukraine. After seeing its bid for independence crushed by the Red Army during the Revolution, the region had remained restive under Soviet rule. The Soviet state did in principle promote a degree of autonomy for its most important nationalities. Soviet Ukrainians, unlike Polish Ukrainians, could go to school in their own native language. But Stalin was determined to crush Ukrainian opposition to his policies, and many historians believe he made use of the famine to do so. Perhaps 50 percent of all Soviet deaths in the great famine occurred in this one region, mostly in 1932–33. Some desperate Ukrainian peasants managed to flee into neighboring Poland. Others took up arms in resistance and were quickly repressed. Even so, while anecdotal reports of the horrors filtered out of the region with them, neither the Soviet population itself nor foreign observers became aware of the famine's full, hideous dimensions until many years afterward.

The first Five-Year Plan came to an end six months early in 1932 with Stalin's planners already gearing up for a second one. Yet despite the considerable progress made toward the goals of industrialization and collectivization, it was clear that ultimate success would take far longer, and involve far greater costs, than the planners had expected. Sympathetic left-wing visitors from abroad, treated to tours of showcase factories and towns but kept far away from the regions of famine, went home convinced that the Soviets really had managed to create "a new civilization" (to quote the title of a long, laudatory book by two English socialists). But Soviet officials themselves felt increasingly frustrated and were prone to blame delays on counterrevolutionary sabotage.

THE GREAT TERROR In the late 1930s, these frustrations, and Stalin's own increasing isolation and paranoia, led to what historians now refer to as the **Great Terror**. At every level of Soviet society, citizens were encouraged to look for signs of counterrevolutionary activity and denounce suspected traitors. In 1936, the secret police began to arrest hundreds of well-known Communists, including the leadership of the former Left Opposition (except for Trotsky, who left the country), and many other leading Old Bolsheviks—party members since before the Revolution. In a series of spectacular public trials, these men admitted that they had spied for Nazi Germany, engaged in industrial sabotage, and much else—the confessions were fantastical, the victims having been browbeaten, tortured, or threatened into making them. Death sentences followed, and quickly the purges widened out, with the head of the secret police himself falling victim.

In July 1937, Stalin issued his infamous secret order 00447, which called for the arrest and execution of 80,000 supposed traitors and the banishment of 193,000 others to the swelling system of labor and punishment camps known by their Russian acronym as the Gulag and located across the Soviet Union, but most notoriously in Siberia. By September, the new head of the secret police reported enthusiastically back to Stalin that 35,434 people had already been shot. But the Terror continued for more than another year and spun even further out of control. Official Soviet records themselves report the execution of a staggering 680,000 people. Millions more ended up in the Gulag, in horrific conditions under which as many as a million more died. It was during this period that the secret police began carrying out sweeps in the major cities, leading to the terrible events on Cannibal Island.

Before it was over, the Great Terror came close to decimating Soviet society. The intelligentsia paid a particularly high price, with a large proportion of leading artists and writers falling victim. The poet Osip Mandelstam (1891–1938), who dared satirize Stalin in a 1934 epigram ("Every killing is for him a delight"), was just one of the thousands to be arrested and die in prison. Even those professions most essential to the Soviet system were purged—in Stalin's paranoid viewpoint, they were also the professions in which treason and sabotage could do the worst damage. The ranks of leading engineers were devastated, as was the high command of the military, including 16 out of the 21 highest-ranking army generals and 8 out of 9 admirals. The Soviet Union would pay a massive price for these purges when facing a Nazi invasion in 1941. But it was the Communist Party itself that suffered the most. Of the 139 people chosen as members of its Central Committee in 1934, fully 98 were dead four years later.

By the end of the 1930s, then, both Nazi Germany and Stalin's Soviet Union had become totalitarian states. Both had power-drunk, unstable leaders possessed of unlimited power and supported by mammoth cults of personality. Both had secret police forces that had crushed all serious political opposition and orchestrated pervasive climates of fear and denunciation. Both had targeted vulnerable minorities for destruction. Both had undertaken vast transformations of public and private life. And both could still count, remarkably, on considerable popular enthusiasm for the regime and the leader. The Nazi revolution had so far occurred without massive damage to the country as a whole—though Jews, homosexuals and political opponents had of course suffered greatly. The damage and destruction in the USSR, however, was already reaching a massive scale. Even as the Five-Year Plans began to manage and mobilize the Soviet Union's vast human and material resources, the accompanying social disruptions, the famine, and the Great Terror had left it reeling from self-inflicted wounds. As the 1930s came to an end, it was in no condition whatsoever for a military showdown with its totalitarian competitor to the west. But it seemed clear to most observers in Europe that such a showdown was coming—and soon.

THE COMING OF WORLD WAR II

Historians have labored endlessly over the origins of the first world war, but there has been no need for comparable debates in regard to the second. Adolf Hitler built much of his political career on the idea that Germany, supposedly betrayed and victimized in 1918–19, should seek revenge on its tormentors and fulfill its destiny by carving out a new empire, by force, in the rich agricultural lands to its east. The point was there for all to read in *Mein Kampf*, published in 1925–26.

HITLER'S EARLY MOVES

Soon after taking power in 1933, Hitler informed his generals that his long-term foreign policy would in fact aim at these expansive goals. For a time, he played a double game, proclaiming his peaceful intentions even while working to prepare Germany for war. Some Allied statesmen, desperate to prevent another frightful cataclysm, grabbed at his words like a life raft in an ocean storm. But the actions

Mussolini and Hitler At a rally in Munich in 1937, Mussolini and Hitler appear together, indicating the close ties between the two totalitarian rulers following their alliance in 1936.

of Germany and its allies between 1933 and 1939 demonstrated all too clearly an accelerating pattern of aggression.

ALLIANCES   From the very start of his rule, Hitler cultivated close relations with Mussolini, and he signed an initial alliance with Fascist Italy in 1936. As early as 1933–34, he took Germany out of the League of Nations and signed a nonaggression pact with Poland—a clear attempt to avoid another two-front war. He moved toward an alliance with authoritarian Japan, which was engaged in a brutal campaign of expansion on the Asian mainland. And while Hitler did not attempt to put Germany's still-weak military into action in his first years in power, he encouraged Mussolini to unleash Italy's forces. In 1935, Italy tried to wipe out the memory of its humiliating defeat in Ethiopia forty years before by invading the country again, this time with the help of an air force and armored vehicles. The capital, Addis Ababa, fell seven months later, after a campaign that caused the death of some half a million Ethiopians. The Allies and the League of Nations responded to the war with empty rebukes and ineffective, short-lived sanctions, which further encouraged both dictators. Italy soon began moving toward an absorption of Albania into its empire as well.

REARMAMENT   In 1935, Hitler openly broke the terms of the Versailles treaty. He reinstated compulsory military service, re-created the German air force (which the treaty had prohibited), and announced his intention to increase the size of his army to half a million men, far above the Versailles-imposed limits. Then, in March 1936, Hitler sent the German army back into the Rhineland, which Versailles had established as a demilitarized zone. At every turn, he insisted to world public opinion that he was merely acting to address the injustices of Versailles and had no aggressive intentions. Had the Allies confronted him forcefully, he probably would have backed down, particularly in the Rhineland.

But Britain and France did not push back. For one thing, their elites had strong fears of another continental bloodbath—in one telltale sign, students at Oxford University's principal debating society had overwhelmingly voted, in 1933, for the proposition that "this House will under no circumstances fight for its King and Country." But they also saw a balanced competition between strong states as Europe's normal historical condition, and they hoped against hope that once Germany had reclaimed its "rightful" place, it would make no further demands. But with Germany's rearmament, the various agreements of the 1920s to limit the size of European militaries largely collapsed.

The Spanish Civil War, 1936–1939 Nationalist forces based in northern Spain attacked the lines of the Republican-held southeast, and with the support of German and Italian forces besieged Madrid and bombed Republican towns such as Guernica. Despite the Soviet Union's support for the Republicans, by 1939 the Nationalists gained control of most of the country—including the key Republican stronghold of Barcelona—when they defeated the Republicans.

THE SPANISH CIVIL WAR

The leaders of Britain and France were terribly wrong, as events in Spain soon showed. Throughout most of the 1920s and early 1930s, the country had lurched from one crisis to another. General Primo de Rivera's erratic dictatorship ended in 1930, as the Depression hit Spain and he lost the confidence of the military and King Alfonso XIII (r. 1886–1931). A year later, after the election of a left-wing majority in the Cortes (parliament), the king abdicated and a new Republic came into being.

Between 1931 and 1936, the Republic's leaders struggled to reduce the power of the Church and wealthy landowners, but not quickly enough to satisfy radical labor unions and nationalists in the northeastern region of Catalonia, whose armed resistance to the central government was bloodily suppressed in 1933–35. A quasi-Fascist party called the Falange took shape; and after the government tried to ban it in the spring of 1936, a right-wing insurrection in the military began, leading to full-fledged civil war.

The Nationalists, led by General Francisco Franco (1892–1975) and supported by the Catholic Church, aimed to replace the Republic with an authoritarian regime. On the other side, a coalition of liberals, socialists, anarchists, and the rapidly growing Communist Party defended the Republic but largely failed to agree on their own ultimate goals. George Orwell, whose *Homage to Catalonia* offers a vivid account of his experiences fighting for the Republic (he barely survived a bullet wound to the neck), noted that the Communists often seemed more concerned with undercutting their own allies than with winning the struggle.

From the larger European perspective, the **Spanish Civil War** was important for the way it served as a proxy war and testing ground for the future combatants in World War II. The German and Italian air forces openly participated on the Nationalist side, transporting men and supplies, and bombing and strafing Republican positions. For the first time, Europe witnessed major cities under sustained aerial bombardment. The small Basque town of Guernica was virtually wiped out by one raid—Picasso illustrated the incident in one of his most famous paintings. Some 100,000 Italian soldiers participated, and both German and Italian advisers were prominent in the Nationalist ranks.

Stalin sent advisers and aid to the Republicans, funneling as much as possible through the Spanish Communist Party, but Britain and France largely adopted a position of non-intervention. Ragged International Brigades drawn from across the Western world, including the Abraham Lincoln Brigade from the United States, helped the Republicans as well; but poorly trained and equipped, they ultimately made little difference. The Nationalists besieged Madrid for much of the war and

Guernica Picasso commemorated the devastating bombing of the Basque town of Guernica in his huge 1937 painting of the same name. The stark black-and-white canvas shows fragmented figures writhing in pain and shocked at the destruction, as if shattered by the attack.

advanced westward along a confused front that ran from the French border to the Mediterranean. After the fall of Barcelona in early 1939, remaining Republican resistance collapsed. The right-wing dictators marked another triumph.

GERMAN AGGRESSION: AUSTRIA AND CZECHOSLOVAKIA

Hitler now felt sufficiently encouraged to turn his sights to the east. The diminished Austrian state created by Versailles, like many of its central European neighbors, had experienced its share of turmoil in the Depression years, including a brief attempt to establish a fascist dictatorship. In the mid-1930s, it remained deeply unstable with a growing and aggressive Nazi Party calling for union with Germany and a weak government largely running the country by dictate. Hitler, Austrian by birth, pushed for union, accused the Austrians of persecuting Nazis, and met every attempt to placate him with further demands.

In March 1938, when the Austrian president refused to make a Nazi the country's chancellor, German troops poured across the border, where in most cases enthusiastic crowds greeted them with German flags. In another clear violation of the Versailles treaty, but without significant French or British opposition, Austria was quickly absorbed into Hitler's Reich, with tens of thousands of socialists and liberals immediately arrested. Over 180,000 more Jews had also fallen under Nazi rule and found themselves subject to the Nuremberg Laws, as well as to forms of ritual humiliation—some were forced by crowds to scrub the streets of Vienna with their toothbrushes.

THE CZECH CRISIS On the map of Europe, greater Germany, engorged with new territory, now menacingly surrounded the western half of Czechoslovakia—the one remaining central European democracy, a major industrial state, and an ally of France and the USSR. The country's

Humiliation of Jews Nazi supporters (including members of the Hitler Youth in the foreground) force Jewish residents of Vienna to scrub a street following the German annexation of Austria in 1938.

mountainous western border regions, known as the Sudetenland, where the population was largely German speaking, had a growing Nazi Party led by a demagogue named Konrad Henlein. Having completed the annexation of Austria, in mid-1938 Hitler turned his attention here, denouncing Czech harassment of the Sudeten Germans and massing his army on the border.

The Allies had by now realized that Hitler's ambitions were unlikely to stop with redressing the supposed injustices of Versailles. Still, they remained reluctant to go to war less than twenty years since the end of the last war, especially since Hitler was claiming to act in favor of the principle of national self-determination and a majority of Sudeten Germans clearly wanted union with Germany. Even as Britain's Conservative prime minister, Neville Chamberlain, reluctantly began organizing civil defense during the Czechoslovak crisis in late September 1938, he gave a speech in which he lamented: "How horrible, fantastic, incredible it is that we should begin digging trenches and trying on gas masks here because of a quarrel in a faraway country between people of whom we know nothing."

MUNICH After several months of ineffective discussions and increasingly aggressive German demands, Hitler, Mussolini, Chamberlain, and French prime minister Édouard Daladier met in Munich, in September 1938, in an effort to settle the crisis. The Czechs were not invited. The resulting agreement gave Hitler virtually everything he wanted: above all, the immediate annexation of the Sudetenland, with its heavy industry and the very fortifications designed to protect the Czech heartland from Germany. Chamberlain returned home to Britain and declared at the airport, waving the agreement in the air, that he had secured "peace in our time." Scarcely half a year later, Hitler replied to Chamberlain with a gesture of undisguised contempt. He sent the German army across the new borders to occupy the now-defenseless western half of Czechoslovakia, turning it into a German protectorate. Slovaks friendly to the Nazis established an independent Slovakia in the eastern half.

PREPARING FOR WAR

The Czech crisis also had a profound effect on Joseph Stalin. Before the Munich meeting, he had pleaded with the British and French to discuss with him a joint stance to contain Hitler's aggression. He even began mobilizing part of his armed forces in the hope that the British and French would follow suit. But the British and

French leaders, driven by their long-standing hatred of communism and their horror at the excesses of Stalin's rule, refused his request for a meeting. Stalin now came to believe that if Hitler attacked him, he could not count on support from the West.

ARMS RACE With war all but inevitable, the major powers began a frantic arms race, producing ships and planes, mobilizing draftees, and stockpiling supplies and munitions. Over the course of 1938, British production of new military aircraft more than doubled to over 330 per month. By June 1939, the figure had doubled again. The French also worked to reinforce a line of fortresses on their eastern frontier—the so-called Maginot Line—in which their military command put a dangerously absolute faith, believing it sufficiently strong to resist even a major armored offensive by the Germans. They did not, however, extend the line to their northern frontier with neutral Belgium, in part because they believed the densely forested frontier zones to be impassable by heavy armored vehicles (they were not, as they would learn to their enormous cost). They also ignored the recommendations of a mid-ranking officer, Charles de Gaulle, to increase their own reliance on tanks and other armored vehicles.

In the spring and summer of 1939, the scene of the developing pre-war tragedy moved to Poland. Hitler had already determined, in accordance with his long-standing plans for eastward expansion, to attack the vulnerable Polish state despite its alliance with Britain and France. Already in the spring, he had given orders to his high command to prepare for a start to hostilities on September 1. Hitler did not just want to recapture the German territories ceded to Poland in 1919 (including the so-called Polish Corridor that now divided East Prussia from the rest of Germany), but to annex sizable new territories, from which Slavic and Jewish "subhumans" would eventually be expelled to make way for Aryan settlers. To justify the attack, the German propaganda machine began to churn out stories about the abuse of ethnic Germans in Poland and the supposed desire of the "free city" of Danzig, in the Polish Corridor, to be reunited with the Reich. Should we "die for Danzig?" asked British and French appeasers.

THE NAZI-SOVIET PACT The major question, throughout the summer, was whether the Nazis would have to fight a war on two fronts. Despite the vast ideological differences between the Soviet Union and the western Allies, most onlookers assumed they would eventually conclude an alliance against the common fascist enemy whom the Soviets had spent the past six years denouncing.

Nazi-Soviet Pact A 1939 British cartoon mocks the shocking revelation of the agreement between Hitler and Stalin. The two meet over the body of a fallen soldier, greeting each other as "the scum of the earth" and "the bloody assassin of the workers."

The German high command of course desperately wanted to avoid a repetition of the two-front war that had proven fatal to them in 1914–18. But Stalin also wanted to avoid an immediate confrontation with the Nazis. The Soviet Union was facing Japanese encroachments into its eastern territory from Japan's new puppet state in Manchuria—the conflicts there even boiled up into a brief border war in 1939, in which the Soviets prevailed. But the USSR remained unprepared for a war in the west, especially after the disruptions of the Five-Year Plans and the Great Terror, and the decimation of the military command. A rapid Nazi offensive into Poland might quickly place them on the borders of Ukraine, whose devastated and resentful population had every reason to rise up against the Communists.

In these conditions, the two dictators had strong incentives to work out a deal of their own. During the summer of 1939, German foreign minister Joachim von Ribbentrop (1893–1946) and Soviet foreign minister Vyacheslav Molotov (1890–1986) came to an arrangement in secret. The Soviets agreed not to respond to a German attack on Poland, and in return the Germans promised them a sphere of influence in the regions the USSR had lost after World War I: eastern Poland and the Baltic states of Estonia, Latvia, and Lithuania.

Only the first part of the deal, the **Nazi-Soviet Pact**, was announced publicly, but the announcement on August 23 caused shock in the west. Never before had a diplomatic switch of such proportions and speed taken place, even in the reversal of alliances that had preceded the Seven Years' War in the eighteenth century. Western Communists who had spent the previous six years dutifully repeating the Soviet line about the demonic Nazis, and who genuinely saw Stalin as the architect of a new socialist society, reeled. Thousands left the party. Millions more westerners who had felt some sympathy for the Soviet experiment now expressed outrage at the Soviet leader's hypocrisy. Across Europe, another generation of young men now knew they would soon have to go off to war, but the realization led to none of the scenes of enthusiasm that had taken place in 1914, and none of the hopes that war might regenerate their societies. A mood of grim determination prevailed.

INVASION OF POLAND

Early in the morning of September 1, 1939, a mass of 1.5 million German troops, accompanied by tanks and supported by the powerful German air force—the Luftwaffe—began to cross the frontier into Poland. Britain and France reluctantly declared war but did not attempt to attack Germany themselves. Instead, they watched as the German troops advanced eastward and German planes subjected Warsaw to the largest aerial bombing Europe had yet seen, killing thousands. The Polish armed forces offered a gallant and determined resistance, but they were no match for the Nazi forces. Then, on September 17, Soviet troops marched into Poland from the east, as permitted by the secret terms of the Nazi-Soviet Pact. On September 27, Warsaw fell to the Germans, and the remnants of the Polish government fled to London. On October 6, the remaining Polish forces surrendered.

In the newly occupied Poland, the two totalitarian regimes showed all too brutally what Europe had to expect from the coming six years of total war. In both occupation zones, thousands of members of the Polish elites—top officials, academics, journalists, army officers—were arrested and sent to prison camps or simply executed outright. The Germans annexed large territories directly to the Reich, while a central area around Warsaw was transformed into a so-called General Government under German military rule. Harsh discipline prevailed, with the slightest resistance to the German occupation forces punishable by the arrest and execution of scores of hostages.

With their sudden conquest, the Germans also now found themselves ruling over a vast new population of Jews. Unlike in Germany, in Poland Jews made up close in secular Polish life. But lower-class urban Jews, and the large majority of rural ones, remained marked off by their orthodox religion, their traditional dress, and their Yiddish language.

Now all these Jews were at the mercy of the Nazis, who quickly began to force them into crowded, walled ghettoes, while publicly humiliating them in the streets. Although the Nazis had not yet come to a formal decision to kill the Jews under their control, let alone attempt to implement such a decision, their ultimate goal was clear to those with eyes to see, that the coming war would not just be a total war, but a war of extermination.

JAPANESE AGGRESSION

And it would be another world war. Japan's violent occupation of Manchuria and invasion of north China had already produced millions of casualties. In 1937–38, Japanese forces committed atrocities against hundreds of thousands of Chinese civilians in the city of Nanjing. Japan had proclaimed the aims of freeing East Asia from Western colonialism and sharing resources among its peoples—what would become known as the East Asian Co-Prosperity Sphere. Its ambitions threatened not just China proper but also French Indochina, the Dutch Netherlands, British Malaysia, and Hong Kong—even the American-dominated Philippines. In the United States, a powerful isolationist movement, which had taken shape over the course of the inter-war period, insisted that the country keep out of the fighting, and for the time being President Franklin Roosevelt went along. But given the close political and economic ties between the United States and western Europe, and the potential for conflict between America and Hitler's ally Japan, eventual U.S. involvement seemed likely.

THE PHONY WAR

But at the end of autumn 1939, not only did the war remain limited to Europe; it had fallen into a strange lull—what would soon be called the Phony War. The guns in Poland had gone silent, and the western front remained largely inactive. Across Europe, the powers continued frantically to arm. The world waited in dread. And the dread was all too justified. Despite the setbacks of the Great Depression, Europe's industrial capacity had reached new heights, which, as the Spanish Civil War had shown, could be deployed all too easily for purposes of mass destruction.

Aggression in Europe, 1936–1939 In the years before war broke out, Hitler's Germany asserted its military power by occupying the previously demilitarized Rhineland, annexing Austria, and ultimately invading Czechoslovakia and Poland in 1938–39. Italy and the Soviet Union also rearmed and asserted their authority over new territories with the aid of non-aggression pacts with Germany.

to 10 percent of the population—and roughly one-third in some major cities, including Warsaw. Assimilation of this population had taken place with relative speed over the previous twenty years as the Jews, freed from tsarist restrictions on their employment, were able to explore new economic opportunities. Particularly in the cities, middle-class Jews generally spoke Polish as a first language, dressed in modern fashion, and did their best, despite continuing discrimination and quotas on their presence in the universities and professions, to take part

Paired with the ideological capacity of the totalitarian dictators to mobilize vast forces for the purpose of all-out conflict, and to demonize enemies as subhumans deserving of death, the peril had no precedent in world history.

CONCLUSION

At this moment, it had been barely twenty years since the end of World War I. And despite the best efforts of men and women across Europe, the Continent had not yet emerged from the dark shadow of the earlier war. In two of the empires that had collapsed at the end of World War I—Germany and Russia—the inter-war period had brought further violence and political chaos that facilitated the emergence of totalitarian dictatorships. In the wreckage of a third empire—Austria-Hungary—the emergence of new national states founded very imperfectly on the principle of national self-determination had not brought peace, but instead sowed the seeds of new conflicts. The economic cost of the war had left all parties depleted, vulnerable to the severe dislocations of the Great Depression, and increasingly dependent on the economy of the United States, an ocean away. Finally, the sense that the devastating death toll of the war had served little purpose fed resentment and cynicism among some, while leading others to embrace extreme ideologies that promised a rebirth of the human species—or at least their own part thereof. In all these ways, the first world war led to the second. Now, in the winter of 1939–40, a storm of blood was about to break.

[CHAPTER REVIEW]

KEY TERMS

Weimar Republic (p. 743)   Bauhaus School (p. 751)   Great Depression (p. 756)   Five-Year Plan (p. 763)

Adolf Hitler (p. 743)   John Maynard Keynes   mandates (p. 757)   collectivization (p. 764)

Nazis (p. 744)   (p. 754)   Mohandas Gandhi (p. 759)   Great Terror (p. 765)

Beer Hall Putsch (p. 744)   corporatism (p. 754)   totalitarianism (p. 761)   Spanish Civil War (p. 767)

Benito Mussolini (p. 746)   fascism (p. 756)   Nuremberg Laws (p. 762)   Nazi-Soviet Pact (p. 770)

Joseph Stalin (p. 747)

REVIEW QUESTIONS

1. What conditions created openings for the rise of Nazism in the Weimar Republic?

2. During the 1920s, what were the causes of political instability in the new states of central and eastern Europe?

3. What were the major characteristics of modernist literature, art, film, and architecture during the 1920s and early 1930s?

4. During the 1920s and 1930s, what were the most significant shifts in life in European cities?

5. What impact did the Great Depression have on Europe?

6. How did colonial peoples challenge Britain and France's control of their newly expanded empires?

7. How did Hitler's Nazi regime establish control over Germany's government and society?

8. What were the successes and failures of Stalin's first Five-Year Plan?

9. In what ways did the Spanish Civil War presage World War II?

10. What methods did Germany use to expand its territory in the late 1930s?

CORE OBJECTIVES

After reading this chapter, you should have a solid understanding of the following core objectives. To strengthen your grasp of the core objectives, use the resources on the Student Site for The West.

- Analyze the causes of social and political instability in the aftermath of World War I.

- Assess the cultural changes associated with modernism, new technologies, and gender roles in the 1920s and 1930s.

- Describe the economic and political struggles in Europe and the European colonies during the inter-war period.

- Compare Germany under Hitler and the Soviet Union under Stalin in the period before World War II.

- Trace the events that led to the outbreak of World War II.

 GO TO inQuizitive TO SEE WHAT YOU'VE LEARNED—AND LEARN WHAT YOU'VE MISSED—WITH PERSONALIZED FEEDBACK ALONG THE WAY.

April–June 1940
German blitzkrieg in
Norway, Denmark,
Low Countries,
and France

　　June 21, 1940
　　France signs armistice
　　with Germany

　　　　Sept. 1940–May 1941　　　　**June 22, 1941**　　　　**December 7, 1941**　　　　　　**Spring 1943**
　　　　The Blitz in London　　　　　Germany invades　　　　Japan attacks　　　　　　　Axis driven from
　　　　　　　　　　　　　　　　the Soviet Union　　　　Pearl Harbor　　　　　　　North Africa

　　　July–October 1940　　**1941**　　　　　　　　　　　**January 1942**　　　　**Aug. 1942–Jan. 1943**　　**September 3, 1943**
　　　Battle of Britain　　　　U.S. Congress　　　　　　Wannsee　　　　　　Battle of Stalingrad　　　Italy attempts to
May 27–June 4, 1940　　approves Lend-Lease　　conference　　　　　　　　　　　　　　surrender to the Allies
Evacuation　　　　　　**1941–1944**
of Dunkirk　　　　　　Siege of Leningrad

The Abyss

WORLD WAR II AND THE HOLOCAUST

1940–1945

February 1945
Yalta conference

January 1945
Red Army liberates
Auschwitz

June 6, 1944
D-Day

August 1945
U.S. government
drops atomic bombs
on Hiroshima
and Nagasaki

August 12, 1945
Japan surrenders

August 23, 1944
Liberation of Paris

May 8, 1945
Germany surrenders

July 1945
Potsdam
conference

n Britain and France, the year 1940 began in a guarded but hopeful mood. In Paris, revelers packed the streets to celebrate the New Year's holiday and thronged to the horse races at Vincennes, which had just reopened after a four-month suspension. At Piccadilly Circus in the heart of London, young men and women obeyed "blackout" rules against fireworks and instead clicked flashlights on and off while singing the popular song of the moment, the "Beer Barrel Polka." British journalists calmly mused that the imminent introduction of food rationing (four ounces of butter and twelve ounces of sugar per week per person) would do wonders for the national waistline. Total war deaths on the western front to date were calculated at 9,604, giving credence to the idea that a Phony War was in progress—with no one sure if or when it would give way to a more intense conflict. The *New York Times* summarized the conventional wisdom as follows:

> No one can fail to notice how much less alarming the outlook seems at the beginning of the new year, after four months of war, than it seemed three or four months ago. In spite of the brilliant success of the *Blitzkrieg* in Poland, there has been no *Blitzkrieg* in the West. Hitler has not dared seriously to attack the Maginot Line…there has been no mass airplane bombing of London and Paris…the Nazi military machine is not as smoothly functioning and irresistible as the Polish campaign made it seem.

A Call to Attack An iconic photograph by the Soviet photojournalist Max Alpert captures a lieutenant of the Red Army on July 12, 1942, raising his pistol to the sky to rally his fellow soldiers to attack the Germans. The lieutenant is thought to be Aleksey Gordeyevich Yeremenko, who was stationed in eastern Ukraine and died shortly after the photograph was taken.

In fact, the Phony War would not last much longer. Within months, the apparent lull would break, and Europe and the world would be plunged fully into the most intense, destructive war that the planet has ever known.

FROM BLITZKRIEG TO THE BATTLE OF BRITAIN

Blitzkrieg—German for "lightning war"—was coming to the west. Now Germany would begin an assault against the full strength of the western Allies, Britain and France. Most observers expected a drawn-out series of titanic battles, but the reality was shockingly different.

THE GERMAN OFFENSIVES IN SCANDINAVIA AND WESTERN EUROPE

In early April 1940, German forces invaded Denmark and Norway, in order to exploit the latter's strategic position in the North Atlantic and to ensure continuing supplies of Scandinavian iron ore. While Denmark was immediately overwhelmed, Norwegian resistance continued, with Allied help, through the spring, but the Wehrmacht—the German army—seized most of its strategic objectives quickly. By the late spring, Germany had occupied and fortified Norway and installed a puppet government under Norwegian fascist leader Vidkun Quisling (1887–1945), whose last name has become a synonym for treasonous collaboration with invaders.

Then, on May 10, the Germans launched a major offensive in the main theater of operations. Using tanks, infantry, paratroopers, and even gliders, they simultaneously attacked France and the three neutral countries of Belgium, Luxembourg, and the Netherlands. The Allies initially seemed in a strong position to push them back. They had more soldiers in the field than Germany, and more tanks as well. Had the Germans followed their initial plan of attacking through central Belgium, they would have run into heavy Allied concentrations. But instead they targeted their forces on the heavily forested Ardennes region, which the Allies had assumed was impassible. Some 1,800 German tanks proved them wrong, pushing through with ease, overwhelming Belgian resistance, and then driving toward the Channel coast. The Germans made full use of airpower, strafing Allied soldiers with Stuka dive-bombers mounted with guns and blaring sirens that panicked the infantry in their path. The French Ninth Army crumbled and surrendered. At one point, German general Erwin Rommel (1891–1944) took 10,000 French prisoners while losing only 41 of his own men. Adolf Hitler was ecstatic: "I could have wept for joy, they had fallen into the trap."

Events now moved with stunning speed. On May 10, 1940, Neville Chamberlain resigned and Winston Churchill became the British prime minister. The Germans completed their occupation of the Netherlands and began to close their "trap" on the Allied forces cut off in Belgium and northern France. Hitler did make one large mistake, however: German tanks stopped for a fateful two days in late May, giving the British time to organize a makeshift flotilla to evacuate its army. Some 337,000 soldiers escaped from the northern French port of **Dunkirk** in an operational success that gave a much-needed boost to British morale. In early June, the French desperately set up a new defensive line across northern France, but the Germans broke through easily. On June 10, the French government declared Paris an "open city" and fled south. Up to 10 million people from northern France fled as well in an exodus of indescribable chaos and fear. They clogged the roads with overloaded cars, carts, and bicycles, hindering the maneuvering of the Allied forces. The Germans deliberately heightened the chaos by strafing the refugees with their horrifying Stukas. Paris seemed empty as the first German soldiers entered on June 14, 1940.

THE FALL OF FRANCE

The Battle of France now came to an inglorious end. When French premier Paul Reynaud refused to surrender, he resigned and was replaced by eighty-four-year-old Marshal Philippe Pétain (1856–1951), a heroic World War I commander. Pétain immediately went on the radio to announce France's surrender: "I give myself to France to assuage her misfortune.... It is with a heavy heart that I say we must end the fight." On June 22, the French signed an armistice in the same railroad coach where German envoys had surrendered in 1918. With Hitler himself looking on exultantly, they agreed to severe terms: German occupation of northern France and the Atlantic coastline; the effective demilitarization of a large unoccupied zone; and the indefinite use of 2 million French soldiers as forced labor in Germany.

Early in the morning of June 23, Hitler landed at Le Bourget airport north of Paris and took a three-hour tour of the city. He loudly admired the ornate nineteenth-century Opera House and tried to tip the French attendant, who refused. At the military monument of the Invalides, he spent many minutes staring silently down at the tomb of Napoleon Bonaparte. In London, five days earlier, a little-known French general named Charles de Gaulle had gone on the radio to defy his own government and urge further resistance. But in France, his appeal was little heard or heeded. The vast majority of the French population rallied to Pétain as their savior.

The blitzkrieg was not quite the inevitable triumph that it appears in retrospect. The French high command had made a number of disastrous mistakes, including restoring normal leave to the army just three days before the start of the German offensive. Worst of all, when defeat stared the French in the face in early June, the conservative military and political leadership cared less about rallying the nation to resist than about ensuring that the German victory would not lead to a left-wing uprising in Paris, as had happened in 1871. When the French National Assembly voted in July to give dictatorial powers to Pétain, they acted not to provide a "shield" for the defeated and divided nation but to allow French ultra-conservatives to exploit the German victory for their own benefit and impose a conservative National Revolution. A new ultra-conservative regime, headquartered in the spa town of **Vichy** in the unoccupied zone, soon took shape.

Fall of Paris German soldiers march through the Arc de Triomphe down the Champs Élysées, in central Paris, following France's surrender to Germany in June 1940.

BRITAIN ISOLATED

In short, just six months after the hopeful New Year's celebrations of 1940, the war had changed beyond recognition. Germany, its allies, and the Soviet Union (which had signed the non-aggression pact with Hitler in 1939) now controlled virtually the entire European continent. After the fall of France, Stalin, taking advantage of the secret provisions of the Nazi-Soviet pact, invaded the three Baltic states of Lithuania, Latvia, and Estonia and annexed them to the USSR. On the Continent only the Balkans, Iberia, and neutral Sweden and Switzerland remained outside of Nazi or Soviet control. With the vast territories of the French Empire now under the uncertain control of France's Vichy regime (under the terms of the armistice, French colonies were bound to neutrality, but both sides tried to gain control of them), and with Japan occupying large stretches of China, the war had truly become a world war. Against the German juggernaut, Britain stood very much alone.

At this decisive moment, the British leadership lay in the hands of a man widely lampooned as a washed-up, unscrupulous, pigheaded drunk. **Winston Churchill**, then sixty-six years old, had led by any account a checkered career as soldier, journalist, adventurer, and maverick, party-switching politician. His reputation remained tarnished in part because of his role as architect of Britain's disastrous Gallipoli expedition in World War I.

World War II in Europe and North Africa At the start of the war, Hitler's blitzkrieg saw numerous territorial gains: Poland in 1939; Scandinavia, the Low Countries, and France in 1940; and the Balkans by 1941. But when Hitler's invasion of Russia faltered in the winter of 1942–43, the Red Army pushed back across swathes of eastern Europe. The British-led Allied invasion from North Africa up through Italy, and then the famous D-Day landings at Normandy in June 1944, ultimately combined with the Red Army to bring down Berlin in 1945.

He had an astonishing ability to avoid seeing certain unpalatable truths, even though he saw others with piercing clarity. Probably no other leading British politician had retained such a romantic view of warfare undiminished by the trauma of World War I. And few other British politicians held as deep and uncomplicated a faith in the British Empire, which had led him resolutely to fight against Indian independence in the 1930s. Yet no other British politician had seen the Nazi threat so clearly.

But in the desperate spring and summer of 1940, Churchill's qualities proved to be exactly what Britain needed. A more "realistic," less stubborn politician would have been more tempted to seek terms with the German colossus, as some in Britain were urging. A more sensitive one, without Churchill's enormous stamina (fueled, as the legend rightly has it, by massive overindulgence in whisky and cigars), could never have borne the strain. And a less romantically minded one could not have so brilliantly

Winston Churchill Britain's new prime minister in 1940, just over two weeks after he became leader of the country and thus of the Allied war effort.

inspired the British to continue fighting. Churchill did inspire the British people in a series of unforgettable speeches—in most cases, broadcast on radio—that matched a sober assessment of the challenge with Shakespearean calls to arms. Upon taking office as prime minister in May, he declared: "I have nothing to offer but blood, toil, tears and sweat." On June 4, as the situation in France went from terrible to catastrophic, he concluded with defiance: "We shall not flag or fail.... We shall defend our Island, whatever the cost may be, we shall fight on the beaches, we shall fight on the landing grounds, we shall fight in the fields and in the streets, we shall fight in the hills; we shall never surrender." Two weeks later, with France surrendering, his eloquence reached new heights:

> The Battle of France is over. The Battle of Britain is about to begin.... The whole fury and might of the enemy must very soon be turned on us.... If we can stand up to him, all Europe may be freed and the life of the world may move forward into broad, sunlit uplands. But if we fail, then the whole world, including the United States, including all that we have known and cared for, will sink into the abyss of a new Dark Age made more sinister, and perhaps more protracted, by the lights of perverted science. Let us therefore brace ourselves to our duties, so bear ourselves that, if the British Empire and its Commonwealth last for a thousand years, men will still say, "This was their finest hour."

During the summer, Hitler made peace overtures to Britain and indicated that he would allow the British Empire to remain intact. Churchill spurned all notion of an agreement, and thanks in considerable part to the success of his oratory, few of his compatriots challenged him.

THE BATTLE OF BRITAIN

As Churchill proclaimed, there followed the Battle of Britain, a duel of aerial forces that Hitler meant as the prelude to a full-fledged invasion across the English Channel. After early attacks on coastal forces, the Luftwaffe attempted to destroy the Royal Air Force in battles that

sometimes involved over a thousand planes. It had some success, shooting down more fighter planes than the British did. But the British could turn out 500 fighter planes a month compared to Germany's 140. They employed a primitive version of radar that gave them early warning of German attacks. And they were fighting over friendly soil and waters from which they could rescue damaged planes and surviving crews. In August, Churchill saluted the Royal Air Force's fighter pilots with forgivable exaggeration as latter-day knights: "Never in the field of human conflict was so much owed by so many to so few."

With the arrival of stormy autumn weather, a frustrated Hitler gave up on the idea of a cross-Channel invasion and began deliberately targeting civilians in the hope of breaking the British population's morale. This bombing, known to the British as the **Blitz**, continued intensively for two months, and more sporadically thereafter, forcing Londoners to take shelter in deep subway tunnels and send their children into the countryside for safety. Between September 1940 and May 1941, the Germans killed 43,000 British civilians and destroyed or severely damaged more than a hundred thousand buildings in London alone. They did not, however, significantly damage British morale or industrial capacity. Initially, the Germans hit the grittier, industrial areas of east London, but their bombs eventually fell all over major cities. When one of them landed on Buckingham Palace, Queen Elizabeth (mother of Elizabeth II) remarked: "It makes me feel I can look the East End in the face."

Although the Nazis failed to break the British with their air war, Britain remained in deep peril from another source. Unlike Germany, which was largely self-sufficient in food and coal (if not in high-grade iron ore and oil),

The Blitz East London families shelter in the London subway during an air raid in September 1940.

Britain depended heavily on imports to keep its economy going: 55 million tons of food, fuel, and other raw materials in 1939, requiring a merchant fleet of some 4,000 vessels. In June 1940, when French Atlantic ports fell under German control, this fleet became vulnerable to German mine-laying and especially to German U-boats, or submarines. By mid-1942, the Germans had 300 in service and were sinking 7 million tons of British shipping per year.

Britain managed, for the moment, to stave off economic strangulation through a combination of American help, superlative intelligence work, and sheer good luck. President Franklin Roosevelt was not prepared to take America into the war, but he did use his considerable political capital to push through substantial aid to the Allies. In early 1941, the U.S. Congress approved the so-called **Lend-Lease** policy, which authorized the United States to supply the Allies with war materiel in return for leases on bases or a promise of eventual repayment. Meanwhile, British intelligence efforts paid off particularly in the cracking of the complex German Enigma ciphers by teams of mathematicians and cryptanalysts, based on work carried out by Polish intelligence in the 1930s. Overall, by the spring of 1941 it had become clear that Britain would survive the initial Nazi onslaught.

OCCUPIED EUROPE

Despite the failure of the Nazi attempt to defeat Britain in 1940–41, there would be no return to the Phony War—and no chance for peace. It was clear that the war would continue until the utter defeat of one side or the other, and that the conflict would require the utmost efforts of all the combatants. This was total war, and a truly global war. In September 1940, Germany, Italy, and Japan signed the Tripartite Pact creating an even closer military alliance among them. They would now be known as the Axis powers, and they seemed on the brink of worldwide domination.

WESTERN EUROPE UNDER NAZI OCCUPATION

In 1940–41, the Nazis consolidated their rule on the European continent. They found support from so-called collaborators whose perception of an inevitable German victory conveniently reinforced existing or newfound pro-fascist convictions. Following the blitzkrieg,

it became fashionable to see Germany as a transcendent agent of History itself. "This collapse of a decrepit world," declared the prominent Belgian politician Hendrik de Man, "far from being a disaster, is a deliverance." In Norway, Denmark, and the Netherlands, collaborators proclaimed their nations' racial kindred to the Germans. In France, conservatives and anti-Semites who had denounced the fragile Third Republic before 1940 now rallied to the Vichy regime's National Revolution.

At this stage of the war, the Nazis preferred in most cases to rule through local authorities such as the Vichy regime. In Denmark, they allowed the king and Parliament to remain in place, and managed the country with a German staff of scarcely 100. In Norway, they tried to rule through their puppet Quisling, and in the rump state of Slovakia through a nationalist priest named Josef Tiso. In the Netherlands and Belgium, German officials supervised the native civil service. In France, Pétain's Vichy government had considerable authority in the occupied zone as well.

VICHY FRANCE Among the conquered western European countries, France mattered the most because of its expanse and population (41,510,000), its worldwide empire, and its powerful fleet. After the fall of France, some possessions (such as Chad and Congo) rallied to the Free French organized by General de Gaulle; some, especially in North Africa, came under the authority of Vichy; and some remained in uneasy limbo. As for the French fleet, in the summer of 1940 the British made it clear that they would not allow it to fall into German hands or be used in the German interest. The largest concentration of French warships lay in the Algerian port of Mers-el-Kébir, and on July 3, 1940, a British squadron sank or damaged most of them, killing 1,250 French sailors. The incident helped turn French public opinion against Britain and led Pétain and his advisers into more active collaboration with Germany.

Vichy's program, which took effect across the entire country and in several French possessions, was remarkably aggressive. It involved authoritarian rule by "the Marshal" and his deputies, an attempt to reorder the economy along corporatist lines similar to those of fascist Italy, and systematic hostility to foreigners and minorities, especially Jews. Within a few months of the 1940 defeat, Vichy, not waiting for German compulsion, banned all French Jews from the army, journalism, and the civil service. There would follow exclusions from the universities, law, and medicine, from commercial and industrial jobs; and confiscation of Jewish businesses. Jewish men and women were forced to sew yellow stars of David onto their clothing. In Indochina, Vichy's authoritarian nationalism helped spur indigenous nationalist resistance movements.

Throughout the war, civilian populations in occupied western Europe suffered considerable hardship. In the occupied zone of France, where conditions were worst, agricultural production fell, and much of what remained was confiscated by the Germans. A corrupt and inefficient rationing system permitted French adults only 1,180 calories a day of food over the course of the war, roughly half the amount needed to maintain their weight and health. Malnutrition caused the average height of French boys to decline by nearly three inches during the war, and that of girls by over four. Desperate Parisians raised an estimated 400,000 rabbits in their apartments as a source of meat. One and a half million French soldiers were transported to Germany as prisoners. Other western countries generally did somewhat better (Dutch civilians had an average of 1,900 calories a day) but still suffered considerably. Everywhere, black markets flourished, often with the enthusiastic collaboration of German occupation officials. With men absent and jobs scarce, women sometimes formed liaisons with German soldiers, producing, in France alone, an estimated 200,000 children during the war years.

OCCUPIED POLAND AND THE JEWS

From the beginning of the war, it was clear that Poland would suffer a cruel fate under occupation. After the German and Soviet invasions in 1939, Hitler and Stalin officially wiped the country off the map. Large chunks bordering Germany and along the Baltic, known as Warthegau and Danzig, were absorbed into the German Reich as part of its plans for racial expansion. The Soviet Union annexed Poland's eastern half, including the cities of Bialystok, Lvov, and Vilnius. The remainder, centered on Warsaw and Kraków, became known simply as the General Government under direct Nazi rule.

By the summer of 1941, the Germans had expelled upward of 1 million Poles and Jews from the annexed regions into the General Government. In this area, they began to establish labor camps for slave laborers, and concentration camps in which to imprison anyone they saw as a threat to their rule. Nazi officials, in keeping with their racial ideology, saw the Poles as subhumans who should be "spiritually sterilized"—that is, be deprived of any but the most rudimentary education and culture. Heinrich Himmler (1900–1945), head of the SS, wrote in May 1940 that Polish schools should teach nothing

Nazi Occupation of Poland In the winter of 1939–40, a man walks past the remains of the city of Lodz's synagogue, which the invading German army had destroyed.

more than "simple arithmetic up to 500 at most; writing of one's name; a doctrine that it is a divine law to obey the Germans." In the fall of 1939, the entire faculty of Kraków University was deported to a German concentration camp, and in the spring and summer of 1940 some 30,000 more Polish intellectuals and civic leaders were arrested, and 7,000 massacred. Food shortages quickly became endemic.

The Nazis reserved their cruelest treatment for the Jews, of whom 3 million (nearly one-third of the European Jewish population) lived within Poland's pre-war borders. Despite Hitler's dreams of extermination and the ferocious anti-Semitism he had cultivated in the German population, through the end of 1940 the German government did not pursue a deliberate policy of genocide. It aimed at expelling the Jews of German Europe to the General Government, and then possibly expelling all the Jews out of Europe altogether (for a time, it seriously considered a mass deportation to Madagascar). Perhaps 100,000 Jews died at Nazi hands during 1940—a horrifying figure, but one that would soon pale before the almost unimaginable totals of the **Holocaust**. But the Nazis engaged in every form of oppression short of genocide at this time. They banned Polish Jews from any but menial professions, stole wealth, and imprisoned entire populations behind the walls and barbed wires of hastily constructed ghettos. In Warsaw, where the Jews had made up one-third of the population in 1939, they were forced into just one-tenth of the city's surface area—400,000 people in 1.3 square miles, packed 7.2 persons per room. Similar patterns repeated themselves in every major Polish city.

OCCUPATION OF EASTERN AND SOUTHERN EUROPE

It was not only German rule that oppressed Europeans in the first years of the war. Soviet rule in eastern Poland and the Baltic states also brought serious disruptions. In these areas, local authorities were dismissed or arrested, and local institutions forcibly integrated into Soviet ones. The Soviet secret police also simply murdered some 22,000 Polish officers, policemen, and civic leaders in the spring of 1940, with the largest number of victims buried in mass graves in the forest of Katyń.

In the fall of 1939, Stalin also tried to return another former Russian province, Finland, to his sphere of influence by force. The Finns ended up surrendering considerable territory. But despite being vastly outnumbered, they fought against Stalin until March 1940 and inflicted a string of humiliating defeats on a Red Army that had been demoralized and stripped of leadership by Stalin's purges. Their successes encouraged Hitler to conclude that the Soviet Union would not stand up to a serious military challenge.

In the second half of 1940, more of Europe fell under hostile occupation. In October 1940, Benito Mussolini's Italy invaded Greece, hoping to add this prize to his expanding Italian empire in the Mediterranean—one he explicitly modeled on the Roman Empire. Instead, the Greeks forced the Italians back and made overtures to the British, raising the possibility that Britain could gain bases from which to bomb the Romanian oilfields on which Germany depended. To prevent this turn of events, and to secure the Balkans in case of war with the Soviet Union, Hitler decided to invade Greece himself and pressured the Balkan countries into giving him full military support. In Yugoslavia, the government's decision to accept this alliance provoked an anti-German coup d'état, whereupon Hitler added Yugoslavia to his invasion list. In the spring of 1940, he carried blitzkrieg into southeastern Europe and again won quick victories. Greece came under German occupation and Yugoslavia itself was dismembered, with large swathes of territory taken by Germany, Italy, Hungary, and Bulgaria. Hitler allowed Yugoslav collaborators to declare a newly independent state of Croatia.

BARBAROSSA

Even with all this fighting, through the spring of 1941 World War II could not yet stand comparison with World War I

as a sheer devourer of human life. The increasing mechanization of warfare—and particularly the dominance of tanks in land warfare, backed by aerial bombers—ensured that Europe would not see a repetition of the grinding slaughter of the trenches of 1914–18. So far, campaigns had moved quickly and ended quickly, limiting the death tolls. The German bombing of British cities, and particularly German and Soviet atrocities in Poland, amounted to crimes on a terrifying but not yet wholly unprecedented scale. In June 1941, most of Poland's pre-war population, Christian and Jewish alike, was still alive.

HITLER'S DECISION TO ATTACK THE SOVIET UNION

The war's real plunge into the abyss began on June 22, 1941, when Germany invaded the Soviet Union in what it called **Operation Barbarossa**, a reference to the Holy Roman emperor who had expanded German power in the twelfth century. From then on, the sheer scale of death would dwarf anything yet seen in human history. The fault lay above all with Adolf Hitler and those, German and otherwise, who turned executioner in his service. But the war led to a general barbarization of conduct that affected all the combatants.

At first glance, Hitler's decision to open a new front to the east seemed suicidal. The Soviet Union dwarfed Germany in population, land, and natural resources. Fighting it at the same time as Great Britain meant taking on both the world's greatest land and the greatest sea empires—and Britain could also increasingly draw on the resources of the United States through Lend-Lease. History offered vivid cautionary tales of conquerors whose ambitions shattered on the rock of Russia: notably, Charles XII of Sweden and Napoleon.

Yet from Hitler's perspective in 1941, attacking the Soviet Union had considerable logic to it. The USSR was Britain's one remaining potential ally on the Continent. Furthermore, Hitler considered an eastern war inevitable in the long run. Not only did the Nazi and Stalinist systems conflict radically in their models of how society and politics should be organized, but both—despite the Soviet slogan "Socialism in one country"—had aggressive agendas that threatened the other. Stalin continued to support Communist parties outside the Soviet Union, while Hitler still dreamed of "living space" (*Lebensraum*) for Germany in the east.

All of this meant that in Hitler's eyes the Nazi-Soviet Pact of 1939 could never be anything more than a

Operation Barbarossa The German army used tanks to move quickly through Russian territory, although they often eventually became bogged down in the snow and mud. This 1941 photograph shows a German tank and soldiers advancing on a village on the outskirts of Moscow.

temporary measure, allowing him to avoid a war on two fronts during the conquest of continental western Europe. A so-called General Plan for the East, worked out in 1941 by German strategists and revised as the war progressed, called for even more massive population transfers than seen in Poland, as well as large-scale German colonization of eastern territories. Hitler spoke of Russia's "immeasurable riches" and told his aides he planned to annex virtually all of Belarus, Ukraine, and European Russia. Finally, from Hitler's perspective, if the conflict was to come, it was better perhaps for it to come early, while the Soviet Union and the Red Army were still reeling from the purges of the 1930s, and before Stalin had the chance fully to rebuild and rearm. By the summer of 1940, Hitler had already made up his mind to attack, and throughout the winter and spring of 1941 the Nazis built up their forces. After many delays, they attacked on June 22 with the largest armed force ever seen in history: some 3 million men, 2,000 aircraft, and over 3,000 tanks.

SOVIET CATASTROPHE

The Soviets should have anticipated the invasion. During the spring of 1941, they received scores of credible warnings from their own intelligence services and from the British. But Stalin, having by now invested so much planning and personal prestige in the Nazi-Soviet Pact, did not want to face the possibility that Hitler would betray him. Nor could he believe that the Germans would undertake

such a costly and dangerous campaign. Instead of fortifying his existing defenses against attack, he ordered them abandoned and began the construction of a new defensive line farther west. It was in a vulnerable position hard up against the new frontier that cut through the middle of pre-1939 Poland. Only in March, as a safety measure, did he agree to the mobilization of reservists and an acceleration of arms production. But the Red Army remained poorly armed and supplied, and its officer ranks remained depleted, disorganized, and demoralized from the purges.

The result, for the Soviets, was catastrophe. Attacking along a front almost a thousand miles long, the Germans crushed initial resistance. Within hours, the Luftwaffe had destroyed a significant proportion of Stalin's aerial forces on the ground. Within five days, the German army was approaching the Belarussian capital of Minsk, some 300 miles east of the frontier. A panic gripped the Soviet population, prompting an exodus that dwarfed the one seen in France the year before: perhaps 25 million people fled east ahead of the advancing Germans.

Stalin himself seemed gripped by panic. At a meeting with his top generals on June 27, he stomped out of the room, allegedly growling: "Lenin founded our state, and we've f***ed it up." For several days, he remained incommunicado at his dacha outside of Moscow. He returned to the Kremlin on July 1 and two days later delivered a radio address in which he described the conflict as a "war of the entire Soviet people." Soviet propagandists appealed forcefully to Russian history and tradition, including frequent evocations of Napoleon's invasion of 1812. But for the moment, the words did nothing. Minsk fell on June 28, Smolensk on July 16, and Kiev, the Ukrainian capital, in mid-September. Also in September the Germans surrounded Leningrad—the former Saint Petersburg, capital of Peter the Great. In the Baltic states and Ukraine, some local populations were welcoming the Germans with flowers, denouncing local Soviet officials (and Jews), and volunteering their services to the new regime.

THE TURN TO MASS MURDER

An upsurge in German barbarity began practically the moment the Germans crossed the frontier, driven by the sheer scale of the hostilities and the Nazis' sense of having entered into a truly apocalyptic struggle. "The war against Russia," Hitler had told his generals in March, "will be such that it cannot be conducted in a chivalric fashion: the struggle is one of ideologies and racial differences and will have to be conducted with unprecedented, unmerciful and unrelenting harshness." His contempt for Slavs as "sub-humans" reinforced his sense that Germany could only control their vast territories and populations with brutality. Following his lead, the German commanders made no attempt to treat the men and women who fell under their rule with even minimal humanity. In any case, they had few resources at their command to do so. Soviet prisoners of war became the largest group of victims yet to suffer Nazi mass murder. Frequently, the Germans made no attempt to keep alive the men who surrendered, but simply herded them into huge pens and left them to die of thirst, starvation, and disease. Of the 3 million Soviet prisoners taken by the end of 1941, as many as two-thirds died by the next summer.

With this mass murder already occurring, and with German forces seemingly on the way to yet another stunning victory, historians believe that Adolf Hitler lost any remaining hesitation about putting into practice his long-held dream of exterminating the Jews. He now believed Germany had a unique opportunity to cleanse the Continent of those he saw as dangerous parasites. Adolf Eichmann (1906–1962), one of the principal organizers of the Holocaust, later testified that it was in July 1941 that he heard, from the deputy head of the SS, that Hitler had decided upon "physical extermination." It would take more than another year for the Nazis to organize the system of transports and extermination camps that today symbolize the Holocaust. But the actual liquidation of the Jews and others began as German forces moved eastward in the summer of 1941. The work was carried out above all by special "task forces" (*Einsatzgruppen*) composed of SS members, ordinary police units from Germany, and local auxiliaries, all under SS command.

These forces had the murder of innocent men, women, and children as their principal purpose, and they received full support from the German army in doing so. In the newly occupied territories, they systematically hunted down and slaughtered the targets of Nazi ideology: Jews, Communists, the mentally handicapped, homosexuals, and Roma, a largely itinerant ethnic group with roots in India who numbered over 1 million in 1939. The Nazis forced the victims to dig mass graves, confiscated their valuables, and then machine-gunned them. At the end of September, the Germans took 33,771 of Kiev's Jews, who believed they were being resettled, to the ravine of Babi Yar at the edge of the city. Over the course of two days, nearly all were killed with the help of Ukrainian collaborators. The reports of the *Einsatzgruppen* themselves suggest that by the end of 1942 they had murdered well over

1.1 million Jews. In almost all cases, the killers took part willingly in the slaughter. In few cases were Germans who refused to participate punished, let alone killed.

TOTAL MOBILIZATION

The German actions quickly pushed the Soviets into seeing the conflict in apocalyptic terms as well, and into total mobilization. "These people without honor or conscience, these people with the morality of animals, have the effrontery to call for the extermination of the great Russian nation," Stalin thundered on November 6, 1941. "Very well, then! If they want a war of extermination, they shall have it!" The Germans found that despite the Soviet lack of arms and supplies, individual Soviet units fought with ferocity and often to the last recruit. Very quickly, the Soviet government conscripted most adult men and women under age forty-five for military service or other defense work. Following the example set by revolutionary Russia in 1917–18, but on a much larger scale, some 800,000 Soviet women served in the armed forces alongside the men. The Soviet air force assembled three regiments of bombers flown and serviced entirely by women, one of which became known as the Night Witches. In August 1941, the USSR declared that it was treason for an officer to become a German prisoner or to retreat under fire. To drive the point home, the Soviet government arrested the

"Night Witches" A group of Soviet women pilots receive orders from their commander—also a woman—for an upcoming bombing raid in 1944. These so-called Night Witches were among the roughly 800,000 women in the Soviet army.

wives of prisoners, including Stalin's own daughter-in-law (his son died in German captivity in 1943).

Under the threat of extinction, the communist command economy that had performed so unevenly in the 1930s finally began to function as its architects had intended. Drawing on the experience of the Five-Year Plans, the Soviets frantically dismantled thousands of factories —as much as 80 percent of the country's industrial capacity— and shipped the pieces eastward to the Ural Mountains, where workers put them back together and began turning out munitions, weapons, and vehicles within a few months. In addition, the United States quickly extended its Lend-Lease program to the USSR and began shipping millions of tons of goods. U.S. trucks, jeeps, high-grade steel, and foodstuffs all played an important role in the Soviet war effort.

THE STRUGGLES FOR LENINGRAD AND MOSCOW

These emergency measures came just in time. The Germans might well have captured Leningrad, but the city's new military commander, a talented peasant-born soldier named Georgi Zhukov, refused to contemplate surrender. Leningraders constructed seventeen miles of barricades and anti-tank ditches throughout the city, and set up 20,000 fortified posts. In late September 1941, the Germans abandoned the idea of a frontal attack on the city and instead began a siege. They still counted on eventual victory and the extermination of Leningrad's inhabitants. "In this war for existence we have no interest in keeping even part of this large city's population," commented Hitler.

The German army kept up merciless bombardments and waited for the Leningraders to starve. During the terrible winter of 1941–42, as many as 1 million of the 3.3 million people caught in the city did in fact die of starvation, cold, and disease. As the siege lengthened to 900 days, the city almost ceased functioning entirely, and the desperate citizenry ate pets, medicines, leather, and even, sometimes, one another. Yet somehow Leningrad did not give in, and during the winter months of the long siege the Soviets managed to open an "ice road" across a frozen lake from unoccupied territory and bring in enough supplies to keep the remaining population alive.

Even as Leningrad held, the Germans pushed hard toward the greater prize of Moscow, where the Soviet situation was also beyond desperate. In mid-October 1941,

the Soviets had just 90,000 men standing between the German army and their capital. Once again, Stalin called on Zhukov, who strengthened a defensive line sixty miles from the capital and used hundreds of thousands of women and children to build a second one just ten miles from the Kremlin. For a time, the weather—early snow that melted and turned the Russian soil into an ocean of mud—slowed the German advance. But by early November, as the soil again hardened, the German vanguard stood just forty miles from Moscow; by the end of November, just twelve. Hitler held a ceremony to declare victory, and Stalin began evacuating the government 500 miles to the east.

But here, finally, before Moscow, the titanic scale of the war and the tremendous material resources of the Soviet Union began to tell on the seemingly invincible German army. The rough terrain led vehicles to succumb to mechanical failure. As early as September, two-thirds of all German tanks could no longer function, and by November one German army group had abandoned half its trucks in favor of horse-drawn wagons. The terrible cold of the Russian winter began to affect men and machines. The army suffered 133,000 cases of frostbite. All in all, by the end of November 1941 fully 25 percent of the German infantry had been killed, wounded, or incapacitated by disease.

The Soviet resistance remained as desperate as ever: soldiers fought tanks with rifles and Molotov cocktails— bottles filled with gasoline, named after Stalin's foreign minister. The Soviets held on to the key city of Tula, south of Moscow, preventing the capital's encirclement. In early December, with the Germans believing that the Soviets had no reserves left, the Soviets launched a surprise counteroffensive that broke the German pincers and drove the Wehrmacht back two hundred miles. It was the first major German defeat of the war. As the year 1941 came to an end, the German army remained in a powerful position, and an eventual victory in Russia still seemed possible. But the day of the blitzkrieg was clearly over.

CRUCIAL POINTS

Up until the end of 1941, the course of the war had depended in large part on the strategic choices made by the different combatants—particularly on the decisions Hitler made in the invasions of western Europe and then of the Soviet Union. But thereafter, increasingly, it would depend on the sheer ability of the contending powers to mobilize natural resources, industry, and soldiers, to organize them, and to deploy them against the enemy. And the number of contending powers expanded as the war turned truly global in scope.

PEARL HARBOR AND THE GLOBAL WAR

Even as Soviet forces were beginning to drive the Nazis back from Moscow, a stunning event took place 7,000 miles away in the middle of the Pacific Ocean. On December 7, 1941, the Japanese Empire launched a surprise attack on the American fleet at **Pearl Harbor** in Hawaii and declared war on both the United States and Great Britain. Hitler greeted the news with exultation. "Now it is impossible for us to lose the war," he burbled to top generals. "Now we have an ally who has never been vanquished in three thousand years." Four days later, over the objections of Foreign Minister Ribbentrop, he declared war on the United States.

Hitler's reaction hinted at a loss of touch with reality

World War II in the Pacific The war in Asia began with the Japanese attack on Pearl Harbor in December 1941, quickly followed by Japanese offensives throughout the South Pacific: Malaya, the Dutch East Indies, the Philippines, New Guinea, and elsewhere. Major engagements between Japanese and U.S. forces took place at sea, such as at Midway in 1942. Despite U.S. offensives in 1944–45, the war dragged on in the South Pacific until the atomic bombs dropped in August 1945 forced Japan's surrender.

that would increasingly afflict him over the next three and a half years. There was little hope that Japan could help him beat the Soviet Union or Britain, even if it managed to expand its Pacific empire at U.S. and British expense. The Soviets had already beaten back Japanese forces during their short border war of 1938–39. And bringing the United States into the war threw its unmatched industrial capacity into the balance on the Allied side. Winston Churchill, on hearing the news of Pearl Harbor, correctly drew the opposite conclusion from Hitler's: "So we had won after all."

With Pearl Harbor, an alliance of the United States, the United Kingdom, and the Soviet Union quickly took shape. Churchill and U.S. president Franklin Roosevelt had already met in the summer of 1941 and signed an Atlantic Charter laying out a vision for a peaceful, postwar world in which the occupied countries would regain their freedom. As we have seen, the United States was already supplying considerable materiel to Britain and the USSR under its Lend-Lease program. During the war the so-called Big Three powers would hold a series of summit meetings to coordinate strategy, including personal meetings among Churchill, Roosevelt, and Stalin.

A WAR OF EMPIRES Even before Pearl Harbor, the war between the European powers had spilled into the far-flung reaches of Europe's colonial empires. The colonies mattered as sources of raw material and men, and also as bases from which to protect supply lines and to disrupt enemy supply lines. Soon after the fall of France, Italian forces in Ethiopia occupied the British colony in what is now Somalia, on the horn of eastern Africa. In 1941, the British counterattacked from their East African colonies, drove Italy out of Ethiopia, and restored to the throne Emperor Haile Selassie. Elsewhere in Africa, British and Free French forces loyal to Charles de Gaulle tried and failed to capture the strategic port of Dakar, in present-day Senegal, bringing them into direct combat with Vichy France.

In the Middle East, the pro-German general Rashid Ali revolted against Iraq's British overlords, with the complicity of the Vichy authorities in neighboring Syria. The British government responded with a costly but successful invasion of Syria from its own bases in Iraq and Palestine. Some of the most vicious fighting took place precisely where Israel and Syria now confront each other, on the Golan Heights. In these various conflicts, as in the sinking of the French fleet at Mers-el-Kébir in 1940, British forces fought the French for the last time in the two nations' long history of belligerency. With the British controlling Egypt

Colonial Troops All of the colonial empires participating in the war drew on their overseas holdings for soldiers; many non-Europeans, but not all, served willingly. A January 1941 photograph shows soldiers from Somaliland (in East Africa) serving in the Italian army in North Africa.

and Italy controlling Libya, fighting also broke out across the deserts of North Africa. And after the shah of Iran flirted with the Germans, Britain and the Soviet Union staged a successful joint invasion of that country in the summer of 1941 to secure its valuable oilfields.

The colonial empires in turn relied more heavily than ever on their subjects to prosecute the war. Britain's Indian holdings provided 2.5 million soldiers, who fought in all the principal theaters of operation, including Europe. The Free French army that formed after France's capitulation in 1940 drew heavily on the French Foreign Legion and on black African troops. The celebrated French Second Armored Division initially included thousands of black African and Muslim North African soldiers. Colonial soldiers felt that their service placed the empires in their debt, and they resented the increased exploitation of colonial resources for the war effort.

Pearl Harbor greatly expanded the global dimensions of the war. It connected the European fighting with the bloody conflict that had been occurring in East Asia since the 1930s as the Japanese Empire gobbled up large areas of China, and it tied events in Europe to a vast struggle for control of the Pacific Ocean. In the days after the attack on Hawaii, Japanese forces took the strategic American islands of Guam and Wake. They also launched devastating attacks on British-held Malaya (present-day Malaysia) and, crucially, the Dutch colonies in the East Indies (present-day Indonesia): a source of oil for the Japanese war machine. In one of the worst defeats for Britain in modern history, its colony of Singapore surrendered to Japan in February 1942, and some 130,000 British, Indian, Australian, and local troops went into Japanese captivity. In ensuing months, Japan conquered the American-held Philippines and moved into British-held Burma, on the doorstep of India.

NORTH AFRICA AND THE QUESTION OF A SECOND FRONT

In the first few months of 1942, the newly enlarged scale of the fighting did little to diminish Hitler's confidence. At the southern end of the eastern front, the Germans continued to score significant victories, occupying nearly all of Ukraine and the Crimean Peninsula. In North Africa, General Erwin Rommel was leading a second German-Italian offensive from Italian-held Libya against British and Allied forces in Egypt. On June 21, 1942, he took the key fortress of Tobruk, along with some 33,000 prisoners—the greatest British defeat of the war after Singapore. Within a month, Rommel's tanks had reached El Alamein, just fifty miles west of the ancient Egyptian port city of Alexandria. North Africa mattered particularly to the British, who controlled Egypt and with it the crucial Suez Canal that allowed for rapid transport to British India.

But at El Alamein, the British finally stopped the German advance, forcing a retreat that would take Rommel's forces all the way back to Vichy-held Tunisia. In November 1942, Churchill famously declared: "The Germans have received back again that measure of fire and steel which they have so often meted out to others. Now this is not the end. It is not even the beginning of the end. But it is, perhaps, the end of the beginning."

Even as Churchill was speaking, the North African campaign took a new turn. British and U.S. forces invaded Morocco, Algeria, and Tunisia, making use of new amphibious technology to land troops quickly on beaches. They easily overcame scattered and confused resistance by the Vichy French, and by the next spring the Allies had driven the Axis from North Africa altogether.

TENSIONS IN THE ALLIANCE This new British-American offensive, however, provoked some objections from the third major Allied power, the Soviet Union.

Stalin, fighting for his country's survival against Hitler, had pushed Roosevelt and Churchill to put all their efforts into an invasion of France that would open up a second, western front for the Germans and relieve some of the pressure on his own country. He made this case in his first meeting with Churchill, in Moscow, in August 1942. Churchill insisted that an invasion of France would require a massive concentration of force that the Allies were not yet capable of deploying. He also believed that the invasion of North Africa would help preserve the British colonial empire by ensuring Britain's connections with India and Africa. While Churchill developed a wary respect for Stalin's cunning, memory, and "crude wit" (Churchill's words), the two men remained suspicious of each other, with Stalin fearing that the British preferred to see the Soviet Union bled white to minimize the threat it might pose after the war. Stalin prompted Communist parties in the west and their sympathizers to adopt "Second Front Now!" as their slogan. The question of the second front would remain a major source of tension among the Allies for the next year and a half.

STALINGRAD

In the summer and fall of 1942, the Soviets felt even more pressure because Hitler's eastern forces were gaining new momentum. Rejecting his generals' desire for another major assault on Moscow, Hitler instead ordered an attack through Ukraine to the city of Stalingrad, some 1,500 miles east of Berlin, and then to follow the Volga River southeast to the Caspian Sea, cutting the Caucasus region and its crucial oilfields off from the Soviet heartland. By the late summer of 1942, the German Sixth Army established a fortification on the banks of the Volga north of Stalingrad.

But once again, the Soviet defenders resisted with unexpected tenacity. The Soviet command economy functioned best under emergency conditions, and by now it was producing war materiel at a stunning pace. In the summer of 1942, Germany was producing 500 tanks a month. A German general told Hitler that the Soviets were doing better, with 1,200 tanks a month. Hitler, pounding the table for effect, insisted the figure was exaggerated. But in fact the Soviets were actually producing 2,200 tanks a month, and 2,600 aircraft.

The Soviet government also demanded total mobilization and obedience from the population. On July 28, Stalin issued his infamous Order 227: "Not a Step Back!"

It commanded all Soviet troops to defend "every meter of Soviet territory to the last drop of blood." Anyone who disobeyed and retreated could be shot out of hand or condemned to serve in penal battalions charged with suicide missions on the front lines. By some estimates, as many as 158,000 Soviet soldiers were sentenced to death by their own side during the war. The formidable propaganda capacity of the Soviet state was also mobilized to inspire the Soviet population and demonize the enemy. Ilya Ehrenburg (1891–1967), one of the most acclaimed Soviet journalists of the war, wrote in the press in 1942: "Do not count days; do not count miles. Count only the number of Germans you have killed. Kill the German—this is your mother's prayer. Kill the German—this is the cry of your Russian earth. Do not waver. Do not let up. Kill."

In what became the most important battle of the entire war, the **battle of Stalingrad**, like Moscow, somehow did not fall. A hugely expansive city filled with factories, Stalingrad stretched for miles along the sandy western bank of the Volga. It was named for Stalin because of his role in securing it for the communists during the Civil War. In late August and early September, as the Germans advanced, Stalin sent his most competent commander, Zhukov, to investigate the situation. He and his colleagues soon devised a plan for a counteroffensive both north and south of the city. Yet even as the Soviets prepared, German divisions surrounded the city center. The fighting defied comprehension: every green leaf was burned off trees; every building was destroyed or heavily damaged, and covered in a thick layer of dust and ash. The Germans advanced over the rubble, capturing the central railroad station seven times, but each time they were driven back by the desperate defenders.

On November 19, a Soviet counteroffensive finally started. Thanks to the factories that had moved to the east in 1941, Lend-Lease aid from the United States, and conscription, the Soviets managed to bring an additional 1,350 aircraft, nearly a thousand tanks, 14,000 heavy guns, and a million more men into the battle. Within days, they broke the German flanks and encircled the German Sixth Army, along with other German and Axis units, numbering some 330,000 soldiers. The tables had been turned. Hitler ordered his forces to stand their ground despite the hopeless situation. Finally, at the end of January 1943, having lost nearly 150,000 dead, they surrendered. The Soviet toll was even higher.

Yet for the Allies overall, the cost was worth it. Stalingrad delivered an immense material blow to Nazi Germany, and an even more important moral one. "Losses

Soviet War Propaganda A bold 1943 propaganda poster shows a Soviet bayonet stabbing and killing a lion emblazoned with a swastika. The caption reads: "Beat the German beasts! Destroy the Hitlerian Army! Can and Must Be Done!"

can never be too high," Hitler raved in 1942. "They sow the seeds of future glory." But fewer and fewer Germans agreed with him. Stalingrad broke the myth of German military superiority and prevented the Germans from strangling the Soviet economy. It also won crucial time for the Allies—above all, the Soviet Union and the United States—fully to exploit their advantages in population and industrial capacity.

HUNGER ON THE EASTERN FRONT

On the eastern front, soldiers on both sides had to learn to survive with scarce rations. Heavy mud and thick snows choked the overextended German supply lines as the Wehrmacht pushed deeper into Russia, while Soviet resources were strained by the destruction wrought by the fighting, although Lend-Lease provided aid from the United States. Field kitchens could be located miles away from the fighting, and fuel for cooking was often scarce. Soldiers generally had to make do with small amounts of stale bread, watery soup, margarine, or horsemeat, with perhaps a small allowance of liquor. In this desperate state, troops seized any opportunities to scavenge, steal, or requisition fresh food to enrich their meager diet.

Willy Peter Reese, from *A Stranger to Myself*

A young German soldier, Reese kept a poetically worded diary of his struggles on the eastern front from 1941 until his death in combat in 1944. In this early passage, he describes staving off hunger by stealing food from Russian civilians.

We were hungry. The cooks slaughtered cattle and pigs on the way and requisitioned peas, beans, and cucumbers everywhere. But a little midday soup wasn't enough to get us through our exertions. So we started taking the last piece of bread from women and children, had chickens and geese prepared for us, pocketed their small supplies of butter and lard, weighed down our vehicles with flitches of bacon and flour from the larders, drank the overrich milk, and cooked and roasted on their stoves, stole honey from the collective farms, came upon stashes of eggs, and weren't bothered by tears, hand wringings, and curses. We were the victors. War excused our thefts, encouraged cruelty, and the need to survive didn't go around getting permission from conscience. Women and children were made to go to the wells for us, water our horses, watch our fires, and peel our potatoes. We used their straw for our horses or for bedding for ourselves, or else we drove them out of their beds and stretched out on their stoves....

... We suffered from diarrhea. Our bellies were a ferment of swamp. We were disgusted and appalled, but we couldn't fast. Hunger hurt too much.

We moved in semipermanently. We drove the women out of their homes and pushed them into the most wretched of the dwellings. Pregnant or blind, they all had to go. Crippled children we shooed out into the rain, and some were left with nothing better than a barn or shed, where they lay down with our horses.... [W]e lived as well as we could and didn't think about the deprivation that would come after us....

...I would give up God and my own humanity for a piece of bread. I had no comrades. Everyone fended for himself, hated anyone who found better booty than himself, wouldn't share, would only trade, and tried to get the better of the other.... The weaker was exploited, the helpless left in his misery.

Vasily Grossman, from *Life and Fate*

Grossman was a Russian war correspondent who drew on his observations at the battle of Stalingrad in writing the novel *Life and Fate* (1959). In this passage, a Major Byerozkin catches his men cooking a fish—a rare treat in the midst of the battle.

Byerozkin said: "So where's this five-kilo pike-perch, comrade Movshovich? The whole division's talking of nothing else."

With the same sad look, Movshovich ordered: "Cook, show him the fish please." The cook, the only man present to have been carrying out his duties, explained: "The comrade captain wanted it stuffed in the Jewish manner. I've got some pepper and bay-leaves, but I haven't any white bread or horse-radish...."

"I see," said Byerozkin. "I once had one done like that in Bobruysk, at the house of one Sara Aronovna—though, to be quite frank, I didn't think much of it."

Suddenly they all realized that it hadn't even occurred to Byerozkin to get angry. It was as though he knew that Podchufarov had fought off a German attack during the night; that he had been half-buried under falling earth during the small hours; that his orderly...had had to dig him out, shouting: "Don't worry, comrade Captain, I'll get you out of there." It was as though he knew that Movshovich and his sappers had crept along one particularly vulnerable street, scattering earth and crushed brick over a chessboard pattern of anti-tank mines.

They were all young and they were glad to be alive one more morning, to be able to lift up a tin mug and say, "Your good health!", to be able to eat cabbage and smoke cigarettes. ...In any case, nothing had really happened—they had just stood up for a moment before a superior and then invited him to eat, watching with pleasure how he enjoyed his cabbage.

QUESTIONS FOR ANALYSIS

1. What reasons does Reese give for his thefts?
2. Why do you think the soldiers fear Major Byerozkin's anger?
3. What are the similarities and differences between the soldiers' interactions in both sources?

Sources: Willy Peter Reese, *A Stranger to Myself: The Inhumanity of War: Russia, 1914–1944*, trans. Michael Hofmann (New York: 2003), pp. 35–36; Vasily Grossman, *Life and Fate*, trans. Robert Chandler (New York: 1985), pp. 61–62.

MIDWAY AND THE TURN IN THE PACIFIC

Even as Stalingrad marked the turning of the war in Europe, the Allies were also managing to push back the Axis powers in the Pacific theater. In a series of critical battles waged largely by airplanes launched from aircraft carriers against enemy ships (in some cases, the opposing fleets did not even see each other), the United States halted the Japanese advance across the ocean. Breaking crucial Japanese codes, the U.S. navy was able successfully to concentrate its forces against a Japanese carrier group at the decisive battle of Midway in June 1942, destroying four Japanese carriers.

Now, even as the Soviets were beginning the long, difficult land campaign to push the Nazis toward Germany, the Americans began an extended naval campaign to push Japan back across strings of small Pacific islands toward Asia. The Americans also developed a submarine fleet to attack Japanese merchant shipping, because Japan had much the same basic vulnerability during the war as Great Britain: it was a small, resource-poor archipelago dependent on oil and food imports. Despite Japanese success in taking the Dutch East Indies and their oil reserves, by the end of 1943 the American submarine campaign had proven so successful that the Japanese did not have enough shipping to get the oil they needed to their military and their home islands.

HOLOCAUST

The turning of the tide in the war provided no immediate relief for most of the millions of men, women, and children under Nazi occupation. Even as the Axis powers reached the limits of their expansion and felt their militaries buckle under the strain, the Nazis fell upon their most helpless victims with hideous fury.

PLANNING GENOCIDE

In January 1942, well before the German thrust toward Stalingrad began, fifteen high-ranking Nazis gathered for a day-long conference at a luxurious villa on the Wannsee Lake west of Berlin. Convened by Reinhard Heydrich, the deputy head of the SS, they discussed in cold-blooded, bureaucratic terms the German government's plans,

already decided upon by Hitler, to exterminate the Jewish population of Europe. As the Nazis conquered new territories in the east after June 1941, they had continued the policy begun in Poland of forcing the Jews to live in densely populated, unsanitary ghettos. In September 1941, they started deporting German, Austrian, and Czech Jews to the eastern ghettos as well. Disease and starvation took their toll in these city-sized prisons, with 83,000 Jews dying prematurely in Warsaw alone between 1940 and mid-1942. At the same time, the *Einsatzgruppen* carried out their grisly mass executions.

The **Wannsee conference** marked the moment at which the Nazis moved toward a more efficient, industrialized process of mass murder. Under the control of Heydrich's Reich Main Security Office, a vast system of

The Holocaust Hitler's plan for the extermination of the Jews included concentration camps and ghettos across Europe, the many sites in eastern Europe where "task forces" perpetrated mass executions, and ultimately the extermination camps in Poland.

transport was designed to move Jews and other populations destined for slaughter to a series of vast concentration camps being built largely in Poland. The most important groups targeted for the camps, other than Jews, were homosexuals, political opponents of the Reich, and the Poles, Soviets, and Roma.

In the camps, the able-bodied would be allowed to live and work as slave laborers for the German war effort. Everyone else was to be killed on arrival. Initially, these killings were done with machine guns. But in the fall of 1941, after members of the *Einsatzgruppen* had complained about the costs of mass shootings—both the psychological toll taken on the executioners and the simple price of ammunition—the Nazis began experimenting with gas as an alternative. At first, they killed with truck exhaust that was modified to empty into sealed containers holding the prisoners. Later, they built stationary gas chambers that they flooded, first with diesel exhaust and then with a poison gas called Zyklon B originally invented for fumigation.

THE DEATH CAMPS

The worst of the killings occurred between mid-March 1942 and mid-February 1943. At the start of this period, over three-quarters of all victims of the Holocaust were still alive. At the end, more than three-quarters were dead.

In the summer of 1942, the Nazis began carrying out mass deportations from Warsaw and other ghettos to the killing centers. The victims were told they were being "resettled" in the east, but those who resisted or fled were shot out of hand, as were hospital patients, the elderly, the insane, and others who could not walk to the designated departure sites. Some Jews cooperated with the Nazis in the vain hope of mollifying them, lowering the death toll, or perhaps just saving their own lives. On arrival at the camps, the victims had to hand over their valuables and present themselves for "selection," during which doctors would choose those fit for slave labor. Those condemned to death were made to undress and were herded into gas chambers disguised as showers. Afterward, prisoners themselves disposed of the bodies, initially in mass graves but later in a sophisticated system of crematoria.

The largest and most infamous concentration and extermination camp was **Auschwitz-Birkenau**, some thirty-seven miles west of Kraków near the old German-Polish border. At its peak in early to mid-1944, it contained more than 100,000 prisoners engaged in slave labor producing synthetic rubber, fuel, and other war materiel.

Death Camps Imprisoned laborers at the Auschwitz death camp were made to pose with an emaciated corpse in front of a furnace that was used to cremate the bodies of the dead.

Its gas chambers and crematoria could dispose of up to 15,000 men, women, and children per day. Between 1940 and 1945, approximately 1.1 million European Jews were deported there, of whom some 960,000 were killed, along with hundreds of thousands of others, especially Poles, Roma, and Soviet prisoners of war.

Auschwitz-Birkenau, however, was only one part of a network of death camps in occupied Poland that included Majdanek, Sobibór, and Treblinka. In the Greek city of Salonika, where Jews had long formed a large percentage of the population, the Germans deported nearly the entire Jewish community to their deaths in Auschwitz. In July 1942, the Vichy police arrested nearly 13,000 Parisian Jews, including more than 4,000 children, and shut them up for days in stifling heat before sending them on to the extermination camps. Some 60,000 more Jews from France would eventually follow.

All in all, at least 5.4 million Jews perished during the Holocaust, along with an estimated 250,000 Roma, tens of thousands of homosexuals and political prisoners, and millions of Soviet prisoners of war. In country after country, a long Jewish history was brutally cut off. Nearly all the 3 million Jews of Poland died. Throughout Europe, the Germans relied not only on their own military forces but also on German police units, prisoners of war (especially Ukrainians, Lithuanians, and Latvians), and local populations that, while suffering from constraint and fear, were also driven by their own anti-Semitic traditions. In one of the most well-documented episodes, Polish Christians in the town of Jedwabne turned on their Jewish neighbors, torturing them and raping women before herding

DEPORTATION FROM THE LODZ GHETTO

The city of Lodz in central Poland was the site of the second-largest Jewish ghetto, with over 200,000 Jews passing through over the course of World War II. In 1942, the Germans began to deport Jews to a nearby extermination camp. When the ghetto was liberated at the end of the war, fewer than 900 Jewish survivors remained.

An inhabitant and archivist of the Lodz ghetto, Josef Zelkowicz (1897–1944) kept a detailed diary of daily life there before he was deported to Auschwitz, where he died in 1944. In this excerpt from September 4, 1942, he describes the ghetto's reaction to the news of the impending deportation of children and the elderly.

The ghetto was dealt a horrific blow this morning. What only yesterday was considered impossible and inconceivable became, tragically, a fact. Children up to age ten are being torn from their parents and siblings and are doomed to deportation....

If it were only a "deportation." If only there were the slightest surety that the deportees would be allowed to continue living—even under the harshest conditions—the tragedy would not be so horrific.... But in this case, no one has even a vestige of doubt that the deportees from the ghetto are not being taken to any other location. They are being led to perdition, at least the elderly.... They are being thrown on the garbage heap....

No house, no apartment, no family is unaffected by this terrible edict. Every-one has a son, an elderly father or an aged mother....

Hearts have turned into ice. Hands pound each other in agony. Facial features are twisted, eyes are lowered to the ground, and all eyes are crying....

The wretched children still know nothing. Infants, incapable of perceiving the sword... suspended over their guileless heads, unwittingly sense the great danger that lurks in their midst and they clutch their fathers' and mothers' skinny, emaciated necks with all the strength in their two little hands....

Mothers race about in the streets, one shoe on and the other off, half of their hair combed and the rest unkempt, kerchiefs half draped over their shoulders and half dragging on the ground. They still have their children. They can still clutch them fiercely to their shriveled bosoms. They can still kiss their clear eyes. But what will happen afterwards, in another hour, tomorrow? Rumor has it that the children will be removed from their parents and sent away on Monday. Sent away—where?

QUESTIONS FOR ANALYSIS

1. How do the inhabitants of the Lodz ghetto respond to the deportation announcement?
2. What do the Jews of Lodz know about the fate that awaits the deportees?
3. What does this excerpt from Zelkowicz's diary reveal about the everyday experience of the victims of the Holocaust?

Source: Josef Zelkowicz, *In Those Terrible Days: Writings from the Lodz Ghetto*, ed. Michal Ungar (Jerusalem: 2002), pp. 261–64.

---

a thousand or more (the numbers remain disputed) into a barn, dousing it with kerosene, and burning it to the ground. In the extermination camps, the Germans made widespread use of Polish and Ukrainian auxiliaries, and also of prisoners, including Jews, willing to serve as *kapos* (low-level guards). In many individual cases, however, Polish Christians sheltered Jews from the Nazis and aided them in the camps.

"Never shall I forget the little faces of the children, whose bodies I saw turned into wreaths of smoke beneath a silent blue sky. Never shall I forget those flames which consumed my faith." The Holocaust survivor Elie Wiesel (1928–2016) wrote these lines in his novel *Night*, about his experiences at Auschwitz. Other former Auschwitz inmates such as the Italian Jew Primo Levi (*The Saved and the Damned*) and the Polish Catholic Tadeusz Borowski (*This Way to the Gas, Ladies and Gentlemen*) also left astonishing literary portraits of the Holocaust, as did the German-Jewish poet Paul Celan. (All three, irredeemably scarred by their experiences, later committed suicide.) Thousands of other victims left memoirs, testimonials, and diaries—notably, the diary of the young German Jew Anne Frank, who went into hiding with her family in Amsterdam, was arrested by the Germans in the summer of 1944, and died at age fifteen in the camp of Bergen-Belsen.

The Holocaust is distinguished from other episodes of genocide in history by the cold-minded, bureaucratic planning that went into the process through which the Nazis rounded up entire Jewish populations, transported them hundreds or even thousands of miles, and then systematically murdered them. Of all the physical evidence from the Holocaust, which includes vast storehouses of possessions taken from the victims—jewelry, suitcases, clothes, shoes, eyeglasses, and toothbrushes—as well as the actual remains of the camps, nothing is quite so chilling as the paperwork. In millions of daily memoranda, invoices, account books, and minutes of meetings, one sees that hallmark modern phenomenon—a large-scale industrial bureaucracy—turned to the purpose of destroying innocent life.

Evidence of the Holocaust Those murdered in the camps had their belongings confiscated and stored in huge warehouses. A modern-day display at the Auschwitz Museum consists of a colossal pile of victims' shoes, a sobering reminder of the scale of the death toll.

TOTAL WAR

Even as Hitler was waging this merciless campaign against millions of innocent victims, the war continued on a worldwide scale. An Allied victory now looked likely, but to achieve it would require enormous expenditures of material resources and blood.

THE ALLIED ADVANTAGE

Historians have often claimed that after the Allied victories in North Africa and Stalingrad, the final defeat of the Axis powers was inevitable. This idea rests particularly on the Allied economic superiority attained once the United States came into the war. After all, in 1942 the combined gross domestic product (GDP) of the Allied countries dwarfed that of the Axis by more than two to one. By 1944, the ratio had reached almost three to one. While the GDP of Germany rose by 13 percent from 1939 to 1944, that of the United States grew by an astonishing 72 percent. The leviathan that was American industry, after having engaged in relatively little military manufacturing before the war, ramped up to produce 141 aircraft carriers, 88,410 armored vehicles, 324,750 aircraft, and 41 billion rounds of ammunition during the war. Even Britain's GDP went up by 20 percent, while the Soviet Union, despite the German invasion and occupation of much of its industrial heartland, had returned by 1944 to its 1939 economic level.

But economics does not explain everything. As the American general Dwight David Eisenhower wrote in his diary in 1942 after meeting with politicians in Washington: "Not one man in twenty in the government realizes what a grisly, dirty, tough business we are in. They think we can buy victory." Economic strength did not translate directly into military effectiveness. The Allies had to learn, often at a steep price, how best to deploy their resources. They had to learn to cooperate with one another—a difficult task given the differences between Soviet communism and western democracy, and the differences in war aims and strategies. The most important of these was Stalin's insistence on the quick opening of a second front in western Europe, and Churchill's reluctance to comply. They also had to learn, within their own militaries, how best to coordinate land, air, and sea power. For their part, the highly militarized societies of Germany and Japan assigned little prestige to the unglamorous but vital tasks of supply and maintenance, and therefore often handled them badly. The German army in the east lost two-thirds of its tanks and half its trucks in the winter of 1941–42, and it never entirely recovered from this loss. As the war went on, it relied increasingly on horses for transport, in what some historians call a demodernization.

THE BOMBING CAMPAIGN

The Allies made particularly deadly use of their superior aircraft production. As early as the summer of 1940, Churchill declared that victory required "an absolutely devastating, exterminating attack by very heavy bombers upon the Nazi homeland." He hoped such attacks would devastate German industry and cripple the Nazi war effort. But through 1942, Allied bombing of German cities achieved relatively little. Daylight raids saw high losses for the attackers—during the war, the British and Americans combined lost 21,000 bombers and 140,000 airmen. Night raids, while safer, were woefully inaccurate. But bombing gradually became more effective as a result of technical innovations designed in consultation with British and American industry.

In July 1943, over a thousand Allied planes attacked the northern German port city of Hamburg, suffering only a 2.8 percent loss rate. Over two days, they dropped high-explosive and incendiary bombs that set off an unstoppable firestorm. Some 40,000 people were killed, and 1 million left homeless. Yet even with destruction on this scale, the bombing did not always achieve the desired results. Although the Allies above all targeted Germany's industrial base, not civilians, as the war progressed they also came to hope that the civilian deaths would break Germany's morale and discipline. There is little evidence that this occurred. Five months after the Hamburg raid, industrial production in the city had returned to 80 percent of the pre-raid level. Germany did see its weapons production and industrial capacity severely damaged by the bombing, but mainly in the last year of the war.

The case of Dresden, capital of the German state of Saxony, has achieved special notoriety because the beautiful baroque city, called Venice on the Elbe, had little strategic or industrial importance. In February 1945, it was crammed with refugees. The attack on the city that month involved 1,300 Allied bombers dropping nearly 4 million tons of explosives that killed between 24,000 and 40,000 civilians and wiped out the baroque center almost entirely. Altogether, bombing raids probably killed somewhere on the order of 600,000 German civilians during the war, including over 100,000 children.

The United States inflicted massive civilian casualties on Japan once it started sustained strategic bombing of

Allied Bombing A solitary statue of an angel looks out over the city of Dresden, largely destroyed by the Allied bombing campaign of February 1945.

the Japanese home islands in mid-1944. Even before the atomic bombing of Hiroshima and Nagasaki in August 1945, the firebombing of Tokyo in March killed over 80,000 people. Debates continue about the Allies' moral responsibility for the deaths of innocents on this scale, and the ways in which the "barbarization" of warfare initiated by the Axis ended up affecting their adversaries as well.

THE EASTERN FRONT

On the eastern front as well, what mattered was not only the Soviet Union's superior economic capacity, reconstructed after the devastation of the initial German offensive, but the way this capacity was deployed and the way the Red Army adjusted its strategy. Owing to the experiences of the 1930s, the Soviets already had the capacity to undertake brutally fast industrial initiatives, but it took time to redirect this capacity to effective military ends. During 1942 and early 1943, the general staff reorganized the army around powerful tank corps, copying the German model that relied on concentrations of tanks to break through enemy lines. At the beginning of the war, the Soviets had lost six to seven tanks for every German one they took out. By late 1944, the ratio was one to one.

These changes were evident in the next great conflict after Stalingrad, centered on the city of Kursk, some 350 miles south of Moscow. The Germans had 3,000 tanks and 1,800 aircraft. The Red Army countered with 3,600 tanks, nearly 2,800 aircraft, and a stunning 1,300,000 infantry. Soviet forces at Kursk held, shattering the Nazi offensive. The Soviets could now continue pushing the Germans back out of their territory, even as they continued to take frightful losses.

THE INVASION OF ITALY

The only way to relieve the ferocious pressure on the Soviets was for the western Allies to open a second front, to divert German resources from the east. But where would the western Allies strike? Stalin continued to urge an attack on German forces in France. The British, however, saw a more immediately tempting target that would distract the Germans without requiring the immense concentration of force necessary for an invasion of France—a concentration they believed was not yet possible. Instead, they looked to Italy. Mussolini had come unwillingly into the war, had gained little from it, and faced weakening support among the Italian population. The Americans initially were reluctant, wishing to conserve resources for the eventual attack through France, but Churchill prevailed upon Roosevelt.

In July 1943, the Allies successfully invaded the island of Sicily. Soon afterward, the Fascist Grand Council turned against Mussolini and arrested him, while King Vittorio Emmanuel III took control over the armed forces. The new government signed an armistice with the Allies on September 3. Five days later, American general Eisenhower began landing his troops near Naples. Italy would not prove so easy to subdue, however, for Hitler immediately sent divisions of his own to occupy the peninsula, and SS officers staged a daring rescue of Mussolini by using gliders. Allied forces only reached Rome in June 1944 and did not liberate parts of northern Italy until nearly the end of the war, at which point the Italian resistance captured and executed the dictator who had launched the fascist movement a quarter of a century before.

HOME FRONTS

The war brought the greatest suffering to the vast areas of the continent under Axis military occupation. But even more than in World War I, conditions of total war also transformed daily life beyond recognition for millions behind the front lines in the combatant countries. Not only did millions of men and women experience the horrific bombing campaigns discussed above; they also found themselves required to participate in the most ambitious mobilization of social resources ever attempted by European states.

WARTIME BRITAIN, GERMANY, AND THE USSR

Although never invaded by the Axis, Great Britain experienced enormous changes in the war. As the Allies carried out their invasion of Italy and planned for an invasion of France, the British Isles became their staging ground. By mid-1944, there were over 1.6 million American personnel in Britain. New military bases proliferated, and the British were exposed to American culture as never before. Over 70,000 British women became brides of American servicemen by the end of the war.

Other changes were reminiscent of what Britain had experienced in World War I. Rationing began almost immediately and affected nearly every consumer product, including foodstuffs, textiles, and fuel. The government urged civilians to donate aluminum cookware to the war effort to produce airplane parts, and millions complied. Blackouts, as a precaution against bombing, left nighttime streets dark and empty. Censorship of the news media and popular entertainment, while not comparable to that experienced in Germany or the Soviet Union, increased dramatically. The film industry in particular became virtually an arm of a new Ministry of Information. Even more quickly than in World War I, government ministries effectively took over large parts of the economy, setting production and consumption quotas, fixing wages, and organizing manufacturing.

In addition to conscripting able-bodied men for the military, in late 1941 Parliament passed a law conscripting single women in their twenties for service in industry, civil defense, or women's auxiliary corps attached to the armed forces. The proportion of women in the civilian workforce rose from 26 percent before the war to nearly 40 percent. Feminists again hailed the evidence that women could perform as well as men in jobs previously closed to them, and expressed the hope that this time the new opportunities would remain in place permanently.

In Germany and the Soviet Union, wartime daily experience more closely resembled that of the pre-war period in some ways. In both countries, totalitarian governments had already attempted massive reconfigurations of society. In the USSR the government already had virtually total control of the economy, and in Germany it set economic policy to an extent unknown in the Western democracies. Both states already exercised total control over the media,

WOMEN OF BRITAIN COME INTO THE FACTORIES

As in World War I, during World War II women were called on to fill jobs in industries that had previously been held by men, working in factories, hospitals, government offices, and on farms. In Britain, many women also served in noncombatant roles in the military as drivers, pilots, clerks, radar operators, and code-breakers.

To encourage women's participation in the war effort, the British government produced hundreds of posters that celebrated women's roles in fighting Nazi Germany. This poster from December 1941 calls for women to work in munitions factories. Flanked by a factory and a pair of advancing tanks, a woman worker assumes a powerful stance, her outstretched arms seeming to command forward a squadron of bombers. The text at the bottom encourages women to ask at centers managed by the Ministry of Labour about employment opportunities in factories. Such posters appealed to women's sense of patriotism and their status as British subjects.

QUESTIONS FOR ANALYSIS

1. What forms of work related to the war effort were available to women in Britain?
2. How does this poster attempt to persuade women to seek employment in factories?
3. How might this poster have tied into feminist views of women's place in society?

engaged in constant large-scale propaganda campaigns, and made use of enormous police apparatuses to stifle any significant dissent. In the USSR, women already participated in the labor force to a higher proportion than any other European state.

But in both countries the war nonetheless brought massive disruptions and changes. Both countries introduced extensive rationing, and in both the specter of malnutrition and even famine soon arose. As we have seen, Soviet women were conscripted along with men, and served extensively in combat positions. Soon after the German attack, Stalin ordered the deportation to the East of hundreds of thousands of "Volga Germans"—descendants of Germans who settled in Russia at the invitation of Catherine the Great in the eighteenth century. During the war, other Soviet nationalities suspected of sympathy for the Nazis suffered a similar fate, including hundreds of thousands of Crimean Tatars (the original Muslim inhabitants of the Crimean Peninsula in the Black Sea), who mostly ended up in Uzbekistan. Germany, meanwhile, made use of millions of slave laborers, including prisoners of war, to keep its domestic economy functioning. By 1944, more than seven million men and women from across Europe were working as forced labor in Germany.

RESISTANCE MOVEMENTS

As the Allies built up their strength in Britain, planning for an eventual invasion of France, Hitler's support outside of Germany weakened. In the occupied countries, collaborations grew more isolated, while resistance movements gained adherents and undertook bolder campaigns. To a large extent, the success of these movements depended on geography. Lowland countries like the Netherlands, Belgium, and Denmark had few territories in which partisans could hide from the Germans. The mountains of Yugoslavia and the deep forests of Russia, Ukraine, Norway, and Poland offered considerably safer terrain. The effectiveness of resistance forces also depended on organizational ability, and here communist groups, in some cases drawing on long experience of covert, underground organization before the war, had a decisive advantage. The Allies attempted where possible to drop supplies as well as personnel to help resistance groups.

In Yugoslavia, communist and non-communist partisans fought Germans, Italians, Croatian and Serbian fascists, and one another, with the bitter conflicts ultimately taking the lives of perhaps a tenth of the pre-war population. The Communist leader Josip Broz, who called

himself Tito (1892–1980), eventually came out on top. Meanwhile, behind German lines on the eastern front, the numbers of partisans fighting in the forests steadily grew: in Ukraine, from 17,000 in mid-1943 to 140,000 a year later. Although poorly armed, these fighters did manage to disrupt German supplies and kill or wound tens of thousands of German soldiers. The Germans responded with vicious scorched-earth tactics and the slaughter of civilians.

It was in France where "the **Resistance**" was most systematically celebrated after the war. It had its heroes and martyrs: most famously Jean Moulin (1899–1943), a high official dismissed by Vichy who fled to Charles de Gaulle's Free French forces in London and then returned to unite and organize the disparate non-communist Resistance forces. Captured by the Germans in June 1943, he was most likely tortured to death. By July 1944, the French Resistance may have numbered as many as 116,000 men and women, but in truth its exploits are often exaggerated. Through most of the war, the Germans, reinforced by an unpopular French Militia, needed no more than a security force of 6,500 to guard against Resistance activity in France. Through at least mid-1942, the majority of the French population continued to support Pétain's Vichy regime.

In some ways, the single most impressive act of resistance to the Nazis was also the most hopeless, and it took place in the heart of Hitler's darkness: the Warsaw Jewish ghetto. In January 1943, as the Germans carried out

Warsaw Ghetto Uprising Following the defeat of the January 1943 uprising, German soldiers round up for deportation the inhabitants of the Warsaw ghetto, who raise their hands in surrender.

yet another sweep aimed at deporting Warsaw's Jews to the death camps, a secret Jewish Combat Organization attacked with a motley collection of pistols, ancient rifles, grenades, and Molotov cocktails. Taken by surprise, the Germans withdrew, enabling the insurgents to fortify themselves in a series of underground bunkers. A German SS and police force counterattacked in force in April, but it finally succeeded only by literally burning the entire section of the city to the ground. Some 13,000 Jews died in the uprising. Of the remaining 50,000 Jews of Warsaw, most ended up in the Treblinka death camp.

LIBERATION

Since 1940, Winston Churchill had made clear that he would only accept one outcome for the war: Germany's unconditional surrender. Stalin and Roosevelt concurred. Adolf Hitler, meanwhile, after invading the Soviet Union, made no further serious peace overtures, even when an Allied victory came to seem inevitable after the battles of Stalingrad and Kursk.

THE BEGINNING OF THE END

In February 1943, after the surrender at Stalingrad, Hitler's propaganda chief, Joseph Goebbels, gave a hallucinatory speech at the Berlin Sports Palace in which he screeched: "I ask you: Do you want total war? Do you want it more total and more radical than we can even yet imagine?" Hitler himself turned increasingly disjointed in his speech and dependent on drugs, including narcotics and amphetamines, administered by his personal physician. More and more he put his faith in a miraculous reversal of fortunes, perhaps thanks to new super-weapons.

BUILDING AN ATOMIC BOMB Both sides attempted to develop such weapons during the war. German scientists managed to develop two important new weapons: a pilotless flying bomb (the V-1), followed by the first workable ballistic missile (the V-2). However, in another triumph of intelligence work the Allies discovered the V-program's center of operation and destroyed it. In 1944, the Germans finally managed to start producing V-1's and V-2's in large numbers and launched them toward London, killing some 2,500 people. But the weapons came too late.

The Germans also worked on atomic weapons, but their efforts were hindered by insufficient coordination and the fact that many Jewish physicists had fled before the war. As a result they fell far behind the large-scale **Manhattan Project** run by British and American physicists in the United States. Even before the war, émigré scientists Albert Einstein (1879–1955) and Leo Szilárd (1898–1964) had urged President Roosevelt to begin a nuclear weapons program, lest Germany develop such weapons first. After Pearl Harbor, the Americans and British devoted massive resources to the project, eventually spending over $2 billion and employing some 130,000 scientists and staff. It was the Allies who would test the first nuclear weapon—in New Mexico in July 1945.

PLANNING A CROSS-CHANNEL INVASION The war now approached its final stages. In the Pacific, the Americans continued their advance and in June 1944 captured the island of Saipan, from which American bombers could strike at the Japanese home islands. Meanwhile, through the first half of 1944 the Red Army continued its own advance westward. By June, it had driven the Germans out of almost all of Russia and eastern Ukraine. Another major offensive would push them back to the 1939 border line by August.

Even as these events were taking place, planning for the second front was reaching fruition. Churchill, Roosevelt, and Stalin agreed at a summit meeting in Tehran in November 1943 to launch an invasion of France across the English Channel the next spring. By this point, Churchill had put aside his earlier reluctance to commit to such a massive project. He and Roosevelt had always wanted to defeat Germany as quickly and decisively as possible, but now they also realized that if they did not soon strike in the west, the Red Army might well end up liberating the entire Continent and install governments sympathetic to Stalin from Poland to Provence. Churchill in particular had few illusions about the durability of the western democracies' alliance with Stalin (he tellingly once remarked: "If Hitler invaded Hell I would make at least a favorable reference to the Devil in the House of Commons"). And so, ironically, he and Roosevelt now acted to restrain Stalin's future success by granting him his long-standing demand: the invasion of France.

D-DAY AND THE INVASION OF FRANCE

The Allied invasion across the English Channel was a massive operation. In November 1943, Hitler had ordered the construction of an Atlantic Wall involving some 3 million mines, half a million obstacles on beaches, and the reinforcement of German divisions in France and the Low

Countries. The Allies, meanwhile, steadily built up their forces in Britain, while doing their best to confuse the Germans about the eventual site of the landing. Overall command of the operation was given to American general Dwight D. Eisenhower (1890–1969), a steady, cautious commander who managed to contain considerable squabbling among his multinational subordinates.

When the invasion force actually appeared off the coast of Normandy on June 6, 1944—**D-Day**—it took the Germans at least somewhat by surprise. The very size of the Allied fleet had shock value: some 5,000 ships ranging from battleships to small landing craft, carrying 100,000 predominantly American and British soldiers to five beaches spread out over some thirty miles, heavily supported by air power. On the beach code-named Omaha, American forces had to advance under murderous German fire. Yet in the end, D-Day casualties numbered around 10,000—far less than the supreme commander, Eisenhower, had feared—and the Allies successfully established a beachhead.

Breaking out of Normandy's small Cotentin Peninsula still took two months of hard fighting. But during July alone, the Allies landed more than 1 million men, 171,000 vehicles, and 560,000 tons of supplies. In early August, the hard-driving American general George Patton (1885–1945) finally cut through German lines to the south, and his Third Army embarked on a virtual blitzkrieg of its own. By late August, Allied forces were approaching Paris. Hitler angrily ordered the city destroyed, but his commander in Paris refused to obey the order. In mid-August, Parisian police and Resistance units rose up in revolt against the Germans, who soon began pulling out. In a gesture

D-Day U.S. soldiers disembarking from a landing craft rush through water to the beaches of Normandy on June 6, 1944.

to the Free French forces under De Gaulle, Eisenhower allowed the actual liberation of Paris to be conducted by the French Second Armored Division, and on August 23 its first three tanks entered the city. By mid-September, the Allies had liberated Belgium and Luxembourg and had penetrated as far as the French border with Switzerland.

In fall 1944, the Allied push to the east briefly faltered. The liberation of the Netherlands took far longer than planned, and German resistance stiffened noticeably as the Wehrmacht retreated back toward its home territory. The success of Hitler's deputy, Albert Speer, in dispersing industrial production to avoid bombing temporarily enabled Germany to manufacture record amounts of war materiel. Between September and December, the Allied front line did not advance significantly, and in mid-December Hitler launched his last major offensive in the west. Still, by New Year's it was clear that the Germans had lost the so-called Battle of the Bulge, and by March 1945 the Allies had captured most of the German Rhineland.

LIBERATION AND POWER STRUGGLES

With the Allies advancing toward Germany from both sides, the countries that had suffered under the Nazi yoke celebrated their liberation. But this liberation came with significant pain and strife. Everywhere, but especially in the east, the front often rolled back over cities and towns like a steamroller, leaving rubble behind. While some occupied cities largely escaped damage in the war—Paris, Prague, Copenhagen, Kraków—they were in the minority. Now, with Nazi rule finally crumbling, the resistance forces throughout occupied Europe achieved their greatest importance as they harried the demoralized Germans and maneuvered to take control of the liberated areas.

The liberation brought bloody score-settling and vicious struggles for power in many countries. In Greece, communist and non-communist resistance forces, who had barely managed to cooperate beforehand, fell into a full-fledged civil war that lasted, with interruptions, until a final communist defeat in 1949. In France, the Resistance took revenge on the more visible and vulnerable collaborators: thousands died, and women who had slept with German soldiers sometimes had their heads shaved as a sign of shame. The restored French Republic Marshal Pétain, now in his late eighties, was put on trial and sentenced to life imprisonment. Other collaborators died in front of firing squads. Still, many highly placed ones, particularly those who had managed to slide over to the

Victory Townspeople flood the streets of Prague to celebrate, here gathering around a soldier playing the accordion, after the Red Army's liberation of Prague in 1945.

Resistance in time, remained in prominent positions in public life, including police officials who had helped round up French Jews for deportation to the death camps.

Where the Red Army advanced in eastern Europe, it sought to place its friends in power. Stalin attached particular importance to Poland, which he insisted become a pro-Soviet buffer against any new invasion of his country. As the Red Army moved into Poland in the summer of 1944, Stalin recognized a pro-communist group in the eastern city of Lublin as the legitimate government, even though the government-in-exile in London had the loyalty of the largest Polish resistance group, the **Home Army**. The Home Army itself desperately wanted to avoid communist rule, and as the Red Army approached Warsaw at the end of July 1944, fully 20,000 of its fighters revolted against the Germans in an attempt to seize the city. They acted prematurely, however. While a German counterattack initially kept the Soviets pinned down across the Vistula River, German army and SS divisions set about systematically destroying Warsaw. By early October, the city center no longer existed, and its population was dispersed or imprisoned. The Soviets, who had little desire to rescue the Home Army, only captured the ruins of Warsaw in the winter.

Amidst these tensions and conflicts, the liberation continued. In the fall, Romania and Bulgaria abandoned their German allies and opened their frontiers to the Red Army. The Germans retreated from Greece, and Yugoslavia fell, with Tito's resistance seizing power. By January 1, 1945, Soviet forces stood inside the boundaries of German East Prussia.

But Germany did not surrender. The last chance for an early end to the war had been lost on July 20, 1944, when a group of high-ranking German officers failed in an attempt to assassinate Hitler and seize power. An aristocratic Catholic officer, Count Claus von Stauffenberg, smuggled a bomb into Hitler's bunker in East Prussia inside a briefcase. But when it exploded, Hitler was on the other side of a heavy oak conference table and suffered nothing but a burst eardrum. The plotters were quickly discovered and killed.

A VIOLENT CONCLUSION

The final chapter of World War II in Europe had an otherworldly quality. Cities that six years before had been a part of the modern world, with electric light and factories, automobiles and department stores, had been reduced to smoking rubble where dazed survivors scrounged for food and fuel, and callous soldiers killed, raped, and stole like a mythical barbarian horde. The British poet Stephen Spender (1909–1995), upon seeing the ruined German city of Cologne in July 1945, wrote:

My first impression on passing through the city was of there being not a single house left. There are plenty of walls, but these walls are a thin mask in front of the damp, hollow, stinking emptiness of the gutted interiors.... The ruin of the city is reflected in the internal ruin of its inhabitants, who, instead of being lives that can form a scar over the city's wounds, are parasites sucking on a dead carcass, digging among the ruins for hidden food.

Refugees choked the roads of Europe. According to some estimates, as many as 10 million people struggled to make their way home in spring and summer 1945. The Allies uncovered crimes so hideous that Europeans did not fully come to terms with them for decades.

Much of the violence that accompanied the fall of Nazi Germany had of course been provoked by the Nazis' own barbarization of warfare. In a speech to his men as they stood on the boundaries of Germany, Marshal Zhukov gave voice to the Soviet people's deep hatred and desire for revenge:

We have not forgotten the pain and suffering done to our people by Hitler's cannibals. We have not forgotten our burned-out cities and villages. We remember our brothers and sisters, our mothers and fathers, our wives and children tortured to death by Germans. We shall avenge those burned in the devil's ovens, avenge those who suffocated in the gas chambers, avenge the murdered and the martyred. We shall exact a brutal revenge for everything.

In their advance, Soviet forces made little attempt to spare the German civilian population. Soviet soldiers routinely raped German women and girls, stole from the population, and killed Germans out of hand. Their officers generally made little attempt to control them.

BORDERS AND REFUGEES

The violence and disruption in 1945 were also shaped by decisions taken collectively by the Allies at their wartime conferences. At the Tehran meeting with Stalin in November 1943, Churchill and Roosevelt had reluctantly agreed that in compensation for the massive Soviet losses, after the war the Soviet Union would keep the territories it had seized in 1939–40: the Baltic states and eastern Poland. In addition, the Allies discussed compensating Poland for this loss with territory taken from Germany.

At the Crimean resort town of **Yalta** in February 1945, the Big Three met again and confirmed these decisions. Roosevelt was especially anxious to please Stalin so as to secure Soviet support for the ongoing war in the Pacific. They further agreed to demilitarize and denazify Germany, to divide both the country as a whole and also Berlin and Vienna into occupation zones, and to restore Austrian independence. At Yalta they also agreed to free elections in Poland to choose between the two competing claimants to power: the government-in-exile that had established

The Big Three Churchill, Roosevelt, and Stalin meet at the Yalta conference in February 1945.

itself in London in 1939, and the Soviet-backed provisional government based in Lublin.

The Allied decisions meant expulsion or worse for the more than 12 million Germans living in what was now Poland and for millions of other ethnic Germans throughout Europe, notably 3 million in the Czech Sudetenland. More than half of them fled ahead of the Red Army, and as many as 2 million died or disappeared in the process amid terrible scenes. On January 30, 1945, as the German passenger ship *Wilhelm Gustloff* steamed into the Baltic from the port of Gdynia carrying more than 9,400 panicked German refugees and also some German military personnel, it was torpedoed by a Soviet submarine and sank. Nearly all the passengers died, close to half of them children, in what still stands as the greatest maritime disaster in history.

The German refugees were just part of a larger flood tide of refugees from every part of the Continent. It included Cossacks and other minority groups in the Soviet Union whom Stalin—with the tacit support of Roosevelt and Churchill at Yalta—ruthlessly expelled to Siberia in revenge for their initial support of the German invasion. It included 5.7 million men and women who had volunteered or been forced into working in Germany, as well as hundreds of thousands of surviving Jews whose homes had been destroyed or who did not dare return to them for fear of further pogroms—a real threat in Poland. To these groups must also be added the millions of Europeans who had seen their homes destroyed. It was human disruption on an unbelievable scale, amid the ruins of a civilization.

THE GERMAN SURRENDER AND THE LIBERATION OF THE CAMPS

The final act of the war in Europe took place in the city where it had started with Hitler's seizure of power twelve years before: Berlin. In the late winter and spring of 1945, the Soviets made a final push for the city. Hitler continued to deny reality, seizing at any wisp of good news (most notably, Franklin Roosevelt's death on April 12) as proof that Germany's deliverance was at hand. The Nazis forced old men, and boys as young as twelve or thirteen, into the fray and hanged suspected traitors and cowards. But the city was lost. In late April, even as American and Soviet troops met on the Elbe River, the Red Army forced its way through Berlin's suburbs, fighting building by building.

In a bunker near the Reichstag where he had lived for much of the year, Hitler finally recognized what had happened, castigated the German people for failing him,

Europe at the End of World War II, 1945 Amid the ruins to which many parts of Europe had been reduced, the Allies redrew the map. They reconstituted Poland, Czechoslovakia, and other countries Hitler had invaded, and they divided Germany into four zones of occupation, with Berlin and Vienna governed jointly by the four Allied powers.

and solemnly prepared his death. "I must now obey the dictates of Fate," he told his aides. "Even if I could save myself, I would not do so." After marrying his long-time mistress, Eva Braun, he shot himself and she took poison. His aides then doused the bodies with gasoline and burned them. Joseph Goebbels, ever the fanatic, along with his wife poisoned their six children as they slept in the bunker, and then committed suicide in their turn. Admiral Karl von Dönitz, named by Hitler as his heir, acceded to Allied demands and after a week signed the acts of unconditional surrender. The war in Europe was over.

Even as this final act of the Third Reich was taking place, on April 15, 1945, British and American troops liberated the concentration camp of Bergen-Belsen in northern Germany. They found thousands of bodies lying unburied on the ground and thousands of prisoners in a state of advanced starvation: hideous living skeletons. The reports shocked even a war-hardened western public. In January, the Red Army had liberated Auschwitz, which the Germans had abandoned shortly before, herding the surviving prisoners back toward Germany in a death march. In May, the Soviets made public what they had found there,

Liberation Survivors liberated by Allied forces at a concentration camp in Ebensee, Austria in 1945.

although they neglected to specify that the large majority of victims had been Jews. In some camps in Germany, Allied commanders forced the inhabitants of nearby towns to come see what had been done in the name of Germany and to help bury the dead.

THE WAR IN ASIA AND THE POTSDAM CONFERENCE

The war was over in Europe. But in Asia, it dragged on and continued to affect European developments. The long and brutal push to dislodge Japanese forces from a series of island fortresses continued, along with saturation bombing of Japan that took lives on the same scale as the bombing of Germany. The Allies began to plan for a massive invasion of the Japanese home islands, while hoping that Japan, starved of resources by the ongoing blockade, might be driven to surrender without it. Britain and the United States continued to press the Soviets to declare war on Japan. Although liberated France now reestablished control over its African colonies, the European colonies in Southeast Asia remained battlefields.

This was the atmosphere in which Churchill, Stalin, and the new U.S. president, Harry Truman, met in Potsdam, outside of Berlin, in mid-July 1945. They finalized the details of the occupation zones of Germany and Austria, agreed on policies to purge Nazis from German government and society, imposed reparations on Germany, and planned to eliminate Germany's industrial war potential. They also agreed to war crimes trials for Germans, including many of the country's leaders.

These trials took place in the German city of Nuremberg from the fall of 1945 to the fall of 1946, and they resulted in long prison terms or death for much of the surviving Nazi leadership. Hermann Goering cheated the hangman by committing suicide, while Heinrich Himmler, head of the SS, killed himself before even coming to trial. During the **Potsdam conference**, the stubborn spirit of democracy expressed itself in an unexpected way: in British elections, voters weary of hardship and rationing threw the governing Conservatives out of office in favor of a Labour Party pledged to sweeping social reforms. Winston Churchill duly departed from Potsdam to be replaced by the new prime minister, Clement Attlee.

It was clear by this point that even as the Allies scrambled to end the Pacific War, they were also preparing for a future shaped by competition between a western bloc led by the United States and an eastern one led by the Soviet Union. These considerations, along with a desire to end the war without further loss of Allied life, fed into the final, momentous American actions of the summer of 1945. On August 6, four days after the end of the Potsdam conference, the United States dropped the first of two **atomic bombs** on Japan, vaporizing the city center of Hiroshima and killing between 60,000 and 80,000 people instantly, with a final death toll over 130,000. Three days later, even as the Americans dropped a second bomb

Hiroshima The devastation wrought by the atomic bomb on Hiroshima on August 6, 1945, included the leveling of most of the city. The Prefectural Industrial Promotion Hall, at right, was one of the very few structures to survive the bombing mostly intact, although everyone inside it was killed.

on Nagasaki, the Soviet Union went to war against Japan and rapidly seized large territories in Manchuria and Sakhalin Island. On August 12, 1945, Japan joined Germany in surrender.

UNPARALLELED VIOLENCE

World War II remains the greatest outbreak of violence in the entire history of humanity. Of the hundred bloodiest battles of modern times, a large majority took place during World War II, with most of those on the eastern front. The colossal death toll almost defies explanation, but it had at least three obvious sources. The first was the rise of an expansionist racial ideology in Germany that placed little or no value on the lives of those it dubbed "subhumans," including Slavs and particularly Jews. The Germans' murderous attempts to translate this ideology into military reality forced Germany's enemies to adopt ruthless means in response, something that came especially easily to Stalin's totalitarian dictatorship, which was faced with challenges far beyond what any other Allied power faced. Second, there was the state of military technology, which, despite the increasing prominence of tank and air warfare, still reserved a crucial place for the mass use of infantry. As a result, the contending powers mobilized a higher proportion of their populations than at any other time in history. Third, there was the ability of advanced industrial economies to produce the means of death on a hitherto unimaginable scale. The result was unimaginable horror. Germany paid a heavy price for unleashing it; but despite losing millions of people and a quarter of its territory, it still did not suffer as much as its victims.

The barbarization of warfare between 1939 and 1945 affected all the combatants. By 1942, the Allies had begun campaigns of "area bombing" against Germany that, despite the concentration on industry, entailed a frightful toll in innocent civilian life. During the war as a whole, the Allies dropped no less than 2.5 million tons of conventional explosives on Germany and Japan. Between 1943 and 1945, almost every major German city was left in ruins.

Still, it was the Germans who inflicted the greatest harm, and the Soviet Union that suffered the most. Of a Soviet population that numbered nearly 197 million in June 1941 (counting the recent annexations), more than one person in eight would lose their life over the next four years—over 27 million men, women, and children. Soviet military losses alone came to a staggering 10.7 million—more than thirty times the corresponding American figure. Soviet birth rates dropped sharply during the war,

and the loss of young men was so severe that among Soviet women in their mid-twenties during the war, fewer than two-thirds ever married. The cities of the western Soviet Union were left, for the most part, smoking ruins. And the same was true of most of central and eastern Europe. This was the essence of World War II. For four evil years, the achievements of European civilization—its ingenious developments in technology, industry, and social organization—seemed to turn to this one terrible purpose of destruction.

UNDERSTANDING THE HOLOCAUST

And then there was the Holocaust, perhaps the single darkest moment in all of European history. Despite the impossibility of ever fully understanding it, historians have nonetheless tried to offer some explanations. Many have argued that the Holocaust was driven by impersonal processes, like some bureaucratic cancer that carried events beyond even the Nazis' conscious intentions. Yet such interpretations tend to distract attention from the men and women who actually carried out the killings. And they also discount the decade or more of intensive ideological indoctrination by which Hitler's state, building on and deeply intensifying long traditions of anti-Semitism, taught its citizens that Jews, Roma, and other "undesirables" were vermin who posed a mortal threat to Germany's survival.

Even this indoctrination might not have been enough to transform ordinary Germans and others into willing executioners. But when combined with the habits of obedience inculcated by an authoritarian state turned totalitarian, in the crisis atmosphere of total war, and with the killers' desire not to show weakness in front of their comrades or to let them down, this indoctrination sufficed to break the human bond and bring about the Holocaust. In October 1943, Heinrich Himmler, head of the SS, told a gathering of his colleagues: "Most of you know what it means to see a hundred corpses lying together, five hundred, or a thousand. To have gone through this and yet—apart from a few exceptions, examples of human weakness—to have remained decent fellows, this is what has made us hard. This is a glorious page in our history that has never been written and shall never be written."

In the face of these crimes, some Europeans did act, often at great risk, to hide the victims or help them escape. The Danish people and government ferried virtually their entire Jewish population to safety in neutral Sweden. The Bulgarian government, in response to widespread popular protest, refused to deport the country's 50,000 Jews. Individual Christians—like the ones in Amsterdam who hid Anne Frank's family—helped individual Jews. The Israeli government's Holocaust monument and museum has recognized 22,000 "righteous" individuals who acted to save Jews, including a disproportionate number of Christian clergy.

Yet at the same time, little was done to help by some who had considerable power to do so. By mid-1943, numerous credible reports of the Holocaust had already appeared in the American, British, and Swiss press. Pope Pius XII and the Catholic Church hierarchy knew well what was happening in German-occupied Europe. But the pope, who still had considerable sway over German and Austrian Catholics, failed to denounce the killings. As for the Allied powers, they did so only weakly, if at all, and made no serious effort to disrupt them—for instance, by bombing the death camps or the railroads leading to them. Many officials continued to dismiss reports of the slaughter, however well documented, as wild rumors, even as attempts by Jews to gain special treatment. Anti-Semitism undoubtedly played a role in these reactions, as did a misguided determination not to let anything interfere with the central goal of Allied victory. But in some cases, Allied inaction also stemmed from an inability to come to terms, even in the face of solid proof, with the enormity of what the Nazis were doing. Could "civilized" Europeans really commit such acts?

CONCLUSION

Overall, World War II marked the culmination of trends in European history that had been developing since the first Industrial Revolution and the almost simultaneous rise of racially tinged romantic nationalism. But the year 1945—what the Germans refer to as their Hour Zero—brought a sudden and definitive end to these trends, and to much else besides. The defeat of Nazi Germany, and the revelation of German crimes, overnight turned fascism and extreme conservatism into pariah ideologies preserved only by tiny fringe movements. The kindling of atomic light over Hiroshima made war of the sort just fought, with its confrontation of massive land, sea, and air forces, impossible to repeat. The joint triumph of the United States and the Soviet Union meant that in place of a continent dominated by a shifting and contentious constellation of native powers, there would now be a continent divided between two great and opposed political forces, led by nations outside the traditional European heartland.

Like the Napoleonic Wars and World War I, World War II would also have tremendous long-term consequences for Europe's relations with the rest of the world. Japan, with its program for an East Asian Co-Prosperity Sphere, tried to cast a veil of anti-imperialism over its own imperialist ambitions. In some of the European colonies that it overran, notably the Dutch East Indies, Japan installed puppet governments that claimed to represent local nationalist aspirations, and thereby strengthened these aspirations. More important, by driving European nations out of large areas of Asia, even as those same nations bled white in the European conflict, it damaged the structures of European colonialism, making them harder to reimpose in the war's aftermath. European authority also suffered in the French colonies left in limbo between Vichy and the Allies.

In Europe itself, amid the ruins, facing this unpredictable future and the long and wearying process of rebuilding, men and women had every reason to be apprehensive. Already in the spring of 1945, tensions between the West and the Soviet Union were clearly visible. In a letter to President Truman, Winston Churchill had already used the phrase *iron curtain* (which he would make famous in a speech a year later) to describe the division of Europe between East and West. Even so, to a remarkable extent this apprehension was *not* justified. The next fifty years would bring much trouble and tension. But overall, it would also bring something surprising: stability, prosperity, and peace. The most horrible chapter in European history was about to give way to one of the brightest.

[CHAPTER REVIEW]

KEY TERMS

blitzkrieg (p. 776)

Dunkirk (p. 776)

Vichy (p. 777)

Winston Churchill (p. 777)

Blitz (p. 779)

Lend-Lease (p. 780)

Holocaust (p. 781)

Operation Barbarossa
(p. 782)

Einsatzgruppen (p. 784)

Pearl Harbor (p. 786)

battle of Stalingrad
(p. 789)

Wannsee conference
(p. 791)

Auschwitz-Birkenau
(p. 792)

Resistance (p. 798)

Manhattan Project (p. 799)

D-Day (p. 800)

Home Army (p. 801)

Yalta conference (p. 802)

Potsdam conference
(p. 804)

atomic bombs (p. 804)

REVIEW QUESTIONS

1. What were the results of the German offensives in western Europe in 1940?

2. In terms of its impact on civilians, how did World War II differ from World War I?

3. How did German occupation practices in Poland compare with those in western Europe?

4. How did the German invasion of the Soviet Union bring a new scale of destruction to World War II?

5. In what ways did the Japanese attack on Pearl Harbor change the global dimensions of World War II?

6. How did the systematic mass murder planned at the Wannsee conference mark a change from earlier Nazi measures against Jews and others deemed undesirables?

7. What factors contributed to the perpetration of the Holocaust?

8. Starting in 1942, how did the Allies harness their economic advantages to achieve military victories?

9. Why did violence follow liberation throughout Europe?

10. How did the Allied leaders decide to reshape Europe during their conferences near the end of the war?

CORE OBJECTIVES

After reading this chapter, you should have a solid understanding of the following core objectives. To strengthen your grasp of the core objectives, use the resources on the Student Site for The West.

- Describe the military tactics and occupation policies employed by Germany in the first two years of World War II.

- Assess the German invasion of the Soviet Union and its horrific impact on the Soviet people.

- Trace the spread of the war around the globe starting in 1941.

- Explain the origins, evolution, and culmination of the Holocaust.

- Analyze the late period of the war leading to Allied victory.

- Identify the major demographic, social, and cultural effects of the war.

 GO TO **inQuizitive** TO SEE WHAT YOU'VE LEARNED—AND LEARN WHAT YOU'VE MISSED—WITH PERSONALIZED FEEDBACK ALONG THE WAY.

CHRONOLOGY

1945
Nuremberg
trials

1947
Marshall Plan
announced

1947
India and Pakistan
become
independent

1948–1949
Berlin blockade and airlift

1948–1949
Communist regimes
established throughout
Eastern Europe

1948
State of Israel created

1948
George Orwell
publishes *1984*

1949
Simone de Beauvoir
publishes *The Second Sex*

1949
NATO formed

1949
Mao Zedong and
Communists take
power in China

1950–1953
Korean War

1954–1962
Algerian War
of Independence

1954
French defeat
in Vietnam

March 1953
Stalin dies

1955
Warsaw Pact
formed

1956
Soviet Union invades
Hungary after the
Hungarian government
attempts to withdraw
from the Eastern bloc.

1956
Suez Crisis

1957
Treaty of Rome
creates the European
Economic Community

1958
Fifth Republic
established
in France

Recovery and Cold War

REBUILDING A DIVIDED CONTINENT

1945–1973

Spring 1968
Student protests
throughout Europe

1962–1965
Second Vatican
Council

1962
Algeria achieves
independence

1961
Berlin Wall
built

January 30, 1972
Bloody Sunday
in Ireland

1964–1975
Large-scale U.S.
military involvement
in Vietnam

n July 1952, an American landing craft—one of the same that had brought American soldiers to Omaha Beach on D-Day seven years before—again hit a European shoreline. The target this time was Finland, a neutral country on the border of the Soviet Union, with which the United States and its allies were now locked in the ongoing confrontation of ideologies, and political and economic interests, known as the Cold War. And this time the craft did not carry soldiers or weaponry. Instead, it was loaded with salesmen, publicity material, and many thousands of bottles of Coca-Cola, all bound for the Olympic Games taking place in the Finnish capital of Helsinki. It was a publicity stunt connected to an aggressive plan by the American soft drink company to establish itself in Europe. The plan called for ninety-six bottling plants in western Germany by 1954, and sales of over a billion bottles a year on the European continent. As early as 1949, rumors had spread in France that Coca-Cola would try to advertise on the side of Notre Dame Cathedral or attach its famous logo to the Eiffel Tower. The French Communist newspaper *L'Humanité*, learning of the French sales goals, accused the company of seeking to replace wine with Coke and stridently asked: "Will we be Coca-Cola-Colonized?"

These incidents, while comic, illustrate a great deal about Europe's recovery from World War II. Coming so soon after the end of the fighting in 1945, they suggest just how

Protest in Prague In August 1968, Czechoslovakian protesters throng the streets to prevent Soviet soldiers in tanks from reaching the headquarters of the national radio station after the Soviets invaded so as to overturn the country's reform-minded Communist government.

FOCUS QUESTIONS

- Why was the aftermath of war so unsettled in Europe?
- What drove the speedy rebuilding of Europe?
- What caused the onset of the Cold War?
- What were the causes of decolonization in the post-war years?
- What were the major social changes in post-war Europe?
- How did the politics of Eastern and Western Europe differ in the 1950s?
- How did the crises of Suez and Algeria affect politics in Europe?
- How did the Cold War turn more threatening in the early 1960s?
- What caused the popular protests that spread across Europe in the late 1960s?

quickly European countries literally cleared away the war's rubble and rebuilt themselves. These incidents point to the new centrality of consumption, and consumers, in post-war European society and economics. And they also underline a startling reversal that Europe experienced in the aftermath of World War II. After several centuries in which the Continent had exported power, technology, and population to the rest of the world, now the currents were moving in the opposite direction.

Most immediately, Europe felt the powerful influence of the United States, whose industrial capacity in 1945 equaled that of the rest of the world put together. America had emerged from the war as the world's sole nuclear-armed power and quickly took on the role of Western Europe's protector against the Soviet Union. In 1949, the United States, Canada, and ten Western European nations would sign a formal military alliance, the North Atlantic Treaty Organization (NATO). At the same time, Central and Eastern Europe felt a different external influence—that of the Soviet Union—as the Cold War split the Continent in half. The Soviet Union and its satellite states would form an economic alliance called Comecon in 1949, and their own military alliance, known as the Warsaw Pact, in 1955. Although in 1945 the

Allies had created a new international organization—the United Nations—as a successor to the League of Nations, these rival Western and Eastern military alliances had greater importance in international affairs throughout the post-war period.

This period also saw a vast, rapid shift in Europe's relationship with the rest of the world. In an often-violent process, the formal European colonial empires almost entirely dissolved as countries around the world gained independence. Decolonization would not just affect the former colonies themselves. It would also have important effects on the societies, cultures, and politics of the former imperial homelands. Notably, it would mark the start of large-scale movements of populations back toward Europe from the overseas empires—both European colonists and also, increasingly, non-European immigrants and refugees seeking a better life for themselves.

THE AFTERMATH OF WAR

Much of Europe in mid-1945 gave the impression of a continent in ruins. Scores of cities—above all, in Germany, Poland, and the Soviet Union—had been largely or partially destroyed by aerial bombing and artillery. Many tens of millions of people were dead. Perhaps 40 million more—refugees, forced laborers, prisoners of war—were displaced and desperate to return to homes that, in many cases, no longer existed. Much of the Continent remained under the effective control of the Allied armies. Both Germany and its capital, Berlin, had been formally divided into American, British, Soviet, and French occupation zones, in accordance with plans finalized at the Potsdam conference in the summer of 1945.

REFUGEES

The speed of Europe's recovery from the war was all the more impressive because violent disruptions did not end with the May 1945 armistice. The cease-fire led to one of the largest movements of European populations in the modern period. The expulsion of German populations from Poland, Czechoslovakia, and other states continued, with the refugees washing into camps in the American, British, and French occupation zones of Germany. Meanwhile, the Soviets were expelling as many as

2 million Poles from the formerly Polish territories they had annexed during the war, with the majority moving west to formerly German cities and towns such as Breslau and Stettin, henceforth known by the Polish names of Wrocław and Szczecin. The Western allies were sending back to the Soviet Union, often forcibly, as many as 2.5 million Soviet citizens who had ended up on their side of the demarcation lines. Fully 20 percent of these men and women were imprisoned in the Gulag or executed, and whole ethnic groups were sent into inhospitable internal exile. Millions more prisoners of war and forced laborers took more months or even years to return home. The USSR, which had taken between 2 and 3 million Germans prisoner during the war, kept hundreds of thousands of them in captivity until as late as 1956.

Jews who had survived the Holocaust faced renewed persecutions and difficulties, despite the worldwide revulsion that had accompanied the exposure of the Nazi crimes. Several hundred thousand Jews hoping to leave Europe for Palestine found themselves trapped in "displaced persons" camps, including one located next to the Nazi concentration camp of Bergen-Belsen. The British government, nervous about aggravating tensions between Jews and Arabs in the Palestinian territory, which it had governed as a mandate since 1918, refused Jews entry there and kept them in limbo. A Palestinian Jewish organization attempted to smuggle refugees past the British blockade, but the British intercepted most of them and imprisoned over 50,000 Jews in camps on Cyprus. The refugee crisis, however, finally helped push the British to surrender control of Palestine. In 1947, it turned the problem over to the new United Nations, which voted to partition the territory into separate Jewish and Arab states. The new nation of Israel came into being in May 1948, succeeded in defeating an invasion by five Arab armies, and expelled Arab populations from many of the areas they controlled. Between 1948 and 1950, over 300,000 Jews from Europe, and another 200,000 from Muslim countries, immigrated to the new Jewish state.

European Refugees, 1945–1950 Mass movement of migrants and refugees followed the post-war redrawing of European borders, of which Jewish survivors of the death camps were a small minority. Ethnic Germans were moved from Poland and Czechoslovakia to Allied-run refugee centers in West Germany, and Soviet citizens were moved back to the Soviet Union. Many spent years in refugee camps (also known as displaced persons camps) across Western Europe.

RECKONING WITH WAR CRIMES

In addition to these massive movements of population, most European countries had internal reckonings to carry out with respect to former Nazis and Fascists, or their collaborators—especially in Germany, Italy, and countries that had suffered under Axis occupation. The Eastern bloc countries tried thousands for war crimes—both Germans and home-grown collaborators. Poland tried and executed or imprisoned former officials from concentration camps—including the former commandant of Auschwitz, who died on a gallows at the camp itself in 1947. Norway, meanwhile, put all 55,000 members of the country's principal pro-Nazi organization on trial, and imprisoned some 17,000, or one out of every 175 of the country's citizens. In France, the immediate aftermath of the liberation saw violent, large-scale settling of scores, with some 80,000 arrests and over 10,000 summary executions. Once the chaos of this initial period passed, however, the desire to impose justice diminished in most countries. In the end, the French imprisoned fewer than one person in a thousand for helping the Nazis, and nearly all of them went free in a 1947 amnesty, although the senile Marshal Pétain received a sentence of life imprisonment and the collaborationist prime minister Pierre Laval was executed.

In the Axis countries, a full reckoning with Nazi and Fascist crimes was not really attempted. The Allies did make a serious effort to punish the most important Nazi leaders, whom they put on trial at Nuremberg in late 1945. While many had died in the war or escaped (including Adolf Eichmann, a chief organizer of the Holocaust, who went into hiding in Argentina), twenty-one were prosecuted at the **Nuremberg trials**. Ten—including former foreign minister Ribbentrop—went to the gallows in October 1946, while Hitler's deputy Hermann Goering committed suicide the night before his scheduled execution. A larger series of trials of leading figures in Nazi Germany followed over the next several years. They ended in more death sentences and established the principle that perpetrators of war crimes could not be exonerated on the grounds they had just "followed orders." But the numbers of defendants remained tiny in proportion to the 8 million Germans who had belonged to the Nazi Party, including the elites of nearly every profession.

The rapid onset of the Cold War increased the incentives for the United States, the Soviet Union, and their European allies to make use of experienced personnel, even those with tainted wartime records. Millions of former Nazis remained in leadership positions in both the Western and Soviet occupation zones of Germany, especially the former. When the Western zones consolidated into the new Federal Republic of Germany in 1949, no less

than 43 percent of its new diplomatic corps had seen service in the SS. In Italy, where a referendum put an end to the disgraced monarchy in 1946, tens of thousands of former Fascists went to prison, but mostly for short periods. As for Austria, which had provided a higher proportion of SS members and war criminals than Germany itself, the Allies preferred, in restoring it as an independent state, to consider it "Hitler's first victim." Fewer people—and a far smaller percentage of the population—went to prison for war crimes in Austria than in Norway.

Most people in the Axis countries thought sufficient punishment had already arrived in the form of defeat, war deaths, territorial losses, and the massive physical devastation they had suffered. Germany, in addition to at least 5 million war dead (possibly many more), over 2 million soldiers still in captivity, and the amputation of its eastern territories, had lost 20 percent of its industrial capacity, 40 percent of its housing stock, and 90 percent of its railways. One American official there spoke of "complete economic, social and political collapse, the extent of which is unparalleled in history unless one goes back to the collapse of the Roman Empire." Of course, even this degree of destruction could not match what the Soviet Union had experienced, with its 28 million dead, and 70,000 villages and 32,000 factories simply wiped from the map. But Germans still refer to the immediate post-war period as Zero Hour.

REBUILDING

Throughout Europe, the immediate focus was less on coming to terms with the war than on simple rebuilding. And in rebuilding, Europeans looked more intently than ever to the guiding hand of the state.

Nuremberg Trials Soldiers guard Hermann Goering, Joachim von Ribbentrop, and two other Nazi leaders as they stand trial for war crimes and crimes against humanity at Nuremberg in 1945.

THE ROLE OF THE STATE

No matter what the prevailing ideology, the war had everywhere led to government taking a larger role than ever before in the management of national economies—capitalist Britain, corporatist Vichy France, fascist Germany, and the communist Soviet Union all had similar experiences in this regard. Now facing the Herculean task of clearing away ruins, restoring infrastructure, and rebuilding homes and factories, few Europeans questioned the need for continued, massive state intervention. In November 1945, the British historian A. J. P. Taylor could write: "Nobody in Europe believes in the American way of life—that is, private enterprise."

But the state role in reconstruction efforts varied greatly. In some countries, elaborate economic planning bureaucracies took shape, such as France's General Planning Commissariat, established in early 1946, which coordinated economic efforts by government, management, and labor. In other cases, what mattered most was state ownership of industry. In Great Britain, the Labour Party government that took power at the end of the war began an ambitious program to bring the "commanding heights" of the economy under state management. Between 1946 and 1949, it nationalized the Bank of England, telephone and telegraph service, the coal industry, iron and steel, the railroads, and electricity generation, with each henceforth run by quasi-independent public boards responsible to Parliament. In Czechoslovakia, even before the Communist takeover there, the state employed 93 percent of all transport workers and 78 percent of industrial workers. Throughout Europe, the state remained by far the largest source of public investment, and in the late 1940s nearly every state concentrated its investment efforts on the rebuilding of basic infrastructure: factories, railroad tracks, power generation stations, and the like.

INDUSTRY OVER CONSUMERS One result of this strategy was a relative neglect of the consumer sector. Food rationing remained in effect throughout much of Europe for years after the end of the war. In Britain, it actually expanded to previously unrationed commodities such as bread and potatoes, and finally came to an end only in 1954. In devastated Germany, the official daily food ration in the American occupation zone fell to only 860 calories per adult in 1945–46: close to starvation level. In the former Axis countries, the difficulties for consumers were worsened by the collapse of currencies, sometimes amid episodes of hyperinflation reminiscent of Germany after World War I. Hungary, in July 1946, experienced a theoretical monthly inflation rate of 42 quadrillion percent—the highest ever in world history (in fact the currency simply collapsed). In Germany, American Camel cigarettes temporarily took the place of the devalued reichsmark as the effective currency. Throughout Europe, real wages rose very little in the late 1940s. Yet the emphasis on infrastructure had the desired effect and was usefully reinforced by the experiences of wartime planning. Industry and transportation networks rapidly recovered from wartime damage. By mid-1946, over 90 percent of Germany's railways were again operational.

THE RISE OF THE WELFARE STATE An expanded role for the state produced many different tangible

UK Labour Party A staff member at Labour campaign headquarters sorts through election posters during the 1955 general election campaign. The photo of Clement Attlee on the wall bears the caption: "You can trust Mr. Attlee."

benefits for ordinary Europeans. Britain, under Clement Attlee's Labour Party, again led the way. While the newly established Coal Board moved to institute paid vacations and sick pay for miners, the government itself put in place enhanced unemployment benefits, retirement plans, and free public health care. The National Health Service, created in 1948, put most doctors and hospital personnel onto the public payroll and transformed medical services into an entitlement for all. Britain here followed the lead taken between the wars by Sweden and Norway, but substantially expanded on it. Similar policies followed across much of the Continent, marking the rise to maturity of the European **welfare state**—that is, a state that aims to guarantee a minimum level of services and subsistence for all citizens. In France, spending on social services as a proportion of gross domestic product rose by 64 percent from 1938 to 1949. A principal difference from earlier efforts was that the policies did not consist principally of "poor relief," but instead benefited the entire population.

BRETTON WOODS AND THE MARSHALL PLAN

The Continent also benefited in its reconstruction efforts from outside aid. Even before the end of the war, American officials, trained in the New Deal ferment of Franklin Roosevelt's Washington, had assumed that the United

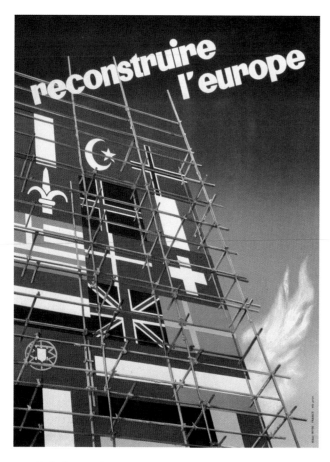

Marshall Plan On this French poster, titled "To Reconstruct Europe," the flags of all the countries receiving Marshall aid hang from scaffolding, suggesting a sense of restored unity.

funded 50 percent of public investment. In Austria, it provided 14 percent of all national income. Overall, however, the Plan amounted to an average of less than 3 percent of national income in the countries that received it.

The program brought European managers and technicians to study in the United States, and it sponsored educational programs in Europe itself, including propaganda that touted the virtues of capitalist consumer societies. But this propaganda had relatively little impact and could even be counterproductive. In France, the Communist Party managed to convince a majority of the public (to judge by opinion polls) that the Marshall Plan was a blueprint for American domination. Similar suspicions led the Soviets to refuse Marshall aid, not only for themselves but for the Eastern and Central European states in their orbit as well. Instead, the Soviets moved toward the creation of Comecon, through which they would provide substantial aid to what became their satellite states.

COLD WAR

Between 1945 and 1949, the tensions between the emerging Western and Eastern blocs steadily worsened and finally brought about the period of prolonged ideological hostility and strategic competition that contemporaries soon came to call the **Cold War**.

TENSIONS BETWEEN THE UNITED STATES AND THE SOVIET UNION

Historians have long debated whether this turn of events was inevitable and who bears principal responsibility for it. Tensions between the Soviet Union and the West of course long predated 1945. As will be recalled, the United States and the United Kingdom had both sent supplies and small detachments of troops to fight against the Bolsheviks after the Russian Revolution. During the war, Stalin had repeatedly clashed with Churchill and, to a lesser extent, Roosevelt, especially over the timing of the Allied invasion of France. But through 1946 the victorious Allies all remained as concerned with the possibility of renewed German aggression as with an East-West confrontation. The United States drastically reduced its defense budget and continued to give considerable diplomatic support to Soviet actions. The Soviets, for their part, did not move immediately to subject the nations liberated by the

States would take a major role in rebuilding post-war Europe. In July 1944, representatives from all the Allied nations met in Bretton Woods, New Hampshire, to set up a new and stable international monetary system, based on a fixed price of gold in American dollars. The Bretton Woods system established fixed exchange rates among the major currencies, although Britain and France did not join the system until the late 1950s. It also created new institutions, located in Washington, to monitor the rules and provide liquidity: the International Monetary Fund and what would soon become the World Bank.

The United States also provided massive direct assistance to Europe, which Secretary of State George Marshall announced in a commencement address at Harvard University in 1947. "Our policy," he declared, "is not directed against any country, but against hunger, poverty, desperation and chaos." The **Marshall Plan** combined loans with $13 billion in direct aid to Europe, including the Western occupation zones of Germany. In France, the program

Red Army to Soviet political control. Yet at the same time, Joseph Stalin saw a certain degree of control as a legitimate spoil of war and also as a necessity for protecting the Soviet Union against future attacks along its western frontier. Millions of Soviet soldiers remained in the liberated nations.

The Western powers viewed Stalin as committed to the expansion of communism as a system. In a speech in Missouri in March 1946, Winston Churchill used memorable language to condemn Stalin for seeking the division of Europe: "From Stettin in the Baltic to Trieste in the Adriatic an iron curtain has descended across the Continent." The Soviets, he insisted, "desire ... the fruits of war and the indefinite expansion of their power and doctrine." A year later, the influential American diplomat George Kennan published, anonymously, an article that laid out a fundamental new goal for U.S. foreign policy: the "long-term, patient but firm and vigilant containment of Russian expansive tendencies." As the only power possessing nuclear weapons, the United States could conceivably have launched a war of massive destruction against the Soviets or used the threat of nuclear attack to cow Stalin. But in the aftermath of the greatest military mobilization in American history, neither the administration of President Harry Truman (1884–1972) nor the American public had any stomach for such extreme measures.

As for Stalin, whatever his desires and tendencies, he was in fact relatively cautious in his immediate post-war policies. But disagreements with the Western Allies, especially over Germany, soon pushed him into a more aggressive stance. In part to avoid a repeat of the post–World War I economic debacle in Germany, the Western Allies wanted German reconstruction to take place as quickly as possible. France needed German coal to fuel its own heavy industries, while all the Western powers wanted Germany to recover as a market for their goods. Stalin, however, sought to strip Germany of its industry and impose heavy reparations. The Soviets actively pursued this policy in their occupation zone, moving thousands of factories eastward to the USSR. Stalin objected loudly to plans for a new German currency and a united economy.

At the end of 1946, after months of stalemate, the British and the Americans finally defied him and fused their two zones into a single economic region, leading Stalin to believe that the two Western powers were trying to transform Germany into an anti-Soviet puppet state. In 1947, he responded to these developments, and to the Marshall Plan, by bringing together Poland, Hungary, Romania, Bulgaria, and Yugoslavia into the so-called Cominform—a

Cold War Europe, 1950s The opposing alliances of NATO, joined by most Western European countries, and the Warsaw Pact of Soviet-allied states created an iron curtain roughly stretching from Stettin to Trieste across the European continent. The Berlin Airlift that followed the Soviet blockade of East Berlin in 1948 represented a rare confrontation along that hard border—and indicative of the particularly charged tensions in divided Germany.

partial revival of the pre-war Communist international organization, the Comintern.

THE SOVIETIZATION OF EASTERN EUROPE

The more Stalin sought to forge a united front against the West, the more he needed to transform the states on his side of the "**iron curtain**" into fully reliable—meaning Communist—allies. In none of them did the move find favor with a majority of the population. In early 1945, the Hungarian Communist Party still had fewer than 5,000 members, and the Romanian one barely 1,000. But just four years later, both of these states and four others (Bulgaria,

Czechoslovakia, Poland and East Germany) had become Soviet satellites, ruled by Communist regimes bent on creating smaller copies of Soviet government and society.

In Hungary, where the Communists still won less than a quarter of the vote in August 1947, despite committing massive election fraud, the Communist interior minister used his office to persecute political opponents and to take control of civil society. In 1946 alone, he banned some 1,500 unofficial civic associations and had hundreds of thousands of political opponents arrested. In 1948–49, the USSR forced the Hungarian Social Democrats to merge with the Communists and created a People's Front that duly passed a new, Soviet-style constitution. In Czechoslovakia, the Communists did better at the polls, but non-Communist President Edvard Beneš resisted a full takeover, forcing the Communists to carry out a coup d'état in February 1948. Romania and Bulgaria moved quickly into close Soviet orbit as well.

YUGOSLAVIA AND POLAND   The extent of sovietization did vary, however. Yugoslavia, led by the charismatic former resistance leader Josip Broz Tito, avoided absorption into the Soviet bloc altogether. Stalin broke with Tito soon after the war and never managed to reinstitute Soviet control over the Balkan state. While Yugoslavia remained dominated by its Communist Party and imposed a command economy similar to those in the Soviet bloc, Tito pursued a neutral foreign policy and abandoned the collectivization of agriculture. In later years, the Yugoslavs experimented with "worker self-management" in many industries. Tito also faced the considerable challenge of keeping intact the fractious union of peoples that constituted Yugoslavia, including Serbs and Croats who had fought bitterly against each other in the war.

Within the Soviet bloc, Poland remained in significant ways an outlier. Although at Yalta Stalin had promised that the Poles could hold free elections, the Red Army brought a Communist-dominated government, the so-called Lublin Committee, back to Warsaw. Then, with the help of a rigged referendum in 1946, the Communists further increased their power, sidelining forces who hoped for a return to democratic pluralism. In 1948, they banned or neutralized competing parties and turned the country into a People's Republic. But Polish agriculture remained largely in private hands, and the Catholic Church retained a large degree of autonomy. The Church continued to play a vital role in Polish life, and its Primate, or leading bishop, despite his opposition to the Communist regime, never suffered anything worse than three years' house arrest.

WESTERN REACTIONS   Western observers most often saw the clampdown on political dissent in what was coming to be called Eastern Europe, and the imposition of the Soviet model there, as confirming Churchill's warning about the iron curtain and fears of Soviet expansionism. The fact that a bitter civil war was continuing in Greece, with the Communists scoring significant gains in 1948, and that Communist parties remained strong in many parts of Western Europe, only added to the Western view.

In 1948, the British writer George Orwell gave lasting expression to Western anxieties in his novel *1984*, which presented a nightmarish vision of a totalitarian Britain ruled by a mustachioed dictator known only as Big Brother. Its miserable inhabitants lived under twenty-four-hour surveillance, while an all-powerful Party controlled every last scrap of information they received and used a sinister Thought Police to enforce its will. The Party aimed not simply at obedience but at the complete subordination of the human spirit. "If you want a picture of the future," a member of the ruling elite tells Orwell's defeated hero, Winston Smith, "imagine a boot stamping on a human face, forever." Orwell himself insisted that despite the obvious resemblance of his dystopia to the Soviet Union, he meant the book as a cautionary tale about all totalitarianisms, fascist as well as communist, and his own staunchly socialist background supports the claim. But in the chill political climate of 1948, most readers read *1984* as a warning of the dangers from the East.

BERLIN

In 1947, American president Harry Truman, in promising significant new aid to anti-Communist forces in Greece, declared defiantly that the United States would provide support to "free peoples" against what he labeled totalitarian regimes. The United States, even before the formation of NATO, was laying claim to leadership of what it called the free world. It faced little competition for the role. In addition to its military dominance, it also possessed by far the largest economy in the world and deserved to be called a superpower. Britain, still recovering from its wartime sacrifices and expenditures, was also confronting in South Asia the first great episodes of decolonization. The USSR lagged behind the United States economically, but owing to its military strength it could also be seen as a superpower. The confrontation between it and the United States would dominate international politics around the globe for the next four decades.

Berlin Airlift Spectators watch as an American military aircraft lands at Berlin's Tempelhof Airport in August 1948, delivering food and supplies to the West Berliners cut off by the Soviet blockade.

If the Cold War had a symbolic opening drama, it took place in the divided capital of defeated Germany. In early June 1948, faced with stalemate on the issue of Germany's future, the United States and Great Britain decided to reorganize the areas of the country under their and France's control into a new, separate state. On June 18, they gave it a currency: the so-called deutsche mark, which replaced the devalued and useless reichsmark. In response, at the end of the month the Soviets began a blockade of the three Western zones of Berlin, cutting off all surface communications with the surrounding, Soviet-occupied territory. By starving West Berlin, Stalin hoped either to force the Western Allies out of the German capital altogether or to abandon the idea of a separate Western German state. But the Allies mounted a huge airlift to supply the city with canned and dried food and other necessities. Over the next eleven months of the **Berlin Airlift**, Allied planes arrived in the city at the astonishing rate of over two per minute—over 278,000 flights in all, many making dangerous landings on hastily built runways next to crowded apartment blocks.

In May 1949, the Soviets finally abandoned the blockade. Soon afterward, with France joining its occupation zone to the British and American ones, the Western-supported Federal Republic of Germany formally came into being, with its capital in the small, sleepy, Catholic Rhineland town of Bonn—socially and culturally the opposite of massive, Protestant, Prussian Berlin.

Its founders gave the new state a democratic constitution and a decentralized governing structure in which ten large regions (*Länder*) possessed considerable autonomy. The Soviets soon matched West Germany with an East Germany, turning their own occupation zone into the German Democratic Republic, built, like the other states in the Soviet bloc, on the Soviet model. The new states quickly received international recognition, although it would take until 1973 for them to join the United Nations. Germany was now officially divided, which did not displease those who feared a revival of German nationalism. "I love Germany so much," the French novelist François Mauriac quipped, "that I am delighted there are two of them."

A DIVIDED CONTINENT IN A DIVIDED WORLD

The splitting of Germany served as the wedge, but the crack that it drove between the Western Allies and the Soviet bloc reached far beyond Central Europe. In April 1949, as we have seen, the United States, Canada, and ten Western European countries came together to form the **North Atlantic Treaty Organization (NATO)**, a new military alliance. The Communist countries constituted a de facto alliance as well, and in 1955 it took official form as the **Warsaw Pact**. Other events in 1949 heightened the tensions between these developing blocs. Communists led by Mao Zedong took power in China, the most populous country on earth, while the Soviets successfully tested an atomic weapon, having acquired the technology in part through espionage. In the United States, partly in reaction to this espionage, a wave of anti-Communist hysteria developed, led by Wisconsin senator Joseph McCarthy, bringing about widespread persecutions of suspected Communists. And a year later, in East Asia, after the USSR's client state North Korea invaded its southern neighbor, Western forces mobilized to repel it, led by the United States and acting under the banner of the new United Nations.

A period had begun in which the earth seemed divided between opposing camps—the Western "First World" and the Communist "Second World"—each armed with steadily expanding arsenals of atomic weapons. Europeans now had to confront the possibility of a new conflict whose horrors might, incredibly, overshadow those of the war just past, a conflict that might literally bring about the extinction of human life on the Continent.

DECOLONIZATION: THE FIRST STEPS

The coming of the Cold War signaled clearly that Europe no longer dominated the world as it had done in the past. The continent's future would now depend in large part on the conflict between the two "superpowers." But the influence of the European states had also begun to fray in regions that, for the moment, still belonged in large part to their colonial empires. France, Belgium, and the Netherlands struggled to reestablish their authority in overseas territories from which Nazi and Japanese occupations had cut them off, such as the French colonies in West Africa, the Belgian Congo, and the Dutch East Indies. But they were resisted by newly powerful independent movements in what would soon come to be called the Third World. Scarcely sixty years after the chaotic "scramble for empire" of the late nineteenth century, an even more chaotic process of decolonization was now beginning.

THE SUN SETS ON THE BRITISH EMPIRE

In the immediate post-war period, the most dramatic episodes of decolonization took place in the most powerful and extensive empire of all: Great Britain's. The

Indian Independence A parade in Bombay (Mumbai) on August 15, 1947, celebrates the declaration of Indian independence. Marchers wearing white carry instruments and the new Indian national flag, while crowds of spectators look on.

desperate fight against Germany and Japan had left the British Empire with vastly reduced strength, and nowhere was this weakness more apparent than in the "jewel in the crown"—India. In the 1930s, British India had roughly one British soldier for every two Indian soldiers; by the end of the war, the ratio had fallen to less than one to six. Britain had also proven woefully unresponsive in face of the great famine in Bengal in 1943, which took some 3 million lives. Meanwhile, the Indian nationalist movement had continued to grow in strength. Britain's Labour Party had a tradition of sympathy for Indian aspirations toward self-rule, and after its victory in the 1945 elections its leaders generally agreed that Indian independence had become inevitable. In early 1947, the British government sent a distant relation of the royal family, Lord Mountbatten, to India with instructions to negotiate the process.

The subsequent British retreat from India exemplified both the promise and the perils of decolonization. In theory, the rise of an independence movement committed to nonviolence, led by the renowned figure of Mohandas Gandhi (1869–1948), should have ensured a smooth transition of power. Gandhi's ally in the Indian National Congress, the suave, Cambridge-educated Jawaharlal Nehru (1889–1964), who spoke Hindi with a British accent, stood poised to become a prime minister with whom Great Britain could work. But not all subjects of the British possessions in South Asia wanted to be part of a united, independent India dominated by Hindus such as Gandhi and Nehru. A Muslim League led by Mohammad Ali Jinnah (1876–1948), who like Gandhi was trained in Britain as a barrister, demanded partition of British India into separate Hindu and Muslim states, and threatened civil war if Britain did not agree. The British, to Gandhi's despair, gave in.

On August 14, 1947, Nehru announced on radio that "at the stroke of the midnight hour, while the world sleeps, India will awake to life and freedom." But well before then, two huge, violent exoduses had begun—of Hindus from Muslim territory (which would become the Republic of Pakistan) and vice-versa. It recalled the bloody forced migrations in Europe after World War I. Eventually, some 11 million people would leave their homes and as many as 1 million would be killed in communal violence. The new, diminished state of India still had a significant Muslim population. The new state of Pakistan (meaning "land of the pure"), divided into western and eastern portions on either side of India, was far more religiously homogeneous. Lord Mountbatten and his wife presided over colorful, dignified independence ceremonies and then sailed serenely

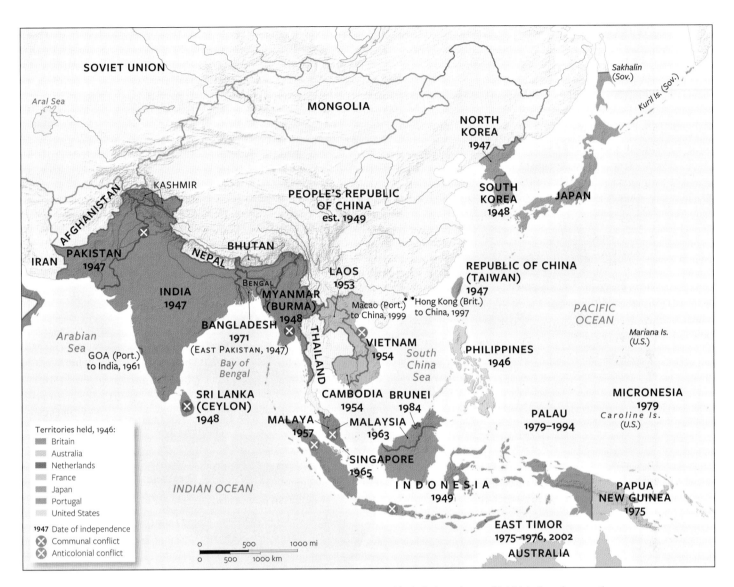

Decolonization in Asia The beginning of the end of European empires in Asia came with the independence of British India, subsequently partitioned into modern-day India and Pakistan. The war's aftermath also brought the end of the Dutch Empire in Indonesia, France's rule in Indochina, and U.S. control of the Philippines. Many smaller colonies did not become independent until decades later.

away from the carnage and chaos. In 1948, Gandhi himself fell victim to a radical Hindu assassin.

Britain quickly washed its hands of communal conflict in many other places as well. In early 1948, it officially granted independence to Ceylon and Burma, and in both these countries massive violence followed, including the assassination of the popular Burmese nationalist Aung San (1915–1947) by political rivals in 1947. On the Malay Peninsula, plans for an autonomous confederation foundered, leading to a long insurgency that the British doggedly worked to repress. The new state of Malaysia only attained independence in the late 1950s. And as we have seen, in 1948 Britain withdrew from the Palestine Mandate,

leading immediately to a full-scale war between the new state of Israel and several large Arab armies. Movements for greater autonomy, or even independence, also gained strength in Britain's African colonies, especially Kenya, leading, as we will see, to considerable violence.

THE DUTCH EMPIRE

The Netherlands saw an even more dramatic collapse of its overseas empire. The Dutch East Indies had long generated wealth for the Netherlands through its exports of rubber, oil, timber, metals, and spices. During World War II, the

Decolonization in Africa French Northwest Africa became a series of independent nation-states beginning in the 1950s and culminating with the end of the bloody and divisive Algerian War in 1962. By 1970, all of the British East African territories that had stretched "from Cape to Cairo" were also independent, though many—most notoriously South Africa—remained riven by racial divides. Portugal was the last European power to leave its colonies, withdrawing from Angola and Mozambique amid anticolonial violence in the 1970s.

Japanese occupied nearly the entire archipelago and sponsored an independence movement under the leadership of a Javanese architect known as Sukarno (1901–1970). As the Japanese position in the islands collapsed, the movement tried to claim full control. On August 17, 1945, just two days after the Japanese surrender to the Allies, Sukarno's forces issued a Declaration of Independence for a new state they dubbed Indonesia. With the Netherlands still recovering from its own occupation by the Nazis, it was the British who initially moved in to reassert Allied control.

They tried to reach an accommodation with Sukarno and his allies; but as Dutch forces returned, these efforts collapsed. The Dutch began a series of aggressive "police actions" to restore their imperial authority, until they had close to 150,000 soldiers bogged down in the islands. In the resulting chaos, the threat of a communist insurgency grew, and as it did the United States put increasing pressure on the Dutch to recognize Indonesian aspirations. Indonesian independence was finally granted at the end of 1949.

THE FRENCH EMPIRE AND THE FRENCH UNION

The French Empire was weakened as well by the disruptions of World War II. Japan had occupied French Indochina (present-day Laos, Cambodia, and Vietnam), while France's massive possessions in sub-Saharan Africa (from present-day Mali and Niger down to Congo and Gabon) had initially come under the rule of Vichy, which tried to impose more explicit forms of white rule on them than France's Third Republic had done. In 1942–43, with Allied victories in North Africa and signs of an eventual German defeat, the French colonies mostly shifted their allegiance to the Free French led by Charles de Gaulle. But it took time for de Gaulle to establish effective control of the empire. In some areas, notably Indochina, movements that originally came together to fight the Axis transformed themselves, upon the Allied victory, into armed movements for national independence.

In 1945–46, the founders of the new French Fourth Republic sought to forestall the growth of these independence movements by transforming the empire into a cumbersome new structure called the French Union. In theory, this entity would give a greater political voice than before to the native peoples under French rule. France also formally designated several overseas possessions, mostly in the Caribbean, as integral parts of the French Republic—coastal Algeria, where political participation remained largely limited to European settlers, already had this status. The new "departments" became bound closely enough to France that they still form an equal, integral part of the French Republic today, much as Hawaii forms part of the United States.

The French Union, however, was most often greeted as an unworkable compromise, or as thin camouflage for the harsh realities of colonial exploitation. In Africa, in 1946 Félix Houphouët-Boigny of the Ivory Coast helped found a new movement that called for greater French support for development and self-government in its African territories. The French government strongly opposed it, especially because it had the support of the French Communist Party. In Vietnam, the Viet Minh movement originally formed to fight Japan proclaimed an independent republic in 1945. Led by the veteran nationalist and Communist Ho Chi Minh (1890–1969), it was launched with a formal declaration modeled after the American Declaration of Independence and the French Declaration of the Rights of Man. Escalating violence would roil Indochina for the next thirty years, with the United States eventually replacing a defeated France as the major outside power struggling to limit the spread of Communist influence. And the Viet Minh's fight in turn made a lasting, powerful impression on the Algerian nationalists who came together in the late 1940s to form a paramilitary organization to fight for independence. So in the French Empire as well the British, it was becoming clear that decolonization would for the most part be a difficult, blood-soaked process.

POST-WAR PROSPERITY

Despite the anxieties of the Cold War and the retreat from empire, in the late 1940s and early 1950s Europe's broad loss of geopolitical dominance had relatively little impact on most day-to-day lives in Europe itself. British prime minister Harold MacMillan (1894–1986) spoke the truth when he declared in 1957: "Let us be frank about it—most of our people have never had it so good." The comment would have applied just as well to most of the Continent, including even the eastern portion.

STRUCTURAL CHANGE

A number of factors drove the quick return to prosperity after World War II. In Western Europe, states, employers, and powerful labor unions reached agreements whereby workers limited their wage demands in return for the entitlements of the new, expanded welfare states that were coming into being, including health care, old age pensions, generous guaranteed vacations, and a significant voice in economic planning. Their restraint freed up capital for high levels of long-term investment in industrial restructuring and new technologies. In addition, in many states the simple need for repairing war damage provided a powerful economic stimulus, as the theories of John Maynard Keynes suggested. Marshall Plan aid helped as well. In some cases, wartime destruction even provided a post-war boon. Whereas the British economy, despite new capital investments, remained hindered by aging, increasingly decrepit industrial plants, reconstructed West Germany could rely on largely new ones. In the Soviet Union, the factors were different because the entire economy was under state control, but the initial result was much the same. Simple reconstruction helped drive economic growth, as did the return to peacetime industrial planning. The Soviets benefited from the services of millions of prisoners of war who remained on its soil as laborers, and also from the industrial infrastructure and raw materials confiscated from Germany.

THE THIRTY GLORIOUS YEARS

The result, throughout Europe, was an economic boom. Just three years after the war, the Soviet economy had returned, amazingly, to its pre-war size. Between 1945 and 1950, the USSR managed an average growth rate of close to 15 percent, which fell to a still-respectable 5.8 percent over the subsequent decade. Eastern Europe took longer to start its recovery, but by the 1950s growth rates in the Soviet satellites had also taken off.

In Western Europe, the economic recovery started strong and remained at a remarkably high rate for decades. Today the French commonly refer to the thirty years following World War II as the Trente Glorieuses—the "Thirty Glorious Years"—and the phrase has resonance for Western Europe as a whole. Between 1950 and 1973, real per capita gross domestic product (GDP) there rose by an astonishing 163 percent. Even in Great Britain, burdened with an aging and inefficient industrial base, it went up by a remarkable 75 percent. Southern Europe managed particularly spectacular figures, with Italy rising nearly threefold between 1950 and 1973 and Spain more than threefold. West Germany's GDP expanded more than threefold as well, giving rise to the phrase "the West German economic miracle."

This growth in wealth and income per person took place in tandem with the greatest population boom in European history. After the war, as soldiers returned home and families were reunited, many countries experienced a **baby boom**. In the period 1945–50, the birthrate in Europe as a whole increased by 23 percent as compared to that of the war years. Overall, the Continent grew over 20 percent between 1940 and 1973, and its economies absorbed this growth without any negative effects on individual wealth. As late as the mid-1960s, the average unemployment rate in Western Europe remained just 1.5 percent.

Throughout this book, we have tried to highlight the continuing effects of economic hardship on European life, but the astonishing fact is that in the post-war period the threat of destitution diminished dramatically. By 1973, the percentage of Western Europeans experiencing real economic hardship had fallen to less than one-fifth. A large majority of the population, for the first time in history, now had the certainty of enough to eat, a roof over their heads, heat in the winter, and steady employment in the family. An increasing number of them could count on free public education, even up to university level; free health care; unemployment insurance, and a pension plan. An increasing number had a disposable income that allowed them to buy consumer products or to travel for recreation. Infant mortality in most European countries fell by more than half during the 1950s and 1960s.

A CONSUMER REVOLUTION IN THE WEST

Immediately after the war, the planners who tried to dictate economic priorities tended to emphasize growth in heavy industry—above all, coal and steel—over consumer goods. In Britain, these policies helped keep daily life feeling relatively pinched and poor, even for the middle class, through the early 1950s. Yet by the late 1950s, when Macmillan's boast became a Conservative Party campaign slogan, a flood of consumer goods, including such quintessentially American products as Coca-Cola, had inundated the Western half of the Continent and reached Britain as well.

The Soviet Union and its East European satellites proved unable to shift so nimbly toward a consumer economy. Their more rigid planning processes, coupled with large-scale economic inefficiency, meant that the consumer sector went largely neglected. Housing also lagged far behind. In Soviet cities, the state allocated all housing, and families faced years-long waiting lists, during which time they often had to share apartments with relatives or strangers, often three or more people per room. Even Tito's Yugoslavia, despite its experiments with worker self-management, could not match the West in consumer products. Throughout the late 1950s and early 1960s, the Eastern economies still continued to grow at a healthy pace, and men and women there had more to eat and better housing than at any time in their history. Nonetheless, they could only look on in envy at a Western prosperity that was beginning to dwarf their own.

The changes in the texture of daily life were radical. By

votre **réfrigérateur**

véritable magasin à domicile, vous met à l'abri des surprises de la dernière minute.
Un RÉFRIGÉRATEUR

— conserve vos provisions plusieurs jours, dans les cuisines chaudes de l'hiver,
— économise votre temps et votre argent en supprimant les fatigues et les soucis quotidiens de l'approvisionnement,
— améliore votre confort en simplifiant votre travail.

N'attendez plus pour bénéficier de tous ces avantages.
Commandez maintenant votre RÉFRIGÉRATEUR,
vous éviterez les délais de livraison, très longs en été.

POUR NOËL...
... un RÉFRIGÉRATEUR
est le plus beau cadeau
que vous puissiez faire
à votre famille...
un cadeau apprécié
365 jours par an.

Votre vendeur vous accordera les plus larges facilités.

Consumer Society A 1957 French refrigerator advertisement speaks to the changes consumer goods brought to post-war society. "Never taken by surprise! Some friends for dinner...no problem!" reads the caption, as a housewife produces a roast from the fridge for her guests.

the 1960s, most Western Europeans had stopped shopping for food on a daily basis. In the Netherlands, the number of supermarkets rose from just seven in 1961 to 520 in 1971. In Italy, the number of households with refrigerators expanded from less than 2 percent in 1957 to 94 percent in 1974. Until the 1950s, European apartment buildings bristled with small storage shelves hung outside windows to keep food fresh during the winter months. By the 1960s, they had largely vanished. Houses in northern Europe gained central heating. Between 1951 and 1970, the temperature inside the average British house rose five degrees Fahrenheit. The numbers of cars on the road in Europe exploded ninefold in just seventeen years: 5 million in 1948; 44 million in 1965. Nearly all this increase came in the West.

The consumption of entertainment changed just as dramatically. If radios and record players (often hand-cranked) had been common in Western Europe before 1945, by 1970 most Western European families owned portable radios and television sets. Cinema attendance began to fall as Europeans increasingly took in their visual entertainment at home. Partly in reaction, and partly because the European film industry could not compete with Hollywood, important film directors such as Italy's Federico Fellini (1920–1993), Sweden's Ingmar Bergman (1918–2007), and France's François Truffaut (1932–1984) deliberately cast themselves as the "authors" of serious, difficult works of art that placed new demands on audiences. Like many other works of avant-garde art, these films often challenged conventional standards of morality and taste. Fellini's 1960 work *La Dolce Vita* ("The Sweet Life") earned condemnations both for irreligion (one scene parodied Christ's second coming) and for its frank depiction of sexuality. In France, Truffaut and other directors connected to the magazine *Cahiers du Cinéma* ("Cinema Notebooks") championed films shot in experimental styles that commented on current social issues, and that came to be known as the "New Wave."

NEW POSSIBILITIES FOR WOMEN

These changes in the texture of life had particularly important consequences for women. In Western Europe, the arrival of such conveniences as running water, central heating, and refrigerators, and later of washing machines and dishwashers, reduced the domestic drudgery that had dominated the lives of most young and married women. The same innovations reduced the need for domestic servants, even as the period's labor shortages enabled women to move out of service into higher-paid industrial jobs as well as office work and teaching. The provision of inexpensive child care as part of the growth of welfare states also contributed to the entry of women into the labor force in record numbers. The number of working women in Britain would more than triple between 1950 and 1990.

As these changes occurred, some formal legal restrictions on women vanished. French women finally received the vote at the end of the war, and by the 1960s they saw other expansions of their private rights. It took until this time for married women, for instance, to gain the right to publish books without their husbands' permission. The Labour Party in Great Britain appointed women to important cabinet positions. In Eastern Europe, the formal commitment of the Communist parties to sexual equalities meant an even higher level of female labor force participation and the rise to political prominence of several important women. Ana Pauker (1893–1960), born into

WOMEN'S INDEPENDENCE IN WEST GERMANY

The many changes in daily life in post-war Europe, from the timesaving conveniences of new housekeeping inventions to the hole in the labor force left by the ravages of war, contributed to shifts in attitudes toward women's roles in society. Immediately after the war, many women were left reeling in the midst of the destruction of their cities and families. At the same time, though, no longer simply confined to the care of their children, husbands, and households, women gained new rights and work opportunities.

In 1946, the West German radio host Walther von Hollander discussed the various ways in which women dealt with post-war life, and he received many letters from women in response—often expressing ambivalence. In the following note, a woman from an industrial region describes her relationship with her husband during the war, her living situation following his death, and her hesitancy about a new suitor.

We got married in 1934. My husband was an engineer in an airplane engine plant, a man highly talented in his field and utterly committed to his work. He had a good income. We had a small house…an hour's drive from the city; we had a car. Very soon we had two children. I saw my husband for an hour in the evening, when he came home from work dead tired. When he occasionally came earlier, he would sit at his drawing table half the night, brooding, and from my bed, I heard him talking to himself and cursing. He was a tough man in every regard. At least that's what those under him said, and his superiors didn't like him because he advocated his views brusquely and told everyone his opinion, even if it was unsolicited; I myself did not suffer from his gruffness. Toward me he was always consistently nice. But never affectionate, and he had no strong bonds with the children. How could he? He hardly ever saw them. Everything got worse during the war. He came out once a week, at most. Since he was working on mysterious weapons and there was nothing in his life other than his work, he became almost mute. Therefore, I don't know what kind of trouble there was in his factory. In any case, he was suddenly drafted into the army, even though he was completely indispensable. As a veteran, he was deployed immediately and was soon killed in action. My life changed little because of it. That may sound harsh, but that's the way it was. We had saved quite a bit. The house is rented out. We are living on the top floor, and I have a job as a secretary in the neighboring town. Everything could be fine. But a man has appeared. Again, a very capable man, an architect who is well employed and full of ideas that will surely lead to an excellent position soon. He loves me and wants to marry me. You are now going to say: Well, then! What good luck for this woman! My mother and girlfriends are saying the same. But I don't want to get married. Or, if I were to marry again, then it would be to a gentle person who needs me, whom I can guide and protect. For where did the men lead us? First, it was bleak working life—and now? Don't you think that the men have done a lot of stupid things and can't find their way out? And here I'm supposed to marry another man like that? Must I do that?

QUESTIONS FOR ANALYSIS

1. How was the letter writer affected by her husband's demanding work?
2. Why did her life change little after her husband's death?
3. How did the letter writer's attitude toward men and marriage change following the war?

Source: Walther von Hollander, "Women's Issues—Women's Worries" (1946), trans. Thomas Dunlap, in *Occupation and the Emergence of Two States (1945–1961)*, vol. 8, *German History in Documents and Images*, eds. Volker Berghahn and Uta Poiger (Washington, DC: n.d.), pp. 1–2.

Expanded Women's Rights Ana Pauker in front of a portrait of herself during her tenure as foreign minister of Romania in 1947–52. This was one very prominent example of a woman benefiting from the Communist commitment to sex equality.

an Orthodox Jewish family in Romania, became the effective leader of the Romanian Communist Party for a time after the war. She served as the country's foreign minister from 1947 to 1952 before falling prey to an anti-Semitic purge.

COUNTRYSIDE AND CITY

Even as women benefited in these diverse ways, the peasantry—the largest component of European society throughout history—began to vanish. A worldwide Green Revolution was taking place, involving the sophisticated use of fertilizers and mechanization, and the introduction of new, high-yield cereal grains. This made it possible to grow food more efficiently than ever before with

much less labor, reinforcing trends in European farming that had begun in the early modern period. By the early 1970s, the percentage of the population engaged actively in agriculture had fallen to less than 10 percent in France and West Germany; less than 5 percent in Belgium, the Netherlands, and Great Britain; and even in relatively undeveloped Spain to just 20 percent. In Spain, France, and Italy, whole villages sometimes stood largely abandoned, their former inhabitants now living in cities and suburbs.

Meanwhile, European cities, both East and West, expanded at a record pace, with newcomers from the countryside (and in some countries, increasingly, from abroad) mostly housed in long rows of nondescript concrete high-rise apartment blocks. These structures, and the office blocks that sprang up as well, had mostly plain, geometrical architecture in line with the aesthetic of the Bauhaus movement and the need for cheap, utilitarian construction. In Western Europe, suburbs around major cities also expanded. In the East, the Communist regimes deliberately drove the process of urbanization forward, with cities such as Bratislava in Czechoslovakia marked for large-scale industrial development. In 1949, the Polish regime founded a new steel city dubbed Nowa Huta next door to the old university town of Kraków, hoping in part to develop a politically reliable proletarian population there. In the next eleven years, its population climbed to 100,000 inhabitants.

POPULATIONS ON THE MOVE

People moved not only between rural and urban areas within the same countries, but across national borders as well. The movement led to rapid and dramatic changes in the demographic makeup of many European states, with important economic, social, and political consequences.

EUROPEANS From early in the 1950s, significant movement took place between European states, mostly from south to north, and into Europe from the crumbling colonial empires. Seven million Italians (mostly men) went abroad in search of temporary work between 1945 and 1970, as did a quarter of active Greek workers. By the early 1960s, Italians made up close to one-quarter of the labor force of neighboring Switzerland, while Germany sought to compete for the same supply of manpower by offering free transportation north. In France, which had led Europe in its openness to immigrants before World War II, waves of newcomers from Portugal and Spain added to existing populations of Poles, Italians, and Jews, while arrivals from France's colonies in Africa and Muslim North Africa steadily increased.

A different sort of population flow took place in the center of Europe, between the two German states that had come into being in 1949. Over the next twelve years—until the construction of the Berlin Wall—no fewer than 2.5 million East Germans, disproportionately young and well educated, left the Communist state for West Germany. In 1960 alone, some 200,000 East Germans emigrated out of a population of less than 18 million. They did so because of the repressive rule of the Communist East German government and the lure of prosperity across the border. By the end of the 1950s, only a tiny percentage of East Germans yet owned cars, televisions, or other consumer products common in the West. Most still heated their houses with coal. The East German state guaranteed employment and free child care to its citizens, but standards of health care lagged behind those in the West, and most East Germans had few opportunities for travel. When the East German state moved to collectivize agriculture, some 20,000 farmers emigrated to West Germany.

GUEST WORKERS European prosperity also lured millions of non-European migrants from former European colonies, and other non-European nations to Europe itself. The phenomenon had deep roots but became particularly significant in the 1960s, when for the first time in modern history more people came to live in Europe from outside the Continent than left it to live somewhere else. Most of the newcomers came as supposedly temporary **guest workers** to fill low-level jobs that prosperous native Europeans increasingly refused to take. The number of foreigners working in West Germany, for example, rose from 1.2 million to 4 million (accounting for 7 percent of the population and 12 percent of the labor force) between 1964 and 1973. Some 600,000 guest workers from Turkey formed the largest migrant group in Germany. In France, the largest numbers came from former colonies in North and West Africa; and in Britain, above all from India, Pakistan, and the Caribbean.

The governments of Western Europe initially gave the migrants a warm welcome, seeing them as crucial to continued economic development. The migrants found it easy to bring families to join them, and in most states they enjoyed the protection of the newly robust European welfare states. This welcoming attitude, however, was not always shared by ordinary citizens, who often greeted the newcomers with considerable suspicion and prejudice. As early as 1958, two weeks of rioting took place in the Notting Hill area of London, where white gangs fought with blacks of West Indian origin.

POLITICAL STABILIZATION

On both sides of the iron curtain, the 1950s saw a stabilization of the political patterns set in motion in the initial post-war period. But whereas in the East this stabilization involved considerable violence and repression, in the West it initially took place with relatively little disruption or even notice. The most important political challenges of the decade in Western Europe involved foreign policy and decolonization. Only at the end of the 1950s, as the collapse of more of France's overseas empire destabilized its government, did the threat of large-scale civil violence again, and only briefly, touch the soil of Western Europe itself.

DESTALINIZATION IN THE EAST

The repression in the East began with Joseph Stalin. By 1950, he was in his early seventies and had wielded absolute power for more than a quarter century. The years after the war did not see a repetition of the horrors Stalin had overseen before 1939, but as he grew old he turned increasingly suspicious, and the horrifying possibility of mass death again loomed over the Soviet population. Even as Stalin continued to support and encourage North Korean dictator Kim Il Sung (1912–1994) in direct military conflict with the United States, at home he started to warn against a dangerous plot by "Jewish nationalist" doctors, whom he called agents of American imperialism. But before he could take any action against the Jews, in March 1953 he suffered a stroke and died. Millions of communists throughout the world, swept up in his cult of personality, mourned his death as if it were that of a family member.

At first, power in the USSR passed in large part to the head of the secret police, Stalin's Georgian crony Lavrenti Beria. Beria stopped the persecution of the Jewish doctors and ordered the release of hundreds of thousands of prisoners from the Gulag. But the other survivors of Stalin's inner circle deemed Beria (quite correctly) psychotic, and within months they conspired to have him arrested and executed. Soon afterward, Nikita Khrushchev (1894–1971), a long-standing party functionary, emerged as the leading figure in the government. A coarse-mannered Ukrainian with a strikingly bald head,

Nikita Khrushchev
The Soviet premier famous for his campaign of destalinization gives a speech to workers in Azerbaijan (a constituent republic of the Soviet Union) in 1960.

Khrushchev quickly followed Beria's lead in what would become known as **destalinization**. He released more prisoners from the Gulag—ultimately, some 5 million. He pursued more stable relations with the West. He also moved carefully toward a repudiation of Stalin himself. It culminated in a highly critical, secret speech delivered to party elites in February 1956. Without abandoning the Communist ideology that had prevailed in its broad outlines since Lenin's day, Khrushchev denounced Stalin's "deviations" from that ideology and his crimes. Within days, newspapers in the West were reporting on the speech, and in the Eastern bloc the electrifying news quickly spread by word of mouth.

EASTERN BLOC REVOLTS

Khrushchev hoped that an end to the most severe Stalinist repression and a dose of moderate, rational reform would stabilize the Communist system, allow it to flourish, and, not least, secure his own power. But Khrushchev found that reform in fact released uncontrollable hopes and created dangerous new pressures. Soon after Stalin's death, thousands of prisoners in Gulag labor camps in Siberia began to strike for better conditions, and in one camp scores died when panicked officials ordered guards to open fire.

EAST GERMANY AND POLAND In June 1953, East German workers began striking for better conditions, and the strikes quickly turned into political protests, with demands raised for the government's resignation. Finally, the East German leadership called on Soviet troops to help quell the nascent insurrection, and they did so at a cost of scores, perhaps hundreds, of deaths. The German poet and playwright Bertolt Brecht (1898–1956), who had returned from the United States to live in East Germany, composed a satirical poem that cited a Communist functionary's statement that the people had forfeited the confidence of the government. "Would it not be easier in that case," Brecht wrote, "for the government to dissolve the people and elect another?"

In the summer of 1956, after Khrushchev's secret speech had become common knowledge, Polish security forces bloodily suppressed riots by workers protesting food shortages. The alarmed government moved to placate the workers, and Władysław Gomułka, a leading Communist reformer whom the party had expelled just a few years before, was installed as party leader. He purged a hard-line Soviet marshal from the Polish politburo, a move that led Khrushchev and his associates briefly to consider an invasion.

HUNGARY These events helped to precipitate a full-fledged revolt against Communist rule in another Eastern bloc country. Since 1948, power in Hungary had swung back and forth between a hard-line faction dominated by Mátyás Rákosi and reformers led by Imre Nagy. Rákosi presided over the execution of nearly 500 political enemies and the imprisonment of more than 1.5 percent of the population. The Soviets ordered him deposed in the summer of 1956, but his Stalined allies remained in power. But in October, after news of events in Poland broke, students in Budapest began staging protests, inspiring much of the city's population to come out into the streets. In the hopes of forestalling an insurrection, the Communist leadership brought back Nagy as prime minister.

The protests, however, only continued to grow, and on October 28 Nagy announced that he would abolish the hated secret police and demand the departure of Soviet troops from the country. Two days later, encouraged by this remarkable cascade of events, Hungarian crowds attacked secret police headquarters, killing some twenty-four agents. Nagy himself now took command of what had become an open revolt against Communism,

Hungarian Revolt A crowd of Hungarian freedom fighters mount a Soviet tank in Budapest in November 1956.

"THE PATH FROM EARTH TO THE STARS"

The successes of the Soviet space program marked a realization of Communist goals for modernization. Following the 1957 launch of the first satellite, *Sputnik*, in April 1961, the Soviet Union successfully sent the first human into space, the cosmonaut Yuri Gagarin. These achievements inspired people living in the East and caused alarm in the West (the first American entered space in May 1961).

This propaganda poster from 1963 is one of many meant to sustain patriotism, optimism, and faith in the Soviet Union. Illustrated in bright Soviet red, it shows a giant hand boosting the launch of a rocket emblazoned with "USSR" and the Communist hammer and sickle. The rousing caption reads: "Be proud, Soviet person, you have opened the path from Earth to the stars."

QUESTIONS FOR ANALYSIS

1. What do you think the hand represents, and why was it was used as a symbol on this poster?
2. Why do you suppose the caption gives Soviet citizens credit for the space program's success?
3. How does this depiction of the space program relate to the Soviet Union's approach to industrialization in the twentieth century?

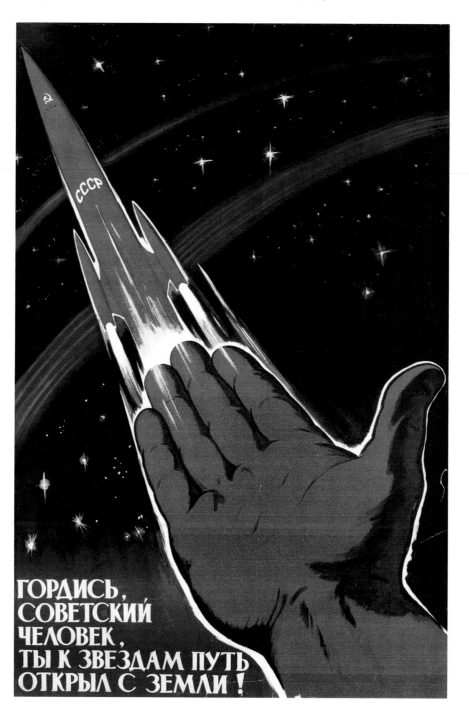

828

declaring an end to one-party rule and the rebirth of a "free, democratic and independent Hungary" that would immediately withdraw from the Warsaw Pact. With this as the final straw, the Soviet Union invaded and within days crushed desperate armed resistance and restored a reliably Communist government. Some 3,000 Hungarians died in the invasion and subsequent executions, while hundreds of thousands fled across the border to neutral Austria. Nagy himself was executed in 1958.

The Soviets' brutal action in Hungary succeeded in mostly stopping the momentum of Eastern European reform, although it did not entirely kill off enthusiasm for the Communist regimes. Improving living conditions and Khrushchev's limited liberalization somewhat increased support for these regimes in the late 1950s, while the USSR's successful 1957 launch of *Sputnik*, the first human artifact ever put into earth orbit, stirred genuine patriotic enthusiasm in the USSR (so did the first launch of a human being, Yuri Gagarin, into earth orbit in 1961). But in Western Europe, news of the invasion of Hungary hurt Communist parties more than anything since the Hitler-Stalin pact of 1939. Thousands resigned their memberships in disgust, and the Italian Communist Party split openly over the event.

WESTERN EUROPEAN STABILITY

In contrast to the violence in the East, most of Western Europe in the 1950s experienced a greater degree of political stability than at any time since the beginning of the century. In Great Britain, Winston Churchill and the Tories returned to power in 1951, but they did relatively little to deconstruct the welfare state put in place by Attlee and the Labour Party. Promises to re-privatize nationalized industries went largely unfulfilled, in part because the industries in question (especially coal and steel) appeared too unprofitable to potential buyers. In Italy, an intellectually lively Communist Party showed great electoral strength, especially in the north, but the right-wing Christian Democrats kept control of the government throughout the decade. Italian corruption was rampant by northern European standards, but the Christian Democrats did manage to divert some of the output from the post-war economic boom toward development of the woefully impoverished south of the country.

In France, the Fourth Republic (1946–58) largely re-created the politics of the Third, with a great deal of surface instability that did little to disrupt the economic progress of the Thirty Glorious Years. The period saw, on average, a new French government every six months, with power shifting back and forth among the old center-left parties, the new center-right Popular Republican Movement, and the Socialists. A new movement led by a shop-keeper named Pierre Poujade briefly emerged as a powerful force in the mid-1950s, appealing especially to the resentments of small business owners feeling threatened by economic transformations. But its appeal soon fizzled. The French Communist Party, rigidly loyal to Moscow, had formidable political appeal, attracting up to a quarter of the electorate, but it never came into power.

In the 1950s, certain parts of Western Europe demonstrated a political stability that verged on petrification. Spain and Portugal remained under their conservative, Catholic, protectionist dictators, Salazar and Franco, and both countries saw little relief from isolation and impoverishment during the decade. Greece, meanwhile, recovered from its brutal civil war and remained a fragile democracy. The Scandinavian countries largely saw steady Social Democratic rule and a further consolidation of their welfare states. Sweden's Social Democratic prime minister held office for a European record-setting twenty-three years, from 1946 to 1969. Finally, the German-speaking countries in the West saw a return to the sort of stability they had not known since before World War I. The Christian Democrats remained in power throughout the decade in West Germany, in alliance with Bavaria's Christian Social Union. The Communist Party, officially banned, had virtually no influence, and even the Social Democrats formally renounced Marxist orthodoxy in 1959. In Austria, the Soviets and the Western powers quietly agreed to an end to occupation in 1955 and a transition to a democratic, limited free-market system.

FIRST STEPS TOWARD EUROPEAN UNITY

Against this background of stability and peace, the Western European countries also moved toward unprecedented economic and political cooperation. In 1951, France, West Germany, Italy, and the Low Countries (Belgium, Luxembourg, and the Netherlands) entered into an agreement to abolish tariffs and create a common market for coal and steel. France in particular saw the move as a means of binding West Germany closely to it and increasing French political influence with Britain and the United States. But all the countries saw benefits for their economies and considered the agreement as only a first step. In 1957, after lengthy negotiations, the same six countries signed the

Treaty of Rome, which created a broader common market known as the European Economic Community—direct predecessor to the present-day European Union. Britain joined in 1973, along with Ireland and Denmark.

While the image of the 1950s as a decade of complacency only came after the fact, and as a caricature, it remains true that the period saw a quick ebbing of the ideological tides that had dominated European politics and culture from the 1930s through the early post-war period. By the middle of the decade, the prospect of Communist takeovers in Western Europe already seemed remote, and the economic boom and rising standards of living had diminished the desire for radical change on the part of millions of Europeans who now saw themselves as comfortably middle class. Even in France and Italy, the powerful Communist parties did not manage winning majorities of the vote. Meanwhile, despite the brief successes of figures like Poujade, the radical right, indelibly associated with fascism, remained a discredited and largely impotent political force throughout most of the West. In 1955, the liberal French sociologist Raymond Aron could write of "the end of the age of ideologies."

CULTURAL FERMENT

In keeping with this new political climate, the leading cultural movements of the 1950s often avoided direct ideological commitments. In the Soviet Union, the period marked a hiatus between patriotic wartime literature and the dissident writing that would flower in the 1960s. The most important Soviet novel of the decade, the melodramatic *Dr. Zhivago* written by Boris Pasternak (1890–1960), did not pass muster with the Soviet censors but nor did it directly challenge the regime. Smuggled to the West, it became one of the great bestsellers of the decade and the basis for a blockbuster film.

Other Soviet writers were at work on masterpieces that would blisteringly depict the crimes of Stalinism, but these did not appear until later. The great poet Anna Akhmatova (1889–1966) was finishing the long, brilliant elegy entitled *Requiem*, centered on the tragic figures of women who stood outside prisons waiting for news of arrested relatives—a role that Akhmatova herself had played after the arrest of her husband and son. Alexander Solzhenitsyn (1918–2008) was completing the harrowing *One Day in the Life of Ivan Denisovitch*—a brilliant account of the struggle to survive in Stalin's Gulag, based on his own experiences. Solzhenitsyn's novel was allowed to appear in print under Khrushchev. *Requiem* was only published abroad.

In the West, many of the most famous intellectuals continued to support the Communist Party, at least in name, until 1956, but without hewing mechanically to any line laid down in Moscow. More intellectual excitement bubbled up over the broad movement known as existentialism, associated above all with France's Jean-Paul Sartre (1905–1980). The existentialist movement explored the need of individuals to become free, willful actors in the midst of the world's absurdity, violence, and unreason. Sartre, the most famous intellectual of the decade, himself retained a fascination with cathartic, cleansing violence, which led him to express sympathy with anti-colonialist guerrilla and terrorist movements. His friend, the Algerian-born novelist Albert Camus (1913–1960), broke with Sartre over this aspect of his thought and over his political loyalty to the USSR. In Camus's own novels, notably *The Stranger* (originally published in 1942), he promoted a more humanist, apolitical ethic of responsible action. Playwrights, meanwhile, pushed the theme of the confrontation with the irrational to an extreme in the so-called theater of the absurd, which sought to provoke, perplex, and unsettle audiences by rejecting conventional notions of plot and character.

Many of the most daring intellectual experiments of the period became major cultural phenomena in the 1960s and 1970s. *The Second Sex*, first published by Sartre's long-time partner **Simone de Beauvoir** (1908–1986) in 1949, became a founding text of modern feminism.

Sartre and de Beauvoir Writers and romantic partners Jean-Paul Sartre and Simone de Beauvoir are caught in conversation in this candid photograph from 1945. Both had a major influence on developing intellectual movements—Sartre on existentialism, de Beauvoir on feminism.

EUROPE'S OTHERS WRITE BACK

In the cultural dislocation of post-war Europe, women, minorities, and other marginalized members of society challenged their exclusion from civil and cultural equality. Feminist writers such as Simone de Beauvoir criticized women's second-class status and demanded equal opportunities for women in political and social life. Artists and writers from racial minorities, both in imperial centers like London and Paris and in the colonies themselves, attacked the racism and hypocrisy of the European empires and demanded democratic reforms. These sidelined groups questioned the justness of the societies that for so long had been centered around and directed by white men.

Simone de Beauvoir, from *The Second Sex*

In this passage from her trailblazing feminist book *The Second Sex* (1949), de Beauvoir argues that throughout history woman has been seen as an inferior "Other."

Woman has ovaries and a uterus; such are the particular conditions that lock her in her subjectivity; some even say she thinks with her hormones. Man vainly forgets that his anatomy also includes hormones and testicles. He grasps his body as a direct and normal link with the world that he believes he apprehends in all objectivity, whereas he considers woman's body an obstacle, a prison, burdened by everything that particularizes it. "The female is female by virtue of a certain *lack* of qualities," Aristotle said. "We should regard women's nature as suffering from natural defectiveness." And Saint Thomas in his turn decreed that woman was an "incomplete man," an "incidental" being. This is what the Genesis story symbolizes, where Eve appears as if drawn from Adam's "supernumerary" bone, in Bossuet's words. Humanity is male, and man defines woman, not in herself, but in relation to himself; she is not considered an autonomous being. "Woman, the relative being," writes Michelet. Thus Monsieur Benda declares in *Le rapport d'Uriel* (Uriel's Report): "A man's body has meaning by itself, disregarding the body of the woman, whereas the woman's body seems devoid of meaning without reference to the male. Man

thinks himself without woman. Woman does not think herself without man." And she is nothing other than what man decides; she is thus called "the sex," meaning that the male sees her essentially as a sexed being; for him she is sex, so she is it in the absolute. She is determined and differentiated in relation to man, while he is not in relation to her; she is the inessential in front of the essential. He is the Subject; he is the Absolute. She is the Other.

Aimé Césaire, from "Discourse on Colonialism"

Césaire (1913–2008) was a poet and a politician from the French Caribbean possession of Martinique. In this excerpt from his 1955 essay "Discourse on Colonialism," he attacks the dehumanizing processes of colonization.

First we must study how colonization works to *decivilize* the colonizer, to *brutalize* him in the true sense of the word, to degrade him, to awaken him to buried instincts, to covetousness, violence, race hatred, and moral relativism; and we must show that each time a head is cut off or an eye put out in Vietnam and in France they accept the fact, each time a little girl is raped and in France they accept the fact, each time a Madagascan is tortured and in France they accept the fact, civilization acquires another dead weight, a universal regression takes place, a gangrene sets in, a center of infection begins to spread....

And then one fine day the bourgeoisie is awakened by a terrific reverse shock: the gestapos are busy, the prisons fill up, the torturers around the racks invent, refine, discuss.

People are surprised, they become indignant. They say: "How strange! But never mind—it's Nazism, it will pass!" And they wait, and they hope; and they hide the truth from themselves, that it is barbarism, but the supreme barbarism, the crowning barbarism that sums up all the daily barbarisms; that it is Nazism, yes, but that before they were its victims, they were its accomplices....

...What [the Christian bourgeois] cannot forgive Hitler for is not *the crime* in itself, *the crime against man*, it is not *the humiliation of man as such*, it is the crime against the white man, the humiliation of the white man, and the fact that he applied to Europe colonialist procedures which until then had been reserved exclusively for the Arabs of Algeria, the coolies of India, and the blacks of Africa.

QUESTIONS FOR ANALYSIS

1. According to de Beauvoir, how are women and men seen in relation to each other?
2. What link does Césaire draw between colonialism and Nazism?
3. How do both of these works expose the assumptions behind Europe's claim to having a superior form of civilization?

Sources: Simone de Beauvoir, *The Second Sex*, trans. Constance Borde and Sheila Malovany-Chevallier (New York: 2010), pp. 5–6; Aimé Césaire, *Discourse on Colonialism*, trans. Joan Pinkham (New York: 1972), pp. 13–14.

Written just as the post-war landscape began to offer new possibilities for European women, the book eloquently denounced traditional sex roles as the social and cultural inventions of men, rather than simple reflections of nature. "One is not born, but rather becomes, a woman," de Beauvoir wrote, and she challenged women to assert different identities and roles for themselves. The work of the black French thinker Frantz Fanon (1925–1961), culminating in his 1961 book *The Wretched of the Earth*, laid the basis for much subsequent thinking about race and violence. A psychiatrist who keenly analyzed the psychological effects of racism on blacks, Fanon spent much of the 1950s in French Algeria, joined the independence movement there, and found justification for extreme violence against colonial oppression.

DECOLONIZATION AND POLITICAL CHANGE

The major international crises afflicting Western Europe in the 1950s involved the continuing wave of decolonization that Fanon supported. Britain successfully tested nuclear weapons in 1952, and France in 1960, but these events had less practical effect on their geopolitical standing than the continuing crumbling of their empires. One dramatic European defeat occurred in Vietnam, where the French lost the battle of Dien Bien Phu to Ho Chi Minh's forces in 1954. The French quickly pulled out of Vietnam altogether, and following an international conference in Geneva, two independent Vietnamese states came into being in 1955: a North Vietnamese state under Ho Chi Minh and a pro-Western South Vietnam.

THE SUEZ CRISIS OF 1956

The most important flashpoint of the decade was Egypt, where young nationalist officers overthrew the pro-British monarchy of King Farouk (r. 1936–1952) in 1952. Egyptian nationalists then started to insist on control of the country's resources, including the **Suez Canal**—the crucial waterway that allowed shipping to pass from the Mediterranean toward the Indian Ocean. In 1954, Britain reluctantly agreed to begin withdrawing its military forces from the canal zone.

Matters came to a head in 1956 when the hot-tempered new Egyptian leader, Gamal Abdel Nasser (1918–1970), abruptly nationalized the Suez Canal. France, Britain, and Israel—which had never signed a peace agreement with Egypt—planned a joint military operation that they hoped would lead to a reoccupation of the canal zone and the fall of Nasser's government. But the Egyptian army put up an unexpectedly tough fight, and then both the United States and the Soviet Union began to pressure the Western countries to withdraw. U.S. president Dwight Eisenhower in particular resented what he saw as the Europeans' selfish and deceptive conduct, and he privately accused them of risking Middle East peace for their own economic benefit. With American financial pressure undermining the stability of the British pound, the British and French gave in by early November and withdrew their forces. The Suez Crisis led Britain to question its imperial role even further.

ALGERIA

In France, Suez—following on the final French defeat in Vietnam in 1954—further damaged a weak Republic that was already struggling with another crisis in the Arab world. Most of the French considered Algeria, which had over a million inhabitants of European descent, an intrinsic part of their nation.

THE WAR FOR INDEPENDENCE That feeling was not shared, however, by the more than 8 million Algerian Muslims who remained largely shut out of political participation and deprived of most chances for social or economic advancement. An armed insurrection against France broke out in 1954, led by young Algerian nationalists inspired in part by events in Egypt. Unable to confront the French army militarily, their **National Liberation Front (FLN)** instead turned to guerrilla and terrorist tactics, including the massacre of 123 civilians in the Algerian town of Philippeville (now Skikda) in 1955. Such actions pushed the French to ever more desperate attempts at counterinsurgency, with the army carrying out massacres of its own and torturing prisoners to uncover the whereabouts of FLN units.

In the so-called battle of Algiers in 1957, the FLN carried out bombings and shootings in the Algerian capital and staged a general strike. French forces finally crushed the Algiers insurgents, but only after a costly campaign lasting the better part of a year. The FLN's attacks continued elsewhere in the territory. Algerians of European descent, known as *pieds noirs* ("black feet"), grew ever more suspicious of the government in Paris and ever more ready to take up arms themselves. Segments of the French army in Algeria openly sympathized with them.

The French leadership desperately considered different options. They granted full independence to the neighboring countries of Tunisia and Morocco, which had been French protectorates. They also developed the idea of giving full French citizenship to Algerian Muslims and introducing affirmative action for them in certain segments of French government. This plan violated the strict individualist principles underlying France's republican constitution. But by 1957–58, these principles mattered less than restoring order in Algeria—and preventing the disorder there from spreading back across the Mediterranean to France itself.

ALGERIA AND THE FALL OF THE FRENCH FOURTH REPUBLIC

The French leadership failed in this goal. In 1957–58, three successive French governments fell because of the Algerian issue. Then in May 1958, a group of army officers in Algiers staged a coup there and took control of the territory, demanding **Charles de Gaulle**'s return to power. When paratroopers loyal to these officers seized control of the French Mediterranean island of Corsica on May 24, the threat of bloodshed in France itself turned very real. To prevent it, the French president appointed de Gaulle, hero of the wartime Free French, as prime minister. The National Assembly voted him extraordinary powers for six months, along with the authority to prepare a new constitution. De Gaulle immediately flew to Algeria, and before a huge crowd he delivered the deliberately ambiguous words: "I have understood you." The new constitution he largely devised, which gave France its Fifth Republic, replaced the country's weak parliamentary system with a strong executive one. In December 1958, de Gaulle himself won election to the newly powerful office of president.

De Gaulle did not, however, save French Algeria. By the time he took office, he already realized that France had little hope of keeping the territory. The FLN continued its resistance campaign, including terrorist attacks in France itself. In October 1961, French police in Paris killed scores—perhaps as many as 200—of peaceful, mostly North African protestors, in a massacre that the French state covered up until the late 1990s. The police prefect who bore ultimate responsibility was Maurice Papon, who during the war had helped organize the deportation of French Jews to the Nazi death camps—like many other such officials, he had avoided post-war punishment and continued his successful administrative career.

But even before these events, de Gaulle had entered into secret negotiations with the FLN that concluded in 1962 with an agreement to give Algeria full independence. Enraged at this supposed betrayal, French generals

Algerian War French soldiers stand guard over members of the FLN whom they have taken prisoner following a confrontation during the Algerian War of Independence.

in Algiers staged another coup and planned to land paratroopers in Paris. The plot failed, and its leaders went underground into the so-called Secret Army Organization, which itself carried out terrorist acts including a failed assassination attempt on de Gaulle in August 1962. Meanwhile, the European settlers in Algeria fled to France, along with significant numbers of Arabs and Berbers associated with the French regime.

The loss of a territory that the French had considered part of their nation for more than a century had a traumatic effect, and ironically led prominent intellectuals to abandon earlier visions of French identity as "universal." In its place, they adopted a more limited, ethnically-exclusive vision of France. This shift would make it much harder for the country to absorb the wave of Muslim immigration that was just beginning.

THE SCRAMBLE OUT OF AFRICA

Even as the crises in Algeria and the Suez shook Western Europe, both France and Britain continued to wrestle with the forces of decolonization in sub-Saharan Africa. In Kenya, a widespread insurrection known as the Mau Mau Uprising took tens of thousands of lives and involved widespread atrocities by British forces, including the forced imprisonment of hundreds of thousands of members of the Kikuyu tribe in camps where torture and sexual assault were common. While the British ultimately suppressed the revolt, the events made clear that Britain could not hold on to its African colonies except at an impossibly high cost in money, blood, and the Britons' own principles.

By the mid-1960s, Britain and France had granted independence to most of their colonies in Africa, including Kenya, where the British government bought out the property of white settlers. Belgium likewise pulled out of its colony in the Congo, where some of the worst excesses of European imperialism had taken place. All in all, between 1957 and 1967 over thirty new African states joined the United Nations. White rule in Africa remained principally in the Portuguese colonies of Angola and Mozambique, and in the racist white settler states of South Africa and Rhodesia. The rulers of the latter unilaterally declared independence from Britain in 1965.

The new African states generally came into existence with democratic, European-style constitutions, grand hopes for development, and promises of aid and assistance from the former imperial powers. In most cases, these hopes and promises were soon largely dashed. In the subsequent fifty years, virtually none of them preserved their original democratic systems, and all had to contend with woeful economic underdevelopment, a catastrophic collapse in physical infrastructure, and a host of other afflictions, including the AIDS epidemic. Historians and social scientists debate the extent to which European imperialism directly caused these problems, but there is no doubt that the combination of imperialism and rapid decolonization left the African continent in desperate straits.

It is worth noting, however, that decolonization did not always mean real disengagement. The United States and the USSR both cultivated allies in Africa and sent advisers and aid to the new states. France retained a strong military presence in its former colonial region of West Africa, and all European states remained deeply involved in exploiting the African natural resources that had drawn them to the continent in the first place. In 1980, France had more citizens living in the Ivory Coast than twenty-five years before, during colonial rule.

SHIFTING COLD WAR DYNAMICS

Even as the former European imperial states continued to confront decolonization, the threat of war again loomed over Europe itself. In the early 1960s, at several frightening moments, it seemed as if the Cold War might turn very hot indeed.

COLD WAR CRISES

On Sunday, August 13, 1961, citizens of Berlin woke up to find the border between the two halves of the city closed. East German soldiers and police were tearing up pavement and erecting barbed wire fences around the enclave of West Berlin. The Communist regime, faced with the continuing flight of its citizens—especially younger, productive adults—had decided to keep them in the country by force. Within a few years, the **Berlin Wall** had evolved into a massive, forbidding symbol of Communism's failure: a 12-foot high, 87-mile-long concrete barrier studded with 116 watchtowers. It was separated from East Berlin by a "death strip" patrolled by armed border troops.

While several thousand East Berliners did manage to escape across the wall during its twenty-eight years of existence—including by tunnel, balloons, and wires stretched over to West Berlin buildings—they did so mostly at the start. At least 136 East Germans died trying to flee. The regime also massively reinforced its entire border with West Germany, laying minefields and setting automatic gun traps. The moves provoked angry rhetoric from the West and particularly from the young American president, John F. Kennedy (1917–1963), who extravagantly promised in his inaugural address in January 1961 to "pay any price, bear any burden . . . to assure the survival and the success of liberty." In 1963, Kennedy came to West Berlin, expressed his solidarity with its citizens, and laid down a stark challenge to the East: "There are some who say in Europe and elsewhere we can work with the Communists. Let them come to Berlin."

In 1962, the United States under Kennedy and the Soviet Union under Nikita Khrushchev came closer to open warfare than at any other time during the Cold War. In October of that year, after the Americans discovered that the Soviets were placing nuclear missiles in Communist Cuba, just ninety miles off the coast of Florida, they imposed a blockade of the island, and for several days the world feared the conflict might escalate into a nuclear exchange. The crisis ended with a deal by which the Soviets removed missiles from Cuba and the Americans secretly promised to do the same from Turkey.

The progress of a Communist insurgency in South Vietnam led the U.S. government to send advisers and material support to the Western-backed regime there. The growing American commitment in Vietnam was influenced by the Cold War strategy often referred to as the domino theory, which held that the fall to Communism of one pro-Western regime in the region would

> Berlin [has] now become—as never before—the great testing place of Western courage and will, a focal point where our solemn commitments stretching back over the years since 1945 and Soviet ambitions now meet in basic confrontation.
>
> *PRESIDENT JOHN F. KENNEDY, TELEVISED SPEECH, JULY 25, 1961*

BUILDINGS
1. Friedrichstrasse Station
2. Soviet Embassy
3. SED headquarters
4. Checkpoint Charlie
5. Brandenburg Gate

Road
Wall
Railroad
Checkpoint
Sector boundary
Plaza
Mixed residential/commercial use
Industrial use
Park or open area

Tegel airport
FRENCH SECTOR
Bernhauer Strasse
Stasi Prison
SOVIET SECTOR
Alexanderplatz
BRITISH SECTOR
Ostbanhof Station
Spree R.
Potsdamer Platz
Berlin Wall, 1961–1989
Treptower Park
Schöneberg Town Hall
Harzer Strasse
Tempelhof airport
AMERICAN SECTOR
Kommandantura headquarters

Cold War Berlin
FRENCH SECTOR
BRITISH SECTOR
AMERICAN SECTOR
SOVIET SECTOR
EAST GERMANY
Checkpoint Bravo

A group of East German workers' militiamen stands, armed, in front of the Brandenburg Gate on August 14, 1961, a day after the borders between East and West Berlin were sealed.

EAST GERMANS FLEEING TO THE WEST

1949–1961	**2.8 MILLION***
May 1961	17,791
June 1961	19,198
July 1961	30,415
August 1–12, 1961	22,000

*16 percent of the German Democratic Republic's population, most of them young and well educated

The Bernhauer Strasse lay directly on the border of East and West Berlin. Many East Germans fled across this street, escaping through their apartment windows to the opposite sidewalk on the Western side.

"OPERATION ROSE," 1961

JULY 6

Soviet premier Khrushchev's approval of "Operation Rose," the East German plan to close the borders to West Berlin

AUGUST 13

"Barbed-Wire Sunday": border sealing begins at 1:00 a.m.; complete by 6:00 a.m.

The Berlin Wall, a symbol of the Cold War, eventually extended for almost 100 miles with 300 watchtowers.

Over two decades later, it was dismantled by Berliners on November 9, 1989.

QUESTIONS FOR ANALYSIS

1. How did the location of a divided Berlin make it a flashpoint in the ongoing hostilities of the Cold War?

2. What connections do you see between the flight of East Germans to the West and the plan of East German and Soviet officials to close off the Western sectors of the city?

3. What evidence do you see that the sealing off of West Berlin disrupted neighborhoods and families in the city?

lead to the loss of others in a series. By the mid-1960s, the United States had started to send troops in large numbers, fighting unsuccessfully against both the insurgent Viet Cong and Communist North Vietnam, with the conflict spilling over into other Southeast Asian states as well. Europeans waited and watched nervously to see which, if any, of these flashpoints might send dangerous sparks flying in their direction.

CHALLENGES TO COLD WAR IDEOLOGIES

Yet the Cold War in the 1960s did not amount to a simple continuation of the conflict that had begun in the late 1940s. Through at least the early 1950s, the ideological stakes on both sides had still seemed enormously high. Western and Soviet leaders each saw the other side as bent on the destruction of the opposing social and political system. Soviet actions in Central and Eastern Europe convinced a large portion of Western public opinion that their leaders were right. Societies, as well as governments, remained psychologically prepared for war. By the early 1960s, however, things had changed.

The Soviet Union continued the retreat from rigid ideology signaled by Khrushchev's secret speech of 1956. Although Khrushchev proclaimed that same year to a group of Western ambassadors that "we will bury you" and frequently predicted that the Soviet Union would soon surpass the West economically, at home he tolerated small but telling retreats from Communist orthodoxy. In the economy, he gave increased freedom to small private farmers who, while only working 3 percent of the country's available farmland, produced a third of its total agricultural output in the early 1960s. He also permitted Hungary greatly to enlarge its private sector. Politically, he allowed the Gomułka regime in Poland to continue cautious political liberalization. And in 1962, the Soviet regime itself allowed a literary magazine to publish Solzhenitsyn's *One Day in the Life of Ivan Denisovitch*. In foreign policy, divisions opened up between the USSR and the more radical Chinese regime of Mao Zedong (1893–1976). The Sino-Soviet split opened in part because of what Mao saw as Khrushchev's overly conciliatory policies toward the West, although it also echoed long-standing historical tensions between Russia and China. A full-fledged split took place in 1964, with Mao denouncing Khrushchev as a capitalist counterrevolutionary.

This major splintering of the Communist bloc, worsened by China's successful test of a nuclear weapon in 1964, undermined the standing of Khrushchev himself with the Soviet party leadership. In October 1964, they removed him from office, and the gray functionary Leonid Brezhnev (1906–1982) replaced him as party general secretary. Despite momentary fears in the West of a return to the Stalin era, Khrushchev's fall did not bring about any major changes of direction in Soviet policy, even if Brezhnev and his cautious colleagues showed less tolerance for dissent.

The idea that Western Europe had to follow the United States unquestioningly in a rigid ideological conflict with the Communist bloc also came in for serious political challenges. In 1958, a group of prominent left-wing British cultural figures founded the Campaign for Nuclear Disarmament, calling for Britain unilaterally to give up nuclear weapons and perhaps disengage from NATO altogether. Its protest marches attracted hundreds of thousands of supporters. French president de Gaulle (1890–1970) repeatedly signaled his disagreements with American policies and sometimes spoke of France as an independent power between East and West. In 1966, he followed through on this rhetoric by withdrawing French military forces from the unified NATO command structure although France remained a part of the overall alliance.

The deepening American involvement in Southeast Asia during the 1960s also stirred opposition in Europe. Although six Western European nations had sent at least token forces to fight in the Korean War in the early 1950s, none participated in the tragic Vietnam conflict (although Australia and New Zealand did). By 1967, polls showed that large majorities of Western Europeans opposed America's actions. Also in 1967, Britain's most prominent philosopher, Bertrand Russell (1872–1970), who had opposed British involvement in World War I fifty years earlier, presided over a mock tribunal in Stockholm that found the United States guilty of "war crimes." By 1968, every major Western European capital had experienced large-scale protest marches against the war.

THE DECADE OF YOUTH REVOLT

The increasing opposition to American policy had its origins not only in the waning of Cold War ideologies but also in the explosive and turbulent youth culture of the 1960s. Europe had of course seen generational tensions before.

They had a particular importance in the era of the French Revolution and at the birth of the romantic movement in art and literature. But in the 1960s, for the first time in European conflict, generational tensions came to be seen as one of the main forces driving political, cultural, and social change.

POST-INDUSTRIAL SOCIETY

As in the United States, the youth culture was linked to the baby boom that had followed the war and the coming to maturity of a huge cohort of men and women raised in unprecedented comfort and prosperity. More explicitly than ever before, the tastes and behavior of people in their teens and twenties—involving music, clothing, hairstyles, drugs, and sexual behavior—became politicized. And while the slogan "Never trust anyone over thirty" came from the youth movement in the United States, it had just as much resonance in Western Europe. Young people in Eastern Europe often aspired to develop their own versions of rebellious youth culture, but they had much less opportunity than their Western counterparts because of the regimented nature of the Eastern political regimes.

The transformation of youth culture would have been unthinkable had economic growth not continued. In the 1960s, it was not only continuing but bringing further structural changes to societies and economies of the West. Just as the proportion of the population employed in agriculture had been falling since the nineteenth century, now the proportion employed in manufacturing began to decline as well, to the profit of service and knowledge industries. Western Europe was experiencing what the sociologist Daniel Bell called "the coming of post-industrial society." The East, as we have seen, had much more difficulty making the transition away from heavy industry.

Educational patterns in Western Europe changed markedly as a result. As late as 1950, most Western European children left school by the age of fourteen to begin vocational training. British grammar schools and public schools (which were actually private), French *lycées*, and German *Gymnasiums* were all elite institutions catering to less than 10 percent of all teenagers. But in the 1960s, the numbers going through secondary education and higher education exploded. In 1950, West Germany had only 108,000 full-time university students. By 1968, the number had increased almost fourfold. Other European countries experienced similar rates of expansion. Nearly all the European universities were public and free, and many were open to anyone with a baccalaureate (high school) degree. Educational bureaucracies shoehorned students into existing facilities and oversaw the construction of new campuses.

THE DECLINE OF RELIGIOUS OBSERVANCE

These students came to universities with different outlooks and habits from even their immediate predecessors. Most striking, they were far less religious than their predecessors. During the 1960s, the number of children enrolled in religious education in Great Britain fell by half, and the number of children baptized fell to under 50 percent. Throughout Europe, weekly attendance at church was declining as well, especially among those under age thirty. In both the Catholic Church and the numerous Protestant denominations, the number of men and women entering religious life fell dramatically, too, forcing religious schools to hire greater numbers of secular teachers. A similar fall in religious observance took place in the officially atheist Eastern European states.

The established churches were trying to adapt to their changing societies, but often in a hesitant or reluctant manner. Most dramatic was the action of the Catholic Church. In 1958, the conclave of cardinals elected the seventy-six-year-old Italian Angelo Roncalli as pope. He was expected to serve as a passive placeholder after the controversial pontificate of Pius XII (r. 1939–1958), whose tolerance of the Fascists in Italy and Germany during the war had earned the Church considerable criticism. Instead, Roncalli, taking the name John XXIII (r. 1958–1963), embarked on an ambitious reform program that culminated in the **Second Vatican Council** of 1962–65. This body produced the greatest change in Church liturgy since the Middle Ages. Henceforth, priests would say the Mass in the local language, not in Latin, and while facing the congregants, not with their backs turned. Congregants no longer kneeled to receive Communion. The Church formally withdrew its accusation that the Jews had killed Jesus Christ.

But Church reform had its limits, as was evident in the explosive issue of birth control. In 1968, a new, more cautious pope, Paul VI (r. 1963–1978), reaffirmed the Church's ban on the practice. Sexual intercourse had only one purpose, he stated in an encyclical: human reproduction.

The declaration deeply disappointed a large proportion of the Catholic population, especially younger people in northern Europe, and hastened the decline of religious observance.

YOUTH CULTURE

The spread of birth control itself amounted to another broad cultural shift with particular significance for European youth. Europeans had employed forms of contraception for centuries—especially coitus interruptus, primitive prophylactic sheaths, and abortion-inducing drugs. While abortion remained illegal in nearly all of Europe through the 1960s, more efficient prophylactics for men were widely available. And starting in Britain in 1961, birth control pills for women became available as well. The risk of unplanned pregnancies fell dramatically, and rates of premarital sex rose just as dramatically. At the same time, many European states began loosening censorship laws on pornography. D. H. Lawrence's explicit *Lady Chatterley's Lover*, which had first appeared in print in Italy in 1928, finally made it to publication in the novelist's native Britain in 1960. Sex, in short, was becoming more visible in the public life of the West.

Beatlemania Young fans excitedly pose with Ringo Starr, John Lennon, Paul McCartney, and George Harrison at a concert hall in Edinburgh in 1964, at the height of the Beatles' fame.

All of these cultural changes left their mark on the vastly increased numbers of students who crammed into European universities in the 1960s—students who already had more free time and disposable income than their predecessors. Companies eagerly competed to sell them distinctive youth products: clothing, much of it marketed as sexually appealing (notably blue jeans and miniskirts), books, magazines, and above all music.

The most famous representatives of the new generation were four young working-class men from the grimy English industrial city of Liverpool, who came together as a band in the early 1960s playing music inspired by American rock and roll. The Beatles exploded onto the British and American music scenes in the fall of 1962. By early 1964, Beatlemania had grown so fevered that as much as half the American population tuned in to television to see the group perform on *The Ed Sullivan Show*. The group would go on to sell over a billion albums. The Beatles were only one of many rock groups to transform popular music in the 1960s, but they were almost certainly the most important. In 1966, John Lennon boasted that the group had become more popular than Jesus Christ—words that had a certain plausibility, given the fall-off in religious practice.

STUDENT REBELLIONS: 1968

Despite being packaged and sold by profit-seeking corporations, rock music and other elements of the 1960s youth culture breathed a spirit of rebellion. The flouting of sexual conventions by the youth culture, and its embrace of recreational drug use—especially marijuana and psychedelic drugs such as LSD—only intensified the tensions it generated. The Beatles boasted of smoking marijuana in the toilets in Buckingham Palace, and their fans widely took the surreal lyrics of "Lucy in the Sky with Diamonds" as a paean to LSD. The uncertain career prospects for the glut of new college graduates contributed to the tensions in a different way. As early as 1955, the British journalist Henry Fairlie had coined the term *the Establishment* to describe the constellation of individuals and institutions that exercised real control over British society. He used the word sardonically, but by the late 1960s it had become a term of abuse, not just in Britain but also throughout Europe and the United States, for young people at odds with their elders.

The tensions exploded in the year 1968. Throughout Western Europe and the United States, university students protested, staged sit-ins, went on strike, occupied

Violent Protests The French protests in May 1968, turn violent when a group of students rip pavement stones out of the Boulevard Saint-Germain, in the Latin Quarter of Paris, to throw at the police.

campus buildings, and took part in violent clashes with riot police. The great common cause was the war in Vietnam. Some 10,000 students in West Berlin held a sit-in to protest American involvement there, and Italian students forced the closure of the University of Rome for twelve days for the same reason. In West Germany, students also protested the continuing presence of former Nazis in prominent positions in government and society. It did not help that in 1966 a former Nazi propagandist had become chancellor of West Germany. In Spain, students protested against the repression of the Franco regime, and in response the regime closed the University of Madrid for a month. At the University of Belgrade, in Communist but non-aligned Yugoslavia, students went on strike for seven days and won some concessions from the Tito regime.

The protests of 1968 were most serious in France, where Charles de Gaulle had now been president for ten years. His Fifth Republic, with its powerful executive, enjoyed a degree of political stability known by no previous democratic regime in France. But this very success had left the elderly president dangerously complacent. On New Year's Eve 1967, he had declared in a national broadcast that "I greet the year 1968 with serenity. . . . It is impossible to see how France today could be paralyzed by crisis as she has been in the past." University students soon taught him a lesson.

Unrest first spread at the desolate, overcrowded, modernist campus in the Parisian suburb of Nanterre and soon spread to the Sorbonne, heart of the University of Paris. In April, the government closed the school and arrested some 600 students. On May 6, the escalating troubles turned bloody—students fought back against riot police, throwing cobblestones and improvised gasoline bombs,

and engaging in that most traditional of Parisian revolutionary actions: building street barricades. The rioting continued for a solid week, with thousands injured, at which point the heavily Communist trade unions took a role as well, declaring a national general strike for better pay and working conditions. A remarkable utopian spirit briefly appeared in Paris, expressed in slogans such as "Be Realistic: Demand the Impossible." In panic, de Gaulle briefly fled the country for a military base in West Germany. However, the students and workers failed to make common cause. De Gaulle called for new parliamentary elections, and on May 30 up to a million demonstrators flowed down the wide boulevard of the Champs-Élysées in support of his government. So in France, as throughout Western Europe, the events of 1968 led to surprisingly little violence, and little permanent political change, although much larger degrees of social and cultural change.

SPAIN AND NORTHERN IRELAND

The worst violence in the late 1960s and early 1970s in Western Europe had relatively little to do with the student movement. In Spain, the slow easing of Francoist repression enabled the regime's most viciously repressed victims—the country's large ethnic minorities—to start organizing and campaigning for greater rights. In the northern Basque country in 1958, radicals founded an armed movement called ETA (for the Basque initials for "Basque Country and Freedom") that aimed at full Basque independence, and in the late 1960s they started a campaign of assassination and bombings against police, government officials, and moderate Basque politicians.

In Northern Ireland, the Catholic minority campaigned for civil rights such as an end to discrimination against them in housing and employment. Growing Catholic support for a violent Provisional Irish Republican Army led to a noisy and brutal backlash from the province's dominant Protestants. In response to these so-called **Troubles**, in 1969 the London government deployed the British army to take over security from the autonomous Northern Irish government. But the army, sent largely to protect the Catholic population, came increasingly into conflict with it, culminating in Bloody Sunday in January 1972, when British paratroopers killed thirteen civilians in the town of Derry. As the so-called Provos gained support and started a full-fledged guerrilla campaign against the army, along with terrorist attacks in mainland Britain, the Conservative prime minister dissolved the Northern Irish government in 1972 and asserted direct control over the province. Political violence in Northern Ireland would continue into the 1990s.

POLAND AND CZECHOSLOVAKIA

The late 1960s also brought considerable turmoil in the Soviet bloc. Students initially led the way in Poland, with protests for more freedom of expression and better living conditions. Police attacked them brutally, leading to much larger protests in Warsaw that were joined by workers. But in response, the relatively liberal Gomułka regime turned repressive, dismissing dissenting intellectuals from academic jobs and closing university campuses. The powerful interior minister, Mieczysław Moczar, blamed the crisis on Jews and used it as an excuse to begin purging them from the universities and the professions. Between 20,000 and 30,000 Jews—the majority of Poland's post-Holocaust Jewish remnant—fled the country. Gomułka himself struggled on for another two years. After police shot and killed protesting shipyard workers in the port city of Gdańsk in 1970, he was forced to resign. Polish workers

Czech Counterculture In 1965, students in costume pose on a festival stage with the American poet Allen Ginsberg (seated), whom they have just crowned King of the May. The gathering indicated the influence of Western counterculture on Czechoslovakian youth radicalism, much to the disapproval of the Communist authorities.

and students would continue to search for ways of putting pressure on the regime, and they received considerable support from the one institution in the country that maintained real autonomy during the decades of Communist rule: the Roman Catholic Church.

A much greater confrontation took place to the south. Czechoslovakia had also felt the currents of youth rebellion, with a vibrant student movement that eagerly embraced symbols of avant-garde Western culture. When the American "beat" poet Allen Ginsberg (1926–1997) visited Prague in the spring of 1965, students elected him King of the May. But the Communist authorities quickly expelled Ginsberg from the country, and students who protested openly against the regime found themselves blacklisted from promising careers or even imprisoned.

In January 1968, the Party Central Committee elected the forty-seven-year-old Slovak Alexander Dubček (1921–1992), a former member of the resistance against the pro-Nazi wartime government of Slovakia, as first secretary. He revived a stalled economic reform program, and this in turn encouraged public demands for greater press freedom. Seeking to build popularity for the regime, Dubček made further concessions, and his supporters began to speak of building "socialism with a human face." Dubček insisted on the primacy of the Communist Party and on remaining within the Warsaw Pact, believing that as long as he made these concessions the USSR would have no reason to fear Czechoslovak reform. But he was wrong.

The Soviets, and Communist leaders elsewhere in Eastern Europe, quickly grew concerned that events in Czechoslovakia would infect their own states. They issued steadily more dire warnings; and when the Czechs proved unwilling to rein in the reform movement, they resorted to force. On August 21, some 500,000 Warsaw Pact troops crossed the Czech frontier and quickly overcame a largely passive resistance. The Soviets allowed Dubček to remain in office, a humiliated figurehead, for one more year and then replaced him. For the next twenty years, Czechoslovakia would strike visitors as the most repressed of all the Soviet bloc states.

In both East and West, then, the youth revolutions failed to live up to the often-apocalyptic fears of conservative critics. The year 1968 did not turn out to be another 1848—a year of revolutions setting one another off across Europe like a chain of firecrackers. They did not even, for the most part, lead to the formation of durable new political parties. Instead, in Western Europe, most of the protesting students left their universities peacefully, accepted the jobs that the still-booming economy was offering them, and moved on into the middle classes. In the East, the protestors mostly withdrew into enforced silence, although a significant minority would become leaders of the growing dissident movements of the 1970s.

TOWARD NEW FORMS OF LIBERATION

Yet the events of 1968 had significance nonetheless, particularly in the West. In universities, and more broadly in national educational systems, they marked a partial collapse in old hierarchies, whether of the powerful bureaucrats who controlled French higher education or of the elite public grammar schools in the United Kingdom. Educational systems removed some of the competitive exams that tended, in practice, to benefit social elites. Teachers sought more explicitly to make schools an instrument not just of social mobility but also of social leveling. Even more important, the shaking up of sexual hierarchies led directly to the birth of movements for the rights of women. In 1970, a group of French women, mostly veterans of the student movement and inspired by the earlier works of figures like de Beauvoir, founded the Movement for the Liberation of Women. As we will see, it would flourish in the 1970s, along with similar groups in other Western European states, and build on the important social changes that the post-war period had already introduced to help bring about a permanent transformation of gender roles.

If most veterans of the youth movement greeted the lack of larger political change with acceptance or resignation, a radical minority did not. Some of them, infatuated with Third World guerrilla movements such as the Palestinian Liberation Organization, became convinced that only terrorist violence could shake existing power structures. In Germany, the year 1970 saw two young radicals, Andreas Baader and Ulrike Meinhof, form the terrorist Red Army Faction, which carried out a haphazard program of bombings, shootings, and kidnappings, especially of prominent businessmen and politicians with Nazi pasts. In Italy, the Red Brigades came into being with similar goals. Throughout the 1970s, as we will see, these and other groups would garner attention far out of proportion to their tiny numbers with a series of spectacularly brutal, if often clumsily executed, actions that harkened back to the anarchist terrorism of the late nineteenth century.

Even as they criticized the greed and materialism of Western society, the student rebels continued to behave as good Western consumers, buying Beatles albums and American blue jeans and swigging Coca-Cola. Some of the more profound and sympathetic artistic portrayals

of the movement pointed to this contradiction: Jean-Luc Godard's 1967 film *La Chinoise* concentrated on a group of self-described Maoist youth who, very much unlike earlier generations of French students who had risked their lives on the barricades, earnestly debated theories of political violence amid middle-class comfort in Paris.

The student protests of the late 1960s found sharp and lasting expression in more intellectual forms of radicalism that were developing within the universities. Centered around forms of cultural analysis known as **structuralism** and post-structuralism, they raised questions about whether fixed, timeless intellectual frames of reference really exist: was there even such a thing as "human nature" that remained essentially the same across different cultures and time periods? They also explored the ways that forms of knowledge, by determining the boundaries of "truth" and "error," can structure relations of power within societies. These new ideas had particular appeal in a decade when fixed frames of reference seemed everywhere to be collapsing and many forms of authority were under assault.

One key figure was the radical French philosopher Michel Foucault (1926–1984). In several works, he advanced the seductively counterintuitive claim that the great Enlightenment movements for more humane treatments of criminals and the insane in fact represented a facet of increasingly insidious, faceless systems of social repression that forced people into rigid and fixed patterns of behavior and belief. This idea found a powerful echo in the youth movement, among those angrily attacking the prosperous, open, democratic societies of Western Europe as in fact deeply repressive of individual expression. In the 1970s and 1980s, the post-structuralists who emerged out of this intellectual climate would eclipse the Marxists as the dominant current in Western European thought. And they would challenge, more effectively than any other intellectual movement of the twentieth century, the idea that European history was a story of progress that would continue indefinitely into the future.

CONCLUSION

Despite the legacy of wartime devastation, the tensions of the Cold War, and the dislocations and violence of decolonization, the decades after the war were still, overall, ones of prosperity, peace, and stability for the European continent. The Thirty Glorious Years had transformed the Continent almost as much as the previous thirty years of war and destruction. In the lands of the Warsaw Pact, the politics of the Cold War weighed much more heavily than in Western Europe; but even here, living conditions had improved dramatically, not just since the war but in comparison with the pre-war period.

But already in the late 1960s, Europeans were being forced to confront the question of whether they could keep all they had rebuilt since the war, or whether their remarkable recovery would now start to crumble between their fingers. Could the prosperity of the post-war boom continue? Could the new welfare states continue to provide generous benefits? Warning signs were already present in the form of higher inflation and slowing rates of job creation. The new terrorist movements, in combination with the disruptions and protests of 1968, raised the question of whether political stability would continue. And the shadow of the Cold War remained deep and menacing.

KEY TERMS

Nuremberg trials (p. 812)
welfare state (p. 813)
Marshall Plan (p. 814)
Cold War (p. 814)
iron curtain (p. 815)
Berlin Airlift (p. 817)

North Atlantic Treaty
 Organization (NATO)
 (p. 817)
Warsaw Pact (p. 817)
baby boom (p. 822)
guest workers (p. 826)

destalinization (p. 827)
Treaty of Rome (p. 830)
Simone de Beauvoir
 (p. 830)
Suez Crisis (p. 832)
National Liberation Front
 (FLN) (p. 832)

Charles de Gaulle (p. 833)
Berlin Wall (p. 834)
Second Vatican Council
 (p. 837)
Troubles (p. 839)
structuralism (p. 841)

REVIEW QUESTIONS

1. In the immediate aftermath of World War II, how did the government's role in the economy change in many European states?

2. How did disagreements over the future of Germany escalate tensions between the Soviet Union and the other Allies?

3. What were the characteristics of the Communist governments that had been imposed in most of Central and Eastern Europe by 1948?

4. What caused the wave of decolonization in the British, Dutch, and French empires?

5. What factors contributed to the spectacular growth in European standards of living in the decades following World War II?

6. Following the Eastern bloc revolts of the 1950s, how did the Soviet Union reassert control over Eastern Europe?

7. Why did post-war Western Europe achieve such unprecedented political stability during this period?

8. What events led to the dissolution of the European empires in the 1950s and 1960s?

9. What challenges to Cold War ideologies arose in the 1960s?

10. What changes in post-war Western society contributed to the emergence of a distinctive, politicized youth culture?

CORE OBJECTIVES

After reading this chapter, you should have a solid understanding of the following core objectives. To strengthen your grasp of the core objectives, use the resources on the Student Site for The West.

- Assess the condition of the nations of Europe in the immediate aftermath of World War II.

- Explain the onset and development of the Cold War.

- Describe the decolonization process around the world in the decades that followed the war.

- Evaluate the economic and political developments that took place in post-war Europe.

- Analyze the social and cultural ferment of the period.

- Trace the evolution of politics and political ideologies in the 1960s and 1970s.

GO TO inQuizitive TO SEE WHAT YOU'VE LEARNED—AND LEARN WHAT YOU'VE MISSED—WITH PERSONALIZED FEEDBACK ALONG THE WAY.

CHRONOLOGY

1967–1974
Military junta
rules Greece

1971
Collapse of the
Bretton Woods
system

1972
Munich
Olympics
massacre

1973–1974
Oil shock

1973
Solzhenitsyn's
The Gulag Archipelago
published in the West

1975
Helsinki Accords

1976
Spain transitions
to democracy

1978
Pope John
Paul II
elected

1979
Soviet Union
invades
Afghanistan

1979
Margaret Thatcher
becomes British
prime minister

1980
Solidarity forms
in Poland

1981
Martial law
in Poland

1985
Mikhail Gorbachev
rises to power
in Soviet Union

April 1986
Chernobyl disaster

1988
Earthquake
in Armenia

October 1990
German reunification

Nov.–Dec. 1989
Velvet Revolution
in Czechoslovakia

November 9, 1989
Fall of the Berlin Wall

1990s
Wars in
Yugoslavia

June 1991
Boris Yeltsin
elected president
of Russian Federation

August 1991
Coup in Soviet Union

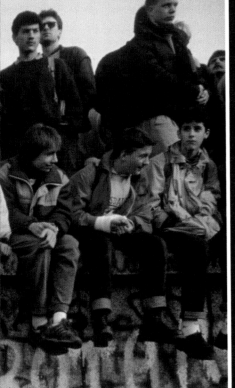

25

Reunion

EUROPEAN UNIFICATION AND THE END OF THE COLD WAR

1973–1999

Dec. 31, 1991
Soviet Union
dissolves

1999
Poland, the Czech
Republic, and
Hungary join NATO

1994–1996; 1999–2000
Chechen Wars

1992
European Economic
Community becomes
European Union

On December 10, 1989, a team of coal stokers working for the Prague metro once again found themselves a man short. For several weeks, fifty-two-year-old Jiří Dienstbier had largely neglected his job. Now he sent word that he was quitting, effective immediately. He explained that an interesting new employment opportunity had come up for him: foreign minister of Czechoslovakia. Dienstbier, a prominent former journalist and dissident whom the Communist regime had forced to work as a stoker since the end of a prison term seven years earlier, was suddenly part of the first Czechoslovak government since 1948 that was not dominated by Communists. Just a week later, he would stand on the Czechoslovak-Austrian border with Austrian foreign minister Alois Mock, the two men together grasping a huge pair of wire cutters, and snip through the strands of barbed wire separating the countries—literally tearing down the iron curtain. Twelve days after that, the most famous Czechoslovak dissident of all, writer Václav Havel, would take the place long held by career Stalinists and become the country's president.

Jiří Dienstbier's rapid job change stands as one of the more remarkable events of the remarkable year 1989. But the truly remarkable thing is that by the time it occurred, it seemed almost humdrum. The year had begun with the Hungarian Communist Party allowing true opposition parties to form. In the spring, the Polish government agreed to allow partially free elections, which took place in June and resulted in the Communists' crushing

Berlin Wall A crowd of people sits atop the Berlin Wall on November 10, 1989, the day after the Wall fell.

- What were the major effects of the economic crisis of the 1970s?
- How did Europe's post-war political and social consensus change in the 1970s?
- What signs of political change were starting to appear in the Eastern bloc nations?
- What were the major causes of the collapse of Communism in Eastern Europe?
- What events led to the fall of Communism in the Soviet Union?
- What divisions led to the fragmentation of Yugoslavia?
- How did the forces of globalization affect Europe in the 1990s?

defeat. The following months only saw events accelerate, with the most momentous of all occurring on November 9: the opening of the Berlin Wall. In mid-November, Czechoslovakia's so-called Velvet Revolution began.

These events, followed two years later by the collapse and breakup of the Soviet Union, remain the most important in European history since 1945. They involved, to be sure, considerable economic dislocation and hardship. They also led directly to the violent breakup of Yugoslavia and to a series of Balkan wars that took hundreds of thousands of lives in the 1990s. Yet overall, the end of Communism and the Soviet Empire took place with relatively little bloodshed and oppression. In a short time, they brought the former states of Eastern Europe toward the unprecedented peace and prosperity enjoyed by their Western neighbors since the immediate post-war period.

Today more than 510 million Europeans live in a twenty-eight-member Union that covers nearly the entire continent west of the former Soviet Union; and despite many challenges, they still enjoy a remarkable degree of comfort and freedom. As we will see in the next chapter, today these achievements seem less durable than they did in the early years of the twenty-first century, but they remain impressive. The events of 1989 both reflect the

Continent's progress toward this goal and helped bring it about.

SEASONS OF DISCONTENT

In the early 1970s, this favorable turn of events seemed almost unimaginable. Indeed, as the decade began, European democracy and prosperity seemed far more fragile than resurgent.

COUPS AND TERRORISM

Spain and Portugal remained under ineffective, authoritarian right-wing rule. Greece had retreated violently from democracy after a 1967 military coup. The new junta of conservative generals there arrested an estimated 8,000 political opponents and banned an almost comic range of supposed threats to Christian Greek culture, including the works of Aristophanes and the academic field of sociology. In Northern Ireland, the continuing Troubles saw terrorist attacks and heavily armed soldiers on the streets of Belfast. And in West Germany and Italy, the home-grown terrorists of the Red Army Faction and Red Brigades carried out a series of spectacular assaults on prominent figures in business and politics. In 1978, a former Italian prime minister was found shot dead in the trunk of a parked car, two months after his kidnapping by

Munich Olympics Massacre One of the terrorists looks down from the apartment in Munich's Olympic Village where nine Israeli athletes were being held hostage on September 5, 1972.

the Red Brigades. Both groups were eventually broken up by police forces.

The event that best symbolized the 1970s' seasons of discontent was the terrorist massacre at the 1972 summer Olympic Games in Munich. For West Germany, the chance to host the Olympics for the first time since the infamous 1936 Berlin Games had initially seemed a chance to demonstrate the country's full return to the company of civilized nations. But on September 5, a team of Palestinian terrorists attacked the Olympic Village, killed two members of the Israeli team, and took nine others hostage. An attempted rescue by the West German authorities went horribly wrong, and in a chaotic confrontation at a military airport all the hostages died. The games would now be remembered for an act of terrorism and the murder of Jews on German soil.

THE OIL SHOCK OF 1973–1974

The next year, strife in the Middle East contributed to European discontent in a more lasting manner and showed that European countries were becoming more economically vulnerable to global events beyond their control. In October 1973, Egypt and Syria launched a surprise attack on Israel during the Yom Kippur holiday, and the United States began an intensive effort to resupply Israel, enraging the Arab states. Within a week, the leading Arab oil exporters declared a complete embargo of oil shipments to the United States, followed by a general cutback in oil production. Over the next two years, the price of crude oil on the world market nearly quadrupled to a then-unimaginable $12 per barrel. Just twenty years before, Western Europe had mostly relied on coal for energy; but now oil, primarily imported from the Middle East, supplied over 60 percent of its energy needs, and the **oil shock** caused serious economic damage. Several European states took drastic measures to cut consumption, including the rationing of gasoline.

Worse, the shock came at a moment of particular economic fragility. In 1971, the Bretton Woods system, which had pegged major currencies to the price of gold and the U.S. dollar at fixed rates, had fallen apart. The value of most major currencies fell, contributing to inflation. The oil shock drove many countries into recession without reducing inflation, a deadly economic combination that afflicted the Continent for many years. Stock markets crashed across the Western world in 1973–74. In London the major stock index fell by 73 percent. Inflation

in Britain reached a height of nearly 27 percent per year in 1974–75. Similar patterns developed over much of the Continent.

WELFARE STATES UNDER PRESSURE

Even before 1971, the expansive welfare states created after World War II had been coming under increased pressure. With generous pension plans in place, European workers were retiring earlier, while advances in health care meant they now lived longer. In France, many workers for the national railroads retired before age fifty-five, even though few of their jobs still required hard physical labor. And at the same time, birthrates across Western Europe were steeply dropping as a result of the cultural changes discussed in the last chapter, including the decline in religious observance and the increased use of birth control. This meant that fewer workers would be available in the future to pay into the system and cover the swelling costs of pensions. A birthrate of 2.1 children per woman is needed for a population to remain stable. By the 1980s, in West Germany the figure had fallen to just 1.4. By the end of the century, in Italy it would hit 1.3. The economic crisis of 1973–74 signaled that the mechanisms Western European states had used to finance welfare-state benefits were no longer sufficient. But it took a long time for European politicians to understand this shift and develop responses to it.

This economic crisis hit most sharply in Great Britain, where after the war unions, industry, and government had developed effective forms of cooperation, and where entitlements such as health care, public education, and mass transit had expanded broadly. Now threats to strike by the country's powerful trade union movement made it difficult for industries, especially nationalized ones, to cut even obsolescent jobs or to reduce benefits for their workers. Although particularly hostile to Edward Heath's Conservative government of 1970–74, the unions came into conflict with Heath's Labour successors as well.

By 1976, the economic crisis in Britain had grown so severe that stringent austerity measures were necessary to restrain inflation—measures that lowered overall economic demand and thereby forced firms to lay off workers. The unions reacted by staging increasingly disruptive strikes. In the city of Liverpool, even gravediggers walked off the job, leading cadavers literally to pile up in the morgues. In many cases, the government gave in to the unions, providing wage increases of as much as

Public Housing Built during the period 1962–75 south of Naples, Italy, the Vele di Scampia housing project was intended as a utopian community. By the 1980s, however, the tower blocks were in poor shape, with many residents living in slum conditions amid drug trafficking and gang violence.

20 percent, which only added to inflationary pressures. Finally, in March 1979 Labour lost a no-confidence vote in Parliament and agreed to hold new elections.

The most visible symbol of the fraying welfare state was public housing. In the 1960s and early 1970s, Socialist and Conservative governments alike were continuing to sponsor the construction of millions of units of cheap residential housing for poor and lower-middle-class families. These mostly took the form of huge agglomerations of Bauhaus-style apartment blocks on the outskirts of major cities, owned and managed by the government. In France, the period saw more than 6 million people move into such housing units, and in Britain, by the mid-1970s, one-third of the population lived in them.

Although these new structures often represented a great improvement over their inhabitants' previous accommodations, critics denounced their stark, unlovely architecture and lack of greenery. More serious, rates of crime and unemployment in these new urban areas quickly rose high above national averages. By 1982, the British rock band The Jam could sing: "They were gonna build communities / It was going to be pie in the sky / But the piss stench hallways and broken down lifts / Say the planners' dream went wrong." Beyond housing, public systems of health care, education, and mass transit remained in place, with overwhelming support from the populations, but they too showed increasing strain as budgets tightened.

SOUTHERN EUROPE'S BUMPY ROAD TO DEMOCRACY

In southern Europe, politics and society in the 1970s moved in a more hopeful direction, but haltingly and

at high cost. In Greece, the rule of the military junta ended in 1974, but in the context of a bloody dispute over the eastern Mediterranean island of Cyprus, where the Greek majority and Turkish minority had shared uneasily in a common government since independence fourteen years before. In the summer of 1974, Cypriot Greek officers, with the support of the Athens junta, staged a coup, triggering a Turkish invasion and occupation of the north of the island, which remains divided to this day between the Greek Cypriot state and a so-called Turkish Republic of Northern Cyprus recognized only by Turkey.

Even worse strife, linked to decolonization, was greeting the return of democracy to Portugal. Unlike France and Britain, Portugal had never given up its major African colonies, and by the early 1970s it found itself embroiled in increasingly costly struggles against insurgents in Angola and Mozambique. As many as one-quarter of adult Portuguese males fought in Africa during the 1960s and early 1970s, and the country lost a higher proportion of soldiers than the United States did in Vietnam. The aged dictator António de Oliveira Salazar (1889–1970) died in 1970, but his regime lingered for another four years until finally left-wing military officers staged a coup. There followed a period of violence in which radical military factions, allied with the Communist Party, threatened to seize power. Finally, in 1976, a democratic government prevailed in free elections and consolidated its authority.

Dictatorship also finally came to an end in Spain. In 1969, the seventy-six-year-old Francisco Franco (1892–1975) had promised to restore the monarchy, and he named as his successor the young prince Juan Carlos, grandson of the last king. Franco did so on condition that Juan Carlos swear to preserve the ultraconservative regime and society that he had built up since the Civil War of the 1930s. When Franco died in November 1975, Juan Carlos quickly broke this promise, legalizing the Socialist and Communist parties and allowing free elections.

Yet even in Spain the transition from dictatorship brought significant turmoil. Basque and Catalan nationalist movements demanded and received considerable autonomy for their regions in northern and northeastern Spain, while the Basque terrorist group ETA continued to carry out bomb attacks and assassinations. Most dangerously, in 1981 renegade officers loyal to Franco's memory took over the Parliament in an attempted coup. But they had little popular support, and the new king gained enormous popularity by insisting, in a television broadcast, on support for Spanish democracy. The coup failed, and Spain has remained a stable democracy ever since.

SHIFTS IN THE POST-WAR SOCIAL CONSENSUS

During the three decades after the end of World War II, the Western European consensus about the proper way to organize a society had seemed almost unchallenged. Its principal tenets were a generous, all-inclusive welfare state, nationalization of major industries, tax policies aimed at a limited redistribution of income, and a significant role for government in managing a country's economy. Economists generally argued that governments could maintain high levels of employment and growth by careful management of the money supply and interest rates, coupled with ambitious spending programs where necessary. Even conservative political leaders in Western Europe did little, if anything, to dismantle the extensive welfare states and planning mechanisms created earlier in the century in part as a result of wartime pressures. By the late 1970s, the top marginal income tax rate in Great Britain stood at 83 percent.

But the consensus was never total. In 1944, the Austrian-born economist Friedrich von Hayek, a refugee from Hitler in Britain, had published a book entitled *The Road to Serfdom,* which insisted that central planning threatened individual freedoms. During the 1950s and 1960s, Hayek's followers developed an extensive critique of close government management and regulation of economies. These **neoliberals**, as their critics would come to call them, advocated something closer to the classical laissez-faire liberalism of the nineteenth century. Through the end of the 1960s, they had relatively little political influence outside the United States—and even there, little outside of the Republican Party. But in May 1979, in Britain, this all changed.

MARGARET THATCHER'S ATTACK ON THE WELFARE STATE

If the British elections that month made headlines around the world, it was less because of the Conservative victory than because, for the first time, a woman had become head of a major European government. But **Margaret Thatcher** had not campaigned on a platform of woman's rights. Her first cabinet consisted of herself and twenty-four men. Her real significance lay elsewhere. Born in 1925, the daughter of a stern Methodist grocer, she won election to Parliament as a Conservative in 1959. An outsider to the party's cozy, wealthy establishment on account of both her sex and her class origins, she developed considerable scorn for it. Thatcher was temperamentally a radical, who once declared that "there is no such thing as Society. There are individual men and women."

Upon her election, she quickly made clear her intention to dismantle the British welfare state and managed economy as they had existed since the war, even if this entailed a very high social cost. Her government slashed income tax rates and began auctioning off state-run industries such as telecommunications and aerospace to the private sector. She also started an ambitious program of selling public housing units to the people who lived in them, arguing that people would take better care of homes they actually owned. In the midst of a deep recession, these actions proved deeply unpopular, and moderate Conservatives urged her to reverse her policies. Speaking to a party conference, she refused to budge: "You turn if you want to. The lady's not for turning."

Thatcher was bolstered by an economic recovery that began in 1982 and also by an unexpected military conflict that developed when Argentina seized the British-owned Falkland Islands in the South Atlantic. A British naval task force quickly defeated the Argentinians, and Thatcher's approval rating nearly doubled. Meanwhile, the Labour opposition underwent a destructive split, which Thatcher capitalized on to hold an election in June 1983. Labour refused to modify its long-established policies, including a demand for "common ownership of the means of production, distribution and exchange." One party member called this platform "the longest suicide note in history," and the Conservatives, despite seeing their share of the vote decline slightly, won a massive parliamentary majority.

During her second term in office, Thatcher grew even more ambitious and confrontational, fully earning her nickname of The Iron Lady. In 1984, when the National Coal Board decided to close inefficient mines and put some 20,000 miners out of work, even as unemployment rates remained high, the National Union of Mineworkers went on strike in protest. But Thatcher refused to make concessions, while railing against the union leaders as "the enemy within." After nearly a year, the miners surrendered. Thatcher won other battles with unions and permanently weakened the British labor movement. She also tried to weaken local governments, in part by replacing their funding with a deeply unpopular, nationally assessed poll tax. Her government deregulated London's financial markets and opened them up to world competition in what financiers referred to as the 1986 Big Bang. Finally, in 1990, Conservative leaders concluded that her policies—especially the poll tax—and her abrasive personal style had become liabilities, and forced her out of office. But the political transformation she had carried out proved enduring. The Labour Party would only regain power in 1997, after abandoning its commitment to public ownership, tacitly accepting many of Thatcher's neoliberal reforms.

IDEOLOGICAL SHIFTS

Elsewhere in Western Europe, the retreat from the post-war consensus was less dramatic. In Sweden, the Social Democrats lost control of the government in 1976 for the first time in forty years, but the new, centrist governing coalition did little to challenge Sweden's formidable welfare state. In West Germany, the government remained in Social Democratic hands through the 1970s and early 1980s, and even after a shift back to the right West German social welfare programs remained essentially intact. Despite neoliberal prophecies of doom, the Scandinavian and West German economies remained robust. And strong growth allowed these states to continue to support their swelling numbers of retirees.

COMMUNISM IN DECLINE Yet the political complexion of Western Europe had nonetheless changed for good, as shown not only by Thatcher's reforms but also by the decline and transformation of Communist political parties. In southern Europe, the Communists attempted to retain their electoral position by renouncing their Stalinist pasts and fidelity to the Soviet Union, and promising to move toward a socialist economy by persuasion rather than force. The Italian Enrico Berlinguer became the embodiment of a so-called Eurocommunism that even tried to reconcile with the Catholic Church. But even he could not stop a steady erosion of popular support after 1976 as the traditional industrial working class shrank in the transition to a post-industrial economy. In France, where the Communist Party refused to budge from its Stalin-era policies, support fell dramatically. To the dismay of mainstream European parties, many Communist voters did not turn toward the center but instead defected to the extreme right parties, which, as we will see, pandered to white working-class resentment of expanding immigrant populations.

Communism was also rapidly losing its appeal to Western European intellectuals—even in countries such as France, where so many leading thinkers and artists, such as Jean-Paul Sartre and the poet Louis Aragon, had belonged to the party or supported its goals. The year 1973 saw the hugely successful publication in French translation of Alexander Solzhenitsyn's devastating portrait of Soviet repression, *The Gulag Archipelago,* which, like his earlier *One Day in the Life of Ivan Denisovitch*, drew on his own experiences. Over the next few years, a succession of young French "New Philosophers" published strong, if not particularly original, attacks on Soviet totalitarianism, also to considerable acclaim. The influential historian François Furet worked to resuscitate a native French liberal tradition. In short, by the early 1980s it had become clear that while social and economic divisions had hardly disappeared from the European scene, orthodox Marxism, as a means for addressing them, no longer attracted much support from European politicians and intellectuals.

FRANCE'S "PARENTHESIS IN THE HISTORY OF SOCIALISM"

Despite these shifts, it initially seemed as if the political currents in France were turning in a very different direction from those in Britain. In 1981, the left-wing Socialist opposition took power for the first time since the 1950s. But the new French leader was no doctrinaire leftist. François Mitterrand (1916–1996), a cultured, sly, long-time politician who enjoyed the nickname The Sphinx, came from a right-wing Catholic milieu in southwestern France and had even flirted with a far-right terrorist group as a student in the 1930s. Only after the war did he become a fixture of the moderate left and eventually forge a "common program" with the fossilized French Communists.

The Mitterrand presidency initially seemed to signal a renewal of French socialism. Upon the 1981 election victory, as ecstatic supporters danced in the streets of Paris, Mitterrand visited the Pantheon, burial place of the "great men of the fatherland." (In one of his last acts as president in 1995, Mitterrand arranged for the first woman, Marie Curie, to be interred there. As of this writing, there are three and soon to be four: in addition to Curie, two were active in the French Resistance during World War II, and the fourth is Simone Veil, Holocaust survivor and minister of health who fought to legalize abortion in France.) At the Pantheon Mitterand laid red roses on the tombs of three of his left-wing idols, including the nineteenth-century abolitionist Victor Schoelcher—an apparent sign of his commitment to serving an increasingly multiracial population. Over the next year, his government (which included four Communist ministers) nationalized numerous large banks and firms. But these actions panicked French

Mitterrand's Paris The president's building projects included I. M. Pei's glass pyramid, installed at the Louvre Museum in 1989. Many Parisians initially saw the structure as ostentatious and unfitting for the site.

financial circles, leading to an abrupt worsening of the French economy.

Scarcely a year after taking office, Mitterrand executed an almost complete policy U-turn, implementing austerity measures, introducing income-tax cuts, and expressing support for private enterprise. Mitterrand himself claimed he was simply introducing a "parenthesis in the history of socialism"—but in fact the parenthesis never closed. And despite Mitterrand's nominal socialism, he grew increasingly regal in his manner during his fourteen years in office, concentrating much of his energy on massive, controversial construction projects such as the gleaming glass and steel pyramid designed by I. M. Pei in the courtyard of the Louvre Museum.

CULTURAL OPENINGS

President Mitterrand intended his grand projects to leave as great a mark on his capital city as those of some of his royal and imperial predecessors, such as Louis XIV and Napoleon Bonaparte. But the projects had little in common with theirs besides grandiosity, and few mustered much public support. Critics complained that European cities were turning into giant museums that no longer added to the glories of the past. Tellingly, the most successful of Mitterrand's projects, the addition to the Louvre Museum, drew millions of new spectators to view collections that dated almost entirely from before the twentieth century.

THE ARTS There was a settled, institutional quality to much of cultural life throughout Western Europe during the period. As had been the case for centuries, relatively few artists and writers managed to earn a living from their work. Now, in place of private or princely patrons, financial support mostly came from government fellowships or teaching positions in universities. No fresh artistic and literary movement or style developed that could compare in coherence, originality, or broad appeal with romanticism or modernism. Some figures, especially in architecture, embraced a post-modern style that resisted definition but

A POST-MODERN SKYSCRAPER

The Messerturm (Market Tower) in Frankfurt, Germany, was completed in 1991, and for several years claimed the title of the tallest building in Europe. The architect, Helmut Jahn (1940–), was born in Nuremberg, Germany, and grew up watching the city rebuild itself in the wake of World War II. He has studied and practiced architecture in both Germany and the United States, and his work is representative of the post-modern style of art and architecture that has in many ways characterized late-twentieth-century art.

This iconic skyscraper is based on the elements of a classical Greek column: with a plinth at the bottom, column shaft in the center, and pinnacle on top. In this case, the pinnacle is a glass pyramid similar to the Louvre Pyramid by I. M. Pei, blending classical and ancient architectural elements in a single, post-modern structure. The exterior façade is constructed of stones quarried in Sweden, polished in Italy, and assembled on the Danube—an international effort designed to look like the traditional Frankfurt sandstone used in many of the city's major buildings for centuries.

QUESTIONS FOR ANALYSIS

1. What elements of post-modernism are visible in Jahn's design?
2. How does the Messerturm reference classical and ancient motifs in its architecture?
3. In what ways does the Messerturm strive to be a primarily German building, and in what ways is it a composite of international efforts?

that usually involved a playful, ironic reintroduction of classical motifs into works that remained fundamentally abstract in form, such as the 1991 Messerturm (Market Tower) in Frankfurt. The so-called New Wave of cinematic *auteurs* such as Jean-Luc Godard who had attracted such attention in the 1950s and 1960s had few clear heirs in subsequent decades, while symphonies and operas overwhelmingly preferred the classical canon to the performance of new works.

In the arts, including film and television, censorship declined rapidly in this period. In 1972, the Italian director Bernardo Bertolucci (1940–) provoked a scandal with his film *Last Tango in Paris*, which graphically depicted the sexual relationship between a middle-aged American and a young French woman. But the film was widely distributed, and by the end of the century similarly graphic depictions of sexuality were commonplace in film and on cable networks. By contrast, the Communist governments of the Eastern bloc continued to impose much stronger restrictions on sexual expression of all sorts.

Many important cultural developments of the period derived from the neighborhoods of large cities where immigrant populations, especially from Africa and the Caribbean, helped to generate distinctive musical, visual, and literary styles. Events like the annual Notting Hill Carnival in London attracted hundreds of thousands of visitors each year to its vibrant displays of Caribbean dancing and musical performances. These developments showed that in culture, just as much as in economics, Europe was growing less isolated from larger patterns of global interaction.

GENDER AND SEXUALITY   Overall, the most important cultural changes of the late twentieth century were linked to changing attitudes toward gender and sexuality. The feminist movements that had taken on such strength in the 1960s continued to evolve and to push further demands for equality. One of their principal aims was the legalization of abortion. Already in 1967, Great Britain had legalized abortion under certain circumstances, including preserving the physical or mental health of the mother. Many other countries, including France and Italy, followed in the 1970s. In Spain, after Franco's death, the Parliament legalized contraception and adultery, which the law had previously forbidden.

Women's professional opportunities continued to expand, although unevenly across the Continent. By 1990, women constituted at least one-third of the members of Parliament in all of the Scandinavian states, but under 10 percent in France and Britain. In response, French feminists succeeded in passing a law, in 2000, mandating that political parties field equal numbers of male and female candidates in most elections or pay fines. The leading parties, however, often chose to pay the fines. In nearly every European country by the year 2000, women made up at least 40 percent of the labor force.

Also by the year 2000, laws against homosexual behavior had almost entirely vanished from the books in most of Europe. Homosexuals, while still disproportionately victims of hate crimes, achieved new levels of toleration and visibility. Prominent intellectuals and artists such as the philosopher Michel Foucault (1926–1984) and the singer Elton John (1947–) no longer hid their sexuality. In 1999, France allowed homosexual couples to enter into formal civil unions, but same-sex marriage would not receive acceptance in Europe until the twenty-first century.

EXTERNAL AND INTERNAL PRESSURES ON THE EASTERN BLOC

Even as these cultural differences between the Western and Eastern blocs were growing, their political relations were again turning confrontational. In the 1970s, following the end of the Vietnam War, U.S. president Richard Nixon had reached out to Communist China and also helped initiate a process of **détente** (relaxation of tension) with the Soviet Union. The two countries signed trade, sports, and arms control agreements and began to reduce their nuclear arsenals. Regular summits continued through the 1970s. But in 1979, the Soviet Union invaded Afghanistan on its southern border so as to shore up the wobbling new Communist government there, and quickly became embroiled in a costly struggle against Muslim insurgents. The U.S. government under President Jimmy Carter reacted strongly. It reinstated draft registration for young men, boycotted the 1980 Moscow Olympics, and moved ahead with a plan to station medium-range nuclear missiles in Great Britain and West Germany to counter the Soviet deployment of similar weapons.

RONALD REAGAN AND THE EUROPEAN PEACE MOVEMENT

In 1981, Ronald Reagan succeeded Carter as president. A long-time advocate of "rolling back" Communism rather than simply containing it, Reagan raised anxiety in much of Western Europe by denouncing the Soviet Union as an "evil empire," vastly increasing the U.S. defense budget, and providing substantial aid to the Afghan insurgents and to right-wing guerrillas in Central America. He also continued the deployment in Europe of medium-range missiles, which had the strong support of both the British and West German governments. Later in his term, he promoted the development of the so-called Star Wars missile shield to defend the United States against Soviet ballistic missile attacks.

The peace movement in Western Europe, which had declined after the end of the Vietnam War, quickly revived in response to these developments. In Britain, large anti-nuclear protest marches took place, and a permanent Women's Peace Camp was founded outside the gates of the Royal Air Force base at Greenham Common, one of the sites for the new missiles. In Germany, a powerful environmental movement, which had already spun off an important new political party known as the Greens, embraced the cause of nuclear disarmament and drew strength from it in turn. West German protest marches in the early 1980s attracted as many as a million people. Berlin, the focal point of Cold War tensions, ironically became the center of opposition to the missile deployment. In the West Berlin district of Kreuzberg, wedged up against the Berlin Wall, street murals portrayed Reagan as a cowboy with a giant missile protruding from his trousers,

while leaflets and posters claimed the deployment would lead to a devastating nuclear exchange on Western European soil. But in the end, the deployment took place.

DISSIDENT MOVEMENTS IN THE EAST

The peace movement had little equivalent on the other side of the iron curtain, despite the valiant attempts of some East German Lutheran churches to organize one. Instead, the most important political developments in the Eastern bloc during the 1970s involved the slow, halting revival of **dissident movements**. In 1974, the Soviet government sent its most prominent dissident writer, Solzhenitsyn (who had won the Nobel Prize for Literature in 1970), into exile abroad. Andrei Sakharov (1921–1989), a noted physicist and father of the Soviet hydrogen bomb, managed to avoid this fate, but his protests against the invasion of Afghanistan led to his arrest and internal exile. Sakharov's celebrity at least ensured him a measure of protection, but the secret police brutally hounded lesser-known dissidents, throwing thousands into labor camps or psychiatric hospitals. It also persecuted Russian Jews who were demanding the right to emigrate to Israel.

The Soviet satellite states, meanwhile, followed different courses on dissent. In Romania and Bulgaria, what little dissident activity that emerged was ruthlessly suppressed. In the former, party leader and president Nicolae Ceauşescu deliberately pursued a maverick, independent foreign policy, and in return the Western powers generally turned a blind eye to his increasingly baroque domestic tyranny. Like despots of legend, he razed large sections of Bucharest to build an elaborate palace for himself, while imposing drastic austerity policies on ordinary Romanians so as to pay off the country's foreign debt. He filled so many positions in the government with relatives that Romanians, referring to Stalin's slogan of "Socialism in a Single Country," joked that Ceauşescu wanted "Socialism in a Single Family."

The East German dissident movement remained weak as well, but for a different reason. After decades of relatively little official contact between the two Germanies, in the early 1970s West German chancellor Willy Brandt (1913–1992), on the view that both states would benefit from a stable relationship, began a series of cautious moves toward reconciliation and coexistence that came to be known as Ostpolitik ("East Policy"). By the early 1980s, West Germany's conservative Christian Democrats had come to agree, and in 1987 they even invited East German leader Erich Honecker (1912–1994) to visit his native

Greenham Common Members of the Women's Peace Camp at Greenham Common in 1983 participate in an "embrace the base" action, joining hands to encircle the perimeter of the Royal Air Force base. The colorful, hand-sewn banners on the fence became emblematic of the camp.

THE INDIVIDUAL AGAINST THE STATE

The social and cultural upheavals of the late twentieth century from both the left and the right emphasized the importance of individual freedom over the strictures of society and government. The economic malaise of the 1970s contributed to a questioning of the power of the state to manage the economy, helping lead to conservative governments in the West and contributing to the eventual collapse of Communism in the East. Dissident movements, such as the Czechoslovakian Charter 77 group led in part by future president Václav Havel, criticized Communist governments for betraying both individual freedoms and the ideals of socialism. Meanwhile, Margaret Thatcher led British Conservatives in attacking what they saw as state overreach and advocated a return to laissez-faire economic principles. Though differing in ideology, both movements aimed to prioritize the needs of the individual over state control.

Václav Havel, from "The Power of the Powerless"

In this passage from a 1978 essay, Havel describes the necessity of dissent within the Communist system.

A spectre is haunting eastern Europe: the spectre of what in the West is called "dissent." This spectre has not appeared out of thin air. It is a natural and inevitable consequence of the present historical phase of the system it is haunting.... The system has become so ossified politically that there is practically no way for such nonconformity to be implemented within its official structures....

...This is why life in the system is so thoroughly permeated with hypocrisy and lies: government by bureaucracy is called popular government; the working class is enslaved in the name of the working class; the complete degradation of the individual is presented as his or her ultimate liberation; depriving people of information is called making it available; the use of power to manipulate is called the public control of power, and the arbitrary abuse of power is called observing the legal code; the repression of culture is called its development; the expansion of imperial influence is presented as support for the oppressed; the lack of free expression becomes the highest form of freedom; farcical elections become the highest form of democracy; banning independent thought becomes the most scientific of world views; military occupation becomes fraternal assistance....

...If living within the truth is an elementary starting point for every attempt made by people to oppose the alienating pressure of the system, if it is the only meaningful basis of any independent act of political import...it is difficult to imagine that even manifest "dissent" could have any other basis than the service of truth, the truthful life and the attempt to make room for the genuine aims of life.

Margaret Thatcher, from "Speech in Finchley"

On May 2, 1979, Thatcher gave a speech to constituents in Finchley, the area of North London that she represented in Parliament. In this excerpt, she presents "independence of the individual" as a favorable alternative to the "big government" of the Labour Party.

...We stand for the independence of the individual, for the fundamental freedom of the individual....I've travelled many miles, visiting many constituencies, and we find everywhere we go that there is an overwhelming feeling throughout the country that it's time for a change. People say, "Look, we can't go on like this. We can't go on as we are. We don't like the decline in Britain. We don't like our neighbors overseas doing very much better than we are. We don't like it that Britain has fallen in the prestige of nations." And so frequently they say to me, "Give us back our national pride."...

...We must remember that Labour has ruled the country for eleven out of fifteen years....It's a philosophy of big government, big battalions, big taxation, big bureaucracy, until the individual says, "Goodness me, do I count for anything? Can I make any of my own decisions? Am I entitled to keep the fruits of my own labour in my own pocket to look after my own children?" And today, people long to be protected from the big battalions, and the world over there is a revolt against heavy taxation by government, there is a revolt against big government, and it is happening too in this country....

...Being Conservative, we found our policies on fundamental individual rights, the rights of families, the rights of men and women and their families, to lead their own lives in their own way with minimum interference by the state, but under a rule of law, under the firm protection of the government and the independence of the judges. So we see the process of recovery in Britain, the recovery of Britain, as the work of individuals.

QUESTIONS FOR ANALYSIS

1. According to Havel, why is dissent based in "the service of truth"?
2. According to Thatcher, how had the welfare state, as represented by the Labour Party, stifled the individual?
3. What are the similarities and differences between Havel's and Thatcher's interpretations of individual freedom?

Sources: Václav Havel, "The Power of the Powerless," trans. Paul Wilson, *International Journal of Politics* 15, no. 3/4 (London: 1985–1986), pp. 23, 30–31, 67; Margaret Thatcher, "Speech in Finchley" (May 2, 1979), Margaret Thatcher Foundation (website), www.margaretthatcher.org/document/104072.

western Germany. West Germany began to pay substantial sums to East Germany to "buy" dissidents and move them to the West, leaving relatively few opposition leaders behind the Wall for long.

In Hungary, and especially in Czechoslovakia, stronger dissident groups slowly emerged. They took particular advantage of the fact that in 1975 the Soviet bloc had joined with the Western states to sign the **Helsinki Accords**, pledging to respect current European borders—including the wartime Soviet annexations—but also fundamental human rights. Initially denounced by many Western conservatives as a propaganda victory for the Soviets, Helsinki in fact gave Eastern bloc dissidents a tool for holding their own governments to account. In January 1977, a group of dissidents in Czechoslovakia published a manifesto—soon called Charter 77—that denounced the Czech government for failing to live up to the Helsinki Accords. More broadly, the Accords marked a moment when states and international organizations increasingly oriented their foreign policies around issues of human rights, claiming the right to act on behalf of people throughout the world in the name of these rights.

"SOLIDARITY" IN POLAND

The biggest changes in the Soviet bloc took place in Poland. In 1976, large-scale protests forced the Communist government to repeal planned food price increases. Two years later, Polish cardinal Karol Wojtyła unexpectedly won election as Pope John Paul II (r. 1978–2005). A charismatic personality as well as a forceful theological conservative, John Paul drew huge, adoring crowds when he visited Poland in 1979, and he greatly strengthened the position of the Church as an autonomous force in Polish society.

These events emboldened ordinary Poles to defy the government, and in the summer of 1980, when the government attempted to raise the price of staple goods such as meat and gasoline, a wave of strikes broke out. In the port city of Gdańsk, striking shipbuilders formed a trade union they named **Solidarity**, led by a then-unknown electrician named Lech Wałęsa, and branches quickly spread across the country. The government retreated in disarray, and in November it tried to ease the ongoing unrest by giving Solidarity unofficial recognition. There followed thirteen astonishing months in which Solidarity, under Lech Wałęsa's charismatic leadership and in partnership with dissident intellectuals and a large section of the Polish clergy, effectively carved out a semi-free civil society in the middle of a Soviet satellite state.

Solidarity Lech Wałęsa takes up a microphone to address a crowd of workers during the shipyard strikes at Gdańsk in the summer of 1980.

All too aware of the suppression of reform movements in Hungary in 1956 and Czechoslovakia in 1968, the leaders of Solidarity proceeded with caution. They did not demand free elections or the dismantling of the socialist system. Nonetheless, the Communist authorities soon came to see the situation as dangerously unstable. General Wojciech Jaruzelski, who became prime minister in early 1981, felt that Solidarity would inevitably end up challenging Communist control and possibly provoke a Soviet invasion. To prevent this, in December 1981 his government outlawed the union, arrested its leaders, and imposed martial law. The crackdown engendered outrage in the West and contributed to increasing tensions between the blocs.

CRACKS IN THE EASTERN BLOC

By the mid-1980s, the rigidity of the Communist systems, to which the previous chapter already drew attention, had reached crisis proportions. In each of the Eastern European states, as in the USSR, the Communists had accomplished a rapid industrialization and urbanization of society. They had also managed to provide employment and basic services—including housing, health care, child care, elder care, and education—to virtually all their citizens. But they had proven unable to put in place the post-industrial shifts to a service and consumer economy that had taken place in the West. Inefficiency and corruption affected the distribution of even basic consumer goods, leading to endless lines for such commodities as bread, fruit, and toilet paper. While Eastern bloc

THE POWER OF LIPSTICK

In the 1970s and 1980s, chronic shortages and long lines for basic consumer goods were commonplace in Eastern Europe. Cosmetics and Western clothing were luxuries, difficult to obtain. In her essay "Make-Up and Other Crucial Questions" (1992), the Croatian journalist Slavenka Drakulić (1949–) describes the lengths to which Yugoslavian women went to appear fashionable, adding a personal dimension to the struggles of planned economies. Official Communist ideology dismissed consumerism as frivolous and decadent, yet, as Drakulić suggests, the wearing of lipstick or jeans could be integral to individual expression. And to present oneself as an individual in a collective state was not only difficult but potentially subversive. Drakulić blends a feminist critique of beauty standards for women with an observation of the Communist system, revealing the power of having control over one's own appearance.

The young communist states at that time— and until they ceased to exist—had more important tasks than producing make-up, tasks like rebuilding countries devastated by war, like industrialization and electrification. …Aesthetics were considered a superficial, "bourgeois" invention.…A nicely dressed woman was subject to suspicion, sometimes even investigation…

…Without a choice of cosmetics and clothes, with bad food and hard work and no spare time, it wasn't at all hard to create the special kind of uniformity that comes out of an equal distribution of poverty and the neglect of people's real needs. There was no chance for individualism—for women or men.…

To avoid uniformity, you have to work very hard: you have to bribe a salesgirl, wait in line for some imported product, buy bluejeans on the black market and pay your whole month's salary for them; you have to hoard cloth and sew it, imitating the pictures in glamorous foreign magazines.…To be yourself, to cultivate individualism, to perceive yourself as an individual in a mass society, is dangerous. You might become living proof that the system is failing. Make-up and fashion are crucial because they are political.…

Walking the streets of Eastern European cities, one can easily see that women there look tired and older than they really are. They are poorly dressed, overweight, and flabby. Only the very young are slim and beautiful, with the healthy look and grace that go with youth. For me, they are the most beautiful in the world because I know what is behind the serious, worried faces, the unattended hair, the unmanicured nails; behind a pale pink lipstick that doesn't exactly go with the color of their eyes, or hair, or dress.…They deserve more respect than they get, simply because just being a woman—not to mention a beauty—is a constant battle against the way the whole system works.

QUESTIONS FOR ANALYSIS

1. Why are such seemingly inconsequential goods as lipstick and blue jeans so important to the women of Eastern Europe, according to Drakulić?
2. How does Drakulić both celebrate and critique the pursuit of fashion?
3. What did women risk in being seen as too fashionable?

Source: Slavenka Drakulić, *How We Survived Communism and Even Laughed* (London: 1992), pp. 22–23, 26, 31–32.

---

consumers did gradually begin to acquire products like televisions and automobiles, they often had to wait years and paid a far higher percentage of their salaries for them than their Western counterparts did.

In their intensive pursuit of industrialization, the Eastern bloc states also ravaged the environment. In Slovakia, by the early 1980s nearly half the rivers were dangerously polluted. In the Soviet Union, the diversion of rivers to provide irrigation for industrial-scale agriculture literally dried up the Aral Sea, which eventually shrank to less than 10 percent of its original size—an unprecedented ecological disaster. In Poland, factories in the new industrial city of Nowa Huta pumped vast quantities of unfiltered smoke and gas into the air, much of it settling on neighboring

Environmental Devastation By the 1990s, much of the Aral Sea had disappeared as a result of Soviet irrigation projects. Here abandoned ships sit rusting on a dry, deserted former seabed.

bloc in the 1980s through its aggressive strategic moves and strong rhetoric. Most give particular credit to Soviet leader **Mikhail Gorbachev** and the policies of liberalization that he set in motion. In the words of the historian Tony Judt: "It was Mr. Gorbachev's revolution."

In fact, these various factors all worked together. The dissidents, by themselves, could never have overturned powerful police states. Yet their activities did more than anything else to discredit these states and to dramatize the need for reform—including to Gorbachev. The U.S. government's military buildup of the 1980s did not, by itself, push the Soviet Union to the breaking point, but it did help convince Gorbachev that his country could not compete with the United States without undergoing fundamental changes. Gorbachev himself did not set out to destroy the system—far from it. But without him, the events of 1989–91 would have been inconceivable.

Cracow, where the facades of beautiful early modern buildings crumbled and turned black from the pollution.

These failures caused support for Communist regimes to fall to the lowest levels ever, which only increased their political rigidity. Communist elites, desperate to stay in power, continued to deny the population both elementary freedoms and the rule of law. Rigged elections routinely ended with 98 percent of the votes supposedly cast for the same slate of career officials. Secret police forces no longer murdered on a vast scale, as in Stalin's USSR, but they could still prove enormously oppressive, and not just toward dissidents. The East German Stasi, or state security service, had some 85,000 employees, who in turn worked with over 650,000 collaborators and informers of various sorts. Altogether, they kept files on 6 million people—one-third of the East German population. Co-workers and neighbors routinely informed on each other, and in some cases so did family members, even spouses.

THE COLLAPSE OF COMMUNISM

The reasons for the collapse of the Communist system are still the subject of lively debate. With hindsight, historians recognize the system's weakness, but they also argue that the repressive state apparatuses of the Soviet bloc, combined with sheer inertia, could have kept the system going for decades more. Why did it fall apart when it did, and so quickly? Some scholars single out the heroic role of dissidents. Others credit the pressure that the administration of U.S. president Ronald Reagan put on the Eastern

NEW SOVIET LEADERSHIP: MIKHAIL GORBACHEV

In the early 1980s, the Soviet Union's decay seemed to express itself most directly in its leadership. Leonid Brezhnev, an aged and infirm seventy-five, died in 1982. He

Reagan and Gorbachev U.S. president Ronald Reagan looks on as Soviet leader Mikhail Gorbachev makes a speech at the signing of a treaty to reduce nuclear armaments, on December 8, 1987.

was succeeded as general secretary of the Communist Party by the sixty-eight-year old Yuri Andropov, a former head of the KGB. Three months later, Andropov's kidneys failed, and he spent most of the next year in the hospital before dying in early 1984. The leadership then fell to the seventy-three-year-old Constantin Chernenko, who also lasted barely a year in the job, much of it in the hospital.

Upon Chernenko's death, a long-awaited generational shift finally took place with the rise to power of Mikhail Gorbachev (1931–). Then just age fifty-four, Gorbachev, from Stavropol in southern Russia, had moved steadily up in the Soviet apparatus since obtaining a law degree from Moscow State University in 1955, gaining a reputation for energy and intelligence. As he rose, the failings of the system became all too clear to him; but on becoming general secretary his immediate goal was to reform the Soviet Union and make it more competitive with the West, not to change it radically. As the Yugoslav dissident Milovan Djilas wrote about him: "Gorbachev, unlike Brezhnev, strikes me as a true believer." His first major initiative was an attack on the perennial Russian phenomenon of alcoholism, in the hope of increasing productivity. He began to develop a program he would later call **perestroika**, or "restructuring"—in this case, of Soviet society and government.

Yet events quickly convinced him of the need for more dramatic action. In April 1986, a nuclear power plant in **Chernobyl** (Soviet Ukraine) suffered meltdown, releasing huge quantities of radiation into the atmosphere, hundreds of times more than the Hiroshima atomic bomb. Scores died, hundreds suffered severe radiation poisoning, over 130,000 were evacuated from the region, and the plant itself had to be encased in a thick shell of concrete. Reports widely attributed the accident to incompetent management, and Gorbachev was reported to have told his wife, the same evening: "We cannot go on like this." Two and a half years later, a horrific earthquake in Soviet Armenia killed at least 25,000 people; their deaths mostly resulted from the widespread collapse of shoddily constructed buildings. Meanwhile, the war in Afghanistan, increasingly called the Soviet Union's Vietnam, dragged on, with the Soviet forces no more able than the British in the nineteenth century to suppress Afghan resistance, despite a massive deployment of personnel. And the Soviet economy, which had become increasingly dependent on oil revenue, was suffering from falling oil prices.

Gorbachev still resisted any major retreat from Communist central planning, concentrating instead on

Chernobyl An aerial photograph shows a cloud of smoke rising from the rubble of the Chernobyl nuclear reactor after the meltdown in April 1986.

political changes. For the first time since Lenin's early days in power, the government encouraged public debate and criticism under the banner of **glasnost** ("openness"). It eased up on the persecution of dissidents, and at the end of 1986 allowed the dissident physicist Andrei Sakharov to return to Moscow. It rehabilitated Stalin's most prominent purge victims and cancelled high school history exams because textbooks could not keep up with the rapidly changing past. By 1988, Gorbachev was experimenting with limited free enterprise in services and small-scale manufacturing. In foreign policy, he forged a surprisingly cordial relationship with President Reagan and negotiated the most important nuclear arms reductions since the start of the Cold War. A 1987 treaty led to the elimination of thousands of intermediate-range nuclear missiles, and the START treaty—which Gorbachev signed with Reagan's successor, George H. W. Bush, in 1991—set a ceiling on the total number of warheads each side could possess. Throughout the reform process, Gorbachev remained confident about keeping it under control. As one of his deputies remarked, after implementing a measure that removed decades-old controls on the Russian Orthodox Church: "Since the power belongs completely to us, I think we are capable of pointing this track in whatever direction is to our interest." In fact, nothing could have been further from the truth.

Collapse of the Eastern Bloc, 1989–1990 One Communist government after another collapsed quickly in the summer and fall of 1989: in Poland, Hungary, Czechoslovakia, Bulgaria, Romania, and East Germany. The Berlin Wall fell in November. Within two years, the Soviet Union and Yugoslavia would experience not only the fall of communism but also the breakup of thier multi-national states.

THE END OF COMMUNISM IN POLAND AND HUNGARY

The most immediate challenge to the system did not come from Gorbachev himself, but from men and women far from Moscow who were encouraged by glasnost and perestroika to push a radical agenda. These men and women were located in the satellite states and also, increasingly, in the constituent republics of the USSR itself. As the grip of the Communist Party loosened, the idea that non-Russian nationalities in the USSR might achieve a greater degree of autonomy—perhaps even independence—suddenly seemed possible. Movements began to form first in the

Baltic states, annexed by Stalin only in 1940. They were then copied elsewhere, including in the six Muslim republics that lay to the south of Russia.

But Soviet control first cracked in what was still called Eastern Europe—a label the Czech dissidents in particular strongly rejected, feeling that they belonged to the heartland of the Continent, Central Europe. On December 7, 1988, Gorbachev spoke before the United Nations in New York and effectively renounced the "Brezhnev doctrine" by which the USSR had reserved the right to keep its satellite states in check by force, as in Czechoslovakia in 1968. In Hungary, the speech gave new confidence and energy to a reform movement that was developing within the Communist Party there. Its new leadership had already moved to legalize opposition movements, authorize free trade unions, and free the press. Now it began to move toward free elections.

The Poles then raced ahead of Hungary. Throughout the late 1980s, the government of General Jaruzelski had struggled without success against a continuing economic crisis. The cause was, above all, Poland's massive foreign debt to the Western countries, which the government had incurred in order to revamp Polish industry and purchase consumer goods. As the inflation rate rose steeply, approaching 1,000 percent in early 1989, labor protests again spread across the country. In desperation, the government entered into negotiations with the banned Solidarity union, leading to the legalization of free trade unions, economic reforms in favor of private enterprise, and partially free elections to be held in June.

These elections effectively marked the demise of Communism in Poland, as Solidarity won all but one of the freely contested seats. From Moscow, Gorbachev indicated his acceptance of the result, and in September 1989 a non-Communist prime minister took power in Poland for the first time since the 1940s. His government immediately began planning for full parliamentary democracy and a transition from Communism to a free-market economy. The handover took place with remarkable smoothness, not least because of the enormous restraint shown by the leaders of Solidarity. In part, Lech Wałęsa and his supporters still feared the possibility of Soviet military intervention, but more broadly these workers and intellectuals wanted to break with an older model of European political change. As the dissident intellectual Jacek Kuroń explained in an article for a French newspaper, what was happening in Poland was *not* a revolution. Revolutions, he insisted, with pointed reference to the bicentennial of the French Revolution of 1789 then being celebrated in Paris, involved too much bloodshed. The age of revolutions was over.

The Hungarian leadership practiced the same restraint. Free elections did not come to Hungary until the spring of 1990, but already in 1989 the Hungarian Communist Party gave up its formal "leading role" in the state, adopted a new constitution with a Bill of Rights modeled on that of the United States, and began planning for the transition to free-market democracy. Its loss of power was already a certainty. The Hungarians carried out another momentous change by removing the electrified fences that had lined its border with Austria. Now Hungarians—and also the citizens of any Eastern bloc country who could travel freely to Hungary—could cross into the West without hindrance.

EAST GERMANY AND THE FALL OF THE BERLIN WALL

The events in Hungary sparked the next major phase of the collapse of Communism. East Germans did not need visas to visit Hungary, and during the summer and early fall of 1989 tens of thousands of them traveled there and simply walked into the West. Tens of thousands more sought refuge in West Germany's embassies in Budapest and Prague. In East Germany itself, dissidents founded an opposition group called New Forum. Encouraged by clear signals of support from Gorbachev, street demonstrations swelled in Berlin and Leipzig, with hundreds of thousands of protestors chanting the slogan "We are the people." Younger Communists forced the elderly party leader Erich Honecker out of office and announced a program of cautious reforms—but these came far too late.

On November 9, in a last attempt to stabilize the situation, the new leaders announced that East Germans could now freely travel into West Germany. At a news conference, an official was asked when the new law would take effect, and, taken off guard, he replied: "immediately." Within hours, huge crowds had converged on the Berlin Wall from both sides. East German border guards, trained to kill anyone who crossed without authorization, stood by in confusion as tens of thousands of East Germans simply walked past them, or climbed up on the Wall in wild celebration, or started to dig into it with hammers and chisels. Fifty thousand East Berliners, most of whom had never seen the Western city that lay just yards away, ambled in delight past the brightly lit, well-stocked storefronts of West Berlin. Televised images of the event spread instantly around the entire world. Commentators correctly interpreted it as Communism's death knell.

CZECHOSLOVAKIA, ROMANIA, AND BULGARIA

With the Wall in ruins, the collapse of Communism in the three other satellite states became a foregone conclusion. True, Czechoslovakia, Romania, and Bulgaria did not have religious and independent organizations like Solidarity that were united in defiance of the Communists, as Poland did. They did not have a reforming Communist Party, as Hungary did. And they did not have a sister state in the West to escape to, as East Germans did. But their regimes had no more support from the population than in those three countries, and it had now become obvious that without support from Moscow, Communist regimes simply could not remain standing.

In Czechoslovakia, where memories of pre-war democracy and of the abortive 1968 experiment with "socialism with a human face" were strong, massive demonstrations quickly began. Veteran dissidents, led by the charismatic **Václav Havel** (1936–2011), a playwright and philosopher who had criticized the regime in absurdist plays and taken on a leading role in Charter 77, founded a broad-based opposition movement called the Civic Forum. On December 10, 1989, as demonstrations swelled, the Czech Communist leaders simply gave up and resigned in favor of a new largely non-Communist government, which Havel would soon head as president. The events had taken place in so quick, nonviolent, and smooth a manner that they were soon dubbed the **Velvet Revolution**.

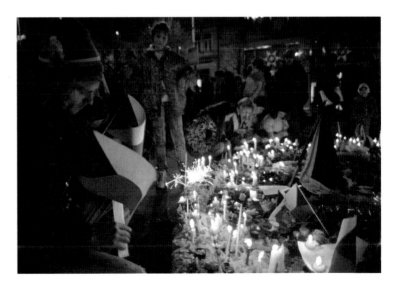

Velvet Revolution Attendees at a vigil in Prague in 1989 light candles and display Czech flags. Such gatherings were typical of the peaceful demonstrations that accompanied the transfer of power in Czechoslovakia.

The transition in Romania was also quick, but in no way nonviolent or smooth. In November, the megalomaniacal Nicolae Ceauşescu could still count on some sixty-seven standing ovations from Party members after his reelection to the office of secretary general. But on December 21, the previously unthinkable happened: during a public speech Ceauşescu was openly booed by protestors, and he visibly faltered as if struck. The next day he fled the capital, while a group from within the government hastily announced the formation of a National Salvation Front. Scores died in street battles that broke out in Bucharest between its supporters and members of Ceauşescu's hated secret police, the Securitate. Ceauşescu himself was captured, hastily tried, and executed by firing squad, along with his wife. During the same period, Todor Zhivkov, longest serving of the East European leaders, fell from office in neighboring Bulgaria. The last Communist "domino," non-aligned Albania, turned out the Communists in 1990–91.

THE "THIRD WAY" REJECTED

Although the formal Warsaw Pact treaty organization would last until 1991, the Eastern bloc had effectively ceased to exist by 1990. American policy-makers had long warned of a domino effect in which the fall of one country to Communism might lead its neighbors to suffer the same fate. But in the end it was the fall of Communism that offered the most dramatic example of the domino effect in the twentieth century. The only real question, by the end of 1989, concerned what path the newly liberated satellite states would follow. Would they simply join the Western bloc and move as rapidly as possible to duplicate its political and economic systems? Or would they attempt to find a "third way" between socialism and capitalism, preserving the state ownership of industry and a comprehensive social welfare system while introducing democracy and limited markets?

Despite the hopes of some intellectuals on both sides of the Continent, the answer was a resounding endorsement of Western European free-market democracy and a decision to erase the Communist past. Solidarity leader Lech Wałęsa made this erasure dramatically clear when, in late 1990, he became president of Poland. Rather than accept the seals of office from his predecessor, General Jaruzelski, he reached out to the Polish government-in-exile in London, which had carried on a lonely and mostly ignored existence since it had refused to accept the Communist government in the late 1940s. Throughout the bloc, and most thoroughly in Czechoslovakia, anyone involved with

the Communist secret services was banned from holding public office. Wałęsa, Havel, and most of the other new Eastern European leaders, who were by no means Thatcherites, wanted to retain strong social services. But they also believed that the path to Western levels of prosperity demanded mainly free markets and the private ownership of most of the economy.

THE REUNIFICATION OF GERMANY

The Germans, meanwhile, took the idea of a return to the past to its logical conclusion: a reunification of Germany. Even before the fall of the Wall, it was already being asked whether the small East German state (population 17 million) could possibly survive on its own as a democracy, or whether it would inevitably merge with its much larger Western neighbor (population 61 million). Erich Honecker's battered successors pushed for a "third way" and were joined, ironically, by many former dissident intellectuals, who had resisted emigration to the West and remained committed to socialism in some form. But a far larger number of East Germans simply wanted the freedom and prosperity of West Germany, as fast as possible. After the Wall came down in 1989, street demonstrations continued, but now the slogan "We Are the People" pointedly became "We Are One People." In March 1990, elections took place, and supporters of reunification won a decisive victory over the newly reformed Communists. The dissidents' New Forum received just 2.8 percent.

It was West German chancellor Helmut Kohl who, above all others, brought about unification. Kohl, a Christian Democrat from the Rhineland, feared that if unification did not take place quickly, it might never come about at all. The former World War II Allies, still nervous about a united, powerful Germany, might block it, or the East Germans themselves might grow reluctant. So Kohl pushed reunification through at breakneck speed, committing the West German state and economy to vast expenditures in the process and risking massive social disruptions in the East. To ensure their support, he allowed East Germans to convert large sums of their nearly worthless currency to solid West German deutsche marks at a rate of 1:1. To assuage the Soviets, he agreed to over $100 billion in direct transfers to their ailing economy. He also won over the Western allies by raising the prospect that anything other than speedy unification might eventually threaten the position of West Germany in NATO. When the American negotiators, President George H. W. Bush and his secretary of state, James Baker, promised that NATO would now become more of a political than a military alliance, Mikhail Gorbachev conceded that a united Germany could be part of NATO.

Under the treaty of unification in September 1990, Berlin finally lost the status of occupied city. The Soviets withdrew the 360,000 soldiers they still had stationed on East German soil. In October, unification formally took place. The Berlin Wall had already become a tourist attraction, with chunks sold off to adorn bookshelves and mantelpieces around the world.

THE END OF THE SOVIET EMPIRE

Less than two months after the fall of the Berlin Wall, a smaller but deeply symbolic event took place on Pushkin Square in the center of Moscow: the opening of a McDonald's restaurant. In order to ensure reliable supplies of beef and potatoes to its new Russian outpost, the company involved itself in every aspect of the food's production and distribution, from field and feedlot to cash register. It also charged higher prices than most competing restaurants. Nonetheless, it was immediately overrun with customers and for years remained one of the busiest McDonald's in the world. Some Soviet citizens craved this literal taste of the West so badly that they had Big Macs flash-frozen in Moscow and shipped by air as far as Vladivostok.

The opening of the restaurant raised the question of whether the USSR, too, could transform itself from an authoritarian state with a command economy into a democracy that allowed the operation of free markets. The hurdles were certainly much greater. In the former Eastern bloc, where the very different pre-war political systems were still part of living memory, Communism could be conveniently stigmatized as an alien imposition. In the USSR, however, Communism not only was home-grown but had been searingly affirmed by the massive sacrifices and ultimate victory of what Russians called the Great Patriotic War against Hitler. In the USSR, no one under age eighty had much recollection of any other sort of social system—and while the Russia of the tsars had permitted private enterprise, it had been no democracy. Soviet society was firmly organized along collectivist lines, with the result that an independent restaurant like McDonald's could not even count on getting a reliable supply of high-grade potatoes from Soviet farms without its own close supervision.

Free Market in Moscow Crowds pack Russia's first McDonald's as supervisors train the cashiers in taking orders shortly after the restaurant's opening in 1990.

NATIONALIST CHALLENGES

Yet even as the Soviet leadership started to grapple with these issues, it was increasingly distracted by the challenge of nationalism. In 1987, Mikhail Gorbachev had unwisely boasted: "We can truly say that for our country the nationalities issue has been resolved." But dreams of independence were already stirring in the Baltic states, encouraged by the collapse of Communism in Eastern Europe. In August 1989, as many as 1.8 million people—one-quarter of the combined populations of Estonia, Latvia, and Lithuania—formed a human chain through the three republics in a demonstration in favor of the republics' independence. In March 1990, the Lithuanian Supreme Soviet unanimously voted to secede and restore the country's pre-war constitution, although it hesitated to implement its decision.

And this nationalist unrest eventually reached into all the republics of the USSR. In the south, it affected Armenia and Georgia, which possessed strong national cultures and a long history of conflict with Russia. It affected Ukraine, which most Russians viewed as the birthplace of their own nation. The eastern half of Ukraine was predominantly Russian in ethnicity, language, and religion; its western half, much of it annexed from Poland during the war, was predominantly Ukrainian in language and ethnicity, and Catholic or other non-Orthodox Christian in religion. The nationalist upsurge even affected Byelorussia, which had never seriously aspired to independent status. And it affected the Muslim republics of Central Asia.

NATIONALISM IN PERSPECTIVE This apparently sudden emergence of nationalism, both in the USSR and beyond, needs some explanation. As we have seen, nationalism, which mostly began to take shape in Europe in the late eighteenth and early nineteenth centuries, had remained a potent political force throughout the twentieth century. It had driven the breakup of the Austro-Hungarian and Ottoman Empires after World War I, and the near breakup of the Russian Empire at the same time. It provided the pretext for Hitler's aggression in the 1930s and shaped the process of decolonization after World War II. But the Cold War, and the division of the Continent into two opposing camps, had muted its presence in Europe between 1945 and 1989.

Commentators in the 1990s overwhelmingly treated nationalism as a timeless, somewhat archaic phenomenon. They therefore interpreted its resurgence as the expression of "ancient" or "natural" ethnic sentiments that Communism had supposedly "frozen" and "suppressed" but that were now bursting out from under its melting ice. Yet there was nothing ancient or natural about nationalism. And the USSR, far from suppressing national identifications, had encouraged them as a means of placating its many non-Russian minorities and managing its vast, multicultural territory. It required that every citizen have a formal nationality, and it divided its territory along national lines, both on the scale of the Union and also within some of its constituent republics.

RUSSIAN NATIONALISM In fact, it was precisely these Soviet policies that helped drive the reassertion of nationalism when central authority in the USSR began to weaken. Until the very end, with the exception of the Baltic states, national independence movements gained relatively little popular support, even in the Muslim republics that bordered Afghanistan. In March 1991, Gorbachev sponsored a Union-wide referendum on whether the USSR should be preserved, and over 70 percent of participants voted yes. In some of the Muslim republics, the figure topped 90 percent. But as central government authority diminished, leaders of the dominant ethnic groups in the non-Russian republics feared challenges to their own privileged positions, both from above (Moscow) and from below (their own ethnic minorities). These fears were reasonable, since each republic was itself a mosaic of ethnic groups, with the largest minority, in most cases, being Russians who had settled there since 1917. In Baltic Latvia, for example, only 54 percent of the population was ethnically Latvian. In these circumstances, members of the different groups quickly started to embrace nationalist ideas, reviving or inventing ethnic traditions as a way to preserve or enhance the status quo.

Nationalism of this sort even emerged in Russia itself. The Russian Federation (RSFSR), which extended from Kaliningrad (the former German city of Königsberg) on the Baltic to Vladivostok on the Pacific, was by far the largest constituent republic in terms of surface area. Its 148 million people made up more than half of the Soviet population. In the period of glasnost and perestroika, Russian opponents of the regime found it increasingly useful to stoke nostalgia for pre-Soviet political forms and symbols—which meant Russian national ones. Peter the Great's red, white, and blue Russian flag, almost entirely forgotten, began to reappear in opposition marches, as did symbols of the long-dead tsarist family, the Romanovs.

Politically, the key advocate of Russian anti-Soviet nationalism was **Boris Yeltsin** (1931–2007), a strong-willed, impulsive, career Communist whom Gorbachev had initially treated as a protégé and appointed both to the Politburo and to head the Communist Party in Moscow. In 1987, after Yeltsin publicly denounced the slow pace of reforms, Gorbachev demoted him. But as central party control over Soviet elections declined, Yeltsin won an office in the Congress of People's Deputies, and then in the spring of 1990 he became chair of the Presidium of the Russian Federation's Supreme Soviet. He then led the RSFSR to declare the supremacy of its laws over those of the USSR, setting up a potential constitutional crisis.

THE CRISIS OF 1990–1991

Throughout late 1990 and early 1991, these nationalist tensions continued to grow, and Gorbachev's authority withered. In January 1991, an attempt to restore central authority in the Baltics led to serious bloodshed, including fourteen dead in the Lithuanian capital of Vilnius. Some 150,000 people marched in Moscow to protest, and Yeltsin defiantly signed bilateral agreements with the Baltic states, recognizing their sovereignty in the name of Russia. Desperately, Gorbachev staged the referendum on the preservation of the Union and then promulgated a new USSR constitution that gave republics the right of secession. In June 1991, in the first free elections ever held for a Russian leader, Yeltsin won the presidency of the RSFSR. The USSR now seemed on the brink of chaos.

At this point, far too late, conservatives within the Communist Party finally decided it was time to overthrow Gorbachev and restore the Soviet system in its entirety. On August 19, 1991, after the Soviet leader had left for his

Boris Yeltsin During the August 1991 coup led by the Emergency Committee, Yeltsin (center) stands on a tank and speaks to reporters in front of the Russian Parliament building.

annual vacation in the Crimea, a self-styled Emergency Committee in Moscow that included the prime minister, the defense minister, and the head of the KGB demanded that Gorbachev surrender his powers to them. He refused angrily, upon which they declared him incapacitated for reasons of health, and announced a state of emergency. They gave out extra pay to all KGB personnel and prepared for wide-scale arrests.

In Moscow, Yeltsin condemned the coup and called for a general strike to support Gorbachev. Ordinary Muscovites immediately flocked to the Russian Parliament building (the "White House") and started to build barricades around it. Yeltsin himself gave interviews to the foreign press while standing atop a tank. The stage was set for a violent conflict. But it never came, owing above all to the farcical incompetence of the coup plotters, at least one of whom allegedly spent most of the crucial period in an alcoholic stupor. The armed forces, rather than rallying to the conservatives, vacillated. Estonia and Latvia joined Lithuania in declaring full independence from the USSR. Yeltsin remained defiant, in full view of the world media, and collected expressions of support from world leaders. After just four days, the plotters gave up and submitted to arrest. One of them committed suicide.

Gorbachev himself quickly returned to Moscow and tried to regain the initiative by suspending the Communist Party. But the coup had already effectively completed the USSR's dissolution. Over the next month, the remaining Soviet republics declared independence, often with long-standing local Communist Party leaders reinventing themselves as anti-Soviet nationalists. The Russian

Federation asserted control of state institutions on Russian soil and gave Leningrad back its original name of Saint Petersburg. In October, the KGB was formally abolished. And in December, the leaders of Russia, Ukraine, and Belarus met in Minsk to propose the formal end of the Union and its replacement by a loose Commonwealth of Independent States. Gorbachev protested and blustered, yet ultimately he had no choice but to agree to the dramatic end of a process that he himself had set in motion. On December 31, 1991, the Soviet Union ceased to exist.

And so, between 1989 and 1991 the borders of Europe, seemingly set in stone by the Cold War, shifted again. The three Baltic states of Lithuania, Latvia, and Estonia that had existed between the wars came back into being. New independent states of Ukraine, Belarus, Moldova, Georgia, Armenia, and Azerbaijan were created and received international recognition, as did the former Soviet republics in Central Asia. The Russian Empire, of which the Soviet Union had been the inheritor, finally ceased to exist.

Communism was simultaneously disappearing as a worldwide force. In China during the 1980s, although the Communist Party remained in power under the leadership of Deng Xiaoping (1904-1997), it abandoned its earlier ideology almost completely and embraced private enterprise. The Southeast Asian states moved away from Communism as well. At the end of the century, only Cuba and North Korea still retained the communist systems they had developed during the Cold War.

"RETURNING TO EUROPE"

Despite the theatrics around the August 1991 coup in Russia and the violence in the Baltics, the USSR met its end in what was, by historical standards, a remarkably orderly manner. Never before in history had such a large, multinational empire come to an end with so little loss of life. Credit belonged in the first place to Gorbachev and Yeltsin, who both behaved with considerable restraint. The Western alliance offered support where possible and otherwise refrained from counterproductive interference. But above all, the peaceful transition showed that in a crucial respect Russia and its neighbors, too, were finally, in a phrase much used in these countries at the time, "returning to Europe." Just as the Western European nations had lived in peaceful coexistence since 1945, so in 1989–91 the nations of the USSR showed themselves ready to observe the same standards.

As a result, the period's surge of nationalism played itself out in a very different manner from earlier periods.

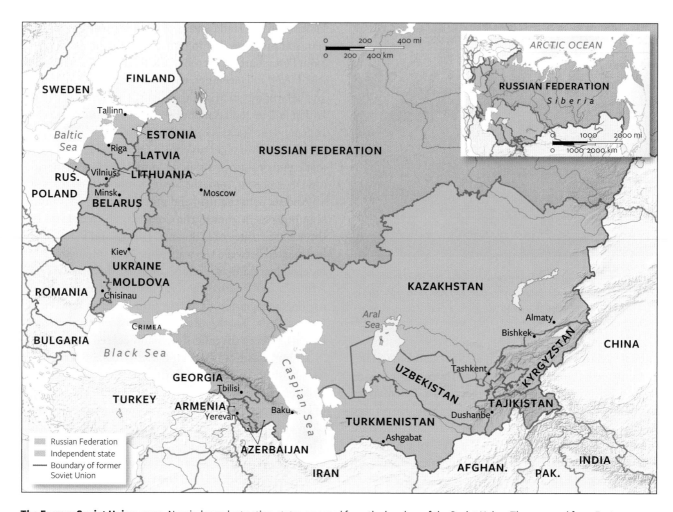

The Former Soviet Union, 1992 New independent nation-states emerged from the breakup of the Soviet Union. These ranged from Eastern European countries like Estonia and Lithuania to those in central Asia bordering China, like Kazakhstan and Kyrgyzstan. The largest new state was the Russian Federation, itself experiencing resurgent nationalism and covering a vast territory.

The existence of large Russian minorities throughout the former Soviet republics did not lead to wide-scale violence or the readjustment of borders (although such violence would occur much later in Ukraine). Even newly independent Moldova, which had never existed as a state of its own and which had deep historical and linguistic ties to neighboring Romania, remained separate. One reason, tellingly, was that if Romania remained desperately poor by Western European standards, Moldova made it look rich in comparison, and few Romanians wanted the burden of absorbing their impoverished cousins. In this corner of the Balkans, as in most of the Continent, the desire for peace and prosperity outweighed national longings.

In the early 1990s, the same logic governed the development of nationalism elsewhere on the Continent. Slovakia and the Czech Republic parted ways without violence—the Velvet Revolution giving way to a Velvet Divorce. And

the example of nationalist success in the former Eastern bloc encouraged renewed pushes for autonomy in areas of Western Europe as well. In Italy, northerners angry at the central government for decades of subsidies to the southern part of the country founded a party called the Lombard League to push for autonomy or even independence. Belgium at several moments seemed ready to split between Flemish-speakers and French-speakers, who worked out ever more complex arrangements for sharing power. In Spain, the Catalans and Basques pressed successfully for a greater degree of local authority. In Great Britain, Scotland gained a Parliament of its own with significant control over education, health, and the justice system, while Wales obtained a less powerful local assembly (these reforms went by the name "devolution"). And in Northern Ireland, protracted negotiations brokered by American senator George Mitchell finally produced an uneasy settlement, the renunciation of violence by the Irish Republican Army, and the establishment of a new Assembly in Belfast, giving the province a degree of political autonomy. The violence that had begun in the late 1960s finally petered out.

The apparent consensus around peace, democracy, and a limited free-market economy was so striking that as early as 1989, the American political scientist Francis Fukuyama could publish an influential article predicting not just the end of empire but "the end of history." By this, he essentially meant an end to conflicts over the proper form of society. As more and more countries agreed that their societies should take the form of representative democracies with limited free markets, their public lives would supposedly turn increasingly dull, with technocrats tinkering with the universally accepted mechanisms for social development rather than ideologues engaging in dramatic struggles. Other social scientists amplified the message, arguing that since democracies (supposedly) did not go to war with one another, the spread of democracy would bring about an age of universal, perpetual peace.

But events did not work out as predicted. Even as the United States drew down its forces in Europe, it was increasingly drawn into conflicts in the Middle East. In 1990–91, it fought its first war since Vietnam, in alliance with several Arab countries, to liberate Kuwait, which Iraqi dictator Saddam Hussein had invaded. And in one corner of Europe, the 1990s saw the worst violence on European soil since World War II. Commentators mostly blamed it on the new nationalism that had burst out following the collapse of Communism. But most of the bloodshed occurred between warring religious groups as well as national ones. The fault line that now threatened the peace of Europe was the divide between Christianity and Islam, along which history returned to the Continent with a vengeance.

THE NEW BALKAN WARS

For much of the forty years after World War II, Yugoslavia, by the standards of Communist Europe, was a success story. Tito, its leader until his death in 1980, ruled with a relatively light hand after breaking with Moscow at the start of the Cold War. He allowed Yugoslavs to travel freely and permitted a wider range of political and cultural expression within the country than his Communist neighbors did. Economically, he broke with the prevailing Eastern bloc model of centralization by experimenting with various forms of worker self-management. And he

helped ensure a degree of coexistence among the country's principal ethnic groups (Serbs, Croats, Slovenes, Bosnian Muslims, Macedonians, Hungarians, and Albanians) by dividing the spoils of government among them and harshly repressing nationalist movements that threatened the arrangement. Intermarriage increased, and with each census a larger share of the population—although still a minority—described themselves simply as "Yugoslav."

YUGOSLAVIA'S COLLAPSE

Still, there were tensions within this composite state, assembled in 1919 after the peace conference at Versailles. The relatively wealthy Slovenes, who had once belonged to Austria and still considered themselves the efficient "Germans of Yugoslavia," resented subsidizing the poorer areas of the south. With just 8 percent of the population, Slovenia produced 29 percent of the country's exports, while the predominantly Albanian autonomous region of Kosovo, with the same-size population, produced 1 percent. Citizens of Serbia, with its powerful nationalist traditions dating to before World War I, resented the fact that despite having the most populous of the six Yugoslav republics and two autonomous regions, the 1974 constitution gave them no more representation in the federal government than tiny Montenegro, with barely one-tenth the population.

Tensions also arose over the boundaries of Yugoslavia's republics and regions, which were mostly derived from nineteenth-century international borders rather than the actual distribution of ethnic groups. Nearly 3 million Serbs lived outside the borders of Serbia. Yugoslavia's religious divisions compounded these tensions. In the regions ruled longest by the Ottoman Empire, Bosnians and Albanians had largely embraced Islam. In return, they had received favors from the Turks, which heightened the resentment felt toward them by the Serbs. Croats and Slovenes were largely Catholic; Serbs, Montenegrins, and Macedonians were largely Orthodox. The combination was potentially explosive.

After Tito's death, the system lumbered on for another eight years, even as the country's huge foreign debt triggered a powerful economic crisis. But by the mid-1980s, the simmering resentments had become more vocal, and the Serbs in particular began to push for a greater influence over federal affairs. In 1986, a memorandum of the Serbian Academy of Sciences and Arts stirred controversy by accusing Slovenes and Croats of systematic oppression and denouncing the genocide of Serbs by the Albanian majority in the region of Kosovo. The site of an

Yugoslavia, 1988–2000 When the composite state of Yugoslavia collapsed in 1991, Slovenia and Macedonia were able to establish their independence quickly. But Serbia responded to the secession of Croatia, and especially of Bosnia-Herzegovina, with bloody and drawn-out conflict.

epic Serbian defeat at Turkish hands in 1389, Kosovo had strong symbolic value for Serbs, many of whom liked to see themselves as the vanguard protecting Christendom from Muslim invaders. The Academy's sentiments were tacitly encouraged by Slobodan Milošević, a fierce nationalist and ambitious Serbian politician who became president of the republic in 1988. Within a year, he destroyed Yugoslavia's constitutional stability by eliminating the autonomy of the regions of Kosovo and Vojvodina within Serbia—thereby increasing Serbia's size and influence within the federation. He also backed a peaceful uprising in Montenegro that put a pro-Serbian government in power there. With Serbia now in control of four of eight republics and regions, independence movements surged in Slovenia, Croatia, Bosnia-Herzegovina, and Macedonia.

Before the late 1980s, unrest of this sort in a neutral state strategically located between the Eastern and Western blocs would have resulted in great-power pressure to preserve the status quo. But now, with the Soviet Union moribund, the United States no longer had as significant a strategic interest in the region as it once did. Calls from the United Nations for peace were ineffectual. And so,

with nationalism sweeping across the region with apparent inevitability, no pressure materialized and Yugoslavia quickly followed the USSR into dissolution. Slovenia and Croatia, where multi-party elections had already turned the Communists out of power, declared independence in 1991, and Macedonia soon followed. A Serbian attack on Slovenia lasted less than two weeks and ended with the Serbians withdrawing and recognizing Slovene independence. Slovenia quickly made the transition to free-market democracy and prospered, subsequently joining NATO and the European Union. In a longer, messier conflict, ethnic Serbs in Croatia attempted to secede, leading to two rounds of large-scale violence.

THE WARS IN BOSNIA-HERZEGOVINA AND KOSOVO

These struggles were dwarfed, however, by the two wars involving the Muslim-Christian fault line: in Bosnia-Herzegovina, and then in Kosovo. In the first of these, the proclamation of independence in March 1992 led to a rebellion by ethnic Serbs—Christians by faith—who declared a separate Serb Republic supported by Milošević's government in Belgrade. Heavily armed bands of Serbian irregular forces aimed less at overturning the Bosnian government than at "**ethnic cleansing**" of the territories they claimed, adding through terrible violence a chilling new phrase to the world's long lexicon of horror. They also carried out a long and bloody siege of the Bosnian capital, Sarajevo.

The UN, the EU, and NATO condemned the violence

Siege of Sarajevo UN peacekeeping forces stand guard as Sarajevo residents take cover from sniper fire behind an armored vehicle in 1993—just a few of the many civilians affected by the ongoing violence in the former Yugoslavia.

but did little to intervene beyond the creation of a series of ineffective "safe areas." European peacekeepers stood by helplessly in July 1995 as Bosnian Serb forces slaughtered 7,400 defenseless Bosnian Muslim men and boys in the town of Srebrenica, part of a supposed safe area. Only in the late summer of 1995, after Bosnian Serbs had shelled the main marketplace in Sarajevo, did the U.S. government finally authorize a sustained bombing campaign by NATO against Serbia, which then agreed to peace talks at the U.S. Air Force base in Dayton, Ohio. The agreement negotiated there and signed in December 1995 ended up preserving a fragile but united Bosnia, in which Muslims, Croats, and Serbs had substantial autonomy.

During the Bosnian War, the Serbs repeatedly appealed to the late medieval struggles of Serbia against the Ottoman Turks and posed as the front-line defenders of Christendom against Islam. Many Muslim countries gave expressions of support to the embattled Bosnian government. Still, for the most part religion mattered in the conflict mostly as a badge of identification, not as a source of fervent belief. Most of the leaders on both sides had grown up in officially atheist, Communist Yugoslavia. But throughout the late 1980s, much of the Serb media presented an unrealistic picture of Serbs in danger of genocide from an expanding Yugoslav Muslim population. Milošević, and the Bosnian Serb leaders, felt threatened by Muslims in a way that they did not feel threatened by Catholic Croats or Slovenes, and at the same time they felt free to treat Muslims more brutally. It was these factors that allowed ethnic strife to explode into all-out violence.

And then, at the end of the 1990s, the former Yugoslavia again became the scene of appalling violence—this time in the region of Kosovo, once the symbolic heartland of Serbia but now home to an Albanian Muslim majority. Milošević, unconcerned with his international reputation as a butcher, turned a blind eye to massacres of Albanians by Serbian police units. Hundreds of thousands of Kosovars fled for safety to Macedonia and Albania. This time, the United States and NATO reacted more quickly. In the spring of 1999, they carried out an intensive, three-month-long bombing campaign against Serbia, at the end of which Milošević gave in and withdrew his forces from the region.

With the conclusion of this last Balkan war, the parts of the former Yugoslavia finally began a slow process of healing and started to follow the former Soviet bloc nations in the path of European integration. In September 2000, after Milošević lost a presidential election and tried to contest the results, popular protests drove him from office. The new democratic government handed him over to a war crimes tribunal in the Hague, set up on the model of the post-war Nuremberg tribunal. He died during his prolonged trial.

CHECHNYA

Several other armed confrontations took place in Europe following the collapse of Communism. Each had its own particular causes, but in broad terms they followed the same pattern of ethnic-religious conflict seen in the Balkans: the worst violence took place on the fault line between Christianity and Islam. In the Caucasus Mountains south of Russia, not far from where the Armenian genocide had occurred during World War I, a war took place between Christian Armenia and Muslim Azerbaijan over a majority-Armenian region within the latter. The conflict badly damaged the new Armenian state and ended with an uneasy truce in 1994.

Even worse fighting erupted to the north, within Russia itself. Although ethnic Russians composed nearly 80 percent of the population of the Russian Federation, scores of other nationalities—Tatars, Chechens, Ossetians, and many others—also occupied portions of its vast territory, with many of them having autonomous republics of their own. In predominantly Muslim Chechnya in the north Caucasus, a serious independence movement had developed during the late 1980s. Stalin had deported virtually the entire Chechen population to Kazakhstan during World War II, and even after their return in the 1950s

Chechen War A team of fighters transports an injured companion on a stretcher, in the midst of the violence in Grozny, in the 1990s. The Russian campaign against the Chechens laid waste to the city and left nearly half of the population dead.

they remained bitter toward the Moscow regime. In the early 1990s, Chechnya tried to secede but President Yeltsin refused to let the Federation suffer the same fate as the Soviet Union. Russia's disorganized military campaign against Chechnya dragged on for two years, left the capital city of Grozny a smoking ruin, and ended indecisively. In 1999, the Russian authorities blamed Chechen terrorists for a series of attacks in Russian cities that killed hundreds of civilians. They then unleashed a more effective campaign that destroyed the Chechen military, killed many of their leaders, and set up a compliant regime in the territory. Altogether, the Chechen War left at least 40,000 civilians and soldiers dead in a region with a population of little over a million and, as we will see, only strengthened hostility toward Russia.

In Chechnya as in Yugoslavia, religious identity did not initially play the decisive role in the conflict. But religious difference and the memory of past conflicts quickly heightened existing tensions and lowered the threshold at which violence could occur. As in Yugoslavia, the orchestration of Christian fears played a greater role in sparking the conflict than radical Islam. But then, in Chechnya, thousands of Muslim volunteers flocked from other countries to join the rebel forces. These fighters had a very strong religious motivation. They saw the conflict as part of a larger battle between Islam and the West, into which they also grouped the Soviet war in Afghanistan, the Bosnian War, and the Arab-Israeli conflict. And so the Chechen War helped to spur the development of radical jihadist movements—dedicated to the struggle against what they considered enemies of Islam—that would become increasingly important over the subsequent decades.

War in the Caucasus, 1998–1999 The Caucasus region was the site of ethnic and religious tensions that erupted into conflict in the 1990s: both on the border between Christian Armenia and Muslim Azerbaijan, and in the majority-Muslim region of Chechnya in the north Caucasus, whose attempts to seek independence from Russia led to reprisals.

CONNECTIONS

The conflicts in the former Yugoslavia and Chechnya, violent as they were, had little direct impact on the everyday lives of most Western Europeans. The refugee crises that accompanied the war mostly did not spill over the borders of the former Yugoslavia. The main challenge for most of Europe in the 1990s was to navigate the more general problems posed by ever thicker, more intense sets of connections between the Continent and the wider world, and within the Continent itself.

THE CHALLENGE OF ECONOMIC GLOBALIZATION

These global connections, as we have already seen, involved the movement of both capital and people. In the 1980s, international bank lending, centered in the United States but flowing across the world, grew nearly twentyfold, and it continued to expand strongly in the next decade as well. Some European countries profited enormously from this change. Ireland, for instance, which did not have an antiquated industrial base dragging down its economy, and which possessed a well-educated population fluent in the main language of international commerce, saw its services and high-technology sectors expand at blazing speed, powered also by low taxes. Between 1990 and 2000, the "Celtic tiger's" economy doubled in size, copying the success of "Asian tigers" such as Taiwan, Singapore, and South Korea. Business centers such as London, Frankfurt, and Hamburg also benefited enormously.

Elsewhere in Europe, however, the same process of globalization made it all the more difficult to support obsolescent economic sectors, and the sort of labor disruptions seen in Britain in the Thatcher years repeated themselves across the map. Companies increasingly moved themselves across borders in search of lower operating costs, especially cheaper labor. Goods and people circulated more intensively. And in the mid-1990s, the development of the World Wide Web began to spark a new revolution in communications and commerce. France had initially taken the lead in new forms of telecommunication, with its state telecom company providing users with free terminals called "Minitels," through which they could access an extensive text-only data network. But the system could not compete with the internet, and the government's attempts to preserve it ended up delaying the spread of internet technology in France

IMMIGRATION AND RIGHT-WING POLITICS

Part of this newly intense phase of globalization involved immigrant communities. In the last quarter of the twentieth century, the populations of non-European origin on the Continent continued to expand, thanks both to high birthrates and to continued immigration. Between 1980 and 1992, fully 15 million immigrants came to Europe from around the globe. In Britain, the proportion of ethnic minorities rose by 50 percent in the 1990s. By 1995, in Germany, Austria, and Belgium, some 9 percent of the population was foreign-born. These new communities mainly fit into patterns set by earlier waves of migration: Turks moved to Germany, South Asians and Caribbean blacks to Great Britain, North Africans and sub-Saharan Africans to France.

Any pretense that the new groups were mere guest workers disappeared as the migrants had children who grew up speaking European languages as their native tongues and retained only distant connections to their parents' birthplaces. In many poorer areas of major industrial cities, such as Brixton in London or the poor suburbs around Paris, these populations became the majority, and right-wing politicians profited from white suspicions and fears of criminality. In France, the National Front of the blustery former paratrooper Jean-Marie Le Pen won over 10 percent of the vote in several national elections, often gaining the support of working-class voters who had previously backed the Communists. In Austria, the anti-immigrant politician Jörg Haider's Freedom Party won 28 percent of the vote in 1997. Both Haider and Le Pen also stirred up the embers of European anti-Semitism, with Le Pen calling the gas chambers a mere "detail" in the history of World War II and Haider expressing admiration for aspects of the Nazi regime.

Most mainstream European politicians denounced these extremists, but at the same time most Western European regimes moved to rein in illegal immigration and place stricter limits on the legal kind as well. Immigration to the Netherlands, mainly from the former Dutch colony of Indonesia and, increasingly, Morocco and the Middle East, became a political target when Pim Fortuyn, an openly gay politician, called Islam a "backwards" religion, in part because of its attitudes toward homosexuality.

Brixton Large numbers of immigrants from Jamaica and other parts of the Caribbean transformed the London neighborhood of Brixton in the 1990s.

Fortuyn founded a mass movement committed to restricting immigration.

TOWARD EUROPEAN UNION

Even as globalization was binding economies around the world closer together, many Europeans believed the destiny of the Continent would be found in its own political and economic integration. In 1985, five European countries signed the so-called Schengen agreement that drastically reduced the extent of border controls between them. The "Schengen Zone" has since grown to 26 countries. By the end of 1986, the European Community had grown to twelve members with the addition of Greece, Spain, and Portugal, but significant economic barriers remained among them. France and West Germany in particular pushed strongly for additional degrees of union, not only to cement their own relationship but also to allow Europe as a whole to compete more effectively with the United States and the rising Asian economies. Britain, where a significant portion of the Conservative Party remained opposed to the nation's membership in the Union altogether, seeing it as an infringement of British sovereignty, was much less enthusiastic. But the desire for closer union prevailed.

In early 1986 the member countries adopted a Single Europe Act, and in 1992 they signed the Maastricht Treaty. Together, these agreements created a fully open European market, opened all borders, renamed the Community the **European Union (EU)**, and committed the member states to adopting a single currency by the end

The European Union, 1995 Three years after the signing of the Maastricht Treaty, the EU comprised fifteen member states, including almost every country in Western Europe—though Norway and Switzerland remained notable exceptions.

of the twentieth century. They gave expanded powers to the executive European Commission in Brussels, which is joined in the constellation of European institutions by a European Parliament and Court of Justice. In 1995, after the end of the Cold War, the formerly neutral countries of Austria, Sweden, and Finland joined the Union as well.

The increasing strength of the EU certainly provoked opposition. British "Euroskeptics" liked to point to the endless bureaucratic regulations that seemed to pour out of Brussels, such as the jargon-filled Regulation 2213/83 that took eleven pages to define standards for onions. They criticized the Union for subsidizing uncompetitive farmers, especially in southern Europe, at a cost of tens of billions of dollars a year and "mountains" of unsold products. At times in the early 2000s, this EU "public stock" included nearly 100 million gallons of alcoholic beverages, mostly wine, sitting in storage.

At the same time, many Europeans, especially wealthy and well-educated ones, benefited from their new freedom of movement. Young French businessmen, stymied by their own country's legacy of heavy regulation, flocked to London's booming financial district. University students across the Continent benefited from the Erasmus exchange program, which gave them the ability to do part of their degrees in another EU state. EU citizens also appreciated the virtual disappearance of physical borders, freely moving back and forth across lines that had once bristled with police and fortifications.

ECONOMIC CONNECTIONS

And it was not only political changes that encouraged increased movement. In 1981, the French national railway inaugurated high-speed train service that cut travel time between Paris and Lyons by half. The so-called TGV (*Train à grande vitesse*, or "high-speed train") initially traveled at over 120 miles an hour—faster than Japan's pioneering bullet train. Since then, high-speed networks have spread over the western half of the Continent (including much of Italy and Spain), and speeds have increased on some lines to 180 mph. In France itself, the trains largely eliminated internal air travel and spawned a new species of long-distance commuters who might, for instance, live in Paris but work in the northern French city of Lille—130 miles away but just an hour by TGV. The best-known TGV line, meanwhile, connected Paris and London: it did so through the Channel Tunnel, an engineering marvel built as a joint effort of French and British companies, subsidized by the two governments. Construction began in 1988, and President Mitterrand and Queen Elizabeth

Reunified Berlin Once divided by the Berlin Wall, Potsdamer Platz in central Berlin now features twenty-first-century office blocks and a new train station, harkening back to the square's pre–World War II importance as a commercial hub and transit center.

II formally opened it in 1994. In the late 1990s, Europe followed the United States in deregulating airline travel. Fares tumbled, and discount airlines proliferated.

Connections grew across the former iron curtain as well. In Berlin, the new, united city government quickly moved to knit the former Eastern and Western cities together, reconnecting streets and subway lines and rebuilding the old central train station in East Berlin, which became the hub of yet more high-speed train lines. The Wall had physically bisected the city's great central square, the Potsdamer Platz, which had lain in ruins since the war. The city now hired a firm of Munich architects to transform it into a vast new commercial complex, including a new headquarters for the auto giant Daimler-Benz.

THE TRANSITION TO CAPITALISM IN THE FORMER EASTERN BLOC

Integrating the former Eastern bloc countries into a democratic, capitalist Europe proved considerably more difficult. These countries had to build new representative institutions even as they opened up their economies to private enterprise and sold off their inefficient state-owned industries—processes that came at considerable human cost. Strategies for accomplishing the transformation varied significantly. Some countries, such as Poland and Estonia, opted for a Big Bang strategy of immediately privatizing industry, allowing inefficient firms to fail, removing subsidies for basic consumer goods, and encouraging new private enterprise. In Poland, where industrial workers and farmers now found themselves competing in a worldwide market, real wages (that is, adjusted for inflation) fell by 40 percent almost overnight, and millions of workers incapable of retraining faced difficult times as they lost their jobs. Whereas the Communist system had guaranteed everyone a job, now unemployment spiked to over 15 percent by 1995. Polish street markets filled with pensioners and the unemployed desperately selling off their valuables to make ends meet. But after several hard years, Poland and Estonia managed the readjustment. In Estonia, economic growth hit 11 percent in 1997 and then remained consistently above 7 percent between 2000 and 2007. Countries such as Slovakia, Romania, and Ukraine, which tried to soften the transition and preserve subsidies to industry and consumer goods, generally lagged behind in terms of growth: by the late 1990s, real wages in Poland were five times that of neighboring Ukraine.

Building up democratic institutions could be just as difficult in the former Eastern bloc countries, which had little experience with genuine multi-party systems and a free press. Moreover, the former Communist parties often retained considerable strength and organization. During the 1990s, many of them took advantage of popular resentment at the economic dislocations to regain support, and in some cases, notably in Hungary, they won elections. But in most of the new states, a common desire to emulate the institutions of the West worked to preserve the new freedoms. In no case did a former Communist Party try to reverse the political and economic changes that had followed the events of 1989. Similarly, outside of the former USSR the dislocations did not threaten the transition to democracy. By the end of the century, the former satellite nations and the Baltic states all had functioning democratic systems with regular, free elections between rival parties.

Ironically, the country that experienced the greatest difficulties in making the transition to capitalism, outside of the former USSR and Yugoslavia, was the one with the greatest apparent advantages: East Germany. Even before its full absorption into the Federal Republic, the territory had received huge subsidies from West Germany, and the common language made it all the more attractive to West German investment capital. But through the transition, West Germans often showed little respect to Ossis ("Easterners") and were in turn angrily denounced as arrogant "colonizers." In the university system, whole cadres of professors were simply dismissed from their jobs if judged unqualified by West German standards and replaced by Western nominees. West German firms setting up or purchasing Eastern firms often sent in their own personnel to manage them. Within a few years, a wave of "Ostalgie" for the former regime had grown up (*ost* is German for "East"). It was gently spoofed in the film *Goodbye, Lenin!*, whose protagonists try to hide the end of East Germany from their fervently Communist but desperately ill mother, who has just awakened from a long coma and who they fear might drop dead from shock if she learns the truth.

RUSSIA'S DECADE OF DISRUPTION

East Germany's troubles paled, however, in comparison to those of Russia. Boris Yeltsin remained president throughout the decade but often seemed to be stumbling from one crisis to another. In the year following the end of the Soviet Union, he promoted an ambitious program of economic privatization, only to run into sustained opposition

Crisis in Russia A soldier stands atop a tank outside the "White House" in Moscow as fires blaze inside after Yeltsin ordered troops to fire on his political opponents in October 1993.

from the Russian Supreme Soviet. In 1993, he demanded special powers to push the program through and barely escaped impeachment. As the conflict with the Parliament escalated, Yeltsin ordered tanks to fire on the same "White House" building he had helped defend during the 1991 coup, and then he ordered elections for a new Parliament. The voters decisively rejected his policies of rapid privatization, giving a plurality to ultra-nationalists, while the Communists made a strong showing as well. However, the voters also approved a new constitution that gave the president expanded powers, which did allow Yeltsin to proceed with the economic transition. The next year, with Russian domestic politics still unstable, the first Chechen War broke out.

Thanks to these troubled conditions and Russia's lack of experience with democratic institutions or private markets (at least within living memory), Russian privatization took place in a chaotic, corrupt manner that enabled a small number of entrepreneurs—mostly with strong connections to the former regime and KGB—to seize control of vast sectors of the economy, including most of the crucial oil industry. By 2004, just thirty-six men—the so-called oligarchs—controlled wealth in excess of $110 billion, or one-quarter of the country's domestic product.

And unlike Poland or the Czech Republic, Russia did not rebound quickly from these immediate difficulties. Indeed, the country suffered an economic and demographic catastrophe in the years that followed the change in regime. In what was a boom decade for most of the Western world, the Russian economy *shrank* by over 40 percent between 1990 and 1996, and by 14.5 percent in

1992 alone. Overall life expectancy in the country tumbled, according to World Bank indicators, from 69.5 years in 1988 to 64.5 in 1994—a decline without parallel in modern history outside of wartime. The number of children born dropped precipitously, while rates of death from infectious disease, cardiovascular disease, and accidents all skyrocketed—all of them linked strongly to alcoholism. Death rates from alcohol poisoning (particularly from cheap homebrew) were estimated at 100 times the American rate. Boris Yeltsin, himself prey to alcoholism, nonetheless won a second term as president in 1996. Ordinary Russians, however, at the same time expressed increasing nostalgia for the Soviet Union and bitterness at Russia's decline. The entry of Poland, the Czech Republic, and Hungary into NATO in 1999 only strengthened these feelings, as did NATO's bombing of Serbia, a fellow Slav country and traditional Russian ally.

CONCLUSION

Russia's troubles, along with the Balkan wars and other episodes of ethnic and religious conflict, provided dark and unsettling codas to the story of Communism's collapse. By the year 2000, the exhilaration that had greeted the end of the Cold War had largely faded. The backlash against immigrant communities and concerns about globalization only darkened the mood further, as did the strains on social welfare systems. Despite a decade of relatively robust economic growth in most of the Continent, and despite the success of many former Eastern bloc countries in transitioning to Western-style limited free-market democracy, most Europeans greeted the new millennium with, at best, muted hopes. The ideological commitments and utopian visions that had flourished between the French Revolution and World War II had largely evaporated.

Even so, the prosperity and social-support systems that had been built up since the war still provided basic levels of comfort and security for most people on the Continent. The violence that followed the collapse of Communism had been contained without anything like the loss of life seen in earlier parts of the twentieth century. Globalization offered the prospect of new wealth and cultural enrichment as well as the threat of economic dislocation. And so, at the start of the twenty-first century, Europeans could still hope that the extraordinary social and political progress made since the war would not soon be reversed.

KEY TERMS

oil shock (p. 847)

neoliberalism (p. 849)

Margaret Thatcher (p. 849)

détente (p. 853)

dissident movements
  (p. 854)

Helsinki Accords (p. 856)

Solidarity (p. 856)

Mikhail Gorbachev (p. 858)

perestroika (p. 859)

Chernobyl (p. 859)

glasnost (p. 859)

Václav Havel (p. 861)

Velvet Revolution (p. 861)

Boris Yeltsin (p. 864)

ethnic cleansing (p. 868)

European Union (EU)
  (p. 871)

REVIEW QUESTIONS

1. In the early 1970s, what developments threatened the long period of prosperity and stability in the post-war West?

2. During the 1970s and 1980s, in what ways did Western European states shift away from the post-war social and political consensus?

3. What characterized the cultural developments of the late twentieth century?

4. How did the dissident movements of Eastern Europe fight against Soviet control?

5. During the 1980s, what Soviet policies and structural weaknesses foreshadowed the collapse of Soviet power in the Eastern bloc?

6. How did the events of 1989 lead to the end of Communism in Eastern Europe?

7. What major factors caused the collapse of the Soviet Union?

8. In the 1990s, why did ethnic violence arise in the former Yugoslavia?

9. From the 1980s onward, what challenges did globalization pose to European states?

10. What new economic connections developed among European countries at the end of the twentieth century?

CORE OBJECTIVES

After reading this chapter, you should have a solid understanding of the following core objectives. To strengthen your grasp of the core objectives, use the resources on the Student Site for The West.

- Examine the economic and political shifts of the 1970s and 1980s.

- Identify the trends that undermined the stability of the Soviet bloc.

- Evaluate the collapse of Communism in Eastern Europe.

- Explain the demise of the Soviet Union.

- Analyze the aftermath of the collapse of Communism.

- Assess the growth of global economic and political connections that transformed Europe in the 1980s and 1990s.

 GO TO inQuizitive TO SEE WHAT YOU'VE LEARNED—AND LEARN WHAT YOU'VE MISSED—WITH PERSONALIZED FEEDBACK ALONG THE WAY.

CHRONOLOGY

2004
French Parliament bans conspicuous religious symbols from schools

2004
European Council proposes constitutional treaty

2004
Seven former Eastern bloc countries join NATO

2001
Same-sex marriage legalized in the Netherlands

January 2002
Euro currency comes into use

2004
Ten countries join the EU, eight from former Eastern bloc

2007–2009
Great Recession

2007
Lisbon Treaty

2010
Conservative-led coalition in Britain ends New Labour era

2001
Afghan War begins

Sept. 11, 2001
Al-Qaeda launches terrorist attacks on the World Trade Center and Pentagon

2003–2011
Iraq War

2005
Angela Merkel becomes German chancellor

2009
Beginning of Greek debt crisis

2011
Syrian civil war begins

26

Under Pressure

EUROPE'S UNCERTAIN PRESENT

Since 2000

November 2016
Donald Trump elected
president of United States

2014
Revolution in Ukraine
leads to war with
Russian-backed militias

2015
All European
states sign Paris
climate accord

June 2016
British citizens vote
to leave the EU
in Brexit

2015
Refugee crisis
explodes in
Europe

Octo ber 2016: On the outskirts of the French town of Calais, on the English Channel, a refugee camp had grown up. At least 7,000 asylum-seekers—a majority of them young men, about 10 percent of them minors—lived in tents, shipping containers, and makeshift huts, waiting for the chance to cross through the Channel Tunnel into Great Britain. Some had relatives there; others believed they would have a greater chance of receiving permanent asylum in Britain than elsewhere in Europe. Many looked for a chance to stow away in a truck or train heading through the tunnel, and already in 2016 at least thirteen had died in the attempt. They came from across the world, but especially from troubled areas of Africa and the Middle East. The British press, in a racially tinged phrase, called the place "the Jungle."

For the moment, the British had refused them entry, but still they waited. Residents of Calais complained about the threats of disease and violence, and about a drop-off in visits from British shoppers. Marine Le Pen (1968–), leader of France's far-right National Front Party, visited Calais and promised to sue the French government to close the camp. Aid workers and the refugees themselves complained about crowding, unsanitary conditions, and insufficient shelter. Finally, in October the French government forcibly dispersed the camp and moved the refugees to reception centers elsewhere in France. But newspapers

Refugee Crisis Volunteers on the Greek island of Lesbos helping refugees on a small boat just arrived from Turkey. In the fall of 2015, over 7,000 refugees, mostly Syrian, landed on Lesbos every day.

FOCUS QUESTIONS

- How did terrorism and war in the Middle East affect European society and politics?
- What were the major gains and setbacks in European integration?
- What impact did the Great Recession have in the EU?
- What were the major causes of the crisis in Ukraine?
- Why did an illiberal populism spread through Europe after 2010?
- What impact did the refugee crisis have in Europe?

soon reported that many of the former residents of the camp—possibly thousands—had ended up sleeping in the streets of Paris.

Calais, owing to its strategic location on the narrowest stretch of the English Channel, has long had a significant place in the European story. It was from here that Julius Caesar set off for his invasion of Britain, and here that England's Richard II landed in France on his way to the Crusades. Captured by England during the Hundred Years' War of the fourteenth and fifteenth centuries, the town remained the last piece of the European continent under English rule, returning to France only in 1558. During World War II, the Allies deceived the Germans into thinking that their cross-Channel invasion would take place at Calais, a ruse that helped the actual invasion, in Normandy, succeed.

But in 2016, the Calais refugee camp stood as an illustration of many of the problems facing Europe in the first decades of the twenty-first century. Most obviously, it illustrated how what is often called globalization—the increasingly intense and interconnected movement of people, goods, capital, and ideas across the world—has affected European communities and governments. In particular, civil wars and economic misery have sent millions of refugees and economic migrants heading toward many different European destinations. Over a million refugees arrived in Europe in 2015 alone, a majority of them fleeing the civil war in Syria. Globalization in turn helped fuel the rise of populist nationalism. The far-right leader Le Pen held up the Calais camp as a supposed example of the ways out-of-touch

French elites were disregarding the will of ordinary people by allowing migrants into the country, and the message resonated in Calais itself. In the French presidential election of May 2017, Le Pen won a large majority there even as she lost the country as a whole by a landslide. A month later, she was elected to a parliamentary seat from the Calais area.

The presence of refugees in Calais demonstrated as well the halting, uneven progress of European unification. As we have seen, by the year 2000 many members of the European Union had adopted the same currency and had virtually dismantled their intra-European border controls. But other countries resisted this trend, including Great Britain, which continued to enforce passport controls for everyone seeking to enter the country. Refugee status in the EU remained governed by a confusing welter of regulations, with ultimate control still belonging to the member states. As a result, the desperate refugees hoping to resettle in Britain found themselves stopped at Calais. The refugee crisis itself, as we will see, proved to be a boon to those in Britain who wanted to leave the EU altogether.

But the crisis in Calais also testified to something else. It showed that in 2016, for all the problems facing the Continent, Europe was seen by people from around the world as a destination worth considerable risk to reach. Throughout most of its modern history, Europe was a place that itself generated refugees. Hunger, war, and religious and political persecution drove desperate men and women to undertake migrations across the Continent and beyond. From the Puritan migrants of the 1600s, to survivors of the Irish potato famine in the 1840s, to victims of Nazism in the 1930s, Europeans fled across the oceans. In the early twenty-first century, the tide was reversed. The refugee issue, a source of crisis in the immediate political context, was also, in longer historical perspective, a sign of success.

In this final chapter, we will survey the history of Europe between 2000 and 2017, showing how the consensus that seemed to develop at the end of the twentieth century around liberal democracy, limited free markets, and strong social safety nets has come under pressure. But we will also consider how the social and political progress of the post-war decades has, at least for the moment, withstood this pressure. We will look briefly at the state of Europe today and offer some thoughts on where the Continent stands at this point in its history.

TERRORISM AND WAR

At the start of the twenty-first century, even as the former Soviet bloc countries were completing the first stage of their transition from Communism and the EU was preparing to introduce its single currency, a new challenge suddenly arose in a distant and unexpected quarter: the mountains of Afghanistan. There the terrorist network known as Al-Qaeda ("the base" in Arabic) planned an audacious attack on the United States. Its members were largely Arabs committed to a radical, violent version of Islam and a hatred of the West that had developed over the course of the Arab-Israel conflict, the Soviet invasion of Afghanistan, the Gulf War, and conflicts in Chechnya.

SEPTEMBER 11 AND ITS AFTERMATH

On September 11, 2001, the attack took place, with terrorists hijacking four American airplanes. They crashed two of them into the twin towers of the World Trade Center in New York City, destroying both with enormous loss of life, and one into the Pentagon in Washington, badly damaging it and killing many more. Passengers fought for control of the fourth plane, targeted either for the White House or for the Capitol building in Washington, and it crashed into a field in rural Pennsylvania. All told, nearly 3,000 people were killed.

Most Europeans reacted to the attack with outrage and sympathy. The headline in the leading French daily, *Le Monde*, ran: "We Are All Americans." True, some European commentators suggested that 9/11 had come as a response to aggressive U.S. policies in the Middle East, and the German composer Karl-Heinz Stockhausen was widely quoted calling the attack "the greatest work of art imaginable for the whole cosmos"; but these were very much minority voices. When U.S. president George W. Bush asked for European support to invade Afghanistan, overturn the Taliban regime that had supported Al-Qaeda, and destroy the terrorist organization itself, he received immediate aid from Britain. Eventually, the NATO alliance itself formally invoked its principle of collective defense (enshrined in Article 5 of the North Atlantic Treaty) and committed itself to the Afghan war. The Western forces met with early success, replacing the Taliban with a pro-Western government. However, these forces subsequently became bogged down in a long guerrilla conflict, and it took until 2011 for U.S. special forces to locate and kill the leader of Al-Qaeda, Osama bin-Laden.

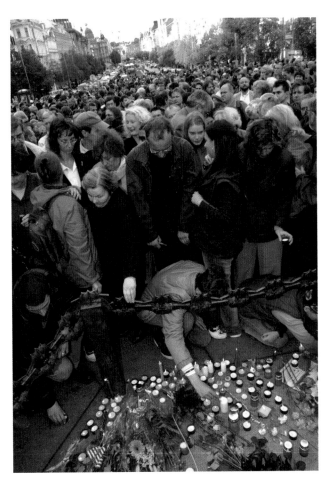

Memorializing Tragedy People worldwide responded with shock and sympathy to the tragedy of the September 11, 2001, terrorist attacks. Here Prague residents flock to an impromptu public gathering on September 12 to remember the victims.

Europe itself had a central part in the story of the rise of jihadist terrorism. Several of the 9/11 attackers had lived for long periods in Germany, including one of the ringleaders, the Egyptian Mohammed Atta (1968–2001), who had studied at the Technical University of Hamburg. Alienated and isolated, feeling at home neither in his birthplace nor in Europe, Atta found meaning for his life, and a cause, in Al-Qaeda's hate-filled doctrines. And while Atta targeted the United States, other terrorists with similar backgrounds sought victims in Europe itself. On March 11, 2004, jihadist terrorists set off explosives on board trains in Madrid, killing 192. On July 7, 2005, four British-born terrorists blew themselves up in London subways and buses, killing 52. Such attacks would continue through the second decade of the century.

Nor did terrorism spare Russia, although in this case it was connected first and foremost to the brutal conflict in Chechnya rather than to a more general jihadist hostility toward the West. The worst incident was the **Beslan attack**: on September 1, 2004, a large group of terrorists, principally from the Muslim-majority autonomous southern Russian republics of Chechnya and Ingushetia, attacked a school in the town of Beslan in the southern autonomous republic of Ossetia. They took over 1,100 hostages, a majority of them schoolchildren. Two days later, Russian security forces attempted to end the standoff by force. In the fighting, much of the school burned and 330 people died, including 186 children.

THE IRAQ WAR

The initial solidarity of the European powers with the United States in what President Bush called the war on terror soon fractured. In 2002, the Bush administration began to plan for a war against Iraq. Although Iraqi dictator Saddam Hussein had no connection to Al-Qaeda and the 9/11 attacks, the Bush administration nonetheless saw him as a threat and charged Iraq with harboring weapons of mass destruction. Both the United States and France had given support to Hussein's regime in the 1980s; but following the Iraqi dictator's attempt to conquer Kuwait in 1990, which a broad Western and Middle Eastern coalition reversed in the Gulf War, he had become one of the United States' chief enemies. Bush and his team also thought that replacing Hussein with a democratic regime could spark a wave of liberalization throughout the Muslim world.

On February 5, 2003, U.S. secretary of state Colin Powell appeared before the United Nations and presented evidence allegedly proving the existence of a dangerous, clandestine Iraqi weapons program. But he did not convince all of America's European allies of the need for war. Britain, under the moderate New Labour government of Tony Blair, agreed to join the United States, as did many of the former Communist bloc countries that had now become part of NATO, including Poland, Hungary, and the Czech Republic. Germany and France refused, leading U.S. defense secretary Donald Rumsfeld to deride these countries as "old Europe." In response, on February 14 French foreign minister Dominique de Villepin delivered a passionate speech to the UN against the war. "This message," he declared, "comes to you today from an old country, France, from an old continent like mine, Europe, that has known wars, occupation, and barbarity."

In March 2003, despite the French and German objections, the **Iraq War** began. And although the U.S.-led "coalition of the willing" initially had great success, it found no weapons of mass destruction and was soon bogged down in a debilitating guerrilla conflict in which the Iraqi civilian population suffered enormously. European governments that supported the war, particularly Blair's in Great Britain, lost popular support. Triumphantly reelected to a second term in 2001, Blair eked out a third victory in 2005, but with a considerably reduced majority in the House of Commons. Two years later, amid accusations that he had deceived Parliament to bring Britain into the war, he resigned.

THE RESPONSE OF THE RIGHT

Only a very small percentage of European Muslims sympathized with terrorism. However, the events that followed from 9/11, particularly the U.S.-led war in Iraq, made it easier for radical Muslim preachers to recruit followers, especially among alienated Muslim youth, by claiming that an apocalyptic conflict between Muslims and unbelievers had begun. Similar rhetoric of a "clash between civilizations" also appealed to some non-Muslim politicians and cultural figures, especially on the far right.

The two countries where the temperature rose the highest were France and the Netherlands. In 2002, the veteran French far-right leader Jean-Marie Le Pen (father of Marine) shocked France by squeaking past a divided left to make his way into the second, run-off round of the presidential election campaign against the conservative Jacques Chirac, who led the party that had descended from the Gaullists. A crushing majority of voters (82 percent) supported Chirac in the second round, rather than vote for a man known for racism and anti-Semitism. Still, Le Pen's initial success raised fears that his xenophobic, anti-immigrant program was becoming more popular in the wake of 9/11.

Then in November 2005, following the deaths of two Muslim teenagers running from the police, a wave of youth rioting broke out throughout the dilapidated suburbs around major French cities in which Muslim immigrant communities were concentrated. The members of these communities, although increasingly French-born and French-speaking, remained subject to discrimination and found it difficult to integrate fully into French life. The rioters burned over 8,000 automobiles, and the French government restored order by imposing a formal state of emergency granting the police extraordinary powers. These events in turn helped Nicolas Sarkozy (1955–), who had gained a hard-line reputation as Chirac's interior minister, win the French presidency in 2007. Sarkozy

Rise of the Far Right National Front leader Jean-Marie Le Pen addresses a gathering of supporters at a rally calling on French voters to say "non" (no) in the 2005 referendum on a constitution for the European Union.

brought his party closer to the **National Front**'s positions on immigration, loudly insisting that French Muslims "integrate" fully despite the difficulties they faced.

In the Netherlands, the early years of the century were marked by two sensational assassinations. In 2002, the populist politician Pim Fortuyn was shot dead by a Dutch Christian who objected to his Islamophobia. Two years later, a Dutch Muslim of Moroccan descent shot the filmmaker Theo van Gogh, who had recently directed a film entitled *Submission* that viciously attacked Muslim treatment of women. These events helped spur the rise of the far-right Party for Freedom, led by the populist Geert Wilders, which in subsequent years became the second-largest party in the Dutch Parliament.

EUROPEAN CONSTRUCTION AND ITS DISCONTENTS

Suspicion of immigrant communities frequently formed part of a more general hostility to globalization in Western Europe. Populist politicians like Jean-Marie Le Pen stoked this hostility, warning that their countries' national identity and sovereignty were at risk. And in the first decade of the new century, this hostility increasingly focused also on the European Union, drawing on and intensifying the Euroskepticism of previous decades.

THE EU AND NATO

For the first few years of the new century, the process of what was widely called European construction had seemed to be continuing apace. On January 1, 2002, a major symbolic threshold was crossed when twelve member countries of the EU began using the same euro coins and bills. The currencies had been effectively joined since 1999, when conversion rates among them were fixed (initially for eleven states; Greece joined later) and control of their monetary policies passed largely to the European Central Bank. From then on, the member countries were in theory bound by a set of strict conditions, including keeping their budget deficits under 3 percent of gross domestic product (GDP). But for most ordinary Europeans the real shift came in 2002, when they could start to use the same physical money in countries from Portugal to Finland. By 2017, nineteen countries had adopted the euro as their currency. Among the largest European economies, Britain remained the major holdout. Many economists criticized the euro as a dangerous and unworkable innovation because it forced countries with very different economies and political systems to follow the same monetary policies. But the desire for political progress outweighed purely economic considerations.

Two years after the introduction of the euro, another major transformation of the EU took place when it admitted ten new member states, all but two from the former Eastern bloc. In terms of population, the expansion was the largest in the Union's history. The new states included Poland, whose 38 million people made it the EU's sixth-largest member. But the expansion also introduced a new level of inequality among EU countries. Latvia, the poorest new member, had a GDP per capita of just $10,000 per year—less than one-third that of the richest members, Denmark and Austria. Poland's was only slightly larger, at $11,000 per year. With citizens of the new member countries eligible to live and work in other member states within a few years, large-scale labor movement began. By 2007, some 2.3 million Polish citizens were living abroad—nearly 400,000 in the United Kingdom alone. The figure of the so-called Polish plumber—willing to work for less than his British competitors—became a fixture of British popular culture, and indeed employment levels among the least skilled elements of the British workforce stagnated during these years. In the decade after 2004, Bulgaria,

Romania, and Croatia also joined the EU, bringing total membership to twenty-eight states.

The first decades of the century also saw a further expansion of NATO. In 2004, seven states from the former Eastern bloc joined the alliance, including the three Baltic states of Estonia, Latvia, and Lithuania. With this enlargement, NATO came to include not only all of the former Soviet satellite states of Central and Eastern Europe, but also these three former republics of the Soviet Union itself. Although the Russian government did not object strenuously to the change at the time, over the next decade Russian resentment of the alliance would grow steadily more powerful.

POLITICAL INTEGRATION

In the Western European states where the EU had been born, the next step in the so-called construction of Europe was a greater degree of political union. In 2002, the European Council convened a constitutional convention, chaired by former French president Valéry Giscard d'Estaing. Some of the participants hoped that the convention might produce a document similar to national constitutions, combining a grand statement of principles with articles that would clearly and simply delineate the powers of the Union and its principal institutional branches: the executive European Council, the Parliament, and the Court of Justice.

However, after protracted negotiations, the participants could not come to a consensus around such a document. Instead, in 2004 they produced a Treaty Establishing a Constitution for Europe, nearly five hundred pages long, which spelled out in far more detail the functions of European institutions and the relation between the Union and its member states. It strengthened the powers of the Union government, but only incrementally, and did not offer a major departure from established practice. Among other things, it created new offices for a president of the European Council and a Union minister for foreign affairs.

To take effect, the new constitutional treaty needed ratification by all members of the Union: at the time, twenty-five separate states. In most cases, the member Parliaments complied without substantial debate. But then something very unexpected took place. In France in 2005, President Chirac decided to submit the decision to a national referendum, hoping that a large "yes" vote would serve as a vote of confidence in his own government. Both his own party and the opposition Socialists announced

their approval. But an unexpectedly strong "no" campaign took shape in response. Dissident Socialists, the Communist Party, and several other small parties on the left opposed the treaty on the grounds that it would make it harder for France to resist Europe-wide free-market policies. Dissident neo-Gaullists and the far-right National Front led by Jean-Marie Le Pen claimed that the treaty would allow the Union to infringe on French sovereignty. Both sets of opponents suggested that increasing European integration would enable yet more migrants from Central and Eastern Europe to take jobs away from French citizens. And on May 29, in a turn of events that shocked most members of the French social elite, 54.7 percent of voters rejected the treaty. Three days later, following a similar debate, an even larger proportion of Dutch voters (61.5 percent) voted "no" in their own referendum.

Following this failure, a different strategy came into play. Instead of proposing a new treaty that would supersede earlier European agreements, in 2007 negotiators from the member countries devised the so-called **Lisbon Treaty** that would function as a series of amendments to those agreements. In practice, many of the changes proposed in the earlier treaty were incorporated into the new one, including the offices of Union president and foreign minister. But it was much harder to characterize the Lisbon Treaty as the foundation stone of a new, pan-Union government threatening the sovereignty of individual member states, and this time the French and Dutch governments prudently declined to hold referenda on ratification. The member states all formally signed the treaty in 2007, and it came into effect in 2009. But given the difficulty of getting any treaty approved, and the opposition in many member states to further European integration, it seemed unlikely that any additional major steps would take place in the construction of Europe for some time. In Great Britain, the Lisbon Treaty strengthened the Euroskepticism that had long flourished in the Conservative Party.

The country that remained most committed to the European ideal was Germany. There, given the weight of the past, a strong commitment to Europe seemed the surest guarantee against any resurgence of xenophobic nationalism. But in addition, as the European country with the largest population (81.9 million people in 2000) and the largest economy ($1.95 trillion in 2000), Germany could count on exercising more influence in the Union than any of its partners. In 2005, after elections that left the center-right Christian Democrats as the largest party, the chancellorship passed to Angela Merkel (1954–): the country's first female leader, and the first leader of the newly united Germany from the former East. A chemist

Angela Merkel Leader of the opposition party in the German Parliament, Angela Merkel campaigns in the days prior to the September 2005 election that made her chancellor.

by training, a cautious and methodical leader, Merkel consistently advocated the strengthening of European cooperation and European institutions. She knew well that Germany, as Europe's leading exporter, benefited disproportionately from the expansion of European markets.

SOCIAL AND CULTURAL CHANGE

The debates over increased European integration took place simultaneously with the ongoing transformation of European countries into post-industrial societies, in which the service and information sectors of the economy came to dwarf manufacturing in importance. In Great Britain, the country that had led Europe's industrial development in the nineteenth century, manufacturing jobs still accounted for 45 percent of all employment as late as 1970. But by 2015, that figure stood at just 19 percent. Most other Western European countries had fallen to similar levels. In Central and Eastern Europe, manufacturing was also in decline, although not as steeply: in the Czech Republic in 2015, for example, manufacturing still accounted for 38 percent of

all jobs. Large areas of Europe were also becoming more educated. In Scandinavia, the British Isles, and the Low Countries, over 40 percent of thirty-year-olds had completed some form of post-secondary education. The same was true in large portions of France, Spain, and Poland.

Among these highly educated Europeans, especially those in the service and information sectors of the economy, support for European integration, and globalization more broadly, was high. In general, these men and women benefited from the free movement of people and capital across borders. But workers attached to the industrial sector feared—often correctly—that this free movement would enable their employers to close factories and outsource their jobs to cheaper labor markets elsewhere. They provided the core of support for the "no" votes in the French and Dutch referenda on the European constitutional treaty.

But not all changes in the economy in this period were so divisive. Some—in particular, those related to new means of communication and information—quickly spread to all sectors of the population. By 2015, an estimated 77 percent of all Europeans had regular Internet access. In most countries, over 50 percent of the population owned a smartphone, and in wealthy Sweden and Switzerland the proportion topped 70 percent. By the end of 2016, over 40 percent of all Europeans used Facebook.

A broad European consensus also spurred the development of renewable energy sources in the face of climate change. Between 2000 and 2016, overall energy production from renewable sources (such as solar, wind, and

Renewable Energy Windmills tower over a power plant in Copenhagen, Denmark, indicative of the country's increasing reliance on renewable forms of energy and on wind in particular.

geothermal) more than doubled in the states of the European Union. Energy from wind power expanded nearly twelvefold, as vast wind farms sprang up in locations ranging from the Baltic Sea to the plains of southeastern Romania. Wind power produced nearly 40 percent of Danish domestic energy consumption and 8 percent of European consumption overall. Consumption from all renewable sources together roughly equaled the consumption from oil. Few voices in Europe challenged the reality of climate change, and all the European states signed on to the 2015 Paris accord, in which nearly all the nations of the world pledged to work to reduce their output of carbon dioxide.

Among cultural changes during this period, one in particular took place with striking speed—and also caused deep divisions. As of the year 2000, not a single European country had yet recognized marriage between members of the same sex. But the Netherlands took this step in 2001, followed by Belgium in 2003 and another twelve countries—including Great Britain, Spain, Germany, and France—by 2017. Eleven other countries, including Italy, recognized some sort of domestic partnership arrangement.

Religion played a part in the conflicts over the issue. Nearly every Protestant country legalized gay marriage, while Catholic ones were split. But the major division occurred across the former iron curtain. Not a single former Communist country recognized gay marriage as of mid-2017, and only three—the Czech Republic, Hungary, and Slovenia—allowed a form of domestic partnership. In fact, between 1990 and 2015 thirteen countries formerly under Communist rule took the step of formally defining marriage as heterosexual. But even in Western Europe, the change did not come without significant opposition. In France, opinion polls as late as 2016 showed 30 percent of respondents disapproving of gay marriage and 40 percent disapproving of adoption by homosexual couples. Large protests erupted after France legalized what proponents called "marriage for all" in 2013, and these protests helped push the cultural conservative François Fillon to the presidential nomination of the conservative party, now called the Republicans, in 2017.

THE GREAT RECESSION AND THE EUROZONE CRISIS

In the midst of these social and cultural changes, in 2007–8 Europe suddenly found itself confronting the largest economic challenge since World War II. As with the Great Depression of the inter-war period, the initial shock came from the United States, where a real estate bubble fueled by lax lending policies collapsed, leading to the failure of a major investment bank, a spectacular stock market crash, and the worst economic downturn since the Depression itself seventy years before. Dubbed the **Great Recession**, this new downturn quickly spread to Europe, whose countries had generally experienced robust growth since the start of the century, but where banks' lending policies had often imitated the dangerous U.S. examples.

In Europe, the effects of the crisis varied considerably from country to country. While Germany experienced a moment of severe economic contraction in 2008–9, by early 2010 its economy had again begun to expand. France experienced only a mild recession, although its economy subsequently went into a long period of stagnation. But small Iceland, whose leading banks had gambled heavily on the continuation of high stock prices and easy access to credit, came close to economic collapse: its GDP declined from $21.3 billion in 2007 to just $12.9 billion two years later. A quarter of the population went into default on their home mortgages. Finland also saw a severe contraction, in part because its economy had become dependent on the success of a single corporation—the cell-phone maker Nokia, which had unwisely dismissed smartphones as a momentary fad. Greece, Spain, Italy, and Ireland, all with overheated economies in the first years of the century, also experienced deep recessions. In Greece, as we will see in a moment, the political consequences—not just for the country itself, but for Europe as a whole—were especially dire.

TENSIONS WITHIN THE EUROZONE

Europe had of course experienced such downturns before, but one particular factor made this economic crisis strikingly different from earlier ones: the existence of the **Eurozone**. By joining the common currency, its member countries had effectively surrendered much of the direction of their own economies to the European Central Bank. They could not devalue their own national currencies to make their exports cheaper, nor could they print more money to pay off their debts. They had no control over interest rates. And keeping their commitment to maintain their budget deficits at less than 3 percent of their GDP would prohibit them from compensating for low economic demand in the classic manner prescribed by John Maynard Keynes: through government stimulus spending.

Worse, the leading country in the Eurozone—Germany—showed little inclination to relax these rules to

MAKING CONNECTIONS

A CRISIS IN UNITY

The end of the Cold War in 1989 presented a utopian moment for the architects and advocates of a unified Europe. For its proponents, the EU represented an opportunity to put a century of wars, ethnic genocide, and political division definitively behind them. The new "United States of Europe" would work toward a free, prosperous, and tolerant society unburdened by the prejudices and horrors of the past. At the same time, many Europeans distrusted the new institution as a bureaucratic power grab that was subservient to the interests of political and economic elites and not responsive to those of ordinary citizens. Disputes culminated in the 2016 referendum in which British citizens voted narrowly to withdraw from the EU. The prospects for a unified Europe, which seemed so certain in 1993, now seemed quite gloomy.

Angela Merkel, from "Speech at the ceremony commemorating the 100th anniversary of the battle of Verdun, 5/29/16"

Angela Merkel (1954–) has served as chancellor of Germany since her election in 2005. She has emerged as Europe's leading politician and an adamant defender of the European Union. In this speech, delivered to commemorate the deaths of hundreds of thousands of French and German soldiers at Verdun in 1916, she emphasizes the importance today of leaving behind "the trenches of enmity" and maintaining full European integration.

Only by opening up to one another can we also learn and benefit from each other. That precisely is the key to Europe's success. It is particularly apparent these days, when we are also witnessing weaknesses in our community. Still, I maintain that the 21st-century challenges we face can only be tackled together.

With European integration, we have left behind us the trenches of enmity. We have gained peace and prosperity. We have overcome quite a number of crises during which we feared the many things we've accomplished through integration may forever be lost. After the recent Franco-German Council of Ministers, President François Hollande said: "We have always managed to overcome the obstacles in our path." That is exactly why today, as well, despite numerous difficulties and setbacks, we can confidently set our sights on the future.

In the European Union, we will at times [have] different opinions on certain issues. That is only natural. However, all sides will benefit if, in the end, we always prove that we are able to reach compromises and adopt common positions. Thinking and acting as pure nation states would set us back. We would not be able to successfully defend our values or promote our interests, neither internally nor abroad. This is true for overcoming the European sovereign-debt crisis, for dealing with the many people who have come to Europe seeking refuge, and for all other great present-day challenges.

We must visibly demonstrate on a daily basis our shared commitment to the fundamental values of freedom, democracy and the rule of law.

Nigel Farage, from "Speech to the European Parliament, 6/28/16"

Nigel Farage (1964–) has been a member of the European Parliament and leader of the United Kingdom Independence Party (UKIP), a Euroskeptic organization. In this address to members of the EU governing body, he speaks on behalf of British voters who rejected what they saw as an unwelcome, imposed political union.

You, as a political project, are in denial. You are in denial that your currency is failing.... Just look at the Mediterranean.... As a policy to impose poverty on Greece and the Mediterranean you have done very well.... You are in denial over Ms Merkel's call last year for as many people as possible to cross the Mediterranean into the European Union, which has led to massive divisions between countries and within countries. But the biggest problem you have got, and the main reason the United Kingdom voted the way that it did, is that you have, by stealth, by deception, without ever telling the truth to the British or the rest of the peoples of Europe, imposed upon them a political union....

... What the ordinary people did, the people who have been oppressed over the last few years and seen their living standards go down, [was] they rejected the multinationals. They rejected the merchant banks, they rejected big politics, and they said, actually, we want our country back. We want our fishing waters back, we want our borders back, we want to be an independent, self-governing normal nation, and that is what we have done and that is what must happen. And in doing so, we now offer a beacon of hope to democrats across the rest of the European continent. I will make one prediction this morning: the United Kingdom will not be the last Member State to leave the European Union.

QUESTIONS FOR ANALYSIS

1. According to Merkel, why is openness so important for Europe's future?
2. In Farage's account, how did the 2016 British referendum vote express the voice of ordinary Europeans?
3. Based on these two speeches, what issues are dividing Europeans and how might the European Union resolve or worsen them?

Sources: Angela Merkel, "Speech at the ceremony commemorating the 100th anniversary of the battle of Verdun, 5/29/16," The Press and Information Office of the [German] Federal Government (website); Nigel Farage, "Speech to the European Parliament, 6/28/16," European Parliament, Debates, Tuesday, 28 June 2016, Brussels (website).

help the countries in greatest difficulty, still less to provide the sort of generous economic bailout that the Germans themselves had benefited from after World War II. German economists, reasoning from their country's own position, believed that the problem with the worst-affected countries lay not in low economic demand but in profligacy and waste stimulated by overly easy access to cheap credit. These economists did not prescribe deficit spending, but rather severe austerity measures to *cut* public spending and restore fiscal responsibility. Chancellor Merkel fully shared these views. In her speeches, she frequently referred to the legendary figure of the so-called Swabian housewife—a frugal domestic manager from the German province of Swabia who hated debt and could always make do with less. Following Merkel's lead, the EU insisted that the countries in economic distress tighten their belts.

THE CRISIS IN GREECE

But in many countries, especially in southern Europe, such **austerity policies**, coming on top of the constraints of the Eurozone, only deepened the economic misery. And in Greece they came close to causing social collapse. Up until 2007, Greece had routinely reported budget deficits of just over 3 percent of GDP—a level in keeping with Eurozone rules. But after the financial crisis, Greek officials confessed that this figure had been calculated using accounting tricks. The true figure was over 15 percent. Fiscal trickery had a long history in Greece, which had been in default on its national debt in over half the years since its independence in 1832.

The new revelations led to the wholesale collapse of the Greek banking sector and one of the worst economic contractions in European history. The country's GDP, which stood at $354 billion in 2008, fell precipitously and kept falling, reaching just $195 billion in 2015. It was unclear whether the country could remain in the Eurozone, even though its withdrawal might prompt other countries such as Spain to follow and ultimately lead to the collapse of the common currency altogether. In the end, European institutions and the International Monetary Fund agreed to a bailout, but—taking the lead from Germany—only on the condition that the Greek government impose even more severe austerity policies. They also overestimated the total amount of the Greek debt, thereby calling for even harsher austerity than their own theories prescribed. For ordinary Greeks, the crisis was punishing. The unemployment rate reached 25 percent, and the youth unemployment rate twice that. State pensions fell by nearly half,

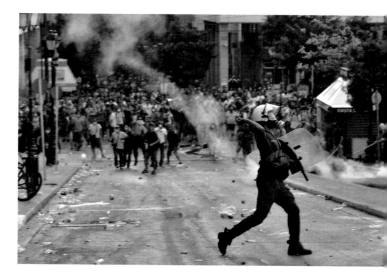

Economic Crisis Protestors and riot police clash on the streets of Athens on June 28, 2011, during a two-day strike against the government's economic failings. The harsh austerity policies occasioned by the Greek economic crisis incited widespread demonstrations and strikes.

while the homelessness rate rose by more than a quarter. The population's suicide rate rose by 45 percent.

It was a testimony to Europe's newfound social and political stability that despite this severe test, even in Greece the Great Recession and Eurozone crisis did not provoke anything like the social and political upheavals that occurred during the Depression of the 1930s. While the downturn grievously stretched social safety nets, they did not break. In England in 2011, the shooting of an unarmed black man by police prompted a wave of riots, with large-scale arson and looting by racially mixed crowds, and five deaths, but no large-scale threat to social order. Greece experienced a wave of violent protests against austerity policies but saw no fundamental challenge to its democratic system. And while the **Greek crisis** spurred the rise of a new left-wing party called Syriza, when its leader came to power in 2015 he continued to cooperate with the European Union, accepted modified austerity policies, and remained committed to Greece's membership in the Eurozone.

CONFLICT IN THE FORMER SOVIET UNION

While the EU countries remained politically stable even under the pressure of the Eurozone crisis, other parts of the Continent did not avoid large-scale violence between

2000 and 2017. As in the 1990s, the trouble broke out along the former internal boundaries of a multi-ethnic Communist state. But this time the state in question was not Yugoslavia, but the Soviet Union. The level of destruction did not approach that of the earlier Balkan wars, but at many points it threatened to do so.

PUTIN'S RUSSIA

The dominant figure in these conflicts—and the most important European political figure of the twenty-first century to date—was the new president of the Russian Federation, Vladimir Putin (1952–). Born in Leningrad, as it was then known, Putin made his early career in the Soviet secret police, the KGB, serving for many years as a high-ranking officer in East Germany. In the 1990s, following the collapse of the Soviet Union, he entered Russian political life and soon became a favorite of President Boris Yeltsin, who named him prime minister in mid-1999.

In this role, Putin made a reputation for ruthless and decisive action by directing a new campaign against the rebellious region of Chechnya after a series of terrorist attacks in Russia that the security services blamed on Chechens. This time, unlike in the earlier Chechen conflict, the Russians won a decisive victory and restored a pro-Russian government there. At the end of 1999, upon Yeltsin's resignation, Putin became acting president and Yeltsin's designated heir. He won election to a full term three months later. He has remained in power ever since, although term limits set by the Russian constitution forced him formally to step out of the presidency between 2008 and 2012, becoming prime minister but retaining real power.

After the chaos, economic disruption, and political freedom of the 1990s, Putin aimed to restore order to Russia, along with a large measure of authoritarianism. And he largely succeeded, thanks to a combination of often-brutal repression and a spike in oil prices that generated massive new wealth for the Russian economy. The repressive tactics included the placing of state media—especially television—firmly under Putin's control, while intimidating and marginalizing independent media. It also extended to beatings of protestors by police and even, allegedly, to the murder of opponents, including a prominent opposition journalist who was mysteriously shot on Putin's birthday in 2006, and the deliberate radiation poisoning—in London—of a former intelligence officer turned dissident. Putin also gave new powers and resources to the police to cut down on crime, and he cultivated an image of personal strength: a physical fitness enthusiast, he liked to pose for pictures bare-chested. Putin cultivated an alliance with the Russian Orthodox Church, reconstructing church buildings destroyed under Communism and banning proselytism by competing Christian denominations. In return, the Church gave him its enthusiastic support.

As for the oil wealth, much of the country saw relatively little of it; but Moscow and Saint Petersburg boomed with new construction, while their streets flooded with new Western automobiles that caused virtually permanent traffic jams. As late as 1980, even in Moscow, fewer than one person in thirty had owned a car. By 2012, nearly half of all Russians owned one. Russians experimented with new tastes and developed a particular love for sushi. By 2014, Moscow had nearly 1,000 Japanese restaurants—twice the number to be found in New York City. A new, capitalist middle class was emerging, and its members largely credited Putin for the country's new stability and prosperity.

Putin did not put an end to the influence of the so-called oligarchs who had siphoned vast state resources into their own pockets after the collapse of the USSR. However, he

Putin's Russia Russian president Vladimir Putin walks with senior Russian Orthodox clerics in Moscow in May 2017. Warm relations with the Russian Orthodox Church have been an important aspect of Putin's distinctive brand of nationalism.

broke the power of the wealthiest and most independent of them, including the head of the Yukos oil company, Mikhail Khodorkovsky, who was arrested in 2003 and spent the next ten years in prison on corruption charges. In their place, Putin developed a new class of oligarchs, loyal to himself and drawn in many cases from a close circle of boyhood friends. Arkady Rotenberg, who had the good fortune to meet Putin in a judo club at age twelve, made a fortune estimated at $2.5 billion from infrastructure contracts awarded by the Russian government. Putin's own personal fortune remained a matter of speculation, but it almost certainly amounted to billions of dollars as well.

From the start of his rule, Putin set as a key goal the restoration of Russian influence over the territory of the former Soviet Union. Although he could not prevent the Baltic states from joining NATO in 2004, over the next few years he successfully put pressure on Ukraine and Georgia, which were dependent on Russian oil and natural gas, to prevent them from taking the same step. In 2008, when Georgia tried to repress an uprising in its pro-Russian region of South Ossetia, Putin sent in the Russian army, which occupied part of Georgia and briefly bombarded its capital city. South Ossetia subsequently declared independence, although only Russia and a few small allies gave it diplomatic recognition.

CRISIS IN UKRAINE

Five years later, a major crisis erupted in the largest of the non-Russian former Soviet republics: Ukraine. After achieving independence at the end of 1991, the country had experienced a difficult transition to democracy. Former Soviet officials remained in positions of power amid widespread charges of corruption. And Ukraine suffered from sharp divisions between Russian-speaking, Russian Orthodox groups, largely in the east, who felt a strong bond of identification with Russia, and Ukrainian-speakers, many of them belonging to other Christian denominations, largely in the west. In 2004–5, after the pro-Russian Viktor Yanukovych (1950–) claimed victory in the presidential election, opponents alleging voter fraud staged a series of large protests. The Ukrainian Supreme Court ordered a second vote, which Yanukovych lost. This bloodless transition of power became known as the Orange Revolution, the color adopted by the opposition campaign.

Yanukovych became president after a fair election in 2010 and tried to steer a middle course between Russia and the West. But in 2013, under pressure from Putin, he decided not to sign a trade agreement with the EU that

Ukrainian Crisis A protestor throws a stone at a police vehicle in a confrontation between protestors and police during outbreaks of violence in Kiev in January 2014—part of widespread popular protest against Viktor Yanukovych's government.

hopeful Ukrainians had viewed as a first step toward the country's membership in the Union. Protests erupted, and student demonstrators set up a protest camp in Independence Square in the capital, Kiev. Police attempts to break up the camp only drew more protestors to what became known as the **Euromaidan** (after the Ukrainian word for "square"). In February 2014, the violence spiraled out of control as police fired on protestors (a small number of whom were armed), causing as many as a hundred deaths. On February 22, Yanukovych resigned and the Parliament set a date for new elections. It seemed that a second post-Soviet revolution had taken place.

THE CRIMEAN PENINSULA But the **Ukrainian crisis** had only begun. The Crimean Peninsula was an ethnically Russian region of Ukraine that traced its Russian history back to its seizure by Catherine the Great from Muslim Tatars in the eighteenth century. Nearly entirely Russian-speaking, and a favorite Black Sea destination of Russians, the Crimea had only been joined to Ukraine in the 1950s by Communist Party leader Nikita Khrushchev. Just days after Yanukovych's resignation, crowds in Crimea flying Russian flags called for the peninsula to secede from Ukraine. Gunmen, most of them Russian army soldiers in disguise, took control of government buildings in the Crimean capital, Simferopol. On March 16, 2014, in the face of international condemnation of this military action, local authorities in Crimea staged a referendum and announced that 96 percent of the voters favored immediate union with Russia. Two days later, President Putin signed a hastily passed law annexing the region. With Crimea tied to mainland Ukraine only by a narrow land bridge, the new Ukrainian government did not attempt to reassert control.

EASTERN UKRAINE In April, the process seemed to repeat itself in Russian-speaking areas of eastern Ukraine, on the Russian border. Protestors in several Russian-speaking industrial cities, such as Donetsk and Luhansk, again supported by Russian soldiers in disguise, seized control of government buildings. In May, two People's Republics in the region (the name a deliberate nod to Communist-era titles) declared independence. But this time, the Ukrainian army responded, and widespread fighting broke out. Over the next year, an estimated 6,000 people would die as the Ukrainians battled local militias aided by the Russian army. International observers fretted that the conflict might explode into a full-scale war and warned that Putin's Russia might attempt similar moves against other former Soviet Republics—notably the Baltic states, which had large minorities of ethnic Russians. The EU and the United States passed a series of stringent economic sanctions to punish Russia for its role in the crisis and to pressure it to withdraw support for the rebels.

In fact, the worst fears of Putin's Western critics, some of whom compared his actions to those of Hitler in the 1930s, did not materialize. The Ukrainian crisis coincided with a 50 percent fall in the worldwide price of oil, which sent the oil-dependent Russian economy into a recession that the Western sanctions worsened. The fighting in eastern Ukraine gradually died down, and a weakened Russia did not make aggressive moves elsewhere in the former USSR. The most blatant Russian aggression did not occur on the ground with troops, but in cyberspace with hackers, as Putin's intelligence services attempted to destabilize the political systems of their adversaries. Most notoriously, in 2016 Russian hackers allegedly interfered with the U.S. presidential election campaign on behalf of Donald Trump, stealing e-mails from Democratic Party and other servers and making them available to leakers.

A RISING ILLIBERALISM

Vladimir Putin, the point bears repeating, was no Hitler or Stalin. He had no ambition to transform Russia—still less other areas of the world—in accordance with any sort of totalitarian ideology, and he did not develop a powerful ideological party apparatus. While his regime flagrantly violated the norms of human rights that had developed in most of Europe by the year 2000, the level of political repression remained well below what Russia had experienced under Stalin's Soviet Union, or Germany under the Nazis.

But Putin nonetheless represented a model of sorts for a new, powerful current of **illiberalism** that flourished in Europe after 2010. Elements of the model included strong doses of nationalism and anti-Americanism, a disdain for democratic constitutionalism, an admiration for the naked exercise of power, and a cultural conservatism that expressed itself especially in hostility to homosexuals and gay marriage. (In 2013, Putin's tame Parliament passed a law outlawing so-called homosexual propaganda that might allegedly influence minors.)

HUNGARY AND POLAND

This current of illiberalism found a strong echo in two states of the former Eastern bloc: Hungary and Poland. In the former, the driving force was the politician Viktor Orbán (1963–), the long-time leader of the Fidesz Party, which had emerged out of dissident student movements at the end of the Communist period. Under Orbán's leadership, the party

Ukraine and Crimea, 2014–2017 Tensions on the Russia-Ukraine border simmered throughout the 2010s. In 2014, Russia occupied and annexed the Crimean Peninsula. Territory on the eastern border of Ukraine changed hands repeatedly, amid fighting between the Ukrainian army and separatist militias aided by Russia.

took on an increasingly conservative, nationalist character. In 2010, in coalition with the Christian Democrats, it won an overwhelming majority in Parliament, bringing Orbán to the premiership and allowing him to pass constitutional changes that, notably, reduced the independence of the Hungarian judiciary and the central bank.

The government then purged the heads of cultural institutions such as the Budapest New Theater, replacing them with strident Hungarian nationalists. It did little to stop right-wing gangs who were assaulting Roma encampments and desecrating Jewish cemeteries. It also passed laws banning gay marriage and defining conception as the beginning of life (although to date it has not banned abortion). During the refugee crisis of 2014–15, as we will see, it attempted to close Hungary's border to prohibit the entry of asylum-seekers from the Middle East. Orbán assumed close control over state-run media, and soon after a leading opposition newspaper criticized his personal corruption, it was closed, most likely because Orbán had threatened its owners. Orbán also attacked the EU, especially after its officials criticized his tendencies toward authoritarianism, and in 2017 the Hungarian Parliament attempted to close Budapest's independent Central European University. In his speeches, Orbán called for Hungary to become a "non-liberal democracy" and expressed admiration for Vladimir Putin.

Poland seemed to embark on a similar course after the conservative, nationalist Law and Justice Party took power after elections in October 2015. Led by Jaroslaw Kaczyński (1949–), the party restricted the independence of the highest Polish court and asserted control over state-run media. The government cracked down on public protests, with the police using tear gas to break up peaceful demonstrations. Kaczyński, like Viktor Orbán, frequently attacked Western cultural attitudes, especially the toleration of homosexuality. The government insisted that state schools and museums convey a strongly nationalist view of Polish history, and it threatened to prosecute a Polish-born American historian, Jan Gross, who had published evidence about the murder of Polish Jews by Polish Christians during the Holocaust. The same strong Polish nationalism, however, kept Kaczyński and other party leaders from seeking a close relationship with the leader of Poland's traditional adversary, Russia.

WESTERN EUROPE

The nationalist **populism** seen in Hungary and Poland bore a striking similarity to that of right-wing populist parties in Western Europe. Populism can take many forms, but it always involves a sharp hostility to social and cultural elites. In recent times, it has also almost always incorporated a bitter opposition to international free trade and international organizations such as the EU.

FRANCE In twenty-first-century Europe, the most prominent European populist party has been France's National Front. In 2011, Jean-Marie Le Pen gave up its leadership and was replaced by his daughter, Marine. She immediately began a process that the French press called the "de-demonization" of the Front, notably by renouncing her father's anti-Semitism. Indeed, she actively cultivated Jewish support while maintaining her father's hostility toward recent immigrant communities, especially those from Muslim North Africa. She was hoping to profit from rising tensions between Jews and Muslims in France and from several cases of anti-Semitic violence by Muslim extremists, including the murder of a rabbi and three schoolchildren outside a school in 2012. She also took an increasingly conservative line on social issues, including gay marriage.

Marine Le Pen called for France's withdrawal from the EU and praised Putin on several occasions. Russia, it was alleged, was providing the National Front with direct financial support. The Dutch populist Geert Wilders did not show the same approval of Putin and took a more liberal line on social issues than Le Pen, but he shared the National Front's stance on immigrant communities and the EU.

BREXIT In Great Britain and Germany, populist movements failed to gain comparable support. The right-wing Alternative for Germany Party, with a program broadly similar to the National Front's, rarely topped 15 percent in opinion polls and by 2017 had fallen to less than half of that. In Britain, the United Kingdom Independence Party (UKIP) campaigned largely on a single issue: British withdrawal from the EU. It did well in the 2014 European elections but never managed to elect more than two members of the British Parliament.

UKIP did, however, play an important role in forcing the British Conservative Party to confront the issue of EU membership. Euroskepticism had long had considerable influence in the party, as we have seen; but for forty years after Britain joined the EU, the skeptics had managed to do little more than limit the extent of Britain's participation in EU and other pan-European initiatives: Britain had remained out of the common-currency Eurozone and the Schengen "open borders" zone created in 1985. But UKIP's

ERASING BRITAIN FROM EUROPE

Banksy is an internationally renowned, but anonymous, artist whose work draws on graffiti and street art traditions to address contemporary social and political concerns. Banksy's work has appeared in cities and locations worldwide and has highlighted issues ranging from mass surveillance to police brutality to consumer capitalism to the rights of Palestinians. This recent piece, which depicts the EU flag, responds to the 2016 Brexit referendum, in which a narrow majority of British citizens voted to leave the European Union. Bansky placed the mural on the side of a building in Dover, England, not far from where the Calais ferry and the so-called Chunnel rail tunnel link Britain with continental Europe. In a crucial twist, Banksy has painted a workman standing on a ladder, chipping away at one of the stars on the EU flag.

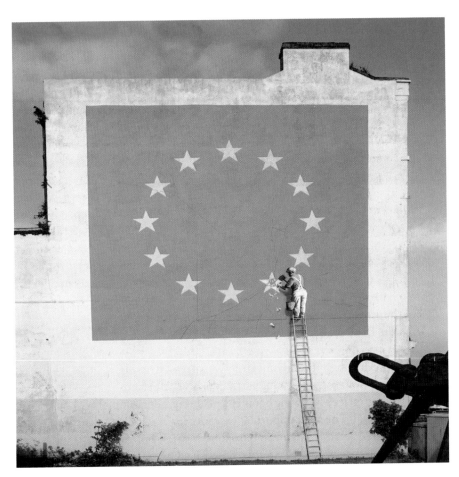

QUESTIONS FOR ANALYSIS

1. What is the significance of the workman's actions in Banksy's mural?
2. Why do you suppose Bansky placed this image in Dover, England?
3. What is Bansky communicating about Britain's decision to leave the EU?

strident attacks on the EU, especially after the Lisbon Treaty came into effect in 2009, strengthened the hand of EU opponents in the Conservative Party and forced the party leadership to take on the issue.

Matters came to a head in 2015, when incumbent Conservative prime minister David Cameron (1966–) promised, in his successful reelection campaign, that the party would hold a referendum on a British exit from the EU, or **Brexit**. In the campaign leading up to the June 2016 referendum, the conservative British tabloid press issued dire warnings about the loss of British sovereignty and

promised that if Britain withdrew it would gain full control of its borders, expel much of its foreign labor force, and save the money that it contributed to the Union. Opponents of Brexit including Cameron vehemently challenged these arguments and emphasized the economic and political benefits Britain received from its EU membership, including the greater weight Britain enjoyed on the world stage as part of this larger whole. The vote, taking place in the middle of the Calais refugee camp crisis, produced a narrow victory for Brexit. Cameron resigned, and a year later his successor, Theresa May (1956–), initiated the

Brexit Demonstrators gather near Parliament to urge the British government to follow through on its promise to leave the European Union following the divisive June 2016 referendum. They hold signs from the "Vote Leave" referendum campaign and from the United Kingdom Independence Party, which supported the campaign.

characteristic of so much earlier European nationalism. In 2007, an alliance with the Scottish Greens allowed the Scottish National Party (SNP) to form a government in the Scottish assembly created as a result of the Blair government's decentralizing initiatives in the late 1990s. In 2011, they achieved an absolute majority, enabling them to push for a referendum on independence, which took place three years later.

In the referendum campaign, the nationalists pledged to develop stronger ties between an independent Scotland and the EU, and to preserve social welfare policies that they accused the Conservative British government of undercutting. The "no" forces warned of possible economic chaos if Scotland seceded from the United Kingdom, while promising a greater degree of autonomy for the Scots. Voters ended up defeating the proposal for independence by 55 percent to 45 percent, but in the next year's general election the nationalists under First Minister Nicola Sturgeon won fifty-six out of Scotland's fifty-nine seats in the British Parliament. And as the possibility of a British exit from the European Union rose, so did the

lengthy process of negotiating Britain's actual withdrawal from the EU.

SPAIN Although populism largely expressed itself through nationalist, right-wing parties during this period, in a few countries a left-wing populism made considerable strides as well. The most important case was Spain, which had suffered terribly from the Eurozone crisis, if not to the same extent as Greece. In 2013, Spanish youth unemployment topped out at more than 55 percent. In 2014, a group of left-wing Spanish academics founded a new political movement called Podemos ("We Can"), which initially committed itself to a repeal of austerity policies and a guaranteed basic income for all citizens. While not favoring Spanish withdrawal from the EU, it called for a democratization of European institutions and opposed the EU's promotion of free-market policies. Its leader, Pablo Iglesias, also criticized the EU's "aggressive" support of Ukraine in the conflict with Putin's Russia. Within a year, Podemos was polling ahead of the Socialists and the conservative Popular Party, and in the 2016 elections in alliance with other left-wing parties it captured nearly a quarter of the vote.

SCOTLAND In Scotland, the nationalist movement that had campaigned for independence from the United Kingdom since well before the start of the century flourished in large part because it moved away from the xenophobia

The European Union, 2017 By the early twenty-first century, the EU had twenty-eight member states, including the former Eastern bloc countries that had joined in 2004. But several members did not participate in the Schengen immigration agreement or use the euro as their currency. One such long-time EU member was the United Kingdom, which in 2016 voted to withdraw from the Union.

Map legend:
- European Union member, 2017
- European Union Eurozone
- Limit of Schengen area
- Scheduled to leave EU in 2019 (Brexit)

possibility that the enthusiastically pro-European Scots might rethink their decision to remain within the United Kingdom.

FROM FRICTION TO VIOLENCE: EUROPE AND ISLAM

The rise of populist movements was fueled in part by continuing disputes over the place of Islamic immigrant communities in European life. France, home to the largest Islamic population in Western Europe—an estimated 5 million people—once again drove these disputes.

CULTURAL CONFLICT

Disputes often arose over cultural and religious practices. For instance, did girls have the right to wear Islamic head coverings in school? Since the 1990s, many leading French cultural critics and politicians had insisted that the practice violated French republican principles of church-state separation, which—more stringently than the U.S. variety—demanded the removal of all forms of religious observance from public spaces. While few schools had actually reported problems with the practice, advocates of a ban on headscarves argued that it would further the "integration" of Muslims into French life, notably by requiring young French-born Muslim women to give up at least one of the allegedly misogynistic customs their parents had brought from their homelands.

In 2004, the French Parliament passed a law banning "conspicuous religious symbols" from schools—presumably including not only the headscarf, or hijab, but also Sikh turbans and Jewish yarmulkes, although nearly all the debates only mentioned headscarves. In 2010, it added a law banning full-face coverings such as the burqa, this time with the argument that obscuring the face did damage to French communal life. In 2016, several French seaside towns also tried to ban so-called burqinis—full-body swimsuits preferred by some Muslim women—even though these garments resembled nothing so much as the wetsuits worn by surfers. Critics insisted that despite the stated purpose of "integration," these measures in fact sent French Muslims the message that if they followed their consciences as to religious observance, they would not be welcome in France.

Other countries pursued different strategies. The Netherlands, home to an increasing number of Muslim

Cultural Conflict Muslim women draped in French flags protest on the streets of Paris on January 17, 2004, rallying against the French government's decision to ban the hijab from schools in France.

immigrants from North Africa as well as from the former Dutch colony of Indonesia, established a new entrance examination for would-be immigrants in 2006. Part of it involved the viewing of a movie that showed gay men kissing and topless women sunbathing as examples of tolerant Dutch values. Denmark, under pressure from a right-wing populist party, significantly tightened its immigration laws, requiring that would-be migrants demonstrate "an active commitment to Danish society" and financial independence, even for those hoping to gain citizenship because of marriage to a Dane. In 2015, in Denmark, social benefits to immigrants and refugees were cut, and the government was empowered to confiscate assets from asylum-seekers to pay for their resettlement.

THE ISLAMIC STATE AND TERRORISM

The challenge that these issues posed for Europe was intensified by terrorism, which became more of a threat thanks to the ongoing crises in the Middle East. Continuing violence in Iraq, followed by the catastrophic civil war in Syria that began in 2011, spurred the birth of the so-called Islamic State, a radical group located across the border of the two countries and south of the border with Turkey. Its leaders declared that they were establishing a new caliphate to rule all Muslims, invoking the examples of the great Umayyad and Abbasid caliphates of the Middle Ages. They also called for Muslims everywhere to strike against "unbelievers" through acts of terrorism. Several thousand European Muslims traveled to Syria to fight for the Islamic State and for branches of Al-Qaeda, and many received terrorist training there.

On January 7, 2015, two young French Muslim brothers of Algerian descent with ties to these Syrian-Iraqi networks walked into the offices of a satirical French magazine, **Charlie Hebdo** ("Charlie Weekly"), which had published obscene cartoons of the Prophet Muhammad. Armed with assault rifles, the men killed twelve people, mostly members of the magazine's editorial staff. Two days later, even as police caught up with the brothers and killed them in a firefight, a companion of theirs shot and killed four more people at a Jewish supermarket in Paris and engaged in a lengthy hostage standoff with police. The attacks deeply shocked the French public and prompted one of the largest demonstrations in the country's history in solidarity with the victims. The slogan "Je suis Charlie" ("I am Charlie") went viral on social media in France and around the world. Socialist president François Hollande (1954–) imposed a state of emergency and declared that France was at war with the terrorists. He also promised, in a choice of words that unwisely recalled late-medieval conflicts between Christians and Muslims in Spain, to "reconquer" the predominantly Muslim suburbs that had allegedly nourished the terrorists' hatreds.

Over the next two years, such attacks continued, and not just in France. Some of the attacks involved men trained in terror tactics in Syria and Iraq. Others involved inexperienced "lone wolves"—mostly alienated and confused young men driven to terrorism by online propaganda from the Islamic State or other jihadist organizations. In the single most bloody episode, several teams of terrorists, from both France and Belgium, killed 130 people in coordinated attacks in Paris in November 2015, including 89 at a rock concert in a theater once owned by Jewish supporters of Israel. On July 14, 2016, a lone wolf drove a heavy truck at high speed into dense crowds celebrating the French national holiday on the seaside promenade in the southern city of Nice, killing 86 and wounding hundreds of others. Bloody attacks occurred in Belgium, Spain, and Britain as well, including a suicide bombing by a Muslim Briton of Libyan descent who blew himself up outside a Manchester concert hall where an American pop star popular with young girls had just finished performing in May 2017. Twenty-two people died, including several girls.

While intelligence services had some success in disrupting terror networks in these countries, they could do little against the lone wolves. Authorities throughout much of Western Europe warned that for the foreseeable future the population would have to expect more such attacks and also tolerate more police presence and possible limits on civil liberties. The attacks did not generally provide immediate electoral benefits for the right-wing populist parties, but they certainly contributed to the atmosphere in which these parties could build support.

THE REFUGEE CRISIS

The Syrian civil war also did more than any other factor to create the **refugee crisis** that threatened to overwhelm Europe's capacity to receive newcomers in 2015. That year, over a million refugees reached Europe, mostly by sea—from Turkey to Greece and from North Africa to Italy and Spain. In the fall of 2015, over 7,000 refugees, mostly Syrian, landed on the small Greek island of Lesbos, just off the Turkish coast, every day. But the EU as a whole managed to approve only 292,000 asylum applications in 2015, with the other applicants kept in limbo, many in temporary camps. At the Keleti train station in Budapest, Hungary, thousands of men, women, and children—mostly from Syria, Iraq, and Afghanistan—crammed into tents and makeshift shelters, hoping for permission to continue on the land route to northern EU nations, especially Germany and Scandinavia. As would be the case in Calais the next year, the plight of the refugees at Keleti received worldwide attention.

In 2015, this plight also provoked a dramatic humanitarian gesture from German chancellor Merkel, who announced that Germany would welcome all Syrian refugees who arrived at its border. Germany did ultimately accept up to 1 million of them. Although controversial, the announcement was also a highly symbolic statement from

"Je Suis Charlie" Demonstrators wave French flags and carry a banner with *Charlie Hebdo*'s logo as a gesture of national unity at a rally in solidarity with victims of the Paris terrorist attacks in January 2015.

DOCUMENTING EVERYDAY LIFE

A REFUGEE'S PERILOUS JOURNEY

Since 2011, millions of refugees from Africa, the Middle East, and Central Asia have undertaken dangerous journeys to reach the relative peace and prosperity of Europe. Thousands have died in the attempt, either drowned in the Mediterranean after overcrowded boats capsized or asphyxiated in sealed shipping containers. The story of Hosein, told to an aid worker with the United Nations Refugee Agency, is sadly typical. An Afghan engineering student fleeing the ongoing Afghan civil war with his mother and sister, he boarded a smuggler's boat bound for Samos, Greece. The boat overturned in rough seas, and although Hosein survived, his family is still missing. Hosein's account speaks to some of the dangers that threaten millions of refugees and migrants seeking safety in Europe.

International organizations have criticized the responses of the European government to the refugee crisis, which is one of the largest humanitarian crises since World War II. Despite being bound under both international and EU law to aid refugees, many governments have responded to fears about Islamist radicalism by expelling migrants or holding them in transfer camps, making the perilous journey to Europe only one hurdle in a long succession of dangers that refugees face.

The past ten days were the most agonizing days of my life. On 10 July, along with my mother Fatme and my sister Shokoufeh, we sailed off in a 12 meter [40-foot] boat after having paid 9,000 Euro for the three of us. It was overcrowded as the smugglers had crammed around 40 men, women and children on that little boat.

After several hours at sea, the captain informed us that he was no longer in command of the boat, which suddenly started taking in water.

Among terrified screams, I tried to elbow myself to reach the small cabin where my mother and sister were, but I was hurled overboard by panicking passengers. I was very desperate. In the sea, the currents were so strong that I could hardly swim. It was only until several hours later, namely on Friday 11 July at noon, that I along with another, almost unconscious passenger, were spotted by an Italian sailing boat and were transferred to Chios Island. Other survivors were brought to Samos. Fifteen Syrians and Afghans have been rescued. The shipwreck so far claims the lives of six persons who were found by the Greek and Turkish Coast Guards while the rest are still missing.

Other family members of missing people with whom we were in the same boat, are in Germany and in Denmark while I am currently in France with my two sisters and their families. I traveled legally on a travel document issued by the French Embassy in Athens. All the families of missing people are appealing that the search and rescue operations of the authorities continue unabated. We urge the Greek authorities to bring up the boat as there were women and small children in the cabin who may have been trapped.

As for my missing mother and sister, another passenger who left the boat after me told me that they were not trapped in the cabin. Since they had very good life jackets, they must have survived. I am sure they are alive. I will not abandon the search. I expect and hope for good news. But even if the news were bad I still want to know!

QUESTIONS FOR ANALYSIS

1. Reading Hosein's story, how would you describe the kinds of conditions that refugees face in their attempt to reach Europe?
2. How have European governments both helped and failed migrants like Hosein?
3. Why does Hosein refuse to give up hope?

Source: UNHCR Stories, "Hosein's Story, Greece," recorded by Ketty Kehayioylou UNHCR/2014 (website), http://stories.unhcr.org/hoseins-story-greece-p13163.html.

---

the leader of the country that had, within living memory, attempted to exterminate minority populations deemed racially inferior.

But Germany also found it difficult to absorb such a vast new number of refugees. Within a year, Merkel was admitting that the country had not properly prepared for the influx and was working to cut down sharply on new arrivals. In 2016, the EU reached an agreement to send refugees landing in Greece back to Turkey, and as a result the numbers reaching Europe fell by two-thirds. But the deal was a fragile one, and with the Syrian civil war still ongoing, the possibility remained that the flood might resume.

A CENTRIST RESPONSE

The events of the new century placed liberal democracy in Europe under greater pressure than at any time since World War II. Despite this, voters in several European countries proved capable of resisting the populist candidates seeking to exploit the pressure and discontent for their own benefit.

In May 2017, as most observers had predicted, Marine Le Pen made it into the second round of the French presidential election campaign. But she faced an unexpected opponent. Following a decade of economic stagnation and political paralysis, the mainstream parties, the Socialists and the neo-Gaullist Republicans, both

saw their support collapse. (The Republican candidate was also mired in a corruption scandal.) Instead of one of their candidates, Le Pen found herself running against the thirty-nine-year-old free-market centrist Emmanuel Macron (1977–), who had never held elective office, although he had briefly served as Hollande's economics minister. Handsome, eloquent, and charismatic, Macron crushed Le Pen in a televised debate and went on to defeat her by a 2 to 1 margin in the second round. Then, in June, his brand-new centrist political party, called Republic On the Move, won a landslide victory in legislative elections.

Like populists across Europe, Macron benefited from popular disgust with politics as usual. But instead of appealing to xenophobic nationalism, he called for further integration of France into Europe while also denouncing his own country's earlier imperialist ventures in Algeria as a "crime against humanity." While promising to renegotiate the conditions of France's membership in the Eurozone, Macron also appeared as a natural partner for Germany's chancellor Merkel. In the same month, June 2017, Britain's Conservative Party lost its majority in a

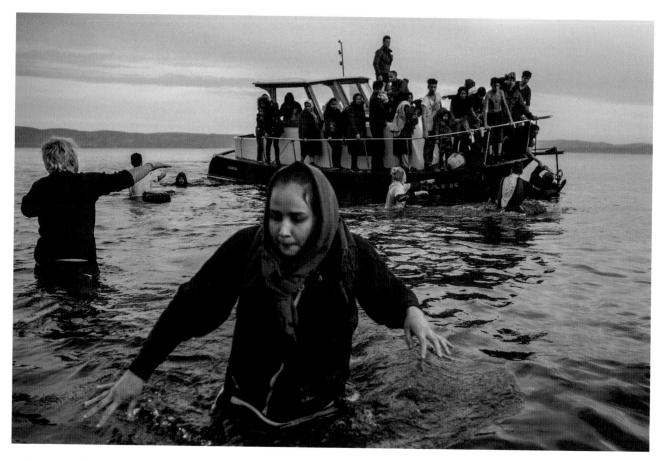

Peril at Sea A Muslim girl wades through the water of the Mediterranean Sea on November 15, 2015, having just disembarked from the small boat that brought her from Turkey to the Greek island of Lesbos.

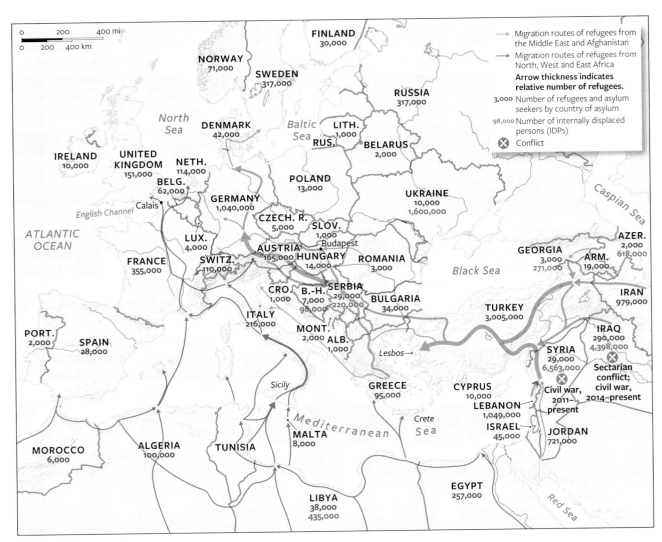

Refugee Crisis, ca. 2016 Fleeing civil war and sectarian conflict in the Middle East, and famine and war in sub-Saharan Africa, millions of displaced people entered Europe in the largest refugee crisis since World War II. Their typical routes involved crossing the Mediterranean or coming by land from Turkey before entering the European Union in Italy, Greece, or Bulgaria, and then traveling northward to Germany, France, and Scandinavia.

general election, weakening its hand in the Brexit negotiations that were just beginning.

European resistance to populism was also strengthened, ironically, by the rise of populism in the United States. In 2016, the winner of the U.S. presidential election, Donald Trump (1946–), criticized European NATO members for not contributing enough financially to the alliance's overall budget. He refused to say whether the United States would come to the aid of European allies under attack, and he hinted that the alliance as a whole had outlived its usefulness. As president, at a NATO summit in May 2017 he again failed to confirm Article 5 of the North Atlantic Treaty, which binds each member state to support others if attacked (he has subsequently confirmed it, however). Trump's remarks spurred new support throughout the Continent for European cooperation on defense matters. Chancellor Merkel declared in a speech that Europe needed "really to take our fate into our own hands." She added: "The times in which we could rely fully on others—they are somewhat over."

CONCLUSION: THE PRESENT MOMENT IN HISTORICAL PERSPECTIVE

Overall, the various pressures on European liberal democracy in the second decade of the twenty-first century reminded Europeans on a daily basis of the changes in the Continent's position in the world and the decline of its influence. Beginning with the voyages of exploration in the fifteenth century, this small corner of the Eurasian landmass had gradually come to dominate much of the globe. During the period that stretched from the beginning of the Industrial Revolution in the eighteenth century to World War I, the European powers and their former settler colonies had come to control 84 percent of the world's land surface area, while a single power, Great Britain, had dominated the oceans. The European powers had dominated the globe economically as well, organizing patterns of trade and resource extraction to benefit their own populations, at the expense of the indigenous peoples they ruled over. European political ideas and cultural forms had inspired adaptations across the world, even as Europe itself adapted ideas and forms it found elsewhere.

The suicidal cataclysm of World War I and the rise of the United States shook this dominance in the early twentieth century, but the European colonial empires remained in place for another forty or more years. And even after a second, greater cataclysm in World War II, Europe remained a focus of global politics throughout the decades of the Cold War: the main theater of confrontation between the rival blocs. But with the end of the Cold War, this centrality, too, was lost.

In a sense, Europe in the early twenty-first century looked surprisingly like Europe in the late Middle Ages: a continent divided into a large number of states, with one very imperfect and limited large union (the Holy Roman Empire in the earlier period, the EU in the present one); a continent that looked like a backwater compared to more populous and powerful states elsewhere on the globe.

But in another sense, Europe in this period, for all the pressures and challenges it was facing, still represented a significant human achievement. For over seventy years since the end of World War II, despite the divisions caused by the Cold War and its troubled aftermath—and despite the bloody conflicts that the Cold War spawned elsewhere in the world—the Continent itself had remained largely at peace. For over seventy years, despite many economic challenges, it had maintained a remarkably high level of material comfort and social welfare. For over seventy years, despite many setbacks, democracy and protection for human rights had advanced across the Continent.

But even as Europe achieved new levels of peace and prosperity, its influence on the global stage waned. Since the time of the Greek city-states, Western power and influence have generally been bound up with competition of many sorts. Except for the brief centuries of Roman hegemony, the West has never possessed the kind of political and cultural unity seen, for instance, in China. It has been divided by political, religious, ideological, and ethnic allegiances. Its different states have competed with one another for influence, even as, within these states, different groups have vied for control. The competition has often been brutally destructive, both within Europe and throughout the world, as Europeans vied for advantage over one another by expanding their reach across continents and seas. In recent decades, as Europe's global influence declined, the fires of competition within the Continent seemed to die down as well. They died down most obviously among the European states, but also within these states as a new consensus developed around the ideals of democracy, human rights, limited free markets, and strong welfare states.

But will the flames of competition remain banked as the twenty-first century unfolds? Patterns of global trade and exchange, and floods of migrants and refugees, have brought new external pressures to bear on European democracies and welfare states. Populist nationalism, harkening back to an older age of strident competition, threatens to undermine European unity. Chancellor Merkel's words about "taking our fate into our own hands" suggest that European states are individually too small to withstand these new pressures separately. They must come together, continuing the process of European construction traced in this volume's last chapters, and without relying on the United States to the degree they did after World War II. But others fear that a more united Europe will inevitably be a Europe dominated by its most populous and economically powerful state: Germany. The long, deeply fraught question of Russia's relation to the rest of the Continent also remains volatile.

In the face of this uncertainty, Europeans have many reasons for discontent and anxiety. They also have reasons to feel shame for what has been done in the name of their societies in the past. But they can take pride in having created societies whose people enjoy more comfort and freedom than at any point in the past. In Europe, the epic story of the West, after a period of almost unfathomable horror in the first half of the twentieth century, took a surprisingly calm and happy turn in the subsequent decades, and even the disturbances of the early twenty-first century have not reversed this turn. The question is whether this achievement can be preserved.

KEY TERMS

9/11 (p. 879)
Beslan attack (p. 880)
Iraq War (p. 880)
National Front (p. 881)

Lisbon Treaty (p. 882)
Great Recession (p. 884)
Eurozone (p. 884)
austerity policies (p. 886)

Greek crisis (p. 886)
Euromaidan (p. 888)
Ukrainian crisis (p. 888)
illiberalism (p. 889)

populism (p. 890)
Brexit (p. 891)
Charlie Hebdo (p. 894)
refugee crisis (p. 894)

REVIEW QUESTIONS

1. In what ways did European countries respond to the rise of terrorism in the wake of 9/11?

2. How did the EU and NATO expand and develop in the early twenty-first century?

3. Why did the Eurozone sharpen the effects of the Great Recession across Europe?

4. What risks did the economic crisis in Greece pose to the EU itself?

5. What factors contributed to increased Euroskepticism in the early twenty-first century?

6. How did Vladimir Putin change the social, political, and economic order of Russia?

7. What factors contributed to the crisis in Ukraine?

8. What were the characteristics of the illiberalism that gained traction in Europe after 2010?

9. In what ways did populism manifest itself in Britain and elsewhere in Europe?

10. What challenges did the refugee crisis present, and how did individual European countries respond to them?

CORE OBJECTIVES

After reading this chapter, you should have a solid understanding of the following core objectives. To strengthen your grasp of the core objectives, use the resources on the Student Site for The West.

- Analyze the conflicts that arose throughout the world in the aftermath of 9/11.
- Consider the evolution of, and disruptions to, the European Union in the last two decades.

- Explore developments in Russia under Vladimir Putin.
- Explain the growth of right-wing populism in Europe.
- Evaluate the crises arising from terrorism.

 GO TO **inQuizitive** TO SEE WHAT YOU'VE LEARNED—AND LEARN WHAT YOU'VE MISSED—WITH PERSONALIZED FEEDBACK ALONG THE WAY.

FURTHER READING

CHAPTER 10 Renaissance Europe (1400–1500)

Andrade, Tonio, *The Gunpowder Age: China, Military Innovation, and the Rise of the West in World History*. Princeton, 2016.

Baxandall, Michael, *Painting and Experience in Fifteenth-Century Italy*, 2nd ed. Oxford, 1988.

Fernández-Armesto, Felipe, *1492: The Year the World Began*. New York, 2009.

Fletcher, Catherine, *Diplomacy in Renaissance Rome: The Rise of the Resident Ambassador*. Cambridge, 2015.

King, Margaret, *The Renaissance in Europe*. London, 2003.

Kraye, Jill, ed., *The Cambridge Companion to Renaissance Humanism*. Cambridge, 2006.

Pettegree, Andrew, *The Book in the Renaissance*. New Haven, 2011.

Rubin, Miri, and Walter Simons, eds., *The Cambridge History of Christianity*. Vol. 4, *Christianity in Western Europe, c. 1100–c. 1500*. Cambridge, 2009.

Skinner, Quentin, *Foundations of Modern Political Thought*. Vol. 1, *The Renaissance*. Cambridge and New York, 1978.

CHAPTER 11 Reformations (1500–1600)

Benedict, Philip, *Christ's Churches Purely Reformed: A Social History of Calvinism*. New Haven, 2002.

Eire, Carlos, *Reformations: The Early Modern World, 1450–1650*. New Haven, 2016.

Greengrass, Mark, *Christendom Destroyed: Europe 1517–1648*. London, 2015.

Holt, Mack, *The French Wars of Religion*. Cambridge, 2005.

Hsia, R. Po-chia, ed., *The Cambridge History of Christianity*. Vol. 6, *Reform and Expansion, 1500–1600*. Cambridge, 2007.

Kaplan, Benjamin, *Divided by Faith: Religious Tolerance and the Practice of Toleration in Early Modern Europe*. Cambridge, MA, 2007.

Kraye, Jill, ed., *The Cambridge Companion to Renaissance Humanism*. Cambridge, 2006.

Pettegree, Andrew, *Brand Luther*. London, 2016.

Richardson, Glenn, *Renaissance Monarchy: The Reigns of Henry VIII, Francis I and Charles V*. London, 2002.

Skinner, Quentin, *Foundations of Modern Political Thought*. Vol. 2, *The Reformation*. Cambridge and New York, 1978.

CHAPTER 12 Things Fall Apart (1600–1640)

Elliott, John H., *The Old World and the New, 1492–1650*. Cambridge, 1970.

Hufton, Olwen, *The Prospect before Her: A History of Women in Western Europe*. New York, 1996.

Parker, Geoffrey, *Global Crisis: War, Climate Change and Catastrophe in the Seventeenth Century*. New Haven, 2013.

Underdown, David, *Fire from Heaven: Life in an English Town in the Seventeenth Century*. New Haven, 1994.

Wilson, Peter H., *The Thirty Years War: Europe's Tragedy*. Cambridge, MA, 2009.

CHAPTER 13 Ordering the World (1640–1680)

Beik, William, *Absolutism and Society in Seventeenth-Century France: State Power and Provincial Aristocracy in Languedoc*. Cambridge, 1985.

Elliott, John H., *Richelieu and Olivares*. Cambridge, 1984.

Rabb, Theodore, *The Struggle for Stability in Seventeenth-Century Europe*. New York, 1975.

Schama, Simon, *The Embarrassment of Riches: An Interpretation of Dutch Culture in the Golden Age*. New York, 1987.

Shapin, Steven, *The Scientific Revolution*. Chicago, 1998.

Worden, Blair, *The English Civil Wars, 1640–1660*. London, 2009.

CHAPTER 14 From Court to City (1680–1740)

Bell, David A., *The Cult of the Nation in France: Inventing Nationalism, 1680–1800*. Cambridge, MA, 2001.

Brewer, John, *The Pleasures of the Imagination: English Culture in the Eighteenth Century*. New York, 1997.

Cracraft, James, *The Revolution of Peter the Great*. Cambridge, MA, 2003.

Harms, Robert W., *The Diligent: A Voyage through the Worlds of the Slave Trade*. New York, 2002.

Israel, Jonathan, *Radical Enlightenment: Philosophy and the Making of Modernity, 1650–1750*. Oxford, 2001.

Pincus, Steve, *1688: The First Modern Revolution*. New Haven, 2009.

CHAPTER 15 Enlightenment (1740–1780)

Brewer, John, *The Sinews of Power: War, Money and the English State, 1688–1783*. London, 1989.

Colley, Linda, *Britons: Forging the Nation, 1707–1837*. New Haven, 1992.

Darnton, Robert, *The Great Cat Massacre and Other Episodes in French Cultural History*. New York, 1984.

Edelstein, Dan, *The Enlightenment: A Genealogy*. Chicago, 2010.

Goodman, Dena, *The Republic of Letters: A Cultural History of the French Enlightenment*. Ithaca, 1994.

Robertson, John, *The Case for the Enlightenment: Scotland and Naples, 1680–1760*. Cambridge, 2005.

CHAPTER 16 Revolution (1780–1799)

Blanning, T. C. W., *The French Revolutionary Wars: 1787–1802*. New York, 1986.

Edelstein, Dan, *The Terror of Natural Right: Republicanism, the Cult of Nature and the French Revolution*. Chicago, 2009.

Hesse, Carla, *The Other Enlightenment: How French Women Became Modern*. Princeton, 2001.

McPhee, Peter, *Liberty or Death: The French Revolution*. New Haven, 2016.

Mokyr, Joel, *The Enlightened Economy: An Economic History of Britain, 1700–1850*. New Haven, 2009.

Thompson, E. P., *The Making of the English Working Class*. New York, 1966.

CHAPTER 17 The Age of Napoleon (1799–1820)

Bayly, Christopher, *The Birth of the Modern World, 1780–1914: Global Connections and Comparisons*. Oxford, 2004.

Bell, David A., *The First Total War: Napoleon's Europe and the Making of Warfare as We Know It*. Boston, 2007.

Englund, Steven, *Napoleon: A Political Life*. Cambridge, MA, 2004.

Hochschild, Adam, *Bury the Chains: Prophets and Rebels in the Fight to Free an Empire's Slaves*. Boston, 2006.

Lieven, Dominic, *Russia against Napoleon: The True Story of the Campaigns of War and Peace*. New York, 2010.

CHAPTER 18 Acceleration (1820–1845)

Beckert, Sven, *Empire of Cotton: A Global History*. New York, 2014.

Blanning, T. C. W., *The Romantic Revolution: A History*. London, 2010.

Evans, Richard J., *The Pursuit of Power: Europe, 1815–1914*. London, 2016.

Pomeranz, Kenneth, *The Great Divergence: China, Europe, and the Making of the Modern World*. Princeton, 2000.

Vick, Brian E., *The Congress of Vienna: Power and Politics after Napoleon*. Cambridge, MA, 2014.

CHAPTER 19 Growing Pains (1845–1880)

Figes, Orlando, *Crimea: The Last Crusade*. London, 2010.

Judson, Pieter, *The Habsburg Empire: A New History*. Cambridge, MA, 2016.

Koven, Seth, *Slumming: Sexual and Social Politics in Victorian London*. Princeton, 2004.

Sperber, Jonathan, *The European Revolutions, 1848–1851*. Cambridge, 2005.

Stern, Fritz, *Gold and Iron: Bismarck, Bleichröder and the Building of the German Empire*. New York, 1977.

CHAPTER 20 Apogee (1880–1910)

Cohen, Deborah, *Household Gods: The British and Their Possessions*. New Haven, 2005.

Hochschild, Adam, *King Leopold's Ghost: A Story of Greed, Terror and Heroism in Colonial Africa*. Boston, 1999.

Hull, Isabel, *Absolute Destruction: Military Culture and the Practices of War in Imperial Germany*. Ithaca, 2005.

Mayer, Arno, *The Persistence of the Old Regime: Europe to the Great War*. New York, 1981.

Schwartz, Vanessa, *Spectacular Realities: Early Mass Culture in Fin-de-Siècle Paris*. Berkeley, 1998.

Walser Smith, Helmut, *The Butcher's Tale: Murder and Anti-Semitism in a German Town*. New York, 2002.

CHAPTER 21 Things Blow Up (1910–1922)

Clark, Christopher M., *The Sleepwalkers: How Europe Went to War in 1914*. London, 2012.

Fitzpatrick, Sheila, *The Russian Revolution*. Oxford, 1982.

Hochschild, Adam, *To End All Wars: A Story of Loyalty and Rebellion, 1914–1918*. Boston, 2011.

Strachan, Hew, *The First World War*. New York, 2001.

Tooze, Adam, *The Deluge: The Great War and the Remaking of Global Order, 1916–1931*. London, 2014.

Winter, Jay, *Sites of Memory, Sites of Mourning: The Great War in European Cultural History, 1914–1918*. Cambridge, 1995.

CHAPTER 22 Ideologies (1922–1940)

Hobsbawm, Eric, *The Age of Extremes: A History of the World, 1914–1991*. New York, 1994.

Kershaw, Ian, *Hitler*. New York, 1991.

Kotkin, Stephen, *Magnetic Mountain: Stalinism as a Civilization*. Berkeley, 1995.

Maier, Charles S., *Recasting Bourgeois Europe: Stabilization in France, Germany, and Italy in the Decade after World War I*. Princeton, 1975.

Mazower, Mark, *Dark Continent: Europe's Twentieth Century*. New York, 2000.

Pedersen, Susan, *The Guardians: The League of Nations and the Crisis of Empire*. New York, 2015.

CHAPTER 23 The Abyss (1940–1945)

Browning, Christopher R., *Ordinary Men: Reserve Police Battalion 101 and the Final Solution in Poland*. New York, 1998.

Hitchcock, William, *The Bitter Road to Freedom: A New History of the Liberation of Europe*. New York, 2008.

Krylova, Anna, *Soviet Women in Combat: A History of Violence on the Eastern Front*. Cambridge, 2010.

Overy, Richard J., *Why the Allies Won*. New York, 1996.

Paxton, Robert O., *Vichy France: Old Guard and New Order*. New York, 1982.

Snyder, Timothy, *Bloodlands: Europe between Hitler and Stalin*. New York, 2010.

CHAPTER 24 Recovery and Cold War (1945–1973)

Elkins, Caroline, *Imperial Reckoning: The Untold Story of Britain's Gulag in Kenya*. New York, 2005.

Judt, Tony, *Postwar: A History of Europe since 1945*. New York, 2005.

Kynaston, David, *A World to Build: Austerity Britain, 1945–48*. London, 2008.

Sheehan, James J., *Where Have All the Soldiers Gone? The Transformation of Modern Europe*. Boston, 2008.

Shepard, Todd, *The Invention of Decolonization: The Algerian War and the Remaking of France*. Ithaca, 2006.

Zahra, Tara, *The Lost Children: Reconstructing Europe's Families after World War II*. Cambridge, MA, 2011.

CHAPTER 25 Reunion (1973–1999)

Ash, Timothy Garton, *The Magic Lantern: The Revolution of '89 Witnessed in Warsaw, Budapest, Berlin, and Prague*. New York, 1990.

Gillingham, John, *European Integration, 1950–2003: Superstate or New Market Economy?* Cambridge, 2003.

Kotkin, Stephen, *Armageddon Averted: The Soviet Collapse, 1970–2000*. New York, 2001.

Sarotte, Mary, *1989: The Struggle to Create Post–Cold War Europe*. Princeton, 2009.

Young, Hugo, *One of Us: The Life of Margaret Thatcher*. London, 1993.

CHAPTER 26 Under Pressure (since 2000)

Bowen, John R., *Why the French Don't Like Headscarves: Islam, the State, and Public Space*. Princeton, 2007.

Camus, Jean-Yves, and Nicolas Lebourg, *Far Right Politics in Europe*. Cambridge, MA, 2017.

Gessen, Masha, *The Man without a Face: The Unlikely Rise of Vladimir Putin*. New York, 2012.

Mueller, Jan-Werner, *What Is Populism?* Philadelphia, 2016.

GLOSSARY

9/11: An attack carried out by the terrorist group Al-Qaeda against the United States on September 11, 2001, destroying the World Trade Center, damaging the Pentagon, and killing nearly 3,000 people. The attack initiated a NATO alliance committed to combating jihadist terrorism.

absolutism: The expansion of royal authority, the dominant political trend among European monarchies of the seventeenth and eighteenth centuries. Absolute monarchies generally reduced the political autonomy of the nobility, limited the role of independent political institutions, and involved the state in broad areas of social and economic life.

Alberti, Leon Battista (1404–1472): A renowned Italian humanist with a wide range of talents and interests, mainly in the arts. He is best known as the author of important and influential fifteenth-century treatises on painting, sculpture, and architecture.

Alexander II (r. 1855–1881): The tsar who ended Russian serfdom in 1861 as part of his program to modernize Russia's economy and society. He remained committed, however, to retaining Russia's autocratic form of government and to expanding the empire's boundaries and influence.

Alhambra Decree (1492): A decree issued by Ferdinand and Isabella that gave Jews four months to convert to Christianity or leave Spain.

ambassadors: Beginning in Italy in the mid-fifteenth century, diplomats sent to capitals to represent their state's interests, gather information, and convey official communications.

American Revolution (1775–1783): The successful revolution of the American colonies against the British, which promoted principles of liberty and the rights of the common man.

Anabaptists: A radical Protestant denomination found primarily in Switzerland and Germany starting in the sixteenth century. Anabaptists constituted an apocalyptic sect that rejected infant baptism in favor of adult baptism and that argued the Bible was a blueprint for creating the perfect society. Members of this faith were often persecuted by both Catholics and more mainstream Protestant groups.

Armenian genocide (1915–1917): In response to an Armenian nationalist movement, brutal repression by the Turks in which at least 600,000 Armenians perished.

atomic bomb: The nuclear weapon dropped by the U.S. government on the Japanese cities of Hiroshima and Nagasaki in August 1945, ending World War II. The Soviet Union tested its first atomic bomb in 1949.

Auschwitz-Birkenau: The largest German concentration camp during the Holocaust. Some of the prisoners deported there were used as slave labor; but the vast majority, including nearly 1 million Jews, were killed in the gas chambers and their bodies burned in crematoria.

austerity policies: Measures taken to significantly curtail government spending and reduce government debt.

Austerlitz: Napoleon's defeat, in 1805, of combined Austrian and Russian forces. The decisive victory permitted Napoleon to impose a peace that greatly diminished Austria's role and increased French influence in Germany.

baby boom: The marked increase in birth rate after World War II as families were reunited and wealth and income per person grew. In the period 1945–50, the birthrate in Europe increased by 23 percent as compared to that of the war years.

Bacon, Francis (1561–1626): A British philosopher and scientist who pioneered the scientific method and inductive reasoning. He argued that thinkers should amass many observations and then draw general conclusions or propose theories on the basis of these data.

Baron Montesquieu (1689–1755): An Enlightenment *philosophe* whose most influential work was *The Spirit of the Laws*, in which he investigated different types of government and connected each to the physical environment, especially climate, in which it predominated. His fictional *Persian Letters* critiqued despotic political authority.

Baroque: A seventeenth-century artistic style that featured dramatic displays of monarchical and religious grandeur, exemplified in the works of Peter Paul Rubens and Gian Lorenzo Bernini.

Bastille: The fortress at the eastern edge of Paris that was destroyed on July 14, 1789 by a crowd of Parisian citizens seeking ammunition to use against troops believed to be threatening the city. The success of the attack heralded the loss of royal control of Paris.

battle of Stalingrad: In the summer of 1942, the Germans launched a major offensive against the Russian city of Stalingrad on the banks of the Volga River. Although the Germans at first captured almost the entire city, a Soviet offensive drove them back and eventually forced the surrender of a large German army—but only after staggering loss of life on both sides.

battle of the Somme: An effort by Britain and France beginning in the summer of 1916 to turn the tide of World War I through a large-scale offensive involving massive artillery bombardment of German positions followed by coordinated infantry assaults. By mid-November, the plan had failed due to the defensive advantages of the German entrenchments.

battle of Verdun: A battle sparked by a major German offensive against a key point in France's defenses in 1916. The battle cost hundreds of thousands of lives on both sides, but by its conclusion the Germans had failed to advance.

Bauhaus School: A school of architecture that emerged in Germany during the 1920s, generally incorporating steel-reinforced concrete, simple geometrical forms, little ornamentation, and large windows.

Bayle, Pierre (1647–1707): A French Protestant who fled to the Netherlands, Bayle edited and wrote for the periodical journal *News from the Republic of Letters*. His *Historical and Critical Dictionary* took a critical approach to biblical texts and used satire to question the compatibility of received doctrines and reason.

Beer Hall Putsch: An unsuccessful Nazi coup launched from a Munich beer hall in 1923. For his role in the plot, Hitler served one year in prison.

Berlin Airlift: In response to a Soviet blockade of the three Western zones of Berlin, the Americans and British airlifted massive amounts of food and other necessities into the city during the period 1948–49.

Berlin Conference of 1884–1885: A meeting at which major European powers divided up African territories and established boundaries for future expansion.

Berlin Wall: The wall built in Berlin in 1961 by the East German Communist regime to prevent citizens of East Germany from fleeing to West Germany. It was torn down in 1989.

Beslan attack: An attack in Russia on September 1, 2004, in which terrorists primarily from southern Russian republics of Chechnya and Ingushetia took over 1,100 people hostage at a school in Beslan, Ossetia, leading to 330 deaths.

Bismarck, Otto von (1815–1898): The prime minister of Prussia and later the first chancellor of a unified Germany, Bismarck was the architect of German unification and helped to consolidate the new nation's economic and military power.

Blitz: The German bombing of London from September 1940 through May 1941. Despite the destruction inflicted on the city, the campaign failed to weaken Britain's industrial capacity or civilian morale.

blitzkrieg: The German "lightning war" strategy used during World War II. The Germans invaded Poland, France, the Soviet Union, and other countries using fast-moving and well-coordinated attacks involving aircraft, tanks, and infantry.

Boers: Ethnically European settlers in South Africa. In the Boer War (1899–1902) with Britain, both sides suffered terrible casualties, with many Boer families being confined to concentration camps.

Bohemians: During the 1830s and 1840s, an ill-defined group of struggling artists and writers who defied middle-class social and moral conventions.

Bolshevik Revolution (1917): Also known as the October Revolution, the 1917 uprising in which Bolsheviks overthrew the Provisional Government and seized control of Russia.

Bolsheviks: Radical former members of the Russian Social Democratic Party who advocated for violent revolution and rule by the proletariat, and who started the Russian Revolution. Prominent Bolsheviks included Vladimir Lenin, Joseph Stalin, and Leon Trotsky.

Bonaparte, Napoleon (r. 1799–1814): The Corsican-born French general who seized power and ruled as dictator and emperor after the French Revolution. Following the successful conquest of much of Europe, he was defeated by Russian and Prussian forces and died in exile.

bourgeoisie: A term for the middle class—people who fell in between those who lived by manual labor and those who had inherited titles of nobility or vast wealth, originally designating non-noble town-dwellers.

Brexit: A referendum passed by British voters in June 2016 to exit from the EU.

Burke, Edmund (1729–1797): A prominent English political figure who argued in his *Reflections on the Revolution in France* (1790) that the French Revolution was doomed to end in bloodshed and the destruction of European tradition. Burke's book had a major influence on modern conservatism.

Calvin, John (1509–1564): An important figure in the Protestant Reformation, Calvin created a branch of the church that came to bear his name. His most important theological contributions were ideas about predestination. Calvin became the de facto ruler of the city of Geneva for twenty years in the mid-sixteenth century.

Carbonari: From the Italian word for "charcoal-burners," Carbonari were members of Italian secret societies, originally formed to resist Napoleonic rule. After 1815, they worked against the restored Austrian rule in the north and the Bourbon monarchy in the south to establish a united Italy based on democratic principles.

di Cavour, Camillo (1810–1861): The prime minister of Piedmont-Sardinia who played a key role in the movement for Italian unification under the Piedmontese king Victor Emmanuel II.

Charles I (r. 1625–1649): The king of England who clashed repeatedly with Parliament, preferring the continental absolutist model of government. Charles tried to rule without Parliament altogether from 1629 to 1640, thereby breeding conflicts that set the stage for civil war throughout the British Isles.

Charles V (r. 1519–1556): Heir to three of Europe's largest royal houses, Charles V was also Holy Roman emperor in the first half of the sixteenth century. Charles saw it as his duty to defend the Catholic faith against the Protestant reform movement. Because of his vast empire, he was in nearly constant warfare with the other major states of Europe.

Charlie Hebdo: A satirical French magazine that was attacked by terrorists in 2015 after publishing offensive depictions of the Prophet Muhammad. The slogan in solidarity with the victims, "Je suis Charlie," echoed across France and around the world, and the event mobilized France to join in the war against terrorism.

Chartist movement: An English radical movement supporting the People's Charter (1838), which called for universal adult male suffrage and annually elected parliaments. Although the Chartists for a time gained considerable public support for their program, the movement failed to achieve its goals.

Chernobyl: A Soviet nuclear power plant that suffered a meltdown in 1986. The accident killed at least thirty-one people, exposed hundreds to severe radiation poisoning, forced the evacuation of more than a hundred thousand more, and raised concerns throughout Europe about the release of nuclear radiation. The disaster highlighted inefficiencies and incompetence in the management of the Soviet economy.

Chmielnicki, Bogdan (1595–1657): A Cossack leader who began a 1648 uprising against the Poles, targeting Jews and Christians.

cholera: A water-borne disease that reached epidemic proportions in the crowded cities of the 1830s and 1840s. Sanitary efforts to reduce outbreaks marked a sharp break with earlier medical models that had focused on the physical or moral characteristics of individual patients.

Churchill, Winston (1874–1965): The British prime minister who led the country during World War II.

Civil Code: Also known as the Napoleonic Code, a national legal system devised under Napoleon and based on Roman law. Although it stated the equality of all citizens before the law and confirmed the redistribution of property, including to peasants, it asserted the legal subordination of married women and recognized Catholicism as the dominant religion in France.

Cold War (1945–1991): The ideological, political, and economic conflict in which the Soviet Union and Eastern Europe opposed the United States and Western Europe in the decades after.

collectivization: The forced replacement of private agriculture with state-managed collective farms in the Soviet Union.

Columbus, Christopher (1457–1506): The Genoese mariner Columbus received a commission from the monarchs of Spain to chart a new route to the East Indies in 1492. Over the course of a decade and four voyages across the Atlantic, Columbus established settlements throughout the Caribbean Sea and ushered in the era of Spanish colonization in the New World.

Comintern: Also known as Communist International, a united party formed by the Soviet Union in 1919 to advocate for international communism.

Committee of Public Safety: An executive authority formed by the French legislature in April 1793 to meet the immediate threats of invasion and counterrevolution. Under the leadership of Robespierre, the Committee exercised almost unlimited emergency authority during the Reign of Terror.

Communist Manifesto: An 1848 political pamphlet by German radicals Karl Marx and Friedrich Engels calling for a new socialist order, driven by an uprising of the proletariat, to replace the inherently unjust capitalist order.

composite monarchies: Early modern empires in which several countries were ruled by a single ruler, who governed each territory separately and distinctly according to the local government, laws, and customs.

Concert of Europe: An agreement among the major powers gathered at the Congress of Vienna to cooperate in the settlement of international disputes. For about forty years, this system prevented any wars among the major powers, and no total war broke out in Europe for one hundred years.

confraternities: Lay Christian associations founded beginning in the Middle Ages as charitable organizations or as groups to conduct rituals and worship.

Congress of Vienna: The international conference held in 1814–15 to reorganize Europe after the downfall of Napoleon. European monarchies restored the Bourbon family to the French throne and agreed to respect one another's borders.

Congress Poland: A sovereign state of Poland created by the Congress of Vienna in 1815. Congress Poland tried unsuccessfully to claim full independence from Russia in 1831, leading to its complete dissolution in 1832.

conservatism: A political and social movement starting in the nineteenth century and opposed to liberalism and revolutionary politics. Conservatives sought stability and incremental change that strengthened structures of authority.

Continental System: The economic embargo of Britain that Napoleon imposed in 1806 on the European territories under French control. Because it proved impossible to effectively patrol thousands of miles of coastline, the boycott failed to trigger the economic collapse of Britain.

Cook, James (1728–1779): An English explorer who undertook three expeditionary voyages during the period 1758–79. During his journeys in the Pacific Ocean, he and the scientists who accompanied him investigated indigenous populations as well as the flora and fauna of these regions.

Copernicus, Nicolaus (1473–1543): The Polish astronomer who advanced the idea that the earth revolves around the sun.

corporatism: The model of social organization, imposed by Mussolini in Italy, in which the various sectors of the economy were managed by corporations that supposedly represented both capital and labor, with the state serving to reconcile the divergent interests.

Cortés, Hernán (1485–1547): The Spanish *conquistador* who defeated the great Aztec Empire of mainland Mexico in the early sixteenth century. His victory enabled the Spanish to claim lands throughout Central America, Mexico, and the area known today as the United States. Cortés was the first governor of the colony known as New Spain.

Council of Constance (1414–1418): A council of the Catholic Church called to end the dispute between French and Italian claimants to the papacy. The result of the Council was the removal of the two rival popes and the ascension of Pope Martin V to the papal throne.

Council of Trent (1545–1563): An ecumenical council of the Catholic Church held in the Italian city of Trent. The Council sought to clarify Catholic doctrine and answer criticisms of the Church brought forth by the Protestant movement.

Court of Star Chamber: An English court of law that met secretly and passed harsh sentences on Puritans and others who were thought to be disloyal to the monarchy. The Court was abolished in 1641 by the Long Parliament under King Charles.

Crimean War (1853–1856): The invasion by Britain and France of Russia's Crimean Peninsula to protect the Ottoman Empire from Russian expansion. Although the British and French were victorious, the peace treaty did not result in any major changes in boundaries.

Cromwell, Oliver (1599–1658): The commander of Parliament's new Model Army during the British Civil Wars and Lord Protector of England following the execution of Charles I.

cult of domesticity: Gender roles connected to the economic and social changes of the nineteenth century. In particular, because middle-class men increasingly worked in larger businesses or government offices, maintaining the home and caring for children became more exclusively the responsibility of women.

Darwin, Charles (1809–1882): A British naturalist whose *On the Origin of Species* (1859) developed the theories of natural selection and biological evolution.

D-Day: The Allied amphibious invasion of Normandy, France, on June 6, 1944, which opened up a long-awaited second front against the Germans.

de Beauvoir, Simone (1908–1986): The French author whose influential book *The Second Sex* (1949) questioned traditional gender roles as cultural norms imposed by men, rather than as reflecting innate differences between the sexes. Her book played a foundational role in the feminist movement following World War II.

Decembrists: Nineteenth-century Russian army officers who were influenced by events in France and formed secret societies that espoused liberal governance. Their protest in December 1825 was put down by Nikolai I.

Declaration of the Rights of Man and Citizen (1789): Issued by the French National Assembly, the Declaration enumerated the rights of all male citizens on the basis of their civic equality. The Declaration also asserted the nation as a whole, rather than just the king, to be the source of all legitimate authority.

Defenestration of Prague: A 1618 event in which Protestant deputies of the Bohemian Estates threw three representatives of the Catholic king Ferdinand from the windows of Prague's royal palace, igniting the Thirty Years' War.

De Gaulle, Charles (1890–1970): The leader of the Free French during World War II and founder of the Fifth Republic of France in 1958. In 1962, de Gaulle and the FLN came to an agreement to give Algeria full independence.

deism: A set of beliefs that holds that a single, non-Christian God figure created the universe and then left it to its own devices.

Democracy in America: The French liberal Alexis de Tocqueville's reflections on his visit to the United States during the 1830s. Unlike most European aristocrats, who saw America as immature in its development, Tocqueville presented American democracy as the wave of the future.

Deroin, Jeanne (1805–1894): A French feminist and socialist who advocated for equal rights for women, founding women's clubs and newspapers and unsuccessfully running for the French Assembly in 1849.

Descartes, René (1596–1650): The French philosopher who maintained that the universe could be understood not on the basis of received truths but, instead, only through principles that could be established without doubt.

destalinization: Following the 1953 death of Joseph Stalin, the Soviet Union's self-distancing from his policies. Destalinization included the release of millions of prisoners from the Gulag, the stabilization of relations with the West, and Soviet premier Nikita Khrushchev's 1956 denunciation of Stalin in his "secret speech."

détente: The relaxation of Cold War tensions between the United States and the Soviet Union during the 1970s.

Diderot, Denis (1713–1784): The French *philosophe* and author who was the guiding force behind the publication of the first encyclopedia. His *Encyclopedia*, edited with Jean le Rond d'Alembert, showed how reason could be applied to nearly all realms of thought and aimed to be a compendium of all human knowledge.

Diet of Worms (1521): A meeting of the imperial parliament called by the Holy Roman emperor Charles V to address the growing Protestant movement. Luther refused to renounce his views and was arrested afterward.

Directory: The five-member executive that governed France from 1795 to 1799. Although it repudiated the egalitarian policies of the Jacobins, the Directory remained committed to maintaining republican government and "exporting" the Revolution through a policy of French expansion.

dissident movements: In the Eastern bloc during the 1970s and 1980s, groups of artists, scientists, politicians, and thinkers, including the famous writer Alexander Solzhenitsyn, who spoke out against the ideology and policies of their states' Communist governments.

Dreyfus Affair: Beginning in 1894, the French scandal surrounding accusations that a Jewish officer, Alfred Dreyfus, had sold military secrets to the Germans. Convicted, Dreyfus was sentenced to confinement for life. However, after a public outcry it was revealed that the trial documents were forgeries, and Dreyfus was fully exonerated in 1906 after a long series of trials.

Duma: The Russian national parliament, created in response to the Revolution of 1905.

Dunkirk: The French port on the English Channel from which a makeshift fleet of British naval and civilian vessels evacuated 337,000 troops surrounded by the Germans between May 27 and June 4, 1940.

Dutch "Golden Age": The period during the mid-1600s when the Dutch Republic dominated European trade and enjoyed the highest standard of living in Europe. The Golden Age gave rise to a new style of painting by artists such as Dirck Hals (1591–1656), Jan Vermeer (1632–1675), and Rembrandt Harmenszoon van Rijn (1606–1669), who drew inspiration from scenes of everyday life.

Dutch Revolt (1566): The largely Calvinist population of the Dutch provinces of the Spanish Empire began a revolt against what they saw as the increasing repression of Philip II's rule. The Dutch broke free and formed the United Provinces in 1581, finally achieving officially recognized independence in 1648.

Edict of Nantes (1598): Signed by the French king Henry IV, the Edict granted the Huguenots substantial rights within the state and allowed for a greater degree of toleration after the French Wars of Religion of the sixteenth century.

Edict of Restitution (1629): Signed by Holy Roman Emperor Ferdinand II, the Edict returned to the Catholic Church all its property that had been seized by Protestants since 1552, stoking Protestant fears and expanding the scope of the Thirty Years' War.

Einsatzgruppen: Special German military task forces whose sole purpose, beginning in the summer of 1941, was to exterminate Jews, Roma, homosexuals, the mentally handicapped, and Communists and other political opponents of the Reich.

Einstein, Albert (1879–1955): The German scientist who posited that time could flow at different rates for different bodies, depending on their relative motion, and whose groundbreaking theory of relativity linked mass and energy, thereby opening up the theoretical possibilities of nuclear fission and fusion.

enclosure: In eighteenth-century Britain, the practice through which wealthy landowners appropriated lands previously used for common grazing. Through the application of new agricultural techniques, these lands contributed to a tremendous growth in agricultural production and productivity.

Engels, Friedrich (1820–1895): A German socialist thinker and journalist who collaborated with Karl Marx on many publications, including *The Communist Manifesto*.

enlightened absolutism: An absolute monarchy, inspired by Enlightenment thought, in which absolute rulers held to the tenets of rationalism and utilitarianism to curtail the power of the Church and introduce Enlightened reforms.

Enlightenment: The intellectual movement in eighteenth-century Europe that reflected a belief in human betterment through the application of reason to solve social, economic, and political problems.

Erasmus, Desiderius (1466–1536): A Dutch teacher, scholar, theologian, and humanist. He is considered one of the most important forerunners of the Reformation owing to his criticisms of the Catholic Church, although he himself did not leave the faith.

Estates General: The representative body of the three estates in France. In 1789, King Louis XVI summoned the Estates General to meet for the first time since 1614 because it seemed to be the only solution to France's worsening economic crisis and financial chaos.

ethnic cleansing: A term coined during the Bosnian War (1992–1995) to describe the systematic murder or deportation of all members of an ethnic or religious group from a region. During the Bosnian War, Serbian troops slaughtered thousands of defenseless Bosnian Muslims.

eugenics: A term devised by the English scientist Francis Galton (1822–1911), referring to efforts to improve the human race through selective breeding, generally of Europeans.

Euromaidan: After the Ukrainian word for "square," a surge of demonstrations in Kiev, Ukraine, in late 2013 through early 2014, protesting President Viktor Yanukovych's refusal to sign a trade agreement with the EU and signaling the start of the Ukrainian crisis.

European Union (EU): The successor organization to the European Economic Community, formed by the Maastricht Treaty of 1992. The member states of the European Union share an open market; open borders among members; a single currency, the euro; and certain political institutions, including a European Parliament and Court of Justice.

Eurozone: The group of nations in the European Union whose currency is the euro. As of 2017, the Eurozone includes nineteen countries.

factory towns: During the Industrial Revolution, towns sustained by factories, mills, mines, and foundries, made notorious by contemporary literature for their cramped and filthy living conditions.

fascism: The doctrine, formulated by Benito Mussolini, that emphasized three main ideas: absolute state control, nationalism, and militarism.

Five-Year Plan: A Soviet effort launched in 1928 in which Stalin set goals for the rapid industrialization of the still largely agrarian Soviet Union. The plan did indeed result in increased industrial production, an explosion of the urban population, and a state-managed economy. But the forced collectivization of the countryside to increase agricultural output led to millions of deaths by execution, deportation, and starvation. Starting in 1933, subsequent Five-Year Plans followed the first.

Fourteen Points: U.S. president Woodrow Wilson's plan to establish peace after World War I on the basis of a new world order. The points included redrawing the map of Europe according to the principle of national self-determination and creating a League of Nations to settle international disputes.

Franco-Prussian War (1870–1871): Following Prussian chancellor Otto von Bismarck's provocations, Napoleon III declared war. Prussia's more mobile army proved victorious, and the southern German states that had supported Prussia formed a German Empire ruled by the king of Prussia.

Freemasons: An eighteenth-century society that developed into a network of "lodges" throughout Europe. Masons engaged in complex rituals and devoted themselves to ideals of the public good derived from radical ideas of the English Civil War.

Freud, Sigmund (1856–1939): The Austrian physician who founded the discipline of psychoanalysis and who suggested that human behavior is largely motivated by unconscious and irrational forces.

Fronde: A revolt against royal authority that began in Paris in 1648, originating in protests by the magistrates of high court against new taxes and centralizing policies.

Fugger, Jacob (1459–1525): A wealthy German banker who lent money to the Habsburgs and other monarchs in exchange for mining and trading rights; lived from 1459 to 1525.

Gallipoli Campaign: The unsuccessful 1915 plan devised by Winston Churchill to knock Turkey out of the war by capturing the Dardanelles. About half of the invasion force of 400,000 were killed or wounded before the Allies withdrew.

Gandhi, Mohandas (1869–1948): The Indian leader who advocated nonviolent noncooperation to protest colonial rule and helped win home rule for India in 1947.

Garibaldi, Giuseppe (1807–1882): The Italian revolutionary leader who led the fight to free Sicily and Naples from the Habsburg Empire.

German Confederation: Founded in 1815, a weak collective of German states led by Prussia and Austria that succeeded the Holy Roman Empire.

Girondins: Members of a Jacobin faction during the French Revolution, led by Jacques-Pierre Brissot. In 1792, they were strong advocates of war against Austria.

Following the overthrow of the monarchy, they opposed *sans-culottes* demands for strict price control and sought to reduce the influence of Parisian radicals on the government.

glasnost: Meaning "openness," the policy introduced in 1986 by Soviet leader Mikhail Gorbachev allowing public debate and criticism, with the aim of reforming the Communist system. Instead, such open discussion undermined the authority of the Communist Party and contributed to the collapse of the Soviet Union.

globalization: The integration of world economic networks. These global exchanges are not limited by nation-states and in recent decades have become associated with new technologies, such as the Internet.

Glorious Revolution (1688): The events surrounding the nearly bloodless overthrow of King James II of England, after which William III and Mary II were granted rule. In the subsequent Bill of Rights, Parliament asserted its indispensable role as part of the government and explicitly limited the monarch's authority.

Gorbachev, Mikhail (1931–): The Soviet leader who attempted to reform the Soviet Union through his programs of glasnost and perestroika in the late 1980s. He encouraged open discussions in other countries of the Soviet bloc, which led to the end of Communism throughout Eastern Europe. Eventually, the political, social, and economic upheaval he unleashed led to the breakup of the Soviet Union.

Great Depression: The global economic crisis following the U.S. stock market crash on October 24, 1929, and ending with the onset of World War II.

"Great Fear": Following widespread rumors of imminent attacks by gangs of brigands in the summer of 1789, this panic caused many French peasants to attack nobles' property and destroy records of the peasants' feudal obligations.

Great Recession: A massive, prolonged economic downturn from 2007 to 2009, sparked by the collapse of the U.S. housing market and risky bank lending policies worldwide.

Great Schism: A divide in the Roman Catholic Church lasting from 1378 to 1417 CE and caused by two—and at one point three—simultaneous claims to the papacy. The division between Italian and French claimants was largely driven by politics as opposed to theology and did great damage to the reputation and power of the Church.

Great Terror: The series of anti-counterrevolutionary purges in the Soviet Union between 1936 and 1938 during which thousands were executed or imprisoned in the Gulag.

Greek crisis: The collapse of the Greek banking sector during the Great Recession in part due to misreported budget deficits, jeopardizing Greece's membership in the EU. Greece was bailed out by European institutions and the International Monetary Fund after agreeing to adopt severe austerity policies.

Grumbach, Argula von (1492–ca. 1554): A Bavarian noblewoman whose pamphlets in defense of Luther and Protestantism were printed as many as 29,000 times.

guerrilla warfare: Spanish for "little war," originally used to describe Spanish irregulars' insurgency against French forces during the Peninsular War. Guerrilla forces generally attack by surprise in small groups and then blend back into the countryside.

guest workers: In the second half of the twentieth century, supposedly temporary workers from former colonies and the Middle East who filled low-level jobs in Europe. These newcomers often encountered suspicion and prejudice on the part of citizens of European countries.

Gutenberg, Johannes (1398–1468): A German metalsmith and printer, Gutenberg is credited with introducing the printing press to Europe in the 1450s. The printing press allowed for the rapid and inexpensive production of books and made them accessible to people at all levels of society.

Habsburg dynasty: One of the most influential royal houses in Europe, the Habsburgs ruled over Austria, Spain, and various other European states from the eleventh to the twentieth century. They also controlled the title of Holy Roman emperor for most of the early modern era.

Havel, Václav (1936–2011): The playwright and philosopher who led an anti-Communist movement in Czechoslovakia, later becoming the last president of Czechoslovakia (1989–1992) and the first president of the Czech Republic (1993–2002).

Helsinki Accords: A 1975 agreement in which nearly all European states as well as the United States recognized the de facto post-war boundaries established in Europe. Although the recognition of wartime annexations seemed a major gain for the Soviet Union, dissident groups soon referred to Helsinki to hold their governments accountable.

Henry VIII (r. 1509–1547): The second monarch of the Tudor dynasty, Henry ruled

England from 1509 until his death in 1547. Although he was famous for his marriages, his most consequential policy was to break with the Catholic Church in the 1530s and establish the independent Church of England.

Hitler, Adolf (1889–1945): The leader of the Nazis who became chancellor and subsequently dictator of Germany. Hitler and the Nazi regime started World War II and orchestrated the systematic murder of over 6 million Jews, 250,000 Roma, and tens of thousands of homosexuals and political prisoners.

Hobbes, Thomas (1588–1679): The English philosopher whose *Leviathan* discussed the origins of government and the effective exercise of political authority. Hobbes maintained that government rests on a social contract with its subjects, formed to prevent the violence and uncertainty of man's natural condition. This contract requires subjects to subordinate themselves to a sovereign authority.

Holocaust: The genocide of 5.4 million Jews and the murder of around 250,000 Roma, tens of thousands of homosexuals and political prisoners, and millions of Soviet prisoners of war by Nazi Germany.

Home Army: The largest Polish resistance group during World War II. Because the Home Army supported the non-Communist government-in-exile in London, the Soviets did not support its unsuccessful July 1944 uprising in Warsaw.

home rule: Self-government sought by Irish nationalists, who in the nineteenth century called for repeal of the 1801 Act of Union between Great Britain and Ireland.

Huguenots: French Calvinists. The Edict of Nantes led to increased toleration of the Huguenots, but Louis XIV reversed it in 1685 when he abolished all legal recognition of Protestantism in France.

humanism: The intellectual worldview held by leading figures of the Renaissance, who were attempting to revitalize classical culture. Humanists celebrated reason and rationality, the liberal arts, and civic engagement. Humanism emphasized the value and potential of mankind.

Hume, David (1711–1776): A leading philosopher of the Scottish Enlightenment who championed rigorous skepticism and argued in *The Natural History of Religion* that belief in God was rooted in superstition.

Hundred Days: The three months in early 1815 during which Napoleon regained control of France following his escape from Elba. After his defeat at Waterloo by the British

and the Prussians, Napoleon was exiled to the remote island of Saint Helena.

illiberalism: An ideology that gained support across Europe after 2010, consisting of fervent nationalist and anti-American sentiment, a disdain for democratic constitutionalism, an admiration for the naked exercise of power, and a cultural conservatism that was most manifest in issues relating to homosexuality.

impressionism: A nineteenth-century artistic movement that experimented with light and color, eschewing the precise forms of realism.

indulgence: A donation made to the Catholic Church for the remission and forgiveness of sins. Abuse of the sale of these indulgences, as well as the question of their validity, was the subject of Luther's Ninety-Five Theses.

Industrial Revolution: The gradual accumulation and diffusion of technical knowledge that accelerated in the nineteenth century, spurred by a state-supported culture of innovation and by developments in coal power, finances, and agriculture. The Industrial Revolution changed the economic landscape of northwestern Europe and North America, catapulting industrialized areas ahead of the rest of the world in manufacturing, agricultural output, and standard of living.

intendants: French royal agents who since the late Middle Ages had been sent to the provinces with powers to act on the king's behalf. In 1635 Cardinal Richelieu, adviser to Louis XIII, made them permanent fixtures of royal administration.

Iraq War (2003–2011): A conflict initiated by a U.S.-led coalition backed by Britain and many former Communist bloc countries in NATO, who attacked on the grounds that Iraq possessed weapons of mass destruction. The alleged weapons were never found, and the war devolved into a taxing and unpopular guerrilla conflict.

Irish famine: The period of agricultural blight in Ireland from 1845 to 1849. Because of inadequate relief efforts by the British government, hundreds of thousands died from hunger or disease. The economic collapse also led to the emigration of another million Irish.

iron curtain: A term coined by Winston Churchill in 1946 to refer to the borders of Eastern European nations that lay within the zone of Soviet control.

Jacobins: Members of a radical political group during the French Revolution that took power after 1792, executed Louis XVI, and sought to remake French culture.

Jansenism: An ascetic Catholic movement in France and the Low Countries during the seventeenth century. Jansenists criticized the lavish decoration of Baroque churches and what they saw as an undue emphasis in the Catholic Reformation Church on the role of free will in the process of salvation.

Jesuits: Officially known as the Society of Jesus, the Jesuit religious order was founded by Ignatius Loyola and recognized by the pope in 1540. The Jesuits were particularly active in education and missionary activity and were leaders of the Catholic Reformation.

July Revolution (1830): A revolt beginning on July 27, 1830, during which Parisians overthrew Charles X and installed his cousin, Louis-Philippe, who ruled in cooperation with bourgeois advisers and expanded the size of the electorate.

justices of the peace: Beginning in the fourteenth century in England, justices of the peace were unpaid local officials, serving terms of one year, that oversaw juries, kept public order, and enforced legislation.

Keynes, John Maynard (1883–1946): An influential British economist who argued that in order to maximize the growth of free markets, public spending by the government is needed to stimulate economic demand.

laissez-faire: Also known as free-market capitalism, an economic system in which the state does not regulate or interfere with the workings of the market, and most economic activity is controlled by private individuals and privately owned corporations.

League of Nations: An international organization founded after World War I to resolve international disputes through arbitration. It was dissolved in 1946 and its assets were transferred to the United Nations.

Lend-Lease: A program, beginning in 1941, through which the United States provided war materiel first to Britain in exchange for leases on military bases and then to other Allied nations on the promise of eventual repayment.

Lenin, Vladimir (1870–1924): Born Vladimir Ilich Ulyanov, Lenin was the head of the Bolshevik Revolution (1917) and the first leader of the Soviet Union.

Levellers: A radical group in the English New Model Army who called for granting all adult men the right to vote.

liberalism: A political and social movement starting in the nineteenth century and adopted by those who favored democratic, representative government, the principle of human rights, and the reduction of government control over the economy.

Lisbon Treaty (2009): A series of amendments to the former European Union agreements, formally establishing the offices of Union president and foreign minister. Ratified by all EU member states in 2007, the treaty took effect in 2009.

Little Ice Age: A period of global cooling from the sixteenth through the early nineteenth centuries, which reached its greatest intensity during the seventeenth century. It played a role in harvest failures that were responsible for the death of millions from starvation and from lowered resistance to epidemic diseases.

Locke, John (1632–1704): The English philosopher and political theorist who maintained that government originated when people formed a social contract to overcome the uncertainties of living in the state of nature, but that the people retained most of their natural rights and thus had the right to resist and even depose tyrannical rulers.

Louis XIV (r. 1643–1715): Known as the Sun King, Louis greatly strengthened the monarchy in France by establishing a highly centralized, absolutist government.

Louis XVI (r. 1774–1792): The well-meaning yet weak-willed king of France who was finally deposed and executed by guillotine during the French Revolution.

Low Countries: The coastal region of northwest Europe, including the area of the modern-day Netherlands and Belgium, which was a center of trade and manufacturing in the fifteenth century.

Luddites: English textile weavers who in the early 1800s organized to destroy the new power looms and workshops that threatened their livelihoods. They claimed to be following the example set by the semi-mythical Ned Ludd, said to have smashed looms thirty years earlier.

Lusitania: A large ocean liner that was sunk by a German U-boat in May 1915. Although the ship was in fact carrying munitions, the heavy loss of civilian life, including many Americans, led to widespread condemnation of Germany by the American press.

Luther, Martin (1483–1546): A monk and professor with a doctorate in theology who was the primary figure in the early Protestant Reformation. Luther's criticisms of the Catholic Church ended that institution's dominance over the religious culture of western Christianity.

Machiavelli, Niccolò (1469–1527): An Italian Renaissance diplomat, historian, and political theorist most famous for his work *The Prince*. Machiavelli is considered one of the most influential political thinkers of the early modern era due to his essays concerning the nature of power and leadership.

mandates: Middle Eastern territories, including Palestine, Iraq, Syria, and Lebanon, ostensibly subject to the League of Nations following World War I but directly administered by Britain and France.

Manhattan Project: The secret American and British government research project that developed the first nuclear bomb, first tested in New Mexico in July 1945.

Marshall Plan: Announced in 1947, an American economic plan pledging billions of dollars in direct aid and loans for the post-war reconstruction of Europe. Suspicion of American motives played a role in the formation of a rival system of cooperation, COMECON, between the Soviet Union and the regimes it had established in Central and Eastern Europe.

Marx, Karl (1818–1883): A German socialist writer, organizer, and economist who believed that a revolution of the working classes would overthrow the capitalist order and create a classless society. Author of *The Communist Manifesto* (with Friedrich Engels) and *Capital*.

Maximillian I (r. 1508–1519): The Holy Roman emperor who established Habsburg claims over much of Burgundy, Aragon and Castile, and Milan, while leading an ambitious effort to reform the empire.

Medici family: An Italian banking family and political dynasty that dominated Renaissance Florence. The Medici were also important patrons of the arts and proponents of civic humanism, which made them instrumental to the Renaissance.

Mehmed I (r. 1413–1421): The Ottoman ruler who expanded the empire's territory throughout Europe and Asia Minor, conquering Constantinople in 1453.

Mensheviks: A moderate faction, formerly of the Russian Social Democratic Party, whose members advocated slow changes and a gradual move toward socialism.

mercantilism: Economic policies shaped by the assumption that one country's commerce could only grow at the expense of another's because of limits in the world's economic resources.

middle passage: The trans-Atlantic route from Africa to the Americas, along which over 11 million Africans were transported in grueling conditions to be sold into slavery.

Mill, John Stuart (1806–1873): An English philosopher whose faith in human reason led him to support a broad variety of civic and political freedoms for men and women, including the right to vote and the right to free speech.

Mississippi Company: A French overseas trading corporation established by the Scot John Law, who became France's finance minister in 1716. The price of shares rose dramatically until 1720, when the investment bubble burst because speculation far outstripped actual profits from Louisiana. The collapse of the company, and with it the banking system introduced by Law, set back French economic development.

modernism: In the late nineteenth and early twentieth centuries, a movement in art, literature, and music that included the following beliefs: that the world had radically changed and that this change should be embraced; that traditional aesthetic values were ill suited to the present; and that art should emphasize expression over representation and value novelty, expression, and creative freedom.

More, Thomas (1478–1535): An English scholar, lawyer, politician, and humanist. More wrote *Utopia* and was the lord chancellor of England before being executed for refusing to recognize Henry VIII's Church of England. He was also one of the most vocal and harshest critics of Luther.

Mountain: A radical Jacobin faction—so named for the high seats its members occupied in the Assembly hall—that held power during the Reign of Terror. Under the leadership of Robespierre, they successfully pushed for the execution of Louis XVI, vigorous prosecution of the war effort, government regulation of the economy, and ruthless suppression of counterrevolution.

Mussolini, Benito (1883–1945): The leader of Italian fascism, Mussolini consolidated his hold on Italy between 1922 and 1925, staging a "March on Rome" with his paramilitary black shirts. After 1925 Mussolini ruled Italy as head of a party dictatorship, until he was deposed in 1943, captured, and executed in 1945.

Mutiny (1857): The British term for the Indian uprising that was sparked when Hindu and Muslim soldiers refused to use rifle cartridges they believed to be coated with beef and pork fat and were harshly disciplined by their British commander. Protests against the cartridges fed into widespread resentment of British policies, and soon the episode became a full-fledged rebellion before being violently suppressed by British troops.

Napoleon III (r. 1852–1870): The nephew of Napoleon Bonaparte, Napoleon III was elected president of the French Second Republic in 1848 and made himself emperor of France in 1852. During his reign, he rebuilt the French capital of Paris. Defeated in the Franco-Prussian War, he went into exile.

National Assembly: The governing body of France that succeeded the Estates General in 1789 during the French Revolution. It was composed of, and defined by, the delegates of the Third Estate.

National Convention: The governing body of France from September 1732 to October 1795, charged with writing a new constitution. It declared France a republic and then tried and executed Louis XVI. The Convention also confiscated the property of enemies of the Revolution, instituted a policy of de-Christianization, and placed a cap on the price of necessities.

National Front: The most prominent political party in twenty-first-century France, known for its conservative policies and anti-immigrant rhetoric; led first by Jean-Marie Le Pen, then by his daughter, Marine Le Pen.

National Liberation Front (FLN): A nationalist Algerian movement founded in 1954, using guerrilla and terrorist tactics to revolt against French control.

nationalism: A movement to unify a country under one government based on perceptions of the population's common history, customs, and social traditions.

Nazis: The National Socialist German Workers' Party, which under Adolf Hitler controlled Germany from 1933 to Germany's defeat in 1945. Nazi ideology was founded on violent anti-Semitism, anti-Marxism, and German nationalism.

Nazi-Soviet Pact: An August 1939 agreement in which Nazi Germany and the Soviet Union declared mutual non-aggression. Secret clauses divided eastern Europe into spheres of influence. The pact paved the way for the German invasion of Poland just a week later.

neoliberalism: The economic belief that free markets and restraints on budget deficits and social welfare programs are the best guarantee of individual liberties.

new imperialism: A push for colonial expansion beginning in the 1880s, in which major western European powers vied for territory in Asia and Africa for economic gain and material resources rather than for settlement. The new imperialism demonstrated Europe's economic and technological clout and led to the severe subjugation of indigenous populations.

Newton, Isaac (1642–1727): An English physicist and mathematician who in his *Principia Mathematica* (1687) showed how objects act on one another through a law of universal gravitation. By using differential calculus, which he invented, he demonstrated how the same forces govern both terrestrial and planetary motion.

Nietzsche, Friedrich (1844–1900): The German philosopher who argued that both Christian morality and rationality had sapped Western civilization of its creative life force. In works such as *Thus Spoke Zarathustra* (1883–85), he maintained that a "superman" not bound by conventional morality could restore the vitality of the life force.

Nightingale, Florence (1820–1910): A British battlefield nurse who served in the Crimean War, established nursing as a profession, and worked to improve healthcare.

Ninety-Five Theses: Penned by Luther in 1517, the theses were a stinging criticism of the Church's practice of selling indulgences and are considered the first event in the Protestant Reformation.

North Atlantic Treaty Organization (NATO): A military alliance created among the United States, Canada, and ten Western European countries in 1949 to counteract the growing influence of the Soviet bloc. Today NATO includes twenty-eight countries, including former members of the Warsaw Pact.

Nuremberg Laws: Laws enacted by the German government in 1935 that stripped Jews of citizenship, denied them entry into most professions, and required them to wear yellow Stars of David on their clothing.

Nuremberg trials: The prosecution of twenty-one leading Nazis in late 1945. Eleven were sentenced to death, including Hitler's deputy Hermann Goering.

oil shock (1973–1974): In retaliation for U.S. support of Israel during the 1973 Yom Kippur War, Arab states halted oil exports to the United States and cut back on oil production. Over the next two years, the fourfold increase in crude oil prices contributed to a severe economic recession in most of the West.

Operation Barbarossa: Germany's invasion of the Soviet Union in 1941.

Opium War (1839–1842): The conflict between Britain and China that was ended by the Treaty of Nanking, which granted Britain access to Chinese ports and markets and control of the port city of Hong Kong.

Ottomans: The Ottomans, first led by Osman I, were a nomadic, warrior people who originated in the area of modern Turkmenistan. By the end of the fourteenth century, they controlled most of Turkey; led by Mehmed II, they sacked Constantinople in 1453. Their empire lasted until their defeat in World War I and the emergence of the modern Turkish state.

pan-German parliament: An assembly, formed in March 1848, to draft a constitution for a united German state. Its goals were never realized, with the most powerful German states, Austria and Prussia, refusing to be governed under a constitutional monarchy.

Pankhurst, Emmeline (1858–1928): A British feminist and the founder of the Women's Social and Political Union, which championed women's suffrage. Pankhurst urged her followers to bring the issue to the fore by taking assertive action, including civil disobedience.

Paris Commune: The revolutionary government in Paris that was formed in the spring of 1871 by the Parisian National Guard, militant workers, and political radicals who were disenchanted with the new French Republic established following the defeat by Prussia and the overthrow of Napoleon III. When the French government sent troops to assert its authority over Paris, the result was a bloody conflict in which both sides killed prisoners.

Pascal, Blaise (1623–1662): The Jansenist mathematician and philosopher whose *Pensées* defended Christian faith and expressed skepticism about conventions regarding society and knowledge.

Peace of Augsburg: The settlement, reached between Charles V and the Schmalkaldic League (an alliance of Protestant German states), that created the policy of *Cuius regio, eius religio*: the rulers of the German states could decide the official religion of their territory.

Peace of Utrecht: Negotiated in 1713–14, an agreement that concluded the War of the Spanish Succession. The settlement left Philip V on the Spanish throne; but by partitioning Spain's European territories, it put an end to Louis XIV's ambitions of French expansion.

Peace of Westphalia: The set of treaties that in 1648 brought an end to the Thirty Years' War. The negotiators in effect replaced the notion of a Europe united by a common Christian religion with one of a continent based on mutual respect for the sovereignty of individual states.

Pearl Harbor: The American naval base in Hawaii that was attacked by Japan on

December 7, 1941, bringing the United States into World War II.

Peasants' War (1523–1525): A widespread popular revolt of the German peasantry. The war was fueled by several factors, primarily centered on issues of class, economics, and the Reformation. The revolt was put down in particularly brutal fashion following Luther's denunciation of the peasants.

Peninsular War (1808–1814): The conflict that raged in Iberia following Napoleon's replacement of Spain's Bourbon monarch with Napoleon's own brother Joseph. Resistance from Spanish royal forces aided by the British and by bands of local irregulars prevented France from securing effective control of Spain, thereby weakening French efforts in Russia and elsewhere.

perestroika: Meaning "restructuring," Mikhail Gorbachev's plan to reform the Soviet Union and increase efficiency to make it more competitive with the West.

Peter the Great (r. 1682–1725): The energetic tsar who transformed Russia into a leading European country by centralizing government, orienting elites more toward the West, modernizing the army, creating a navy, and reforming the economy.

Peterloo Massacre: The brutal attack by British cavalry on peaceful demonstrators in Manchester, England, on August 16, 1819. The incident occurred in response to a large popular demonstration demanding parliamentary reform and the repeal of laws that restricted foreign imports and kept cereal prices high.

Petition of Right (1628): A declaration by Parliament that limited royal power, establishing that only Parliament had the authority to levy taxes, that the king could not declare martial law during peacetime, and that prisoners had the right to appeal their detention before a court or judge.

Petrarch: Often referred to as the "Father of Humanism," Petrarch was an Italian scholar, linguist, and poet who was an important figure in the beginning of the Renaissance. He rediscovered many lost texts, which inspired him to work at revitalizing the study of classical Latin.

philosophe: One of a group of leading public intellectuals who sought to teach as well as implement the ideas of the Enlightenment, especially religious toleration.

Picasso, Pablo (1881–1973): A Spanish painter and leading modernist artist, whose 1907 masterpiece *The Young Ladies of Avignon* incorporated African influences and reduced figures to basic shapes, a technique that he developed further in later cubist works.

pietism: A Protestant religious movement that began in Germany in the seventeenth century and flourished in the eighteenth. Pietists, such as Methodists, supported an emotional, enthusiastic form of religion that focused on the individual experience of salvation.

pogroms: Anti-Jewish riots, typically occurring in nineteenth- and twentieth-century Russia.

Poor Law Amendment of 1834: An attempt by the British Parliament to address the problem of poverty by instituting a national policy designed to impose more discipline on the poor through a nationwide system of residential workhouses.

populism: A political orientation that champions the common person, usually in bitter contrast to social and cultural elites, and often demonstrates a fierce opposition to international organizations and international free trade.

portolan chart: A detailed rendering of the coastlines, ports, and trade routes of Europe, Africa, and Asia created by fourteenth- and fifteenth-century European cartographers using compasses. These maps were incredibly accurate and helpful for establishing trading posts.

Potsdam conference: The 1945 conference where U.S. president Harry Truman, British prime minister Winston Churchill, and Soviet premier Joseph Stalin met to discuss making territorial changes to Germany and its allies and the question of reparations following World War II.

proletariat: A term for the industrial working class—people who worked for wages—beginning in the nineteenth century.

protectorate: A form of imperial rule that was ostensibly created to protect indigenous populations but that in reality granted imperial governments even more power. Established by European colonizers including the British, French, and Germans during the scramble for Africa.

Protestant Reformation: The movement, starting in 1521 and inspired by Martin Luther, that called into question the theology and practices of the Catholic Church. Due to the decentralized nature of reform, many different Christian denominations emerged under the umbrella of Protestant churches.

Provisional Government: Following the abdication of Tsar Nikolai II in 1917, the unelected Russian government led by Alexander Kerensky that failed to gain widespread popular support.

"putting out" system: An eighteenth-century textile manufacturing system in which urban merchants delivered wool to peasants in rural areas, who were paid for processing the wool into coarse cloth.

Quakers: A Christian group that emerged during the English Civil Wars. They refused any role for a clergy, rejected displays of social deference, and renounced military service.

Queen Victoria (r. 1837–1901): The influential queen of Great Britain who presided over the expansion of the British Empire as well as the evolution of English politics and social and economic reforms.

realism: A nineteenth-century artistic and literary style that sought to portray common situations as they would appear in reality.

Realpolitik: A political strategy based on advancing power for its own sake, with no regard for moral or ideological concerns.

Reform Bill of 1832: In response to strong popular support for electoral reform, the British Parliament passed this bill to expand the electorate, provide for free elections, and redraw the country's electoral map more fairly.

refugee crisis: The movement of over a million refugees—mostly from Syria, Iraq, and Afghanistan—to Europe, beginning in 2015. Such a large influx created tension across Europe as different countries responded to the humanitarian crisis in different ways.

Reign of Terror (1793–1794): The campaign at the height of the French Revolution in which violence, including systematic executions, was used to purge France of its "enemies" and to extend the Revolution beyond its borders. Radicals executed as many as 40,000 people who were judged to be enemies of the state.

Republic of Letters: An informal international community of intellectual figures that included the English scientist Francis Bacon, the French philosopher René Descartes, and the Dutch scholar Anna Maria van Schurman. Starting in the late sixteenth century, members of this community shared their ideas through correspondence in Latin.

republicanism: An Enlightenment current of thought inspired by ancient republics and developed by Rousseau and other writers; it called for austerity and a strict separation of sexes.

Resistance: Anti-Vichy French resistance forces during World War II.

Richardson, Samuel (1689–1761): An English novelist whose most famous novels *Pamela* (1740) and *Clarissa* (1748), written in the form of letters by the protagonists, had a strong influence on European culture.

Robespierre, Maximilien (1758–1794): The former lawyer who became a leader of the Jacobins and the Committee of Public Safety, and also the architect of the Reign of Terror during the French Revolution. He was executed at the beginning of the Thermidorian Reaction.

Robinson Crusoe: Published in 1719 and widely regarded as the first modern realist novel. In this purportedly factual account of the resourcefulness of a man who survives a shipwreck, author Daniel Defoe provided both an exotic adventure story and a protagonist with whom ordinary readers could identify.

romanticism: An artistic and literary movement that started in the late eighteenth century and was inspired by nature and sentiment rather than by science and reason.

Rousseau, Jean-Jacques (1712–1778): The French *philosophe* and radical political theorist whose *Social Contract* attacked privilege and inequality. Rousseau argued that true freedom could only be attained by submission to the "general will."

Saint Bartholomew's Day Massacre: The mass murder of French Protestants (Huguenots) instigated by Queen Catherine de' Medici of France and carried out by Catholics in Paris on August 24, 1572 (Saint Bartholomew's day).

salons: Beginning in eighteenth-century Europe, gatherings in urban aristocratic homes, frequently hosted by elite women, for discussion of new literature, current events, and more generally ideas associated with the Enlightenment.

sans-culottes: Working-class Parisians, so named for wearing trousers rather than breeches (*culottes*), who during the French Revolution formed a militant political movement led largely by educated professionals and artisans.

Schlieffen Plan: A German military plan developed by Count Alfred von Schlieffen in 1905, calling for a quick defeat of France by invading through Belgium and then a longer war against Russia. The plan nearly succeeded in August–September 1914 but failed in part because of unexpectedly heavy resistance by the Belgians.

scramble for Africa: The European rush to colonize parts of Africa at the end of the nineteenth century.

Second Industrial Revolution: The technological developments of the last third of the nineteenth century, which included new techniques for refining and producing steel; increased availability of electricity for industrial, commercial, and domestic use; advances in chemical manufacturing; and invention of the internal combustion engine.

Second Vatican Council: A meeting of the Catholic Church convened by Pope John XXIII during 1962–65 that introduced far-reaching changes in practices and teachings, including having the Mass read in local languages instead of Latin and ceasing to blame Jews for the death of Jesus Christ.

September Massacres (1792): The name given to the week during which vigilante mobs of *sans-culottes* raided the jails of Paris and summarily tried and executed hundreds of alleged counterrevolutionaries.

Seven Years' War (1754–1753): A conflict involving fighting in Europe, North America, Africa, and India. Britain's naval superiority as well as its ability to raise funds to equip and move armies contributed to its victory over France and its allies.

Sevi, Shabbetai: A Greek Jew who during the 1650s and 1660s identified himself as the Messiah before being ordered by the Ottoman sultan to convert or face execution. His movement collapsed when he chose to accept Islam.

ship money: A medieval custom in England established by King Charles I that required coastal towns to supply ships, or the money to build them, to the crown as a means of generating royal income.

Smith, Adam (1723–1790): The Scottish philosopher and economist who proposed in *The Wealth of Nations* that competition among self-interested individuals led naturally to a healthy economy and that a division of labor would increase productivity and prosperity.

socialism: Originally meaning a social system that guaranteed decent living conditions and work for all people, a political ideology that calls for a classless society with collective ownership of all property.

Solidarity: Beginning in 1980 as an independent trade union formed by Polish shipyard workers under the leadership of Lech Wałesa, Solidarity grew into a political movement tolerated by the Communist government. Solidarity's dominance in elections in 1989 heralded the end of Communism in Poland.

soviets: Local councils elected by workers and soldiers in Russia that formed in the early twentieth century. In the midst of World War I, the Petrograd soviet in the capital emerged as one of the centers of power after the Russian monarchy collapsed in 1917. Thereafter, the soviets became increasingly powerful, pressing for social reform and the redistribution of land.

Spanish Armada: The fleet of warships sent against England by Philip II of Spain in 1588 but vanquished by the English fleet and bad weather in the English Channel.

Spanish Civil War (1936–1939): A military conflict between conservative Nationalists, led by General Francisco Franco (1892–1975), and leftist Republicans, a coalition of liberals, socialists, communists, and anarchists. Franco and the Nationalists triumphed by 1939.

Spinoza, Baruch (1632–1677): The Dutch philosopher of Jewish descent who shocked Jews, Protestants, and Catholics when he rejected the distinction between spirit and matter and propounded that the universe comprises only one substance. He further maintained that the workings of the universe could be understood only through scientific observation and logic.

Stalin, Joseph (1879–1953): The Bolshevik leader who succeeded Lenin as leader of the Soviet Union and ruled until his death in 1953.

structuralism: A form of cultural analysis that emerged in the 1950s, positing that language and culture have no inherent meaning apart from their cultural setting. Michel Foucault, a French philosopher associated with structuralism, maintained that changes in "epistemological regimes" were arbitrary.

Suez Crisis (1956): A conflict following Egyptian leader Gamal Abdel Nasser's sudden nationalization of the Suez Canal, in which Britain, France, and Israel launched coordinated attacks to reoccupy the canal zone and destabilize the new regime. Unexpectedly strong Egyptian resistance as well as condemnation of the attacks by both the Soviet Union and the United States forced the British and French to withdraw.

syndicalism: A movement that flourished in France during the late nineteenth and early twentieth centuries in which unions took militant political action against capitalism through general strikes.

taille: Established as early as 1439 in France, a permanent tax used to support the military, collected from all those who were neither clerics nor nobles.

Talleyrand, Charles-Maurice de (1754–1838): The French foreign minister under the Directory, Napoleon, and Louis XVIII. Talleyrand played an important role in persuading France's allies to restore the Bourbon dynasty under Louis XVIII following Napoleon's first abdication.

Tennis Court Oath: An oath taken by the French National Assembly in June 1789 pledging to create a new, written constitution.

Thatcher, Margaret (1925–2013): Prime minister of Great Britain during the period 1979–1990, Thatcher led a conservative government that emphasized individuality and limited government.

Thermidorian Reaction: The phase of the French Revolution, starting July 27, 1794, in which Robespierre was executed and the Reign of Terror was ended, marking the close of the most radical period of the Revolution.

tolerationists: Beginning in the seventeenth century, thinkers who argued for tolerance of other religious beliefs.

total war: First described during World War I, a war effort drawing on all of a society's military, economic, and civilian resources.

totalitarianism: A system of government based on complete state control over all aspects of public and private society.

trade unions: Beginning in the nineteenth century, collectives of workers that pushed for better working conditions and expanded suffrage.

treaties of Tilsit: Negotiated in July 1807 by Napoleon and the Russian emperor Alexander I, two agreements that divided Europe into mutually recognized spheres of influence, reduced Prussian territory, and established new satellite states in Westphalia and Poland.

Treaty of Rome (1956): The agreement in which six Western European states established the European Economic Community, a common market without trade barriers.

Treaty of Tordesillas (1494): A treaty to divide the newly explored, non-Christian lands of the New World between the Spanish and the Portuguese in the wake of Columbus's first voyage.

trench warfare: Weapons such as the machine gun and barbed wire gave tremendous advantages to defensive positions in World War I, leading to prolonged battles between entrenched armies in fixed positions. Eventually, thousands of miles of trenches and tunnels stretched across the western front.

triangle trade: The eighteenth-century commercial Atlantic shipping pattern that involved transporting rum from New England to Africa, trading it for slaves taken to the West Indies, and bringing sugar back to New England to be processed into rum.

Triple Alliance: An 1882 alliance among Germany, Austria-Hungary, and Italy.

Triple Entente: An alliance that by 1907 included Britain, France, and Russia.

the Troubles: Decades of political and sectarian violence in Northern Ireland between the Protestant majority and the minority Ulster Catholics, led at times by the Irish Republican Army. The Good Friday Agreement, signed April 10, 1998, which provided for representation of Catholics and Protestants in a National Assembly, paved the way to a reconciliation.

Turgot, Anne-Robert (1727–1781): A physiocrat, or "economist," who advocated for a series of unpopular reform programs, including edicts that freed price controls on grain, ended the conscription of peasants, abolished guilds, and formed an elected assembly to advise the monarch.

Ukrainian crisis: A crisis that erupted in Ukraine after the pro-Russian president, Viktor Yanukovych, resigned following a series of protests known as the Euromaidan, which called for Ukraine to align with the EU rather than Russia. Yanukovych's resignation ignited violence in Crimea and later in parts of eastern Ukraine, as rebels aided by Russian soldiers called for secession from Ukraine and union with Russia.

utilitarianism: A liberal school of thought that measures political good according to the welfare of individuals and holds that a government should always act to benefit the majority.

Velvet Revolution: Led by Václav Havel in November–December 1989, the peaceful transition in Czechoslovakia from a Communist to a mostly non-Communist government.

venality of office: The sale of government offices in France, especially judgeships, starting in the fifteenth century in response to the increased need for agents of the central government. The practice brought both income and noble status to the purchasers, while at the same time providing revenue to the French state.

Vendée: The department of western France that served as home to the counterrevolutionary Royal and Catholic Army. During the Reign of Terror, government forces ruthlessly exterminated not only the rebels but also much of the civilian population of the region.

Versailles Peace Conference: The peace conference held by the victors of World War I; it resulted in treaties that redrew the map of Europe, forced Germany to pay reparations and to give up its colonies to the victors, and broke up the Austro-Hungarian Empire.

Versailles: The enormous palace built by Louis XIV outside of Paris and the new center of French government in the late seventeenth century.

Vichy: The French government established after the surrender to Germany in June 1940, led by World War I hero Marshal Philippe Pétain (1856–1951). The authoritarian regime sought to remake France by pursuing ultra-conservative, anti-Semitic policies.

Voltaire (1694–1778): The French *philosophe* and satirist who championed the cause of human dignity against oppression by the state and the Church. His masterpiece, *Candide*, took aim at the belief of optimism.

Wannsee conference: A meeting of high-ranking Nazi officials in January 1942 to plan the systematic extermination of the Jews of Europe. Jews, as well as Roma, homosexuals, and those accused of political crimes were now to be deported to concentration camps, where most would be killed in gas chambers.

war communism: Radical economic policies adopted by the Bolshevik government during the Russian Civil War of 1918–1921. The policies included a top-down system of central planning, the virtual abolition of cash, and the nationalization of heavy industry.

War of the League of Augsburg: An alliance formed in the 1680s by Protestant and Catholic powers, including Sweden, England, the Netherlands, Austria, Spain, and Bavaria, to resist France's expansionist policies. The ensuing war ended in a compromise peace in 1697.

War of the Spanish Succession: A conflict beginning in 1702 when, through the will of Charles II, the entire Spanish Empire was offered to Louis XIV's grandson, who became Philip V of Spain. The prospect of Spain's European and American territories coming under French control led Austria, the Netherlands, England, and other European powers to form a Grand Alliance to contest the succession.

Warsaw Pact: A military alliance among the Soviet Union and other Communist states, established in response to the formation of NATO.

Wars of the Roses (1455–1487): A series of wars waged between the Houses of Lancaster and York during the years 1455–87 CE for control of the English crown. The Lancastrian Henry Tudor emerged victorious and established his family's dynasty for the next century.

Weimar Republic: The democratic German government established after World War I, so named for the town in which the constitution was drafted in 1919. The Republic came to an end with Hitler's rise to power in 1933.

welfare state: A state structure, adopted by states such as Sweden, Norway, Britain, and France in the twentieth century, that aims to guarantee a minimum level of services and subsistence for all citizens.

What Is the Third Estate?: A widely distributed pamphlet, written by Emmanuel Sieyès, that attacked the idea of France as a kingdom comprising different orders, or estates. The pamphlet asserted that the Third Estate—the vast majority of French who were neither clergy nor nobility—constituted a complete nation with the authority to decide for the whole.

Wilkes affair: The controversy following Parliament's removal of John Wilkes, a radical critic of the government, from his seat. The affair and subsequent movement to seat Wilkes led to British public opinion gaining a voice in politics.

Yalta Conference: The 1945 meeting among U.S. president Franklin D. Roosevelt, British prime minister Winston Churchill, and Soviet premier Joseph Stalin in which they planned for the post-war order.

Yeltsin, Boris (1931–2007): A strong advocate of Russian anti-Soviet nationalism and the first president of Russia (1991–1999) following the collapse of the Soviet Union.

Young Turks: Members of the Committee of Union and Progress who launched a successful coup in 1908 with the goal of bringing constitutional government and modernization to the Ottoman Empire.

Zwingli, Ulrich (1484–1531): The leader of the Reformed church in Zurich, Zwingli broke from Luther over differing interpretations of the Eucharist. He argued that public behavior should be regulated by the Christian magistrate.

TEXT CREDITS

CHAPTER 10

Documenting Everyday Life, p. 328 "The Declaration of Lorenzo Ghiberti, sculptor" from *The Society of Renaissance Florence: A Documentary Study*, edited by Gene A. Brucker (Toronto: University of Toronto Press, 1998). Reprinted by permission of Gene A. Brucker.

Making Connections, p. 332 "The Plight of the French Poor," translated by James Bruce Ross, from *The Portable Renaissance Reader*, edited by James Bruce Ross and Mary Martin McLaughlin, copyright 1953, 1968, renewed © 1981 by Viking Penguin Inc. Used by permission of Viking Books, an imprint of Penguin Publishing Group, a division of Penguin Random House LLC.

CHAPTER 11

Making Connections, p. 383 Excerpts from "The Twelve Articles of the Peasants" from Lowell H. Zuck, ed., *Christianity and Revolution: Radical Christian Testimonies, 1520–1650* (Philadelphia: Temple University Press, 1975). Reprinted with permission from the Estate of Lowell H. Zuck.

Excerpts from "Admonition to Peace" by Martin Luther, translated by Charles M. Jacobs in *Luther's Works: The Christian in Society III, Vol. 46*, edited by Robert C. Schultz. Copyright © 1967 Fortress Press. Reproduced by permission of Augsburg Fortress Press. All rights reserved.

CHAPTER 12

Documenting Everyday Life, p. 430 Excerpts from *The Essential Thirty Years War: A Documentary History*, edited and translated by Tryntje Helfferich (Indianapolis: Hackett Publishing Company, 2015), pp. 47–49. © 2015 Hackett Publishing Company, Inc. Reprinted with permission of Hackett Publishing Company.

Making Connections, p. 437 Excerpts from *The Galileo Affair: A Documentary History*, edited and translated by Maurice A. Finocchiaro (Berkeley: University of California Press, 1989). Copyright © 1989 by The Regents of the University of California. Reprinted by permission of the University of California Press.

CHAPTER 14

Making Connections, p. 491 "The Code Noir" reprinted from *Slave Revolution in the Caribbean, 1789–1804: A Brief History with Documents*, by Laurent Dubois and John D. Garrigus (New York: Palgrave Macmillan, 2006), pp. 51–54, © 2006 by Bedford/St. Martin's, with permission of Springer Nature.

CHAPTER 15

Making Connections, p. 526 Excerpts from "Sketch for a Historical Picture of the Progress of the Human Mind: Tenth Epoch," by Marquis de Condorcet, translated by Keith Michael Baker. *Daedalus* 133:3 (Summer 2004), pp. 74, 77–78. © 2004 American Academy of Arts & Sciences. Reprinted by permission of MIT Press Journals.

CHAPTER 16

Documenting Everyday Life, p. 558 Excerpt from *Women in Revolutionary Paris, 1789–1795*, edited and translated by Darline Gay Levy, Harriet Branson Applewhite and Mary Durham Johnson. Copyright © 1979 by the Board of Trustees of the University of Illinois. Used with permission of the University of Illinois.

CHAPTER 19

Making Connections, p. 656 Excerpts from *From Supplication to Revolution: A Documentary Social History of Imperial Russia*, edited by Gregory L. Freeze. Copyright © 1988, Oxford University Press, Inc. Reprinted by permission of Oxford University Press, USA.

CHAPTER 21

Documenting Everyday Life, p. 734 "Letter from a peasant to Bolshevik Leaders, 10 January 1918" from *Voices of Revolution, 1917*, edited by Mark D. Steinberg, translated by Marian Schwartz, pp. 302–303. Copyright © 2001 by Yale University. All rights reserved. Reprinted by permission of Yale University Press.

CHAPTER 22

Making Connections, p. 755 "The Doctrine of Fascism" by Benito Mussolini, from Michael Oakeshott, ed., *The Social and Political Doctrines of Contemporary Europe* (Cambridge: Cambridge University Press, 1939), pp. 166–168, 170–171, 177–178. © 1939 Cambridge University Press.

Documenting Everyday Life, p. 762 Excerpt from *Account Rendered: A Dossier on my Former Self* by Melita Maschmann, translated by Geoffrey Strachan. Copyright © Melita Maschmann. English translation copyright © 1964 by Harper & Row. Reprinted by permission of HarperCollins Publishers and Plunkett Lake Press; paperback and eBook editions at http://plunkettlakepress.com/ar.

CHAPTER 23

Making Connections, p. 790 Excerpts from "Russian Passion" from *A Stranger to Myself: The Inhumanity of War, Russia 1941–1944* by Willy Peter Reese, translated by Michael Hofmann. Copyright © 2011 by Hannelore Kern and Stefan Schmitz. Translation copyright © 2005 by Michael Hofmann. Reprinted by permission of Farrar, Straus and Giroux.

Excerpt from *Life and Fate* by Vasily Grossman, translated by Robert Chandler. Published by Collins Harvill. Reprinted by permission of The Random House Group Limited.

Documenting Everyday Life, p. 793 "Friday, September 4, 1942" by Josef Zelkowicz from *In Those Terrible Days: Writings from the Lodz Ghetto* (Jerusalem: Yad Vashem, 2002), edited by Michal Unger. Reprinted by permission of Yad Vashem Publications.

PHOTO CREDITS

Bridgeman Images; p. 482: Bibliotheque Nationale, Paris/Bridgeman Images; p. 484: Château de Versailles, France/Bridgeman Images; p. 485: Historisches Museum der Stadt, Vienna/De Agostini Picture Library/G. Dagli Orti/Bridgeman Images; p. 488: Gianni Dagli Orti/The Art Archive /Shutterstock; p. 492: Private Collection/Photo © Christie's Images/Bridgeman Images; p. 493: De Agostini Picture Library/A. Dagli Orti/Bridgeman Images; p. 494: Granger, NYC; p. 495 (left): Private Collection/Photo © Tarker/Bridgeman Images; (right): © The Trustees of the British Museum/Art Resource, NY; p. 497: © Look and Learn/Peter Jackson Collection/Bridgeman Images; p. 498: Private Collection/The Stapleton Collection/ Bridgeman Images; p. 501: © Courtesy of the Warden and Scholars of New College, Oxford/Bridgeman Images.

Chapter 15: Pages 504–505: Archives Charmet/ Bridgeman Images; p. 508: Archives de l'Ecole Nationale des Ponts et Chaussees, Paris/ Archives Charmet/Bridgeman Images; p. 514: akg-images; p. 516: National Gallery of Art, Washington DC/ Bridgeman Images; p. 517: Musee Conde, Chantilly, France/Bridgeman Images; p. 518: Musee National du Chateau de Malmaison, Rueil-Malmaison, France/Bridgeman Images; p. 520: British Library, London/© British Library Board. All Rights Reserved/Bridgeman Images; p. 522: HIP/Art Resource, NY; p. 523: "The Cruel Death of Calas"/Elizabeth Nesbitt Room Chapbook Collection/Hillman Lib Special Collections /Call Number: f BX9459.C3 V613 1800z/ Information Sciences Library /University of Pittsburgh; p. 524: Erich Lessing/Art Resource, NY; p. 525: De Agostini Picture Library/M. Seemuller/ Bridgeman Images; p. 527: Erich Lessing/Art Resource, NY; p. 529: State Hermitage Museum, St. Petersburg, Russia/Bridgeman Images; p. 530: Dagli Orti/REX/Shutterstock; p. 531: Granger NYC; p. 532: State Hermitage Museum, St. Petersburg, Russia/Bridgeman Images; p. 533: Hanley Museum & Art Gallery, Staffordshire, UK/Bridgeman Images; p. 534: Granger NYC; p. 535: Bibliotheque Nationale, Paris/ Bridgeman Images.

Chapter 16: Pages 538–539: The Taking of the Bastille, 14 July 1789 (oil on canvas), French School/Chateau de Versailles, France/Bridgeman Images; p. 542: Musee de la Ville de Paris, Musee Carnavalet, Paris, France/Bridgeman Images; p. 543: Courtesy of The Lewis Walpole Library, Yale University; p. 544: © RMN-Grand Palais/Art Resource, NY; p. 546: Dagli Orti/ REX/Shutterstock; p. 548: Musee de la Ville de Paris, Musee Carnavalet, Paris/Bridgeman Images; p. 549: Granger, NYC; p. 550: Musee de la Ville de Paris, Musee Carnavalet, Paris/Archives Charmet/Bridgeman Images; p. 552: Bibliotheque Nationale, Paris/Bridgeman Images; p. 553: Archiv Gerstenberg /ullstein bild via Getty Images; p. 554: akg-images; p. 555: Scala/ White Images/Art Resource, NY; p. 556:

Erich Lessing/Art Resource, NY; p. 557: The Art Archive /REX/Shutterstock; p. 559: Album/Art Resource, NY; p. 560: Private Collection/© Leemage/Bridgeman Images; p. 561: Photo © Tallandier/Bridgeman Images; p. 562: Photo © Tarker/Bridgeman Images; p. 566: Atlaspix/ Alamy Stock Photo.

Chapter 17: Pages 570–571: Heritage Images/ Getty Images; p. 573: Musee National du Chateau de Malmaison, Rueil-Malmaison, France/ Bridgeman Images; p. 575: London Metropolitan Archives, City of London/Bridgeman Images; p. 577: Château de Versailles, France/Bridgeman Images; p. 580: Private Collection/Bridgeman Images; p. 581: The Art Archive /REX/Shutterstock; p. 582: Prado Museum, Spain, Alamy Stock Photo; p. 583: Chronicle/Alamy Stock Photo; p. 585: Louvre, Paris/Bridgeman Images; p. 587 (top): © Fine Art Images/Heritage/ The Image Works; (bottom): De Agostini Picture Library/M. Seemuller /Bridgeman Images; p. 590: Clemens Lothar Wenzel, Prince Metternich, 1815 (oil on canvas), Lawrence, Thomas (1769–1830)/Royal Collection Trust © Her Majesty Queen Elizabeth II, 2017/Bridgeman Images; p. 592: Dagli Orti/REX /Shutterstock; p. 593 (top): INTERFOTO/Alamy Stock Photo; (bottom): Imagno/Getty Images; p. 597: Chronicle/Alamy Stock Photo; p. 598: Manchester Art Gallery, UK/Bridgeman Images.

Chapter 18: Pages 600–601: DeAgostini/Getty Images; p. 605: Granger, NYC; p. 606: National Gallery, London/Bridgeman Images; p. 607: ART Collection/Alamy Stock Photo; p. 608: Universal History Archive/UIG /Bridgeman Images; p. 613: Granger, NYC; p. 614 (left): Heritage Image Partnership Ltd/Alamy Stock Photo; (right): British Library, London/Bridgeman Images; p. 617: CCI/REX/Shutterstock; p. 618: Chronicle/ Alamy Stock Photo; p. 619: Private Collection/ The Stapleton Collection/Bridgeman Images; p. 620: De Agostini Picture Library/Getty Images; p. 621: Hamburger Kunsthalle, Hamburg, Germany/Bridgeman Images; p. 622: Louvre, Paris/ Bridgeman Images; p. 624: Josse Christophel/ Alamy Stock Photo; p. 625: Private Collection/ Archives Charmet/Bridgeman Images; p. 626: Leemage/Corbis via Getty Images; p. 629: Peter Horree/Alamy Stock Photo; p. 633: Private Collection/Peter Newark Pictures/Bridgeman Images.

Chapter 19: Pages 636–637: Images Group/ REX /Shutterstock; p. 639: Private Collection/© Look and Learn/Bridgeman Images; p. 641: Private Collection/© SZ Photo/Sammlung Megele/Bridgeman Images; p. 642: Roger Viollet Collection/Getty Images; p. 643: Dagli Orti/ REX/Shutterstock; p. 645 (left): Granger, NYC; (right): Christophel Fine Art/UIG via Getty Images; p. 648: Pictorial Press Ltd/Alamy Stock Photo; p. 649: Pictures From History/akg-images; p. 652 (left): Florence Nightingale Museum, London/Bridgeman Images; (right): Private Collection/Bridgeman Images; p. 653:

Schloss Friedrichsruhe, Germany/Bridgeman Images; p. 655: Granger, NYC; p. 657: Universal History Archive/UIG/ Bridgeman Images; p. 659: Granger, NYC; p. 660: Granger, NYC; p. 661: Private Collection/Bridgeman Images; p. 662: Kharbine-Tapabo/ REX/Shutterstock; p. 663: Bibliotheque Marguerite Durand, Paris/ Archives Charmet/Bridgeman Images; p. 667: Musee d'Orsay, Paris/Bridgeman Images; p. 668: Niday Picture Library/Alamy Stock Photo.

Chapter 20: Pages 670–671: Art Collection 3/ Alamy Stock Photo; p. 673: ullstein bild via Getty Images; p. 676: Heritage Image Partnership Ltd/ Alamy Stock Photo; p. 680: Archives Charmet/ Bridgeman Images; p. 681: akg-images; p. 683: Museum of the Revolution, Moscow/Sputnik/ Bridgeman Images; p. 685: Baker Street Scans/ Alamy Stock Photo; p. 686: Granger, NYC; p. 689: Private Collection/Photo © Ken Welsh/Bridgeman Images; p. 691: World History Archive/Alamy Stock Photo; p. 692: Sueddeutsche Zeitung Photo/Alamy Stock Photo; p. 694: Library of Congress/Corbis/VCG via Getty Images; p. 697: © 2017 Artists Rights Society (ARS), New York/ADAGP, Paris; Les Demoiselles d'Avignon, 1907 (oil on canvas), Picasso, Pablo (1881–1973)/Museum of Modern Art/ Bridgeman Images; p. 698: Heritage Image Partnership Ltd/Alamy Stock Photo; p. 699 (left): INTERFOTO/Alamy Stock Photo; (right): ANL/ Vienna, LW 73.623-C; p. 700: Rue des Archives/ Granger, NYC; p. 701: Images Group/ REX/Shutterstock; p. 702:© Ludwig Meidner-Archiv, Jüdisches Museum Frankfurt. akg-images.

Chapter 21: Pages 704–705: *The Menin Road*, 1919 (oil on canvas), Nash, Paul (1889–1946)/ Imperial War Museum, London/Bridgeman Images; p. 709: Mary Evans Picture Library/ Alamy Stock Photo; p. 710: Dagli Orti/REX/Shutterstock; p. 712: akg-images/Jean-Pierre Verney; p. 714: Trinity Mirror/Mirrorpix/Alamy Stock Photo; p. 715: Photo © Bonhams, London/ Bridgeman Images; p. 716: The Stapleton Collection/Bridgeman Images; p. 717: Everett Collection Historical/Alamy Stock Photo; p. 719: The Stapleton Collection/Bridgeman Images; p. 720: Science History Images/Alamy Stock Photo; p. 721: Granger, NYC; p. 722: *'Over the Top' 1st Artists' Rifles at Marcoing, 30th December 1917*, 1918 (oil on canvas), Nash, John Northcote (1893–1977)/Imperial War Museum, London, UK/© IWM (Art.IWM ART 1656)/Bridgeman Images; p. 723: James Kerr/Alamy Stock Photo; p. 725: Pictures from History/Bridgeman Images; p. 729 (top): Images Group/REX / Shutterstock; (bottom): The Print Collector/ Alamy Stock Photo; p. 735 (top): Granger, NYC; (bottom): Universal History Archive/UIG/ Bridgeman Images; p. 736: Granger, NYC.

Chapter 22: Pages 740–741: © 2017 Artists Rights Society (ARS), New York/ADAGP, Paris. *Fireside Angel* 1937 Max Ernst classicpaintings/Alamy Stock Photo; p. 744 (top): Godot13/ National Numismatic Collection, National

INDEX

Page numbers in italics refer to illustrations, maps, and tables.

The ABC of Communism, 733–34, 755
Abdulhamid II, Ottoman sultan (r. 1872–1909), 708
abortion, 838, 850, 853
absolutism, 404, 431, 443, 459–63, 479–82, 502
  in Austria, 532
  in Brandenburg, 459, 480
  conduct of warfare and, 482–85
  in Denmark, 459
  enlightened, 531–33
  in France, 460–63, 479, 532–33
  in Germany, 431, 532
  peasant life in, 481–82, 483
  in Portugal, 531
  in Prussia, 480–81, 532
  religious toleration and, 499, 531, 532
  in Russia, 474, 479–80, 532
Abyssinia, kingdom of, 691, 692 *See also*
  Ethiopia.
Account Rendered (Maschmann), 762
Action Française ("French Action"), 681
Act of Settlement (1701), 477
Act of Union (1707), 488
Acts of Union (1800), 567, 575, 684
Admonition to Peace Concerning the Twelve Articles of the Peasants (Luther), 383
aerial warfare
  in Spanish Civil War, 767
  Stuka dive-bombers in, 776, 777
  in World War I, 719, 719, 779
  in World War II, 770, 775, 776, 782, 783, 791, 795, 795
Affair of the Placards (1534), 388
Afghanistan
  Al-Qaeda in, 879
  British Empire in, 632, 633, 633, 649
  Muslims in, 853
  refugees from, 894, 895
  Soviet Union in, 853, 854, 859, 870
  United States in, 879
Africa. *See also specific African countries.*
  and artistic modernism, 697
  decolonization in, 820, 832–34, 848
  France and, 688, 689, 691, 693, 821, 832–34
  Germany and, 671–72, 673, 691, 693
  Great Britain and, 688, 689, 690–92, 693, 833–34
  Italy and, 691, 692
  malaria in, 689
  missionary activities in, 692–93
  in Ottoman Empire, 394
  partition of, 690, 690–91
  Portugal and, 346, 351, 688, 689, 834, 848
  post–World War I, 758
  refugees from, 895

  in Renaissance era, 329, 345, 346, 347–49, 351
  scramble for, 672, 689–93
  scramble out of, 833–34
  slavery and slave trade in, 347–49, 415, 416, 489–92, 509, 689
  in triangle trade, 415, 416, 489, 509
  in World War I, 717
  in World War II, 787, 787
agriculture
  in American settlements and colonies, 417, 417, 418, 492, 494, 507–8
  collectivization of, 764–65, 826
  cotton and, 507–8, 603, 605–7, 632
  enclosure movement and, 507, 604
  in England, 494
  in Enlightenment era, 506–7, 508
  in France, 482, 483, 486, 545, 609
  in Great Britain, 507, 586, 604, 678, 825
  Green Revolution in, 825
  increased productivity in, 507, 604, 678–79
  in Ireland, 646–47
  in Little Ice Age, 411, 413, 482
  in Renaissance era, 332
  in Russia, 657, 678
  in Second Industrial Revolution, 678–79
  slavery and, 509–10
  in Soviet Union, 764–65, 836
  tobacco in, 355, 415, 417, 417, 489
AIDS, 834
Akhmatova, Anna (1889–1966), 712, 830
Albania, 708, 766, 869
Albert of Brandenburg, 378
Albert von Saxe-Coburg (1819–1861), 646
Alberti, Leon Battista (1404–1472), 361, 364–65, 365, 367
Albizzi family of Florence, 327
alcohol
  in Soviet Union and Russia, 859, 874
  and temperance movement, 613, 615
Alexander, king of Yugoslavia (r. 1921–1934), 746
Alexander I, tsar of Russia (r. 1801–1825), 576–77, 578, 579, 592, 593, 596, 625
Alexander II, tsar of Russia (r. 1855–1881), 651, 655–57, 663, 682
Alexander III, tsar of Russia (r. 1881–1894), 682, 728
Alexander VI, Pope (r. 1492–1503), 325, 338
Alexandra, queen of England (r. 1901–1910), 682
Alexandra, tsarina of Russia, 707, 727
Alexei I, tsar of Russia, 480
Alfonso XIII, king of Spain (r. 1886–1931), 767
Algeria
  France and, 603, 633, 644, 688, 689, 691, 693, 821, 832–33, 896
  independence movement in, 821, 832–33, 833

  Muslims in, 633, 832, 833
  in World War II, 788
Algiers, 693, 693, 832
Algonquian Indians, 417
Alhambra Decree, 335
Allied powers
  post–World War I, 766, 769
  post–World War II, 810, 812
  in World War I, 711, 712, 713, 715–20, 723–25, 730–34, 736–38, 742
  in World War II, 776, 780, 787–89, 791, 794–96, 799–802, 804–5, 806
All Quiet on the Western Front (Remarque), 752
almanac printing, 350–51
Alpert, Max, 774–75
alphabet books, 351, 351
alphabets
  Latin, 349
  Turkish, 745
Alps, Napoleon crossing, 573, 573
Al-Qaeda, 879, 880, 894
Alsace, 457, 463, 653, 681, 687, 712
Alternative for Germany Party, 890
Amazon River, European exploration of, 352, 353
ambassadors of Renaissance Italian states, 329–30
American Civil War (1861–1865), 707
American Revolution (1776–1783), 514, 535–36, 541, 542
  and French Revolution compared, 547, 552–53
Amiens, Peace of (1802), 575
Amsterdam
  in Golden Age, 466, 467
  Jewish community in, 468
  literacy rate in, 422
  Oude Kerk (Old Church) of, 402
  population growth in, 414, 467
  vegetable markets in, 467
Anabaptists, 385, 385–86, 394
anarchism, 662, 680
The Anatomy Lesson of Dr. Nicolaes Tulp (Rembrandt), 469
Andropov, Yuri, 859
Angell, Norman (1872–1967), 679
Anglican Church, 400, 418, 443, 464
Anglo–Dutch Wars, 458, 466, 468, 470
Angola, 834, 848
Anne, queen of England (1655–1714), 478, 488
Anne of Austria, 446, 460
anthrax, 665
Anti-Corn Law League, 627
anti-immigration policies in France, 871, 880–81
antipope, Clement VII as, 339, 339
antirealism, 667–68, 668
Anti-Semitic League, 682
anti-Semitism, 871
  in Austria-Hungary, 684

in France, 681–82, 757, 780–81, 890
in Germany, 684, 743, 744, 745, 759,
  760–63, 768, 768, 805
in Great Britain, 648
Holocaust and, 805–6. *See also* Holocaust
in Poland, 781
in post-Napoleonic Europe, 596
in Russia, 681, 682, 683
antislavery movement, *534,* 534–35
in France, 534, *534,* 549, 642–43
in Great Britain, 633–34, 643
antiwar movement
  post-World War I, 766
  in World War I, 721–23, 725–27, 752
Apocalyptic Landscape (Meidner), 702, *702*
Aquinas, Thomas (1225–1274), 343
Aragon, 334–35, 391, 399
Aragon, Louis, 850
Arc de Triomphe, 583, *583,* 638, *777*
architecture
  Bauhaus School influence on, *750,* 751, 825
  of Messerturm skyscraper of Jahn, 852,
    853
  postmodern, 851, 852
  post-World War II, 825
  of public housing, 848
  of Renaissance, *361,* 361–62, 366
Argentina, 582, 849
aristocracy. *See* nobility
Aristotle (384–322 bce), 343, 527
Arkwright, Richard (1732–1792), 507
Armada, Spanish, 401, 419
Armenia, 859, 863, 866, 869
Armenians in Turkey, 708
  genocide of, 725, *725,* 743
arms control, post-World War I, 754, 766, 769
Army of England of Napoleon, 576
Arndt, Ernst Moritz (1769–1860), 589
arquebus gun, 336–37, *337*
*The Arraignment of Lewd, Idle, Forward, and
  Unconstant Women,* 423
Arras, Treaty of (1482), 331
art and artisans
  in antirealism, 667–68, *668*
  avant-garde, 697, 823
  Baroque art, *433,* 433–34, *434,* 462
  in confraternities, 510
  cubist, 698
  in Dada group, 750
  in Dutch Golden Age, 441–42, *468,* 468–70
  in Europe (1400–1500), *324–25,* 356, 359,
    361–67
  in Europe (1680–1740), 494
  in Europe (1740–1780), 517, 520, 529, *529,*
    530
  in Europe (1799–1820), 583–84
  in Europe (1820–1845), 603, 606
  in Europe (1845–1880), 666–68
  in Europe (1880–1910), 696–98, 701, 702,
    702
  in Europe (1910–1922), *704–5,* 709, 722
  in Europe (1922–1940), *740–41,* 748, 749,
    750
  in Europe (1973–2000), 851–53
  Futurist, 709
  and guilds, 596
  impressionist, 667–68, 696, 698
  in modernism, 696–98, 748, 749, 750
  neoclassical, *530*

patrons of, 362–64, 435
in Peninsular War, 582
portrait painting, 359, 494
in realism, 666, *667*
in romanticism, 620, *621,* 622, 666–67
in Soviet Great Terror, 765
surrealist, *740–41, 750*
at Versailles palace of Louis XIV, 462
Aryans in Nazi Germany, 760
Ashkenazi Jews, 344
Ashley, Lord, earl of Shaftsebury, 609
Asia. *See also specific Asian countries.*
  British expansion in, *632,* 632–33, 649,
    688, 693
  decolonization and, *819,* 819–21
  European imperialism and, 693–95, *695*
  France and, 693
  World War II in, 804–5, 806
Askew, Anne, 387
Asquith, Herbert (1852–1928), 711
Assembly of Notables (France), 543
assignats, 557
Astrakhan, 403
astrology, 343, 351
astronomy
  Copernicus on, 397, *397,* 435, 436, 437
  Galileo on, 435, 436, 437
  Kepler on, 436
  Newton on, 501
Atatürk, Kemal Mustafa, president of Turkey
  (1881–1938), 745
atheism, 522, 561
Atlantic Charter, 787
atomic weapons, 799
  at Hiroshima and Nagasaki, 795, *804,*
    804–5
  of Soviet Union, 817
Atta, Mohammed (1968–2001), 879
Attlee, Clement, 804, 813
Augsburg, Peace of (1555), 392–94, *393,* 398,
  421, 458
Augustine, Saint, 422, 449
Augustine Canons, 375
Augustus (Octavian) (63 bce–14 ce), Roman
  emperor, 358
Aung San (1915–1947), 819
Aurora in Bolshevik Revolution, 729
Auschwitz-Birkenau concentration and death
  camp, 792, *792,* 793, 803
Auschwitz Museum, *794*
Austen, Jane (1755–1817), 615, 622
austerity policies, 886, 892
Austerlitz, battle of, 577, 578, 587
Australia, 688, 693
  in Vietnam, 836
  in World War II, 788
  in World Word I, 705, 717, 718
Australian and New Zealand Army Corps, 705,
  718
Austria and Austrian Empire (pre-1867)
  absolutism in, 431, 532
  in Austro-Prussian War (1866), 651, 707
  Carbonari in, 597, 630
  and Congress of Vienna, 593
  Czechs in, 630, 641, 643, 684
  and France, 582–83
  in French Revolution era, 550, 553, 554,
    555, 557
  in Holy Alliance, 628
  Hungarians in, 638–640, 641, 643

in international balance of power, 628, 629
in Italy, 650
and Napoleon, 564–65, 567, 573, 576–77,
  582–82, 589–90
and Ottoman Empire, 448, *485,* 485–86
and revolutions of 1848, 640–41, 643, 644
in Seven Years' War, 514
in Thirty Years' War, 428
War of Succession in (1740–1748), *511,* 512
Austria (post-1918)
  border with Hungary, 861
  in European Union, 872, 881
  Great Depression in, 756
  immigrant population in, 871
  Jews in, 768
  Marshall Plan in, 814
  Nazi Germany annexation of, 768, *768*
  post-World War I, 745
  post-World War II, 829
  Versailles Peace Conference and
    settlement on, 736
  voting rights in, 753
  war crimes trials in, 812
Austro-Hungarian Empire (1867–1918)
  and Bosnia-Herzegovina, 708
  city life and culture in Vienna, 698–99
  ethnic conflict in, 684
  and Servia, 710, 732
  in Triple Alliance, 687, 707
  Versailles Peace Conference and
    settlement on, 736, 745
  in World War I, 707–8, 710–11, 712, 717, 718,
    724, 728, 732
Austro-Prussian War (1866), 651, 707
autocracy in Russia, persistence of, 682–83
automobiles, 677–78, 680, 751, 752, 823, 887
avant-garde culture, 697, 823, 840
Avicenna (Ibn Sina; ca. 980–1037), 397
Avignon, Babylon Captivity in, 339, 340
Axis powers in World War II, 788, 789, 791,
  794, 796, 812
Azerbaijan, 866
Aztecs, *353,* 354, *354,* 415

Baader, Andreas, 841
Babeuf, François-Noël (1760–1797), 564
baby boom, post-World War II, 822, 837
Babylonian Captivity of Avignon papacy, 339,
  340
Babylonian Captivity of Jews, 339
Bacon, Francis (1561–1626), 435, 436, 438, 501
Bacon, Roger (ca. 1214–ca. 1292), 343
Bahamas, Columbus landing in, 351–52
Baker, James, 863
Baker, Sidney Harold, 726
Bakunin, Mikhail (1814–1876), 662, 680
balance of power, in government,
  Montesquieu on, 528
balance of power, international, 485–88
  French Revolution affecting, 563
  in Napoleonic Wars, 572
Balboa, Vasco Núñez de (1475–1519), 352
Balfour, Arthur (1848–1930), 725, 759
Balkan League, 708
Balkans
  Bismarck on, 654
  imperial competition in, 708
  independence in, 655, 708, *708*
  Ottoman Empire in, 485, 655, 708
  religious and ethnic groups in, 708

Balkans (continued)
    Russia and, 629, 651, 655, 687
    slaves from, 347
    in World War I, 718
Balkan Wars, 708, 718, 725
ballistic missile development, 799
Balzac, Honoré de (1799–1850), 612, 622
Bank of Amsterdam, 414, 432, 478
Bank of England, 478, 495, 533, 813
banks
    in Dutch Republic, 414, 432
    in economic globalization, 870
    in economic recession (2008), 885
    in France, 495, 574, 586, 658–59
    in Great Britain, 478, 495, 533, 586, 676
    in Greece, 886
    in industrial growth, 603–4, 658–59, 676
    interest charges of, 380, 399
    warfare costs financed by, 398–99, 716
Banks, Joseph (1743–1820), 519
Banksy (British artist), 891
baptism, 377, 385
Baptistery of Florence, bronze doors of, 362, 365
Baptists, 476
Barbados, 489
barbarization of warfare, 801, 805
Barbarossa Operation, 782–85
Barcelona, 447, 768
Baroque art, *433*, 433–34
Barrès, Maurice (1862–1923), 681
Basque independence movement, 839, 848, 866
Bastille fortress, 539
    storming of, *538–39*, 539–40, 545
Battle of the Nations (1813), 590
Baudelaire, Charles, 637, 638, 668, 697
Bauer, Ida, 700
Bauhaus School, *750*, 751, 825
Bavaria
    miracle-working image in, 380–81, *381*
    and Napoleon, 583
    post–World War II, 829
    revolutions of 1848 in, 641
    Soviet Republic established in, 735
Bayezid I, Ottoman sultan, 335
Bayle, Pierre (1647–1706), 498, 499, 500, 524
Beagle (HMS), 665
Beatlemania, 838, *838*
Bebel, August, 686
Beccaria, Cesare (1738–1794), 534
Beer Hall Putsch, *744*, 744–45
Beethoven, Ludwig van (1770–1827), 589, 622
beguines, 343
Belarus, 783, 866
Belcampius, Otto, 467
Belgium, 628
    in Congo, 672, 677, 691, 692, *692*, 818, 834
    in European Economic Community, 829–30
    French invasion of, 564, 593
    German atrocities in, 712, *712*
    immigration to, 871
    nationalism in, 866
    post–World War II, 825, 829
    same-sex marriage in, 885
    terrorist attacks in, 894
    in United Netherlands, 593
    in World War I, 711, 712, 714, 715, 716, 717, 727, 730

    in World War II, 776, 780, 798, 800
Bell, Daniel, 837
Belleau Wood, battle of, 731
Bellini, Giovanni (ca. 1430–1516), 362
Benedictines, 374
The Benefits of a Good Education (Greuze), 529
Beneš, Edvard, 816
Bengal, famine in, 818
Bentham, Jeremy (1748–1832), 623, 663
Benz, Karl (1844–1929), 677–78
Bergen-Belsen concentration camp, 803
Bergman, Ingmar (1918–2007), 823
Beria, Lavrenti, 826
Berlin
    airlift of supplies to, 817, *817*
    city life in (1922–1940), *751*, 751–52
    in Cold War era, 816–17, *817*, 834, 835
    German surrender at, 802–4
    modernism in, *670–71*, 752
    occupation zones in, 802, 810, 817
    Olympic Games in (1936), 761, 847
    Potsdamer Platz in, *751*, 751–52, 753, *872*, 873
    in reunification of Germany, 863, *872*, 873
    revolutions of 1848 in, 641, *641*
Berlin Airlift, 817, *817*
Berlin Conference (1884–1885), 691
Berlin Wall, 826, 834, 835, *844–45*
    fall of, 835, 846, 861, 862, 863
Berlioz, Hector (1803–1869), 622
Bernadotte, Jean-Baptiste, 596
Bernini, Gian Lorenzo (1598–1680), 433–34, *434*
Berruguete, Pedro, *344*
Bertolucci, Bernardo (1940–), 853
Beslan attack (2004), 880
Bessemer, Henry (1813–1898), 658
Beveridge, Albert, 693
Beyle, Henri (Stendhal) (1783–1842), 622
Bible
    English translation of, 391
    Erasmus study of, 375–76, 377
    Gutenberg, *349*, 350
    in Latin, 340, 350, 377, *380*, 396
    Luther studies of, 372, 373
    plays based on, 342
    printing of, 377, 380, *380*
    Simon writing on, 499–500
    Vulgate, 377, *380*, 396
Big Push in World War I, 723
Big Three powers, 787
Bill of Rights (England), 477, 491
bin-Laden, Osama, 879
birth control, 521, 753, 838, 853
birthrate, 847
    in age of industry, 617
    baby boom in, 822
    and contraception, 521
    in post–World War I era, 753
    in Russia, 874
    in Second Industrial Revolution, 679
    in World War II, 805
Bismarck, Otto von (1815–1898), 651, 653, *653*, 654, 684
Black Army of Hungary, 337
Black Code, 490–92
Black Death, 341, 345, 347, 411, 466, 706
Black Hand, 708, 710
Black Magic, 524

black shirts (Italy), 744, 747
Black Square (Malevich), 698
Blair, Tony, 880, 892
Blake, William, 586, 608
Blanc, Louis, 640, 642
blank slate, Locke on, 502, 524
Blitz in Britain, 779, *779*
blitzkrieg (lightning war), 775, 776, 777, 780, 782
Bloody Sunday (1905), 683, *683*
Bloody Sunday (1972), 839
Blum, Léon (1872–1950), 757
Boccaccio, Giovanni (1313–1375), 357
Boccioni, Umberto (1882–1916), 701
Bochkareva, Maria (1889–1920), 717, *717*
Bodin, Jean (1530–1596), 404, 443
Boer War (1899–1902), 691–92, 696
    British concentration camps in, 691, *691*
Bohemia, 426, 643, 737
    Hussites in, 340–41, 374
    in Thirty Years' War, 426, 427, 428, 429
Bohemians, 662, *662*, 666, 667
Böhm, Hans, 384
Boleyn, Anne, 390
Bolívar, Simón (1783–1830), 631
Bolivia, silver mining in, 354
Bolotsky, Avrom-Meir, 677
Bolshevik Revolution (1917), 729, 729–30
Bolsheviks, 683, 728–30, 733–36, 765
    peasant criticism of, 734
    Stalin in, 747
    war communism of, 733, 736
Bonald, Louis de (1754–1840), 624
Bonaparte, Jerome (1784–1860), 578
Bonaparte, Joseph (1768–1844), 578, 579, 580, 581, 590
Bonaparte, Louis (1778–1846), 578
Bonaparte, Louis-Napoleon (1808–1873), 644
Bonaparte, Napoleon. *See* Napoleon I
Boniface IX, Pope (r. 1389–1404), 339
Bon Marché department store, 660, 661
Le Bon Marché (Vallotton), 661
Book of Common Prayer, 443
The Book of the City of Ladies (Christine de Pizan), 360
books
    alphabet books, 351, *351*
    Catholic censorship of, 396, 398
    chapbooks, 434–35, 514
    in Europe (1400–1500), 343, 349–51, 357
    in Europe (1600–1640), 434–35
    in Europe (1740–1780), *516*, 516–17, 520, 521, 525–27
    in Europe (1820–1845), 612, 614
books of hours, early printing of, 350, 351, 374, *374*
Bora, Katharina von (1499–1552), 387, *387*
Borgia, Cesare (1475/6–1507), 325
Borgia, Rodrigo (Pope Alexander VI), 325
Boris Godunov, tsar of Russia (r. 1598–1605), 424
Borowski, Tadeusz, 793
Borromeo, Charles, archbishop of Milan, 394–95
Borromini, Francesco (1599–1667), 433
Bosnia-Herzegovina, 684, 708, *868*, 868–69, *869*
Bosnian War, 868, 870
Boston Tea Party, 535
botany, Fuchs study of, 397, *398*

Bougainville, Louis-Antoine de (1729–1811), 519
Boulainvilliers, count of (1658–1722), 479
Boulanger, Georges, 681
Bourbon dynasty, 479, 486
    and Napoleon, 580, 581, 592
    reforms of, 531–32
    restoration of, 592
bourgeois/bourgeoisie, 611
    in age of industry, 611–15
    challenges to culture of, 662–63
    Marx and Engels on, 642, 657, 662, 728
The Bourgeois Gentleman (Molière), 462
Bourgogne, Adrien, 588
Boxer Rebellion, 693
Boyle, Robert (1627–1691), 455, 456
Boyle's Law, 455
Boyne River, battle of (1690), 478
Boyraionne, Catherine, 424
Bracciolini, Gian Francesco Poggio (1380–1459), 357, *357*
Bramante, Donato (1444–1514), 366
Brandenburg, 459, *459*, 480
Brandenburg Gate, 835
Brandt, Willy (1913–1992), 854
Braun, Eva, 803
Brazil
    Dutch capture of, 429
    European exploration of, 346, 348, 352
    Portugal and, 348, 415, 489, 631
    slavery in, 631
    sugar cultivation in, 489
Brazza, Pierre Savorgnan de (1852–1905), 689
bread, in France, 482, *482*, 483, 497, 533, 545
    in French Revolution era, 554, 557, 558
    riots in shortage of, 548, 558
breaking on the wheel, 523, *523*, 527, 534
breastfeeding in Enlightenment era, 529
Brébeuf, Jean de (1593–1649), 417
Brecht, Bertolt (Berthold) (1898–1956), 752, 827
Breitenfeld, battles at, 429, 456
Brest-Litovsk, Treaty of, 730
Bretton Woods system, 814, 847
Brexit vote, 890–92, *892*, 897
Brezhnev, Leonid (1906–1982), 836, 858, 860
Brienne, Étienne Charles de Loménie de (1727–1794), 527
Bright, John (1811–1889), 627, 634, 679
Brissot, Jacques-Pierre (1754–1793), 554–55, 556, 557, 559
British East India Company, 415, 478, 512, 632, 633, 647, 648
British Expeditionary Force in World War I, 712, 714
British Isles civil wars (1639–1649), 442–46, 465
British Society for the Promotion of Temperance, 615
British Union of Fascists, 757
"The Bronze Horseman" (Pushkin), 621
Brooke, Rupert (1887–1915), 711, 726
Brothers and Sisters of the Common Life, 342–43, 375
The Brothers Karamazov (Dostoyevsky), 666
Broz, Josip (Tito) (1892–1980), 798, 801, 816, 822, 839, 867
Bruegel, Pieter (the Elder), 412
Brunel, Isambard Kingdom (1806–1859), 652, 660

Brunelleschi, Filippo (1377–1446), *361*, 361–62, 364–65
Bruni, Leonardo (ca. 1370–1444), 357, 358
Brunswick, duke of (1735–1806), 555, 556
Brusselton-Stockton railway, inaugural trip on, 601–2
bubonic plague, 411, 466, 482
Buckingham Palace in World War II, 779
Budapest, 659, 827, *827*
Bukharin, Nikolai (1888–1938), 755
Bulgaria, 629
    in Balkan Wars, 708
    dissidents in, 854
    end of communism in, 861, 862
    in European Union, 882
    independence of, 655, 708
    post–World War II, 815–16
    sovietization of, 815–16
    in World War I, 712, 718, 731
    in World War II, 782, 801, 805–6
Bulge, Battle of, 800
Bundesrat (Germany), 654
Buonarotti, Philippe, 624
Burgundy in Renaissance era, 330, 331
Burke, Edmund (1729–1797), 550, 551, 562, 596, 624, 663
Burma, 632, 788, 819
burqa and burqinis, 893
Bush, George H. W., 860, 862–63
Bush, George W., 879, 880
Byelorussia, 863
Byron, George Gordon, Lord (1788–1824), 621, 629
Byzantium, 335

Cabaret, 752
The Cabinet of Doctor Caligari (film), 750
Cabot, John (ca. 1450–ca. 1499), 352, *353*
Cabral, Pedro Álvares (1467/8–1520), 346
Cádiz constitution (1812), 582
Il Caffè periodical, 517
cahier of Estates General, 332
Caillebotte, Gustave, *636–37*, 662
Calabria revolt, 579–80, *580*, 581
Calais refugee camp, 877–78, 891, 894
Calas, Jean, 523, *523*, 527, 534
Calas, Marc-Antoine, 523
Callot, Jacques, *413*, 429, *429*
Calonne, Charles-Alexandre de (1734–1802), 543
Calvin, John (1509–1564), *388*, 388–90, 402, 449
Calvinism, 388–90, 391, 394, 398, 418, 421, 422, 424
    in Dutch Republic, 468
    in England, 443, 476
    in France, 399, 400–401, 428
    and Jansenism, 449
    and Oude Kerk in Amsterdam, 402
Cambrai, battle of, 722
Cambridge University, 675
cameralism, 532
Cameron, David (1966–), 891–92
Cameroon, 691
Campaign for Nuclear Disarmament, 836
Campbell, Henry, 693
Canada, 688, 692, 693
    French settlers in, 492, 493, 512
    in NATO, 810, 817

    in Seven Years' War, 512
    Ursuline monastery and schools in, 451
    in World War I, 717, 724
Canal du Midi waterway, 460
canal systems
    in Amsterdam, 467
    in Dutch War, 463
    of Louis XIV, 460
    in Mexico City, 415
    in Milan, 329
    in Saint Petersburg, 474
    at Versailles, 462, 463
Candide (Voltaire), 509–10, 524, 525
Cannibal Island, 741–42
cannibalism, 405
cannons in Renaissance warfare, 336–37
The Canon of Medicine (Avicenna), 397
Capetian dynasty, 330
Capital (Marx), 662
capitalism
    in Eastern bloc countries, 873
    free-market, 528
    in Industrial Revolution, 604
    Marx on, 662
    and socialism, third way between, 862
Capuchins, 394
Carafa, Gian Pietro, 394
Carbonari, 597, *597*, 624, 630
Caribbean
    British colonies in, 688
    European exploration of, 352, *352*
    French colonies in, 512, 549, 574, 688, 693, 758, 821
    slavery in, 489–92, *550*, 550–52, 574, 605
    sugar production in, 489–92, 605
    and War of the League of Augsburg, 486, 489
Carlist Wars, 625
Carlo Alberto, king of Piedmont-Sardinia (r. 1831–1849), 642, 645
Carlos, Juan, 848
Carlos IV, king of Spain (r. 1788–1808), 580
Carmelite order, 395
Carracci, Annibale (1560–1609), *348*
Carter, Jimmy, 853
Carvalho e Melo, Sebastião José de, marquis of Pombal (1699–1782), 531
Casas, Bartolomé de las, 633
Castagno, Andrea del, *356*
Castile, 334–35, 391, 399
Castlereagh, Viscount (1796–1822), 593
Catalonia, 432, 447, 458, 767, 866
catasto (census) in Florence, 327, 328, 358
Cateau-Cambrésis, Peace of (1559), 399
Cathedral of Santa Maria del Fiore, Florence, 361, *361*, 363
cathedrals, 361, *361*, 363
Catherine I, empress of Russia, 473
Catherine II (the Great), empress of Russia (r. 1762–1796), 514, 527, 532, *532*, 550, 564, 888
Catherine of Aragon, 390, 398
Catherine of Genoa, 394
Catholic and Royal Army, 557, 559, 560
Catholic Church
    and British civil wars, 443, 444, 464
    celibacy in, 521
    confessions in, 371–72, 396
    in Europe (1500–1600), 399–401, *400*
    in Europe (1600–1640), 421–24, 426

Catholic Church (continued)
  in Europe (1640–1680), 443, 444, 447, 449–51, 458, 464
  in Europe (1680–1740), 475, 476, 477–78
  in Europe (1740–1780), 521, 523, 527, 531, 532
  in Europe (1820–1845), 619–20
  in Europe (1845–1880), 645–46, 665–66
  in Europe (1945–1973), 837–38, 839
  in France, 475, 552, 557, 574, 578–79, 592, 619–20, 645–46, 666, 682
  on Galileo as heretic, 436, 437
  in Germany, 654, 760
  and Gun-powder Plot (1605), 410
  in Holocaust, 806
  in Holy Roman Empire, 426
  humanist critics of, 375–77
  indexes of forbidden books issued by, 396, 398
  in Ireland, 444, 477–78, 627, 684, 685, 725
  in Italy, 645, 850
  and Jansenists, 449–50
  and Luther, 372–74
  in Northern Ireland, 839
  in Poland, 447, 816, 840, 856
  in Portugal, 829
  renewal and reform of, 394–96, 424, 449
  and rights of women, 685, 686
  role of priests in, 377
  and same-sex marriage issue, 885
  in Spain, 399, 581, 767, 829
  and Thirty Years' War, 421, 426–30, 450, 456, 458
  women in, 394–95, 450–51
Catholic League, 426, 430
Caucasus region, 869, 870
Cavaignac, Eugène (1802–1857), 643–44
Cavaliers in British civil wars, 444, 445, 465
Cavell, Edith, 716
Cavendish, Margaret (1623–1673), 453, 453–54
Cavour, Camillo di, 649–51
Ceaușescu, Nicolae, 854, 862
Celan, Paul, 794
Cenotaph war memorial (London), 752, 752
censorship, 515, 525, 838, 853
  in Austria, 644
  by Catholic Church, 396, 398
  by Napoleon, 574
  in Nazi Germany, 760
  in Prussia, 625
  in Soviet Union, 830
  during World War II, 796
census taking in Renaissance era, 327, 328
Central America, Spanish and Portuguese presence in, 415
Central Asia
  Muslims in, 863, 865
  refugees from, 895
  Soviet republics in, 863, 865, 866
Central powers in World War I, 711–12, 713, 716–18, 723–25, 731–33, 736
Cervantes, Miguel de (1547–1616), 434, 497
Césaire, Aimé (1913–2008), 758, 831
Ceylon, 819
Cézanne, Paul (1893–1906), 698
Chad, 780
Chamberlain, Joseph (1836–1914), 685
Chamberlain, Neville (1869–1940), 769, 776
Chambord, count of, 655
Champlain, Samuel de (1567–1635), 417

Channel Tunnel, 872
chapbooks, 434–35, 514
Chaptal, Jean-Antoine (1756–1832), 611
Charcot, Jean (1825–1893), 700
charivari, 422
Charles I, king of England (r. 1625–1649), 410, 419, 420, 432, 433, 443–45, 464, 557
Charles II, king of England (r. 1660–1685), 464, 476, 477, 478, 494
Charles II, king of Spain (1661–1700), 486
Charles III, king of Spain (r. 1759–1788), 531–32
Charles IV, king of Bohemia and Holy Roman Emperor (r. 1346–1378), 340
Charles V, Holy Roman Emperor (r. 1519–1556), 378, 378, 391–94, 392, 398, 399, 429
Charles VI, Holy Roman Emperor (r. 1711–1740), 512
Charles VI, king of France (r. 1380–1422), 339
Charles VII, king of France (r. 1422–1461), 331, 332
Charles VIII, king of France (r. 1483–1498), 337
Charles IX, king of France (r. 1560–1574), 400, 405
Charles X, king of France (r. 1824–1830), 624, 626
Charles XII, king of Sweden (1682–1718), 488
Charles Edward Stuart (Bonnie Prince Charlie) (1720–1788), 512
Charles the Bold (1433–1477), 330, 331
Charlie Hebdo magazine, 894, 894
Charter 77 (Czechoslovakia), 856, 861
Chartist movement, 627, 646
Chassériau, Théodore, 624
Chateaubriand, François-René de (1768–1848), 596, 620
Château-Thierry, battle of, 730
Châtelet, Emilie du (1706–1749), 529
Chechen War, 869, 869–70, 874
Chechnya, 869, 869–70, 879–80, 887
checks and balances in government, Montesquieu on, 528
Cheka (Russia), 730, 736
chemical weapons in World War I, 720, 720, 727, 730
Chemin des Dames, battle of, 725
Chernenko, Constantin, 859
Chernobyl nuclear accident, 859, 860
children
  alphabet books for, 351
  Congolese, 692
  in Enlightenment era, 529
  in France, during World War II, 781
  in France, rural, 483, 508
  Freud theories on, 700
  in Holocaust, 793
  in Jesuit schools, 396
  labor of, 608, 609, 675–76
  in Lodz ghetto, 793
  in Nazi Germany, 762, 784
  playing cards, Dutch painting of, 440–41, 441
  as reign of terror victims, 560, 560–61
  religious education of, 386
  in Renaissance era, 327, 332
  in slavery, 347, 490, 491, 494, 520
  in Soviet famine, 764
  in Thirty Years' War atrocities, 429, 430
  in urban poverty, 332, 496, 510, 617
  of working poor, 617
"Children Playing Cards" (Hals), 440–41, 441

China
  book printing in, 349
  Boxer Rebellion in, 693
  Communist Party in, 866
  European trade with, 693–95
  Great Britain in, 688
  Japanese invasion of, 771, 777, 787
  Mao Zedong in, 817, 836
  Opium Wars in, 632, 633, 639, 653, 693
  in Sino-Japanese War (1894–1895), 693
  and Soviet Union relations, 836
  and United States relations, 853
La Chinoise, 841
Chirac, Jacques, 880, 882
chlorine gas as weapon in World War I, 720
Chmielnicki, Bogdan (1595–1657), 447, 448, 458
chocolate in New World, 355
cholera, 617, 617, 678
Christian III, king of Denmark and Norway (r. 1534–1559), 388
Christian Democrat Party (Hungary), 890
Christian Democrat Party (Italy), 829
Christian Democrat Party (West Germany), 829, 854, 862
Christianity. See also confessions.
  in Bosnia-Herzegovina, 868–69
  and British civil wars, 443–44, 445
  in Europe (1500–1600), 371–406
  in Europe (1600–1640), 418, 421–24
  in Europe (1640–1680), 443–44, 445, 447, 449–51, 458
  in Europe (1680–1740), 475–76, 498–500
  in Europe (1740–1780), 521–23, 531–32
  in Europe (1845–1880), 665–66
  and European monarchs, 390–94
  Great Schism in (1378–1417), 339–40, 341
  humanist critics of, 375–77
  Luther on, 371–74
  marriage beliefs in, 378, 382
  and missionary activities in Africa, 692–93
  and natural world studies, 396–98
  in New World, 354–55, 355, 417, 418–19
  Orthodox, 341–42, 447, 651–52
  in Ottoman Empire, 336, 708, 725
  reforms of, 340–42, 379–90
  religious life in, 342–43
  and religious wars across Europe, 399–401, 400
  in Renaissance, 336, 339–44
  suppression in French Revolution, 561
  and witch trials, 343–44, 403–4
  women in, 394–95
Christian Social Union (Bavaria), 829
Christina, Queen of Sweden, 438
Christina of Tuscany, Grand Duchess, 437
Christine de Pizan (1364–1430), 358–60, 360
Christmas customs in Scotland, 389
Christmas Day truce (1914), 723
Chrysoloras, Manuel (d. 1415), 357
Churchill, Winston (1874–1965), 696, 706, 734, 758, 779, 795
  in Cold War era, 815, 816
  letter to Truman, 806
  at Potsdam Conference, 804
  at Tehran Conference, 799, 802
  in World War I, 718, 777
  in World War II, 776, 777–79, 787, 788, 799, 814
  at Yalta Conference, 802

Church of England, 390–91, 400, 619
    and British civil wars, 443, 444, 445
    and Glorious Revolution, 477
Church of Scotland, 443
Cicero, Marcus Tullius (106–43 bce), Petrarch
    reading letters of, 356
Le Cid (Corneille), 434
cities. *See also specific cities.*
    automobiles in, 678
    coffeehouses in, *495,* 495–96, 515
    cosmopolitanism in, 520
    in Europe (1680–1740), *495,* 495–97
    in Europe (1740–1780), 508–9, 510, 517
    in Europe (1845–1880), 659–60, 661
    in Europe (1880–1910), *670–71,* 674, 678,
        701
    in Europe (1922–1940), 745, 746, *751,*
        751–54
    in Europe (1945–1973), 825
    and factory towns, 608, 609–10
    industrial lower classes in, 615–18
    in Industrial Revolution, 607–8
    literacy in, 514–15
    middle class in, 510, 613, 659–62
    poor population in, 332, 496–97, 508–9,
        510, 615–18
    in Reformation era, 380–81
    reform movements in, 613, 615
    in Renaissance era, 332, 363
    in Second Industrial Revolution, 678
citizenship
    in France, in French Revolution era, 552
    in mandate and colonial territories, 758
    in Nazi Germany, 762
    Rousseau on, 529–30
    in Spanish colonies, 582
The City Rises (Boccioni), 701
Civic Forum (Czechoslovakia), 861
Civil Code (Napoleonic Code), 574, 575, 579,
    591, 615
Civil Constitution of the Clergy (France), 552
civil service in Brandenburg, 459
civil wars. *See also specific wars.*
    in British Isles (1639–1649), 442–46, 464,
        465
    in continental Europe (1640–1668),
        446–48
    in Russia (1918–1921), 730, *733,* 733–36, 743
    in Spain, 625, 628, *767,* 767–68
    in Ukraine and Poland-Lithuania (1648–
        1668), 447
    in United States (1861–1865), 707
Clarissa (Richardson), 516
class
    in Europe (1820–1845), 611–18
    in Europe (1845–1880), 659–62
    Marx and Engels on, 642, 662
    middle class. *See* middle class
    of native royalty, 696
    of notables, 541, 585
    in Soviet Union, 764
    working class. *See* working class
Clausewitz, Carl von (1780–1831), 590
Clemenceau, Georges (1841–1929), 736
Clement VII, Pope (antipope) (r. 1378–1394),
    339, *339,* 391
clerical work of women, 675–76
climate change, 883, 885
clocks, pendulum-driven, 414
cloth industry. *See* textile production

clothing and dress
    of Bohemians, 662
    in Eastern Europe, 857
    in European cities (1845–1880), *636–37,*
        659, 660, 662
    in European cities (1922–1940), 753, *753*
    of Muslims, 893, *893*
coal, 415, 603, 604, 605
    in Great Britain, 603, 604, 605, 609, 610,
        611, 673, 849
    and industrialization in Europe, *610,* 674
    mining for, 605, 609
    and Second Industrial Revolution, 673, 675
Cobbett, William, 591, 597
Cobden, Richard (1804–1865), 627, 634, 679
Coca-Cola, 809, 822
coffee, 489
    coffeehouses in London, *495,* 495–96, 515
Colbert, Jean-Baptiste (1619–1683), *455,*
    460–61, 463, 492
Cold War era, 809–42, 898
    Berlin in, 816–17, *817,* 834, 835
    challenges to ideologies in, 836
    Cuban missile crisis in (1962), 834
    decolonization in, 818–21
    domino theory in, 834
    North Atlantic Treaty Organization in,
        815, 817
    prosperity in, 821–26
    shifting dynamics in, 834–36
    sovietization of Eastern Europe in, 815–16
    superpowers in, 816, 818
    Warsaw Pact in, *815,* 817
Colet, John (1467–1519), 375
Colette (1873–1954), 754
collectivization of agriculture, 764–65, 826
Collins, Anthony (1676–1729), 500
colonialism and imperialism
    Césaire on, 831
    and decolonization, post–World War II,
        810, 816, 818–21, 826, 832–34, 848
    of Europe (1400–1500), 347, 348, *353,*
        354–55, *355*
    of Europe (1500–1600), 399, 401, 402
    of Europe (1600–1640), 413, 415–19
    of Europe (1640–1680), 451, 466, 470
    of Europe (1680–1740), *472–73,* 478, 488,
        489, 492–93, 494
    of Europe (1740–1780), 509–10, 512,
        519–20, 535
    of Europe (1780–1799), 549, 550–52, 566
    of Europe (1799–1820), 574
    of Europe (1820–1845), 631, *631,* 632,
        632–33
    of Europe (1845–1880), 647–49, 653
    of Europe (1880–1910), 671–73, 686–96
    of Europe (1910–1922), 717, 737–38
    of Europe (1922–1940), 757–59
    of Europe (1940–1945), 777, 787, 788
    of Europe (1945–1973), 810, 818–21, 826
    scramble for Africa and, 672, 689–93
    and scramble out of Africa, 833–34
    slave trade in, 415, *472–73,* 488, 489–92,
        509–10, 605, 633–34
The Colossus, 582
Columbian exchanges, 355–56
Columbus, Christopher (1457–1506), 338,
    351–52, *352, 353*
Combination Acts (1824), 628
Comecon alliance, 810, 814

Comédie Française, 622
Cominform, 815
Comintern (Communist International),
    734–35, 747
commemoration of World War I, *752,* 752–53
commerce. *See* trade
Committee of Public Safety (France), 559,
    560, 561, 562
Committee of Union and Progress, 708
commoners and elites in Europe (1600–1640),
    422
Common Sense (Paine), 535, 536
Commonwealth, English, 445, 447, 464
communication
    in age of industry, 607
    radio transmission in, 678
    telegraphs in, 607, 640, 652
    telephones in, *676,* 678, 883, 885
communism, 850, 856–63
    domino theory and, 834
    Engels on, 642
    Fascism compared to, 755
    Marx on, 642, 728, 734
    Proudhon on, 619
    war communism, 733, 736
    women in, 735, *735*
Communist International (Comintern),
    734–35, 747
The Communist Manifesto, 642
Communist Party
    in China, 866
    in Czechoslovakia, 816, 840, 861
    in France, 745, 757, 829, 830, 850
    in Germany, 735, *735,* 743, 759, 760, 827
    in Great Britain, 745
    in Hungary, 815, 816, 827–29, 845, 860, 861
    in Italy, 829, 830
    in Poland, 816, 827, 845, 860
    in Russia, 728–30, 733–36, 755
    in Soviet Union, 747–48, 763–65, 784, 865,
        866
    in Spain, 767
    in Yugoslavia, 816
composite monarchies, 411, 421
comuneros, 391
concentration and death camps
    of British in Boer War, 691, *691*
    of Nazi Germany, *791, 792,* 792–94, 799,
        803–4, *804*
Concert of Europe, 593–95
Conciliarists (1409–1449), 341
Condé, prince of (1621–1686), 446, 463
The Condition of the Working Class in England
    (Engels), 616
Condorcet, Marquis de, 526
Confederation of the Rhine, 577
confessions, religious, 371–72, 396
Confessions (Rousseau), 516
confraternities
    of artisans, 510, 519
    religious, 342, *342,* 374, 521
Congo
    Belgium and, 672, 677, 691, 692, *692,* 818,
        834
    France and, 691, 780
Congress Kingdom of Poland, 593, 628, 655
Congress of Berlin (1878), 655, 687
Congress of Vienna (1814–1815), 592–95, *593,*
    594, 628, 707, 711
Conrad, Joseph (1857–1924), 692

Conservative Party (Great Britain), 596, 648, 649, 685, 757, 822, 847
    and Brexit vote, 890–91, 897
    and Scotland, 892
    Thatcher in, 849–50, 855
conservatives, political, 624
    in France, 549
    in post-Napoleonic Europe, 596
    reaction to revolutions of 1848, 642–44
Constant, Benjamin, 563, 589
Constantine, Roman emperor (r. 306–337), 360, 377
Constantinople, 335, 361–62, 652
Constituent Assembly (France), 643
Constitutional Democrats (Russia), 683
constitution of France
    in Bourbon Restoration, 592
    under Louis XVIII, 596
    under Napoleon, 574
    National Assembly writing, 548–49, 552
    National Convention elected to write, 555
    Tennis Court Oath on, 545
constitution of Poland, 549, 550
Constitution of United States, 528, 536, 717
consubstantiation doctrine, 382
consumerism
    and department stores, 660, 661
    in post-World War II prosperity, 822–23, 823
Contagious Diseases Acts, 663
Contarini, Gasparo (1483–1542), 394
Contat, Nicolas, 510
Continental Congress (1775), 535
Continental System of Napoleon, 579, 580, 586, 587, 588
contraception, 521, 753, 838, 853
convents in Reformation era, 387
Cook, James (1728–1779), 519–20
Cook, Thomas (1808–1892), 614
Copernicus, Nicolaus (1473–1543), 397, 397, 398
    and Galileo, 435, 436, 437
Coppard, George (1898–1984), 721
copper mining, 391
Corneille, Pierre (1606–1684), 434
Corn Laws (Great Britain), 597, 627, 647
Coronation of Napoleon (David), 584
corporatism, 754–56
Corsican spider, Napoleon as, 575
Cortés, Hernán (b. 1485–1547), 354, 354
Cortes (courts) in Spain, 335
cosmetics in Eastern Europe, 857
cosmopolitanism, 520
    and anti-cosmopolitanism, 520–21
Cossacks, 447
cotton gin invention, 605
cotton production, 507, 603, 605–7, 632
Council of Constance (1414–18), 340, 341
Council of Florence (1439), 341
Council of Nicea, 377
Council of Trent, 396, 396
counterrevolutionaries in French Revolution, 553, 554, 555, 555–56, 560
    rebellion of (1793), 560
Courbet, Gustave (1819–1877), 666
courtiers, 484, 484–85
Court of Star Chamber (England), 444
Coverdale, Myles, 390–91
Cranach the Elder, Lucas (1472–1553), 373, 380, 387

Cranmer, Thomas, archbishop of Canterbury, 391, 398
Crédit Mobilier, 658
creoles, 582, 631
crime
    and deportation to American colonies, 492, 509
    in European cities (1680–1740), 496–97, 497
    in European cities (1740–1780), 508–9
    in European cities (1820–1845), 615, 617–18
    and social reforms, 617–18
Crime and Punishment (Dostoyevsky), 666
Crimea, 888–89, 889
    Ottoman Empire in, 335, 447, 532, 651–52
    Russia in, 532, 651–52, 655, 888–89
    in World War II, 788, 798
    Yalta conference in (1945), 802
Crimean War (1853–1856), 594, 651–52, 652, 655, 659
    battlefield medical care in, 652, 652, 721
    casualties in, 724
Critical History of the Old Testament (Simon), 499–500
Croatia, 643, 868, 869, 882
Cromwell, Oliver (1599–1658), 445, 464, 464, 465
Cromwell, Richard (1626–1712), 464
Cromwell, Thomas (ca. 1485–1540), 390
Cruikshank, George (1792–1878), 598, 613
Crusades, Fourth (1202–4), 335
Crystal Night (Kristallnacht), 763
Crystal Palace, 660, 660
Cuba, 866
    European exploration of, 352
    missile crisis in (1962), 834
    as Spanish colony, 688, 693
    sugar production in, 489
cubist art, 698
cult of domesticity, 614, 614–15
cult of personality, 765, 826
cult of the supreme being, 561, 561
culture
    and absolutism, 433–38
    avant-garde, 697, 823, 840
    Bohemian, 662
    Dutch, 441, 468
    of elites and commoners, 422, 422
    in Europe (1400–1500), 340, 344, 348, 356–68
    in Europe (1500–1600), 372–79
    in Europe (1680–1740), 495, 495–99
    in Europe (1740–1780), 514–21, 529, 534, 536
    in Europe (1780–1799), 541–42, 551, 552
    in Europe (1799–1820), 583–84
    in Europe (1820–1845), 603, 604, 612–14, 615
    in Europe (1845–1880), 659–68
    in Europe (1880–1910), 696–98, 699
    in Europe (1922–1940), 748–54
    in Europe (1945–1973), 809–10, 822–23, 830–32, 836–37, 838
    in Europe (1973–2000), 851–53
    in Europe (2000–2017), 883–85
    Islamic, 893
    middle class, 612–14, 615, 659–62, 667
    modernist, 748–54
    of native peoples, 493
    in post-industrial society, 837

    at Versailles under Louis XIV, 462
    visual. *See* visual culture
    youth culture of 1960s, 836–37, 838–41
Cunard, Samuel (1787–1865), 607
Cunard Line, 675
Curia, Roman, 358, 396
Curie, Marie (1867–1934), 685, 700, 850
Curie, Pierre (1859–1906), 700
currency
    in Bretton Woods system, 814, 847
    British, 676
    Dutch, 414
    in European trade (1680–1740), 495
    in European Union, 871–72, 878, 881, 885, 886, 891
    in France, 557
    in Germany, 744, 744, 817, 862
    gold standard in, 676, 716, 756, 814, 847
    in Napoleon era, 583
    post-World War II, 813, 814
    in Russia, 727
The Customs of American Savages Compared to the Customs of Early Times (Lafitau), 493
Cyriac, 360
Czech language, 630, 684
Czechoslovakia, 734. *See also* Czech Republic.
    Charter 77 in, 856, 861
    Civic Forum in, 861
    Communist Party in, 816, 840, 861
    dissidents in, 855, 856, 861
    ethnic tensions in, 746
    Nazi Germany in, 768–69
    post-World War I, 745, 746, 768–69
    post-World War II, 813, 816, 825
    Prague protest in (1968), 808–9
    sovietization of, 816
    Velvet Revolution in, 846, 861, 861, 866
    Versailles Peace Conference and settlement on, 736, 737
    youth culture and rebellion in, 840, 840
Czech Republic, 866, 874, 880, 883, 885. *See also* Czechoslovakia.
Czechs in Austrian Empire, 630, 641, 643, 684, 732

Dachau prison camp, 760
Dada group of artists, 750
daily life
    in age of industry (1820–1845), 607–8, 608, 609
    in cities (1740–1780), 510
    in cities (1880–1910), 678
    in cities (1922–1940), 751–54
    in Cold War Berlin, 835
    in Eastern Europe, 857
    in home fronts during World War I, 716, 717
    in home fronts during World War II, 796–99
    in Little Ice Age, 412
    in Lodz ghetto, 793
    in Nazi Germany, 762, 796, 798
    in post-World War II prosperity, 821, 822–26
    putting out system affecting, 507
    of refugees, 895
    and religion in Europe (1600–1640), 421–24
    in Renaissance, 328

in retreat of Napoleon's soldiers from Russia, 588
in Scotland during Reformation, 389
in trench warfare during World War I, 721–23
Velázquez painting of, *408–9*
at Versailles palace of Louis XIV, 462
Daladier, Édouard, 769
d'Alembert, Jean le Rond (1717–1783), 496, 524, 527
Dante Alighieri (1265–1321), 359, 622
Danton, Georges (1759–1794), 556, 562, 565
Darwin, Charles (1809–1882), 665, 695
Daughters of Charity, 450
David, Jacques-Louis (1748–1825), *530, 559*
    Napoleon paintings by, 573, *573,* 584, *585*
    Oath of the Horatii, *530,* 546
    The Tennis Court Oath, 546, *546*
d'Azeglio, Massimo, 657
D-Day (1944), 799–800, *800*
death camps in Holocaust, *791, 792,* 792–94
death penalty, 534
de Beauvoir, Simone (1908–1986), *830,* 830–32, 841
De Man, Hendrik, 780
Debussy, Claude (1862–1918), 697
Decameron (Boccaccio), 357
Decembrist Revolt (1825), *625,* 625–26
Declaration of Independence (American), 535, 536
Declaration of the Rights of Man and Citizen (France), 547, 552, 561, 563
Declaration of the Rights of Man and Citizen (Southern Netherlands), 549
"Declaration of the Rights of Woman" (Gouges), 549
decolonization, post-World War II, 810, 816, 818–21, 826, 832–34, 848
Defenestration of Prague, 426, *426*
Defoe, Daniel (1660–1731), 497, 516
de Gaulle, Charles (1890–1970), 769, 777, 780, 787, 798, 821, 833, 836, 839
deism, 522
Le Déjeuner sur l'herbe (Manet), 667, *668*
Delacroix, Eugène (1798–1863), 622, 626, *626, 629*
de Launay, Bernard-René, 539, 540
democracy, 898
    in Africa, 834
    communist threat to, 733, 738
    in Czechoslovakia, 768, 861
    in England, 464, 476, 757
    fascism compared to, 755, 756
    in former Eastern bloc countries, 873
    in France, 541, 547, 552–53, 563, 585, 654, 757, 839
    and free market policies, 862, 867, 868, 874
    in Germany, 684, 744, 817, 862, 884
    in Great Depression era, 756–57, 759
    in Greece, 829, 846, 848, 886
    in Hungary, 829, 861, 890
    and illiberalism, 889
    in Italy, 597
    liberal, 596, 634, 897
    in Netherlands, 543
    in Poland, 860
    in Portugal, 848
    post-World War I, 745, 746–47
    post-World War II, 831

    in Prussia, 579
    Rousseau on, 530, 531
    in Slovenia, 868
    social vision of, 745
    in Spain, 848
    Tocqueville on, 624, 663
    in Turkey, 708
    in Ukraine, 888
    in United States, 535, 624
    in World War II era, 794, 796, 799, 804
    in Yugoslavia, 869
Democracy in America (Tocqueville), 624, 663
The Demons (Dostoyevsky), 666
Deng Xiaoping (1904-1997), 866
Denmark
    absolutism in, 459
    in European Economic Community, 830
    in European Union, 881
    in Great Northern War, 488
    immigration to, 893
    Little Ice Age in, 459
    populism in, 893
    Prussia at war with, 651
    renewable energy in, 885
    in Thirty Years' War, 428, 456, 458, 459
    in World War II, 776, 780, 798, 805
Dentière, Marie, 387
department stores, 660, 661
Deroin, Jeanne (1805–1894), 663, *663*
Descartes, René (1596–1650), 438, 499, 502
The Descent of Man (Darwin), 665
Despard, Charlotte (1844–1939), 721
destalinization, 826–27
Detaille, Edouard, *645*
détente policy, 853
de Vieira, Antonio (1682–1745), 473, 474, 479, 480, 497, 502
devolution, 866
de Witte, Emanuel, 402
Dialogue Concerning the Two Chief World Systems (Galileo), 437
diamonds, 689, 691
Dickens, Charles (1812–1870), 612, 615, 622, 750
dictatorship of the proletariat, 662, 733–34, 755
Diderot, Denis (1713–1784), 516, 519, 524, 527, *529,* 534
Dien Bien Phu, battle of, 832
Dienstbier, Jiří, 845
Diet of Speyer (1529), 379
Diet of Worms, *378,* 378–79, 393–94
Diggelmann, Otto, 705
Diggers, 449, 465
Directory regime (France), 564, 566, 567
"Discourse on Colonialism" (Césaire), 831
Discourse on Method (Descartes), 438
Discourse on the Origins of Inequality (Rousseau), 524
diseases
    AIDS, 834
    cholera, 617, *617,* 678
    in Columbian exchanges, 355
    in European cities (1820–1845), 615, 617
    in European cities (1880–1910), 678
    in European cities (1922–1940), 752
    of Europeans affecting Native Americans, 417, 418
    in Irish famine, 647
    leprosy, 360
    Pasteur study of, 665

    plague. *See* plague
    Spanish flu (1918–19), 738
    syphilis, 338, 355, 394
    venereal, 663–64
    in World War I, 718, 721
Disraeli, Benjamin (1804–1881), 647–49, *649*
dissident movements in Eastern Europe, 854–56, 861
Diverse Thoughts on the Comet of 1680 (Bayle), 499
Djilas, Milovan, 859
Dmitri Ivanovich, 424
    and false Dmitris, 424
Dobrovský, Josef (1753–1829), 630
Dr. Zhivago (Pasternak), 830
"The Doctrine of Fascism" (Mussolini & Gentile), 755
La Dolce Vita (Fellini), 823
domesticity
    cult of, *614,* 614–15
    and feminism, 687
domestic service, work of women in, 414, 675
Dominican Republic, 489
Dominicans, 343–44, *344,* 354–55, 374
domino effect, 834, 862
Donation of Constantine, 360
Donatists, 385
Dönitz, Karl von, 803
Donne, John, 356, 434, 438
Don Quixote (Cervantes), 434, 497
d'Orléans, Philippe, 493
Dostoyevsky, Fyodor (1821–1881), 666
Doyle, Arthur Conan (1859–1930), 696
Drakulić, Slavenka, 857
Dreadnoughts, 709, *709*
Dresden, Allied bombing of, 795, *795*
Dreyfus, Alfred (1859–1935), *681,* 681–82
Drumont, Édouard (1844–1917), 681, 684
Dryden, John, 464
Dubček, Alexander (1921–1992), 840
Dubois, François, *401*
Duchamp, Marcel (1887–1968), 750
Ducos, Roger, 567
Duma, 683
Dunkirk, battle of, 776
Dunlop, John Boyd (1840–1921), 677, 678
Dupin, Amantine-Lucile-Aurore (1804–1876), 662
Durand, Marguerite (1864–1936), 676
Dürer, Albrecht (1471–1528), 334, *334,* 356, *375*
Durkheim, Émile (1858–1917), 700
Dutch East India Company, 415, 417, 466
Dutch Golden Age, 441–42, *466,* 466–70
Dutch Patriot Revolt (1781–1787), 543, *543*
Dutch Reformed Church, 476
Dutch Republic, 413–15, 432. *See also* Netherlands.
    in Anglo–Dutch Wars, 458, 466, 468, 470
    banks in, 414, 432, 466
    disaster year of (1672), 470
    France at war with, 463, 470
    Golden Age in, 441–42, 466–70
    Grotius writing on, 435
    independence of, 427
    naval strength of, 419, 458
    North American settlers from, 418, 489
    and privateering, 413, 435
    in South America, 419
    in Thirty Years' War, 428, 429
    toleration and creativity in, 468–70

Dutch Republic (*continued*)
    trade of, 414–15, 432, 458, 466, 467, 468
    wealth in, *466,* 466–68
Dutch Revolt (1566–1648), 399–400, 401
Dutch War, 463, 470
Dutt, Romesh Chunder (1848–1909), 696
dynamite, 678
Dzhugashvili, Josef, 747. *See also* Stalin, Joseph

earthquake in Lisbon (1755), 506
East Africa, 691, 717, 787, *787*
East Asian Co-Prosperity Sphere, 771, 806
East Berlin, 834, 835, 861, 873
Eastern Europe
    collapse of communism in, *859*
    daily life in, 857
    destalinization in, 826–27
    dissidents in, 854–56, 861
    economy of, 822, 856–57, 873
    environmental issues in, 857–58, *858*
    under Khrushchev, 827–29
    sovietization of, 815–16
    urbanization of, 825
    women in, 823, 857
Easter Uprising in Ireland (1916), 725, 743
East Germany, 817
    and Berlin Wall, 834, 835, 861
    dissidents in, 854–56, 861
    economy of, 826, 873
    immigration from, to West Germany, 826, 834, 835
    New Forum in, 861, 862
    Ostpolitik (East Policy) toward, 854
    protests and repression in, 827
    reunification with West Germany, 862–63
    sovietization of, 815, 816
    state security service and collaborators in, 858
Ebensee concentration camp, *804*
Eck, Johann (1486–1543), 378, *378*
economy
    in corporatism, 754–56
    in Dutch Golden Age, 466–68
    of Europe (1400–1500), 327, 328
    of Europe (1500–1600), 391
    of Europe (1600–1640), 411–15, 419, 421, 431, 435
    of Europe (1680–1740), 478, 490, 493–95, 496
    of Europe (1740–1780), 506–10
    of Europe (1780–1799), 541, 542–43, 545, 557–59
    of Europe (1799–1820), 586–87
    of Europe (1845–1880), 639, 658–59
    of Europe (1910–1922), 715–16
    of Europe (1922–1940), 744, *744,* 745, 754–57, 759
    of Europe (1940–1945), 794, 796
    of Europe (1945–1973), 815, 821–22
    of Europe (1973–2000), 847–48, 849, 850–51, 856–57, 860, 870, 873, 874
    of Europe (2000–2017), 883, 885–86
    globalization of, 676, 870–71
    government role in, 754–56, 796
    in Great Depression, 756–57, *757*
    in Great Recession, 885
    in Industrial Revolution, 611
    Keynes on, 754
    liberal view of, 623–24

    Marx on, 642, 662, 728
    mercantilist policies in, 478
    in neoliberalism, 849, 850
    in oil shock (1973–1974), 847
    of Russia, 682, 727, 733, 735–36, 873–74, 887, 889
    Smith on, 528
    of Soviet Union, 735–36, 836, 859, 863
    of Spain, 822, 885, 892
    in third way between capitalism and socialism, 862
    Thirty Glorious Years in, 822
    of United States, 489, 794
Ecstasy of Saint Teresa (Bernini), 433–34, *434*
Edgar, John, 615
Edict of Nantes, 401, 420
    revoked by Louis XIV, 475, 479, 498
Edict of Restitution (1629), 428
The Ed Sullivan Show, 838
education
    in African colonies, 693
    in Europe (1600–1640), 422, 423, *423*
    in Europe (1740–1780), 514, 516, 517, 526, 531, 532
    in Europe (1880–1910), 675
    in Europe (1945–1973), 822, 837, 841
    in Europe (2000–2017), 883
    in European Union, 872
    in France, *423,* 612, 675, 837, 841, 883
    in Germany, 612, 675, 837
    in Great Britain, 612, 675, 837, 841
    and impact of book printing, 350
    of industrial working class, 617
    in Jesuit schools, 396, 422, 531
    in Lutheran schools, 386, *386*
    in Marshall Plan, 814
    of middle class, 612
    musical training in, 517, *517*
    in Napoleon era, 584, 585
    in post-industrial society, 837
    religious, 837
    in Renaissance, 343, 358
    and Second Industrial Revolution, 675
    and student rebellions (1960s), 838–41
    of women, 423, *423,* 454, 675
Edward IV, king of England (r. 1461–1470, 1471–1483), 333
Edward VI, king of England, 398
Edward VIII, king of England (r. Jan. 1936–Dec. 1936), 757
Egypt, 629
    in Arab–Israeli War (1973), 847
    Great Britain and, 690–91, 787, 788, 832
    Napoleon campaign in, *566,* 566–67
    in World War I, 725
    in World War II, 787, 788
Ehrenburg, Ilya (1891–1967), 789
Eichmann, Adolf (1906–1962), 784, 812
Eiffel Tower, 675, 680, 692
Einsatzgruppen (special operations) in Nazi Germany, 784, 791, 792
Einstein, Albert (1879–1955), 702, 799
Eisenhower, Dwight David (1890–1969), 794, 796, 800, 832
Eisenstein, Sergei, 750
Elba, Napoleon in, 593, *593,* 595
electricity, 658, 675, 678
Eliezer, Israel ben (1698–1760), 522
Eliot, George (1819–1880), 666
Eliot, T. S. (1888–1965), 748

elites
    and commoners, 422
    and cosmopolitanism, 520
    in France prior to French Revolution, 541
Elizabeth, tsarina of Russia (r. 1741–1762), 513
Elizabeth I, queen of England (r. 1558–1603), 400, 401, 410, 415
Elizabeth II, queen of England, 779, 872
Ellis, Sarah Stickney, 613
Emile (Rousseau), 529
Enabling Act (1933), 760
enclosing of common lands for agriculture, 507, 604
encomiendas and *encomenderos* system, 354, 355
Encyclopedia (Diderot & d'Alembert), 524, 525, 527, 528
Encyclopedia Britannica, 521
energy, scientific studies on
    of Einstein, 702
    of Planck, 770
energy sources
    coal as, 415, 603, 604
    in Dutch Republic, 414
    electricity as, 658
    in Industrial Revolution, 603
    oil as, 678. *See also* oil production
    renewable, *883,* 883–85
    in Second Industrial Revolution, *674,* 675
    steam engine as, 508, *508,* 601–2, 603
Engels, Friedrich (1820–1895), 611, 616, 642, 654, 662
England, 464–66
    Act of Union with Scotland, 488
    American settlements and colonies of, 416–19, 466, 475, 489, 493, 512, 514, 535–36
    in Anglo–Dutch Wars, 458, 466, 468, 470
    antislavery movement in, 534–35
    Bill of Rights in, 477, 491
    Christianity in, 340, 390–91, 398, 400, 464
    city life and culture in (1680–1740), *495,* 495–97
    civil war in (1639–1649), 442–46, 464, 465
    coffeehouses in, *495,* 495–96
    as Commonwealth, 445, 464
    constitution of, unwritten, 464
    Court of Star Chamber in, 444
    French Huguenots in, 475
    gender roles in seventeenth-century, 454
    Glorious Revolution in (1688), 474, 476–78, 486, 494, 533
    growth of political parties in, 464
    Little Ice Age in, 411
    mercantilist policies in, 478
    middle class in, 510
    monarchy in, 333–34, 390–91
    as Netherlands ally, 478
    in Peace of Utrecht, 487–88
    periodicals and newspapers in, 496
    Petition of Right in (1628), 432
    pietism in, 522
    political equality in, 465
    Poor Law Amendment in (1834), 618
    Protestant persecution in, 476
    Reformation Movement in, 388, 390
    in Renaissance, *331,* 333–34, 340
    riots in (2011), 886
    rise in power of, 488

ship money as source of revenue in, 419, 420, 431, 443
in slave trade, 417, 493, 494
Speenhamland system in, 509
taxes in, 479
trade of, 415, 417, 478, 493–95
in War of Austrian Succession, 512
Wars of the Roses (1455–87) in, 333, *333*
English Letters (Voltaire), 525–27
Enlightenment (1740–1780), 475, 504–36
citizenship in, 529–30
cultural transformation in, 514–21
economic changes in, 506–10
impact of changes in, 541–42
literature in, 506, 516–17, 519, 521, 525–28, 529–30
politics of, 531–36
reason in, 523–24, 542
religious change in, 521–23
republicanism in, 530–31
science in, 524, 527–28
Scottish, 528
sentimentality in, 529
society in, 527–28
warfare in, 511–14
entertainment and leisure activities
in Enlightenment era, 516, 517
in middle class culture, 614, *614*, 659, 660
movie theaters in, 678
post–World War II, 822, 823
reading in, 350, 516
vacations and travel in, 614
of women in cities, 753
environmental issues
in climate change, 883, 885
in Eastern Europe, 857–58, *858*
equality
in Britain after civil wars, 465
in feminism, 687
as French Revolution principle, 547, 563, 579
in Napoleon reforms, 579
Erasing Britain from Europe (Banksy), 891
Erasmus, Desiderius (1466–1536), *375*, 375–76, 377, 381
Eritrea, 691
Ernst, Max (1891–1976), *740–41*
Essay Concerning Human Understanding (Locke), 502, 525
Essay on the Inequality of Human Races (Gobineau), 665
Essays (Montaigne), 405
Estates General (France), 331, 332, 391, 404, 443, 479, 539–41, 543–45, 624
Estates General (Prussia), 480
Estonia, 770
capitalism in, 873
independence of, 732, 866
nationalism in, 863
in NATO, 882
post–World War I, 745
Soviet invasion of, 777
Ethiopia, 691, 766, 787. *See also* Abyssinia.
ethnic cleansing in Bosnia-Herzegovina, 868
Eucharist, 377, 381–82
eugenics, 695–96, 753
Eurocommunism, 850
euro currency, 881
Euromaidan, 888

Europe. *See also specific European countries.*
in age of Napoleon (1799–1820), 571–98
at apogee (1880–1910), 671–702
balance of power in (1680–1721), 485–88
as continent in crisis (1600–1640), 408–39
emerging cultures in (1680–1740), 473–502
Enlightenment in (1740–1780), 504–36
French Revolution in (1780–1799), 539–68
ideological extremism in (1922–1940), 741–72
maritime regions of, 413–14
military revolution in, 419–20
new forms of authority and knowledge in (1640–1680), 441–70
post-Napoleonic, 595–98
in post–World War II and Cold War era (1945–1973), 809–42
under pressure (2000–2017), 877–98
Reformation era in (1500–1600), 371–406
religious intolerance in, 475–76
religious wars across, 399–401, *400*
Renaissance in (1400–1500), 324–69
return to, 866–67
and scramble for Africa, 672, 689–93
settlements and colonies in North America, 416–18, 489–95
state building in, 420–21
Thirty Glorious Years in, 822
Thirty Years' War in, 426–33
unification of (1973–1999), 845–74
in World War II (1940–1945), 775–806
European Central Bank, 881
European Community, 871
European Council, 882
European Economic Community, 829–30
European Union, 830, 846, 871–72, 881–82, 884, 898
British exit from (Brexit), 890–92, *892*, 897
constitutional treaty in, 882
currency in, 871–72, 878, 881, 885, 886, 891
economic recession in, 885–86
Euroskepticism on, 872, 881, 882, 884, 890
and Eurozone crisis, 885–86, 892
France in, 872, 882, 883, 890, 896
Germany in, 882–83, 884, 885–86
Great Britain in, 871, 872, 878, 881–82, 890–92
and Hungary, 890
members of, 872, *872*, 892
refugee crisis in, 894–96
renewable energy in, 883–85
Slovenia in, 868
Spain in, 886, 892
and Ukraine, 888, 889
and violence in Bosnia-Herzegovina, 868
Euroskepticism, 872, 881, 882, 884, 890
Eurozone, 885–86, 892
evangelization in Europe (1600–1640), 422–23, 424
Evans, Elizabeth, 408
Evans, Mary Ann, 666. *See also* Eliot, George.
An Evening with Madame Geoffrin (Lemonnier), 518
evolution theory of Darwin, 665, 695
existentialism, 830
Experimental Academy (Florence), 455
extermination camps in Holocaust, *791*, *792*, 792–94

Eyck, Jan Van (ca. 1395–ca. 1441), 350, 362, *364*
Eylau, battle of (1807), 578

Facebook, 883
Factory Acts on child labor, 608, 675–76
"The Factory Town" (Jones), 608
factory towns, 608, 609–10
Fairlie, Henry, 838
Falange (Spain), 767
Falkenhayn, Erich von (1861–1922), 720–21, 724
Falkland Islands, 849
false Dmitris, 424
family
and cult of domesticity, *614*, 614–15
in Little Ice Age and famine, 482
middle class, 612–15
in Reformation era, 387
in Renaissance Europe, 327, 332, 358
in Second Industrial Revolution, 676, 679
of working poor, 615–17
work of women in, 614–15, 676
famine
in Bengal, 818
in France, 482, *482*, 486, 508, 545
Irish potato famine, 617, 646–47
in Little Ice Age, 411, 424, 429, 482
in Netherlands, 399
in Ottoman Empire, 425
refugee crisis in, 878, *897*
in Russia and Soviet Union, 403, 411, 424, 735, 743, 764–65, 798
in Serbia, 718
in Thirty Years' War, 429
and witch trials, 403, 404
Fanon, Frantz (1925–1961), 832
Fantastic Symphony (Berlioz), 622
Farage, Nigel (1964–), 884
"Farewell to the Year 1790" pamphlet, 551
Farouk, king of Egypt (r. 1936–1952), 832
fascism, 738, 754–56
communism compared to, 755
in Italy, 743, 744, 746–47, 754–56, 766, 767
in Nazi Germany, 760
fashions, 753, *753*. *See also* clothing and dress
The Fat Kitchen (Steen), *467*
Faust (Goethe), 621
Fawcett, Millicent Garrett, 687
February Revolution in Russia (1917), 727–28
Febvre, Lucien, 342
Federal Republic of Germany. *See* West Germany.
Fellini, Federico (1920–1993), 823
The Female Instructor or Young Woman's Companion (1811), *614*
femininity, 359, 529
feminism, 501, 615
and domestic life, 687
in Europe (1640–1680), 453–54, 462
in Europe (1820–1845), 619
in Europe (1845–1880), 643, 663, 664
in Europe (1880–1910), 685–86, 687
in Europe (1940–1945), 796
in Europe (1945–1973), 830–32, 841
in Europe (1973–2000), 853
in France, 453, 462, 619, 663, 664, 830–32, 841
Fénelon, François de (1651–1715), 479
Ferdinand I, emperor of Austria (r. 1835–1848), 641, 644

Ferdinand II, Holy Roman emperor (r. 1619–1637), 426, 427, 428
Ferdinand and Isabella of Spain, 334–35, *335*, 351
Ferdinand of Styria, archduke of Inner Austria (1578–1637), 426
Fernando VII, king of Spain (r. 1808; 1813–1833), 580, 581, 590, 624, 625, 631
Ferry, Jules, 680
Festival of Federation (France), 552
Ficino, Marsilio (1433–1499), 356, 358, 360–61, 375
Fidesz Party (Hungary), 889
field hospitals in World War I, 721, *721*
Fifth Monarchy Men, 449
Fifth Republic of France, 833, 839
Fifth Symphony (Beethoven), 622
Fiji, 696
Fillon, François, 885
films
    from Hollywood, 750, 823
    and movie theaters, 678, 750
    New Wave, 823, 853
    post-World War II, 823
fin de siècle ("end of the century")
    artistic modernism in, 697, 698
    feminism in, 685–86
    France in, 680
    Germany in, 683–84
    liberal worldview in, 679–80
    Vienna in, 698, 699
Finland
    economic recession in, 885
    in European Union, 872
    independence of, 736
    Russian rule of, 588, 594
    Soviet Union in, 782
Fireside Angel (Ernst), *740–41*
First Estate (France), 545
First French Republic (1792–1793), 555–59, 561
First Maroon War, 492, *492*
First World countries, 817
First World War. *See* World War I
Five Year Plans in Soviet Union, 763–65, 770, 785
Flaubert, Gustave (1821–1880), 666
Fleury, André-Hercule (1653–1743), 479, *479*
flooding in Mexico City, canal project in prevention of, 415
Florence
    catasto (census) in, 327, 328, 358
    Experimental Academy in, 455
    Habsburg control of, 392
    Medici family of, 326, 327, *327*, 337–38, 435
    oligarchy in, 327
    patrons of art in, 362–64, 435
    in Renaissance, 326–29, 330, 337–38, 361–62, 363
"flour war" in France (1775), 508
Fontenelle, 496
foods. *See also* famine
    in age of industry (1820–1845), 604, 617
    and bread in France, 482, 483, 497, 533, 545, 548, 554, 557, 558
    in Columbian exchanges, 355
    in Dutch Golden Age, 466–68
    in Ireland, and potato famine, 617, 646–47
    post-World War II, 813
    in Soviet collectivization of agriculture, 764–65

on transatlantic passenger ships, 675
    in World War I, 716, 724
    in World War II, 779–80, 781, 785, 790, 796
forms, Plato on, 343
Fortuyn, Pim, 871, 881
Foucault, Michel (1926–1984), 841, 853
Fouquet, Nicolas (1615–1680), 460
Fourier, François-Charles (1773–1837), 618–19, 623, 624
Fourteen Points, 732
Fourth Republic of France (1947–58), 821, 829
Fox, George (1624–1691), 449
Fragonard, Jean-Honoré (1732–1806), *516*
France
    abortion in, 853
    absolutism in, 460–63, 479, 532–33
    in age of industry (1820–1845), 609, 611, 626–27, 628
    and Algeria, 603, 633, 688, 689, 691, 693, *693*, 832–33, 896
    and American Revolution, 536, 541, 542
    anti-immigration policies in, 871, 880–81
    antirealism in, 667–68
    anti-Semitism in, 681–82, 757, 780–81, 890
    antislavery movement in, 534, *534*, 549, 642–43
    antiwar movement in, 766
    banks in, 495, 574, 586, 658–59
    birthrate in, 679, 753
    Black Code of, 490–92
    Bourbon Restoration in, 592
    Calais refugee camp in, 877–78, 891, 894
    Catholic Church in, 475, 552, 557, 574, 578–79, 592, 619–20, 645–46, 666, 682
    cholera epidemic in, 617, *617*
    city life and culture in (1680–1740), 495, 496, 497
    city life and culture in (1740–1780), 517
    city life and culture in (1845–1880), *636–37*, 637–38, 659, 660
    city life and culture in (1922–1940), 752
    Civil Code of Napoleon in, 574
    civil strife in, 425–26, 428
    Communist Party in, 745, 757, 829, 830, 850
    in Congress of Vienna, 594
    constitution of. *See* constitution of France
    cosmopolitanism in (1740–1780), 520
    in Crimean War, 652, 659
    D-Day in, 799–800, *800*
    Directory regime in, 564, 566, 567
    Dreyfus Affair in, *681*, 681–82
    economy of (1780–1799), 541, 542–43, 545, 557–59
    economy of (1910–1922), 715–16
    economy of (1922–1940), 745, 754, 756, 757
    economy of (1945–1973), 822, 829
    economy of (1973–2000), 850–51
    economy of (2000–2017), 885
    education in, *423*, 612, 675, 837, 841, 883
    enlightened reform in, 532–33
    Estates General in, 331, 332, 391, 404, 443, 539–40, 624
    in European Economic Community, 829–30
    in European Union, 871, 872, 882, 883, 890, 896
    famine in, 482, *482*, 486, 508, 545

feminism in, 453, 462, 619, 663, 664, 830–32, 841
    Fifth Republic of, 833, 839
    First Republic of, 555–59, 561
    flag of, 547
    "flour war" in (1775), 508
    food rationing in, 781
    Fourth Republic of, 821, 829
    in Franco-Prussian War, 594, 653, 687
    in Franco-Russian alliance, 578
    in Franco-Spanish War, 447
    Fronde revolt in, *446*, 446–47, 458, 460, 463
    and German invasion of Poland, 769, 770
    in German occupation zone, 817
    government bankruptcy as threat in, 542–43, 545
    in Great Depression, 756, 757
    Great Fear in, 547
    guest workers in, 826
    Huguenots in, 399, 475
    hyperinflation in, 557
    immigration to, 752, 825–26, 871, 880–81, 882
    intellectual changes and culture in (1780–1799), 541–42
    in international balance of power, 628, 629, 651, 653
    Internet technology in, 870–71
    and Iraq War, 880
    in Italian Wars, 337–38
    Italy as ally of, 650, 652
    Jews in, 475, 549, 680, 681–82, 780–81, 792, 801, 833
    June Days in (1848), *643*, 643–44
    liberals in, 596
    literature in, 434, 462, 525–27, 830–32
    Little Ice Age in, 482
    mandate and colonial territories of, 757–58, *758*
    Marshall Plan in, 814
    in Mexico, 653
    middle class in, 612
    monarchy in, 331–33, 391, 474
    in Morocco, 691, 707
    at Munich meeting (1938), 769
    Muslims in, 880–81, 890, 893, *893*, 894
    Napoleon Bonaparte in, 564–67, 571–98
    National Front in, 871, 877, 881, 882, 890
    in NATO, 836
    in New World exploration, 352, 417, 492
    North American settlements and colonies of, 489, 492–93, 512
    in Opium War, 639
    Paris Commune in, 654–55, 662, 664, 680
    Paris University in, 350
    and Peace of Utrecht, 487–88
    and Peace of Westphalia, 456, 457, *457*
    and Peninsular War (1808–1814), 580–83
    populism in, 890
    post-Napoleonic, 595–98
    post-World War I, 745, 752, 753, 756, 757–58
    post-World War II, 813, 825
    poverty in, 332, 508
    printing and publishing in, 496, 515
    public culture in (1740–1780), 517
    public housing in, 848
    railways in, 872
    Reformation Movement in, 388, 390

reign of terror in (1793-1794), 559-64
religious intolerance in, 475, 499
religious observance in, decline of, 521-22, 527
religious wars in (1562-1589), 399, *400*, 400-401
in Renaissance, *331*, 331-33
republicanism in, 530, 638
resistance to Nazis in, 798, 800, 801
resistance to World War I, 725-27
revolution of 1789 in, 539-68. *See also* French Revolution
revolution of 1830 in, 626-27, 628, 639, 640
revolution of 1848 in, 639-40, 642-43, 645-46
Richelieu in, 431-32, 434
rights of women in, 420, 547, 549, *549*, 643, 685
romanticism in, 622, 666
rural, 483, 508, 825
salons in, 496, 517, 518
same-sex marriage in, 885
Second Empire of, 646
in Second Opium War, 653
Second Republic of, 639-40, 642-43, 657
in Seven Years' War, 512-14, 536
skepticism and political authority in, 500
socialism in, 655, 680, 709, 711, 745, 757, 829, 850-51
social protections in, 685
social transformations in, 541
in Southeast Asia, 693, *695*
and Spanish Civil War, 625, 628, 767, 768
student protests in (1968), 839, *839*
in Sudan, 691, 707
in Suez Crisis (1856), 832
syndicalism in, 680
taxes in, 421, 429, 446, 479
terrorist attacks in, 894, *894*
Third Estate in, 540, 541, 544, 545, 547, 554
Third Republic of, 653, 654-55, 680-82
Thirty Glorious Years in, 822
in Thirty Years' War, 428, 429, 446, 456, 458, 530
trade unions in, 680, *680*, 685
trade with American colonies, 493-95
in Triple Entente, 687, 707
ultra-conservatives in, 777
unification of, 420
venality of office in, 420, 461
in Versailles Peace Conference and settlement, 736, 738
Vichy regime in, 777, 780-81, 787, 788, 792, 798, 821
in Vietnam, 653, 821, 832
voting rights in, 552, 564, 639, 753, 823
war crime trials in, 811-12
war financing in, 716
wars under Louis XIV, 463, *463*, 470, 479, 483, 484, 485, 486-88
welfare state in, 813, 847, 848
in West Africa, 691, 693, 818
White Terror in, 564
in World War I, 706, 707, 711-21, 725-27, 730, 732, 736
in World War II, 776-77, 779-81, 796, 798-801, 804, 814
and World War I mandates, 757-58, *758*

Francesca Romana, Saint (1384-1440), 342
Francis I, Holy Roman Emperor, 483
Francis I, king of France (r. 1515-1547), 391
Francis II, emperor of Austria (r. 1804-1835), 577
Franciscans, 354, 374, 417
Franco, Francisco (1892-1975), 767, 829, 848, 853
Franco-Prussian War (1870-1871), 594, 653, 687
Franco-Spanish War, 447
Frank, Anne, 794, 806
Frankenstein (Wollstonecraft), 621
Franklin, Benjamin, 517
Franz Ferdinand, archduke of Austria (1863-1914), 709-10
    assassination of, 710, *710*
Franz Josef, emperor of Austria (r. 1848-1916), 644, 710
Frederick I, king of Bohemia, 427-28
Frederick I, king of Denmark and Norway (r. 1523-1533), 388
Frederick I, king of Prussia (1657-1713), 480, 495
Frederick II "the Great", king of Prussia (r. 1740-1786), 481, 499, 512, 513, 527, 532
Frederick III, elector of Brandenburg (1657-1713), 480
Frederick III, elector of the Palatinate (r. 1559-1576), 424
Frederick III, Holy Roman emperor, 334
Frederick III, king of Denmark (r. 1648-1670), 459, *459*
Frederick V, elector of the Palatinate, 427, 428
Frederick the Wise, elector of Saxony (r. 1486-1525), 374, 378
Frederick William, elector of Brandenburg (r. 1640-1688), 459, 480
Frederick William I, king of Prussia (r. 1713-1740), 480-81, 495
Frederick William II, king of Prussia (r. 1786-1797), 543
Frederick William III, king of Prussia (r.1797-1840), 577-78, 579, 590
Free, John, 375
freedom
    as French Revolution principle, 547
    Mill on, 663
    of press, 468, 496, 544, 625, 626
    and rights of man, 534-35
    Rousseau on, 529-30, 534
    of worship, 477
Freedom Party (Austria), 871
Free French army, 787
free market policies
    and democracy, 862, 867, 868, 874
    in French enlightenment, 533
    post-World War I, 754, 756
    Smith on, 528, 756
Freemasons, 519
French, John (1852-1925), 714, 721
French Academy of Sciences, 456
French Foreign Legion, 787
French language, 434, 462, 520, 521, 561, 583
French Revolution (1780-1799), 539-68
    and American Revolution compared, 547, 552-53
    Bastille storming in, *538-39*, 539-40
    beginning of, 543-47
    Burke on, 550, 551

civil war in, 557-59
Committee of Public Safety in, 559
counterrevolutionaries in, 553, 554, *555*, 555-56, 560, *560*
economic crisis in, 557-59
émigré army during, 553, 554, 555
and First French Republic, 555-59
Great Fear in, 547
hopes and fears in, 551
international impact of, 549-52, 563-64, 640
lack of national consensus on, 552-53
Mountaineers in, 556, 558-59, 560, 564
and Napoleon Bonaparte, 564-67, 578-79
October Days in, 548
Old Regime in, 540, 544, 545, 548, 549, 552, 554
origins of, 540-43
political and ideological responses to, 550
radicalization of, 547-55
sans-culottes movement in, 554, 555, 556, 557-59, 560, 562, 564
September massacres in, *555*, 555-56
and slavery, 549, 550-52
Tennis Court Oath in, 545, 546, *546*
The Terror in (1793-1794), 559-64
Thermidorian Reaction in, 562, *562*
as treason, 553
Valmy battle in, 556, 557
Vendée peasant rebellion in, 557, 559
violence in, 552-53
women in, 548, *548*, 549, *549*, 550, 558, 615
French Revolution (1830), 626-27, 628, 639, 640
French Revolution (1848), 639-40, 642-43, 645-46
French Union, 821
Freud, Sigmund (1856-1939), 700, *700*, 750
Friedrich, Caspar David (1774-1840), *621*
Friedrich III, kaiser of Germany (r. March-June 1888), 683-84
Friedrich Wilhelm IV, king of Prussia (r. 1840-1861), 641, 644
From the Earth to the Moon (Verne), 666
Fronde revolt (1648-1653), *446*, 446-47, 458, 460, 463
Fuchs, Leonhart, 397, *398*
Fugger, Jacob, 391
Fugger family in banking, 355, 391
Fukuyama, Francis, 867
fundamental laws in France, 420
Fundamental Rights of the German People, 644
Furet, François, 850
fur trade, 415, 417, 418, 492
Futurist group of artists, 709

Gagarin, Yuri, 828, 829
Galápagos Islands, 665
Galen, 397
Galileo Galilei (1564-1642), 435, 436, 501
    Inquisition trial, 435, 436, 437
    telescope of, 436, *436*
Gallipoli Campaign, 705, 706, 718, 724, 777
Galton, Francis (1822-1911), 695-96
Gama, Vasco da (ca. 1460-1524), 346-47, *347*
Gambetta, Léon (1838-1882), 655
Gance, Abel, 750
Gandamak, last stand of British at, 633, *633*

Gandhi, Mohandas (1869–1948), 694, 696, 759, 818–19
Garibaldi, Giuseppe (1807–1882), 645, *645*, 650, *650*
Garrick, David, 517, 521, 525
gas and chemical weapons in World War I, 720, *720*, 727, 730
gas chambers in Holocaust, 792
Gaspard II de Coligny, 400
Gauguin, Paul (1848–1903), 696, 698
gay population. *See* homosexuality
Gdańsk, Solidarity in, 856, *856*
gender roles
    Cavendish on, 453–54
    in cult of domesticity, *614*, 614–15
    in Europe (1600–1640), 414, 423, *423*
    in Europe (1640–1680), 453–54
    in Europe (1820–1845), *614*, 614–15, 619
    in Europe (1845–1880), 660, 663–64
    in Europe (1880–1910), 675–76, *676*, 687, 696
    in Europe (1922–1940), 753
    in Europe (1940–1945), 797
    in Europe (1945–1973), 823–25, 831, 832, 841
    in Europe (1973–2000), 853
    Fawcett on, 687
    Poulain on, 453
    in socialism, 663
    in textile production, 414, 610
General Confederation of Labor, 680
General Government (Poland), 781
General Maximum law (1793), 560
Geneva, Calvinism in, 388–90, 401
Genius of Christianity (Chateaubriand), 620
genocide
    of Armenians in World War I, 725, *725*, 743
    in Holocaust, 791–94. *See also* Holocaust
    of Serbs by Albanians, 867
Gentile, Giovanni (1875–1944), 755
Geography (Ptolemy), 351, 357
George, David Lloyd (1863–1945), 736, 745
George I, king of England (1660–1727), 478
George II, king of England, 512, 533
George III, king of England (r. 1760–1820), 519, 533, 535
George V, king of England (r. 1910–1936), 724
Georgia, 863, 866, 888
Géricault, Théodore (1791–1824), 622
German Confederation, 630–31, 641–42, 644, 651
German Democratic Republic. *See* East Germany
German Empire, 653–54, *654*
German language, 520, 641, 644
German Southwest Africa, 671–72, 673, 691, 717, 737
German Workers' Party, 743–44
Germany
    absolutism in, 431, 532
    in age of industry (1820–1845), 605, 609, 620, 625
    agriculture in, 678, 825
    Allied bombing of, 795, *795*, 805
    anti-Semitism in, 684, 743, 744, 745, 759, 760–63
    antiwar movement in, 721
    atrocities in Belgium, 712, *712*
    Beer Hall Putsch in, *744*, 744–45
    birthrate in, 679

    British blockade of, 716, 718, 720, 724
    Catholics in, 654, 760
    city life in (1922–1940), *751*, 751–52
    Communist Party in, 735, *735*, 743, 759, 760, 827
    East. *See* East Germany
    economy of, 744, *744*, 756, 794, 873, 885
    education in, 612, 675, 837
    in European Union, 882–83, 884, 885–86
    Federal Republic of. *See* West Germany
    fin de siècle ("end of the century") in, 683–84
    food rationing in, 716, 813
    French Huguenots in, 475
    in French Revolution era (1780–1799), 554, 563, 567
    Great Depression in, 756, *757*
    Greens party in, 854
    Grosz painting of society in, 749
    hyperinflation in, 744, *744*, 756
    immigration from, 647
    immigration to, 871
    industrialization in, 658, *673*, 673–75
    and Iraq War, 880
    Jews in, 684, 743, 744, 760, 761–63
    Messerturm skyscraper in, 852, 853
    military in, 673, 684, 687, 709, 766, 794–95
    in Namibia, 671–72, 673
    and Napoleon, 576, 577–78, 579, 589–90
    nationalism in, 521, 630–31, 684, 817
    Nazism in, 743–45, 759–63. *See also* Nazi Germany
    North American settlers from, 489
    occupation zones in, 810, 812, 814, 815
    Peasants' War in (1524–1525), 382–85
    philosophy of history in, 623
    pietism in, 522
    post-Napoleonic, 596
    post-World War I, 743–45, 754
    post-World War II, 804, 810, 815, 822
    public culture in (1740–1780), 517, 519
    refugee crisis in, 894–96
    religious movements in, 620
    reunification of, 862–63, *872*, 873
    revolutionary movements in (1848), 640–42
    romanticism in, 589, 621–22, 667
    same-sex marriage in, 885
    Second Industrial Revolution in, *673*, 673–75, 676
    in Seven Years' War, 513, 514
    socialism in, 654, 662, 684, 709, 721, 743, 759
    social protections in, 685
    in Spanish Civil War, 767
    in Thirty Years' War, 428, 429, 430, 456
    trade of, 696
    in Triple Alliance, 687, 707
    unification of, 630–31, 638, 641–42, 644, 651–52, *653*, 653–54
    Versailles Peace Conference and settlement on, 736, 738, 743, 744, 766, 769
    voting rights in, 753
    Weimar Republic of, 743–45, 759, 761
    West. *See* West Germany
    witch trials in, 424
    women's independence in (1945–1773), 824
    work of women in, 676

    in World War I, 706, 707, 711–24, 730–33, 736
    in World War II, 711, 766, 768–71
Gerson, Jean, 343
Ghiberti, Lorenzo (ca. 1378–1455), 328, 362, 363
Ghirlandaio, Domenico (1449–1494), 359
Giberti, Gian Matteo, 394
Gide, André (1869–1951), 754
Gilbert, Eliza, 641
Gillray, James, 557, *557*
Ginsberg, Allen (1926–1997), 840, *840*
Giotto di Bondone (d. 1337), 362, *362*
Girl with a Pearl Earring (Vermeer), *468*
Girondins, 554, 556, 557, 558–59, 562
Giscard d'Estaing, Valéry, 882
Gladstone, William Ewart (1809–1898), 648, 684
glasnost, 859, 860, 865
glass pyramid at Louvre Museum, 851, *851*, 852
The Gleaners (Millet), *667*
globalization, 874, 898
    economic, 870–71
    immigration and refugees in, 871, 878, 881
    and nationalism, 878
    in Second Industrial Revolution, 676
Glorious Revolution (1688), 474, 476–78, 486, 494, 533
Gobineau, Arthur de (1816–1882), 665
Godard, Jean-Luc, 841, 853
Godoy, Manuel, 580
Goebbels, Joseph (1897–1945), 759, 760, 799, 803
Goering, Hermann, 760, 804, 812
Goethe, Johann Wolfgang von (1749–1832), 521, 589, 620, 621
Gogol, Nikolai, 666
gold
    as currency standard, 676, 716, 756, 814, 847
    in South Africa, 691
Golden Age (Dutch), 466–70
    Amsterdam in, *466*, 467
    decline of, 470
    painting in, 441–42, *468*, 468–70
    toleration and creativity in, 468–70
Golden Freedoms in Poland, 425, 549
Gomulka, Wladyslaw, 827, 836, 840
Gonzalo Fernández de Córdoba, "Great Captain" (1453–1515), 335, 338
Gorbachev, Mikhail (1931–), 858, 859–60, 865
    and East Germany, 861
    on nationalism, 863
    and Reagan, *858*, 859
    and reunification of Germany, 863
    and Yeltsin, 865–66
Gordon, Charles (1833–1885), 692
Gordon riots (1780), 523
Gorky, Maxim, 728
Gouges, Olympe de (1758–1793), 549, 550, 615
government
    archives established in, 623
    conservative view of, 624
    liberal view of, 623
    Mill on, 663
    Montesquieu on, 528
    Napoleon on, 585
    in post-World War II rebuilding, 812–15
    Rousseau on, 529–30
    in welfare state. *See* welfare state

Goya, Francisco de (1746–1828), 581, *581*, 582, 584

Graffigny, Françoise de (1695–1785), 516–17

Grand Canal at Versailles, 462, *463*

Grand National Consolidated Trades Union, 628

Grand Remonstrance (England), 444

"The Grave of Countess Potocki" (Mickiewicz), 621

gravitation, universal, Newton on, 501

Great Britain, 898

    abolition of slavery in, 633–34, 643

    abortion in, 853

    in Afghanistan, 632, 633, *633*, 649

    in Africa, 688, 689, 690–92, 693, 694, 833–34

    agriculture in, 507, 586, 604, 678, 825

    American colonies of, 512, 522, 535–36

    American Revolution against, 514, 535–36, 541, 542

    anti-nuclear protests in, 854

    antiwar movement in, 721, 766

    ascendance in power and influence of, 646–49

    in Asia, *632*, 632–33, 649, 688, 693

    blockade of Germany by, 716, 718, 720, 724

    in Boer War (1899–1902), *691*, 691–92

    Brexit vote in, 890–92, *892*, 897

    child labor in, 608, 609, 675–76

    civil violence in (1791), 550

    coal in, 603, 604, 605, 609, 610, 611, 673, 849

    and Congress of Vienna, 593

    and Cook expeditions, 519–20

    Corn Laws in, 597, 627, 647

    in Crimean War, 652

    cult of domesticity in, 615

    currency of, 676

    and Czech crisis (1938), 769

    Dreadnoughts built by, 709, *709*

    economy of (1799–1820), 586–87

    economy of (1910–1922), 715–16

    economy of (1922–1940), 754, 756, 757

    economy of (1940–1945), 794

    economy of (1945–1973), 822

    economy of (1973–2000), 847–48, 849

    economy of (2000–2017), 883

    education in, 612, 675, 837, 841

    in Egypt, 690–91, 787, 788, 832

    enclosure movement in, 507, 604

    in European Economic Community, 830

    in European Union, 871, 872, 878, 881–82, 890–92

    Euroskeptics in, 872

    factory towns in, 608, 609–10

    in Falkland Islands, 849

    financing of industry in, 604, 611

    food rationing in, 716, 796, 813

    in French Revolution era (1780–1799), 550, 557, 564, 566, 567

    and German invasion of Poland, 769, 770

    German occupation zone of, 817

    in Great Depression, 756, 757

    growth of cities in, 607

    guest workers in, 826

    immigration from, 688

    immigration to, 871, *871*, 877

    imperial expansion of, *632*, 632–33, 672

    in India, 512, 632, 633, 647–48, 649, 693, 696, 759, 818–19

    industrialization in, 586–87, 602, 604–5, 606, 617, 658, 673, 675–76

    in international balance of power, 628, 629, 651, 687–89

    in Iraq War, 880

    and Irish home rule, 684–85, *685*

    Japan declaring war on, 786, 787

    in Kenya, 833–34

    in liberation of concentration camps, 803

    local governments in, 866–67

    mandate and colonial territories of, 757–59, *758*

    in Manhattan Project, 799

    middle class in, 510, 611–15

    military in, 597, 715, 717, 769

    Montesquieu on government in, 528

    at Munich meeting (1938), 769

    and Napoleon, 566, 567, 573, *575*, 575–76, 579, 586

    national identity in, 520–21

    nationalism in, 866–67

    in NATO, 836

    nuclear weapons in, 836, 853, 854

    oil shock in (1973–1974), 847

    in Opium War, 639

    origin of political parties in, 596

    penal laws in, 521

    Peterloo Massacre in, 597–98, *598*

    in post-Napoleonic era, 596, 597–98

    post-World War I, 743, 745, 752, *752*, 753–54, 756, 757–59

    post-World War II, 813, 822

    at Potsdam Conference, 804

    printing and publishing in, 515, 516

    propaganda campaigns in, 716

    public culture in (1740–1780), 517, 519

    public housing in, 848

    railways in, 601–2, 604, 606

    Reform Act of 1832 in, 627, 646, 648

    reform and repression in, 597–98, 627–28

    religious movements in, 619

    and revolutions of 1848, 646

    rights of women in, 686, *686*

    romantic movement in, 621, 622

    Second Industrial Revolution in, 673, 675–76

    in Seven Years' War, 512–14, 533, 536

    sexuality in, 646, 664

    social protections in, 685

    in South Africa, *691*, 691–92, 694

    in Soviet-American alliance, 787, 788, 802

    and Spanish Civil War, 767

    in Sudan, 691, 692, 707

    in Suez Crisis (1856), 832

    temperance movement in, 613, 615

    terrorist attacks in, 894

    Thatcher in, 849–50, 855

    trade of, 509, 604–5, 632, 696

    trade unions in, 627–28, 648, 685, 754, 847, 849

    in Triple Entente, 687, 707

    in United Kingdom, 478, 488, 567

    urbanization of, 659

    in Versailles Peace Conference and settlement, 736, 738

    Victorian Age in (1837–1901), 646–48

    voting rights in, 597, 627, 648, 686, *686*, 687, 717, 753

    war financing in, 716

    in War of 1812, 587

    in War of Austrian Succession, 512

    welfare state in, 813, 829, 847–48, 849–50

    Wilkes affair in, *533*, 533–34

    Women's Peace Camp in, 854, *854*

    work of women in, 675–76, *676*, 717, 796, 797

    in World War I, 706–7, 711–27, 730, 732, 736

    World War I commemoration in, 752, *752*, 753

    in World War II, 775–80, 786–88, 794–96, 799–800, 803, 804

    and World War I mandates, 757–59, *758*

    at Yalta Conference, 802, *802*

    youth culture of 1960s in, 838

Great Council of Venice, 329

Great Depression, 756–57, *757*

Great Exhibition (1851), 646

Great Fear in France, 547

Great Fire of London (1666), 466

The Great Illusion (Angell), 679

Great Northern War (1700–1721), 488, *488*

Great Patriotic War of USSR against Hitler, 863

Great Plague of London (1665), 466

Great Recession, 885

Great Schism (1378–1417), 339–40, 341

Great Terror (Soviet Union), 765, 770

Great War, 706. *See also* World War I

Grebel, Conrad (ca. 1498–1526), 385

Greece, 743

    ancient, 530, 542, 561, 563

    austerity policies in, 886

    in Balkan Wars, 708

    economic crisis in, 885, 886, *886*

    in European Community, 871

    in European Union, 881, 886

    independence of, 629, 630

    military coup in (1967), 846, 848

    in post-Napoleonic era, 597

    post-World War II, 816, 825, 829

    protests in, 886, *886*

    Versailles Peace Conference and settlement on, 737, 738

    in World War II, 782, 792, 800, 801

Greek crisis, 885, 886

Greek Orthodox Church, 341–42

Greeley, Horace, 660

Green Revolution, 825

Greens party (Germany), 854

Gregory XI, Pope (r. 1370–1378), 339

Greuze, Jean-Baptiste (1725–1805), 529, *529*

Grey, Edward (1862–1933), 706–7

Grimmelshausen, Hans von (1621–1676), 458

Groot, Geert (1340–1384), 342

Gropius, Walter (1883–1969), 751

Gros, Antoine-Jean (1566), *566*, 570–71

Gross, Jan, 890

Grossman, Vasily, 790

Grosz, George (1893–1959), 749

Grotius, Hugo (1583–1645), 435

Grozny, violence in, *869*, 870

Grumbach, Argula von (1492–ca. 1554), 386–387

Guadeloupe, 574

guaiacum bark as syphilis treatment, 355

Guam, 787

Gude and Godlie Ballatis, 422

Guericke, Otto von, 430

Guernica (Picasso), 767, *767*

Guernica bombardment in Spanish Civil War, 767, *767*
guerrilla warfare
    in Algeria, 832
    in Boer War, 691
    in Germany, 590
    in Iraq, 880
    in Peninsular War, 581, 582
guest workers, 826, 871
guilds
    under Louis XIV of France, 461
    in post-Napoleonic Europe, 596
    in Renaissance, 361, 362, 365
Guizot, François (1787–1874), 627, 639–40
Gulag (Soviet Union), 765, 826, 827
The Gulag Archipelago (Solzhenitsyn), 850
Gulf War, 880
Gulliver's Travels (Swift), 497–98
Gun-powder Plot (1605), 410
guns and gunpowder, 336–37, *337, 419,* 419–20, 484
Gustavus Adolphus, king of Sweden (r. 1611–1632), 421, 428–29, 430, 438
Gutenberg, Johannes (1398–1468), 349–50
    Bible printed by, *349,* 350
Guyart, Marie, 450–51

habeas corpus right in Britain, 464–66, 557
Habsburg dynasty, 334, 391–92, *392,* 411, 486
    and Bosnia-Herzegovina, 708
    feuds in, 426
    and Napoleon, 577
    in Peace of Westphalia, 457, *457*
    revolts against, 447
    and revolutions of 1848, 644
    territorial possessions of, *420,* 420–21
    in Thirty Years' War, 428, 429, 456
    in World War I, 706, 707, 718
Hagia Sophia, church of, 361–62
Hague Conventions, 679, 720
Haider, Jörg, 871
Haig, Douglas (1861–1928), 720, 724, 727
Haiti, 489, 490, 574. See also Saint-Dominque
Half Moon, 417
Hall of Mirrors (Versailles), 463, 548
Hals, Dirck (1591-1656), *440–41,* 441
Handel, George Frideric (1685–1759), 517, 519
Hanseatic League, 388
Hardenberg, Karl von (1750–1822), 579
Hardie, Keir (1856–1915), 709
Hardy, Thomas (1840–1928), 697
Harvey, William, 397
Hasidism, 522
Haskalah (Jewish Enlightenment), 522, 620
Haussmann, Georges-Eugène (1809–1891), 638, 654, 659, 662
Haussmannization, *636–37,* 638, 659
Havel, Václav (1936–2011), 845, 855, 861, 862
Hawaii, 520
    Pearl Harbor attack in, 786–87
Hawkwood, John (1320–1394), 336
Haydn, Joseph (1732–1809), 517
Hayek, Friedrich von, 849
headscarf (hijab) of Muslims, 893, *893*
Heart of Darkness (Conrad), 692
Heath, Edward, 847
Hebrew language, 620
Hebrews. *See* Jews
Hegel, Georg Wilhelm Friedrich, 578, 623, 646
Heidegger, Martin (1889–1976), 761

Heine, Heinrich (1797–1856), 602–3
heliocentric view of universe, Galileo on, 436, 437
Helsinki Accords, 856
Henlein, Konrad, 769
Henry, Emile, 680
Henry II, king of France (r. 1547–1559), 393, 398, 399
Henry III, king of France (r. 1574–1589), 401
Henry IV, king of France (r. 1589–1610), 401, 420, 421, 425, 433, *433*
Henry VI, king of England (r. 1422–1461, 1470–1471), 333
Henry VII, king of England (r. 1485–1509), 333, 352
Henry VIII, king of England (r. 1509–1547), 377, 390, 390–91, 398
Henry of Navarre, 400, 401, 405
Henry the Navigator (1394–1460), 345–46, *346*
Herder, Johann Gottfried (1744–1803), 521, 589
Herero, German massacre of, 671–72, 673, 692, 725
heresy, 398
    of Hus, 341, *341*
Hernani (Hugo), 622
Herzl, Theodor (1860–1904), 682
Heydrich, Reinhard, 791
hijab (headscarf) of Muslims, 893, *893*
Hildegard of Bingen (1098–1179), 374, 394
Himmler, Heinrich (1900–1945), 781, 804, 805
Hindenburg, Paul von (1847–1934), 712, 724, 754, 760
Hinduism, *498,* 647, 648, 818
Hiroshima bombing, 795, 804, *804*
Hispaniola, 352, 489
Historical and Critical Dictionary (Bayle), 499
history
    humanist study of, 360
    systematic study of, 622–23
History of the Inquisition (Limborch), 498–99
History of the Two Indies, 534, *534,* 633
Hitler, Adolf (1889–1945), 711, 742, 743–45, 766, 768–71
    and Allied invasion of France, 799–800
    and Allied invasion of Italy, 796
    assassination attempt on, 801
    Atlantic Wall and, 799
    and Austria annexation, 768
    and battle of Britain, 779
    and Beer Hall Putsch, *744,* 744–45
    and Czechoslovakia, 768
    at end of World War II, 799, 800, 802–3
    and fall of France, 777
    as Führer, 760
    Great Patriotic War of USSR against, 863
    and Holocaust, 805
    international alliances of, 766
    and Japanese attack on Pearl Harbor, 786–87
    in Munich Conference (1938), 769
    and Mussolini, 766, *766*
    and Operation Barbarossa, 782–85
    and Poland invasion, 769, 770–71
    resistance to, *798,* 798–99
    seizure of power, 759–60
    Soviet Union alliance with, 769–70, *770,* 777
    Soviet Union attacked by, 782–85

suicide of, 803
    war preparations of, 766, 769–70
Hitler Youth, 760, *761,* 762
Ho Chi Minh (1890–1969), 758, 821, 832
Hobbes, Thomas (1588–1679), *451,* 451–52, 477, 524, 529, 534, 623
Hoffmann, Melchior, 385–86
Hofmannsthal, Hugo von, 699
Holbein, Hans, *374*
Holland, 401, 593
Hollande, François (1954–), 884, 894
Hollander, Walther von, 824
Hollywood film industry, 750, 823
Holocaust, 781, 784, 791–94, 805–6, 890
    concentration camps in, *791,* 803–4, *804*
    deportation from Lodz ghetto in, 793
    evidence of, *794*
    factors contributing to, 805–6
    Wannsee conference on, 791
    war crime trials on, 811–12
Holy Alliance, 628
Holy Roman Empire
    civil strife in, 426
    independent states in, 421
    and Napoleon, 577
    in Peace of Westphalia, 456, 457
    Peasants' War in, 384
    Reformation Movement in, *380,* 380–81, 390
    in Renaissance, *331,* 334
    in Thirty Years' War, 429, 456
"Home and Politics" speech (Fawcett), 687
Home Army (Poland), 801
home fronts
    during World War I, 715–17
    during World War II, 796–99
home rule, Irish, 684–85, *685*
homosexuality, 497, 664, 752, 754, 853
    in Hungary, 890
    in Nazi Germany, 761, 792
    in Poland, 890
    in Russia, 889
    and same-sex marriage, 853, 885, 890
Honecker, Erich (1912–1994), 854, 861
Hong Kong, 632, 688
Hooper, John, 391
Horace, 727
horseless carriage, 677–78
horses in New World, 355
Hottentots (Nama), German massacre of, 672, 673
Houphouët-Boigny, Félix, 821
House of Commons, 685, 753
House of Lords, 685
House of Orange, 470
housing/homes
    in consumer revolution, 823
    in Dutch Republic, 414, *414*
    and high-rise apartments, 825
    lending policies on, and Great Recession, 885
    and public housing, 848, *848,* 849
Hudson, Henry (ca. 1565–1611), 417
Huexotzinco people, *355*
Hugo, Victor (1802–1885), 622, 638, 640, 666, 750
Huguenots, 399, 400–401, 475
The Human Comedy (Balzac), 622
humanism
    criticism of Church in, 375–77

of Erasmus, 375–76, 381
in Renaissance, 358–62
human nature
Enlightenment thought on, 524, 525, 526, 528–29
Locke on, 502, 524, 525
structuralism on, 841
human rights. *See also* rights
Helsinki Accords on, 856
and rights of man concept, *534,* 534–35, 536, 550
Hume, David (1711–1776), 528
The Hundred Days, 595, *595*
Hundred Years' War (1330–1453), 336
Hungarians
in Austrian Empire, 638, 640, 641, 643
in Austro-Hungarian Empire, 651, 684, 707, 732
Hungary, 426, 743
border with Austria, 861
Communist Party in, 815, 816, 827–29, 845, 860, 861
dissidents in, 856, 889
Great Depression in, 756
illiberalism in, 889–90
in Little Ice Age, 411
marriage in, 885
nationalism in, 630, 890
in NATO, 874, 880
post–World War I, 745, 746
post–World War II, 815–16, *827,* 827–29, 836
Protestant persecution in, 486
refugees in, 894
serfs in, 413
sovietization of, 815–16
Soviet Republic established in, 735
Versailles Peace Conference and settlement on, 736
in World War II, 782
Hunters in the Snow (Bruegel), 412
Huron tribe, 417
Hus, Jan (ca. 1372–1415), 340–41, *341*
Hussein, Saddam, 867, 880
Hussites, 340–41, 374
Hutter, Jacob (d. 1536), 386
Hutterites, 386
Huxley, Julian (1887–1975), 760
Huygens, Constantijn, 467
hyperinflation, 744, *744,* 756, 813

Iberian Peninsula, and Napoleon, 580–83
Ibn Sina (Avicenna; ca. 980–1037), 397
Ibrahim I, Ottoman sultan, 448
Ibsen, Henrik (1828–1906), 666
Iceland, 885
Iglesias, Pablo, 892
Ignatius Loyola (1491–1556), 395, *395*
illiberalism, 889–93
immigration, 676–77, *677*
and anti-immigration policies, 871, 880–81
within European Union, 871–73
to France, 752, 825–26, 871, 880–81, 882, 893
from Germany, 647
from Great Britain, 688
to Great Britain, 871, *871,* 877
of guest workers, 826, 871
to Hungary, 890
from India, 693, 694
from Ireland, 647
of Jews, 677, *677,* 682, 758, 762, 763, 811
in Little Ice Age, 411
of Muslims, 833, 871, 893
post–World War II, 810–11, *811,* 825–26
and refugee crisis, 894–96
and right-wing politics, 871, 880–81
to South Africa, 693, 694
to United States, 647, 677, *677,* 682
imperialism. *See* colonialism and imperialism
impressionist art, 667–68, 696, 698
Incas, 354, 415
Independent Labour Party (Great Britain), 685, 709
indexes of forbidden books issued by Catholic Church, 396, 398
India
British Empire in, 512, 632, 633, 647–48, 649, 693, 696, 759, 818–19
British trade with, 415, 632, 647
cotton production in, 632
famine in (1943), 818
French Revolution impact in, 563
immigration from, 693, 694
independence movement in, 759, *818,* 818–19
Mutiny of 1857 in, 647–48, *648*
nationalism in, 759, 818
Portuguese expedition to, 346
Seven Years' War in, 512
textile production in, 605–7
War of Independence (1857–1858), 647–48, 759
in World War I, 714, 727
in World War II, 787, 788
Indian Ocean, Portuguese exploration of, 346–47
indigenous populations
in Africa, 671–72, 673, 688, 692–93
Enlightenment era view of, 519–20, *520*
enslavement of, 415, 419
European diseases affecting, 417, 418, 688, 692
French contact with, 417, 492, 493, *493*
in Jamestown, 417
in Latin America, 631
Manhattan Island purchased from, 417
in Namibia, German massacre of, 671–72, 673
in New England, 418–19
in new imperialism, 672
in New Zealand, 688
in Plymouth, 418
royalty status in, 696
in Seven Years' War, 512
in Spanish colonies, 582, 631, 633
Indochina, France in, 781, 821
Indonesia
immigration from, 893
independence of, 821
Netherlands in, 688, 819–21, 893
in World War II, 788
indulgences, 373, *373,* 374
Luther on, 371–72, 373, 377
industrialization
armament production in, 679, 709, 716, 785, 794, 795, 805
banks and financing in, 603–4, 658–59, 676
child labor in, 608, 609, 675–76
coal- and iron-producing regions in, *610,* 658, 673, *674*
in Europe (1740–1780), 507–9
in Europe (1799–1820), 586–87
in Europe (1820–1845), 602, 603–11, 617
in Europe (1845–1880), 638, 658–59
in Europe (1880–1910), 673–79
increased scale of operations in, 674–75
and scramble for Africa, 689–93
social impact of, 616, 676, 678–79
in Soviet Union, 763, 764, 765
and urbanization, 659
and women in factory work, 797
Industrial Revolution, 602, 603–11
cotton and textile production in, 605–7
daily life and working conditions in, 607–8, *608,* 609
factors promoting industrial development in, 603–4
in Great Britain, 604–5
growth of cities in, 607
pace of change in, 608–11, *610*
Second (1880–1910), 673–79
transportation and communication in, 601–2, 607
use of term, 602
industrial working class, 611, 615–19, 642, 654. *See also* working class
industrious revolution in Dutch Republic, 414
industry, age of (1820–1845), 601–34
Industrial Revolution in, 602, 603–11
international order and nationalism in, 628–34
lower classes in, 615–19
middle classes in, 611–15
political patterns in, 623–24
railways in, *600–601,* 601–2, 606, 607
religious reform in, 619–20
repression and reform in, 624–28
romanticism in, 620–23
steam engine in, 601–2
inflation
in France, 745
in Germany, 744, *744,* 756
in oil shock (1973–1974), 847
post–World War I, 744, *744,* 745, 756
post–World War II, 813
in World War I era, 716, 727
infrastructure projects
in Enlightenment era, 508
of Haussmann in Paris, 638
Innocent XI, Pope, 486
Inquisition, 344, *344,* 396, 399, 400, 423
Galileo trial in, 435, 436, 437
In Search of Lost Time (Proust), 748
Institutes of the Christian Religion (Calvin), 388
intellectual property in Renaissance, 362
intendants (France), 431–32, 446, 460, 461, 479
interest charges, 380, 399
The Interior of the Oude Kerk (de Witte), 402
internal combustion engine, 677–78
International Congress on Women's Rights and Feminine Institutions (1889), 686
International Monetary Fund, 814, 886
International Workingmen's Association, 680
Internet technology, 870–71, 883
The Interpretation of Dreams (Freud), 700
investment banks, rise of, 658–59

Iran, 787
Iraq, 867
    Great Britain in, 757, 758, 787
    refugees from, 894
    search for weapons of mass destruction
        in, 880
    in World War II, 787
Iraq War, 880
Ireland
    in British civil wars, 464
    Catholics in, 444, 477–78, 627, 725
    Easter Uprising in (1916), 725, 743
    in economic globalization, 870
    economic recession in, 885
    in European Economic Community, 830
    in French Revolution era, 567
    home rule of, 684–85, 685
    Northern, 478, 839–40, 846, 866–67
    post–World War I, 743
    potato famine in, 617, 646–47
    resistance to World War I, 725
    revolt in (1641), 444, 444
    Sinn Féin Party in, 743
    Swift on food shortages in, 498
    in United Kingdom, 567, 575
Irish National League, 684
Irish Republican Army, 684, 743, 839, 867
iron, 605, 658
iron curtain, 806, 815
Iron Lady, Thatcher as, 849
Iroquois tribe, 417
Isabella and Ferdinand of Spain, 334–35, 335,
    351
Isabella d'Este, Marchesa of Mantua (1474–
    1539), 364, 364
Isherwood, Christopher, 752
Islam, 893–94. See also Muslims
Islamic State, 893–94
Israel, 811, 819, 832, 847
Italian Wars (1494–1517), 337–39, 338
Italy
    abortion in, 853
    absolutism in, 431
    in Africa, 691, 692
    alliance with France, 650, 652
    alliance with Nazi Germany, 766
    Allied invasion of, 796
    birthrate in, 753, 847
    Calabria revolt in, 579–80, 580
    Carbonari in, 597, 597, 624, 630
    Catholic Church in, 645, 850
    Communist Party in, 829, 830
    and Congress of Vienna, 593, 594
    economy of, 822, 829, 885
    and Ethiopia, 691, 766, 787
    Eurocommunism in, 850
    in European Economic Community,
        829–30
    Fascists in, 743, 744, 746–47, 754–56, 766,
        767
    and Greece, 782
    Habsburg control of, 391–92, 447
    Jews in, 344
    language in, 657
    and Libya, 708
    Lombard League in, 866
    and Napoleon, 564–65, 567, 573, 573–74,
        578, 579–80, 580
    nationalism in, 630, 642, 667
    opera in, 435, 667

    post-Napoleonic, 596, 597
    post–World War II, 825, 829
    railways in, 600–601
    rebirth of (Risorgimento), 650
    Red Brigades in, 841, 846–47
    Reformation Movement in, 388
    in Renaissance, 325–30, 337–39
    revolution movement of 1848 in, 642, 645
    romanticism in, 667
    slavery in, 347
    in Spanish Civil War, 767
    state control in, 754–56, 761
    in Triple Alliance, 687, 707
    unification of, 642, 649–51, 650
    Versailles Peace Conference and
        settlement on, 736
    in World War I, 711, 712, 716, 718, 731
Ivan IV, tsar of Russia (1533–1547), 403, 424
Ivory Coast, 691, 821, 834

Jacobin Club, 552, 563
    closing of, 564
    Girondins in, 554
    Robespierre speech at, 555
Jacobins, 552, 553, 554, 556, 562
    international impact of, 563, 575
    and Napoleon, 578
    nationalism of, 630
    in Paris Commune, 654–55
Jahn, Helmut (1940–), 852
Jamaica
    Columbus in, 352
    First Maroon War in, 492, 492
    slavery in, 415, 490, 492, 492, 509
    sugar production in, 489, 509
Jamerey-Duval, Valentin, 483
James I, king of England (r. 1603–1625),
    409–10, 417, 420, 427, 432
James II, king of England, 464, 476–77, 478,
    486
James VI, king of Scotland (r. 1567–1625), 420
Jamestown settlement, 416–17
Jan III Sobieski, king of Poland (1629–1696),
    486
Janissaries, 448, 448
Jansen, Cornelius, 449
Jansenism, 449–50, 450, 453, 499, 500
Japan
    alliance with Nazi Germany, 766, 771, 786
    Allied bombing of, 795, 804, 804–5
    China invasion by, 771, 777, 787
    Pearl Harbor attack, 786–87
    in Russo-Japanese War (1904–1905), 683,
        693, 707
    in Sino-Japanese War (1894–1895), 693
    and Soviet Union, 770, 787, 805
    in World War I, 717
    in World War II, 786–88, 791, 794, 795,
        799, 804–5, 806, 819–20
Jaruzelski, Wojciech, 856, 860, 862
Jaurès, Jean (1859–1914), 711
Jefferson, Thomas (1743–1826), 535
Jerusalem, 725
Jesuits, 395, 395–96, 399, 423
    baroque style of churches, 433
    European educational missions of, 422
    expulsion in Enlightenment, 531, 531,
        532–33
    on free will, 449
    as New World missionaries, 417, 419, 493

Jewish Combat Organization, 799
Jewish France (Drumont), 681
Jews
    Alhambra Decree on, 335
    in American colonies, 492
    in Austria, 768
    in Austria-Hungary, 684, 698
    Babylonian Captivity of, 339
    in Dutch Republic, 468
    in England, 478
    in Enlightenment era, 522, 620
    in France, 475, 549, 680, 681–82, 780–81,
        792, 801, 833
    in Germany, 684, 743, 744, 760, 761–63
    in Holocaust, 784, 791–94, 803–4, 804,
        805–6
    immigration of, 677, 677, 682, 758, 762,
        763, 811
    in Italy, 344
    in Lodz ghetto, 793
    Napoleon reforms concerning, 579
    Orthodox, 620
    in Ottoman Empire, 336, 344
    in Palestine, 758, 759
    in Poland, 447, 448, 522, 770–71, 781, 791,
        792–93, 798–99, 840, 890
    in Poland-Lithuania, massacre of, 447, 448
    in post-Napoleonic Europe, 596
    Reformed, 620
    and Reformed Judaism, 620
    in Renaissance era, 335, 336, 344
    resistance to Nazis, 798, 798–99
    ritual-murder trials of, 344
    in Russia, 596, 681, 682, 683
    and Sevi as Messiah, 448
    in Soviet Union, 784, 802, 826
    in Spain, 335, 344
    university education of, 612
    in Warsaw ghetto uprising, 798, 798–99
jihadist movements, 870, 879, 894
Jiménez de Cisneros, Francisco, 377
Jinnah, Mohammad Ali (1876–1948), 818
Joffre, Joseph (1852–1931), 709, 715
John IV, king of Portugal (r. 1640–1656), 447
John VIII, Byzantine emperor (r. 1425–1448),
    335, 341
John XXIII, Pope (r. 1958–1963), 837
John, Elton (1947–), 853
John Frederick I, Elector of Saxony, 393
John of Leiden, 385, 386
John of the Cross, 395
John Paul II, Pope (r. 1978–2005), 856
Johns Hopkins University, 675
Jones, Ernest, 608
Jordan, 758
José I, king of Portugal (r. 1750–1777), 531
Joseph II, king of Austria (r. 1780–1790), 512
Joseph Bonaparte (1768–1844), 578, 579, 580,
    581, 590
Josephine, empress of France, 583, 585
Journal of Bonaparte and Virtuous Men, 565
Joyce, James (1882–1941), 748, 750
Judaism. See Jews
Julius II, Pope (r. 1503–1513), 366
July Monarchy (1830–48), 626, 639
July Revolution (1830), 626, 628, 633, 639
June Days (1848), 643, 643–44
Junkers, 459, 480, 651, 654
Jupiter, Galileo discovering moons of, 435, 436

justices of the peace in Renaissance England, 333

Jutland, battle of, 718

Kaczyński, Jaroslaw, 890
Kadets (Russia), 683, 730
Kafka, Franz (1883–1924), 748, 750
Kant, Immanuel (1724–1804), 523
Karl I, emperor of Austria (r. 1916–1918), 732
Karlstadt, Andreas (1486–1541), 378, 385
Katikati (New Zealand), and World War I, 705–6, 717
Kazakhstan, 869
Kazan, 403
Keats, John (1795–1821), 621
Kellogg-Briand Pact, 754
Kennan, George, 815
Kennedy, John F. (1917–1963), 834
Kenya, 833–34
Kepler, Johannes (1571–1630), 436, 501
Kerensky, Alexander (1881–1970), 728, 729
Kérouaille, Louise de, 494
Kershaw, Patience, 609
Keynes, John Maynard (1883–1946), 754, 756, 821, 849, 885
KGB, 730, 865, 866
Khodorkovsky, Mikhail, 888
Khrushchev, Nikita (1894–1971), 826–27, 827, 834, 836, 888
Kiev, violent protests in, 888, 888
Kikuyu tribe, 833
Kim Il Sung (1912–1994), 826
King Lear (Shakespeare), 409–10, 433, 438, 445
Kipling, Rudyard (1865–1936), 672, 692, 693, 696
Kirchner, Ernst Ludwig, 670–71
kirk sessions in church courts of Scotland, 389
The Kiss (Klimt), 698, 698
Kitchener, Herbert (1850–1916), 692
Kleist, Heinrich von (1777–1811), 589
Klimt, Gustav (1862–1918), 698, 698
Knox, John, 389
Kohl, Helmut, 862
Köprülü, Mehmet (1575–1661), 448
Korea, 836
    book printing in, 349
    North Korea, 817, 826, 866
Korean War, 836
Kosovo, 867, 868, 869
Kossuth, Lajos (1802–1894), 640, 643, 644
Krafft-Ebing, Richard von (1840–1902), 664
Kraków University, 781
Kristallnacht (Crystal Night), 763
Kronstadt mutiny, 736, 736
Krupp Steel Works, 673, 674–75, 679, 716, 719
Kun, Béla (1886–1938), 735
Kuroń, Jacek, 860
Kursk Salient, battle of, 795–96
Kuwait, 867, 880

labor unions. See trade unions
Labour Party (Great Britain), 685, 686, 745, 754, 847, 848
    post-World War II, 813, 813, 818, 823, 829
    under Thatcher, 849, 850
Lady Chatterley's Lover (Lawrence), 753, 838
Lafayette, in French Revolution, 554
Lafitau, Joseph-François, 493, 493
laissez-faire system, 528, 648

Lamennais, Hugues de (1782–1854), 619
La Mettrie, Julien de (1709–1751), 524
Lancastrian family in Wars of the Roses (1455–87), 333
Lang, Fritz, 750
language
    Czech, 630
    in Europe (1600–1640), 420, 422, 434
    in Europe (1845–1880), 657
    French, 434, 462, 520, 521, 561, 583
    German, 520, 641, 644
    Hebrew, 620
    Hungarian, 684
    Latin. See Latin language
    and nationalism, 630
    Russian, 682
L'An 2440 (Mercier), 526
La Salle, René-Robert Cavelier de (1643–1687), 492
Las Casas, Bartolomé de (1484–1566), 354–55
Last Tango in Paris (Bertolucci), 853
Latin America, 354, 355, 631
    impact of Peninsular War in, 582, 587
    independence movements in, 631, 687–88
    native population of, 631
Latin Church, Hussite treaty with, 341
Latin empire in Fourth Crusades, 335
Latin language
    alphabet in, 349
    Bible written in, 340, 350, 377, 380, 396
    Catholic Mass in, 342, 378
    in England, 333
    printing books in, 349, 350
    in Reformation era, 372, 375, 377, 379
    in Renaissance culture, 356, 357, 358, 360
Latvia, 770
    in European Union, 881
    independence of, 732, 866
    nationalism in, 863, 865
    in NATO, 882
    post-World War I, 745
    Soviet invasion of, 777
Laud, William, 443
Laval, Pierre, 812
law
    in Europe (1400–1500), 333, 340, 356
    in Europe (1600–1640), 420
    in Europe (1799–1820), 574
Law, John (1671–1729), 479, 493, 495
Law and Justice Party (Poland), 890
Law of Suspects (1793), 560
Lawrence, D. H. (1885–1930), 753, 838
League of Augsburg, war of (1688–1697), 484, 486
League of Cognac, 391–92
League of Nations, 738
    arms control efforts in, 754
    creation of, 732, 736
    Germany leaving, 766
    mandate system, 757–58, 758
    in Poland, 746
    United Nations as successor of, 810
League of the Public Weal, 330
Lebanon, 757
Lebensraum (living space), 745, 760, 782
Leeuwenhoek, Antonie van (1632–1723), 455–56
Left Opposition to Stalin, 748, 765
left-wing parties, 548
Legislative Assembly (France), 554

Leibniz, Gottfried Wilhelm (1646–1716), 501
Leipzig, Battle of the Nations at (1813), 590
leisure activities. See entertainment and leisure activities
Lemonnier, Anicet-Charles-Gabriel, 518
Lend-Lease policy, 780, 782, 785, 787, 789, 790
Lenin (Vladimir Ilich Ulyanov) (1870–1924), 728–29, 729, 730, 733
    death of, 748
    New Economic Policy of, 735–36, 764
    and Stalin, 747, 747–48
Leningrad, 783, 785, 866
Lennon, John, 838, 838
Leo X, Pope (r. 1513–1521), 372, 378
Leonardo da Vinci (1452–1519), 365–66, 366, 367
Leopold I, Holy Roman Emperor (1640–1705), 485–86
Leopold II, emperor of Austria, 553
Leopold II, king of Belgium (r. 1865–1909), 672, 692
Le Pen, Jean-Marie, 871, 880, 881, 881, 882, 890
Le Pen, Marine (1968–), 877, 878, 890, 896
leprosy, 360
Lermontov, Mikhail (1814–1841), 626
Lessing, Gotthold (1729–1781), 525
Letters from a Peruvian Woman (Graffigny), 516–17
Leutwein, Theodor, 671, 673
Levellers, 445, 447, 449, 465, 533
Levi, Primo, 793
Leviathan (Hobbes), 451, 451–52, 529
Lewis, Wyndham (1882–1957), 748
Liberal Party (Great Britain), 648, 649, 684–85, 686, 691
liberals, political, 623–24, 679–86
    classical, 623
    in France, 548–49, 680–82
    in Great Britain, 627, 684–85
    in post-Napoleonic Europe, 596
    in revolutions of 1848, 640, 644
    and rise of nationalism, 630
Liberal Unionist Party, 685
Liberia, Republic of, 691
liberty, as French Revolution principle, 563
Liberty Leading the People (Delacroix), 626, 626
libraries, 358, 517
Library Company of Philadelphia, 517
Libya, 708, 787, 788
Liebknecht, Karl (1871–1919), 735
Life and Fate (Grossman), 790
life insurance, 510
The Life of Gargantua and Pantagruel (Rabelais), 497
Lima (Peru), 354
Limborch, Philipp van, 498–99
Lincoln, Abraham, 767
Lippi, Filippino, 363
lipstick and cosmetics, 857
Lisbon, earthquake in (1755), 506
Lisbon Treaty, 882, 891
Liszt, Franz (1811–1886), 620, 620, 621
literacy
    in Europe (1400–1500), 350–51
    in Europe (1600–1640), 422, 434–35
    in Europe (1740–1780), 514–17
    in Europe (1820–1845), 612, 617
    in Europe (1845–1880), 667

literacy (*continued*)
    and impact of book printing, 350–51
    of middle class, 612
    in Prussia, 612
    of working poor, 617
literature
    in Europe (1400–1500), 356–60
    in Europe (1600–1640), 434–36
    in Europe (1640–1680), 451–53, 458
    in Europe (1680–1740), 408–502, 496
    in Europe (1740–1780), 506, 516–17, 519,
        521, 525–28, 529–30
    in Europe (1799–1820), 589
    in Europe (1820–1845), 603, 608, 612, 615,
        620–21
    in Europe (1845–1880), 666
    in Europe (1880–1910), 681, 696, 697
    in Europe (1922–1940), 748–50, 753–54
    in Europe (1940–1945), 793–94
    in Europe (1945–1973), 830–32, 838
    in Holocaust, 793–94
    in modernism, 697, 748–50
    in realism, 666
    in romanticism, 589, 620–21
    on travel, 506, 519, 614
Lithuania, 770
    independence of, 732, 866
    Jews in, 522
    nationalism in, 863, 865
    in NATO, 882
    post–World War I, 745
    Soviet invasion of, 777
    union with Poland, 425
Little Ice Age, 410, 411, 412, 429, 459
    in France, 482, 486
living space (*Lebensraum*), 745, 760, 782
Livingstone, David (1813–1873), 689, *689*
Locarno Treaty (1925), 754
Lochnagar Crater, *723*
Locke, John (1632–1704), 477, *477*, 498, 500,
    525, 623, 663
    Essay Concerning Human Understanding,
        502, 525
    on human mind, 502, 524
    and rights of man concept, 534
Lodi, Treaty of (1454), 329, *329*
Lodz ghetto, 793
Lollards, 340
Lombard League (Italy), 866
Loménie de Brienne, Étienne Charles, 543
London
    in British civil wars, 444
    Cenotaph war memorial in, 752, *752*
    city life and culture in (1680–1740), *495*,
        495–97, *497*
    city life and culture in (1740–1780), 517,
        519
    city life and culture in (1845–1880), 660,
        660
    city life and culture in (1922–1940), 752
    coffeehouses in, *495*, 495–96, 515
    French Huguenots in, 475
    Gordon riots in (1780), 523
    Great Fire (1666) in, 466
    Great Plague (1665) in, 466
    literacy in (1740–1780), 514–15
    in Little Ice Age, 411
    middle class in, 613, *614*, 660
    Pentonville Prison in, 618, *618*
    Piccadilly Circus in, 752, 775

    population growth in, 466, 607, 659
    poverty and crime in, 496–97, *497*, 508–9
    riots in (1958), 826
    terrorist attacks in, 879
    World Exhibition in (1851), 660, *660*
    as world financial center, 754
    in World War II, 775, 779, *779*
London University, 612
London Zoo, 614, *614*
Long Parliament (England), 443–44
Lorraine, 457, *457*, 653, 687
Lotzer, Sebastian, 383
Louis IX, king of France, 485
Louis XI, king of France (r. 1421–1483), 331–33
Louis XII, king of France (r. 1498– 1515), 338
Louis XIII, king of France, 425–26, 428, 433,
    446
Louis XIV, king of France (r. 1643–1715), 474,
    520
    absolutism of, 460–63, 479
    balance of power politics of, 563
    and Colbert, *455*, 460–61
    death of, 479, 495
    Edict of Nantes revoked by, 475, 479
    and Fronde revolt, 446, 460
    military of, 484–85
    portrait of, *460*
    on religious uniformity, 498, 500, 521
    as Sun King, *461*, 461–62
    supporting Ireland and James II, 478, 486
    taxes under, 541
    Versailles palace of, 462–63, 484–85, 495
    wars of, 463, 470, 479, 483, 484, 485,
        486–88
Louis XV, king of France (1710–1774), 479, 495,
    500, 532–33, 542
    death of, 533, 542
    taxes under, 541
Louis XVI, king of France (r. 1774–1792), 533
    death of, 592, 640
    in French Revolution, 540, 542–45, 548,
        550, 553–54, 556–57
    portrait of, *542*
    trial and execution of, 556–57
Louis XVIII, king of France (1755–1824), 592,
    594, 595, 596, 626
Louis Bonaparte (1778–1846), 578
Louis-Napoleon Bonaparte (Napoleon III),
    emperor of France (1808–1873), 583, 638,
    639, 644, *645*, 645–46, 650, 652–53, 657,
    658
Louis-Philippe, king of France (r. 1830–1848)
    (1773–1850), 556
    abdication of, 640
    caricature of, 639, *639*
    as citizen king, 626, 639
    as king, 626–27, 633
    and Second French Republic, 639–40
Louis, Pierre (1787–1872), 617
Louise de Marillac, Saint (1591–1660), 450
Louisiana, 492, 512, 574
Lourdes, as religious site, 666, 681, 686
Louverture, Toussaint (1743–1803), 552, 574
Louvre, 517, 614, 637
    glass pyramid at, *851*, *851*, 852
Low Countries, 330
    agriculture in, 507
    Catholics and Calvinists in, 399
    in French Revolution era, 567

    Renaissance culture in, 362
    textile production in, 507
lower classes in industrial economy, 615–18
LSD, 838
Lublin Committee (Poland), 816
Lucian (Greek satirist), 376
Ludd, Ned, 586, *587*
Luddites, 586–87, *587*
Ludendorff, Erich von (1865–1937), 724, 730,
    731, 732, 744
Ludwig I, king of Bavaria (r. 1825–1848), 641
Lueger, Karl (1844–1910), 684
Luftwaffe, 770, 779, 783
Lully, Jean-Baptiste (1632–1687), 462
Lusitania, 675, 719
Luther, Martin (1483–1546), 371–74, 377–79,
    383, 402, 421
    critics of, 381–82
    and Diet of Worms, *378*, 378–79
    and education, 386, *386*
    and Erasmus, 377, 381
    marriage of, 387
    message of, 377
    and Peasants' War, 382–85
    portrait of, *373*
    and Reformation Movement, 379–88, 523
    on sinfulness of mankind, 449
Lutherans, 422, 424, 654
Luxembourg, 776, 800, 829–30
Luxemburg, Rosa (1871–1919), 735, *735*

Maastricht Treaty, 871
Macaulay, Thomas (1800–1859), 646
Macbeth (Shakespeare), 445
MacDonald, Ramsey (1866–1937), 745, 754, 756
Macedonia, 868, 869, *869*
Machiavelli, Niccolò (1469–1527), 325–26, *367*,
    367–68
MacMahon, Patrice (1808–1893), 655
MacMillan, Harold (1894–1986), 821, 822
Macron, Emmanuel (1977–), 896
Madagascar, 691, 758, 781
Madame Bovary (Flaubert), 666
Madrid, 413, 581, 879
magazines and periodicals, 496, 498, 515, 516,
    517
    mail delivery of, 508
Magdeburg, sack of, in Thirty Years' War, 429,
    430
Magellan, Ferdinand (1480–1521), 352, *353*
Maginot Line, 769, 775
Magna Carta, 445
Magnitogorsk, 763
Mahomed, Frederick Akbar (1849–1884), 696
mail service in Enlightenment era, 508
Maistre, Joseph de (1753–1821), 624
"Make-Up and Other Crucial Questions"
    (Drakulić), 857
malaria, 689
Malaya, 787, 819
Malaysia, 787, 819
Malevich, Cazimir (1879–1935), 698
Mallarmé, Stéphane (1842–1898), 697
Malplaquet, battle of, 484
Mameluke military caste (Egypt), 566
Man: A Machine (La Mettrie), 524
Manchuria, 770, 771
mandate system, 757–58, *758*
Mandelstam, Osip (1891–1938), 765
Mandeville, Bernard (1670–1733), 528

Manet, Édouard (1832–1883), 667, *668*
Manhattan Island, New Amsterdam founded on, 417
Manhattan Project, 799
manufacturing
    in age of industry, 605, 607–8, *608*, 609–10
    of armaments and military supplies, 679, 709, 716, 785, 794, 795, 800, 805
    British, Napoleon boycott of, 579, 580
    comparative advantage in, 623
    daily life of workers in, 607–8
    Dutch, 414, 466, 468
    energy usage for, 414, 415, 675
    of paper, 612
    in post-industrial society, 837, 883
    in Second Industrial Revolution, 675
    of textiles. See textile production
    trade in goods from, *490*, 509, 689, 696
    working conditions in, 607–8, 616
Manutius, Aldus (1449–1515), 375
Maori, 688, 705
Mao Zedong (1893–1976), 817, 836
Marat, Jean-Paul (1743–1793), 553, 554, 556, 559, *559*, 584
"March on Rome" (1922), 747
Marconi, Guglielmo (1874–1937), 678
Marengo, Battle of, 573, 587
Margaret of Parma, 399
Margaret of Valois, 400
Maria-Louise, empress of France (1791–1847), 583
Maria Theresa, empress of Austria (r. 1740–1780), 512, 532
Marie-Antoinette, queen of France (1755–1793), 542, 548, 550, 555
    death of, 562
    flight and capture of, 553, *554*
Marie de' Medici, Queen of France, 425–26, 433, *433*
Marie of the Incarnation (1599–1672), 450–51
Marinetti, Filippo Tommaso (1876–1944), 709
Market Tower (Messerturm) skyscraper, 852, 853
Maroons, 492, *492*
Marpeck, Pilgram, 386
marriage, 423
    in Christianity, 378, 382
    of Mexicans and Europeans, 355
    political alliances by, 334
    in Reformation Movement, 378, 382, 387
    in Renaissance, 334, 355, 358, 360
    same-sex, 853, 885, 890
    in second serfdom, 413
Marseilles, "Farewell to the Year 1790" pamphlet from, 551
Marshall, George, 814
Marshall Plan, 814, *814*, 815, 821
Martin V, Pope (r. 1417–1431), 340
Martinique, 574
Marvell, Andrew (1621–1678), 468
Marx, Karl (1818–1883), 611, 625, 642, *642*, 646, 654, 657, 662, 734
    on religion, 733
    on socialist movement in France, 655
Marxists, 683, 684
Mary I, queen of England (r. 1553–1558), 398, 399, 476
Mary II, queen of England (1662–1694), *476*, 476–77, 484, 488

Masaccio, *361*, 362
Maschmann, Melita (1918–2010), 762
Masonic lodges, 519, 520, 521
Massachusetts Bay Colony, 418, *418*, 492
Matthias, Archduke of Upper Austria (1557–1612), 426, 427
Mau Mau Uprising, 833–34
Mauriac, François, 817
Maurice of Nassau (1567–1625), 401, 419, *419*
Mauritania, 675
Maxim, Hiram (1840–1910), 679
Maximilian, emperor of Mexico, 653
Maximilian I, Holy Roman emperor (r. 1508–1519), 334, *334*
May, Theresa (1956–), 892
Mayflower, 418
Mayflower Compact, 418
Mazarin, Jules (1602–1661), 446, 460
Mazzini, Giuseppe (1805–1872), 630, 645, 650
McCarthy, Joseph, 817
McDonald's restaurant in Moscow, 863, *863*
means of production, Marx on, 728
medical care on battlefield, 652, *652*, 721, *721*
Medici, Catherine de', 399, 400
Medici, Cosimo de' (1389–1464), 327, *327*
Medici, Cosimo II de', 437
Medici, Lorenzo de' (1449–1492), 327, 330, 337
Medici, Piero de' (1416–1469), 327, 337
Medici family, 326, 327, *327*, 337–38, 363, 367
    patronage of, 435, 437
Mehmed I, Ottoman sultan (r. 1413–1421), 335
Mehmed II, Ottoman sultan (r. 1451–1481), 335–36, *336*, 342
Mehmet III, Ottoman sultan (r. 1595–1603), 425
Mehmet IV, Ottoman sultan (r. 1648–1693), 448
Mehmet Ali, ruler of Egypt (r. 1805–1848), 629
Meidner, Ludwig, 702, *702*
Meinhof, Ulrike, 841
Mein Kampf (Hitler), 745, 762, 766
Meissonier, Ernest (1815–1891), *643*
Melanchthon, Philip, 379, 386, 387
Memoirs (Rémusat), 591
mendicants, 342, 374
The Menin Road (Nash), 704–5
Mennonites, 386
Menno Simons, 386
Mensheviks, 683
mercantilism, 415, 478, 493
The Merchant of Venice (Shakespeare), 415
Mercier, Louis-Sébastien, 526
mercury as syphilis treatment, 355
Merici, Angela, *394*, 394–95
Merkel, Angela (1954–), 883, *883*, 884, 886, 897, 898
    and refugee crisis, 894–96
Mesopotamia, 724
Messerturm skyscraper, 852, 853
Messiah, Sevi proclaiming self as, 448
messianism, 448–49
mestizos, 355, 417
Methodism, 522, 619
Metternich, Klemens Lothar von (1773–1859), 590, *590*, 592, 593, 628, 641
Mexico
    Christian missionaries in, 354–55, *355*
    European exploration of, *353, 354,* 354–56
    France and, 653
    Spain and, 415
Mexico City, 354, 415

Michael VIII, Byzantine emperor (r. 1261–1282), 335
Michael Romanov, tsar of Russia, 424
Michelangelo Buonarotti (1475–1564), *365,* 365–66, 392
Michelet, Jules, 547
Mickiewicz, Adam (1798–1855), 621
middle class, 638
    in age of industry, 611–15
    culture of, 612–15, 659–62, 667
    definition of, 611–12
    and department stores, 660, 661
    in Dutch Republic, 414
    in French Revolution, 547
    Mill on, 663
    as model in reform movements, 615, 618
    in Nazi Germany, 761
    post-World War I, 758
    post-World War II, 830
    urban, 510, 520, 659–62
Middle East
    mandate system in, 757–58, *758*
    oil in, 724–25, 758, 787, 847
    refugees from, 895
    Suez Crisis in (1856), 832
    United States in, 867
    Versailles Peace Conference and settlement on, 737–38
    in World War II, 787
middle passage in slave trade, 490
Midway, battle of, 791
Mies van der Rohe (1886–1969), 751
Mignard, Pierre, 494
Milan, in Renaissance, 326, 327, 329, 330
military
    aristocracy in, 484–85
    battlefield medical care for, 652, *652*, 721, *721*
    daily life in, during retreat from Russia, 588
    desertion from, 725–27, 732
    in Europe (1600–1640), *419,* 419–20
    in Europe (1680–1740), 480, 481, 483–84
    in France, 458, 463, 484–85, 486, 717, 769
    in France, during French Revolution, 553, 554, 555, 559, 560, 561, 564, 567
    in France, under Napoleon, 564–67, 571, 576, 578, 579, 585–89, 595
    in Germany, 673, 684, 687, 709, 766, 794–95
    in Great Britain, 597, 715, 717, 769
    industrial production of supplies for, 679, 709, 716, 785, 794, 795, 805
    New Model Army in, 445, 464
    in Prussia, 480, 481, 579, 590, 651, 653
    Quakers as conscientious objectors to service in, 449
    recruitment in, 715, *715*
    in Russia, 655
    in Soviet Union, 783
    violence and discipline in, 483–84
    women in, 717, 783, *783*, 798
Mill, John Stuart (1806–1873), 662, 663
Millet, Jean-François (1814–1875), 666, *667*
millet system in Ottoman Empire, 336
Milošević, Slobodan, 868, 869
Mines and Collieries Act (1842), 609
mining
    coal, 605, 609
    copper, 391

mining (*continued*)
    diamond, 689, 691
    silver, 391
Mirabeau, Honoré Riqueti de (1749–1791), 544, 545, 565
Les Misérables (Hugo), 638, 666
"The Miseries and Misfortunes of War" (Callot), 429, *429*
missionary activities, 422
    in Africa, 692–93
    in Canada, 451, 492, 493
    in China, 693
    of Jesuits, 395–96, 417, 419, 493
    in New World, 354–55, *355*, 417, 418–19, 421
Mississippi Company, 493
Mitchell, George, 866
Mitterrand, François (1916–1996), 850–51, 872
Mock, Alois, 845
Moczar, Mieczyslaw, 840
Modern Devotion, 375
modernism, *670–71*, 696–702, 748–54
modernity, 603
"A Modest Proposal" (Swift), 498
Moldova, 866
Molière (Jean-Baptiste Poquelin) (1622–1673), 462
Molotov, Vyacheslav (1890–1986), 770
Molotov cocktails, 785
Moltke, Helmuth von (1800–1891), 653, 709, 710
monarchy
    absolute, 443, 474, 479–82
    and Church balance, 390–94
    composite, 411, 421
    conservative view of, 624
    in humanism, 358
    Machiavelli on, 367–68
    in Renaissance era, 330–35, *331*, 358
monasteries, 374
Monck, George, 464
Mondrian, Piet (1872–1944), 750
Monet, Claude (1840–1926), 667, 696
Mongols, 335
Monroe Doctrine, 631
Montaigne, Michel de (1533– 1592), 404–5, *405*
Montefeltro, Federigo da, 330, *330*
Montenegro, 655, 708, 867, 868
Montesquieu, Baron (1689–1755), 496, 500–501, 502, 525, 530, 536, 663
    portrait of, *527*
    on society, 527–28
Montez, Lola (Eliza Gilbert), 641
Montezuma (Aztec ruler), 354, *354*
"Moonlight" Sonata (Beethoven), 622
morality, Rousseau on, 542
Moravia, 386
More, Thomas (1478–1535), 374, *374, 376*, 376–77, 381, 390, 405
Moriscos, 344, 399, 423, *423*
Morocco
    crises in (1905/1911), 707, 708, 709
    France and, 691, 707, 833
    German interest in, 707
    independence of, 833
    Rif War in, 743
    Spain and, 743
    in World War II, 788
Morse, Samuel (1791–1872), 607

mortality rates, 659, 679
Morton, John, 333
Moscow
    French burning of, *587*
    McDonald's restaurant opening in, 863, *863*
    Olympic Games in (1980), 853
    population growth in, 763
    under Putin presidency, 887
    "White House" in, 865, 874, *874*
    in World War II, 785
Mosley, Oswald (1896–1980), 757
Moulin, Jean (1899–1943), 798
Mountaineers in French Revolution, 556, 558–59, 560, 564
Mountbatten, Lord, 818
Movement for the Liberation of Women, 841
movie theaters, 678, 750
Mozambique, 834, 848
Mozart, Wolfgang Amadeus (1756–1791), 517
Munich Olympic Games (1972), *846*, 847
Murad II, Ottoman sultan (r. 1422–1451), 335
Murad III, Ottoman sultan (r. 1574–1595), 425
Murat, Joachim, 567, 580
Muscovy, 413, *424*, 424–25
Muscovy Company, 403
music
    in Enlightenment era, 517, 519, 520
    in middle class culture, 612
    in modernism, 697–98, 750, 752
    in Protestant religious practice, 386
    in romanticism, 589, 620, *620*, 622, 667
    in youth culture of 1960s, 838, *838*
Music for the Royal Fireworks (Handel), 519
muskets in warfare, 484
Muslims, 632, 633, 893–94
    in Afghanistan, 853
    in Algeria, 633, 832, 833
    in Bosnia-Herzegovina, 868–69
    in Central Asia, 863, 865
    in Chechnya, 869–70, 880
    in Crimean Peninsula, 798
    in France, 880–81, 890, 893, *893*, 894
    immigration of, 833, 871, 893
    in India, 647, 648, 818
    in jihadist movements, 870, 879, 894
    and Moriscos, 344, 399, 423
    in Netherlands, 881, 893
    in Ottoman Empire, 342, 447, 448, 499, 708
    and Portuguese expeditions, 346–47
    in Renaissance, 336, 344
    response of political right to, 880–81, *881*
    in Russia, 880
    in Spain, 399, 423
    in Sudan, 692
    in Turkey, 745
    in Yugoslavia, 867, 868
Mussolini, Benito, 738, 743, 744, 746–47
    and Allied invasion of Italy, 796
    "Doctrine of Fascism," 755
    on economic planning, 754–56
    and Greece, 782
    and Hitler, 766, *766*
    "March on Rome" (1922), 747
    at Munich meeting (1938), 769
    promotion of domesticity and motherhood, 753
    totalitarianism under, 761
Mustafa, Vizier Kara (1635–1683), 486

mustard gas as weapon in World War I, 720
Mutiny of 1857 in India, 647–48, *648*

Nagasaki bombing, 795, 804–5
Nagy, Imre, 827, 829
Nanking, Treaty of (1842), 632
Nama (Hottentots), German massacre of, 672, 673, 692, 725
Namibia, 737
    German massacre of Herero and Nama in, 671–72, 673
Nantes, reign of terror in, 560, 560–61
Napoleon I (Napoleon Bonaparte) (1769–1821), 564–67, 571–98
    Civil Code of, 574, 575, 579, 591, 615
    communication system of, 607
    and Congress of Vienna, 592–95, 628
    Continental System of, 579, 580, 586, 587, 588
    coronation of, *585*, 596
    as Corsican spider, *575*
    crossing Alps, 573, *573*
    David portrait of, 573, *573*
    death of, 595
    downfall of, 587–92
    Egyptian campaign of, *566*, 566–67
    European attitudes toward, 591
    in exile, 593, *593*
    Gros paintings of, *566*, 570–71
    Hitler at tomb of, 777
    and the Hundred Days, 595, *595*
    in Italy, 564–65, 567, *573*, 573–74
    military coup of, 567, 573, 574
    peace attempts of, 575–76
    Peninsular War of, 580–83
    and post-Napoleonic Europe, 595–98
    resistance to, 579–80
    rise to power of, 564–67, 573
    Russian campaign of, 587–89
    society under, 579, 584–87
    surrender at Waterloo, 595
    territory in empire of, 583, *584*
Napoleon III (Louis-Napoleon Bonaparte), emperor of France (1808–1873), 583, 638, 639, 644, *645*, 645–46, 650, 652–53, 657, 658
Napoleonic Code (Civil Code), 574, 575, 579, 591, 615
Napoleonic Wars, 564–67, 571–83, 639
    and Congress of Vienna, 592–95
    France in, 590–92
    German national resistance in, 589–90
    and post-Napoleonic Europe, 595–98, 687
    Russian campaign and retreat in, 587–89
    social and economic impact of, 586–87
Narragansett Indians, 418
Nash, John (1893–1977), 722
Nash, Paul, *704–5*
Nasser, Gamal Abdel (1918–1970), 832
Nathan the Wise (Lessing), 525
National Assembly (France), 540, 545, 547, 550
    constitution written by, 548–49, 552
    counterrevolutionaries in, 553
    Declaration of the Rights of Man and Citizen, 547
    social privileges abolished by, 547
    in Third French Republic, 654
National Bank of France, 574
National Chartist Association, 627

National Coal Board, 849
National Convention (France), 555, 556, 557, 558–59
National Covenant, Scottish, 443
National Fascist Party (Italy), 747
National Front (France), 871, 877, 881, 882, 890
National Guard (France), in French Revolution, 547, 548, 552, 554, 555, 558–59
National Health Service, 813
nationalism
    in Europe (1740–1780), 520–21
    in Europe (1820–1845), 630–31
    in Europe (1845–1880), 638, 640, 657, 667
    in Germany, 521, 630–31, 684, 743, 817
    and globalization, 878
    in India, 759, 818
    Jewish, 682
    in Napoleonic era, 589, 630
    post–World War I, 743, 745, 758–59
    revolutionary movements in, 640
    and romanticism, 630, 667
    in Soviet Union, 863–65
Nationalists in Spanish Civil War, 767–68
nationalization
    in Great Britain, 813, 829
    of Suez Canal, 832
National Liberation Front (Algeria), 832, 833, *833*
National Revolution (France), 777, 780
National Salvation Front (Romania), 862
National Socialist German Workers' Party, 744. *See also* Nazi Germany
National Workshops (France), 642, 643
native populations. *See* indigenous populations
NATO (North Atlantic Treaty Organization), 810, *815*, 817, 836, 874, 882
    and Bosnia-Herzegovina, 868, 869
    collective defense principle of, 879
    Germany in, 862–63
    and Iraq War, 880
    and Serbian bombing campaign, 869, 874
    Slovenia in, 868
    United States in, 810, 817, 897
The Natural History of Religion (Hume), 528
natural selection, 665
natural world
    Galileo on, 437
    and Little Ice Age, 411, 412
    Newton on, 502
    Reformation era study of, 397–98
Navarino, battle of (1827), 629
navigation
    portolan charts in, 345, *345*
    and Renaissance expeditions, 345–47
Nazi Germany, 759–63
    anti-Semitism in, 759, 760–63, 768, *768*
    Austria annexation by, 768
    barbarization of warfare, 801
    collaborators with, 780, 798, 800, 811
    in Czechoslovakia, 768–69
    daily life in, 762, 796, 798
    fall of, 801–6
    Holocaust in, 784, 791–94, 803–4, 805–6
    international alliances of, 766
    and Italy alliance, 766
    and Japan alliance, 766, 771, 786
    Lebensraum (living space) in, 745, 760, 782

and mass murder in Soviet Union, 783–84
    at Munich meeting (1938), 769
    in Nazi-Soviet Pact, 769–70, *770*, 777, 782–83
    origins of, 743–45
    Poland invaded by, 769, 770–71, 775
    propaganda campaigns in, 759, 760–61, *761*, 762, 769
    rearmament of, 766
    resistance to, *798*, 798–99, 800, 801, 805–6
    seizure of power in, 759–60
    slave laborers in, 798
    society in, 760–61
    Soviet Union alliance with, 769–70, *770*, 777, 782–83
    Soviet Union attacked by, 782–85, *783*
    in Spanish Civil War, 767
    surrender of, 802–4
    totalitarianism in, 761, 765, 805
    Wannsee conference in, 791
    war crimes of, 804, 811–12
    war preparations in, 766, 769–70
Nazino Island, 741–42
Nazi-Soviet Pact, 769–70, *770*, 777, 782–83
Necker, Jacques (1732–1804), 542, 543, 545, 547
Négritude, 758
Nehru, Jawaharlal (1889–1964), 818
neoclassicism, *530*, 531, 583–84, 620
neoliberalism, 849
Nero, Roman emperor (r. 54–68 ce), 358
Netherlands, 415
    in Anglo-Dutch Wars, 458, 466, 470
    assassinations in, 881
    books as sign of prosperity in, 435
    decolonization of, 819–21
    domestic service of women in, 414
    Dutch Patriot Revolt in (1781–1787), 543, *543*
    Dutch Revolt in (1566–1648), 399–400, 401
    England as ally of, 478
    in European Economic Community, 829–30
    in European Union, 882, 883
    France at war with, 463, 564, 576
    as French territory, 583
    German occupation of, 776
    immigration to, 871, 893
    in Indonesia, 688, 819–21, 893
    mortality rates in, 659
    Muslims in, 881, 893
    Party for Freedom in, 881
    in Peace of Westphalia, 457, *457*
    in post-Napoleonic era, 596
    post–World War II, 825, 829
    printing and publishing in, 515
    religious intolerance in, 476
    same-sex marriage in, 885
    States General in, 468
    in World War II, 776, 780, 798, 800
Neuve Chapelle, battle of, 714
New Amsterdam, 417, 466
New Deal, 813
New Economic Policy (Russia), 735–36, 747, 764
The New Eloise (Rousseau), 529
New England, 418–19, 489
New Forum (East Germany), 861, 862

New France, 417, 418, 492
New Instrument (*Novum Organum*) (Bacon), 438
New Lanark, as model town for social reform, 619, *619*
New Model Army in British civil wars, 445, 464
New Netherland, 417, 418, 466
New Philosophy, 438
New Rochelle (New York), 475
News from the Republic of Letters, 498, 499
New Spain, 354
newspapers
    censorship of, 574, 625
    Crimean War news in, 652
    in Dutch Golden Age, 468
    in Europe (1680–1740), 496
    in Europe (1740–1780), 515
    in Europe (1780–1799), 553, 554
    in Europe (1799–1820), 574, 596
    in Europe (1820–1845), 612, 625
    in Europe (1845–1880), 643, 667
    feminist, 643, 676
    in Nazi Germany, *763*
New Testament
    Erasmus study of, 375–76, 377
    Luther on, 373, 378
    Simon on, 500
    Welsh publication of, 422
Newton, Isaac (1642–1727), *501*, 501–2, 524, 525, 529, 702
New Wave films, 823, 853
New World, 351–56, 415–19, 489–95
    France in, 352, 417, 492
    missionaries in, 354–55, *355*, 417, 418–19, 421
    Portugal in, 351–52, *353*, 415, 417
    Spain in, 346, 351–52, *353*, 354–55, 413, 415, 419, 581–82, 631
New York, 417, 466, 475, 492
New York Herald, 689, *689*
New Zealand, 688
    Maori in, 688, 705
    in Vietnam, 836
    in World War I, 705–6, 717, 718
Niboyet, Eugénie, 643
Nietzsche, Friedrich (1844–1900), 698–700
Nightingale, Florence (1820–1910), 652, *652*
Night of the Long Knives, 760
Night (Wiesel), 793
Night Witches, 783, *783*
Nikolai I, tsar of Russia (r. 1825–1855), 620, 625–26, 628, 644, 646, 651
Nikolai II, tsar of Russia (r. 1894–1917), 682–83, 710, 727
    abdication of, 728
    death of, 733
9/11 terrorist attacks, 879, *879*, 880
1984 (Orwell), 816
Ninety-Five Theses, 378
Ninth of Thermidor, 562, *562*, 564
Nivelle, Robert (1856–1924), 725, 727
Nixon, Richard, 853
Nobel, Alfred (1833–1896), 678, 679
Nobel Prizes, 678, 685, 854
nobility
    in absolutist states, 459, 460, 479, 480
    Calvinism of, 399
    in France, 331, 400, 420, 460, 462–63, 479, 484–85
    in Germany, 426

nobility (*continued*)
    in military, 484–85
    in Poland, 447, 514
    in Prussia, 459, 480
    in Russia, 480
    in Spain, 334
    in Sweden, 428
noble savagery, 519, 524
Nokia cell phones, 885
Nördlingen, battle of (1634), 484
Norman Conquest (1066), 477
Normandy, Allied forces landing at (1944), 800, *800*
North Africa
    France in, 633, 758, 780, 821
    Muslim immigration from, 893
    Napoleon campaign in, *566*, 566–67
    in World War II, 787, 788
North Atlantic Treaty Organization. *See* NATO
Northern Ireland, 478
    political violence in, 839–40, 866–67
    Troubles in, 839, 846
North German Confederation, 651
North Korea, 817, 826, 866
North Vietnam, 832
Norway, 630, 753
    war crime trials in, 811, 812
    welfare state in, 813
    in World War II, 776, 780, 798
notables, 541, 585
Notre Dame Cathedral, 561, 575
Novalis (1772–1801), 620
novels, 434, 435
    of Defoe, 497
    in Europe (1740–1780), 516, 525, 526, 529, 534
    in Europe (1799–1820), 588
    in Europe (1845–1880), 666
    in Europe (1880–1910), 697
    in Europe (1922–1940), 748
    in middle class culture, 612
    in modernism, 697, 748
    of Montesquieu, 500–501
    romantic, 622
    women as readers of, 516, *516*
Novum Organum (New Instrument) (Bacon), 438
nuclear accident at Chernobyl, 859, *860*
nuclear weapons, 853
    in Cold War era, 815, 832, 836
    in Great Britain, 836, 853, 854
    START treaty on, 859–60
    in World War II, 799
Nuremberg Laws (1935), 762–63, 768
Nuremberg trials, 804, 812
nursing care on battlefield, 652, *652*
nutmeg, Dutch trade in, 414–15

Oath of the Horatii (David), *530*, 546
Occitan language, 422
Ochino, Bernardino, 388
O'Connell, Daniel (1775–1847), 627
October Days in French Revolution, 548
October Manifesto (Russia), 683
October Revolution (1917), *729*, 729–30
Of the Demonomania of Sorcerers (Bodin), 404
oil production, 678
    in Middle East, 724–25, 758, 787, 847
    in Russia, 887, 888, 889

and Second Industrial Revolution, *674*
oil shock (1973–1974), 847
Oldcastle, John, 340
Old Church (Oude Kerk) of Amsterdam, 402
The Old Regime and the French Revolution (Tocqueville), 663
Old Regime in French Revolution, 540, 544, 545, 548, 549, 552, 554
Old Testament, 373, 377, 499–500
Old Woman Cooking Eggs (Velázquez), *408–9*
oligarchy
    in Florence, 327
    in Russia, 874, 887–88
    in Venice, 329
Olivares, Gaspar de Gúzman, Count-Duke (1587–1645), 409, 429, 431, 432, 447
Oliver Twist (Dickens), 615
Olympic Games
    in Berlin (1936), 761, 847
    in Helsinki (1952), 809
    in Moscow (1980), 853
    in Munich (1972), *846*, 847
On Crimes and Punishments (Beccaria), 534
One Day in the Life of Ivan Denisovitch (Solzhenitsyn), 830, 836, 850
On Liberty (Mill), 663
On the Law of War and Peace (Grotius), 435
On the Origin of Species (Darwin), 665
opera, 435, 667
Operation Barbarossa, 782–85, *783*
Operation Rose, 835
Opium Wars, 632, 633, 639, 653, 693
Oprichnina, 403
Orange Free State, 691
Orange Revolution (Ukraine), 888
Orangist Party (Netherlands), 543
Oratory of Divine Love, 394
Orban, Viktor (1963–), 889–90
Order of the White Feather, 715, *715*
Orthodox Christianity, 341–42, 447, 651–52
Orthodox Judaism, 620
Orwell, George (1903–1950), 756, 816
Osiander, Andreas (1498–1552), 398
Osman I, Ottoman sultan (1258–1326), 335
Ostpolitik (East Policy), 854
Ottoman Empire, 393, *393, 487*
    Armenian genocide in, 725, *725*
    in Balkan Wars, 708
    and Bosnia-Herzegovina, 708
    in Crimean War, 651–52
    ethnic and religious groups in, 707, 708
    Greek independence in, 629
    instability and civil conflicts in, 425, 448
    Italy at war with, 691
    Jews in, 335, 336, 344
    Muslims in, 342, 447, 448, 499, 708
    Napoleon campaign in, *566*, 566–67
    Orthodox Christianity in, 341–42, 651–52
    persecution of Christians in, 708, 725
    in Renaissance, *331*, 335–36
    Russian expansion in, 629
    in Russo-Turkish Wars, 629, 655
    as Sick Man of Europe, 707
    siege of Vienna (1683), 485, 485–86
    Spain at war with, 399
    territories of, 448
    Treaty of Sèvres on, 745
    in World War I, 706, 707–8, 717–18, 724–25, 737
    Young Turks in, 708, 717, 725, 737

Oude Kerk of Amsterdam, 402
Over the Top (Nash), 722
Owen, Robert (1771–1858), 619, *619*, 624, 628
Owen, Wilfred (1893–1918), 720, 727
Owens, Jesse, 761
Oxenstierna, Axel (1583–1664), 428, 431, 432
Oxford University, 350, 675, 696, 766

pacifism, 385, 709, 711, 721, 755
Paine, Thomas (1737–1809), 535, 536, 550
Pakistan, 818
Palatinate, 424, 427, 428, 483, 485
Palestine, 682
    Great Britain in, 757, 758, 759, 819
    Jewish immigration to, 682, 758, 811
    Jewish national state in, 725, 759, 811
Palestine Liberation Organization, 841
Pamela (Richardson), 516
Panama, expedition of Columbus to, 352
pan-German parliament, 641–42, 644
Pankhurst, Emmeline (1858–1928), 686, *686*, 711, *717*
Pan-Slav Congress, 643
papacy. *See also* Catholic Church; *specific popes*
    Babylonian Captivity of, 339, 340
    Great Schism in (1378–1417), 339–40, 341
    infallibility of, 666
    in Renaissance humanism, 358
Papal States in Renaissance, 326, 329
Papen, Franz von, 760
Papon, Maurice, 833
Paracelsus, Theophrastus Bombastus (1493–1541), 397
Paris
    anarchists in, 680
    automobiles in, 678
    Bastille fortress in, *538–39*, 539–40, 545
    Bon Marché department store in, 660, 661
    book printing in, 350
    bread riot in, 548, 558
    city life and culture in (1680–1740), 495, 496, 497
    city life and culture in (1740–1780), 517
    city life and culture in (1845–1880), *636–37*, 637–38, 659, 660, 661
    city life and culture in (1922–1940), 752
    city zoo of, 653
    Commune in, 654–55, *655*, 662, 664, 680
    Eiffel Tower in, 675, 680, 692
    French Revolution battle in, 555
    Fronde revolt in, 446, *446*
    Haussmann renovations in, *636–37*, 638, 654, 659, 662
    immigrant population in, 871
    Jews in, 792
    June Days in (1848), *643*, 643–44
    liberation of, 800
    literacy in, 514–15
    massacre of protesters in (1961), 833
    modernist culture and art in, 698, 752
    in Napoleon era, 583, *583*
    National Guard of, 654
    Pont Neuf (New Bridge) in, 425, *425*
    Reformation Movement in, 388
    revolutions of 1848 in, 640, 643
    Saint Bartholomew's Day Massacre (1572) in, 400–401, *401*, 404
    student protests in (1968), 839, *839*
    terrorist attacks in, 894, *894*

Third Estate control in, 547
in Third French Republic, 654–55
Universal Exposition in (1889), 680
university established in, 350
in World War I, 719, 730
in World War II, 776–77, *777*, 781, 792, 800
Paris accord on climate change, 885
Paris Commune, 654–55, *655*, 662, 664, 680
Paris Gun in World War I, 719
Paris Street; Rainy Day (Caillebotte), *636–37*, 662
parlements (France), 420, 446, 479, 500, 532, 533, 541
under Louis XVI, 542, 543, 544
Parliament, British
in age of industry, 611, 627, 628
Bill of Rights issued by, 477
and British civil wars, 443–45, 464, 465
and Cromwell, 464
and Glorious Revolution, 477, 478
political parties in, 464, 478
and revolutions of 1848, 646
and Wilkes affair, 533–34
parliament, pan-German, 641–42, 644
Parliamentarians in British civil wars, 444
Parnell, Charles Stewart (1846–1891), 684
Party for Freedom (Netherlands), 881
Pascal, Blaise (1623–1662), 453, 455
Passion of Christ fresco (Giotto), *362*
Pasternak, Boris (1890–1960), 830
Pasteur, Louis (1822–1895), 665, 666
patents on intellectual property, 362
"The Path from Earth to the Stars," 828
patriotism, 531, 556, 597
Patriot Party (Netherlands), 543
patronage, 362–64, 435
Patton, George (1885–1945), 800
Pauker, Ana (1893–1960), 823, 825, *825*
Paul III, Pope (r. 1534–1549), 394
Paul IV, Pope (r. 1555–1559), 394
Paul VI, Pope (r. 1963–1978), 837–38
Pazzi family of Florence, 330
peace movement in Europe, 853–54
Peace of Amiens (1802), 575
Peace of Augsburg (1555), 392–94, *393*, 398, 421, 458
Peace of Cateau-Cambrésis (1559), 399
Peace of Utrecht (1713–1714), 487–88, *488*
Peace of Westphalia (1645–1648), 456–59, *457*, 593, 736
Pearl Harbor attack, 786–87
Pearse, Pádraig (1879–1916), 725
peasants
in Europe (1524–1525), 382–85, *384*
in Europe (1680–1740), 481–82, 483
in Europe (1740–1780), 507, 508, 514
in Europe (1799–1820), 585, 596
in Europe (1945–1973), 825
in Great Fear of France, 547
literacy of, 514
in Russia, 481–82, 656, 682, 730, 734
in Soviet collectivization of agriculture, 764–65
view of city-dwellers on, 657
work of, 507, 508
Peasants' War (1524–1525), 382–85, *384*
Peel, Robert, 627
Pei, I. M., glass pyramid designed by, 851, *851*, 852
penal reform, 618, *618*

penance in Christianity, 342, 377
Peninsular War (1808–1814), 580–83
Penn, William (1644–1718), 449, 489
Pennsylvania, 489
Pensées (Thoughts) (Pascal), 453
Pentagon, terrorist attack on, 879
Pentonville Prison, 618, *618*
"People's Charter" (Great Britain), 627
People's Republics (Ukraine), 889
The People's Will (Russia), 682
Pepys, Samuel (1633–1703), 466
Pequot tribe, 418
perestroika, 859, 860, 865
periodicals and magazines, 496, 498, 515, 516, 517
mail delivery of, 508
persecution
of Anabaptists, 385, *385*
of Christians in Ottoman Empire, 708, 725
Descartes fear of, 438
of dissidents, 859
of Jansenists, 500
of Jews, 344, *677*, 811, 826. *See also* Holocaust
of Lollards, 340
of Protestants, 399, 476, 486, 534
of Puritans, 443
of Quakers, 449, 476
refugees in, 878
of socialists in Russia, 683
of suspected Communists, 817
of Waldensian church, 394
of witches, 423–24
Persian Letters (Montesquieu), 500–501, 525
personality cults, 765, 826
Peru, 354, 411
Pétain, Philippe (1856–1951), 727, 777, 780, 798, 800, 812
Peter I (the Great), tsar of Russia (1672–1725), 473, 474, 479–80, 495, 514
in Great Northern War, 488
peasant life under, 481–82
at Poltava battle (1709), *480*
religious toleration under, 499
and Russian nationalism, 865
territorial acquisitions of, *481*
Westernization projects of, 480, 520
Peter III, tsar of Russia (r. Jan 1762–July 1762), 513, 532
Peterloo Massacre (1819), 597–98, *598*
Petition of Right (1628), 432
Petrarch (Francesco Petrarca) (1304–1374), *356*, 356–57, 358, 359
Petrograd
and Kronstadt mutiny, 736, *736*
Revolutions of 1917 in, 727–28, 729, *729*
petroleum, 678. *See also* oil production
Philadelphia, 517, 520
Philip I, king of Spain, 391
Philip II, king of Portugal, 420
Philip II, king of Spain (r. 1556–1598), 398, 399, 400, 401
Philip III, king of Spain (r. 1598–1621), 420, 423, 428
Philip IV, king of Spain (r. 1621–1665), 429, 433
Philip V, king of Spain (1683–1746), 486, 493
Philip of Hesse (1504–1567), 390, 393
Philip of Orléans (1674–1723), 479
Philip the Good (1396–1467), 330
Philipon, Charles, *639*

Philippines
Spain in, 419, 459, 581, 688, 693
in World War II, 788
philosophes, 527, 529, 531, 532, 533, 534
in age of industry, 618, 620
in French Revolution era, 542, 554
on primitive peoples, 633
and romantic movement, 620
and utopian reformers, 618
philosophy
in Europe (1400–1500), 360–61
in Europe (1680–1740), 499–500
in Europe (1740–1780), 525, 527, 542
in Europe (1880–1910), 698–700
Philosophy of Manufactures (Ure), 616
Phony War, 771–72, 775, 776
photography, 750
physics, Newton study of, 501–2
Picasso, Pablo (1881–1973), 697, *697*, 698, 750, 767, *767*
Piccadilly Circus (London), 752, 775
Pico della Mirandola, Giovanni, 361
Piedmont-Sardinia, 642, 645, 649, 650, 652
Piero della Francesca, *330*
Pierre-Auguste Renoir (1841–1919), 667
pietism, 522, 619
Pilgrims, 418
Pillars of Society (Grosz), 749
Pilsudski, Józef (1867–1935), 746
piracy, 413, 633
Pitt, William (1759–1806), 557, 575, 596
Pius II, Pope (r. 1458–1464), 341–42, 375
Pius VII, Pope, 578–79, *585*
Pius IX, Pope (r. 1846–1878), 645, 666
Pius XII, Pope (r. 1939–1958), 806, 837
Pizarro, Francisco (ca. 1475–1541), 354
plague, 344, 345, 410
Black Death in, 341, 345, 347, 411, 466, 706
bubonic, 411, 466, 482
in France, 482
Great Plague of London (1665), 466
in Ottoman Empire, 425
in Russia, 403
in Thirty Years' War, 429
in troops of Napoleon, 567
Planck, Max (1858–1947), 700
Plantagenet family in Wars of the Roses, 333
Plato (429/8–348/7 bce), 343, 357–58, 360, 376
plays
Bible as basis of, 342
of Ibsen, 666
of Molière, 462
in romanticism, 622
of Shakespeare, 409–10
of Voltaire, 527
Plymouth Harbor, 418
Podemos movement in Spain, 892
Podosinovka, petition to Alexander II from peasants in, 656
poetry
post-World War I, 748
in Renaissance, 356
romantic, 620, 621
pogroms, 682, 683
poison gas in World War I, 720, *720*, 727, 730
Poland
border conflicts with Russia, 743
capitalism in, 873
Catholic Church in, 447, 816, 840, 856
civil strife in, 425

Poland (*continued*)
Communist Party in, 816, 827, 845, 860
Congress Kingdom of, 593, 628, 655
constitution of, 549, 550
Cossack uprising in, 447
economic crisis in, 860
ethnic tensions in, 746
in European Union, 881
General Government of, 781
German invasion and occupation of, 769, 770–71, 775, 781, *781*, 782, 802
Golden Freedoms in, 425, 549
in Great Northern War, 488
Holocaust in, 792–93
Home Army in, 801
illiberalism in, 889, 890
independence of, 733
Jews in, 447, 448, 522, 770–71, 781, 791, 792–93, 840, 890
Lodz ghetto in, 793
and Napoleon, 578
nationalism in, 890
in NATO, 874, 880
partition of, 514, *514*, 549, *563*, 564
post–World War I, 743, 745
post–World War II, 815, 816, 825, 827
protests and repression in, 840
resistance to Nazis in, 798–99
romantic movement in, 621
and Russia, 447, 458, 514, 550, 564, 628, 651, 655
Sejm in, 425, 431
Solidarity in, 856, *856*, 860
Soviet Union in, 770, 781, 782, 801, 802, 836
Sweden at war with, 425, 447, 514
union with Lithuania, 425
uprising in (1830–32), 628, 630
Versailles Peace Conference and settlement on, 736
war crime trials in, 811
Yalta Conference on, 802
Poland-Lithuania, 424, 425, 428, 447, 448
and Congress of Vienna, 594
French Revolution impact in, 549–50, *563*, 564
police
in Russia, 730, 736, 887
in Soviet Union, 765
Polish Corridor, 769
political parties. *See also specific parties.*
in Britain, 464, 478, 596, 648
in France, 548–49, 553
in Nazi Germany, 760
politics
in age of industry, 603
in Enlightenment era, 531–36
Hobbes on, 452
Machiavelli on, 367–68
in post-Napoleonic Europe, 596
in Renaissance humanism, 358
Rousseau on, 530
Spinoza on, 452
women in, 849–50, 853
Politics (Aristotle), 527
Politique party, 421
pollution in Eastern Europe, 857–58
Poltava, battle of (1709), *480*, 488
Pont Neuf (New Bridge) in Paris, 425, *425*
Poor Law Amendment (1834), 618

Pope, Alexander, 502
popular culture, 434–35
anti-Semitism in, 681
interactions with non-Europeans affecting, 696
Popular Front (France), 757
Popular Republican Movement (France), 829
populist movements, 890–93, 894, 896, 898
in United States, 897
Poquelin, Jean-Baptiste (Molière) (1622–1673), 460, 462
portolan charts, 345, *345*
Portrait of a Lady (Ghirlandaio), 359
Portrait of Louise de Kérouaille (Mignard), 494
portrait painting, 359, 494
Portugal
and Africa, 346, 351, 688, 689, 834, 848
Brazil as colony of, 348, 415, 489, 631
Catholic Church in, 829
democracy in, 848
dictatorship in, 756–57
enlightened absolutism in, 531
in European Community, 871
exploration and expansion by, 345–47, *347*, 351–52, *353*
independence from Spain, 447, 458
and Napoleon, 573, 580–83
in New World, 351–52, *353*, 415, 417
post–World War II, 825, 829
in Renaissance, 334–35, 345–46, 348, *348*
and slave trade, 348, *348*, 415
post-industrial society, 837, 883
postmodern architecture, 851, 852
post-structuralism, 841
post-traumatic stress disorder, 721
potatoes, 507, 604
and famine in Ireland, 617, 646–47
Potocki family (Ukraine), 482
Potsdam Conference (1945), 804, 810
Potsdamer Platz (Berlin), *751*, 751–52, 753, *872*, 873
Poujade, Pierre, 829, 830
Poulain de la Barre, François (1647–1725), 453, 456, 462
Pound, Ezra (1885–1972), 697
Poussin, Nicolas (1594–1665), 433
poverty
and criminality, 617–18
in Europe (1400–1500), 332
in Europe (1600–1640), 411, 413, *413*
in Europe (1680–1740), 496–97
in Europe (1740–1780), 508, 510
in Europe (1820–1845), 617–18
in France, 508, 558
of Russian serfs, 655, 656
social protections in, 685
Powell, Colin, 880
"The Power of the Powerless" (Havel), 855
Prague
Defenestration of Prague, 426, *426*
protest in (1968), *808–9*
Praise of Folly (Erasmus), 376, 377
prayer, Christian, 374
predestination doctrine, 388
Preobrazhensky, Evgenii (1886–1937), 755
Presbyterian Church, 443, 445
Priestley, Joseph, 550
Primo de Rivera, José Antonio, 767
The Prince (Machiavelli), 326, 367

Princip, Gaurilo (1894–1918), 710, *710*
Principia Mathematica (Newton), 501, 502, 529
printing
of Bible, 377, 380, *380*
of books of hours, 350, 351, 374, *374*
by Brothers of the Common Life, 375
Catholic censorship of, 396, 398
of chapbooks, 434–35, 514
in Europe (1400–1500), 343, 348, 349–51, 352, 357
in Europe (1500–1600), 375, 377, 379–80, 384, 386–87, 396, 398
in Europe (1600–1640), 422, 434–35
in Europe (1680–1740), 496, 498
in Europe (1740–1780), 514, 515–17, 521
in Europe (1780–1799), 544
in Europe (1820–1845), 612
and freedom of press, 496
of newspapers, 468, 496
and peasant unrest, 384
of periodicals, 496, 498
of prayers and meditations, 343
and religious education in Europe, 422
printmakers, 334, *334*, 429, *429*
prisons, 534, 618, *618*
Pritt, Henry, 705
privateers, Dutch, 413, 435
privatization in Russia, 865–66
progress, idea of, in Enlightenment, 526
proletariat, 611
dictatorship of, 662, 733–34, 755
Marx and Engels on, 642, 657
propaganda campaigns
in Marshall Plan, 814
in Nazi Germany, 759, 760–61, *761*, 762, 769
in Soviet Union, 763, 788, *788*, 798, 828
in World War I, 716, *716*, 721
property
intellectual, in Renaissance, 362
Marxist theory on, 728
and rights of women, 420, 615, 685
"The Protecting Brewer," 465
protectorates in Africa, 691
Protestant churches, 372
in American colonies, 418, 419, 489, 492
and British civil wars, 443, 444, 464
in Dutch Republic, 468
education in, 386
in England, 390–91, 398, 399, 400, 443, 444, 464, 476, 477–78
in Europe (1500-1600), 390–91, 398, 399–401
in Europe (1600–1640), 420, 421–24, 426
in Europe (1640–1680), 443, 444, 456, 458, 464, 468
in Europe (1680–1740), 475–76, 477–78, 486, 492, 498
in Europe (1740–1780), 521–23
in Europe (1820–1845), 619–20
in Europe (1945–1973), 837, 839
in France, 420, 475, 492, 498, 521, 549
freedom of worship for, 477
in Holy Roman Empire, 426
in Hungary, 486
in Ireland, 478, 684–85, 839
and same-sex marriage issue, 885
and Thirty Years' War, 421, 426–30, 456, 458

Protestant Reformation, *379, 379–90, 421*
    Calvinism in, 388–90
    influence on art, 442
    women in, 386–87, *387*
    Zwingli in, 382, 385
Protestant Union, 426
Proudhon, Pierre-Joseph (1809–1865), 619
Proust, Marcel (1871–1922), 748, 750, 754
Provisional Government (Russia), 728, 729
Prussia, 459, *459, 495*
    absolutism in, 480–81, 532
    in Austro-Prussian War (1866), 651, 707
    Bismarck in, 651, 653
    and Congress of Vienna, 593
    Denmark at war with, 651
    and Dutch Patriot Revolt (1781–1787), 543, *543*
    in Franco-Prussian War (1870–1871), 594, 653, 687
    in French Revolution era (1780–1799), 550, 554, 555, 556, 563–64
    and Germany, 630–31, 653–54, *654*
    in Holy Alliance, 628
    in international balance of power, 628, 651
    military of, 480, 481, 651, 653
    and Napoleon, *577,* 577–78, 579, 589–90, 595
    reforms in, 579
    and revolutions of 1848, 641, 644
    serfs in, 579
    in Seven Years' War, 513–14
    in War of Austrian Succession, 512
Prussian Home Army, 590
psychiatry, Freud theories on, 700
Ptolemy of Alexandria, 351, 357
public housing, 848, *848,* 849
Public Record Office Act (1838), 623
public works projects, 460, 524
Puerto Rico, 688, 693
Puffing Devil, 602, 603
punishment
    in Bastille fortress, 539
    breaking on the wheel in, 523, *523,* 527, 534
    death penalty in, 534
    human rights in, 534
    imprisonment in, 534, 618, *618*
    in Soviet Gulag, 765
purges in Soviet Great Terror, 765
Puritans, 400, 418, 449
    in American colonies, 489
    and British civil wars, 443, 444, 445
    and Cromwell, 464
Pushkin, Alexander (1799–1837), 621
Putin, Vladimir (1952–), *887,* 887–90
putting out system, 507
Pym, John (1584–1643), 443, 444
Pyrenees, Treaty of (1659), 458

Qing Empire, 695
Quakers, 449, 450, 464, 476
    in antislavery movement, 534, 633
    in antiwar movement, 721
    in North American colonies, 489
Québec, 417, 451, 512
quinine, 689
Quisling, Vidkun (1887–1945), 776, 780

Rabelais, François (1494–1553), 497
racial issues
    in Darwinism, 665, 695
    in eugenics, 695–96
    Fanon on, 832
    in Germany, 743, 744, 760, 761, 762, 805
    "science" of, 695–96
    in South Africa, 692, 834
Racine, Jean (1639–1699), 462
radar, 779
Radetzky, Josef, 642, 645
radicals, political, 596–98, 624
    communist, 642
    in Great Britain, 627
    in revolutions of 1848, 642, 644
radioactivity, Curie research on, 770
radio stations, commercial, 750, 823
railways
    in Europe (1820–1845), *600–601,* 601–2, 604, 606, 607
    in Europe (1845–1880), 658
    in Europe (1880–1910), *674,* 680
    in European Union, 872
    in India, 693
    in Russia, 658, 677, 682, *693*
Rákosi, Mátyás, 827
Rambouillet, marquise of (1588–1655), 462
Rapallo Treaty, 744
Raphael Santi (1483–1530), 365–66, *366*
Rashid Ali, 787
Rasputin, Grigori (1869–1916), 727
Rathenau, Walter, 744
Raynal, Guillaume-Thomas-François (1713–1796), 534
reactionaries, political, 624
Reagan, Ronald, 853–54, 858, *858,* 859
realism, 666, *667*
    and antirealism, 667–68, *668*
Realpolitik, 651
reason, in Enlightenment era, 523–24, 542
Reconquista, 334–35
Red Army, 733, 736, *774–75*
    in Russian Civil War, 733, *733,* 735
    in World War II, 782, 783, 795, 799, 801
Red Army Faction, 841, 846
Red Brigades (Italy), 841, 846–47
Red Cross, founding of, 652
Red Shirts, 650, *650*
Reed, John (1887–1920), 728
Reese, Willy Peter, 790
Reflections on the Revolution in France (Burke), 550, 551
Reform Act of 1832 (Great Britain), 627, 646, 648
Reformation Movement, *379,* 379–90
Reformed Church, 382
Reformed Judaism, 620
refugees, *876–77*
    from Afghanistan, 894, 895
    in Calais camp, 877–78, 891, 894
    crisis in, 894–96
    in Hungary, 890
    perilous journey of, 895, *896*
    from Syria, *876–77,* 878, 894–96
    in World War II, 801, 802, 810–11, *811*
Regensburg (Bavaria), 380–81, *381*
Reichstag (Germany), 654, 684, 743, 759, 760
reign of terror in France (1793–1794), 559–64
    Thermidorian Reaction to, 562, *562*
religion. *See also specific religions.*
    and British civil wars, 443–44, 445
    campaign for toleration in, *498,* 498–500
    in Chechen War, 870
    conservative view of, 624
    and cult of the supreme being, 561, *561*
    and cultural conflicts, 893
    decline in formal observance, 521–22, 837–38
    Descartes on, 438
    and discipline of daily life, 421–24
    in Europe (1500–1600), 371–406
    in Europe (1600–1640), 418, 421–24, 426–30, 437
    in Europe (1640–1680), 443–44, 445, 447, 448–51, 456, 458, 468, 498–500
    in Europe (1680–1740), 475–76, 477–78
    in Europe (1740–1780), 521–23, 524, 528, 531, 532, 541
    in Europe (1780–1799), 549, 561
    in Europe (1799–1820), 574, 578–79, 596
    in Europe (1820–1845), 618–19
    in Europe (1845–1880), 665–66
    in Europe (1945-1973), 837–38
    Galileo on, 437
    Marx on, 733
    and missionary activities. *See* missionary activities
    new enthusiasms in, 522–23
    in New World, 354–55, *355,* 417, 418–19
    Pascal on, 453
    and same-sex marriage issue, 885
    Spinoza on, 452–53
    and Thirty Years' War, 426–30, 456
    and weekly church attendance, 837
    in Yugoslavia, 867, 868, 870
Religious Customs and Ceremonies of All the Peoples of the World, 498
Remarque, Erich Maria (1898–1970), 752
Rembrandt Harmenszoon van Rijn (1606–1669), 468–70
Rémusat, Madame de, 591
Renaissance (1400–1500), 324–69
    Burgundy in, 330
    Christianity in, 336, 339–44
    culture in, 356–68
    discovery of New Word in, 351–56
    England in, *331,* 333–34, 340
    France in, *331,* 331–33
    Holy Roman Empire in, *331,* 334
    Italy in, 325–30, 337–39, 361–62, 363
    Ottoman Empire in, *331,* 335–36
    poverty in, 332
    slavery and slave trade in, 347–49, *348*
    Spain in, *331,* 334–35, 344, 346
    technology advances in, 343, 345–51
    warfare in, 327, 330, 335, 336–39
    witchcraft in, 343–44
    women in, 343–44, 348, *348,* 358–60, 364, *364*
renewable energy, *883,* 883–85
repentance in Christianity, 371–72, 373, *373,* 377, 396
The Republic (Plato), 376
republicanism, 530–31, 638
Republicans in Spanish Civil War, 767–68
Republic of Letters, 435–36, 456, 498, 499, 500, 502, 506, 523, 525
Republic On the Move party (France), 896
Requiem (Akhmatova), 830
The Return of the Hero play, 567
"return to Europe," 866–67

Revere, Paul, 475
Revolutions of 1848, 639–46
Reynaud, Paul, 777
Rhine, Confederation of, 577
Rhodes, Cecil (1853–1902), 691
Rhodesia, 834
Ribbentrop, Joachim von (1893–1946), 770, 786, 812
Ricardo, David (1772–1823), 623–24, 642
Richard III, king of England (r. 1482–1485), 333
Richardson, Samuel (1689–1761), 516
Richelieu, Cardinal (Armand-Jean du Plessis) (1585–1642), 428, 429, 431, 431–32, 434, 446
    intendants of, 431–32
    portrait gallery of, 432, 433
Rif War in Morocco, 743
rights
    American Declaration of Independence on, 535
    Black Code in France on, 490–92
    Declaration of the Rights of Man and Citizen on, 547
    English Bill of Rights on, 491
    and French Revolution, 547, 549
    of habeas corpus, 464–66, 557
    Helsinki Accords on, 856
    liberal view of, 623, 630
    and rights of man concept, 534, 534–35, 536, 550
    voting. See voting rights
    of women. See women's rights
The Rights of Man (Paine), 550
right-wing parties, 548
    anti-immigration policies of, 871, 880–81
Rilke, Rainer Maria (1875–1926), 697
Risorgimento (rebirth of Italy), 650
The Rite of Spring (Stravinsky), 697
rituals
    of artisan confraternities, 510
    of Freemasons, 519
    of Louis XIV at Versailles, 462
    for social discipline, 422, 422
road building in Enlightenment era, 508
The Road to Serfdom (Hayek), 849
The Road to Wigan Pier (Orwell), 756
Roanoke Island, English colony on, 416
Roberts, Richard, 603
Robespierre, Maximilien (1758–1794), 553, 553, 554–55, 556, 559, 565
    on cult of the supreme being, 561, 561
    in reign of terror, 562
Robinson Crusoe (Defoe), 497, 516
Röhm, Ernst, 760
Roma ethnic group, 784, 792, 805, 890
Romania, 629, 630, 734
    capitalism in, 873
    dissidents in, 854
    end of communism in, 861, 862
    in European Union, 882
    independence of, 655, 708
    and Moldova, 866
    post-World War II, 815, 816, 825, 825
    Versailles Peace Conference and settlement on, 736, 737
    in World War II, 801
Romanov dynasty, 424
Romanov, Fedor, 424
romanticism
    in Europe (1799–1820), 589

    in Europe (1820–1845), 603, 620–23, 630
    in Europe (1845–1880), 666–67
    and nationalism, 630, 667
Rome
    revolutionary movement of 1848 in, 645
    in unification of Italy, 650
Rome, ancient, 530, 530
    French Revolution influenced by, 542, 545, 546, 561, 563, 564, 565
    Napoleon influenced by, 575, 583–86
Rome, Treaty of (1957), 829–30
Rommel, Erwin (1891–1944), 776, 788
Roncalli, Angelo, 837
"A Room of One's Own" (Woolf), 754
Roosevelt, Franklin, 771, 780, 787, 799, 813, 814
    death of, 802
    at Tehran Conference, 799, 802
    at Yalta Conference, 802, 802
Rosenberg, Alfred, 744
Rosetta Stone, 566
Rossini, Gioacchino (1792–1868), 630
Rotenberg, Arkady, 888
Roundheads in British civil wars, 444
Rousseau, Jean-Jacques (1712–1778), 516, 520, 522, 524, 527, 529–30, 561, 620, 623, 663
    entering essay contest, 505–6, 519, 525
    political theory of, 544
    portrait of, 524
    and rights of man concept, 534
    on role of women, 531
    Social Contract, 529–30, 531, 534
    on virtue, 542
Royal Academy of Sciences (France), 455, 455
Royal Air Force (British) in World War II, 779
Royalists in British civil wars, 444, 445, 465
Royal Navy (British), 576, 718–19
Royal Society (British), 455, 519
rubber, 677
    in tires, 677, 678
Rubens, Peter Paul (1577–1640), 433, 433
Rucellai, Giovanni, 363
Rudolf II, Holy Roman emperor (r. 1576–1612), 421, 426
Rump Parliament (British), 445, 464
Rumsfeld, Donald, 880
rural areas, 746
    childhood in, 483
    in France, 483, 508
    post-World War II, 825
    poverty in, 508
    in Second Industrial Revolution, 678–79
    view of urban residents on peasants in, 657
Rus, Chmielnicki as ruler of, 447
Russell, Bertrand (1872–1970), 721, 836
Russia
    absolutism in, 474, 479–80
    in age of industry (1820–1845), 602, 609, 625–26, 628
    agriculture in, 657, 678
    Alexander II in, 651, 655–57, 663, 682
    autocracy in, 682–83
    and birth of USSR, 735–36
    Bloody Sunday in (1905), 683, 683
    Bolsheviks in, 728–30, 733–36
    border conflicts with Poland, 743
    Civil War in (1918–1921), 730, 733, 733–36, 743
    communism in, 728–30, 733–36, 755
    and Congress of Vienna, 593, 594

    in Crimea, 532, 651–52, 655, 888–89
    Decembrist Revolt in (1825), 625, 625–26
    economy of, 682, 727, 733, 735–36, 873–74, 887, 889
    education in, 612
    ethnic groups and nationalities in, 869
    expansion into Ottoman Empire, 629
    in Franco-Russian alliance, 578
    in Great Northern War (1700–1721), 488, 488
    in Holy Alliance, 628
    industrialization in, 673–74
    in international balance of power, 628, 651, 687, 688–89
    Ivan IV in, 403, 424
    Jews in, 596, 681, 682, 683
    in Little Ice Age, 411
    migration within, 677, 677
    and Napoleon, 570–71, 571–72, 576–77, 578, 587–89, 590, 625
    nationalism in, 865
    New Economic Policy in, 735–36, 747
    oil in, 887, 888, 889
    Orthodox Church in, 341, 482, 587, 620, 733, 887, 887
    peasants in, 481–82, 656, 682, 730, 734
    and Poland, 447, 458, 514, 550, 564, 628, 651, 655
    population growth in, 659
    in post-Napoleonic era, 596
    privatization in, 865–66
    propaganda campaigns in, 716
    Provisional Government in, 728, 729
    Putin in, 887, 887–90
    railways in, 658, 677, 682, 693
    realism in, 666
    revolution of 1905 in, 683, 693, 727
    and revolutions of 1848, 644, 646
    revolutions of 1917 in, 706, 727–30, 734, 738
    romantic movement in, 621
    Russification policies in, 655, 682
    in Russo-Japanese War (1904–1905), 683, 693, 707
    in Russo-Turkish Wars, 629, 655
    serfs in, 481–82, 532, 596, 655–57
    in Seven Years' War, 513
    territory of (1689–1725), 481
    territory of (1910), 682
    terrorist attacks in, 879–80, 887
    in Triple Entente, 687, 707
    and United States presidential election (2016), 889
    war financing in, 716
    wealthy oligarchs in, 874, 887–88
    Westernization projects of Peter I in, 480, 520
    "White House" in, 865, 874, 874
    women in, 663, 717, 733, 735
    working class in, 674
    in World War I, 706, 707, 710–12, 716–18, 720, 724–25, 727–36
Russian Federation, 865, 866, 869
Russian language, 682
Russian Orthodox Church, 341, 482, 587, 620, 733, 887, 887
Russian Revolutions (1917), 706, 727–30, 738
    Bolsheviks in, 728–30, 734
    of February, 727–28
    Lenin in, 728–29

Marxism in, 728
of October, 729–30
peasant criticisms in, 734
Russification policies, 655, 682
Russo-Japanese War (1904-1905), 683, 693, 707
Russo-Turkish Wars, 629, 655

Sadoleto, Jacopo, 394
Saint Andrews kirk session (1573/74), 389
St. Augustine, Spanish colony at, 416
Saint Bartholomew's Day Massacre (1572), 400–401, *401*, 404
Saint Basil's Cathedral, Moscow, 403
Saint-Domingue. *See also* Haiti
cosmopolitanism in, 520
independence of, 574
slavery in, 490, 509, 520, 550–52, 557, 574, 586
sugar production in, 509
Saint Helena, Napoleon exiled to, 595, 597
Saint-Just, Louis-Antoine (1767–1794), 556, 560, 562, 565
Saint Peter's Basilica, Rome, 366, 372
Saint Petersburg
Bloody Sunday in (1905), 683, *683*
Decembrist Revolt in (1825), *625*, 625–26
de Vieira in, 473, 474, 480, 502
founding of, 474, 480, *481*, 495, *495*
during Putin presidency, 887
renamed as Leningrad, 783, 866
renamed as Petrograd, 727–28
St. Sergei monastery, serfs owned by, 482
Saint-Simon, duke of (1675–1755), 479
Saint-Simon, Henri (1760–1825), 618, 623, 642
Saipan, 799
Sakharov, Andrei (1921–1989), 854, 859
Salazar, António de Oliveira (1889–1970), 756–57, 829, 848
Salisbury, Lord, 690
salons, 496, 500, 517, 518, 519, 529
Salutati, Coluccio (1331–1406), 357
same-sex marriage, 853, 885, 890
Sand, George, 662
San Martín, José de (1778–1850), 631
San Romano, battle of (1432), *324–25*
sans-culottes movement in French Revolution, 554, 555, 556, 557–59, 560, 562, 564
Santa Maria del Fiore Cathedral, Florence, 361, *361*, 363
Saragossa, in Peninsular War, 581
Sarajevo, siege of, 868, *868*
Sarikamiş, battle of, 725
Sarkozy, Nicolas (1955–), 880–81
Sartre, Jean-Paul (1905–1980), 830, *830*, 850
Satie, Erik (1866–1925), 697
Sattler, Michael, 385
Saudi Arabia, 758
Saussure, César de, 515
The Saved and the Damned (Levi), 793
Savonarola, Girolamo (1452–1498), 325, 337–38, *338*, 351, 374, 379
Scandinavia, 594, 747, 776, 829
Schappeler, Christoph, 383, 384
Schengen Zone, 871, 891, *892*
Schleiermacher, Friedrich (1768–1834), 620
Schleitheim Confession, 385
Schlieffen, Alfred von (1933–1913), 707
Schleicher, Kurt von, 760
Schlieffen Plan, 707, 711, 712, 720

Schmalkaldic League, 393
Schoelcher, Victor, 850
Schoenberg, Arnold (1874–1951), 697–98
scholarly academies, *455*, 455–56, 517–19
scholasticism, 343
scholastic theology, 343, 344
School of Athens fresco (Raphael Santi), 365–66, *366*
Schubert, Franz (1797–1828), 622
Schurman, Anna Maria van (1607–1678), *435*, 436
Schwarzenberg, Felix von (1800–1852), 644
science
in Dutch Golden Age, 469
in economic planning, 754
in Enlightenment, 524, 527–28
in Europe (1845–1880), 665, 666
in Europe (1880–1910), 675, 685, 700–702
in Europe (1922–1940), 753
of Newton, *501*, 501–2
of race, 695–96
of society, 527–28
women in, 685
scientific method
Bacon on, 435, 438
in Enlightenment, 524
scientific revolution, 455–56
academic societies in, *455*, 455–56
early stages of, 436–38
Scotland, 410, 443
Act of Union with England, 488
in British civil wars, 443, 444, 445, 464
Enlightenment in, 528, 530
independence movement in, 892–93
kirk sessions of Church courts in, 389
local government in, 866
National Covenant in, 443
romanticism in, 622
in War of Austrian Succession, 512
Scott, Walter (1771–1832), 622
Scottish Green party, 892
Scottish National Party, 892
scramble for Africa, 672, 689–93
scramble out of Africa, 833–34
sculpture, Baroque, 433–34, *434*
Second Empire of France, 646
Second Industrial Revolution (1880–1910), 673–79
scramble for Africa in, 689–93
Second International socialist alliance, 679–80
Second Opium War (1860), 639, 653
Second Republic of France (1848–1852), 639–40, 642–43, 657
second serfdom, 413
The Second Sex (de Beauvoir), 830–32
Second Treatise of Government (Locke), 477
Second Vatican Council (1962–65), 837
Second World countries, 817
Second World War. *See* World War II
Secret Army Organization (France), 833
secret order 00447 of Stalin, 765
Sehestad, Hannibal (1609–1666), 459
Sejm in Poland, 425, 431
Selassie, Haile, 787
self-determination principle
in French Revolution, 563, 564
post-World War I, 758, 769
in World War I, 732, 736, 737
Selim II, Ottoman sultan (r. 1566–1574), 399
Seneca, 358

Senegal, 787
Senghor, Léopold (1906–2001), 758
sentimentality in Enlightenment, 529, *529*
Sephardic Jews, 344
September 11, 2001 terrorist attacks, 879, *879*, 880
September massacres in French Revolution, *555*, 555–56
Serbia, 629, 630, 710, 867–68, *869*
in Balkan Wars, 708
bombing campaign in, 869, 874
independence of, 655, 708
in World War I, 718, 732
Serbian Academy of Sciences and Arts, 867–68
Serbs
in Bosnia-Herzegovina, 708, 868–69
in Yugoslavia, 867–68
serfs, 413
in Enlightenment, 532
in Prussia, 579
in Russia, 481–82, 532, 596, 655–57
in second serfdom, 413
in Ukraine, 482
Servetus, Michael (ca. 1511–1553), 398
Seven Years' War (1756–1763), 512–14, *513*, *514*, 521, 533, 536, 770
Sevi, Shabbetai (1626–1676), 448, 450
Sèvres, Treaty of, 745
sexuality
Catholic Church on, 837–38
in cult of domesticity, 615
in Europe (1600–1640), 423
in Europe (1845–1880), 646, 663–64
in Europe (1922–1940), 752, 753–54, 761
in Europe (1945–1973), 837–38
in Europe (1973–2000), 853
Freud theories on, 700
in Nazi Germany, 761
in Victorian Age, 646, 663
Sforza, Ludovico, Duke of Milan, 337, 338, 367
Shakespeare, William (1564–1616), 409–10, 415, 434, 438, 521
Shelley, Percy Bysshe (1792–1822), 598, 621
shell shock in World War I, 721
shipbuilding, 419
of Dreadnoughts, 709, *709*
Renaissance advances in, 345
of steamships, 607, *607*
ship money, 419, 420, 431, 443
Siberia, 415, 677, 741–42
Sieyès, Emmanuel (1748–1836), 544, *544*, 545, 567
Sigismund III, king of Poland (r. 1587–1632), 425, 431
silk industry, 329
silver, 354, 391
Simon, Richard Simon (1638– 1712), 499–500
Simplicissimus (Grimmelshausen), 458
Singapore, in World War II, 788
Single Europe Act, 871
Sinn Féin Party, 743
Sino-Japanese War (1894–1895), 693
Sistine Chapel frescoes of Michelangelo, *365*, 366
Skawronska, Marta, 473
skepticism, 499–501, 521
and Euroskepticism, 872, 881, 882, 884, 890

Sketch for a Historical Picture of the Progress of the Human Mind (Condorcet), 526

slavery
    Africa as source of slaves in, 347–49, 415, 417, 689
    and antislavery movement, 534–35, 549, 633–34, 642–43
    and Black Code, 490–92
    in Brazil, 631
    children in, 347, 490, 491, 494, 520
    Christians as slaves in, 448
    in cotton production, 507, 605
    and England in slave trade, 417, 493, 494
    and French Revolution, 549, 550–52
    in French territories, 492, 642–43
    and middle passage, 490
    Native Americans as slaves in, 415, 419
    Quaker opposition to, 449
    in Renaissance, 347–49, *348*
    resistance and revolts of slaves in, 492, *492*
    in Saint-Domingue, 490, 509, 520, 550–52, 557, 574, 586
    in second serfdom, 413
    in sugar production, 348, 415, 473, 489–92, 509–10, 586, 605
    in tobacco farming, 417, *417*
    and transatlantic slave trade, 348, 415, *416*, 417, 489–92, *490*, 509, 509–10
    and trans-Saharan slave trade, 347–48
Slovakia, 643, 780, 866, 873
Slovenia, 867, 868, *869*, 885
smallpox, 353, 417, 542, 545
smartphones, 883, 885
Smith, Adam (1723–1790), 528, 623, 756
social contract, Hobbes on, 452
The Social Contract (Rousseau), 529–30, 531, 534
social Darwinism, 665
Social Democratic Party (Germany), 654, 684, 732, 759, 850
Social Democratic Party (Sweden), 747, 829, 850
Social Democratic Workers' Party (Russia), 683
socialism, 611, 619, 624, 662, 679–80
    and capitalism, third way between, 862
    Fascism opposed to, 755
    in France, 655, 680, 709, 711, 745, 757, 829, 850–51
    in Germany, 654, 662, 684, 709, 721, 743, 759
    in Great Britain, 685
    in Russia, 728–29, 730
    women in, 663
    and World War I, 709, 711, 721
social sciences, 700
social welfare policies, 745, 747. *See also* welfare state
society
    Durkheim on, 700
    in Europe (1680–1740), 502
    in Europe (1740–1780), 517–19, 527–31
    in Europe (1780–1799), 541
    in Europe (1799–1820), 579, 584–87
    in Europe (1820–1845), 603, 611–19
    in Europe (1845–1880), 657, 659–68
    in Europe (1880–1910), 673–79, 700
    in Europe (1922–1940), 748–54, 760–61
    in Europe (1945–1973), 821–26, 837

    in Europe (2000–2017), 883
    Marx on, 728
    modernist, 748–54
    in Nazi Germany, 760–61
    post-industrial, 837, 883
    and Reformation Movement, 380
    in Renaissance humanism, 358
    Weber on, 700
Society of Antiquaries, 521
Society of Friends of the Blacks, 549
Society of Jesus, *395*, 395–96
Soderini, Piero, 338
solar system
    Galileo on, 435, 436, 437
    Kepler on, 436
Solidarity (Poland), 856, 860
Solzhenitsyn, Alexander (1918–2008), 830, 836, 850, 854
Somalia, 787
Somme, battle of, *723*, 723–24
Sons of Liberty, 535
Sorbonne (Paris), printing at, 350
Sorel, Georges (1847–1922), 680
Sorgh, Hendrick Martenszoon, 467
Soubirous, Bernadette, 666
South Africa
    Boer War in (1899–1902), *691*, 691–92, 696
    discrimination against Indians in, 694
    Great Britain in, *691*, 691–92, 694
    immigration from India to, 693, 694
    racial inequality in, 692, 834
    in World Word I, 717
    Zulu uprising in, 649
South America
    effects of Peninsular War in, 581–82
    European exploration of, 346, 348, 352, *353*, 355, 419
    independence movements in, 631
    silver mining in, 354
South Carolina, 492
Southeast Asia, 866
    France in, 693, *695*, 758
    United States in, 834–36
Southern Netherlands, 549, 628
South Ossetia, 888
South Sea Company, 493, 495
South Vietnam, 832, 834–36
Soviets (councils), 728, 729, 730
Soviet Union, 734, 735–36
    in Afghanistan, 853, 854, 859, 870
    in Africa, 834
    in British-American alliance, 787, 788, 802
    and China relations, 836
    in Cold War, 809, 810, 814–17, 834, 836
    collapse and breakup of, 846, 863–70, *864*
    collectivization of agriculture in, 764–65
    in Comecon alliance, 810, 814
    crisis in (1990–1991), 865–66
    and Czechoslovakia, *808–9*
    deportation to Nazino Island in, 741–42
    détente policy of United States with, 853
    dissidents in, 854
    in Eastern Europe, 815–16
    economy of, 754, 794, 822, 836, 859, 863
    in Finland, 782
    Five Year Plans in, 763–65, 770, 785
    food shortages during World War II, 790, 798
    in German occupation zone, 817
    glasnost in, 859, 860, 865

    Gorbachev in, *858*, 858–60
    in Great Patriotic War against Hitler, 863
    Great Terror in, 765, 770
    and Helsinki Accords, 856
    Hitler pack with, 769–70, *770*, 777, 782–83
    Hitler attack on, 782–85, *783*
    industrialization in, 763, 764, 765
    iron curtain in, 806, 815
    and Japan, 770, 787, 805
    Jews in, 784, 802, 826
    Kursk battle in, 795–96
    Lend-Lease program in, 785, 787, 789, 790
    literature in, 830
    losses in World War II, 805, 812
    military in, 783
    nationalism in, 863–65
    Nazi mass murder in, 783–84
    in Nazi-Soviet Pact, 769–70, *770*, 777, 782–83
    Night Witches in, 783, *783*
    and Operation Barbarossa, 782–85, *783*
    perestroika in, 859, 860, 865
    and Poland, 770, 781, 782, 801, 802, 836
    in post-World War II occupation of Germany, 815
    post-World War II rebuilding of, 822
    at Potsdam Conference, 804
    propaganda campaigns in, 763, 788, *788*, 798, 828
    and second front question in World War II, 788
    secret order 00447 in, 765
    space program in, 828, 829
    in Spanish Civil War, 767
    Stalingrad battle in, 788–89, 790, 799
    Stalin in, 747–48, 763–65, 826
    state control in, 754, 755, 796–98, 822
    in Suez Crisis (1856), 832
    as superpower, 816
    totalitarianism in, 765, 796, 805
    in violent conclusion of World War II, 801–2
    in Warsaw Pact, 810
space program in Soviet Union, 828, 829
Spain
    Armada of, 401, 419
    bankruptcy of (1627/28), 413
    Basque independence movement in, 839, 848, 866
    Catalonia region of, 432, 447, 458, 767, 866
    Catholic Church in, 399, 581, 767, 829
    civil wars in, 625, 628, *767*, 767–68
    democracy in, 848
    economy of, 822, 885, 892
    education in, 675
    enlightened absolutism in, 531–32
    in European Community, 871
    in European Union, 886, 892
    in Franco-Spanish War, 447
    in French Revolution era (1780–1799), 557, 564
    Inquisition in, 344, *344*, 396, 399, 400, 423
    in Italian Wars, 338
    Jews in, 335, 344
    language and literature in, 434
    in Little Ice Age, 411
    military of, 335
    monarchy in, 334–35, 391, 399
    Moriscos in, 344, 399, 423, *423*
    and Morocco, 743

and Napoleon, 573, 576, 580–83, 587, 590, 625, 631
  in New World, 346, 351–52, *353*, 354–55, 413, 415–17, 419, 581–82, 631
  Olivares in, 409, 429, 431, 432, 447
  in Peace of Utrecht, 487–88
  in Peninsular War (1808–1814), 580–83
  and Philippines, 419, 459, 688
  Podemos movement in, 892
  post–World War II, 825
  Reformation Movement in, 388
  religious intolerance in, 499
  in religious wars, 399–400, 401
  in Renaissance, *331*, 334–35, 344, 346
  same-sex marriage in, 885
  in slave trade, 415
  in Spanish-American War (1898), 693
  student protests in (1968), 839
  terrorist attacks in, 879, 894
  in Thirty Years' War, 428, 429, 458–59
  transatlantic trade of, 411, 413
  War of Succession in (1702–1714), 486, 488
Spanish-American War (1898), 693
Spanish civil wars, 625, 628, *767*, 767–68
Spanish flu (1918–19), 738
Spanish Netherlands, 420. *See also* Belgium
  French claims on, 463
  in Thirty Years' War, 428, 429, 458
The Spectator, 516
"Speech in Finchley" (Thatcher), 855
Speenhamland system, 509, 618
Speer, Albert, 800
Speght, Rachel, 423
Spencer, Herbert (1820–1903), 665
Spender, Stephen (1909–1995), 801
Spice Islands, 414, 415
spice trade, 346, 414–15, 466
Spinoza, Baruch (1632–1677), *452*, 452–53, 456, 468, 499, 500, 524, 525
The Spirit of the Laws (Montesquieu), 527, 529
Spring Offensive (1918), 730–31
Sputnik, 828, 829
Squinobal, Albert, 705
Staël, Germaine de, 584
stained glass windows in churches, 382
Stalin, Joseph, 742, *747*, 747–48, 763–65, 860
  in Cold War, 814–17
  death of, 826
  deportation of Chechen population, 869
  and destalinization post–World War II, 826–27
  and Finland, 782
  Great Terror of, 765
  Hitler pack with, 769–70, *770*, 777
  Hitler attack on, 782–85
  Left Opposition to, 748, 765
  and Lenin, *747*, 747–48
  at Potsdam Conference, 804
  secret order 00447 of, 765
  in Spanish Civil War, 767
  at Tehran Conference, 799, 802
  in World War II, 787, 788, 794, 799
  at Yalta Conference, 802, *802*
Stalingrad, battle of, 788–89, 790, 799
Stalinism, 763–65
Stanislaw August Poniatowski, king of Poland (r. 1764–95), 549–50
Stanley, Henry Morton (1841–1904), 689, *689*
START treaty, 859–60

Star Wars missile defense system, 854
States General (Netherlands), 468
Stauffenberg, Claus von, 801
steam engine, 508, *508*, 586
  in age of industry, 601–2, 603
  in textile production, 603, *605*
steamships, 607, *607*
steel production, 605, 658
  in Second Industrial Revolution, 673, 674, *674*
Steen, Jan, *467*
Stein, Karl Vom (1757–1831), 579
Stendhal (Henri Beyle) (1783–1842), 622
Stöcker, Helene (1869–1943), 753
Stockhausen, Karl-Heinz, 879
Stolberg, Anna von, abbess of Quedlinburg, 387
Stopes, Marie (1880–1958), 753
The Stranger (Camus), 830
A Stranger to Myself (Reese), 790
Stravinsky, Igor (1882–1971), 697
Strozzi, Filippo, 363
structuralism, 841
Stuart dynasty, 410, 464, 512
student rebellions (1960s), 838–41
A Study in Scarlet (Doyle), 696
Stuka dive-bombers in World War II, 776, 777
Sturgeon, Nicola, 892
Der Stürmer, 761, *763*
The Subjection of Woman (Mill), 663
submarine warfare, 718–19, 724, 780, 791
Submission (van Gogh), 881
sub-Saharan Africa, 833–34
suburbs, post–World War II, 825
Sudan, 691, 692, 707
Sudetenland region of Czechoslovakia, 769, 802
Suez Canal, 649, 690–91, 832
  crisis of (1956), 832
  Egyptian nationalization of, 832
  in World War I, 718
  in World War II, 788
sugar production, 346, *472–73*
  slavery in, 348, 415, 473, 489–92, 509–10, 586, 605
Sukarno (1901–1970), 820, 821
Suleiman the Magnificent, Ottoman sultan (r. 1520–1566), 393, 485
Supplement (Diderot), 519
surrealism, *740–41*, 750
Surrender of Breda (Velázquez), 432
survival of the fittest, 665, 680
swastika, 744
Sweden, 596, 805
  in European Union, 872
  Finland seized from, 594
  in Great Northern War, 488
  literacy rate in, 422
  military of, 432, 458
  Oxenstierna in, 432
  in Peace of Westphalia, 457, *457*
  Poland at war with, 425, 447, 514
  post–World War I, 747, 756
  post–World War II, 829
  in Thirty Years' War, 428–29, 456
  welfare state in, 813, 850
Swift, Jonathan (1667–1745), 497–98
Switzerland, 825
Sylvester I, Pope (r. 314–335), 360
Symposium (Plato), 357

syndicalism in France, 680
syphilis, 338, 355, 394
Syria
  in Arab–Israeli War (1973), 847
  civil war in, 893, 894–96
  France and, 757, 787
  Muslims in, 893, 894
  refugees from, *876–77*, 878, 894–96
  in World War II, 787
Syriza party (Greece), 886
Szilárd, Leo (1898–1964), 799

Table of Ranks (Russia), 480
Taborites, 341
Tahiti, 519, *520*
taille (France), *331*, 332, 429, 432, 479, 543
Taliban, 879
Talleyrand, Charles-Maurice de (1754–1838), 592, *592*, 594
tank warfare, 769
  in World War I, 720, 727, 731
  in World War II, 776, 782, *783*, 785, 795
Tannenberg, battle of, 712, 718
Tanzania, 691, 737
Target, Guy, 541
Tatler, 496
Tauler, Hans, 388
taxes
  in Europe (1400–1500), 327, 331, 333
  in Europe (1600–1640), 419, 421, 425, 429, 431, 432
  in Europe (1680–1740), 479, 481
  in France, 541, 543, 579
  in Great Britain, 533, 535, 541
Taylor, A. J. P., 812
Taylor, Frederick Winslow (1856–1915), 754
Taylor, Harriet (1807–1858), 663
technological innovations
  and age of industry (1820–1845), 601–34
  and economic globalization, 870–71
  in Enlightenment, 507–8, *508*
  Internet in, 870–71, 883
  and Luddites, 586–87, *587*
  in military, 419, 719–20
  in Napoleon era, 586–87
  in Renaissance, 343, 345–51
  in Second Industrial Revolution, 677–78
  in textile production, 507–8, 586–87, 603, 610
  in World War I, 719–20
Tehran Conference (1943), 799, 802
telegraph, 607, 652
telephones, *676*, 678
  smartphones, 883, 885
telescope of Galileo, 436, *436*
television, 823
temperance movement, 613, 615
Tencin, Claudine Guérin de (1682–1749), 496, 500, 524
Tennant, Charles, 607, 608
Tennis Court Oath, 545, 546, *546*
Tenochtitlán, 354
Teresa of Ávila (1515–1582), 395
The Terror in France (1793–1794), 559–64
terrorism, 879–81
  Islamic State and, 893–94
  in Russia, 879–80, 887
Tetzel, Johann, 372
textile production, 461, 466, 478, 494
  child labor in, 608

textile production (*continued*)
    in Enlightenment era, 507–8
    in France, 586
    gender roles in, 414, 610
    in Great Britain, 586–87, 610, 632
    and growth of cities, 607
    Industrial Revolution in, 603, 605–7
    "putting out" system in, 507
    in Renaissance, 333
    steam power in, 603, 605
    technological innovations in, 507–8,
      586–87, 603, 610
Thanksgiving holiday, 418
Thatcher, Margaret, 849–50, 855
Theatines, 394
theology, scholastic, 343, 344
Thermidorian Reaction, 562, *562*
Thermidorians, 564
Thiers, Adolphe (1797–1877), 654–55
Third Estate (France), 540, 541, 544, 545, 547,
    554
The Third of May (Goya), 581, *581*
Third Republic of France, 653, 654–55, 680–82
third way between capitalism and socialism,
    862
third way between Catholicism and
    Protestantism, 426
Third World countries, 818
Thirty Glorious Years, 822, 829, 841
Thirty Years' War (1618–1648), 410, 411, 421,
    426–33, 446, 482, 484
    atrocities and mass death in, *429*, 429–30
    map of, *427*
    outbreak of, 427–28
    and Peace of Westphalia, 456–59
    population killed in, 706
This Way to the Gas, Ladies and Gentlemen
    (Borowski), 793
Thoughts (Pensées) (Pascal), 453
The Three-Penny Opera (Brecht), 752
Thus Spoke Zarathustra (Nietzsche), 700
Tilsit, treaties signed at (1807), 578, 579, 582
Timur, Mongol leader, 335
Tindal, Matthew (1657–1733), 500
Tiso, Josef, 780
Titian (painter), *364*
Tito (Josip Broz) (1892–1980), 798, 801, 816,
    822, 839, 867
Tlaxcalans, 354
tobacco, 355, 415, 417, *417*, 489
Tocqueville, Alexis de (1805–1859), 544, 596,
    624, *624*, 663
Togo, 691
The Toleration Act (1689), 477
tolerationists, 499
Tolstoy, Leo (1828–1910), 588, 666, 759
Tone, Theobald Wolfe (1763–1798), 567
Tordesillas, Treaty of, 352
Tories, 464, 478, 533, 596, 627
torture, inquisition or inquiry by, 344
totalitarianism, 742, 759–65
    in Italy, 761
    in Nazi Germany, 761, 765, 796, 805
    in Soviet Union, 765, 796, 805
total war
    in World War I, 715–23, 732
    in World War II, 794–96
Toulouse, Calas broken on wheel in, 523, *523*,
    527
tourism, as middle class leisure, 614

trade, 411–15
    in agricultural products, 507, 678–79
    with American settlements and colonies,
      416–17, 418, 419, 493–95
    of China and Europe, 693–95
    in Continental System of Napoleon, 579,
      580, 586
    Corn Laws on, 597, 627, 647
    in cotton and textiles, 605–7, 632
    of Dutch Republic, 414–15, 432, 458, 466,
      467, 468
    of England, 415, 417, 478, 493–95
    of France, 493–95
    in fur, 415, 417, 418, 492
    globalization of, 676
    of Great Britain, 509, 604–5, 632, 696
    in Industrial Revolution, 604, 605–7
    liberal view of, 623–24
    maritime advances in, 345
    in mercantilism, 415, 493
    Napoleonic Wars affecting, 586
    New World products in, 355
    in opium, 632, 639
    post-World War I, 754
    in Renaissance, 345, 346–47
    in Second Industrial Revolution, 676
    in slaves, 347–48, 415, *416*, 417, 489–92,
      509–10
    Spanish, 399, 411, 413
    in spices, 346
    in tobacco, 417, *417*
    transatlantic triangle trade, 415, *416*, 489,
      509
Trades Union Congress, 754
trade unions
    in France, 680, *680*, 685
    in Germany, 685
    in Great Britain, 627–28, 648, 685, 754,
      847, 849
    in Hungary, 860
    in Poland, 856, 860
    post-World War II, 821
    strikes of, 680, 685
    women in, 717
    in World War I era, 717
Trafalgar, battle of, 576, 580
transportation
    automobiles in, 677–78, 680, 751, 752, 823,
      887
    Cunard Line in, 675
    and infrastructure development in
      Enlightenment, 508
    railways in, 600–601, 601–2, 606, 607
    shipbuilding advances in, 345
    steamships in, 607
    subway and transit systems in, 678
Trans-Siberian Railroad, 677, 682, *682*, 693
Transvaal, 691, 694
travel literature, 506, 519, 614
Treatise on the Three Impostors (Spinoza),
    500
Treaty Establishing a Constitution for Europe,
    882
Treblinka death camp, 799
Treitschke, Heinrich von (1834–1896), 684
trench foot, 721
trench warfare in World War I, 714, *714*, 718,
    720, *720*, 721–23
Trevithick, Richard (1771–1833), 602, 603
triangle trade, 415, *416*, 489, 509

Triple Alliance, 687, 707, 709
Triple Entente, 687, 707, 709
Tristan, Flora (1801–1844), 619
Trithemius, Johannes (1462–1516), 374
Trotsky, Leon (1879–1940), 729–30, 733, 735,
    736, 747–48, 765
Troubles, 839, 846
The True Levellers Standard Advanced
    (Winstanley), 465
Truffaut, François (1932–1984), 823
Truman, Harry (1884–1972), 804, 806, 815, 816
Trump, Donald (1946–), 889, 897
tuberculosis, 665
Tudor dynasty, 333
Tunisia, 691, 788, 833
Turgot, Anne-Robert (1727–1781), 533, 542
Turkey, 708, 743. *See also* Ottoman Empire
    in Balkan Wars, 708
    in Cold War era, 834
    in Cyprus, 848
    guest workers from, 826
    post-World War I, 745
    in Russo-Turkish Wars, 629, 655
    Versailles Peace Conference and
      settlement on, 737–38, 745
    in World War I, 711, 717–18, 724–25, 731
Turkish Republic of Northern Cyprus, 848
Turner, J. M. W. (1775–1851), 606, *606*, 607
turnip winter (1916–17), 724
Twelve Articles of the Peasants (1525), 383
20,000 Leagues under the Sea (Verne), 666
Two Sicilies, kingdom of, 597, 630, 640, 642,
    650
Tyers, Jonathan, 519
Tyndale, William, 390, 391
typhus epidemic in World War I, 718
Tyrol, 583

U-boats, German, 719, 780
Uccello, Paolo, *324–25*, 362
Ukraine, 424, 447, 730, 770
    capitalism in, 873
    Chernobyl nuclear accident in, 859
    and Crimea, 888–89, *889*
    crisis in, *888*, 888–89, *889*
    Euromaidan camp of protesters in, 888
    independence of, 732, 733, 866, 888
    map of, *447*
    nationalism in, 863, 888
    Orange Revolution in, 888
    People's Republics in, 889
    during Putin presidency, 888–89
    serfs in, 482
    Soviet collectivization of agriculture in,
      764–65
    in World War II, 783, 788, 798, 799
Ukrainians in Poland, 746
Ulster Temperance Movement, 615
Ulyanov, Vladimir Ilich (1870–1924), 728–29,
    729. See also Lenin
Ulysses (Joyce), 748
unemployment
    in Eastern bloc countries, 873
    in Europe (1922–1940), 745, 754, 756, 759
    in Europe (1945–1973), 822
    in France (1780–1799), 545
    in Great Depression, 756
    in Greece, 886
    Keynes on, 754
Union of South Africa, 691–92

Union of Soviet Socialist Republics (USSR). *See also* Soviet Union
unions. *See* trade unions
United Irishmen, 567
United Kingdom, 478. *See also* Great Britain
    Brexit vote in, 890–92, *892,* 897
    creation of, *487,* 567, 575, 684
    Scottish independence movement in, 892–93
United Kingdom Independence Party, 884, 890–91
United Nations, 810, 868
    African nations in, 834
    and Bosnia-Herzegovina, 868, *868*
    Germany in, 817
    Gorbachev at, 860
    and Iraq War, 880
    and Israel, 811
    and Korea, 817
    Refugee Agency of, 895
United Netherlands, 593
United States
    and Afghanistan, 879
    and Africa, 834
    anti-communism in, 817
    and Berlin Airlift, 817, *817*
    and Bosnia-Herzegovina, 868
    and China relations, 853
    Civil War in (1861–1865), 707
    and Cold War, 809, 810, 814–17, 834, 836
    Constitution of, 528, 536
    cotton production and slavery in, 605
    cultural influence in Europe, 750, 809–10, 822
    détente policy with Soviet Union, 853
    economic recession in, 885
    education in, 675
    English settlements and colonies in, 416–19, 466, 475, 489, 493, 512, 514, 535–36
    French Huguenots in, 475
    German occupation zone of, 817
    Great Depression in, 756
    gross domestic product of, 794
    Hollywood film industry in, 750, 823
    immigration to, 647, 677, *677,* 682
    in Iraq War, 880
    isolationism in, 771
    and Korea, 817
    as leader of free world, 816
    and League of Nations, 738
    Lend-Lease policy of, 780, 782, 785, 787, 789, 790
    and liberation of concentration camps, 803
    Manhattan Project in, 799
    Marshall Plan of, 814
    middle class culture in, 612
    in Middle East conflicts, 867
    in NATO, 810, 817, 897
    oil shock in (1973–1974), 847
    Pearl Harbor attack in, 786–87
    populism in, 897
    post–World War I, 754, 756
    in post–World War II rebuilding, 813–14
    at Potsdam Conference, 804
    presidential election of 2016 in, 889, 897
    Reagan administration in, 858
    revolution against Britain, 514, 535–36
    rising international power of, 693

    September 11, 2001 terrorist attacks in, 879, *879,* 880
    in Serbian bombing campaign, 869
    and Seven Years' War, 512
    in Spanish-American War (1898), 693
    and Spanish Civil War, 767
    and START treaty, 859–60
    Star Wars missile defense system of, 854
    steamships in, 607
    and Suez Crisis (1856), 832
    as superpower, 816
    at Versailles Peace Conference, 736
    and Vietnam, 821, 834–36, 839, 853
    voting rights in, 717
    and War of 1812 against Britain, 587
    in World War I, 716, 719, 724, 730, 732, 733, 736
    in World War II, 780, 785, 786–91, 794, 795, 799–800, 803
    at Yalta Conference, 802, *802*
Universal Exposition (1889), 680, 692
universe
    Descartes on, 438
    Galileo on, 436, 437
    Newton on, 501–2
    Spinoza on, 452
universities
    in age of industry, 612
    book printing in, 350
    in Germany, 873
    historians in, 623
    in Paris, 350
    in post-industrial society, 837
    religious education in, 386, 390
    in Renaissance, 340, 343, 350, 357
    revolutionary movements in, 640
    and Second Industrial Revolution, 675
    student rebellions in (1960s), 838–41
    studies of natural world in, 396–97
    youth culture of 1960s in, 837, 838–41
University of Belgrade, 839
University of Cambridge, 376
University of Chicago, 675
University of Madrid, 839
University of Marburg, 390
University of Paris, 839
University of Rome, 839
The Uprooted (Barrès), 681
Ural, 763
Urban VI, Pope (r. 1378–1389), 339
urbanization, 659. *See also* cities
Ure, Andrew (1778–1857), 616
Ursuline Order, 394–95, 450, 451
utilitarianism, 524, 623
utopia, Enlightenment idea of, 526, 618–19
Utopia (More), *376,* 376–77
Utrecht, Peace of (1713–1714), 487–88, *488*
Uzbekistan, 798

vacations, as middle class leisure, 614
vaccinations, 665, 678
Valla, Lorenzo (1407–1457), 360, 375
Vallotton, Félix (1865–1925), 661
Valmy, battle of, 556, 557, 639
Valois dynasty, 330
van Gogh, Theo, 881
Van Gogh, Vincent (1853–1890), 698
Vasily II, Grand Prince of Moscow (r. 1425–1462), 341

Vatican, 650
    library of, 358
Vauxhall Gardens, *504–5,* 519
The Vegetable Market (Sorgh), 467
Veil, Simone, 850
Velázquez, Diego (1599–1660), *408–9,* 432
Velvet Revolution (Czechoslovakia), 846, 861, *861,* 866
venality of office, 420, 431, 461
Vendée
    peasant rebellion in, 557, 559
    reign of terror in, 560–61, 580
Venice in Renaissance era, 326, 329
Verdi, Giuseppe (1813–1901), 667, 698
Verdun, battle of, 706, 720–21, 723, 727, 884
Vermeer, Jan (1632–1675), 468, *468*
Verne, Jules (1828–1905), 666–67
Versailles, palace of Louis XIV at, *462,* 462–63, 495
    court life in, 462, *484,* 484–85, 542
    Estates General meeting at (1789), 545
    Hall of Mirrors in, 463, 548
    women's march on, 548, *548*
Versailles Peace Conference and settlement, 736–38, 758
    and ethnic tensions, 736, 745–46, *746*
    Germany in, 736, 738, 743, 744, 766, 769
    Yugoslavia in, 736, 737, 867
Vesalius, Andreas (1514–1564), 397
Vespucci, Amerigo (ca. 1454–1512), 352, *353*
Vichy regime in France, 787, 788, 792, 798, 821
    and National Revolution, 777, 780
Victoria, queen of England (r. 1837–1901), 615, 646
    as empress of India, 649, *649*
Victorian Age (1837–1901), 646–48, 663
Vienna
    city life and culture in, 698, 699
    modernism in, 698
    Ottoman siege of (1683), *485,* 485–86
Viet Cong, 836
Viet Minh, 821
Vietnam, 758
    division of, 832
    France and, 653, 821, 832
    protests against war in, 836, 839
    United States in, 821, 834–36, 839, 853
Villepin, Dominique de, 880
Villermé, Louis René (1782–1863), 617
Vincent de Paul, Saint (1581–1660), 450
Vindication of the Rights of Women (Wollstonecraft), 550
Virgil (70–19 bce), 356
Virginia Colony, 417, 418, 419
The Virgin of the Rocks (Leonardo da Vinci), 365, 366
virtue, Rousseau on, 542
Visconti family of Milan, 326, 329
visual culture. *See also* art and artisans
    An Evening with Madame Geoffrin (Lemonnier), 518
    Le Bon Marché (Vallotton), 661
    The City Rises (Boccioni), 701
    The Colossus, 582
    Erasing Britain from Europe (Banksy), 891
    Hunters in the Snow (Bruegel), 412
    The Interior of the Oude Kerk (de Witte), 402
    Messerturm skyscraper of Jahn, 852
    "The Path from Earth to the Stars," 828

visual culture (*continued*)
    Pillars of Society (Grosz), 749
    Portrait of a Lady (Ghirlandaio), 359
    Portrait of Louise de Kérouaille (Mignard), 494
    Rain, Steam and Speed—The Great Western Railway (Turner), 606, *606*
    Tennis Court Oath (David), 546
Vitruvius (d. after 15 ce), 361
Vittorio Emmanuele II, king of Sardinia and Italy (r. 1849–1861), 645, 650
Vittorio Emmanuele III, king of Italy (r. 1900–1946), 747, 796
Vives, Juan Luis, 332
Voltaire, François-Marie Arovet (1694–1778), 509–10, 522, 524, 525–27, 528, 529
    and Frederick II of Prussia, 532
    portrait of, *525*
    and rights of man concept, 534
voting rights, 544, 630, 685
    in France, 552, 564, 639, 753, 823
    in Great Britain, 597, 627, 648, 686, *686*, 687, 717, 753
    liberal view of, 623
    of women, 549, 643, 685, 686, *686*, 687, 753, 823
Vulgate Bible, 377, *380*, 396

Wagner, Otto, 699
Wagner, Richard (1813–1883), 667, 684, 698
Wagram, Battle of (1809), 583, 587
Wake island, in World War II, 787
Waldensian Christians, 475–76
Wales, 618, 866
Wałęsa, Lech, 856, *856*, 860, 862
Wallace, Alfred Russel (1823–1913), 665
Wallenstein, Albrecht von (1583–1634), 428, 458
Waller, John, 496–97
Walpole, Robert, 533
Walter, Jakob, 571, 572, 588
Wanderer above the Sea of Fog (Friedrich), *621*
Wannsee conference, 791
War and Peace (Tolstoy), 588, 666
war communism, 733, 736
war crimes
    of Milošević, 869
    in World War II, 804, 811–12
Ward, Mary (1851–1920), 715
warfare. *See also specific wars.*
    barbarization of, 801, 805
    conduct of, 458, 482–85
    in Europe (1400–1500), 327, 330, 335, 336–39
    in Europe (1500–1600), 398–403
    in Europe (1600–1640), *419*, 419–20, 426–30
    in Europe (1640–1680), 458, 463, *463*, 470
    in Europe (1680–1740), 479, 482–88
    in Europe (1740–1780), 511–14
    financing cost of, 398–99
    guerrilla. *See guerrilla warfare*
    Hague Conventions on, 679, 720
    of Louis XIV of France, 463, *463*, 470, 479, 483, 484, 485, 486–88
    medical care on battlefield in, 652, *652*, 721, *721*
    professional soldiers in, 336–37

war crimes in, 804, 811–12, 869
weapons in. *See weaponry*
War of 1812, 587
War of Austrian Succession (1740–1748), *511*, 512, 519
War of Independence in India (1857–1858), 647–48, 759
War of Spanish Succession (1702–1714), 486, 488
War of the League of Augsburg (1688–1697), 484, 486, 489
Warsaw
    and Congress of Vienna, 593
    German-Soviet battle at, 801
    Jews in, 781, 791, *798*, 798–99
    uprising in (1944), *798*, 798–99
Warsaw Pact, 810, *815*, 817, 829, 840, 841, 862
Wars of the Roses (1455–87), 333, *333*
War Sonnets (Brooke), 726
Warwick the Kingmaker, 333
Washington, George, 512, 535
"The Waste Land" (Eliot), 748
Waterloo, battle of (1815), 595, 628, 651
water wheels as source of power, 507
Watt, James (1736–1819), 586
    steam engine of, 508, *508*, 602, 603
Waverly (Scott), 622
The Wealth of Nations (Smith), 528
weaponry
    atomic weapons in, 795, 799, *804*, 804–5, 817
    chemical weapons in, 720, *720*, 727, 730
    in Europe (1680–1740), 484
    industrial production of, 679, 709, 716, 785, 794, 795, 805
    and international arms control, 754
    in Nazi Germany, 766, 769, 799
    nuclear weapons in. *See nuclear weapons*
    in Renaissance, 336–37, *337*
Weber, Friedrich, *744*
Weber, Max (1864–1920), 700
Weill, Kurt, 752
Weimar Republic, 743–45, 759, 761
welfare state, 847–50
    in France, 813, 847, 848
    in Great Britain, 813, 829, 847–48, 849–50
    and post-World War I policies, 745, 747
    post-World War II rise of, 813, 829
    public housing in, 848, *848*, 849
    in Sweden, 813, 850
Wellesley, Arthur, 581
Wellington, Lord and Duke of (1769–1852), 581, 590, 593, 595, 627
Wells, H. G. (1866–1944), 711
Wentworth, Thomas (1593–1641), 443, 444
Wesley, John (1703–1791), 522
West, Rebecca, 686
West Africa, France in, 691, 693, 818, 834
West Berlin, 834, 835
    and fall of Berlin Wall, 861
    student protests in (1968), 839
West Germany, 812, 817, 822
    agriculture in, 825
    and Berlin Wall, 834, 835, 861
    birthrate in, 847
    economy of, 822, 826
    education in, 837
    in European Community, 871
    in European Economic Community, 829–30

    guest workers in, 826
    immigration to, 826, 834, 835
    Munich Olympic Games in (1972), *846*, 847
    nuclear weapons in, 853, 854
    Ostpolitik (East Policy) of, 854
    political stability in, 829
    Red Army Faction in, 841, 846
    reunification with East Germany, 862–63
    social welfare programs in, 850
    student protests in (1968), 839
    women's independence in, 824
Westphalia, Peace of (1645–1648), 456–59, *457*, 593, 736
What is the Third Estate (Sieyès), 544
Whigs, 464, 478, 533, 627, 648
White armies in Russian Civil War, 733, *733*, 735
white-collar work in Second Industrial Revolution, 675, 676
White Company, 336
Whitefield, George (1714–1770), 522
"White House" in Moscow, 865, 874, *874*
"The White Man's Burden" (Kipling), 692
White Mountain, battle of (1620), 421, 428, 433
White Terror (France), 564
Whitney, Eli, 605
Wiene, Robert, 750
Wiesel, Elie (1928–2016), 793
Wild, Jonathan, 496
Wilders, Geert, 881, 890
Wilhelm Gustloff (German passenger ship), 802
Wilhelm I, king of Prussia (r. 1861–1888), 651, 653
    as kaiser of Germany, 653, 653–54, 683, 684
Wilhelm II, kaiser of Germany (r. 1888–1918), 671, 684, 687
    in World War I, 707, 710, 718, 732
Wilkes, John, 533–34, 597
Wilkes affair, *533*, 533–34, 535
William III of Orange (1650–1702), *476*, 476–77, 478, 488
    as Dutch stadholder, 470, 476
    military of, 484
William IV, king of Great Britain (r. 1830–1837), 627
William of Occam (ca. 1287–1347), 343
William the Silent, Prince of Orange (1533–1584), 400, 401
Williams, Helen Maria, 549
Wilson, Woodrow (1856–1924), 719, 724, 732, 736, 738
windmills in Dutch Republic, 414
Winstanley, Gerrard, 465
witchcraft, 343–44, *403*, 403–4, 405
    Bodin on, 404
    and witch trials in Europe, 423–24
Witte, Emmanuel de, *466*
Wittenberg, 374, 378–79
Wojtyla, Karol, 856
Wollstonecraft, Mary (1759–1797), 550, 615, 621
Wollstonecraft, Mary (1797–1851), 621
women
    in academic salons, 496, 517, 518
    African, in Europe, 348, *348*
    in battlefield nursing, 652, *652*
    as beguines, 343
    in Catholic Church, 394–95, 450–51

in communism, 735, *735*
Congolese, 692
in cult of domesticity, *614*, 614–15
in Eastern Europe, 823, 857
education of, 423, *423*, 454, 675
in Europe (1400–1500), 343–44, 348,
    358–60, 364
in Europe (1500–1600), 386–87, *387*
in Europe (1600–1640), 414, 420, 423–34,
    430, 435–36
in Europe (1640–1680), 450–51, 453–54,
    462
in Europe (1740–1780), 516–19, 529, 531
in Europe (1780–1799), 547, 548, 549, 550,
    558, 560–61, 562
in Europe (1799–1820), 574, 585, 591
in Europe (1820–1845), 615, 619
in Europe (1845–1880), 660, 663, 663–64
in Europe (1880–1910), 675–76, *676*
in Europe (1922–1940), 752, *753*, 753–54,
    760, 762
in Europe (1945–1973), *823*, 823–25, *825*,
    830–32, 841
in Europe (1973–2000), 849–50, 853
French, deported to Louisiana, 492
in Lodz ghetto, 793
in middle class, 612, 660
in military, 717, 783, *783*, 798
in Nazi Germany, 760, 762, 784
in North American settlements, 417
in Paris Commune, 664
in politics, 849–50, 853
in Protestant religious movements, 619
in republicanism, 531
in Republic of Letters, 435–36
rights of. *See* women's rights
in Russia, 663, 717, 733, *735*
in sack of Magdeburg, 430
in slavery, 347, 490, 491
in socialism, 663
in Soviet Union, 783, *783*
in Turkey, 745
as witches, 343–44, 403–4, 423–24
work of, 414, 608, 610, 617, 675–76, 717,
    796, 797, 798, 823–25
in World War I, 715, *715*, 717, *717*
in World War II, 796, 797, 798
Women's Battalion of Death, 717
Women's Peace Camp, 854, *854*
women's rights, 420, 547, 549, 550, 574, 615,
    663, 823–25
    property rights in, 420, 615, 685
    voting rights in, 549, 643, 685, 686, *686*,
        687, 717, 753, 823
Women's Social and Political Union, 686, 711
Women's Voice, 643
Women under Socialism (Bebel), 686
wool, 329
Woolf, Virginia (1882–1941), 754
Wordsworth, William (1770–1850), 550, 621
work
    of Africans in Europe (1400–1500), 348
    of children, 608, 609, 675–76
    in Eastern bloc countries, 873
    in European Union, 881–82, 883
    gender roles in, 414, 610
    of guest workers, 826
    in Industrial Revolution, 607–8, *608*, 609,
        610
    under Louis XIV of France, 461

of middle class, 612, 613
of peasants, 481–82, 507, 508
post–World War II, 821, 823, 825, 826
in putting out system, 507
scientific approach to productivity in, 754
in Second Industrial Revolution, *673*, 674
in Soviet Union, 763–64
and trade unionism, 627–28
in urban areas (1740–1780), 510
in urban areas (1820–1845), 607–8, *608*,
    615–17
in urban areas (1880–1910), 701
of women, 414, 608, 610, 617, 675–76, 717,
    796, 797, 798, 823–25
workhouses for indigent, 618
working class, 611, 615–19
    Engels on, 642, 662
    in France, 680, 745
    in Germany, 654
    in Great Britain, 648, 745
    Marx on, 642, 662, 728
    post–World War I, 745
    in Russia, 674, 682
    social protections for, 685
World Bank, 814
World Exhibition (1851), 660, *660*
World Exposition (1867), 638
The World's Olio (Cavendish), 454
World Trade Center, terrorist attack on, 879
World War I, 898
    airplanes used in, 719, *719*
    Allies in, 711
    Armenian genocide in, 725, *725*
    armistice in (1918), 732–33
    arms race and military mobilization prior
        to, 708–9
    Balkan front in, 718
    battlefield tactics and weapons in, 714–15,
        719–21
    Big Push in, 723
    breaking points in (1916–1917), 723–27
    British blockade in, 716, 718, 720, 724
    Central powers in, 711–12, *713*, 716–18,
        723–25, 731–33, 736
    chemical weapons in, 720, *720*, 727, 730
    Christmas Day truce in (1914), 723
    commemoration of, *752*, 752–53
    desertion and mutinies in, 725–27, 732,
        736, *736*
    early German successes in, 712
    eastern front in, 718, 728
    economic impact of, 715–16
    expanding theater of, 717–19
    field hospitals in, 721, *721*
    Gallipoli Campaign in, 706, 718, 724, 777
    German ambitions in, 707
    home front during, 715–17
    ideological extremism after, 741–72
    Italian front in, 718
    Lusitania attack in, 719
    military manpower in, 709, 715, 717
    military plans on, 706–7
    modernist depiction of destruction in,
        704–5
    naval battles in, 718–19
    opposition to, 721–23, 725–27, 752
    origins of, 706–11
    outbreak of, 710–11
    propaganda campaigns in, 716, *716*, 721
    public attitudes toward, 711–12, 726

and Russian civil war (1918–1921), 730, *733*,
    733–36
and Russian Revolutions, 706, 727–30
Schlieffen Plan in, 707, 711, 712, 720
Somme battle in, *723*, 723–24
Spring Offensive in (1918), 730–31
stalemate in, 712–14, *713*
submarines in, 718–19, 724
total war in, 715–23, 732
trench warfare in, 714, *714*, 718, 720, *720*,
    721–23
turnip winter in (1916–17), 724
United States in, 716, 719, 724, 730, 732,
    733
Versailles Peace Conference and
    settlement in, 736–38
as "war to end all wars," 711
western front in, *713*, 714, 715, 718, 722,
    723, 724, 730
women during, 715, *715*, 717, *717*
World War II, 711, 742, 775–806, 898
    aftermath of, 810–12
    Allied bombing campaign in, 795, *795*,
        804–5
    atomic bomb in, 795, 799, *804*, 804–5
    barbarization of warfare in, 801, 805
    blitzkrieg in, 775, 776, 777, 780, 782
    British Blitz in, 779, *779*
    crucial points in, 785–91
    D-Day in, 799–800, *800*
    decolonization after, 810
    Dunkirk battle in, 776
    eastern front in, 790, 795–96, 805
    France in, 776–77, *777*, 779, 780–81
    German surrender in, 802–4
    Great Britain in, 775, 776, 777–80
    Holocaust in, 784, 791–94, 803–4, 805–6
    home fronts in, 796–99
    hunger in, 790
    Lend-Lease policy in, 780, 782, 785, 787,
        789, 790
    liberation in, 799–801
    long-term impact of, 806
    maps of European territories in, *778*, *803*
    Midway battle in, 791
    North Africa in, 787, 788
    occupied Europe in, 780–82
    Operation Barbarossa in, 782–85
    origins of, 766–72
    in Pacific, *786*, 786–88, 791, 804–5
    Pearl Harbor attack in, 786–87
    phony war in, 771–72, 775, 776
    Poland in, 769, 770–71, 775, 781
    Potsdam Conference in, 804
    prosperity after, 821–26
    rebuilding after, 812–14
    refugees in, 801, 802, 810–11, *811*
    resistance movements in, 798–99, 800,
        801, 805–6
    Scandinavia in, 776
    second front question in, 788, 794, 796
    Stalingrad battle in, 788–89, 790
    Tehran Conference in, 799, 802
    total war in, 794–96
    unparalleled violence in, 805
    violent conclusion of, 801–6
    war crimes in, 804, 811–12
    women in, 796, 797, 798
    Yalta Conference in, 802, *802*
Worms, Diet of, *378*, 378–79, 393–94

The Wretched of the Earth (Fanon), 832
Wycliffe, John (ca. 1330–1384), 340

Yalta Conference (1945), 802, *802*
Yanukovych, Viktor (1950–), 888
Yeats, William Butler (1865–1939), 697, 725, 748
Yeltsin, Boris (1931–2007), *865*, 865–66, 870, 873–74, 887
Yeremenko, Aleksey Gordeyevich, *774–75*
Yom Kippur War (1973), 847
Yorktown, battle of, *535*
Young, Arthur (1741–1820), 508
Young Italy, 630, 645
The Young Ladies of Avignon (Picasso), 697, *697*, 698

Young Turks, 708, 717, 725, 737
youth culture (1960s), 836–37, 838
    student rebellions in, 838–41
Ypres, battle of, 713–14, 720, *720*
Yugoslavia, 732, 867–68
    breakup of, 846, 868, *869*
    Communist Party in, 816
    ethnic tensions in, 746, 867–68
    Muslims in, 867, 868
    post–World War I, 745, 746
    post–World War II, 815, 816, 822
    shortage of consumer goods in, 857
    student protests in (1968), 839
    Versailles Peace Conference and
        settlement on, 736, 737, 867
    in World War II, 782, 798, 801

Yukos oil company, 888
Yule Day customs in Scotland, 389

Zaïre (Voltaire), 529
Zelkowicz, Josef (1897–1944), 793
Zero Hour, 812
Zetkin, Clara (1857–1933), 686
Zhivkov, Todor, 862
Zhukov, Georgi, 785, 789, 801
Zionism, 682
Zola, Émile (1840–1902), 682, 697
Zollverein, 651
Zulu in South Africa, 649
Zurich, Reformation Movement in, 382, 385
Zwingli, Ulrich (1484–1531), 382, *382*, 385, 402

ARCTIC OCEAN

Franz Josef Land (Russia)

Severnaya Zemlya

Ostrova Anzhu

Svalbard (Norway)

Novaya Zemlya

Kara Sea

Laptev Sea

East Siberian Sea

wegian Sea

Barents Sea

NORWAY

SWEDEN

FINLAND

L. Onega

L. Ladoga St. Petersburg

RUSSIA

Bering Sea

Stockholm ⊕ ESTONIA
Baltic Sea LATVIA
NMARK LITHUANIA
Moscow ⊕

Berlin ⊕ POLAND BELARUS
ERMANY
CZECH REP. Kiev ⊕ UKRAINE
SLOVAKIA
AUSTRIA HUNGARY
TZ. CROATIA ROMANIA
ITALY SERBIA BULGARIA
Rome ⊕ *Black Sea*

KAZAKHSTAN

Aral Sea

L. Balkhash

L. Baikal

MONGOLIA

Urumqi

Sea of Okhotsk

Sakhalin

⊕ Istanbul
Athens ⊕ TURKEY
nis GREECE
Mediterranean Sea
TUNISIA CYPRUS
LEBANON SYRIA
ISRAEL Baghdad
JORDAN IRAQ
Cairo ⊕

Caspian Sea
UZBEKISTAN
Tashkent ⊕ KYRGYZSTAN
TURKMEN. TAJIKISTAN
Tehran ⊕ AFGHAN. ⊕ Kabul
IRAN PAKISTAN

Beijing ⊕
N. KOREA
Seoul ⊕ JAPAN
S. KOREA
⊕ Tokyo
Sea of Japan

CHINA
Chengdu Shanghai
East China Sea
Osaka

LIBYA EGYPT
SAUDI ARABIA
QATAR
Riyadh ⊕ U.A.E.
OMAN
KUWAIT

New Delhi
NEPAL BHUTAN
INDIA
Kolkata ⊕ Dhaka
BANGLADESH
MYANMAR

Hong Kong
⊕ Taipei
TAIWAN
Philippine Sea

PACIFIC OCEAN

NIGER CHAD
ERITREA
SUDAN
Khartoum YEMEN
DJIBOUTI

SOUTH
GERIA CENTRAL SUDAN
AFRICAN REP. ETHIOPIA
os CAMEROON
Addis Ababa

Mumbai
Arabian Sea
Bangalore
Bay of Bengal
SRI LANKA

MALDIVES

LAOS
THAILAND VIETNAM
Bangkok CAMBODIA
South China Sea
Manila
PHILIPPINES

FEDERATED STATES
OF MICRONESIA
MARSHALL
ISLANDS

PALAU
KIRIBATI
NAURU

SOMALIA

L. Victoria
UGANDA
CONGO KENYA
DEM. REP. Nairobi
OF THE RWANDA
CONGO BURUNDI
ME TANZANIA
GABON
PE Kinshasa
Luanda ⊕

SEYCHELLES

BRUNEI
MALAYSIA
SINGAPORE
Sumatra INDONESIA
Jakarta ⊕
Java *Java Sea*
Borneo

EAST TIMOR

New Guinea

PAPUA NEW
GUINEA

SOLOMON
ISLANDS
TUVAL

ANGOLA
MALAWI
ZAMBIA COMOROS
ZIMBABWE
NAMIBIA MOZAMBIQUE
BOTSWANA Antananarivo
MADAGASCAR MAURITIUS

INDIAN OCEAN

Coral Sea VANUATU

New Caledonia (France)

FIJ

Johannesburg ⊕ Maputo
SWAZILAND
SOUTH LESOTHO
AFRICA
Cape Town ⊕

AUSTRALIA

Sydney
Melbourne

Tasman Sea NEW
ZEALAND

Tasmania

Kerguelen Is. (France)

SOUTHERN OCEAN

Antarctica